THEORIES
OF LEARNING
Fourth Edition

Ernest R. Hilgard
Gordon H. Bower

Both of Stanford University

PRENTICE-HALL, INC., *Englewood Cliffs, New Jersey*

Library of Congress Cataloging in Publication Data

HILGARD, ERNEST ROPIEQUET, 1904–
    Theories of learning.

    (The Century psychology series)
    Includes bibliographies.
    1. Learning, Psychology of. I. Bower, Gordon H.,
joint author. II. Title.
LB1051.H52 1974   153.1'5   74-5087
ISBN 0-13-914457-9

THE CENTURY PSYCHOLOGY SERIES

Gardner Lindzey and Kenneth MacCorquodale, Editors

To the loving memory of my father and mother, Clyde and
Mabelle Bower, who raised me to revere life and love knowledge;
and to my sister, Shirley Bower Montgomery, who taught me to
appreciate talent and the hard work that brings it forth.—G.H.B.

Printed in the United States of America

10   9   8   7   6

Table 10-4 is from *Studies in Cognitive Development: Essays in Honor of Jean
Piaget* by David Elkind and John Flavell. Copyright © 1969 by Oxford
University Press, Inc. Reprinted by permission.

Prentice-Hall International, Inc., *London*
Prentice-Hall of Australia, Pty. Ltd., *Sydney*
Prentice-Hall of Canada, Ltd., *Toronto*
Prentice-Hall of India Private Limited, *New Delhi*
Prentice-Hall of Japan, Inc., *Tokyo*

Contents

Preface to the
Fourth Edition

Psychology seems to be constantly in a state of ferment and change, if not of turmoil and revolution. In attempting to understand mental life, thousands of psychologists are continually proposing new perspectives, ideas, phenomena, experimental results, and investigative methods at a pell-mell pace. The professional often feels that he is drowning in a torrential flood of information; the new student doesn't know where to enter the waters or in which direction to swim. In such situations of information overload, a time-tested method for reducing cognitive strain is to examine the genesis of major, integrative perspectives and to study their development into the contemporary research scene. The historical perspective provides a major organizing scheme for student and professional alike, since many of the "big questions" about mental phenomena were posed long ago, and the answers to the questions advanced by the historically prominent positions serve as prototypes, of which contemporary hypotheses can often be seen as sophisticated variations.

The aim of this text is to provide the student with an understanding of modern learning theory, its historical context and background. To this end we review the theories of learning expounded by the major "schools" of psychology—behaviorism, gestalt, functionalism, information-processing— as well as the learning theories associated with major intellectual figures such as Thorndike, Pavlov, Guthrie, Hull, Tolman, Skinner, Piaget, and Freud. Each theory is expounded in terms of its historical setting and the scientific problems which the theorist was addressing. The salient experimental evidence associated with each theory is also surveyed.

Comparing this new edition with the prior (third) edition, the reader will note many changes. The first chapter includes new material on the philosophical precursors of psychology, contrasting the theories of mind advocated by philosophical empiricism and rationalism; these contrasting themes recur frequently throughout the contemporary scene (for example, in the Skinner versus Chomsky debates). The next chapters review the theoretical work associated with the figures of Thorndike, Pavlov, Guthrie, Tolman, Hull, and Skinner; these chapters have been substantially revised and updated to show the contemporary relevance of these positions by citing current research which builds on the previous ideas. The chapters describing the "schools" of gestalt and functionalism have been thoroughly rewritten in terms relevant to their modern advocacy: the organizational approach to human memory (gestalt), and the interference theory of forgetting (functionalism). The chapter on Piaget, which is entirely new, is included because of the current salience of Piaget's view of learning and cognitive development. The chapter on Freud has been appreciably revised by inclusion of new studies on repression. The chapters on "specialized areas"—mathematical learning theory, information-processing theories, and neurophysiology of learning—survey new developments since the previous edition. The chapter on "recent developments" is new; it surveys the more salient lines of recent work in conditioning, social learning theory, and information-processing models of human memory. The final chapter on the technology of instruction provides up-to-date coverage of developments in learning as applied to the schools. We hope that with these changes, the text will provide a firm foundation for the student to understand and perhaps contribute to modern learning theory or its applications.

Revising a comprehensive text is a large job, and we are pleased to acknowledge the help of many people. First, the Center for Advanced Study in the Behavioral Sciences provided GHB with a fellowship while he worked on this book. We were aided by our secretaries, Joan Warmbrunn, Joyce Lockwood, and Myrna Valdez, who cheerfully endured the retyping of the several drafts of this manuscript. The manuscript was substantially improved by the high-quality copy editing of Miriam Gallaher of the Center staff. Joyce Lockwood patiently suffered the frustrations of tracking down all the permission rights. The final shepherding of the manuscript into print was overseen by our production managers, Linda Harms and Carolyn Davidson. So to all those to whom we are indebted, we extend our sincere thanks.

G.H.B.

Appearing in its first edition in 1948, this book has been periodically revised to reflect new knowledge and changes in approaches to the psychology of learning, without losing the advantage of recognizing historical roots in some earlier positions that were, at the time they were advanced, somewhat clearer and more confident than their contemporary representations. Gordon Bower joined me in the third edition, adding the capabilities of a vigorous younger participant in experimentation and theory construction. In that edition, he took primary responsibility for the authorship of five of the sixteen chapters, and each of the chapters bore the initials of one of us to indicate its authorship. I was pleased to have Dr. Bower take the major responsibility for the revision of this (fourth) edition, my only primary contributions being the new chapter on Piaget and the chapter now bearing the title "Theories of Instruction." The designation of authorship by chapter is therefore no longer appropriate; what is new is primarily his.

E.R.H.

The Nature of Learning Theory:

Origins and Characteristics

It is no secret that psychology developed out of philosophy. The really fascinating and absorbing questions of psychology were not "discovered" by modern psychologists, but rather have been matters of deep concern to philosophers for many centuries. And these are not trivial "academic" questions of only historical interest; on the contrary, they center upon the most vital motives and forces underlying Western thought and civilization: What am I to believe? What can I trust? How do we know? What kind of life is worth living? What is man's role and what is his destiny in this universe? What is Justice, the Good, the Truth? What government, if any, is worth having? What is the nature of man? Is man free? What is Mind and what is its relation to nature?

These are not sterile questions because the answers we give to them impinge in countless ways upon our daily lives, providing the motives for our personal and social conduct, the rationale for systems of legal and governmental control over our lives, and our modes of thinking about our personal identity and about the meaning of our lives. The serious thinkers of each generation have aimed at the systematic consideration and clarification of such questions and of proposed answers to them. Philosophical psychology began as an attempt to deal with the nature of man; later, psychology split off to become the "science of mental life." The questions were: What is mind, consciousness, awareness? What is the relation of the mind to the body? How does the mind develop from birth? How does it acquire knowledge of the world? How does it come to know other minds? To know itself? What drives us to action? What is the self? What produces continuity of personal identity? These and many other questions have provided the intellectual underpinnings of modern psychology.

Memory and Knowledge

This is a textbook about *learning* or *memory,* which is a branch of modern psychology. But the study of learning and memory really stems and originally had its impetus from two philosophical sources: the analysis of knowledge (how we come to know things), and the analysis of the nature and organization of mental life. The first issue concerns what philosophers call epistemology, the theory of knowledge. The second issue concerns the nature and contents of our concepts, thoughts, images, discernments, reminiscences, creative imaginations, and other mental constructions; the further question here concerns what operations, rules, or laws may be supposed to underlie these mental phenomena. The study of learning may aptly be characterized as experimental epistemology, since learning and knowing seem related as a process is to its result, as acquiring is to a possession, as painting is to a picture. The close relation between the meanings of *learn* and *know* are obvious in any dictionary. The following definitions (slightly edited) from the *American heritage dictionary* represent common usage:

to learn (verb): (1) to gain knowledge, comprehension, or mastery of through experience or study. (2) To fix in the mind or memory; memorize. (3) To acquire through experience. (4) To become informed of, to find out.

to know (verb): (1) To perceive directly with the senses or mind; apprehend with clarity or certainty. (2) To be certain of; accept as true beyond doubt. (3) To be capable of, have the skill to do. Used with *know how* to do something. (4) To have a practical understanding through experience with something. (5) To experience, to be subjected to. (6) To have firmly secured in the mind or memory. (7) To be able to distinguish, recognize, discern. (8) To be acquainted or familiar with. (9) *Archaic*: To have sexual intercourse with, as in *"Adam knew Eve his wife; and she conceived."*

Dictionaries help systematize the way concepts are used in everyday life, and such definitions illustrate that *learn* and *know* are closely related in their primary senses. To *learn* means "to gain knowledge through experience"; but one of the meanings of "experience" is "to perceive directly with the senses" which, of course, appears initially in the definition of *know*. So we complete one side of the chain. But *knowledge* is defined, among other things, as *learning* (erudition) and as familiarity or understanding gained through experience, and learning is defined as acquired knowledge. So we come full circle.

Consider the two further terms *memory* and *remembering. Memory* is the faculty of retaining and recalling past experiences, or the ability to remember, and *remembering* is defined as recalling an experience to mind or thinking of it again. These clearly form an interconnected cluster of concepts. More than that, in our everyday dealings, memory (or remembering) is one of the primary ways by which we know things and by which we support knowledge-claims. The status accorded in the law courts to testimony from firsthand witnesses attests to the evidential power-to-persuade of direct memories: "How do I know that John stole the money? Because I *remember* seeing him with his hand in the till." The existence of such memories constitutes a *prima facie* case for the knowledge-claim—unless other considerations enter to cause doubts. In fact, one of the earliest "applications" (if it may be called that) of the psychological study of memory had the effect of undermining its validity for supporting knowledge-claims; such studies illustrated just how inaccurate, distorted, and subjectively biased were many of the memories of remote events remembered in personal testimonies on the witness stand, especially memories connected with emotionally laden episodes.

ALTERNATIVE EPISTEMOLOGIES

Beyond this specific relation of memory to knowledge-claims, however, lie the more general and deeper questions of epistemology. One of the most engaging issues within the theory of knowledge is the question of how our concepts and knowledge arise, and what is the relation between experience and the organization of the mind. Historians of philosophy have discerned two major but opposing positions on this matter which may be labeled *empiricism* and *rationalism*. These have been constant combatants within the intellectual arena for centuries and strong forms of them are still perfectly recognizable on the contemporary scene of "scientific psychology." Therefore, it is appropriate to give a thumbnail sketch to characterize these two positions.

Empiricism

Empiricism is the view that *experience* is the only source of knowledge. Special emphasis is given to sensory experience, although some allowance is made too for knowledge derived from intellectual reflections regarding relations among a number of experiences. Furthermore, our concepts or ideas are derived from sense impressions: either they are direct copies of sensory impressions (so-called simple ideas) or they are combinations of several simple ideas or several complex ideas. The sensory impression of an object (say, an orange) is decomposable into a set of sensory qualities—sensations corresponding to its color, smell, size, texture, taste, and so on. These sensory qualities all become connected (or "associated") in the mind because they occur closely together in time or in space as we interact with the object. The idea of an orange is then a complex one, but is reducible to interassociations among a bundle of more primitive, simple ideas. Further "knowledge" acquired about oranges can be expressed in terms of associations of this complex to the other relevant ideas—for example, that oranges are fruits, are edible, cost a dime each, and so forth. Such knowledge may be acquired verbally, by someone telling us such facts; still, the linguistic device of predication is supposedly analyzable in terms of contiguity of ideas aroused in the mind of the listener.

These beginning remarks suffice to characterize empiricism by the following features: (1) *sensationalism,* the hypothesis that all knowledge is derived through sensory experience; (2) *reductionism,* the thesis that all complex ideas are built up out of a basic stock of simple ideas, and that they are in turn reducible to these primitive elements; (3) *associationism,* the thesis that ideas or mental elements are connected through the action of association by contiguity in experience; and (4) *mechanism,* the belief that the mind is like a machine built out of simple elements with no mysterious components; simple, additive rules will serve to characterize the properties of complex associative configurations by sole use of the properties of the underlying simple ideas.

Learning in Empiricist Doctrines

There are two basic learning assumptions in this approach: (1) internal representations of simple ideas ("memory images") originate by simply *copying* their corresponding sense impressions into the memory store; and (2) complex ideas are formed by connecting together in memory simple ideas that are experienced contiguously; they are connected by an associative bond. The memory that event A was followed immediately by event B is recorded in memory as an association from idea *a* to idea *b*. This is in effect copying into memory the fact of the co-occurrence of mental contents *a* and *b*.

Within the classical empirical philosophy, this law of association was the only mechanism by which knowledge could be acquired. The doctrine was elaborated, fleshed out, and applied to many different cases, primarily by the British philosophers Thomas Hobbes, John Locke, David Hume, James Mill, and his son, John Stuart Mill. For example, David Hume provided a classical "skeptical" analysis of inductive inference, more specifically the premise of causality, in terms of association between mental events. He asserted, for instance, that the only evidence we have that boiling water causes steam (or that any event A causes any event B) is that these events have been seen to occur invariably in this temporal order without exception, so that the *a-b* association is very strong. Probable knowledge and the limits of certainty regarding inductive inferences were explicated in terms of the mind recording (by means of strengths of associations) the relative frequency with which event A tended to be followed by B rather than some other event X.

The Order of Mental Events

Just as association was to be the principle of knowledge acquisition, so was it also presumed to govern the flow of mental contents during thinking or imagination. The ancient philosophers of mind were concerned with accounting for the order of succession of ideas during either idle or goal-directed thinking. Their touchstone again was "records of experience" from memory. To illustrate how old are these basic notions, the following quotations are taken from the book *Human nature,* written by Thomas Hobbes in 1650 (note the year!), and they provide the full flavor of the approach, albeit in Elizabethan English. (Hobbes used *sense* as "sensory impressions," and he used *coherence in sense* to denote contiguity.)

The cause of the coherence or consequence of one conception to another, is their first coherence or consequence at that time when they are produced by sense. . . . The mind may run almost from anything to anything. But as in the sense the conception of cause and effect may succeed one another so may they after sense in the imagination. . . . The remembrance of succession of one thing to another, that is, of what was antecedent and what consequent, and what concomitant, is called an experiment. . . . To have had many experiments, is [what] we call experience, which is nothing else but remembrance of what antecedents have been followed by what consequents. . . . When a man thinketh on anything whatsoever, his next thought after is not altogether so casual as it seems to be. Not every thought to every thought succeeds indifferently. But as we have no imagination, whereof we have not formerly had sense, in whole, or in parts; so we have no transition from one imagination to another, whereof we never had the like before in our senses. The reason whereof is this. All fancies are motions within us, relics of those made in sense: and those motions that immediately succeeded one another in the sense, continue also together after sense.

Hobbes goes on in this passage to distinguish two modes of thought or "mental discourse": (1) unguided, idle reverie wherein conceptions follow one another freely without restrictions; this "stream of consciousness" thinking is easily indulged in by any of us, and can be terribly revealing of our belief structure, which is why the technique is still actively used by Freudian psychoanalysts to have their patients "dredge up" psychodynamically relevant material; and (2) regulated goal-directed thinking, wherein we try to figure out how to achieve some goal (Hobbes said "desire") or how to avoid some feared consequence. Hobbes believed that the goal-representation (e.g., "I want to eat ice cream") called to mind an immediate precursor of it (e.g., "Buy some at the shop"), and that thought in turn brought to mind the cause of that (e.g., "Get money and go to the shop"), and so on, unwinding an effect-to-cause sequence backwards from the goal "till we come to some beginning without our own power," which then initiates action of the thought-out sequence. He saw reason to distinguish only two kinds of regulated thought trains or "seekings"—"a hunting out of the causes of some effect, present or past; or of the effects, of some present or past cause." These, of course, are involved in the psychological activities of, on the one hand, *explaining* why something came about or describing how to bring it about; and, on the other hand, *expecting*, anticipating, or predicting future events, effects, or consequences of a given event or action that is presently occurring.

Reflection

The empiricist John Locke (1690)[1] explicitly included in his account the idea that the mind has the power of "reflection" whereby it can call up from memory several ideas, compare them, arrange them in some logical order, and thence remember that "imaginary" conclusion. The mental phenomena which he felt justified this assumption were those associated with knowledge gained by abstraction, inference, and deduction. In abstraction, we form a general concept of a type of thing (e.g., *boy, whiskey, knife*) from experience with a set of widely varying examples, by "abstracting" the common, cri-

[1] References cited can be found by author and date in the list at the end of the book.

terial attributes of the concept out from the varying accidental, nonessential properties. In modern psychology this process is called either stimulus discrimination, or concept formation, or pattern recognition. Inductive inference is like abstraction but refers more to the search for lawful regularities among series of events or different properties of an event: the regularity or correlation between cause and effect may be obscured in particular cases because of multiply varying, accidental accompaniments of the particular events in particular observations. Thus, one may observe on separate occasions that too much beer-drinking made a teenage boy drunk, wine-drinking made a young girl drunk, whiskey-drinking made a middle-aged man drunk, and gin-drinking made a very old woman drunk. Arrival at the appropriate causal law from memory of these particular instances requires both abstraction (that beer, wine, whiskey, and gin are alcoholic beverages) and correlation of descriptions of contiguous events (namely, "X is sober," then, "X drinks a lot of alcohol" and then "X is drunk"). Locke figured that all such calculations can be carried out in one's head with the faculty of "reflection" poring over the contents of memory. He did not make clear when or why these reflections would take place without explicit questions being put to the mind.

The third job performed by reflection in Locke's mental system is deduction, by which he included deduction of both factual and logical information. As a simple example, I can use the fact that Jim is 6 feet tall and John is 5 feet 10 inches tall to "deduce" the relational fact that Jim is taller than John. More complex examples would be the successive lines or statements in a logical proof sequence, generated while deducing a theorem in geometry, mathematics, or logic. In either case, Locke would suppose that these statements or thoughts obtained by reflection could be stored in memory just as though they were perceptual inputs from the external world. Within the empiricist doctrine of mind, this mechanism is the only means available for freeing the mind from being a totally passive recorder of sequences of sensory impressions.

Empiricism and Experimental Psychology

The following remarks will close this brief review of empiricism as an epistemology and as a philosophy for reconstructing mental life. Empiricism has a very long and rich history which is reviewed in books by Boring (1950), Murphy (1949), and Warren (1921). These tell the developments of associationism over the years. As just one example, considerable attention was given during the 1800s to the question of the laws of association. Assuming contiguity of experienced events to be the necessary and sufficient condition for association-formation, the empiricists proposed that the *degree* of association (or amount of memory) would vary directly with the *vividness* of the experience, its *frequency*, its *duration,* and its *recency* (closeness in time) to the retention test. Such conjectures have generated much experimental research on learning and memory, and every learning theory deals with these factors in one way or another.

Associationism led to the experimental investigation of learning. The first experiments on human memory, by the German scientist Hermann Ebbinghaus (1885), explicitly set out to test certain proposals within associationist doctrine; the first experimental monograph on animal learning, by Edward Thorndike (1898), was titled *Animal intelligence: An experimental study of the associative processes in animals.*

Developments within the American "schools of psychology" over the next 60 years have done little to alter that associationistic approach. Things have become far more precise, of course, and much more detailed information has been accumulated. Also, the important roles of motivation, reward, and punishment in learning and performance have received greater systematic treatment than was accorded them in the classical associationist tradition. The behavioristic revolution, led by John Watson, substituted observable stimuli and responses for the mentalistic ideas and images of the earlier times. But the associationistic cast of the "acquisition mechanism" (or learning device) remained. (These points are developed in greater detail in a recent review by Anderson and Bower [1973].) It is thus fair to say that empiricism and associationism laid down the mold (the rut?) into which contemporary learning theory has flowed and jelled, perhaps even solidified. Unfortunately, there appear to be several basic flaws in the fundamental assumptions of classical associationism, considered either as an epistemology or as a means for reconstructing the contents of mental life. These critiques are brought together in the Anderson and Bower book (Chapters 2 and 3), which should be consulted for details since they cannot be quickly summarized here. The general drift of some of these critiques can be seen by examining the opposing epistemological position, that of Rationalism. We turn now to that topic.

Rationalism

Rationalism is the general philosophical position that reason is the prime source of knowledge, that reason alone rather than authority or spiritual revelation, or intuition, or sense data is the only valid basis for knowledge, belief, and action. Understanding, the comprehension of knowledge from reason, should be the aim of empirical as well as philosophical investigations.

Rationalist philosophers such as Descartes, Leibniz, and Kant confront empiricism at almost every turn of a phrase. First of all, rationalists have an entirely different perspective on the role of "sense data" in our construction of reality. For the empiricist, our ideas are passive copies of sense data. For the rationalist, sense data are unstructured, undifferentiated chaos that only provide raw material to an interpretive mechanism that considers these raw data as clues regarding their probable source and meaning. The raw data can be interpreted only according to certain forms—more precisely, according to certain classes of innate perceptual assumptions with which the mind begins. Regarding these interpretive activities of the mind in dealing with sense data, Immanuel Kant has this to say in his *Critique of pure reason* (1781):

That element in the phenomenon which corresponds to sensation I call the *matter,* while that element which makes it possible that the various determinations of the phenomenon should be arranged in certain ways relative to one another is its *form.* Now, that without which sensatioris can have no order or form cannot itself be sensation. The matter of a phenomenon is given to us entirely *a posteriori*; but its form must be *a priori* in the mind, and hence must be capable of being considered by itself apart from sensation.

In this quotation, Kant uses *a posteriori* to denote things known empirically, and *a priori* to denote things given prior to experience.

What are these forms, these interpretive assumptions? Here, the rationalists differ among themselves, but tend to mention a common class of abstract but "self-evident" truths. One of these is the assumption of "substance," of the substantiality of physical objects. David Hume, the skeptical empiricist, had argued before Kant that we can know a physical object only as a cluster of associated properties (e.g., a candle as wax of a particular shape, weight, texture, color, and odor). But the rationalists would argue that our *a priori* (or *innate*) makeup projects the notion of physical object into that array of particular qualities—the substance is the thing which possesses these various qualities, which holds them together. The substance will still maintain its ideal identity despite certain changes in the properties (e.g., the same piece of wax melted down to a liquid).

The Temporal-Spatial Framework

Another example of an *a priori* interpretive assumption is that events always come to us embedded in a temporal-spatial framework: physical events (and even most things we call "mental events") occur at a particular time and at a particular place—or, at least, we cannot prevent ourselves from interpreting them in that way. Kant and Descartes thought that our *a priori* knowledge of space was simply the projection onto the world of the "self-evident truths" of Euclidean geometry with which we were born; Kant would have none of Bishop Berkeley's earlier empiricistic attempt to *derive* the perception of depth (of objects in three dimensions) from empirical correlations between sensations on the two-dimensional retina and the sense of touch (e.g., reaching the hand to the object in view). This issue still absorbs the interest of psychologists studying perceptual development (see T. G. R. Bower, 1965, 1966; Gibson, 1969; Hochberg, 1964), and recent evidence appears rather to favor the "innate" hypothesis regarding depth perception.

Another *a priori* for Kant is the presupposition of causality of recurrent events in the temporal-spatial manifold. This is such a basic hypothesis that our very perceptual interpretation of the world "projects" causality into observations of temporal succession of events. Again, modern experiments by Michotte (1954) suggest that causality is as much a salient perceptual relation as are relations like *brighter than, to the left of,* or *taller than.*

Perceptual Organization and Relations

A general criticism that rationalists have leveled against classical empiricism is that the empiricist theory of perception provides an inadequate account of the unitariness of percepts and the role that relations play in creating perceptual unities. The relations among elementary sense points are just as primary and psychologically vivid as the sensa themselves; we do not hear a series of tones but a coherent melody (based on successive sense ratios); we do not see a particular brightness but the ratio of reflectances between a spot and its surround; we do not see successive stills of an object's changing locations but its "continuous motion" through visual space. The color of an object "adheres" or sticks to its surface as an inalienable property of a unity: we do not sense "redness" and "apple," but rather the attributive unity of "a red apple." Gestalt psychology, reviewed in Chapter 8, began as a revolt against the elementaristic and reductionist analyses of perceptual experience provided by classical empiricism. The Gestalters supposed that perceptual experience revealed "emergent" properties (e.g., apparent motion) not derivable from additive combinations of the properties of its elements (e.g., sequences of stills). Perceptions were said to become *organized* according to certain laws of segmentation, relational grouping, and simplicity; perceptual processes were said to seek out "good forms" and to impose such organizations and interpretations upon chaotic or amorphous "matter," to use Kant's term. These issues will be clarified in our later discussion of Gestalt theory, but the important point now is that Gestalt psychology really began as a brand of philosophical rationalism.

Rationalism and the Order of Mental Events

In its attack upon associationism as a doctrine of mental contents, rationalism has been eminently successful (see Anderson & Bower, 1973; De Groot, 1965; Duncker, 1945; Mandler & Mandler, 1964). For one thing, it is clear that "associations" between ideas carry with them information regarding the *type of relation* involved. For example, in our mind a restaurant is associated with eating, a glutton with eating, a fork with eating, and a steak with eating. But the unadorned "associative link" of the classical doctrine does not explain our knowing that the relation between the first pair of ideas is that of *location* to action, the second pair of *actor* to action, the third pair of *instrument* to action, and the fourth pair of *object* to act. The mind requires a representation of knowledge wherein interassociated ideas are *labeled* according to their type: for example, that *animal* is labeled as a superordinate of *bird*, that *canary* is a subordinate, that *wings* or *feathers* are possessive properties of *birds*, and that *sings* or *flies* are possible actions of birds. Such labeling seems utterly necessary in order to direct efficient searches through memory for information that meets certain requirements. For instance, it is not clear, according to classical associationist principles, how the associationists' mental apparatus could have answered questions like "What has relation R to concept X?" (e.g., "What is an instance of a bird?"). If associations are tagged with relational labels, then restricted searches and retrievals are possible. This point was made explicitly by Selz in 1927. Ach (1905) had earlier made the point that the direction of associations can be determined by background instructions stating general goals (e.g., "Give me the opposite association of each word—up-*down*, left-*right*,

tall-*short* . . .'') and that after a short while these "determining tendencies'''
became unconscious and automatic, and were not a conscious element in the
associative process as it operated on the stimulus words (taking *heavy* into
light and so on).

Well-Formedness Conditions on the Input

A further criticism regards the lack of structural organization imposed
upon incoming perceptual data by the associative theory of the mind. That
is, the theory provided no restrictions or constraints on what could be associated with what; there were no inherent principles for determining the
"belongingness" of items of experience (see Thorndike's treatment of "belongingness" in Chapter 2), no restrictions regarding "well-formedness" of
input structures. If Locke's hypothetical mind heard the word salad "Colorless ideas wailingly green in suitcase our snooze," it would patiently begin
associating the idea of *colorless* to that of *ideas,* and that complex in turn to
wailingly, thence to *green,* and so forth. Why? Because the theory has no
mechanism which shouts "Garbage!" and refuses to operate on ill-formed
inputs. The illustration is from grammar (or rather, ungrammaticality), but
it applies as well to the structuring of perceptual input. The Gestalters, as
did the rationalists before them, were arguing for well-formedness conditions—that the perceptual mechanisms organize the sense data into certain
groupings which are in turn organized into hierarchical structures. For
instance, the perceptual apparatus applied to a visual scene would yield a
segmentation and hierarchical description in terms of clusters of objects
in particular spatial relations, the clusters decomposable into individual
objects and their interrelations, and the individual objects in turn describable in terms of their locations, contours, and properties. Such a hierarchical
description was beyond classical associationist principles for several reasons
—not the least of which was that Locke et al. had no way to represent
abstractly any arbitrary collection of objects in order to predicate something
about ("comment upon") that collection. The issue of constraints on well-
formedness is brought out by Katz, a modern linguistic philosopher writing
on the empiricism-rationalism debate:

The basis for the controversy is not, as it is often conceived in popular discussions, that empiricists fail to credit the mind with any innate principles, but rather
that the principles which are accorded innate status by empiricists do not place
any substantive restrictions on the ideas that can qualify as components of complex
ideas or any formal restrictions on the structure of associations which bond component ideas together to form a complex idea. On the empiricist hypothesis, the
innate principles are purely combinatorial devices for putting together items from
experience. So these principles provide only the machinery for instituting associative bonds. Experience plays the selective role in determining which ideas may be
connected by association, and principles of association are, accordingly, unable to
exclude any ideas as, in principle, beyond the range of intellectual acquisition.
(1966, pp. 240–241)

Katz is giving the rationalist's critique, that "raw experience" plus associative learning principles are not sufficient to prevent the accumulation of a

disorganized mass of accidental vagaries that collapse in a booming, buzzing chaos of overwhelming particulars. Rather, certain "constraints" must be imposed (as innate forms or principles) in interpreting events; only hypotheses of particular forms are acceptable by the human mind.

Language Acquisition: A Rationalist's Example

Nowhere is this advanced more vigorously than in certain modern accounts of first-language acquisition by children. Linguists such as Chomsky (1972), Katz (1966), Lenneberg (1967), and McNeill (1970) argue that empiricistic assumptions are simply inadequate in principle to account for the learning of linguistic competence shown by any native speaker of a language. The language learner must learn an apparently fantastically complex and abstract set of rules for transforming strings of speech sounds into meanings, and vice versa. Modern analyses of linguistic competence illustrate just how abstract are the grammatical rules that the speaker exemplifies in his dealings with language—in judging the grammaticality of utterances, the synonymity of two utterances, the ambiguities of an utterance, and transformational equivalents of a complex proposition. The problem for the empiricist is that this abstract and complex competence at language seems to be learned more or less uniformly by all children at about the same age level, with relatively little variation in basic grammatical competence (ignoring dialects). The problem is further compounded by the fact that recordings of adult utterances to a preverbal child (his input evidence) show an egregious frequency of halts, slips, grammatical mistakes, fragmentary utterances, hems-and-haws, changing of sentence in mid-utterance, and utter nonsense. In short, from a grammatical point of view the speech input to the child is noisy slop. Moreover, the parent-as-trainer tends to react to the child's utterance according to its truth or falsity rather than its approximation to good grammar. A typical scenario is: "Daddy went store?" "No, he went to the office"; "Daddy office?" "Yes, that's right: Daddy office."

The paradox is how our linguistic competence, which seems characterized by this very abstract set of grammatical rules, could ever be learned from such sloppy linguistic inputs. In rejecting empiricist accounts, Chomsky (1972) argues that the child must begin life innately endowed with a small set of *linguistic universals* as regards both some basic concepts and some basic principles. Examples of basic concepts would be the twenty-odd distinctive features of speech-sounds (see Jakobson, Fant, & Halle, 1963), out of which all known languages compose their vocabulary; or the grammatical concepts of sentence and of subject and predicate; or the principles that distinguish deep ("logical") structure of an utterance from its surface phonological (sound) form, or the principles that constrain the class of grammatical transformations that relate deep and surface structures (see Chomsky, 1972, for discussions of these terms). Similar components—concepts and rules—are found in all natural languages studied so far: they appear *universal* to human languages. The theory is that this universal grammar is part of the child's innate endowment, that it provides an interpretive schema to which any particular language must conform. Chomsky states this argument as follows:

. . . it seems that knowledge of a language—a grammar—can be acquired only by an organism that is "preset" with a severe restriction on the form of grammar. This innate restriction is a precondition, in the Kantian sense, for linguistic experience, and it appears to be the critical factor in determining the course and result of language learning. The child cannot know at birth which language he is to learn, but he must know that its grammar must be of a predetermined form that excludes many imaginable languages. Having selected a permissible hypothesis, he can use inductive evidence for corrective action, confirming or disconfirming his choice. Once the hypothesis is sufficiently well confirmed, the child knows the language defined by this hypothesis; consequently, his knowledge extends enormously beyond his experience and, in fact, leads him to characterize much of the data of experience as defective and deviant. (1972, p. 91)

Chomsky makes no pretense of having discovered a full set of linguistic universals (see Greenberg, 1962) or of having provided the details of how specific linguistic hypotheses are formulated (in what language?) and tested. He does argue, however, that such a framework has much more chance of advancing our understanding of language acquisition than the empiricist-associationist account, which has impressed him and other linguists as simply false.

Final Comments on Rationalism

Here, then, we have specific examples of rationalism and their persuasive force. As Kant (1781, p. 1) wrote: "Although all our knowledge begins *with* experience, it by no means follows that it all originates *from* experience." For real knowledge it is necessary to presuppose a certain framework of thought relationships over and above the raw sense data. For Descartes, self-evident truths having little relation to sensory experience must be inherent in the mind; we do not learn them through the senses, but perceive them instinctively because they have been part of our mental equipment from birth. The rationalist theory of knowledge says, then, that it is not Nature which imposes its necessary truths upon us; it is we who project laws onto Nature. The truths of the rationalist are not revelations of existence regarding a world beyond the senses; they reveal, instead, our own intellectual makeup. They provide the framework and the forms of experience, as over against its contents. You may ask, How did the mind come to acquire these innate structures that one is led to attribute to it? Either one can answer, "Natural selection," on the premise that the mind is the way it is because it helps the individual adapt to the way the world truly is (less fortunate innate endowments having been crushed in the juggernaut of biological evolution); or one can answer at a deeper level that the exact processes by which the innate organization of the human organism evolved are a total mystery.

Rationalism, Empiricism, and Modern Learning Theory

The foregoing discussion of empiricism and rationalism provides valuable background for comparing and classifying modern learning theories. All behavioristic theories of learning are also associationistic: they include those of Thorndike, Pavlov, Guthrie, Hull, Skinner, and the school of functionalism. These schools developed out of the combination of associationism with hedonism.[2] Gestalt psychology and the newer information-processing approaches to psychology are clearly at the rationalist end of the spectrum, as is modern "cognitive psychology" and psycholinguistics. Tolman's brand of cognitive psychology straddles the fence on several important matters. Mathematical psychology, at least stimulus-sampling theory, is empiricistic, although nothing inherent in the use of quantitative theories requires that orientation.

Before moving on, however, we would be well advised to return to the central topic of this chapter, namely, learning, and begin to stake out some of the important distinctions that have grown up around this concept. Concept formation in science progresses by drawing distinctions and classifying cases, and so it is with the concept of learning. Necessarily, too, some terminology ("jargon") accompanies these distinctions, but these do not extend much beyond usage familiar to the average layman.

CHARACTERIZATION OF LEARNING

Learning, as we noted before, is often concerned with the acquisition of knowledge. Let us think for a moment about what that means. *Acquisition* refers basically to a *change* in "possession"; at one time, the organism did not "possess" a given bit of knowledge; at a later time, it did. What caused that acquisition? At a minimum, something had to happen to the organism to change its state of knowledge. Typically we suppose that the organism had some specific experience which caused or was in some way related to the change in its knowledge state—either the world put some sensory information into it, or it may have tried out some action and observed the consequences, or it may have thought out a proof of Fermat's last theorem, or any number of other events.

What is the nature of the knowledge that the organism learns? This can be fantastically varied—as different as there are different ways of knowing and different things to be known. The simplest knowledge in memory is merely a biographical "event record": an event of a particular description occurred to me at such-and-such a time in such-and-such a place. This is frequently misphrased as storage of a "copy" of sensory experiences (*that* metaphor is so old even Plato used it) or an internal description of an event. One problem (among several) with the copy, or "image," theory of memory is that in remembering a scene, one usually sees *himself* as an actor in the scene—which, of course, could not have been the sense impression he experienced on that occasion. Perhaps it is better to say merely that the organism can be conceived of as "storing a description" of the event that

2 In the seventeenth and eighteenth centuries, there actually was a great deal of thought regarding human interests, values, and motivations as reasons for action. This is connected with developments in utility theory (see Bernoulli, 1738; Bentham, 1789) as extensions of the doctrine of *hedonism*, which asserts that each individual is motivated by the desire for pleasures and by aversion from pain and deprivation. Modern learning theories like Hull's (Chapter 6) can be regarded as the offspring of the intellectual traditions of associationism and hedonism.

occurred. Typical events might be "My dog Spot bit the postman," "Henry laughed last," or "The word *pencil* was presented to me by the experimenter." In the make-believe world of talking animals, Pavlov's dog might say to itself, "The bell was followed by food" and the giant axon of a squid might say, "Irritation of my nerve ending is followed by a hell of a shock." Suppose that such event descriptions are stored in memory: although they are not profound items of wisdom, they are nonetheless bits of knowledge about the world of our organism; its memoirs have a new entry.

So the experience causes a change in the state of knowledge. Does it always? Well, no; not always: we know the organism might have "failed" to learn for any number of reasons—perhaps he was not paying attention when the event occurred. So perhaps we had better relax the conditions to say that the experience *may* cause (probably causes) a change in the state of knowledge.

But Doubting Thomas asks: how do you know that your subject has changed his state of knowledge? Good question: how can you tell what somebody knows? Well, you could ask him: "Ahh, please sir, would you mind telling us everything you know?" If the subject is a college professor, you will get no end of blather (sometime next week you'll have forgotten what the question was); if it's the giant axon of a squid, a deadly silence answers back. The question was poorly framed: you want rather to know whether the subject's knowledge about a *specific* event has changed as a result of a specific experience. So you try to frame specific questions—or specific "retrieval cues" as we say. You ask: What did Spot do? Who laughed last? What word was presented to you by the experimenter a few moments ago? What event follows the bell? What follows axonal irritation?

After asking the question, you wait for the subject to answer. How? He responds: he says something, nods his head, licks his chops, or flexes his stomach muscles. Question, answer; stimulus, response. From his response, we *infer* whether or not he has available the specific information of interest —or, at least, we find out whether our question gains access to that stored information. The word *infer* is used advisedly; whether or not somebody possesses a bit of information is not uniformly guaranteed either by our having presented the information to him or by his saying that he knows it (he could be lying or mistaken or have misunderstood the question). So we infer someone's knowledge from inputs to him and outputs from him, and we *infer* learning caused by an experience because of before-to-after changes in his inferred knowledge.

We may summarize our discussion by the sequence of events charted in Table 1.1.[3] This isolates the important happenings within a single learning trial, going from a possible pretest through presentation of the information to be remembered, and trace formation, through retention, to retrieval and utilization of the stored information. We speak of the "memory trace" as being whatever is the internal representation of the specific information stored at time 2 in Table 1.1. The experiencing and new knowledge state at times 2 and 3 are usually relegated to "perception," whereas memory, or

---

[3] Tables and figures have double numbers, the first referring to the chapter number and the second to the figure or table within the chapter.

Table 1.1 **Flow chart of the important events within a trial and inferred states of the subject's knowledge. The terms at the right are the labels psychologists use to refer to the theoretical processes going on at particular times during this sequence. S and E refer to the subject and the environment (or experimenter), respectively.**

Time	Inferred States and Events	Psychologist's Labels
0	S's prior state of knowledge	"Pretest"
1	E presents Event X to S	
2	S experiences Event X	Trace formation (Acquisition)
3	S's new state of knowledge	
•		
•		Trace retention
•		
n	S's "altered" state of knowledge	
n+1	E cues S to test S's knowledge	Trace retrieval
n+2	S answers or responds	Trace utilization

(handwritten margin notes: "perception (2–3)"; "memory or retention (3–N)")

"retention," of the perceived information is tested after the retention interval spanning time 3 to time n. In different experiments, this interval can vary from several seconds to several years; when this interval is varied, we may be said to be studying *"forgetting."* What is forgetting? That's simply your failing to remember something on a current test when we had reason to believe that you knew the information earlier. Different other events can be presented to the subject (are said to be "interpolated") during the retention interval from time 3 to time n; if we vary these and notice how retention of the original target item is affected, we are said to be studying "interference" effects on retention.

At time $n+1$ we test the subject's retention by presenting one or more "retrieval cues" which act as questions whose purpose is to assess what the subject knows about the target item. Trace retrieval is the process by which the test cue gains access to the information the subject has stored about a given target item. The test cue can come in a variety of forms, can even be systematically altered from the "natural" cue for the target information. At the simplest level we may ask a human subject to describe or name the to-be-remembered event, or to recognize its recurrence. At a more complex level, say with propositional material, we may ask for meaningful paraphrases of the learned proposition, for use of it in an argument, or any of a number of other "behaviors" we take as illustrating comprehension of a text. Experiments which systematically vary the retrieval cue are said to be studying either "stimulus generalization" or "transfer of training." The transfer notion refers to the fact that the knowledge the subject acquires in one task may be found to be useful in a second task, so that that knowledge would appear to have been "transferred" and applied to the second task. Of course, transfer may be detrimental ("negative") insofar as earlier learning may go against and interfere with new learning. Analysis of specific cases is required.

A final terminological note as to the terms *repetition* and *practice*: we may present the same information repeatedly to the subject, and he may practice remembering it many times over. Successive repetitions of the same event are typically separated by several minutes and by presentations of other information to be learned. Elementary conditioning experiments with animals may use several hundred "trials," on each of which two events occur in temporal contiguity (e.g., the sounding of a bell to Pavlov's dog, then its eating of food placed in its mouth). In such animal experiments, of course, the experimenter measures some response (like amount of saliva) made to the retrieval cue (the bell), which is considered to be a reliable index of the animal's knowledge of the temporal order of events (that bell is followed by food). A behaviorist would not describe matters this way: he would say that it is the response itself which is learned to the bell rather than some knowledge about the temporal order of events. But that is a matter to be discussed much later.

The text surrounding Table 1.1 provides a preliminary characterization of learning events and their terminology. But the characterization is actually incomplete because there are other learning activities which seem not fully captured by the description in Table 1.1. The main class of these has to do with the learning of *skills*, perceptual-motor skills as well as intellectual skills. Examples of skills are typewriting, swimming, bicycling, grading term papers, writing poetry, evaluating the relevance of possible evidence for a hypothesis, drawing facsimiles, constructing a proof-picture in plane geometry, piano playing, brushing your teeth properly, and so on and on. Most skilled activities are in fact a vast set of interrelated component responses (consider typing as an example; seeing or thinking "M" gets translated into striking a particular key); we may suppose that practice provides feedback information for all of these components. In the case of skills, we describe the person's (or animal's) knowledge in terms of his *knowing how* to do something rather than his being able to describe events to us. The remembering is exemplified in the performance. One can well imagine how an early and excessive concern with motor skills learning could lead a psychologist into behavioristic biases, where "having learned" means "being able to do it well." More intellectual skills (e.g., organizing a speech to be given) do not lend themselves at all to such seductions. An important point to make about intellectual skills is that, once acquired, they have the power to enhance the learning capability of the subject beyond what he had before he acquired the skill (e.g., consider reading as one such skill). This is part of the cumulative nature of knowledge and illustrates how the intellect can bootstrap itself into encyclopedic proportions. The mental encyclopedia of most adults includes not only vast amounts of particular facts but also many theoretical question-answering or problem-solving schemas which can be applied profitably to large classes of problems, all these along with a vast array of efficient procedures or skilled "action-recipes" for how to produce certain types of results or achieve certain types of outcomes. But we digress; more on such matters later (Chapter 13).

A POSSIBLE DEFINITION OF LEARNING

To return, then, to our beginning problem of characterizing learning, experimenters working with animals or nonverbal humans need some kind of working definition of learning which does not require verbal instructions, verbal questions, and verbal answers. They obviously have to observe some kind of overt behavior of the animal, presumably one indexing the specific learning for him. Framing such an operational definition turns out to be rather a difficult business. A peculiar but nonetheless serviceable one is the following:

Learning refers to the change in a subject's behavior to a given situation brought about by his repeated experiences in that situation, provided that the behavior change cannot be explained on the basis of native response tendencies, maturation, or temporary states of the subject (e.g., fatigue, drugs, etc.).

The definition has the import of allowing an inference regarding "learning" only when a case cannot be made for another explanation. It does not state sufficient conditions for learning, since some cases of repeated experience with a situation do not produce much in the way of observable changes in responses. But let us go on to consider some of the behavioral changes that are excluded by this provisional definition.

NATIVE RESPONSE TENDENCIES VERSUS LEARNING

The older catalogs of native or innate behavior usually included among unlearned activities the reflexes (such as pupillary constriction to light), the tropisms (such as a moth's dashing into a flame), and the instincts (such as a bird's nest-building). We may continue to acknowledge such activities as characteristic of various species, and those more nearly idiosyncratic to one species as *species-specific*. The concept of instinct has been the most controversial of these terms, partly because of a vagueness of connotation, partly because of a tendency to use the word as explanatory, hence as a cloak for ignorance.

Such species-specific behavior is said to be innate, meaning that its form is set down in the nervous system of all members of that species independent in some ways from experience. But it turns out to be very difficult to classify behaviors as altogether innate or altogether learned. One finds that expression of some so-called instinctive behavior depends very much upon variations in experience or learning (Beach, 1955; Hinde & Tinbergen, 1958; Hinde, 1966). For example, the development and expression of sexual behavior or of maternal behavior in monkeys depends critically upon the young monkey's having "normal" contacts with its mother and "normal" opportunities for play with age mates (see Harlow & Harlow, 1966; Sackett, 1967). The development of the characteristic song of many species of birds depends upon the young bird's hearing that song during its early life (see Marler, 1970; Nottebohm, 1970). For instance, the development of the song of the chaffinch or of the white-crown sparrow appears to be as follows: during its first springtime of life, the young male must be exposed to the singing of males of its species, although the young bird does not itself sing during this time. During the mating season the following year the young bird (even if now in total isolation) begins to sing: his initial songs are of rather poor quality and phrasing, but are nonetheless recognizable as the song dialects of the males of his species. But the really fascinating result is this: by sheer practice alone, plus listening to himself, the young bird comes eventually to sing a very good reproduction of the older birds' song. The puzzle is how can this bird, in total isolation, improve the match between his singing and the model he heard a year ago? Apparently we must suppose that something like a memory record is made of a genetically selected song, and that the stored record can serve the following year as a template and an "internal tutor" for correcting the initial poor-quality productions of the young bird, by the bird's comparing its feedback from singing with the stored template. But what an utterly astounding accomplishment for a mere bird-brain!

Another illustration of the in-between nature of behavior with large instinctive components stems from the experiments on imprinting (e.g., Lorenz, 1952; Hess, 1958). A young duckling, for example, is prepared instinctively to accept a certain range of mother-figures, characterized by size, movement, and vocalization. Once such a mother-figure has been accepted and followed about, only this *particular* mother can satisfy the instinctive demand. The selected mother (who may be Professor Lorenz crawling on hands and knees) has become imprinted, and is the only "mother" the duckling will follow. Imprinting is then a form of learning, but a form very closely allied to the instinctive propensities of a particular kind of organism of a particular age. (We lack at present clear evidence for imprinting except in fowls.) The task of distinguishing between the instinctive and learned components of the behavior illustrated by imprinting is an experimental problem, depending for its clarification upon the ingenuity of the experimenter in designing appropriate control experiments.

Students of ethology, the study of natural behaviors of species in their natural habitats, have cast off the "innate versus learned" distinction as an exclusive "either-or" affair; the received opinion is that it is a poorly framed distinction. Behavior and its development are simply too complex to be sliced up by such an artificial category. Ethologists strive rather for analysis and understanding of the various components of a given species-specific pattern and how it develops out of experimental interactions. The innate constitution of the animal, like Kantian *a priori* forms, imposes a slight selective bias to develop in certain ways given the "standard normal" form of stimulation for that species, but the bias can be overridden by extreme variations in environmental stimulation.

Maturation versus Learning

Growth is learning's chief competitor as a modifier of behavior. If a behavior sequence matures through regular stages irrespective of intervening practice, the behavior is said to develop through maturation and not through learning. If training procedures do not speed up or modify the behavior, such procedures are not causally important and the changes do not classify as learning. Relatively pure cases such as the swimming of tadpoles and the flying of birds can be attributed primarily to maturation. However, as indicated before, many activities are not as clear-cut, but develop through a complex interplay of maturation and learning. A convenient illustration is the development of language in the child. The child does not learn to talk until old enough, but that development depends critically upon appropriate stimulation from his verbal community at the critical times. The "wolf children" found in the wilds or babies brutally locked in attics for years have no language and develop rudimentary and primitive forms only very slowly by patient tutoring (see Itard, 1932; Lenneberg, 1967).

Fatigue and Habituation versus Learning

It has been common practice to distinguish motor fatigue or sensory habituation from learning proper. Let us describe these phenomena and then come back to the distinction. When a motor act is repeated in rapid succession, there is often a loss in efficiency—it becomes slower and weaker in amplitude until eventually the subject may refuse to perform it. We say the response has suffered "fatigue" or that its performance shows "work decrement." The fatigue occurs faster the greater the effort of the response. Recovery from fatigue occurs mainly as a simple function of "rest time." In terms of sheer performance curves, fatigue and recovery curves look very much like curves of experimental extinction and spontaneous recovery; however, common practice has been to apply the "learning" label to the latter but not to the former case. Why? Because fatigue, unlike extinction of a conditioned reflex, is presumed not to induce enduring and relatively *permanent* changes in the behavior. But a moment's reflection will show this defense is useless, since extinction effects can also be reversed—an extinguished response can be trained, and with little effort. So what is the crucial difference? There really is none as long as we remain solely at the behavioral level of measuring the elicited response. Other information has to be brought into the decision—namely, all those behavioral consequences that would be implied by the descriptions (for the human) that in the one case he stopped "because he was tired" versus, in the other case, he stopped "because he learned that food no longer followed the bell." From the response decrement alone we can not make this decision regarding "hypothetical causes."

Consider a second kind of change, that called *habituation*. Presentation of a stimulus produces a certain perceptual reaction (what Pavlov called the "orienting reflex" or OR). This reaction can be recorded electrically throughout the nervous system. If the stimulus is repeated over and over in a monotonous series, the OR aroused by each presentation becomes less and less, eventually declining to an almost undetectable level.[4] The subject is said to have *habituated* to that stimulus; he has "gotten used to" it. Now, habituation displays many of the same functional properties we ascribe to learning (or to extinction): it dissipates with time (like "forgetting" or "spontaneous recovery"); it is easily disrupted or dishabituated by interpolation of a novel, interfering event; a recovered OR to a stimulus can be habituated again and again, and each time it habituates a little faster than before (like relearnings of a forgotten response); and habituation generalizes to other similar stimuli as a function of their similarity to the habituated stimulus. (Chapter 14 discusses habituation in more detail.) Thus, habituation displays engaging similarities to the dynamic laws of learning.

Do we want to call habituation learning? We equivocate: in some cases, yea; in others, nay. It depends really on the "complexity" of the stimulus to which habituation occurs. If it is an electric shock feeding into a sensori-motor synapse in the spinal cord of a decerebrate ("headless") cat, we would rather label it as sensory adaptation. However, if it is a more complex stimulus (e.g., a tone pattern, a picture) requiring higher brain centers for its discrimination, we would prefer to label it as learning. In these latter cases, habituation seems to index (inversely) the development of internal representations of the stimulus event or of its general class. Habituation of this kind seems to be a crude form of *stimulus recognition,* which probably depends upon the organism's having learned or stored a replica or model of the habituated stimulus. Once the model is formed, the incoming stimulus is compared to it, with dishabituation ("surprise") occurring in case the mismatch between the two is extensive enough. In fact, theories of cortical habituation (see Sokolov, 1963, reviewed in Chapter 3) use just such concepts of internal models and mismatching processes. And surely, we would want to say that stimulus recognition is a result of learning. So habituation is one of those cases that straddle the boundaries of the semantic domain of this loose concept of "learning" we are trying to characterize.

Performance versus Learning Factors

As indicated earlier, learning must always remain an inference from performance, and only confusion results if performance and learning are identified. The concepts of learning versus performance parallel the concepts of disposition versus actualization, of knowing how to do something versus

---

4 Habituation is distinguished from sense-organ *adaptation,* such as that occurring within the retinal cells during light adaptation; or the differential bleaching of color pigments in the retina causing us to see different colors in succession as we stare continuously at a high intensity yellow light (Cornsweet, 1970). In these cases, the reduced or altered responsiveness can be traced directly to changes at the receptor surface.

actually doing it. Performance may fail on a retention test for many reasons other than lack of earlier learning. The topic of motivation or drive is relevant here: motives or drives are supposed to be those psychological factors which are responsible for converting knowledge into action. A rat who knows how to thread his way through a maze to find food at a goal-box may nonetheless be loath to do this if he is currently stuffed with food. He must first be put in an appropriate state of relevant deprivation if he is to show us what he knows. Another illustration is provided by performance under the influence of drugs, intoxicants, or illness. The fact that performance of a learned act fails when the organism is in such a state does not mean that it did not learn originally nor that it has forgotten what it learned. When the normal state has been restored, the performance may return to normal levels without intervening training. Labeling of the drug or the illness or food satiation as a "performance reducer" rather than as an "unlearning" factor seems to depend logically upon the *reversibility* of the effect of the factor. The behavior returns when the organism "comes out from under the influence" of the drug or sickness. If, on the other hand, the original learned behavior could not be recovered after the immediate effects of the drug wear off, then we would say that that drug has some kind of "anti-memory" effect, either blocking the "consolidation" of a memory trace, or destroying the trace, or preventing its expression. In Chapter 14 we review just such literature regarding the anti-consolidation effects of drugs like ether and metrazol.

Definition Not a Major Source of Disagreement between Theories

While it is extremely difficult to formulate a satisfactory definition of learning so as to encompass all the activities and processes we wish to include and to eliminate all those we wish to exclude, the difficulty does not prove to be embarrassing because it is not a source of controversy as between theories. The controversy is over fact and interpretation, not over definition. Everyone realizes that satisfactory definitions really flow from satisfactory scientific theories. Learning is one of those loose, "open-textured" concepts that include a variety of very different species. Some psychologists feel that we should stop using the general label to gather together so many different kinds of effects of experience. However, in casual conversation, it is satisfactory to continue to mean by learning that which conforms to the usual socially accepted meaning that is part of our common heritage. Where distinctions have to be made with greater precision, they can be made through carefully specified types of inference from experiments.

SOME TYPICAL PROBLEMS CONFRONTING LEARNING THEORIES

The preferences of the theorist often lead him to concentrate upon one kind of learning situation to the neglect of the others. His theory is then appropriate to this situation, but becomes somewhat strained in relation to other problems of learning. A comprehensive learning theory ought to answer the questions which an intelligent nonpsychologist might ask about the sorts of learning which are met in everyday life. A few such questions will be listed here, and then used later in appraising the theories different writers present.

1. What are the limits of learning?   Here is raised the question of the capacity to learn, of individual differences among learners of the same species and of unlike species. There are questions not only of persistent differences in capacity, but of change in capacity with age. Who can learn what? Are the limits set at birth? Do people get more or less alike with practice? These are the sorts of questions it is natural to raise.

2. What is the role of practice in learning?   The old adage that practice makes perfect has considerable historical wisdom behind it. Surely one learns to roller skate or to play the piano only by engaging in the activity. But what do we know about practice in detail? Does improvement depend directly on the amount of repetition? If not, what are its conditions? What are the most favorable circumstances of practice? Can repetitive drill be harmful as well as helpful to the learner?

3. How important are drives and incentives, rewards and punishments?   Everybody knows in a general way that learning can be controlled by rewards and punishments, and that it is easier to learn something which is interesting than something which is dull. But are the consequences of rewards and punishments equal and opposite? Is there a difference between intrinsic and extrinsic motives in their effect upon learning? How do goals and purposes affect the process?

4. What is the place of understanding and insight?   Some things are learned more readily if we know what we are about. We are better off as travelers if we can understand a timetable or a road map. We are helpless with differential equations unless we understand the symbols and the rules for their manipulation. But we can form vowels satisfactorily without knowing how we place our tongues, and we can read without being aware of our eye movements. Some things we appear to acquire blindly and automatically; some things we struggle hard to understand and can finally master only as we do understand them. Is learning in the one case different from what it is in the other?

5. Does learning one thing help you learn something else?   This is the problem of formal discipline, as it used to be called, or of transfer of training, to use a more familiar contemporary designation. Some transfer of training must occur or there would be no use in developing a foundation for later learning. Nobody denies that it is easier to build a vocabulary in a language after you have a start in it, or that higher mathematics profits from mastery of basic concepts. The question is really one of how much transfer takes place, under what conditions, and what its nature is.

6. What happens when we remember and when we forget?   The ordinary facts of memory are mysterious enough, but in addition to familiar remembering and forgetting, our memories may play peculiar tricks on us. Some things we wish to remember are forgotten; some things we would be willing to forget continue to plague us. In cases of amnesia there are often gaps in memory, with earlier and later events remembered. Then there are distortions of memory, in which we remember what did not happen, as is so strikingly demonstrated in testimony experiments. What is taking place? What control have we over processes involved?

These six questions will serve as useful ones to ask of each of the major theories. They suffice to illustrate the kinds of questions which give rise to theories of learning.

ISSUES ON WHICH LEARNING THEORIES DIVIDE

The preceding section posed certain common-sense questions about learning on the assumption that a good learning theory should have something to say about each of them. Such questions can be raised before we know anything about actual learning theories. Now we turn, however, to certain issues that have arisen in the formulation of actual theories. By being alerted in this way to what is to follow, we are better prepared for some of the differ ences in flavor that we shall meet as we review one theory after another.

As indicated earlier, the major conceptual division within psychological approaches is that between empiricism and rationalism. A major thesis of empiricism is that learning occurs through contiguous association of events or ideas. This associationistic framework was accepted by almost all learning theories and theorists of the first half of this century: functionalism, Pavlov, Guthrie, Thorndike, Hull, Skinner, and Tolman. The only real opposition was (is) to be found among Gestalt psychologists (Chapter 8), Piaget (Chapter 10), those using the modern information-processing framework (Chapter 13), and those working in contemporary cognitive psychology (last half of Chapter 15). Some recent work (e.g., Anderson & Bower, 1973; Kintsch, 1972; Rumelhart et al., 1972) attempts to synthesize these two approaches.

A second division is one that has been the basis of contention even within associationistic theories, and this is the conflict between *stimulus-response* theories and *cognitive* theories. This division produced much controversy during the "middle years" of learning theory, from approximately 1925 through 1965. The stimulus-response theories and theorists include those mentioned above as being associationistic, except for Tolman, who was the first systematist of cognitive theory. The rationalist theories are all cognitive theories.

General Issues Producing a Cleavage between Stimulus-Response and Cognitive Theories

The cleavages between the theorists of opposing camps are difficult to understand because some of the distinctions which at first seem to contrast sharply later are found to be blurred in the light of subsequent experimental knowledge. All reputable theorists accept a common logic of experimentation, so that disagreements over experimentally obtained facts are readily arbitrated. In the end, all the theorists accept a common body of demonstrated relationships at the factual or descriptive level; any theorist who denied an established fact, a reproducible experimental finding, would stand accused of intellectual dishonesty by his scientific colleagues, and his theories would no longer command respect. The first rule as we judge the relative merits of different theories is this: *all the theorists accept all of the facts.* Some experimental findings are doubted when they are first announced, and the status of findings *as fact* may for a long time be doubted; replications and systematic extensions may be tried. But once the status as fact is established, all accept the fact as true. Hence the differences between two theorists are primarily differences in interpretation. Both theories may fit the facts reasonably well, but the proponent of each theory believes his view to be the more fruitful. We shall be better prepared later on to discuss the ways in which theories are validated or modified after we are acquainted with them in more detail. For the present, we must be prepared to accept the historical truth that opposing theories have great survival value, and that an appeal to the facts as a way of choosing between theories is a very complex process, not nearly as decisive in practice as we might expect it to be.

We may begin by examining three kinds of preferences on which stimulus-response theorists tend to differ from cognitive theorists.

1. "Peripheral" versus "central" intermediaries. Ever since Watson promulgated the theory that thinking was merely the carrying out of subvocal speech movements, stimulus-response theorists have preferred to find response or movement intermediaries to serve as integrators of behavior sequences. Such movement-produced intermediaries can be classified as "peripheral" mechanisms, as contrasted with "central" (ideational) intermediaries. The stimulus-response theorist tends to believe that some sort of chained muscular responses, linked perhaps by fractional anticipatory goal responses, serve to keep a rat running to a distant food-box. The cognitive theorist, on the other hand, more freely infers central brain processes, such as memories or expectations, as integrators of goal-seeking behavior. The differences in preference survive in this case because both kinds of theorists depend upon *inferences* from observed behavior, and the inferences are not directly verified in either case. It is potentially easier to verify tongue movements in thinking than it is to discover a revived memory trace in the brain, but in fact such verification is not offered with the precision necessary to compel belief in the theory. Under the circumstances, the choice between the peripheral and the central explanation is not forced, and favoring one or the other position depends upon more general systematic preferences.

2. Acquisition of habits versus acquisition of cognitive structures. The stimulus-response theorist and the cognitive theorist come up with different answers to the question: what is learned? The answer of the former is "habits"; the answer of the latter is "cognitive structures." The first answer appeals to common sense; we all know that we develop smooth-running skills by practicing them; what we learn is *responses*. But the second answer also appeals to common sense: if we locate a candy store from one starting point, we can find it from another because we "know where it is"; what we learn is *facts*. A smooth-running skill illustrates a learned habit; knowing alternate routes illustrates cognitive structure. If all habits were highly mechanical and stereotyped, variable nonhabitual behavior would force us to admit cognitive structures as part, at least, of what is learned. But the stimulus-response psychologist is satisfied that he can deduce from the laws of habit formation the behavior that the cognitive theorist believes supports his interpretation. Hence we cannot choose between the theories by coming up with "decisive" illustrations of what we learn, for both groups of theorists will offer explanations of all our examples. The competing theories would not have survived thus far had they been unable to offer such explanations.

3. Trial and error versus insight in problem-solving.   When confronted with a novel problem, how does the learner reach solution? The stimulus-response psychologist finds the learner assembling his habits from the past appropriate to the new problem, responding either according to the elements that the new problem has in common with familiar ones, or according to aspects of the new situation which are similar to situations met before. If these do not lead to solution, the learner resorts to trial and error, bringing out of his behavior repertory one response after another until the problem is solved. The cognitive psychologist agrees with much of this description of what the learner does, but he adds interpretations not offered by the stimulus-response psychologist. He points out, for example, that granting all the requisite experience with the parts of a problem, there is no guarantee that the learner will be able to bring these past experiences to bear upon the solution. He may be able to solve the problem if it is presented in one form but unable to solve it if it is presented in another form, even though both forms require the same past experiences for their solution. According to the cognitive theorist, the preferred method of presentation permits a perceptual structuring leading to "insight," that is, to the understanding of the essential relationships involved. The stimulus-response psychologist tends, by preference, to look to the past history of the learner for the sources of solution, while the cognitive psychologist, by preference, looks to the contemporary structuring of the problem. His preference for the past does not require the stimulus-response psychologist to ignore the present structuring of the problem; nor does his preference for the present require the cognitive psychologist to ignore the past.

These three issues—peripheral versus central intermediaries, acquisition of habits versus acquisition of cognitive structures, and trial and error versus insight in problem-solving—give something of the flavor of the differences between these two major families of theories.

Specific Issues Not Confined to the Major Families

Some issues lie outside the conflict between the stimulus-response and the cognitive theories. Thus, two stimulus-response psychologists may differ as to the role of reinforcement in learning, and two cognitive theorists may differ regarding the interpretation of extinction. Four of these issues will suffice to alert us to the many problems that learning theorists face.

1. Contiguity versus reinforcement.   The oldest law of association is that ideas experienced together tend to become associated. This has come down in one form or another to the present day as the principle of association by contiguity, although stimulus-response psychologists describe the association as between stimuli and responses rather than as between ideas. Some theorists have accepted the principle of contiguous association, for example, Guthrie (a stimulus-response psychologist) and Tolman (a cognitive psychologist). Other theorists insist that learning does not take place through contiguity alone, unless there is some sort of reinforcement, some equivalent of reward or punishment.

2. *Extinction of learned responses.*   After a rewarded response is well learned it may be extinguished by letting the response occur repeatedly without reinforcement. A variety of factors related to training conditions are known to systematically influence the persistence with which the organism continues responding during the extinction series. There are several plausible theories of extinction, and they do not divide along "cognitive versus S-R" lines. One plausible theory is that during extinction the animal simply learns to expect no reward, and stops responding because of that expectancy. An alternate theory suggests that nonreward is actually aversive (frustrating) and that it sets up active inhibitory processes which compete with performance of the formerly rewarded response. Both theories have several variants, and both are easily elaborated to handle the major findings regarding extinction.

3. *Learning as jumpwise or by small increments.*   The possibility that learning takes place at its most basic level in all-or-none fashion was early proposed by Guthrie, and it has received support from several sources. The alternative is, of course, that learning takes place gradually, modifications taking place even below threshold, so that several trials may be necessary before the results of learning reach threshold and begin to be revealed in performance. This was Hull's position. The issue, then, is not one between S-R and cognitive psychologists; psychologists within either major camp can take opposing positions on this issue of all-or-none learning.

4. *One or more kinds of learning?*   The contiguity-reinforcement dilemma may be resolved by accepting both learning processes, thus defining two varieties of learning. This solution has appealed to theorists such as Thorndike and Skinner and Mowrer. But these two varieties are not the only possibilities. Perhaps by using the common name "learning" to cover the acquisition of motor skills, the memorization of a poem, the solving of a geometrical puzzle, and the understanding of a period in history, we are deceiving ourselves by looking for basic laws that explain processes that have little in common. We should recognize more than one kind of learning. Tolman at one time pointed to the possibility of seven kinds of learning. Gagné (1970) has argued for similar distinctions.

This brief introduction to three contrasts between stimulus-response theories and cognitive theories, and four issues that are not confined to the two major families, should make it clear that what seem to be diametrically opposed points of view may turn out to be based on differences in preference, each being possible of persuasive statement, and to a point justifiable. We shall have to wait until later to consider how a more unified outlook may eventually be achieved.

The Plan of This Book

The student of learning, conscientiously trying to understand learning phenomena and the laws regulating them, is likely to despair of finding a secure position if opposing points of view are presented as equally plausible, so that the choice between them is made arbitrary. He may fall into a vapid eclecticism, with the general formula, "There's much to be said on all sides."

This is not a necessary outcome of a serious attempt to understand opposing points of view. Science ought to be systematic, not eclectic, but a premature systematic position is likely to be dogmatic and bigoted just as an enduring eclecticism is likely to be superficial and opportunistic. It is possible to have systematization of knowledge as the goal without permitting the desire for system to blind the seeker to the truths unearthed by those with views unlike his own.

Throughout the chapters that follow, in presenting, one after the other, a variety of systematic positions with illustrative experiments testing their assertions, the effort is made to show that there is something to be learned from each of them. Each has discovered phenomena which move us forward in our knowledge about learning. At the same time, no one has succeeded in providing a system invulnerable to criticism. The construction of a fully satisfactory theory of learning continues as an uncompleted task. But this is in the nature of science. The only completed research field is a dead one.

SUPPLEMENTARY READINGS

General sources on the psychology of learning:
BUGELSKI, B. R. (1956) *The psychology of learning.*
DEESE, J., & HULSE, S. H. (1967) *The psychology of learning* (3rd ed.).
GAGNÉ, R. M. (1970) *The conditions of learning* (2nd ed.).
HALL, J. F. (1966) *The psychology of learning.*
HALL, J. F. (1971) *Verbal learning and retention.*
KIMBLE, G. A. (1961) *Hilgard and Marquis' conditioning and learning* (2nd ed.).
KINTSCH, W. (1970) *Learning, memory, and conceptual processes.*
McGEOCH, J. A., & IRION, A. L. (1952) *The psychology of human learning* (rev. ed.).

Contrasting points of view toward learning:
ANDERSON, J. R., & BOWER, G. H. (1973) *Human associative memory.*
ESTES, W. K., KOCH, S., MacCORQUODALE, K., MEEHL, P. E., MUELLER, C. G., JR., SCHOENFELD, W. N., & VERPLANCK, W. S. (1954) *Modern learning theory.*
GOLDSTEIN, H., KRANTZ, D. L., & RAINS, J. D. (1965) *Controversial issues in learning.*
HILL, W. F. (1971) *Learning: A survey of psychological interpretations* (rev. ed.).
KOCH, S. (Ed.) (1959) *Psychology: A study of a science.* Vol. 2.
MARX, M. H. (Ed.) (1963) *Theories in contemporary psychology.*

The *Annual Review of Psychology*, appearing first in 1950, each year reviews critically the current experimental and theoretical literature on learning. The reviews are valuable not only as indexes to the literature but also for the trends in experiment and theory detected by the reviewers.

The psychology of learning and motivation: Advances in research and theory, edited by G. H. Bower, has been published annually in a series since 1967; each volume contains numerous research chapters written by eminent learning theorists (of all persuasions) reviewing their own and others' research centered around some general topic in learning or motivation.

Thorndike's Connectionism

For nearly half a century one learning theory dominated all others in America, despite numerous attacks upon it and the rise of its many rivals. It is the theory of Edward L. Thorndike (1874–1949), first announced in his *Animal intelligence* (1898). Its preeminence was aptly assessed by Tolman:

> The psychology of animal learning—not to mention that of child learning—has been and still is primarily a matter of agreeing or disagreeing with Thorndike, or trying in minor ways to improve upon him. Gestalt psychologists, conditioned-reflex psychologists, sign-gestalt psychologists—all of us here in America seem to have taken Thorndike, overtly or covertly, as our starting point. (1938, p. 11)

The basis of learning accepted by Thorndike in his earliest writings was association between sense impressions and impulses to action (responses). Such an association came to be known as a "bond" or a "connection." Because it is these bonds or connections between sense impressions and responses which become strengthened or weakened in the making and breaking of habits, Thorndike's system has sometimes been called a "bond" psychology or simply "connectionism." As such, it is the original stimulus-response or S-R psychology of learning.

While more recent versions of S-R psychology have reduced the prominence given to Thorndike's interpretations of learning, it must not be supposed that his views are of historical interest only, for they continue to influence much recent experimentation. Nearly a quarter of a century after Tolman made the statement just quoted, Postman, another active worker in the field of learning, had this to say:

> The picture of the learning process which Thorndike sketched more than fifty years ago is still very much on the books. No comprehensive theory of human learning can afford to ignore the heritage left to us by Thorndike. (1962, p. 397)

Connectionism before 1930

There were few changes in Thorndike's theory between 1898 and 1930. During these years Thorndike devoted himself largely to applications of his established theory to problems of educational social importance. Because of the stability of the concepts during these years, it is possible to select any one of Thorndike's many publications to serve as a guide to his theory. The major work, from which most of the quotations in what follows have been taken, is the three-volume *Educational psychology* (1913–1914), which represents the system at the height of its popularity.

The most characteristic form of learning of both lower animals and man was identified by Thorndike as trial-and-error learning, or, as he preferred to call it later, learning by selecting and connecting. In this paradigmatic situation, the learner is confronted by a problem situation in which he has to reach a goal such as escape from a problem-box or attainment of food. He does this by selecting the appropriate response from a number of possible responses. A trial is defined by the length of time (or number of errors) involved in a single reaching of the goal. Thorndike's earliest experiments were of this kind, done chiefly with cats, although some experiments with dogs, fish, and monkeys were included (1898, 1911).[1] When Thorndike began his early work, a very common explanation for animal "intelligence" was that the animal would "think through" or reason to a solution of a problematical situation. The literature of comparative psychology at that time was filled with anecdotes (about pet dogs and cats) which were presumed to show that animals would reason and deliberate before choosing that act which fulfilled their purposes.

Thorndike despised such theorizing about animal behavior; he viewed it as a shoddy kind of anthropomorphic projection of the layman's mentalistic concepts into the mind of the beast, giving one the smug satisfaction of having explained something when in fact only a fanciful analogy had been drawn. Like a true mechanist of his day, Thorndike sought to provide a *mechanistic* account of animal learning, one that could be stated in terms of elementary events and operations which were not more complex than the behavior they were supposed to explain. For instance, deliberate reasoning is not an elementary concept, but requires analysis into simpler terms. As Thorndike says (1898, p. 39), he began his work "to give the *coup de grace* to the despised theory that animals reason."

The typical experiment is one in which a hungry cat is placed in a confining box such as that shown in Figure 2.1, which is reproduced from Thorndike's very first paper (1898). Some sort of unlatching device—a loop of wire, a handle, a knob—would be mounted inside the box; when it was manipulated, the door would fall open, permitting the animal to escape confinement and get a bite of food just outside the door. In Thorndike's analysis, the interior of the problem-box constitutes the "stimulus situation"; to this stimulus situation, the animal would bring a repertoire of possible behaviors or responses it would try out in attempting to escape from the box. Thus, typically the initial trials would be characterized by much irrele-

---

[1] When years only are given, the name of the author can be understood from the context.

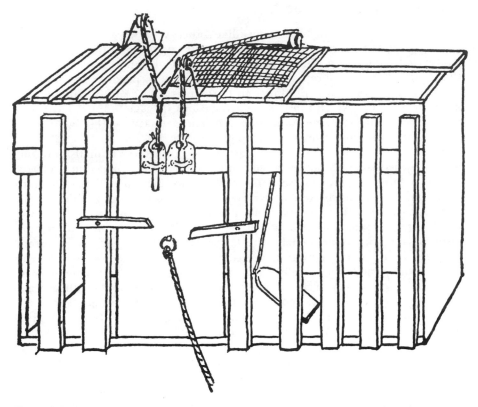

Figure 2.1.   Drawing of one of Thorndike's puzzle-boxes. The animal would be confined inside. The door could be opened if the animal pulled on a latch mounted inside the box. (From E. L. Thorndike, Animal Intelligence, *Psychol. Rev. Monogr.* Supple. 2, No. 8, 1898. Copyright 1898 by the American Psychological Association. Printed by permission.)

vant, unsuccessful behavior—a great amount of clawing, biting, rubbing, vocalizing, dashing about, clinging to the ceiling, etc., before the door latch would be tripped, in almost an "accidental" fashion. The performance score recorded was the amount of time elapsed before the animal performed the correct response and escaped. Initially, these times are very high due to so much random, irrelevant behavior. However, on succeeding trials the time scores get lower, but slowly and irregularly. This gradual learning is typically graphed as a "learning curve," with "time elapsed before successful response" plotted on the vertical axis and successive practice trials on the horizontal axis. Such response time curves typically show high values initially, declining to low, relatively stable values near the end of 10 or 20 practice trials.

It was this gradualness which suggested to Thorndike that the cat does not really "catch on" to the method for escaping, but learns it instead by the gradual stamping in of correct responses and stamping out of incorrect responses. For Thorndike, the important point was that the gradual stamping in of rewarded responses and stamping out of unsuccessful ones was an automatic, *mechanistic* explanation for the change in the animal's performance from the early to the later trials of training. No great intelligence was required to mediate such mechanistic learning. After recounting his diverse experiments with several species of animals and many types of problem-boxes, he concluded that he had "failed to find any act that even *seemed* due to reasoning."

Experiments like this have become so commonplace that the importance of their introduction by Thorndike is easily overlooked. By contrast with the other laboratory arrangements within which learning was studied, the problem-box brought to the fore the problems of motivation, rewards, and punishments. The typical laboratory experiments on learning before Thorndike were either the experiments introduced by Ebbinghaus on the memorization and recall of verbal materials or the experiments on acquisition of psychomotor skill exemplified by the Bryan and Harter studies of learning telegraphy (1897, 1899). In both of these, motivation remains in the background as one of the contextual features, along with learning capacity and other factors not entering as manipulated variables. But in his "law of effect" Thorndike brought motivation and reward into the foreground. Trials were defined not by a repetition of a list (Ebbinghaus) or by so many minutes of practice (Bryan and Harter) but by the string of unsuccessful responses occurring prior to successful goal attainment.

Thorndike formulated his mechanistic law of effect in the following terms: responses to a situation which are followed by a rewarding state of affairs will be strengthened or stamped in as habitual responses to that situation; responses which are unsuccessful will be weakened or stamped out as responses to that situation. Rewards, or successes and failures, were thus introduced as providing a mechanism for selection of the more adaptive response. The principle bears much resemblance to the mechanism of "natural selection by successful adaptation" or "the survival of the fittest," which was the basis for Darwin's theory of the evolution of species. Thorndike, as well as other comparative psychologists of his era, was influenced by the intellectual attractiveness of the Darwinian analysis of species selection.

Thorndike saw that in his law of effect he had added an important supplement to the familiar law of habit formation through repetition:

But practice without zeal—with equal comfort at success and failure—does *not* make perfect, and the nervous system grows *away* from the modes in which it is *exercised with resulting discomfort*. When the law of effect is omitted—when habit-formation is reduced to the supposed effect of mere repetition—two results are almost certain. By the resulting theory, little in human behavior can be explained by the law of habit; and by the resulting practice, unproductive or extremely wasteful forms of drill are encouraged. (1913, p. 22)

The interest in rewards and punishments which grew out of his experiments with animals continued naturally enough as he turned his attention to learning as it occurs in schools. There the arguments over punishment, promotion, school marks, and other incentive devices were rife, even though academic psychologists had not yet awakened to the centrality of motivational concepts.

Thorndike's experiments on animals had a very profound influence upon his thinking about human learning. He became convinced, contrary to the then popular beliefs, that animal behavior was little mediated by ideas. Responses were said to be made directly to the situation as sensed. While he did not go so far as to totally deny ideation among animals, he was convinced that the great bulk of their learning could be explained by the direct binding of acts to situations through the automatic action of the law of effect, unmediated by ideas. A comparison of the learning curves of human subjects with those of animals led him to believe that the same essentially mechanical phenomena disclosed by animal learning are also the fundamentals of human learning. Although always aware of the greater subtlety and range of human learning, he showed a strong preference for understanding more complex learning in terms of the simpler, and for identifying the simpler forms of human learning with that of animals.

Both theory and practice need emphatic and frequent reminders that man's learning is fundamentally the action of the laws of readiness, exercise, and effect. He is first of all an associative mechanism working to avoid what disturbs the life-processes of the neurones. If we begin by fabricating imaginary powers and faculties, or if we avoid thought by loose and empty terms, or if we stay lost in wonder at the extraordinary versatility and inventiveness of the higher forms of learning, we shall never understand man's progress or control his education. (1913, p. 23)

The Law of Readiness

The law of readiness is an accessory principle which characterizes the circumstances under which a learner tends to be satisfied or annoyed. Thorndike tended to state these conditions in terms of neuronal units "conducting" impulses, but his neurophysiology was exceedingly speculative. If we interpret his "conduction units" as action tendencies, then the three characteristics subsumed under Thorndike's law of readiness can be paraphrased roughly as follows:

1. Given the arousal of a strong impulse to a particular action sequence, the smooth carrying out of that sequence is *satisfying*.
2. If that action sequence is thwarted or blocked from being completed, that is *annoying*.
3. If a given action is fatigued (tired out) or satiated, then forcing a further repetition of the act is annoying.

What Thorndike had in mind with the first two laws was the running off of complete chains of consummatory behavior, such as a child going to the refrigerator for ice cream or a baby reaching for a bright toy or a cat chasing a mouse. The "impulse" for food or touching attractive things brings into *readiness* the early responses of the action sequence; similarly, performance of the early components of the chain enhances the organism's readiness for the next response in the action sequence. The third law above refers to fatigue or satiation effects; if you are already stuffed with food, being forced to take another bite is positively aversive.

In these laws, Thorndike was pointing to the fact that satisfaction and frustration (annoyance) depend upon the state of readiness (or preparation) the organism is in when a particular "response" occurs or is blocked. There is another kind of readiness familiar to educators. This is illustrated by the use of "reading readiness" to refer to the child's reaching a level of maturity appropriate to the beginning of reading. Thorndike was referring to totally different matters, and it would be historically inaccurate to construe his law of readiness as anticipating a relation between the two kinds of readiness, because interests and motives mature along with capacities. Thorndike's readiness was a law of preparatory adjustment, not a law about growth.

The Earlier Law of Exercise

The law of exercise refers to the strengthening of connections with practice (law of use) and to the weakening of connections or forgetting when practice is discontinued (law of disuse). Strengthening is defined by the increase in probability that the response will be made when the situation recurs. This probability may be either a *greater* probability of occurrence if the situation is repeated immediately, or an *equal* probability persisting longer in time. That is, a stronger connection is in a favored competitive position relative to other habits, either at the time of its strengthening or if tested after there has been opportunity for forgetting. The definition of strength by probability of occurrence (1913, p. 2) has a very contemporary ring.

The kinds of phenomena falling under the law of exercise are chiefly those of repetitive habits, as in rote memorizing or the acquiring of muscular skills. The belief was simply that "practice makes perfect." Thus, learning curves plotting excellence of performance against practice trials should increase in accord with the law of use. On the other hand, forgetting curves showing loss of skill over various intervals of disuse gave quantification to that law. During the period under discussion, Thorndike accepted uncritically the prevailing principle of learning by doing, even though he had criticized the use of the principle independent of the law of effect. He later altered his position and greatly reduced the emphasis upon the law of exercise.

The Earlier Law of Effect

As noted previously, the law of effect refers to the strengthening or weakening of a connection as a result of its consequences. When a modifiable connection is made and is accompanied by or followed by a satisfying state of affairs, the strength of the connection is increased; if the connection is made and followed by an annoying state of affairs, its strength is decreased.

Two chief objections were made to the law of effect by its critics at the time of its early formulation. At the height of behaviorism it was objected that satisfaction and annoyance were subjective terms, inappropriate for use in describing animal behavior. But Thorndike was in reality ahead of his critics, for he had early stated what he meant by such states of affairs in what would today be called operational terms:

By a satisfying state of affairs is meant one which the animal does nothing to avoid, often doing things which maintain or renew it. By an annoying state of affairs is meant one which the animal does nothing to preserve, often doing things which put an end to it. (1913, p. 2)

These definitions are not circular, so far as the law of effect is concerned. That is, the states of affairs characterized as satisfying and as annoying are specified independently of their influence upon modifiable connections. The law of effect then states what may be expected to happen to preceding modifiable connections which are followed by such specified states. The objection that Thorndike was lacking in objectivity in the statement of satisfying and annoying states of affairs is not a valid one.

The second objection was that the backward effect of a state of affairs on something now past in time is not conceivable. Since the stimulus-response event occurs before the reward (or punishment), how could the latter exert an influence upon the earlier event? The past is gone, whereas effects can be felt only in the present. The criticism, like the first, is a faulty one. The effect is revealed in the probability of recurrence of the response when the situation next occurs; whether or not such an effect occurs is a matter of observation and experiment, not something to be denied on *a priori* grounds.

Translated into more familiar words, Thorndike is saying in this law that rewards or successes further the learning of the rewarded behavior, whereas punishments or failures reduce the tendency to repeat the behavior leading to punishment, failure, or annoyance. So much would merely be a reassertion of common observations. But he went further and insisted that the action of consequences is direct, mechanical, automatic, and need not be mediated by conscious ideas. It is precisely with respect to these technical addendums to common sense that later critics were to attack Thorndike's statement of the law of effect—as we shall see presently. In this insistence on mechanical action, Thorndike's law of effect anticipates the reinforcement principle adopted in later conditioned-response theories. The later changes in theory reduced the importance of annoyers relative to satisfiers (see the truncated law of effect, below) and added some new phenomena, but the central importance of a modified law of effect persisted in Thorndike's final statements of his position.

Subordinate Laws

The major laws of readiness, exercise, and effect were said to have five subsidiary laws applicable to both animal and human learning (1913, pp. 23–31). Among these occurs one, associative shifting, which is so similar to one variety of conditioned-response theory that it deserves special mention, even though it was listed as the fifth of the subordinate principles.

In a short account of Thorndike's views, the impression may be given that he was a very systematic writer. His "system," apart from a few persistent preferences, is in fact a rather loose collection of rules and suggestions. What was called a "law" at any one time was a statement which at the time appeared to Thorndike to have some generality of application. Today psychologists would call it a "hypothesis" or "a significant variable" in reference to some phenomenon. No effort was made to retain internal coherence among the concepts used, or to establish any genuine relationship of coordination or subordination among the laws. The five "subordinate laws" to be discussed are principles which seemed to Thorndike somewhat less important than the major laws of readiness, exercise, and effect. They are not related to the major laws in any clear manner, and in later writings they were occasionally omitted, occasionally revived.

1. Multiple response. The first of the five principles is that of multiple response or varied reaction. In order for a response to be rewarded, it must occur. When the learner faces a problem, he tries one thing after another. When the appropriate behavior is stumbled upon, success follows and learning is possible. Were the organism unable to vary its responses, the optimum solution might never be elicited. Even when a response to a given situation is found to yield some reward, there is still adaptive value to some variation around that response, since reward may be larger or more frequent for other responses.

2. Set or attitude. The second principle is that learning is guided by a total attitude or "set" of the organism. Responses are determined in part by enduring adjustments characteristic of individuals raised in a given environment or culture. The attitude or set determines not only what the person will do, but what will satisfy or annoy him. For instance, a professional golfer will be annoyed by shots which the amateur would cherish. This illustration, from Thorndike, antedates by years the construct of "level of aspiration" which came into prominence in personality theory in later years. Roughly, the notion is that an individual has his own internal standard regarding how well he should perform a given task, and he judges and reinforces (or punishes) his own performance accordingly as it is above or below his standard in quality.

3. Prepotency of elements. The third principle states that the learner is able to react selectively to prepotent or salient elements in the problem. That is, a man can pick out the essential item and base his responses upon it, neglecting other adventitious features which might confuse a lower animal. This ability to deal with the relevant parts of situations makes analytical and insightful learning possible. In other theories, this selection of the critical element is described in terms of either attention or abstraction.

4. Response by analogy. The fourth principle is that of assimilating, comparing a new situation to a previously learned one, and thus giving a response by analogy. How does man react to novel situations? He responds to a new situation as he would to some situation like it, or he responds to some element in the new situation to which he has a response in his repertory. Responses can always be explained by old acquisitions, together with inborn tendencies to respond; there is nothing mysterious about responses to novelty, since "novel situations" can always be decomposed into new arrangements of mainly familiar features and parts.

5. Associative shifting. The fifth of these subsidiary laws is called associative shifting. The fundamental notion is that if a response can be kept intact through a series of changes in the stimulating situation, it may finally be given to a totally new stimulus. The stimulating situation is changed first by addition, then by subtraction, until nothing from the original situation remains. Thorndike illustrates this principle by the act of teaching a cat to stand up at command. First a bit of fish is dangled before the cat while you say, "Stand up." After enough trials, by proper arrangement, the fish may be omitted, and the oral signal will alone evoke the response. The general statement of the principle of associative shifting implies that we may "get any response of which a learner is capable associated with any situation to which he is sensitive" (1913, p. 15). This is obviously related to that type of conditioning in which the process is described as substituting a conditioned stimulus for an unconditioned one. Thorndike, while noting the similarity, believed the Pavlovian conditioned response to be a more specialized case under the broader principle of associative shifting. More to the point is the resemblance of Thorndike's principle to that which Skinner (see Chapter 5) has called "fading" or "vanishing," whereby discriminative control of a response is shifted from one stimulus to a second. This principle is now in wide use in teaching-machine programs. An elementary example is that of a child's being taught to spell a new word by pairing presentation of the spoken with the written word (which he copies); after successive trials in which progressively more visual letters (as prompts) are deleted, the child must spell the complete word when it is spoken. Eventually the response of spelling the word, which was originally controlled only by copying a visual word, becomes shifted to control by the spoken word alone. Such educational applications, however, flowed from Skinner's ingenuity, and were not part of Thorndike's many suggestions regarding practical problems.

Controlling Learning

There is always some danger of misunderstanding a systematic writer's influence if attention is confined to the more abstract and generalized laws which he proposes, to the neglect of accessory details which give both flavor and comprehensible substance to his teaching. Thorndike as early as 1913 was giving much more attention to the dynamics of learning than the formal consideration of his laws suggests.

Within the framework of his primary laws, he saw three considerations which affected the teacher's problem in using them in the classroom. These were: (1) ease of identification of the bonds to be formed or broken; (2) ease of identification of the states of affairs which should satisfy or annoy; and (3) ease of application of satisfaction and annoyance to the identified states of affairs (1913, pp. 213–217). The teacher and the learner must know the characteristics of a good performance in order that practice may be appropriately arranged. Errors must be diagnosed so that they will not be repeated. When there is lack of clarity about what is being taught or learned, practice may be strengthening the wrong connections in place of the right ones. At the same time, needed connections may be weakened by disuse. Thorndike believed that it is especially hard to teach imagination, forcefulness, and beauty in literary expression because it is difficult to be specific about the conduct which should be made satisfying at the time it occurs; in this regard,

Skinner and Guthrie differ sharply from Thorndike, believing that specific behavior objectives can be formulated for teaching of "fuzzy" or "ill-defined" artistic subject matters or skills. The importance of specificity runs throughout Thorndike's writings. As we shall see later, this is at once a source of strength in his system and one of its points of vulnerability.

But Thorndike's advice was not limited to the application of his major laws. He refers also to a number of motivational features not readily deducible from the laws of readiness and effect. The active role of the learner, who comes to the learning situation with needs, interests, and problems which determine what will be satisfying to him, is recognized implicitly by Thorndike. He lists five aids to improvement in learning as the *interest* series (1913, pp. 217–226). These he believes to be commonly accepted by educators:

1. Interest in the work
2. Interest in improvement in performance
3. Significance of the lesson for some goal of the student
4. Problem-attitude in which the student is made aware of a need which will be satisfied by learning the lesson
5. Attentiveness to the work

The Identical-Elements Theory of Transfer

Schools are publicly supported in the hope that more general uses will be made outside the school of knowledge and skills learned in school. To some extent, all schooling is aimed at a kind of transfer beyond the school. Whether the proper way to achieve this end may turn out to be to teach more formal subject matter, such as mathematics and the classics, or to give more attention to practical subject matter, such as manual training and social studies, the problem is a central one for educators.

Thorndike early interested himself in the problem. His theory began to take form in an experimental study done in collaboration with Woodworth (Thorndike & Woodworth, 1901), and was formally stated in his early *Educational psychology* (1903). The theory proposes that transfer depends upon the presence of identical elements in the original learning and the new learning which it facilitates. These may be identities of either substance or procedure. For example, the ability to speak and write well are important in all schoolroom classes and many tasks of ordinary life. Hence mastery of these skills will serve in different pursuits, and transfer will be effected through what the different situations require in common. The substance of what is required in different situations may be unlike, but there may be procedures in common. The procedures of looking things up in such diverse sources as a dictionary, a cookbook, and a chemist's handbook have much in common, despite the unlike contents of the three kinds of book. If an activity is learned more easily because another activity was learned first, it is only because the two activities overlap. Transfer is always specific, never general; when it appears to be general, the fact remains that new situations have much of old situations in them.

Intelligence as measured by tests may be thought of as, to some extent, a measure of the transfer capacity of an individual. That is, the test measures the ability to give right answers in relatively novel situations. It is logically sound that Thorndike's theory of intelligence was, like his theory of transfer, a matter of specific connections. The more bonds the individual has which can be used, the more intelligent he is.

Thorndike's specificity doctrines of transfer and of intelligence have been highly influential and have led to a great deal of experimental work. Although the problems of the nature and measurement of intelligence lie outside the scope of this volume, there will be occasion later to consider some of the alternative explanations of transfer.

During the stable period of Thorndike's system there were many changes in psychological climate, but these left him unruffled. The rise of behaviorism and the new importance attributed to the conditioned response affected him but little, because the new enthusiasts were talking what was to him a congenial language, even when they included him in their sweeping attacks on everything which preceded them. The attacks by the Gestalt psychologists in the twenties were more telling, and he began later to meet some of their criticisms. But it was his own experiments which led him to come before the International Congress of Psychology in New Haven in September 1929 with the statement, "I was wrong." He there announced two fundamental revisions in his laws of exercise and effect which became the basis for a number of publications dating from 1930.

Connectionism after 1930

The revisions of his original laws (hypotheses) were reported by Thorndike in a number of journal articles and monographs with various collaborators, the main results being gathered in two large volumes under the titles *The fundamentals of learning* (1932a) and *The psychology of wants, interests, and attitudes* (1935). The law of exercise was practically renounced as a law of learning, only a trivial amount of strengthening of connections being left as a function of mere repetition. The law of effect was revised, with the weakening effects of annoying consequences being renounced.

Disproof of the Law of Exercise

The type of experiment used to disprove the law of exercise was that in which repetition of a class of responses to a given situation occurred under circumstances which minimized the operation of the law of effect. For instance, a blindfolded subject would be asked to attempt to draw a 4-inch line, and to do so hundreds of times over many days, but never with any feedback information from the experimenter. Thorndike was here interested in whether the initially more frequent responses (e.g., line lengths, say, between 4.1 and 4.6 inches long) would slowly "drain off" strength from the less frequent responses, so that eventually the high-frequency responses become ever more probable and the low-frequency responses are driven out. This was, he supposed, the implication of the law of exercise whereby a response to a situation is strengthened by its sheer occurrence; and since probabilities over all responses must sum to 1.00, increasing the probability of one class of responses must decrease the probability of another class.

The results in this and several similar experiments by Thorndike were distinctly negative; the probability distribution of line lengths drawn on the twelfth practice day was in essentials the same as the distribution on the first practice day. Without information or rewarding feedback, there was relatively little change in the response distribution. In full contrast, if, each time after his attempt to draw a 4-inch line, the person is informed as to whether his product was too long or too short, his response productions improve rapidly to be tightly distributed at about 4 inches (Trowbridge & Cason, 1932).

The line-drawing experiment shows that repetition of a *situation* without knowledge of the correct response produces little or no change in the relative response frequency. However, Thorndike was well aware that some varieties of repetition ("exercise") are important, and they are precisely those occurrences of a stimulus-response connection of a simple kind in which the person knows he is remembering correctly. For instance, a pupil who has been told to remember "The capital of Oregon is Salem" is well advised to subvocally rehearse the sentence or pairings "capital of Oregon—Salem" even though the teacher is not standing by delivering a series of verbal reinforcements. Such implicit "exercise" of the connection is well known to promote long-term retention of the connection. Thorndike would explain the effect of implicit rehearsal as due to an internal "confirming reaction" (or satisfier) which the person supposedly interposes after each S-R rehearsal, as though he were saying to himself "capital of Oregon—Salem—okay."

The Truncated Law of Effect

A number of experiments yielded data which Thorndike interpreted as showing that the effects of reward and punishment are not equal and opposite, as had been implied in earlier statements on the effects of satisfiers and annoyers. Instead, under several conditions, reward appeared to be much more powerful than punishment. This conclusion, if it is ever confirmed, would be of immense social importance in such fields of application as education and criminology.

One of these experiments was done with chicks (1932b). A simple maze gave the chick the choice of three pathways, one of which led to "freedom, food, and company"—that is, to an open compartment where there were other chicks eating. The wrong choices led to confinement for 30 seconds. Statistics were kept on the tendencies to return to the preceding choice if it had led to reward, and to avoid the preceding choice if it led to punishment. Thorndike interpreted his findings as follows: "The results of all comparisons by all methods tell the same story. Rewarding a connection always strengthened it substantially; punishing it weakened it little or not at all" (1932b, p. 58).

The corresponding experiment with human subjects consists of a multiple-translations arranged in the same manner. The subject guesses the translation word, underlines it, and then hears the experimenter say *Right* ("rewarded" response) or *Wrong* ("punished" response). How will he change his choice vocabulary test. For example, a Spanish word is given with five English words, one of which is its correct translation. A second and a third Spanish word follow, and so on through a list, each word with alternative responses the next time through the list? As with the chicks, reward led to repetition of the rewarded connection, but punishment did not lead to a weakening of the punished connection. In six experiments of this general sort, Thorndike concluded that the announcement of *Wrong* did not weaken connections enough to counterbalance the slight increase in strength gained from their just occurring (1932a, p. 288).

Thorndike and his staff went on to collect a series of testimonials about the relative efficacy of rewards and punishments from published biographies and other sources, going back many years. The almost universal evidence of the greater beneficial effect of reward rather than punishment gave practical support to the findings of the experiments, which otherwise could be criticized as too far removed from ordinary life (1935, pp. 135–144, 248–255).

There were some statistical difficulties in Thorndike's interpretations of his data which caused him to underestimate the significance of punishment. In a later section, we shall take up some of these criticisms of Thorndike's interpretation of his results, as well as counterevidence.

As in the disproof of the law of exercise, Thorndike's repudiation of the principle of weakening by annoying aftereffects was not absolute. It was only direct weakening which was denied. Punishments do, according to Thorndike, affect learning indirectly. He said that their indirect effect comes chiefly from leading the animal to do something in the presence of the annoyer which makes him less likely to repeat the original connection. But this is not necessarily the case.

An annoyer which is attached to a modifiable connection may cause the animal to feel fear or chagrin, jump back, run away, wince, cry, perform the same act as before but more vigorously, or whatever else is in his repertory as a response to that annoyer in that situation. But there is no evidence that it takes away strength from the physiological basis of the connection in any way comparable to the way in which a satisfying after-effect adds strength to it." (1932a, pp. 311–313)

Thorndike was less successful in his attempts to explain the action of effect than in demonstrating that there are phenomena to which his principles apply. He distinguished between a direct *confirming influence* and the *informative influence* of rewards. Control of behavior according to the information supplied by its consequences implied for Thorndike mediation by ideas of the sort, "If I do this, I get fed; if I do that, I get slapped." Thorndike believed that he kept this kind of deliberation at a minimum in his experiments, so that what he had to explain was the direct confirmatory reaction which he said was responsible for the strengthening of responses through reward. This confirming reaction is vaguely described as an "unknown reaction of the neurones" which is aroused by the satisfier and strengthens the connection upon which it impinges (1933c). The confirming reaction is said to be independent of sensory pleasures, and independent of the intensity of the satisfier. It is highly selective, depending upon aroused drives or "overhead control in the brain." While such an account is far from satisfactory, it at least helps to show where Thorndike stood. He was against mediation by ideas, as an interpretation of effect according to information would seem to imply. At the same time, he recognized the complexity of the reinforcement process and was not committed to a simple hedonism. The law of effect was not interpreted by Thorndike as necessarily involving a conscious feeling of pleasure or emotion.

Belongingness

In addition to the revisions of the laws of exercise and effect, several new terms entered as Thorndike's system was revised. One of these, *belongingness*, by its recognition of an organizational principle foreign to the structure of Thorndike's theory of specificity and mechanical action, made slight concessions to the Gestalt psychologists. According to this principle, a connection between two units or ideas is more readily established if the person perceives the two as belonging together or going together. For example, if the person hears a repetitive series of sentences such as "John is a butcher. Harry is a carpenter. Jim is a doctor" and so on, the association "butcher-John" will be a much stronger one than is "butcher-Harry," despite the fact that "butcher" occurs closer in time to "Harry" than to "John." Obviously, the person is perceiving, grouping, and rehearsing the flow of words as subject-predicate constructions; our knowledge of syntax groups the words together in a manner differing from their surface contiguity, and assigns the predicate of a sentence to the subject of the same sentence rather than to the next sentence. There are hundreds of examples of this principle at work, illustrating how various perceptual variables (like temporal or spatial proximity) determine which units will be perceived and rehearsed together, and consequently connected. Thorndike recognized this "belongingness" factor without being very clear on how to accommodate such phenomena showing "perceptual determination of association" into his mechanistic system.

The other use of "belongingness" Thorndike recognized was that the reward or punishment which follows a stimulus-response event should be perceived as "belonging" to that S-R event, or interpreted by the person as being related to his response. For instance, if during learning of a paired-associate item, the subject were suddenly to be given a big payment by the experimenter with an offhand remark like "This is the wage I was going to pay you later," or if a shock were delivered to the subject but the experimenter said, "Oops, sorry; that was an accident of my equipment," then those rewarding or punishing events would not be seen as *contingent* on the person's response. Therefore, the response which precedes such an aftereffect without belonging will not have its associative connection altered very much by the experience. These belongingness effects clearly have to do with how the subject has perceived or grouped together units which are to be rehearsed as an associative unit.

While the principle of belongingness may be interpreted as something of a concession, the principle of *polarity* was emphasized as defying Gestalt principles (1932a, p. 158). Thorndike's principle of polarity stated that connections act more easily in the direction in which they were formed than in the opposite direction. If you have learned German vocabulary items by always testing yourself in the German-to-English direction, you are likely to fail in a test in the English-to-German direction. Thorndike's "polarity principle" amounts to the presupposition that associations can be unidirectional between two terms rather than necessarily bidirectional. He contrasted this with the "associative symmetry" view (which he attributed to Gestalt theory) that a connected pair of items forms a new whole or unit; according to this view, since the holistic trace is redintegrated to the recall cue, it makes no sense to say that an association could exist in one direction but not in the other.

This issue of associative symmetry is still very current among contemporary workers in human learning. The resolution of the symmetry issue seems to depend on: (a) the subject's mode of rehearsal—Merryman (1969) has shown that subjects can be led to rehearse in such manner as to form mainly unidirectional or mainly bidirectional associations; and (b) the *availability* of the two units as recallable responses (see Horowitz, Norman, & Day, 1966). If we are assured of the person's familiarity with each unit, specifically of his ability to recall the unit by itself, then his recall of that unit when cued with the other member of the associated pair will be high. The two elements of a pair will tend to show associative symmetry to the extent that both units are equally available as responses *per se*. For instance, in our German-English illustration given above, the English speaker would be more familiar with the English than with the German word, and hence his recall in the two directions would appear asymmetric, but, according to Horowitz et al. (1966), only because of the different availability of the German and English words.

Identifiability and availability.   Among several other learning variables identified by Thorndike, we select for comment his notions of "stimulus identifiability" and "response availability," since both of these relate closely to contemporary work. The principle of identifiability is that a situation is easy to connect to a response to the extent that the situation is identifiable, is distinguishable from others in a learning series. Thorndike is here recognizing the issue of stimulus discrimination or perceptual learning which play a large role in later theories of associative learning. He talks about stimulus identification as follows:

> Learning as a whole includes changes in the identifiability of situations as well as changes in the connections leading from them to responses. . . . Elements of situations which are hard to identify because they are hidden qualities or features are analyzed out into relief, and made identifiable by having attention directed specifically to them and by the action of varying concomitants and contrast (1931, pp. 88–89)

Thorndike thus recognized the importance of stimulus recognition to association formation; he also describes the typical procedure by which the relevant distinctive feature is to be abstracted from a series of complex stimulus patterns, namely, by variation of irrelevant features and contrasting appearances of the relevant feature. These ideas, of course, have a quite modern ring to them.

Thorndike's use of the response-availability variable is illustrated by the following:

> Consider now the principle of availability as get-at-able-ness of the response, which is that, other things being equal, connections are easy to form in proportion

as the response is available, summonable, such that the person can have it or make it at will. (1931, p. 89)

The kind of distinction Thorndike had in mind here was that some responses are overlearned as familiar acts (e.g., touching our nose, tapping our toes) which are readily executed upon command, whereas more finely skilled movements (e.g., drawing a line 4 inches as opposed to 5 inches long while blindfolded) may not be so readily summonable. In this matter, Thorndike seems to be discussing what today we would call "response differentiation," the ease with which the person can distinguish two or more responses which are to be paired with corresponding stimuli. The terms *response availability* or *response learning* came to be used in the later literature to refer to acquisition of a complex chain of items, for example, to say the sequence "HXDFR" to a particular signal.

The Spread of Effect

In 1933 a new kind of experimental evidence was offered in support of the law of effect, evidence described as the *spread of effect* (1933a, 1933b). The experiments purported to show that the influence of a rewarding state of affairs acts not only on the connection to which it belongs but on temporally adjacent connections both before and after the rewarded connection, the effect diminishing with each step that the connection is removed from the rewarded one. The effect acts to strengthen even punished connections in the neighborhood of the rewarded one. The experiments lent support to the automatic and mechanical action of effect. A characteristic experiment was that in which the subject was asked to state a number from 1 to 10 following the announcement of a stimulus word by the experimenter. The experimenter then called his response *Right* or *Wrong*, these "rewards" and "punishments" conforming either to a prearranged assignment of correct numbers to each word, or to some systematic pattern of *Rights* or *Wrongs*. In either case, the assignment of numbers from the point of view of the subject is arbitrary, and the cue to repeat the number he first gave to the stimulus word or to change it comes from the experimenter's reaction following each number. The lists are so long that the subject cannot recall very well on the second trial just what was done on the first.

After the list has been read a number of times in this manner, the responses of the subject are classified to find the number of times the responses were repeated to the same stimulus. Not only are the rewarded responses repeated more often than the others, but responses followed by *Nothing* (the experimenter says nothing) are repeated beyond chance expectancy *if* they occur close in time to a response called *Right*.

An example experiment is that by Tilton, earlier an associate of Thorndike; he repeated the spread of effect experiment with careful controls to determine what the empirical level of repetition would be without the saying of *Right* and *Wrong* (i.e., the experimenter saying nothing following the subject's response). He then proceeded to plot the spread of effect on either side of an isolated rewarded and an isolated punished response (Tilton, 1939, 1945). He found that the effects of *Right* and *Wrong* are about alike, the announcement of *Wrong* decreasing repetitions about as much as *Right* increases them. A replotting of Tilton's results is shown in Figures 2.2 and 2.3.

Tilton's study shows that there is a tendency for punished responses in the neighborhood of reward to be repeated more frequently than such responses remote from reward. Their punishment (being called *Wrong*) suffices, however, even one step from reward, to lead to *less* repetition than would occur if the response were neither rewarded nor punished (Figure 2.2). Similarly, when a response called *Wrong* (punished) occurs in the midst of a series of rewarded responses, the neighboring rewarded responses are repeated less frequently than they would have been had they not been in the neighborhood of the punished response. Again, however, their reward (being called *Right*) is enough to lead to their repetition at a *greater* frequency than that represented by the neutral baseline (Figure 2.3).

The important point here for Thorndike is the apparent "gradient" of repetition probability for pairs occurring close in time to the rewarded or punished pair. This continuous function was presumed to demonstrate the spreading of the automatic strengthening effect of a reward to temporally contiguous connections, and similarly for the spread of the weakening effect of a punishment (note the declining curves in Figure 2.2 and the rising curves in Figure 2.3 with increasing distance from the critical pair which was rewarded or punished, respectively). The startling and counterintuitive nature of such results led to much experimentation, a good deal of which

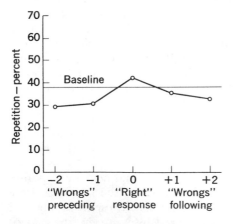

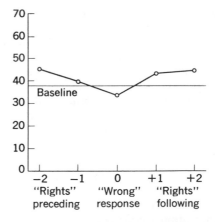

Figure 2.2.   Gradient of effect around a *Right* response. Calling a response *Right* increases its repetition, calling a response *Wrong* decreases its repetition. The decrease from being called *Wrong* is less, however, when the response called *Wrong* is near an isolated *Right*. (Redrawn from Tilton, 1945. By permission.)

Figure 2.3.   Gradient of effect around a *Wrong* response. Calling a response *Wrong* decreases its repetition, calling a response *Right* increases its repetition. The increase from being called *Right* is less, however, when the response called *Right* is near an isolated *Wrong*. (Redrawn from Tilton, 1945. By permission.)

was an attempt to explain away the "spread of effect" gradients (such as Tilton's) as being caused by one or another artifact or contaminating variable in the task. And indeed a fair number of other factors—such as recurrent number-guessing sequences, nonrandom guessing habits altering the repetition baseline, the influence of set or intention to learn, etc.—were shown to influence the "spread of effect" data and consequently to cast in doubt its original interpretation. The array of conflicting evidence on the issue was reviewed in the prior edition of this volume (Hilgard & Bower, 1966, pp. 28ff.) and by Postman (1962), who was basically sympathetic to Thorndike's position on the spread of effect.

THORNDIKE AND CONTEMPORARY ISSUES

It will help place the contribution of Thorndike into perspective if we examine a few of the contemporary strands of research that are related specifically to his systematic positions on important issues. It is indeed remarkable how much of Thorndike is still very contemporary. The following section will review some modern work on the interpretation of the spread of effect, on the law of effect as applied to human learning, and on the topic of learning without awareness. On each of these topics, Thorndike's views have served as the impetus for much systematic experimentation and theorizing. In our opinion, the fates of time and scientific evidence have not smiled on Thorndike's earlier positions; yet, although we here take issue with him, it should be recognized that criticism is the highest form of scientific flattery. Insignificant theories are rarely criticized; they are simply ignored, thus to die a quiet death from neglect.

AN ALTERNATE EXPLANATION OF THE SPREAD OF EFFECT

Weighing the evidence for one or another artifact, the present authors come to the conclusion that the spread of effect is very likely the result of the operation of much simpler processes than Thorndike had supposed. First, we might note that the spread of effect as a theoretical principle was evoked solely to explain the particular data collected under this rubric, and the old law of effect is actually logically independent of whether or not spread occurs. Second, we believe that the spread-of-effect data are probably the result of stimulus generalization among serial positions within a list, and may have nothing whatsoever to do with spreading aftereffects of a reward. To illustrate this analysis, consider the paradigmatic list in a Thorndikean experiment as illustrated below (Table 2.1) for a miniature list of eight arbitrary items: on trial 1, the list of words (*cup, scissors, . . .*) is presented, to each of which the person guesses a digit from 1 to 10, following which the experimenter always arbitrarily says "Wrong" except for (let us say) the fifth item in the series. Following the first cycle, a second cycle through the series occurs, with the items being presented in the same serial order, and the subject making a trial-2 guess, as listed in the last column. Our hypothetical data illustrate repetition of the response 3 to *pencil*, which had been directly

Table 2.1   Illustrative events on two trials of a Thorndikean associative learning task.

| | | Trial 1 | | Trial 2 |
Serial Position	Cue Word	S's Guess	E's Feedback	S's Guess
1.	cup	7	wrong	2
2.	scissors	9	wrong	1
3.	plate	5	wrong	5
4.	sky	6	wrong	6
5.	pencil	3	RIGHT	3
6.	book	1	wrong	1
7.	house	8	wrong	8
8.	chair	2	wrong	6

rewarded on trial 1 and also repetition of responses given to stimuli presented two steps before and after the rewarded *pencil-3* connection. These
illustrate "spread of effects," of course.

The "stimulus generalization" explanation for such data might proceed
as follows (suggested by Estes, 1969a). Within any given trial of a stimulus-
response-outcome (S-R-O) sequence, there is some likelihood that the subject
learns any and all of the three pairwise associations, namely, S-R, S-O, and
R-O. These are presumed to be learned independently. An index of an S-O
association, for example, would be that the person could later recall that to
the word *pencil* the experimenter had said "Right" to the subject's response.
Moreover, and relevant to the spread-of-effect issue, we may suppose that the
person identifies the serial position of each item in a rough and imprecise
way, but nonetheless enters this serial position into associations with the
S-R-O events that occur at that position in the list. For the list illustrated
above, this would mean that the person might associate (during trial 1) an
implicit "serial position 5" to *Right* as an outcome. This would be evident,
for example, in his later ability to say after studying the list that a pairing
approximately in the *middle of the list* had been called *Right* by the
experimenter (note that the *Right* was a salient event, isolated among a
series of *Wrongs*—which arrangement is necessary for spread-of-effect experiments).

The further assumption of Estes's theory is that the person's memory of
the outcomes associated with a stimulus complex controls whether or not
he will perform the response he remembers having made to that stimulus.
If he remembers the response he made to *pencil* and remembers either that
the response to *pencil* or to serial position 5 was called *Right*, then he will
repeat the response he remembers having made. This is the basis for the
repetition effect for connections followed by *Right*. If the person remembers
that the outcome for a stimulus (or serial position) was called *Wrong*, then
he will make a different response from that which he remembers having
made on the prior trial. This is the basis for why *Wrong* will, other things
being equal, reduce repetition of responses below an appropriate control
baseline (which is response-repetition given a neutral event, neither *Right*
nor *Wrong*, after the response on trial 1).

To deal with the spread of effect, we need suppose only that the person's memory for the serial position that was correlated with a *Right* is imprecise, so that "serial position 5→*Right*" *generalizes* to neighboring serial positions SP3, SP4, SP6, and SP7, according to their distance from the correct location. Such stimulus generalization is a well-documented phenomenon, so it is not an unreasonable supposition. This principle suffices to explain the "spread of effect." To illustrate, consider the S-R-O event *"book-1-Wrong"* which occurs in serial position 6 just following the *Right* in serial position 5. Suppose that the person remembers what he said—that is, the S-R event. If he recalls *"book-Wrong,"* then he will not repeat the *"book-1"* connection (as Tilton's data show in Figure 2.2). If he forgets the *Wrong* for *book*, then he might recall, incorrectly as a generalization error, "serial position 6-*Right*" because SP6 is very similar to SP5. If this generalization or confusion occurred among adjacent serial positions, then the spread of effect would result as a *performance* factor (rather than a learning factor, as Thorndike had interpreted it), essentially amounting (crudely) to the subject's strategy to "repeat S-R connections that you can remember having made to a context that was approximately serial position 5."

Several implications follow from this "position generalization" hypothesis regarding the spread of effects. First, if subjects are asked on trial 2 to recall the response made on trial 1 *and* whether it was called *Right* or *Wrong*, one finds that responses recalled are the same for the several aftereffects but that there is a "generalization spread"; pairs called *Wrong* but in proximity to a pair called *Right* are likely to be later misrecalled as having been called *Right*; the opposite occurs for a pair called *Wrong* surrounded by pairs called *Right* (see Nuttin, 1949, 1953). This is exactly as expected by the generalization theory.

Furthermore, the spread of effect should be markedly reduced in magnitude if the stimuli are presented on trial 2 in a new, scrambled serial order. Zirkle (1946) in fact found a reduction in the spread of effect with rescrambling of the test list; there was no increase in the tendency to give an R to an S which had occurred close to an "S-R *Right*" connection unless that S recurred in the same or a nearby serial position as it had during trial 1.

The illustration above has used a short list (eight items) and assumed a fortuitous pattern of associations to explain the spread of effect; under more realistic circumstances (e.g., long lists), these factors will have lesser effects. But it must be realized that the "spread of effect" was at best a small effect, usually of only a few percentage points in repetition probabilities (reexamine Figures 2.2 and 2.3). What is perhaps so annoying in retrospect is that so much experimental effort was diverted into the controversy over the "reality" of the spread of effect. But this illustrates the seductive allure of a theoretical issue in attracting experimentalists.

Law of Effect in Human Learning

The two hypotheses which seem presently to be more in keeping with the facts about rewards and learning were, surprisingly, formulated clearly by Thorndike himself; but he rejected them on the basis of what today appear inadequate arguments. These alternate interpretations of why aftereffects strengthen S-R connections were dubbed the "rehearsal" and the "ideational" (or "informational") hypotheses by Thorndike. Thorndike formulated the "rehearsal" hypothesis as follows:

The next doctrine or hypothesis to be considered is that when a certain connecting has been followed by a satisfier, the individual concerned *repeats the connection* or something more or less equivalent to it. He thus strengthens the right connections himself by repetition. The wrong connections he may simply dismiss, or he may strengthen their negatives as by saying to himself *Four cross lines, don't turn head to left.* (1931, p. 51)

Current research on human learning gives much support to this differential rehearsal viewpoint, especially in learning situations in which the learner is presented with many more items than he can learn and these vary in their monetary value when learned. For example, the person might be presented with a number of paired-associates to study and told for each one how much money he will receive if he can remember that pairing on a later cued recall test. In such a situation, recall will vary directly with the expected payoff for remembering a given item. However, it appears likely that this is largely due to more rehearsal time allotted by the subject to the high-payoff items to the detriment of the low-payoff ones (see Atkinson & Wickens, 1971). If the person has strategic control over which items are entered into or deleted from a small set of items undergoing active rehearsal in his short-term memory as the list of pairs are presented serially, then high-payoff items receive the highest priority in remaining in the active rehearsal set. It is this rehearsal which is alleged to be the causal variable promoting better learning of high-value items.

A similar "rehearsal-like" effect has been found for simple recognition memory for single pictures (of naturalistic scenes) which were presented as pairs for study but with monetary values (of 9, 3, or 1 point) assigned to each picture of the pair (Loftus, 1972). For example, a given pair of pictures might have 9 points assigned to the left-hand picture and 3 points for the right-hand picture; these were the points to be earned if the subject could later recognize this presented picture from among a set of similar pictures. As expected, Loftus found that higher-valued pictures were remembered better than lower-valued pictures on a recognition test. The interesting and significant results came from recordings of concurrent eye movements as the subject studied the pair of pictures for 3 seconds. The significant variable proved to be the number of eye fixations on a given picture. Later recognition memory for a given picture increased directly with the number of eye fixations on it during the study trial. Valued pictures received more eye fixations, on the average. Significantly, however, there was no residual effect on memory of monetary value once the number of eye fixations was held constant. That is, for all pictures receiving, say, six eye fixations, the person's later recognition memory was equally good irrespective of how many points that picture was worth. The conclusion is that monetary value affects memory only through the intermediary of affecting the amount of visual processing of the picture. This may be analogous to rehearsal of verbal materials.

So rewards (anticipated or delivered) surely act in human learning by promoting differential exposure to and rehearsal of the connections to be learned. Of course, Thorndike did not deny this. He said:

Such strengthening by repetition does, of course, occur in many acts of learning. Everybody must admit this. The question is whether it is the *essential* and general method by which satisfiers and annoyers following connections strengthen or weaken them, or only an accessory or occasional procedure. (1931, p. 51)

From consideration of several experiments in which rewards had their usual positive effects but which precluded the subject's carrying out much conscious postreward rehearsal, Thorndike concluded that differential rehearsal was not an *essential* or necessary feature determining the influence of rewards. In this, we cannot but agree with him; one can get reward effects even when differential rehearsal is obviated, although permitting the operation of differential rehearsal assuredly magnifies the observed effects. The remaining issue is then how to interpret such reward effects as are found when rehearsal is minimized or equalized among conditions. We next take up the "information" hypothesis.

The Information Hypothesis Regarding Aftereffects

Thorndike's formulation supposed that satisfiers act directly to strengthen S-R connections they follow. The main alternative hypothesis supposes that S-R-O may be remembered simply by virtue of their occurring together (with "belonging"), and that the person's memory of the outcome causes him on the next trial to carry out the same response or to alter it according to whether he does or does not want that same outcome again. This viewpoint, given briefly in the preceding section, has been promoted recently by Buchwald (1967, 1969) and by Estes (1969a). It was anticipated by Thorndike as the following lines demonstrate:

The first of these theories declares that [aftereffects influence connections] by calling up ideas of themselves or some equivalents for themselves in the mind. For example, in our experiments in learning to choose the right meaning for a word, the person has these experiences: Seeing word A, response 1, hearing 'Wrong'; seeing word A, response 2, hearing 'Wrong'; seeing Word A, response 3, hearing 'Right'. When he next sees word A, any tendency to make response 1 or response 2 calls to his mind some image or memory or ideational equivalent of 'Wrong', whereas any tendency to make response 3 calls to his mind some image or memory or ideational equivalent of 'Right'. So this theory would state. It would further state that such memories or ideas of wrong associated with a tendency must *inhibit* the tendency, and that such memories and ideas of right associated with a tendency must *encourage* it to act, and so preserve and strengthen it.

In the same way this theory . . . would explain the learning of a cat who came to avoid the exit S at which it received a mild shock and to favor the exit F which led to food, by the supposition that the tendency to approach and enter S calls to the cat's mind some image or idea of the painful shock, whereas the tendency to approach and enter F calls to its mind some representation of the food, and that these representations respectively check and favor these tendencies. (1931, pp. 47–48)

The first paragraph of this quotation contains the essentials of the current Estes-Buchwald theory of how reward operates in human learning; the second paragraph contains the hypothesis, subscribed to by Kenneth Spence and Clark Hull in his later writings (see Chapter 6), that responses are selected by the anticipation of rewards or frustration consequent on the responses.

Having formulated this ideational theory of aftereffects, Thorndike rejected it on the basis of three arguments which appear, with the wisdom of hindsight, to have been inadequate. First, he said that his subjects rarely report introspectively recalling the *Right* or *Wrong* announcements of the experimenter from the previous trial. But he seems not to have collected any systematic data on such matters and relied merely on volunteered reports, which are often unreliable. More recent experiments which ask subjects to recall prior outcomes as well as to give correct responses (e.g., Allen & Estes, 1972) find appreciable recall of the outcomes.

Second, Thorndike argued that some learned, skilled movements occur so very quickly that there simply would not be enough time to bring up an image of the outcome before firing off the response (e.g., a boxer flicking a left jab through a momentary opening in his opponent's defense). The criticism fails, however, if the alternate theory provides for direct S-R connections which can be fired directly by short-circuiting the usual deliberate intervention of S-O memories. Estes's theory has exactly such a short-circuiting option available to handle high-speed execution of habitual S-Rs. Third, Thorndike argued that the ideational theory would expect symmetrical effects of *Right* versus *Wrong*, since each was just an "informational stimulus," whereas in fact Thorndike had found that *Wrong* apparently had a much smaller effect in weakening connections than *Right* had in strengthening them. But Thorndike's conclusion can be faulted: he typically used an incorrect baseline for computing repetition effects (the correct baseline is the repetition probability when the subject's initial response is followed by neither *Right* nor *Wrong*); when the correct baseline is used, the effects of *Right* and *Wrong* appear more symmetrical (e.g., see the results of Tilton in Figures 2.2 and 2.3).

Having dealt with Thorndike's criticisms of the informational hypothesis, let us briefly review a few experiments on human learning which seem to support that hypothesis in contradiction to Thorndike's interpretation of the law of effect.

Buchwald's delayed-information experiment.   An ingenious experiment by Buchwald (1967) tested a rather critical difference between the "satisfier" versus "information" theories of reward. Consider the standard Thorndikean two-trial experiment in which words are presented and the subject guesses digits, as illustrated before. Some subjects received immediate feedback of *Right* or *Wrong* following each S-R event on trial 1. A novel procedure was used with the other subjects; on trial 1, they made guesses to each stimulus word but were told nothing (neither *Right* nor *Wrong*) at that time. But on the trial-2 test which followed some minutes later, when shown a stimulus word, they were then told "The response you made to this word on the previous trial was Right (or Wrong)." They then gave their trial-2 response. Let us call this the delayed-information condition.

Thorndike's analysis expects that subjects receiving immediate feedback for their response on trial 1 will show larger changes in response probability than will those subjects receiving very delayed information; for Thorndike, the satisfier or annoyer had to occur just after the S-R connection to influence its strength. But the Buchwald-Estes analysis predicts just the opposite result, that subjects receiving delayed information will show greater changes due to being told *Right* or *Wrong* than will the subjects receiving immediate feedback. The reasoning goes as follows: consider the case where the word is *sky*. The subject's response is 4, and the experimenter immediately says *Wrong*. The possible connections formed here are *sky*-4, *sky-Wrong*, and 4-*Wrong* (the latter association is useless, since, with so many items, any specific response such as "4" would be often right and often wrong). On the next trial, in order to show an effect of *Wrong* in reducing repetition of *sky*-4, the person has to remember *sky*-4 and *sky-Wrong*, and use the latter to inhibit response 4 to *sky*. To the extent that the immediate-feedback subject forgets the *sky-Wrong* association, he will repeat *sky*-4 at the baseline probability. Consider now the case with delayed information; here the subject may remember that he said 4 to *sky* on trial 1 and now is told before he responds on trial 2 that his earlier response was wrong. He can therefore inhibit response 4 to *sky*. Clearly, the delayed-information subject need only remember his earlier S-R association in order to inhibit that R, whereas the immediate-feedback subject needs to remember both his earlier S-R association and the S-O association from the prior trial in order to inhibit that R to that S. Since they need to remember more to reject 4 to *sky*, the immediate-feedback subjects are therefore expected to show less of an effect of *Right-Wrong* than the delayed-information subjects.

The results of Buchwald's experiment (1967) and of a replication (noted in Estes, 1969a) confirmed the predictions from the informational analysis: repetition of the trial-1 response was increased for the delayed-*Right* over the immediate-*Right* condition, whereas repetition was reduced more for the delayed-*Wrong* than for the immediate-*Wrong* condition. The upshot, then, is a strong confirmation for the information hypothesis in contrast to Thorndike's interpretation of satisfiers as directly stamping in S-R connections which they follow.

Estes's "never-right" experiment.   In the typical trial-and-error learning experiment, the stimulus-response and reward events typically occur together so that the learning of the S-R unit and that of the S-R-O unit are inextricably confounded. Estes contrived a situation "in which the subject could learn relationships between stimulus-response combinations and reward values without any possibility of a direct strengthening effect of the latter upon the former" (Estes, 1969a, p. 75). In the experiment, the subjects were shown eight pairs of nonsense syllables over repeated trials; within each pair, one syllable (*i* through *p* in Table 2.2) had a value of zero whereas the other syllable (*a* through *h* in Table 2.2) was worth a certain number of points (1, 2, 3, 4) when chosen. The various assignments are shown in Table 2.2. The syllables are represented in the table by alphabetic letters. Syllables *e* through *p* are easily understood; they were uniformly paired with 1, 2, 3, 4, or 0 points, respectively, as indicated in the table. Now in order to win the indicated number of reward points, the subject had to first select the correct syllable (as contrasted to the 0-point alternative in each pair) and then indi-

Table 2.2   Design of "never-right" experiment. Alphabetic letters stand for distinct nonsense syllables, and digits represent the monetary points assigned. (From Estes, 1969a.)

Stimulus	Value Assigned	Informational Condition	Reward on Correct
a	1, 2	Random	1, 2
b	3, 4	Random	3, 4
c	1, 2	Never right	0
d	3, 4	Never right	0
e	1	Uniform	1
f	2	Uniform	2
g	3	Uniform	3
h	4	Uniform	4
i, j, ⋯, p	0	Uniform	0

cate correctly how many points the chosen syllable was worth. For example, in a typical trial, syllable f (worth 2 points) might be presented along with syllable n (worth 0 points); the person could receive 2 points only if he chose f *and* said it was worth 2 points; any other sequence (e.g., f and 3 points) was penalized by receiving no points. The correct value for the chosen syllable was always displayed at the end of the trial. This procedure obviously induces the subject to learn the payoffs associated with each syllable.

Along with these uniform-payoff syllables, four other stimuli a, b, c, d have two different point values associated with them as indicated in Table 2.2. For the "random" stimuli, a and b, the experimenter decided in advance to say one or the other values on a random half of the trials regardless of the subject's guess; on the average, once the subject learned the two values associated with syllables a and b, he would receive reward half the time.

The critical items are c and d, the never-right items which were also assigned two point values. For a test card like c-k, if the subject chose c and guessed any value other than 1 or 2, then he received no points and a value of 1 or 2 was indicated randomly as the correct value for that trial. But if the subject chose c and guessed 1 point, the assigned points were said to be 2 on that trial; if he had said 2 points for c, the experimenter would have said that 1 was the correct value for that trial. In either case, the subject received no reward on trials when he chose c or d; it was just that he was led to expect that c and d are "valuable" syllables (in comparison to the uniform-0 syllables), but that he had been unlucky in not guessing the correct value on the training trials.

It will be recalled that this unorthodox procedure was used to avoid the usual confounding between the learning of information about what outcomes follow given S-R events versus the strengthening effect of that outcome on the S-R connection. The never-right items give the subject information about possible reward magnitudes but never give him the "satisfaction" of receiving that reward.

The subjects were trained on this eight-item list until they completed two trials of choosing the correct syllable of each pair and correctly anticipating its value (or one of its two values). A first result worth noting is that rate of learning (to choose the correct syllable) was the same for the random and the never-right conditions. The more critical results come from a series of test trials, in which the syllables used in training would be recombined into various choice sets; the same point assignments were used, only they were not shown during the test series. The person was told to choose so as to maximize the points he would earn, which he was to be paid at the end of the test series. The variety of different test pairs is summarized in Table 2.3 along with the percentage in a direct choice pair. The marginal entry gives the average proportion of time that the row stimulus was chosen over all the competitors with which it was paired.

The information theory supposes that subjects will select that alternative which they anticipate will lead to the larger reward. Such is clearly upheld for the uniform items (see the marginal entries in the last column); frequency of choosing an item increases directly with its assigned payoff. Even the random items appear to fall (in choice value) at about the average of the values for the corresponding uniform items.

The significant data for the information theory concern how the never-right items c and d are treated during the test series. The important result is that the never-right items seem to behave almost exactly like the random items with the same point values. For example, R(3, 4) and NR(3, 4) have about the same average preference, neither being preferred over the other (see the .56 of row 4, column 2, where .50 would indicate equality of prefer ence for the two alternatives). NR(1, 2) is preferred to U1, but NR(3, 4) beats NR(1, 2) by about the same degree as R(3, 4) beats R(1,2). Finally, averaging the two comparisons of random with never-right items, the mean preference is only .52 for the random conditions. In all respects, then, subjects appear to treat these two classes of items as equal.

The test data in Table 2.3 show that reward value is very effective in producing systematic differences in the responses selected; the subjects were acutely sensitive to relatively slight variations in reward values. Therefore, the absence of a difference between the random and never-right conditions makes all the more credible the informational analysis of reward effects. For items in these two conditions, the subject had equal opportunities to asso-

Table 2.3   Choice proportions of row over column stimulus in the "never-right" experiment. The matrix is symmetric about the main diagonal. (From Estes, 1969a.)

Stimulus	Reward Condition	a	b	c	d	e	f	g	h	Average
a	R(1, 2)	—	.02	.61	.05	.85	.19	0	0	.25
b	R(3, 4)	.98	—	1.00	.44	1.00	.95	.79	.05	.74
c	NR(1, 2)	.39	0	—	.01	.76	.04	0	0	.17
d	NR(3, 4)	.95	.56	.99	—	.95	.92	.74	.01	.73
e	U1	.15	0	.24	.05	—	.04	0	0	.07
f	U2	.81	.05	.96	.08	.96	—	0	.01	.41
g	U3	1.00	.21	1.00	.26	1.00	1.00	—	.02	.64
h	U4	1.00	.95	1.00	.99	1.00	.99	.98	—	.98

ciate the same reward values with choice of the syllable. The only feature that differed between the two conditions is that for the never-right items the subjects in fact never received the satisfying aftereffect of any monetary pay-off. Thus, the notion of "satisfiers" cannot be evoked to explain any direct strengthening of the subject's choosing a never-right syllable. Learning occurs and anticipated rewards have their appropriate selective function in performance, all without the aid of any direct satisfying aftereffects of a rewarded connection.

The conclusion of this and several other studies by Estes (1969a) is that the informational (or "ideational") interpretation of the law of effect is consistently supported. Learning of S-R, S-O, and R-O associations seems to proceed independently of the value of the outcome, O. The assigned value of the outcome influences performance; that is, the anticipation of a highly valued outcome provides facilitative feedback to energize an S-R connection; anticipation of nonreward or punishment to a stimulus provides inhibitory feedback that blocks or prevents the S-R connection from firing the response. Along with such a theory, of course, one needs some ideas about what kinds of outcomes will be valued or what causes their relative values to change depending on the subject's state. Such matters are usually discussed under the heading of "motivation."

Although the data confirming the information hypothesis have been presented only for experiments involving human verbal learning, the presumption is that a similar analysis of reward-punishment effects can be made for conditioning experiments with animals (see the earlier Thorndike quotation stating the ideational hypothesis). In fact, many recent theories of instrumental (operant) conditioning do make just this analysis of reward effects (e.g., Logan, 1960; Mowrer, 1960; Spence, 1956): contiguity of experience (with "belonging") between a stimulus and a response is presumed to suffice to strengthen the association between the two; rewards and punishments act to influence performance of the instrumental response by virtue of being anticipated just prior to occurrence of the response. These views, which have been arrived at after much sifting of experimental data, make central use of the distinction between learning (of an S-R connection) and performance—roughly, between *knowing how* to do something versus actually *doing* it. At the time Thorndike was working and thinking, this learning-performance distinction was neither well formulated nor believed to be critical. Later, Tolman (see Chapter 5) was one of the first major theorists to give the learning-performance distinction a central position in hypotheses regarding learned behavior.

Learning without Awareness?

One final issue will be discussed because it stems from Thorndike's views and still excites the curiosity of modern experimentalists. This issue regards the alleged "automatic" action of a reward or punisher in influencing the S-R connection which it follows. Thorndike believed that aftereffects exerted their influence in this automatic fashion, acting to strengthen behavior whether or not the subject was consciously aware of the temporal contingency between his response and the rewarding outcome. The "ideational" or "informational" theory would seem more compatible with the opposite view, that subjects would learn about rewarding consequences and alter their performances according to these expectations.

This issue has cropped up and been argued most vigorously in "verbal conditioning" studies. In the typical experiment, the subject is asked to do some verbal task, such as to say simple words, or compose sentences around a list of critical words. Usually, some irrelevant pretext is fabricated to elicit the subject's support in this task, for example, he is told that the experimenter is recording intonation contours in the subject's production of different phonetic combinations. The experimenter monitors the words spoken for a while, to establish a baseline rate for productions of a given kind; then he begins unobtrusively to say *good* or *umm-hmm* (indicating approval) whenever the subject says a particular kind of word (e.g., a plural noun of any sort). Usually during this period, the subject's rate or probability of producing instances of the reinforced response class increases. In some experiments, the reward contingency may be terminated for a period, during which time the response rate drops back to the baseline rate. This basic sort of experiment has by now been done many times, using many different types of responses, different types and scheduling of reinforcers following the critical responses, with variations in instructions, etc.

The procedure in such experiments, with free-flowing speech, ill-defined response categories, and subtle, unobtrusive, symbolic rewards, is not highly conducive to high levels of conditioning. Roughly speaking, it is difficult for the subject to isolate and rehearse the relevant S-R-O events. There are indeed rather wide individual differences in sensitivity to the reinforcement contingencies, with some subjects conditioning very readily and others not at all. It turns out that this degree of conditioning correlates fairly well with the subject's "awareness" as measured by his self-reports on a questionnaire administered at the end of the conditioning session. The questionnaire probes for the person's knowledge of what was really happening in the experiment: "Was the experimenter saying anything? If so, what? When? Were you selecting your words according to any particular rule? What? Why? Did you notice yourself saying particular words more than others? If so, why? Do you feel as though the experimenter were trying to influence what you said? If so, how?" Such questions can vary from general and vague to detailed and leading, and experimenters have varied in the type and extent of questioning.

To illustrate how "awareness" of the response-reinforcement contingency may relate to the extent of verbal conditioning, Figure 2.4 shows results from a "plural-noun" study by DeNike and Spielberger (1963) where the experimental group was divided on the basis of their answers on the post-experimental questionnaire into aware and unaware subjects. Data on the two groups are plotted separately in the figure. The control subjects simply emitted words without the experimenter's reinforcing any responses, and these subjects show a steady base-rate of plural noun productions throughout the experiment.

The significant feature is the high level of conditioning for the aware subjects in contrast to the virtual absence of conditioning for the unaware subjects; the unaware subjects do not differ from the nonreinforced control

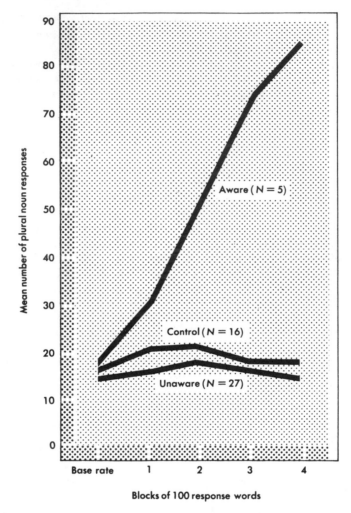

Figure 2.4.   The role of awareness in the effectiveness of verbal conditioning procedures. Subjects who showed awareness of the experimenter's saying "Good" show
increases in giving plural nouns. Other subjects who were not aware showed no change
in rate, but behaved just like the control group. (From DeNike & Spielberger, 1963. By
permission.)

subjects. Such results as these suggest that human subjects try to figure out
what is going on in such experiments, and if they can get the right hypothesis (i.e., infer that the experimenter says "Good" whenever they say a plural
noun), then they will "instruct themselves" to produce plural nouns if they
want the experimenter to say "Good" to them. The most detailed formulation of this volitional hypothesis is given by Dulany (1968).

The alternative position is that learning *can* occur without awareness of
reinforcement contingencies, although it may not be such a dramatic performance change as is produced by an explicit self-instruction to produce

responses of a specific class. The proponents of this view (e.g., Kanfer, 1968) point to the less than perfect correlation between verbal reports of awareness and level of conditioning, or they emphasize cases in which the critical response rates clearly change without much awareness apparent in the subject's introspections. They take the position that the primary response (e.g., plural nouns) *and* the verbal self-reports are both to be viewed as dependent variables that are functionally related to all sorts of experimental variables, and that concurrent learning of the two types of responses (to say nouns *and* to describe the reinforcement contingencies) could proceed independently but both be related to the same experimental variables.

Upon closer analysis, the verbal conditioning paradigm is quite ill-suited for settling this issue of awareness and learning, since the response to be influenced is known to have one source of "volitional" control and since the response and its outcomes are both quite observable to the subject. The issue can be answered more decisively by studies in which the reinforced responses or their effects are not attributable to awareness for the simple reason that the action itself (or its outcome) is not observable. The former conditions have been arranged in experiments with human subjects by Hefferline and his associates (Hefferline & Keenan, 1963; Hefferline, Keenan, & Harford, 1959) and by Sasmor (1966). In these studies, very tiny, unobservable muscular responses (e.g., tension in a thumb muscle), detected by the experimenter through electronic amplification, were shown to be modifiable when these responses were made to produce a positive reinforcer or avoid a negative reinforcer. The frequency of this unseen response increased and decreased appropriately during conditioning and extinction; and yet none of the subjects could verbally identify the response that was producing the reinforcers. They were being conditioned without their ability to state correctly what they were doing to cause the reinforcer to appear. Often they were not able to state that anything about their behavior was being modified.

It seems clear now that these two views are not so terribly different; once one encounters the problems of measuring "awareness," of specifying exactly how the subject ever comes to be aware of (or able to verbalize) the reinforcement contingencies, of specifying exactly how his describing to himself the reinforcement contingencies leads to control of his overt responses once all these issues have been squarely faced and answered, it then seems that the "automatic S-R" and the "volitional" interpretation are very similar except for differing emphases. This is not an infrequent happening in psychological theorizing. The question of whether rewards exert their influence in an "unconscious, automatic manner" turns out to be a rather poorly framed research question that has generated much experimentation and relatively little light. This judgment is not to denigrate the value of the verbal conditioning paradigm as a possible model for how reinforcement operates in all sorts of social settings involving verbal behavior, such as job interviews, psychiatric interviews, opinion polling, mental testing, personality probing, and psychotherapeutic sessions (see Krasner, 1962). For instance, studies illustrating how a psychotherapist selectively reinforces and punishes particular remarks of a patient, albeit often in an unwitting manner, are significant in revealing effective variables in interpersonal influence and attitude change within psychotherapy.

Estimate of Thorndike's Position

Before proceeding to an appraisal of the contemporary significance of Thorndike's position, let us summarize his answers to the standard problems of learning. Attempting such a summary for each of the several leading learning theorists will make it easier to keep perspective on their similarities and differences.

Thorndike's Position on Typical Problems of Learning

Thorndike's answers are briefly summarized according to the six typical problems discussed in the first chapter.

1. Capacity. Learning capacity depends upon the number of bonds and their availability. The differences between bright and dull are quantitative rather than qualitative, although intelligence has dimensions of magnitude as well as of breadth (Thorndike et al., 1927). The theory of intelligence is consonant with the identical-elements theory of transfer.

2. Practice. Repetition of situations does not in itself modify connections. Repetition of connections leads to a negligible increase in strength, unless the connections are rewarded. Practice is important because it permits rewards to act upon connections.

3. Motivation. Reward acts directly on neighboring connections to strengthen them; punishment has no corresponding direct weakening effect. Punishment may work indirectly, however, through making the learner do something else which may confront him with a reward. "Ideas" need not intervene; connections may be strengthened directly, without awareness.

4. Understanding. The role of understanding is minimized, not because it is undemonstrable, but because it grows out of earlier habits. The best way to get understanding is to build a body of connections appropriate to that understanding. When situations are understood at once, it is a matter of transfer or assimilation, that is, there are enough elements in common with old situations to permit old habits to be used appropriately.

5. Transfer. The theory of identical elements is espoused. Reaction to new situations benefits by the identity of these new situations, in part, with old situations, and also by a principle of analogy described as assimilation.

6. Forgetting. The original law of disuse assumed forgetting to take place in the absence of practice in accordance with the empirical findings of studies such as those of Ebbinghaus. Later books did not deal with the problem in any detail; the law of disuse was not mentioned, but some forgetting with disuse was still assumed.

The flavor of Thorndike's theory was all along that of the automatic strengthening of specific connections directly, without intervening ideas or conscious influences. While Thorndike was not an avowed behaviorist, and was willing occasionally to use subjective terms, his emphasis was certainly behavioral.

It would be unfair to leave the discussion of Thorndike without referring to his insistence on measurement, and through that insistence, his contribution to the improvement of the learning of skills in the schools. There was an energetic empiricism about Thorndike's experimenting and theorizing which compensated for their lack of systematic elegance.

The Specificity Doctrine, a Source of Both Strength and Weakness

Thorndike gave great impetus to what has sometimes been called the scientific movement in education—the movement which suggests that educational practices be regulated according to verified outcomes of specific practices. His tremendous drive led to enormous output in fields as varied as handwriting scales, dictionary-writing, methods in teaching arithmetic and spelling, intelligence tests, and vocational guidance. But the secret of his output was not only energy: the output stemmed also from his matter-of-fact conception of science, the notion that, in order to do something about anything, you have to know specifically what you are about.

The specificity doctrine helps you to roll up your sleeves and get to work. Consider, for example, all the complications involved in the teaching of reading. What is it that the child is to be taught? Philology? Grammar? Semantics? It took a Thorndike to give the simple answer: "Words." With that answer, he proceeded to count the frequency with which each word occurs in English, by tabulating millions of printed words from all manner of sources. He then arrived at the most common words. These are the words which must surely be understood. He made available lists and dictionaries to facilitate teaching the most needed words. A specificity theory like Thorndike's tells the educator where to look and how to measure in a baffling field such as schoolroom practices.

The specificity doctrine is also a source of weakness, and it has been the target of the most severe attacks upon Thorndike. The illustration above shows the kinds of criticisms Thorndike invites. Is language no more than words? Are the most frequent words really what we wish to teach? Perhaps we need to think of language as a means of expression, as logic in action, and must therefore equip the child with the minimum set of tools necessary for adequate communication. That this approach is a possible one has been shown by the development of Basic English, wherein the central vocabulary of 850 words overlaps only in part with Thorndike's most frequent words. The approach of Basic English takes into account the organized character of language as an instrument of meaning. Thorndike, true to association tradition, tended to think of language as a collection of words, which he set out to treat quantitatively. As did all psychologists at that time and for some time after, Thorndike gave a very superficial and inadequate analysis of language acquisition and language functioning. Part of the revolution in modern linguistics was the demonstration of complexities in language of a sort beyond the wildest dreams of behavioristic psychologists.

In Thorndike, the analytical emphasis of association theory also pervaded the conception of rewards and punishments, and weakened somewhat the analysis of these phenomena. The notion that the law of effect works mechanically on all connections in the neighborhood of the rewarded one makes of reward something extrinsic to the activity in question. In showing that the law of effect may work this way, he slighted the internal relationships between success and what the individual is trying to do, goals which satisfy aroused motives or needs. Again, texts may be cited in proof of the fact that Thorndike knew all this—he early quoted the "interest series" as we have shown and later added the notion of "belongingness"—but that does not alter the conclusion that his scientific preoccupations led him away from the internal relations of effort and success to the external relationship of any satisfying state of affairs strengthening any connection which happened to be near it.

Perhaps more heat has been generated over Thorndike's subordination of insight and understanding to drill and habit than over any other aspect of his writings. While he thought insight very rare in animals—perhaps rarer than it actually is—he did not deny insight in man. He was not awed by it, and thought it best understood by the same associative laws as applied in other situations. Just as erroneous inferences are made because of habitual associations which throw the learner off his course, so the insights of the genius are made by appropriate habitual associations and analogies. He had this to say of reaction to novel situations:

> There is no arbitrary hocus pocus whereby man's nature acts in an unpredictable spasm when he is confronted with a new situation. His habits do not then retire to some convenient distance while some new and mysterious entities direct his behavior. On the contrary, nowhere are the bonds acquired with old situations more surely revealed in action than when a new situation appears. (1913, p. 29)

Although this comment is true enough, Thorndike's failure to give real concern to the way in which past habits are utilized in problem solution, to consider what arrangement makes a problem hard, what easy, when the same essential bonds are involved, is a genuine limitation. The difference is a real one for school practice. It is possible to learn number combinations first (establish the "bonds"), then acquire some glimmer of understanding later, or it is possible to achieve some understanding of what numbers are for, to comprehend the situation as a problem, and then to learn the combinations in this context. In the end, you come out at the same place, knowing the tables and knowing how to use them, but it is not a foregone conclusion that the one method of teaching will be more efficient than the other, either for the student's knowing precisely what has been taught or for his being able to apply it in new situations. Thorndike's preoccupation with bonds has insured that we turn to others, not Thorndike's followers, for a more careful appraisal of the role of meaning and understanding.

SUPPLEMENTARY READINGS

Thorndike was a prolific writer. His bibliography appears in two parts in the *Teachers College Record*: for the years 1898 to 1940 in volume 41 (1940), pages 699–725; for the years 1940 to 1949 in volume 51 (1949), pages 42–45. The total comes to more than 500 items.

The following books contain his major contributions to learning theory, with much supporting experimental data:

THORNDIKE, E. L. (1911) *Animal intelligence.*
THORNDIKE, E. L. (1913) *Educational psychology: The psychology of learning,* Vol. II.
THORNDIKE, E. L. (1922) *The psychology of arithmetic.*
THORNDIKE, E. L., et al. (1928) *Adult learning.*
THORNDIKE, E. L. (1931) *Human learning.*
THORNDIKE, E. L. (1932a) *The fundamentals of learning.*
THORNDIKE, E. L., (1935) *The psychology of wants, interests, and attitudes.*
THORNDIKE, E. L. (1949) *Selected writings from a connectionist's psychology.*

The following is a recent biography of Thorndike:

JONCICH, G. (1968) *The sane positivist: A biography of Edward L. Thorndike.*

Pavlov's Classical Conditioning

One cannot mention conditioned reflexes without thinking of the distinguished Russian physiologist, Ivan Petrovich Pavlov (1849–1936), who gave them their name. Although he did not begin his investigations of conditioned reflexes until he was 50 years old, he spent the rest of his long life in laboratory investigations of them, eventually with a research staff that numbered well over 100 professionals and assistants. His influence upon learning theory has been considerable outside the Soviet Union as well as within it; the prominent place of conditioned reflex concepts in American theories will become abundantly clear in the ensuing chapters presenting the views of Guthrie, Skinner, and Hull.

The classical experiment is by now familiar to every schoolboy. When meat powder is placed in a dog's mouth, salivation takes place; the food is the *unconditioned stimulus* and the salivation the *unconditioned reflex.* Then some arbitrary stimulus, such as a light, is combined with the presentation of the food. Eventually, after repetition and if time relationships are correct, the light will evoke salivation independently of the food; the light then becomes the *conditioned stimulus* and the response to it is the *conditioned reflex.* American psychologists have tended to use the words *conditioned response* instead of *conditioned reflex,* on the ground that all that gets conditioned is not reflex, but the difference in terms is not very important.

Pavlov began his scientific career with investigations of circulation of the heart, then turned to the study of the physiology of digestion, for which he was awarded the Nobel Prize in 1904. This came as something of a surprise to him, for he had not felt that his book *The work of the digestive glands* (Russian, 1897; German, 1898; English, 1902) had been very enthusiastically received. The main work on conditioned reflexes began in 1899 with the publication of Wolfson's thesis, done under Pavlov's direction, entitled "Observations upon salivary secretion" (Pavlov, 1927, p. 412). The newly discovered reflexes were then called "psychic secretions" to distinguish them from the unlearned physiological reactions. The term which has come to be translated *conditioned reflex* was first used publicly by Tolochinov, one of Pavlov's associates, in a report to the Congress of Natural Sciences in Helsingfors in 1903, based on investigations begun in 1901. Pavlov wrote two books on this work in the next quarter of a century, translated into English under the titles *Conditioned reflexes* (1927), and *Lectures on conditioned reflexes* (1928). At the time these books were written, Pavlov was already 75, but he now became interested in psychiatry, and in the remaining years of his life spent a good deal of time making observations in mental hospitals and attempting to parallel some of his observations with experiments upon dogs in his laboratory. The final papers were collected by Gantt, translated, and published in a volume entitled *Conditioned reflexes and psychiatry* (1941), although many other topics are covered in the translated lectures. The Russians themselves, in later years, translated some of his Wednesday lectures, as they were called; some of these appear with other papers in the volume *Selected works* (1955). In addition to secondary accounts of Pavlov's work, of which there are a number (e.g., Frolov, 1937; Babkin, 1949), there is one other collection in English of Pavlov's own writings, entitled *Experimental psychology and other essays* (1957). Although this chapter is being written nearly 40 years after his death, it is evident that Pavlov's scientific influence is still current; we are fortunate that most of what he had to say about conditioned reflexes is available to us in English.

Anticipations of Conditioning

Modern experimental psychology developed under the influence of association theory which had its origins in the philosophical school of English empiricism: Locke, Hobbes, Berkeley, Hume, Hartley, and the Mills. Ever since Aristotle, the laws of association have tended to be stated as those of temporal contiguity, similarity, and contrast of the elements to be associated, although later associationists, such as Thomas Brown (1820), designated these as primary or qualitative laws, and added a number of secondary or quantitative laws. When the laws were stated in quantitative form (effects of frequency, etc.), there came a strong tendency to emphasize contiguity of elements as having priority over the principles of similarity and contrast. Physiological explanations tended to rest primarily on contiguity:

> When two elementary brain-processes have been active together or in immediate succession, one of them, on reoccurring, tends to propagate its excitement into the other. (James, 1890, I, p. 566)

If, as in this statement from William James, we emphasize contiguous

---

[1] Much of what follows is adapted from Hilgard and Marquis (1940) and Kimble (1961).

events and state their association as one between brain states, we are not far from Pavlov's conditioned reflex.

The fundamental facts of conditioning were known before anyone attempted to do what Pavlov did, that is, to study exactly what happened, and to vary the parameters that controlled the events. Whytt recognized "psychic secretion" over a century before Pavlov:

> We consider . . . that the remembrance or *idea* of substances formerly applied to different parts of the body produces almost the same effect as if these substances were really present. Thus the sight, or even the recalled *idea* of grateful food, causes an uncommon flow of spittle into the mouth of a hungry person; and the seeing of a lemon can produce the same effect in many people. (1763, p. 280, as quoted by Rosenzweig, 1962)

Pavlov's own work was greatly influenced by Sechenov, known as the father of Russian physiology, whose *Reflexes of the brain* was published in journal form in 1863 and as a book in 1866; selections are available in English (Sechenov, 1935). He freely used the expression "psychic reflexes" and interpreted man's voluntary behavior in reflex terms. Pavlov acknowledged the importance of having read Sechenov as he began to study psychic processes by physiological means.

Pavlov was apparently in some conflict during the years 1899–1902, not yet having turned his back on the study of gastrointestinal function, but becoming more interested in the physiological approaches to psychic functioning. Apparently he resolved this conflict around 1903, when he lectured on experimental psychology and psychopathology in animals, defended the study of psychic reactions by physiological means, and discussed the conditioned reflexes to which he was thereafter to devote his exclusive attention (Pavlov, 1928, pp. 47–60).

PAVLOV'S EXPERIMENTS AND THEORIES

Some Empirical Relationships

Pavlov's contribution rests not so much on his discovery of the conditioned reflex, or even on his theorizing about it, as in the care with which he explored numerous empirical relationships, thus determining the essential parameters and providing the background and the terminology for countless succeeding experiments by others as well as by his own colleagues and disciples.

Reinforcement, extinction, spontaneous recovery. The history of a simple conditioned reflex begins with its acquisition through repeated *reinforcement*, that is, the repeated following of the conditioned stimulus by the unconditioned stimulus and response at appropriate time intervals. Pavlov presented data from often-conditioned dogs, so that the course of original acquisition is not commonly available from his data, but comparable experiments show some tendency for an S-shaped curve, an initial portion with little or no response, then a rapid increase, then some falling off in rate of increase. The curve of Figure 3.1 shows the initial acceleration, but the experiment was not continued long enough for the slowing down to occur as an asymptotic level of responding is achieved.

When reinforcement is discontinued and the conditioned stimulus is presented alone, unaccompanied by the unconditioned stimulus, the conditioned response gradually diminishes and disappears, a process that is called *experimental extinction*. Pavlov gave numerous tables showing such extinction; the data from one of them are plotted in Figure 3.2. Note, however, that, after elapsed time without further repetition of any kind, the conditioned salivation has returned; this is called *spontaneous recovery* of the extinguished reflex. Pavlov's explanation of these effects will be discussed later.

Generalization of excitation and inhibition.   In the process of conditioning, the response comes to be evoked by a broad band of stimuli centered around the specific conditional stimulus. The CR will occur on a test to a neighboring stimulus to an extent dependent upon the similarity of the test stimulus to the training stimulus. This is called *stimulus generalization*. Figure 3.3 shows an example: in that study by Hovland (1937), human subjects were conditioned to give a galvanic skin response (GSR, sweating of the palm) to a tone by pairing it with an electric shock. Following training, the subjects were tested with three tones varying in frequency (pitch) and lying

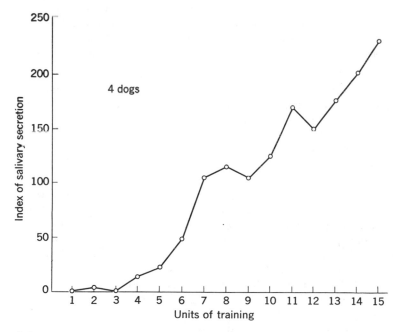

Figure 3.1.   The course of acquisition of a conditioned salivary response. The salivation anticipated injection of morphine in four dogs. (Plotted by Hull [1934b, p. 425] from the data of Kleitman & Crisler [1927]. By permission.)

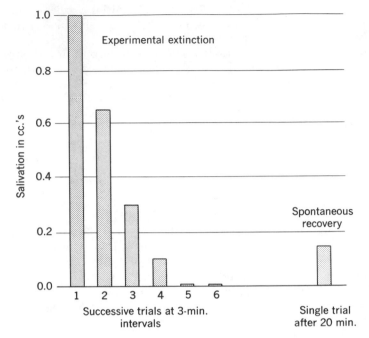

Figure 3.2.   The course of extinction and of spontaneous recovery. The decreasing heights of the bars at the left indicate the fall off in conditioned salivation as the conditioned stimulus (the sight of meat powder) was repeated without reinforcement. The bar at the right shows spontaneous recovery after a rest of 20 minutes. (From Pavlov, I. P., Conditioned reflexes, 1927, p. 58, by permission of The Clarendon Press, Oxford.)

differing distances from the training CS. This distance is measured by counting up the number of just-noticeable-differences (JNDs) between the CS and the test stimulus. Figure 3.3 plots the results, namely decreasing generalization of the CR to tone stimuli that are progressively more distant from the training CS.

Not only is there generalization of excitation following training, there is complementary generalization of inhibition following extinction. Although first discovered by Pavlov, the effect can be illustrated much more clearly by another part of Hovland's (1937) experiment shown in Figure 3.4. In this case, subjects were first conditioned through intermixed trials to give a GSR to all of four pitched tones. Then an extreme tone was presented alone repeatedly without shock, so that the GSR to that tone extinguished (or became inhibited). Thereafter, the subjects were tested without reinforcement with all four tones, yielding the results in Figure 3.4. This shows the lowest response amplitude to the extinguished stimulus (above zero JND), but progressively less decrement (generalized inhibition) the farther is the test stimulus from the extinguished stimulus.

As we shall see farther on, Pavlov tried to explain generalization phenomena in terms of the irradiation of excitation (or inhibition) in the

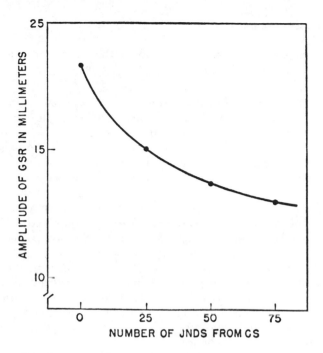

Figure 3.3.   Stimulus generalization gradient for the galvanic skin response conditioned to a tone of 1,000 cycles per second. (From Hovland, 1937. By permission.)

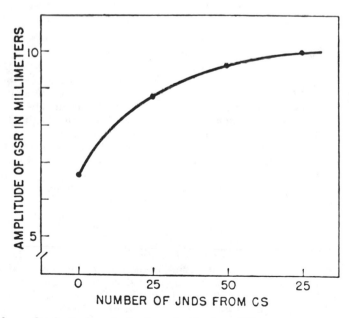

Figure 3.4.   Gradient of generalization of extinction. GSR was conditioned to all tones and then extinguished to an extreme tone (at 0 on scale). Finally tests were conducted with all tones. (From Hovland, 1937. By permission.)

cortex between the neural sites of action of the CS and the test stimulus. But more on that later.

Differentiation. A conditioned response that generalized to a wide range of stimuli could be quite maladaptive in situations requiring a precisely tuned reaction sensitive to subtle or critical features of a stimulus situation. Consequently, *differentiation*, the complementary process to generalization, has great adaptive significance. Pavlov demonstrated repeatedly this process of differentiation, of how initial generalization from a reinforced CS to a test stimulus could be overcome by contrasting the two stimuli alternately over trials. That is, the subject receives a series of trials randomly alternating between presentations of the positive CS (called CS⁺) paired with reinforcement versus trials of the negative CS (called CS⁻) not paired with reinforcement. Eventually, after some fluctuations, the conditioned reflex occurs mainly to CS⁺ and little or not at all to CS⁻. The subject now *discriminates* between CS⁺ and CS⁻, whereas previously he had *generalized* his conditioned response between the two. Just as Pavlov discussed generalization in terms of underlying irradiation in the cortex, so did he also think of differentiation as the corresponding *concentration* of excitation at the CS⁺ cortical site and of inhibition at the CS⁻ cortical site.

Favorable and unfavorable time relationships between conditioned and unconditioned stimuli. The temporal relations within conditioning, as defined and discussed by Pavlov, were summarized as follows by Hilgard and Marquis (1940, pp. 44–45).

A. Conditioned and unconditioned stimuli overlap temporally.
　1. *Simultaneous conditioned response.* The conditioned stimulus begins from a fraction of a second to 5 seconds before the unconditioned stimulus, and continues until the latter occurs. The conditioned response tends to follow the beginning of the conditioned stimulus almost immediately.
　2. *Delayed conditioned response.* The conditioned stimulus begins from 5 seconds to several minutes before the unconditioned stimulus, and continues until the latter occurs. Although the conditioned response begins before the unconditioned stimulus, it follows the onset of the conditioned stimulus by a delay proportional to the length of the interval between the two stimuli. Delayed conditioned responses are difficult to form unless a simultaneous conditioned response has already been established.
B. Conditioned and unconditioned stimuli do not overlap temporally.
　3. *Short-trace conditioned response.* The conditioned stimulus is removed for a few seconds before the unconditioned stimulus begins.
　4. *Long-trace conditioned response.* The interval between the cessation of the conditioned stimulus and the beginning of the unconditioned stimulus is 1 minute or more. The conditioned response does not begin at the onset of the conditioned stimulus, nor at its cessation, but after an interval proportional to the time elapsing before the presentation of the unconditioned stimulus. Long-trace conditioned responses are formed with greater· difficulty than delayed conditioned responses.
　5. *Backward conditioned response.* The conditioned stimulus does not begin to act until after the cessation of the unconditioned stimulus.
C. Time interval functions as the conditioned stimulus.
　6. *Temporal conditioned response.* An unconditioned stimulus is presented at

regular intervals of time. If it is now omitted, a conditioned response will occur at approximately the usual interval. Intervals as long as 30 minutes have been used successfully with dogs.

American experimenters have tended to follow Pavlov's classificatory scheme, except that "simultaneity" for them means 0–0.5-second CS-US intervals; and many of the studies of interstimulus interval use 2–4 seconds, well within what Pavlov considered "simultaneous" conditioning. These studies have been summarized by Kimble (1961, pp. 155–160). They typically use phasic, quick responses (e.g., an eye blink CR to an airpuff US) rather than a slow response like salivation.

Varieties of inhibition. The inhibitory phenomena within conditioning, first described in connection with extinction, became of great interest to Pavlov, and a classification of various types of empirical manifestations of inhibition was arrived at. The summary by Hilgard and Marquis of these types of inhibition follows:

A. External inhibition.
   Temporary decrement of a conditioned response due to an extraneous stimulus, as when a loud sound reduces conditioned salivation to a light.
B. Internal inhibition.
   Internal inhibition develops slowly and progressively when a conditioned stimulus is repeatedly presented under one of the following conditions.
   1. *Experimental extinction.* The weakening of response to a conditioned stimulus which is repeated a number of times without reinforcement.
   2. *Differential inhibition.* A conditioned response given originally to either of two stimuli is restricted to one of them through the reinforcement of one and the nonreinforcement of the other. The nonreinforced negative stimulus becomes inhibitory.
   3. *Conditioned inhibition.* A combination of stimuli is rendered ineffective through nonreinforcement, although the combination includes a stimulus which alone continues to evoke the conditioned response. The other stimuli in the combination are conditioned inhibitors.
   4. *Inhibition of delay.* If a regular interval of sufficient duration elapses between the commencement of a conditioned stimulus and its reinforcement, during the early portion of its isolated action the conditioned stimulus becomes not only ineffective, but actively inhibitory of other intercurrent activities. (There may be temporary disinhibition at the onset of the conditioned stimulus, so that there is a slight conditioned response before the inhibition is manifested.)
C. Disinhibition.
   Temporary reappearance of an inhibited conditioned response due to an extraneous stimulus. This may be considered as an external inhibition of an internal inhibition.

Irradiation and concentration apply to inhibition as well as to excitation. These are matters of theory, and to these theories we now turn.

Pavlov's Cerebral Physiology

Pavlov commonly talked of the "higher nervous activity," by which he meant the physiological processes going on within the cerebral cortex. An early experiment in which conditioning was attempted in a decerebrate dog convinced Pavlov that conditioned reflexes could not be formed in the absence of the cerebral cortex.[2]

Although many extirpation experiments were conducted and some anatomical localization of function was recognized, the main physiological processes described by Pavlov are inferences from behavior, not the result of direct studies of particular centers. When the "visual analyzer" or the "auditory analyzer" are mentioned, they are assigned vague anatomical localizations, but are primarily inferred from the kinds of visual or auditory discriminations of which the animal is capable. The same is true of "pathological cortical cells" or other references to quasi-anatomical portions of the brain. Contemporary Russian neurophysiologists, although followers of Pavlov, use modern electrophysiological, pharmacological, and other techniques for direct study of the brain, but at this point we are considering the theories Pavlov first enunciated years ago.

Association.   The connection between the excitation produced by the conditioned stimulus and the center aroused by the unconditioned stimulus is a result of a kind of attraction or drainage of impulses from the first aroused center to the second, similar to the suggestion quoted above from William James. Presumably the direction of attraction is a matter both of time order (the conditioned stimulus arriving first and serving a signaling function) and of relative intensity (the unconditioned center normally being more highly excited). Pavlov is clear that what he calls conditioning is what psychologists have called association:

> Thus, the temporary nervous connection is the most universal physiological phenomenon, both in the animal world and in ourselves. At the same time it is a psychological phenomenon—that which the psychologists call association, whether it be combinations derived from all manner of actions or impressions, or combinations derived from letters, words, and thoughts. Are there any grounds for differentiation, for distinguishing between that which the physiologist calls the temporary connection and that which the psychologist terms association? They are fully identical; merge and absorb each other. (1955, p. 251; original date, 1934)

Irradiation, concentration, and reciprocal induction.   Two fundamental nervous processes, excitation and inhibition, manifest themselves in various ways; their interactions provide the essential basis for the operation of the cerebral hemispheres. Incoming impulses by way of afferent nerves and the lower centers finally reach some special cells of the cortex appropriate to the sensory system (analyzer) to which the afferent nerves belong. From these special cells the excitatory process irradiates to various other cells over a greater or lesser area. It is this irradiation that provides the basis for generalization of conditioned reflexes among similar stimuli, through the overlap of the fields of excitation produced by the differing stimuli. The idea was that stimuli which are physically alike will also activate neighbor-

---

[2] Experiments done much later showed, in fact, that relatively crude sorts of conditioned reflexes could be formed in dogs without their cortex; however, especially simple stimuli that require little processing (e.g., the flashing of a bright light) must be used. Such studies are reviewed in Chapter 15.

ing places in the cerebal cortex. Hence, in addition to the association or coupling of excitations, we need the notion of irradiation. However, finer analysis would be destroyed if irradiation were not corrected by *concentration* of excitation back to the original special cells. This comes about most promptly if aided by *inhibition*. This differentiation by the method of contrasts, in which the positive stimulus is reinforced and the negative one not, develops an inhibitory process in relation to the negative stimulus that reduces the irradiation of excitation from the positive stimulus and concentrates it where it belongs. The inhibition irradiates also, which can be demonstrated by showing that immediately after presenting the negative stimulus, the response to the positive one is also weakened. This is true in the early stages of the establishment of a differentiation; later, when both excitation and inhibition have been concentrated, *reciprocal induction* takes place. This phenomenon was rediscovered and renamed *behavioral contrast* in modern times (see Hilgard & Bower, 1966, pp. 514–518). In reciprocal induction, the effect of the positive conditioned stimulus becomes stronger when applied immediately or shortly after the concentrated inhibitory stimulus; the effect of the inhibiting stimulus likewise proves to be more exact when it follows the concentrated positive one. Thus the eventual cortical patterns are determined by the interplay of excitation and inhibition through irradiation, concentration, and reciprocal induction.

It should be noted that the evidence Pavlov used in favor of his ideas about cortical irradiation, concentration, and reciprocal induction was entirely behavioral; he never directly measured cortical electrical fields (it was technically infeasible at the time Pavlov was active), so his "brain theorizing" was purely at a conceptual level, based on inferences from behavior. As the behavior of his dogs showed irregularities or greater complexities, so would Pavlov merely complicate the presumed operations of irradiation and concentration of excitation and inhibition (e.g., that they waxed and waned in peculiar temporal waves and patterns following a conditioning session). By and large, the complexities of behavior that Pavlov described have not been securely replicated or accepted (see, for example, Loucks, 1933), and most psychologists regard Pavlov's "brain theorizing" as fanciful but without much conceptual power for making novel predictions.

Types of nervous system. Pavlov recognized four types of genotypical nervous systems based on the strengths of excitatory and inhibitory processes, their equilibrium and mobility. These types turned out to be coordinated with the ancient classification of temperaments that has come down from Hippocrates. Where excitation and inhibition are both strong, but equilibrated, two types arise. If the states are labile, the *sanguine* temperament results; if they are inert, then the *phlegmatic* temperament is found. If, however, excitation overbalances inhibition, so that the processes are unequilibrated, then the temperament is *choleric*. Finally, when both excitation and inhibition are weak, whether the states are labile or inert, a *melancholic* temperament ensues.

While each animal belongs to one or another of these temperament classes, his actual character (the phenotype) depends upon his experiences with the environment so that character is "an alloy of the characteristics of type and the changes produced by external environment" (Pavlov, 1955, p. 260; original date, 1934). Pavlov was dissatisfied by Kretschmer's typology of mental diseases (Kretschmer, German, 1921; English, 1925) for several reasons: it was too simple (two types only), it was based on pathology, and it failed to distinguish between genotype and phenotype (Pavlov, 1955, pp. 616–619; original date, 1935).

Second signal system.   While in his own work Pavlov did not give strong emphasis to the point, he recognized that the ability to speak greatly enlarged man's potentialities, and later Soviet scientists have made much of this. The conditioned reflex mechanisms that man shares with lower animals are grouped together as the *first signal system*; speech in man provides a *second signal system*.

When the developing world reached the stage of man, an extremely important addition was made to the mechanisms of nervous activity. . . . speech constitutes a second signalling system of reality which is peculiarly ours, being the signal of the first signals. On the one hand, numerous speech stimulations have removed us from reality, and we must remember this in order not to distort our attitude toward reality. On the other hand, it is precisely speech which has made us human, a subject on which I need not dwell in detail here. However, it cannot be doubted that the fundamental laws governing the activity of the first signalling system must also govern that of the second, because it, too, is activity of the same nervous tissue. (Pavlov, 1955, p. 262; original date, 1934)

Pathological states.   The discovery in Pavlov's laboratory of the "experimental neurosis," and Pavlov's concern with psychiatric patients late in life, led Liddell repeatedly to refer to Pavlov as "the psychiatrist of the future" (Liddell, 1936, 1961). Whether or not this view was justified, Pavlov was quite interested in investigating behavioral disturbances. His initial discoveries of "experimental neuroses" in dogs were made quite by accident. A dog was taught to salivate to presentation of a circle but not to presentation of an elongated ellipse. Then, over a series of trials, the radius of the ellipse was shortened, making it progressively harder to discriminate from the circle with which it continued to be contrasted. As the discrimination became exceedingly difficult, the dog's behavior became erratic, his discriminative performance became very poor, and he began to show signs of "emotional disturbance." Whereas he had formerly been trained to stand quietly in the restraining harness of the conditioning apparatus, he now began to struggle, moan, and bark. Eventually the dog became quite violent and resisted being taken into the conditioning laboratory. He had acquired what Pavlov called an "experimental neurosis"; Pavlov thought such disturbed states could be produced by a conflict within the cerebral cortex of the antagonistic forces of excitation and inhibition at closely adjacent sites.

Although difficult discriminations (involving reward versus nonreward) have not proved in later work to be the most reliable procedure, "experimental neuroses" of this general sort are easily produced in laboratory animals by placing rewarded approach behavior into direct conflict with punished avoidance behavior. For example, a very hungry cat who has been trained to press a lever for a food reward can then be punished with a severe electric shock for pressing, with the result that he shows disturbed, conflicted behavior (see Masserman, 1943; Dollard & Miller, 1950). The study of such conflict and disrupted, neurotic behavior has been an interesting sidelight in the literature of learning theory.

This is not the place to go into Pavlov's views with respect to psychiatric pathology in any detail. He felt that the experimental neuroses in his animals were similar to neurasthenia in man, that persecution delusions corresponded to something like hypnotic states in the dog, that catatonic schizophrenia was a hypnotic-like state of *protective inhibition*,[3] that manic-depressive reactions represented a derangement of the normal relations between excitatory and inhibitory processes. Obsessional neuroses and paranoia he felt must be due to a pathological inertness of the excitatory processes of different motor cells.

On the whole, the leap from his speculative brain physiology to confident statements about neuroses and psychoses appears much too pat to be taken seriously as scientific explanation. In summary, then, we find Pavlov accounting for a myriad of relationships on the basis of a clash of excitation and inhibition in the cerebral hemispheres, their irradiation and concentration, plus some characteristics of cortical cells, including their occasional inertness or pathological excitability.

POST-PAVLOVIAN DEVELOPMENTS

Extension of the Empirical Base

Pavlov was a centrally significant figure in the development of American behaviorism; behaviorists like John B. Watson (1916) took inspiration from Pavlov's work to use the conditioned reflex as the basic building block for their theoretical reconstruction of behavior. In Russia, Pavlov was an imposing, powerful intellectual giant who throughout his very long and active life heavily influenced the course of Russian psychology and physiology. A good deal of the research stemming from Pavlov's work concerned simple extension of the conditioning paradigm to new responses, new sorts of stimuli, new sorts of animals. With a little ingenuity, a decent psychologist can think of literally thousands of small problems to investigate, the results of all of which conceivably will be collated in some encyclopedia concerning all that is known about conditioning or learning of one or another species of organism.

One interesting development was the investigation of *interoceptive conditioning* within either man or higher animals. In interoceptive conditioning, the usual conditioning procedure is used, except that either the CS or

---

[3] When a conditioned stimulus exceeds a certain strength, instead of the expected increase in response with increasing strength, there follows a decrease in response, to which Pavlov gave the name *protective inhibition*. He believed that this mchanism protected the organism from overstimulation. This is part of the rationale for "sleep therapy" as used by the Russians (Gantt, 1965, pp. 135f). Modern learning theorists are more likely to explain Pavlov's original observation in terms of interfering pain reactions brought on by the extremely intense conditioned stimulus.

the US (and UR), or both, involve stimulation of an internal organ such as the kidney, heart, or pancreas. It turns out that a fantastically large variety of internal organs can be conditioned to respond in the Pavlovian manner to a variety of internal signs. Bykov (1957) reports a number of such experiments. For example, a physiological stressor can be applied to a dog (as a US) producing hypertension as a UR, and this hypertensive response can become conditioned to any of a variety of either external or internal stimuli. Similarly, by use of drugs or special implanted electrodes, enhancements in normal activity can be reliably elicited from and conditioned in such organs as the pancreas (insulin release), the liver (glycogen uptake), the kidneys (urinary extraction), the bladder (urination), the heart, the stomach (flow of secretions), and the gall bladder, as well as in various and sundry endocrine glands (e.g., adrenals and salivary) and in blood conditions (e.g., hypoglycemia). It would seem that almost anything that moves, squirts, or wiggles could be conditioned if a response from it can be reliably and repeatedly evoked by a controllable US.

The fact that such interoceptive conditioning is possible is suggestive for interpretations of many so-called psychosomatic symptoms. For example, the man who becomes hypertensive when he thinks about a hated boss is understandable, as is the child who gets "sick to his stomach" at the thought of eating some food which earlier made him nauseous. Conceivably, the delicate balance in which our physiological systems maintain our inner milieu in constant equilibrium is coordinated in part by cross-conditional adjustments between the activities of interrelated organs or systems, i.e., a departure of one system from its equilibrium acts like an internal CS for an anticipatory adjusting CR in a compensatory system. In any event, these studies have shown that the organs inside an animal are just as conditionable as are those outside (albeit a bit slower because they have their "natural rhythms"). As we shall see in Chapter 15, this generalization also includes special activities of brain cells themselves.

Inhibitory Conditioning

Pavlov proposed that, during experimental extinction, an active inhibitory process was building up, becoming associated to the nonreinforced CS, so as to overcome and impede the positive response to the CS. He thought of this inhibition as becoming conditioned to the CS during extinction (or to the negative CS⁻ during differentiation training) and as being an *antiresponse* factor. American psychologists, especially Skinner (1938), looked at such data and questioned whether one really needs an active inhibitory notion: why would not simple *loss of excitation* account for all of Pavlov's data? Hearing no convincing answer, most psychologists held in abeyance their judgments on the utility of behavioral inhibition constructs.

In recent experimentation, much evidence has been forthcoming showing the existence of conditioned inhibitory factors in classical and operant conditioning. Some experiments by Rescorla (reviewed by him, 1969a) are particularly clear in demonstrating conditioned inhibition of "fear" or "anxiety" in dogs and rats. A necessary component of such demonstrations is an already conditioned response to some base stimulus (call it S₀) to which we then add an excitatory or an inhibitory stimulus, in order to assess the change in responding to S_0. In one demonstration by Rescorla (1966), three groups of dogs were first trained to avoid electric shock in a two-compartment shuttle-box by running back and forth across a middle barrier. The shock was reprogrammed to start 30 seconds after each jump, with the shock coming on the side in which the dog was sitting. This contingency suffices to keep the animals shuttling back and forth to avoid the shock. The rate of shuttling (i.e., number of crossings per unit-time) is the measure of conditioning, and after much training the dogs settle into a fairly steady rate of responding (about seven responses per minute in Rescorla's experiment). This is the baseline response to S_0 (the shuttle-box situation) which will be used to test later excitatory or inhibitory stimuli.

Following the avoidance training, the three groups of dogs underwent a phase of Pavlovian conditioning involving a tone and an electric shock. Each dog was penned into one side of the shuttle-box and given tones and electric shocks for several sessions. For one group, designated P for positive contingency, the 5-second tone was always followed by a shock; for a second group, called N for negative contingency, shocks occurred frequently unheralded by any stimulus, but a 5-second tone was never paired with nor followed within 30 seconds by a shock, so that for these subjects the tone served as a safety signal; for a third group, called R for random, the tones and shocks occurred independently of one another, at random times; for these subjects, the tone had no predictive validity for the occurrence of the shock, either positive (as for group P) or negative (as for group N).

Following these tone-shock sessions, the dogs were returned to the shuttle-box and continued their avoidance training. After stability of avoidance rates had returned, a series of probe-stimulus tests were given: the tone would be sounded for 5 seconds (not systematically related to the ongoing shock schedule) and shuttle responses recorded in 5-second periods for half a minute before and for a minute after the tone probes. The results averaged over several such tests are shown in Figure 3.5, showing average rate of barrier crossing in 5-second periods for six pre-CS (tone) periods, for the one tone period (marked CS), and for eleven 5-second periods following the tone period.

The important thing to note is that group P (which had the "excitatory" conditioning of fear to the tone) about doubles their response rate during the tone, while group N (which had the "inhibitory" conditioning of fear) reduces their response rate to about one-third the baseline. Group R which had no specific correlation between tone and shock shows no change in response rate to the tone. Following the tone probe, the response rates return gradually to the baseline level of avoidance maintained by the shuttle-box shock schedule.

The obvious interpretation is that for group P the tone had become a reliable predictor of shock occurrence, conditioned to a fear reaction; when the probe tone elicits this anticipation of shock, that alone suffices to kick off the shuttle-avoidance response. For group N, the tone had become a reliable predictor of absence of shock; it had become a safety signal, conditioned to inhibition of fear or relief from anxiety. Therefore, the probe reduces the dog's level of fear and thus reduces his rate of shuttle-avoidance, which is based on such fear.

There are other recent demonstrations of conditioned inhibition, using

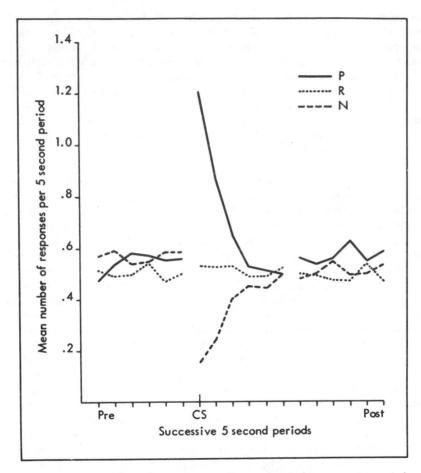

Figure 3.5. Mean number of responses per 5-second period in successive periods prior to CS onset, during the CS and the subsequent 30 seconds of differential conditioning treatment, and after the expiration of that period. (From Rescorla, 1966. By permission.)

both classical and instrumental responses, so it is no longer possible to doubt the reality of such opposing or "antiresponse" factors that arise from negative correlations between presence of a "neutral stimulus" (the CS) and appearance of a reinforcing stimulus. What is even more remarkable is that recent experiments have confirmed some of Pavlov's earlier observations that the positive conditioned stimulus (correlated with occurrence of reinforcement) comes to acquire certain *inhibitory* characteristics of its own! In a review of such paradoxical inhibitory factors in conditioning, Kimmel (1966, p. 238) writes:

The studies reviewed . . . support the conception that the acquisition of classical conditioning involves a distinctly negative component side by side with its more well-known positive characteristics. After the formation of an initial association of an excitatory nature, the CS gradually begins to develop inhibitory properties that result in attenuation and delay of the CR and even its ultimate total loss under continued reinforcement, as well as diminution of the UCR in the presence of the CS. The latter is revealed particularly by the technique of omitting the CS and comparing the resulting UCR with UCRs observed (both before and after) when the CS is present.[4]

The research reviewed by Kimmel mainly involved human subjects and noxious unconditioned stimuli like shock or an airpuff to the eye. In these cases, the person may come to steel himself or get prepared to receive the noxious US when the CS comes on, with a consequent reduction in UCR magnitude; the occasional US given without prewarning by the CS catches him unprepared, and elicits the full UCR it did at the onset of training. Such informal ideas might account for the adaptation of the aversive UCR when it is preceded by a CS.

With appetitive conditioning (e.g., food eliciting salivation in a hungry dog), one can still find a gradual lengthening of the latency of the CR (its time of occurrence between the CS and US), with the CR sometimes totally disappearing, "receding" to that temporal point of the interval when the US is delivered. Pavlov (1927) mentioned such phenomena, which he called "inhibition of delay." Sheffield (1965) and Ellison (1964) have observed such effects recently in salivary conditioning with dogs. A usable analysis of the situation proposed by Skinner (1937a) is that "inhibition of delay" results from the experimental subject's acquiring a more precise temporal discrimination regarding the time of delivery of the US (food) following the onset of the CS. The interval from CS-onset to US-onset may be conceived of as a stimulus continuum, with early-interval cues being associated with non-reinforcement while late-interval cues are associated with reinforcement. This analysis would then lead us to expect that eventually early-interval cues (just after CS-onset) would become conditioned inhibitors; the inhibition could extend so far along the time (implicit stimulus) continuum as to nearly make the actual CR disappear. This was Pavlov's position on the matter. In such circumstances, the simplest way to demonstrate the CR is to either delay or omit the US on test trials. When this is done, a large CR appears at almost precisely the time when the US should have been delivered (see Ellison, 1964).

CLASSICAL AND INSTRUMENTAL CONDITIONING

Although many writers, especially physiologists, imply that learning and Pavlovian conditioning are essentially synonymous, this position is no longer generally held among psychologists. One kind of distinction that has arisen is between conditioning of the type studied by Pavlov, which has come to be called *classical conditioning*, and another variety that has come to be known as *instrumental conditioning*, or, within the arrangements studied by Skinner, *operant conditioning*. Actually, much of the work within the Soviet Union also follows the paradigm of instrumental conditioning, so that it is appropriate to call attention to the distinction between classical and instrumental conditioning.

Konorski's two types of conditioned response. Working in Warsaw, Miller and Konorski (1928) began studying a kind of conditioned reflex which they felt to be a second type, Pavlov's salivary conditioning being the first type. The experiments were repeated in Pavlov's laboratory, with his approval. A typical experiment was that in which the dog was trained to lift its paw to a conditioned stimulus. The leg was passively flexed after a signal, and then the dog was fed. This "reward" type of training soon led to conditioned leg flexion at the signal. This type of conditioning was called "instrumental conditioning" by Hilgard and Marquis (1940) because the leg flexion was "instrumental" to the receiving of the reinforcement; the same term was applied by them to the operant conditioning of Skinner (1938). Konorski (1964) later adopted the terms *classical* and *instrumental conditioning* when writing in English, and has continued to show in what respects the two types of conditioned reflex differ. The two types have provided the basis for a good deal of Russian experimentation (Razran, 1961b).

Classes of conditioned reflex according to American psychologists. The distinction between two classes of conditioned reflex, as first proposed by Miller and Konorski (1928), has had a number of reflections in classificatory schemes by American psychologists. Kimble (1961) has drawn up a table showing a number of these twofold classifications of learning (Table 3.1).

At least in prototypical cases, classical conditioning and instrumental conditioning clearly differ in procedures, or in the scheduling of stimulus events. In classical conditioning, the US or reinforcing stimulus is contingent on presentation of the CS, and is applied independently of any response the subject may make (although the subject himself may not think so). Also, the conditioned response that is measured is a fractional part of, or resembles, the unconditioned response elicited by the US. In instrumental conditioning, presentation of the reinforcer is typically contingent upon a specified response; for example, a hungry rat depresses a lever in order to get a bite of food. A discriminative stimulus may enter into this correlation: food may be given for a lever-press, for instance, only when a tone is sounding in the conditioning chamber, and not when the tone is off (Skinner calls this a "discriminated operant").

The procedures differ somewhat in their obvious manipulable variations; for example, the CS-US interval is an inherent variable in classical condi-

Table 3.1   Twofold classifications of learning proposed by different authors. (From Kimble, 1961, p. 66.)

Author(s)	Term for Classical Conditioning	Term for Instrumental Conditioning
Thorndike (1911)	Associative shifting	Trial-and-error learning
Miller and Konorski (1928); Konorski and Miller (1937a, 1937b)	Type I	Type II
Skinner (1937a)	Type S, or respondent	Type R, or operant
Schlosberg (1937)	Conditioning	Success learning
Hilgard and Marquis (1940)	Classical conditioning	Instrumental conditioning
Mowrer (1947)	Conditioning	Problem-solving

tioning, whereas the response-to-reinforcement interval (so-called delay of reinforcement) is inherent in the instrumental conditioning paradigm. Along with these procedural differences, it was earlier believed (primarily by Schlosberg, 1937; Skinner, 1937a; and Mowrer, 1947) that somewhat different response systems were typically implicated in the two forms of conditioning. Thus, behaviors were divided into those mediated by large skeletal muscles (e.g., movements of the limbs) versus those mediated by smooth muscles (e.g., glands, heart) by means of the autonomic nervous system. It was conjectured that responses of this latter sort were elicited by unconditioned stimuli (e.g., shock elicits activities throughout the autonomic nervous system) and were conditionable only in the classical manner. On the other hand, skeletal responses are rarely under control of unconditioned stimuli, are "emitted voluntarily" rather than elicited by a US, and are conditionable primarily by instrumental conditioning procedures. This was the standard "two-factor" theory which dominated learning theory in America for approximately 30 years following 1936. We shall have much to say about it in later parts of the book (see Chapters 7 and 15), the research surrounding it, and how it is being modified in the light of new conceptualizations. Suffice it to say that some persuasive arguments can be made that the distinction has outlived its usefulness (see Staddon & Simmelhag, 1971; Terrace, 1973). But we are getting far ahead in our story. Let us return to some of the work issuing from Pavlov's beginnings.

THE SECOND SIGNAL SYSTEM: THE DIFFERENCES THAT WORDS MAKE

It has already been noted that, toward the end of his life, Pavlov had things to say about the importance of words to man, and about some of the differences between the first and second signaling systems. It is worth commenting somewhat further on this matter, because the psychologists within the Soviet Union have found this a permissible way in which to state a great many facts about child development and human psychology generally without violating the current Pavlovian theories.

A distinction should be made between those experiments concerned with the genuine difference between the organization of verbal and other behavior and those which treat verbal responses merely as an alternate form of response. The ordinary arrangements of classical conditioning are followed in many of the experiments on *semantic conditioning*; some, for example, study the generalization from actual objects to their verbal equivalents (or study the equivalence of one word to another as conditioned stimuli). While some referential characteristics of language are illustrated by such studies, they do not necessarily reflect the unique properties of language behavior. A review of a good deal of the Russian experimentation along these lines can be found in the work of Razran (1961a), who, working in America, originated the term *semantic conditioning* (Razran, 1939). Another form, known as *verbal conditioning*, attempts to influence the words that a subject uses by reinforcing certain of his utterances and extinguishing others. This practice has become incorporated into some forms of psychotherapy (Krasner, 1965). Some of this research was discussed in the preceding chapter. Neither *semantic conditioning*, as such, nor *verbal conditioning* gets at the full flavor of the differences between the first and second signaling systems as they have been studied by, for example, Luria and his associates (Luria, 1961). Luria's interest has been in the development of the child, particularly in the development of voluntary control, and here he finds language of central importance.

The tie to classical conditioning is by way of an experiment originally designed by Ivanov-Smolensky (1927). A child is instructed to press a rubber bulb whenever a given signal (say, a tone) comes on; this is equivalent to an unconditioned response. A second signal, say a colored light, is now regularly presented just a fraction of a second before the tone. The child, who has been instructed to respond as fast as he possibly can to the tone, now begins to "jump the gun" and will actually begin his response to the light which precedes the tone. This conditioning occurs almost unwittingly, since, because of the closeness of the two stimuli, the subject may not consciously realize that he is in fact beginning his response to the light preceding the tones. Kimble and Perlmuter (1970) illustrate just how "automatized" such simple acts can become. Ivanov-Smolensky and other Russian investigators have shown that the usual laws about reinforcement, extinction, and discrimination apply to these "voluntary" conditioned reflexes. Actually, the experiment is transitional to instrumental conditioning, but no point is made of this by Luria or those who work with him. For them anything that is learned is conditioned and they are interested in how learning is controlled rather than in what goes on inside the human organism as he relates himself to the environment. Luria points out that the laws Pavlov discovered for the gradual development of conditioned reflexes and for their resistance to change are fundamental ones, but that they do not apply in full force to the human learner because of speech—the second *signaling system*. Speech makes possible a new *information system* which modifies considerably the laws according to which new responses are learned by man. For one thing, new responses in man usually are not acquired gradually but instead are incorporated at once into some existing category and regulated by a rule that can be stated in words. Learned behavior no longer requires reinforcement to sustain it, because it is sustained by a behavior rule, and behavior thus becomes self-regulating.

Let us consider four stages in the development of the child's control of behavior through language, and see what kinds of experimental evidence bear on each stage. These stages are the following, according to Luria (1961):

1. Speech has first an *impellant* or *initiating* function. This is easily demonstrated in the child of 18 months. Say "Clap hands," and the action follows.
2. The *inhibitory* function of speech develops later. At first it is not possible to alter an action once it gets started, for example, by asking the child to take his stockings *off* while he is pulling them *on*; he finishes what he starts.
3. The *regulatory* function of speech then develops, as in following the instruction, "When you see the light, squeeze the balloon."
4. *Self-regulation* follows, as gradually *internal* speech develops.

A number of very ingenious experiments show how differently the motor and the speech systems operate in the child between the ages, say, of 18 and 36 months. Some illustrative observations follow.

If a child of 18 months is told to squeeze a rubber balloon, he is likely to respond, and to continue to respond, even if told "Stop" or "That's enough." The inhibitory statements may even lead to further intensification of squeezing. It is possible to teach the child of this age (or a little older) to master a "stopping" technique ("When there is no light, don't squeeze") by using the principle of conflicting positive actions to produce the necessary inhibition. Thus, the child is easily taught to do *two* things when the light comes on: to squeeze the bulb briefly and then to place his hand on his knee. Once he has learned to terminate the squeezing, it is possible to shorten the distance the hand moves from the bulb (to the tabletop instead of to the knee) and gradually to eliminate the second act. Now the child is able to squeeze only when the light is on, and to inhibit the tendency to keep on squeezing when it is off.

The regulatory function of speech shows many interesting complexities. For example, children of 3 or 4 who could not follow the self-instruction "I shall press twice!" readily pressed twice to their self-repeated "Go!" "Go!" Luria believes that the original control through speech is based more on impulse control than on signification, but it is worth noting that the speech control is more adaptable, even at this age, than motor control. The limits of control through signification are illustrated by modifying the "Go!" "Go!" experiment to one in which, following a positive signal (a red light), the child is to say "Press!" and then press a bulb, whereas, following a negative signal (a blue light), he is to say "Don't press!" and resist pressing the bulb. This is too much for him; he tends to err by pressing while saying "Don't press." If he keeps *quiet* (*viz.*, says nothing) at the negative signal, he is then able to inhibit pressing to the negative signal.

The ultimate control through signification and through internal speech comes more gradually; then we have the highest form of self-regulation.

The Orientation Reflex

Pavlov early talked about the "what-is-it reflex" or the "reflex of curiosity," and this came to be called the *orientation reflex* in his laboratory. It referred to the tendency to orient toward (or pay attention to) any novel stimulus, without regard to its significance. This tendency was found to interfere with conditioned reflexes (illustrating external inhibition), but as the conditioned reflexes became stronger, the orientation reflex tended to disappear.

The orientation reflex has in recent years become a matter of major interest in the Soviet Union, with numerous investigators being concerned with its physiological and behavioral manifestations. Interest in America has been furthered through the overlap between the functioning of orientation and arousal, as controlled to some extent by the reticular formation in the brain stem.

The *physiological* indicators that have been most used in the study of the orientation reflex have been EEG activity, plethysmographic responses, recordings of blood pressure or blood flow (through, say, a finger) and galvanic skin responses (GSRs). The behavioral correlates are adjustments of the sense organs, such as head turning or pricking up ears; this alertness is also revealed in a lowering of sensory thresholds (Berlyne, 1960a; Sokolov, 1963).

The *adaptive* significance of the orientation response is twofold: first, in preparing for environmental events that may call for swift action ("emergency reactions"), and, second, through a process of habituation, in preventing the animal from orienting repeatedly to monotonous repetitive stimuli of no biological significance to it. In general, it is found that the orienting response habituates (extinguishes) fairly soon to predictable stimulus sequences if the stimulus has no signaling value, is not paired with a US, or does not require some reaction. If, following habituation, the stimulus is altered slightly (e.g., a beeping tone is changed in pitch), *dis*habituation occurs, and the orienting reflex returns to take in the novel stimulation.

Habituation is one of the most primitive forms of stimulus learning or pattern perception; in habituating to a recurrent stimulus, the organism is in effect saying, "I know that stimulus, and it bores me." Dishabituation follows the rules of stimulus generalization; the farther removed a test stimulus is from a habituated one, the more likely it is to evoke a full orientation reflex. Habituation is a widespread phenomenon, present in many forms of lower animals, and even in short neuronal circuits (e.g., a spinal reflex). In Chapter 14, habituation will be discussed in greater detail. For the moment, we might point out that the orienting reflex is the concession Pavlovian psychologists make to the subjective phenomenon of "attention."

Phylogenetic Comparisons

The conditioned reflex provided a usable methodology for the comparative study of forms of learning across many different species of organisms. It can be in principle a powerful tool in the hands of a comparative psychologist. Once a reliable unconditioned stimulus has been found and isolated, the technique can be used to see whether a given organism is at all sensitive to a given dimension of stimulus variation (e.g., to discover if rats are color-blind), or whether it can learn conditional discriminations of a given complexity. Certain sorts of cross-species comparisons are prone to misinterpretation inasmuch as learned behavior is a function of a large number of variables (temperature, drive level, distracting stimuli, reward preferences) for which optimal values could well vary drastically across species. Therefore, comparative psychologists tend not to be so concerned with, for example, relative "intelligence" of different animals in learning mazes of different complexities. They are rather concerned with how behavior of a single species is affected by variation in a single learning parameter; they are also concerned with whether organisms at a particular level of phylogenetic development are capable of showing one or another type of learning under the most optimal circumstances one can create for that animal.

Certainly since the days of Darwin, comparative psychology has worked on the implicit belief that there are various "levels" of learning abilities and different types or kinds of learning, ordered from simple forms (like "habituation") to the complex (like learning verbal problem-solving). The belief, too, has been that these levels or types of learning are added progressively as one moves up the evolutionary scale, from simple one-celled organisms through various lower phyla to the primates and man. Comparative psychologists, particularly the Russians, as well as ethologists have been patiently collecting and classifying such experimentation for many years.

A recent review and theoretical perspective on that vast catalogue of data has been completed by Razran (1971). He organizes his presentation around an evolutionary hierarchy of learning types which we have summarized in Table 3.2. To indicate just briefly some of the learning types not yet discussed here, *sensitization* refers to a great sensitivity (lower threshold) of a UCR due to its having been evoked recently; *configuring* refers to differentiation of specific patterns of compound stimuli; *eductive learning* is like predictive learning which makes use of notions of object permanency; *symbosemic, sememic,* and *logicemic* are three stages of linguistic learning, from single words, to simple predications, to propositional connectives.

Lower organisms are supposed to show only lower forms of learning, but evolutionary forces selected out variations in the species and so developed more highly structured organisms that can display higher forms of learning. A few of Razran's generalizations from the experimental studies are:

Coelenterates are readily habituated but cannot be conditioned.
Prevertebrate chordates and spinal mammals habituate, become sensitized, but likewise are not conditionable.
Sensory preconditioning and learned stimulus configuring is possible only in birds and mammals.
Eductive learning is possible with more intelligent birds and mammals (crows, magpies, dogs, and cats) but not in less intelligent ones (pigeons, chickens, ducks, and rabbits).
Oddity and learning sets are largely primate behaviors, and symboling is an exclusively human achievement.

The general evidence clearly supports Razran's thesis of a hierarchical development of learning skills. Thus, not all organisms can be trained by classical conditioning techniques, although all seem capable of habituation. It is to Razran's credit that he undertook the painstaking job of collating

Table 3.2   **Evolutionary levels of learning according to Razran (1971, pp. 310–311).**

> A. *Reactive (Nonassociative)*
>> 1. Habituation
>> 2. Sensitization
> B. *Connective (Conditioning)*
>> 3. Inhibitory (punishing)
>> 4. Classical
>> 5. Reinforcing (instrumental, operant, reward conditioning, etc.)
> C. *Integrative (Perceiving)*
>> 6. Sensory-sensory learning (sensory preconditioning)
>> 7. Configuring
>> 8. Eductive learning
> D. *Symboling (Thinking)*
>> 9. Symbosemic
>> 10. Sememic
>> 11. Logicemic

and organizing the myriad facts available in the relevant Russian and English literature.

Equivalence of Associability

Another recent interest of psychologists is in species-specific variation in what stimuli and what responses are readily conditionable (by classical or instrumental procedures) and which are difficult or impossible to condition. Previously, the standard position of learning theorists on this issue was what Seligman (1970) has termed the assumption of "equivalence of associability." Roughly, it is the supposition that any stimulus the organism can perceive can be linked up to any response it can make, according to the standard laws of learning and with relative indifference to what is being linked to what. Some quotes from Pavlov suggest the position:

It is obvious that the reflex activity of any effector organ can be chosen for the purpose of investigation, since signalling stimuli can get linked up with any of the inborn reflexes. (1927, p. 17)

Any natural phenomenon chosen at will may be converted into a conditional stimulus . . . any visual stimulus, any desired sound, any odor, and the stimulation of any part of the skin. (1928, p. 86)

It is essentially this principle of equivalence of associability that accounts for the very arbitrary, almost bizarre and unnatural, choices of stimuli and responses which learning psychologists have used over the past 80 years; if the principle is true, then any stimulus or response lying conveniently at hand will do, since the same general laws will apply no matter what is used. Or so it was believed.

A number of learning theorists are now beginning to doubt this position; certain critical data have begun to appear which clearly break the rule and do so with no dispute possible. Inklings of the matter came long ago in Thorndike's (1911) original puzzle-box investigations; although his cats readily learned to pull strings and handles and to push buttons to escape the confining puzzle-box, they had an inordinately difficult time learning to lick (wash) themselves in order to escape, despite the fact that coat-washing has a fairly high operant level. Seligman (1970) reviews many other examples; for instance, it is next to impossible to teach a hungry dog to yawn for food reward or a rat to groom in order to get reward, or to reduce a rat's "rearing on hind legs" by punishing it with a loud noise. Part of the laboratory folklore for many years has been that rats and cats will seldom learn or maintain lever-pressing avoidance responses, whereas allowing them to jump out of the apparatus to avoid shock is readily conditionable. Such matters can be passed off to one or another disturbing contaminant—a too-low operant level, or incompatibility of the US-eliciting behavior with the response to be conditioned, or whatever. Psychologists are rarely at a loss for *post hoc* excuses to salvage a cherished general principle.

Meanwhile, however, the evidence continues to grow that evolution has innately endowed certain species with an affinity or "preparedness" for connecting certain stimulus and response events and not others. The connections that are learned readily seem almost to have a clear evolutionary basis (e.g., fleeing to escape aversive stimulation); those for which the organism is "contraprepared" (to use Seligman's term) seem arbitrary and "unnatural." They are either unnatural in the sense of taking a response involved in one consummatory sequence (e.g., the courtship dance of mating doves) and trying to link it into a different motivation-reward system ("dancing" to get food to eat); or unnatural in the sense that a part of the organism's innate reaction to the reinforcing stimulus (or natural series of acts leading up to its consummation) are required to be eliminated and short-circuited in order to have efficient conditioned performance. Breland and Breland (1960) provided several striking illustrations of how their various animals kept intruding species-specific behavior patterns into the arbitrary operant conditioning tricks they were trying to teach them. To take an even further leap regarding species preparedness, Lenneberg (1967) has conjectured that the human child is naturalistically prepared or preprogrammed for language acquisition. All children learn language despite the typical absence of carefully arranged training contingencies. He would suppose that language preparedness is a peculiarly human characteristic; but this is disputed by such scientists as Gardner and Gardner (1971) who have taught a chimpanzee rudiments of American sign language for communicating with her human trainers.

A rather clear-cut case of selective preparedness has been demonstrated in experiments by Garcia and his associates (e.g., Garcia & Koelling, 1966). Thirsty rats drank saccharine-flavored water from a drinking spout which caused lights to flash and noises to sound with each lick. During the session, the rats were X-irradiated; this makes the animals sick, but not until about an hour later. Subsequently, the rats were tested for their learned dislike (or conditioned sickness) to the light-plus-noise stimuli and to the saccharine-flavored water. It was found that the rats had acquired a strong aversion to saccharine-water but none whatever to the flashing light plus noise. The brain had picked out the novel saccharine taste rather than the "bright noises" to selectively associate to the "unconditioned reaction" of feeling sick.

It might be argued that for rats the saccharine taste is just a more salient stimulus than the light-noise combination. To rule out this simple excuse, Garcia and Koelling also ran a complementary experiment in which licking at "bright noisy saccharine water" was the CS whereas a painful electric shock to the feet was the US. On a later test of the elements, the bright noise was now found to have acquired aversive properties, whereas the saccharine water had acquired relatively little association to the shock US. It thus appears that externally applied USs are readily conditioned to external cues like flashing lights and buzzers, whereas internal UCRs like stomach upsets, nausea, and sickness become selectively associated to novel tastes. Garcia has shown in later work that this selective association of a novel taste to an induced sickness can occur over very long time delays (up to many hours), which is well beyond the range of CS-US intervals at which conditioning can be made to occur in the typical situation involving an arbitrary, phasic stimulus. When an animal becomes sick he is selectively biased, so to speak, to remember or "call to mind" the last novel thing he ingested and to associate that taste with his current sickness. In Seligman's terms, the taste-to-nausea connection is one which is highly prepared by the innate wiring of the organism.

Such facts clearly argue for abandonment of the assumption of equivalent associability. The facts themselves are not "explained" in any sense by saying that the organism is "prepared" or "unprepared" to make a given association, since that merely relabels the observation that his conditioning rate was fast or slow in particular cases. The more probable explanations, as Seligman admits, are likely to be of an evolutionary-developmental type, which illuminate the adaptive significance of certain pre-set biases on classes of events likely to be associated in the natural environment.

ESTIMATE OF PAVLOV'S CONTRIBUTION TO LEARNING THEORY

How the Theory Bears on the Typical Problems of Learning

As in the other chapters, we may see what Pavlov's theory has to say about the various questions that are put to each of the theories.

1. Capacity.   The capacity to form conditioned reflexes is in part a matter of the type of nervous system; hence, there are some congenital differences in learning ability. (Such capacity differences between normal and retarded children have interested Luria, who has studied them particularly in relationship to language development—the second signal system—and the orientation reflex; little is made of anything resembling Pavlov's types, however.)

2. Practice.   In general, conditioned reflexes are strengthened with repetition under reinforcement, but care always has to be taken to avoid the accumulation of inhibition, for inhibition may appear even within repeated reinforcement.

3. Motivation.   In the usual alimentary reflexes, in which salivation is reinforced by food, the animal has to be hungry; drive is particularly important in the case of instrumental responses. Because of the "signaling" function of conditioned stimuli, it is presumed that some sort of drive reduction is usually involved; mere contiguous stimulation does not appear to be the basis for learning, although there is some lack of clarity on this point.

4. Understanding.   Subjective terms are to be avoided, so that Pavlov finds no use for terms such as understanding or insight. Yet his conception of reflex activity is so broad that he does not hesitate to say such things as:

When a connection, or an association, is formed, this undoubtedly represents the knowledge of the matter, knowledge of definite relations existing in the external world; but when you make use of them the next time, this is what is called insight. In other words, it means utilization of knowledge, utilization of the acquired connections. (1955, p. 575; original date, 1934)

This is the characteristic associationist view of understanding: the utilization of past experience through some kind of transfer. The problem of novelty is not raised.

5. *Transfer*.   Transfer is best considered to be the result of generalization (irradiation) whereby one stimulus serves to evoke the conditioned reflex learned to another. Particularly in the language system, words substitute readily one for another, and thus permit wide generalization.

6. *Forgetting*.   Pavlov did not deal systematically with the retention or forgetting of conditioned reflexes over time, partly because the same animals were used over and over again, their conditioned reflexes were greatly overlearned, and forgetting was not a laboratory problem. The decline of conditioned reflexes through experimental extinction, or other forms of inhibition, was always recognized, and he always spoke of conditioned reflexes as temporary. It is important to distinguish between extinction and forgetting, however, for there is spontaneous recovery following extinction, and a weakened conditioned reflex is therefore not a forgotten one.

A RECENT APPRAISAL OF PAVLOV'S INFLUENCE

Razran (1965) has summarized Pavlov's influence in the form of six summary paragraphs, which may be paraphrased as follows:

1. Pavlov stimulated an enormous number of experimental investigations using the paired-stimulus method, with all kinds of organisms, throughout their life span and with a great variety of stimuli and responses. Razran estimated that there had been some 6,000 experiments using his exact paradigm (i.e., classical conditioning), reported in at least 29 different languages, predominantly Russian and English.

2. Pavlov converted the general notion of associative learning by way of conditioning into a highly parametric area of study, that is, the quantitative influences upon conditioning interested him from the beginning. One illustration of this is the persistence of his terms to define the significant variables. In Kimble's (1961) glossary of terms relevant to conditioning and learning, 31 terms are attributed to Pavlov, and 21 others to all American and Western psychologists combined.

3. Pavlov succeeded in getting the conditioned reflex adopted as the most convenient basic unit for all of learning. Although the desirability of this is a matter of some dispute, and other units compete with it (while some authorities question that there *is* any such basic unit at all), there is no doubt that it has taken a leading place in this respect.

4. By introducing the notion of the second signal system, unique to man, Pavlov prevented the system from being frozen at an unprofitable reductionist level, in which no distinction would be made between animal and human learning. Oddly enough, he accused the American psychologists of oversimplifying, and of not being in tune with the complexity of actual events.

5. Pavlov's continuing interest in psychopathology, beginning in 1903 but evidenced particularly in his later years, opened up fruitful rapprochements between learning theory and psychiatry, including such functional matters as sleep and drug therapy. Razran notes that of the six volumes in Russian reporting Pavlov's Wednesday seminars, three volumes, comprising 1,716 pages, are reports of clinical demonstrations in which he participated.

6. Even when a second paradigm of conditioning was introduced by Miller and Konorski (1928) and Skinner (1935), it was found that most of the parameters held. While there are some differences, as has been pointed out, the basic facts of reinforcement, extinction, generalization, and so on, are found to hold. Skinner, scarcely a Pavlovian, has found it possible to use many of Pavlov's terms in describing the functional relations within his variety of operant conditioning. While he went much farther than Pavlov on schedules of reinforcement, the first experiments on intermittent reinforcement were indeed done in Pavlov's laboratory. Because rewarded learning, which fitted the instrumental paradigm more nearly than the classical one, was characteristic of American studies of animal learning, Pavlov's work became more acceptable when it was found that most of the principles held within instrumental conditioning.

Pavlov's Influence on Psychologists

Pavlov, in trying to make his studies purely objective, anticipated American behaviorism and later contributed to the behaviorist tradition in America. While he remained strictly within physiology, as he understood it, he was not unaware that he was dealing with essentially psychological problems, and in his Wednesday seminars he made a good many references to the writings of those psychologists he had read. He thought particularly well of E. L. Thorndike, and felt that in some respects Thorndike's work had anticipated his own.

As far as influence upon American psychology is concerned, by testimony of the American psychologists themselves, Pavlov ranks with Freud and Wundt as a major influence (Coan & Zagona, 1962). It therefore behooves the student of learning theory to know something about the man who is responsible for so many of the concepts of contemporary psychology, especially in the field of learning.

SUPPLEMENTARY READINGS

The following English sources cover most of Pavlov's major writings:
PAVLOV, I. P. (1927) *Conditioned reflexes* (Anrep translation).
PAVLOV, I. P. (1928) *Lectures on conditioned reflexes* (Gantt translation).
PAVLOV, I. P. (1941) *Conditioned reflexes and psychiatry* (Gantt translation).
PAVLOV, I P. (1955) *Selected works* (Edited by Koshtoyants and translated by Belsky).
PAVLOV, I. P. (1957) *Experimental psychology and other essays*.

For shorter introductions to Pavlov's work, the interested reader can do no better than to read some of Pavlov's own summaries. His very early essay (1903) "Experimental psychology and psychopathology in animals" gives much of the later flavor; it can be found in Pavlov (1928), pages 47–60, and in Pavlov (1955), pages 245–270. A chapter by a devoted follower is Gantt, W. H. (1965) "Pavlov's system," in B. B. Wolman and E. Nagel (Eds) *Scientific psychology*, pages 127–129.

Books that carry on the experimental tradition started by Pavlov, but make their own contributions, include:
BYKOV, K. M. (1957) *The cerebral cortex and the internal organs*.
GRAY, J. A. (Ed.) (1964) *Pavlov's typology*.
KONORSKI, J. (1948) *Conditioned reflexes and neuron organization*.

LURIA, A. R. (1966) *Higher cortical functions in man.*

RAZRAN, G. (1971) *Mind in evolution: An East-West synthesis of learned behavior and cognition.*

For biographical material on Pavlov:
BABKIN, B. P. (1949) *Pavlov, a biography.*
FROLOV, Y. P. (1937) *Pavlov and his school.*

While much of the experimentation in American laboratories has departed from the classical conditioning paradigm, that there is still vigorous interest in it is shown by the following books:

GEIS, G. L., STEBBINS, W. C. & LUNDIN, R. W. (1965) *Reflexes and conditioned reflexes: A basic systems program.*

KIMBLE, G. A. (1961) *Hilgard and Marquis' conditioning and learning* (2nd ed.).

PROKASY, W. F. (Ed.) (1965) *Classical conditioning: A symposium.*

MACINTOSH, N. J., & HONIG, W. K. (Eds.) (1971) *Fundamental issues in associative learning.*

Guthrie's Contiguous Conditioning

In some respects, the system proposed by Edwin R. Guthrie (1886–1959) follows naturally from those of Thorndike and Pavlov. It is an objective stimulus-response association psychology, and uses the conditioned response terms coming from Pavlov, while being practical and relevant in the spirit of Thorndike. But in other respects the interpretations of learning are very different. It is such similarities and differences which pose issues for learning theory.

GUTHRIE, THORNDIKE, PAVLOV, AND BEHAVIORISM

Thorndike accepted two kinds of learning: selecting and connecting (under the law of effect), and associative shifting. For him associative shifting was originally the fifth of some subsidiary principles, and by far the major burden was carried by selecting and connecting (or trial-and-error learning). For Guthrie, on the contrary, a conception very like associative shifting became the cornerstone of his system. Guthrie did not accept the law of effect in Thorndike's sense, and this was the basic cleavage between their systems.

Guthrie was an early behaviorist. Behaviorism as a "school" of psychology is usually thought of as originating with John B. Watson (1878–1958), who in 1913 announced the behaviorist position, and became thereafter its most vigorous spokesman. There were other varieties of behaviorism, however, and Guthrie was led to his position by way of the philosopher Singer (1911), with whom he had studied. The behaviorists, then and now, had and have in common the conviction that a science of psychology must be based upon a study of that which is overtly observable; physical stimuli, the muscular movements and glandular secretions which they arouse, and the environmental products that ensue. The behaviorists have differed among themselves as to what may be inferred in addition to what is measured, but they all exclude self-observation (introspection) as a legitimate scientific method (except that if studied as verbal behavior, much formerly called introspection can be saved for science). Partly as a protection against an indirect use of introspection, behaviorists have tended to prefer experimentation on animals and infants. They conceive of themselves as biologists who happen to be interested in how organisms behave under various circumstances.

Watson's *Behavior: An introduction to comparative psychology* (1914) was the first book to follow the announcement of his new position. In it were his attempted refutation of Thorndike's law of effect and his substitution of the laws of frequency and recency in place. He believed that animal learning, as in the maze or problem-box, could be explained according to what the animal had most often been led to do in the situation, with the most recent act favored in recall. Because the successful act was both most frequent and most recent (it occurs at the end of each trial in the puzzle-box), its recurrence on the next trial could be explained without recourse to an added principle of rewarding effects. This denial of effect was part of his program of getting rid of the residual subjectivity which he felt was implied in Thorndike's concepts of satisfiers and annoyers. While the frequency-recency theory did not survive its criticism (Peterson, 1922; Gengerelli, 1928), it serves to point up Watson's desire to find objective laws to substitute for those with even a tinge of subjective flavor.

The behaviorist knows that other events intervene between measured stimuli and the responses to them. In order to preserve a systematically coherent position, these intervening events are posited to be much like the observed ones, that is, *implicit* or *covert* stimulus-response sequences. In his early studies on the control of the maze habit, Watson (1907) had attributed great importance to kinesthetic stimuli as integrators of the maze-running habits involved. Because kinesthetic stimuli are aroused as a result of the organism's movements, they fit well into a behavioral or response-oriented psychology. Even the unobserved processes inferred to be going on between stimuli and responses are said to be comprised of subliminal movements and movement-produced stimuli. This emphasis upon kinesthesis as the integrator of animal learning served Watson well when he became puzzled about human thought processes. He decided that thought was primarily a matter of implicit speech, that is, talking to oneself. Sensitive enough instruments, he conjectured, would detect tongue movements or other movement accompaniments of thinking. He was thus able to hold to his consistent behaviorist position without denying that thinking goes on.

It was somewhat later that Watson discovered that the conditioned reflex of Pavlov and Bekhterev might serve as a useful paradigm for learning (Watson, 1916). Because it grew out of the objective tradition that had happened to develop within Russian physiology, it fitted his temper and he adopted it enthusiastically. In Watson's later writings, the conditioned reflex was central to learning, as the unit out of which habits are built.

Watson's general textbook, *Psychology from the standpoint of a behaviorist*, appeared in 1919. It was soon followed by other books written from an avowedly behavioristic standpoint. Among these was Smith and Guthrie's

General psychology in terms of behavior (1921). Like Watson's book, it treated all of psychology from a behavioral viewpoint and made use of conditioning principles. It, too, laid great stress upon movement-produced stimuli. Hence, there is a family relationship between the two books, although they differ greatly in expository style. Watson laid far more stress upon the details of physiology and anatomy, and upon appropriate methods for the behavioral study of psychological relationships. Smith and Guthrie showed less concern for experimental and neurophysiological detail, but instead gave a plausible interpretation of ordinary experience as described consistently from the behavioristic standpoint. Guthrie's later writings preserved the flavor of the Smith and Guthrie book. Despite their similarities, Guthrie's point of view must be considered as something other than a working out of Watson's position.

Doubtless influenced by Watson, Guthrie began to use the language of conditioning in his behavioristic psychology, but he chose to use what was learned from conditioned reflexes in a manner very different from Watson. Watson used the Pavlov experiment as a paradigm of learning, and made the conditioned reflex the unit of habit, building his whole system eventually on that foundation. Guthrie, unlike Watson, started with a principle of conditioning or associative learning, a principle which is not dependent strictly on the Pavlov kind of experiment. Pavlov, in fact, criticized Guthrie for his emphasis on the one principle of contiguity, without sufficient concern for the many complexities within conditioning (Pavlov, 1932). Guthrie (1934) stuck to his guns in a reply, arguing that Pavlov's was a highly artificial form of learning, and what was found to occur within Pavlov's experiments needed explanation according to more general principles.

CONTIGUITY OF CUE AND RESPONSE: THE ONE LAW OF ASSOCIATION

The Lowest Common Denominator of Learning

Guthrie's one law of learning, from which all else about learning was to be made comprehensible, was stated by Guthrie as follows: "A combination of stimuli which was accompanied by a movement will on its recurrence tend to be followed by that movement" (1935, p. 26).[1]

There is an elegant simplicity about the statement, which avoids mention of drives, of successive repetitions, of rewards or punishments. Stimuli and movements in combination: that is all. This one principle serves as the basis for a very ingenious and intriguing theory of learning.

A second statement is needed to complete the basic postulates about learning: "A stimulus pattern gains its full associative strength on the occasion of its first pairing with a response" (1942, p. 30).

This somewhat paradoxical statement, in view of undeniable improvement with practice, is a necessary adjunct to the theory, because it makes possible a number of derivative statements about learning and forgetting.

---

[1] Where the quotations from Guthrie remain unchanged between the 1935 and 1952 editions of his book, the earlier only will be cited.

It can be thought of as a kind of *recency principle*, for if learning occurs completely in one trial, that which was last done in the presence of a stimulus combination will be that which will be done when the stimulus combination next occurs.[2]

How could Guthrie demonstrate that more complicated forms of learning conform to these simple principles? Like other sophisticated theorists, he did not proceed by denying familiar forms of learning. His problem was to show that complex learning can, in fact, be derived from these basic principles along with auxiliary suppositions. He did not deny that there is learning which may be described as insightful or purposive or problem-solving. It was Guthrie's task to show that each of these forms requires no new principles of explanation beyond the primary law of association by contiguity.

Why Strict Contiguity of Measured Stimulus and Response Is Not Essential

One of the standard experiments in the literature of conditioning is that of showing the importance of the time interval between the conditioned stimulus and unconditioned response. The empirical results suggest a gradient, with a most favorable interval and less favorable intervals on either side of this optimal interval (Kimble, 1961, pp. 155–160). The optimal interval varies from half a second to many seconds, depending on the response system conditioned and the measure of conditioning.

Guthrie was able to defend strict simultaneity of cue and response in the face of such data by proposing that the true cue being conditioned is not the stimulus as measured. An external stimulus will give rise to movements of the organism. These movements, in turn, produce kinesthetic stimuli. When associations appear to be made between stimuli and responses separated in time, it is because these intervening movements fill in the gap. The true association is between simultaneous events. The same analysis would be used to explain how an animal learns to deliberately delay its response to a signal in order to get reward; the signal cues off a *chain* of adjunctive behaviors that usher the animal directly into the point of reinforcement.

There is a strong preference for *movement-produced* stimuli as the true conditioners in Guthrie's system. They permit the integration of habits within a wide range of environmental change in stimulation, because these stimuli are carried around by the organism. It appears that some of this preference dates from the early emphasis of Watson (1907) on kinesthesis as the basis of control of the maze habit, a position no longer tenable.[3] Such covert movement-produced stimuli provide ever-present explanations for conduct which cannot be inferred from external stimulus-response relationships. The same emphasis on response-produced stimuli and their conditioning to reward-expectations is still prevalent in the "neo-Guthrians" Sheffield and Estes, as we shall review later.

---

[2] Because it refers to the last response of a succession rather than to recency in time, Voeks (1948, 1950) suggested that it be called the *principle of postremity*.

[3] Honzik (1936) found kinesthesis to be one of the least useful of several sensory controls of the maze habit.

Why Repetition Brings Improvement

The reason that practice brings improvement is that improvement and other forms of success refer to acts, to outcomes of learnings, rather than to *movements*. Guthrie believed that his interest in movements, and the prediction of movements, was almost unique among learning theorists; others, he said, were interested in goal achievements and results of one sort or another. One difference between him and Thorndike was that Thorndike was concerned with scores on tasks, with items learned, pages typed, or correct responses attained. Guthrie was concerned only with the movements of the organism, regardless of whether they led to error or success.

A skill, such as getting the ball into the basket in a game of basketball, is not one act but many. It depends not upon a single muscular movement but upon a number of movements made under a number of different circumstances. Any one movement may be learned in any one trial, but to learn all the movements demanded by the complicated skill calls for practice in all the different situations: while near the basket and far away, on one side and on the other, with and without a guard nearby. Practice is necessary; but it produces its consequences, not according to a law of frequency, but according to the simple principle of the attachment of cues to movements. The more varied the movements called for in a given act of skill, and the more varied the cues which must become assimilated to these movements, the more practice is required. There is no mystery about the length of time it takes to learn to operate a typewriter: there are so many keys in so many combinations, calling for the attachment of a great many cues to a great many responses. It is concomitantly necessary to get rid of the faulty associations which lead to what, from an achievement point of view, is an error. This is done by having the correct behavior occur to the cue which previously gave rise to the faulty behavior. When finally all the cues lead to acceptable behavior, the task is mastered. The apparent contradiction between single-trial learning and the actual experience of painstaking fumbling before success is achieved is resolved when the skilled task is seen to be composed of a large number of habits.

Associative Inhibition, Forgetting, and the Breaking of Habits

The fact of extinction is one of the findings of conditioning experiments that is in need of explanation. Because responses should remain faithful to their cues, Guthrie could not agree to extinction as a decay in habit strength due to mere nonreinforced repetition. According to him, extinction always occurs as associative inhibition, that is, through the learning of a different, incompatible response. His is an interference theory and hence requires no new principles, because the original learning and the interfering learning follow the same rules.

He explained forgetting in the same way. If there were no interference with old learning, there would be no forgetting. Guthrie's position is but an extreme form of the retroactive inhibition theory of forgetting, to be discussed in greater detail later. It has been shown, for example, that conditioned responses, even though in some respects they appear fragile, are actually quite resistant to forgetting (e.g., Hilgard & Campbell, 1936; Wendt, 1937; Skinner, 1950). The long-lasting character of these laboratory conditioned responses is to be understood as intrinsic to learning that is highly specific to cues not confronted in the learners' daily life outside the conditioning situation. If the learners lived in the conditioning situation, their responses would be subject to more interferences. Furthermore, in the typical conditioning experiment, the subject receives a large number of trials in associating a particular CS with a single US. Undeniably, much more forgetting of simple CRs would occur with less practice and concurrent learning of, say, 20 different CSs paired with presence versus absence of 10 different USs. This more closely approximates the task complexity of multiple verbal associations which is known to lead to much forgetting.

If it is desired to break a habit (that is, to accelerate its replacement), it is only necessary to cause countermovements to occur in the presence of the cues to the habit. The problem of locating the cues and substituting counterbehavior often takes time, because many cues may lead to an undesirable habit.

Drinking or smoking after years of practice are action systems which can be started by thousands of reminders. . . . I had once a caller to whom I was explaining that the apple I had just finished was a splendid device for avoiding a smoke. The caller pointed out that I was at that moment smoking. The habit of lighting a cigarette was so attached to the finish of eating that smoking had started automatically. (Guthrie, 1935, p. 139)

Guthrie suggested three methods by which activities are commonly weakened:[4]

1. The first is to introduce the stimulus that you wish to have disregarded, but only in such faint degree that it will not call out its response. This is the method of training a horse to the saddle by starting with a light blanket and gradually working up to full equipment, at no time permitting the horse to become so startled that it plunges or struggles. This is called the "toleration" method, because it presents the CS at just that level (the current "threshold") the subject will tolerate without evoking the response.

2. The second is to repeat the signal until the original response is fatigued, and then continue it, so that new responses are learned to the signal. The "bronco-busting" of the western ranches followed essentially this technique. It is called the "exhaustion" or "flooding" method.

3. The third is to present the stimulus when other features in the situation inhibit the undesirable response. One illustration given by Guthrie is that of training a dog not to catch and eat chickens by tying a dead chicken about its neck. As it struggles to get rid of the corpse, it develops an avoidance response to chickens at close quarters. Another example, illustrating learning, is the disobedience learned by the child whose mother calls him when he is too occupied with what he is doing to obey. This is called "counterconditioning" or "reciprocal" inhibition.

[4] Paraphrased from Guthrie (1935), pages 70–73.

These techniques for breaking unwanted habits have been picked up and applied with much ingenuity by modern psychotherapists in helping their patients overcome certain debilitating behavior problems. One example is called "systematic desensitization" (Wolpe, 1958) and is used to relieve (extinguish) a patient's severe anxieties or phobias regarding some situation or action. A typical case might be a businessman with a debilitating phobia about riding on airplanes, which he wishes to overcome. With the patient, the therapist first identifies a crude hierarchy or generalization gradient of situations ordered according to their "psychological closeness" to the dreaded event, in this case flying in an airplane. These might include distant situations which evoke little anxiety such as looking at airplane travel brochures, holding a toy airplane, or seeing an airplane overhead; nearer things like driving to the airport, walking into the terminal building, approaching the check-in desk, talking to the stewardess, walking up to the door of the plane, going inside the plane, moving around or sitting inside the stationary plane, taxiing, taking off on short trips, going on longer trips, flying in turbulent weather, etc. The items in this generalization hierarchy are rated by the patient according to how much anxiety they arouse.

In the second phase, the therapist teaches the patient the techniques of deep muscle relaxation—that is, how to relax all muscles completely, how to get the relaxation under nearly immediate verbal control (saying "relax" as a CS for a relaxation response pattern), and how to discriminate between when he is tense and when he is relaxed.

In the third phase, the fear aroused by the patient's *imagining* the various situations in his stimulus hierarchy is then extinguished by a combination of the toleration and counterconditioning methods. While deeply relaxed, the patient is asked to imagine the least fear-arousing situation in his hierarchy (e.g., ordering airline tickets). This is done for several extinction trials, then is repeated with the next higher fear-arousing item in the hierarchy, etc. The patient moves on to the next item in the series only if he can remain thoroughly calm and relaxed while imagining himself in that situation. After several one-hour therapeutic sessions with this procedure, the patient eventually will be imagining himself in the phobic situation but feeling no fear.

Fourth, if possible, concurrent with the imaginal counterconditioning in the therapist's office, the patient is also put through a graded series of real-life situations arranged in a fear hierarchy leading up to flying. For example, the therapist might accompany the patient to the airport, while he talks with a stewardess, sits inside a stationary plane, and so on. During these activities, the therapist would be urging the patient to remain calm and verbally reinforcing him for doing so. In case these "dry runs" in the field cannot be arranged, there is still substantial transfer or generalization of the fear extinguished in the imaginal situation to reduce the fear in the real-life setting.

This procedure for extinguishing phobias is now one of the standard tools in the armamentarium of the "behavior therapist." Wolpe (1958) and many others have reported spectacularly high "cure" rates with the procedure (over 90 percent), applied to a variety of phobias such as fear of heights, of animals, of public-speaking, of being outdoors, of autos, of sexual encounters, and so on. The components of the clinical procedure are easily studied (and have been much studied) in the laboratory setting using the common localized phobias of college students—excess fear of snakes, spiders, public-speaking, etc. The procedure—which is undeniably successful in eliminating a high percentage of unwanted phobias—has two components: the fear is elicited at first by only a very weak cue for it, and the imaginal cue is also paired with deep relaxation; the relaxation "response" is presumed to be antagonistic to the anxiety reaction (it "reciprocally inhibits" fear). There-fore, in theory the weak cue becomes connected to the relaxation response. Because of stimulus generalization, the anxiety-inhibitor conditioned to the weakest cue will also reduce the fear now aroused by the next cue in the hierarchy, and it, too, can then be overlaid or replaced by the antagonistic relaxation response. The idea is that if the cues are introduced in slow pro-gression, one could optimally extinguish the phobic reaction throughout the stimulus hierarchy without an anxiety reaction once being experienced by the patient.

One may ask how the various extinction methods compare, say, in their effectiveness in reducing a CS-CR habit within a fixed number of trials or a fixed period of time. A study by Poppen (1968) provides a rather complete comparison of various pure techniques, and combinations of techniques, in extinguishing in rats the fear evoked by a tone that had been paired with electric shock. Poppen found that the toleration-plus-counterconditioning technique was most effective, whereas the typical extinction procedure (sim-ply presenting the CS briefly without shock) was the least efficient. These are just a few of the sequelae of Guthrie's speculations on how to break habits.

Some Derivative Explanations and Applications

Motives.   The motivational state of the organism, its hunger, thirst, or state of comfort or discomfort, had no formal place in Guthrie's learning theory: the motivational state is important only because it determines the presence and vigor of movements that may enter into associative connections. The motive is important only for the stimulus-response sequences that occur, specifically the consummatory response sequences like eating, drinking, mat-ing, etc. The movements that occur get associated to the coincident cues; if a hungry cat acts differently from a well-fed cat, its movements are different and so its learning may be different. It learns what it does; what it does is more important than what its motivational state happens to be. In the Guthrie and Horton (1946) experiments to be described later, the cat often did not eat the salmon provided as a reward in the dish outside the cage. This did not matter, for *leaving the cage* was the important behavior as far as Guthrie was concerned.

Motives are, however, important in one of the derivations from the basic theory of contiguous association: they are important in providing *maintain-ing stimuli*, keeping the organism active until a goal is reached. The goal removes these maintaining stimuli, and brings the activity to an end (Guthrie, 1942, p. 18). We shall see how these maintaining stimuli, along with movement-produced stimuli, tend to keep a series of acts integrated, and account for anticipation of goal-objects (e.g., food to satisfy hunger), for behavior characterized by intent or purpose.

Reward. While Guthrie believed as everyone else does that rewards influence outcomes, his rejection of the law of effect and of the principle of reinforcement in conditioning was based on the position that nothing new is added to associative learning by reward except a particular sort of mechanical arrangement. This mechanical arrangement, which places reward at the end of a series of acts, removes the organism from the stimuli (internal as well as external) acting just prior to the reward. Hence, being removed from the stimuli, the behavior to these stimuli is preserved intact. Instead of behavior's being strengthened by reward, reward protects it from new associations being formed to the *same* stimuli. The successful response was just as strong before the reward occurred, but, if there had been no reward, new behavior in the same situation would have been evoked, resulting in the displacement of the correct response with other, irrelevant responses becoming associated to the experimental stimuli. The act leading to the reward, since it is the last act in the problematic situation, is the one favored when the situation next repeats itself. Guthrie was very explicit about this. Of an animal's escape from a problem-box he said:

> *The position taken in this paper is that the animal learns to escape with its first escape.* This learning is protected from forgetting because the escape removes the animal from the situation which has then no chance to acquire new associations.
>
> (Of latch-opening followed by food.) *What encountering the food does is not to intensify a previous item of behavior but to protect that item from being unlearned.* The whole situation and action of the animal is so changed by the food that the pre-food situation is shielded from new associations. These new associations can not be established in the absence of the box interior, and in the absence of the behavior that preceded latch-opening. (1940, pp. 144–145)

Although this is the fundamental position with respect to reward, and frequently reiterated in opposition to the law of effect and related interpretations, the action of reward is found to be somewhat more complicated when one examines the totality of Guthrie's system. The first (and primary) role of reward is to remove the animal from the problem situation and thus prevent unlearning. But by the principle of association, the animal also learns the activity that he carries on in the presence of the reward (chewing and salivating to food, for example), and this behavior tends to be evoked by renewed hunger and by any of the cues from the problem that may have persisted while the rewarded behavior was going on.

> . . . There is one act, however, to which hunger may remain a faithful conditioner. That is the act of eating; and the faithfulness of hunger to this association derives from the fact that hunger dies when eating occurs. As Stevenson Smith and I pointed out in our *General Psychology*, elements of the consummatory response tend to be present throughout a series of actions driven by a maintaining stimulus. (1935, pp. 151–152)

Not only do general movements of eating tend to be aroused by hunger contractions, but the specific movements demanded by the particular nature of the food are possibly in evidence. Hence when the rat runs the maze he is ready for whatever reward has been received in the past, sunflower seed or bran mash. This readiness is an actual muscular readiness. . . . (1935, p. 173).

In this passage Guthrie states some aspects of the drive-reduction hypothesis, that rewards (at least eating) act by changing internal drive states (hunger cues are removed), and some aspects of the "anticipatory reward" interpretation of the action of reinforcement. Guthrie's interpretation of reward was at once ambiguous, provocative, and a source of frequent attacks upon his position. Some reinforcing events clearly are interpretable in terms of stimulus change following the critical response. For example, in human associative learning, the subject typically rehearses the correct response to each stimulus before the next item occurs, thus insuring that the correct response was the last one to the stimulus before it changed.

As a second illustration, consider an experiment by Bower, Starr, and Lazarovitz (1965), who trained rats in a two-compartment shuttle-box to run into the opposite compartment when a loud tone sounded in order to avoid a painful electric shock. If the rat had not run within 5 seconds, the shock came on and drove it into the opposite compartment. Immediately following the response, the intensity of the tone (the CS) was reduced to some new level at which it was left for 10 seconds (during which time the rat was sitting still following his shuttle response) before being turned off entirely. According to Guthrie's theory, those subjects receiving less change in the CS following the response would have an opportunity to learn new responses (of sitting, relaxing) antagonistic to the shuttle-run CR; these antagonistic responses would generalize to the tone CS and compete with running to the CS, in proportion to the similarity of the postresponse stimulus to the preresponse stimulus. In this manner, Guthrie would predict that successful shuttling would be learned to a higher level by those rats receiving greater changes in the CS contingent on their response. The results of one experiment are shown in Figure 4.1 for subjects receiving no CS change, a moderate CS change, and substantial CS change immediately following the response; the results clearly confirm the Guthrie analysis. A later experiment showed that it was not necessary for the post response stimulus to be close to the between-trials "safety signal"; comparable effects could be produced by several different stimulus changes immediately following the response (e.g., turning on a light or increasing the pitch of the CS tone).

The problem with such demonstrations of "stimulus change as reward" is that they are easily interpretable with other theories. Thus, for example, the theory which supposes that avoidance responses are reinforced by anxiety reduction would also handle the results above; the greater the change away from that CS directly conditioned to fear, the greater the generalization decrement, hence the greater the fear-reduction and reinforcement following the response. Thus such results do not provide differential evidence in favor of Guthrie's reinforcement hypothesis.

Moreover, Guthrie's hypothesis suggests a variety of experimental operations which turn out to be not the least bit rewarding. We can arrange for certain radical changes in the stimulus environment to occur immediately after a rat depresses a lever, such as an electroconvulsive shock, or having

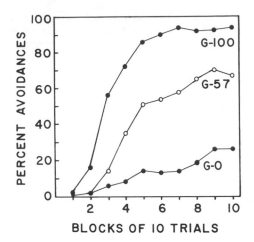

Figure 4.1.   Group mean percentage of avoidance responses in 10-trial blocks. For Group 100, the CS terminates immediately after R; for Group 57, the CS reduces 57 percent in intensity after R and then goes off after 10 seconds; for Group O, the CS remains unaltered before going off 10 seconds after R. (From Bower et al., 1965.)

the floor drop out from under him, or suddenly jiggling the box, or stuffing him in a black cloth bag, etc.; such events simply do not act as rewards, although psychologists have argued that Guthrie's theory predicts that they should. The number of such elementary embarrassments have led contemporary Guthrians—in particular Sheffield and Estes—to abandon the stimulus-change hypothesis of reward in favor of a "conditioned excitement" or motivational interpretation of the action of rewards. We will discuss this theory later in this chapter.

Punishment.   The primary interpretation of punishment was for Guthrie that of all associative learning: you tend to do what you did under the same circumstances:

. . . Sitting on tacks does not discourage learning. It encourages one in learning to do something else than sit. It is not the feeling caused by punishment, but the specific action caused by punishment that determines what will be learned. To train a dog to jump through a hoop, the effectiveness of punishment depends on where it is applied, front or rear. It is what the punishment makes the dog do that counts or what it makes a man do, not what it makes him feel. (1935, p. 158)

What we can predict is that the influence of stimuli acting at the time of either satisfaction or annoyance will be to reestablish whatever behavior was in evidence at the time. (1935, p. 154)

If Guthrie had stopped with statements such as these, it would appear that he treated reward and punishment in a symmetrical fashion. Certainly punishment changes a situation very strikingly, as reward does. Hence one might infer that all antecedent behavior would remain intact, being protected from new learning by the altered conditions of punishment as much as by the altered conditions of reward.

The symmetry in treatment of reward and punishment, as implied in the foregoing quotations, is somewhat illusory, for "doing what you last did" refers to very different parts of the behavior cycle when the reference is to reward than it does when the reference is to punishment. "What you last did" that remains in your behavior repertory because of reward is what you did *just before* the reward appeared; "what you last did" in the case of punishment refers to what you did *just after* the punishment, leading to escape. Punishment produces "maintaining stimuli" relieved by a later movement that brings relief:

. . . An animal on a charged grid, a barefoot boy on a hot pavement, a man sitting on a tack have as their goals mere escape from the intense stimulation that causes general tension and restlessness as well as specific movement. These stimuli continue to act as what Stevenson Smith and I called maintaining stimuli until some movement carries the subject away from the source of stimulation, or the source of stimulation away from the subject. (1935, p. 165)

When these stimuli are removed, we have the circumstances defining reward in Guthrie's theory, and so, if that were the whole story, the prior behavior should remain intact. This kind of relief from punishment has come to be known as *escape learning* to distinguish it from *avoidance learning*. To move from escape learning to avoidance learning, we require an anticipatory response, conditioned to some cue, so that the punishment is circumvented. As we saw in relation to reward, Guthrie's system makes provision for anticipatory responses, and these can, of course, be used to explain avoidance learning. The animal merely makes the escape response to some cue present at the time of punishment—a cue which, fortunately, makes its appearance before the threatened punishment. Hence what happens at the end of a sequence of acts leading to punishment does something *in addition to* and *other than* removing the organism from the scene; it also sets up some conditioned anticipatory responses.

This idea, that the avoidance response is an anticipatory form of the escape response elicited by the noxious stimulus, has implications of varying empirical truth value. One curious set of implications concerns a set of studies on what has come to be called "experimental masochism" in which it appears that a rat actively seeks to give itself a painful electric shock (see Gwinn, 1949; Brown, 1969). As always, the terminal behavior depends upon a particular training history. For instance, the animal is first trained to run down a long alleyway having an electrically charged grid floor to get to the safety box at the end of the runway. Then he is taught, when placed in the alley without shock on the floor, to run rapidly to the end-box in order to avoid the shock which comes on after 4 seconds. In this second phase, when the subject gets shocked, he is in the process of running to the end-box, and the effect of the shock when it does come on is to impel him forward even faster into the safety box. Once this running pattern is established, one can then alter the contingencies as follows: if the rat will just sit still when placed in the start-box of the alleyway, he will receive no shock and will be removed from the alley after 30 seconds; however, if he moves out of the start-box by 12 inches, he will step onto the electrically charged grill and "punish himself." Such training suffices to trap the subject into a vicious cycle: he has been taught to run before shock comes on, and to run when the shock hits him; therefore, despite the change in contingencies from the experimenter's point of view, from the subject's perspective the contingencies (during "punished extinction") are the same as in avoidance training as long as he keeps on running. Rats may continue this self-punitive behavior for many hundreds of trials, as Guthrie's theory would predict, until on some random trial they happen to sit still in the start-box or happen to lurch back to safety rather than dashing forward when they step on the shock grill. Once these novel responses occur, "extinction" proceeds precipitously, perhaps in a trial or two—also as Guthrie would have predicted (see Dreyer & Renner, 1971).

However, it should be mentioned that, in apparent opposition to Guthrie's analysis of avoidance learning, one can train animals and people to make one response to avoid a noxious event but a different response to terminate that state of affairs if it should happen. For instance, in anticipation of a possible house fire, we buy fire insurance and check wiring insulation and the furnace; but if the house is actually burning around us, we run to the nearest exit or assist others to get out. Obviously we can discriminate between and act differently to the threat of our house burning down and the actual event. In less complicated surroundings, it has been demonstrated that a rat can be trained to make one response (e.g., rear up on its hind legs) to avoid a shock when a tone sounds; but if that fails, to make a different response (e.g., depress a lever in his chamber) should the shock come on and have to be terminated by the subject (e.g., Mowrer, 1947).

Noxious stimuli may lead not only to escape and avoidance learning but to a third subvariety, more properly called punishment, that is, to the inhibiting of otherwise rewarded behavior. We may try to stop the child's doing something he enjoys; we may try to break a "bad habit." Punishment of this kind always involves conflict.

Guthrie's position with respect to this subvariety of punishment has been aptly summarized by Sheffield:

(a) Punishment works only if the last response to the punished situation is incompatible with the response that brought on the punishment.
(b) Punishment works only if the cues present when the incompatible response is performed are present when the punished response is performed.
(c) Punishment that produces only emotional excitement will tend to fixate the punished response. (1949)

The main point is that punishment is effective in conflict situations where incompatible responses have a tendency to occur. The statement about the presence of cues is not as decisive as it sounds, in view of Guthrie's acceptance of anticipatory responses and movement-produced stimuli as cues. The third point is a useful one: in some cases, what appears to the trainer to be punishing may not be punishing to the learner; in still other cases, punishment, even though annoying, may accentuate stereotyped behavior.

Intentions.   Conduct is organized into sequences in which people make plans and carry them out, or at least start to carry them out. Guthrie was aware of this and devoted a chapter to learning with and without intention (1935, pp. 202–211).

He and Smith had earlier followed the lead of Sherrington and Woodworth in considering sequences of behavior as composed of precurrent or preparatory responses followed by consummatory responses (Smith & Guthrie, 1921; Sherrington, 1906; Woodworth, 1918). Such acts appear from the outside to be intentional, for the earlier adjustments clearly are in readiness for the consequences that are to follow. These anticipatory responses or readiness reactions are said to be conditioned to maintaining stimuli.

The typical case is that of the hungry rat running down an alleyway to food at the end. The activity is maintained by the internal stimuli aroused by food deprivation to which running and eating behavior have been conditioned in the past. That is, the rat found food at some previous time in this situation after running while hungry. These internal stimuli, plus the stimuli from the runway (if it has been previously a path to food), maintain the running of the animal against competing responses, such as stopping to explore. Anticipatory salivation or chewing movements give directional character to the behavior. All this food anticipation is fulfilled if there is food at the end of the maze. Because the stimuli of hunger and anticipation are now removed, and the animal is out of the maze, all the learning is intact for a new trial at a later time. This paradigm provides a way of talking about human intentions and purposes also.

> The essence of an intention is a body of maintaining stimuli which may or may not include sources of unrest like thirst or hunger but always includes action tendencies conditioned during a past experience—a readiness to speak, a readiness to go, a readiness to read, and in each case a readiness not only for the act but also for the previously rehearsed consequences of the act. These readinesses are not complete acts but they consist in tensions of the muscles that will take part in the complete act. (Guthrie, 1935, pp. 205–206)

This statement goes a long way toward the point of view which those with very different theories of learning accept. The only feature which keeps it within the bounds of Guthrie's theory is that all the readinesses, including the readiness for the "previously rehearsed consequences of the act," are said to consist in tensions in the muscles. This assumption, characteristic of the behaviorist position regarding cognitive events, remains in the realm of conjecture rather than of demonstration.

Neo-Guthrian Interpretations of Rewards and Intentions

Among the many contemporary experimental psychologists influenced by Guthrie, F. D. Sheffield has been not only one of the more persuasive defenders of the theory but a proponent of innovations in it. One of the more salient changes has been in Sheffield's reinterpretation of how reward operates to guide instrumental responses, especially in appetitive situations. Sheffield's account was first made available in 1954 in a mimeographed version of a colloquium speech, and later in publications (Sheffield, 1965). Let us consider the simple situation in which a hungry rat, say, is running through a T-maze for food reward in one of the end-boxes, or is depressing a lever which delivers ·a bite of food. The first notion is that the proprioceptive stimuli from the critical response (e.g., lever-pressing) are in an optimal temporary relationship to the unconditioned response (eating), so that fractional parts of the consummatory response will become conditioned to these critical proprioceptive cues as well as to those precursor movements preceding the critical response (e.g., approaching the lever, rising up to press the lever, etc.). It is further supposed that when early components of this successful behavior chain are begun, they produce stimuli causing anticipation of consummatory activity; this anticipation produces "excitement" which feeds into invigorating the ongoing segment of the successful response chain, making it compete more successfully against interfering distractors. By the end of sufficient conditioning trials, the rat is "pulled" through the successful behavior chain by his selecting those precursor responses which produce those stimuli that maximize the conditioned arousal of the consummatory response (i.e., anticipation of reward). Sheffield used these ideas to explain a great deal of the action of positive rewards on learning. It is significant that a similar account of reward effects was adopted by Spence (1956) and other Hullians in their concept of incentive motivation (which was the intervening variable affected by reward in Hull's system, see Chapter 6). Sheffield's ideas were also largely adopted by Mowrer (1960) in later accounts of his theorizing regarding reward effects.

Another innovator in the Guthrian tradition, W. K. Estes, has recently also adopted somewhat the same hypothesis for how rewards influence instrumental responding. Estes writes:

It is assumed that . . . response evocation depends upon the joint action of stimulus input from receptors and input from drive mechanisms. . . . Originally, these specific mechanisms are activated by unconditioned stimuli, for example, the mechanism associated with hunger is activated by the taste of food, the mechanism associated with pain by impinging traumatic stimulation. The result of activity of a drive mechanism is to generate what may be termed facilitatory or inhibitory feedback. . . . By associative learning, . . . control of these positive and negative drive mechanisms is extended to stimuli which have preceded the original unconditioned stimuli. . . . The result of this combination of motivational and associational mechanisms is that after some learning experience the organism's behavior is continuously modulated by anticipations of rewards or punishments, behavior sequences leading to increases in positive feedback being preferentially selected and behavior sequences leading to decreases in positive feedback or to punishment being inhibited. (1970, pp. 10–11)

If for "facilitative drive feedback" in Estes's statement one substitutes the phrase "excitement by conditioned arousal of the consummatory response," the similarity of the two formulations is heightened. The new addition by Estes is the notion of reciprocal inhibition between the general "positive" and "negative" drive centers. Thus, if while performing an appetitive response sequence the animal sees or hears a signal associated with anxiety, that will activate the negative or inhibitory drive mechanism, reciprocally inhibit the positive drive mechanism, and thus lower performance of any appetitive response while the anxiety signal is present. This type of effect, termed "conditioned suppression," was observed long ago by Estes and

Skinner (1941), and has been repeated since many hundreds of times. Estes's assumption of reciprocal inhibition between positive and negative motives seems reasonable and appears to enable us to interpret a number of different results of punishment (see Estes, 1969b).

The Control of the Learning Process

It is part of the charm of Guthrie's writing that it was closely in touch with life and provided amusing but cogent suggestions for meeting the problems of animal training, child-rearing, and pedagogy.[5] This practicality is not a necessary characteristic of the system, for if one seriously attempted to provide evidence for the theory he would be buried in the midst of the precise movement correlates of measurable stimuli and the muscular tension accompaniments of preparatory adjustments. But the system was not intended to be taken seriously in that sense. As long as a convenient way of talking about things could be found without seeming to contradict the system, quantitative precision was presumed not to be essential. It was Guthrie's conviction that scientific laws, to be useful, must be approximately true, but that they must also be stated coarsely enough to be teachable to freshmen (1936).

Most of the practical advice Guthrie gave was good advice, and he succeeded in making it flow from the theory. Consider the following:

> The mother of a ten year old girl complained to a psychologist that for two years her daughter had annoyed her by a habit of tossing coat and hat on the floor as she entered the house. On a hundred occasions the mother had insisted that the girl pick up the clothing and hang it in its place. These wild ways were changed only after the mother, on advice, began to insist not that the girl pick up the fallen garments from the floor, but that she put them on, return to the street, and re-enter the house, this time removing the coat and hanging it properly. (1935, p. 21)

Why was this advice given? Behavior is in response to stimuli. Hanging up the coat and hat had been a response of the girl to her mother's pleading and the sight of the clothing on the floor. In order that the desired behavior be attached to its proper cues, it was necessary for her to go outside and come into the house, so that entering the house became the cue for hanging up the coat and hat.

The following represent the kind of suggestions which recur in Guthrie's writings:

1. If you wish to encourage a particular kind of behavior or discourage another, discover the cues leading to the behavior in question. In the one case, arrange the situation so that the desired behavior occurs when those cues are present; in the other case, arrange it so that the undesired behavior does not occur in the presence of the cues. This is all that is involved in the skillful use of reward and punishment. A student does not learn what was in a lecture or a book. He learns only what the lecture or book caused him to do.

2. Use as many stimulus supports for desired behavior as possible, because

---

[5] The same comments apply to his collaborative books as well: Smith and Guthrie (1921), Guthrie and Horton (1946), Guthrie and Edwards (1949), Guthrie and Powers (1950).

any ordinary behavior is a complex of movements to a complex of stimuli. The more stimuli there are associated with the desired behavior, the less likely that distracting stimuli and competing behavior will upset the desirable behavior. There would be fewer lines confused in amateur theatricals if there were more dress rehearsals, since the cues from the stage and the actors are part of the situation to which the actor responds. Another way of putting this is to rule that we should practice in the precise form later to be demanded of us.

EXPERIMENTS ON THE PUZZLE-BOX

One of the serious defects in the early versions of Guthrie's proposals was the failure to set up convincing experiments. Such an experiment was completed by Guthrie and Horton (1946) between the two editions of Guthrie's book on learning and provides a much more tangible ground on which to come to grips with both the strengths and the weaknesses of Guthrie's position.

It is fitting that Guthrie and Horton should have chosen as a characteristic experiment the behavior of the cat in escaping from a puzzle-box, because this situation had already been the occasion for both experiment and theory. Thorndike's classical experiment has already been cited (p. 30). This gave the send-off to Thorndike's theory by convincing him that little of the cat's behavior was mediated by ideas and much of it controlled by the influence of rewards.

The Guthrie and Horton Experiment

Because of their wish to record details of movement rather than to score achievement in a gross manner, a special problem-box was designed which permitted the cat to be fully observed during the period prior to solution and its exact posture to be recorded photographically at the moment it activated the release. The release mechanism was a small pole set in the middle of the floor of a cage having a glass exit door in the glass front. The animal entered through a start-box and tunnel at the rear. If it touched the pole in any manner at all, the front door was opened and the animal could escape into the room. A camera was operated as the door was opening, so that a photograph of the animal was obtained at the moment of release, while it was still in contact with the pole.

In each of three preliminary trials, the animal entered the box through the tunnel and made its way out the front door, which was left ajar, to find a bit of salmon on the tabletop in front of the box. The first of the regular trials followed. During the regular trials, the experimenters kept notes of the animal's behavior as it entered the box through the tunnel at the rear, and the camera recorded the exact time and position when it struck the release mechanism.

The results are remarkable for the amount of repetitiousness in each cat's successive releases. A cat which bites the pole may do so time after time; one which has escaped by backing into the pole may back almost endlessly in its efforts to escape by the same movement. Others use front paws or hind paws, or roll against the pole. The cat, in full agreement with the theory, learns the method of escape in the first trial and then repeats what is essentially the same solution time after time. Some cats have several modes of escape which they use at different times, or they have one type of escape for a long time and then shift to another. These exceptions to the principle of doing what was done the last time are accounted for on the basis of a different entrance, which changes the stimulating conditions; as the result of accidental distractions; or because, having been in the box a long time and having failed to operate the release by a familiar method, the cat may find some method to supersede the familiar one. The fact that the last movement—the movement at the time of release—is the most stereotyped is in agreement with the principle that such an act will remain intact because nothing has interfered with it, since the cat left the situation as soon as he struck the release mechanism. The fact that the food reward is inconsequential is shown by the cat's frequent failure to eat the fish or to lap the milk provided for it after it escapes the puzzle-box.

Guthrie and Horton say that they have seen in the behavior of their cats all that Thorndike reported. But they have also seen a degree of stereotypy which points strongly to the tendency for behavior to repeat itself under similar conditions. Some of the tracings of photographs of Guthrie and Horton's cats are shown in Figure 4.2. This behavior is so convincing that it must be acknowledged. It is coherent with all that Guthrie had been proposing in his theory. That is surely as much as could be wished for by a theorist from a series of experiments.

Why did these cats learn so much more readily than Thorndike's? The answer given is plausible. First, these cats were somewhat habituated to the apparatus and to the presence of the salmon outside the box; also, they always found the release mechanism available in exactly the same form, and readily operable. Thorndike's release mechanism was more difficult to operate and was probably not always in precisely the same position. Hence Thorndike's cats had to learn a series of habits rather than a single habit. When Guthrie and Horton's cats failed to operate the mechanism by a familiar method, they, too, adopted a new method. Stereotypy was shown because stereotypy worked.

Guthrie and Horton make it clear that they are not proposing a test of the cat's intelligence. They could easily have devised an experiment in which there would have been much less sterotypy. But the point is that as far as the learning of movements is concerned, the animal tends to do pretty much what it last did in the situation. If the situation forces it to do something else, it will do something else. Cats do not jump at the place where a bird was previously caught if there is no bird there, though they may lie in wait at the same spot.

The experiments were accepted by the authors as fully justifying the theory that Guthrie had all along expounded:

It has been our conclusion from our observation of this series of experiments that the prediction of what any animal would do at any moment is most securely based on a record of what the animal was observed to do *in that situation at its last occurrence*. This is obviously prediction in terms of association. (Guthrie & Horton, 1946, p. 42)

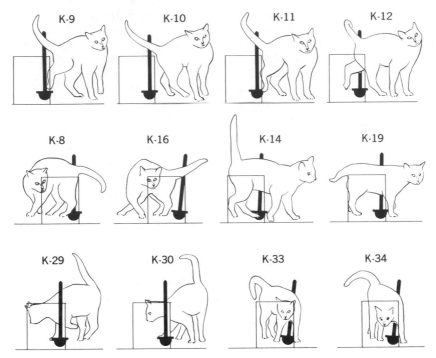

Figure 4.2.   Alternative stereotyped responses of a single cat escaping from the puzzle-box by touching the pole. Responses K-9 through K-12 illustrate one type of response used frequently by cat K. The remaining pictures show four other response types used by the same cat. Reproduced from tracings of photographs taken automatically at the time of release. (From Guthrie & Horton, 1946. By permission.)

Some Objections to the Guthrie and Horton Experiments as Representative of Animal Learning

The experiments of Guthrie and Horton are appropriate ones for showing that, under limiting conditions, learned responses may exhibit a high degree of stereotypy. To go beyond this and assume that these experiments provide the typical case for animal learning is misleading.

According to the authors themselves, varied behavior supervenes if the response of the animal does not release it from the box fairly quickly. The stereotypy appears to result at least in part because the problem is an easy one and the dominant response to the situation succeeds. It may be mastered in a single trial, and the later trials are then merely the repeated performances of a learned act. There is little remarkable about easy learning taking place promptly, or about its being repeated when there is nothing to block it and there is reward to sustain it.

Some critics have argued that the restrictions on the photographs violate Guthrie's insistence that learned behavior should not be defined by outcome or effect, because the moment at which the picture was snapped was defined by the consequences of the activity, namely, releasing the door.

The effect of this restriction in picture taking could be seen more clearly in an experiment that required the animal to stand on his hind legs and reach out of the upper corner of the cage in order to press a button to release the door and take the picture. In this way we further restrict the set of possible responses and achieve added stereotypy. On the other hand, other experimental situations could be constructed, which would reduce stereotypy. In either case, however, what is procured are data concerning responses defined in terms of effect. (Mueller & Schoenfeld, 1954, p. 358)

It is not quite clear how much Guthrie and Horton wished to make of the amount of stereotypy they observed. Commenting on an earlier and related experiment done with guinea pigs by Muenzinger, Koerner, and Irey (1929), Guthrie wrote:

These authors conclude that the mechanization of habitual movement "is still accompanied by variability of its pattern . . ." and that accessory movements, "while on the whole exhibiting much plasticity, show some mechanization of a brief and unstable kind."

The account given by Muenzinger, Koerner, and Irey is quite consistent with what Horton and I observed in our cats. We were interested in the routinizing, they in the exceptions and new behavior. We were convinced that whole segments of movement appear and are repeated all-or-none on succeeding trials. (1952, pp. 271–272)

Guthrie and Horton certainly succeeded in showing a considerable amount of repetitiveness and stereotypy in learned behavior. This led them to conclude, as indicated in the earlier quotation, that prediction is best made on the basis of the last prior occurrence, and that such a prediction is obviously one in terms of association. We may question this last conclusion. To prophesy that a man who owns and wears only blue ties will wear a blue tie tomorrow is an actuarial prediction pure and simple, with no theory in it. It is logically similar to the prediction of an insurance company that a given percentage of people will die at a given age. The only assumption is a certain uniformity of events when taken en masse—an assumption scarcely attributable to associationism.

To account for learning, rather than for the repetition of learned acts, one has to account not for uniformity but for change. Upon learning in this sense the Guthrie and Horton experiments throw little light. Most of the change in behavior took place in the neglected early trials in which the cats learned to find their way out of the box through the glass door. There was, to be sure, the supplementary learning to use the pole to open the door. A harder but possibly clearer problem, of the type used in "insight" experiments, perhaps would be solved by fewer animals, but those that solved it would be able to use the solution in novel situations. Thus the chosen learning situation has a great deal to do with what aspects of behavior will be revealed. The problem-box of Guthrie and Horton, which at first appears to lay bare the primitive nature of learning, may in fact be a highly specialized situation poorly designed to show the behavior of the cat as it goes about solving a problem; perhaps a more difficult problem but with clearer cue-response relationships would be more appropriate for studying learning.

GUTHRIE'S FINAL REFLECTIONS UPON HIS THEORY

Shortly before his death, Guthrie was invited to prepare a chapter giving the background, orienting attitudes, and general systematic characteristics of his learning theory. This he did, and the chapter appeared in his last year (Guthrie, 1959).

He repeats his arguments for the need for simplicity. Thus, in the statement of scientific laws, or rules for regularities in nature, the requirement that these must be communicable and teachable makes simplicity desirable (1959, p. 162). He denies that nature was set up in a pattern of simple laws, waiting to be discovered—the requirement of simplicity is a human requirement. "It is men that are simple, not nature" (p. 162).

This orientation implies that psychology must choose an appropriate level for its categories of stimulus and response. Guthrie notes that human behavior is highly predictable in our daily interactions, and that our lives would be intolerable if this were not so. It is therefore rather remarkable that we have been so unsuccessful as psychologists in formulating general rules of behavior. Perhaps we have been going at it the wrong way. When we describe behavior changes that are predictable, we do so according to the presence or absence of specific stimuli and responses to be observed, not according to their intensity or degree. In our scientific efforts, however, we often try to abstract measurable attributes of response, such as latency, vigor, or time to extinction. These measurements, Guthrie notes, fail to agree with one another, the most promising measure being probability of occurrence. He cites Estes' (1950) development of a probabilistic theory, which, in favoring association by contiguity, is in some respects like his own. Yet he objects strongly to two of Estes' assumptions: first, that the elements that make up a situation have independent probabilities; second, that the effects of elements are additive (Guthrie, 1959, p. 167).

The Revised Law of Association

The main supplement to his earlier formulations was an emphasis on the role played by the organism's own activity in *selecting* the physical stimuli to which it would attend. There is a certain amount of "scanning" that goes on before association takes place. The new rule can be succinctly stated:

What is being noticed becomes the signal for what is being done. (1959, p. 186)

Guthrie went on to list eight assumptions concerning what takes place in associative learning, although he denied these the status of formal postulates (1959, pp. 187–189):[6]

1. Patterning of physical stimuli is effective as such, as distinct from the effects of degrees of intensity or the summation of the effects of stimulus elements.
2. A given pattern of physical stimuli is accepted by the observer to be a cue for the observed organism only on the basis of supplementary data available to the

---

[6] These have been somewhat abbreviated and paraphrased.

observer, either data from the past history of the organism or from present observation of the perceptual response to the cue.

3. The effectiveness of physical stimuli is governed by a class of responses called attention.

4. When two cues that have been associated with incompatible movement patterns are both present, action is withheld and the movements involved in attention become pronounced, including that which may be called scanning.

5. At any moment the class of movement responses possible is limited by the ongoing action.

6. Rules which do not take into account what the animal is doing when stimulated will not be descriptive of the phenomena of association.

7. The complexity of the determiners of action requires that prediction allow for high degrees of error.

8. What is being noticed, as a response is elicited, becomes a potential cue for that response.

What this amounts to is, in the first place, a warning against defining effective stimuli in physical terms. Of course, stimuli can be analyzed into physical changes taking place, but these are only changes that the observer *expects* to become stimuli until he has some evidence of the organism's reaction to them. Hence the attention (scanning) behavior becomes important because it in some sense converts the physical patterns into stimuli for the organism. In the second place, the law of association by contiguity, of single-trial association, is modestly reaffirmed with respect to the attended stimuli.

STEPS TOWARD FORMALIZATION AND ADDITIONAL EXPERIMENTAL TESTING

Some of Guthrie's students have undertaken the task of clarifying and formalizing his theory, and of designing new experiments crucially related to it. The theory has gained support also from other quarters, such as studies in verbal memory.

Voeks's Postulates

Guthrie's statements were collected and cast into postulational form by Voeks (1950). She stated eight theorems open to experimental test, and provided some confirming experimental results. Her four basic postulates are here quoted verbatim:

Postulate 1: Principle of Association

(a) Any stimulus-pattern which once accompanies a response, and/or immediately precedes it (by $\frac{1}{2}$ seconds or less) becomes a full strength direct cue for that response. (b) This is the only way in which stimulus-patterns not now cues for a particular response can become direct cues for that response.

Postulate 2: Principle of Postremity

(a) A stimulus which has accompanied or immediately preceded two or more incompatible responses is a conditioned stimulus for only the last response made while that stimulus was present. (b) This is the only way in which a stimulus now a cue for a particular response can cease being a cue for that response.

Postulate 3: Principle of Response Probability

The probability of any particular response's occurring (P) at some specified time is an increasing monotonic function of the proportion of the stimuli present which are at that time cues for that response.

Postulate 4: Principle of Dynamic Situations

The stimulus-pattern of a situation is not static but from time to time is modified, due to such changes as result from the subject's making a response, accumulation of fatigue products, visceral changes and other internal processes of the subject, introduction of controlled or uncontrolled variations in the stimuli present. (1950, pp. 342–348)

These four postulates (and the theorems related to them) deal with isolated responses as the essential core of Guthrie's theory. Unfortunately Voeks's theorem system was not extended to deal systematically with the puzzling problems posed by various arrangements of reward and punishment, with anticipatory responses, or with the integration of acts through movement-produced stimuli. Nevertheless, the start made by Voeks is a very useful one, and her experimental tests are cogent.

Her first experimental test (Voeks, 1948)—completed before the system was formalized, but consistent with the formalization—deals with the prediction of behavior in a maze. She studied the individual responses at each choice point of 57 human subjects learning a raised relief finger maze and also a punchboard maze. She tested which of two predictions was the more accurate: (1) prediction based on the *frequency* of prior choices at the point of choice, and (2) prediction based on *postremity* (i.e., the last choice that was made). Postremity won out easily. The success of prediction by postremity was most striking when the prediction disagreed with that on the basis of frequency. For 56 of the 57 subjects, postremity predicted better than frequency for those choices in which the predictions disagreed. These results are, of course, in agreement with Guthrie's theory, especially as stated in Voeks's postulate 2.

The major puzzle is why the maze was learned at all. Why was not the last trial chiefly a repetition of the first, with some minor fluctuations according to postulate 4? The explanation is not very difficult for the high-relief maze, for the last response was always leaving the choice point by the true path. The explanation is more difficult for the punchboard maze, because a "noncorrection" method was used. That is, if the "wrong" hole was punched, this was signaled to the subject, but he went on to the next choice without punching the "right" hole. Let us look at Voeks's explanation of the learning of the punchboard maze:

. . . Now, in the learning of the punch-board maze, S may insert his stylus into the wrong hole of a pair, e.g., pair 8. A stimulus then is presented (the sound of the buzzer in our experiment, E saying "wrong" in others, etc.) which may cause S to withdraw his stylus and make additional responses on that trial to that choice point. These responses may involve, for instance, the S's saying to himself "Eight, not this hole, that one is right," or even making incipient or possibly overt movements toward the correct hole while looking at the pair. If this has been the case, the next time S comes to the pair of holes, he will say "Eight" (as instructed), and it is expected he will start toward the incorrect hole, draw his stylus back, say "No, not this hole; that one is right," and then make the previously established conditioned response to the stimulus "That-is-right," i.e., the response of inserting his stylus into the hole at which he has just looked and said "That is right." Thus another error may be eliminated. This again is in accordance with the principle of postremity.[7] (1948, p. 505)

It may be pointed out that this change of response, from error to correct, would have been *recorded* as a failure of prediction by postremity, although on the basis of her theoretical analysis it was no failure at all. Hence her successful predictions by postremity are on the conservative side. The explanation offered for the actual learning (the elimination of an error) seems to come very near to an explanation according to knowledge of results or effect, and gives somewhat specialized meaning to the concept of "doing what you last did." It includes, in particular, implicit rehearsal of the correct response after being told of one's error.

The second experiment (Voeks, 1954) studied conditioned eyelid responses of human subjects, measuring both the occurrence of the responses and their amplitudes. The question asked was this: "Is a stimulus-response connection gradually strengthened by reinforcement, or is a stimulus-response connection established suddenly, in all-or-none fashion?" Hull is said to favor gradual strengthening, Guthrie all-or-none appearance of responses, according to Voeks's postulates 1 and 2.

Two tests were made of the theory of gradual strengthening, the first studying amplitude, the second frequency. Beginning with the first conditioned response (CR), succeeding responses for each subject were divided into fourths. For only 6 of 32 subjects was there a progressive increase in *amplitude* of CR from quarter to quarter. In general, increases from quarter to quarter were not statistically significant, although for 25 of the 32 subjects the last CR was larger than the first (a significant difference). Amplitude changes thus gave only little support to Hull's theory of gradual increase in strength with repeated reinforcement. The *frequency* results were more strikingly in Guthrie's favor, because a response was required in all-or-none fashion. No subject showed an increase in frequency of CR from quarter to quarter following his first CR. Half the subjects gave CRs on every trial after their first one, and there were only a few lapses for the others.

How do Voeks's results compare with the many acquisition curves published for CRs? It is well known that curves for groups of subjects show characteristics very different from curves for individual subjects. Voeks has very convincingly shown that response acquisition may be all-or-none for each individual and yet the group average learning curve will show a gradual slope. The accompanying learning curve (Figure 4.3) results, for example, when the probability of response is plotted as a group function for 15 subjects, all of whom had jumpwise curves, that is, all of whom responded consistently with CRs after their first CR was made. The form of the curve is determined solely by the trial on which the first CR happened to appear for different subjects.

[7] Copyright 1948 by the American Psychological Association. Reprinted by permission.

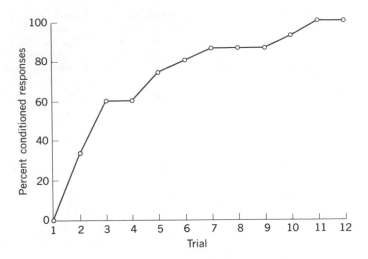

Figure 4.3.   Misleading effect of combining individual learning curves. The group curve results from combining the curves of 15 subjects, all of whom had jumpwise curves, i.e., a run of no responses followed by consistent responding. (From V. W. Voeks, Acquisition of S-R connections: A test of Hull's and Guthrie's theories, *Journal of Experimental Psychology*, 1954, 47, p. 145. Copyright 1954 by the American Psychological Association. Reprinted by permission.)

Voeks predicted jumpwise curves of learning under the very uniform conditions of stimulation that she arranged, and her predictions were well borne out. However, not all individual conditioning curves are of this jumpwise type. For example, Hilgard (1931) and Cohen, Hilgard, and Wendt (1933) early published eyelid conditioning curves for individual subjects which showed rather gradual conditioning. Why the difference? It probably concerns the greater degree of control over extraneous stimuli in the extreme situation arranged by Voeks, for it is known that conditioning occurs more rapidly with less distracting variability in the conditions surrounding CS presentation. Also, Voeks used a very strong airblast to the eye as a US, and it is likely that many of her subjects learned what would today be classified as a "voluntary avoidance" response rather than a "true conditioned" response. Furthermore, to reduce variability of muscular kinesthesis at the time of CS presentation, Voeks had her subjects bite on a bite board and squeeze a hand dynamometer; but it has since been discovered that such heightened general muscle tone sensitizes many reflexes, particularly ones like an eyeblink. Finally, Spence (1956) showed that such jump-type conditioning curves would be implied by a theory (like Hull's) which assumed gradual accumulation of associative strength, a low degree of fluctuating variability in strength from moment to moment, and the assumption that CRs occur only when the momentary strength of the S-R habit exceeds some "threshold" for response evocation. Considerations such as these lead one to regard the original interpretation of Voeks's data with suspicion.

How is gradual learning of S-R connections to be accommodated within Guthrie's system? According to Guthrie:

The strengthening of an S-R connection with repetition may very possibly be the result of the enlistment of increasing numbers of stimuli as conditioners. (1930, p. 420)

But why should practice make the effect increasingly certain? Is it not quite possible that on successive practice periods more and more conditioners are enlisted, so that after twenty periods there is a high probability that the cue will have enough support to be effective? (1935, p. 100)

This hedge on gradual learning says that it results from the fact that the stimulus situation consists of many different parts that do or do not occur in random constellations over successive trials, and it takes many trials to cycle all of these cues through the conditioning procedure. These notions were formalized and stated more clearly later by Estes (1950) in his "stimulus sampling theory" of learning. Estes regarded the stimulus situation as a population of relatively small, independent environmental events or stimulus components, of which only a sample is effective on any given trial of the learning experiment. On each reinforced trial, all active stimulus elements in that trial's sample become conditioned to the response elicited at the termination of the trial. However, the overall proportion of conditioned stimulus-elements in the total situation may grow either very rapidly or very slowly depending on the proportion of stimulus components that are sampled on each trial. In Estes's theory, the more variable is the stimulus situation from trial to trial, the lower is the percentage of stimuli of the total situation present on each trial, so the slower will be the rate of conditioning the whole population of stimuli. These arguments will be elaborated further in Chapter 12 when we take up stimulus sampling theory. In that context, the issue of whether learning in a particular instance is gradual or all or none (jumpwise) depends upon an unknown "variability parameter" which cannot be estimated until after the experiment has been run and the results are in. Effectively, Guthrie's particular formulation of the all-or-none learning principle has been superseded by later theoretical developments and distinctions.

The work of Voeks and of Estes illustrates a few of the formalizations needed by Guthrie's theory as well as a few of the early experimental tests. A number of other experiments critical of Guthrie's position have been done. For example, experiments showed that animals tended to learn a large equivalence class of responses that achieve a certain end result rather than learning a rigid specific movement (see Lashley, 1924). A rat taught to run through a maze for food will under altered test conditions swim through the same maze when it is flooded, or roll on the floor (if inner-ear damage has upset its coordinated running), doing so unerringly to get to the goal-box. Or a person who has been conditioned to *extend* his resting index finger to a CS in order to avoid a shock to the fingerpad will now *flex* his finger to the CS when his hand is turned over; he has learned to "move away from" the shock pad, not to flex or to extend his finger (Wickens, 1938). Such experiments stand as testaments against ready adoption of Guthrie's claims of specific cue-muscle movement habits as the basis for all learned behavior. It might appear instead that any available response is called into service as needed to achieve a certain end result, such as getting to the food-box or avoiding the shock.

SHEFFIELD'S EXTENSION OF CONTIGUOUS CONDITIONING TO PERCEPTUAL RESPONSES

Those influenced by Guthrie's theories are not limited, of course, to the formalizing and testing of what Guthrie said, but are free to extend the theory through making use of its orientation in novel ways. An interesting and important extension was made by F. D. Sheffield (1961) in developing a theory to explain the learning of complex sequential tasks from demonstrations and practice.[8]

The faithfulness of Sheffield's general orientation to that of Guthrie is clear:

A fundamental assumption underlying all of the theoretical considerations is that learning *per se* requires only association by contiguity. This process will usually be referred to as "conditioning." (1961, p. 14)

An important additional assumption is that *sensory responses* ("images") exist which are completely central in locus ("nonmuscular") and need not have any motor components. These responses are, in their substance, un-Guthrian (since Guthrie's behaviorism allowed only for movements and glandular secretions as responses) but in their functional relationships they are completely Guthrian:

Such sensory responses are assumed to be subject to the learning principles of association by contiguity and are assumed to have cue properties as well as response properties. That is, a sensory response can not only be connected to a cue, but also is a cue to which other responses can be connected. (1961, p. 14)

The position taken here is that what is usually called "perception" refers to cases in which the immediate sensory stimulation is not only eliciting its innate sensory responses, but is also eliciting other sensory responses which have been conditioned to the immediate stimulation in past experience. (1961, p. 15)

What consequences flow from the introduction of these sensory responses? For one thing, they allow for the occurrence and utilization of what historically have been called memory images. Thus perceptual responses commonly give a full representation of a distinctive stimulus *object*, even in the absence of that object, or when the given stimuli incompletely represent it.

---

[8] The bearing of Sheffield's theory on practical aspects of instruction will be considered in Chapter 16. For the present it may be noted that not only Sheffield but Lumsdaine, the editor of the volume in which Sheffield's paper appeared, and Maccoby, a collaborator with Sheffield in some of the experimentation, were all Guthrie's students as undergraduates; although each took his Ph.D. degree elsewhere, the theoretical orientation of each of these three men has remained close to this original imprinting.

[A] wristwatch is completely "transparent" to a skilled watch repairman. From the outside he can note the distinctive brand and model; this is sufficient for him to "fill in" all the internal parts—their sizes, shapes, arrangements, and so forth. When he takes the watch apart, he is completely prepared for everything he sees because his anticipatory conditioned sensory responses correspond with immediate unconditioned sensory responses when he opens it and makes the inner works visible. (1961, p. 16)

This manner of speaking frees this kind of behaviorism from the necessity of finding movement intermediaries for sensing and thinking, and makes it simpler to deal with the problems of patterned perception than it was when behaviorism required that such patterns be carried by speech mechanisms or other movements.

Some of the implications of introducing sensory or perceptual responses follow (1961, pp. 16–25):

1. Because sensory responses have both cue and response properties, the various sensory responses associated with an object become "cross-conditioned" so that as soon as one sensory response is elicited by an object, the total perceptual response appropriate to that object tends to be aroused. Such a response was earlier called a redintegrated response (e.g., Holling-worth, 1928). This relatively stable patterned response also serves as a cue, as, for example, in eliciting the name "orange" from the olfactory orange as well as from the visual orange.

2. In addition to the formation of stable perceptual patterns through experience, sensory conditioning provides also for the integration of response sequences or chains. All those later portions of a sequence which can occur simultaneously with earlier portions tend to move forward, so that the sequence is more highly patterned and stable than it would be if events were simply chained in an *a-b-c* order. Such integration of sequences applies both to well-coordinated motor habits and to perceptual sequences whose responses are presumably central.

3. Supraordinate sequences can be formed in which the subordinate sequences are themselves "natural units" which serve as "elements" in the new sequence. This is like the notion of a hierarchy of units. A "natural unit" has a distinctive context, different from other parts of the task. Thus, in the game of golf, "putting" is in the context of the putting green, whereas "driving" is in the context of tees, fairways, and the rough. "Learning to play golf" is therefore divisible into at least the two "natural units" of putting and driving. A sensible solution of the part-whole problem (i.e., whether it is more efficient to study the parts of a problem separately, or to study the whole task all at once) requires the identification of such "natural units."

4. Some perceptual mediation occurs without the formation of an overt serial chain, that is, without requiring the acquisition of a perceptual sequence. Learning from demonstrations is often of this sort in which *perceptual "blueprints"* are formed and followed in reconstructing the responses called for. Sheffield recognized the similarity here to the "cognitive maps" of Tolman (1948). It may be noted that "natural units" facilitate perceptual "blueprinting."

Sheffield lists a number of related hypotheses (1961, pp. 25–30), but the four principles given here suffice to show the flavor of his supplement to Guthrie.

The two main points to be noted are: (1) the many references to the possibility that sensory responses may be central, without involving peripheral movements, and (2) the emphasis upon "perceptual patterning" and "natural units." While the Gestalt-like nature of these references is recognized, Sheffield believes that, by contrast with Gestalt theory, he has not *assumed* perceptual structure, but has *deduced* it from such principles as cross-conditioning (1961, p. 18).

It is unimportant whether or not Sheffield's emendations of Guthrie's theory have made concessions to other theories, such as those of Tolman and the Gestalt theorists. In any case, he has brought the theory into contact with important aspects of learning which the theory had not dealt with earlier in any such detail.

ESTIMATE OF GUTHRIE'S POSITION

Guthrie's Position on Typical Problems of Learning

By way of comparative summary, we shall briefly state Guthrie's position on the several representative problems of learning.

1. Capacity. Problems of capacity are not formally treated, although species differences are recognized and allowance is made for maturation as a determiner of many classes of acts (1935, pp. 18, 38). Presumably any response which the organism can make may become associated with any stimulus to which he is sensitive—this generalization about the possibility of learning is reminiscent of what Thorndike says about associative shifting. It is a presupposition which now appears to be false, based on evidence reviewed in Chapter 3. If pressed, Guthrie could find a basis for differences in capacity both in the differentiation of movement and in the discrimination among proprioceptive cues. All animals are not equally versatile and equally equipped with receptors.

2. Practice. Practice assimilates or alienates cues to specific movements until a whole family of stimulus combinations comes to evoke a whole family of responses, which lead to the outcome socially described as successful performance. Because skill represents a population of habits, learning appears to accumulate with repetition, although basically each individual habit or atomic unit is learned at full strength in a single repetition.

3. Motivation. Motivation affects learning indirectly through what it causes the animal to do. Reward is a secondary or derivative principle, not a primary one as in Thorndike's system. Reward works because it removes the animal from the stimulating situation in which the "correct" response has been made. It does not strengthen the "correct" response, but prevents its weakening because no new response can become attached to the cues which led to the correct response. Thus there is a relative strengthening, because responses to other cues get alienated. We illustrated a few of the difficulties of this idea, and showed how reward effects are now being treated by the neo-Guthrians, Sheffield and Estes.

Punishment does several different things at once. In general, its effects for learning are determined by what it causes the organism to do, according to the principle that the best predictor of learning is the response in the situation that last occurred. We may distinguish four cases:

a. Mild punishment may be merely exciting, and enhance ongoing behavior rather than disrupt it.
b. More intense punishment may break up a habit by leading to incompatible behavior in the presence of the cues for it.
c. Continuing punishment acts like a drive, producing maintaining stimuli that keep the organism active until it finds relief. Then the consequence for learning is really like that of reward: the act that leads to safety is rewarding because it terminates the punishment, and, by removing the maintaining stimuli, protects from unlearning the activities carried on in the presence of those stimuli.
d. Stimuli that have previously accompanied the punishment produce behavior that formerly occurred following the punishment itself. Here we have an illustration of anticipatory response, essential to avoidance behavior. The cues to avoidance must earlier have been present at the time of punishment for this anticipation to occur. A problem with this view is explaining how organisms learn avoidance responses which differ from the escape response given to the noxious stimulus.

1. Understanding. Concepts like "insight" are handled in a derisive manner, although it is recognized that learning with foresight of its consequences may occur. Guthrie's tendency was to talk down such learning, however, just as Thorndike did, and to emphasize the mechanical and repetitive nature of most human as well as animal learning. Such learning with intention and foresight as does occur is explained on the basis of conditioned anticipatory or readiness reactions, based upon past experience and hence not contradicting association principles.

5. Transfer. Learning transfers to new situations because of common elements within the old and new. In this the position is rather like Thorndike's. Stress is laid, however, on the identity being carried by way of common responses evoked, the proprioceptive stimuli being sufficiently similar in the case of responses to a variety of stimuli to evoke common conditioned responses. The emphasis upon movement-produced stimuli thus represents Guthrie's supplementation to Thorndike.

Because of his principle of responses being conditioned to all adventitious contiguous stimuli, Guthrie expected rather little transfer and was, in fact, rather extreme about it. The only way to be sure to get desired behavior in a new situation is to practice in that new situation as well. To be able to perform in a variety of situations, you have to practice in a variety of situations.

6. Forgetting. Learning is said to be permanent unless interfered with by new learning. Hence all forgetting is due to the learning of new responses which replace the old responses. It may take place gradually for the same reason that skills may be acquired gradually: remembering depends upon many habits to many cues, and subhabits may drop out gradually as subcues become attached to new responses.

In contrast to Thorndike, Guthrie was an avowed behaviorist who made it a matter of some importance to get rid of subjective terms, to refer, for example, to inner speech instead of to thinking. The emphasis upon movement-produced stimuli was part of the older behaviorist tradition of Watson which Guthrie carried on. While he was an orthodox behaviorist in these respects, his was an informal behaviorism, with little of the brittleness of earlier Watsonianism. We have already seen how it permitted itself in Sheffield's hands to adapt itself to nonmovement response learning.

Invulnerability of the Theory—A Cause for Skepticism

The uncertainty that exists in practically all learning experimentation makes the fact-minded psychologist suspicious of a finished system at this stage of our knowledge. While scientific truth must eventually have exceptionless validity—if its laws are truly lawful—the history of our most advanced sciences shows that their theories move by successive approximations, and the most advanced theories do not emerge full blown from the head of the theorist. Even as loose a system as Thorndike's went through revisions on the basis of evidence regarding the effects of punishment; Hull's system was continuously being revamped to meet experimental fact. One of the sources of uneasiness about Guthrie's system lies in its assured answers to the problems of learning—answers that remained unchanged through more than a quarter of a century of the most active psychological experimentation we have ever known. Experimental controversies finally get resolved as we learn more about the independent variables that modify the measured consequences. No matter how these issues get resolved, Guthrie's system remains unchanged. Either the theory is a miraculously inspired one or it is not stated very precisely, and hence is not very sensitive to experimental data.

The Simplicity of the Theory May Be Illusory

Certainly much of the fascination of Guthrie's theory rests upon his ability to deduce a wide range of phenomena from the single principle of one-trial contiguous association. Parsimonious scientific theories are attractive, and this is the ultimate in reductionist theories. Although Voeks found it convenient to state four postulates, with proper definitions of the stimuli and responses entering into association, she could have found one to be enough, with the other three as corollaries.

A painstaking search through Guthrie's writings for careful definition of stimulus and response, for distinctions between observables and constructs, for statements taking the form of predictions and those taking the form of *a posteriori* explanations, led critics to conclude:

> While the principles of conditioning which he expands seem to have a parsimony that would be desirable in a theoretical formulation of behavior, a closer analysis reveals that a formidable set of additional assumptions and constructs are required

if his theory is to possess any real applicability to experimental data. (Mueller & Schoenfeld, 1954, p. 377)

It is undoubtedly true that many reviews of Guthrie in the literature have mistaken incompleteness for simplicity. (Mueller & Schoenfeld, 1954, p. 368)

Guthrie was without peer in the use of anecdote and illustration to make pertinent comments about the activities of everyday life, including symptoms found in the psychological clinic. This complicated material he talked about in dramatically simple terms, and his theory makes this kind of talk possible. There is much to be learned from Guthrie's type of psychologizing, a type that is appealing enough to have led many promising young men and women to enter upon productive careers in psychology—a contribution to the field not to be overlooked.

At the experimental level, Guthrie's greatest contribution was to call attention to the large element of repetitiveness and stereotypy in behavior when the opportunities are favorable to such stereotypy. But Guthrie was at heart an associationist with a strong behavioristic bias. Although the associationist tradition will doubtless continue on, the particular set of behavioristic renditions of it given by Guthrie seem to have lost their appeal to succeeding generations, with the advent in recent times of "cognitive psychology."

SUPPLEMENTARY READINGS

The two following books, available also in more recent paperbound editions, give Guthrie's own theory:
GUTHRIE, E. R. (1935) (1952) *The psychology of learning.*
GUTHRIE, E. R. (1938) *The psychology of human conflict.*

His own shorter summaries, which show how little the theory changed over the years, can be found in the following three accounts:
GUTHRIE, E. R. (1930) Conditioning as a principle of learning. *Psychological Review*, 37, 412–428.
GUTHRIE, E. R. (1942) Conditioning: A theory of learning in terms of stimulus, response and association. Chapter 1 in *The psychology of learning.* National Society for the Study of Education, 41st Yearbook, Part II, 17–60.
GUTHRIE, E. R. (1959) Association by contiguity. In S. Koch (Ed.) *Psychology: A study of a science*, Vol. 2, 158–195.

For a critical review of Guthrie's contributions from the point of view of the logic of science and system making, see:
MUELLER, C. G., JR., and SCHOENFELD, W. N. (1954) Edwin R. Guthrie. In W. K. Estes et al. *Modern learning theory*, 345–379.

5

Tolman's Sign Learning

The theory of Edward C. Tolman (1886–1959) was called purposive behaviorism in his major systematic work, *Purposive behavior in animals and men* (1932). Later he (and others) called it a sign-gestalt theory, a sign-significate theory, or an expectancy theory. These later terms all emphasize the *cognitive* nature of the theory, which distinguishes it in certain respects from the stimulus-response theories of Thorndike, Guthrie, Skinner, and Hull. The designation *sign learning* provides a satisfactory short name, abbreviating sign-gestalt.

Tolman was a behaviorist, but one cast from a completely different mold from a Watson or a Pavlov or a Guthrie. Tolman was concerned with how behavior theory was to make contact with such notions as *knowledge, thinking, planning, inference, purpose,* and *intention.* He was a sort of "layman's behaviorist," often describing an animal's behavior in terms of its motives, bits of knowledge (cognitions), expectations, intentions, and purposes, in much the way an intelligent layman would describe another person's behavior. Tolman's major influence was in opposing and partially counteracting certain restrictive premises adopted by his more strictly behavioristic predecessors and contemporaries. He was not a "systematist," but rather a very astute observer of animal behavior and critic of the prevailing S-R reinforcement theory of his day. The measure of his success is how much his opponents' theories (notably Hull's, see Chapter 6) were forced to acknowledge and deal with the phenomena and conceptual distinctions drawn by Tolman.

Despite some shifts in vocabulary, Tolman held firm to his main tenets during the 27 years between the time his initial book appeared and his death.

1. His system was a genuine *behaviorism,* and as such rejected introspec-

tion as a method and "raw feels" as data for psychological science. When he made reference to consciousness, to inventive ideation (thinking), and the like, he was talking about interpretations of observed behavior.

2. The system was a *molar*, rather than a *molecular*, behaviorism. An act of behavior has distinctive properties all its own, to be identified and described irrespective of muscular, glandular, or neural processes. As Tolman said (1951, p. 417), "behavior has emergent patterns and meanings which are other than the patterns and meanings of the gland secretions and muscle contractions which underlie it, though no doubt they are completely dependent upon the latter." Behavior is to be described in terms of acts or actions, which include what is the purpose and the achievement of the act. A marketing psychologist interested in consumer buying behaviors, for instance, is concerned only with whether an individual consumer buys a particular product, not the precise, detailed manner in which the purchase is made. Tolman argued that the achievement of the act, not the sequence of muscle twitches, should be the fundamental unit of a psychological analysis. In effect, this is the level of "behavioral description" embodied in our natural language vocabulary for describing action episodes.

3. The system referred to the *purpose* of behavior, always pointing to the fact that an act sequence seemed integrated and held together by the fact that it was striving toward a particular goal. In contrast to a simple stimulus-response machine which simply emits a hierarchy of responses in accordance with their strength to the stimulus situation, the organism of Tolman's conception made use of its knowledge of "stimulus-act-consequence" relations in order to achieve satisfaction of its current demands (needs). The purposivism implicit in Tolman's theory did not embrace a teleological metaphysics; with the modern advent of servomechanisms, we now know that "goal-seeking" machines can be built without requiring some occult spirit inside the device. Cybernetics has made "purposive explanations" acceptable to mechanistic psychologists.

We will elaborate upon these brief comments in the sections which follow.

Behavior as Molar

The descriptive properties of molar behavior are the most general characteristics of behavior which would impress themselves upon an intelligent onlooker without presuppositions and before any attempt to explain how the behavior comes about.

First, behavior is goal-directed. It is always a getting toward something, or a getting away from something. The most significant description of any behavior is what the organism is doing, what it is up to, where it is going. The cat is trying to get out of the box, the carpenter is building a house (or earning a living), the musician is seeking acclaim for his virtuosity. The particular movements involved are less descriptive of the molar behavior than is the goal toward which or away from which the movements lead. This feature characterizes molar behavior as *purposive*.

Like most complex phenomena (e.g., rainbows, football games), an organism's behavior can be described at several different levels (as can a corresponding stimulus situation). For example, a sentence uttered by an actor in a play may be described in terms of movements of his tongue, oral cavity, diaphragm, and vocal cords; or it can be described in terms of the sequence of phonemes emitted, or the words said, or the meanings or ideas conveyed, or the prosodic expertise of the delivery, or the function of the line in the playwright's development of a character or of the plot, and so on *ad infinitum*. A similar set of onion-layers characterizes the possible analyses of what a listener in the audience is "doing." It is pointless to ask, "But which of these various things is he *really* doing?"; clearly, in one sense, he is doing all of them. Rather, the issue is which level of analysis will prove more fruitful for answering particular questions of interest. Tolman clearly came down on the side of using molar ("large unit") descriptions of behavior, referring to its supposed *purposes*. What was upsetting about this program to the other comparative (animal) psychologists of that time was that it seemed anthropomorphic (projecting human traits onto lower animals) and unparsimonious (the "purposes" immanent in behavior were to be *derived* from simpler conditioning principles rather than taken as a basic postulate at the outset). It also resembled teleological and vitalistic explanations then current in biology, some of which were clearly fallacious, had been roundly discredited, and were thence automatically suspect among biologists at that time. It was because of these "surplus meanings" that Tolman's brand of purposive behaviorism received a critical hearing from the other behaviorists of his day.

Second, in Tolman's view, behavior frequently makes use of environmental props or supports as means-objects toward the goal. A man fetches a ladder in order to climb onto his roof; Kohler's chimp (see Chapter 8) used a stick in order to reach a banana that was just out of arm's reach. The world in which behavior goes on is a world of paths and tools, obstacles, and bypaths with which the organism has commerce. The manner in which the organism makes use of paths and tools in relation to its goals characterizes molar behavior as planful as well as purposive. Knowledge of the world is used in planning out efficient action sequences.

Tolman conceived of the organism's knowledge as organized into a sort of "cognitive map" of the environment rather than being a simple listing of local stimulus-response pairs. He characterized this organization of knowledge in the following way:

> [The brain] is far more like a map control room than it is like an old-fashioned telephone exchange. The stimuli, which are allowed in, are not connected by just simple one-to-one switches to the outgoing responses. Rather, the incoming impulses are usually worked over and elaborated in the central control room into a tentative, cognitivelike map of the environment. And it is this tentative map, indicating routes and paths and environmental relationships, which finally determines what responses, if any, the animal will finally release.[1] (1948, p. 192)

Third, Tolman supposed that there would be a selective preference for short or easy means to a goal as against long or difficult ones, called the *principle of least effort*.

Fourth, behavior, if it is molar, is *docile*. That is, molar behavior is

---

[1] Copyright 1948 by the American Psychological Association. Reprinted by permission.

characterized by teachableness or plasticity. If it is mechanical and stereo-typed, like a spinal reflex, it belongs at the molecular level.

Intervening Variables

Tolman was one of the first learning theorists to give a systematic account of "intervening variables," which are constructs presumed to represent processes or variables mediating the effects of stimulus (or input) variables on performance. A cognition or expectancy or even the construct of "learning" itself is an intervening variable, a theoretical concept (or state) which is presumed to be a function of certain experiences and which determines, in turn, a set of behaviors. Tolman conceived of the task of a molar psychology as that of inventing the right intervening variables, of relating them in the appropriate way among themselves and to input (stimulus) and output (response) variables, thus to capture the significant determinants of behavior.

The precise intervening variables entering into Tolman's analyses were constantly changing as he updated his system. An early sample (Tolman, 1938) was the following:

Intervening Variable	*Environmental Variable*
Demand	Maintenance schedule
Appetite	Appropriateness of goal object
Differentiation	Types and modes of stimuli provided
Motor Skill	Types of motor response required
Hypotheses	Cumulative nature and number of trials in a situation

For example, *demand* for food was conceived as a measurable quantity which increased with period of deprivation of food, and which would have specific effects on behavior—in particular, increasing demand for food would raise to prominence those behavioral sequences which had led to food in this situation in the past.

It will be noted that even in this short list Tolman's "intervening variables" are a mixed bag conceptually. It was characteristic of theorists at that time to list experimental and individual-difference ("capacity") variables presumed to be important in determining behavior in particular situations. Today such mixed enumerations would not be characterized as serious theorizing, although in Tolman's day they were. Several of these listings of variables concerning the learner, the learning situation and materials, and the various types of learning considered by Tolman were reviewed in the earlier edition of this volume (Hilgard & Bower, 1966) and it may be consulted for details. For clarity and conciseness of statement of Tolman's final theory, however, the summary interpretation by MacCorquodale and Meehl (1953, 1954) will be introduced as a didactic device. Tolman's writing is discursive, anecdotal, and poorly organized for simple exposition. MacCorquodale and Meehl undertook the task of making explicit what expectancy theory would be like were it formalized, much as in the fashion that Clark Hull formalized his theory.

MacCorquodale and Meehl's Postulate System

To begin with, an expectancy is said always to have three terms: (1) something initially perceived, called an *elicitor* of the expectancy (S_1); (2) something to be done following this perception, a response (R_1); and (3) something that will be perceived as the goal of the expectancy, the *expectandum* (S_2). The process can be symbolized as S_1-R_1-S_2 in the defining of an expectancy, just as the process S-R is used to define an association. The best way to remember the process is to think of some ordinary sentence, such as: "When this *button* (S_1) is *pressed* (R_1), I expect to hear the *ringing doorbell* (S_2)." This three-termed associative unit, prior to doing anything to the button right now, is the expectancy. If ringing the doorbell becomes a goal (becomes positively *valenced*), then the expectancy is *activated*. I *push* the button only if I want to ring the doorbell; I may have the expectancy without doing anything about it. Capital letters are used to describe the significant environmental events S_1-R_1-S_2, and the same letters may be used for the inferred construct, the expectancy ($S_1R_1S_2$). The letters are enclosed in parentheses when reference is to the construct rather than to events themselves.

Twelve postulates are stated, often with guesses as to the form of mathematical function involved. To introduce the flavor of the system, the postulates are here paraphrased, with much of the quantitative detail omitted.

1. Mnemonization. The occurrence of the sequence S_1-R_1-S_2 results in an increase in the strength of an expectancy ($S_1R_1S_2$). The *rate* of growth increases with the valence of S_2. The *limit* of growth depends on the probability (P) with which S_2 regularly follows S_1-R_1. That is, the growth approaches P as a limit.

This is the basic acquisition postulate. It is a contiguity theory, in that mere occurrence of the sequence stimulus-response-outcome presumably leads to an increase in expectancy. But it is also a kind of reinforcement theory, because the expectancy is influenced by the valence of the terminal item (S_2) in the sequence. Valence refers to something like value or utility of the S_2 stimulus. The theory is not a stimulus-response theory in the usual sense.

2. Extinction. The occurrence of a sequence S_1-R_1, if not followed by S_2, tends to produce a decrement in the expectancy.

Two cases must be distinguished. If P has been 1.00 (that is, S_1-R_1, always followed by S_2) a single omission of S_2 will lead to a prompt decrement, depending both on the current strength of ($S_1R_1S_2$) and the valence of S_2. If, however, P has been less than 1.00, the course of decrement will be slower; and, if the new probability of S_2 following S_1-R_1 is P', then the S_1-R_1-S_2 expectancy will approach the value of P' as an asymptote.[2]

---

[2] This postulate is remarkably like the "probability matching" theorem derivable from Estes's stimulus-sampling theory (see Chapter 12). Roughly, it says that the likelihood that the organism expects outcome S_2 following S_1-R_1 comes eventually to match (be equal to) the objective probability of that outcome following that S_1-R_1 sequence.

3. Primary-stimulus generalization. When an expectancy $(S_1R_1S_2)$ has been strengthened, other expectancies $(S'_1R_1S_2)$ will also have received some strength, depending upon the similarity of the elicitors S'_1 and S_1.

Similarity gradients are an empirical matter, and there is no point in trying to distinguish these functions from those used by stimulus-response psychologists. The postulate simply recognizes that stimulus generalization occurs.

4. Inference. When an expectancy $(S_1R_1S_2)$ exists at some strength, the presence of a valenced object S^* in close contiguity with S_2 gives rise to a new expectancy $(S_1R_1S^*)$.

5. Generalized inference. Even though $(S_1R_1S_2)$ is originally of zero strength, the occurrence of a valenced object S^* in close contiguity with S_2 may give rise to a new expectancy $(S_1R_1S^*)$, provided $(S_1R_1S'_2)$ is of some strength, and S'_2 is similar to S_2.

These are the kinds of postulates which contribute heavily to the identification of an expectancy theory. They describe a hypothetical process by which events at a goal (S_2) can work back to have effects on subsequent response selection. The inference postulate is relevant to the work to be reviewed later under the heading of latent learning. The generalized inference postulate was relevant to some deductions concerning "reasoning" by rats in putting together related pieces of information.

The next six postulates have to do with motivation, described according to needs, cathexes, and valences. They have been renumbered for expository purposes. They can easily be identified in the original source because their titles are unchanged. The three following postulates state the fundamental position with respect to motivation.[3]

6. Cathexis. The cathexis (C^*) of a valenced stimulus situation (S^*) is a function of the number of contiguous occurrences between it and the consummatory response.

7. Need strength. The need (D) for a cathected stimulus (S^*) is an increasing function of the time interval since satiation for it.

8. Valence. The valence of a stimulus S^* is a multiplicative function of the correlated need D and the cathexis C^* attached to S^*.

The term *cathexis* was borrowed by Tolman from psychoanalytic theory. Tolman uses the term to refer to an acquired relationship between an object and a drive, mediated through occurrences of the consummatory response. If a hungry child wants a banana, it is supposed that the child has a learned cathexis between its hunger drive and a banana as a preferred goal-object. But note that in postulate 6 above a cathexis can include the stimulus situation in which consummatory responses occur, such as the goal-box of a maze. This postulate presumably underlies the phenomenon called "sec-

---

[3] The treatment covers rewarding (appetitive) motivation only. Pain and avoidance are not treated explicitly by MacCorquodale and Meehl.

ondary reinforcement" or "acquired reward" by Hull, Skinner, and others. That is, a neutral stimulus (e.g., a poker chip) paired repeatedly with a consummatory response (like eating by a hungry monkey) thereby acquires positive reinforcing powers of its own. In Tolman's terms, the poker chip would be a "cathected" stimulus.

Postulate 7 is the basic motivational postulate and it is to be noted that needs (drives) do not activate habits, responses, or expectancies, nor do they impel the organism directly to action. Rather, needs have their influence by increasing the valence of cathected stimuli relevant to the particular need (postulate 8). Thus, for example, an object or stimulus repeatedly paired with eating and hunger reduction would nonetheless not appear to be strongly valenced unless the animal was hungry during the test trials. As we shall see later, this valence notion is closely paralleled by the "$D \times K$" motivational complex used in the theories of Hull and Spence (see Chapter 6), which theories combine drive and reward variables multiplicatively in determining performance.

Some additional postulates concerning some further relationships between experience and cathexes are the following:

9. *Secondary cathexis.* The contiguity of S_2 and S^* (a valenced stimulus) increases the cathexis of S_2.

This is a kind of "secondary reinforcement" or acquired incentive value, whereby the valence of one expectandum (stimulus) is given to a contiguous expectandum just by sheer stimulus-stimulus contiguity, with no overt responses required.

10. *Induced elicitor-cathexis.* The acquisition of valence by an expectandum S_2 belonging to an existing expectancy $(S_1 R_1 S_2)$ induces a cathexis in the elicitor S_1.

11. *Confirmed elicitor-cathexis.* The confirmation of an expectancy $(S_1 R_1 S_2)$, when S_2 has a positive valence, increases the cathexis of S_1.

These two postulates mean that an elicitor, as a discriminative stimulus, comes to have reinforcing power. This can be easily demonstrated. Suppose a chimpanzee, when given a poker chip (S_1), can get a raisin (S_2). After such training the chimp can be readily trained to perform some new response (like climbing on a box) in order to get the poker chip as a "reward." Postulate 11 simply says that such subgoals increase in cathexis whenever they lead to the positively valenced goal.

12. *Activation.* The reaction potential $_sE_R$ of a response R_1 in the presence of S_1 is a multiplicative function of the strength of the expectancy $(S_1 R_1 S_2)$ and the valence of the expectandum.

This final postulate says that the tendency to make a particular response in a particular situation depends on the expectancies and their valences. This postulate gets around the jibe of Guthrie (1952, p. 143) that Tolman "leaves the rat buried in thought." The parallel with the Hull-Spence basic formulation is striking:

Hull-Spence: $_sE_R = f(_sH_R) \times f(D, K)$
MacCorquodale-Meehl: $_sE_R = f(S_1R_1S_2) \times f(D, C^*)$

In the Hull-Spence formulation, $_sH_R$ refers to the associative strength between the current stimulus and the response under consideration, D refers to drive level, and K to incentive motivation.

MacCorquodale and Meehl go on to relate reaction potential, $_sE_R$, to performance indices such as response probability, response latency, and so forth, using the same calculational devices as did Hull in his theory. As MacCorquodale and Meehl point out, there is no reason to handle these matters differently in the expectancy model and the stimulus-response model.

Several comments are appropriate regarding the MacCorquodale-Meehl interpretation of expectancy theory. First, writing in 1953, they had the advantage over Tolman's 1932 formulation of 20 years of research and conceptual distinctions, so they could make clear several issues on which Tolman had been vague. Second, Tolman's views changed progressively over the 30-odd years of his active career, and the MacCorquodale-Meehl postulates tend to capture only the later, more refined versions of Tolman's ideas. Third, some of the "postulates" of the system are little more than direct translations of empirical phenomena into the vocabulary of the theoretical constructs (e.g., stimulus generalization, secondary reinforcement). Such postulates (translations) are not to be interpreted as suggesting that Tolman in any sense "discovered" these psychological principles; they were known long before he began his systematic writings (the same remark applies to many of Clark Hull's theoretical postulations, which are considered in Chapter 6). Fourth, enumeration of the several postulates does not do justice to the reams of psychological experimentation and evidence which lie behind them; this we try to sketch in the next section. Fifth, the enumeration does not mention many of the informal, more programmatic suggestions which were scattered throughout Tolman's writings and which provided a valuable stimulus for research into particular areas. Again, we can only briefly mention a few of these auxiliary hypotheses at the end of the next section.

EVIDENCE RELEVANT TO TOLMAN'S VIEWS

Sign Learning as an Alternative to Response Learning

Stimulus-response theories, while stated with different degrees of sophistication, imply that the organism is goaded along a path by internal and external stimuli, learning the correct movement sequences so that they are elicited under appropriate conditions of drive and environmental stimulation. In traditional S-R theory, the organism is supposed not to have, at the time of response selection, any representation of the goal; all that the organism "knows," according to a strict Watsonian interpretation, is that certain responses have particular strengths in particular situations. Reinforcement conditions are not represented in the subject's knowledge of the situation; rather, they are merely reflected in the relative strengths of particular S-R connections.

The alternative possibility propounded by Tolman is that organisms learn goals ("rewards"), so that they come to know what stimuli (significates, S_2s) will follow particular S_1-R_1 combinations. In this sense, Tolman's S-R-S formulation ascribes to the subject an internal representation of the goal, or the next stimulus in the sequence. According to this approach, then, during learning of a complex response sequence (e.g., running a complex maze) the learner is following signs to a goal, is learning his way about, is following a sort of map—in other words, is learning not movements but meanings. This is the contention of Tolman's theory of sign learning. The organism learns sign-significate relations; it learns a behavior route, not a movement pattern. Many learning situations do not permit a clear distinction between these two possibilities. If there is a single path with food at the end and the organism runs faster at each opportunity, there is no way of telling whether its responses are being stamped in by reinforcement or whether it is guided by its increasingly stronger goal cathexis and expectations of food.

Because both stimulus-response and sign learning so often predict the same behavioral outcome, it is necessary to design special experiments in which it is possible to favor one theory over the other. Three situations give strong support to the sign-learning alternative. These are experiments on reward expectancy, on place learning, and on latent learning.

1. Reward expectancy. One of the earliest and most striking observations on reward expectancy was that of Tinklepaugh (1928). In his experiment, food was placed under one of two containers while a monkey was watching but was prevented from immediate access to the containers and food. A few seconds later, the monkey was permitted to choose between the containers and he invariably demonstrated his memory by choosing correctly. This is the standard "delayed response" situation. The behavior which is pertinent here occurred when, after a banana had been hidden under one of the cups, the experimenter, out of the monkey's view, substituted for it a lettuce leaf (a less preferred food). Upon turning over the correct container and finding the lettuce leaf instead of the preferred banana, the monkeys would show "surprise" and frustration, would reject the lettuce leaf, and would engage in definite searching behavior, as though looking for the expected banana. Somewhat the same sort of behavior was found by Elliott (1928) when the food in the goal-box of a rat maze experiment was changed from bran mash to sunflower seed. More systematic experiments were carried out later with chimpanzees (Cowles & Nissen, 1937). There is little doubt that animals have some sort of expectancy for specific goal-objects. Under those circumstances, other goal-objects produce signs of behavior disruption. Such behavior means that the sign-learning theory is appropriate; it does not, of course, mean that other theories may not attempt to deduce the behavior from other principles. Hull's theory tried to represent reward expectancy in terms of the "fractional anticipatory goal response" (r_G), a mechanism about which we shall have more to say later. Moreover, Amsel (1958, 1962), a neo-Hullian, introduces his hypotheses about *frustration* by considering it to result from a discrepancy between an expected and obtained reward for responding. So the later Hullians basically accepted Tolman's notion that the organism has some representation of the expected reward at the time it responds.

2. Place learning.   Experiments on place learning were designed to show that the learner is not moving from start to goal according to a fixed sequence of muscular or turning movements, such as would be predicted from the idea that responses are to be defined with reference to the exact musculature involved. Tolman believed rather that the animal is capable of behavior which is varied appropriately according to altered stimulus or response situations, as though he "knows" where the goal is. For example, a monkey who has been rewarded with a raisin for choosing a black triangle in preference to a white square when they are presented alternately to the left or right in a horizontal row will continue to choose the black triangle when the objects are presented in a novel vertical array, one above the other on the panel. The organism has learned to "approach black triangle" rather than to "choose right to the configuration of white left-black right."

There are several subtypes of experiments revealing such "place" or "goal" learning. The first subtype of the place-learning alternative to response learning leaves the form of the path intact but interferes with the movement sequences in getting from start to goal. In one experiment, rats that had learned to run a maze straight on were then given cerebellar lesions; although they were now unable to move through the maze except by small circling movements, they nonetheless were still able to make their way through the maze without error (Lashley & Ball, 1929). They could not have been repeating the earlier learned sequences of kinesthetic habits. In another study, rats were able to demonstrate what they had learned by swimming through the correct path after having been trained in wading it (Macfarlane, 1930). Still later, it was shown that rats who had been merely drawn repeatedly through a water-maze on a raft to the goal, repeatedly observing the correct sequence of turns at signaled choice points to a food-rewarded goal, were then able to run through the maze almost errorlessly when finally given a chance to perform. They had apparently learned the correct sequence of signs or cues to follow leading to the rewarded goal-box, all this without any overt "running movements" at all.

The second subtype of place-learning experiment sets a movement habit against a spatial habit and determines which is the more readily learned. Tolman and his collaborators (Tolman, Ritchie, & Kalsh, 1946, 1947) arranged an elevated maze in the form of a cross, as shown in Figure 5.1. The response-learning group was started in random alternation from either S_1 or S_2, always finding food by turning to the right; that is, food was at F_1 when the start was S_1 and at F_2 when the start was S_2. The place-learning group, by contrast, always went to the same place for food. This meant that if running to F_1, a right turn would be required when starting from S_1, but a left turn when starting from S_2. In this arrangement, the place-learning group was much the more successful. The eight rats of the place-learning group all learned within 8 trials, so that the next 10 trials were without error. None of the eight rats of the response-learning group learned this quickly, and five of them did not reach the criterion in 72 trials. Under these circumstances (an elevated maze with many extra-maze cues), it was clearly demonstrated that place learning is simpler than response learning.

However, other experimenters soon found conflicting results (e.g., Blodgett & McCutchan, 1947, 1948), discovering "response" learning to be sometimes

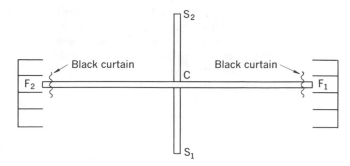

Figure 5.1.   Maze used to test the relative ease of learning either a response which brings reward or the place at which reward is found. By starting irregularly at S_1 and S_2, but finding reward at the same food-box each time, one group of rats turns now to the right, now to the left, to find food always at the same location. These are the place learners. By starting at either S_1 or S_2, but always finding food as a result of turning the same way (right or left), another group is taught always to make the same response, but to find food at different places, depending upon the starting point. Place learning, under the conditions of the experiment, is found to be easier than response learning. (From Tolman, Ritchie, & Kalish, Studies in spatial learning. II. Place learning versus response learning. *Journal of Experimental Psychology*, 1946, 36, p. 223. Copyright 1946 by the American Psychological Association. Reprinted by permission.)

faster, sometimes slower, or sometimes equal to "place" learning depending on the presence and distinctiveness of extra-maze cues relative to left-right positional cues. Some resolution of a spate of conflicting literature on the topic was provided by Restle (1957), who suggested that subjects can learn to respond with respect to either sort of cue ("place" or "response"), and that the relative learning rates depend on the relative salience or distinctiveness of the two types of cues in the total maze situation. For example, one can reduce the distinctiveness of "place" cues (e.g., by having the arms of the maze radiate in a V at angles progressively less than 180°). Such manipulations have the desired effect in slowing acquisition of subjects who are required to learn with respect to the manipulated cue. Restle carried the analysis further with a mathematical model of discrimination learning which permitted quantitative assessment of the "salience" or "distinctiveness" of the place and/or the "response" cues. A significant prediction that was confirmed was that when subjects learn a problem in which "place and response" are always correlated and redundant (e.g., in Figure 5.1, the subject always starts from S_1 and always finds food at F_1), their learning rate will be the sum of the learning rates for subjects learning by "place" alone and for subjects learning by "response" alone. That is, learning rates are higher for redundant relevant cues. Furthermore, Restle showed that in a conflict test given following "place + response" learning, when the two modes of responding are placed in opposition, the percentage of animals choosing the "place" alternative on the test trials was predictable from the earlier estimates of the relative saliences of the place and response cues—with the more salient cue receiving the predominant choices. Altogether then, Restle's analysis seemed to have satisfactorily resolved the "place versus response controversy," and showed how in some respects the controversy was misguided or at least based on too simplistic an analysis of what is (or can be) learned.

The third subtype of place-learning experiment involves the use of alternative paths when a practiced path is blocked. An early form of the blocked-path experiment is that of Tolman and Honzik (1930a), which is said to demonstrate inferential expectation, or insight, in rats. The main features of the arrangement are as follows. There are three paths (1, 2, and 3), in that order of length from shortest to longest and hence in that order of eventual preference (Figure 5.2). In preliminary training, when path 1 was blocked at A, a preference was established between paths 2 and 3 for the shorter of these paths. Only when path 2 was blocked also did the rats run to path 3. We may somewhat oversimplify by saying that a familiarity with all paths and a preference for them in the order 1, 2, 3 was established in preliminary training. An important feature of the maze design, crucial for the test, was that paths 1 and 2 had a common segment leading to the goal. Previously the block in path 1 had been placed before this stretch of common path; then the rat, after backing up from the block, ran to path 2. Now in the

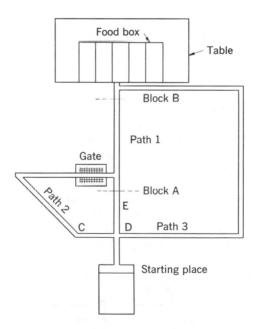

Figure 5.2. Maze used to test insight in rats. The paths become established as a hierarchy according to length, path 1 preferred to path 2, path 2 to path 3. If path 1 is closed by block A, the rats run by path 2. If path 1 is closed by block B, the rats run by path 3 if they have "insight" that the barrier closes path 2 as well as path 1. (From Tolman & Honzik, 1930a, p. 223. Originally published by the University of California Press; reprinted by permission of The Regents of the University of California.)

critical test trial, the block was placed farther along path 1, so that it fell in the common path, at point B. The question was whether the' rat, in backing out again, would choose the second preference, path 2, and be frustrated, or would "infer" that path 2 was also blocked. What the rats did, predominantly, was to avoid path 2, and to take the path ordinarily least preferred, the long path 3, but the only one open, given the block at point B. Again the hypothesis is supported that the rat acted in accordance with some sort of "map" of the situation, and not according to blind habit, or according to the automatic performance in hierarchical order of habits elicited by choice-point stimuli.

The Tolman and Honzik experiment was criticized by other experimenters who showed that the results, while reproducible, were easily disturbed by the manipulation of experimental variables such as alley width which theoretically should not affect the animal's "reasoning ability"—see Evans (1936), Harsh (1937), Keller and Hill (1936), and Kuo (1937). A successful repetition was reported in an alley maze by Caldwell and Jones (1954). An ingenious variation was introduced by Deutsch and Clarkson (1959), to which further reference will be made.

3. Latent learning.   In addition to the experiments on reward expectancy and on space learning, a third variety of experiment bears importantly on sign learning: the latent-learning experiments. These show that an animal can learn by exploring the maze, without food reward, so that, when reward is later introduced, performance is better than that of rats without this exposure, and is sometimes as good as that of rats with many previously rewarded trials. The "latent learning" consists of knowledge of the maze, not revealed in choice of the shortest path from entrance to exit until the rat is motivated to make that choice. The experiments, beginning with those of Blodgett (1929), were critical of the hypothesis that reinforcement was necessary before any associative learning could occur at all. This popular hypothesis had been propounded by Thorndike (see Chapter 2), by Pavlov, and by Hull in his early writings.

Following up the work started by Blodgett (1929), Tolman and Honzik (1930b) studied the effect of introduction of reward in a rat-maze experiment after the animals had been allowed to wander through the maze for ten trials without food. The control group, fed each day in the maze, reduced their error and time scores much more rapidly than the nonfed group, but when food was introduced for the latter group, error scores and time scores abruptly became alike for both groups. Thus the nonfed group had apparently profited as much by its earlier trials as the fed group. Since this profiting did not show in earlier performance, the learning taking place is said to be "latent." The results for error elimination are shown in Figure 5.3. There were three groups: two control groups, one rewarded throughout, the other nonrewarded throughout, and the experimental group, nonrewarded until the eleventh trial. On the twelfth day, the experimental group, having been fed but once in the maze, made as few errors as the group which had received food in the maze each of the preceding days.

There are several comments to make on this situation, in its bearing on other theories as well as Tolman's. The maze used was a 14-unit one of

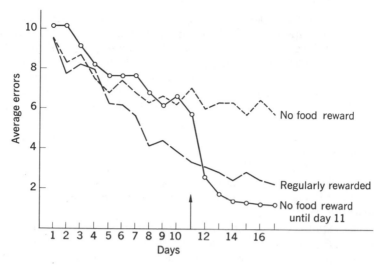

Figure 5.3.   Evidence for latent learning in the maze. With no food reward there is some reduction in errors, but not as great a reduction as with regular food reward. Despite the higher error scores prior to the introduction of food, the group rewarded only from the eleventh trial immediately begins to do as well as the group that had been regularly rewarded. The interpretation is that some learning went on within the first ten trials which did not show in performance until the food incentive activated it. (From Tolman & Honzik, 1930b. Originally published by the University of California Press; reprinted by permission of The Regents of the University of California.)

multiple-T type (Stone & Nyswander, 1927), arranged with doors between each unit to prevent retracing. Even without food at the end, the rat still progressed through the maze, so that, according to a reinforcement theory such as Guthrie's, learning conditions were ideal. The rat had no opportunity to unlearn what it last did in each segment, which was, of course, to go through the correct door to the next one. The results are critical of Guthrie's reinforcement theory not because the rat shows latent learning but because it does not show *enough* learning when there is no food at the end of the maze. The Guthrie explanation is not sufficient, because the fed rats learned much better than the unfed ones.

Reinforcement theories, in their older form, were also at a loss to explain latent learning. In the older forms of "law of effect" theories, the presumption was that reinforcement worked directly upon response strength, so that all that was learned should be revealed in performance. But this appeared to be contradicted by the instances of latent learning; as Tolman had conjectured, some learning (i.e., knowledge of the maze) might occur and be available without being *used* until motivational or reward conditions make it profitable.

In their defense against latent-learning experiments, reinforcement theorists usually made much of the decrease in errors during nonrewarded trials in latent-learning experiments as evidence that *some* reinforcement was present before reward was introduced. For example, since an incorrect choice in the maze resulted in the rat's bumping its nose against a locked door, perhaps correct choice responses became relatively stronger simply because incorrect choices were mildly punished. But such defenses could really only account for *that much* gain by reinforcement; any previously concealed gain, shown when reward was introduced, remained unaccounted for. In Hull's later theory, however, in which habit strength ($_sH_R$) is acquired independently of the magnitude of reinforcement, this difficulty no longer holds. Under minimum values of incentive magnitude K (such incentives as are present without food reward, including exploration, return to home cage, etc.), habit strength will be practically "latent," to be revealed in reaction potential when large values of K are created by introducing the food reward. But this change in Hull's theory was forced partly to handle the latent-learning results.

Tolman's explanation is that the nonreward situation was a good one for learning the spatial relations of the maze. Every unit had one dead end and another end with a door. The last thing done in each case was to go through the door. Recency (which is accepted as favoring sign-gestalts) would strengthen the cognition that the door was the way from one segment to the next, though under nonreward conditions there were no reasons for the rat to show what it "knew." The substitution of the food at the end of the maze, a highly demanded goal-object, led the rat to use its cognitive map, to take the turns which led from one unit to the next. Hence the sudden reduction in errors.

An upsurge of interest in the issues opened up by the latent-learning experiments led to a great many experimental reports, chiefly in the 1940s and 1950s. These were reviewed by Thistlethwaite (1951), again by MacCorquodale and Meehl (1954, pp. 199–213), and also in the second edition of this book (Hilgard, 1956, pp. 211–215). While different varieties of latent-learning experiments led to somewhat different scores, of the 48 studies reviewed by MacCorquodale and Meehl, 30 were reported as positive, 18 as negative. There is little doubt that, under appropriate circumstances, latent learning is demonstrable.

Following their review of the latent-learning literature, MacCorquodale and Meehl concluded:

In spite of the preceding difficulties of interpretation, it seems safe to say that the current state of the evidence is at least encouraging to the theorist oriented to some form of expectancy theory. We were, frankly, somewhat more impressed by the overall trend of the evidence than we had expected to be. (1954, p. 213)

Direct Alteration of Valence of the Goal

Recall the inference postulate (no. 4) given previously, namely, that if expectancy ($S_1R_1S_2$) exists and we pair a valenced object S^* with S_2, then a new expectancy ($S_1R_1S^*$) will arise (or will be inferred). The latent-learning experiments reviewed above are relevant, since they are derivable from this postulate plus the postulate that ($S_1R_1S_2$) knowledge units are acquired as a function of contiguity of experience. Other evidence relevant to the inference postulate is that in which, following learning of an $(S_1 R_1 S_2)$ unit, the valence of S_2 is altered by directly placing the subject into the S_2 situation but with a different incentive, S^*. If, for instance, a positively valenced S_2 is replaced by a negatively valenced S^*, then by the inference postulate the expectancy $(S_1 R_1 S^*)$ arises, and $S_1 R_1$ will lose in strength due to the negative valence of S^*.

There have been two general classes of tests of this sort. A classic experiment is by Tolman and Gleitman (1949), who first familiarized rats with a homogeneous T-maze with food rewards provided in both distinctive end-boxes, so that their "habit strengths" to the two maze arms were equal. Then, on a critical day, the animals were placed directly into one of the distinctive end-boxes and given painful electric shocks. On the crucial free-choice tests which followed, the animals now predominantly chose the maze arm leading to the other end-box, avoiding the arm leading to the shocked end-box. Since the differential goal-box cues were not perceptible from the choice point of the maze (they were hidden behind curtains), the animal, in choosing, must have "known" that one maze arm led to that place where he had been shocked, and so avoided that arm and chose the other.

A second sort of experiment of this type is called "latent extinction." The first such experiment was done by Seward and Levy (1949), and the literature on the topic was reviewed by Moltz (1957). In these experiments, animals are first trained on a simple instrumental response, say, depressing a lever in order to operate a food-dispensing mechanism or running down a runway to receive food in the goal-box. After the performance is well established, the subject is given direct exposure to the goal situation without reward; the lever might be removed from the cage and the experimenter operate the food-dispensing mechanism many times without actually delivering any food, or the animal might be placed directly in the goal-box of the runway repeatedly without any food's being there. Such experiences inevitably result in extinction of the terminal members of the behavior chain established earlier; the animal stops going to the food-well when the dispenser clicks. But the critical observations occur when the animal is placed again in the first part of the runway, or when the response lever is reinserted in the cage. Invariably, that initial response has now been seriously weakened, often not occurring at all. The rat in the start-box is no longer so eager to run down to the end-box because he now "infers" that it will be empty of food; or in the lever-pressing type of experiment, the animal is not very eager to press the reinserted lever to sound the dispensing mechanism because he "infers" that the noise of the mechanism is no longer associated with food (the originally valenced object).

These are sort of "common-sense" results; but their unique property is that they imply that the strength of an "S-R habit" can be altered without *that response* occurring and receiving the altered conditions of reinforcement. The rat did not press the lever, get the dispenser sound, and receive no food; only the final link in the chain was broken. Yet the influence of that event was "passed back" to earlier members of a behavior sequence. Such results create difficulties for an S-R reinforcement theory which supposes that responses can have their habit strengths altered only when they occur and are then explicitly punished or nonrewarded. The results seem to call for two assumptions; that at the start of a behavior sequence, organisms have available some representation of what goal they expect to achieve at the end of the response sequence; and that that goal expectation can be altered by direct experience with the goal situation without execution of the prior response sequence leading up to it. These, of course, are exactly the assumptions embodied in Tolman's (or really MacCorquodale and Meehl's) postulates 4 and 9, regarding secondary cathexis and inference. It was such results as these which forced Hull and Spence to greater reliance on r_G, the anticipatory goal response, as a theoretical representation of the organism's goal expectation.

Confirmation versus Reinforcement

Because Tolman was at such pains to protest against the law of effect and the principle of reinforcement as essential to learning, it is appropriate to inquire what role he assigned motivation in learning.

One role assigned to motivation was in relation to performance. Learning is *used* when drives are active. When drives are aroused a state of tension ensues, expressed as demands for goal-objects. These demands lead to activity, guided by the expectancies or cognitive structures available. In this role, then, motivation is not really a factor in learning at all. It is related to performance, not to acquisition. Because this role of motivation is made much of in Tolman's criticisms of reinforcement theories, the impression is given that learning, the acquiring of cognitive structures, is independent of motivation. This is not true in fact, nor is it true in Tolman's theory.

The second role of motivation is in the acquisition of cognitive structures. In one of the experiments critical of the law of effect, the suggestion was made that what appeared to be the principle of effect might better be considered the influence of *emphasis* (Tolman, Hall, & Bretnall, 1932). That is, motivation determines which features of the environment shall interest the learner, and thus those to which he pays attention. Such factors are influential in perceptual acquisitions, which are the genuine substance of place learning. The goal-object, by its presence or absence, verifies or refutes hypotheses regarding its location. Hence the goal-object is essential for the establishment of some features of cognitive structure. Latent learning, which dramatizes a relatively unmotivated, incidental type of learning, is an extreme instance of the relationship of goal behavior to learning and is probably not a typical case.

The importance of something like emphasis was suggested in some experiments by Muenzinger (e.g., Muenzinger, 1935; Muenzinger et al., 1952) in which punishment or obstacles to be overcome in the maze, even on the side of the correct choice, aided learning. Whether or not punishment will be an aid to learning thus depends upon what influence it has on the cognitions of the learner. It may be helpful as an emphasizer or harmful as a distractor.

This emphasizing function is also suggested by more recent interpretations of reward in human verbal learning (e.g., Atkinson & Wickens, 1971). In verbal-learning experiments in which subjects are informed that they will receive one or another sum of money for remembering different items, it is clear that they give preferential rehearsal to the high-valued items at the expense of low-valued items. Similar results can be produced by assigning to items differential punishments or penalties to be extracted in case they are forgotten. In all such cases, the role of the incentive is to act as an informational stimulus, selecting out particular S-R relations to be worked on, elaborated, and learned. Rewards are thus acting as *emphasizers* of particularly useful bits of knowledge which the subject would do well to acquire.

Confirmation Probability and Expectancy

The principle in Tolman's system that most nearly replaces reinforcement is the principle of *confirmation*. An expectancy $(S_1R_1S_2)$ is confirmed every time the consequent, S_2, in fact follows the occurrence of the event S_1R_1. The expectancy $(S_1R_1S_2)$ is *disconfirmed* whenever event S_1R_1 is followed by some new consequent, S_3, different from S_2. Confirmation of an expectancy increases its probability value, whereas disconfirmation decreases the probability value. In this manner, the expectancy value can track the probability with which particular outcomes (S_2s) are given as consequences of S_1R_1 events.

This "learning of probabilistic expectations" was developed in a stimulating paper by Tolman and Brunswik (1935); they pointed out the adaptive significance of probability learning, arguing that the causal texture of the environment (e.g., the correlation between the proximal and the distal stimulus pattern, or between appearance and reality) is such that probabilistic rather than uniform zero-one expectancies should prove more adaptive. In experimental tests, Brunswik (1939) presented his rats with probabilistic reinforcement in a T-maze, with reward found sometimes in the right, sometimes in the left arm of the maze. He found good agreement between the asymptotic choice probability of the rat and the probability that food would be where he went for it. Thus, for example, if three-quarters of the rat's runs ended with reward in the left goal-box and one-quarter in the right goal-box, then the rats would come eventually to distribute their choices about .75:.25 to the left and right arms of the maze. That is, the probability of choosing a given response came to match the probability with which that response was reinforced (or "confirmed").

Humphreys (1939) and later Estes and Straughan (1954) used a similar probabilistic situation for what they called "verbal conditioning" with human subjects. In its simplest arrangement, the task for the subject is to predict on each trial which one of two events is going to occur (for example, the lighting of a left or a right bulb). After the subject has made his predictive response, the actual event is shown. The events occur in a random, unpredictable sequence, with, say, one event occurring two-thirds of the trials and the other event the other one-third. This situation routinely leads to the subject's matching his response probabilities to the corresponding event probabilities.

An observation made by Humphreys and since confirmed by many others concerns the rate of the person's *shifting* of his response probabilities when the objective event probabilities are shifted between a training and a test series of trials. Suppose we let π_1 denote the probability that the left light comes on during the training series ($1 - \pi_1$ is the likelihood of the right-light event), and let π_2 denote the likelihood of the left lamp's lighting during the test series. The simple observation is that the behavioral probabilities (of left versus right predictions) shifted more rapidly the greater the shift in the event probabilities, from π_1 to π_2. The most extreme shift, of course, would be from a training series with $\pi_1 = 1$ where the left lamp always comes on, to a test series with $\pi_2 = 0$ where the left lamp never comes on (while the right lamp lights on every trial). Such a shift in event probabilities is readily discriminated, and the subject readily adjusts his behavior in accord with the prevailing reinforcement (event) probabilities of the test series. Much as occurs with discrimination of sensory magnitudes, the discrimination of the training series from the test series depends on the difference between π_1 and π_2. Such results were found to apply not only to human "verbal conditioning" but to eyelid conditioning, to rats' pushing of levers or running down alleyways for food, and so on.

Humphreys and Tolman, as well as many others, saw the relevance of such results to classical theories of extinction. Thus, a response reinforced on only 50 percent of the training trials proved to be much more resistant to extinction (i.e., 0 percent reward) than was a similar response trained with uniform, 100 percent reinforcement. This so-called partial reinforcement extinction effect created a long-standing dilemma for S-R reinforcement theory, since how could a response reinforced only part of the time ever come to be "stronger" and more resistant to extinction than a response reinforced all the time during training? A variety of ingenious solutions to this puzzle have been proposed and researched over the years, several of which will be discussed throughout this volume. But one of the prominent hypotheses suggested by Humphreys, Tolman, and others was the *"discrimination"* hypothesis suggested by the early probability-learning experiments. The hypothesis, in brief, is that expectancies and behavior change at a faster rate the greater the discriminability of the change of conditions between the training and testing series. This hypothesis has reached its most refined statement and elaboration in the recent theorizing of Capaldi (1967), to which we will refer in Chapter 15. The discrimination hypothesis was a most congenial one for Tolman, and the partial reinforcement extinction effect (or its variants) never proved a thorn in his side as it did for the S-R reinforcement theorists who were his contemporaries.

Provisional Expectancies as Hypotheses

In Tolman's view, prior to solving a learning problem, the learner is actively trying out various "hypotheses" regarding the nature of the (SRS*) relationships existing in the problematic environment. A given hypothesis conjectured about the correct solution to a discrimination problem might be considered as a provisional expectancy. When the situation is not yet structured and path-to-goal relationships are not yet known, behavior would still be "systematic" based on these provisional hypotheses or guesses.

The initial evidence for this view was provided by Krechevsky (1932a, 1932b, 1933a, 1933b), a colleague of Tolman's. Krechevsky found that prior to learning a four-unit maze (with light versus dark cues plus left-right position cues at each choice point) his rats adopted systematic modes of response which they would "try out" for a while, then switch to a different systematic pattern. For instance, an animal might begin by consistently trying a "turn left" hypothesis, follow it for ten trials or so, then shift to an "alternate positions in successive maze units" mode for a while, finally hitting upon a "go to the dark side" hypothesis, which was correct. Krechevsky called these systematic modes of attempted solutions "hypotheses," and contrasted them with the "blind, random trial and error" which was commonly supposed to be the prediction of the Thorndikean position for trial-and-error learning. Krechevsky showed convincingly that averaging time or error scores across groups of individuals tends to conceal the systematic nature of each individual's mode of attack. It was supposed that, rather than gradually stamping in the correct response, the effect of reinforcement was to consistently confirm the correct hypothesis, whereas nonreinforcement was used as an informative signal for abandonment of a provisional but incorrect hypothesis. The correct solution would be hit upon all at once, when the animal abandoned a hypothesis based on an irrelevant cue and then selected the correct hypothesis based on the relevant cue. The solution to the problem was sudden and apparently "insightful." These experiments and associated ideas furnished the opening shots in a long-standing but fruitful controversy over "continuity" and "discontinuity" in discrimination learning by animals, with the "hypothesis experiments" furnishing initial evidence for the discontinuity hypothesis. The controversy will be mentioned frequently throughout this volume.

The clearest statement of "hypothesis" theory has been made by Restle (1962) and Levine (1965, 1969, 1970), and the clearest evidence for it has been collected by Levine (summarized in Levine, 1970) using human adults learning simple "concept identification" problems. A typical set of stimuli in one of Levine's experiments is shown in Figure 5.4. The stimulus patterns here vary in four binary dimensions: shape (X or T), size (large or small), color (black or white), and position (left or right). Each card contains a pat-

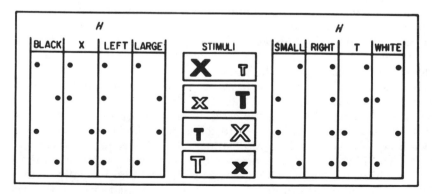

Figure 5.4.   Eight patterns of choices corresponding to each of the eight hypotheses (H) when the four stimulus pairs are presented consecutively without feedback. (From M. Levine, Human discrimination learning: The subset sampling assumption. *Psychological Bulletin*, 1970, 74, p. 398. Copyright 1970 by the American Psychological Association. Reprinted by permission.)

tern alongside its full complement—for instance, a large black X on the left versus a small white T on the right. The experimenter elects to say *Right* whenever the subject selects that pattern having a particular property—for instance, those having the T shape. The subject's task is to learn always to select the correct pattern as each pair is shown.

Hypothesis theory supposes that a learning problem such as this is representable by saying that the subject at the outset of training entertains a small population of possible hypothesis (Hs) regarding the solution (e.g., one H would be "choose the left pattern"). The subject presumably selects an H and responds to the card according to that H; if his response is correct or if he is given no feedback regarding the correctness of his choice, he continues using the same H for the next trial. If his response is called *Wrong*, then it is assumed that he samples a different H from the pool of hypotheses. This "win-stay/lose-shift" strategy for H selection will guarantee eventual solution if the correct H is available in the subject's repertoire, since all incorrect hypotheses eventually lead to errors and are discarded, whereas only the correct hypothesis leads to consistently correct responses.

Levine assesses hypothesis behavior in humans by the use of test blocks of nonfeedback trials interspersed among feedback trials when the person is told *Right* or *Wrong* for his response. It is assumed that nonfeedback trials cause no change in the subject's H, simply preserving the status quo for another trial. The arrangement of feedback (F_i) trials and nonfeedback trials (assessing H_i) is shown in Figure 5.5. Here F_1 denotes the initial feedback trial, H_1 the initial hypothesis as assessed, F_2 the second feedback trial, H_2 the hypothesis assessed following F_2, and so on. The cards in the test block are so arranged that each of the eight different, simple hypotheses can be uniquely identified by the pattern of choices to the test cards. In Figure 5.4, for instance, with the sequence of four test cards as shown, the sequence of choices "left, left, right, right" would indicate that the person was testing out or holding a "choose X" hypothesis during that test block. Another eight of the possible $2^4 = 16$ response sequences (not shown in Figure 5.4) would not correspond to any of the simple one-attribute hypotheses, and would be denoted by Levine either as "more complex" Hs or as "random" behavior. Importantly, the technique permits the experimenter to inspect the subject's "hypothesis behavior" (if any) throughout the course of acquisition of the identification, relating H_{n+1} to H_n and F_n.

In such conditions, adults' behavior conforms almost exactly to the postulates of H-theory. First, most of their test blocks (over 95 percent) reveal the use of systematic, simple Hs; the occasional lapses are likely to be the result of stray "oops" errors, as Levine calls them. Second, subjects tend very much to follow the "win-stay/lose-shift" strategy for H-selection following a feedback trial. That is, if F_n is "correct," then H $_{n+1}$ very probably is the same as H_n. Third, the correct H is eventually selected and typically maintained "all at once," and one can notice that it was never used prior to the trial on which it was selected. All of these are the sorts of results that Krechevsky was claiming to find for his rats learning their mazes back in 1932. One may take issue with the restrictive arrangements of Levine's experiments or note some opposing data from lower animals regarding the "continuity" position. But it is undeniable that the "hypothesis-testing" approach propounded by Krechevsky and Tolman has very strong experimental support and theoreti-

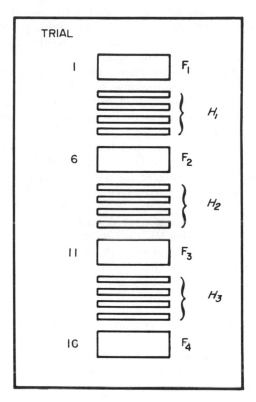

Figure 5.5.   Schema of a 16-trial problem showing the feedback trials (F_i) on which the experimenter says *Right* or *Wrong* and the blank trials from which the hypotheses (the H_i) are inferred. (From M. Levine, Human discrimination learning: The subset sampling assumption. *Psychological Bulletin,* 1970, 74, p. 399. Copyright 1970 by the American Psychological Association. Reprinted by permission.)

cal devotees on the current scene (see Trabasso & Bower, 1968). The theory is still very much on the books.

Vicarious Trial-and-Error Behavior

Another set of observations cited by Tolman as consonant with his approach concerned so-called vicarious trial-and-error (VTE) behavior of animals at a choice point. This behavior, studied by Muenzinger (1938) and Tolman (1939) among others, is the hesitation, vacillation, and comparison of the alternative stimuli by the animal at a choice point before he "commits himself" to one or the other choice. This active scanning over and comparing of discriminative stimuli appeared to Tolman to support the view that perceptual-cognitive processes are prominent in controlling behavior at a choice point.

Bower (1959, 1962b) and Spence (1960b) later provided mathematical descriptions of choice-point behavior in terms of a "random walk," with the organism orienting to each of the discriminative stimuli in turn and approaching or not approaching them with measurable probabilities. Bower showed how such a model fit the probabilistic structure of rats' VTE behavior during learning of a simple discrimination.

Later, Mowrer (1960) and Estes (1962, 1969a) developed the idea of a "response-scanning" or "stimulus-response scanning" mechanism to account for selection of rewarded responses and inhibition of punished responses. The thought was that in an instrumental conditioning situation, the organism internally scans through a limited repertoire of responses (either incipiently or entirely centrally). If the anticipated outcome for a response is negative (e.g., is associated to punishment and fear), then that response is inhibited. If the anticipated outcome for a scanned response is a high positive reward, then positive facilitative feedback is provided to "push" that incipient response on through to completion. These ideas arose earlier in our discussions of Estes's theory of reward (in Chapter 2) and the Sheffield-Estes theory of incentive motivation (in Chapter 4). But clearly the notions of stimulus scanning, prediction of rewards, comparison of anticipated outcomes, and so forth, are all ideas that Tolman would have found quite congenial to his "cognitive" account of the components of decision-making.

TOLMAN'S POSITION ON THE TYPICAL PROBLEMS OF LEARNING

Because it is a system with some aspirations toward completeness, there are statements within Tolman's writings relevant to most of the problems raised by other writers.

1. Capacity. Tolman recognized the need for capacity laws. The matter interested him chiefly because of the possible gradation of learning tasks from those requiring least to those requiring most intelligence. It is natural that one who makes predictions about what animals will do in problem-solving situations is confronted with the limitations of one organism as compared with another.

2. Practice. The law of exercise is accepted in the sense that the probability of an S_1-R_1-S_2 sequence affects the strength or value of that expectancy. Exercise is not the cause of the initial selection of the right response. Mere frequency without "belonging" of the significate with that response does not establish a connection.

3. Motivation. Rewards and punishment tend to regulate performance, rather than acquisition, although they are related to acquisition also because they serve as "emphasizers" and because goal-objects confirm or refute hypotheses. Because of the demonstration of latent learning, the law of effect in its usual sense (reward as a strengthener of response tendencies) is not accepted, although a few concessions were made by Tolman later on.

4. Understanding. Cognitive processes are of the very essence of molar behavior and learning. Hence Tolman was friendly to learning by creative inference, inventive ideation, and so on. He repeatedly stated, however, that he did not wish to endorse "introspectively get-at-able conscious contents." The prototype of learning is sensible, reasonable adjustment according to the requirements of the situation; stupid learning occurs as a limiting case when the problem is unsuited to the learner's capacities or is set up in inaccessible form. Insightful learning is not limited to the primates; it is characteristic of rat behavior as well.

5. Transfer. The problem of transfer as such has been of relatively slight interest to those experimenting with animals. To some extent all of the experiments on change of reward, change of drive, place learning, and latent learning are experiments on problems related to transfer, that is, the ability to use something learned in one situation in relation to another. All cognitive theories expect a large measure of transfer, provided the essential relationships of the situation are open to the observation of the learner.

6. Forgetting. As he had earlier experimented in the field of retroactive inhibition (1917), it is probable that Tolman was friendly toward some theory of retroactive inhibition, and he indicated that he accepted the Freudian mechanism of repression (1942, pp. 63–64). These conceptions were not prominent in his writings on learning theory, although in 1949 (see pp. 211–213) he speculated about the relative permanence of various subvarieties of learning. Thus, he asserted the resistance of cathexes and equivalence beliefs to forgetting, and the susceptibility of field expectations to the kind of forgetting emphasized by Gestalt psychologists.

When Tolman announced his purposive behaviorism (1922), ten years before his major book appeared, American psychology was still excited over the new behaviorism of Watson. It was Tolman's contribution then to show that a sophisticated behaviorism can still be cognizant of all the richness and variety of psychological events, and need not be constrained by an effort to build a "telephone switchboard" model of the learning machine.

With the diversification of behaviorism under the influence of Tolman and others, the old brittleness of Watsonian behaviorism has largely disappeared, and what virtues there are in the behavioristic position have now become part of the underlying assumptions of most American psychologists— although most of them do not think of themselves as "behaviorists" at all.

Tolman's catholicity and his friendliness to new ideas prevented his developing a "tight" or "elegant" system, even though he all along made suggestions as to what such a system would be like. He kept his prominent place in the forefront of learning theorists by his sensitivity to important problems, by his inventiveness in experimentation, and by his way of keeping others on their mettle.

Related Systematic Ideas

As intellectual climates change, ideas formerly expressed in one form tend to turn up in others, and may be unrecognized. As we have repeatedly emphasized throughout this chapter, Tolman anticipated many of the later significant developments in learning theory.

Thus, *decision processes* have become very interesting in contemporary psychology, growing out of the theory of games as proposed by von Neumann and Morgenstern (1944). As the theory has been adapted by psychologists (Edwards, 1954, 1962) increasing interest arises in *subjective probability* and *subjective utility*, terms rather similar in meaning to Tolman's notions of expectancy value and object valence. The importance both of probabilities and of risk was explicit in the paper by Tolman and Brunswik (1935), in which their separate views were harmonized. Pointing this out does not mean that the ideas in decision theory came historically from Tolman and Brunswik. It is rather that if related ideas appear in new forms, with appropriate experimental and mathematical procedures, there is no special point in pushing for the earlier ideas, except to point out that they had a measure of validity. Rotter (1954), in a book designed to provide a theory for clinical psychology, evolved an expectancy-reinforcement theory, with some points of contact with Tolman's views. His basic formula for *behavioral potential* (BP) makes it a function of *expectancy of reinforcement* (E) and the *reinforcement value* of the expected reinforcement. The expectancy of reinforcement is close to Tolman's means-end-readiness, and the reinforcement value corresponds roughly to valence.

The *structural model* proposed by Deutsch (1960) and used in connection with a great variety of experiments appears a far cry from Tolman, yet in many respects it represents a kind of thinking about psychological problems quite consonant with that of Tolman. Even though Deutsch proposes a "machine" type of model, in which such a machine has memory storage and feedback mechanisms, it can show insightful behavior of the order of Tolman's rats (Deutsch, 1954). In fact, one of the more ingenious experiments is a repetition, with changes, of the Tolman and Honzik (1930a) experiment, as reported by Deutsch and Clarkson (1959).

As in the Tolman and Honzik experiment (see Figure 5.2) the maze was arranged with longer and shorter alleys, and the various portions could be blocked. The pattern is shown in Figure 5.6. Three problems were set, problems A, B, and C, but only after the rats were familiar with the maze and had found food in both goal-boxes whenever they reached them.

In problem A, the near goal-box (goal-box 1) was left empty. Nearly all the rats ran to the near goal-box first. Now, having found it empty, the rat could return by the same short route, take the alternate short route, or take the long route. According to the "insightful" interpretation, the rat would take the long path to goal-box 2; 9 of 12 rats made this choice, and in view of the oft-repeated habit of running to the near box via the short path, the result is highly significant statistically.

In problem B, one of the short paths was blocked as shown (actually, both paths were blocked, but the rat had no way of knowing this). Now the rat has the choice of taking the other short path or the long one. In this case, 9 of 12 rats chose the other short path, rather than the long one as in problem A. The results for both problems A and B support Tolman's interpretation, as well as the predictions (made on somewhat similar grounds) by Deutsch and Clarkson.

Problem C is really the crucial one, for here the Deutsch-Clarkson prediction goes opposite to common sense. A wire-mesh barrier was placed within

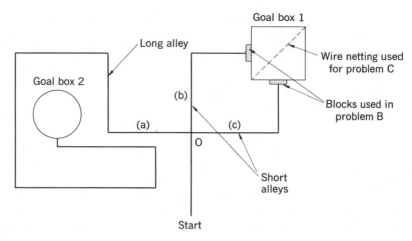

Figure 5.6.   A reasoning experiment. The maze is actually an alley maze, but has been diagrammed for simplicity. For explanation, see text. (Modified from J. A. Deutsch and J. K. Clarkson, Reasoning in the hooded rat. *Quarterly Journal of Experimental Psychology*, 1959, 11. Copyright 1959 by the American Psychological Association. Reprinted by permission.)

the near box (diagonal broken line in goal-box 1 in Figure 5.6). No blocks were used. The animal entered the box by way of one of the short paths and perceived food beyond the wire netting, but could not eat it. The rat was observed while in the box and was not removed until it had made distinct attempts to thrust its snout through the wire mesh to get the food on the other side. Now common sense (and the latent-learning predictions of Tolman) would predict that the rat, knowing the maze and knowing where the food was, would take the other short path the next time. But Deutsch and Clarkson predicted that this would not take place. The reasoning is that the food-seekings via the two short paths are very closely linked, especially at the terminal link. When the block occurs prior to any commerce with food, the linkages are not involved as they are when there has been some commerce with food, even though frustrating as in problem C. This frustration now affects both the short-path behaviors, and raises the potency of the long path. Hence the long path will be chosen in preference to the alternate short path. This turned out to be the case, again with 9 of 12 rats choosing the long path.

The theory proposed by Deutsch is more complex than this short description suggests, but the point being made here is that we have a very Tolman-like experiment, critical of S-R reinforcment theory, yet guided by a theory that predicts results somewhat different from those that Tolman would predict. This is exactly the kind of development to be expected in an experimental science.

Some experiments with a Tolman-like interpretation (though not designed particularly in relation to his theory) were presented by Lawrence and Festinger (1962) to test predictions based on Festinger's concept of cognitive dissonance (Festinger, 1957). This is a type of motivational theory deriving from the level of aspiration experiments of Lewin, with which Festinger had been earlier associated (Festinger, 1942). The interpretation can be thought of as Tolman-like because of the inference to cognitive processes in rats.

The finding of the Lawrence and Festinger experiments is that animals who have been induced to perform an effortful response under insufficient reward conditions (e.g., small, infrequent, or delayed rewards relative to the effortfulness of the response) will reveal greater resistance to extinction of that response than will their more amply rewarded confreres. The interpretation is that the occurrence of an insufficient reward following an effortful performance induces a momentary state of "cognitive dissonance" which is unpleasant to the animal. One method to reduce that dissonance is to seek out intrinsic attractions in the activity or the insufficient goal situation itself, which will justify the action just taken. Thus a man who moves a long distance to take a disappointingly low-paying job may begin to justify his staying with the job because he "likes the work" or "is getting good experience" or "the community is a great place to live." In a series of inventive experiments, Lawrence and Festinger (1962) showed the viability of this cognitive dissonance analysis of what was influencing rats to continue performing an insufficiently rewarded response during an extinction series. As Festinger (1961) has summarized the theory, "we come to love those things for which we have suffered." The results of Lawrence and Festinger surely sound the death knell for any theory that attempts to explain "resistance to extinction" of a response in terms of a simple construct of "habit strength" that increases the more favorable is the reward condition prevailing during its acquisition. Yet this was the predominant theory for many years, promulgated by Thorndike, Hull, and their followers.

Modern Cognitive Psychology

The kind of behavior theory that Tolman dimly foresaw began to appear during the 1960s in American psychology under the name of "cognitive psychology" or "information-processing" approaches to theorizing. Beginning with the seminal writings of Chomsky (1957) and Newell, Shaw, and Simon (1958), with the arguments forcibly marshaled by Miller, Galanter, and Pribram (1960) and by Neisser (1967), the "cognitive psychology" movement has by now become a major, if not the dominant, force in contemporary experimental psychology, especially that concerned with human memory and attention. Some of the work carried out in this newer tradition will be described in Chapter 13 on information-processing models and in Chapter 15 on recent developments. Very little of this recent work derives directly from the specific hypotheses promulgated by Tolman. However, most of the work is congenial to the spirit of the kind of theory for which Tolman was arguing.

The Miller, Galanter, and Pribram book *Plans and the structure of behavior* (1960) has become a classic in the current Zeitgeist of cognitive psychology, and is required reading for serious students of modern theoretical psychology. The authors reject the S-R reflex as a basic unit in behavioral analysis and replace it with a TOTE unit, a sort of feedback cycle whereby

(a) a goal is pursued by testing a stimulus condition for congruity with that goal, (b) if a discrepancy is detected, control shifts to an "operate" loop which performs some act designed to reduce the discrepancy from the desired goal, (c) the outcome of the operation is again tested for congruity to the goal and the process exits (stops) if that particular goal is achieved. Figure 5.7, for instance, illustrates a TOTE (test-operate-test-exit) hierarchy for the simple act of hammering a nail down so that it is flush with a board. The process begins by testing the state of the nail; if it sticks up, then control flows to the "hammer" routine which has as its first component a test for where the hammer is (up or down); if it is down, it is lifted; if it is up, a command to "strike nail" is executed, whereupon the "hammer" routine momentarily stops and control returns to the "test nail" routine which tests whether the nail still sticks up or is flush to the board; in the latter case, this particular process terminates and control is passed along to some higher unit of a plan which the person is executing.

Although this gives just the barest sketch of the basic unit of behavioral analysis, the TOTE diagram of Figure 5.7 illustrates several things. First, the elementary parts are like "instructions" in a computer program, either to compare one thing to another or to execute some operation (act). Second, the arrows in the diagram correspond to the flow of control (or the order of succession of instructions carried out) rather than referring to energy or S-R bonds. Third, the "program" could loop or recycle indefinitely until the desired goal state is achieved. Fourth, one or more TOTEs can be arranged within a higher-order TOTE, in a sort of hierarchy. Thus, one's overall plan might be to build a table, which would require many subplans

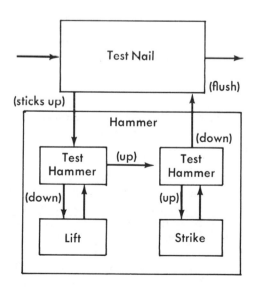

Figure 5.7.   A hierarchical plan for hammering a nail. (From *Plans and the Structure of Behavior* by George A. Miller, Eugene Galanter and Karl H. Pribram. Copyright © 1960 by Holt, Rinehart and Winston, Inc. Reprinted by permission of Holt, Rinehart and Winston, Inc.)

(TOTEs) requiring collection of materials, then preparation of materials, then, say, nailing together of wooden parts, and finally at the lowest level of the overall plan would be the repeated activation of the "Test Nail" TOTE of Figure 5.7. This overall plan can be recognized as being *hierarchically organized*, as having multiple parts that follow one another, but with multiple pieces or subcomponents within each part. But this analysis of "what the person is doing" at any one time gives us a new perspective on the "molar versus molecular" behavior distinction; such terms describe the level within a hierarchical program on which we are focusing. In molar terms, the person is "building a table," but in molecular terms the muscles of his right arm are contracting so as to lift a hammer.

Miller, Galanter, and Pribram suppose that all behavior is organized according to such hierarchical plans, that the succession of plans executed depends upon the organism's current values and needs, and that during execution of the plans his mind draws continuously upon a large storehouse of skills, procedures, and knowledge (cognitions) that he has filed away in his memory, including past plans and their evaluated successfulness. The accumulated knowledge possessed by a person is termed his *image* of the world, and it is conceived much along the lines of Tolman's "cognitive maps." But Miller, Galanter, and Pribram also devote much attention to an analysis of motor skills and to rule-governed behaviors like speaking or problem-solving. Much attention is given to strategies as components of problem-solving plans, and they discuss a diverse set of mnemonic strategies used by adults as "plans for remembering." This surely antedates the current interest in mnemonic strategies among investigators of human memory (see, for example, Bower, 1970a; Norman, 1965; Tulving & Donaldson, 1972). These ideas have been developed in much greater detail than can be presented here. The entire enterprise is very much in the spirit of the sort of cognitive theory which Tolman was urging some 30 years earlier, albeit obscurely and imprecisely at times.

Final Comment

While it is true that there have been very few recent experiments showing their direct origin in Tolman's original theory, we have been at pains to point to a number of contemporary developments that can be traced back to Tolman and his influence. He clearly posed for standard stimulus-response theories many of the enduring problems with which it has struggled— for example, the distinction between learning and performance, latent learning, goal anticipation and incentive motivation, hypothesis-testing behavior, sharpening of the characterization of "what is learned," and so forth. Stimulus-response theorizing developed and matured well beyond Watson, Thorndike, and Pavlov because of the vigorous challenges provided by cognitive theorists who frequently were the first to call attention to some new problem area regarding learning. This was entirely wholesome, and in our time has led to a kind of coalescence of the competing learning theories in a synthesis of a sort not envisioned by the original protagonists.

We may ask, what kind of contribution by a scientist is likely to endure? A global system, unless it is very successful in grouping together a number of well-established empirical facts (Newton's law, Einstein's relativity theory), is less likely to endure than a single well-established relationship (Archimedes' principle, Ohm's law, the Weber-Fechner law). Tolman's system was not tight enough to endure, and there is no "Tolman law" to give him immortality; perhaps the latent-learning experiment is as uniquely his as is the nonsense syllable uniquely Ebbinghaus's. Some of these less dramatic contributions, as they work their ways into the stream of science, may be enough to win a rightful place in the history of science for the man who made them.

The hope, however, is for something more than this, and that is for the march of science (in our case, psychological science) to be evident either in firm factual relationships upon which future theories are built, or in the introduction of new paradigms which give science a fresh look, as emphasized by Kuhn (1962). In retrospect, Tolman's contribution may have been of this latter kind, giving a new cast to behaviorism by insisting that it be open to the problems created by cognitive processes, problem-solving, and inventive ideation. The sort of program Tolman envisioned seems now to be coming to fruition in modern cognitive psychology.

SUPPLEMENTARY READINGS

The only major book on Tolman's system is
TOLMAN, E. C. (1932) *Purposive behavior in animals and men.*

Fortunately, his shorter writings have been assembled in book form:
TOLMAN, E. C. (1951) *Collected papers in psychology.*

A final summary and overview of his theorizing was published in the chapter:
TOLMAN, E. C. (1959) Principles of purposive behavior. In S. Koch (Editor). *Psychology: A study of a science.* Vol. 2.

An interesting little book, which started out to be a book on motivation but was retitled because of World War II (and remains a book on motivation despite its title), is:
TOLMAN, E. C. (1942) *Drives toward war.*

For a thorough review of Tolman's position, with some suggestions as to possible steps in systematization, see:
MacCORQUODALE, K., & MEEHL, P. E. (1954) Edward C. Tolman. In W. K. Estes et al. *Modern learning theory*, 177–266.

Hull's Systematic
Behavior Theory

Clark L. Hull (1884–1952), greatly impressed by the appearance of Pavlov's *Conditioned reflexes* (1927), began thereafter a long series of theoretical and experimental studies that in their totality comprise the best example of hypothetic-deductive system-making in psychology to appear during the first half of the century. The system is a behaviorism, and as such falls into the family of theories which also includes those of Guthrie and Skinner. Each of these three systems represents in its own way a fulfillment of the behavioristic program originally proposed by Watson. Like Watson's, Hull's theory is avowedly mechanistic and studiously avoids reference to consciousness. Its central concept is habit, and it derives most of its information about habit from experiments with conditioned responses, primarily with animals. Complex behavior, furthermore, is assumed to be derivable step by step from what is known about more elementary forms of learning. In these respects the theories of Watson and Hull are alike, but in other respects Hull's system represents a great advance over Watson's. Hull took the detailed findings of conditioning experiments much more seriously than Watson, who was satisfied to make use of the general paradigm provided by conditioned responses as a base for his speculative analyses. Hull adopted (and adapted) Thorndike's law of effect, whereas Watson had rejected it. For Watson's policy of denials and negations, Hull substituted a positive program of trying to explain purposes, insights, and other phenomena difficult for a behaviorism to encompass.

The Basic Orientation

Before turning to the more formal system, expressed in postulates, corollaries, and theorems, we may do well to examine the broad framework within which the system operates.

Intervening variables and their anchorage in observables.   In the first revision (1929) of his widely used textbook, Woodworth suggested that we substitute the formula S-O-R for the earlier recommended S-R formula. The stimulus (S) affects the organism (O), and what happens as a consequence, the response (R), depends upon O as well as upon S. Hull's system may be thought of as a herculean elaboration of this S-O-R formula.

In experiments we measure environmental influences upon the organism (the input), and then measure the organism's responses (the output). These events that we can observe, record, and measure provide the "groundwork" over which theories are constructed. But input and output are not comprised exclusively of the experimentally studied stimuli and responses. Other influences upon the organism can be treated as experimental variables, such as its history of prior training, deprivation schedules, injection of drugs, and past and present contingencies of reinforcement. These influences can be described as objectively as can stimuli and responses. What goes on within the organism we have to infer, and in the course of making these inferences we postulate certain *intervening variables* or *symbolic constructs*. If we tie these inferences firmly to the input-output terms by way of quantitative mathematical statements, we lose nothing in objectivity and gain something in convenience, understanding, and fertility of deducing new phenomena. This is the basic logic of a system involving reference to unobservable, theoretical concepts.

Reinforcement, the primary condition for habit formation.   In his choice among the three major possibilities (contiguity alone, reinforcement alone, or a dual theory), Hull stood firmly for a reinforcement theory. As early as 1935 he suggested that the Pavlov experiment might be considered a special case under Thorndike's law of effect, and in 1937 he published a formal derivation of Pavlovian conditioning on the basis of a reinforcement principle (Hull, 1935; 1937). In Hull's view, "reinforcement" acted in the same way in Pavlovian as in instrumental conditioning, namely, by providing a "satisfying" effect following a response. In this view of Pavlovian conditioning, the food (US) which followed the bell (CS) was not only an unconditional *elicitor* of salivation but also a *satisfier* which would reward any ongoing response, including the salivation produced by the food. Especially when the salivary response occurred in anticipation, the food would act as a strong reward for the response. According to this view, then, learning in the Pavlovian as in the instrumental conditioning situations involved a "reward" or "satisfaction" principle. What differed between the two procedures was that the Pavlovian procedure used the US to *force* the correct response (salivation) to occur in proper contiguity to the CS, whereas no similar arrangement could be enforced for "emitted" operant responses.

Reinforcement theory of the kind Hull espoused requires, in the specification of a primary reinforcing state of affairs, drive reduction, as in need satisfaction (e.g., food reduces a hunger drive, escape from pain reduces the pain drive). Later, for various reasons, Hull shifted his position slightly and identified reinforcement with drive-stimulus reduction, which was assumed to be more like satisfaction of a "craving" than a need. There is a subtle distinction between cravings and biological needs. Most needs lead to cravings or "appetites," but some do not—for example, asphyxiation by carbon monoxide (i.e., need for oxygen) is not painful. And we have many cravings that are not based on real needs—the obese person may eat when already full. Also, a craving can be reduced without a reduction of a biological need: a hungry rat will be rewarded by saccharine water, which is sweet but utterly nonnutritive; a hungry baby can be pacified by nonnutritive sucking on a pacifier. These would be examples of what Hull intended by "drive-stimulus reduction" rather than "need reduction." In primary reinforcement the two events (drive and drive-stimulus) are so closely associated that it does not matter very much which is assumed to be reduced. But needs may require time for their satisfaction (as in the time required to digest food) whereas incentives (including food) work promptly as reinforcers, more as stimuli might be expected to work. Furthermore, as secondary reinforcement came into greater and greater prominence in reinforcement theories, the stimulus-reduction theory became even more attractive. This follows because secondary reinforcement value is attached to stimuli that can be introduced quickly and phasically.

Integration of behavior sequences through anticipatory responses.   Most of the primary behavioral laws in Hull's system were derived from either classical or instrumental conditioning (both interpreted as illustrations of learning under the control of reinforcement). But the appeal of the system rests upon the detailed explanation it provides of many phenomena of learning in experiments not classifiable as simple conditioning: more complex trial-and-error and discriminatory learning, maze learning, all varieties of rote verbal memorization, tool-using, and so on. In order to make these further deductions, Hull proposed a number of intermediate mechanisms, derivable from the basic laws of his system but, once derived, of very wide applicability. An example of these intermediaries is the notion of anticipatory goal-responses; illustrations of other intermediate mechanisms will be presented later in this chapter.

Many of the stimuli present at the time the goal is reached are present earlier as well. These include the stimuli from the internal drive (what Guthrie called maintaining stimuli), environmental stimuli present both earlier and during reinforcement, traces from earlier stimuli persisting to the goal, and stimuli aroused by the animal's own movements. Hull assumed that all of these stimuli become conditioned to the goal-response (eating and salivation) to a degree dependent on their trace availability at the time the goal-response occurred. Hence in reactivating a sequence of acts leading to a goal, as in running through a maze, there are always enough of these stimuli conditioned to the goal-response to elicit fractions of the goal-response prior to reaching the goal. These fractional, antedating goal-responses (r_G's) are very important integrators in Hull's system, and he made very ingenious use of them. While they were prominent all along in Guthrie's system, Guthrie never did formalize their use as Hull did.

The fractional anticipatory responses give rise to stimuli (s_G). These response-produced stimuli can be assigned several functions. First, these s_G stimuli can become conditioned to differential responses and so aid in eliciting them. Thus, a rat can be taught more readily to turn left in a white maze and right in a black maze if the reward is qualitatively different in the two situations to be discriminated (e.g., food powder versus sucrose solution). The discrimination of which turn to make in which maze is helped by the different r_G's leading to different s_G's in the two situations, and the different s_G's become differentially associated to the two turning responses. Second, the s_G's can serve as the equivalents of "directing ideas," "purposes," or "intentions." In such illustrations, Hull referred to r_G as a "pure-stimulus act," that is, an act that serves functionally merely to provide a stimulus which maintains a steering role in guiding a sequential chain of behavior. An illustration would be that of a child thinking or saying "Cookie" to himself as he assembles and goes through the complex steps required to pull up a chair and climb on it to reach the cookie jar.

Furthermore, these r_G-s_G stimuli are used by Hull in describing the further mechanisms of *secondary reinforcment*, the *gradient of reinforcement*, and the *habit-family hierarchy*, concepts we shall meet later on.

The important point, however, is that on the basis of a simple conditioning principle (namely, r_G getting connected to earlier stimuli in an instrumental sequence), Hull derived a mechanism of wider generality (e.g., the directive role of s_G).

The Requirements for a Quantitative, Deductive System

Hull knew very clearly what he wanted in the way of a formal system. Such a system should begin with adequately defined terms, and then state a few (as few as possible) basic postulates. Either these postulates may be very general empirical findings, and thus independently verifiable, or, if not directly testable, they must be subject to indirect verification. Their purpose is to relate the fundamental intervening variables by strict logic (or mathematical equations) to each other and to their anchorages in environmental events. These postulates, taken together with the definitions, will generate new testable deductions or predictions. These are the corollaries and the theorems of the system.

In this view, the progress of science comes about through the experimental testing of theorems. When agreement is found, the postulate system generating the theorem is confirmed and remains in the running; when disagreement is found, a search is made for the faulty postulate, if such there be, and the postulate is then revised. Possibly, if no faulty postulate can be found, a new postulate may have to be added. The procedure is self-correcting, and only those features of the theory survive that have stood the scrutiny of meticulous experimental testing.

Systems of this kind begin as "miniature" ones. That is, they encompass at first only a limited range of data. Even these limited data put the early system under strain, and the next steps consist in trying to secure a better fit between the theory and these data. Then additional data from related experimental paradigms are incorporated through extensions of the system. Sometimes two or more "miniature systems" may be combined as appropriate bridging concepts are developed. There may be major shifts in the systematic formulations, as when, in physics, Newtonian theory became a special case under Einstein's more general theory. Thus theory construction proceeds by successive approximations, and finality in a theory is often a sign that the theory is intellectually moribund.

Earlier Sets of Postulates

Hull's theoretical system evolved gradually. He habitually wrote down various conjectures and plans for experiments in bound notebooks, 73 notebooks between 1902 and 1952.[1] Many of his later publications were foreshadowed in these notes and in the frequent mimeographed memoranda that he circulated. His first paper addressed specifically to the subject matter of his final system was in 1929, entitled "A functional interpretation of the conditioned reflex" (Hull, 1929). In it he acknowledged his great indebtedness to Pavlov and began on an informal basis to make the kinds of theoretical deductions he later sought to formalize. Another important influence on his later theorizing arose out of a summer's teaching at Harvard in 1930, when he was invited to lecture on aptitude testing because of the favorable reception of his recent book on that topic (1928). There he met C. I. Lewis and other philosophers, and read Newton's *Principia* and Whitehead and Russell's *Principia mathematica*. These raised his sights as to the kind of hypothetical deductive theory to which he might aspire. The first formal system, using definitions, postulates, and theorems, appeared in 1935 (Hull, 1935). It was what he called a "miniature system" concerned with rote learning (memorization of a verbal series), and was to be elaborated later in the most detailed of Hull's formal systematic efforts, the collaborative book entitled *Mathematico-deductive theory of rote learning* (Hull et al., 1940).

The true ancestor of the later postulate sets, however, was contained in Hull's presidential address before the American Psychological Association at Dartmouth in 1936 (Hull, 1937). This new "miniature system" was concerned with adaptive behavior of the kinds reflected in *Principles of behavior* (1943), *Essentials of behavior* (1951), and *A behavior system* (1952a). The last book was completed only a few weeks before Hull's death and appeared posthumously. The system was by no means a finished one, and Hull was the first to acknowledge this; the final book is full of qualifications and reservations.

The 1940 Theory of Rote Learning

In a thoroughgoing study with the forbidding title *Mathematico-deductive theory of rote learning: A study in scientific methodolgy*, Hull and his col-

---

[1] He mentioned these in Hull (1951), page 120. A number of excerpts from these notebooks have been published, and they provide an interesting glimpse into the private thinking of a scientist (Hull, 1962).

laborators attempted a rigorous systematization of rote memorization, in which interrelated hypotheses would be subjected to empirical testing (Hull et al., 1940). It is called a mathematico-deductive theory to indicate not only that it uses the hypothetico-deductive method, but that it uses it in a strictly quantitative way. The approach is very formal, beginning with primitive concepts and definitions, and proceeding to postulates, corollaries, theorems, and problems.

The book covers three main bodies of factual material: (1) serial position effects, relating the learning rate to the ordinal position of a nonsense syllable in a series being memorized; (2) reminiscence and forgetting, relating the initial rise in the curve of retention to other factors, such as distributed practice, serial position, and length of list; and (3) reaction thresholds and the course of memorization.

As was prevalent at the time, Hull et al. conceived of a serial list of verbal units (nonsense syllables) as a sequence of stimuli and responses. Figure 6.1 shows the chain of stimuli and responses for the series symbolized as *ABCD*. Presentation of syllable *A* is a stimulus, S_A, eliciting its name as a response, R_A. In the conventional anticipation method of serial learning, the elements are presented one by one in fixed order, with presentation of each syllable being the cue for the subject to anticipate in advance the next syllable in the series. Thus, each syllable in the series serves first as a response (to the prior cue) and then as a cue for the next syllable in the series.

Hull postulated that associations (habits) develop between the stimulus S_A and the anticipatory response for the next syllable, R_B; the S_A-R_B habit would be reinforced, of course, by the subject seeing that R_B is the "correct" response following S_A. The same principle applies to the remaining adjacent pairs in the series. These correct adjacent habits, $S_n \rightarrow R_{n+1}$ (shown as straight arrows in Figure 6.1), must eventually become strong enough to "win out" over various competing and extraneous factors which were presumed to degrade performance, introducing difficulties into serial learning.

These extraneous factors are of several kinds. First, as illustrated in

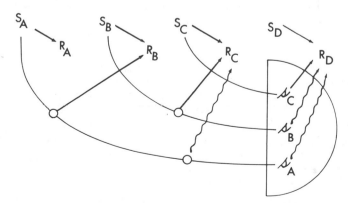

Figure 6.1.   Stimulus-response representation of the series A, B, C, D, ... Presentation of each stimulus leads to its pronunciation. Traces of the stimuli (small s's) perseverate and become associated (wiggly lines) to more remote responses in the series.

Figure 6.1, presentation and removal of a stimulus was assumed to set up a perseverative stimulus trace, characteristic of that stimulus, which persisted for several seconds (say, 10 seconds). Since later responses were reinforced during this time of active perseveration, these later responses were presumed to become associated to some degree to the perseverating stimulus trace. In Figure 6.1 this is symbolized by the wavy line connecting the s_A trace to R_C and R_D, or the s_B trace to R_D. To the extent that the trace of stimulus A, s_A, is similar to actual presentation of S_A, these later responses R_C and R_D will tend to be elicited by S_A and to compete with the correct response R_B. Assuming that the stimulus trace weakens and changes over time after presentation of the stimulus, there would be less generalization and hence weaker competition from responses that are more remote in time from the point of the correct response. Thus, use of the notion of the perseverative stimulus trace enables one to "derive" the phenomena of *anticipatory errors* and a *gradient* of remote intrusions, both of which are known phenomena of serial learning.

In order to overcome these anticipatory-error tendencies and reach eventually perfect performance, the subject was presumed (by Hull et al.) to develop an inhibition ("negative habit") to prevent each specific remote association. Thus, corresponding to each "wiggly line" or response association in the series of Figure 6.1, there would develop a corresponding tendency *not* to give that response to that stimulus; these inhibition tendencies presumably arise because remote anticipatory responses are nonreinforced ("extinguished") when they do occur. Hull et al. assumed specific rates of growth of these various excitatory (positive) and inhibitory (negative) associations, made particular assumptions about how these factors vary with time (e.g., that inhibition declines rapidly between trials), and made assumptions about how a response is determined by all the positive and negative habits operative at that time at that point in the series.

The theory was rather complex, with something like 18 postulates and 10 corollaries. However, it enabled Hull et al. to derive a number of "theorems" about serial learning, most of which they proceeded to verify in a set of experiments on rote serial learning. Among the derivations were that syllables learned at a similar rate would conform to an ogival (S-shaped) learning curve, that the number of errors before learning the syllable at a given serial position would vary with its position in the characteristic "bowed serial position curve," and that the serial position curve would vary in steepness as a function of the rest interval between trials (which was alleged to permit dissipation of inhibition). Altogether, about 55 percent of the derivations or theorems of the theory were confirmed, 28 percent were marked by conflicting evidence, and 17 percent were disconfirmed by the data.

Mathematico-deductive theory of rote learning met with a curious reception in the psychological world. It was both hailed as a monumental achievement of formal, miniature theorizing and described as a crashing bore. Many people referred to it but few read it or were influenced by it in their research.

This curiously flat reception of the book tempts one to speculate on why. One reason may have been that many of the substantive hypotheses—regarding remote associations, use of inhibition, summation of inhibitory connections spanning a location to explain the serial-position curve—were not original with Hull and this book. These were common ideas current in the rote learning literature since Ebbinghaus's original work. Hull et al. had simply added formal (and formidable!) machinery to permit calculations to be made with what were previously informal ideas. Second, and more importantly, the Hull et al. set of hypotheses about serial learning were not seminal because other experimentation soon began to show that the basic form of analysis was probably mistaken. For example, Hull did not separate learning of the nonsense syllables as response units and learning to order the syllables correctly in series, but this is clearly an important distinction to be mirrored in any theory. Further, later experiments questioned seriously whether the preceding item, S_n, was the functional stimulus for response R_{n+1}; rather, much later experimentation (summarized in Young, 1968) began to show that the *position* the item holds in the series can in many cases be the effective cue. Moreover, Hull's particular formulation of the rote learning theory led to a number of predictions regarding reminiscence (improvement in performance over a rest interval, the opposite of forgetting), and these proved through a series of controversial experiments not to be replicable or reliable phenomena. So the final verdict on *Mathematico-deductive theory of rote learning* was the empiricists' judgment: the basic analysis of serial learning was wrong, and no amount of formalization could cure that fatal illness. The fact that a number of "derived theorems" were confirmed had to be looked at with an extremely critical eye; one must always inquire regarding a number of auxiliary conditions such as whether the experimental result provides a crucial differentiation between the proposed theory and a strong competitor, or whether a given result is but a "trivial" extension of a known generalization that has been adopted as a "postulate" of the theory. In the case of the Hull et al. book, these side conditions were not convincingly met. If this were all that Hull's theorizing had amounted to, he would hardly have had the impact he did have on learning theory. That comes from his more general behavior system, first presented in 1943.

The 1943 Postulate System

In his *Principles of behavior* (1943) Hull's general system was presented at the height of his confidence in it, and many of his followers continue to refer to this book when comparing their views to his.

The general plan is straightforward. The complete behavioral event begins with stimulation provided by the external world and ends by a response, also part of the interplay with the environment. Everything else lies within the organism, influencing in one way or another what response will occur, if any, following the onset of the stimulus. The set of intervening processes, which are theoretical constructs rather than observables, are anchored, as Hull says, at both ends—at the stimulus end and at the response end.

The postulates.   In order to make it easier to grasp the system as a whole, in what follows the postulates have been paraphrased and assigned titles. The more exact statement can be found in the pages of Hull (1943) to which reference is made in each case.

A. *The external cues which guide behavior, and their neural representation.*
Postulate 1. *Afferent neural impulses and the perseverative stimulus trace.*

Stimuli impinging upon a receptor give rise to afferent neural impulses which rise quickly to a maximum intensity and then diminish gradually. After the termination of the stimulus, the activity of the afferent nervous impulse continues in the central nervous system for some seconds (1943, p. 47).

Postulate 2. *Afferent neural interaction.*

Afferent neural impulses interact with other concurrent afferent neural impulses in a manner to change each into something partially different. The manner of change varies with every impulse or combination of impulses (1943, p. 47).

B. *Responses to need; reinforcement and habit strength.*
Postulate 3. *Innate responses to need.*

Organisms at birth possess a hierarchy of need-terminating responses which are aroused under conditions of stimulation and drive. The responses activated by a given need are not a random selection of the organism's responses, but are those more likely to terminate the need (1943, p. 66).

Postulate 4. *Reinforcement and habit strength.*

Habit strength increases when receptor and effector activities occur in close temporal contiguity, provided their approximately contiguous occurrence is associated with primary or secondary reinforcement (1943, p. 178).

C. *Stimulus equivalence.*
Postulate 5. *Generalization.*

The effective habit strength aroused by a stimulus other than the one originally entering into conditioning depends upon the remoteness of the second stimulus from the first on a continuum in units of discrimination thresholds (just noticeable differences) (1943, p. 199).

D. *Drives as activators of response.*
Postulate 6. *Drive stimulus.*

Associated with every drive is a characteristic drive stimulus whose intensity increases with strength of drive (1943, p. 253).

Postulate 7. *Reaction potential aroused by drive.*

Habit strength is sensitized into reaction potential by the primary drives active at a given time (1943, p. 253).

E. *Factors opposing responses.*
Postulate 8. *Reactive inhibition.*

The evocation of any reaction generates reactive inhibition, a disinclination to repeat that response. Reactive inhibition is spontaneously dissipated in time (1943, p. 300).

Postulate 9. *Conditioned inhibition.*

Stimuli associated with the cessation of a response become conditioned inhibitors (1943, p. 300).

Postulate 10. *Oscillation of inhibition.*

The inhibitory potential associated with every reaction potential oscillates in amount from instant to instant (1943, p. 319).

F. *Response evocation.*
Postulate 11. *Reaction threshold.*

The momentary effective reaction potential must exceed the reaction threshold before a stimulus will evoke a reaction (1943, p. 344).

Postulate 12. *Probability of reaction above the threshold.*

The probability of response is a normal (ogival) function of the extent to which the effective reaction potential exceeds the reaction threshold (1943, p. 344).

Postulate 13. *Latency.*

The more the effective reaction potential exceeds the reaction threshold, the shorter the latency of response (1943, p. 344).

Postulate 14. *Resistance to extinction.*

The greater the effective reaction potential, the more unreinforced responses of striate muscle occur before extinction (1943, p. 344).

Postulate 15. *Amplitude of response.*

The amplitude of responses mediated by the autonomic nervous system increases directly with the strength of the effective reaction potential (1943, p. 344).

Postulate 16. *Incompatible responses.*

When reaction potentials to two or more incompatible responses occur in an organism at the same time, only the reaction whose effective reaction potential is greatest will be evoked (1943, p. 344).

These 16 postulates, as summarized from an exposition that requires upwards of 300 pages of text, cannot convey any hint of the effort that went into stating them in precise mathematical form, and with their empirical justification. In order to write equations, Hull adopted a special notation which has been omitted in the statement of the postulates. The chief symbols he used are given and defined in Figure 6.2.

The System as a Chain of Symbolic Constructs

The diagram in Figure 6.2 may be read from left to right as a chain of six major processes going on when a learned response is evoked; some of these are processes guided by environmental events; mostly the processes are inferred intervening variables.

1. Reinforcement. Habit strength ($_sH_R$) is the result of a reinforcement of stimulus-response connections in accordance with their proximity to need reduction (Postulates 3 and 4).

2. Generalization. Generalized habit strength ($_s\overline{H}_R$) depends both upon direct reinforcement of an S-R connection and upon generalization from other similar S'-R' habits (Postulate 5).

3. Motivation. Reaction potential ($_sE_R$) depends upon the interaction of habit strength and drive (Postulates 6 and 7).

4. Inhibition. Effective reaction potential ($_s\overline{E}_R$) is reaction potential as reduced by reactive inhibition and conditioned inhibition (Postulates 8 and 9).

5. Oscillation. Momentary effective reaction potential ($_s\dot{\overline{E}}_R$) is effective reaction potential as modified from instant to instant by the oscillating inhibitory factor associated with it (Postulate 10).

6. Response evocation. Responses are evoked if the momentary effective reaction potential is above the threshold of reaction. Such responses may be measured according to the probability of reaction, latency of reaction, resistance to extinction, or amplitude (Postulates 11–16).

We thus see how the system fulfilled Hull's desire for an inferential system firmly anchored to the physical world. It is anchored to antecedent observable events in the physical environment and the organism, and, on the consequent side, to observable and measurable reactions.

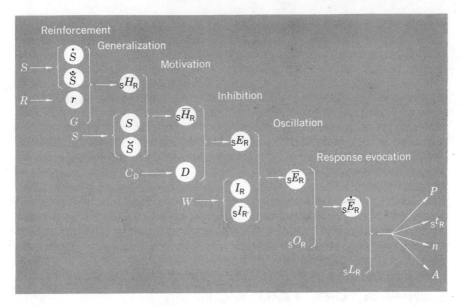

Figure 6.2. Diagram summarizing the major symbolic constructs in Hull's system of behavior. After Hull (1943a, p. 383).

A, amplitude of reaction
$\dot{S}$, the physical stimulus energy
R, the organism's reaction
$\dot{s}$, the neural result of the stimulus
$\breve{s}$, the neural interaction arising from two or more stimulus components
r, the efferent impulse leading to reaction
G, occurrence of reinforcing state of affairs
$_sH_R$, habit strength
S, evocation stimulus on same stimulus continuum as $\dot{S}$
s, the neural result of S
$\breve{s}$, neural interaction
$_s\overline{H}_R$, the generalized habit strength

C_D, the objectively observable phenomena determining the drive
D, the physiological strength of the drive
$_sE_R$, the reaction potential
W, the work involved in the evoked reaction
I_R, reactive inhibition
$_sI_R$, conditioned inhibition
$_s\overline{E}_R$, effective reaction potential
$_sO_R$, oscillation
$_s\dot{\overline{E}}_R$, momentary effective reaction potential
$_sL_R$, reaction threshold
p, probability of response evocation
$_st_R$, latency of reaction evocation
n, number of unreinforced reactions to extinction

Habit Strength ($_sH_R$) and Influences upon It

Paraphrasing Hull's postulates in the foregoing account has necessarily lost much of their detail and elegance. To illustrate, the fourth postulate, concerning reinforcement and habit strength, was stated by him as follows:

Whenever an effector activity ($r \rightarrow R$) and a receptor activity ($S \rightarrow s$) occur in close temporal contiguity ($_s^rC_R$), and this ($_s^rC_R$) is closely and consistently associated with the diminution of a need (G) or with a stimulus which has been closely and consistently associated with the diminution of a need (G), there will result an increment to a tendency ($\triangle_s H_R$) for that afferent impulse on later occasions to evoke that reaction. The increments from successive reinforcements summate in a manner which yields a combined habit strength ($_s H_R$) which is a simple positive growth function of the number of reinforcements (N). The upper limit (M) of this curve of learning is the product of (1) a positive growth function of the magnitude of need reduction which is involved in primary, or which is associated with secondary, reinforcement; (2) a negative growth function of the delay (t) in reinforcement; and (3) (a) a negative growth function of the degree of asynchronism (t') of $\dot{S}$ and R when both are of brief duration, or (b), in case the action of $\dot{S}$ is prolonged so as to overlap the beginning of R, a negative growth function of the duration (t'') of the continuous action of $\dot{S}$ on the receptor when R begins. (1943, p. 178)

In this postulate, and the developments growing out of it, we have the essence of the learning theory: the fundamental operation of rewards, the effects of repetition, and the gradients of reinforcement. To restate what it implies requires at least the following three statements:

1. Learning depends upon contiguity of stimulus and response closely associated with reinforcement defined as need reduction (or in secondary reinforcement, associated with a stimulus that itself has been associated with need reduction). This is essentially a restatement of Thorndike's law of effect, with reward specified in terms of need reduction.

2. The course of learning described as a simple growth function is based on the implied assumption that the increment of habit strength with each reinforcement *is a constant fraction of the amount remaining to be learned.* Because more remains to be acquired early in learning and little remains late in learning, the result is a curve of decreasing gains, very familiar in laboratory studies of learning.

3. The upper limit M of the association between S and R depends on the amount of reward (need reduction) and the delay of reward. The third part of this postulate concerns temporal relationships between CS onset and the UR in classical conditioning wherein particularly favorable intervals may be enforced. The initial parts of the postulate commit Hull to a reinforcement theory of association; some reinforcement (at a short delay) is necessary in order for an R to become associated to an S. Contiguity of the two events with belonging will not suffice.

Because in many experiments everything is kept constant but the number of reinforcements, the form of learning curve equation that has remained familiar from the 1943 book is as follows:

$$_s H_R = M(1 - e^{-iN}) \qquad \text{(1943, p. 119)},$$

where N is the number of reinforced trials and M is the limit dependent on the magnitude and delay of reward.

The Role of Drive

The concept of drive was very important in Hull's theorizing. It had three distinct functions, all implied in Postulates 6 and 7:

1. Without some drive there could be no primary reinforcement, because primary reinforcement requires the rapid diminution of some D. There could, of course, be no acquisition of secondary reinforcement value to a neutral stimulus either, for secondary reinforcement originates in the association of a stimulus with primary reinforcement.

2. Without drive there could be no response, for drive activates habit strength into reaction potential. Hull assumed that drive (D) multiplied habit strength, so that a "zero-drive" state implied that no $_sE_R$ could exceed the reaction threshold.

3. Without the distinctiveness of the drive stimulus S_D there could be no regulation of habits by the need state of the organism, no way for it to learn to go one place for water when thirsty, another place for food when hungry (see, e.g., Hull, 1933).

The first of these conditions describes *which* types of "goal-objects" will be reinforcing when the subject is in a particular need state, and describes *why* these particular stimuli will be reinforcing. The second condition attributes energizing potential to a drive; it goads the animal into action in the direction of need satisfaction. The third condition attributes to drives a discriminative or steering role in behavior.

The equation that expresses the relationships among reaction potential, habit strength, and drive is based on the assumption that drive interacts with habit strength in some multiplicative fashion to produce reaction potential:

$$_sE_R = {_sH_R} \times D.$$

Hull encountered some difficulties, however, in trying to get precise about this notion of drive. He thought of all drives from all sources as contributing to a general pool of energy, which was indexed by D, the energizer (multiplier) of all habits. Thus, a response trained under one drive (hunger) might still be energized and goaded to action during special tests conducted while the animal was operating under a different drive (say, thirst). He recognized the problem, however, that some habits were relevant to some drives but irrelevant or antithetical to others. For example, it did not seem right intuitively that aversive drives (pain, fear) should activate food-seeking habits. And when drive interactions began to be studied directly, it was found that hunger and thirst were intimately interlocked; for example, a thirsty man with a parched throat is not inclined to eat dry rolls unless his "hunger" has reached severe limits. Although Hull was cognizant of these problems (he felt some could be handled by the selective function of drive stimuli), he nonetheless went ahead and postulated a particular equation for pooling "relevant" and "irrelevant" drive strengths so as to come up with an effective multiplier index. The conjectured equation is of solely mathematical interest since it ignores the basic conceptual difficulties of his hypothesis of a generalized drive pool. It was that notion—reminiscent of the Freudian notion of "libido" or the layman's simple notion of "nervous energy"—which encountered grave conceptual problems.

The Inhibition Postulates

Hull's notions about inhibition were an amalgam of ideas about fatigue (reactive inhibition, I_R) gathered from the literature on fatigue factors in repetitive performance of motor reactions, and Pavlov's ideas (see Chapter 3) about "internal" (or conditioned) inhibition generated by conditions of non-reinforcement, specifically during an extinction series following reinforced training. For Hull, as for Pavlov, $_sI_R$ was a *learned* form of active inhibition, a learned opposition to a particular response. There was even some attempt to maintain a drive-reduction interpretation of how the habit of "not-responding," $_sI_R$, came about. Supposing the reaction R were very effortful, generating much aversive drive (fatigue, I_R), then stopping or quitting the response would be reinforced by the immediate reduction in fatigue. There-fore, the $_sI_R$ would really be based on an associative habit for the "stopping of R." But if I_R were like a drive state it should enter into D, or it should multiply *its* habit $_sI_R$, as in the $H \times D$ formula; instead Hull assumed that I_R and $_sI_R$ simply add together to form an inhibitory composite that was subtracted from the excitatory potential for making the response.

Hull used the I_R and $_sI_R$ concepts to derive several phenomena of interest, for example, that heavily massed trials on an effortful response would pro-duce the well-known phenomenon called "work decrement," that a rest period following such massed elicitations would produce some recovery ("reminiscence") of the motor response, and that somewhat similar effects could be found in nonreinforced extinction of simple conditioned reflexes. These were hardly surprising "deductions," given the basis for postulating these principles.

The specific inhibition postulates of Hull have fared rather badly in light of subsequent conceptual and empirical attacks (Koch, 1954; Gleitman, Nachmias, & Neisser, 1954). For example, Hull for some inexplicable reason related "resistance to extinction" (n in Figure 6.2) to $_sE_R$ by a direct equa-tion rather than deriving such a relationship from $_sE_R$ and his postulates regarding nonreinforced trials and the buildup of $_sI_R$. No matter, since it is clear that an unelaborated inhibition theory could not begin to explain the increased resistance to extinction provided by partially reinforced training. Furthermore, the postulates as stated imply the absurd conclusion that con-ditioned inhibition for a response should eventually overtake the positive habit tendency for the response. For one thing, for on-off responses, "stop-ping" the response (say, halting at the end of a runway) is always in a closer temporal relation to reward (e.g., eating) than is the positive response (run-ning), therefore "stopping" should be more favorably reinforced than the positive response. So on that ground conditioning should be impossible. Second, to mention another flaw, although Hull indicated a limit, M, on the growth of habit strength, the limit of growth of $_sI_R$ was just the prevailing level of the positive habit. But this means that as training continues and $_sH_R$ reaches its limit, each trial builds up some I_R and $_sI_R$ so the $_sI_R$ should theoretically accumulate up to the current value of $_sH_R$. Since performance ($_sE_R$) is the difference between the positive and inhibitory tendencies, the above derivation suggests that learning curves should increase and then, with continued practice, turn over and decrease—which is absurd. These deficiencies are perhaps small matters that could be patched up with closer attention to details of formulation of the inhibition assumptions, or the laws of chaining, etc.

There were two other major conceptual problems with the inhibition postulates: (a) the fact that relatively effortless responses (e.g., eye blinks, GSRs, pupil dilation) undergo relatively rapid extinction, whereas Hull's postulates would have expected such responses to extinguish very slowly; and (b) the notion of a "not-response" was ill-defined, and seemed to lead into a tangle of conceptual puzzles. For any given R, what is its "not-R"? How many different "not-Rs" is an organism performing at any one time? One? Five? Five thousand? It would seem better to identify extinction, as had Guthrie, with acquisition of particular competing (interfering) behaviors—although, to be sure, Guthrie was typically never very explicit about what these competing responses might in general be.

As these comments suggest, Hull's specific formulation of I_R and $_sI_R$ was not generally acclaimed, although the need for some kind of inhibitory construct was clearly recognized from the outset. For example, Spence (1936) gave a rather general, noncommittal formulation of inhibition due to non-reinforced responding in discrimination learning which has stood the test of time. Amsel (1958, 1962) later identified "frustration" as the underlying basis for conditioned inhibitory factors in appetitive conditioning. We shall be meeting these terms later on.

The Final Behavior System (1952)

The book *Principles of behavior* (1943) was intended as an exposition of the most basic aspects of the system, and stopped short of the derivations of more complex behavior at which Hull was very skillful. He began immediately thereafter to work on a more thorough quantification of the postulated processes, revising the postulates as necessary, and then turned to the derivations of other kinds of behavior on the basis of these basic principles. The quantitative program in which he took most satisfaction was an elaborate effort to arrive at a measurement of habit strength.[2] The revised postulates were published first in 1950, again in 1951, and finally in *A behavior system* in 1952 (Hull, 1950, 1951, 1952a). The final book, appearing just after Hull's death, contains not only the new postulates with evidence related to them, but many derivations of other behavior familiar in the writings of Hull from 1929 on.

The differences between the 1943 and 1952 books are readily apparent. The whole of the 1943 book (or nearly all of it) is concerned with developing the system of postulates and corollaries, whereas these are condensed into the first chapter of the 1952 book. The remainder of the final book is devoted to applying the principles to a variety of more complex behavior, such as trial-and-error learning, discrimination learning, maze learning, and problem-solving.

Rather than review the new postulates in detail, some differences between

[2] The pertinent papers are: Hull, Felsinger, Gladstone, and Yamaguchi (1947), Felsinger, Gladstone, Yamaguchi, and Hull (1947), Gladstone, Yamaguchi, Hull, and Felsinger (1947), and Yamaguchi, Hull, Felsinger, and Gladstone (1948).

the 1943 and 1952 sets will be noted, and then attention will be directed to some of the derivations.[3]

Changes in the Postulates between 1943 and 1952

While there are a number of minor changes in detail, such as the inclusion of mathematical statements within the postulates themselves, only a few changes that represent major theoretical alterations will be noted here.

The first change is in the conception of primary reinforcement. While in the 1943 postulates primary reinforcement depended upon need reduction (hence reduction in D), it came in 1952 to depend chiefly on the reduction of drive-produced stimuli (S_D), or on the decrease of the goal stimulus (s_G) produced by the fractional anticipatory goal-response (r_G). While favoring drive-stimulus reduction, Hull left the matter somewhat open, having vacillated between drive reduction and drive-stimulus reduction as essential to reinforcement (1952a, p. 153).

The second important change is that the quantitative aspects of reinforcement have no influence upon habit strength, provided there is some unspecified minimum amount; what counts is only the frequency with which reinforced trials have occurred. This was basically, then, a contiguity theory of association formation.

The third important change is the addition of a number of nonassociative factors affecting reaction potential. While some of these had been recognized in the 1943 book, they were now incorporated in a different manner, all as multipliers affecting reaction potential through the multiplication of habit strength. The constitution of reaction potential now becomes

$$_sE_R = {}_sH_R \times D \times V \times K \qquad \text{(1952a, p. 7)},$$

where V is the stimulus-intensity dynamism of the evoking stimulus (particularly CS-intensity in a Pavlovian situation), and K is the incentive motivation based on the weight of the food or quantity of other incentive given as reinforcement.

The new roles for stimulus intensity (V) and for the amount of incentive (K) deserve a little discussion. Because all associative learning is based solely on the number of reinforcements (and not on the amount of drive reduction involved in any one reinforcement) all the nonassociative factors now become equivalent to drive as multipliers of habit strength. In the 1943 version, the amount of incentive entered into an equation limiting the maximum amount of habit strength that could be acquired under given incentive conditions; in 1952, the amount of food reinforcement on the prior trial determines the vigor of response (reaction potential) on the next trial, while not affecting habit strength. The same applies to the newcomer, stimulus-intensity dynamism (V), which states merely that a stronger stimulus will evoke a greater response, habit strength remaining equal. While other changes in detail occurred, one is worth citing, because it reflects a change

---

[3] A critical exposition of the postulates can be found in the second edition of this book (E. R. Hilgard, 1956, pp. 127–150). Hull's own treatment of them is more thorough in his *Essentials of behavior* (1951) than in *A behavior system* (1952a), although the reader must be warned that there were a few modifications between 1951 and 1952.

in interpretation: this is the conception of the influence of delay in rein-forcement. In the first place, delay in reinforcement now produces less reaction potential $(_sE_R)$, while earlier it produced less habit strength $(_sH_R)$. But also the time intervals have shrunk: in the 1943 version, the primary gradient for a single reinforced response extended up to perhaps 60 seconds (1943, p. 145); in the 1952 version, it extended not more than 5 seconds (1952a, p. 131). The shortening of the gradient came about as secondary reinforcement gained more prominence for Hull as a theoretical mechanism for generating longer gradients of reinforcement. Hull was influenced by Spence's (1947) suggestion that all gradients may be generated through immediate secondary reinforcements or other intermediate mechan-isms.

The Final System Summarized

The set of postulates and corollaries became somewhat formidable, and in places somewhat fragmented, as Hull attempted to work into the basic principles not only all manner of quantitative relationships found to hold in classical and instrumental conditioning, but other kinds of phenomena needed to deal with types of problems beyond these reference experiments. Even so, it is possible to cut through some of the specific detail, and to summarize the system in rather direct fashion as a chain of constructs begin-ning with the antecedent conditions (input), and moving through the inter-vening variables to the response (output). Such a summary is given in Figure 6.3, to be compared with Figure 6.2, page 162.

In column 1 we have input conditions, all except $_s^;H_R$ defined by objective experimental conditions. ($_s^;H_R$ is habit strength from a related habit, to become expressed as generalized habit strength, $_s\bar{H}_R$.)

In column 2 we find the intervening variables most closely tied to the antecedent conditions. In column 3 we assemble, in an intermediate step, the consequences of the simultaneous presence of the variables in column 2. The net reaction potential, $_s\bar{E}_R$, is the final intervening variable determined by experimental variables. The constructs $_sO_R$ (oscillation of $_sE_R$) and $_sL_R$ (reaction threshold) are purely "calculational fictions" invented to convert a single strength measure into a probability of response or into a probability distribution of reaction latencies, amplitudes, or resistances to extinction. Also when two responses are in conflict—when the organism has a choice—that reaction whose $_s\bar{E}_R$ is momentarily dominant at the moment of choice will win and determine the response made. The terms $_sO_R$ and $_sL_R$ have no further function (they derive essentially from Thurstone's [1927] theory of comparative judgment). It will be noted, contrary to the spirit of Hull's other intervening variables, that $_sO_R$ and $_sL_R$ are not "anchored" into any determining antecedent variable. They are simply cal-culational devices to convert a deterministic variable, $_s\bar{E}_R$, into a proba-bilistic dependent variable. This is needed since behavior of a single organism across trials or of a group within any single trial is typically vari-able and probabilistic. This fact itself motivated later attempts to build "stochastic learning models" (see Chapter 12), in which response probabili-ties enter into the initial representation of the organism's performance.

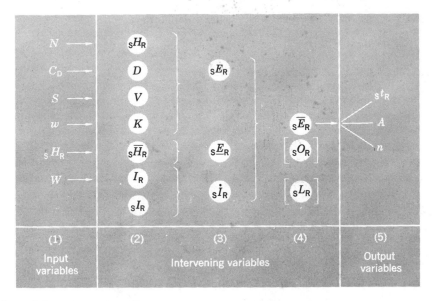

Figure 6.3. Summary of Hull's final system.

Column (1)

N, number of prior reinforcements
C_D, drive condition
S, stimulus intensity
w, amount (weight) of reward
$_sH_R$, strength of a habit based on same response conditioned to another stimulus
W, work required in responding

Column (2)

$_sH_R$, habit strength
D, drive
V, stimulus-intensity dynamism
K, incentive motivation
$_s\bar{H}_R$, generalized habit strength from related habit

I_R, reactive inhibition
$_sI_R$, conditioned inhibition

Column (3)

$_sE_R$, reaction potential
$_s\underline{E}_R$, generalized reaction potential
$_s\dot{I}_R$, aggregate inhibitory potential

Column (4)

$_s\bar{E}_R$, net reaction potential
$_sO_R$, oscillation of reaction potential
$_sL_R$, reaction threshold

Column (5)

$_st_R$, reaction latency
A, reaction amplitude
n, number of nonreinforced responses to extinction
P, probability of reaction

The diagram falls short in not listing the several important stimulus components making up the complex of traces when a response is evoked, important among which are the drive-stimulus (S_D) and the fractional antedating goal-stimulus (s_G). The kinds of items serving as components of the stimulus trace are listed in Table 6.1. Because these components are not all contemporary in origin, some of them representing the subsiding residues of just prior stimulation, others (on the basis of acquired antedating responses) representing events still to come, the complex pattern of stimuli makes possible the linking together of response patterns covering large seg-

Table 6.1   The components of a complex stimulus trace.

Origin of Stimulus-Trace Component, with Symbol		Resulting Component of the Stimulus Trace
Environmental stimulus S	s	Molar afferent impulse
Compound stimuli $S_1, S_2, \cdots$	$\breve{s}$	Molar afferent impulse modified by afferent interaction
Drive D	S_D	Drive-stimulus
Response R	s_R	Proprioceptive consequence of response
Fractional antedating goal-response r_G	s_G	Fractional antedating goal-stimulus

ments of time and space. The stimulus complex contains traces that both activate behavior and guide it.

Derived Intermediate Mechanisms

Hull's system was characterized by him as molar, by which he meant non-physiological. That is, the inferences to intervening variables do not depend upon the discovery of the physiological substratum which is causal in a "molecular" way. The assertions about molar stimulus traces, or afferent interaction, need not include specification in terms of the constitution of nerve bundles or the characteristics of the nervous impulse. Hull vacillated somewhat by including physiological *language* in his postulates. In any case, Hull's system classifies as a *reductive* system, in that more complex phenomena are deduced on the basis of presumably simpler, more basic phenomena and relationships. In this sense the more complex are "reduced" to the simpler through analysis. It is characteristic of all systems of this kind *that they intend to explain behavior that is superficially unlike the behavior from which the postulates are derived.* In other words, Hull did not intend merely to systematize the account of hungry rats pressing levers for food, from which most of the data for his later set of postulates derived. He intended to arrive at the basic laws of behavior, at least the laws of the behavior of mammalian organisms, including the social behavior of man.

In order to bridge the gap between the simple laboratory experiments furnishing the constants in the postulates and corollaries, and the more familiar behavior of organisms adapting to a complex environment, he derived a few *intermediate mechanisms*. Once these mechanisms were available, they presumably would open the way to the explanation of many more varieties of behavior. We shall consider two of the mechanisms: the gradient of reinforcement (originally called the goal gradient), and the habit-family hierarchy.

We have to distinguish between the historical and the logical order of postulates and intermediate mechanisms. Many of Hull's most brilliant deductive accounts of complex phenomena were made in early papers, prior to the postulate systems.[4] Many of these early accounts were essentially

---

[4] For an introduction to the deductions available before 1940, see the summaries in E. R. Hilgard and Marquis (1940): maze learning, 216–221; serial verbal learning, 221–226; reasoning experiments, 236–241; circumventing a barrier, 242–243.

unchanged when they were reworked for the 1952 book, even though in the meantime the postulate system had undergone substantial revision. From a logical point of view, however, once the system has been constructed, the postulates take priority. The same applies, of course, to predictions. An experimental fact may be "predicted" by a system, even though the fact has long been known. The only advantage in predicting new (unknown) facts is that, in predicting them, there is less temptation to include the facts in the postulates used as a basis for their prediction.

The Gradient of Reinforcement (The Goal Gradient)

There are two chief kinds of time gradients involved in conditioning experiments. The first (found primarily in classical conditioning) is based on the time between the conditioned stimulus and the unconditioned stimulus, short forward intervals being found most satisfactory. Hull took this interval into account in developing a postulate regarding the stimulus trace. The assumption was that conditioning is actually simultaneous, but the gradient is produced by a rising and falling neural trace set in motion by the external stimulus. Apparently he felt that by assuming a neural-trace function whose temporal shape was identical to then-available parametric curves relating level of conditioning to the CS-US interval, he would have "explained" those parametric curves. But we now know this is surely a fallacious approach (see N. H. Anderson, 1959; Bitterman, 1965); "conditioning" is a rather complex function of the CS-US interval, of the organism and the exact response system involved, and even quite different "behaviors" may be occurring at differing moments while the organism is "waiting for the US." Therefore, any simple, single measure of "level of conditioning" is likely to misrepresent the behavioral facts. This is hindsight, of course; Hull had no way to know of these matters at the time he was writing.

The second kind of time gradient (found chiefly in instrumental conditioning) is based on the time between the occurrence of the response to be strengthened and the reinforcement. This second gradient is considered in a corollary concerned with delay in reinforcement. The measurement of the gradient is done in instrumental conditioning situations (e.g., lever-pressing or running down an alleyway for a food reward) or in a selective learning situation (e.g., a monkey presses a red or green button, and receives a sugar pellet at some delay interval later). In such experiments, delaying the reward typically retards learning or degrades performance, and more so the longer the delay. Based on some early results from lever-pressing experiments with rats, Hull had conjectured a declining delay of reinforcement gradient that was fairly short, "possibly no more than thirty seconds and very possibly less than sixty seconds."

But all sorts of complications began to arise for this postulate, because in further experimentation it was found that the specific values of delay at which learning could or would not be produced depended critically upon the experimental arrangements, specifically on the nature of the stimulus changes correlated with the correct response and the nature of the activities induced in the subject during the delay interval. Spence (1947) pointed out the crucial role of the presence versus absence of secondary reinforcing stimuli following the correct response, particularly in selective learning. To the extent that the subject's response immediately produces a distinctive stimulus situation which has been associated with primary reward (regardless of its delay) whereas an error response produces a different stimulus, the former distinctive stimulus will act as an immediate confirmer or satisfier for the correct response, and it will reinforce this response. For instance, an experiment by Wolfe (1934) used a T-maze leading to distinctively different goal-boxes with reward provided in the correct one after a 20-minute delay; despite this delay, conditions were still adequate for the operation of *immediate* secondary reinforcement for the choice response of turning into the correct end-box; therefore, rapid learning could still be shown at a 20-minute delay of reward. As a second example, in the lever-pressing situation proprioceptive traces from having pressed the lever were presumed to persist for many seconds and, being paired with later food reward, to thus be converted into secondary reinforcing stimuli which will occur immediately, of course, upon any later recurrence of the lever-press. Spence (1947) showed further that if one could eliminate external "stimulus props" or interfere with internal props as possible sources of immediate secondary reinforcement, then the "true gradient" of delay of primary reinforcement was around 5 seconds for a rat. This seems somewhat close to what one might expect for immediate memory of an earlier "S-R" event.

By combining recognition of a short "primary gradient" and secondary reinforcing stimuli scattered along the route of a maze or other route to a goal, Hull and Spence derived the "goal gradient," whereby earlier components of a long chain of behaviors will be reinforced and strengthened to a lesser degree than will behavioral components closer to the goal (in time). One of the original applications of this principle was to account for the orderly elimination of errors by rats learning long multiple-T mazes. According to the principle, responses nearer to the goal would be more strongly conditioned than those farther removed, so that short paths would be preferred to longer ones, blinds (incorrect choices) nearer the goal would be eliminated more readily than blinds farther away, longer blinds would be more readily eliminated than shorter ones, and so on (Hull, 1932). The goal gradient principle was later applied to field-force problems as studied by Lewin (Hull, 1938; also 1952a, pp. 262–268). For example, in experiments involving the circumventing of barriers between the learner and a visible goal, Hull proposed that the approach behavior to the perceived goal-object should vary according to the goal gradient. That is, the nearer the learner came to the goal, the stronger should be its response-evoking power. Thus Hull, by way of the gradient of reinforcement, came to conclusions similar to those described by Lewin as goal attraction in relation to distance.

The Habit-Family Hierarchy

A second derived principle is that of the habit-family hierarchy. This is not included among the postulates because, like the gradient of reinforcement, it is a principle at intermediate level, being itself derived from more basic principles. It carries great weight, however, in the deduction of further behavioral phenomena.

Because in the natural environment there are typically multiple routes between a starting point and a goal, the organism learns alternative ways of moving from a common starting point to a common goal-position where it finds need satisfaction. These alternatives constitute a "family" of equiva- *transfer* lent responses—called a "habit family"—because of an inferred integrating mechanism. The integration into a family is by way of the *fractional ante-dating goal reaction*, present as each alternative response is performed. The fractional antedating goal reaction provides a stimulus (s_G) to which all overt responses are conditioned. Through the differential action of the derived gradients of reinforcement, some responses are less strongly conditioned to s_G than others. The starting responses of longer routes, for example, are more remote from reinforcement than the starting responses of shorter routes. Hence the latter are more strongly reinforced, and more strongly conditioned to s_G. As a consequence, the alternative behavior patterns are arranged in a preferred order. The less favored routes are chosen only when the more favored are blocked. It is this set of alternative habits, integrated by a common goal-stimulus, and arranged in preferential order, that constitutes a *habit-family hierarchy.*

It was further deduced by Hull that if one member of a habit-family *transfer* hierarchy is reinforced in a new situation, all other members of the family ✕ share at once in the tendency to be evoked as reactions in that situation (Hull, 1937). This makes possible the explanation of response equivalences and other appropriate reactions in novel or problematic situations, such as those found in insight and reasoning experiments.

The principle was first applied to maze learning (Hull, 1934a), serving chiefly to explain the tendency for the rat to enter goal pointing blinds, even though such blinds may not have been entered previously and so had never been reinforced in the maze situation. Goal orientation was taken to represent an inappropriate transfer of spatial habits acquired in free space. Another application was in relation to the detour experiments (Hull, 1938). The amount of difficulty in turning away from a perceived goal beyond a barrier depends on the presence of habit-family hierarchies as well as upon goal gradients. In the usual experience of free space, the favored path is the straight line between the learner and the goal. The next-favored starting response is that making least angle with the goal. The greater the angle the less favored is the starting response in that family of habits built up in previous experience. Hence, when blocked, the learner prefers a path which goes off at a right angle to one which requires that he turn his back on the goal. In some objective situations he may come to prefer a longer path over a shorter one, if the habit-family hierarchy proves to be misleading.

Hull's Quantitative Emphasis

Although our exposition has tended to minimize the matter, Hull became increasingly enamored in later years with *quantitative* aspects of his theory —trying to scale or measure $_sE_R$ in quantitative terms, trying to determine the precise numerical value of particular constants in the equations relating the intervening variable to an independent variable or dependent variables. Most notably, he tried to derive quantitative predictions for the results of new behavioral experiments beyond those involved in inferring the original postulate set. His final book (1952a) consisted essentially of one quantitative derivation after another concerning performance in a variety of experiments on serial chaining of responses, stimulus discrimination learning, latent learning, spatially oriented behavior in open fields, "detour" or "umweg" problems, incentive shifts, approach-avoidance conflict, motor skills, and many other situations studied by psychologists. Hull would start his derivations by taking his postulates and assigning certain initial hypothetical values to the many intervening variables of the theory, and then restrict himself to a very "idealistic" (uncomplicated, unrealistic) characterization of the behavioral situation, making up new rules for quantitative combinations as they were needed, and eventually coming out with some final "calculations" in terms of $_s\bar{E}_R$ which could be compared with some measure of the animals' behavior in the experiment being modeled. If he had predicted the correct *qualitative* (ordinal) trends in the data, he felt satisfied and said the "theorem had been verified." Hull would frequently summarize the successfulness of his theorizing in terms of the number of "confirmed theorems" or in like terms.

Despite Hull's love for the quantitative aspects of his theory, the consensus judgment of the subsequent generation of psychologists, both inside and outside the "Hullian camp," was that the specific quantitative details were the most arbitrary, least important, least interesting, and least enduring features of Hull's theorizing (see Amsel, 1965, for this viewpoint expressed by a neo-Hullian). By modern standards in mathematical learning theory (see Chapter 12), Hull did not have a tractible mathematical system —he had far too many parameters to be measured and far too weak a measurement theory to really get much leverage on the quantitative details of his data. His mathematical derivations are also suspect in detail (see the discussion of cases by Cotton, 1955; Koch, 1954; or in the earlier edition of this book, E. R Hilgard & Bower, 1966, pp. 170–180), since they typically involved a plethora of idealizing assumptions, arbitrary assignments of values to intervening variables, and *ad hoc* rules invented to handle special problems arising in each derivation. In such circumstances, it is doubtless wiser to consider Hull's theory at the informal, "verbal" level, with the concepts and interrelated ideas being of more enduring significance. However, we would be remiss not to point out that it was the quantitative ambitions of Hull's program, and the arguments for it which he so persuasively stated, that set the stage for later developments in mathematical learning theory.

The Neo-Hullians

For some 20 years, roughly between 1930 and 1950, Hull was a very important person in the Institute of Human Relations at Yale University, where he not only influenced successive generations of graduate students and colleagues in psychology, but also left his mark on colleagues in related fields of the behavioral sciences, particularly anthropology and psychiatry. The richness of his contributions is not fully represented in his published papers and books, as sets of *Seminar notes* and *Memoranda* from 1934 to 1950 fully attest.

Among those influenced more or less directly by Hull who have continued to write in the field of learning, Neal E. Miller (1959) and O. Hobart Mowrer (1960) have adopted styles of their own, and although remaining within the tradition of S-R reinforcement theory, they never did use Hull's more formal approach. Kenneth Spence perhaps represented a more direct continuation of Hull's general type of theorizing, but with reasoned alterations. His point of view is best presented in two books, *Behavior theory and conditioning* (1956) and a volume of collected papers entitled *Behavior theory and learning* (1960b). Spence, who was chairman of the psychology department at the University of Iowa for nearly 25 years, influenced a large number of students in his neo-Hullian tradition, among them Abram Amsel and Frank Logan. We shall now briefly discuss the contributions of all these men.

N. E. Miller

Miller drew inspiration and major concepts from Hull's theory, but developed them informally and applied them to a wide range of behavioral phenomena. He was the foremost advocate for many years of the strict "drive-reduction" hypothesis of reinforcement, alternately attacking and defending it as a heuristic spur to progress in our conceptualization of what causes rewards to be reinforcing. Miller also developed the notion of "acquired drive," referring to stimuli which through a conditioning process come to possess the functional properties of a drive. The best example of an acquired drive is fear or anxiety. In Miller's analysis (1951), fear is an innate response to painful stimulation, and as a response it can be conditioned to an antecedent stimulus.[5] But the fear response also has stimulating effects, which are twofold: first, these can serve as discriminative cues so that differential responses may be attached to them; second, when these fear stimuli become sufficiently intense, they act as driving, motivating stimuli which will energize particular responses instrumental in escaping or avoiding those unpleasant, aversive situations which are arousing the fear. Finally, when the conditioned stimuli arousing the fear response are removed, the fear drive is reduced, thus affording reinforcement for any instrumental responses just preceding the removal of the fear stimuli. This set of hypotheses became the basis for the analysis of avoidance conditioning which was to dominate that research area for several decades. Only recently have major emendations been required in the theory (see Bolles, 1972).

Another contribution of Miller (1944) was to elaborate and develop a precise formulation of "conflict theory," beginning with some ideas of Lewin (1935). Consider two different places in space, *A* and *B*, and suppose that, with respect to each place ("goal"), the subject has either an approach tendency, an avoidance tendency, or a combination of approach and avoidance to one or another or both places. The situation is so contrived that the organism is forced to make a choice, or at least behave preferentially with

---

[5] Incidentally, a problem for Miller was how the fear response was reinforced; to be consistent with his drive-reduction position, he had to argue that the onset of fear was reinforced by the later offset of the aversive painful stimulation—a position over which he and Mowrer were to disagree.

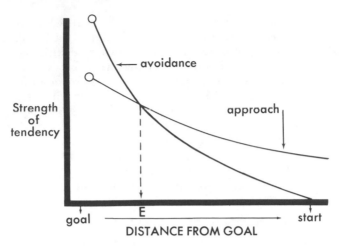

Figure 6.4.   Illustration of spatial generalization gradients of strength of approach and avoidance tendencies plotted against distance from the goal back toward the start of a straight alleyway.

respect to the two goals. Miller proceeds to classify these situations and to indicate the behavior expected, given particular strengths of the approach and avoidance tendencies. Thus, for example, pure approach-approach conflicts are expected to be unstable and quickly resolved in favor of the stronger or more attractive alternative, avoidance-avoidance conflicts lead to stable immobilization at an intermediate point between A and B, whereas double approach-avoidance situations (involving two ambivalent choices) lead to oscillations, hesitations, false starts, beginning movement in one direction but then return, and so on.

The more frequently analyzed situation concerns Miller's theory of a simple approach-avoidance conflict, the components of which are diagrammed in Figure 6.4. Here the goal-object is at once a source of attraction and repulsion, tempting the subject toward it but deterring him from full commerce with the goal. A typical experimental arrangement to study such conflict would be that involving a hungry rat trained to run down a straight alleyway to food reward, but after training, subjected to a series of painful electric shocks in the goal-box. His approach tendency to the food is offset by his fear of shock at the goal-box.

Miller supposed that the avoidance gradient had a steeper slope than the approach gradient,[6] and that the net tendency to approach the goal depended on the algebraic difference between the approach and avoidance tendencies. Under appropriate circumstances, such as those diagrammed in Figure 6.4, when the strength of avoidance exceeds that of approach at the

[6] As Miller and Murray (1952) have shown, this assumption is in fact derivable from the idea that the net avoidance tendency is based on a learned drive (fear) which suffers generalization decrement, whereas the approach tendency is typically based on an internal drive which is constant, with only habit, $_sH_R$, revealing stimulus generalization.

goal, the theory predicts true *conflict* behavior. When placed at the start of the alleyway, the rat will run toward the goal, but then stop, move back and forth, advance some, retreat some, and generally "oscillate" around the equilibrium point, E. This equilibrium point is where the two gradients cross; it is "stable" in the sense that any deviation of the animal from the point E will bring to bear forces which will tend to drive him back toward E.

Miller listed a set of variables which should affect the strength of the approach tendency and another set that should affect the strength of the avoidance tendency. Variations in these should have predictable effects upon conflict behavior. For example, an increase in approach drive should bring the subject closer to the goal (the point E moves to the left), as should a lowering of the avoidance tendency, although in either case the subject should experience greater anxiety at the new points of equilibrium than formerly was the case.

Miller carried out an admirable series of studies confirming and extending this analysis of conflict (summarized in Miller, 1959). He also extended the same theory to analysis of the Freudian notion of "displacement behavior" (Miller, 1948b), in which a person selects a similar goal-object (in Freud's theory, a "displaced love-object") when he is ambivalent and full of conflict regarding choice of an original goal-object. We return to this topic in Chapter 11 when we discuss Freud's theories.

Along with a colleague, John Dollard, Miller applied these hypotheses regarding learning, acquired drives, and conflict to the analysis of thinking, language, personality, neurosis, psychotherapy, imitation, and social behavior. Stimulus-responses concepts were considerably "liberalized" in such analyses. For example, in their analysis of "matched dependent behavior" (a "copying" type of imitation), Miller and Dollard (1941) carried out something like a *cybernetic* analysis of several simple behavioral examples. One illustration was that of a student learning to sing on key, learning in particular to sing a musical note so as to match a voice teacher's sung note. The perceived discrepancy between the student's and teacher's notes was conceptualized as a graded cue motivating an appropriately graded, directional alteration in "vocal response," so that the altered note sung by the student appeared closer to that of the teacher. This is a relational response guided by feedback of a relational cue. Reducing the discrepancy was conceptualized by Miller and Dollard as a secondary reward for the student's learning to match his sung note to a heard note. Such analyses, and similarly ingenious ones appearing in the book *Personality and psychotherapy* (Dollard & Miller, 1950), went a long way toward convincing psychologists that a liberalized version of the stimulus-response-reinforcement approach was a viable and healthy alternative for learning theory.

In more recent times, Miller has turned his attention to analysis of the physiological and biochemical substrates of motivation and reward, areas in which he has also made signal contributions (1958, 1965). He has recently been at the forefront of research demonstrating the "operant conditioning" of a host of alleged "involuntary" responses of the autonomic nervous system. We save for a later chapter (Chapter 15) discussion of this important work.

O. H. Mowrer

Mowrer, a colleague of Hull and Miller at Yale during the mid-1930s, was greatly influenced by them but also developed his own set of unique hypotheses. Among his many pursuits, Mowrer has maintained a constant interest in the interpretation of conditioned anxiety (conditioned drives generally) and conditioned reinforcement. An early position of his (Mowrer, 1947) was that two "principles of reinforcement" are required: (1) instrumental responses involving the skeletal musculature mediated by the central nervous system are reinforced and strengthened by drive reduction; (2) such emotions as fear, nausea, and so forth involving the smooth musculature (glands, viscera, vascular tissue) mediated by the autonomic nervous system are learned by sheer temporal contiguity of a CS to the elicitation of the emotional response. Thus, for example, the simple pairing of a buzzer with painful shocks was sufficient to associate fear to the buzzer, but some active avoidance response (like jumping across a barrier between two compartments) was reinforced because it reduced a fear drive. This was dubbed "two-factor learning theory," and was a view subscribed to by many learning theorists (including, for instance, Skinner) for a number of years.

Following Miller and Dollard (1941), Mowrer offered and researched a particular analysis of *punishment* which was to prove pivotal in later altering his conception of learning and habit formation. To illustrate this analysis of punishment, consider the case of a hungry rat who has been trained to depress a lever to obtain a bit of food, and who then begins to receive a painful electric shock every time he presses the lever. After a few presses and shocks, he slows his rate and eventually stops pressing altogether; punishment has suppressed the formerly strong behavior. But why? How are we to interpret this matter? Mowrer's interpretation was that the proprioceptive feedback stimuli of lever-pressing were in appropriate temporal contiguity to the shock, so that cues associated with the lever along with those response-produced cues of pressing it became conditioned to fear. On later trials, if the rat begins to approach the lever and rises up to press it, these incipient movements present him with a proprioceptive stimulus pattern which arouses anxiety. Those anxiety-provoking stimuli deter him from carrying through the incipient response; the way to "escape" these fear-arousing cues is to cease and desist from the punished act—to do nothing. Thus, whereas in the *active* avoidance situation the animal reduces fear and avoids shock by doing something (e.g., jumping out of the shock-box), in the punishment situation the animal reduces fear and avoids shock by doing nothing. This was to become the generally accepted analysis of how punishment operates to inhibit responses (e.g., Bolles, 1972; J. S. Brown & Jacobs, 1949; Dinsmoor, 1954).

But Mowrer thought over the asymmetry implicit in this position: as posited, positive rewards directly strengthen the habits of instrumental responses, whereas punishments operate indirectly, not by reducing the habit but by having the cues of beginning the response conditioned to fear, which inhibits the "putting through" of the response. He noticed (1956) that the asymmetry was unnecessary if one simply reinterpreted the notion of a "positive habit," such as that of our hungry rat pressing a lever for food reward. Why not interpret "positive habits" in the same way as he had been interpreting punishments, except "reverse the sign" of the anticipated outcome? The proprioceptive feedback from making the correct response is in favorable contiguity to the positive reinforcement (drive reduction) so that it should acquire secondary reinforcing capabilities by contiguity conditioning. And by analogy to the way incipient punished responses are deterred, incipient rewarded responses should be "pushed on through" to completion, because their proprioceptive response pattern is conditioned to "hope," to the anticipation of reward. In this conception, then, there is not a direct associative connection between the external stimulus and the instrumental response, not an S-R bond in the traditional sense. Rather, feedback stimulation from the correct response has become conditioned (in the Pavlovian manner) to a positive emotion ("hope" or secondary reinforcement), which excites or feeds energy into the putting through of that response.

As noted in Chapter 4, this theory is similar to Sheffield's and, later, Estes's analysis of the role of reward in instrumental conditioning. However, since Mowrer excludes direct S-R habits, one is left wondering how the organism ever selects which responses to "begin incipiently." Mowrer (1960) proposes that the brain carries out a rapid *scan* over the central representations of a repertoire of responses, inhibiting those associated with fear and facilitating those associated with hope. But this mechanism has not been elaborated in detail. What is the scanning mechanism? What is scanned over? How many possible responses are there? Five, a hundred, a million? How does the device temporarily store the values of the anticipated reward for each scanned alternative and how does it then compare (or even discriminate) the many hundreds of values scanned? Moreover, how is this all to be done with the quick dispatch that characterizes well-practiced habits? These are the hard questions that Mowrer has not really answered in his tentative "feedback" analysis. These are *not* problems for the particular formulations of "anticipatory reward scanning" by Sheffield and Estes (outlined in Chapter 4)—since they assume direct S-R connections, they assume that reward-scanning is involved in decisions in initial learning before correct habits have been selected and well learned.

Because of this conception of habit as the classical conditioning of a "reinforcing emotion" to some response-produced cues, Mowrer (1960) has been quite concerned with systematizing the several classes of conditionable emotions as to their reinforcing aspects. Figure 6.5 shows the several possibilities considered by Mowrer, beginning with the primary reinforcing events of electric shock or eating for a hungry organism. The diagram is to be read as the flow of events in time (from left to right) within a conditioning trial. The cue *A* preceding shock (which brings about an *increment* in the drive of pain) will become conditioned to a fraction of that drive-increment, which fraction we call "fear" or "anxiety." A cue *C* paired with onset of a positive reinforcer like eating by a hungry baby will become conditioned to the ensuing drive reduction; "hope" is Mowrer's name for the emotion underlying secondary reinforcement. The novel types of conditionable relations pointed out by Mowrer are cues *B* and *D* in Figure 6.5. Cue *B* is one that signals the imminent termination of pain or "drive reduc-

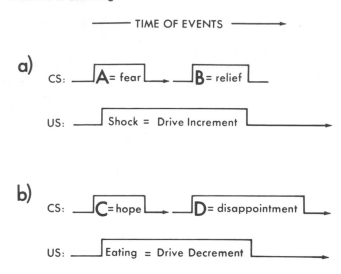

Figure 6.5.   Various pairing arrangements for conditioning. In panel (a), a cue A preceding a drive increment caused by painful shock will become associated with *fear*, whereas a cue B heralding the offset of pain becomes associated with *relief* from anxiety. In panel (b), a cue C preceding a drive decrement caused by a hungry animal's eating becomes associated with *hope*, whereas a cue D preceding the removal of reward becomes associated with *disappointment* or *frustration*.

tion"; therefore, on Mowrer's hypotheses, cue *B* will become associated with *relief* from pain. The validity of the phenomenon of relief, or reassurance that pain is about to stop, is subjectively apparent to anyone who has endured prolonged pain (e.g., of a dentist's drill). There is also an accumulation of behavioral evidence for such a "relief" effect, in particular evidence that frightened animals or animals experiencing shock can be reinforced by stimuli which have been associated with safety or with shock termination.

The other novel arrangement in Figure 6.5 is cue *D*, paired with the removal or withdrawal of a positive reinforcer. Examples would be cues that precede "taking candy away from a baby" or withdrawing a licking tube of sugar water from a hungry rat. The idea is that such cues come to act as "secondary punishers" themselves.

Figure 6.5 has shown the expected "emotions" conditioned by various arrangements between neutral cues and the onsets or terminations of primary reinforcers. Once conditioned, these various stimuli can be made contingent upon some instrumental response so as to increase or decrease its frequency. Figure 6.6 diagrams the six possible outcomes following occurrence of the instrumental response, and assigns to these the labels which Mowrer uses. A "decremental reinforcement" in Mowrer's conception is one which reduces (decrements) a drive, having a positive effect on the prior instrumental response; an "incremental reinforcement" increases (increments) a drive, having an inhibitory or punishing effect on the prior response. It should be realized, of course, that these outcomes will have their specified effects on behavior only when the organism is in the appropriate

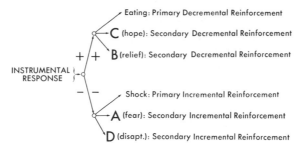

Figure 6.6.   Mowrer's classification of the six types of reinforcers which may follow an instrumental response; those outcomes on the "++" branches act as positive reinforcers (drive reducers) for the response; those outcomes on the "— —" branches act as negative reinforcers or punishments for the response.

drive state. Thus, an animal satiated on food cannot be rewarded by food or by stimuli (C) associated with food or punished by stimuli (D) associated with withdrawal of food. Similarly, an animal who is not frightened will not be reinforced by presentation of a cue (B) associated with relief from fear or pain.

Mowrer (1960) reviews evidence indicating the heuristic value of this symmetric classification system, and a fair amount has appeared since. An example of an experiment showing punitive effects of cues (like D) paired with reward removal is a study by Stea (1964). During an initial "disappointment conditioning" phase, Stea would insert a drinking tube into the cage of a thirsty rat; after it had begun drinking from the tube, Stea would sound a tone and then withdraw the drinking tube from the cage (the tone preceded and followed the tube withdrawal by 5 seconds). After a number of such trials, the second phase of the experiment began during which the rats received a number of free and forced trials to both arms of a T-maze, being rewarded with water from a dish on both sides. This established a baseline performance of "equal preference" for the two arms of the maze. In the third phase of the experiment, Stea now sounded the "disappointing" tone whenever the rat went to a particular side (say, the left side) of the maze to get its water. As a result, the animals developed a significant preference for the opposite side, where they avoided the "disappointing" tone. Control subjects receiving the same treatment, except that tone and water removal (or water presentation) were only randomly related in the first phase, showed no preference in the third phase for the nontone side. The conclusion appears to be that for the experimental subjects the tone has acquired negative value and acts like a punisher because it has been associated with the withdrawal of water, or with the frustration of a consummatory response. Such a result is, of course, consonant with Mowrer's identifying cues of type D as punishers. Although such classification systems have their usefulness, they should not be viewed as "proving" the underlying drive-reduction view of reward on which Mowrer based his classification. Any simple hedonic conception of "pleasant versus unpleasant" activities could have been substituted for Mowrer's theoretically loaded terms "drive incremental" or "drive decremental" reinforcement. As a matter of fact, it now

appears very likely that the drive-reduction hypothesis is empirically inadequate (see E. R. Hilgard & Bower, 1966, pp. 481–487 for our earlier discussion of its problems). However, this does not affect the classification system
for reinforcers which Mowrer has proposed.

K. W. Spence

Kenneth Spence was assuredly closer to being Hull's "collaborator and
successor" than any of the other learning theorists whom Hull influenced.
Following Hull's death, Spence was clearly the leader of the tradition of
Hullian theory, although he was constantly rethinking and altering significant parts of the theory. There was a reciprocal influence between
Spence and Hull. Actually, Hull gained much from Spence, borrowing his
ideas regarding discrimination learning, transposition, the use of intervening variables in theorizing, the notion of incentive motivation, the derived
gradient of reinforcement, and many other hypotheses. In the following,
we will merely touch on a few of Spence's contributions.

Discrimination learning theory. Spence's initial work (1936) was with a
theory of discrimination learning, called the "continuity" theory for reasons
to be explained shortly. In the simplest discrimination setup, called the
"go–no go" type, the subject, usually an animal, is positively reinforced for
responding in the presence of one stimulus (called the positive stimulus,
conventionally denoted as S⁺), and not reinforced for responding in the
presence of another stimulus (the negative stimulus, denoted S⁻). With differential training, the subject comes to respond promptly to S⁺ but not to S⁻;
changes in the stimulus control changes in his behavior—he discriminates.
A slightly different version of the experiment presents S⁺ and S⁻ simultaneously, and the subject makes a preferential choice between the two stimulus
patterns. Learning is revealed when the subject selects S⁺ unerringly on such
choice trials.

In his classic paper of 1936, Spence provided what was to become the
"classical" or "traditional continuity" view of discrimination learning, a view
which withstood many strong tests and many vigorous critics, and provided
a foil for most related developments in studies of discrimination learning.
The basic approach asserted that analysis of discrimination learning should
require no new concepts beyond the notions of simple conditioning, extinction, and stimulus generalization. It was assumed that cumulative effects
from reinforced responding to the positive stimulus would build up a
strong excitatory tendency at S⁺. Similarly, it was assumed that conditioned
inhibition would accumulate at S⁻ from the frustration consequent upon
nonreinforced responses made in the presence of S⁻. These excitatory and
inhibitory tendencies established at S⁺ and S⁻ are assumed to generalize to
similar stimuli, with the amount of generalization decreasing with decreasing similarity. The net tendency to respond to any stimulus is then given
by the generalized excitation minus generalized inhibition to that particular
stimulus (see Figure 6.7 on p. 184). This simple theory has proven extremely
serviceable and has provided decent accounts of much that we know about
discrimination learning (see G. A. Kimble, 1961, for a summary). Over the

years, its inadequacies have been slowly unearthed—they often amount to incompletenesses rather than incorrect assumptions of the theory. A review of several of these failings of the theory was contained in the previous edition (E. R. Hilgard & Bower, 1966, Chapter 15), and they will not be recounted here.

Transposition of relational responding. All theoretical approaches to discrimination learning begin by trying to specify, either formally or intuitively, what it is that a subject has learned in his discrimination training. How are we to characterize the subject's knowledge gained by this educative procedure? For behaviorists, this question gets translated into one about stimulus control of responses: what is the *effective stimulus* controlling the subject's discriminative performance? At one level of analysis, practically all theories answer this general question in a similar manner: the effective stimulus variable that comes eventually to control discriminative performance is that feature (cue, attribute, etc.) or set of features present in S+ and absent (or different) in S-. Such features are called relevant cues because their variations correlate with presence or absence of reinforcement for responding. Cues not so correlated are termed irrelevant.

But let us consider a problem where the relevant cues consist of different values along some ordered stimulus continuum (such as size, brightness, heaviness, etc.). For example, suppose a monkey is trained to use size as a cue for securing a food reward. The setup may consist of simultaneously presenting two boxes between which the monkey is to choose; the one containing the reward has a top with an area of 160 square centimeters, whereas the other box, containing no reward, has a smaller top 100 square centimeters in area. The *relational* theory supposes that, in this situation, the subject would learn the relation "the *larger* area is correct." The *absolute* theory supposes that the subject has learned specific stimulus-response connections; in particular, that the reaching response is conditioned positively to the specific value of the rewarded stimulus (160) whereas the response is inhibited to the value of the nonrewarded stimulus (100).

Which mode of description of "what is learned" is better is more than a matter of taste, because transfer tests with new stimuli provide us with data for inferring what the subject has learned in the 160 versus 100 situation. If the subject had learned a relation ("choose the larger one of the stimuli"), then he should in some degree be able to transfer his response to this relation to new stimulus pairs differing from those used in training. That is, the relation he has learned is one that transcends the specific stimulus pair used to exemplify the relation. Thus, if we test the animal with the new pair 256 square centimeters versus 160 square centimeters, he should still choose the larger stimulus in this pair, namely, 256, in preference to 160, despite the fact that 160 was rewarded in the prior training series. The usual experimental result is that animals do choose the 256 stimulus in preference to the 160 stimulus. That is, they *transpose* the relation "larger" along the size continuum. Such studies are thus called transposition experiments.

This kind of transposition has been found with fair regularity in experiments, and it has been offered as evidence for the relational view of what the animal learns (e.g., Köhler, 1918). It was formerly thought that such a transposition was inconsistent with the absolute theory, since, on that basis, how could one ever predict that a new stimulus (256 square centimeters) would be chosen in preference to the one (160 square centimeters) that had been so often rewarded in prior training?

It was in this context that Spence published another classic paper in 1937 demonstrating that transposition and several related phenomena are perfectly predictable from an absolute stimulus theory of what is learned. All that is required, according to Spence, is the assumption that the generalization gradients of habit strength and inhibition around the specific S⁺ and S⁻ values of training have a certain reasonable form. This view is best illustrated in Figure 6.7, which depicts a theoretical view of the situation established by the 160 versus 100 size discrimination training. The figure shows a habit gradient set up around the reinforced stimulus of training (160), and an inhibition gradient set up around the nonreinforced stimulus (100). The net tendency to respond to any size stimulus is given by the difference between the generalized habit and inhibition at that point. These difference scores are indicated in Figure 6.7. In a choice test between two stimuli, that stimulus having the larger net response tendency will be chosen. For example, for the training pair of 160 versus 100, the net tendency to respond to 160 is 51.7 and to 100 is 29.7; so in this pair, the 160 stimulus would be chosen.

A number of implications follow from this "absolute" stimulus theory. It does predict transposition over a short range of stimulus pairs close to the training pair, e.g., from the difference scores shown in Figure 6.7, the animal would be expected to choose the 256 stimulus (which has a difference score of 72.1) in preference to the 160 stimulus (difference score of 51.7). Thus, a stimulus near S⁺ but on the side opposite S⁻ is expected to actually be stronger or more attractive than is S⁺ itself. Examination of Figure 6.7 shows too that prediction of how the animal will choose on a given test pair of stimuli depends critically on how far the pair is from the training pair. As the test pair is moved above and away from the training pair, the theory first predicts transposition for near test pairs, then reversal of transposition (choosing the smaller) for pairs of intermediate distance (e.g., as in 409 square centimeters versus 256 square centimeters), and then random choices

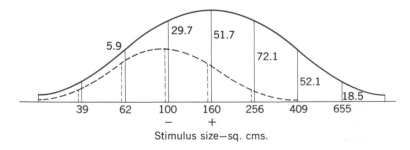

Figure 6.7.   Hypothetical generalization gradient for habit (solid curve) around 160 (+) and inhibition (dashed curve) around 100 (−). The difference, habit minus inhibition, is indicated numerically at various points. The stimulus values are equally spaced on a logarithmic scale. (From Spence, 1942.)

for test pairs very far removed from the training pair (as in, say, 900 square centimeters versus 1300 square centimeters). This decline in transposition with distance has indeed been found many times and it provides a difficulty for the relational view. Furthermore, according to Spence's theory, S⁺ and S⁻ need not be simultaneously present for comparison in order to establish the conditions required by the theory to predict transposition in later pairwise tests. Single stimulus presentation of S⁺ and S⁻ with reinforcement and non-reinforcement of responding should serve suitably to produce later trans-position choices on paired tests. Transposition is found following such single-stimulus training, although various procedural changes generally cause it to be somewhat less than that following simultaneous-presentation discrimination. Several other predictions are derivable from Spence's theory; for example, the test stimulus range over which transposition is observed should be less when S⁻ is even farther below the S⁺ of training. In general, the effects predicted by Spence's theory have been confirmed by experiments. A study by Honig (1962) is particularly clear in showing several of these effects within a single experiment. Owing to confirmation of its deter-minate predictions, and because no similarly developed relational theory was then advanced to explain the facts, Spence's absolute-stimulus theory won the day.

Carrying matters a step further, Spence (1942) extended his theory to cover cases involving three training stimuli. In the *intermediate size* prob-lem, the animal would be trained to choose the 160 stimulus from the triad consisting of 100, 160, and 256 square centimeters. Figure 6.8 depicts Spence's analysis of the situation in terms of his specific stimulus theory. An inhibi-tion gradient is set up around both nonreinforced stimuli, with the two gradients being summated (see Hull's "behavioral addition") at points where they overlap. From this diagram, several implications are evident. First, the intermediate size problem should be much more difficult to learn than a two-choice problem. This may be seen by comparing Figure 6.8 with 6.7, noting that the net differential reaction tendency to S⁺ is much less for the intermediate size task. Second, learning to choose the intermediate stimulus should prove more difficult than learning to choose either of the end stim-

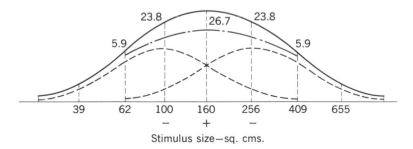

Stimulus size—sq. cms.

Figure 6.8.   Hypothetical gradients following learning of the middle-size problem, where 160 was rewarded and 100 and 256 were nonrewarded. The inhibition gradients (dashed curves) around 100 and 256 are summated to yield a single net inhibition curve with a peak at 160. The difference, habit minus net inhibition, is indicated numerically at various points. (From Spence, 1942.)

uli of the three (largest or smallest). This is true and is easily derived, although it is not shown in Figure 6.8. Third, there should be no transposition following training on the middle-size problem but there should be transposition after training on one of the end stimuli of the triad. In Figure 6.8, for example, following training on the middle-size stimulus, a test with the triad 160, 256, and 409 should lead to choice of 160, the specific positive stimulus of training. In fact, for any test triad, the preferred stimulus should be that one closer in size to 160. Spence (1942) reported data showing indeed that his subjects (chimpanzees) did not transpose the middle-size relation to the test triad (160, 256, 409) following training on 100, 160, 256.

Despite the attractive parsimony of Spence's theory and the evidence that can be marshaled for it, reports of other results that have continued to appear suggest that it either is incomplete or is inadequate in some other way. Some of these studies, such as those by C. B. Smith (1956) and Riley (1958), have emphasized, at least for the brightness continuum, the importance of the background contextual stimulation surrounding the focal stimulus patches to which the subject responds. Thus, a test patch of a particular brightness may be seen as lighter or darker depending on whether its surrounding background is darker or lighter, respectively, than the test patch. Riley, for example, showed that the decline in transposition on the "far tests" did not occur if the test-patch-to-surround-brightness ratio was kept the same in training and testing, although absolute intensity levels were changed for the tests. In other work, Lawrence and DeRivera (1954) demonstrated that rats apparently learned relational cues when the training situation promoted the effectiveness of cues involving brightness-contrast. Moreover, in various follow-up experiments on the middle-size problem, transposition has often been found (contrary to Spence's result), although not in every instance.

It was upon this scene of increasingly confusing results that Zeiler (1963) proposed a theory that appears to account beautifully for most of the results, including those cited for and against Spence's theory. Zeiler developed his theory for the middle-size problem, although judging from the prior work by H. James (1953) the theory can easily be extended to cover the two-choice problems as well. Zeiler's is a ratio theory involving the adaptation-level concept. His basic proposition is that the subject's perception of a stimulus depends upon its ratio to an internal norm or standard called the adaptation level (AL), a concept due to Helson (1964). The AL is assumed to be an average value (actually geometric mean) obtained by pooling the focal and background stimulation currently present and the stimulation that has been effective in the recent past. Without going into details here, Zeiler's theory assumes that the three training stimuli establish a particular AL, and that the subject learns to choose that stimulus (the middle-size one) bearing a particular ratio (call it r^+) to the prevailing AL. When later tested with a new set of three stimuli, a new test adaptation level (call it AL^*) has to be computed from the theory: it is a weighted average of the training AL and the different AL that would be appropriate were only the three test stimuli acting. In the test, the subject is expected to choose that stimulus whose ratio to the test AL^* is closest to r^+, the stimulus ratio reinforced during training. If neither test stimulus ratio is close to r^+, in a special sense defined by Zeiler, then random responding on the test is predicted.

This theory can predict transposition, transposition reversal, or random responding in the middle-size problem depending on the precise set of training and test stimuli involved. In general, the theory does a remarkably good job of accounting for most of the previous data on the middle-size problem. In addition, it predicts fairly well the results of an extensive series of experiments Zeiler carried out with 4- and 5-year-old children. Part of the beauty of the theory is the manner in which it nicely integrates parts of the "relational" and "specific stimulus" theories. According to the specific stimulus theory, the response tendency to any stimulus is established in a definite way by the training conditions and is assumed to be aroused independently of the alternative test stimuli that are present; according to the relational approach, the specific stimuli of the test set are irrelevant, since the relation that the subject has learned supposedly transcends particular elements. But in Zeiler's account, the attractiveness of a stimulus depends upon the context in which it is embedded. It is the composition of the test set that partly determines the new norm, AL*, in relation to which the stimuli are judged. Just as the relational theory would have it, Zeiler supposes that the subject has indeed learned to respond to a particular ratio. However, contrary to the strict relational viewpoint, the test stimulus ratio most similar to that reinforced in training depends on both the current (test) stimulation and the previous (training) stimulation, since both influence the current adaptation level. Zeiler's theory is moderately complex, but this would be true of any adequate theory, since the patterns of the experimental results that have to be accounted for are also complex.

As is often the case in the evolution of scientific explanations, the initial alternative hypotheses (relational versus absolute) are both eventually proved to be inadequate or insufficiently comprehensive. The new explanation, emerging dialectically, involves some novel concepts but also retains certain of the features of the previously competing theories. The transposition phenomenon engendered a controversy only in regard to the behavior of animals and possibly preverbal children. Spence himself restricted his theory's application to nonverbal organisms, believing that the human's use of symbolic language introduces novel factors not covered by his theory. It is indeed true that humans learn and use relational concepts in abundance and our language is replete with relational or comparative terms which we use properly hundreds of times each day (*greater, above, farther, to the west of,* etc.). Several investigators have been concerned with how transposition responding varies as the human child develops and becomes more proficient in the use of language. The general trend of the findings is that transposition improves with the mental age and/or linguistic proficiency of the child, although there have been a few discrepant reports (see Hebert & Krantz, 1965, for a review).

Continuity theory.   One issue requiring mention is the manner in which Spence (in his 1936 paper) treated discrimination learning with respect to compounds or bundles of stimulus cues. The typical discrimination task involves multiattribute or multidimensional stimulus patterns. For instance, in a typical simultaneous discrimination task, a monkey might be required on a particular trial to choose between "a large white triangle on the left" versus "a small black square on the right." By convention, "large-small" are called the *values* of the size *dimension*. In this illustration, there are four binary (two-valued) dimensions, so there are $2^4 = 16$ possible stimulus patterns (and 8 complementary pairs). The experimenter will select the value of one of the dimensions as "correct" (e.g., triangle), so that choice of any pattern having that value will be rewarded. If "triangle" were correct, then *shape* would be called the relevant dimension, whereas size, color, and position would be *irrelevant* dimensions. The various values of the irrelevant dimensions are usually paired equally often with the reinforced value as with the nonreinforced value. For example, the triangle is on the left for half of the trials, and the square is on the left for the other half of the trials. With such arrangements, consistent choice of an irrelevant value (e.g., left) would result for half the trials in reward and for half in nonreward.

With this as background structure to the issue, the nature of Spence's learning and composition rules can now be stated. Roughly speaking, he assumed that every value of a stimulus pattern could be assigned a net reaction tendency for approach (its excitatory minus inhibitory tendencies), and that the total tendency to approach a given pattern was approximated by the algebraic sum of the reaction tendencies of the component values comprising it. When the subject was to choose between two patterns (habit bundles), he was expected to choose that one with the larger summated reaction potential. A further assumption was that, following response to a pattern with consequent reward or nonreward, at the end of that trial the reaction tendencies of each of the components of the chosen pattern were appropriately increased (if it was a rewarded trial) or decreased (if it was a nonrewarded trial). Thus, the subject bases his selection on *all* perceived components of the chosen stimulus, and he learns (alters net habit strengths) with respect to *all* perceived components. Moreover, it was presumed that the changes in habit tendencies to particular cues occurred gradually, by the *continuous* accumulation of increments and decrements due to rewards and nonrewards. This is what earned it the title of "continuity theory."

On this view, for example, a subject might begin with a set of habitual preferences for what prove to be irrelevant cues in the discrimination problem at hand, so that a rat may show systematic position preferences in a maze before the effects of training gradually "turn its attention" to the relevant cue (say, the color of the maze arms). In this theory, differential approach tendencies accrue to the positive versus negative values within the relevant dimension, whereas the approach tendencies toward the two values within irrelevant dimensions tend to gradually become equalized (but with trial to trial variability in strengths due to favorable or unfavorable runs of rewarded correlations with the positive value). The animal comes to respond errorlessly when the habit differential favoring the positive over the negative value is sufficiently great to offset any and all combinations of habit differentials from the irrelevant cues; that is, the summated habit for any positive pattern (bundle) exceeds the summated habit for its complementary (opposite) negative pattern.

These sets of assumptions—regarding the composite determination of choice, and gradual learning with respect to all perceived components—were the core of the continuity theory. Almost all of these assumptions were denied by Spence's "opponents," such as Krechevsky or Lashley or Tolman, who espoused a type of "hypothesis-testing" theory of discrimination learning. Details of the hypothesis-testing theory, particularly Levine's recent work on human discrimination learning, were reviewed earlier (Chapter 5, pp. 140–143). The key kinds of assumptions of H-theory would seem to be these:

(a) The subject's response on a given trial is based on only one (or at most, very few) value of the total pattern. If you will, he "selectively attends" to only that one feature of the pattern.

(b) The rewarding or nonrewarding outcome on that trial causes the subject to learn primarily only about that cue (hypothesis) that dominated his choice for that trial. Mainly, the outcome acts like information enabling confirmation or disconfirmation of a conjecture (hypothesis) regarding the correct solution to the discrimination task.

(c) The solution tends to occur suddenly, "insightfully," in all-or-none manner rather than by the gradual accumulation of strength.

There are differing forms of such noncontinuity theories, varying according to their rules for altering the "attentional" process and the "S-R learning" process. There has been a very lengthy and productive history of research on the details of formulations of such discrimination theories. Recent partial summaries of the vast literature on the topic are contained in Lovejoy (1968), Sutherland and Mackintosh (1971), and Trabasso and Bower (1968). It is a credit to Spence's theorizing that his classic formulation (and experimental argumentation) has held center stage for so many years in the analysis of discrimination learning. Few miniature theories for specific subphenomena in psychology have proven so robust and viable in the light of subsequent research.

Incentive motivation. Another area in which Spence significantly influenced Hullian theorizing was in conceptualizing the actions of rewards and nonrewards upon instrumental behavior. In 1943, Hull had originally assumed that habit strength, the primary associative factor in the theory, was affected by the conditions of reinforcement. Spence had argued, however, that reward should be conceptualized as having a motivating or energizing effect on habits rather than directly affecting the associative factor itself. In fact, in Spence's formulation (1956, 1960a), habit strength was assumed to be a function of the number of S-R contiguities (trials), whereas reward conditions (reward magnitude and number of rewarded trials) were assumed to affect reaction potential through an incentive motivational factor, K. It was assumed moreover that incentive motivation combined additively with drive, D, to comprise the full motivational complex which multiplied habit strength. Thus, dropping subscripts,

$$\text{Hull:} \quad E = H \times D \times K - I$$
$$\text{Spence:} \quad E = H \times (D + K) - I.$$

These different combination rules for D and K lead to somewhat different predictions. Consider, for instance, a choice situation (T-maze) between responses R_L and R_S, in which R_L leads to a large food reward whereas R_S leads to a small food reward. This should result in a differential in incentive motivation for the two responses (call these K_L and K_S). Suppose, further, that we arrange a sequence of forced choices and free choices in the maze so that the subject has equal experience (trials) with the two responses. In either theory, then, this equates the two habit strengths, so $H_L = H_S$.

Consider now the question of how preference (revealed on the free choice trials) varies with drive level, D. Preferential choice increases with the difference in reaction potential favoring the larger reward side. The difference is therefore as follows:

$$\text{For Hull:}\quad E_L - E_S = (H_L \times D \times K_L - I) - (H_S \times D \times K_S - I)$$
$$= H \times D \times (K_L - K_S); \tag{1}$$

$$\text{For Spence:}\quad E_L - E_S = [H_L \times (D + K_L) - I] - [H_S \times (D + K_S) - I]$$
$$= H(K_L - K_S). \tag{2}$$

In these equations, we have used the fact that $H_S = H_L = H$, due to the forced trial procedure. Comparing the two equations, we notice that Hull's multiplicative formula implies that preference for the large reward side of the maze will be a function of the subject's drive level, D, with higher drive (hunger) leading to more extreme preference. On the other hand, Spence's additive formula implies that preference will be independent of the drive level of the subject (the D factor has canceled out in the difference).

To test these predictions, G. H. Bower (1964) conducted an experiment using rats maintained at two different levels of hunger drive. The animals chose in a T-maze between a large reward of .180 grams of food and a smaller reward of .135 grams. In this situation, over 138 training trials, rats performing under different drive levels nonetheless behaved similarly; the asymptotic preference for the large reward side estimated from the last 28 free-choice trials was 83 percent for the high-drive subjects and 84 percent for the low-drive subjects. In this instance (as in several others), the additive formula proposed by Spence appears to be supported.

As always, however, the conclusion depends on the validity of other assumptions. In the present instance, it depends on the assumption that preferential choice is a function of the difference in reaction tendencies, $E_L - E_S$. But another plausible rule—proposed and developed in detail by Luce (1959)—is that choice is a function of the ratio of the two strengths,

$$p(R_L) = \frac{E_L}{E_L + E_S} = \frac{1}{1 + \dfrac{E_S}{E_L}}$$

With this ratio formulation, we now find that the multiplicative assumption $(E = HDK)$ implies that asymptotic choice is independent of drive level, whereas the additive assumption $(E = H(D + K))$ implies that preferential choice of the larger reward regresses toward 50 percent chance the higher the drive level. So the theory that is supported by the data of this experiment depends on the rule that is assumed to govern choices. That rule is very much like a "measurement axiom," allowing one to infer ratios (or differences) in response strengths given the particular choice probabilities observed in an experiment. The equivocation in this instance illustrates how "intervening-variable" types of theories can encounter ambiguities and difficulties unless they have a valid way to measure the intervening variables (see Suppes & Zinnes, 1963, for elaboration of this point).

To return to Spence's theorizing, it was he who first promoted the idea of relating the incentive motivation construct, K, to the strength of the fractional anticipatory goal-response (r_G-s_G). The r_G is viewed as a classically conditioned response which moves forward in the instrumental chain. Its early occurrence in the chain is presumed to channel excitement into performance of the response. This analysis seems plausible since variables which affect r_G amplitude (e.g., amount or quality of reward) or extent of r_G conditioning (e.g., number of trials, delay or probability of reward) are assumed also to have corresponding effects on the theoretical construct, K. As indicated in Chapter 4, this is essentially the way Sheffield and Estes relate rewards to performance of instrumental responses.

There has recently been some disenchantment with this identification between incentive motivation and r_G amplitude, or some peripheral component of the response to the rewarding outcome. The arguments are summarized by Logan (1968). For one thing, one needs something like "incentive motivation" to account for how animals run to escape shock (see e.g., G. H. Bower, 1960), yet in such cases it is difficult to imagine what is the classically conditioned "goal-response" whose anticipation is "exciting." Another argument takes literally the remarks concerning r_G as a peripheral response, and then shows that direct attempts to manipulate r_G for food by drugs which facilitate or inhibit salivation have not had the expected effect on performance of food-rewarded habits (see, e.g., Lewis & Kent, 1961). Another argument is that offered earlier against Mowrer's "response-scanning" theory of habit; a theory which relies on feedback from incipiently initiated responses to provide motivation or inhibition for that response does not have a way to let incentive motivation operate at the moment of choice. For example, assume a rat has had experience with a maze which has (to be absurd) 100 discriminably different alleyways leading off from one choice point, each associated with rewards of slightly different magnitudes or delays. Assuming equal experience with all alleyways (so that H's are equal), the r_G theory would have us believe that the rat can make his choice only by orienting to all alleyways in turn, getting a particular "reading" of r_G for each alley, storing that reading, withholding response until all responses have been scanned, then comparing the "r_G readings," and finally deciding upon that response with the highest reading. But this all seems a bit implausible. If 100-choice mazes strike the reader as too absurd, it should be recalled that at each moment in time throughout performance of a response chain, the organism may be conceived to be choosing from among a vast repertoire of possible responses. For instance, the micromolar theory of Logan (1960), which we shall meet later, supposes that for even the simplest qualitative response the animal is selecting its intensive characteristics—its speed, its amplitude, its forcefulness. As Logan (1968, p. 8) says, "It seems improbable that any organism has the time or resources to make momentary decisions on the basis of implicit monitoring of all possible courses of action." He then concludes, "At the present time, it appears preferable to conceptualize incentive motivation as specific to different S-R events and immediately given as a basis for choice *before* the choice is made" (p. 8). In Logan's view, then, incentive motivation is specific to particular S-R events and is a major determiner of response selection. He supposes (see, e.g., Logan, 1969) that $_sIN_R$ (or K) is scalable upward or downward according to the joint actions of rewards and punishments. Rewards have positive incentive value, punishments have negative incentive value, and the net incentive for a given response depends on the difference between the positive and negative factors. Readers familiar with economics or "value theory" in philosophy will note that incentive motivation is being used here by Logan very much like the concept of subjective utility in those disciplines. Indeed, this is no accident, since Logan wants the theory about "decision-making" or response selection by lower organisms (see, e.g., Logan, 1965) to be consistent with the way we view decision-making by intelligent humans; and utility theory was developed to account for (or normatively prescribe) the choices of "rational" men.

Abram Amsel

Abram Amsel, a student of Spence's, is a prominent contemporary worker within the Hullian tradition. Amsel has concentrated his efforts on an analysis of nonreward and extinction of instrumental behavior. Earlier interpretations of nonreward had assigned to it an essentially passive role. For example, Tolman (Chapter 5) supposed that nonreward served simply to disconfirm and weaken an S-R-S_G expectancy. In Hull's earlier theory, nonrewarded trials were conceived as permitting inhibitory factors to build up without being offset by a corresponding increase in H or K. In contrast to this passive role of nonreward, Amsel's frustration hypothesis views nonreward of a previously rewarded response as an actively punishing and aversive event. In consequence, many of the effects of nonreward upon responding are now seen as analogous to the effects produced upon that same behavior by punishment.

In numerous papers (e.g., 1958, 1962, 1967), Amsel has developed and argued persuasively for this hypothesis; additional significant contributions to its development have come from Wagner (1963, 1966) and Spence (1960a). We shall first state the hypothesis as directly as we can, and then describe the kinds of experiments that have been adduced in support of it. The hypothesis is:

The occurrence of nonreward at a moment when the subject is expecting a reward causes the elicitation of a primary frustration reaction (R_F). The feedback stimulation from this reaction is aversive and has short-term persisting motivational effects upon subsequent instrumental behavior. Fractional parts of this primary frustration reaction become conditioned in the classical manner to stimuli preceding its elicitation. Occurrence of this fractional response in anticipatory form is denoted r_f–s_f. The cues, s_f, from anticipatory frustration are principally connected to avoidance responses, but these connections can be modified through training.

Within the Hullian framework, the phrase "is expecting a reward" is translatable into statements about r_G, their mechanism for representing anticipatory reward. Recall that r_G is a learned variable differing in its amplitude with trials and with the characteristics of the reward (its amount, sweetness, etc.).

The alleged motivational effect of frustrative nonreward may be seen in the intensifying or speeding up of responses occurring within a short time after the animal experiences nonreinforcement. The standard situation for studying this is a two-link runway. The rat is trained to run to a first goal-box for a reward; after a few seconds there, the entrance is opened to a second runway, which he traverses for a second reward. After training on this two-link sequence, omission of the first reward produces a momentary increase in subsequent speed of running down the second runway on that trial. The difference in running speeds in the second runway following nonreward versus reward in the first goal-box is taken as an index of the size of the frustration effect (FE). As Amsel's theory would predict, the factors that influence the size of the FE tend to be those which would make for stronger arousal of the r_G in the first link of the runway. That is to say, the greater the anticipation of reward, the greater the frustration produced by nonreward. A particularly important finding is that, with 50 percent rewarded and nonrewarded trials at the first goal-box, the FE does not appear during the initial trials but it develops gradually with training, presumably reflecting the further conditioning of anticipatory reward. A second important finding (Amsel & Ward, 1965) is that the FE to nonreward in the first goal-box diminishes and eventually disappears if discriminative cues are provided in the first runway (e.g., it is black or white) predicting reward or nonreward in the first goal-box. Thus, if no reward is expected, then nonreward is no longer frustrating. Third, it was claimed that the FE occurs when the amount of reward is merely reduced to a lower (nonzero) level, with the size of the FE graded according to graded reductions in the test reward below the amount customarily expected (G. H. Bower, 1962c). However, recent evidence (Barrett et al., 1965) makes it appear that these graded effects are in fact confounded with the temporary depressive effects upon running speed of the rat related to his having eaten more or less food in the first goal-box.

Wagner (1963) presents data to support the assumption that frustration may be conditioned and that it acts like an aversive drive-stimulus. Rats were run down a runway with half the trials rewarded and half nonrewarded in a haphazard order. A buzzer was presented just a moment before they looked into the empty food cup on nonrewarded trials. This procedure was presumed to associate the buzzer with the frustration reaction elicited when the rat looked into the empty food cup. Later, this buzzer was shown to enhance the startle reflex to a gunshot, a measure which has proved sensitive to acquired motivational effects of cues. Also, the buzzer could be used effectively to train and maintain a response which produced escape from the buzzer. The interpretation is that the escape response is reinforced because it terminates the buzzer, which is associated with aversive frustration. Recent research by Daly (1969, 1970) has shown particularly effective forms of learning presumably reinforced by "frustration reduction."

As applied to extinction of rewarded instrumental responses, frustration is presumed to act like punishment. Since extinction involves repeated frustration at the goal, the animal comes to anticipate frustration (the r_f-s_f mechanism) just as it would anticipate with fear a painful electric shock at the goal. Anticipatory frustration initially produces avoidance of the goal, by evoking responses which interfere with continued approach to the place where frustration occurs. However, it is argued that partial reinforcement effectively trains the animal to "tolerate frustration." In particular, the circumstances of such training result in the s_f cues becoming connected to approach rather than avoidance. Thus, extinction is supposed to be slower following partial reinforcement training because the normal means for arousing interfering (avoidance) responses has been temporarily preempted by the approach habit itself.

This hypothesis regarding extinction and partial reinforcement has received a fair amount of experimental support. There is little doubt that the conditions under which extinction occurs and their associated stimuli are aversive, and that the animal is reinforced by escaping them. For example, in a Skinner box animals will learn a new response to remove a stimulus that has been associated with extinction. Azrin (1964) has further shown that during extinction of a food-reinforced response, pigeons will learn a new response for which the payoff is a brief opportunity to aggress against (fight) another pigeon. Under "neutral" control conditions such fighting does not occur. The relevance of this observation to the frustration hypothesis is that such aggressive responses are known to be highly probable mainly when the bird is in pain or otherwise discomforting circumstances. These results are thus explicable if it is assumed that nonreinforced responses produce frustration and that frustration is aversive.

Another related fact is that tranquilizing drugs, which presumably reduce emotional consequences of frustration, will retard extinction and also partially release a response formerly inhibited by frustration. Additionally, Wagner (1966) has shown large transfer between training animals to resist the stress of punishment (electric shock) and training them to resist frustration for approach to a goal. In particular, if rats have been trained to continue approaching despite punishment at a rewarded goal, then the number of trials required to reach extinction is greater when food and punishment are stopped. Also, animals trained under partial reinforcement will continue responding longer once punishment is introduced at the goal. These results suggest that electric shock and nonreward have common properties, so that learning to withstand one of them transfers in some degree to the other. And this supports the interpretation of nonreward as a frustrating, aversive event.

The studies cited plus several others would appear to provide conclusive evidence that nonreward (when reward is expected) has an aversive effect much like a punishment. One should realize, however, that acceptance of that proposition does not logically entail belief in the particular interference theory of extinction which Amsel proposes. That theory says that anticipation of frustration at the goal is initially connected to avoidance of the goal (elicits responses interfering with goal-directed movement); by arranging circumstances so that the subject is induced to keep running under partial reinforcement training, the cues from anticipatory frustration become associated with approaching the goal rather than avoiding it.

One of the more convincing demonstrations of this *associative role* of r_f-s_f is an experiment done in Amsel's lab by Ross (1964). Table 6.2 outlines the design of the experiment. During phase 1, six groups of rats were trained in a short, black, wide box with either continuous (100 percent) or partial (50 percent) reinforcement using one of three responses: running, jumping across a gap in the floor, or climbing a wire-mesh wall to get to the food well. These three responses had been selected by pretesting to be about equally difficult, and the animals did learn them at about the same rate. The crucial idea here is that during this phase 1 training, the partial reinforcement groups are presumably having anticipatory frustration r_F-s_F conditioned to their approach response, whether that be running, jumping, or climbing. This presumption is tested in phase 3 of the experiment.

Phase 2 of the experiment took the animals, operating under thirst for water rewards (rather than hunger), to a new apparatus and trained them with continuous reinforcement on a running response. The idea here was to use a situation quite dissimilar to that in phase 1 so that differential transfer in phase 3 can arguably arise from internal (mediated) rather than external stimulus similarity.

The critical phase is the third, during which the response learned in phase 2 is extinguished. The question concerns how the various groups will rank-order themselves in extinction. The data are shown in Figure 6.9 relating group mean running speed for the six conditions for the last block of acquisition trials and over 32 (8 blocks of 4) extinction trials. Amsel's theory predicts that during phase 3 extinction the animals will be frustrated and begin to experience anticipatory frustration. What they *do* in the face of this anticipatory frustration depends upon what, if any, response they had been trained to make to it in phase 1 of the experiment, *and* the compatibility of that response with the running response being measured during phase 3. In particular, subjects who had had phase 1 partial reinforcement with a running response (RP) should now show much superior resistance to extinc-

Table 6.2   Outline of the Ross (1964) experiment. (From Amsel, 1967.)

Phases of Experiment	(1) Preliminary Learning	(2) Acquisition Running Response	(3) Extinction Running Response
Apparatus	*(A) Short, black, wide box*	*(B) Long, white, narrow runway*	*(B)*
Motivation	*Hunger*	*Thirst*	*Thirst*
Experimental Conditions	*Running* Continuous (RC) Partial (RP) *Jumping* Continuous (JC) Partial (JP) *Climbing* Continuous (CC) Partial (CP)	*Running* Continuous Reward	*Running* Continuous Nonreward

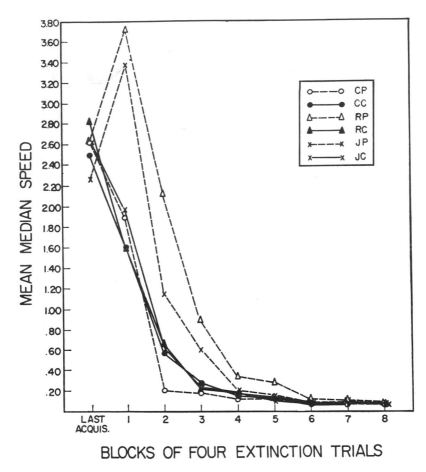

Figure 6.9.   Data from the Ross (1964) experiment showing performance on last acquisition block and over all extinction trials. Data are plotted here as speeds; times were plotted in the original report. The symbols denoting groups refer to climbing, running, or jumping (C, R, J) under continuous or partial reinforcement (C or P). (From Amsel, 1967. By permission.)

tion than their continuously reinforced mates (RC). Subjects trained in phase 1 with a jumping response should show somewhat less of a partial reinforcement effect (JP versus JC). Paradoxically, the group receiving partial reinforcement for a climbing response in phase 1 are expected to be *less* resistant to extinction in phase 3 than their continuously reinforced controls (CP versus CC). This was clearly the case for trial blocks 2, 3, and 4 during extinction. Amsel's theory predicts this "reverse" effect on the assumption that reintroduction of frustration cues in phase 3 brings back the particular responses associated earlier to r_f-s_f, namely, climbing; and these responses are supposedly incompatible with running to the goal, thus hastening extinction of running in comparison to the continuously reinforced controls. Ross in fact observed a high incidence of "climbing" (up the wire-mesh walls of the runway) during extinction in phase 3 by the CP rats, a response that was practically nonexistent during extinction of the other subjects.

The significance of this experiment is that it shows both positive and negative partial-reinforcement effects transferring from a training situation to a greatly altered test situation, and enables us to identify the "response learned to anticipatory frustration" as the critical mediating element. It shows that frustration aroused by nonreward when the animal is hungry and expecting food is very much like that aroused by nonreward when the animal is thirsty and expecting water. The result shows too that we cannot characterize the effect of partial reinforcement as teaching the animal simply to "tolerate frustration" and to "persist responding" in the face of frustration. Rather we must distinguish rather carefully exactly what response the subject has learned to make to anticipatory frustration and its relationship to the criterion response on which the subject's "frustration tolerance" is being assessed. Ross's experiment is of unquestionable significance for Amsel's theory. Because of its critical value, the experiment should be repeated to check its reliability.

More recently, Amsel (1967) has been developing his frustration theory in discrimination-learning situations, for example, having the subject experience continuous reinforcement when run in a white alley and partial reinforcement when run in a black alley. This situation produces a "generalized partial reinforcement effect" wherein resistance to extinction of the discrimination animal in his 100 percent alleyway is considerably greater than that of a control mate which had received continuous reinforcement initially in both alleyways. In some cases (see, e.g., Pavlik & Carlton, 1965), a "reverse" partial reinforcement effect may be found in which the discrimination animal is more resistant to extinction in his continuously reinforced situation than in his partially reinforced situation. This would be expected in Amsel's theory if incentive motivation were higher in the continuously reinforced situation, whereas the frustration mechanism r_f-$s_f \rightarrow$ R is equally available to retard extinction in both situations.

Since it is one of the dominant conceptions of extinction, frustration theory requires critical analysis, because it clearly has a few failings. First, there is the suggestion in experiments by Levy and Seward (1969) that in the two-link runway no FE occurs if the rat is expecting different incentives (food and water) in the two goal-boxes—which is a most puzzling observation. Second, Amsel's extinction theory really applies only to instrumental, appetitive responses, and leaves untouched extinction phenomena (such as partial reinforcement effects) in paradigms such as classical conditioning or instrumental escape conditioning (see, e.g., G. H. Bower, 1960). Partial reinforcement in classical defense conditioning (e.g., eyelid conditioning) enhances its resistance to extinction, yet it is difficult to imagine what could be frustrating about not receiving an anticipated aversive stimulus. Third, Capaldi and his associates (reviewed in Capaldi, 1967) have been able to produce differential amounts of resistance to extinction by variations in the sequential pattern of reinforced and nonreinforced trials the animal experiences during the acquisition series—a set of facts with which Amsel's theory can make no contact. Furthermore, there is now ample evidence (see Robbins, 1971, for a review) for a partial reinforcement effect on extinction following even very short training series (five to ten trials), far too abbreviated to bring to completion the successive stages (of r_G conditioning, then r_f, etc.) envisioned by Amsel's theory. These latter points suggest that extinction is a process with multiple determinants, that Amsel's frustration hypothesis is probably one component of a viable explanation, but that the total range of phenomena other mechanisms will have to be invoked. The currently most popular alternative is Capaldi's "sequential" hypothesis, which is a sophisticated elaboration of the early "discrimination hypothesis" mentioned in Chapter 5. We shall be reviewing Capaldi's interesting work later, in Chapter 15.

Frank Logan

Frank Logan is another dominant figure working with the Hullian approach, and he has written extensively from that viewpoint (e.g., Logan, 1959; 1960; 1970; Logan & Wagner, 1965). He was Spence's student at Iowa and was at Yale during Hull's last years. He has made a number of contributions in both experimentation and theoretical work. His main concern (illustrated in his 1965, 1969 papers) has been with determining how incentive motivation regulates behavior and how it is, in turn, regulated by the conditions of reward and punishment. His viewpoint in this regard was mentioned earlier in discussing the problems encountered by identifying incentive motivation with r_G amplitude.

Perhaps Logan is best known for developing the "micromolar" approach to behavior theory. This adopts a particular viewpoint of what it is that is reinforced, or what is learned, when we say that a "response" is reinforced. The micromolar approach promoted by Logan (1956, 1960) begins with an argument for expanding the definition of response to include its intensive characteristics (its speed, amplitude, volume, etc.). In the classical view, exemplified by Hull's 1943 theory, response classes are defined in terms of their achievements—running down a runway, pressing a lever, etc. The rule is to aggregate together all instances of behavior which achieve the same end result (e.g., getting the lever down); they are so aggregated because they are not differently reinforced by the experimenter. Variations in speed or amplitude of the response during training were taken to be indices of the strength of the response tendency. Hull formalized this idea in his reaction-potential construct $_sE_R$ which presumably determined the probability, speed, amplitude, and resistance to extinction of the response.

This classical approach runs into difficulties at several points, as Logan, among others, has pointed out. First, these various response measures frequently fail to be well correlated. During training, a measure such as response probability may improve monotonically with practice whereas speed and/or force of the response may at first increase and then decrease over trials. One example is the lengthening latency of the CR in classical conditioning (Pavlov's "inhibition of delay" mentioned in Chapter 3); a second is that forcefulness of lever-pressing first increases and then decreases during training, stabilizing at just above that minimal force required to operate the feeder. The second main difficulty of the classical approach results from the fact that one can differentially reinforce intensive characteristics of the response. Skinner (1938) was the first to show this experimentally, demonstrating in the free operant situation differential shaping of slow or fast rates of bar-pressing, weak or strong forces of bar-pressing, and long or short durations of bar-holding. The method is simplicity itself: simply reinforce only responses whose intensive properties fall within a specified criterion range, possibly advancing to stiffer criteria as the animal's performance follows along. It is clear that many skilled performances are differentiated in this way. It is also clear that through such differential reinforcement (e.g., of slow response speeds), the intensive properties of the response (a) may or may not increase monotonically with training, and (b) may be put in any relation to other intensive properties that we choose to reinforce (e.g., talking slowly and loudly, talking fast and softly, etc.).

Logan broadened the notion of "differential reinforcement" to include any variation in some parameter of reinforcement such as its amount, quality, delay, or probability. In conditions of correlated reinforcement, one or more dimensions of reinforcement are correlated with some intensive property of the observed behavior, e.g., its speed. The *terms function* specifies what reinforcement the subject receives for particular response speeds; it is similar to the terms of a contract between the subject and a reinforcing agent (the environment or the experimenter). A tremendous variety of terms functions are imaginable, only a few of which have been investigated. Examples in a runway situation might be: the faster the rat runs to the goal-box, the longer his reward will be delayed, or the faster he runs, the greater will be the amount of reward he receives; or reinforcement may be provided only when the speed falls in the interval x to y, and not otherwise, and so forth. In general, it is found that subjects adjust to such reward conditions, coming eventually to respond at a near optimal level (see Logan, 1960, for some results and a more detailed discussion).

To deal with the behavior of subjects under such conditions, Logan proposed the micromolar approach, that is, one which identifies different speeds as different responses, selectively influenced by differential reinforcement. Logan proposes essentially a "utility analysis" to deal with this approach, although he specifies the components of utility in terms of the intervening variables of habit, drive, incentive, and so on, of Hullian theory. The net utility (or $_sE_R$) of a particular response speed is given by its positive utility minus its associated negative utility. The main component of positive utility is incentive, which increases with the amount of reward provided for that speed and decreases with the total interval of reinforcement for that speed (total interval = duration of response + delay of reward following that response). The subject is viewed as learning through experience the incentive associated with each speed; however, the incentive for a given speed is influenced also by generalization of incentive learned for similar speeds. The main component of negative incentive for a particular speed is its effortfulness, fast responses requiring more effort. The profile of net utility across the speed continuum is then used to calculate the probability distribution of the various speeds. Generally speaking, the expected probability of a particular response speed depends on its net utility relative to that of alternative speeds.

Thus, the sole dependent variable of the theory is response probability, but here, response refers to intensive properties of the behavior.

Suffice it to say that such a theory will account qualitatively for the more or less optimal performance subjects achieve under conditions of correlated reinforcement. Because incentive is specific to particular response speeds, the terms function gets mapped into the model's incentive profile, distorted somewhat because of generalization of reinforcement effects among similar responses. Thus does the model take account of and adjust its behavior in relation to the terms function.

Besides accounting for correlated reward conditions, the approach also gives a creditable account of why Hull's conventional approach (called "macromolar") worked when it did and failed when it did. Logan points out that almost all conditions of "constant" reward involve an implicit correlation between response speed and interval of reinforcement: the faster the rat runs to the goal-box, the sooner he gets the reward. The micromolar theory predicts that a particular response dimension will improve monotonically with practice only if some dimension of reinforcement improves with that response dimension. Thus, although speed of lever-pressing increases with practice because faster responses bring rewards sooner, the forcefulness of the lever-press does not increase because more forceful responses require more effort and bring no better reward. Logan has also shown how the micromolar theory implies the usual effects upon response speed of variations in drive, amount of reward, and delay of reward in "constant" reward situations. Many more details might be cited in connection with the theory, but we will not elaborate further.

The importance of the micromolar theory has been primarily that of conceptual housecleaning within learning theory. By virtue of Logan's analysis, several conceptual puzzles connected with the problem of how reinforcement shapes behavior have been unraveled and understood. The micromolar approach is general and applies to classical conditioning as well as instrumental conditioning, and it influences the way we talk and think about variables. For example, in cases of classical conditioning the micromolar theory says that the response amplitude learned will be that amplitude elicited by the unconditioned stimulus. This provides a direct interpretation of the fact that amplitude of the conditioned reflex correlates very highly with amplitude of the unconditioned reflex. Thus, the satiated dog that gives a feeble salivary CR has learned his response amplitude just as well as the hungry dog that gives a large CR amplitude; the first dog is merely learning a smaller amplitude response. Similarly, the dog will tend to learn to salivate with a particular latency proportional to the CS-US interval. The micromolar approach has been quite useful too in interpreting the influence of various Skinnerian schedules of reinforcement upon rate of responding (see Chapter 7). At least some schedules may be viewed as more or less inexact terms functions which correlate probability of reinforcement with interresponse time. For example, variable interval schedules generate slow response rates, and this may be explained as due to the differential reinforcement of long interresponse times. Recent theoretical work by Shimp (1969) provides a "utility" sort of account of schedule performance, which supposes the animal to select among a set of interresponse times so as to maximize his momentary expected utility.

Moreover, the micromolar approach makes somewhat better contact than did the older approach with the learning involved in so many of our everyday performances. Reinforcing consequences typically depend not only upon whether a response is made but also upon whether it is made at the right time, at the right place, at the correct pace or intensity, and so on. In fact, it is difficult to imagine human situations in which the payoff does not depend in some way—such as in amount, delay, or probability—upon the skillfulness with which the response is made. The micromolar theory treats these temporal and intensive aspects of responding as part of what gets learned. In this respect, the treatment of the response is made more comparable to the conventional treatment of the stimulus, where we distinguish quantitative as well as qualitative variations. Just as an 80 decibel and a 50 decibel sound are different stimuli, so also a shout and a whisper are different vocal responses. In this manner, the descriptive level of our theory is brought more in line with the realities of many learning situations. The micromolar theory of Logan now provides us with the means of analyzing how the learning of differentiated, skillful responses occurs, where previously within the classical tradition no relevant theory had been articulated.

With this section, we close out the discussion of neo-Hullians and their contributions. Hullian theory has clearly been very successful in gaining the allegiance of many productive contemporary psychologists. The ones explicitly mentioned here are but a handful of a rather significant group of scientists working with a Hullian orientation. It is still to a rather high degree a theory based on "animal-learning" results and has not played a large role in current approaches to human memory. But that may be because of predispositions of the respective investigators and because different problems are being attacked in the main by the two areas. We turn now to our final section evaluating Hull's position.

ESTIMATE OF HULL'S POSITION

Hull's Position on Typical Problems

Because he was willing to face the problems of learning posed by others as well as those which he set himself, it is possible to assign Hull a position on the representative problems chosen as the basis for comparing the different points of view.

1. Capacity. A volume on individual differences which Hull had been working on was not completed by the time of his death. He published but a single paper on the problem (1945), and did not carry the analysis much further in his final book. Individual differences in capacity will be reflected in the constants that appear in the behavioral laws. Once these are under control, it will be possible to make fundamental attacks on such problems as that of the relationship between learning and persistent individual differences.

2. Practice. Mere contiguous repetition does nothing but generate inhibition; all improvement depends upon reinforcement. Hull is in this respect in agreement with Thorndike and Skinner, and opposed to Guthrie. Because the *amount* of reinforcement does not affect habit strength, provided some minimum amount is present, the number of reinforcements is the basic variable in acquiring habit strength. Spence, in contrast, held to a strict Guthrian contiguity position.

3. Motivation.   The basic paradigm for reinforcement lies in need reduction, as when food relieves the body's need for sustenance, or when escape saves the organism from injury. Thus the primary reinforcing quality of reward and of punishment is the same: food reward relieves hunger tension, escape from shock reduces shock tension. While these are the underlying biological facts, the reinforcement itself is mediated by stimulus reduction, that is, by reducing the stimuli associated with the drive, rather than by satisfying the drive itself. Secondary reinforcement can be provided by any stimulus regularly associated with primary reinforcement. More complicated relationships involving anxiety, avoidance, expectation, frustration, conflict, may be derived from the more primitive principles of primary and secondary reinforcement.

Drive is related in a complex way to learning: (1) it provides the basis for both primary and secondary reinforcement, (2) it activates habit strength into reaction potential, and (3) it provides differential internal stimuli that guide behavior.

4. Understanding.   The organism's own responses furnish the surrogates for ideas. The fractional antedating goal-response (r_G) provides stimuli (s_G) whose sole function, in some instances, is to guide behavior. Responses that provide such stimuli are called "pure stimulus acts." Ideas thus have the substantive quality that Guthrie also assigns to them. Two intermediate mechanisms emerge as important in meeting the problems of behavior in spatial contexts and in problem-solving generally. These are the principle of the gradient of reinforcement, extended to include objects perceived at a distance, and the habit-family hierarchy which permits the maximum utilization of past experience in the solving of present problems. Both principles depend for their effectiveness upon aroused fractional antedating responses, and upon discriminations among the stimuli that these responses produce.

5. Transfer.   There are two aspects to transfer: equivalence of stimuli and equivalence of responses. Hull explains equivalence of stimuli either on the basis of primary generalization, or by means of secondary generalization mediated by stimulus-producing responses. Equivalence of responses depends in part upon response oscillation, and the generalization there involved. It depends also on the organization of responses into hierarchies by way of the habit-family hierarchy; all responses in the hierarchy have in the past led to the same goal, so that they are in that respect equivalent.

6. Forgetting.   In the volume on rote learning, the decay of excitation is postulated by Hull and his associates to occur according to a kind of law of disuse, making forgetting a function of time. He reaffirmed this position in one of the corollaries of the 1943 book, but did not provide for it in his postulate set (1943, p. 296). There is no reference to forgetting as such in the

1952 book—the only references are to the *rise* in the curve of reminiscence, without discussion of the subsequent fall. The only acquired function that decays systematically with the passage of time is reactive inhibition (I_R). However, Hull's theory is capable of representing the "response competition" and "unlearning" mechanisms popular in the contemporary interference theory of forgetting (see Chapter 9).

It is pertinent to refer here to Hull's own summary of the basic principles as he perceived them, after completing the system reported in his final book. He listed and described eight *automatic adaptive behavior mechanisms* (1952a, pp. 347–350):

1. Inborn response tendencies $(_sU_R)$ provide the first automatic mechanisms for adapting to emergency situations.
2. The primitive capacity to learn is the second mechanism, "a slightly slower means of adaptation to less acute situations."
3. The antedating defense reaction, which is learned and then moved forward by stimulus generalization, provides the third adaptive mechanism.
4. The extinction of useless acts, negative response learning, is the fourth mechanism.
5. Trial-and-error learning is the fifth mechanism.
6. Discrimination learning is the sixth mechanism.
7. A second type of antedating defense reaction, depending on the persistence of stimulus traces (rather than upon generalization, as in the case of a perceived dangerous object), is the seventh mechanism.
8. The fractional antedating reaction (r_G), with its proprioceptive stimulus correlate (s_G), provides for the "automatic (stimulus) guidance of organismic behavior to goals." Hull ascribes particular importance to this mechanism when he writes:

> Further study of this major automatic device presumably will lead to the detailed behavioral understanding of thought and reasoning, which constitute the highest attainment of organic evolution. Indeed the $r_G \rightarrow s_G$ mechanism leads in a strictly logical manner into what was formerly regarded as the very heart of the psychic: interest, planning, foresight, foreknowledge, expectancy, purpose, and so on. (1952a, p. 350).

How Satisfactory a System Did Hull Leave?

Hull's system had many points of superiority over other contemporary psychological systems. It was at once comprehensive and detailed, theoretical yet empirically quantitative. It is easy to locate faults within it because it is so carefully worked out, so explicit and mathematical that its errors of incompleteness or inconsistency are easily brought into focus. A theory expressed solely in the ordinary literary language may sound very plausible because the gaps are glossed over through cogent illustrations. A theory such as Hull's calls attention to itself whenever it jumps a gap. A severe critique by Koch (1954) capitalizes on this relative explicitness of Hull's theory. In criticizing Hull's theory we must not lose sight of the fact that, with all its weaknesses, it was a major achievement.

We do well to think of Hull's system as really twofold. On the one hand, he embarked on a bold and comprehensive theory of behavior, a theory he hoped would serve as a basis for much of social science. On the other hand, he was experimenting with a very precise miniature system, with determinate constants based on controlled experimentation. He attempted to combine these two enterprises at once, and was not very skilled at distinguishing between what he accomplished on a large scale and what on a small scale, for he wanted the whole to be one system.

On the large scale, when dealing with behavior in free space, problem-solving, and ideas, Hull made skillful use of peripheral mechanisms, particularly the hypothesized r_G-s_G sequence. By interlocking these goal anticipations into other features of his system, particularly through the gradient of reinforcement and the habit-family hierarchy, he was able to make large-scale deductions of familiar forms of behavior. When moving on this large-scale level, the theory was very "molar" indeed, and almost no efforts were made to pin down precisely the kinds of anticipatory movements (chewing movements, bodily postures) that would serve as the tangible base for the important fractional antedating response. The large-scale deductions, built on r_G, do not require any one special theory of learning, so long as goal anticipation can be achieved by that theory.

When Hull was operating on a smaller scale and attempting to become precise and quantitative, he became highly particularistic, confining many of the later postulates and corollaries to the results of single experiments done with rat bar-pressing in a Skinner box modified so that a latency measure could be secured. He became so preoccupied with this quantification that he failed to distinguish between this exercise in miniature-system construction and the larger task on which he was simultaneously engaged. It would have been preferable to present the tentative generalization and then separately to offer the quantitative evidence as illustrative. But this is a stylistic defect of Hull as a system-maker, not a basic conceptual defect of the theory.

It must be acknowledged that Hull's system, for its time, was the best there was—not necessarily the one nearest to psychological reality, not necessarily the one whose generalizations were the most likely to endure—but the one worked out in the greatest detail, with the most conscientious effort to be quantitative throughout and at all points closely in touch with empirical tests. Furthermore, it may well be said to have been the most influential of the theories between 1930 and 1950, judging from the experimental and theoretical studies engendered by it, whether in its defense, its amendment, or its refutation.

Various objective estimates exist of Hull's influence upon psychology. For example, during the decade of 1941–1950 in the *Journal of Experimental Psychology* and the *Journal of Comparative and Physiological Psychology*, 40 percent of all experimental studies and 70 percent of those in the areas of learning and motivation referred to one or more of Hull's books or papers (Spence, 1952), while in the *Journal of Abnormal and Social Psychology* during the years 1949–1952 there were 105 citations of Hull's *Principles of Behavior*, and the next most frequently cited book was mentioned but 25 times (Ruja, 1956).

Perhaps the most striking testament to Hull's influence is the talent and productivity of the large number of "neo-Hullians" whom he enlisted into the task of developing, extending, and applying his theory. Men such as

Spence, Miller, Mowrer, Judson Brown, Grice, Amsel, Wagner, and Logan (and their students) have been dominating figures in American psychology over the years since 1940; they have significantly altered the intellectual landscape of learning theory. Their achievements and accomplishments are a tribute to the inspirational example set by Clark Hull and to the theoretical fertility of the system of concepts he molded together.

SUPPLEMENTARY READINGS

The four books which represent Hull's behavior theory are:
HULL, C. L. et al. (1940) *Mathematico-deductive theory of rote learning.*
HULL, C. L. (1943) *Principles of behavior.*
HULL, C. L. (1951) *Essentials of behavior.*
HULL, C. L. (1952a) *A behavior system.*

A review of the theory is:
LOGAN, F. A. (1959) The Hull-Spence approach. In S. Koch (Ed.), *Psychology: A study of a science.* Vol. 2.

A popular paperback explaining learning from a Hullian viewpoint is:
LOGAN, F. A. (1970). *Fundamentals of learning and motivation.*

For a detailed and searching criticism of Hull's system from the standpoint of the logic of science, see:
KOCH, S. (1954) Clark L. Hull. In W. K. Estes et al. *Modern learning theory*, pp. 1–176.

A rare opportunity exists to follow the course of Hull's thinking through excerpts from the 73 "idea books" that he left. The first of these was begun in October 1902, when Hull was only 18, and the last entry was made on April 21, 1952, 18 days before he died. They were intensely personal, and not intended for publication; as Ammons (1962) points out, it is instructive to compare the passages with the autobiographical sketch, which was of course intended to be read. The pertinent references are:
HULL, C. L. (1952b) Autobiography. In H. S. Langfeld et al. *A history of psychology in autobiography.* Vol. 4, pages 143–162.
AMMONS, R. B. (1962) Psychology of the scientist: II. Clark L. Hull and his "Idea books." *Perceptual Motor Skills*, 15, 800–802.
HAYS, RUTH (1962) Psychology of the scientist: III. Introduction to "Passages from the 'Idea Books' of Clark L. Hull." *Perceptual Motor Skills*, 15, 803–806.
HULL, C. L. (1962) Psychology of the scientist: IV. Passages from the "Idea Books" of Clark L. Hull. *Perceptual Motor Skills*, 15, 807–882.

Skinner's Operant Conditioning

In a series of papers beginning in 1930, B. F. Skinner (b. 1904) proposed a formulation of behavior which arose out of observations of animal performance in a type of experiment that he invented: the bar-pressing activity of a rat in a specially designed box called (by others) the Skinner box. Skinner believed that, in this setting, most of the important concepts of behavioral control could be examined and revealed. The success of his analytic procedures and demonstrations has appealed to a generation of experimental psychologists, and has attracted a very productive band of "followers." What Skinner did was to isolate a few highly repeatable phenomena in conditioning—many of which Pavlov and Thorndike had studied and named before him—and then proceed to use these phenomena as a basis for concepts used in analyzing more complex forms of behavior. It is this collection of concepts, principles, and distinctions along with a particular philosophy of science and research strategy which characterizes the "Skinnerian" approach to psychology. A basic faith is that complex behavior (thinking, problem-solving), when properly analyzed, will be interpretable in terms of the complex interplay of these elementary concepts and principles. This faith is very much like that which motivated Clark Hull's efforts or those of most other learning theorists. But whereas Hull was attracted to intervening variables and hypothetico-deductive theorizing, Skinner has rejected "theoretical constructs" as unnecessary and has instead pursued either informal analyses (e.g., of cultural practices) or experimental analyses of various complex behaviors (e.g., reading).

Skinner is also one of the most sophisticated and persuasive protagonists of the *behaviorist methodology* that psychology has ever seen. He rejects mentalistic or "cognitive" explanations of behavior, or explanations attributing behavior causation to "inner psychic" forces of any kind. Skinner argues that we understand a piece of behavior only when we have learned how to predict and control that behavior. Mentalistic explanations are worthless, according to Skinner, because they do not tell us how to manipulate variables so as to control the behavior. Such mentalistic explanations are incomplete, and their acceptance simply postpones doing a proper functional analysis of the behavior. A "functional analysis" of a given behavior means that we attempt to identify and isolate the environmental variables of which the behavior is a lawful function.

Although the early experimental work by Skinner was carried out with rats pressing levers for food pellets in a Skinner box, the experimental base of the analysis has been gradually extended to other animals, to humans of all ages, and to situations and behaviors differing increasingly from the original base (e.g., to "teaching machines" and "behavioral psychotherapy"). Skinner has also defended a particularly compelling behavioristic position regarding the analysis of common-sense psychological terms such as *self, self-control, awareness, thinking, problem-solving, composing, will power*, and many of the psychodynamic concepts such as *repression, rationalization*, and other ego defense mechanisms. He has, in addition, propounded a particular analysis of *verbal behavior*, for the listener as well as for the speaker, which has been quite controversial. He has taken his ideas a step further in the analysis of the notions of *free will, inner determination*, and *social values*, and has discussed how one might arrange cultural practices by design so as to engineer a society that is "better" according to certain humanitarian values. For this reason, and for his books *Walden two* and *Beyond freedom and dignity*, he is probably better known by the public at large than any other contemporary psychologist.

We cannot hope to review in this chapter Skinner's many contributions from a career spanning over 40 years of scientific activities. We will tend toward the historical view, emphasizing Skinner's early collection of concepts and principles. Later we shall delve briefly into the Skinnerian analysis of several complex skills. Skinner's earlier book was *The behavior of organisms* (1938), which introduced the main ideas he was to apply with only slight variation to more complex cases over the next 35 years. The first part of our review refers mainly to this historically significant book.

RESPONDENT AND OPERANT BEHAVIOR

A significant departure from traditional stimulus-response psychology within Skinner's system was the distinction between respondent and operant behavior. Since Watson, stimulus-response psychology had enforced the dictum "no stimulus, no response" by assuming the presence of stimuli when a response occurred even though no stimuli were identifiable. It was not doubted that stimuli were present to elicit such responses, if the experimenter only had means of detecting them. Skinner found this method of forcing facts both undesirable and unnecessary. He proposed that two classes of response be distinguished, a class of *elicited* responses and a class of *emitted* responses.

Respondent and Operant Distinguished

Responses which are elicited by known stimuli are classified as *respondents*. Pupillary constriction to light and the knee jerk to a blow on the patellar tendon serve as convenient illustrations. There is a second class of responses which need not be correlated with any known stimuli. These *emitted* responses are designated *operants*, to distinguish them from respondents. Because operant behavior is not elicited by recognized stimuli, its strength cannot be measured according to the usual laws of the reflex, which are all stated as functions of their eliciting stimuli. Instead, rate of response is used as a measure of operant strength.

An operant may, and usually does. acquire a relation to prior stimulation. In that case it becomes a *discriminated operant*; the stimulus becomes an occasion for the operant behavior, but is not an eliciting stimulus as in the case of a true reflex. A simple illustration of an operant coordinated with a stimulus would be a reaction-time experiment as commonly conducted in the psychological laboratory. The correlation between stimulus and response may easily be changed, as by instructions to depress the key instead of lifting the finger from it. Most human behavior is operant in nature. The behavior of eating a meal, driving a car, writing a letter, shows but little of respondent character.

Two Types of Conditioning

Related to the two types of response are said to be two types of conditioning. The conditioning of respondent behavior is assigned to Type S, because reinforcement is correlated with stimuli. The conditioned stimulus (e.g., a tone) is presented together with the unconditioned stimulus (e.g., food) and thus comes to elicit the response (e.g., salivation). The reinforcing event that interests Skinner is the presentation of the unconditioned stimulus, not the response to it. Pavlov's classical conditioning experiment is said to be of Type S.

Type R is believed to be much more important. This is the conditioning of operant behavior, and the letter R is used to call attention to the important term in the correlation with reinforcement. In this case it is a *response* which is correlated with reinforcement. The experimental example he originally used was lever-pressing. For a hungry organism this response may be strengthened by following it with food. It is not the *sight* of the lever which is important; it is the *pressing* of the lever. The conditioned response does not resemble the response to the reinforcing stimulus; its relationship to the reinforcing stimulus is that the response causes the reinforcer to appear. In operant conditioning, reinforcement cannot follow unless the conditioned response appears; reinforcement is *contingent* upon the response. This is what came to be called instrumental conditioning to distinguish it from the arrangements of classical conditioning (E. R. Hilgard & Marquis, 1940, pp. 51–74). The laws of Type R are not unlike those of Type S, including a law of conditioning and a law of extinction. The law of conditioning of Type R may be compared to Thorndike's law of effect: *if the occurrence of an operant is followed by presentation of a reinforcing stimulus, the strength is increased* (Skinner, 1938, p. 21). Note that the reinforcing situation is defined by its stimulus; nothing is said about satisfying aftereffects or about drive reduction. Skinner suggests further (1938, p. 112) that conditioning of Type S may be limited to autonomic responses, Type R to skeletal behavior.

Recent Doubts

The operant-respondent distinction drawn above was to dominate learning theory for some 30 years. It was called "two-factor" theory, and it laid claim to a number of correspondences. Responses of glands and internal organs (*respondents*) were distinguished (by hypothesis) by being (a) elicited by innate, unconditioned stimuli, (b) controlled by the autonomic nervous system, (c) "involuntary," (d) characterized by minimal response-produced feedback, and most importantly (e) able to be classically conditioned (Type S) but not operantly conditioned (Type R). In stark contrast, responses of striated, peripheral muscles (*operants*) were distinguished by being (a) sometimes emitted, without identifiable stimuli, (b) controlled by the central nervous system, (c) under "voluntary" control, (d) characterized by distinctive proprioceptive feedback, and (e) able to be operantly conditioned but not classically conditioned.

This conceptual cleavage and set of correspondences has come under increasing scrutiny, criticism, and reformulation in recent years (see Rescorla & Solomon, 1967; Terrace, 1973; Staddon & Simmelhag, 1971). Specifically, it is now known that a variety of visceral responses mediated by the autonomic nervous system can be successfully altered by operant conditioning techniques (see N. E. Miller, 1969). Thus, for example, a thirsty dog can learn to salivate or to withhold salivation in order to get a drink of water, or a rat can be taught to make intestinal contractions to an external signal when such contractions are followed by a positive reward. These important findings, of the operant conditioning of allegedly involuntary respondents, will be reviewed in detail in Chapter 15. The present conclusion, however, is that such data indicate the operant-respondent distinction may have outlived its usefulness. Terrace, a "Skinnerian" himself, argues persuasively for modifying "two-factor" theory.

A close analysis of classical conditioning (e.g., the salivary conditioning paradigm) reveals that various skeletal ("operant") responses become associated to the conditioned stimulus, such as orienting to the food well, anticipatory chewing movements, ducking the head down to the food dish, etc.—all of these in addition to the salivary flow that Pavlov measured and talked about (see Zener, 1937). Similarly, in instrumental conditioning, it is clearly established that components of the response elicited by the reinforcer become conditioned and occur in anticipation of it. Thus, as a dog begins to press a lever several times to get food, it will also start to salivate (see Shapiro, 1961; D. R. Williams, 1965). Thus, both operant and respondent behaviors seem to be conditioned in either type of experiment.

The main difference between instrumental and classical conditioning then reduces primarily to one of the *experimental procedure*, the way in which reinforcements (read "unconditioned stimuli") are scheduled. But there are intermediate procedures and undecidable test cases. A nice example is what is called conditioning of "superstitions," a phenomenon first reported by Skinner (1948b) which he discussed in terms of operant reinforcement. Suppose that a hungry pigeon is adapted to eating from a grain hopper in an enclosed box; the feeder is then operated periodically (say, for 3 seconds every 30 seconds) throughout several long experimental sessions. Although reinforcement (feeder presentation) is not contingent upon any particular behavior, the pigeon nonetheless eventually acquires some ritualistic, stereotyped chain of responses which it emits between reinforcements (see also Staddon & Simmelhag, 1971). This is explained as follows: when reinforcement is first delivered, the pigeon is behaving in some way, so this "operant" will be strengthened. It is then more probable that this same behavior, perhaps with small elaborations, will be in progress when the next reinforcement arrives. If so, it is strengthened even further; if not, some other behavior will be strengthened. Eventually the pigeon gets "trapped" into a particular operant sequence, which occurs and is reinforced at just that frequency which will maintain it. Conspicuous superstitious behaviors for a pigeon might include items like "turning sharply to one side, hopping from one foot to the other and back, bowing and scraping, turning around, strutting, and raising the head" (Skinner, 1953, p. 85). There have been many demonstrations of the learning of "superstitions" by human adults exposed to random, noncontingent reinforcement (Wright, 1960), so there is little doubt regarding the effect.

The significance of the "superstition" experiments is to point out that whenever a reinforcement is delivered to an organism, it strengthens whatever operant behavior is in progress at the time. The strengthening effect occurs regardless of whether or not the prevailing operant is truly instrumental in causing the reinforcer; from the organism's viewpoint, temporal contiguity between response and reinforcement is the important factor. Temporal coincidence is interpreted as causality. It is as though the organism believed its superstitious actions were producing the reinforcer.

Curiously, Pavlov (1927) also studied and reported on similar reinforcement contingencies with his dogs, except that he recorded salivation. Every so many minutes (say, 5 minutes) the dog in the experimental stand would be fed, and this cycle was repeated often. Pavlov found that the animal learned eventually to salivate near the expected time for arrival of the food. Because Pavlov thought the sheer passage of time since the last reinforcement became a conditioned stimulus for evoking conditioned salivation, he referred to this arrangement as *temporal conditioning*, a form of classical conditioning.

But since the schedule of events in the superstition experiment and in temporal conditioning are identical, why should we call one "classical" and the other "instrumental" conditioning? Because of the types of responses recorded in the two experiments? But we have just said earlier that many so-called respondents (like salivation) can be conditioned by use of operant reinforcement; similarly, some skeletal responses (like the eye blink and the knee jerk) can be conditioned according to the classical conditioning routine. Thus, the response systems *per se* do not necessarily dictate different laws of learning.

The laws of Type S and Type R conditioning may even be pitted against one another by rewarding the subject for withholding a response to a signal, but in a situation in which the rewarding US elicits the response which is to be withheld. An example of this contingency, devised by F. D. Sheffield (1965), is to reinforce a hungry dog with food only if he does *not* salivate to a signal. Herendeen and Shapiro (1971, 1972) have found successful "operant conditioning" with this procedure. Their dogs learned to "keep their mouth dry" in order to get food. By the end of training, the dogs were withholding salivation and being fed on about 80 percent of the CS trials. A two-factor theorist might argue either that 80 percent reinforced trials are insufficient to sustain a classical CR or that the classical CR that does develop will be weak and will oscillate through small acquisition-extinction cycles in tracking the occurrence and nonoccurrence of the US across trials. But Herendeen and Shapiro ran controls which excluded such explanations. First, yoked control animals receiving the same sequence of food and nonfood trials as their experimental mates earned nonetheless showed a high level of salivary conditioning, so the 80 percent reinforcement schedule was rich enough to sustain a very good classical CR when the negative-response contingency was not in force. Second, trial-by-trial analyses revealed that animals trained with the negative-response contingency were increasingly likely *not* to salivate to the signal the longer was the preceding run of trials on which they were reinforced for not salivating. This is just the reverse of the sequential effect expected by the law of Type S conditioning. It would thus appear that Type S conditioning is not a necessary consequence of CS-US pairings in time; nor is the "last response" performed to the CS (viz., salivation) the one that is strengthened.

The view that seems to be suggested by these considerations (see Terrace, 1973) is a return to the one-factor theory of reinforcement advocated originally by Hull (see Chapter 6). That is, classical conditioning involves the same principle of reinforcement ("reward learning") as does operant conditioning, except that the recorded response and its means of initial elicitation differ in the two cases. There are several ways to conceive of how food as a reward could strengthen anticipatory salivation. First, one could simply say that eating food both elicits and simultaneously reinforces ("rewards") salivation. Second, we could suppose that the anticipatory CR is differentially reinforced because it makes the following US more rewarding (than if the CR had not occurred). Thus, on this hypothesis, anticipatory salivation enhances the taste, palatability, and rewarding value of the food which follows. This view, proposed earlier by Perkins (1955), has much to recommend it, especially in those cases where the preparatory act reduces the unpleasantness of an aversive stimulus. Perkins also shows how this assumption, of appropriate preparatory responses enhancing reward values, can explain the learning of "observing responses" which have no obvious utility other than to provide information about upcoming reinforcing events which prepares the animal for them (see G. H. Bower, McLean, & Meacham, 1966). A third hypothesis is to suppose that the anticipatory CR in the appetitive reward situation is like a superstitiously reinforced operant, except that it has the additional advantage of having a higher "operant level" than other behaviors because the US is directly eliciting the CR as one of its components. For instance, since the dog may still be salivating somewhat from eating on the preceding trial, the next CS-plus-reward trial occurs while some salivation is in progress, and this will strengthen salivation much as it does the rituals in the "superstition" experiments.

The student may be wondering why there is this continual insistence on "reward"-like effects in these interpretations of classical conditioning. Why, he will ask, do we not just say that, following pairings, the bell makes the dog think of the food which is to follow, and that this thought or image makes his mouth water? The problem with this anthropomorphic view is that it does not explain enough difficult cases—for instance, that invertebrates with most elementary nervous systems ("incapable of thoughts or images") can be classically conditioned; or that responses of internal organs can be classically conditioned (as CRs) to stimulation of other internal organs (as CS) without the apparent intervention of cognitive awareness (Bykov, 1957); or that in conditioning experiments with humans, verbal descriptions of the CS-US contingencies (presumably an index of subjects' awareness) can bear almost any trial-by-trial relation to the development of the CR measured as a fractional part of the response to the US—preceding it in time or following it, or one occurring without the other at all (see Razran, 1971). As an example of the latter, if we repeatedly present a tone paired with a light flash (which elicits pupillary constriction), it is exceedingly difficult to obtain reliable pupillary conditioning despite the fact that the person can cognitively describe the tone-light pairings. In order to get conditioning, the US must apparently be "emotional" in some sense, either positive or negative; neutral events which simply reliably elicit a response apparently do not produce reliable classical conditioning (see G. A. Kimble, 1961, p. 51 for some review). For such reasons, psychologists are somewhat skeptical of the "ideational" theory of classical conditioning.

REINFORCEMENT OF AN OPERANT

To study the quantitative relationships within operant conditioning, Skinner designed a special apparatus suitable for use with white rats. It consists essentially of a darkened soundproof box in which the rat is placed. There is a small brass lever within the compartment which, if pressed, delivers a pellet of food. The lever is connected with a recording system which produces a graphical tracing of the number of lever-pressings plotted against the length of time the rat is in the box. By a carefully controlled handling of the animals, remarkably consistent and "lawful" results can be obtained. Modifications of the experiment can be introduced so that food is not delivered every time the lever is depressed. The consequences of doing this and of making other changes in the situation have been systematically reported. The "pigeon box" is a corresponding arrangement for obtaining a response record as a pigeon pecks at a lighted plastic key mounted on the wall at head height and is reinforced by receiving grain.

The consequence of reinforcing the operant is an increase in its rate or probability of occurrence per unit time. Response rate is an appropriate measure in the "free responding" situation in which the lever or response key is continuously available. Depending on the scheduling of reinforcements and many other factors, this response rate can vary over a large range, and one is interested in what will be the "steady-state" level of performance produced and maintained by particular reinforcement contingencies. We shall return to this topic later.

Regarding acquisition of this simple operant, Skinner offered the opinion that it would occur in "one trial" or instantaneously if the extraneous factors were eliminated and if the animal were appropriately prepared for the "one trial." For example, earlier experiences in the box would habituate irrelevant exploratory or fearful behaviors, and earlier "feeder training" would condition the hungry animal to approach the food cup and eat at the sound of the food dispenser discharging a food pellet into the cup. If these behavioral components have been taken care of before the lever is introduced and connected to the feeder, then conditioning of lever-pressing is indeed very rapid, if not instantaneous. According to Skinner (as for Guthrie, see Chapter 4), lever-press conditioning typically appears gradual because it is a chain of component behaviors, and "learning curves" reveal more about the "problem-box" and the conditions of prior preparation than they reveal about basic "laws."

Just as reinforcing an operant strengthens it, so nonreinforcement following the response is alleged to weaken it, and a prolonged series of nonreinforced responses results in a gradual lowering of response rate in the process called "experimental extinction." The animal stops pressing because this action is no longer followed by reinforcement. Skinner, as did others, at first (1938, p. 26) thought that the number of responses emitted during extinction would be a measure of operant strength; however, his own studies of intermittent reinforcement led him to abandon that idea. He came to realize (e.g., 1950), perhaps sooner than others, that we can differentially train an organism either to "resist" or to "desist quickly" in extinction depending on how rewards and nonrewards are scheduled during training.

Positive and Negative Primary Reinforcers

A reinforcer is defined by its effects. Any stimulus is a reinforcer if it increases the probability of a response. The stimuli that happen to act as reinforcers fall into two classes (Skinner, 1953, p. 73):

1. A *positive reinforcer* is a stimulus which, when applied following an operant response, strengthens the probability of that response. Food, water, sexual contact, classify as positive reinforcers for appropriately deprived individuals.

2. A *negative reinforcer* is a stimulus which, when removed following an operant response, strengthens the probability of that response. A loud noise, a very bright light, extreme heat or cold, electric shock, classify as negative reinforcers. They are also called *aversive stimuli*. Notice that the types of reinforcers are classified according to whether their presentation or their removal strengthens a preceding operant. A negative reinforcer or aversive stimulus is one for which the organism will learn something to escape it. As defined here, punishment is *not* negative reinforcement. Punishment is rather an experimental arrangement in which presentation of an aversive stimulus is contingent upon a designated response. The effects of punishment were interpreted by Skinnerians (see Dinsmoor, 1954, 1955; Azrin & Holz, 1966) in terms similar to those of Mowrer and Miller described in Chapter 6; the punishing aversive stimulus converts the proprioceptive feed-

back from the punished response into "conditioned aversive stimuli," so that when the response begins to occur later, the feedback from the incipient movements are aversive, and therefore the response is interrupted. There has been recent disenchantment with this viewpoint (see Herrnstein, 1969; Schoenfeld, 1970), but this is not the place to detail these recent developments. Skinner noted, of course, that the arrangement of contingencies in punishment is just the opposite of reinforcement (although the *effects* are not opposite), so that two main cases arise: (1) the presentation of a negative reinforcer, and (2) the removal of a positive reinforcer.

Other psychologists have been interested in the question, Why is a reinforcer reinforcing? But this question has not been of much interest to Skinner. He is interested in why behavior changes, and finds reinforcers importantly involved. He rather tentatively accepts an explanation of reinforcement in terms of evolutionary biology, but he does not find it of much help in the detailed functional analysis of what actually occurs (1953, pp. 81–84).

Schedules of Reinforcement

The reinforcement of operant behavior in ordinary life is not regular and uniform. The fisherman does not hook a fish with every cast of the line, and the farmer does not always receive a harvest from his planting, yet they continue to fish and to plant. Hence the problem of maintaining or strengthening a response through *intermittent reinforcement* is more than a laboratory curiosity. Skinner has explored extensively two main classes of intermittent reinforcement, now called *interval schedules* and *ratio schedules.*

Fixed interval schedules are arranged using a clock: reinforcement is provided for the first response to occur after the lapse of a designated (fixed) interval of time, measured from the preceding reinforcement or from the onset of a "trial stimulus." Typical intervals studied range from 30 seconds to 10 minutes or so. This arrangement, earlier named "periodic reconditioning" or "periodic reinforcement" (both archaic now), virtually controls the number of reinforcements delivered per hour to the animal. Fixed interval (or FI, as it is abbreviated) schedules produce lawful and orderly results. A first result found by Skinner (1938) was that his rats tended to put out an approximately constant number of responses per reinforcement (about 18–20 lever-presses in one study). Thus the average rate of responding, expressed as responses per minute, would be about twice as high when the animal is working on a 2-minute FI (abbreviated FI 2′) as when he is working on a 4-minute FI. A second finding was what is called the "FI scallop," indicated by a zero rate of responding immediately after a reinforcement, then a gradual acceleration to a high response rate just near the time at which a reinforcement becomes available. The FI scallop develops gradually with continued exposure to a given FI, and is a clear indication of time discrimination. That is, on an FI, reinforcement is not available right after a reinforcement; but as "subjective" time goes by since the previous reinforcement, the animal's response becomes increasingly likely to be reinforced. With continued training, the temporal discrimination becomes sharper, but there are rather clear limitations on how closely a time interval can be estimated. This scalloping can be eliminated by *variable interval* (VI) schedules, in which a range of intervals from very short to very long are used in a random, variable order. In VI, average performance depends mainly on the arithmetic average interval, varying in inverse proportion. The pause after reinforcement tends to be eliminated in VI, especially if very short intervals are included in the set. Under such schedules, the average performance is remarkably stable and uniform. An illustration is found in Figure 7.1. Because of the stability and reproducibility of VI performance, it tends to be used as a baseline in assessing behavioral effects of diverse variables that may be introduced into the situation (e.g., drive level, punishment, drugs, etc.). Responses trained on VI schedules are also unusually resistant to extinction; it is not unusual, for instance, to observe pigeons responding more than 10,000 times during extinction following VI training. Resistance to extinction depends roughly on the mean and maximal interval in the VI program.

The other major class of reinforcement schedule is *fixed ratio* (abbreviated FR), in which reinforcement is provided for the n-th response after the preceding reinforcement. Typical values of n are in the range of 10 to 200, although ratios as high as 1000 or more can be achieved with responses that are relatively effortless. Typically, an animal is not placed directly onto a high-ratio schedule, but rather is gradually "worked up" to it from lower ratio requirements to prevent early extinction.

Responding on ratio schedules tends to be very fast (called "bursts" in laboratory jargon), because the faster the animal responds the sooner he gets the reward (or the higher is his rate of reinforcement per unit time). As with the FI scallop, responding within an FR segment tends to be two-valued: a long pause after reinforcement followed by resumption of a very high response rate that is maintained until the ratio requirement is fulfilled and reinforcement is attained. The pause after reinforcement is longer with larger ratios, and is affected by many variables (emotion, drive level, drugs, etc.), whereas the terminal response rate seems relatively fixed and insensitive to such variables. The pause after reinforcement is likened by Skinner to "abulia," the inability to expend effort. An analogy would be the student who has just finished a term paper, perhaps in a burst of speed as the dead-

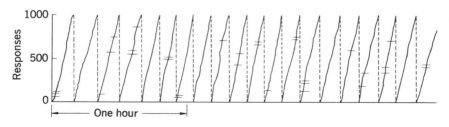

Figure 7.1. Responses within variable interval reinforcement. The curves are of the pecking responses of an individual pigeon reinforced at intervals ranging from 10 seconds to 21 minutes, but averaging 5 minutes. Each of the sloping lines represent 1000 responses; the pen resets to zero after each 1000. The whole record represents some 20,000 responses in about 3 hours, with an average of 12 reinforcements per hour. Each reinforcement is represented by a horizontal dash. (From B. F. Skinner, Are theories of learning necessary? *Psychological Review*, 1950, *57*, p. 208. Copyright 1950 by the American Psychological Association. Reprinted by permission.)

line approaches, and then finds it difficult to start work on a new assignment. In fixed ratio performance, response-produced feedback accumulated by the current response count becomes a discriminative predictor of reinforcement for the organism. A variety of experiments (e.g., Mechner, 1958) shows that animals can use their response count on lever *A* as a discriminative stimulus for switching over to pressing lever *B* in order to get a reinforcer made available by completion of the count on *A*.

As with the fixed interval, the pause after reinforcement on FR may be eliminated by adopting a *variable ratio* schedule, in which the ratio varies randomly from small to large. Because the probability of reinforcement for any response is approximately constant independent of the count, a uniform rate of responding ensues. The rate is typically high because fast bursts of responses tend to "run into" reinforcement quicker, and so are differentially reinforced. For example, on such schedules a pigeon may respond as rapidly as five pecks per second and keep up this rate for hours.

The possible variations in schedules of reinforcement are almost unlimited; Ferster and Skinner (1957) investigated the long-term effects of a large number of schedules in their book *Schedules of reinforcement*. Table 7.1 lists 18 of these schedules along with their code designations. It is difficult to briefly summarize the tremendous catalog of systematic data which Ferster

Table 7.1   **Schedules of reinforcement. (After Ferster & Skinner, 1957, pp. 3– 7; also Chapter 13.)**

Name and Code Abbreviation	*Characterization of Program of Reinforcement*
I. *Nonintermittent schedules*	
1. Continuous reinforcement (crf)	Every emitted response reinforced
2. Extinction (ext)	No response reinforced
II. *Schedules of intermittent reinforcement*	
3. Fixed ratio (FR)	A given ratio of response to reinforcements is indicated by the addition of a number to the letters FR. Thus in FR 100 the one-hundredth response after the preceding reinforcement is reinforced.
4. Variable ratio (VR)	A random series of ratios lying between arbitrary values with a fixed mean (as in VR 100).
5. Fixed interval (FI)	The first response occurring after a given interval of time since the preceding reinforcement is reinforced. The designation, as in FI 5′, is normally in minutes.
6. Variable interval (VI)	A random series of intervals lying between arbitrary values and with a fixed mean, as in VI 5′, expressed in minutes.
7. Alternative (alt)	Reinforcement is delivered according to a fixed ratio or fixed interval schedule, whichever is satisfied first; designated as in alt FI 5′ FR 300. If 300 responses occur before 5 minutes is over, reinforcement will occur; if not, reinforcement will occur when 5 minutes have elapsed.

Name and Code Abbreviation	*Characterization of Program of Reinforcement*
8. Conjunctive (conj)	The requirements of both the fixed ratio and the fixed interval must be satisfied; for example, in conj FI 5' FR 300, reinforcement is contingent on at least 5 minutes of time and at least 300 responses.
9. Interlocking (interlock)	This is a decreasing ratio program in which the number of responses required per reinforcement decreases steadily with time after each reinforcement. The organism is, in effect, penalized for responding rapidly enough to be reinforced early, for then more responses are required for reinforcement than if his responses are spread out in time.
10. Tandem (tand)	A single reinforcement is contingent upon the successive completion of two units, each of which would have been reinforced according to a single schedule. Thus in FI 10' FR 5, reinforcement depends upon a response after 10 minutes have passed, followed by 5 additional responses, whatever their spacing.
11. Chained (chain)	In a tandem schedule there is no change in the stimulus when one of the programs is completed, while in chaining a conspicuous change is introduced. Thus the color of the spot being pecked may change after the FI requirement has been satisfied, but reinforcement is delayed until the FR component has been satisfied.
12. Adjusting (adj)	The value of the interval or the ratio changes systematically as a consequence of reinforcement. (Distinguished from an interlocking schedule because there the change occurs according to responding *between* reinforcements.)
13. Multiple (mult)	Reinforcement is programmed by two or more schedules, usually alternating at random. Change from one schedule to another is signaled by a change in the stimulus that endures as long as the schedule is in force.
14. Mixed (mix)	Similar to multiple, except that no stimuli are correlated with the schedules; the shift from one schedule to another has to be detected from the pattern of reinforcement.
15. Interpolated (inter)	A small block of one schedule may be introduced into a background of another schedule, substituting for that other schedule for a few minutes within, say, a 6-hour period under other standard conditions.
16. Concurrent (conc)	Two or more schedules independently arranged but operating at the same time, reinforcements being set up by both.
III. *Differential Reinforcement Schedules*	
17. Of low rates (DRL)	A response is reinforced only if it follows the preceding one by at least a criterion time.
18. Of high rates (DRH)	A response is reinforced only if it follows the preceding one by less than a criterion time.

and Skinner collected, although the asymptotic performance maintained by a given schedule is typically easily understood in terms of familiar concepts of stimulus discrimination and of reinforcement strengthening the specific momentary *rate* of response (or interresponse time) which prevailed at the moment reinforcement was delivered.

To illustrate just a few examples of schedule-induced performances, let us consider a DRL schedule and a tandem FIFR schedule. On DRL, say of 10 seconds, a response will be reinforced only if at least 10 seconds have elapsed since the last response. If the response occurs too soon, the timer is reset and another wait of at least 10 seconds must occur before a response will be rewarded. DRL schedules generate *timing behavior*; the animal typically learns to go through a variety of superstitious rituals, which eventuate in a response at around the criterion time. The usual analysis of DRL performance as well as other schedule performances (see Morse, 1966; Shimp, 1969) treats the time between successive responses—the interresponse time or IRT —as the micromolar unit of analysis, as Logan (1960) does in his micromolar theory (see Chapter 6). That is, most schedules are presumed to impose a "terms function," relating some differential probability of reinforcement to the different IRTs. This reinforcement probability, along with other factors, affects the "strength" of each IRT, and the animal is viewed as choosing (following each response) which IRT will be the next one he will emit. Without going into details, such theories expect obvious sorts of "adjustments" to DRL schedules, since only IRTs exceeding the criterion time are reinforced.

Consider next performance on tandem FIFR. Suppose the initial FI component is long, say 6 minutes, after which the first response terminates the FI component and begins a fixed ratio, say a small one of 5 responses, after the completion of which reinforcement occurs, and the program resets to the long FI component. Now, on a simple FI 6′ schedule, a hungry pigeon might average, say, 100 responses per 6-minute interval (just to pick a hypothetical figure for illustration). But when the small FR 5 is added as a requirement at the end, as the tandem FI 6′ FR 5 does, the response rate does not simply go up to 105 per 6-minute interval; rather it increases almost threefold, to around 300 responses per 6-minute interval. How are we to understand such a huge effect on behavior of what appears to be a trivial change in the requirements for reinforcement? Again, we must attend carefully to the differences between the FI 6′ and the tand FI 6′ FR 5 schedules in terms of the momentary rate of reinforcing that is likely to prevail at the moment of reinforcement. A simple FI schedule differentially reinforces long IRTs, since the longer one waits after his prior response the more likely it is that the interval has timed out. The small ratio requirement tacked onto the end of the fixed interval alters matters: now reinforcement is most likely when a burst or run of fast responses occur, since they will meet the FR 5 requirement. The result is that "bursts" of 3 to 8 responses get strengthened as a unit. Thus, in the FI 6′ portion of the tandem schedule, the bird still shows an FI scallop ("timing"), except that now when he responds he does so in bursts of key-pecks. The result is thus a large increase in the overall rate of responding when it is counted according to single pecks.

These are just a few examples of schedule-induced performances and how they can be reasonably analyzed in terms of S-R reinforcement theory. Just as one can examine performance maintained by a given schedule, so can one examine *preferential choice* between two schedules, each correlated with a different response key. Herrnstein (1970), using "response strength" constructs somewhat like those of Hull, has shown how percentage choice between two concurrent VI schedules (each associated with two different keys) comes to match the relative rates of reinforcement for pecking on the two keys.

It is worth noting that the reliability and regularity of long-term schedule performance is striking. The performance is also repeatable—that is, one can shift the animal temporarily to other schedules, but when he is shifted back to the original schedule he eventually attains nearly the same steady-state ("asymptotic") performance as he had before. It is because of this "recoverability" of the steady-state performance induced by a given schedule that the favored experimental procedure for Skinnerians is to run each of a few animals through all experimental conditions repeatedly in blocked sequence (see Sidman, 1960). In this way, for example, one might map out a complete function for each individual subject relating the independent variable (say, size of the fixed ratio requirement) to a dependent variable (say, the average pause after reinforcement in steady state). The procedure has a great deal to recommend it when one is dealing with steady states rather than acquisition ("transient") phenomena. Sidman (1960) provides the most persuasive arguments for use of this research strategy throughout *all* behavioral studies, not simply studies of schedules.

A further behavioral technique of widespread usefulness is what Ferster and Skinner (1957) call "multiple schedules." This simply means that the organism can be trained concurrently to respond appropriately to several different schedules, each occurring many times in random alternation with the other schedule components and each associated with a distinctive discriminative stimulus, such as differently colored lights back-projected onto the pigeon's pecking key. Skinner has trained a pigeon to as many as *nine* different performances (key-pecking patterns) controlled successively during the same session by nine different stimuli. For example, in a three-component multiple schedule, a pigeon might have an FI 1' when the key was green for 2 minutes, an FI 2' when the key was white, and an FI 4' when the key was red, these three components occurring in random order in, say, 8-minute blocks. Because the animals tend to behave discriminatively and appropriately to each schedule component, one can in this way plot out a functional relation for each individual, say relating responses per reinforcement to length of the FI. The procedure has much to recommend it (see Sidman, 1960). The problem with the method, clearly recognized by all, is that it is unusable when there are clear *interactions* between the several schedules which are successively controlling the response. An interaction means that performance on schedule *A* depends on what is the schedule *B* with which it alternates within an experimental session. Although such interactions are themselves a topic of interest (as in "behavioral contrast"), they do call into question the interpretation of the functional relations observed by use of multiple schedules.

Conditioned Reinforcement

The principle of conditioned reinforcement is simply this:

A stimulus that is not originally a reinforcing one . . . can become reinforcing through repeated association with one that is. (F. S. Keller & Schoenfeld, 1950, p. 232)

That is, through conditioning, a stimulus acquires the power to act as a reinforcer. This is often referred to by the phrases *secondary reinforcement* or *acquired reward*. Consider, for example, the acquisition of reinforcing power by the light in the following experiment. When a rat presses a bar, a light comes on. After 1 second a pellet of food falls into the tray, reinforcing the bar-pressing. The light remains on for 2 seconds after the food appears. Several groups of animals are conditioned in this way, for 10, 20, 40, 80, and 120 reinforcements, respectively. After conditioning, the rate of responding is reduced to a low level by extinction in the dark. Then the contingencies are changed so that pressing the bar again turns on the light for 1 second, but does not deliver food. Under these circumstances responses again appear, showing that the light has acquired reinforcing properties. The number of responses emitted in a 45-minute period increased with the number of prior pairings of light and food (Bersh, 1951).

Other experiments suggest that the light will acquire secondary reinforcing properties only if it appears *before* the reinforcing stimulus, and is thus either part of a chain or a discriminative stimulus (Schoenfeld, Antonitis, & Bersh, 1950; Webb & Nolan, 1953).

The following summary of conditioned reinforcement shows its systematic importance in operant behavior:

1. A stimulus that occasions or accompanies a reinforcement acquires thereby reinforcing value of its own, and may be called a conditioned, secondary, or derived reinforcement. A secondary reinforcement may be extinguished when repeatedly applied to a response for which there is no ultimate primary reinforcement.

2. A secondary reinforcement is positive when the reinforcement with which it is correlated is positive, and negative when the latter is negative.

3. Once established, a secondary reinforcement is independent and nonspecific; it not only will strengthen the same response which produced the original reinforcement, but will also condition a new and unrelated response. Moreover, it will do so even in the presence of a different motive.

4. Through generalization, many stimuli besides the one correlated with reinforcement acquire reinforcing value—positive or negative. (F. S. Keller & Schoenfeld, 1950, p. 260).

One of the most important consequences of the development of secondary reinforcement is the emergence of a class of *generalized reinforcers* (Skinner, 1953, pp. 77–81). This generalization comes about because some secondary reinforcers tend to accompany a variety of primary reinforcers. Money is a convenient illustration, because money provides access to food, drink, shelter, entertainment, and thus becomes a generalized reinforcer for a variety of activities. The so-called social needs (need for attention, need for affection, need for approval) lead to the kinds of persistent behavior best understood as a consequence of intermittent reinforcement, and the kinds of reinforcement sought are the generalized ones implied in the words *attention, affection,* and *approval.* Language behavior, such as calling objects by their correct names, tends to be reinforced by the generalized reinforcement from the listeners, who show in indirect ways whether or not they understand and approve. According to Skinner, eventually generalized reinforcers are effective even though the primary reinforcers on which they are based no longer accompany them (1953, p. 81). This is close to the functional autonomy of motives, as proposed by Allport (1937).

OTHER INFLUENCES AFFECTING OPERANT STRENGTH

In the effort to remain descriptive and positivistic, Skinner has attempted to avoid the postulating of intermediaries not observed in his experiments, and to deal instead with a procedure that he calls *functional analysis.* A functional analysis is concerned with the lawfulness of relationships and the manner in which these relationships fluctuate under specified conditions. We have just reviewed one very important class of events in the functional analysis of behavior: reinforcements and how their scheduling affects operant strength. Two other classes of events are significantly correlated with responses in the problems that Skinner studies. These are the classes known as *drive* and *emotion.*

Drive

Hours of food deprivation are important in determining the rate of responding in a Skinner box. The variable actually plotted is exactly that; hours of deprivation. Is it necessary to say anything further? Is it important to talk about physiological needs, or hunger? Let us first cite some typical experimental results and then return to these questions.

Eight rats learned to press a lever under interval reinforcement. They practiced daily but received the main portion of their rations on alternate days. The correlation between responding and hours of deprivation showed up in high and low rates on successive days. Two subgroups were created, matched according to their response rates during conditioning. They were now extinguished on alternate days, one group when hunger was high, the other when hunger was low. The high-hunger group yielded nearly double the responses of the low group on successive daily periods, although the two extinction curves show similar curvature (Skinner, 1950, pp. 201–202).

Does deprivation affect the strengthening effect of each reinforcement, or does it merely affect the rate of responding during extinction? In a test of these relationships, rats were trained with reinforcement after various durations of food deprivation, from $\frac{1}{2}$ hour to 47 hours. Various subgroups of animals received training amounting to 1, 10, and 30 reinforcements, respectively. Then the strength of conditioning was tested by resistance to extinction, at a common level of deprivation (23 hours). Resistance to extinction correlated with the number of prior reinforcements, but *not* with the level of deprivation during reinforcement (Strassburger, 1950).

These studies suffice to illustrate the kinds of relationships between drive and operant conditioning that are open to investigation. In a narrative account of the results we tend to move back and forth between describing the rats as "deprived of food" or as "hungry." The two expressions are operationally equivalent, though when we assign the results to "hunger" instead of to "hours without food" we tend to imply a theory. This leads us back to the problem of the status of "drive" as a concept.

Skinner is quite clear that he means by "drive" merely a set of operations (such as the withholding of food for a certain number of hours or reducing an organism's weight to a certain percentage of its "normal" weight) which have an effect upon rate of responding. He is interested in the lawfulness of these effects under various circumstances. He objects to most of the current psychological uses of "drive" by arguing for the following assertions (1953, pp. 144–146):

A drive is not a stimulus.
A drive is not a physiological state.
A drive is not a psychic state.
A drive is not simply a state of strength.

By these negatives he makes it clear that he does not accept the stimuli from stomach contractions as the prototype of drives, nor does he accept physiological needs, or pleasures or pains, or desires or wishes. For the purposes of the systematic study of behavior, the word *drive* is used only to acknowledge certain classes of operation which affect behavior in ways other than the ways by which reinforcement affects it. Skinner does not believe inference to an intermediary (intervening variable or hypothetical construct) to be necessary in order to carry out the functional analysis. The main arguments against Skinner's rejection of "drive" have been marshaled by N. E. Miller (e.g., 1969). Miller points out the parsimony of postulating an intervening variable like "thirst" or "hunger" when we have to summarize a large number of input-output relations, relating a number of "thirst-inducing" independent operations (t) to a number of "thirst-related" behaviors (b). There are in principle tb (the product) input-output functions to be determined. Postulating an intervening variable of thirst can reduce this number requiring determination to $t+b$ functional relations, showing how thirst (the intervening variable) is functionally related to the t independent variables and the b dependent variables. Miller also states ways of testing this formulation, and laments that we have far too few successful tests of the "unitariness" of all the intervening variables which psychologists postulate.

Emotion

Just as drives are inappropriately classified as stimuli, so, according to Skinner, emotions are often unwisely classified as responses. Weeping at a bruised shin or over the loss of a game is ordinarily said to be an emotional response, but weeping because of a cinder in the eye is not. This way of treating emotion is rejected in favor of referring it to a set of operations, in many ways like drive. Its importance arises because of the accompanying or ensuing changes in response.

An example of this view of emotion is in the study of *conditioned suppression* or the *conditioned emotional response* (abbreviated CER), a phenomenon first demonstrated by Estes and Skinner (1941). It is known that painful electric shock causes a cessation or suppression of appetitive behaviors like eating or drinking or of instrumental responses reinforced by such consequences. What Estes and Skinner found was that a formerly neutral stimulus that is paired repeatedly with shock can then exert this same suppressive effect upon any appetitive behavior. A typical experiment uses a hungry rat trained to lever-press for food reinforcement on a variable interval schedule (which generates a very steady rate of response). Then a series of Pavlovian conditioning trials are given during which a tone comes on for 5 minutes and terminates with electric shock. Later, after the animal has returned to lever-pressing steadily on the VI schedule, the tone is sounded, say, for 5-minute periods. During the tone, the animal will often "freeze," reduce his pressing rate, crouch, and show signs of a conditioned emotional response; objectively, the tone has "suppressed" lever-pressing. Once the tone-shock event terminates, the rat will soon resume lever-pressing. These tone-on and tone-off periods can be repeatedly alternated throughout the experimental session. Eventually the animal's performance exhibits two average lever-pressing rates, one high average when the tone is off and another, lower one when the tone is on. The degree of suppression is typically reported in terms of some kind of "suppression ratio," such as the drop in the response rate caused by the tone divided by the tone off baseline rate. This index varies from 0 to 1 as tone-controlled suppression of response rate varies from nil to total suppression.

Most psychologists interpret the CER as due to *motivational* competition between conditioned anxiety and appetitive motives (e.g., Estes, 1969b; Stein, 1964). Moreover, the conditioning of anxiety by the tone-shock pairings is conceived of as a Pavlovian or classical conditioning paradigm. Therefore, the CER or suppression ratio provides a convenient technique for studying classical conditioning, and it has been much exploited for just that purpose (e.g., Kamin, 1965, 1969a; Rescorla, 1969b). Indeed, for many purposes, the suppression ratio can be treated as though it were "drops of saliva" in salivary conditioning.

The CER is just one example of "emotion" and, needless to say, there are many others. An emotional reaction that has been much studied recently by Skinnerians (e.g., Ulrich & Azrin, 1962) is reflexive aggression or fighting in animals, elicited by pain caused by an electric shock or a physical blow (Azrin, Hake, & Hutchinson, 1965) or even by the frustration resulting from nonreinforcement of a response previously receiving positive reinforcement (Azrin, 1964). This seems to be a widespread response, found throughout many species; the aggression is not aimed discriminatively, but rather "hits" any available suitable target, including "innocent bystanders."

Punishment

In punishment, a negative reinforcer is made contingent upon a response which typically had some prior source of strength. Some early studies by Skinner (1938, p. 154) using a mild punisher (the lever slapped upward against the rat's paw when it was pressed) came to the conclusion that punishment was a relatively ineffective means to produce any permanent change in behavior. It was claimed that punishment did have a suppressive effect on behavior while it remained in force, but that when punishment was removed the former response "recovered" and was emitted nearly as much during extinction as was a nonpunished response. This interpretation that punishment is relatively ineffective in altering behavior has been widely quoted and used for various "liberalizing" arguments in practical applications of behavior modification.

But the interpretation, in retrospect, is rather odd. By this strange logic, one might also claim that positive reinforcement is ineffective, is "only temporary with no lasting effects," because the response extinguishes when reinforcement is withdrawn. More recent studies and analyses of punishment by Azrin and Holz (1966) show how very effective punishment can be in suppressing appetitive behavior, how it varies in a lawful way with the parameters of punishment, and also how behavior recovers (or "punishment effects extinguish") after punishment is removed and reinforcement is continued. Azrin and Holz summarize their extensive investigations in the following set of statements:

Let us summarize briefly some of the circumstances which have been found to maximize its effectiveness: (1) The punishing stimulus should be arranged in such a manner that no unauthorized escape is possible. (2) The punishing stimulus should be as intense as possible. (3) The frequency of punishment should be as high as possible. (4) The punishing stimulus should be delivered immediately after the response. (5) The punishing stimulus should not be increased gradually but introduced at maximum intensity. (6) Extended periods of punishment should be avoided, especially where low intensities of punishment are concerned, since the recovery effect may thereby occur. Where mild intensities of punishment are used, it is best to use them for only a brief period of time. (7) Great care should be taken to see that the delivery of the punishing stimulus is not differentially associated with the delivery of reinforcement. Otherwise the punishing stimulus may acquire conditioned reinforcing properties. (8) The delivery of the punishing stimulus should be made a signal or discriminative stimulus that a period of extinction is in progress. (9) The degree of motivation to emit the punished response should be reduced. (10) The frequency of positive reinforcement for the punished response should similarly be reduced. (11) An alternative response should be available which will produce the same or greater reinforcement as the punished response. For example, punishment of criminal behavior can be expected to be more effective if noncriminal behavior which will result in the same advantages as the behavior is available. (12) If no alternative response is available, the subject should have access to a different situation in which he obtains the same reinforcement without being punished. (13) If it is not possible to deliver the punishing stimulus itself after a response, then an effective method of punishment is still available. A conditioned stimulus may be associated with the aversive stimulus, and this conditioned stimulus may be delivered following a response to achieve conditioned punishment. (14) A reduction of positive reinforcement may be used as punishment when the use of physical punishment is not possible for practical, legal, or moral reasons. Punishment by withdrawal of positive reinforcement may be accomplished in such situations by arranging a period of reduced reinforcement frequency (time-out) or by arranging a decrease of conditioned reinforcement (response cost). Both methods require that the subject have a high level of reinforcement to begin with; otherwise, no withdrawal of reinforcement is possible. If non-physical punishment is to be used, it appears desirable to provide the subject with a substantial history of reinforcement in order to provide the opportunity for withdrawing the reinforcement as punishment for the undesired responses. (1966, pp. 426–427)

Discrimination and Differentiation

One further kind of learning is called stimulus discrimination. In behavioral terms, we say that an organism discriminates among two or more stimuli when it can learn to respond differentially (in different ways or with different rates) to each of the stimuli. This is referred to as *stimulus control* since presentation or removal of a given discriminative stimulus controls the occurrence of a particular response pattern or its rate. A second kind of learning is *response differentiation,* in which the form of the response (its topography) or its intensity, amplitude, or latency is altered by differential reinforcement. Skinner presumes that the complexities of behavior can be understood according to stimulus discriminations and differentiated responses arranged into appropriate chains or patterns.

Discrimination of stimuli. The standard lever-pressing experiment may serve the purposes of discriminatory conditioning if the lever-pressing delivers a pellet of food in the presence of a positive stimulus (e.g., a light) and fails to deliver in the absence of this discriminative stimulus. The rat learns to respond only when the light is on, but the light does not actually elicit the response in the sense in which a cinder in the eye elicits tears or touching a heated pan elicits withdrawal. The difference between a discriminative stimulus as an occasion for a response and actually eliciting a response is clarified by an example. I reach for a pencil lying on the desk, but I reach only when the pencil is there, and I do not reach for it just *because* it is there. While the pencil does not elicit reaching, it has something to do with my reaching. If it were dark and there were no pencil there, I might grope for it because the discriminative stimuli would be lacking. The pencil does not elicit reaching in the light any more than in the dark. It is only the occasion for reaching (Skinner, 1938, p. 178) given appropriate conditions.

When the food is delivered only in the presence of the light, the situation is a sort of controlled intermittent reinforcement, for lever-pressing is reinforced only part of the time. Eventually the response occurs almost exclusively when the light is on, so that nearly every response is reinforced. The resistance to extinction that is built up at this stage is not that of interval reinforcement, but that of ordinary every-trial reinforcement. There are two operants with the same form of response, one with the light on, one with the light off; they are selectively reinforced and extinguished. There is an interaction called *induction* by Skinner which corresponds to Hull's generalization: whatever happens to one operant affects the other to some extent. Skinner, like Spence and Hull, offers the usual analysis of discrimination learning in terms of the concepts of reinforcement, extinction, and generalization (see Chapter 6).

Errorless discrimination learning. According to this classical view, discrimination is achieved by extinguishing generalized responses in the nonreinforced stimuli, S⁻. In Spence's theory, for example, the repeated frustration by nonreinforcement of responding to S⁻ causes the inhibition to become associated to S⁻.

Terrace (1963a), a student of Skinner's, has devised a procedure for teaching a pigeon a perfect discrimination in such a manner that it never responds to S⁻ throughout the entire experiment, in other words, it never makes an "error." The initial studies have been done with different colored lights on the pecking key serving as S⁺ and S⁻. The procedure involves (a) introducing S⁻ very early before the response to S⁺ is well conditioned, and (b) introducing S⁻ gradually, initially for very brief durations and at very dim intensities. Over successive trials, the intensity and duration of S⁻ are gradually increased to their full values. The method hinges in part upon certain peculiarities of pigeons such as the fact that they are unlikely to peck a darkened key. However, similar methods have been used with humans.

By using this simple procedure, Terrace proved that it is possible to get perfect discrimination without the occurrence of a nonreinforced response to S⁻. In contrast, suppose that S⁻ is introduced, as it usually is, for the full duration and at full brightness after the pigeon has had several sessions of exposure to S⁺ and has become well conditioned. Under these conditions, the pigeon may emit several thousand responses to S⁻ before learning acceptable differential behavior. Thus, the difference produced by Terrace's simple procedure is truly enormous whether one thinks only in terms of ease of training a discrimination or also, by inference, of the amount of emotional frustration that the subject has been spared.

In a related experiment, Terrace (1963b) was able to show that an errorless discrimination learned to, say, red versus green key colors could be transferred to two new stimuli (a white vertical bar as positive and horizontal bar as negative) by a special method. The special method consisted in (a) first superimposing the vertical bar on the positive red key, and the horizontal bar on the negative green key, and (b) after several sessions of such superimposed conditions, gradually fading out (dimming) the red and green colors on the key, eventually ending up with only the vertical or horizontal bar on a dark key. By this procedure stimulus control is transferred from red versus green to vertical versus horizontal bars, and here, again, no errors occur in the course of the gradual transfer. It is of significance that Terrace was unable to train a vertical versus horizontal discrimination from scratch without errors (by manipulating brightness of S⁻). This suggests that if a difficult discrimination is to be trained, an optimal method is to train without errors another discrimination that is inherently easy for the subject (as colors surely are for pigeons), and then superimpose and fade into the more difficult stimuli. It is of interest, too, that if following the superimposition phase the colors were abruptly removed, the animals did make a number of errors on the vertical versus horizontal discrimination. Moreover, when later retested on the red versus green discrimination, the animals that had the abrupt change started to make errors (responses to S⁻) despite their initial errorless training on red versus green. Terrace points out the relevance of all his results to Skinner's claim that the optimal arrangement of programmed instruction sequences (in teaching machines) is the one in which the student never makes an error in answering questions during learning.

There are several intriguing auxiliary features of errorless discrimination performance as compared to what is obtained under the customary, error-spotted procedure. First of all, the discriminative performance itself is far superior. Animals trained by the errorless method never respond to S⁻, whereas birds whose training routine is spotted with errors continue indefinitely to put out sporadic bursts of responses to S⁻. Second, observation reveals that the error-prone birds display a large amount of emotional behavior in S⁻, suggesting that it is probably an aversive stimulus for them, apparently because of the frustration generated by nonreinforced responding. In comparison, an errorless-trained bird displays little or no emotional behavior in S⁻. Third, giving the animal an injection of the tranquilizing drug chlorpromazine "releases" large quantities of responses to S⁻ in the error-prone trained birds but not in the errorless-trained birds. Presumably, the tranquilizer dispels some of the frustration which had been inhibiting responses to S⁻ for the animals trained with errors. Fourth, the errorless-trained birds do not show a "behavioral contrast" effect (faster rates to S⁺ because it is alternated with S⁻), whereas the error-prone birds do; however, if an errorless-trained bird is induced to start making errors in S⁻ (say, by the abrupt transfer mentioned above), then it begins to show contrast by speeding up its response to S⁺. Fifth, a generalization gradient taken following discrimination training shows a "peak shift" for the error-prone birds but not for the errorless birds. Peak shift refers to the fact that the peak (maximum) rate of responding is produced not at S⁺ but at a value displaced from S⁺ in a direction away from S⁻. Figure 7.2 (p. 228) shows this effect in Terrace's experiment (1964). The stimulus continuum is wavelength of light (corresponding to color changes to the human eye) measured in millimicrons. The S⁺ was at 580 and S⁻ at 540 millimicrons. The peak rate of responding during generalization testing is at 580 (the S⁺) for the errorless-trained birds, but is shifted over to 590 for the error-prone-trained birds.

What does all this mean? How is it best interpreted? A possible account might go somewhat as follows. Errorless discrimination is possible because of conditioning by sheer contiguity of the last response made before a stimulus terminates. Because the pigeon does not peck a dark key and because the S⁻ color is presented initially dim and for short durations, the likely response to these initial S⁻ presentations is either withdrawal or just "sitting still," and this behavior is what gets conditioned to S⁻. This is roughly the account Guthrie or Spence would give for the phenomenon, since both are contiguity theorists. Behavioral contrast and peak shift are effects that depend upon the conversion of S⁻ into an aversive stimulus, and this is ordinarily achieved by the frustration generated by nonreinforced responding to S⁻. Since the errorless procedure produces no frustrated responses, no aversion is conditioned to S⁻, and so contrast and peak shift do not occur in this case. In line with this reasoning, Grusec (1965) found that errorless-trained birds did show peak shift if they received electric shocks in association with S⁻, thus converting it into an aversive stimulus.

Whether or not this hypothesis is correct, the significance of the errorless result still stands. It shows that the conventional extinction procedure can

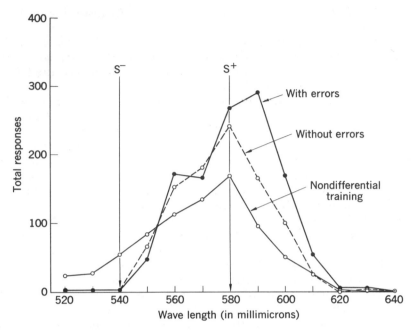

Figure 7.2.   Generalization gradients obtained under three different conditions, relating response output to variations in the wavelength (color) of a light projected on the pecking key. The lower gradient was obtained following simple conditioning at 580 millimicrons without a discrimination procedure. The other two gradients followed discrimination training on 580 millimicrons as S$^+$ and 540 as S$^-$, one procedure involving errors to S$^-$, the other none. A peak shift appears in the former gradient since responding to 590 millimicrons was greater than to 580, the S$^+$ of training. (From Terrace, 1964. Copyright 1964 by the American Association for the Advancement of Science.)

be sidestepped in establishing a discrimination and that the performance thus obtained is better than the ones usually established. Terrace's procedure brings out strikingly a point of view on learning research that has often been lacking in the past. The viewpoint is one concerned with optimality, and asks questions regarding the best arrangement of training conditions, one that permits the subject to achieve some criterion of good performance. The strategy here would be to devise training sequences to optimize or minimize some such variable as the skillfulness of the eventual performance achieved, the speed of effecting a given change in performance, the production of a desired change with a minimum of errors, or a minimum of frustration or of difficulty, and so forth. Such a research strategy will assuredly yield results of practical relevance to educators, psychotherapists, and others whose concern is with practical behavioral engineering.

Differentiation of a Response: Shaping

Among a number of novel and useful distinctions made by Skinner is that between discrimination of stimuli and differentiation of response. In operant

conditioning, reinforcement can be made contingent on either (a) the properties of accompanying stimuli (as just noted, the result is called stimulus
discrimination), or (b) the properties of the response (the result is called
response differentiation).

Response differentiation refers to reinforcement of intensive aspects of a
qualitative response. For example, Skinner (1938) trained some rats to press
and hold down the lever for a long time in order to get reward; he trained
others to press the lever with a forcefulness above a certain criterion. Similarly, as we saw in our earlier analysis of performance on schedules, we can
train the subject to respond selectively at a fast or slow rate. The principle
is that of operant reinforcement, but it is applied at the level of intensive
variations of the response (what Logan calls "micromolar responses," reviewed in Chapter 6). For example, in differentiating a forceful lever-press,
one first reinforces any lever-presses, thus providing a distribution of variable forces. One then establishes a low criterion, and rewards only those
presses which exceed that criterion. The effect of this restriction is to extinguish weaker presses and strengthen forceful presses, so that the entire force
distribution shifts to higher values. The experimenter's criterion may then
be increased again, and again, and thus gradually "shape" the animal's
lever-presses to higher values. An upper limit, of course, can also be imposed
such that forces above that limit are not reinforced; and responses of different forces can be conditioned to several differential stimuli (Notterman &
Mintz, 1962). The relevance of such results to the learning of complex
human skills is obvious. For example, our social community shapes up a
particular speed and loudness to our speaking in particular settings, and
severe deviations from that norm are punished.

Another type of "shaping" occurs when a new qualitative response or
novel sequence of behavioral components is assembled into a unitary performance. This makes use of the notion of *chaining* which played a role in
Skinner's analyses.

Response Chains

Skinner (1938, 1953) argues that most complete acts are in fact a sequence
of movements in which the n-th segment provides feedback stimuli (external
and internal) which become discriminative for the next segment of the
response. Thus the act may be thought of as a chain of small $S^D \rightarrow R$ units.
Even the simple lever-pressing response can be conceived to be a chain. In
their discussion of chaining, F. S. Keller and W. N. Schoenfeld (1950, pp.
197–208) gave a lucid account of the problem of determining the degree of
analysis desirable in order to remain at the level of experimental specification. They began with six distinct operants describing what the rat actually
does in a Skinner box (see Table 7.2, next page).

It would be possible, as they suggest, to lengthen this list to include the
several responses making up the approach to the bar location, and the several ingestion responses that follow upon the chewing of food. Instead,
however, they find it equally legitimate to reduce the list, as shown in
Table 7.3, next page.

The advantage of this reduction lies in the clearly observable and regularly recurring sequence or chain of responses, with identifiable (and con-

Table 7.2   Listing of the stimulus-response components in the response chain
of bar-pressing and eating.

Operant Number	Discriminative Stimulus	Response of the Rat
1	Bar location	Approach of rat to front of box
2	Visual bar	Rising on hind legs; placing paws on bar
3	Tactual bar	Pressing of bar, thus activating food magazine
4	Apparatus noise	Lowering foreparts to food tray
5	Visual pellet	Seizing of pellet by teeth and paws
6	Pellet in mouth	Chewing of pellet

Table 7.3   An abbreviated listing of the links in the reinforced response chain.

Operant Number	Discriminative Stimulus	Response of the Rat
1	Visual bar	Rising
2	Tactual bar	Pressing
3	Apparatus noise	Lowering
4	Visual pellet	Seizing

trollable) stimuli. In this chain each response produces the discriminative stimulus for the next response.

Does the chain operate as a unit? The well-conditioned rat makes the transitions so smoothly that it seems to be giving one response, not four. But the independence of the units of the chain can be tested experimentally.

1. If we eliminate only the stimulus for the final unit of the chain (the pellet), as is done in one form of extinction, the first three links of the chain are gradually weakened, but the last is unaffected. That is, the rat will seize and eat a pellet exactly as before.

2. If we now eliminate both the third and fourth links in the chain (the apparatus noise as well as the pellet), and carry out extinction, we can find out more about the chain. Reintroducing the noise after extinction again reinforces bar-pressing. Hence, during conditioning the stimulus for the third link had become a conditioned reinforcer. Furthermore, the extinction of the preceding two links in the chain did not extinguish the reinforcing properties of the third link.

This kind of functional and experimental study isolates units of the chain which preserve some independence in the whole. These units are part of a chain, and their distinctiveness as units is not entirely arbitrary. It would be possible to record the separate responses, and not only the final one. The unit appropriate for experimental study turns out, in fact, to have a measure of arbitrariness about it. If it is a matter of convenience whether to measure one response of the chain, or four responses, or many more than that, there is evidently some selectivity exercised by the experimenter. This is always true: *all* description is partial description.

This analysis of chaining suggests not only laws for "breaking down" established chains, but also a means for training the organism to new chains, stringing together novel sequences of behavioral components much as one might string together differently colored beads to create novel designs in a necklace. The basic rule is to develop the chain one S^D-R unit at a time, starting from the reinforcement and working backward. The "reinforcement" for learning the next response in the chain is presentation of the S^D for the rest of the chain. If the exact response form does not occur initially at any appreciable rate, then reinforce any behavior which *approximates* the form desired; then when that variation occurs, require an even closer approximation to the form desired before giving reinforcement. Through successive approximations, the shaping method permits the finally learned behavior to be very different from that originally emitted.

Animal trainers are well versed in this method. As a sort of *tour de force* I have trained a rat to execute an elaborate series of responses suggested by recent work on anthropoid apes. The behavior consists of pulling a string to obtain a marble from a rack, picking the marble up with the forepaws, carrying it to a tube projecting two inches above the floor of the cage, and dropping it inside. Every step in the process had to be worked out through a series of approximations, since the component responses were not in the original repertoire of the rat. (Skinner, 1938, pp. 339–340)[1]

There have been a number of demonstrations of all sorts of novel and complex skills taught to various animals by means of shaping by successive approximations. Skinner believes that this is the way most of our complex skills have been synthesized.

LABORATORY TECHNOLOGY

That which is the source of substantive principles in one area of scientific knowledge may become a method or technology for another. Thus the transistor is of interest to the physicist for what it tells about solid-state physics, but it is a technological assist to the person constructing hearing aids or pocket-sized radios. Operant conditioning, similarly, is of interest for what it tells about learning, but it is also very useful for many whose interests are not primarily in learning at all.

One use that interests experimental psychologists is in animal psychophysics. It is possible, by using operant methods, to produce visual sensitivity curves for pigeons that show the course of adaptation to darkness with all the precision of experimentation with trained human subjects (Blough, 1961). A whole range of perceptual phenomena can be investigated with animals, including visual illusions, adaptation level effects, and so on (Blough, 1966).

Another widespread use has been in the testing of drugs. Because the response rates that are recorded in the standard Skinner apparatus are very sensitive to the influence of drugs, these methods become useful for calibration experiments in pharmacology. Thus, for example, most of the new

[1] For other accounts of animal training, see Breland and Breland (1951), Skinner (1951).

drugs and medications which we receive today have already been "screened" through extensive animal testing (typically in operant conditioning tasks), in a search for undesirable side effects on behavior. The technologies of behavioral control are also widely used by physiological psychologists, whereby they assess reinforcing or motivating effects of electrical or chemical stimulation of the brain, behavioral alterations (e.g., overeating) caused by neurological damage (e.g., hypothalamic lesions), and so on.

The wide applicability of the technologies associated with stimulus control and reinforcement contingencies is recognized by many who are testing theories departing widely from those of Skinner. Thus much of the contemporary work in animal learning and motivation makes use of the Skinner box. A recent summary (Honig, 1966) shows the many uses that have been made of the method in the study of a variety of psychological and physiological topics. It is a fair statement that the Skinner box has displaced the maze as the favorite apparatus among American students of animal behavior.

Programmed Instruction

Skinner in 1954 announced and embarked upon a series of investigations and inventions designed to increase the efficiency of teaching arithmetic, reading, spelling, and other school subjects, by using a mechanical device expected to do some things much better than the usual teacher can do them, while saving the teacher for tasks that the teacher can do better. An early form of the device presented number combinations for the teaching of addition. The child punches his answer in a kind of adding-machine keyboard; if the answer is correct, "reinforcement" occurs by having the machine move on to the next problem. This is functionally the same as following the student's response with the teacher's announcement of *Right*. Skinner early pointed out that no teacher can be as discriminating a reinforcer as the machine, for the teacher cannot be with every child in a class at once, commending proper responses and correcting erroneous ones. Furthermore, the teacher may not be as skilled in determining the proper order and rate of presentation of problems as has been determined by empirical studies of the content material.

Skinner's devices, and others modeled after them, soon came to be called *teaching machines* or *autoinstructional devices*, and the materials that became the basis for instruction came to be called *programs*. Some of them began to appear as programmed books (e.g., Holland & Skinner, 1961).

An important summary paper by Skinner in *Science* in 1958 catalyzed the interest that had been mounting, and *programmed instruction* presently became a major education and commercial enterprise that flourishes today. The important issues for Skinner were the following: (1) first, get a clear, detailed, objective specification of what it means to "know" the given subject matter; for Skinner, this typically consists of a detailed list of "stimulus-response" connections; (2) write a series of "stimulus" (question)–"response" (answer) *frames* which expose the student to the material in graded steps of increasing difficulty, frequently retesting the same fact from many different angles; (3) require that the learner be active—for example, require that a response be composed for each frame in the program; (4) provide immediate feedback for each response (answer); (5) try to so arrange the questions that the correct response is very likely to occur and be reinforced; thus, learning is not always accompanied by punishing consequences; (6) let each student proceed through the teaching program at his own pace; and (7) provide plenty of backup reinforcers (praise, candies, wages) for diligent and effective work on the program.

While Skinner believed that the rationale for his proposals was derivable from the principles of operant conditioning, his theoretical interpretations have been the subject of some controversy.[2] Whatever the verdict may be with regard to the essence of programmed instruction, there is no doubt that the upsurge of interest since the 1950s was due to Skinner, and there is no doubt either that he arrived at his methods through an attempt to generalize to education what he had learned through the study of operant conditioning in the laboratory.

Verbal Behavior

Language most clearly distinguishes human behavior from that of other mammals. Knowledge of how we acquire language, and how we use it, is essential to an understanding of human learning. Skinner has long been interested in verbal behavior. As early as 1936 he produced a phonograph record composed of chance groupings of speech sounds, which because they were chance were inherently meaningless. The record, called a "verbal summator," was used to study the words "read into" sounds by the listener. It was a kind of projective technique, similar in the auditory field to the inkblots used in the visual field (Skinner, 1936). Within the next few years Skinner reported studies of word association, alliteration, and other kinds of sound patterning.[3] His William James Lectures, delivered at Harvard University in 1948, appeared in revised form as a volume entitled *Verbal behavior* (1957), in which he approached verbal behavior as an empirical problem.

The main point of the analysis is that speech sounds are emitted (and reinforced) as are any other bits of behavior. Some speech utterances make demands upon the hearer and get reinforced as the hearer complies. A child's utterance of "Milk, please" is reinforced when the parent complies and provides the requested commodity. This function (called the "mand" function) appears early in the language behavior of the child. A second function is concerned largely with naming discriminative stimuli (the "tact" function). A naming repertoire comes about in the "original word game" which the child constantly plays with his parents and others in his verbal community: "What's that?" "It's a car." "Is this a car?" "No, that's a wagon." And so on and on. Because objects and events are multifaceted, acquisition of a tact typically requires discrimination, wherein the same tact is reinforced to the "relevant" feature despite variation in irrelevant features. Thus the tact *red* comes to be controlled by the color of red apples, red cars, red dresses, and so on. This is really an elliptical way of talking: the utterance "red" actually is controlled by a complex of stimuli including the

---

[2] Programmed learning is discussed in greater detail in Chapter 15.
[3] Skinner (1937b), Cook and Skinner (1939).

object (or our "memory" of it) and a request to name its *color* rather than its shape or palatability, and so on. Abstracting or generalizing means that a tact has come under the control of a single property of a whole class of complex objects. Thus, the concept of *sharp object* may be learned by experience with razor blades, knives, and so on. Moreover, acquisition of a new rule such as "Sharp objects can cut you; you should avoid them" will mediate immediate changes in responses to a whole range of stimuli which elicit the same label. Moreover, those avoidance responses will occur to new stimulus patterns (e.g., broken glass, sabres) which are labeled "sharp" by the community.

A third term introduced by Skinner is that of *autoclitic* behavior, intended to suggest verbal behavior that is a comment upon or a description of other verbal behavior by ourselves (1957, p. 315). The speaker is commonly talking in part about his own role when he emits autoclitic behavior: "I was about to say...," "I don't believe that...," "John did *not* do...," or "I hesitate to say that..." are example frames in which autoclitics occur. Thus, autoclitics can comment upon other verbal responses they accompany, or can specify the strength of that behavior, or can identify the effect on the speaker of the fact stated (as in "I was delighted that..." or "Happily, he..."), or negate the truth of another assertion.

Ordering of words is another large class of autoclitic phenomena. Traditionally called grammatical rules, these make use of what Skinner termed "partially conditioned autoclitic frames" (1957, p. 336). Following learning of such possession frames as "The lady's dog," "The lady's car," and "The man's car," the first appearance of the dog with the man can be tacted as "The man's dog" by tacting the objects and their relation using the "possessive" frame. It is proposed that similar word-position frames apply to the ordering of tacting adjective-noun relations and actor-action relations. These are, of course, the basis for predication, which is a primary function of language. Braine (1963) and Staats (1968) have developed this view that the information about syntactic structure primarily concerns the grammatical properties of *locations* within sentence frames (e.g., the first position in an English sentence is characteristically a noun, the second a verb, etc.). Thus, the syntactical relation between words provided by a novel ordering ("The lady's cat" versus "The cat's lady") controls the right interpretation because of "contextual generalization" of the function of words filling certain slots in the frame. This permits some degree of "generative productivity" in the sense that it allows the child to "understand" novel combinations and orderings of words. Braine (1963) reported several positive experiments with children, as did Staats (1968). Premack (1969) and Gardner and Gardner (1971) have utilized these principles in building a sizable linguistic repertoire in two chimpanzees.

However, Skinner's book *Verbal behavior* has not been very influential. This may have come about because it was not well received by professional linguists, and was given a renowned and relentlessly negative review by Chomsky (1959). Largely due to Chomsky's linguistic analyses, modern studies of grammar and language have developed quite extensively beyond the relatively imprecise suggestions of Skinner. Also, the notion of contextual generalization was criticized as being unable in principle to account for most forms of linguistic productivity (Bever, Fodor, & Weksel, 1965a; 1965b). These arguments were accepted by most psychologists studying language, and so other performance models of syntax learning are being pursued presently. However, there have been several attempts to resurrect Skinner's analysis of verbal behavior as a performance theory that would repay serious experimentation (e.g., MacCorquodale, 1969). Skinner's account of syntax and its acquisition is undoubtedly the weakest part of his analysis, whereas grammatical analysis is the strong suit of modern linguistics.

Some Functions of Verbal Responses

According to the behavioristic position, verbal behavior consists of "responses" under stimulus control and with stimulus consequences. But these behaviors can perform a variety of services for the organism. Many S-R psychologists (e.g., Dollard & Miller, 1950; Skinner, 1953; Staats & Staats, 1963) have been concerned with stipulating a few of these functions.

Let us note just a few of the roles of verbal responses in an S-R analysis. Verbal labels and utterances can be used as discriminative stimuli for our own and for others' behavior (as when we shout, "Run, Fire," or "Stop it"); they can be used as reinforcing stimuli for our own or for others' behavior, and used to provide anticipatory incentive or motivating stimuli (e.g., as when we say "I'll be paid tomorrow for this work" or "I'm being paid now for the work I did yesterday"). Also, sequences of cue-producing responses which parallel some external event sequence can be verbally rehearsed to strengthen the chain, thus "remembering" an external event sequence or a verbal proposition. Also, chains of cue-producing responses ("words or sentences") are selected and utilized in relevant ways to solve problems.

A typical Skinnerian analysis of problem-solving is that given by Staats and Staats (1963, p. 204) in interpreting an experiment by Judson, Cofer and Gelfand (1956). Their subjects had been given Maier's two-string problem to solve; the situation is a bare room with two widely separated strings hanging down several feet from the ceiling. The subject's job is to tie the two strings together. The strings are too far apart for the subject to hold one and reach the stationary other one. However, the other string could be reached by stretching if it were swung in motion as a pendulum. The solution therefore requires tying any available object on the end of one rope and setting it in pendulum motion in the direction of the other string; this enables the person to grab both strings at once and tie them together.

In their experiment, Judson, Cofer and Gelfand (1956) showed that solution of this two string problem could be facilitated if subjects were first taught a verbal serial list in which the words *rope-swing-pendulum* appeared in that order. In their reconstruction of this experiment, Staats and Staats use the diagram in Figure 7.3, and they analyze three aspects of the overall behavior. First is the discriminative "tacting" (labeling) of the problematic situation in terms of a relevant stimulus (attending to and saying "rope"). Second is the running off of the verbal response sequence which was learned earlier, *rope-swing-pendulum*; this was made available to experimental sub-

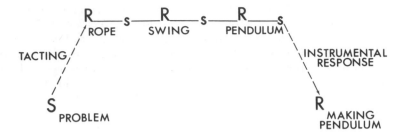

Figure 7.3.   Schematic representation of problem-solving sequence. The problem situation is tacted, then a verbal chain occurs leading to an implicit stimulus which controls occurrence of the correct response, which solves the problem.

jects by the prior verbal-learning task, whereas it is less available to the control subjects. Third are the instrumental behaviors of making a pendulum that are cued off by the implicit cue of saying *pendulum*.

The solution to the problem may fail if any one of these three components is lacking: the person may attend to irrelevant features of the problem situation; or he may notice the rope but not think of it as usable for a pendulum; or he may run off the verbal chain, but not know what *pendulum* refers to or how to make one. These components are identified in rather gross fashion here; they surely require a much finer functional analysis (e.g., *why* does the person, after saying *pendulum*, stop and construct one rather than continuing on with his verbal associative chains?); but Staats and Staats believe that this finer analysis can be pushed through, and they illustrate the matter with many hypothetical cases (see also Staats, 1968). However, from the viewpoint of others working on complex problem-solving (e.g., Newell & Simon, 1972), this type of analysis is far too simplified, ignoring the vast amount of fruitless "searching" among irrelevant possibilities and ignoring the means for directing the search process along paths ("associative chains") likely to lead to success. This issue is discussed in more detail in Chapter 13.

SELF-ATTRIBUTION AND SELF-AWARENESS

Probably more than any other behaviorist, Skinner has been concerned with how a person comes to "know himself," how he becomes "aware of" his feelings and of other private happenings going on inside his own skin. For Skinner, "being aware of certain feelings" is a special kind of readiness to verbalize or act upon a complex of stimuli (internal and external) which are discriminative for that "feeling." Thus, when I say, "My tooth aches," I am labeling a particular internal stimulus; when I say, "I am courageous," I am reiterating an earlier judgment (e.g., about specific acts) made about me by myself or by others.

In discussing the "original word game," we mentioned how the child learns tacts (verbal labels) for objects and events through discriminative reinforcement provided by a verbal community. The same community can train a child to describe his own behavior; for instance, a child might be trained to report "I wet my pants" or "I hit the cat" or "I'm eating a lot." The problem arises when the community tries to teach the child to label private events, internal stimuli, or "feelings." Private events exclusively affect the experiencer; so how is the community to know when to "point and name" the event?

In teaching a child to describe pain, for instance, an observer must teach him the label at a time when it is likely that the critical stimuli are imping-ing on him. The verbal community identifies these critical times on the basis of observable stimuli affecting the child (e.g., he bumps his head) or from his behavior (e.g., crying and holding his head). A description like "That's painful" or "That hurts" may thus be established in the child's repertoire by the observer's saying, "Ouch, that's painful; I know it must hurt," when he sees the child bump his head and cry. Once established, this verbal response will generalize to a large class of "painful" events which produce similar internal stimuli. Skinner identifies two other, minor ways to learn descriptions for private events. One is when I have learned to describe my overt behavior (e.g., my own talking), but that behavior then becomes covert; following a covert verbal sequence I can then say, "I've just been thinking that . . ." or something similar. Another way to learn descriptions for private events is through metaphorical extensions or analo-gies, as when we quickly understand and apply expressions like "butterflies in the stomach" for fright, "churning insides" for anger, and "pinpricks" or "ginger ale bubbles" for a foot that has fallen asleep. But these are minor methods that cover few cases; the main means of learning self-descriptive terms is by the trainer's inferring what is happening inside the child and then labeling it.

These resources of the community for teaching the child a self-descriptive repertoire are relatively meager compared to his finely tuned, discriminative labeling of publicly available stimuli. But then the result is frequently inad-equate. The individual as well as the community typically have faulty or inadequate knowledge of his internal states. For example, a person may never learn to label his neck muscles as "tense" or his palms as "sweaty"; similarly, the community never knows when to trust a reported "headache" or "upset stomach" when that is used as an excuse with obvious instru-mental value (as in "malingering"). Internal identifications we have not been taught remain as ones we are unable to make and are "unaware of." The potential of recent research on biofeedback of physiological measures like the electroencephalogram (EEG or "brain waves") and electromyograph (EMG or "muscle tension") is that these make public what otherwise are exclusively private events or states, and responses involving these systems can now be labeled and consciously controlled through differential rein-forcement of the amplified feedback (Kamiya, 1969; reviewed in Chapter 15).

Significantly, in the original training the child learns to label his own feelings or emotional reactions partially on the basis of the same observable evidence that the community itself uses, namely, the impinging external stimuli (the situational context) and his own reactions to them or his sus-tained behavior. In fact, when the internal events, feelings, or attitudes are vague, amorphous, and unclear, the person's self-descriptions may rely more than usual upon these external circumstances or his responses. This has been illustrated in an experiment by Schachter and Singer (1962), who were able to evoke such widely disparate "emotional feelings" as euphoria and bitter anger from subjects in the same physiological state of drug-induced arousal depending on whether they were placed with a "stooge" ("fake subject") who displayed euphoria or one who displayed rage reactions.

This line of analysis forms the basis for "self-attribution" theory, which is presently a leading theory among social psychologists working on attitude change (Bem, 1967, 1972; Jones et al., 1971). The cornerstone of Bem's theory is that a person's attitudes correspond to his self-perceptions. The two main assumptions of self-perception theory are as follows:

(1) Individuals come to "know" their own attitudes, emotions, and other internal states partially by inferring them from observations of their own overt behavior and/or the circumstances in which this behavior occurs.

(2) To the extent that internal cues are weak, ambiguous, or uninterpretable, the individual is functionally in the same position as an outside observer, an observer who must necessarily rely upon those same external cues to infer the individual's inner states. (Bem, 1972, p. 2)

This kind of theory has proved useful in interpreting the results of numerous attitude-change experiments done originally to support "cognitive dissonance" theory—for example, that subjects who are induced to role-play and argue against their initial opinion on some topic will consequently shift their "true opinion" drastically in the direction of the position they role-played. The references cited may be consulted for information relevant to these hypotheses. But it is interesting that the hypotheses currently salient in social psychology derive in large part from Skinner's behavioristic analysis of private experience.

PERSONALITY AND PSYCHOTHERAPY

Traditional psychodynamic theories of personality such as Freud's (see Chapter 11) assume that the person possesses a set of personality traits, motives, and basic conflicts that are enduring and persistent over time and across different situations. Behavior, whether normal or disturbed, is alleged to be a symptomatic expression of these underlying traits and motives. When the inner conflicts and anxiety become too intense to deal with, the mental apparatus "breaks down" and expresses the inner turmoil in terms of an irrational, neurotic symptom.

Skinner (1953 and elsewhere) specifically rejects this psychodynamic interpretation. For him, motives, wishes, or desires are not explanations of behavior. To explain that a man spends an excessive amount of time cleaning and grooming himself neatly because he "has a compulsive need or wish for cleanliness" is to explain nothing at all. It merely moves the question back a step: *Why* does he have it? *What* determines that wish? To go beyond such useless "motive explanations," Skinner proposes that we analyze the observable events, conditions, situational variables, and past history which regulate the behavior in question.

For Skinner, behavior is to be accounted for in terms of the present stimulus complex and the past training history of the person with respect to similar situations. The past history provides the person with a large fund of information, skills, and values (analyzable in objective terms). Mental-trait descriptions of a person are relatively useless, first because they correlate very poorly with how a person actually behaves across a range of social settings (see Mischel, 1968), and second because the trait description suggests no independent variables we can manipulate to control the behavior.

According to this view of matters, then, what is a neurotic? Why do we classify a person as being abnormal or mentally sick? Social learning theory (see Bandura, 1971a; Mischel, 1971) suggests that this judgment is based on a "social comparison." The neurotic has learned to behave in ways that are personally, legally, or socially disapproved, and considered deviant. Of course, whether a given behavior is judged to be deviant (and evidence of "craziness") depends on the social norms of the group doing the comparison; it also depends on the stimulus context of the act rather than the act itself (e.g., killing other people is approved during wartime).

The function of psychotherapy, in this view, is to remove or replace the deviant behavior which is causing misery for the "neurotic." That behavior is alleged to be controlled by certain social stimuli and by certain reinforcement contingencies. To eliminate deviant behaviors (or to replace them with approved behaviors), the therapist is to find the controlling stimuli or reinforcers, and remove them or alter them so that the deviant behaviors are extinguished or so that approved behaviors are strengthened in their place. The immediate goal of therapy should be to change the deviant behavior directly.

This general strategy is now called *behavior modification* or *behavior therapy*, and it is becoming a dominant approach to disturbed behavior in clinical psychology (e.g., Bergin & Garfield, 1971). It is now being used successfully to treat all kinds of behavioral disturbances in all kinds of populations and institutional settings. Some examples of problems treated are mutism, withdrawal, hyperactivity, self-injury, echolalia, bedwetting, encropresis, eating problems, temper tantrums, constipation, stuttering, excessive vomiting, social deficits in autistic children, hostile attacks, and bizarre speech. The list is hardly exhaustive. Similarly, behavioral treatment programs are used in individual and group psychotherapy, in management of entire psychiatric wards, in prisons, in homes for juvenile delinquents, in institutions for mentally retarded children, for deaf-mute children, and for mentally disturbed children, in normal nursery schools, in primary schools, in the home setting, and so on. The simple procedure is to so arrange contingencies as to cease rewarding undesirable behavior and start reinforcing desired behaviors. Prosaic and banal as that sounds, the fact is that in specific situations identification and manipulation of the relevant variables can be an exceedingly subtle matter requiring some technical sophistication. A frequent problem is that important social agents—for example, those around a child—are not aware that they are subtly reinforcing the deviant behavior, most commonly with solicitous "attention" to the person when he behaves in the deviant manner. An autistic child may bang his head repeatedly against the wall. When he does this, the ward nurse runs and hugs him, partly to prevent his injuring himself. But if the nurse's reinforcing behavior is rescheduled so that she ignores the child when he bangs his head but pays attention to him and hugs him when he is not banging his head, then the frequency of head-banging extinguishes to zero. There are numerous similar examples in the behavior modification literature.

As indicated above, behavior modification procedures are being used effectively in group settings such as classrooms and wards. A study by Packard (1970) illustrates some of the standard principles in operation. This was a class-room experiment with primary school children in which a general class of behaviors referred to as "paying attention to the teacher's instruction" was shaped through managing reinforcement contingencies. Noisy, inattentive disruptions and disturbances are a continual irritant and impediment to teaching and learning in the primary grades. The experiment was carried out by a teacher during each daily 30-minute reading lesson with four different classes (spanning kindergarten to sixth grade).

First, a *token economy* was instituted in the classroom. The children and teacher drew up a list of reinforcers and agreed upon how many tokens (poker chips) each reinforcer was to cost. Typical reinforcing activities were to be 10 minutes' access to playing with an electric typewriter, sitting next to a friend in the next class, 15 minutes' playtime in the gym, serving as teacher's assistant the next period, or 10 minutes' access to play on a piano. These activities could be purchased with tokens the child won by "being good," as stipulated below. The tokens would thus serve as conditioned reinforcers. During this time, the baseline frequency of "inattentive behaviors" by class members was estimated on several occasions, and these were considerable. Attentive behaviors were clearly defined and mainly consisted of sitting quietly, looking at and listening to the teacher, and doing one's lessons; inattentive behaviors included standing up and walking around the classroom, talking to one's neighbor, singing, sleeping, doodling idly, making and throwing paper airplanes, and so on.

Next, the group contingency was instituted and carefully explained to the class; tokens would be given to everyone if the class as a whole were all "paying attention" to the teacher for more than a specified percentage of the 30-minute reading lesson. The specific behaviors that counted as "paying attention" were carefully gone over several times with the children.

Finally, a cue-light prominently displayed on the teacher's desk served to inform the class when the teacher thought they were all paying attention (the green light) as contrasted to when she judged one or more children not to be (the red light). She would flick the light switch to red or green without comment or remarks to the offending pupils. The students knew that as long as the cue-light was green, a recording clock accumulated "attention time" toward their goal for the session; when the cue-light was red, the whole class was losing time and liable not to get their tokens for that day's lesson. The green and red lights served as conditioned reinforcers and punishers, respectively. Needless to say, there were strong group pressures (threats of punishment) brought to bear upon the inattentive member by the others.

Let us call the percentage of the 30-minute lesson during which the whole class was attentive the "percent attentiveness." Initially, the percent attentiveness required for group reinforcement was set very low, but was then advanced to stiffer criteria by means of shaping. In the beginning each child received, say, three tokens if the percent attentiveness for the group exceeded 40 percent (or 12 minutes of the 30-minute lesson). If the class exceeded that amount by 10 percent, they each received a two-token bonus. Tokens were always delivered at the end of each lesson, and the child could "cash these in" immediately for a low-valued reinforcer or save up several days' worth of tokens for a high-valued reinforcer. After several successful sessions at one criterion, it would be increased so that higher percentages of group attention time were required for token reinforcement; moreover, a group total falling as much as 5 percent below the day's criterion was penalized by taking a token from each child.

This field experiment showed spectacular success in shaping up classroom attention and work habits. Most classes were attending around 90 percent of the time by the end of the procedure; this was judged by independent behavior observers as well as by the teacher. In the experiment, this explicit reinforcement procedure was followed by several others, including simple verbal instructions to pay attention along with repeated reprimands; however, when the token reinforcers were removed, the class attention soon extinguished to around 10–20 percent of the time. When token plus backup reinforcers were reinstated, the class's undivided attention to the teacher returned to the 90 percent level.

This study illustrates principles of shaping, conditioned reinforcers, and punishment for a complex set of behaviors, with contingencies programmed for the group as a whole. The method was so successful that it was adopted by other teachers in the school, despite their earlier resistance to "behavior management" programs. Clearly, attention to the teacher and good study habits are needed for learning, and their control is obviously important in education.

There are many such illustrations of practical application of contingency management. For example, group contingencies have also been used in industry, rewarding workers with money as a function of the total productivity of an assembly line. Reports of many such applications appear quarterly in the recently established *Journal of Applied Behavior Analysis*. A number of experiments and case studies are reported in *Behavioral counseling* (Krumboltz & Thoresen, 1969) and in volumes of collected readings by Ulrich, Stachnik, and Mabry (1966, 1970). This is a truly revolutionary movement within the field of psychotherapy and behavior management. However, it would be a mistake to suppose that the success of these technical applications "proves" that all of Skinner's analysis of psychological phenomena is correct and true. They do show what benefits can be reaped by judicious applications of reinforcement contingencies and techniques of stimulus control; but then the empirical law of effect or the facts about stimulus discrimination have never been in much dispute within learning theory.

A current dispute within the "behavior modification" field separates those who adopt the strict Skinnerian approach from those adopting the "social learning theory" viewpoint (see Bandura, 1969; Mischel, 1971); the dispute concerns their interpretation of "cognitive learning" and "cognitive processes." Skinnerians tend to adopt a peripheral-response-oriented viewpoint of thinking, problem-solving, and learning by observation. Social learning theory, on the other hand, does not deny direct stimulus-response learning, but shows more concern for mediational events (Bandura, 1971a)— how the subject encodes the stimulus or the nature of his internal representation of events (e.g., as images rather than as verbal responses). But the issues here are similar in nature to the controversial assumptions which divided Tolman and Guthrie in the 1930s. The question fundamentally is whether observable behavior is to be the subject matter of psychology, or whether behavior is simply to be *evidence* of the operation of cognitive ("mental") processes which are the proper subject matter of psychology. We will return to this issue in Chapter 15.

ESTIMATE OF SKINNER'S SYSTEM

Skinner's Position on Typical Problems of Learning

The existence of general textbooks written from the standpoint of Skinner's position makes possible a summary in relation to problems that do not fit directly into his conceptual scheme.

1. Capacity. In a descriptive system, it is to be expected that the laws will contain empirical constants differing for various species and for different members of each species. The eating rate, for example, cannot be expected to remain the same for young and old animals, and for animals unlike in their food preferences. Because *lawfulness* rather than *laws* is what the systematist insists upon, differences in capacity are not of central importance. There is no suggestion that at higher capacity levels the laws are essentially any different; verbal behavior in man, for example, is said to conform to the general principles of operant behavior.

Skinner argues against the usefulness of a "trait" description in studying individual differences. A trait name does not refer to any unit of behavior suitable for study through the functional analysis that he recommends (1953, pp. 194–203). Thus, Skinner would reject most "personality tests," saying that they provide useless characterizations of the person. Intelligence tests might be useful for educational decisions, since they sample directly the problem-solving skills they purport to measure; but the tests do not tell us how to *remedy* specific educational disabilities or deficits.

2. Practice. Something like a simple law of exercise (practice under conditions of contiguity of stimulus and response) is accepted for Type S conditioning. The conditioning that occurs under Type R depends upon repeated reinforcement. The possibility is favored that maximum reinforcement may occur in a single trial for the single operant, but the single operant is difficult to achieve experimentally. Usually, the accumulation of strength with repeated reinforcement depends upon a population of discriminated stimuli and a chain of related operants, more or less after the manner of Guthrie's interpretation of the acquisition of skill with practice.

3. Motivation. Reward or reinforcement is necessary to increase operant strength. Punishment has a diverse range of effects, although typically it suppresses the response. The common usage of human motivational terms like *interest, apathy, happiness, depression,* and so on, refer typically to the consequences of effective or ineffective reinforcement contingencies. Internal drives are generally viewed by Skinner as relatively useless explanatory constructs, similar to personality traits. Skinner recognizes the effects of explicit deprivation variables on strength of operants reinforced by that restricted commodity, but he claims that nothing is added to a functional analysis by talking about a "drive" intervening between deprivation operations and changes in strength of operant responses.

4. Understanding. The word *insight* does not occur in the indexes of Skinner's books. Keller and Schoenfeld identify insight with verbal description of learning contingencies, which typically produce subsequent behavior change under the stimulus-control of that verbal description. Problem-solving typically involves tacting (labeling) the problematical situation properly, then activating an appropriate verbal response sequence leading up to a mediated cue for the solution behavior (as in the Staats and Staats analysis of solving the two-string problem). The emergence of the solution is to be explained on the basis of (1) similarity of the present problem to one solved earlier, or (2) the *simplicity* of the problem (F. S. Keller & Schoenfeld, 1950, p. 60). The technique of problem-solving is essentially that of manipulating variables (internal or external "hints" or stimuli) which lead to emission of the response. It is possible to teach people to "think" or "be creative" by these methods (Skinner, 1953, pp. 252–256).

5. Transfer. Skinner used the word *induction* for what is commonly called generalization in the conditioning literature. Such induction is the basis for transfer. As do others, he recognizes both primary and "secondary" or "mediated" generalization. The reinforcement of a response increases the probability of that response or similar ones to all stimulus complexes containing the same elements. Included is feedback stimulation from verbal labels; thus, an overt response will occur to a novel object if some property of it controls a verbal label which in turn controls the overt response. Therefore, having learned to shoot a revolver at soldiers in green uniforms in a particular fire zone, a man will also fire a rifle at any new soldier he sees in a green uniform in the same place. This general interpretation of transfer is, in spirit, very similar to Thorndike's.

DIFFICULTIES FOR SKINNER'S POSITION

As psychological science and thought grows, it is expected that new phenomena will be uncovered and new concepts invented in such manner as to make specific historical positions untenable. This has occurred with several of Skinner's earlier ideas over the ensuing years, and a balanced evaluation of Skinner requires mention of these difficulties with the approach. The discussions here will be brief; for elaboration of each point, the articles cited should be consulted.

1. Operant-respondent distinction.   As we noted earlier in our review of the operant-respondent distinction, this is now undergoing reformulation (see N. E. Miller, 1969; Terrace, 1973). A clear operational criterion no longer suffices to separate operant and respondent conditioning. And the issue has apparently been resolved that so-called respondent behavior can be conditioned by the law of Type R. The issue then is whether any "true" Type S is possible, or whether it always involves some "reward" in subtle form. Skinner's earlier position on these matters is no longer tenable.

2. Preparedness.   As reviewed in Chapter 3, increasing evidence is refuting the *equipotentiality* postulate to which Skinner and other learning theorists have implicitly subscribed (which justified the use of such arbitrary responses as a lever-press by a rat). This assumes that any response the organism is capable of can be attached to any discriminable stimulus for any reinforcing stimulus; and the learning of the three-term contingency depends only on the independent identities of the three terms, not their relation of natural fittingness or belongingness. Evidence reviewed by Seligman (1970) shows counterexamples; a stimulus may elicit innate responses which strongly compete with the one to be learned; or a given species-specific response (e.g., yawning in a dog) may occur only to specific stimuli and not be conditionable to other stimuli; or a reinforcer may recruit a set of instinctual activities which compete with the arbitrary operant which is to be established in the three-term contingency. For example, Breland and Breland (1960) reported many cases of instinctive behavior closely linked to food which began to intrude in advance of food delivery, interfering with the correct operant response and delaying reinforcement. Seligman proposes a classification of S-R-S contingencies in terms of whether individuals of a given species are *prepared* or *contraprepared* to make those attachments. An illustration of a prepared connection is the relating of an intestinal upset and nausea to an earlier novel taste, whereas the animal is contraprepared to relate that same upset to a flashing light. Another illustration is that pigeons are highly prepared to peck objects for food reinforcement; pecking is an innate response recruited by food foraging in pigeons. So powerful is this relation that it produces a strange phenomenon recently discovered and called *autoshaping* by P. L. Brown and H. M. Jenkins (1968). They showed that hungry pigeons can be trained to peck a lighted response key simply by illuminating the key for a few seconds before food delivery. No response-reinforcement contingency is needed at all. D. R. Williams and H. Williams (1969) increased the paradox by showing that autoshaped key-pecking was maintained even if the key-peck turned off the key light and thus prevented food delivery on that trial. (On other trials, when the peck did not occur, the key light was followed by food.) In terms of the simple law of effect, it would seem that the animal ought to learn to avoid key-pecking. Autoshaping is thus a good example of behavior recruited by the reinforcer which violates the principle of reinforcement. These are difficulties not anticipated within the principles of operant conditioning.

3. Learning-performance distinction.   Skinner has always considered reinforcers as strengthening S-R connections directly, and has had little use for the learning-performance distinction which has been central to other learning theorists. But this issue clearly comes to the fore when it can be shown that someone has learned something quite well and knows how to do it, but does not perform for lack of reinforcement. For example, Bandura, Grusec and Menlove (1966) had children observe a child model in a film perform a series of novel aggressive acts, and then the model received either rewarding, neutral, or punishing consequences in the film from a "teacher." When the child was later allowed to perform in the same situation, the frequency of aggressive responses imitating those of the model varied directly with the reinforcement of the model shown in the film. However, when incentives were offered in a second test for reproduction of the model's behaviors, the differences in imitation virtually disappeared between subjects exposed to differently rewarded models. Apparently, the children had learned the same amount from observing the model's behavior; they performed more or less of that behavior depending on whether they "expected" to be reinforced for it. Although Skinner can make this distinction (e.g., in terms of two levels of learning, one regarding the behaviors, and a controlling one regarding the consequences of that behavior), the fact is that he frequently does not, so that learning and performance concepts are rather confusedly intertwined in his discussions. Other psychologists are coming to the conclusion that reinforcement affects mainly performance (by means of "incentive motivation" or "anticipatory reward") rather than learning.

4. Observational learning. Related to the above point is the belief of cognitive psychologists that information about perceptual events can be learned by observation without the implicit verbalization or recitation of words (or other discriminating responses) referring to the observed events. The differing approach shows up in their analysis of how perceptual information is "remembered" over a retention interval before the organism is allowed to respond on the basis of that information. For instance, in "delayed matching to sample," a pigeon first sees a red or a green sample color, then has a short delay, followed by the lighting of two keys, one red and the other green, with reinforcement provided if he pecks the color which matches the sample color shown earlier in the trial. During the retention interval, how does the pigeon "remember" which sample color was presented? A standard Skinnerian reply would suppose that each sample color becomes gradually converted into a discriminative stimulus which immediately starts the animal running off two different chains of ritualistic behaviors which "code and carry" the discriminative information over time so that it is available to guide the delayed choice (viz., if chain 1 is in progress, choose the red key; if chain 2, choose the green key). But this claim of adventitious mediating chains has not always been substantiated by observation; often the discriminating animal simply seems to sit during the delay interval, or at least behave similarly during the two types of delay intervals. Apparently he just "remembers" as a central event, rather than remembering in his peripheral musculature.

5. Chomsky's critiques. Perhaps the most effective critiques of Skinner's systematic position and his extrapolation of it to human affairs have been provided by the linguist Noam Chomsky, first in his critical review of Skinner's book *Verbal behavior* (Chomsky, 1959), and later in a similar critical review of Skinner's *Beyond freedom and dignity* (Chomsky, 1971). Chomsky attacks Skinner on a number of different fronts. First, he argues that knowledge of a multitude of input-output (or S-R) relations provides no explanation for behavior in any sense; rather, our task should be to understand the internal structure, states, and organization of the device (organism) that produces this set of input-output relations. To restrict one's theoretical enterprise to observable stimuli and responses is, for Chomsky, to place unwarranted fetters on the development of the science, and to condemn it to be a "monumental triviality" (Arthur Koestler's description of "behaviorism"). "By objecting, a priori, to this research strategy [postulating a theory of internal structure], Skinner merely condemns his strange variety of 'behavioral science' to continued ineptitude" (Chomsky, 1971, p. 19). At issue here is whether behavior is to be the subject matter of psychology or is to be taken only as evidence for the operation of the mind.

Second, Chomsky adopts the standard lines of arguments of cognitive psychologists against the objectivity or validity of Skinner's concepts of stimulus, response, reinforcement, and response strength. Is any and every sensory event presented in the environment a stimulus, or just those to which the subject attends and reacts? What makes two stimulus patterns equivalent or similar? How can a "mediating pure stimulus act" be defined in objective terms? What responses are equivalent? Is the response not better defined as an action directed at a place? How do we distinguish topographically different responses which "mean" the same thing (e.g., proper names versus definite descriptions) and so are interchangeable instances of an operant class, from topographically identical responses which "mean" entirely different things depending on the context (e.g., answering "Yes" to "Did you kill George?" or to "Are you innocent of killing George?"). Similarly, regarding "reinforcements," recent evidence with human subjects (Dulany, 1968; Estes, 1969a) suggests that reinforcements function largely as informational events rather than as "response strengthening" events, and that a given event (e.g., electric shock, a blast of hot air) can be assigned positive or negative "reinforcing value" depending on the cognitive instructions given to the person. Further, research on "hypothesis-testing" behaviors by humans (e.g., M. Levine, 1970) suggests that "reinforcers" serve as information, confirming or disconfirming entire hypotheses which are equivalent to a full range of specific "S-R connections." So there are many difficulties with Skinner's position just at this most elementary level.

Third, Chomsky comes down very hard on Skinner's casual attempts to extrapolate his concepts from the relatively restricted "rat-in-a-Skinner-box" domain to interpretations of processes and phenomena of human mental life. He argues that in Skinner's analysis of common-sense terms such as *want, intend, like, plan,* and *persuade,* those concepts are rather inadequately translated into the three-term contingencies countenanced by Skinner's system. Chomsky's claim is that when Skinner's extrapolations are interpreted literally (in the original laboratory meanings of the terms), they are clearly false; and when these assertions are interpreted in Skinner's vague and metaphorical way, they turn out under analysis to be merely a poor substitute for common-sense usage. Because Chomsky is a linguist, he is particularly astute at showing the absence of clear reference of Skinner's allegedly scientific terms when he is discussing speech behavior. To take just one example, Skinner discusses verb endings (tense markers) by saying that for the speaker the past tense suffix -*ed* is controlled "by that subtle property of stimuli which we speak of as action-in-the-past" (Skinner, 1957, p. 121), whereas the -*s* in *The lady walks* is under the control of such specific features of the situation as its "currency." As Chomsky says (1959), "No characterization of the notion of 'stimulus control' that is remotely related to the bar-pressing experiment (or that preserves the faintest objectivity) can be made to cover a set of examples like these [Chomsky lists about seven or eight—*ed.*], in which, for example, the 'controlling stimulus' need not even impinge on the responding organism." Chomsky provides a number of specific criticisms of the specific examples of verbal behavior analyzed by Skinner.

Fourth, Chomsky argues that the empiricistic (read "behavioristic") approach to language analysis must perforce fail because it proposes to analyze only so-called surface features of utterances, whereas most regularities in language are revealed only when the grammatical "deep structure" is extracted by some complex syntax analyzer in our heads. The "deep structure" of a sentence is something like the logical propositions which it asserts. The same surface string of words may have different deep structures. Thus the phrase *They are eating apples* (and thousands like it) is grammatically ambiguous since it has two possible deep structures, depending on whether *eating* is interpreted as a verb (so *they* means *agent*) or as an adjective (*eating apples* as contrasted to *cooking apples*). Another example is *Time flies, which* is about three ways ambiguous depending on whether *time* and *flies* are independently interpreted as nouns or verbs (as in *The official timed the race*). The deep-structure analysis is also important in illuminating the underlying similarity of a set of surface strings which are otherwise quite distinct. Thus, the passive voice sentence *The boy was bitten by the snake* has a different surface form but the same deep structure as the active-voice sentence *The snake bit the boy*. The two surface forms are derived, according to Chomsky (1957, 1965), by two different *transformations* from the same deep structure or logical proposition. In the same manner, the sentence *Harold and Maude like to attend funerals and burials too* is derived by successive "deletion transformations" from the full conjunction *Harold and Maude like to attend funerals, and moreover, Harold and Maude like to attend burials.*

Chomsky argues that these similarities and regularities among surface utterances cannot be understood without the speaker's or listener's having tacitly acquired a well-developed "theory" of English grammar enabling him to perform something like these translations. Chomsky and his colleagues (e.g., Bever, 1968; Bever, Fodor, & Garrett, 1968) have argued that theories of language which deal only with the observable ("surface") features of the utterance cannot in principle provide an illuminating explanation of our linguistic abilities (e.g., in detecting ambiguities, in recognizing similarities of underlying forms, in generating recursive embeddings of subpropositions, etc.). Rather we must postulate more abstract concepts and assign to the language understander an "internal grammatical theory" which is tacit and exceedingly complex.

This is hardly the place to discuss these claims in detail. The main idea to be gotten across is the revolutionary nature of Chomsky's arguments and claims against the rising tide of behaviorism, and the fact that he is partly responsible for the return of cognitive psychology (and "psycholinguistics") to a position of prominence. In later commenting on his review of *Verbal behavior*, Chomsky had this to say:

Rereading this review after eight years, I find little of substance that I would change if I were to write it today. I am not aware of any theoretical or empirical work that challenges its conclusions; nor, so far as I know, has there been any attempt to meet the criticisms that are raised in the review or to show that they are erroneous or ill-founded.

I had intended this review not specifically as a criticism of Skinner's speculations regarding language, but rather as a more general critique of behaviorist (I would now prefer to say "empiricist") speculation as to the nature of higher mental processes . . . I do not see any way in which [Skinner's] proposals čan be substantially improved within the general framework of behaviorist or neobehaviorist, or, more generally, empiricist ideas that has dominated much of modern linguistics, psychology, and philosophy. The conclusion that I hoped to establish in the review—was that the general point of view is largely mythology, and that its widespread acceptance is not the result of empirical support, persuasive reasoning, or the absence of a plausible alternative. (1967, p. 142)

Although MacCorquodale (1969, 1970) later attempted to answer Chomsky's critique, the tide in psycholinguistics had long since turned to a transformational approach to studying linguistic competence and performance, and the answers simply did not register as effective or persuasive. It is a truism today that experimental psycholinguistics is a branch of linguistics (or "cognitive psychology") rather than an extension of behavioristic learning theories (see, e.g., Slobin, 1971, for a representative presentation of psycholinguistics).

THE CLASH WITH TRADITIONAL VIEWPOINTS

Skinner's "fresh start" approach to psychology has made it difficult for him to use the data collected by others outside the "operant conditioning" camp, and he rejects on principle the sorts of theoretical constructions to which other learning theorists are prone. Skinner and his followers have felt no responsibility for the task of coordinating their work closely with that of others studying learning (and the indifference is regrettably often mutual). For instance, in his most systematic book, *Science and human behavior* (1953), Skinner used no literature citations at all, and of those writers with some place in learning theory, he mentions by name only Thorndike, Pavlov, and Freud.

This insularity is carried forward in pages of the *Journal of the Experimental Analysis of Behavior (JEAB)*, which is in essentials the house organ of the operant conditioning movement. As an index of what literature is being taken into account, an analysis of the papers cited in the bibliography of *JEAB* articles shows that nearly 40 percent of citations are to work previously published in *JEAB*, whereas a comparable specialized journal, the *Journal of Verbal Learning and Verbal Behavior*, shows less than 20 percent self-citations (see Krantz, 1971). Moreover, proportionate citations to *JEAB* articles in other journals devoted to analysis of conditioning and learning have actually fallen somewhat over the years. This tends to create two isolated camps or "schools," the operant conditioners versus the remainder of learning psychologists, who go their separate ways, tilling their independent soils.

Why is there this isolation, particularly the rejection of most of the rest of psychology by the operant conditioners? Krantz (1971) has proposed that strongly different experimental methodologies separate the two camps. The Skinnerian (see Sidman, 1960) argues that traditional experimental design (in learning studies), using trial-by-trial data averaged over trials and over different subjects, "destroys, confounds, or omits the significant data of moment to moment rate changes in a single organism's behavior" (Krantz, 1971, p. 62). In the conventional experimental design, a single subject receives typically a few learning trials in only one condition; in operant conditioning, a single subject may receive thousands of "trials" on any one experimental condition (reaching "steady-state behavior," as they say) before being switched to another value of a schedule variable or to a different experimental condition where he will again receive thousands of trials. A single subject may thus be successively cycled through nearly all values of the independent variable (e.g., mean VI length), his successive steady-state behaviors "tracing out" the functional relation as it exists for him. But the conventional design would use different subjects at the different values— the so-called "between-subjects" design.

This procedural difference is quite transparent in statistics (Krantz, 1971) on the relative usage of between-subjects versus within-subjects designs in *JEAB* and the comparable *Journal of Comparative and Physiological Psychology (JCPP)*; for the years 1967 and 1969, only about 3 percent of *JEAB* articles used a between-subjects design, whereas 89 percent of *JCPP* studies did so; on the other hand, only 6 percent of *JCPP* studies used an exclusively within-subject design, whereas about 90 percent of *JEAB* articles did. (These percentages do not add to 100 because of mixed designs.)

Sidman (1960, p. 53 ff.) sees these two design strategies as incommensurate. The key to use of the within-subject design is *reversibility* of a behavioral phenomenon, particularly steady-state behavior. Reversibility means that a particular steady-state behavior under specified contingencies can be recovered over and over again after the subject has been shifted temporarily to other conditions and then returned to the original contingencies. Other psychologists may shy away from within-subject experiments because of general "transfer" effects, afraid that the subject's behavior in a condition will depend on earlier conditions experienced and their order. The typical remark is that performance on later schedule parameters is "confounded" by general transfer effects, with unknown contaminating influences.

Sidman's reply is, first, to assert that such transfer effects are rare in steady-state experiments; and second, that if they exist, then they are themselves important objects for study. Irreversibility or "transfer" from one to another learning condition cannot be gotten around by running independent groups on the separate values of the independent variable and plotting a curve through the group average. As Sidman says:

> . . . the function so obtained does not represent a behavioral process. The use of separate groups destroys the continuity of cause and effect that characterizes an irreversible behavioral process.
>
> If it proves impossible to obtain an "uncontaminated" relation in a single subject [because of interactions], then the "pure" relation simply does not exist. The solution to our problem is to cease trying to discover such a pure relation, and to direct our research toward the study of behavior as it actually exists.
>
> . . . [W]here irreversibility is met, there is no individual curve that can answer the questions one may put to the group curve, or vice versa. The student should not be deceived into concluding that the group type of experiment in any way provides a more adequately controlled or more generalizable substitute for individual data.
>
> If my point strikes home, it should lead the student to re-evaluate much of the supposedly systematic data of experimental psychology. . . . When this is done, the student may find that he must abandon many of psychology's cherished generalizations. He is also likely to find himself faced with a choice. For the two types of data represent, in a real sense, different subject matters. (p. 53)

It may be noted that the split between the two methodologies depends on the focus of interest—in particular, whether transitional (and transitory) behavior is of primary concern, as when the animal is *acquiring* a new skill or *extinguishing* an old habit; or whether asymptotic steady-state behavior is of central concern. The older learning theories tended to concentrate on acquisition and its rate, whereas operant conditioners are much more concerned with the steady-state behavior maintained by given contingencies. Their methodology rather resembles that of the psychophysicist who tests a single subject repeatedly. Similar designs are now common in studies of human memory (e.g., Atkinson & Shiffrin, 1965) and information processing (e.g., Sternberg, 1969). Therefore, there is really no reason for methodological segregation of these fields any longer. The main division thus remains theoretical preference—or, rather, a preference for theorizing on one side versus an active antipathy to theorizing within the operant conditioning group. This comes down to the matter of deciding what are the proper goals of a scientific psychology. And here we come again upon the empiricism-rationalism schism of antiquity. There is a fundamental opposition between scientists who believe that progress is to be made only by rigorous examination of the actual behavior of organisms and those who believe that behavioral observations are interesting only insofar as they reveal to us hidden underlying laws of the mind that are only partially revealed in behavior. Is psychology to be the science of the mind, or the science of behavior? Is physics the science of physical things, or the science of meter readings? Do behaviorists confuse the subject matter of the field with the evidence available for drawing inferences about this subject matter? Skinner opts for behavior as the subject matter; cognitive psychologists who form the current opposition (e.g., Neisser, 1967) suppose that one uses behavior as *evidence* for the operation of cognitive processes. This contemporary clash between alternative views illustrates how very fundamental are these essentially historic and philosophic assumptions.

SUPPLEMENTARY READINGS

The following books contain Skinner's own accounts of his work:
SKINNER, B. F. (1938) *The behavior of organisms.*
SKINNER, B. F. (1953) *Science and human behavior.*
SKINNER, B. F. (1957) *Verbal behavior.*
SKINNER, B. F. (1968) *The technology of teaching.*
SKINNER, B. F. (1969) *Contingencies of reinforcement.*
SKINNER, B. F. (1971) *Beyond freedom and dignity.*
FERSTER, C. B., & SKINNER, B. F. (1957) *Schedules of reinforcement.*
HOLLAND, J. G., & SKINNER, B. F. (1961) *The analysis of behavior: A program for self-instruction.*

A collection of Skinner's experimental and theoretical papers, selected by him as representative of his contributions, is found in:
SKINNER, B. F. (1961) *Cumulative record.*

A retrospective appraisal of some of Skinner's work, along with some autobiographical material, is:
DEWS, P. B. (1970) *Festschrift for B. F. Skinner.*

Skinner's novel *Walden two* (1948), also available as a paperback, is worth reading along with *Science and human behavior* (1953) for a comparison between the scientific system and its imaginary application in an experimental utopia. His *Beyond freedom and dignity* argues for application of "behavioral technology" to the ills of society. It has had a very controversial reception among intellectuals and social critics. The ethical implications of Skinner's proposals for social control were the subject of a debate between him and Carl Rogers (Rogers & Skinner, 1956).

For the methodological positions of Skinner, an inspiring book is by M. Sidman (1960) *Tactics of scientific research.* For illustrations of various applications, a useful source is W. K. Honig (Ed.) (1966) *Operant behavior: Areas of research and application.* Note also T. Verhave (Ed.) (1966) *The experimental analysis of behavior: Selected readings.*

Gestalt Theory

During the first quarter of the century in America the quarrels within academic psychology lay chiefly inside the framework of association psychology. Structuralism, functionalism, and behaviorism were all members of the association family. They are all examples of the working out of an *empiricist* methodology of science, whereby the accumulation of facts was supposed to lead one to the proper conception of nature. This complacency was disturbed by the new Gestalt doctrine which influenced the early American learning theories chiefly through the appearance in English of Wolfgang Köhler's *The mentality of apes* (1925) and Kurt Koffka's *The growth of the mind* (1924). The theory had been developing in Germany since it was first announced by Max Wertheimer in 1912, but these books, and the visits of Köhler and Koffka to America about the time of their publication, brought the new theory vividly to the attention of American psychologists. Gestalt theory is one of the few examples of a *rationalist* theory in psychology. Gestalters begin with certain rather abstract ideas, concerning the nature of perception and thinking and the structure of psychological experience; they then proceed to *interpret* familiar observations in terms of these novel concepts as well as to arrange striking *demonstrations* of the operation of the alleged organizing forces to which their theory refers.

It must be remembered that Gestalt psychologists were primarily interested in perception and in problem-solving processes. Learning was viewed as a secondary, derivative phenomenon of no special interest; what was learned was a product of and determined by the laws of perceptual organization; what was performed depended on how current problem-solving processes analyzed the present situation and made use of traces of past experience. It is easy to see why, with this orientation, Gestalters did relatively few studies of learning *per se*, or at least would prefer to study human learning.

However, the strong "conditioning and animal learning" bias of early American psychology forced the Gestalters to undertake their discussions and controversies in America within the arena of animal learning and the special problems of interpreting it which were engaging the imaginations of psychologists at that time. Therefore, from its very first importation to America, Gestalt psychology was forced to defend itself on alien scientific territory.

For instance, Koffka's and Köhler's books had an important effect upon early American learning theory because of their detailed criticism of trial-and-error learning as conceived by Thorndike—a thrust at the very heart of the currently popular theory. The vigorous attack on Thorndike (and upon behaviorism) was supported by Köhler's well-known experiments on apes, described in detail in his book. Köhler's book brought the notion of insightful learning into the foreground, as an alternative to trial and error. He showed how apes could obtain rewards without going through the laborious processes of stamping out incorrect responses and stamping in correct ones, as implied in Thorndike's theories and as displayed in the learning curves of Thorndike's cats. Apes could use sticks and boxes as tools; they could turn away from the end of the activity toward a means to the end.

Köhler's Insight Experiments

Köhler's experiments with apes were done in the years 1913–1917, on the island of Tenerife off the coast of Africa. His book about these experiments (Köhler, 1917) appeared in English a few years later and immediately was widely read and quoted. Two main series of experiments interested the American psychological public in the problems of insight. These were the box problems and the stick problems.

In the single-box situation, a lure, such as a banana, is attached to the ceiling of the chimpanzee's cage. The lure is out of reach but can be obtained by climbing upon and jumping from a box which is available in the cage. The problem is a difficult one for the chimpanzee. Only Sultan (Köhler's most intelligent ape) solved it without assistance, though six others mastered the problem after first being helped either by having the box placed beneath the food or by watching others using the box. The problem was not solved by direct imitation of others. What watching others use the box did was to lead the observer to attempt to use the box as a leaping platform, but sometimes without making any effort whatsoever to bring it near the lure. When the problem was mastered, a chimpanzee alone in a cage with box and banana would turn away from the goal in order to seek the box and to move it into position. This "detour" nature of insightful behavior is, according to Köhler, one of its important features.

The box-stacking problem, requiring that a second box be placed upon the first before the banana can be reached, is much more difficult. It requires both the incorporation of the second box into the pattern of solution, and a mastery of the problem of building a stable two-box structure. While the emphasis in secondary accounts of Köhler's work is usually upon the intelligence his apes displayed, he himself was at pains to account for the amount of apparent stupidity. In the box-stacking experiment, for example, he believed that the apes had shown insight into the relationship of "one box upon another," but not into the nature of a stable two-box structure. Such physical stability as was achieved in later structures was essentially a matter of trial and error.

The stick problems required the use of one or more sticks as tools with which to rake in food out of reach beyond the bars of the cage. The beginning of insight occurs as the stick is brought into play, although often unsuccessfully, as when it is thrown at the banana and lost. Once it has been used successfully, it is sought after by the chimpanzee and used promptly. The most dramatic of the stick-using experiments was in a problem mastered by Sultan, in which eventually two sticks were joined together after the manner of a jointed fishing pole in order to obtain a banana which could not be reached with either stick alone. The process was a slow one, and the first placing of the sticks together appeared to be more or less accidental. Once having seen the sticks in this relationship, however, Sultan was able to "get the idea" and to repeat the insertion of one stick into the end of the other over and over again in order to reach a distant banana.

Köhler's interpretation of such performances by his apes was that they were intelligent attempts at problem-solving; that confronted with a problem, the animal could survey the relevant conditions, perhaps "think through" the probable success of a given act, then test it out as a possible solution to the problem. Köhler was particularly concerned with the way his apes might suddenly "see" the instrumental value of a tool (the stick as an extended arm) as a means to the goal. Because of these perceptual interpretations of the "Eureka!" experience, they were dubbed *insight* experiments and the repetition of the successful act following insight was called *insight learning*.

Although the attack by Köhler and Koffka was chiefly upon Thorndike, it came at a time when American psychology was in the grips of a confident but somewhat sterile behaviorism. It is hard to see at this distance why such a common-sense and familiar notion as intelligent problem-solving (insight) should have created such a stir. But at the time Watsonian behaviorism had, in fact, won support for a fairly "hard-boiled" view of learning, according to which the organism was played upon by the pushes and pulls of the environment and reacted in ways essentially stupid. Lloyd Morgan's canon which had seriously undercut the attributing of higher mental processes to animals had fairly well succeeded by means of behaviorism in excising them from man also. Therefore the return to a more balanced view, represented by the insight experiments, gave new hope to teachers and others who saw thinking and understanding returned to respectability. Insight was not a new discovery—it was a return to a conception laymen had never abandoned. Nobody uninfluenced by peculiar doctrines would ever have denied insight as a fact—yet it took Köhler to restore it as a fact in American psychology. It was, in some respects, time for a change, and Köhler's experiments dramatized release from the negatives of Thorndikian and Watsonian thinking.

That the more enthusiastic reception for the new learning theories should have come first from the educators is not surprising.[1] There had already

---

[1] It was an educator-psychologist, R. M. Ogden, who translated Koffka (1924).

been a rift growing between Thorndike and the more progressive group within education, who, under Dewey's leadership, had made much more than Thorndike of the capacity of the individual for setting and solving his own problems. The child should learn by understanding the structure of a problem, not by rote repetition of an incomprehensible formula. The new insight doctrine fitted nicely their slogan of freeing intelligence for creative activity.

The visible opposition between Köhler and Thorndike was over insight and trial and error, that is, over intelligent learning as contrasted with blind fumbling. But the opposition between Gestalt psychology and association psychology goes much deeper. In order to understand this opposition, it will be necessary to examine the Gestalt views in greater detail.

There are a number of variants within the Gestalt movement and among those strongly influenced by Gestalt conceptions. Köhler and Koffka were closest to Wertheimer, the official founder of the school. This chapter is devoted to their treatment of learning. Lewin, while originally from Berlin and definitely within the ranks, broke new ground. All four of these men, originally German, eventually settled in America, where they all have since died. They are the leaders of what is historically Gestalt psychology.

The fullest and most systematic treatment of the problems of learning from the Gestalt viewpoint is found in Koffka's *Principles of Gestalt psychology* (1935). It was written after a period of acclimatization to America, and so meshes somewhat better than earlier writings with the concerns of American psychologists. Most of the direct references will be made to this source.

Gestalt psychology had its start and achieved its greatest success in the field of perception. Its demonstrations of the role of background and organization upon phenomenally perceived processes are so convincing that only an unusually stubborn opponent will discredit the achievement. The primary attack upon association theory was an attack on the "bundle hypothesis" sensation theory—the theory that a percept is composed of sensation-like elements, bound together by association.

When the Gestalt psychologists turned later to the problems of learning, the concepts brought to the study of learning were those which had succeeded in the field of perception, and the arguments previously used against the sensation were turned against the reflex. In spite of the attention which Köhler's ape experiments received, Gestalt psychologists can be fairly said to have been only moderately interested in learning. This does not mean that their few experiments are without significance; it means only that they have considered the problems of learning secondary to the problems of perception. Perhaps in America the shoe was on the other foot, and in preoccupation with learning American psychology had for too long been neglecting the relationship between the two fields.

The starting point for the Gestalter's treatment of learning is the assumption that the laws of organization in perception are applicable to learning. What is stored in memory are traces of perceptual events. Since organizational laws determine the structuring of perceptions, they also determine the structure of what information is laid down in memory. In the case of "trial-and-error" learning in which the learner is confronted with some problem (e.g., to escape from the puzzle-box), Gestalt theory assigns great importance to the way the subject structures or "sees" the problem situation and how salient the correct action is within that structure. The ease or difficulty of the problem is thus largely a matter of perception. In this sense, Köhler's apes were presented with perceptual problems; if they literally "saw" the situation correctly, they had insight.

LAWS OF ORGANIZATION

Below we shall describe a few of the "laws" of perceptual organization as first proposed in a classic paper by Wertheimer (1923, translated and reprinted in 1938). He describes certain stimulus variables that determine how we "group" together certain stimuli, and thus how we structure or interpret a visual field in a certain way. Wertheimer mentioned a number of subsidiary factors, but we shall illustrate here only the factors of proximity, similarity, common direction, and simplicity. There were various attempts by the Gestalters to formulate a more general law stipulating the common features of these subsidiary laws of grouping. This more general formulation was called the law of *Prägnanz* (translatable not as "pregnant" but as "compact and significant"). This "law" in essentials says simply that psychological organization (read "perceptual groupings") tends to be "good gestalts" or "good figures," as determined by the subsidiary laws, and that this organization has the properties of regularity, simplicity, stability over time, and so on. Although Köhler and Koffka tried to explain the operation of this law of *Prägnanz* in terms of dynamic distributions of "fields" of energy in the brain, subsequent generations have considered such explanations as relatively nonsensical (see, e.g., Madden, 1962) and they will not be repeated here. However, we will try to show with each perceptual law an illustration of how it has been or could be used in a learning experiment.

1. The law of proximity. Elements of a field will tend to be grouped together according to their nearness or proximity to one another. The closer together two elements are, the more likely they are to be grouped together. A few illustrations are given in Figure 8.1 using dots. In panel (a), the dots are perceived in groups of three, as *abc/def/ghi*, rather than another grouping like *ab/cde/fgh*. In panel (b), we group the dots as three rows of three dots rather than as three columns of dots. In panel (c), we aggregate the dots into groups *a/bcd/efghi/jklmnop* on the basis of their relative proximities.

These illustrate the proximity factor with visual stimuli distributed about in space. But we may also define proximity with discrete auditory stimuli distributed in time. In tapping on a drum, one will notice "auditory groups" emerging as a result of alternating short and long time intervals ("proximities") between taps. These groupings, of course, elaborated into complex hierarchies of groupings within groupings, form the basis for musical rhythms.

These illustrations with dots and drum taps demonstrate the law with relatively neutral or meaningless stimuli. But this factor of proximity is in constant use when we communicate in reading, writing, or talking. We *hear* ("organize") speech as a series of distinct words with pauses between words and sentences, even though a spectrogram shows in actuality an almost continuous flow of sound (which *is* the way we hear an unfamiliar foreign language). In reading, spaces are used between words in order to se-gr-eg-at-et-he-wo-rd-si-nt-ou-ni-ts, and reading is very disrupted when this familiar segregation is broken. Strings of familiar letters or acronyms may not even be recognized if they are presented rapidly to the subject grouped into novel units.

Examples of the use of this grouping factor occur in recent research on memory by G. H. Bower and D. Winzenz (1969) and G. H. Bower and F. Springston (1970). They had their subjects (college students) immediately recall a number of 12-letter series (or 12 digits) read to them according to a particular pause structure. With dashes to indicate temporal pauses, a typical series for recall might be *IC–BMF–BIJ–FKCO*. An important feature of such recall is that the pause-defined groups tend to behave as all-or-none units in recall; that is, the person tends to recall either all of the "chunk" or none of the "chunk." This means, for example, that the *J* in the third chunk is much more closely tied (or associated) to *B* and *I* than it is to the *F* which follows it in order. Bower and Springston (1970) showed also that recall of a letter series was also very much better if the pauses segregated it into familiar acronyms. Thus, the former series was better recalled if presented according to the pause structure *ICBM–FBI–JFK–CO* in which the pause-defined ("perceptual") groups correspond to familiar acronyms the person already knows.

You have met this law of grouping before in the guise of Thorndike's principle of "belongingness" (see Chapter 2). Two events would become associated only if they "belong together," and one of the determinants of this belongingness of *A* with *B* is that the two occur close together in time or space. For example, suppose a student is told to learn from sight the following associations:

CUF–NUX
PEL–JER
DEQ–PEM
SOQ–RIL

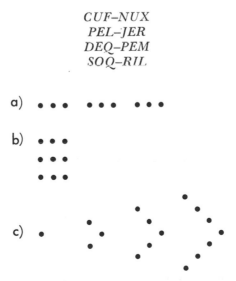

Figure 8.1. Illustrations of proximity as a grouping factor.

It will be found on later tests that he treated these as pairs, rehearsing and associating *CUP* to *NUX*, and *PEL* to *JER*, and so on. However, he has not formed associations from *NUX* to *PEL* or from *NUX* to *JER*, despite the fact that all these elements are spatially proximate to one another. The latter pairings are not seen as "belonging together." This illustrates the fact that the paired-associate learning procedure capitalizes on the "law of proximity" for defining the groups to be learned, and for setting them off from one another.

2. The law of similarity.   The law of similarity states that items similar in respect to some feature (shape, color, etc.) will tend to be grouped together, provided this is not overridden by proximity factors. A few illustrations of this factor are given in Figure 8.2. Panel (a) is organized into successive triplets of black and white dots. Panel (b) is seen as successive columns of white and black dots in alternation. These similarity factors can be put into opposition or supplementation to the groupings suggested by proximities of the elements. Panel (c) shows opposition of the two factors in which spatial proximity clearly wins; these are seen as spatially segregated pairs with black and white dots alternating in their left-right order. Panel (d) shows "addition" of the two factors, both suggesting the same groupings.

A similar factor operates in the perception of auditory groups, say of tones differing in pitch. Thus two notes (C and F) played in pairs will be heard as CC/FF/CC/FF rather than as C/CF/FC. This factor also contributes to the perception of musical rhythm.

This factor is utilized constantly when we read or speak. For example, at a cocktail party, we can pick out and listen to a particular speaker against a noisy background because of the similarity of the speaker's voice quality from one moment to the next. Our shadowing or following of a spoken message becomes exceedingly difficult if the voice quality is constantly altered (e.g., by splicing in on a tape recorder a different voice for each word in the message). A similar result occurs with reading WhErEaLlThElEtTeRs within a word are usually about the same size and color, making for ease of grouping.

A learning experiment by G. H. Bower (1972a) illustrates the potency of

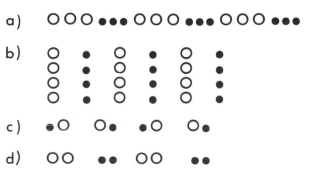

Figure 8.2.   Illustration of grouping by similarity (of color and size in this instance).

this similarity factor in promoting chunking of letter groups in recall. College students were shown flashcards on each of which were printed 12 equally spaced letters which in fact comprised four familiar acronyms. The letters varied in size, on some cards the large and small groupings corresponding to the acronym series, on other cards not corresponding. An example of a corresponding series is *YMCAtwaIBM tb*, whereas a noncorresponding series would be *YAleuSAIbmgi*. Such a series was shown for only a few seconds before the subject was asked to recall it from memory. As expected, when successive letters of an acronym were presented in the same size, they tended to be seen together as a group, and to be recognized and recalled as the familiar group that they were. In the noncorresponding cases, however, subjects tended to adopt the groupings (by similarity) into unfamiliar chunks, and so recalled the string more poorly. Thus, for instance, in the above illustration, the person would tend to recall the letters *SAI* as an all-or-none unit (albeit poorly) rather than breaking the perceptual groupings to recall *USA/IBM* as units. A similar effect on recall was produced by only varying the *colors* of the successive letters on the card. The first four letters might be red, the next three yellow, the next three brown, and the last two blue. If the acronyms of different lengths were also arranged in this order, first the acronym of length 4, then two of length 3, finally the acronym of length 2, then the letters of a given acronym would be of the same color, which aided their unitization and boosted their recall. But if the order of acronym lengths conflicted with the colors, recognition of familiar abbreviations was poorer and recall of the briefly shown series was much worse.

3. The law of common direction.   A set of points will tend to be grouped together if some appear to continue or complete a lawful series or extrapolate a simple curve. This is best illustrated with some examples as shown in Figure 8.3. Consider panel (a) for instance. By a measure of physical proximity, the dots comprising lines *A* and *B* are closer together than the dots comprising lines *A* and *C*. And yet our eye tends to assign *A* and *C* to the same group, namely, as parts of the simple line *AC*, and *B* is just an appendage sticking off this line. However, by moving line *A* closer to *C*, as in the right-hand figure of panel (a), the organization is now altered so that *A* and *B* go together to make up a line unit, whereas *C* now becomes the appendage. In this latter case, *B* is an *extrapolation* of the curve (line, rule) begun in part *A*.

Panel (b) is simply a set of dots arranged in a saw-toothed line by a "directional interpretation" of the dots. But alternative "views" are logically possible; for example, the second row of dots could have been organized as three sets of dot pairs in a row. But they are not; common, simple direction of the dots dictates the saw-toothed organization.

In panels (c) and (d), the principle of good continuation is illustrated somewhat differently. Panel (c) is seen (organized by our perceptual system) as a wavy curve (*AD*) cut by a line (*BC*); but we logically could have seen it as the wave-plus-line *AC* attached to the line-plus-wave *BD*. In the same manner, panel (*d*) is organized as a series of square teeth intersected by a continuous wavy line, whereas it logically could have been seen as a top-half *C, D, G, H, K, L* drawn above the bottom half *A, B, E, F, I, J, M*. The

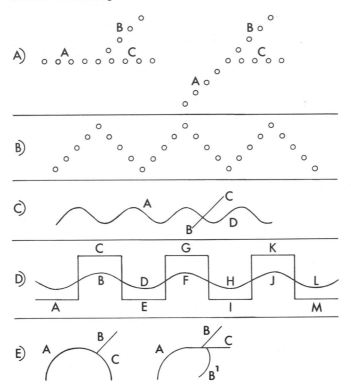

Figure 8.3.   Illustrations of common direction or good continuation.

factor of common direction or "common fate" determines the former "natural" descriptions of these drawings.

Panel (e) illustrates a point similar to that in panel (a), namely, that our eye pairs line segment A with C because one is a regular, smooth continuation or extrapolation of the other, whereas segment B or B^1 alters the direction of the curve, putting a "kink" or discontinuity in the curve.

It is relatively easy to arrange for demonstration of "learning effects" due to the factor of good continuation. One elementary demonstration is by Kaswan (1957), who tested subjects' ease of "associating together" pairs of geometric figures, A with B, where segment B either was or was not a "good continuation" of segment A. After seeing many different A-B pairs, the subject was tested by presentation of part A of each pair for his recall (in drawing) of part B. Looking, for instance, at panel (c) of Figure 8.3, the subject would be shown segment A and have to recall the part it was paired with, either D (if it had exemplified "good continuation") or C (if it had not). As expected, Kaswan found that pairs exemplifying the "good continuation" principle were learned and recalled much better than pairs not exemplifying this principle.

This demonstration incidentally raises the issue of whether the "responses" in the continuation and noncontinuation cases convey the same amount of "information" given the stimulus as a recall cue. Given extrapolation of the cue, there are no more than a few "good continuations," or possibly only one, to produce in response to a cue segment, but there are literally an infinite variety of possible noncontinuations. Perhaps the important feature is that, for good continuation pairs, the stimulus constrains the possible responses to one or a small number. If this is the correct analysis, then differences in performance should disappear with a recognition memory test in which the response alternatives for the "good continuation" pairs were *all* plausible good continuations of the stimulus cue for the pair. That experiment has yet to be done.

The principle of good continuation can be shown with alphabetic or numerical materials, whenever there is some possibility of inducing a *rule* for extrapolating a series of items. This kind of extrapolation is involved in "letter-completion problems" of the sort often found on intelligence tests. A few letters are given in a series, generated by some periodic rule by cycling through the alphabet (forward or backward); the person is to infer what the rule is and apply it to generate the next element. Thus, the series *abcbcdcdede* has a period of three, and cycles through the forward alphabet; the series therefore is completed by the letter *f*. Similar problems of inducing a generating rule occur with mathematical series; thus, the series 1, 3, 7, 13, 21 is "recognized" as the series $n^2 + n + 1$ and has 31 as the next successor.

Also illustrating "good continuation" in the learning context are experiments by Restle and Brown (1970) on the learning of serial patterns, in which subjects learn to predict recurrent periodic sequences of digits such as 3454543. It is shown that subjects conceptually break the sequences down into "runs" (like 345) and "trills" (like 454), and learn the pattern as an organized hierarchy of such parts or subsequences. The "run" in numbers as in the musical scale is defined by continuation of a series of elements in a given direction.

4. The law of simplicity. This law says that, other things being equal, the person will see his perceptual field as organized into simple, regular figures. That is, there will be a tendency toward the "good gestalts" of symmetry, regularity, and smoothness. Again, this notion is easier to illustrate than to make precise; Figure 8.4 shows a few examples. For instance, our eye tends to divide the figure of panel (a) into an ellipse (*AC*) overlapping with a square (*BD*), although another logically possible decomposition is *AB* (an ellipse with a chunk missing) abutting to *DBC* (a square with an interior curve). Similarly, in panel (b), the figure on the left appears as two overlapping icicles, whereas the figure on the right appears as a diamond inscribed inside a long icicle; yet the latter is logically (though not psychologically) decomposable into the same two overlapping icicles oriented differently. In panel (c), the pressures toward simplicity persuade us to structure the design as "a circle in front of a triangle," inferring the occluded triangle rather than describing the matter as "three small spurs at 4, 8, and 12 o'clock on a circle."

In these cases, and hundreds of others of the same general type, figural simplicity is an overriding principle dictating the way in which the picture will be "parsed" or decomposed into constituents. Pictures are always ambiguous in this sense of having multiple logical decompositions; they are

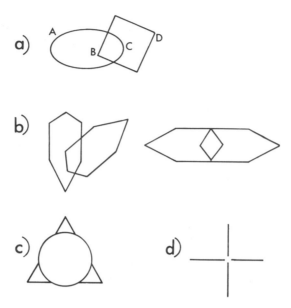

Figure 8.4.   Some illustrations of figural simplicity as a factor in perceptual organization.

also ambiguous insofar as a two-dimensional array can be the projection of a large variety of three-dimensional objects and relations. But the Gestalt principle of simplicity (or "good gestalt") goes a long way toward prescribing which decomposition or which interpretation of the ambiguous picture will dominate.

Another demonstration of the law of simplicity is shown by the "blind-spot" experiment schematized in panel (d) of Figure 8.4. Everyone has a blind spot in each eye; it is that spot on the retina from which the optic tract emanates. A point stimulus projected precisely on this spot is not seen; it is a "blind spot." With this as background, the crucial observation can be explained. Suppose we have discovered that when a person stares at a certain spot to one side of the figure in panel (d), his blindspot is located in space precisely at the intersection of the four lines of the figure. If the figure in panel (d) is now presented to the person in such a way that its center is located at his blind spot, he will "fill in the gap" and see the lines in peripheral vision as a complete cross. Other figures with gaps yield similar perceptions of closed, complete figures. What the brain has done is to fill in the gap with the redundant, predictable extrapolation of the simplest description of the figures. This is sometimes referred to as the phenomenon of "closure." The principle is that closed areas or complete figures are more stable than unclosed areas or incomplete figures.

These principles of perceptual organization can be put to use in the art of *camouflage* (Wertheimer, 1923), wherein a particularly significant figure is hidden or buried by extending and supplementing its lines so that attention is totally distracted from the original shape. We have now made a

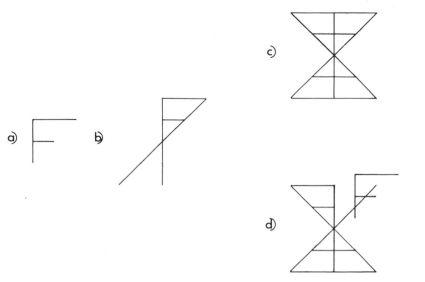

Figure 8.5.   Example of successive stages in camouflaging a shape, the letter F.

particular "parsing" of the pattern unlikely. A simple example of such a transformation of the letter F is shown in panels (a), (b), and (c) in Figure 8.5. The F is totally hidden or "embedded" in the hour-glass figure (c) on the right. On the other hand, if the lines are added but not touching or continuing the lines of F, as in figure (d), the F still stands out as a distinct unit.

THE SPECIAL PROBLEMS OF LEARNING

The general point of view of Gestalt psychology is expressed in the statement that the laws of organization apply equally to perception and to learning. There are, however, special problems within learning upon which Gestalters especially elaborated their ideas. They were most at ease in discussing human memory rather than animal conditioning experiments, and so most of the following illustrations deal with human memory. An initial problem is how to represent a memory, that is, how to conceptualize the way past experiences persist into the present. This is the concern of their trace theory, to which we now turn.

The Trace Theory

The Gestalt conception of a memory is not very different from that of Aristotle, who believed that perception stamped in a corresponding memory trace. Gestalters hold that the neural processes active during perception can endure in a "subdued" form as a trace. Thus, information is stored in substantially the same form, by the same neural processes, as in the original perception. As Köhler describes the matter:

Neural events tend to modify slightly the state of the tissue in which they occur. Such changes will resemble those processes by which they have been produced both in their pattern and with respect to other properties. (1938, p. 236)

Recall or remembering involves the reactivation of a given memory trace; in effect, it is a revival of the same perceptual processes that corresponded to the original perception. The trace continues to exist as an active process in the nervous system; but it is of too low an intensity to enter consciousness. In recall, a cue selects out and amplifies the intensity of a particular trace to raise it over the threshold of consciousness.

The empirical phenomena of association, or *coherence* of elements A and B in memory, is viewed by Gestalters as a by-product of A and B becoming fused into a single unit, a unitary percept. The elements A and B do not remain as independent, separate, neutral facts connected by an indifferent "bond" like a piece of string between two distinct objects. Rather, A and B become organized or fused into a "single object," a unit, a chunk. The laws of organization help prescribe how these units will be formed and how easily they can be formed. The ancient laws of association delineated by philosophers—contiguity, contrast, similarity, cause-effect, and so on—were seen as corresponding to Gestalt laws governing the formation of organized units—namely, proximity, similarity, good continuation, and closure.

Solomon Asch (1969; Asch, Ceraso, & Heimer, 1960) has produced several compelling demonstrations of the role of perceptual relations in promoting coherence of two items in memory. He has collected evidence regarding the visual relations of figure-ground, constitutive, and part-whole. In the figure-ground experiment, the person was exposed to a set of ten nonsense shapes paired with ten colors. There were several conditions corresponding to different relations between the color and the shape with which it was paired. Four of these conditions are illustrated in the top panel of Figure 8.6. The frame represents the $3'' \times 5''$ card on which the form was shown. In case (a), the color (C) was seen as belonging to the surface of the figure against a white background (W), whereas panel (b) shows the figure as white against a colored background. In case (c), the color is seen as belonging to the outlined contour of the nonsense shape, whereas in case (d) the whole card is colored and the shape is outlined in black (B). After exposure to ten such figures, each subject was given a memory test: a duplicate of each contour, drawn in black on a white background, was to be matched to one of ten colored patches identical to the colors used in the exposure series. The results were that when the color was presented as belonging to the figure—was its surface or contour color as in panels (a) and (c)—matching on the memory test was about twice as good as when the color belonged to the background rather than to the figure, as in panels (b) and (d). In this manner, Asch established that coherence of an attribute and object in memory was controlled by its coherence in perception. These results were replicated and extended by Arnold and Bower (1972).

Another relation, illustrated in the middle panels of Figure 8.6, is the *constitutive* relation in which a given form is composed or constituted of another set of smaller forms. For example, Figure 8.6 shows a sort of figure-eight constituted of black dots, and a rhombus constituted of small pluses.

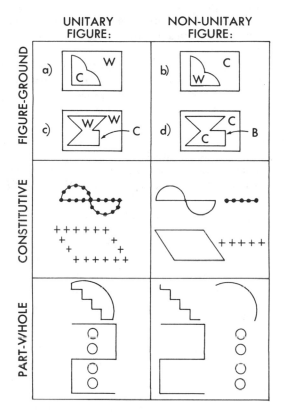

Figure 8.6.   Examples of unitary and nonunitary relations between perceptual items. (Adapted from Asch, 1969.)

The pluses and the dots are the *modes* in which the larger forms are expressed. As in the previous experiment, a subject would be exposed to a set of ten nonsense forms expressed in particular modes, and then would later be given a memory test to assess the coherence in memory of the form with its mode. The control condition involved nonunitary presentation of the same two forms: the form (e.g., rhombus) would be shown on the left in outline paired with a line of pluses (the mode) on the right of the study card. The two groups would be compared on a matching test in which each outlined, larger form was to be matched up with its paired smaller form (the "mode"). Again, subjects exposed to the unitary figures, in which the two shapes were related as "form *X* constituted of mode *Y*," showed about twice as much coherence in memory of the shape pairs than did control subjects exposed to the nonunitary pairs.

A similar effect was produced by the part-whole relation, illustrated in the bottom panel of Figure 8.6. As can be seen, a unitary picture would be divided into two subparts, separated horizontally to make up the non-unitary control pairs. Subjects who had studied the unitary pictures nearly always recalled the subparts together accurately, whereas control subjects were likely to recall only one subpart or to mispair subparts when several were recalled. So again, perceptual unity of subparts made for urity of these subparts in memory.

The significant point here is that the simple law of "association by contiguity" is inadequate to handle these several illustrations. Asch and his predecessors have emphasized the *relation* between two elements or features as a means for cementing them together into a unit or chunk. Temporal or spatial contiguity (*A* before *B*, or *A* beside *B*) is not by itself a particularly compelling or salient relation; it is rather a necessary condition for other, more useful relations to be manifested. This emphasis goes counter to the elementarism of some forms of associationism which regarded relations not as primary facts but as decomposable into nonrelational facts occurring in contiguity.

The examples above use visual geometric stimuli to illustrate unitization effects in memory. However, similar types of effects can be shown with verbal or linguistic materials. As one example (Asch, 1969), two nonsense syllables can be more quickly associated together if they are pronounced together, blending and fusing like a two-syllable word (e.g., *JATPIR* or *FUBNOL*) instead of being treated and pronounced separately in cyclic pairs (e.g., *JAT–PIR*). As a second example, a list of three-word clichés (e.g., Happy New Year, ham and eggs, birth control pill) will be better recalled (and coherently recalled) if they are presented as the set of familiar clichés they are than if all the words are scrambled and presented in unfamiliar triplets. The cliché is a unitary chunk for purposes of memory; it is recalled in all-or-none manner. As a final example of unitization, many mnemonic devices for improving one's memory require the learner to associate two items by imagining the two in some kind of unique relation, typically some vivid interaction. For instance, to remember a list of errands in which I am to buy milk after I buy a pair of shoes, I can associate *shoes* with *milk* by imagining my shoes filled with milk and myself drinking the milk from the shoes. Such bizarre elaborations demonstrably improve our memories (e.g., G. H. Bower, 1970a; Paivio, 1971). Gestalters would claim that such elaborations improve memory because they serve to relate and organize the two items (*shoes* and *milk*) into a single conceptual or imaginal unit, and "association" is a by-product of relating. Without some such hypothesis, it is difficult to understand why adding supplemental material to a complex of elements to be associated should facilitate rather than compete with formation of associations between the critical elements.

The Höffding Step: Retrieving Old Traces

It was Höffding (1891) who pointed to a particular problem previously overlooked by association theories, namely, the question of how perception of a current stimulus can selectively retrieve past memories of specific relevance to that stimulus. From the vast file of memories we carry about with us, how does the present situation make contact with that specific memory which is appropriate to the occasion? Suppose stimulus objects *A* and *B* become associated, which means that some neuronal processes *a* and *b* have (in Gestalt theory) become fused into an interdependent unit *ab*. Due to changes in the prevailing psychological milieu, the later presentation of stimulus *A* is a different event than before, giving rise to a somewhat different perceptual process, *a'*. The question is how *a'* selectively retrieves the trace *ab* rather than any of thousands of alternatives; this hypothetical gap between presentation of *A* and retrieval of the trace *ab* is called the "Höffding step," since he was the first to discuss this problem.

It is important to recognize that this was a problem with classical associationists. They gave explicit attention to association but relatively little to stimulus recognition; Höffding pointed out that stimulus recognition, retrieving *a* from *a'*, would seem to be psychologically prior to activation of an *a* to *b* association. Associative recall will surely fail unless the cue is recognized as something about which something has been learned.

Höffding suggested that *a'* made contact with the *a* in the *ab* memory trace on the basis of *similarity*; because *a'* was more similar to *a* than to (say) *x*, the trace *ab* would be retrieved rather the trace *xy*. The Gestalt psychologists picked up this idea, and argued further (e.g., Koffka, 1935) that it was their version of the law of similarity that explained how *a* and *a'* became "grouped together" at the time of retrieval.

A basic problem with this "similarity" approach to retrieval is that it is essentially vague and unrevealing. Stimuli or situations have multiple descriptions; so between any three situations *A*, *B*, *C*, there can be a multitude of similarities and differences—on some dimensions of description, *A* is closer to *B*; on other dimensions, *A* is closer to *C*. The problem thus becomes one of weighting the various components of "similarity" so as to come out with unambiguous predictions. Without independent assessment of "psychological distances," explanations of phenomena in terms of the similarity of the cue and the trace tend to be *post hoc* rather than predictive before the fact.

Some illustrations of retrieval cues of differential effectiveness are shown in Figure 8.7 for four different examples of inputs to be learned. For each input pattern, two different cues are illustrated. In each case, the top member of the two would be the more effective retrieval cue for recall (reproduction) of the original input pattern. The first two panels, with geometric patterns (a) and (d), show that the better retrieval cue is not necessarily the one which physically overlaps more with the input pattern; for example, cue (c) overlaps more with input (a) than does cue (b). Rather, the difference is that in (b) and (e), the cue is a relatively *articulated* subpart of the input pattern; in other words, the good cue would correspond to a distinctly articulated but integral part in the description (memory representation) of the original pattern. On the other hand, the poorer retrieval cues (c) and (f) comprise only noninformative fragments that would not have been distinguished and articulated in the initial description or "encoding" of the input patterns into memory. In fact, patterns such as (c) may themselves become organized into new patterns (e.g., pair of vertical bars) whose descriptions are completely at variance with the description of the input pattern. Thus a simple "similarity" notion for retrieval requires considerably further specification of the representation of the input and probe as stimulus events.

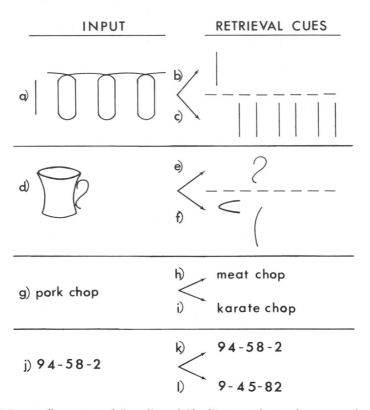

INPUT   RETRIEVAL CUES

Figure 8.7.   Illustrations of "good" and "bad" retrieval cues for inputs of geometric forms, verbal phrases, and grouped digit series.

The third panel illustrates the point with verbal memory. A subject may be shown a series of phrases, with the word to be remembered in capital letters (*CHOP*) whereas the other context word (*pork*) is explained as simply a possible aid to remembering the capitalized word. Later the person receives a recognition test for the words to be remembered (capitalized words). A new context word placed alongside the word to be remembered biases its *semantic* interpretation (meaning) to be either the same as or different from the input meaning. Although the subject is supposed to concentrate his decision on whether or not he has seen the word form to be remembered (e.g., *CHOP*) before in the experimental list, the context word has a strongly controlling effect upon his recognition memory (see Light & Carter-Sobell, 1970). Specifically, the *CHOP* studied in the context *pork CHOP* is not recognized at all well when tested in the context *karate CHOP*. The word *CHOP* is *encoded* or interpreted differently in the two contexts. In this case, the "similarity" of relevance to the recognition decision is similarity of meaning rather than identity of the physical grapheme *CHOP*. Tulving and Thomson (1971) find similar effects even when the word to be remembered does not appear to have obvious multiple meanings; it is as though different context words selectively emphasize different semantic features of the word to be remembered. Thomson and Tulving (1970) also show that this encoding at the time of input drastically alters the ability of certain other words to cue recall of the words to be remembered. For instance, in example (g) of Figure 8.7, following study of a list of such pairs, if the person is tested with the cue "food" or "something to eat," he would quickly recall *CHOP*; but a cue like "a striking blow" (related to "karate *CHOP*") would not elicit recall of *CHOP*. Thus, the interpretation of *CHOP* at input determines what stimuli will or will not serve as effective retrieval cues for the memory of that event.

The fourth panel of Figure 8.7 illustrates how the grouping of an indifferent series of digits is part of its characteristic description or representation in memory. If a series like 94582 is grouped at input (by temporal pauses) into a 2-2-1 structure, that string of underlying digits will be recognized far better on a later recognition-memory test if the test series is grouped precisely in the same way as the input series (see G. H. Bower & Winzenz, 1969). The input series is not coded and stored by the person as a string of digits; rather it is represented as a sequence of chunks or groups, and these chunks are not re-presented when the test series has an altered group structure.

These last are just a few examples of the role of retrieval in memory; they illustrate how the "Höffding step" can slip and fail. The Gestalt psychologists did not specifically work on this problem, either experimentally or by theoretical elaboration. But they did point to the significance of the problem, and to the role of stimulus recognition in associative recall. Those were problems that had been neglected in earlier stimulus-response associationistic theories; researchers have subsequently turned increasing attention to just such problems, as is attested by the recent references in this chapter.

Forgetting

The Gestalters also used their ideas regarding perception in trying to deal with *forgetting* of learned material. The same "dynamic laws of organization" that are alleged to impose structure upon the elements of a perceptual field would also tend to transform incoherent and poorly organized traces over time into traces exhibiting better organization. There were thus autonomous "forces" acting upon memory traces slowly transforming their contents into a form more closely resembling a "good gestalt"—a simple, well-organized, and stable structure. If the trace transformation were too extreme, then all semblance of the initial veridical trace would disappear so that a retrieval cue could not make contact with such an altered trace; in operational terms, the person would be said to have forgotten the original event. On the other hand, if the autonomous transformation were not too extreme, recall or reproduction of the trace should reveal systematic and progressive distortions in the direction of better organization.

This particular hypothesis was first proposed and researched by Wulf (1922), a Gestalt psychologist. He showed subjects a set of geometric forms that were incomplete or irregular in some way—in Wulf's terms, they deviated in an obvious way from an obviously "better figure" which was simpler, or more regular, or more symmetric, etc. Wulf had his subjects reproduce (draw) the memorized set of figures at successive weekly intervals, and tried to score their drawings for progressive and systematic distortions. He claimed to have found evidence for the progressive alterations of the reproductions (i.e., memory traces) in the direction of the "good gestalt" figures.

Because of the striking nature of such a finding and the hoopla made over it by the Gestalters, there was a flurry of experiments directed at the issue over the ensuing years. There were also attempts to extend the basic result from geometric forms to recall of thematic stories (Bartlett, 1932) and to the spreading of rumors within a social group (Allport & Postman, 1947). The later experiments using Wulf's design uncovered an unending series of complications and problems in performing and interpreting such experiments—complications in identifying a subject's reproduction with his memory, complications due to multiple reproductions (in making his n-th reproduction of a figure the subject is actually trying to remember his previous reproduction of it), complications due to verbal encoding (labeling) of the input figures in terms of familiar objects ("looks like a *bowtie*"), and so on and on. A good definitive review of the research on the issue, as well as a methodological critique of many of the experiments, was done by Riley (1963). His conclusion was that the mass of empirical evidence on the issue is largely *against* the Gestalt position. There are, to be sure, distortions in people's memory for geometric forms (or stories or rumors), but they seem to be predictable not so much by biases toward Gestalt "good figures" as by either (a) assimilation of memory of an input figure to a common cultural stereotype (an effect explicable in terms of associative interference), or (b) fusion and confusion of two or more figures in the memory set, so that hybrid reproductions occur by the piecing together of fragments of several figures, or (c) assimilation of the input form to that corresponding to a common label (e.g., "bowtie") used at the time of input, which coding distorts the reproduction of the form in a relatively constant manner over varying retention intervals. The upshot, then, is that Wulf's Gestalt analysis of such changes in memory has been replaced by a more refined and more firmly supported associative analysis of the phenomena.

Another view on forgetting expressed by Gestalt psychologists (e.g., Köhler, 1929, 1941) was that a trace could become distorted through its interactions with a mass of related traces similar to it. The idea was that a trace A will be more distorted by traces $B, C, D \ldots$, the more similar are the perceptual processes underlying A and the other traces. This was their basic way of explaining why associative interference in forgetting experiments was related to the similarity of the interfering material to the material to be remembered. Experiments by von Restorff (1933) and Köhler and von Restorff (1935) demonstrated this "similarity" effect upon memory for a single item within a list. Von Restorff showed that part of the difficulty of learning a list of nonsense syllables (e.g., paired-associates) stems from their homogeneity; they are all undistinguished and equally confusable with one another. However, if one item is made to stand out perceptually by being presented in red letters or in a different type font, or is of different materials (e.g., digits instead of syllables), then that unique item will be remembered better than the other items. A variety of ways can be used to distinguish an item from the rest of a homogeneous list of items to be learned, and they all produce some enhancement in memory for the distinguished item. This has been called the "von Restorff effect" in honor of its discoverer.

How is the von Restorff effect to be explained? She and Köhler thought of the unique item as standing out like a figure against a ground of all the homogeneous items. Being thus distinguished, the trace laid down for the unique item would be isolated from the traces of the rest of the items, and therefore not be distorted by interactions with those traces. Accounts of the von Restorff effect by stimulus-response associationists have proceeded along similar lines, using concepts of stimulus generalization and associative interference. More recently, it has been found that unique items have an advantage in memory because they are typically attended to and rehearsed more fully than are the homogeneous control items (see Rundus, 1971). Also, in free recall tests it can be said that the distinguishing feature of the unique item (e.g., red letters) can serve as a unique retrieval cue for the word, whereas the physical characteristic of the homogeneous background items (e.g., black letters) is connected to multiple interfering responses. Regardless of how associative theorists analyze the von Restorff effect, the original experiments were motivated by testing of some Gestalt ideas regarding forgetting.

Rote Memorizing versus Understanding

One of the basic tenets of Wertheimer and other Gestalt psychologists was that rote memorization—the learning of senseless material by repetitive drill—was an inefficient and rarely used mode of learning in real-life situations. Instead, it was claimed that people in fact learned most things in everyday life by "understanding" or comprehending the meaning of some event or by grasping the principle underlying a sequence of episodes. Rote memorization is a last-resort, inefficient strategy adopted in those few cases (e.g., learning the psychologist's lists of nonsense syllables) when meaning and natural organizing factors are absent.

Research by Katona (1940) published in his book *Organizing and memorizing* provided several illustration of the differing properties characterizing tasks learned by rote versus those learned by understanding a principle or rule. Katona's experiments were designed so that it was possible to commit the same material to memory with or without understanding, and then to test for later retention or for transfer to a new, similar task.

To illustrate, subjects might be asked to study and learn the number series 816449362516941 or the letter series *REKAEPSDUOL*. Half the subjects would learn the series by rote; the others were given various hints that a principle or rule underlay the generation of the series (e.g., think of squared numbers, or backwards words). Those subjects who "figured out" the rule for generating the series—who "understood its meaning," to use Katona's terms—were able to reproduce the series better than their rote-memory companions both on an immediate and on a delayed retention test. Furthermore, once a student had grasped the principle generating the series, he was able to transfer his problem-solving set to new tasks involving similar problems. Thus, having "solved" the problems illustrated above, the subject would readily learn (exhibit "positive transfer" to) a new series such as 256225196169144 or *YRTSIMEHCOIB*. Throughout a variety of problem-solving tasks and learning procedures, Katona illustrated his points relating learning-with-understanding to more rapid learning, superior retention, and superior transfer of learning to similar tasks.

The basic results in Katona's type of experiment are indisputable. At issue is how to characterize the outcomes scientifically. It appears in retrospect that the subject who has the rule (either because he discovered it himself or was told it) has a very much simpler description or representation of the series to be memorized. That is, the series is essentially characterized as a simple transformation or rearrangement of something that is already familiar and well-known (e.g., "spell *LOUDSPEAKER* backward"). By thus making use of known material, the total number of *new* things (associations) to be learned is much smaller than if the problem is attacked at the level of rote memorization. By the same token, a series learned by a rule will be better retained weeks later because there are fewer elements and relations to remember and they are better organized than in the case of rote memory. What is varying in these two cases is the internal description of the stimulus series to be learned: one description is succinct, compact, meaningful; the other is long, clumsy, meaningless. Although Katona would not have agreed with exactly this characterization of the issue, the experiments do serve to illustrate the Gestalt concern with how the current organization of the perceptual field makes contact with older memories.

In the ensuing years there have been many further demonstrations that getting the person to learn (or "see") a rule or principle for generating the material results in much faster learning than does treating the material as a collection of independent, unrelated items. For a recent review of some of this material, see G. H. Bower (1970b, 1972c). The basic fact that "understanding" promotes learning and retention has never been doubted. What was in doubt is the interpretation of "understanding" (what does it denote for a behaviorist?) and whether the relation of understanding to learning has the revolutionary significance that it was once thought to have. Unfortunately, Gestalters and S-R psychologists became embroiled in disputes over educational practices (recall that Thorndike, an educationist, had proposed "stamping-in" drills), and were seemingly at loggerheads over whether to advocate teaching by drill or by understanding. Although the issue is still somewhat alive today in schools of education, the controversy has become resolved for psychologists by their getting an increasingly better representation of what is learned in differing cases, so that conflicting prescriptions can be avoided. In tasks that have underlying principles, one obviously teaches the simplest representation of the problem and rules for generating the solution; but if there are many such tasks with differing principles and procedures, then some repetitive drill is required to learn these higher-level descriptions well.

Problem-Solving and Insight

We would be remiss if in our review of Gestalt psychology we did not mention, albeit briefly, the work of the Gestalters on productive thinking, problem-solving, and insight. It will be recalled that Köhler's experiments with apes were controversial because he supposed that when confronted with a problem the ape would often try implicitly to "think through" the problem's solution "in his head" before responding overtly. Insight might be characterized as implicit problem-solving activity which is successful. Based on his analysis of photographic evidence of the problem-solving behavior of apes, Yerkes (1927), following Köhler, had laid out the following sorts of behavioral criteria for insight:

In acts which by us are performed with insight or understanding of relations of means to ends, we are familiar with certain characteristics which are important, if not differential. The following is a partial list of features of such behavior. It is presented here with the thought that the comparative study of behavior with insight, in different organisms, may reveal common characteristics.

(1) Survey, inspection, or persistent examination of problematic situation. (2) Hesitation, pause, attitude of concentrated attention. (3) Trial of more or less adequate mode of response. (4) In case initial mode of response proves inadequate, trial of some other mode of response, the transition from the one method to the other being sharp and often sudden. (5) Persistent or frequently recurrent attention to the objective or goal and motivation thereby. (6) Appearance of critical point at which the organism suddenly, directly, and definitely performs the required adaptive act. (7) Ready repetition of adaptive response after once performed. (8) Notable ability to discover and attend to the essential aspect of relation in the problematic situation and to neglect, relatively, variations in non-essentials. (Yerkes, 1927, p. 156)

Subsequent analysis of problem-solving by primates and other mammals showed it was a rather complex assemblage of past habits joined with various learned strategies for trying hypotheses. For example, an experienced ape is more likely to achieve insightful solution of a problem than is an inexperienced one. Prior experience with using sticks as tools or boxes as ladders to climb upon enables a chimpanzee to solve later problems using these component skills (e.g., Birch, 1945). The difference between association theories and Gestalt theories lies in the implication of association theories that the possession of the necessary past experience somehow guarantees the solution. While Gestalt theorists would agree that past experience will facilitate solution, they object to explanations in terms of previous experience without taking organization into account. More is needed than the necessary amount of information. Just knowing enough words does not enable one to write a poem. Thus experience alone does not solve the problem.

A second fact that became readily apparent in subsequent research is that some experimental arrangements are more favorable than others for promoting insightful solutions. Both hypotheses inherent in the organism and perceptual structuring in the environment contribute to organization. Insight is more likely when the problematic situation is so arranged that all necessary aspects are open to observation. Moreover, solution occurs more quickly if all the parts which need to be brought into relationship are simultaneously present in perception; for example, it is harder for an ape to learn to use a stick which lies on the side of the cage opposite the food than to learn to use one which lies on the same side as the food (Jackson, 1942).

These and many other facts came out of research on problem-solving with animals. The research area rather lost its steam and petered out in the 1940s because the extant theories simply seemed inadequate to predict or explain the terrifically variable types of behavior elicited in different organisms by the same situation and in the same organism by different situations. That is, experimenters began to despair that perhaps most problem-solving situations were too complex, and the behavior too unpredictable, to make any scientific progress at that level of analysis. It would be like Galileo trying to figure out the laws of falling bodies by studying the paths of falling snow-flakes in a snowstorm; it was decided that the situation was not appropriately simplified to lay bare the elementary laws of behavior. That, at least, is a plausible explanation for the abrupt cessation of research on complex "problem-solving" by animals, and the shift to study of learning in somewhat simpler situations.

Productive Thinking

Wertheimer lectured on thought processes for many years, but published only a few fragmentary papers during his lifetime. He had, however, completed the manuscript of a small book just before his death. This was edited by his friends and appeared under the title *Productive thinking* (1945, 1959). In it a number of his experimental studies are summarized in his characteristic way, with penetrating qualitative analysis of simple situations serving to illustrate the differences between his approach and other approaches to which he was objecting.

The two chief competing alternatives to adopting the Gestalt approach to thinking and problem-solving were said to be formal logic, on the one hand, and association theory, on the other. Both of these alternatives were believed to be too limited to encompass what actually happens when an individual confronted with a problem finds a sensible solution.

The distinction is made throughout between a blind solution in which the learner applies a formula, and a sensible solution in which the learner understands what he is doing in relation to the essential structure of the situation. The blind solution is often an unsuccessful application of the formula to a situation not seen to be inappropriate. Experiments are cited, for example, in which schoolchildren are taught to find the area of a parallelogram by dropping lines from two corners perpendicular to the base, thus converting the figure to a rectangle, whose area can be found. Children who could do the examples perfectly were baffled, however, when a parallelogram was presented in a new orientation, so that the "correct" steps of the procedure led to confusing results. They had learned the solution according to a blind procedure. By contrast, the solution of a 5½-year-old child is reported.

Given the parallelogram problem, after she had been shown briefly how to get at the area of the rectangle, she said, "I certainly don't know how to do *that*." Then after a moment of silence: "This is *no good here*," pointing to the region at the left end; "and *no good here*," pointed to the region at the right. [Figure 8.8.]

"It's troublesome, here and there." Hesitatingly she said: "I could make it right here . . . but . . . " Suddenly she cried out, "May I have a scissors? What is bad there is just what is needed here. It fits." She took the scissors, cut vertically, and placed the left end at the right. [Figure 8.9.] (Wertheimer, 1945, p. 48)

Figure 8.8. Troublesome parts in child's attempt to apply rectangle theory to parallelogram. (Figure from p. 48 in *Productive Thinking*, Enlarged Edition, by Max Wertheimer, edited by Michael Wertheimer [Harper & Row, 1959].)

Figure 8.9. Child's solution of parallelogram problem with a scissors. (Figure from p. 48 in *Productive Thinking*, Enlarged Edition, by Max Wertheimer, edited by Michael Wertheimer [Harper & Row, 1959].)

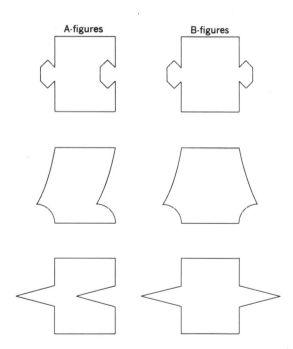

Figure 8.10. Applicability of solution of parallelogram problem to new figures. It is possible to change the A-figures sensibly so that they form rectangles. It is not possible to change the B-figures in this way. The ability of schoolchildren to solve the A-figures and to reject the B-figures is said to depend on something other than the familiarity of the figures. (Figure from p. 19 in *Productive Thinking*, Enlarged Edition, by Max Wertheimer, edited by Michael Wertheimer [Harper & Row, 1959].)

Another child, given a long parallelogram cut out of a piece of paper, remarked early that the whole middle was all right, but the ends were wrong. She suddenly took the paper and made it into a ring. She saw that it was all right now, since it could be cut vertically anywhere and made into a rectangle.

In cases such as these, the solutions appear in an orderly way, in line with the true "structure" of the situation. It is this structural approach which Wertheimer emphasizes. Children readily grasp such "structural" solutions unless they are badly taught in an atmosphere of blind repetitive drill. Given figures such as those on the left in Figure 8.10 and those on the right, they can easily sort out the unsolvable ones from the solvables. It is futile to argue, says Wertheimer, that these distinctions are made on the basis of familiarity, as the associationist seems to believe. Children make the distinction because they know the essential nature of the solution. The structural features and requirements of the situation itself set up strains and stresses which lead in the direction of improving the situation, that is to say, to solving the problem.

The implications of Wertheimer's point of view for teaching are fairly clear. It is always preferable to proceed in a manner which favors discovery of the essential nature of the problematic situation, of the gaps that require filling in, so that, even at the cost of elegance or brevity, the proof is "organic" rather than "mechanical" (Duncker, 1945).

ESTIMATE OF GESTALT THEORY OF LEARNING

Gestalt Theory and the Typical Problems of Learning

The Gestalt psychologists saw a somewhat distorted emphasis in conventional treatments of learning, so that the problems typically emphasized are not the most natural selection of problems from their standpoint. In order to maintain the symmetry of comparative study of the different positions, however, the same list will be followed as was used to summarize the stimulus-response positions.

1. Capacity.   Because learning requires differentiation and restructuring of fields, the higher forms of learning depend very much on natural capacities for reacting in these ways. Increasing capacity for perceptual organization or the ability to "understand" problems leads to increases in learning ability.

2. Practice.   Our memories are allegedly traces of perceptions; association is a by-product of perceptual organization. The laws of perceptual groupings also determine coherence of elements in memory. Repetition of an experience builds cumulatively on earlier experiences only if the second event is recognized as a recurrence of the earlier one. Successive exposures to a learning situation provide repeated opportunities for the learner to notice new relationships so as to provide for restructuring the task.

3. Motivation.   The empirical law of effect, regarding the role of rewards and punishments, was accepted by Gestalt psychologists, but they differed from Thorndike in interpreting it. They believed that aftereffects did not act "automatically and unconsciously" to strengthen prior acts. Rather, the effect had to be perceived as *belonging* to the prior act—a position also emphasized by Thorndike. Motivation was viewed as placing the organism into a problem situation; rewards and punishments acted to confirm or disconfirm attempted solutions of problems.

4. Understanding. The perceiving of relationships, awareness of the relationships between parts and whole, of means to consequences, are emphasized by the Gestalt writers. Problems are to be solved sensibly, structurally, organically, rather than mechanically, stupidly, or by the running off of prior habits. Insightful learning is thus more typical of appropriately presented learning tasks than is trial and error.

5. Transfer. The Gestalt concept most like that of transfer is *transposition*. A pattern of dynamic relationships discovered or understood in one situation may be applicable to another. There is something in common between the earlier learning and the situation in which transfer is found, but what exists in common is not identical piecemeal elements but common patterns, configurations, or relationships. One of the advantages of learning by understanding rather than by rote process is that understanding is transposable to wider ranges of situations, and less often leads to erroneous applications of old learning.

6. Forgetting. Forgetting is related to the course of changes in the trace. Traces may disappear either through gradual decay (a possibility hard to prove or disprove), through destruction because of being part of a chaotic, ill-structured field, or through assimilation to new traces or processes. The last possibility is familiar as a form of theory of retroactive inhibition. Traces which continue to exist may at a given moment be unavailable because of momentary failure in the "Höffding step."

In addition to such forgetting, there are the dynamic changes which take place in recall, so that what is reproduced is not earlier learning with some parts missing, but a trace distorted in the direction of a "good gestalt."

General Aspects of Gestalt Theory

In discussing Gestalt psychology solely as a theory of learning, some of its more general features have been sidestepped, especially its philosophical orientation and its relation to biology.

The objection to association theory of learning is part of the *holistic* emphasis within the general theory, and coherent with the Gestalt opposition to "atomistic" explanations according to connections between parts. The objection to sensations as elements of perception ("the bundle hypothesis") is carried over in the objection to stimulus-response connections as elements of habits.

The *phenomenological* standpoint, often stated by Gestalt psychologists as opposed to the prevailing *positivistic* position, is not easy to characterize satisfactorily. Phenomenal observation is more "subjective" than behaviorism, and less sophisticated and specially trained than the introspection recommended by Titchener. The recommended variety of observation is natural and childlike, appreciative rather than analytical. For example, Köhler's later accounts of insight depended upon such a phenomenological description of events.

The interpretation of Gestalt psychology as a *field theory* rests largely on the evidence assembled by Köhler in his *Physische Gestalten* (1920), showing the relationship between Gestalt laws of organization and well-established principles in physics and biology.

Köhler all along advocated that a principle he called *isomorphism* was central to the understanding of Gestalt psychology. This is the principle that the underlying brain fields correspond in their dynamic aspects to phenomenal experience. If there is perceived separation in space there will be separation in centers of excitation in the brain; if there is perceived movement, there will be some sort of movement of excitation patterns in the brain. It is not a "copy" theory; that is, the neural representation need not be direct, but it must be dynamically equivalent. In the experiments conducted late in his career, Köhler appeared to find some physiological support for his theories. Working with amplifiers that could record resting potentials or slowly varying ones, he and his collaborators detected some changes at the surface of the skull corresponding in some ways to the patterns of movement of visual stimuli (Köhler & Held, 1949; Köhler, Held, & O'Connell, 1952).[2]

As we mentioned at the outset, Gestalt psychologists were primarily concerned with perception and cognitive (problem-solving) processes. Their approach to learning and memory therefore emphasized a combination of these factors in learning situations—how memory mirrored perceptual organization and how problem-solving abilities were brought to bear in understanding a learning task, or in reconstructing a vague memory, or in transferring a learned principle to a new situation. These emphases were appropriate antidotes and challenges to the S-R associationism that prevailed in America.

Gestalt Psychology in the Present

The excitement created by the introduction of Gestalt psychology to America in the late 1920s and early 1930s had largely subsided by the 1950s. Yet much remains valid in what the classical Gestalt psychologists taught. There were always several features to their writings: an experimental or demonstrational part in which one or another psychological phenomenon would be shown, and then a polemical, almost philosophical part in which the ancient elementarism of Titchener's (or Watson's) analyses was flogged to death and some relatively incomprehensible "field theory" of the phenomenon would be advanced. In sensory psychology, the Gestalters easily proved

---

[2] The theory that the experiments supported was criticized experimentally by Lashley, Chow, and Semmes (1951), who placed silver foil on the cortex, thus short-circuiting such "fields" as might exist, without thereby destroying the discrimination that, according to the theory, should have depended upon these fields. Also, Sperry and Miner (1955) implanted mica sheets (insulators) into the visual cortex of their monkeys; such insulators should have seriously disrupted "electrical fields" in the brain, according to Köhler's isomorphism hypothesis. Yet the monkeys of Sperry and Miner suffered no impairment in their visual performance.

their points, their data were accepted and explained in less inflammatory terms, and the area moved forward. So in the domain of sensory perception, Gestalt psychology sort of died by its successful absorption into the mainstream. In the area of learning, following publication of Katona's experiments in 1940, relatively little experimental work was done from the Gestalt viewpoint. None of the Gestalters went into the study of conditioning and animal learning, which were the research areas dominating the interests of learning theorists during the period 1930–1960.

In the 1960s there was a resurgence of interest in the Gestalt approach to human learning. One of these research lines, by Asch and his associates, was reviewed earlier, and it concerns the way perceptual organization influences coherence of elements in memory. Those demonstrations, along with related work by Bower and his associates, have kept in the forefront the idea that associating is relating of elements, and that contiguity is simply a precondition within which other relations operate. Another idea that has proved very useful in analyses of human learning is the notion of unitization or "chunking" of discrete elements into an integrated unit.

Within the last five years, a viewpoint on human learning that has acquired several strong advocates is the "organizational" view (e.g., G. H. Bower, 1970b; Mandler, 1968; Tulving, 1968). The organizational view of memory bears a strong resemblance to certain premises of Gestalt psychology, particularly those explored by Katona. Most of the research in this "new look" in verbal learning has been done on *free recall*, an experimental setup in which the subject is exposed to a large set of items (e.g., common nouns) and then is asked to recall as many of them as he can in any order. On first glance, it is not obvious how a stimulus-response-association theory can even begin to analyze performance in the free-recall task (although see a model by J. R. Anderson, 1972, to illustrate how this can be done). Nonetheless, the organizational theorists (e.g., Mandler, 1968) suppose that the free-recall subject tries to relate the individual items together into subjective units or chunks, which then serve as effective groups that cluster together in his free recall. Recall is limited in terms of a constant number of chunks, although the chunks can be of large or small size. The more highly organized and more stable the organization of the list items the person achieves, the better will be his recall of that list. The chunks typically adopted for word lists are semantic categories. Indeed, Tulving (1962) finds very high correlations between amount recalled and measures of subjective organization in the recall protocol. Procedures which try to facilitate or interfere with stable organization of the list items produce corresponding increments or decrements in amount recalled (e.g., G. H. Bower, Lesgold, & Tieman, 1969). In case the number of subjective units proves to be larger than the optimal number, it is supposed that the person recategorizes his chunks into a smaller number of superordinate categories which is within the memory limit (see Mandler, 1968). In recall, then, the person is presumed to have immediate access to the superordinate categories or chunks, which he unpacks into their subordinate units during recall. This is an efficient recall strategy when the material clearly allows it, as G. H. Bower, M. C. Clark, D. Winzenz, and A. Lesgold (1969) have shown. We will not go further here into the recent interest in organizational factors in memory.

Suffice it to say that the amount of recent research on the topic has led to a research review volume *Organization of memory* edited by Tulving and Donaldson (1972).

The ideas of Gestalt theory still live in learning theory. Along with the emphasis on perceptual factors in memory and organizational factors in free recall, J. R. Anderson and G. H. Bower (1972b) have recently contrasted a Gestalt versus an "elementaristic" analysis of how a person might learn and recall meaningful sentences. The issue is whether memory about a proposition can be decomposed into a number of quasi-independent associative relations, or whether the entire proposition organizes all its elements into a single chunk which is recalled as an all-or-none chunk. The evidence, however, clearly favored an associationist analysis, subject to certain constraints (detailed in J. R. Anderson & Bower, 1973).

In general, Gestalt psychology has had a stimulating and salutary effect on the study of learning and memory. It is interesting that its ideas about human learning have only come to be appreciated and exploited in the past few years. Similarly, Gestalt studies on thinking and problem-solving, particularly the work of Duncker (1945) and of Wertheimer (1945, 1959), are being appreciated once again by scientists such as Allen Newell and Herbert Simon (1972) working on computer simulation of human problem-solving. Thus, the influence of a small band of German Gestalt psychologists has lived on long after their deaths. They were, in fact, the intellectual forefathers of much of what is today called "cognitive psychology," which is indeed a dominant viewpoint currently in American experimental psychology.

SUPPLEMENTARY READINGS

The books by the "big three" of Gestalt psychology are as follows:
Koffka, K. (1924) *Growth of the mind.*
Koffka, K. (1935) *Principles of Gestalt psychology.*
Köhler, W. (1925) *The mentality of apes.*
Köhler, W. (1929) (1947) *Gestalt psychology.*
Köhler, W. (1940) *Dynamics in psychology.*
Wertheimer, M. (1945) (1959) *Productive thinking.*

Although not treated in this chapter, the most relevant book by Lewin is:
Lewin, K. (1935) *A dynamic theory of personality.*
His chapter most directly concerned with learning is:
Lewin, K. (1942) Field theory and learning. Chapter 4 in *The psychology of learning.* National Society for the Study of Education, 41st Yearbook, Part II, pp. 215–242.

For a sympathetic yet critical account of Gestalt psychology, the following is pertinent:
Prentice, W. C. H. (1959) The systematic psychology of Wolfgang Köhler. In S. Koch (Ed.) *Psychology: A study of a science.* Vol. I, pages 427–455.

A good collection of readings, including many translated classic papers formerly available only in German is:
Henle, M. (1961) *Documents of Gestalt psychology.*

Functionalism

The seven approaches to learning that we have examined in the preceding chapters include one stimulus-response theory that antedated behaviorism (Thorndike), four varieties of stimulus-response behaviorism (Pavlov, Guthrie, Hull, Skinner), and two cognitive-type theories (Tolman, Gestalt). Later we shall examine the views on learning provided by a developmental theory (Piaget) and a psychodynamic theory (Freud). In this chapter we review the "functionalist" approach to psychology. Functionalism began around the turn of the century as a revolt against the "structuralism" of Titchener's brand of psychology; it was a doctrine and research program which seemed suited to the American temperament, and it became the informal set of assumptions of its day. Behaviorism grew out of functionalism, but the parent continued to subsist alongside the child. Functionalism is a loosely formulated position, somewhat a combination of empiricism and the common-sense mentalism of the layman; it is eclectic and is free to learn from all the other theories of learning. It has been characterized as the "middle-of-the-road" psychology, not really a formal "school" of precepts and dogma. Perhaps that is why it may be said that many contemporary experimental psychologists are functionalists.

Antecedents of Functionalism

As fate would have it, the program of functionalism was first clearly formulated by an opponent, Titchener, who, while promoting his ideas regarding structuralism, sought to contrast that approach with its opposite, functionalism. Having illustrated the standard classification of biological studies into the three interdependent sciences of morphology (structural anatomy), physiology (function), and ontogeny (growth and decay), Titchener notes that parallel approaches can be taken to the study of the mind. One can analyze the structure of the mind, "to ravel out the elemental processes from the tangle of consciousness, or . . . to isolate the constituents of the given conscious formation." Like the anatomist, the structuralist tries to discover what there is in the mind and in what quantity. For contrast, Titchener outlines the following:

> There is, however, a functional psychology, over and above this psychology of structure. We may regard mind, on the one hand, as a complex of processes, shaped and moulded under the conditions of the physical organism. We may regard it, on the other hand, as the collective name for a system of *functions* of the psychophysical organism. . . . "descriptive" psychology is chiefly occupied with problems of function. Memory, recognition, imagination, conception, judgment, attention, apperception, volition, and a host of verbal nouns . . . connote . . . functions of the total organism. That their underlying processes are psychical in character is, so to speak, an accident; for all practical purposes they stand upon the same level as digestion and locomotion, secretion and excretion. The organism remembers, wills, judges, recognizes, etc., and is assisted in its life-struggle by remembering and willing. Such functions are . . . rightly included in mental science, inasmuch as they constitute, in sum, the actual working mind of the individual man. (1898, p. 451)

While Titchener goes on to argue that such a functionalist analysis is logically subordinate to and incomplete without a thorough investigation of the mental structures subserving these functions, his arguments did little to stem the tide of a research movement for which he himself had helped formulate a coherent goal.

Psychologists became interested in the function of the mind as it is used in adaptation of the organism to its environment. Around the turn of the century, the concepts of *adaptation* or *adaptive value* played a large role in discussions of biology and psychology. This was a consequence of the astounding success of Charles Darwin's theory of natural selection which appeared to explain the origin and descent of species by organic evolution. Darwin's theory rested on three basic interlocking concepts:

1. *Variation:* members of a biological species vary among themselves in many physical attributes, and this variation has a largely hereditary (genetic) basis.
2. *Struggle for existence:* in nature, each species (plants and animals) typically produces many more offspring than can possibly survive on the limited resources available. Consequently, there will be a struggle for survival among individuals of the same species, between different species, and against the physical conditions of the environment.
3. *Natural selection:* in this struggle, any variation that increases *adaptation* (e.g., affords more life-sustaining resources) will be "naturally selected" in that individuals exhibiting that variation will live longer and reproduce more offspring that are genetically similar to themselves. The principle operates with even a minor variation and a slight adaptive advantage because the advantage becomes progressively selected or amplified across succeeding generations (rather like compound interest on loans).

By these principles, Darwin claimed, nature selects those species variations best suited for survival. If one views man in the light of evolutionary theory, he is led rather naturally to questions concerning the *adaptive value* of particular mental faculties, and this, of course, was the program of functionalism. The question became, What is the use of this particular mental ability? Why has evolution selected an organism whose mind has this function? What is the adaptive significance of this mental mechanism?

It may be noted that this functionalist program was particularly suited to the American Zeitgeist around the turn of the century. America was just ending a century of pioneering expansion; it was rough, direct, highly practical, and aggressively ambitious. The frontiersmen and pioneers who daily wrested a living from a frequently hostile environment were living examples of the principles of natural selection and survival of the fittest. The philosophy of America was based on individual ambition, a strong pragmatic spirit, and a practical, "success-oriented" attitude. Knowledge is worthwhile only insofar as it enables the successful solution of practical problems. American psychology reflected these same qualities, and in so doing rejected the structuralism which Titchener was trying to import from German laboratories. The "colonial" psychologists revolted against the land of psychology's origins, Germany; structuralism was overthrown by functionalism in America.

Many of the early functional psychologists engaged in "applied" research, particularly in educational psychology. John Dewey (1859–1952), an early advocate of functionalism, saw the relevance of the psychology of learning to schoolroom teaching and learning. He founded an experimental elementary school at the University of Chicago and was largely responsible for the development of what in its heyday was called "progressive education" (see Mayhew & Edwards, 1936, for a description of Dewey's school). Dewey emphasized the role of the child's interests and his motivation to solve his own problems as positive factors promoting school learning. Another development within functionalism was a concern for individual differences (recall Darwin's "variation") in mental abilities. Beginning with Francis Galton and then James Cattell, functional psychologists became interested in differential mental abilities, what they were good for, and how to measure them with "mental tests." The mental testing movement received a large boost with the demand from school systems for devices for classifying children into different "intellectual groupings," and from the armed services, which during World War I required a rapid means for intelligently assigning thousands of new personnel to particular military jobs. Although mental testing began within functionalism as an objective way to evaluate differences in cognitive functioning, its practitioners gradually drifted away from the strong experimental biases which characterized the other functionalists.

Functionalism at Chicago and Columbia

Functionalism rose to prominence at the University of Chicago and at Columbia University between about 1900 and 1930. The psychologists primarily responsible for this growth, besides John Dewey, were James Angell and Harvey Carr at Chicago, and Robert Woodworth and James Cattell at Columbia. These men trained some very prolific psychologists such as

Edward Robinson and John McGeoch, who in turn influenced the current generation of psychologists working in learning. In an early statement of the functionalist position, Angell (1907) made three points:

1. Functionalism is interested in the *how* and *why* of mental operations as well as in the *what* (i.e., a descriptive content). It is a cause-and-effect psychology, or in modern terms, an input-output psychology, concerned with mental operations in their context.

2. Functionalism is essentially a psychology of the adjustment of the organism to its environment. Consciousness evolved to serve some biological purpose, to help the organism solve its problems, especially when conflicts arise and habits no longer suffice. Once this position was taken, the way became open to welcome applied psychology: educational psychology, industrial psychology, mental hygiene.

3. Functionalism is interested in mind-in-body, and so studies the physiological substratum of mental events. The implied dualism is a purely practical one (as in current psychosomatic medicine) and does not imply a special position on the mind-body problem. The only position that must be rejected, if one is to stress the adaptive role of consciousness, is that known as epiphenomenalism, the view that consciousness is a useless by-product of neural activity.

The belief was fostered that functional psychology was simply "American" empirical psychology, not a "school" distorted by the exaggerations of psychoanalysis, Gestalt theory, or behaviorism. The subject matter of psychology was mental activity, whose function is to acquire, fixate, retain, organize, and evaluate experiences, and to make use of these experiences in guiding later effective actions. The role of motivation in the learning and utilization of knowledge was stressed particularly by Woodworth (1918, 1958).

An appreciation of the functionalist can be gained by noting a few strategies he routinely adopts in psychological research.

1. The functionalist is tolerant but critical.   He is free from self-imposed constraints that have shackled many other systematists. He uses terms from diverse vocabularies, borrowing words freely from other traditions. He is not forbidden the use of older words because today they sound subjective (e.g., *idea, meaning, purpose*), or because they have occasionally been given systematic connotations that he does not accept (*sensation, image, ego*). His definition of the field of psychology is also a tolerant one, and he is ready to accept information obtained by introspection, by objective observation, from case studies, from mental tests, if he finds them converging into some valid interpretation. He is tolerant as to method, and he is also tolerant as to content. The distinction between pure science and applied science seems to him trivial, as long as either is good science.

It is a mistake to confuse this broad tolerance with looseness, as though functionalism were merely an uncritical eclecticism. On the contrary, the functionalist is commonly a very astute critic. Because he has his eyes open for variables that may be ignored by more dogmatic systematists, he is not easily trapped into accepting "pat" systematic solutions for intricate problems.

2. The functionalist prefers continuities over discontinuities or typologies.
The mathematical statement of a functional relationship usually implies gradual changes in the dependent variables. While extremes may differ so markedly as to appear qualitatively unlike, the functionalist looks for connecting in-between cases. This continuity of function was made the basis for a dimensional principle by McGeoch (1936) and the suggestion was elaborated by Melton (1941, 1950).

For example, although psychologists typically recognize such experimental tasks as rote learning and problem-solving to be qualitatively different, the functionalist would inquire into the critical features distinguishing the two types of tasks and try to create and study intermediary tasks involving varying mixtures of the component processes allegedly involved in the two pure tasks. Similarly, a variable like *intentional* versus *incidental learning set* would be conceived as ends of a continuum, with intermediate cases provided by degrees of information about the reinforcement contingencies, orienting or rehearsal procedures, and the like.

3. The functionalist is an experimentalist. In its modern form, functionalism is dedicated to the experimental method. The issues upon which the functionalist is so tolerant become a part of his science only when they are translated into experimentable form. He is free of constraint in his choice of dimensions, and may choose to set up a dimension of items graded for similarity or a dimension of tasks graded according to degree of understanding. He prefers to drive general issues back to specifics before he is led into controversy over them, for he believes that many linguistic difficulties fade when reference is made to the specific findings of experiments. Experimental psychology so generally accepts the three points above which characterize functionalism (viz., a preference for continuities, for experimentation, for openminded criticism) that such functionalism has become an almost unnoticed ground for mutual understanding.

4. The functionalist is biased toward associationism and environmentalism.
A lingering bias is detectable among leading functionalists that tempers the judgment that functionalism is neutral with respect to the major quarrels among learning theorists. This is the bias toward association theory, and the environmentalism that so often accompanies association psychologies. The affiliation with historical association theory has been recognized by leading functionalists.[1] Although these biases are not absolute ones, when there is room for doubt (as in some aspects of perception) one can predict that the functionalist will be on the side of empiricism and against nativism.

In summary, we find the functionalist tolerant but critical, favoring continuities over discontinuities, seeking to translate his problems into experimental form. Within the free, eclectic atmosphere, he nevertheless has a preference for interpretations coherent with historical association theory as against holistic or nativistic interpretations.

[1] Carr (1931), Robinson (1932a). Melton (1950) described his position as an "associationistic functionalism."

FUNCTIONAL ASPECTS OF THE LEARNING PROCESS

Because the functionalist does not have a highly articulated learning theory, we can best understand his approach by following a functionalist's analysis of the problems facing an experimental psychology of learning. In what follows we shall accept Melton's (1950) summary of learning as a representative functionalist statement, using his analysis of learning and his outline of topics.

Melton begins with Dashiell's diagram of the readjustive process (Figure 9.1). The diagram shows how a problem arises when ongoing activity (1) is blocked by an obstacle (2). Eventually the organism, through varied behavior (3), solves the problem (4) and proceeds on his way (5). If the process is repeated, the adequate response (4) recurs in less time, with less excess and irrelevant activity.

Thus the learning process is primarily a matter of the discovery of the adequate response to a problem situation and the fixation of the satisfying situation-response relationship. (Melton, 1950, p. 670)

From this analysis, Melton is led to state several major experimental problems of learning. Expressed as topics, these are:

1. Motivation
2. Initial discovery of the adequate response
3. Fixation and elimination
4. Factors determining the rate of learning
5. Transfer of training and retention

We can follow this outline in characterizing the functionalist approach to these topics.

1. Motivation. Woodworth was the first functionalist to give a treatment of motivation in modern form, in a small book entitled *Dynamic psychology* (1918). It was this book that gave currency to the term *drive* as an alternative to *instinct*, Woodworth set the stage for the prominence that drives and motives were presently to have within psychology.

The cycle of aroused activity and quiescence is discussed according to *preparatory* and *consummatory* reactions, with Woodworth crediting Sherrington (1906) for the distinction. Consummatory reactions are those which satisfy basic drives or needs, activities such as eating or escaping from danger. They are directly of value to the organism. Their objective mark is that they terminate a series of acts, leading either to rest or to the turning by the organism to something else. A preparatory reaction is only indirectly or mediately of value to the organism, its value resting on the fact that it leads to or makes possible a consummatory reaction. The objective mark of the preparatory reaction is said to be that it occurs as a preliminary stage leading to the consummatory reaction.

Preparatory reactions are of two kinds. One kind represents alert attention, "a condition of readiness for a yet undetermined stimulus that may

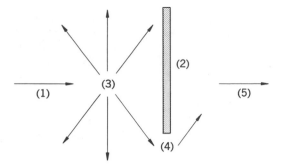

Figure 9.1.   The readjustive process. (After Dashiell, 1949, p. 26.)

arouse further response." Another is the kind of preparatory adjustment evoked only "when the mechanism for a consummatory reaction has been aroused and is in activity." The latter sort of reaction is goal-directed, and evokes seeking behavior, as when a hunting dog, having lost a trail, explores about in order to get back on it.

Another facet to Woodworth's motivational theory was the abiding interest that he showed in the concept of "set," dating from his early experiments on imageless thought. This new emphasis on the role of directional set in thinking provided one feature distinguishing functionalism from traditional associationism. The sets and intentions emphasized by the students of imageless thought and the preparatory reactions oriented toward consummatory responses are concepts with a similar dynamic loading. They are both directional, and they are both inferred from the manner in which behavior sequences are organized. In a later development of his conception of set, Woodworth introduced what he called the *situation-set* and the *goal-set* (1937). The situation-set refers to adjustments to environmental objects; the goal-set refers to the inner "steer" which gives unity to a series of varied but goal-directed activities.

The important suggestion in the concept of situation-set is that the environment must be brought into the psychological account in a manner not suggested by the traditional stimulus-response theories. This notion seems to have antedated the Hullian notion of "incentive motivation" (see Chapter 6), which is something like a goal-directed motive aroused by stimuli preceding the goal.

Carr's interpretation of motivation in his textbook (1925) was influenced by Woodworth's views, but he restated the preparatory-consummatory adjustment in new terms. He accepted the principle that all behavior is initiated by stimuli, so that his point of view is similar to other stimulus-response psychologies, with the difference that responses may be ideational as well as motor. He is concerned with activities, not movements. An adaptive act is described as involving a motivating stimulus, a sensory situation, and a response that alters that situation in a way that satisfies the motivating conditions. The external object by which the organism satisfies its motives is called the incentive, or the immediate objective or goal of the response. (The more remote goal, such as maintaining the life of the organism by preventing starvation, does not enter directly into the control of the act.) More specifically, a motive is described as a relatively persistent stimulus that dominates the behavior of an individual until he reacts in such a manner that he is no longer affected by it. This makes of a motive what Smith and Guthrie call a maintaining stimulus. The adaptive act is organized to obtain certain sensory consequences (i.e., the termination of the motivating stimuli) and the act can be interpreted as completed only when the consequences are attained. The interpretation of the end phase as a sensory change became Carr's way of talking about the empirical law of effect (1938).

Melton, accepting Carr's definition of motivation as a stimulating condition, pointed out that motivating conditions have three functions: (1) they energize the organism, making it active, (2) they direct the variable and persistent activity of the organism, and (3) they emphasize or select the activities that are repeated (fixated) and those that are not repeated (eliminated). Stated in this way, the functionalist's interpretation of motivation is consistent with Hull's, but it is coherent also with the position of Tolman.

2. *Initial discovery of the adequate response.* Melton noted that initial discovery of the correct response may be the main problem in some kinds of learning (e.g., in the problem-box), while it plays little part in others (e.g., in serial rote memorization). The controversy between trial and error and insight in the interpretation of learning hinges in part on the nature of this initial discovery of the correct solution.

Melton saw that two other forms of initial discovery have played less systematic roles in learning theories, yet should not be neglected. One of these is *guidance*. The discovery of the correct response can be facilitated by the teacher or trainer through appropriate manipulation of the environment or the learner. Hence, guided learning is intermediate between rote learning (with no discovery) and problem-solving (with unguided discovery). An extensive research program on guided learning was carried out by Carr and his students and later summarized by him (1930). Such a program illustrates the freedom with which the functionalist selects his experimental variables.

The other form of initial discovery mentioned by Melton is *imitation*. He believed it could be subsumed under guidance, however, for it helps the learner to discover the solution by observing the solution by another organism.[2]

3. *Fixation of adequate responses and elimination of inadequate responses.* Melton accepted the *empirical law of effect* as stated by McGeoch: "Other things being equal, acts leading to consequences which satisfy a motivating condition are selected and strengthened, while those leading to consequences which do not satisfy a motivating condition are eliminated" (McGeoch, 1942, p. 574). When it came to explaining effect, Melton was cautious in choosing between a contiguity theory and a reinforcement theory:

---

[2] The importance of imitation in learning has received a new impetus from the experiments of Bandura and others, as cited in Bandura (1969).

Two alternatives seem to be available to the student at this time: (a) The issue of contiguity vs. effect will be decided at some distant time in terms of the over-all fruitfulness of one or the other postulate, as judged by the application of Hull's theoretical methodology; (b) It may be that *mere* contiguity and reinforcement are extremes of some as yet undefined dimension of the neurophysiology of the organism, such that associations may be formed through mere contiguity *or* through reinforcement. Meanwhile, it is necessary to recognize the experimental findings which make the complete generality of one or the other untenable, for these are actually the fruits of the research on this problem during the forty years. (1950, p. 677)

This quotation well illustrates the functionalist's unwillingness to prejudge the outcome of a controversy whose resolution ultimately must be determined by experiment.

4. Factors determining the rate of learning.   Whatever may be the underlying principles of learning when learning is reduced to the barest essential relationships between stimulus and response, it is not difficult to arrange situations under which learning occurs. By long established convention we plot performance scores against learning trials and come out with a "curve of learning." The search for a "typical" or "true" form of the learning curve has not proven profitable, but learning curves have helped in the search for the parameters of learning. Through a great many experiments we have learned much about the relationship between rate of learning and the amount of material to be learned, about the effects of length and distribution of practice periods, about how the characteristics of the learner affect the rate of progress. These problems have all been inviting ones to the functionalist who sets as his task the exploring of the many dimensions influencing learning.

Some guiding principles are needed to establish order in an empirical program of such vast scope as accounting for everything that affects all kinds of learning by all kinds of learners under all kinds of circumstances.

Some of these guiding principles were inherited from the preexperimental association psychologists. A useful list had been provided by Thomas Brown as early as 1820. He had classified the *laws of association* (or laws of suggestion, as he called them) into *primary* or *qualitative* laws (the laws of similarity, contrast, and contiguity) and *secondary* or *quantitative* laws (frequency, vividness, emotional congruity, mental set, etc.). The primary laws represent the essential general conditions for associative formation or associative revival, whereas the secondary laws determine which of many possible associates is formed or recalled.

After Ebbinghaus (1885) had shown that associations could be studied experimentally, writers such as Müller (1911) and Pilzecker (1900) in Europe and Carr (1931) and E. S. Robinson (1932a) in America began to rewrite associative laws in quantitative form. Carr and Robinson were quite explicit that *all* associative laws could be made quantitative, and they gave lists of laws that they thought expressed our twentieth-century knowledge about associative learning.

Here is Robinson's list of laws (1932a, pp. 62–122):

Law of contiguity
Law of assimilation
Law of frequency
Law of intensity
Law of duration
Law of context
Law of acquaintance
Law of composition
Law of individual differences

While some of Robinson's laws sound qualitative, he attempts to show how all qualitative distinctions can be subjected to a dimensional analysis. He himself raised the question of whether or not in isolating these factors as important he had really stated "laws." He summarized his discussion of "laws" as follows:

> It is my firm conviction that the facility of associative fixation is a function of all of the factors enumerated. Probably several specific relationships are involved for each named factor and almost certainly there are other factors that have been included in this list. But, if the assumption that these factors are important determiners of association be correct, then there are "laws" of these factors whether our knowledge of them is definite or not. (1932a, p. 124)

It turns out that Robinson's position is much like Skinner's, in that he points out the relevant variables and makes a claim for "lawfulness" rather than for "laws." Because of these limitations in the list of "laws," the Carr-Robinson laws did not catch on, even among their students, as a means of ordering the factors determining the rate of learning, although there are occasional mentions of isolated laws from the list. The issues expressed in the laws were somewhat too general. The empirical role of contiguity, for example, breaks down into the study of several varieties of temporal and spatial relationships between events, with their corresponding gradients. Thus the separation of a conditioned and unconditioned stimulus in classical conditioning yields one kind of empirical law of contiguity, while the delay of reward at the end of a maze yields another. Today we tend to name such relationships more concretely (e.g., gradient of reinforcement, spread of effect) rather than to refer them to a more general law of contiguity. So, too, the law of frequency, as a law of relative frequency, covers too many topics, including the form of the learning curve, the form of the work-decrement curve, the effects of distributed and massed practice, the consequences of degree of overlearning. Frequency is only a general topic, within which a number of very different laws are discoverable.

Contemporary functionalist writers, instead of setting up basic laws of learning, tend to use classificatory schemes derived directly from experimental arrangements and results. That is, for each experimental setting (e.g., paired-associate learning) the functionalist will classify and list the vast number of independent variables that can be manipulated in that situation and try to indicate how these affect performance of the learner. For example, in paired-associate learning, one can distinguish among training conditions (e.g., massed versus distributed practice, type of reinforcing feedback), type of material (e.g., meaningfulness, imageability), and list-structural variables (e.g., intralist similarity, S-R correspondence rules). Such a classificatory scheme is not in itself a theory of learning; it simply organizes the effective variables which a functional analysis would have to recognize.

5. *Transfer of training and retention.* Once something has been learned, it can be used, provided it has not been forgotten and provided new situations recur in which the previously learned behavior is called forth. The study of the relative permanence of learning, when tested in situations essentially duplicating those of the original learning, is the study of *retention*, while the study of the effects of old learning in new situations is often discussed as *transfer of training*. Because recurring situations always recur with differences, there is obviously an intimacy between retention and transfer. Because transfer effects may be positive, negative, or indeterminate, one view of forgetting is that it is but an illustration of transfer.

The study of the laws of transfer and forgetting in verbal learning has become a major and continuing enterprise of modern functionalists. Because these studies represent the flavor of the functionalist approach, we will discuss the two research areas in more detail, emphasizing historical developments.

STUDIES OF TRANSFER AND FORGETTING

We may begin with a paper by McGeoch (1932) providing an early functionalist's account of conditions affecting transfer and forgetting of verbal materials. Melton (1950) followed McGeoch in accepting two major laws of forgetting and transfer. The first is the *law of context* (from Robinson's list), which asserts that the degree of retention, as measured by performance, is a function of the similarity between the original learning situation and the retention situation. The second is the *law of proactive and retroactive inhibition*, which asserts that retention is a function of activities occurring prior to and subsequent to the original learning. Proactive and retroactive inhibition have been major topics of research for many decades, ever since the problem was first opened up by Müller and Pilzecker (1900).

The paradigm for retroactive inhibition is *A-B-A*, where the learning of material *B* is interpolated between the learning and the retention of material *A*, and interferes with the retention of *A*. The paradigm for proactive inhibition is *B-A-A*, where the learning of *B* prior to the learning of *A* interferes with the later retention of *A*. Both retroactive and proactive interference with learning are readily demonstrable and the empirical relationships have led to a number of hypotheses. Studying the development of one of these hypotheses about retroactive inhibition will help us to understand not only retroactive inhibition but the manner in which functionalists construct their theories.

One set of problems concerns the *similarity* between the interpolated material and the material originally learned. E. S. Robinson (1927), arguing from some earlier results of his own and of Skaggs (1925), formulated a hypothesis later christened by McGeoch as the Skaggs-Robinson hypothesis.

With the usual functionalist preference for stating dimensions, Robinson, following Skaggs, proposed relating the amount of retroactive inhibition to the dimension of degree of similarity between the original and the interpolated material or activity.

With the similarity dimension in mind, Robinson argued that the interpolation of identical material (material B the same as material A) would simply provide additional practice on material A, and hence lead to increased retention on the test trials during which retroactive inhibition is usually shown. Because retroactive inhibition with dissimilar materials was already an established fact, the natural conjecture on the assumption of continuous variation is that starting with identity the amount of retroactive inhibition would increase gradually as dissimilarity was increased. Now, asks Robinson, what is likely to happen at the other end of the scale, as the original material (material A) and the interpolated material (material B) become *extremely* unlike? Presumably retroactive inhibition represents some sort of interference based on similarity between the original and interpolated activity. If there is very little similarity, there should be very little retroactive inhibition. Putting all these considerations together, it is reasonable to expect a maximum of retroactive inhibition at some intermediate point of similarity between materials A and B. Robinson formulated the whole generalization in words as follows: "As similarity between interpolation and original memorization is reduced from near identity, retention falls away to a minimum and then rises again, but with decreasing similarity it never reaches the level of obtaining with maximum similarity." He expressed this graphically by the figure reproduced as Figure 9.2.

His own experimental test of the generalization was very simple. By the memory span method he studied the recall of the first four of a series of eight consonants as this recall was interfered with by the last four of the

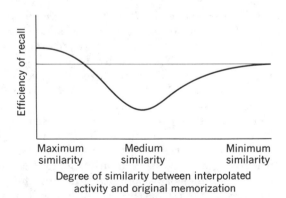

Figure 9.2.   Similarity as a factor in retroactive inhibition. The curve is intended to show that retroactive inhibition bears a quantitative relationship to the degree of similarity between the interpolated activity and the material originally memorized. With maximum similarity, the interpolated activity provides positive transfer, hence increases the efficiency of recall. Maximum interference with recall is predicted to fall at some intermediate value of similarity. (After E. S. Robinson, 1927, p. 229. By permission.)

consonants. That is, the first four were considered to be material A, the last four material B, and the similarity and dissimilarity of materials A and B were controlled. Similarity was defined in terms of common letters in the two halves of the series. Maximum similarity means that the second four consonants were exactly the same as the first four; maximum dissimilarity meant that all the last four differed from the first four.

The results confirmed the hypothesis only partially. Starting with near-identity, retroactive inhibition increased as the interpolated material became increasingly dissimilar. This was part of the conjecture. But the decrease in the amount of retroaction (increase in recall) with maximum unlikeness was not found. In fact, with the materials totally dissimilar, retroactive inhibition was at a maximum.

Later investigators had no better luck than Robinson did in confirming his transfer curve. In fact, later analyses of verbal learning tasks began to uncover several distinct *sources* of "similarity" between two tasks as well as several distinct *kinds* of similarity. For example, in paired-associate learning, the two successive lists of pairs may be schematized as S_1-R_1, then S_2-R_2; at least two sources of similarity are stimulus similarity (of S_2 to S_1) and response similarity (of R_2 to R_1). Second, the kinds of similarity may be in terms of overlap of common elements in nonsense syllables (e.g., *VAX* and *VAS* are said to be "formally similar") or in terms of semantic or associative meaning of two words (e.g., *elated* is somewhat similar to *high*, less to *low*, and the opposite of *sad*). Recognition of these complexities spelled the demise of the Skaggs-Robinson hypothesis. In reviewing the history of studies of transfer and retroaction, Postman (1971, p. 1083) has this to say:

In retrospect it becomes apparent that the Skaggs-Robinson hypothesis failed because it was essentially a nonanalytic formulation, which did not specify the locus of intertask similarity. The hypothesis lapsed into disuse as the analysis of similarity relations in retroaction, as in transfer, shifted to the investigation of stimulus and response functions.

Osgood (1949) proposed a more complex formulation of the relationships involved in transfer. His proposed mapping of similarity effects in paired-associate transfer is diagrammed in the three-dimensional surface shown as Figure 9.3. What Osgood's surface states is that the amount of transfer in positive or negative directions is a function of shifts in similarity of *both* the stimulus conditions *and* the response required. Shifts in stimulus similarity are from front to rear as noted on the right-hand margin, moving from identical stimuli (S_I) through similar stimuli (S_S) to neutral stimuli (S_N) that are far distant on a generalization gradient. Shifts in response similarity are represented from left to right, as noted along the back margin, with identical responses (R_I) being at the left, and moving progressively through similar responses (R_S), neutral responses (R_N), partially opposite responses (R_O) to directly antagonistic responses (R_A). For meaningful verbal materials, the "antagonistic response" was defined as the antonym, a word having the opposite meaning (e.g., *elated–sad*).

The best way to read the diagram is to read its edges first. The rear edge says that stimuli bearing *no* resemblance to those used in original learning

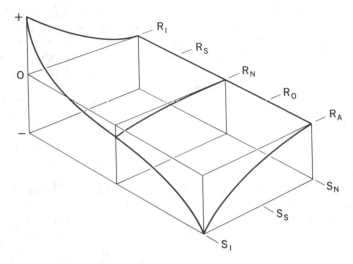

Figure 9.3. Osgood's transfer and retroaction surface. Vertical dimension, amount of transfer (+) or interference (−), with neutral zone represented by a plane (0). Left to right, amount of shift in response similarity between original task and new task, from identity (R$_I$) to antagonism (R$_A$). Front to rear, amount of shift in stimulus similarity between original and new task, from identity (S$_I$) to neutrality (S$_N$). (From C. E. Osgood, The similarity paradox in human learning: a resolution. *Psychological Review*, 1949, 56, p. 140. Copyright 1949 by the American Psychological Association. Reprinted by permission.)

lead to new responses without any transfer effect, positive or negative, regardless of the degree of resemblance between the required responses and responses that have been used in earlier experiments. The front edge says that with *identical* stimuli there will be maximum positive transfer with *identical* responses (for this is merely overlearning), whereas with directly *antagonistic* responses there will be maximum interference, for the earlier responses will have to be completely unlearned or overcome. The left edge says that, with identical responses, shifts in stimulus similarity from identity to neutrality will result in decreasing transfer, but no interference in new learning. The right edge says that, for antagonistic responses, shifts in stimulus similarity from identity to neutrality will produce decreasing interference, but no positive transfer. The diagram is a surface, and yields a curve wherever it is cut by a vertical plane.

Although Osgood's surface represented an important systematic attempt to integrate a large range of transfer and retroaction phenomena, it soon became clear that it, too, was inadequate for a number of reasons. First, there never was any firm evidence that antagonistic responses were associated with more negative transfer than were unrelated responses, even in Osgood's own data. Second, although the verbal learning data give evidence of differences in transfer between identical, similar, and unrelated stimuli (or responses), they have not shown a *continuous gradient* of effects as similarity is varied over the intermediate range (see Postman, 1971, p. 1054).

This graded effect, of course, is implied by the smooth curves drawn. Third, the surface implies that transfer will always be zero when unrelated stimuli are used in successive tasks (see the "rear edge" of the surface in Figure 9.3). However, subsequent work has shown that this arrangement can produce positive transfer when the response term itself is novel and requires much learning. For example, to give nonsense syllables as responses to neutral stimuli requires that the syllables be learned as integrated response units *per se*. Thus, a transfer design like *A-B, C-B* (dissimilar stimuli, identical responses) obviates the necessity of learning the second-list responses, and so can produce positive transfer on this account. Fourth, a fact brought out by a design like *A-B, B-C* (the verbal response of the first list is the stimulus in the second list) is that the so-called *backward* association is established (from *B* to *A*) at the same time that the person is learning the forward association (from *A* to *B*). This backward association then intrudes and causes negative transfer in the *A-B, B-C* paradigm, but causes positive transfer in the *A-B, B-A* design (one just reverses which items serve as cues and which as responses). Fifth, the similarity relations treated in Osgood's surface deal with relations among individual items (pairs) across successive lists, and not with the overall structural relations between successive lists. But it is known that the greatest degree of negative transfer in verbal learning occurs when the stimuli and responses of the first list are simply *re-paired* in new ways to compose the items for the second list. In symbolic notation, this is denoted as the *A-B, A-Br* paradigm. Within the framework of Osgood's surface, this *A-Br* condition can only be represented as *A-B, A-C* with identical stimuli and different responses. Nevertheless, it is known that the *A-Br* paradigm produces much more negative transfer (largely due to competing backward associations) than does the *A-C* design. Sixth, Osgood's surface implies that negative transfer in rate of learning a second list would be perfectly correlated with the amount of forgetting ("retroactive interference") of the first list caused by the subject's learning of the second. The correlation between these two measures is frequently present. However, some discrepant cases are now well known. One of these discrepancies is that whereas *A-B, C-D* (unrelated stimuli and responses) serves as the baseline for defining "zero transfer" in second-list learning, it is clear that *C-D* interpolation causes extensive forgetting (or "retroactive interference") of *A-B* (e.g., Newton & Wickens, 1956). The loss of *A-B* for such *C-D* subjects is quite large compared to that of control subjects who learn *A-B* and then simply rest for an appropriate interval before a retention test. Adopting the usual terminology, then, the *C-D* condition produces zero negative transfer but considerable retroactive interference. This observation, in fact, has been one of the strong reasons for recent doubts regarding the existence of retroactive interference specific to particular paired-associate stimuli (see Postman & Stark, 1969).

Quite clearly, transfer in paired-associates is not a unitary process, but is rather composed of a number of distinct components which come into play during initial learning and transfer testing. As stimulus or response similarity is varied, different aspects or components of the transfer task will vary, although the net effect on performance may be unclear because different components contribute positive or negative effects which may cancel or nullify one another. Martin (1965) has published a more recent attempt to specify transfer surfaces for three different components carried over in transfer; this is shown in Figure 9.4. The three components of transfer considered are response learning (R, in the left-hand panel), forward associations (F, in the middle panel), and backward associations (B, in the right-hand panel). For response learning, the degree of positive transfer is high for identical responses, decreasing to zero for more dissimilar responses, and is independent, of course, of stimulus similarity. The surface for forward associations (F) is the same as Osgood's except that Martin suggests that the response continuum should extend only to unrelated responses (*A-B, A-D*); although antonyms are opposites in meaning they are associatively close to one another and this relation, more than their meaning opposition, dominates so as to produce slightly positive transfer when antonymic responses are used (see Postman, 1971). The results for backward associations (B) are rather symmetrical to those for forward associations except for an interchange of stimulus and response axes. In particular, interpolation of *C-B* following *A-B* learning produces maximal loss of the backward association from *B* to *A*, as indicated in the subject's failure to recall the first-list stimulus *A* when cued with the response term *B*.

Martin's hypothesis does not indicate specifically how these several factors will combine to determine the net transfer effect. It is clear, too, that even further factors have been identified which can influence transfer and forgetting, and these features are not depicted in Martin's surfaces. Thus, for example, a number of experiments have shown that there are some positive benefits from prior attentive exposure to the stimulus or the response terms since this serves to "predifferentiate" these items prior to the commencement of the criterion paired-associate task. To the extent that the subject has already learned to identify and discriminate among the stimuli, it is that much easier for him to continue discriminating while attaching particular responses to the predifferentiated stimuli. Although the normal *A-B*, *A-D* paradigm involves this predifferentiation factor, the competing response

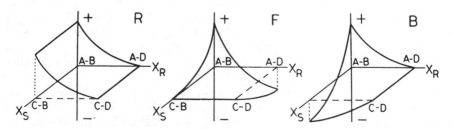

Figure 9.4.   Component surfaces for response availability (R), forward associations (F), and backward associations (B). Degree of stimulus similarity is spaced along the X_S axis, and degree of response similarity along the X_R axis. The point of origin represents identity of both the stimulus and the response. Direction and degree of transfer are indicated along the vertical axis. (From E. Martin, Transfer of verbal paired associates. *Psychological Review*, 1965, 72, p. 328. Copyright 1965 by the American Psychological Association. Reprinted by permission.)

factor seems to override it and to determine net negative transfer in most circumstances.

Another factor missing in this transfer surface is what has been called *list differentiation*, the ability of the subject to identify the list membership of responses which he recalls. Thus during *A-D* learning following *A-B*, the person may intrude the *B* response, although he knows both responses, because he confuses the two lists. Or he may think of but withhold response *D* because he erroneously identifies it as coming from the first list. In like manner, following interpolation of *A-D*, if the person is asked to recall the first-list response, he may withhold *B* or intrude *D* due to a failure of list differentiation. List differentiation as a process is closely analogous to re-membering the time and context in which events occur, a topic which is becoming of increasing interest (e.g., J. R. Anderson & Bower, 1972a; Hin-richs, 1970; G. H. Bower, 1972d). List identification will clearly be a factor in transfer, since confusions about list membership will increase with simi-larity of the stimuli or responses. Thus, for example, if the list 2 responses are digits whereas the list 1 responses are nouns, there would probably be perfect "list differentiation" and the subject would almost never intrude a digit response while trying to recall a list 1 noun.

Martin's hypothesis does encompass the massive negative transfer pro-duced by the re-paired *A-Br* transfer task, since Figure 9.4 shows negative transfer for the forward association (at *A-D* in the middle panel) and nega-tive transfer for the backward association (at *C B* in the right hand panel). What it fails to show or illuminate is that the *A-B*, *C-D* paradigm produces zero negative transfer but nonetheless appreciable forgetting relative to a rest control condition. This is an issue we will touch upon later.

Let us retrace the evolution of these hypotheses (or guessed-at "empirical generalizations") so as to account for the range of similarity effects. First we have the early experiments demonstrating retroactive interference, and some that demonstrate the possible role of similarity as a factor. Next we have Robinson's somewhat crude dimensional hypothesis, leading to a series of experiments which reveal multiple sources and kinds of intertask similari-ties, requiring a generalization more complex than the Skaggs-Robinson hypothesis. At the same time these investigations of forgetting are occurring, a series of related experiments on transfer effects are being conducted, but as though the two phenomena had little in common. Presently Osgood offers his new synthesis, covering the data that have accumulated since Robinson's hypothesis was announced, incorporating in one stroke the results on transfer and on retroactive interference. But a series of analytical studies reveals that the Osgood surface is too simplistic, that there are even more components or independent factors involved in transfer. These more detailed analyses lead to Martin's proposed "component transfer" surfaces for three of the important bits of learning that are now known to be carried over in transfer. Although Martin's proposals are the most adequate integrative summaries yet seen, it is clear that several isolable factors are being ignored, and the weighting of the magnitude of the independent factors and their interactions in determining net transfer is left for future specification. This sort of succession of hypothesized generalizations, with an interplay between data, analytical criticism, and theory, seeking a deeper analysis but a more revealing integration, is exactly what might be expected in a maturing functional analysis. This history also illustrates some of the potential frustrations of a functionalist approach; upon closer analysis, more and more variables or independent factors are discovered to influence the behavior under investigation, and the possibility of strong interactions between one variable and the functions obtained for other variables is a likely prospect. For example, the transfer as a function of response similarity probably varies in quantitative shape depending on whether one is dealing with "formal similarity" (overlapping elements of nonsense materials) or with "meaningful similarity" (e.g., synonymous words); and it is unclear yet whether the latter variable should be anchored to conceptual overlap of dictionary definitions of two words or to overlap of the associative hierarchies elicited by each word (see, for example, Deese, 1965).

The complexities of the behavioral phenomenon of transfer make some investigators despair (e.g., to say "nature couldn't be *that* complicated"), give it up as a poorly formulated scientific question, and move on to work on other issues in psychology with greater prospects of quick progress. The dyed-in-the-wool functionalist would argue that he was simply doing the yeoman's work of elucidating a phenomenon, and claim that no one is ever guaranteed simplicity in his findings and that, although the subproblems shift with the maturity of his analysis, the overriding phenomenon with which the area began (viz., transfer of training) is undeniably a central problem for all of learning theory. If it truly is a central issue, then, the functionalist would claim, it must be studied, analyzed, and understood with the only experimental and conceptual tools we presently have available. We must analyze and understand complexity because "that's the way the world is."

ANALYSIS OF FORGETTING

The foregoing account of research on negative transfer and retroactive interference was carried out at the level of empirical description and generalization. There was little in the way of theoretical constructs which were being manipulated or interrelated to explain the results. However, by far the most significant portion of the research of modern functionalists concerns the analysis of theoretical mechanisms of forgetting. The character of the functionalists' theoretical approach can perhaps be best appreciated by tracing the evolution of their ideas regarding forgetting. Most of this research has been done on verbal-learning experiments with human adults. Of course, animals forget too, even simple conditioned responses, and the study of forgetting in animals is just beginning to enlist serious efforts (see Honig & James, 1971). To reduce the difficulty of the task of understanding, recent experiments on forgetting have concentrated on fairly standard verbal-learning situations to yield the main evidence on forgetting.

If one asks the layman why he forgets things, he has a ready answer: he forgets things because he hasn't used them, or "thought of" them, for some time. He has forgotten the Spanish he learned in high school because he hasn't used it for the past ten years. But he remembers things he continues to use, such as the names of his friends.

The problem with this popular account is that it is vacuous. Lapse of time is not itself a causal variable, although causal events happen in time. If I leave an iron hammer outside, it will progressively rust with time. But it is not the lapse of time that rusts the hammer. Rather, it is the reaction of chemical oxidation that occurs in time.

We can give the layman's proposal a more neurological *sound* (if not sense) as follows: each learning experience establishes a neurological trace whose integrity is gradually obliterated by random neuronal noise that occurs at a fixed rate, eroding away the retrievability of the memory trace as the retention interval increases. Does this formulation buy us anything? The answer is "not really." Unless much more is added regarding relevant variables and their influence on the hypothetical process (and forgetting), the new proposal is worse than vacuous; it is dangerous because someone is likely to consider it seriously due to its apparent technical jargon.

A variety of substantive proposals concerning the causes of forgetting have appeared, differing considerably in their scope and the range of variables of which forgetting is said to be a function. For example, Freud supposed that some forgetting results from active repression of certain materials in the unconscious. This notion will be discussed further in Chapter 11, along with the conflicting data surrounding the hypothesis. Another conjecture, contributed by Gestalt psychologists and reviewed in Chapter 8, was that memories were multifaceted systems continually undergoing dynamic change, moving toward some better organization (or gestalt). This notion became translated in laboratory experiments into the question of whether a subject's recall of an asymmetric or incomplete figure or line drawing tends to move with retention time toward a "good" or "better" gestalt figure. Riley (1963), in his review of this extensive literature, concluded that there was little consistent support for the Gestalt idea. Recall of a figure pattern, more often than not, does tend to move toward cultural stereotypes but such trends as are found turn out more often to be explainable by verbal associations (to the original figure) or proactive interference from prior cultural learning than by Gestalt laws of perceptual organization.

The most serviceable theory of forgetting that has emerged from laboratory experiments is called the *interference* theory. This is closely tied in to the functionalists' analysis of negative transfer and interference. Currently, interference theory has far more adherents, because of more evidence in its favor, than any or all alternative theories of forgetting, so it is fair to call it the current dominating theme of experiments on forgetting. This is an association theory; that is, its basic primitive concept is the notion of an associative bond (functional connection) between two or more elements, the elements being ideas, words, situational stimuli and responses, or whatnot. As indicated earlier in our discussion of transfer paradigms, the conventional notation uses letters A, B, C . . . ., to represent such elements or items, and the notation A-B to represent an associative bond between A and B established by some past training. It is presumed that these associative bonds can vary widely in their strength depending on amount of practice. The experimental situation that best illustrates the theory is paired-associates learning, wherein the subject is taught a set (list) of pairs A-B, C-D, E-F, and so on, and then is tested later for retention. The theory applies as well to most other learning tasks, but the paired-associates task makes the expositional mechanics easiest to implement.

Interference Theory

The basic ideas of interference theory were first stated explicitly by McGeoch (1932), but through the succeeding years changes in the theory have gradually occurred. New concepts have been added, unsupported conjectures pruned away, and new experimental methods devised to measure more exactly the relevant dependent variables. The changing character of interference theory may be seen by comparing McGeoch's early statements with Postman's (1961, 1971) recent formulations. In what follows, we shall indicate some of the changes and the shifts in emphasis.

The first principle of McGeoch's statement seems an absurd one for a theory of forgetting: it says that forgetting does not occur in an absolute sense. The strength of an association between two items, A-B, is established by training, and it is maintained at that level despite disuse of the association. The cause of a measurable retention loss over time is not that the strength of A-B decays, but rather that alternative associations, A-C or A-D, have by some means (to be specified) gained strength in the absence of continued training on A-B. Thus, on a retention test, the subject may give C or D as the associate to A, so we record a retention loss for the A-B association. The A-B association has not been lost or forgotten in any absolute sense; it is still there, but B has been temporarily displaced, losing out in competition with elements C and D at the moment of recall.

On the basis of this theory, then, an association once learned is permanently stored, and forgetting is due to declining accessibility, a lessening probability of retrieval from the storehouse. And this declining accessibility results from competing associations. Such an approach has at least the substrate required to account for the clinically puzzling instances of hypermnesia in which a person demonstrates exceptional recall or believes his recall is genuine, of experiences from long before. Such heightened recall may occur in manic states, in the hours anticipating some emotionally exciting event (e.g., soldiers about to go into combat), in a hypnotic trance (see Reiff & Scheerer, 1959), or while following a line of free associations when on the psychoanalyst's couch (see Stratton, 1919; Pascal, 1949; Stalnaker & Riddle, 1932).

According to this theory, the A-B association may be tested by presenting one of the elements, say A, whereupon the subject tries to produce the associated B. We may think of A as a stimulus term and B as a response. As indicated in our earlier review of transfer, this suggests manipulating the degree of similarity of a test stimulus (call it A') to the original training stimulus A. The principle of stimulus generalization predicts that A' is less likely to activate the A-B association in proportion as A' is dissimilar to A. Moreover, McGeoch suggested that we expand our conception of A to include any background contextual stimulation that is present when the

A-B association is learned. Changes in such contextual stimuli have been found to result in poorer recall (Pan, 1926; Abernethy, 1940; Falkenberg, 1972). Thus, if the subject is tested for recall in a different room than that in which he learned, or with a different type of stimulus-presenting device, or with the material presented on different backgrounds, or when he adopts a different posture, or whatever, his recall is poorer than when, during testing, precisely the original stimulating context is reproduced. Such results seem consistent with the analytic position of interference theory.

Earlier we mentioned that retention loss on a learned *A-B* association results from competition of alternative associations, *A-C*, and so forth, at the moment of recall. If we ask where these conflicting associations come from, the logical answer is that they (or ones similar to them, *A'-C*) come from learning either before or after the *A-B* learning but before the retention test. This faith has led to the intensive investigation of situations in which the *A-B* and *A-C* learning is explicitly controlled. The two basic paradigms are called retroaction or proaction depending on whether the experimenter's interest is in retention of the first-learned or the second-learned material. These paradigms, together with the appropriate control conditions and some hypothetical recall data, are illustrated in Table 9.1. In the retroaction paradigm, the control group first learns the *A-B* associations, then rests, and later is tested for recall of *B* when given the *A* term. The experimental group learns *A-B*, then learns new pairs *A'-C*, and then tries to recall *B* when given *A*. The retroactive interference index calculated for the hypothetical data is 67 percent. The proaction conditions may be read similarly.

A variety of task variables can be studied in this context, and on the whole the recall results fall in line with what would be expected from interference theory (for reviews, see Slamecka & Ceraso, 1960; Postman, 1971). For example, retroactive interference increases with trials on *A-C* and decreases with trials on *A-B*, whereas proactive interference shows just the opposite functional relations, as expected. Consider just one example, namely, the effect of the number of training trials on the *A-B* list (original learning, abbreviated OL) prior to *A-C* learning upon the relative dominance of the *A-B* and *A-C* associations. An experiment by Briggs (1957) illustrates the procedure and results (see Figure 9.5). Four different groups of subjects received 2, 5, 10, or 20 trials of *A-B* learning followed by 20 trials

Table 9.1

	Retroaction		Proaction	
	Experimental	*Control*	*Experimental*	*Control*
List 1	A-B	A-B	A'-C	rest
List 2	A'-C	rest	A-B	A-B
Recall test	A-B	A-B	A-B	A-B
Percent correct recall	20	60	60	80
Effect	$\dfrac{60-20}{60}=0.67$		$\dfrac{80-60}{80}=0.25$	

of *A-C* learning. The lists were ten paired adjectives. After intervals of 0, 2, 5, 10, and 20 trials of *A-C* learning, each subject received a "modified free-recall" test with the stimulus terms. On such tests the subjects were instructed to give whatever response first came to mind (including extralist intrusions), and there was no feedback from the experimenter to indicate which response was wanted. Such a test assesses the relative dominance of *A-C* over *A-B*.

The curves in Figure 9.5 provide a graphic description of the frequency of the new *C* response and the old *B* response after varying numbers of *A-B* and *A-C* trials. At the beginning of second-list learning, the frequency of *B* recall depended directly upon the number of OL trials. During the course of *A-C* training, *B* responses decreased in frequency while *C* responses increased to a dominant role. After 20 trials of *A-C*, the amount of OL still exerted some influence, both in terms of a higher *A-B* recall frequency and a lower *A-C* recall frequency. This picture is exactly what one would expect

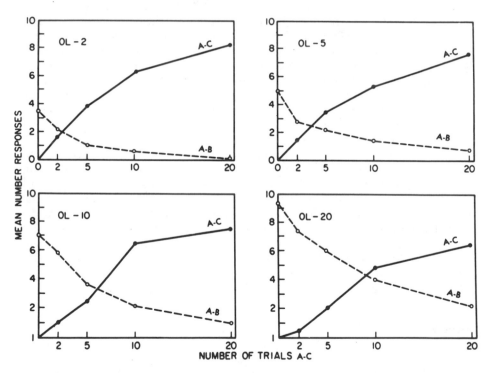

Figure 9.5.   Relative response frequencies of the originally learned response (A-B) and the newly learned response (A-C) during learning of the the new response as measured by modified free recall. The four graphs come from four different groups of subjects given 2, 5, 10, or 20 trials of original learning. (From G. E. Briggs, Retroactive inhibition as a function of original and interpolated learning. *Journal of Experimental Psychology*, 1957, 53, p. 64. Copyright 1957 by the American Psychological Association. Reprinted by permission.)

from McGeoch's earlier ideas of response competition, since the "modified free-recall test" permits only one response.

McGeoch's hypotheses predict a perfect correlation between retention loss of *A-B* and the occurrence on testing of intruding associates, *C* or *D*. This correlation is not always found: on the *A-B* retention test following the *A-C* learning, the subject often is unable to respond with any associate. Two hypotheses were proposed to account for this and both probably have some validity. One notion that we mentioned earlier, proposed by Thune and Underwood (1943), is that the subject can discriminate the list membership (first or second) of associates that come to mind; to the extent that he does this, he will censor and reject response *C* when trying to recall the first-list response, *B*. This is plausible since it is known (Yntema & Trask, 1963) that it is possible to judge with fair accuracy which of two events has occurred more recently in the past. Another idea, first expressed by Melton and Irwin (1940), is that during the *A-C* interpolated learning, the first pair *A-B* is unlearned or extinguished. If so, then, when the test occurs soon after the *A-C* learning, *B* is temporarily unavailable as an associate.

The clearest evidence for unlearning comes from a recall method first used by Barnes and Underwood (1959). Using the *A-B*, *A-C* paradigm, the subject was asked on the later test to recall both list responses to stimulus *A* and to indicate their list membership. This is a noncompetitive recall situation, and failures are ascribed to unavailability of the responses. The results of Barnes and Underwood are shown in Figure 9.6. This shows that recall of *C* responses increased with trials of *A-C* learning but, more importantly, recall of *B* responses decreased with trials on *A-C*. Thus, as the *A-C* training is extended, the first-list associates become increasingly unavailable, presumably due to unlearning. A variety of follow-up experiments confirmed and extended these results, so that the concept of unlearning was widely accepted.

More recently, some doubts have been cast by Postman and Stark (1969) on the validity of the associative unlearning concept. They noted that the *A-B*, *A-C* paradigm produced little if any negative transfer if the *A-B* pair was tested by multiple-choice *recognition* (i.e., recognizing that B_1 but not B_2 was paired with A_1).[3] Furthermore, although this paradigm produced the customarily large *recall* decrement for *A-B*, the forgetting was not very much greater than that produced by an *A-B*, *C-D* paradigm. For these and other reasons, Postman and Stark offered the tentative hypothesis that retroactive interference was not being caused by stimulus-specific associative unlearning, but rather was due primarily to a suppression of the entire set of first-list responses, a suppression that develops during second-list learning and persists awhile into a later retention test for *A-B*. On this hypothesis, *C-D* interpolated learning would cause suppression of the *B* response set (as does *A-C* interpolation) and thus these items would be unavailable as

[3] Pair recognition shows strong RI in the *A-B*, *A-C* paradigm if the interfering response, *C*, is included among the distracting lures on the multiple-choice test for *A-B* (R. C. Anderson & Watts, 1971). However, this RI could be explained by response competition and loss of list differentiation rather than by specific unlearning of *A-B*.

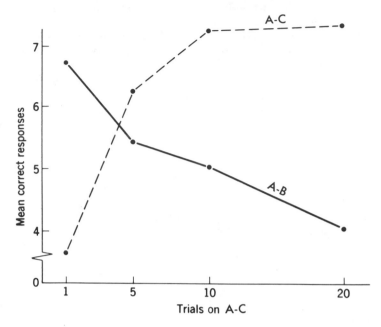

Figure 9.6.   Mean number of responses recalled and correctly identified with stimulus and list in the A-B, A-C paradigm. Eight is the maximum possible score in each case. (From J. M. Barnes and B. J. Underwood, Fate of first-list associations in transfer theory. *Journal of Experimental Psychology*, 1959, 58. Copyright 1959 by the American Psychological Association. Reprinted by permission.)

responses on the *A-B* recall test. But if the *B* responses were made available as on the pair recognition test, then the person would show that he had not unlearned the *A-B* association.

Evidence for stimulus-specific unlearning was not long in coming following the Postman and Stark challenge. A spate of experiments soon reported demonstrations of this effect (see Birnbaum, 1972; Delprato, 1972; Weaver et al., 1972). A typical one was that by Delprato (1972). He used a "within-list" design in which, across two lists, different items within the list learned by a subject exemplified an *A-B, C-D* relation and other items exemplified an *A-B, A-C* relation. The important point about such a design is that a factor like "suppression of first-list responses" should operate equally on all first-list pairs whether the corresponding second-list item is *C-D* or *A-C*. Therefore, any differences among items in recall of *A-B* could probably be attributed to stimulus-specific learning (i.e., learning *A-C* specifically weakens *A-B* in some absolute sense). Delprato's experiment showed exactly this result, with more forgetting on those specific pairs followed by *A-C* than those followed by *C-D*.

The first part of the Postman-Stark hypothesis can then be dismissed; under appropriate circumstances, including even pair-recognition testing (see Merryman, 1971), stimulus-specific unlearning can be demonstrated.

However, there does seem to be something to the notion of a general loss of availability of first-list responses due to second-list learning. One may think of this loss of first-list responses as the unlearning of associations between general contextual stimuli and the first-list responses (see McGovern, 1964; Keppel, 1968). It has been proposed that this loss of availability to contextual cues can be studied in the multilist "free-recall" situation where there are no explicit cues for recall of each item on the list. In any event, experimental evaluation of the response-set suppression hypothesis is just now getting underway.

Proactive Interference

Proactive interference is the decrement in recall of *A-C* by prior learning of *A-B* (or *D-B*, for that matter). Proactive effects are minimal immediately after *A-C* learning, but they increase over a retention interval. It is almost as though the person became confused at the retention test between the two lists he had studied earlier. So one likely explanation of proactive interference is that it involves progressively more confusion between the two lists learned some time before; let us call this the "list-differentiation" idea. It is quite plausible that ability to discriminate between second-list items occurring t hours ago and first-list items occurring $(t + \Delta)$ hours ago will decrease as t becomes larger, a sort of Weber-Fechner law for time discrimination.

But a second explanation has been offered for this increase in proactive interference with an increase in the retention interval following *A-C* learning. This second hypothesis supposes, first, that the original *A-B* associations are extinguished, unlearned, or inhibited during *A-C* learning, and, second, that these *A-B* associates spontaneously recover some of their prior strength over the retention interval. The analogy is to Pavlov's observation (see Chapter 3) that conditioned responses recover during a rest period after a series of extinction trials. Clearly, if the *A-B* associates spontaneously recover, they will compete with *A-C* recall, providing increasing proactive interference as recovery increases over time.

Several lines of evidence support this idea of *A-B* recovery following *A-C* learning. One is an earlier experiment by Briggs (1954), who studied the relative dominance of the *A-B* and *A-C* habits over varying retention intervals using the modified free-recall (MFR) test. In this experiment, subjects learned a first list of 12 paired adjectives (*A-B*) to a criterion of one perfect recitation, rested 24 hours, then learned a second list (*A-C*) to a once-perfect criterion, then received a final MFR test after either 4 minutes or 6, 24, 48, or 72 hours. At various stages during the course of both original and interpolated learning the subjects received an MFR test, in which they were free to say the first response that came to mind as they were shown each stimulus term. The results are shown in Figure 9.7. In the left panel is shown the relative frequency of first-list responses (*A-B*) as contrasted to preexperimental associates (*A-E*) from outside the list when tests were given after various levels of first-list performance, the criteria specified in terms of the percentage of pairs correct on the training trial just preceding the MFR test (0, 1/4, 2/4, 3/4, 4/4 of the list). As expected, extralist associates decline, whereas list 1 responses increase. After the 24-hour rest interval, the MFR test revealed

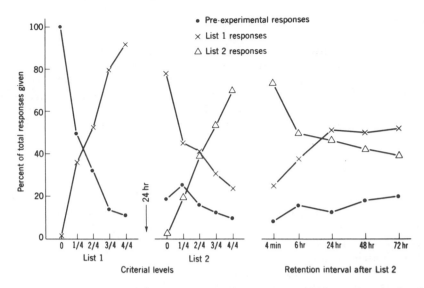

Figure 9.7.   The left and center sets of curves are the acquisition and extinction functions when lists 1 and 2 are learned successively in an RI paradigm. Recall as a function of time from the end of list 2 learning is shown in the right-hand set of curves. (Adapted from G. E. Briggs, Acquisition, extinction and recovery functions in retroactive inhibition. *Journal of Experimental Psychology*, 1954, 47. Copyright 1954 by the American Psychological Association. Reprinted by permission.)

some rise in extralist associates and loss of first-list associates (see the 0 point on list 2, the middle panel). Then during list 2 learning to various criteria, list 1 responses and extralist associates declined, whereas list 2 responses increased.

The data of interest to the spontaneous recovery hypothesis are in the third panel (from separate groups of subjects), showing the relative percentages of *B*, *C*, or *E* responses at differing retention intervals. This graph clearly shows a gradual recovery over time of the *A-B* and *A-E* associates, with a corresponding loss of the most recently learned *A-C* associations. These curves are exactly what would be expected if *A-B* and *A-E* associates were recovering in strength following their unlearning during *A-C* training.

The problem with this interpretation, of course, is that the MFR is a measure of *relative* response strengths of *B*, *C*, and *E*; Briggs's results could have been produced merely by a greater absolute loss in *A-C* rather than an absolute recovery in *A-B* or *A-E*. The obvious way to proceed is to try to demonstrate absolute recovery of *A-B* in a noncompetitive recall situation, specifically the "modified modified free-recall" (MMFR) tests of the type used by Barnes and Underwood. That is, the subject is to try to recall both *B* and *C* responses when cued with stimulus *A*.

But the evidence for spontaneous recovery in studies of temporal changes using MMFR tests have been equivocal, particularly for longer retention intervals ranging from several hours to several days. However, the possibility remains that a small absolute recovery of *A-B* is being masked by progressively greater recovery of preexperimental associates (*A-E*), which are edited out by the subject in the typical MMFR test. If so, then recovery of *A-B* should be most likely in MMFR tests given at reasonably short intervals after *A-C* learning. In these conditions, positive evidence for absolute recovery of *A-B* has been obtained (see Postman, Stark, & Fraser, 1968; Postman, Stark, & Henschel, 1969). Figure 9.8 shows some recovery data from an experiment by Postman, Stark, and Henschel (1969, their Experiment III). The experimental subjects learned three successive lists, having either an *A-B*, *A-C*, *A-D* relation or an *A-B*, *C-D*, *E-F* relation for different subjects, and then received an MMFR test either 2 or 18 minutes after the final learning trial. Two control groups learned the *A-B* list, then were tested for its recall after a time interval equal to that occupied by the interpolated learning plus 2 or 18 minutes. Figure 9.8 shows significant absolute recovery over the retention interval for both first-list and second-list responses; the third-list response was not unlearned and shows a high level of recall at both retention intervals. Significantly, the amounts of recovery are comparable for the *A-B*, *A-C* group and the *A-B*, *C-D* group. This fact suggests that this

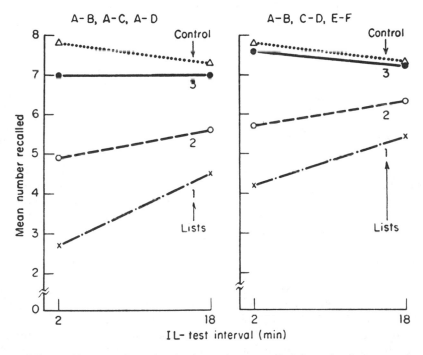

Figure 9.8.   Mean number of paired-associates recalled from the first, second, and third lists after 2 or 18 minutes' delay for subjects receiving either the A-B, A-C, A-D paradigm (left panel) or the A-B, C-D, E-F paradigm (right panel). Recalls of control groups who rested for an equivalent time following list-1 learning are also shown. (From L. Postman, K. Stark, and D. Henschel, Conditions of recovery after unlearning, *Journal of Experimental Psychology Monograph, 82*, Whole No. 1, 1969. Copyright 1969 by the American Psychological Association. Reprinted by permission.)

recovery of early list responses may be due to the dissipation over time of "response-set suppression" rather than to spontaneous recovery of stimulus-specific associative unlearning. To indicate this idea just briefly, during interpolated learning the person makes available the responses being used in that list while selectively suppressing the entire set of responses used in earlier lists. But this suppression dissipates with time, allowing earlier repouses to become progressively available for recall in MMFR tests. This issue of the source of recovery, whether of response availability or stimulus-response associations, is one currently under investigation.

One major shift in interference theory that has occurred consists in the powerful role now assigned to proactive sources of interference in forgetting. In a major paper, Underwood (1957) employed the proactive idea to clear up what had been a major source of embarrassment to interference theory. Most of the earlier studies of retention had shown rather massive forgetting —about 80–90 percent—over 24-hour intervals. The claim that this was due to interference from casual interpolated learning seemed unconvincing since it was difficult to imagine much everyday learning that would interfere with nonsense materials learned in the laboratory. By collating various reports, Underwood determined that those studies reporting massive forgetting had used the same subjects under many list-learning conditions. The more lists a subject had learned, the more he tended to forget the last one when recall of it was measured the next day. Thus, proactive effects presumably accumulated over the lists learned earlier. If a subject learned only a single list of verbal material, then his recall was fairly high—around 75–80 percent after 24 hours.

A particularly apt illustration of massive proactive effects is provided by an experiment by Keppel, Postman, and Zavortink (1968). They had five college students learn and recall 36 successive lists (*A-B, C-D* relations) of ten paired-associates at 48-hour intervals. Each test session began with a recall test on the prior list learned, followed by the learning of a new list to a criterion of one perfect recitation. The recall percentages are shown in Figure 9.9 plotted in successive blocks of three lists; this shows a dramatic decrease in recall from around 70 percent on the first list to around 5 percent on the last two lists. This illustrates the powerful effects that can be produced by proactive interference. It does not, of course, illuminate the mechanism underlying proactive interference in the *A-B, C-D, E-F* design. Presumably it is loss of availability of the final list's responses; if so, then there should be no cumulative proactive effects demonstrable in pair-recognition tests, or if the response words from successive lists came from distinguishably different (but memorable) semantic categories.

Underwood and Postman (1960) attempted to account for the remainder of what is forgotten by appealing to extraexperimental sources of interference. They point out that in learning arbitrary verbal associations or nonsense material in the laboratory, the subject probably has to unlearn the prior verbal habits which he shares with other members of his particular linguistic community. These prior verbal habits may be one of two types— letter sequence associations or unit (word) sequence associations. To give a transparent example, a subject is certain to enter the experiment possessing prior word associations like *table-chair* and *light-dark*. Suppose the learning

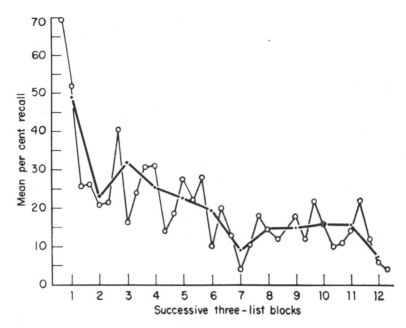

Figure 9.9. Mean percentage of recall of the immediately prior list at a 48-hour interval as a function of the number of prior lists, in blocks of three lists. The heavy black line averages larger blocks of nine lists. (From Keppel, Postman, & Zavortink, 1968. By permission.)

task requires him to form the new associates *table-dark* and *light-chair*. During a rest interval, spontaneous recovery of the unlearned prior associates will produce a decrement in the probability of his recalling the associations learned in the laboratory. The experiments by Underwood and Postman plus related follow-up studies show some merits of this analysis. New materials that clash with prior verbal habits are forgotten more readily, usually being distorted in the direction of agreement with the prior habits. However, the evidence on this hypothesis has been somewhat conflicting, and it appears that a variety of complicating factors can enter to obscure the hypothesized relationship.

A novel demonstration of proactive interference due to prior linguistic habits is to be found in a study by Coleman (1962). He took a 24-word passage of prose from a book and scrambled the words into random order. This order was given to a subject for brief study, and the subject then tried to reconstruct verbatim the serial order of the words he had studied. This reconstructed order was then given to a second subject to study and recall, and his reconstructed order was then studied by a third subject and recalled, and so on. The passage was successively filtered through 16 subjects. As it went from subject to subject, its recall (reconstructed order) was distorted more and more from the original jumble in the direction of sensible English sentences. One of Coleman's original passages and the sixteenth reconstruction of it is given in Table 9.2. The amount of change is dramatic, espe-

Table 9.2

Original passage studied by first subject:	"about was good-looking way and treating made of that a him the quiet youngster nice he manners a them girls wild go with . . ."
Reproduction of sixteenth subject in the chain:	"he was a youngster nice quiet with manners good-looking and a way of treating them that made the girls go wild about him . . ."

cially so considering that each subject was trying to reproduce verbatim the exact order of words he had studied. The change illustrates vividly the powerful effect of prior verbal habits in distorting recall of conflicting associations.

Interference with Meaningful Text

The laboratory studies of interference reviewed above have used "meaningless" materials, either nonsense syllables or random unrelated words. However, recent research provides extensive evidence that similar interference processes operate in the learning and forgetting of meaningful text materials, both at the level of single sentences and at the level of interrelated sets of sentences (text paragraphs). Although some doubts about interference processes had been raised by a few early nonanalytic experiments, recent positive demonstrations show retroactive interference or retroactive facilitation depending in a very lawful manner upon the exact arrangement of materials and the retention measure used for assessing losses (see J. R. Anderson & Bower, 1973; R. C. Anderson & Myrow, 1971; R. C. Anderson & Carter, 1972; Crouse, 1971; Myrow & Anderson, 1972).

We may illustrate the issues with recall of simple active declarative sentences of the form subject-verb-object (e.g., "The mechanic repaired the refrigerator"). We may view this proposition in either of two ways: the sentence establishes in memory a serial chain of associations between the successive words, or it establishes labeled functional connections between groups of semantic concepts which are instantiated by these specific words. A variety of considerations suggest that the latter view is more nearly correct and more fruitful. We may now treat the semantic concepts corresponding to the subject, verb, and object (call them S, V, O) just like terms in a "triplet" association learning task, except that there are a tremendous number of syntactic constraints and semantic selectional restrictions which forbid certain word combinations (e.g., "The night bounced the running" is literal nonsense).

Treating the concepts as terms in an associative triplet, we are then led to expect interference at this level if a given concept co-occurs with different concepts in new predications. Thus, following learning of S_1-V_1O_1, interpolation of S_1-V_2O_2 or S_2-V_1O_1 will lead to an associative loss between S_1 and V_1O_1, when the cueing is done in either direction. This loss would be assessed relative to a control interpolation symbolized as S_2-V_2O_2. Evidence that the interference is occurring at the level of conceptual meaning can be demonstrated by using synonymous paraphrases, say of the V_1O_1 verbal construction. Suppose S_1-V_1O_1 is the sentence "The sheriff aroused the slumbering patient"; letting $P(V_1O_1)$ denote synonymous paraphrase of the verb phrase, then an S_2-$P(V_1O_1)$ sentence might be "The nurse awakened the sleeping sick person." It has been found that interpolation of such paraphrase constructions produces just as much retroactive interference as does use of the verbatim V_1O_1 paired with a new subject-noun, S_2 (see R. C. Anderson & Carter, 1972). Apparently, the cue V_1O_1 contacts a similar trace in memory as does its paraphrase $P(V_1O_1)$, and the S_2 associated with $P(V_1O_1)$ competes with recall of the S_1 associated earlier with the same predicate by use of the words V_1O_1.

Of course, this paraphrase effect could be used to good advantage if one wished to facilitate conceptual (meaning) associations. Thus, a two-list experiment in which S_1-V_1O_1 in list 1 is followed by S_1-$P(V_1O_1)$ in list 2 will result in enhanced recall of the correct gist (meaning) to the S_1 cue of list 1, but probably with some loss in verbatim recall of V_1O_1. For the same reason, a paraphrased sentence $P(S_1)$-$P(V_1O_1)$ (e.g., "The policeman awakened the sleeping sick person") will be readily learned with high positive transfer following learning of S_1-V_1O_1. It is important to remain clear on this distinction between verbatim and gist recall, since it is possible to facilitate associations between general concepts (gist) at the same time one is interfering with verbatim recall.

A particularly striking example of the separation of these two levels was provided in an experiment by S. A. Bobrow (1970). He showed that if the subject and object nouns of a sentence were repeated as a pair in a second sentence, the association between them was or was not enhanced depending on whether the meanings of the nouns were maintained across the two sentence contexts. To illustrate, suppose a sentence in the initial study list were "The milk *pitcher* was splattered with sweet *jam*." A sentence in the second list which preserved a similar conceptual meaning would be "The lemonade *pitcher* was sticky with strawberry *jam*," whereas a sentence which totally altered the conceptual meaning would be "The baseball *pitcher* got caught in a traffic *jam*." The retention test, given at the end of the second study list, involved presentation of the subject noun (*pitcher*) for recall of the object noun (*jam*). As our intuition suggests, the subject-to-object association was greatly enhanced by interpolation of an identical or conceptually similar predication. But there was no accumulative learning when the meanings of the words were changed; performance was similar to what would have occurred if the *pitcher-jam* pair had been presented only once.

Although the illustrations above are for recall of single, isolated sentences, interference effects have been shown for paragraphs, stories, "science lessons," and the like. In such experiments, one must attend carefully to what are the atomic assertions that relate concepts in the initial text, and how these specific predications about these concepts are altered in the interpolated learning. For example, Crouse (1971) and J. R. Anderson and G. H. Bower (1973) have used short biographies of fictional persons as experimental passages. These comprise essentially a listing of life-history facts about the person. An interpolated passage which will produce little interference might concern, say, an art exhibit, whereas a passage causing maximal interference would be a second biography which systematically changes some of the facts contained in the first biography (e.g., names, dates, places, occupations, etc.). Anderson and Bower found that specific facts which remained the same in the two biographies were facilitated in recall of the first biography whereas specifics which were changed (e.g., father's occupation) were forgotten, even though the subject was likely to remember to say something about the right general class of facts. That is, the subject might remember to say something about the father's occupation but would get the specific details wrong. This suggests, as mentioned earlier, that by appropriate interpolation one can selectively facilitate recall of the conceptual "macrostructure" of a passage while at the same time interfering with memory for the specific "micro-structure" of the material.

SUMMARY COMMENTS

This brief tour through interference theory will have to suffice as an indication of its major features. The main shifts that have occurred in it have been acceptance of the notions of unlearning and of response-set suppression, a new emphasis on proactive interference, and identification of a potent source of proactive effects in those prior language habits that conflict with the temporary verbal associations set up in a laboratory experiment. Increasingly, research is being directed at understanding interference and the forgetting of meaningful sentences and larger bodies of text. There have also been changes in the experimental techniques employed. For example, Barnes and Underwood's modified recall procedure mentioned earlier is now widely used because of the additional information it yields on what the person remembers. Pair recognition is used to assess associative learning, whereas free recall is often conceived as an index of pure "response availability." This is an active field of research and no brief discussion can do justice to the range of variables that have been investigated in relation to forgetting. For more comprehensive reviews, see McGeoch and Irion (1952), Adams (1967), J. F. Hall (1971), or Postman (1971).

Current studies of human learning and forgetting appear to be in a highly analytical phase, with attention progressively on finer analysis of smaller aspects. As happens during analytical phases in other specialties, synthesis of the knowledge into a broader conception of the phenomena has been shunted aside temporarily. As a result, the possible uses of our scientific knowledge for solving practical problems have been only cursorily explored, and then in an often stumbling fashion. To mention just one major applied problem: educators or anyone engaged in training personnel would surely like to know how best to teach a student something so that he will retain it for a long time. The laboratory work relating retention to the conditions under which training has occurred is clearly relevant; but it is often so far removed from the kind of task, background, and other variables that make up the applied situation that some ingenious extrapolation is required before the principles can be put to use. Writings by Voeks (1964), Gagné (1970), Bugelski (1964), and a collection of papers edited by E. R. Hilgard (1964a) represent a few attempts at reasonable extrapolations. It is a hope, possibly forlorn, that more work will be done in the future bridging the gulf between the laboratory, on the one hand, and the classroom, shop, or office, on the other.

Current functionalism is not a unified theory such as those earlier discussed. What bonds of unity there are lie in a tolerant acceptance of a wide range of psychological phenomena and a conviction that the task before psychology is to subject the many variables to quantitative study. Such a methodological unity permits wide diversity in content. In earlier days, functionalism was distinguished by a particular philosophical analysis of "the mind." The mind was regarded not as a container of sundry simple elements or constituents (sensations, images, etc.) which combined with different forces to cause a man to behave in some specific manner, but partly as a set of purposive activities and partly as a set of dispositions and capabilities which underlay these activities. The activities of the mind—thinking, remembering—were not to be invariantly identified with a particular content, but rather with a type of function. We may make the analogy of an idea being like a chess piece (e.g., a rook or a king) which is ultimately identified by its function in the game rather than by its shape or appearance. A further feature of the functionalist approach was a "dispositional" analysis of mentalistic terms; "mind" was the collective name for the set of dispositions to behave in particular ways in particular circumstances. To describe a person's mind as brilliant or dull, quick or slow, honest or dirty is not to refer to some inner entity which causes him to act in certain ways; rather, it is to refer to his abilities and tendencies to act in these characteristic ways. This position has been picked up and elaborated by behaviorists (at one extreme) and has been eloquently argued by modern analytic philosophers such as Ryle (1949) or Wittgenstein (1953). In a strong sense, the functionalist revolt against structuralism in psychology set the stage for behaviorism; it also set forth the philosophical orientation which has endured throughout modern experimental psychology (e.g., see A. R. White, 1967).

The Functionalist Position on the Typical Problems of Learning

Within such an unstructured system as functionalism, there is no one clear answer to most problems of learning. The answer to be expected is that "it all depends on conditions," which is indeed perhaps the most accurate generalization about psychological laws. In practice the situation is not quite as free as this implies, for gradually there accumulate some commonly accepted generalizations.

1. Capacity. Robinson recognized individual and species differences in his laws of individual differences and of composition. It is in line with functional developments for McGeoch and Irion to include in their book a chapter on learning as a function of individual differencese. They believe that the increase of learning ability with age is best accounted for on the basis of two hypotheses: first, organic maturation; second, changing psychological conditions (transfer, motivation, personality traits).

2. Practice. The law of frequency was to Robinson a law of relative frequency, which therefore recognizes the losses in score when practice is over-crowded, along with the gains when trials are more appropriately spaced. There is a tendency to emphasize the form of the learning curve and to seek the conditions under which one form rather than another is to be found. There is, however, no diatribe against a law of exercise.

3. Motivation. Woodworth's dynamic psychology placed motivation at its core. Carr accepted in principle the preparatory-consummatory sequence, assigning motivation the role of a continuing stimulus to be terminated by the goal-response. The concept of set enters into the more conventional experiments on memorization and skill as a motivational supplement to the more familiar laws of association. It was the preoccupation of the early func-tionalists with such taks as the learning of rote verbal series which tended to place motivation in the background rather than the foreground of theories such as Robinson's.

4. Understanding. While the functionalist recognizes that meaningful ma-terial is more readily learned than nonsense material, degree of meaning is but one of the dimensions upon which materials can be scaled. Hence he does not believe that problem-solving or insight requires interpretations beyond ordinary associative learning. The organism uses what it has learned as appropriately as it can in a new situation. If the problem cannot be solved by analogy, the behavior has to be varied until the initial solution occurs. Insight is perhaps an extreme case of transfer of training (McGeoch & Irion, 1952, p. 53).

A distaste for holistic or organization concepts (of which "understanding" is one) is evident in the treatment of meaningfulness by Underwood and Schulz (1960) in their book *Meaningfulness and verbal learning.* They dis-avow concern for meaning in any ultimate sense:

> More specifically, meaningfulness as used here should not be confused with the term "meaning." As is well known, meaning has been a focal point of argumentation for generations of philosophers and, in recent years, semanticists. It will be seen that there are no ultimates in the meaning ascribed to meaningfulness by the operations of the learning laboratory, and there need not, therefore, be any cause for confusion with philosophical problems of meaning. (1960, p. 5)

They also dissociate themselves from the "semantic differential" concept of meaning (Osgood, Suci, & Tannenbaum, 1957). Hence, when they arrive at a quantitative theory of meaningfulness (a frequency theory: those items are most readily associated which are most available because of their fre-quency of occurrence in the past), they have produced significant relation-ships in their laboratory exercises, without coming to grips with what to many would be the more interesting problems. Meanings in the real world have some kind of reference. It would be interesting to speculate how it comes about that meaningfulness in rote learning can be treated without regard to reference; may there not be something about significant referential meaning that lies behind this frequency relationship? By being strictly "operational," functionalists did not have to raise such interesting questions at all, yet they remain interesting—and answerable.

5. *Transfer.* Following Thorndike, transfer falls chiefly under the law of assimilation. That is, transfer depends upon degree of likeness between the new situation and the old. Woodworth (1938) reinterpreted the theory of identical elements to mean only that transfer is always of concrete performances.

What the theory of identical elements demands is that transfer should be of concrete performance, whether simple or complex makes no difference to the theory (p. 177)
... Perhaps anything that can be learned can be transferred. But does not everything that can be learned have the concrete character of an act or way of acting? (p. 207)

6. *Forgetting.* The favorite theory of forgetting is that of retroactive and proactive interference, but the functionalist does not insist that this is the whole story. There may be some forgetting according to passive decay through disuse, and there may be forgetting through repression, as pointed out by Freud (E. S. Robinson, 1932b, pp. 113–118). But the functionalist does insist that these processes be demonstrated rigorously in the laboratory before they are accepted.

Does Functionalism Have a Systematic Theory of Learning?

Functionalism is empiricist rather than systematic. It eschews inference in favor of established experimental relationships between demonstrable variables. Its laws are quantitative, directly descriptive of data. There is a healthy respect for data, and there is a commendable urge to state issues specifically in a form subject to test. The relativism brings with it a freedom from bigotry. Before his untimely death, Robinson had turned to social problems, with the conviction that the same methods would work there. So long as people were forced to think in terms of specifics, he believed that they could often reach agreement, even though on larger issues they were swayed by prejudices and preconceptions (E. S. Robinson, 1935).

The disadvantage of an extreme empiricism and relativism lies in its lack of articulating principles to cut across empirical laws. What results is a collection of many "laws," without hierarchical structure. There is no economical multidimensional apparatus for fitting together the various two-dimensional functional relationships, each of which is necessarily cast in the form: "other things being equal." If the dimensional program of the functionalists were fulfilled, we should have a large handbook of data, with each of the several laws illustrated by a number of graphs showing the variations of associative strength under specific conditions. Empirical multidimensionality would be achieved through experimental designs testing several variables at once, but unless some simplifying steps were taken, the possible combinations and permutations of conditions would mount astronomically. Dimensional analysis puts data in order for exposition and for verification, but in itself does not connect the data into an economical scientific system. Such a system has to be logically structured as well as empirically sound.

Functionalism is in some respects an eclectic position. It is eclectic on the problem of introspection versus behavioral description, by accepting both in the account of psychological activity. A favorite illustration is that less attention to details is required after a skill is mastered. Note that this assertion uses an introspective report about the representation of details in awareness, although the mastery of the skill may be studied by observation of the overt movements. Functionalism is eclectic on the problem of blind versus intelligent learning, accepting a continuum between these extremes according to the dimensional analysis of McGeoch and Melton. Any point of view which is pragmatic and pluralistic can easily incorporate concepts from alien systems; hence functionalism is well suited to play the mediating role. Functionalism is, however, an eclecticism with a bias—the bias of associationism in favor of analytic units, historical causation, environmentalism. New data may be accepted but forced back into older concepts not fully appropriate. Thus some of the novelty of the observations made in insight experiments is lost when insight is treated as merely another illustration of the familiar transfer of training experiment. Similarly, what goes on in the reasoning process is not fully encompassed by treating reasoning as trial-and-error learning merely a little further out on the dimension of explicit-implicit response. Those who disagree with the associationist position object to the functionalist's incorporating of new experimental findings without accepting the theoretical implications of these findings. This is a problem the eclectic always has to wrestle with: how much can be taken over without incorporating the material's systematic context? The functionalist has not been greatly concerned about the inner consistency of his borrowings because he is less concerned than others about the inner consistency of his own concepts. What consistency there has been is provided by the framework of associationism within which the functionalist works.

Perhaps Melton's position is the best to take on the matter of functionalism's systematic position: the functionalist does not have an articulated system, but he would like to have one, and is not antitheoretical. His breadth and self-criticism prevent his embracing a comprehensive system until facts are better ordered.

Whatever the systematic limitations may be, it must be recognized that great energy for experimental study has been released within the functionalist group. The books of McGeoch and Irion (1952), Osgood (1953), Woodworth and Schlosberg (1954), J. F. Hall (1971), and Adams (1967) amply attest to this. Out of the large number of research investigations on memory and skill, done largely within this group, there has come a rich body of data and factual relationships with which anyone interested in learning must be familiar.

Convergence toward Functionalist Interpretations

Because there is so much room within functionalism, because it is an experimentalism, because it fits the American temper, it provides a kind of framework appropriate to much of American psychology. Many of the trends in contemporary theory and experiment, while not explicitly related to functionalism as a school of psychology, nevertheless are in accord with its historical orientation.

1. The scientific logic of *operationalism*, whereby scientific facts and concepts are related to the concrete operations through which they are produced, has been widely espoused by psychologists of the most divergent theoretical backgrounds (see, for example, Stevens, 1939). To the functionalist, operationalism is a very natural development from James's pragmatism and Dewey's instrumentalism (e.g., Dewey, 1929, p. 111).

2. Mathematical models that are "neutral" with respect to many historical controversies are essentially "functional" models, in the mathematical sense of function. This mathematical sense of function is coherent with the psychological meaning of function. Hence it is not surprising to find Skinner (1953) writing about the need for a functional analysis (meaning essentially a dimensional analysis), or to find Brunswik (1955) describing his system as a "probabilistic functionalism." The mathematical models to be discussed in Chapter 12 can properly be described as functional ones.

3. Miniature systems, in which restricted realms of data are summarized according to a few special theories, are also congenial to the functionalist. There is a heuristic pluralism involved in functionalism. That is, in order to move forward in the interpretation of data, it is sometimes necessary to accept provisional (heuristic) interpretations that permit one's moving ahead as the analysis progresses.

Contemporary psychology, to the extent that it is increasingly operational and increasingly concerned with mathematical models and miniature systems, reflects the general outlook that has, in one form or another, characterized the functionalist all along.

SUPPLEMENTARY READINGS

The following books are functional in content, although only Robinson's and Woodworth's are designed to state systematic positions:

ADAMS, J. A. (1967) *Human memory.*

COFER, C. N. (Ed.) (1961) *Verbal learning and verbal behavior.*

HALL, J. F. (1971) *Verbal learning and retention.*

KLING, J. W., & RIGGS, L. A. (1971) *Experimental psychology.*

McGEOCH, J. A., & IRION, A. L. (1952) *The psychology of human learning.*

MELTON, A. W. (Ed.) (1964) *Categories of human learning.*

OSGOOD, C. E. (1953) *Method and theory in experimental psychology.*

ROBINSON, E. S. (1932a) *Association theory today.*

UNDERWOOD, B. J. (1966) *Experimental psychology* (2nd ed.).

WOODWORTH, R. S. (1958) *Dynamics of behavior.*

WOODWORTH, R. S. & SCHLOSBERG, H. (1954) *Experimental psychology.*

Piaget's Developmental Psychology

Although Jean Piaget (b. 1896) is the dominant figure in contemporary developmental psychology, he is not usually recognized as a learning theorist. His views belong in a survey of learning theories, however, for the same reason that Freud's do: Piaget provides, as does Freud, a larger context in which to view the acquisition of knowledge and competence as a consequence of growth and interaction with the physical and social environment. Piaget forces the student of learning to be aware of age-specific abilities and to contemplate the interplay between logic and psychology as problems get solved at any age. These concerns with development and logic are of course not new to the learning theorist, but in studying Piaget they become both more specific and more important.

PIAGET'S THEORY OF COGNITIVE DEVELOPMENT

Before attempting to relate Piaget's views to learning theory, we may begin by outlining his position from his own standpoint, and in relation to the aspects of cognitive development that he believes to be most significant.

A General Theory of Development

Postponing for the present the consideration of "stages," for which Piaget is best known, let us examine his views regarding psychological development in general. Piaget notes that classical theories of development consider three aspects:[1]

---

[1] The exposition of this section follows Piaget (1970b).

1. Biological maturation
2. Experience with the physical environment
3. Experience with the social environment

He then proceeds to show how his theory deals with these aspects, and how it differs by adding a fourth consideration:

4. Equilibration

1. Biological maturation. When the theory of instincts came under attack in the 1920s, investigators (uninfluenced by Piaget) turned to two other, less controversial topics. The first of these was the concept of *drive*, so that the former "instincts" based on food-seeking, sex, or mothering could be studied empirically according to "hunger drive," "sex drive," or "maternal drive." The drives could be measured by studying the effects of deprivation of food or sex opportunities, or by separating the mother temporarily from the young. The empirical relationships established lay outside the controversy over instincts. The second substitutive concept was *maturation*. Instead of arguing about the instinctive nature of walking or flying or of a cat's catching mice, the experimenter merely noted the schedule according to which familiar behaviors developed. The position was that much postnatal behavior was as orderly as embryological and fetal development. The orderly changes up to and through adolescence provided a useful illustration of such maturation long after birth. Those advocating attention to maturation, prominent among whom were Coghill (1929) and Gesell (1929), did not think of it as completely independent of learning, and in this respect differed from those who emphasized the unlearned nature of instinctual behavior. For example, it was noted that while children, when they learned to talk, spoke the language they had heard, the *age* at which they learned to talk was independent of the language spoken. Hence maturation indicated a sequence characteristic of the species, without specifying the particular content of that behavior.

In educational psychology the concept of maturation led to the related concept of "readiness to learn," as in "reading readiness," and educators tried to specify the developmental levels at which different kinds of learning might be most efficiently undertaken.

Although Piaget argues against a maturational theory, and confuses some of his interpreters,[2] his concept of stages is indeed a maturational theory. In objecting to maturation he is really objecting to the earlier instinct doctrines which maturation was designed to replace.

2. Experience with the physical environment. All learning theorists are aware of the child's development of sensorimotor skills that permit locomotion and manipulation as the child explores and interacts with the environment. Exercise, trial and error, reinforcement and extinction, and many other learning concepts apply to this interaction. Piaget, in common with

---

[2] Hunt (1961), for example, interprets Piaget as providing a strictly nonmaturational theory. At about the same time, and in dealing with many of the same topics, Vernon (1961) interprets Piaget as having too strong a maturational position!

all the rest, acknowledges that such experiences are important in development, but he has further things to say that he believes distinguish his position from classical ones. He calls attention to three kinds of experiences with the physical environment: exercise, physical experience, and logicomathematical experience. He believes that the classical writers on learning have ignored especially the third of these, the significant logical achievements of the child in dealing with his physical environment.

Exercise leads to a refinement of movement, a matter upon which all can agree: the sucking reflex, for example, becomes more efficient with practice. But even in very early interchanges the child is not passive in meeting environmental demands: his own self-regulated activity is important in a manner not sufficiently recognized by the conventional theorist. Such self-regulation, although present even in exercise, is more evident in the other two types of experience.

The second, called *physical experience*, has to do with extracting information from objects in the environment, including discovering weight while experiencing color. Conventional learning experiments, of course, include learned discriminations, transpositions, and concept formation, but the tasks tend to be artificially imposed upon the learner, and the experimenter may fail to note how spontaneously the necessary information arises through the child's discoveries in the course of his object-manipulation. Educators will recognize that such an assertion is coherent with an emphasis upon "discovery-learning" (e.g., Shulman & Keislar, 1966).

Finally, *logico-mathematical experience* depends on special properties of subject-object interaction, and does *not* depend on the physical properties of the object. In his treatment of this concept we have an opportunity to become familiar with Piaget the logician, adding a viewpoint less familiar among experimental psychologists. The contrasts between them and him are somewhat as follows. The non-Piaget experimenter will set up a situation in which the subject has to perform a logically difficult operation. He may be ingenious in working out approximations so that the child will ultimately be "reinforced" for yielding the correct answer to the problem. The Piagetian investigator, by contrast, is concerned with "what it takes" to meet the demand, that is, with the particular cognitive abilities that are involved. He will thus study the development of these abilities rather than count the percentages of correct answers in tasks set by the experimenter. Here we enter upon the most difficult territory in attempting to understand Piaget. An illustration may help. Suppose a child is shown six red marbles and is told to match their number with some white blocks. To do this he has to abstract the series of integers from color and quality, so that a red marble comes to equal a white block as a "counter." This requires a kind of cognitive "know-how," which Piaget calls *structure*, a product of earlier development. Piaget thus sees a difficult logical problem in what most of us have seen as a readily acquired operation of counting; it is this perceptiveness regarding the nature of familiar performances that gives Piaget a special uniqueness. At the same time, however, this perceptiveness poses such an unfamiliar way of looking at development that some of his readers get lost in the process. As one goes beyond simple counting, there are other problems that do not reside in the nature of the objects themselves, such as the fact that number is independent of order. If pebbles are arranged in a row, they can be counted from either the left or the right, and the same answer will result. This is enough to hint at the later concept of *reversibility*, which will turn out to be a very important property of advanced thought processes. The pebbles can even be arranged in a circle before counting, and one can start anywhere and go in either direction, and still get the same answer. It is pretty obvious to the child that circles and rows are not properties of the pebbles themselves, but that the order has been imposed on them. The order can be ignored (as in the counting problem) or made use of if the problem demands it. If the beads in a chain have to reproduce a sequence of colors, then order has to be respected. These illustrations show that the child's experience of the physical environment must include what he contributes to that environment, and depends upon what he has learned in interaction with it.

3. Experience with the social environment. The social environment provides an opportunity to learn many kinds of activities, concepts, and relationships, such as cooperation and competition, mutual respect, folkways, and mores. Of all these complex interactions with the environment, Piaget—in his cognitive theory—is interested primarily in one: language. This does not mean he is unaware of other social processes, but as he summarizes his views on cognitive development, language becomes the essence of the socialization experience. He attempts to show, in discussing the relation between language and thought, that the origin of logical operations is both deeper than and logically prior to language. Of course, language plays a major part through permitting the child to represent action in thought. However, language, as learned from the social environment, does not *produce* the evolutionary stages of intelligence but is instead an agent *in the service of* intelligence.

4. Equilibration. Having accounted for what truths there may be in the conventional categories, Piaget finds them to be somewhat inappropriate or at least insufficient; he therefore adds a fourth term from his own theory: *equilibration.* He believes that equilibration, if understood as he means it, is the fundamental factor in development, and necessary to coordinate the other three factors.

A full understanding of what he means by equilibration requires knowledge about and use of the logic of classes and relations (see pp. 329–333). An understanding sufficient for our purposes can be achieved by way of examples. The examples are designed to show that equilibration is a progressive, self-regulating process. As we shall see, it leads step by step to a final state of *reversibility* that characterizes higher cognitive structures.

Piaget's favorite illustration is the child's progressive manipulation and understanding of a lump of clay.

a. If two equal lumps of clay are rolled out into sausages, one longer than the other, the young child begins by believing that the longer one contains more clay. At this stage he considers only one dimension, usually length, as in this illustration. This interpretation (unequal amounts of material) is not reversible, because the "unequal" quantities will again be seen as equal when both sausages are remade into rounded lumps of clay.

b. If a sausage is made longer and longer, the child may tire of using the same argument ("The longer the more clay") and shift to another dimension, thinness. Now he argues that the thinner of two sausages will contain *less* matter. This contradicts his first argument, but it is again the result of attending to one dimension at a time, and again the interpretation is not reversible. The child may actually fluctuate between the two interpretations ("The thinner the less clay," "The longer the more clay").

c. When this fluctuation or oscillation occurs, he begins to notice something that will advance him to a new stage of thinking. Note that advances seem to come about in this way, through the child's own actions in relation to his environment. This advancement is not forced, but becomes more probable following such fluctuations of interpretation. The child notices that, as the sausage becomes longer, it becomes thinner. Having made this observation, he moves from a static *configuration* ("a long thin sausage") to the notion of a *transformation*: the sausage can *become* longer and thinner. This transition from configuration to transformation serves as an illustration of equilibration; such equilibration is necessary if development from one stage to the next is to occur.

d. Once the child's thought includes the concept of a transformation, he is prepared for the next stage. This "preparation" consists in an increased probability that the next stage will soon be reached. If the sausage can become longer, it can become shorter. Furthermore, length and thickness can compensate for each other, so that the understanding of the *solidarity* or substantive mass of the clay becomes more firmly fixed. (The child began to glimpse this solidarity when at the previous stage he noticed the correlation between length and thinness.) This solidarity or invariance in the midst of transformation is what Piaget has described as *conservation* (see pp. 327–328), and illustrates reversibility because a transformation does not change the quantity of matter.

What we have seen in these examples is the gradual evolution, through the child's own activities, of increasingly probable equilibrations. These increasing probabilities, once reversibility has been achieved, lead to logical necessity at the higher stages of rational inference.

This brief exposition suffices to show the intimacy between logic and psychology in Piaget's developmental theory—a theory commonly referred to as a *genetic epistemology*, or developmental theory of knowledge. Piaget believes that this intimacy between logic and psychology has been neglected in the classical theories of development.

Two additional concepts are needed in order to understand what Piaget means by *equilibration*, a term often met in his writings. These are *assimilation* and *accommodation*.

The concept of assimilation is very similar to that of *apperception* in the psychology of Herbart (1776–1841). That is, knowledge derived from the environment is not a mere passive registration through perception but depends on the prior experiences producing a background into which the new environmental experience fits. This previous background Herbart called an *apperceptive mass*, and Piaget calls it the child's *schemes* or *structures*. Piaget uses the term *assimilation* for this process of "fitting in" or becoming a part of existing cognitive organization. Such assimilation is then the first part of the two-part process of interaction between external reality and the child's own attained cognitive structure. The second part of the process consists in the child's changing his scheme or structure somewhat so as to conform to the new external reality. This is the process of *accommodation*.

An adjustive process is needed to fit external reality into an existing structure (assimilation), and to modify that structure while this is taking place (accommodation). We may, then, call this adjustment *equilibration*, and recognize it as the essential basis for mental growth. Of course, such an interaction, in broad outlines, has been familiar all along in American functional psychology, where it has been described as adjustment between the organism and the environment. The novelty in Piaget's position does not arise through calling attention to what he terms assimilation and accommodation, for these processes are familiar under other names; it consists rather in the illumination that he brings to the details of the processes as they occur in development.

THE STAGES OF INTELLECTUAL GROWTH

We are now prepared to examine in greater detail the central doctrine for which Piaget is noted, the doctrine of *stages* in intellectual or cognitive growth.

How Piaget views other stage theories. In a more purely maturational theory, such as that associated with the name of Arnold Gesell (1880–1961), the inherent biological growth factors determine a regular order of succession in a preestablished pattern of unfolding, so that the infant crawls, stands, and toddles along with support before it walks freely. Special training can temporarily hasten the appearance of some behaviors, or, if inappropriate, can retard their appearance, but within a wide range of "normal" environmental stimulation the temporary facilitation or inhibition of development is set aside, and the child's development falls back or advances again to the expected pace of normal growth. Gesell and his co-workers demonstrated this in a number of studies using his method of co-twin control, in which one of a pair of monozygotic twins was trained to move ahead of the other in various behaviors such as stair-climbing or reproducing digits from memory. The restricted twin, later given the opportunity, tended to "catch up" promptly, as the advanced one dropped back to the normal growth pattern (Gesell & Thompson, 1941; J. R. Hilgard, 1933). Novel learning can, of course, be imposed upon the readinesses provided by maturation, so that, as in the case of language development, performances are age-specific but the child learns the particular language of his social environment.

A succession from one level of activity to another is implied in Gesell's descriptions of behavior, but he tended to emphasize the continuities rather than the discontinuities. His aim was normative, so that he described development according to age ranges in which certain responses may be expected to appear. Normative studies have continued to appear, such as that illustrated in Figure 10.1. From such a chart a parent can determine how his child's development compares with that of other children.

Piaget objects to such a descriptive sequential interpretation of maturation chiefly because it leaves out any clear recognition of the progressive constructions by which the child participates in moving his behavior from one stage to the next; the progression implied in this descriptive account is too much preformed to satisfy Piaget's liking.

Freud's theory of developmental states (anal, oral, phallic-oedipal, latency, genital) is more stage-specific than the maturational theory of Gesell. Each stage is associated with bodily zones as sources of pleasurable stimulation, each has its special anxiety components, and the problems of each stage must be resolved if normal (mentally healthy) development is to be achieved as one stage succeeds the other. This is brought out most clearly in the somewhat modified Freudian theory proposed by Erikson (1963), in which tasks associated with each stage are listed as dichotomies between a healthful and an unhealthful outcome. Sensitivity to pathological development, characteristic of Freud and Erikson, is foreign to Piaget, who concentrates on normal development culminating in rational behavior. Piaget is uneasy about the psychoanalytic theory precisely because the later stages are often foreshadowed earlier, and previous stages also continue to intrude later on. Hence, a later stage does not have the unequivocal dominance in Freud's theory that it has in Piaget's. This area of disagreement between Piaget's and Freud's theories of development is in part an empirical matter, and Piaget may well be at fault in paying so little attention to pathological development, especially if his views are to be helpful to parents and teachers. For the present purpose, however, we are not debating the merits of Piaget's position relative to other maturational theories such as those of Gesell and

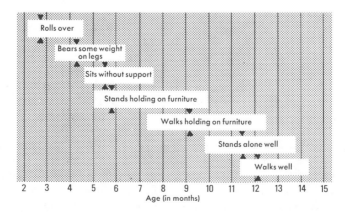

Figure 10.1.   Maturation of the human infant. (From William K. Frankenburg and Josiah B. Dodds, The Denver Developmental Screening Test, J. *Pediatr.*, 1967, 71, pp. 181–91.)

Freud. The purpose is rather to make clear where he stands, before going on to the details of this theory.[3]

Piaget believes that a stage theory must satisfy two requirements:

1. The stages must be so defined as to guarantee a constant order of succession. There must be nothing arbitrary about this order.
2. The definition of stages must allow for progressive construction by the child, without entailing total preformation.

The first of these requirements meshes with the logical development of the stages, so that a later stage cannot be achieved before a previous one has been accomplished; the second is the argument against a purely maturational conception of stage. Experience does not merely *capitalize* on a stage but plays a role in *preparing for* and *making probable* the transition from one stage to the next.

The three periods of intellectual development.   The developing child moves through an orderly sequence in which one stage is logically prior to the next, so that the appearance of any particular operation is *stage-dependent.* It is not, however, *age-dependent* in a manner that can be specified precisely for any one child. Ages are assigned to stages merely for expository convenience. Piaget has been little concerned with age "norms," and there are, in fact, some disagreements over the age ranges that he has assigned. These disagreements leave him unmoved inasmuch as his claim is that operations are stage-specific and not age-specific.

The main periods of development, each of which may include several stages, are the following three:

1. The period of sensorimotor intelligence (birth to roughly $1\frac{1}{2}$ years)
2. The period of representative intelligence and concrete operations ($1\frac{1}{2}$ to 11 or 12 years)
3. The period of formal operations (11 to 15 years)

An understanding of these periods can best be obtained by considering some of the detailed behavior that appears within them.

The period of sensorimotor intelligence.   Through three kinds of circular reaction (primary, secondary, and tertiary) the infant moves from blind repetition to repetition designed to make something last, and then on to active experimentation and some inventiveness. The six stages of sensorimotor intelligence including the circular reactions (response-feedback loops) are described briefly in Table 10.1.

It may be noted that the child achieves invariance of the object during this period—represented by object constancy (e.g., T. G. R. Bower, 1967)— but has not yet achieved the invariance of its attributes, something that awaits the next period.

---

[3] For some contrasts between Freud and Piaget in their discussions of the first two years of life, see Wolff (1960).

Table 10.1   The six stages of the period of sensorimotor intelligence. (After Piaget, adapted from various sources.)

Stage	Approximate Age	Brief Description
1. Exercising ready-made sensorimotor equipment	0–1 month	Sucking, crying, elimination, gross bodily activity; assimilation and accommodation are not differentiated.
2. Primary circular reactions	1–4 months	Stumbles on a new activity; repeats over and over. Example: grasps and lets go. Assimilation and accommodation become differentiated.
3. Secondary circular reactions	4–8 months	Acts, and waits for result to occur; shakes a rattle to hear the noise; brief search for absent object. Moves toward intentionality or goal orientation.
4. Coordinations of secondary schemas	8–12 months	Turns bottle to reach nipple; sets an obstacle aside to reach desired object visible behind it. Imitates a novel response.
5. Tertiary circular reactions	12–18 months	Explores new object in a kind of experimentation to find out in what respects object is new. Learns use of means to an end, such as reaching a watch on a pillow by pulling the pillow toward himself.
6. Invention of new means through mental combinations	18–24 months	Solves a detour problem by going around a barrier even if it means temporarily moving away from the goal; infers causes from observing effects; predicts effects from observing causes; invents new applications of something learned in a different context.

The period of representative intelligence and concrete operations. It is not possible to order the second period in a set of stages quite as distinctive as the six of the first period. In general, the period may be divided into two main parts: the preoperational phase (roughly 2 to 7 years), and the phase of concrete operations (roughly 7 to 11).

The early preoperational phase begins with the internalization of imitation, in the form of images. Once the child can manipulate his images as "signifiers" he is on the road to symbolic thought. But this road is not a smooth one. There are all sorts of impediments such as egocentrism, animism, and irreversibility that the child must overcome before he achieves rational thought processes. He classifies an object at first by some salient feature, and assumes that if A is like B in one respect it must be like B in other respects.

As the child begins to notice more regularities, and his assimilations and accommodations become more differentiated, he moves into a phase transitional to concrete operations, a phase well illustrated by the achievement of conservation of matter, weight, and volume. Matter, weight, and volume are derived physical dimensions, not as immediately observable as geometrical dimensions such as length, width, and height. They depend upon transformations, according to which they may stay the same under some circumstances when length, width, and height change.

The child has to learn this, and he finds it difficult until he has gone through the earlier stages of development. The notion of invariance was one that Piaget arrived at early, especially with respect to the achievement of object constancy, but the specific demonstrations of conservation, to which later references are so frequently made, began in earnest with the work of Inhelder, one of Piaget's associates (Inhelder, 1936), and became central after 1941 (Piaget & Inhelder, 1941).

One of the problems that have beset psychology as a science is that there are so few discoveries of genuinely new phenomena. This comes about in part because the experiences of everyday life have already taught us so much about learning, perception, and emotion. What scientific psychology often does is to find ways of quantifying familiar experience, in which case the excitement of discovery is lacking. Everybody knows that an inch on the nose is more perceptible than an inch on height, so that something like the Weber-Fechner law is not very excitingly new. People know that forgetting takes place over time, so that Ebbinghaus's logarithmic curve is simply a matter of precision with respect to something not totally novel. Some people are evidently mentally quicker than others, so that measured intelligence is again an elaboration of the familiar. Of course, the ordering of the familiar into lawful quantitative statements is one of the marks of science, as in the laws of physics. Still, one hopes for the discovery of something new and unsuspected, and this happens very seldom in psychology. In the field of development, everyone expects more of the older child than of the younger; that is one reason why Binet's age-scale of intelligence was so readily understood. With this background, it is worth noting that the facts of conservation, as pointed out by Piaget and his associates, represent one of the genuine "discoveries" within his experimental observations. We all knew that children made errors in estimation and in classification. As children, many of us played with the riddle: "Which is heavier, a pound of feathers or a pound of lead?" A primitive phenomenology told us that a pound of lead felt heavier than a pound of feathers, and we expected some confusions in the answers. Psychologists have dignified this as the size-weight illusion, but it is not altogether age-specific, and is found in adults as well as in children. To be sure, it was noted long ago that the illusion reached its height at about age 9 and decreased slowly thereafter (J. Gilbert, 1894). The reason conservation counts as a "discovery" is that specific confusions were demonstrated as affecting matter, weight, and volume, and it was found that these tend to be overcome in a particular order over about a 3-year period.[4]

---

[4] Cross-cultural studies have since shown limitations with respect to the universality of this orderliness (e.g., de Lemos, 1969). The popularity of Piaget's conservation studies has rested, however, on the generality of his findings in Western cultures.

The familiar transformations of a lump of clay illustrate the problem with matter or substance invariance. If two balls of the clay, recognized as equal, are divided in various ways, they become unequal. For instance, if one is made into a number of small balls, these seem to contain "more clay" than the remaining large ball. The effects of rolling them out into longer or thinner sausages have already been discussed. To achieve conservation the child must recognize that changes in shape of the clay, or dividing it into parts, will not change the amount of clay. Hence the transformations are eventually reversible, because if the parts are put back together again the two originally equal balls will again be alike. The fact that when back together again the balls are alike is not the important point; the child may recognize this and still not have achieved conservation. He must be able to predict this from his understanding of the problem. Piaget and Inhelder (1941) reported that most children have achieved the conservation of matter at 8–10 years of age, though most studies done outside of Geneva find these ages too high. In one of these it was found that half of a group of bright American children had achieved such conservation at the age of 5 (Kooistra, 1963). Piaget, as previously noted, is little interested in exact normative statements; such ages as he states must not be accepted uncritically.

To study conservation of weight, a balance may be used. Two balls of clay are shown to be of equal weight by being balanced on the pans of a scale. Now one is divided or otherwise changed, and the child is asked whether or not its weight is the same as or different from that of the comparison ball of clay that has remained unchanged. The child believes that the many small pieces of clay weigh more than the single ball. This turns out to be a harder problem than the conservation of mass, and is assigned by Piaget and Inhelder to ages 10–12, although Kooistra found that half the bright children in her sample achieved it at age 6.

Finally, to study the conservation of volume, the investigator must present materials to the child in special ways. For example, the child may be asked to build "houses" of different shape from an identical number of cubes of common size. He is then asked how much "room" there is in each of the houses, and unless the "room" is alike he has failed to conserve volume. Or a number of metal cubes can be arranged in different forms in two bowls. One bowl is now filled with a standard amount of water, to cover the blocks. The child is then asked to predict what the water level will be in the second bowl if the same amount of water is used to cover the blocks. To conserve volume is harder than to conserve weight, and is assigned by Piaget and Inhelder to 12 years and over, although the Kooistra study found half the children able to conserve volume at age 7.

Differences in findings from one experiment to another may rest in part on different criteria according to which conservation is said to have been demonstrated. The important point in Piaget's position is that *order* tends to be invariant. A number of studies have confirmed the order of difficulty, including studies with mentally retarded children (e.g., Inhelder, 1944; Woodward, 1959). Because of the clarity of the conservation measurements, we shall return later to consider their importance in relating learning to development (pp. 333–336).

The achievement of the early stage of conservation is the hallmark of what Piaget characterizes as *concrete operations*. A tortuous logical path has been followed by the child in working his way through the logic of groups and the achievement of *grouping structures*. These grouping structures are the abstractions lying behind the child's concrete operational thought. They represent Piaget's primary interest in his later years, and their exposition is the most difficult feature of his system of genetic epistemology.[5]

Learning by doing is the essence of concrete operations, and achievements can be made that satisfy logical rules without the child's readiness to state these rules abstractly. The whole story here is complex, but we may sample some of the operations discussed in order to gain increased familiarity with Piaget's thought. During the level of concrete operations, we may distinguish the tendencies to seriate, to classify, and to establish correspondence.

To *seriate* means to arrange objects in some sort of order, for example according to increasing size. The child goes through a developmental sequence in handling this task, but when he is finally successful, at around age 7, say, with sticks differing only slightly in length, he has mastered the logic of not only the relationship "greater than" but simultaneously the relationship "smaller than." That is, even though he cannot put it into words, he must know that every stick on one side of a reference stick is shorter than it, while every stick on the other side must be longer than it.

To *classify* is to sort according to some quality, such as putting all blocks of one color in one box and of another color in another box. Very young children can make piles of objects sorted into those of the same shape—distinguishing, say, triangles and circles—but sorting operations of this kind can become more complex, as in sorting together not only things that are alike but things that are similar. Then eventually structures that can be represented *algebraically* are achieved, such that $(A + A') + B' = A + (A' + B') = C$. This is merely a symbolic way of describing inclusive classes; the child does not, of course, use algebraic representation. For example, let C be "all animals," A "blackbirds," A' "other birds," and B' "animals not birds." Then the class $(A + A')$ is the inclusive class of "all birds." If the blackbirds are in the woods and the nonblackbirds are in the field with the other animals, then $(A' + B')$ will be "all the animals in the field." The algebraic expression shows that more than one kind of inclusive grouping can be made ("all birds" and "all animals not birds" or "all animals in the woods" and "all animals in the field") but that the total of "all animals" remains the same regardless of the groupings. To group in these alternative ways is a higher-order achievement at the stage of concrete operations.

At still another level, the child achieves the grouping operation described as *correspondence*. The simplest form of correspondence is the one-to-one correspondence, in which each element of one set is placed into correspondence with an element of a second set. This should logically guarantee that the elements of the two sets are numerically equal, but this does not follow for the preoperational child. Piaget goes beyond such simple one-to-one correspondences to describe the fit between a mathematical model and an

---

[5] For an introductory discussion, see Piaget (1970b), pages 722–732; Flavell (1963), pages 168–201.

empirical situation (as between mathematics and physics) as a correspondence. Sometimes to achieve correspondences it is necessary to bring into association more than one attribute, and hence to achieve what is logically a multiplicative structure. That is, if objects are double-classified, say by color and shape, the relationship can be represented by multiplying the color classification (A_1) by the shape classification (B_1), yielding the double classification (A_1B_1), as in the matrix shown in Table 10.2. There are many degrees of complexity of such matrices, and they have a number of logical properties that need not concern us here. How such matrices define some of the operations performed by children in the later stages of concrete operations can be illustrated by the kind of problem assigned a child at this stage.

There are only three knives in a store. Two of these knives have two blades: they cost 8 francs and 10 francs. Two of these knives have a corkscrew: they cost 10 francs and 12 francs. I choose the one which has two blades and a corkscrew: how much does it cost? (Flavell, 1963, p. 192; cited from Piaget & Inhelder, 1941)

The solution of this problem implies the matrix of Table 10.3. Only three of the four cells are filled, one by each of the three knives of differing cost. The one that solves the problem is double-classified as having two blades and a corkscrew (A_1B_1), which therefore is the 10-franc knife. Of course the child who solves this problem concretely does not go through the formal steps of constructing the matrix, but the structure of his thought processes is represented there. Younger children have trouble with this problem because it is at the upper level of difficulty for concrete operations.

Table 10.2 **Matrix illustrating double classification (bi-univocal multiplication).**

Classes of Color \ Classes of Shape	B_1	B_2	B_3
A_1	A_1B_1	A_1B_2	A_1B_3
A_2	A_2B_1	A_2B_2	A_2B_3
A_3	A_3B_1	A_3B_2	A_3B_3

Table 10.3 **Matrix for solving knife problem (see text).**

Classified by Corkscrews \ Classified by Number of Blades	B_1 two blades	B_2 unspecified
A_1 with	A_1B_1 (10 francs)	A_1B_2 (none in store)
A_2 without	A_2B_1 (8 francs)	A_2B_2 (12 francs)

Brainerd (1973) studied the order of emergence of three concrete-operational skills (transitivity, conservation, and class inclusion) in the two concept areas of length and weight. His subjects were both American and Canadian children, 7 and 8 years of age. He found an order different from that predicted by Piaget: transitivity, conservation, and class inclusion emerging in that order. He believed his results to challenge Piaget's analysis of seriation. Because the results also disagree with some empirical findings of others, the only firm conclusions are that Piaget's system is by no means of exceptionless validity, and that difficulties in measurement procedures allow for some contradictory findings.

The period of formal operations. As the child moves from middle childhood to adolescence, his thought processes move from concrete operations to formal, propositional thinking. At its best such thinking is that which characterizes the scientific method: considering all possibilities, making "if-then" hypotheses subject to verification, organizing the principles into some sort of network. The tasks that Piaget sets may indeed be essentially scientific ones. For example, the child can be given four flasks containing colorless liquids, the flasks numbered 1 to 4, with a test reagent *g*. Adding *g* to a mixture of 1 and 3 will produce a yellow color. This is demonstrated to the subject (without his knowing which liquids have been mixed before the reagent was added). One of the remaining flasks contains pure water, and another a bleaching agent that will remove or prevent the yellow color's resulting when *g* is added to 1 and 3. The subject is asked to reproduce the yellow color by using the flasks 1, 2, 3, and 4, and *g* as he wishes (Inhelder & Piaget, 1958). To produce a superior performance the subject tries each with *g*, and then (because no yellow color is produced) decides that it must be necessary to mix them. In an orderly procedure he will mix them in pairs, trying all combinations. In this way he will produce the yellow color (having mixed 1 and 3 and *g*), but this is really a concrete solution. To achieve a truly formal solution he must be curious to find out more about the liquids and their interactions, going beyond merely answering the question set for him by trying out all possible combinations, and then reflecting on his findings.

Two important changes from the concrete operational structures of seriation, classes, and correspondences will have taken place when the stage of formal operations has been reached. First, instead of dealing with the concretely presented options or groupings, several of the grouping operations are combined, so that a much more generalized classification scheme is reached. Second, a new structure emerges, what Piaget commonly calls a *four-group*, representing *identity*, *negation*, *reciprocal*, and *correlative* transformations (abbreviated by the initials INRC group).[6]

Without going into the details, it can be said that the main characteristic of a physical system having the four-group structure is that it must contain two distinct and equivalent operations which have exactly equivalent outcomes or effects. One can think of pans balanced on the arms of a scale so

---

[6] For those interested in an able and more thorough analysis of Piaget's four-group, a useful summary and review is that by Parsons (1960).

that weights can be added or subtracted from either pan, and the pans can be set at different distances from the fulcrum. Then moving a pan away from the fulcrum (increasing its leverage) will be equivalent to adding weights to the pan. These two operations (changing the length of the lever arm or changing the weight) satisfy the requirements for equivalent operations. The next requirement is that the system must have for each of these operations two more, both of which nullify the preceding operation. One of these, called *negation*, is an inverse operation that cancels the first. In the case of the weights, we can bring about an imbalance by adding weight to the left pan. To restore the equilibrium, we can negate the effect by removing the weight that had been added. Or we can use another operation, the *reciprocal*, by compensating for the change in weight of the left pan by moving the right-hand pan farther away from the fulcrum. These are the important transformations, the kind that enter into experiments with children. Piaget likes them particularly because they give further illustration of his concept of reversibility, inasmuch as the negation and reciprocal transformations can reverse prior operations. The physical system can be represented by a corresponding set of transformations expressed in the language and symbols of logic. Piaget apparently believes that there is an isomorphism (correspondence) between the physical and logical systems that is somehow reflected in the cognitive structure of the adolescent.

Having reached the stage of formal operations, the adolescent mind is equivalent to the adult mind, and the development of cognitive processes has been completed. This account, sketchy as it has been, suffices to provide a background against which to consider the relevance of Piaget for learning theory.

EMPIRICAL TESTS OF PIAGET'S THEORY

Piaget and his collaborators in Geneva have, of course, produced abundant observations, both naturalistic and experimental, in support of his theories. We turn now to some illustrations of attempts by those in other parts of the world to test his theories in their own kinds of studies.

The Periods of Cognitive Development Converted to Test Form

Those accustomed to devising standardized tests for assessing development, as in the many derivatives of Binet scales for measuring intelligence, turn naturally to the testing of Piaget's theories by preparing test batteries based on his observations and experiments. This is a slow process, and although a number of such attempts have been under way for some time, the available evidence is still somewhat sketchy. The method has not been neglected in Geneva, where Vinh-Bang (1957) many years ago reported beginning on such a scale, although not much has been made of it.

A fairly extensive study was undertaken some years ago by Pinard in Montreal, with a standardization sample of 700 French-Canadian children 2–12 years of age (Pinard & Laurendau, 1964). The battery consists of 62 subtests on time, movement, and velocity; space; causality and chance; the child's beliefs about the world (realism, animism, and artificialism); and logical deduction and the logic of relations. Some of the results from early phases have been reported by Laurendau and Pinard (1962). These, consonant with the results of others, show wide disagreement with Piaget's assertions as to ages at which the various stages occur, but this has never been a matter of any importance to Piaget. As for the rest, most of the differences from the Piaget theories are minor.

The data in the study by Laurendau and Pinard (1962) bear primarily on earlier aspects of Piaget's theory, on the child's early egocentricity and animism prior to more objective explanations of causality. In his preface to that book, Piaget raises some doubts about relying on verbal methods for getting at the appropriate facts, and indicates that, had he been consulted, he might have dissuaded the researchers from this approach. Although the results seem, in general, to support Piaget, the authors point out how very difficult it is to be precise about where any one child stands in his developmental career (Pinard & Laurendau, 1969).

A number of other studies are reported as underway, involving some sort of scaling of responses to Piaget-type items (e.g., Tuddenham, 1966; Corman & Escalona, 1969), but full accounts are slow in appearing. Once such scales have been properly standardized and available it should be possible to get better answers to a number of problems. Among these is the issue of gradualism versus sudden spurts when a new stage is reached, a more precise knowledge of the longitudinal development of individual children, and the degree of generality of the abilities tested. For example, there is obviously a correlation between the intellectual status on a Piaget-type test and that on a Binet-type intelligence test, but precise knowledge of the overlaps and the differences is of practical importance if both types of test are to be used diagnostically. K. Feigenbaum (1963) and Goodnow and Bethon (1966) have shown definite relationships between IQ and advancement on Piaget tasks, but more information is needed for analyzing the relationship at different ages and among different socioeconomic groups.

Experiments on Conservation

Within the stage theory, conservation of mass, weight, and volume (in that order) has been so consistently demonstrated that conservation becomes a good target for experimental attack, particularly from the point of view of learning. Can the child *learn* what is needed for the conservation task instead of waiting for the natural development to occur?

Conservation as the criterion of accomplishment.   A fair test of the empirical basis for Piaget's theory about conservation is to attempt to change the performance of the child through some sort of reinforcement procedure. Piaget likes to distinguish between learning and equilibration on the ground that learning is to bring thought in accord with things in the external world, while equilibration is to produce an accord of thought with itself (Smedslund, 1964). The learning practitioner, through selective reinforcement, brings habit in relation to external reality, but according to Piaget it takes the self-regulatory activity of the learner to produce equilibration.

So the lines are drawn, and experiments can be undertaken to see which view prevails with respect to conservation.

In a series of seven studies appearing in 1961 and 1962, Smedslund (1961, 1962) went systematically about attempting to modify conservation. On the whole, he found conservation performances quite resistant to change, although he was able to produce some changes, particularly if the training went on in the presence of conflicting cues. For example, when the child saw the clay (plasticine) rolled into an elongated shape, he was inclined to interpret it as "more clay"; if at the same time a bit of it was removed (making it obviously "less clay"), the child had to reflect on what was happening, and he moved in the direction of greater conservation. However, children who acquired the concept of conservation naturally, rather than by training, tended to hold to it against experimental conditions that challenged the new interpretation. If the experimenter removed a bit of clay from the ball of clay without the child's seeing him do so, after the child had learned that the sausage-shape and the ball should be alike, a test could be made of the firmness of his interpretation. The test was to place the ball of clay on one pan of a balance and the sausage-shaped piece on the other. When the elongated piece was shown to weigh more, those who had newly come to conservation reverted to their nonconservation explanation, while those who had come naturally to conservation said that some must have fallen off before the pieces were weighed.

Many others have performed related experiments. Uzgiris (1964), for example, broadened out the conservation tasks somewhat, using not only the familiar plasticine balls but also metal nuts, wire coils, and straight pieces of insulated wire. For each of these substances she found the usual order of conservation achievement: substance or mass first, then weight, and then volume. Deviation from this order on even one of the four materials was shown by only 8 of her 120 subjects.

When it is asserted that conservation is achieved "naturally," it is assumed (by Piaget as well as by others) that experience with the environment has made its contribution along with the internal maturational processes. However, granting a fairly wide range of interactions with the environment, the specifics of schooling, for example, are not expected to make much difference. These expectations have been challenged by the Harvard investigators Bruner, Olver, and Greenfield (1966). Particularly in her study of children in Senegal, West Africa, Greenfield (1966) found differences that she attributed to the kind and amount of schooling. The Wolof children studied had a common biological heritage, but could be found in either the rural bush setting or the cosmopolitan capital city of Dakar. In Dakar the children received a French-style education; in the bush some had such an education, others did not. The most interesting finding was that the unschooled bush children, after the age of 8 or 9, failed to go on to the achievement of conservation of a quantity, and they persisted with perceptual rather than intellectual-type explanations much longer than did the children who had gone to school (Figure 10.2). Her results are interpreted to support the belief that the child internalizes some culturally transmitted technologies in achieving conservation, so that all is not quite as spontaneous as the Geneva group appears to believe. With proper instruction, some of the unschooled bush children acquired conservation easily.

Other criteria for the significance of conservation. Most of the studies of conservation have taken for granted that it is a great gain intellectually for the child to achieve conservation, but the evidence is primarily internal. That is, conservation is something that can be demonstrated; older children show more of it than younger children; there is a logical advance involved; hence it is a "good thing" to achieve conservation and a "handicap" if conservation has not been achieved. For Piaget the issue was essentially a theoretical one, not requiring empirical validation. From what we know about other aspects of competency, however, we know that there are many ways of compensating for particular deficiencies; one gets by being color-blind, even though many discriminations are made on the basis of color. It is seldom shown that the children have any difficulty in using a balance to determine differences in weight, even before they are able to "pass" a conservation test on the conservation of weight. It might be that conservation is a particular, but possibly isolated, aspect of development—true, but not very important. Its importance is an empirical matter. The discovery many years ago of a blind spot in the eye of every person was interesting, but not very important in the daily economy of the child. The discovery of conservation is interesting, and well confirmed, but how important is it?

It is curiously difficult to get a straightforward answer to this question, partly because the criteria, once one departs from conservation, are not clear. It is like asking, How much is an adult handicapped by the persistence into adult life of visual illusions? The size-weight illusion persists, which is in some ways a denial of adult conservation; yet it is probably not very handicapping.

Among the criteria that might be used would be other kinds of intelligence test performances. For example, when the child crosses into a higher stage in conservation, is there a spurt in his IQ on Binet-type tests? Or it might affect school performance. Is he able to write a longer sentence or

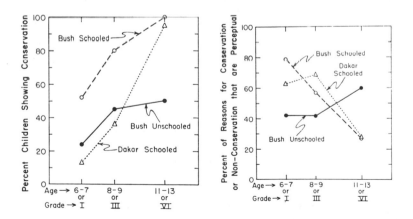

Figure 10.2. Effect of schooling on the attainment of conservation of quantity, and reasons associated with conservation and nonconservation. (From Greenfield, 1966, pp. 233, 237. By permission.)

(a) Percent of children of different backgrounds and ages exhibiting conservation.

(b) Percent of reasons for conservation or nonconservation that are perceptual.

one grammatically more involved shortly after he achieves his new level? (That he will gradually do better is not the issue, for this has been known as long as anyone was interested in asking the question; it is the *stage* issue that is debatable.)

Kohnstamm (1967), for example, showed that it was possible to teach young children that the whole includes the parts and is therefore greater than the part $(B > A$, if $B = A + A')$, without waiting for the appropriate developmental stage. Piaget warns about this, not that it is impossible but that it may be detrimental:

Remember also that each time one prematurely teaches a child something that he could have discovered for himself, that child is kept from inventing it and consequently from understanding it completely. (1970b, p. 715)

One would like to know whether or not in the context of broader school problems (other than specifically logical ones tied closely to the conservation criterion) it makes any difference whether the child has reached some stage of conservation.

There are two major reasons why, after all these years, such questions remain unanswered:

1. The move from one stage to another is gradual—a matter of increasing probability—hence it is difficult to assert with confidence just where a given child belongs. This difficulty is at the base of a controversy between Braine (1959, 1964) and Smedslund (1963, 1965). Braine criticized Piaget for relying too much on verbal methods, and proceeded to develop a nonverbal test. While many of his results were actually in line with Piaget's expectations, he did show that terminological difficulty may be present to mask what a child can otherwise do. Braine thus placed transitivity at ages 4 to 5, whereas Smedslund placed it later, at 7 or 8. The same issue naturally arises in those studies in which acceleration is claimed through training. The study by Kohnstamm (1967) previously cited is in this respect contradicted by Pascual-Leone and Bovet (1966), but there is little basis on which to choose between them.

2. The major test of the stage theory lies, in principle, in the concurrent emergence of a number of abilities when some sort of threshold is crossed and the child is at the next stage. There are a number of ways of studying the breadth of applicability of the newfound gains, in relation to sequential development, but the problems turn out to be enormously complex (e.g., Flavell & Wohlwill, 1969; Pinard & Laurendau, 1969).

The stage of concrete operations is not fully reflected in the conservation task in any case, so that undue attention to conservation is likely to distract from consideration of other fundamental issues.

THE RELEVANCE OF PIAGET TO LEARNING THEORY AND EDUCATIONAL PRACTICE

While Piaget has had a number of remarks to make about the contrast between learning as something imposed from without and development that is self-regulated, he has shown little direct interest in the empirical problems that have been most studied by investigators of learning in the laboratory: rote learning, motor skills, conditioning and extinction, remembering and forgetting. At the same time, his interest in the intellectual development of the child and in the bearing of child development upon pedagogy cannot be thought to lie outside the boundaries of a psychology of learning. Only a learning theorist unduly narrowed by his preoccupations with a particular specialization will fail to recognize that what Piaget has to say must be taken into consideration, whether or not it is accepted. His theory will not bear upon all of the problems with which learning theorists deal, but it will obviously be relevant to some of them, as is so well pointed out by Montada (1970).

Piaget and the Learning Theorists

Most things Piaget has to say about the work of learning theorists are negative. He protests against association theory in both its classical and, as represented, for example, in Hull's theory, its later form (Piaget, 1970a, p. 28). He believes that such theories imply a "copy" theory of knowledge, in which learning consists in reflecting as accurately as possible the sequences of events in external reality. (The rat learns to run the "true path" of the maze, without error.) He also disdains a purely positivistic conception of science, in which the aim is to choose between training methods on the basis of statistically compared outcomes, without any attempt to understand at a deeper level what is going on.

Piaget's objections to association theory do not ally him with the Gestalt theorists, who also attack associationism. He believes that the perceptual model, so dear to Gestalt psychology, is nonadditive and irreversible, in contrast to the operational structural wholes that he favors (Piaget, 1970a, p. 75). Through the years Piaget and his associates have made numerous studies of perception, and the basic conclusions have been summarized (Piaget, 1969b). The major emphasis can be said to be on the differences between perceptual development and cognitive development.

Berlyne's Hullian Version of Piaget's Theory

There is little point in attempting to extract a formal learning theory from Piaget's writings, parallel to the theories of those whose primary concern is with habit formation and the derivatives of a habit-based understanding of learning. Berlyne (1960b, 1965), following a Yale Ph.D. in the general S-R orientation under Hull's influence there, spent some time with Piaget in Geneva and made a serious effort to translate Piaget's theories into a form closely approximating Hull's theory. His translation of Piaget into S-R terms is a patient and nonpolemical effort to see if two systems of thought about learning and thinking can be coordinated. In the following account much of the detail is necessarily sacrificed in order to show the major thrusts of Berlyne's systematic approach to his task.

The general position he espouses is called "neoassociationist behavior theory." What he means by this is that the basic relationships with which he begins are input-output variables consisting of S-R associations. Although he uses mediating variables and may refer to hypothetical processes within the organism, the system, to use an expression of Hull's, is "anchored to the environment" on both the input and the output side. In common with other association theories, there is insistence on reliance on the historical roots of present behavior. That is, a present "program" or "model" accounting for behavior is incomplete unless we know something about how it came to be, both phylogenetically and ontogenetically. When mediating processes are inferred, they tend to be described as "internal stimuli" or "implicit responses." This is not a hollow use of the familiar stimulus-response language, but is intended to mean that these internal processes follow the same "laws" attributed to the stimulus-response relationships that are observable.

The prior statements are appropriate to neoassociationist theories in general; Berlyne's constructive aim is to produce an integrative form of the theory that will encompass the empirical (and logical?) evidence from Piaget. To this end he is ready to temporarily sacrifice precision to generality, waiting for further developments to attain the precision that is ultimately to be desired.

In order to achieve this integrative generality, Berlyne has to rely upon and extend the most general features of Hull's theory. Without going into details, we may say that Berlyne builds up his argument in essentially these steps:

1. Stimulus generalization. From independent association we move to primary stimulus generalization, then to secondary stimulus generalization (such as represented in stimulus chaining), and finally to semantic generalization. A large step is taken when Piaget's conservation, which requires quantitative invariants, is explained as secondary stimulus generalization (Berlyne, 1965, p. 81).

2. Response generalization. Response generalization moves through steps from primary response generalization to secondary response generalization, including response chaining, short-circuiting, and mediated response generalization.

3. Habit-family hierarchies. The habit-family hierarchy is taken directly from Hull (see pp. 172–173). It consists of a set of behavior chains all associated with a common starting point and ending in the same goal situation. Hull found this derived mechanism useful in accounting for free-field experiments, such as the detour experiments of Köhler and some of the experiments of Lewin. Even as used by Hull, the concept was put under some strain to treat cognitive processes as though they were linked together like a rat's running movements in a maze, and in Berlyne's hands it has to carry even heavier burdens.

One specific burden is to explain how a child learns the meaning of "equivalence" for an equation in which both sides are equivalent, such as:

$$(x+y)^2 = x^2 + 2xy + y^2.$$

Berlyne is cautious enough in his analysis to show that this kind of equivalence cannot be accounted for on the basis of derived stimulus equivalences, because too many transformations are involved.

The habit-family provides the solution for him, although the derivation is somewhat strained.

First he indicates that $(x+y)^2$ represents one behavior chain ("Add x to y and calculate the square of this sum"), and $x^2+2xy+y^2$ represents another behavior chain ("Calculate the square of x, store the results of this calculation, multiply x by y, double and store this product, calculate the square of y, add this square and the results of the two previous calculations"). Then his explanation of the equivalence follows: "The equivalence between these two behavior chains resides in their common membership in a number of habit-family hierarchies" (Berlyne, 1965, p. 93).

The habit-family hierarchy is also taken to represent the essentials of what Piaget means by "operation," that is, actions that are internalizable, reversible, and coordinated into systems. "If we therefore say that Piaget's operations are implicit responses organized in habit-family hierarchies, we have apparently captured the fundamentals of his conception" (Berlyne, 1965, p. 113).

4. Transformational habit-family hierarchies.   Berlyne found an essential aspect of Piaget's thinking unrepresented in Hull's system, and impossible to represent without extending Hull's notions into a new area. It is a matter of preference whether or not to consider this a concession to Piaget; Piaget has some doubts whether, even with this addition, the theory is sufficient to cover his evidence (Piaget, 1970b, p. 713). Berlyne finds it necessary to recognize the ability both to imagine a situation that preceded a transformation ("situational thoughts") and to imagine a possible transformation ("transformational thoughts"). The kinds of transformation he has in mind are shown in some experiments of Piaget and Inhelder (1962). A child watches two toy cars, traveling at different speeds, so that one overtakes and passes the other. Then the cars enter a long tunnel. When asked what they saw happen, young children can readily report the witnessed transformation ("situational thoughts"), but they are less successful at anticipatory imagery (anticipating which car would leave the tunnel first). In this experiment, half the subjects at the age of 7 or 8 could report accurately what they actually saw, but success on the anticipatory task did not reach 50 percent until the age of 10 or 11 years.

To work all of this into systematic thinking coherent with his neoassociationist theory, Berlyne has proposed some conditions for transformational habit-family hierarchies:

With respect to transformational hierarchies (as we shall call those that are composed of transformational chains), the particular conditions are (1) that each situational stimulus (that is, the feedback stimulus from a situational response) must belong to the domain of the following transformational response, (2) that each situational stimulus must be associated with the following transformational response, and (3) that each situational stimulus must be the image of the preceding situational stimulus under the preceding transformation. (1965, p. 117)

This is asking a good deal of a stimulus-response system, but if the conditions are met the subject is presumably able to indulge in directed thinking, both in the form of a *transformation-applying habit* and a *transformation-selecting habit*. When he can do this, he can do what Piaget would want him to be able to do: "to represent to himself, and communicate to others, the stimulus situation that would result from a series of transformations, even when the transformations are not actually effected" (Berlyne, 1965, p. 123).

What Berlyne has attempted to do, in addition to seeing how what Piaget describes can be translated into the S-R language, is to achieve an integration between the basic structures that underlie the simplest forms of behavior and those that underlie the most complex forms of thought.

Although Berlyne is to be commended for the care with which he carried out his self-assigned task of translation and integration, two troublesome questions remain for the critic:

1. Are the additions to the Hull-type theory legitimate within that type of theory? Perhaps there has been some inadvertent addition of new "emergents" within the theory, so that the more complex derivations do not arise strictly from the basic definitions and postulates of the system. Adding the transformational habit-family hierarchies may be like adding "insight" as a postulate within an S-R theory.

2. Would an S-R type theory ever have led to investigations of the type that Piaget has conducted? A theory must be judged not only by the possible translation of other findings into its vocabulary, but by its fertility in pointing up new problems and directing new investigations.

Piaget and Appropriate Methods of Teaching

Piaget rightly warns that practical problems of education are not solved by moving directly from theory to practice; that is, an educational psychology is not merely a deductively applied child psychology. An experimental pedagogy must confront problems different from those of psychology itself because it cannot limit itself to the general and spontaneous characteristics of the child and its intelligence, but must necessarily try to modify developmental processes, as, for example, in the teaching of reading.

Generally speaking, since every discipline must include a certain body of acquired facts as well as the possibility of giving rise to numerous research activities and activities of rediscovery, it is possible to envisage a balance being struck, varying from subject to subject, between different parts to be played by memorizing and free activity. In which case, it is possible that the use of teaching machines will save time. . . . (Piaget, 1970a, p. 78)

One of Piaget's followers, Aebli (1951), early made some suggestions about how to use Piaget's theory in relation to teaching. He gave prominence to the epigram *Penser, c'est opérer*, which may be translated, "To think is to operate." Hence all teaching should stress pupil initiative, an active experimentation with the environment in which overt actions gradually become translated into mental operations, with the consequence that eventually less support is needed from external objects. A second important point is that interaction with peers is important, if for no other reason than to liberate the child from his egocentrism. In group activities he must eventually learn to take the perspective of the other, leading to what Piaget calls decentration.

Piaget has made direct educational references on a number of occasions; his 1935 account of the psychological foundations of new methods in education was reissued in 1969 along with eight chapters giving his comments on education and teaching since 1935 (Piaget, 1969a; English ed., 1970a).

Many English and American educators have been influenced by Piaget, and a number of books have appeared summarizing their views (e.g., Furth, 1970; Lovell, 1962; Lunzer, 1960; Phillips, 1969; Wallace, 1965). These vary from summaries of his writings, with derived suggestions for curriculum and educational practices, to serious experimental efforts to apply his views. One summary, containing chapters by Piaget and by a number of others, appeared in 1964 under the title *Piaget rediscovered* (Ripple & Rockcastle, 1964). In this a special effort was made to relate a number of ongoing curriculum studies in the United States to the cognitive development theories of Piaget.

A later paper by E. G. Sigel (1969) may serve to summarize some of the educational implications for training procedures in light of Piaget's concepts (e.g., I. E. Sigel & Hooper, 1968). E. G. Sigel makes a number of points, and the following discussion leans heavily on his interpretation.

1. Through a knowledge of Piaget a teacher may become alerted to changes in development with age.   Many teachers are little aware of the changes that take place, and tend to be more formalistic in their training than is desirable before the child is old enough. However, merely having some acquaintance with Piaget's views may not be enough. It remains to be shown that a teacher familiar with these views in detail has better success as a teacher than one not familiar with them.

2. Those responsible for curriculum construction can base the sequence of expected learnings upon the sequences discovered by Piaget.   This is essentially a restatement of the notion of appropriate development, but stated in such a manner that the teacher would be helped to apply Piaget to, say, a given subject matter such as mathematics or science. Earlier attempts to use "readiness" concepts for the age-placement of materials were not altogether successful; it remains to be seen whether or not experiments can lead to the construction of better curriculum sequences on the basis of Piaget's work. Cronbach (1964) has noted that the bridge between the theory of cognitive development and the aims of the curriculum is still pretty obscure.

Tronick and Greenfield (1973) have developed a curriculum for infants and very young children that illustrates how Piaget's emphasis upon developmental sequences can provide a framework for planning experiences appropriate to stages of development. What they have produced is inventive and derives from their own experiences and those of others, but Piaget's theories and observations provide a background.

3. Specific teaching strategies can in part be derived from Piaget's theories.   By giving the child multiple experiences, as in the classification and categorization of objects, "a more extensive and varied world could be opened up to the child, which he could approach with increased flexibility" (E. G. Sigel, 1969, p. 479).

Piaget has himself dealt with particular subject matters in a chapter entitled "Development of some branches of teaching" (Piaget, 1970a, pp. 43–64). He notes three factors of importance: (a) internal developments of the disciplines taught, (b) new teaching methods, and (c) use of the data provided by child and adolescent psychology. It is to be noted that he does not make the improvement of teaching dependent solely upon developments in the field of psychology.

The topics that he chooses to discuss are "The didactics of mathematics," "Fostering the spirit of experiment and introducing the child to the physical and natural sciences," "The teaching of philosophy," and "The teaching of 'classics' and the problems of the humanities." In case there are those who might think of Piaget as narrowly encapsulated within his studies of child development and genetic epistemology, it is refreshing to find in these essays his essential breadth and concern for educational substance independent of his own special theories.

Piaget and Montessori's Methods

The effort to make something practical out of Piaget has apparently been in part responsible for the recent upsurge of interest in Montessori schools, especially in the United States. The link is, of course, Piaget's emphasis upon sensorimotor intelligence and Montessori's practical emphasis upon the child's manipulation of objects, forms, and textures. Piaget notes that there has for many years been a residue from the notion that thought arises from perception, as in the "sensory education" exercises that Froebel introduced into his kindergartens; according to Piaget, Montessori did somewhat better —but on the basis of intuition and without theory—in providing a fair amount of action, but the action was too much constrained by channeling it according to her previously assembled apparatus (Piaget, 1970a, p. 98). While this is scarcely an endorsement of Montessori's schools as a way of producing Piaget's results in practice, Piaget does give Montessori credit, along with Decroly and Dewey, for bringing to the fore the notion that interest and active effort go together, and that activity provides training for thought (Piaget, 1970a, p. 148).

Elkind (1967) has compared Montessori's views with those of Piaget, without attempting to assess the practical successes of Montessori schools. Among the overlaps is the biological orientation of both standpoints.

Montessori was a medical doctor—the first woman to receive a medical degree in Italy—and it was natural for her to see intellectual development as a form of growth, requiring nourishment just as physical growth does. The "prepared environment" of the Montessori school is designed to provide this "nourishment" (Montessori, 1964). Piaget uses the same figure of speech, for example, "assimilation is essentially the utilization of the external environment to *nourish* his hereditary or acquired schemata" (Piaget, 1954, p. 351; emphasis added).

The concept of the environment nourishing hereditary potential leads to a dual process in growth: on the one hand, native potential is realized under the influence of environment, so that *capacity to learn* is a product of this interaction; on the other hand, this capacity to learn is applied to a content of learning that owes to the environment, and to which natural ability must be subservient. In this Montessori and Piaget are in agreement. They are also alike in being essentially normative in outlook, that is, seeking what can be expected of all children; while both recognized individual differences, neither was ever preoccupied with them. There appears, however, little justification for assuming, by way of these similarities, that a Montessori school represents an applied version of Piaget's theory.

ESTIMATE OF PIAGET'S CONTRIBUTIONS TO LEARNING

Piaget's Position on Typical Problems of Learning

1. Capacity.   In a theory such as Piaget's whereby development rests very largely on maturation, differences in potential are set at least in part by native differences. Development may be retarded by unfavorable environment, and advanced, at least to some extent, by more favorable environment.

2. Practice.   The essence of practice is active *discovery*, and passive learning is ineffective, at least in early childhood. Repetitive practice may assist in the learning of some basic information (figurative), but it is not the way in which inventive transformations are learned (operative). The role of practice varies with developmental stage.

3. Motivation.   Motivational conceptions are little emphasized, although there is considerable admiration for a position such as Dewey's that relates interest and effort. The theory of equilibration suggests that the learner desires to reduce his internal conflicts, thus keeping his thoughts harmonious. In this, the motivation implications are similar to those of tension-reduction theories (homeostasis), or, in the cognitive sphere, of dissonance reduction (Festinger, 1957).

4. Understanding.   Understanding is the very aim of operative intelligence, and, as a logician, Piaget wants the learner to make rational inferences from givens. The notion of "structure" is basic, classifying Piaget's as a "centralist" theory.

5. Transfer.   As a result of assimilation and accommodation, the growing child can comprehend an increasingly wide sphere of relationships. Although the concept of transfer of training is not focal, certainly problem-solving competence is, and this implies generalization of what is learned. One of the empirical problems is that of the concurrent emergence of a number of abilities when a new stage is reached (see p. 336).

6. Remembering and forgetting.   Very often a test of the firmness of a new acquisition is provided by how well it is retained. Inhelder (1969) has devoted a chapter to the problem of memory in relation to intelligence, based on a larger study (Piaget, Inhelder, & Sinclair, 1968). This larger study is reminiscent of the work of Bartlett (1932), to whom acknowledgment is made. It was Bartlett's contention that memory is productive as well as reproductive, and this is brought out in relation to Piaget's concept of development.

For example, children of 3 to 8 years were shown 10 sticks, 9 to 15 centimeters in length, arranged in serial order from the shortest to the longest. A week later, they were asked to draw what they had seen, and then to arrange the sticks as they remembered them to have been arranged. The same requests were repeated some months later. If the children were assigned to four operational stages, on first testing they yielded essentially correct responses (a series of sticks in ascending serial order by size) by stages as shown in Table 10.4. Although these results are somewhat contaminated by having the seriation enter into the stage classification, other, more complex experiments led to the same conclusion. Memory is not simply a residue of the perception of what the child has seen; it is instead a symbolic representation of how the child has schematized what he saw.

In some cases, in which causal relationship lies at the basis of what is perceived and remembered, memory improves over time, because the child's schemes become clearer to him. Of course, the outcome is not always improvement; an improper scheme can distort. In any case, memory cannot be treated as an ability separate from the functioning of cognitive processes as a whole.

The Significance of Stage Theory

Piaget's theory of stages calls attention strongly to new ways of dealing with problems as the child develops. This conception has gradually been forced upon those who began with other orientations, and some sort of hierarchical categorization of learning tasks and of learning abilities is now common. Although some issues remain as to the sharpness or suddenness of the transitions from one stage to another, and as to how widespread the changes are when they occur, at least over a few years the changes are so pronounced that all must recognize them, however they interpret them.

Logic and Psychology

In calling his theory of cognitive development a theory of genetic epistemology, Piaget has brought to the fore the intimacy between logic and psychology (e.g., Piaget, 1957, 1971). Many profound questions arise here, particularly when productive or imaginative thinking is under consideration. On the one hand, Piaget may be said to have psychologized logic, in showing how logic arises out of the cognitive development natural to the child. On the other hand, he has logicized psychology, by showing that much

Table 10.4   Memory for seriation. (Adapted from Inhelder, 1969, p. 341.)

Operational Stage	"Correct" Seriation after a Week
Preoperational	0%
Transitional	35%
Empirical seriation	73%
Operational seriation	100%

of the logic of relations is appropriate to the analysis of empirical problems confronting the learner. We are not prepared to guess what the ultimate influence of Piaget will be in this general direction.

The Special Role of Imagery

With the recent upsurge of interest in imagery as providing mediating processes for learning and memory (see pp. 588–589), psychologists not previously influenced by Piaget are likely to note with greater interest the special role he assigns to imagery in the transition from perception to thought. Imagery is said to arise from imitation. An action is quite likely to have terminated before it is imitated, or part of the action at least is often imitated while it is not occurring. Hence the imitated movement has to be reconstructed in imagery before the child can produce it. Eventually imagery becomes a vehicle for transformation, serving not only to review past transformations (Berlyne's situational thoughts) but to anticipate future transformations (Berlyne's transformational thoughts). In making imagery thus constructive rather than reproductive of perception, Piaget's use of imagery is coherent with that of some contemporary learning theorists.

Discovery Learning

Emphasis on discovery learning, on learning that comes through free activity in a rich environment, only mildly structured by the teacher to facilitate learning, has had an appeal to educators for many years, in America particularly to the followers of John Dewey. Piaget gives such a strong lift to this position that it is likely to be picked up again by those who may have cooled somewhat in their enthusiasm for it. Despite a usual lip-service to the discovery method, formal cognitive-content emphases have been prominent in the rational curriculum projects of recent years (Wittrock, 1966).

A symposium devoted to discovery learning (Shulman & Keislar, 1966) did not give it unanimous support, at least not without many qualifications. The general orientation of discovery learning is clear enough: the subject finds out something for himself, especially some generalization or principle, without its having been explained initially to him by someone else. Usually he puts it in his own words, and if he has acceptably understood, these words communicate clearly to the teacher as well. The arguments against reliance on discovery are chiefly two: (a) that one of the roles of education is the transmission of culture, and this cannot be wholly a matter of free discovery, and (b) that maybe a little discovery goes a long way, and would be inefficient if it had to carry all the burden (Cronbach, 1966). We cannot expect every student to be a combination of Galileo, Newton, and Einstein in discovering the laws of physics. While no believer in discovery learning expects anything like this to happen, stating such an extreme expectation implies the need for careful specification of the limits of discovery to be expected. The student may very well come to some understanding of elementary physical phenomena by designing a few experiments for himself, but after that, the critics say, he may have to learn the way other scientists do—by studying what others have found out.

The issue for Piaget is not set in these terms, for once the higher stages of intellectual development are reached, one can be an inquirer while studying the experiments of others. Piaget is more concerned with the early stages, in which he would have us not hurry the child, allowing him the pleasure of learning to enjoy discovery and to come to respect himself as a problem-solver. If we do not help him a little by arranging things for him, however, he may end up not having this happy experience, but instead may be frustrated (Kagan, 1966). Again, in fairness to Piaget, he does not believe that educational practices can be developed deductively from his theory, but believes that pedagogical science is one in its own right, to be studied in conjunction with psychology but not dictated exclusively by psychology.

SUPPLEMENTARY READINGS

Piaget is a prolific writer. A bibliography through 1966, prepared in honor of his seventieth birthday, listed more than 400 items, including the numerous translations of his books into many languages (Bresson & de Montmillon, *Psychologie et epistemologie genetique*, 1966).

For the student of learning who wishes to read some of Piaget in the original (in English translation) the following sources are recommended:

PIAGET, J. (1950) *The psychology of intelligence.*
PIAGET, J. (1957) *Logic and psychology.*
PIAGET, J. (1970a) *Science of education and the psychology of the child.*
PIAGET, J. (1970b) Piaget's theory. In P. H. Mussen (Ed.) *Carmichael's manual of child psychology.* Vol. 1, pages 703–732.
PIAGET, J., & INHELDER, B. (1969) *The psychology of the child.*

For secondary accounts of Piaget's work, the following are particularly helpful, the first three as compendia and the fourth as an introduction largely in outline form.

ELKIND, D., & FLAVELL, J. H. (Eds.) (1969) *Studies in cognitive development: Essays in honor of Jean Piaget.*
FLAVELL, J. H. (1963) *The developmental psychology of Jean Piaget.*
FLAVELL, J. H. (1970) Concept development. In P. H. Mussen (Ed.) *Carmichael's manual of child psychology.* Vol. 1, pages 983–1059. (This brings Flavell's 1963 bibliography up to date.)
PHILLIPS, J. L., Jr. (1969) *The origins of intellect: Piaget's theory.*

Piaget's autobiography appears in E. G. Boring, et al. (Eds.) (1952) *A history of psychology in autobiography*, Vol. 4, pages 237–256. A brief chronology of his life, including the scientific societies to which he belongs and the names of the 14 universities which by that time had awarded him an honorary doctor's degree, may be found in Bresson and de Montmillon (1966), mentioned above.

Freud's Psychodynamics

Sigmund Freud (1856–1939) so influenced psychological thinking that a summary of theoretical viewpoints, even in the psychology of learning, is incomplete without reference to him. Boring has this to say of Freud's place in the history of psychology:

> It was Freud who put the dynamic conception of psychology where psychologists could see it and take it. They took it, slowly and with hesitation, accepting some principles while rejecting many of the trimmings. It is not likely that the history of psychology can be written in the next three centuries without mention of Freud's name and still claim to be a general history of psychology. (Boring, 1950, p. 707)

It is not easy to extract a coherent theory of learning from Freud's writings, for while he was interested in individual development and the reeducation that goes on in psychotherapy, the problems he worked on were not those with which learning theorists have been chiefly concerned. Psychoanalytic theory is too complex and too little formalized to be presented as a set of propositions ready for experimental testing. Therefore, instead of attempting an orderly exposition of a psychodynamic theory of learning, we shall rest content with examining in somewhat piecemeal fashion suggestions from psychoanalysis that bear upon learning. Some of the suggestions have already influenced experimentation in learning.

PARALLELS BETWEEN PSYCHOANALYTIC THEORY AND CONVENTIONAL LEARNING THEORY

The Pleasure Principle and the Law of Effect

Hedonistic theories—holding that man seeks pleasure and avoids pain—are among the oldest interpretations of human conduct, and any theory of learning must come to grips with the commonsense facts to which they refer.

There is no doubt that we can control learning by way of reward and punishment. The details sometimes elude us, but the gross facts cannot be denied.

Freud's pleasure principle is in accord with these facts, and his interpretation of the pleasure principle represents one of the first points of correspondence between his views and those of learning theorists. The corresponding principle in contemporary learning theory is the *law of effect* or *reinforcement theory*. The broad conception, common to both psychoanalysis and learning theory, is that a need state is a state of high tension. Whether we describe this in terms of instincts seeking gratification or of drives leading to consummatory responses, we are talking about similar events. What controls the direction of movement is a tendency to restore a kind of equilibrium, thus reducing tension. Freud talked about a return to a constant quiescent state, and the physiologists, after Cannon, refer to homeostasis. The principle goes back at least to Claude Bernard, but in any case it is shared by Freud and the learning theorists whose views have already been considered.

One of Freud's concise statements of this position is found in the introductory paragraph of his *Beyond the pleasure principle*:

> In the theory of psychoanalysis we have no hesitation in assuming that the course taken by mental events is automatically regulated by the pleasure principle. We believe, that is to say, that the course of those events is invariably set in motion by an unpleasurable tension, and that it takes a direction such that its final outcome coincides with a lowering of that tension—that is, with an avoidance of unpleasure or a production of pleasure. (Freud, 1920b, p. 1)

There is an important aspect of Freud's tension reduction theory less well represented in the law of effect. This is the basic principle that an aroused need that remains unsatisfied produces a fantasy of the goal-object that could satisfy the need. Particularly in their unconscious expressions, instincts were presumed to arouse an image of the absent goal-object. This is a bit like Tolman's ideas (see Chapter 5) regarding the "cathexis" of particular goal-stimuli given a particular level of need.

The first area of correspondence, then, between learning theories and psychoanalysis is the family resemblance between the tension reduction interpretation of the law of effect (reinforcement theory in one of its forms) and the pleasure principle, with the caution, however, that learning theories have not fully incorporated the fantasy production feature of the Freudian principle.

The Reality Principle and Learning

As the young baby grows and matures, it finds that its biological needs are not automatically satisfied by a nurturant mother. The child is led into simple instrumental acts in order to satisfy its needs; progressively, the motoric and perceptual skills develop which enable the child to deal with an increasingly demanding, uncompromising social and physical environment. Beginning as a primitive savage, the child matures and learns to adjust to the realities around him. He learns to walk to get things he wants, or to ask politely for objects to satisfy his needs, or to outmaneuver his parents' attempt to keep him from watching TV. Freud supposed that a part of the mind he called the *ego* contained all the skills of social and physical adjustment learned by the child—strategies of postponing small immediate gratifications in order to gain larger delayed rewards, coping strategies of planning, reasoning, making rational decisions, and so on. As Freud would say, any behavior instrumental in adjusting the person to reality is done in the service of the "reality principle."

Conflict, Anxiety, and Defense Mechanisms

According to Freud, our personality evolves through a continual clash between selfish impulses seeking immediate gratification and the restraining forces of a moralistic society or the realistic instrumentalities of the physical world. The reciprocal interplay of these urging and restraining forces produces frustration, anxiety, and conflict. For instance, a child may want all the available candy in the house without sharing it with others. Because he is scolded and punished by his parents for such piggish acts, this impulse to "have all of it" becomes associated with anxiety, so that upon later, similar occasions the child will experience conflict. The drive for immediate gratification of impulses follows the pleasure principle; the clash with the social and physical environments, creating frustration, anxiety, and conflict, also leads (according to Freud) to two further sets of beliefs and processes, the *superego* and the *ego*. One set, denoted collectively as the *superego* by Freud, corresponds to a set of moralistic beliefs for judging behavior as good or bad, as moral or immoral. These moral beliefs or rules of conduct correspond to the older notion of a conscience. Freud supposed that the child acquires these moral rules from his parents, by a process he labeled *identification*. The child partly "identifies with" the moral, judging parent and adopts the parent's standards for scolding himself. The superego is thus the internalization of parental control in the form of self-control.

Much recent research on imitation learning by children has shown the plausibility of at least something like what Freud had in mind. For example, Bandura and his associates (reviewed in Bandura, 1969) demonstrated how readily children will imitate principles of moral judgment exhibited by an adult model they have observed. The principles may apply to judging and differentially rewarding one's own behavior (e.g., an internal standard for what is a good versus a bad performance) or to judging other people's behavior. In a study on the latter (by Bandura & McDonald, 1963), for instance, a set of hypothetical situations and episodes involving a child would be described to the subject, who then judged whether the child in the story had done wrong and why.

So the superego adopts the moral beliefs of the society (as exemplified by the parents) and applies them to the impulses and actions of the personality. The term *ego* was used by Freud to denote a set of adjustment skills acquired by the individual, enabling him to deal realistically with his physical and social environment. As noted before, the ego is characterized by adherence to the reality principle and involves realistic, logical thinking and planning through the instrumental use of the knowledge one has acquired about the world.

Freud thought of the ego, superego, and id (the collection of instincts) as metaphorical agents in perpetual conflict with one another. The id seeks pleasure through impulse expression; the superego demands moral puritanism; the ego mediates between these warring forces and the demands of the environment. This continual conflict is fraught with frustrations, punishments, fears, and anxieties. Freud thought that when anxiety could not be handled (reduced) effectively by realistic methods, the individual would resort to unrealistic *defenses*. These ego defenses might be thought of as instrumental behavior designed to avoid anxiety created by the conflict between an impulse seeking expression and the restraining forces of the environment and the superego.

One of the most elementary defenses against anxiety is simply to consciously *deny* the cause of its existence; this happens particularly when the person cannot easily escape the threat by any other means. Especially for children whose reality-testing skills have not yet developed, denial may be a favored method for canceling out unpleasant events. Thus, an orphan may deny that his parents have abandoned him, and believe instead that they will soon return to take him home.

Another defense against anxiety associated with a thought or an idea is to *repress* it from conscious consideration. *Repression* has been defined as "the forgetting, or ejection from consciousness, of memories of threat, and especially the ejection from awareness of impulses in oneself that might have objectionable consequences" (R. W. White, 1964, p. 214). This notion of motivated forgetting has captured the interest of many researchers, and we shall later review some of the experimental work concerning repression.

Other ego-defense mechanisms will be listed only briefly (adapted from Mischel, 1971, p. 28).

Projection: the blocking of the person's own unacceptable impulses and the attribution of the source of the resulting anxiety to another person.

Reaction formation: replacement in consciousness of an anxiety-producing impulse by its opposite impulse.

Intellectualization: the tendency to transform emotional conflicts into abstract, intellectual terms; rationalization or making of excuses rather than admitting "true feelings."

Sublimation: a redirection of impulses from an object that is sexual and prohibited to one that is socially approved.

In each of these instances, the mechanism helps the person to defend himself against anxiety and also to give some expression to his unacceptable impulses in indirect, disguised form. Academic psychologists would describe them as instrumental acts or thoughts reinforced by relief from anxiety and conflict. As illustrated in Chapter 6, Neal Miller has given a very plausible learning theory reconstruction of conflict and displacement.

These illustrations from Freud have been selected to show some parallels between Freudian theory and the discussions by learning theorists. There are many such parallels; Dollard and Miller (1950), in fact, devoted an entire volume to drawing ingenious parallels and effecting translations from psychoanalytic principles to learning theory principles.

PSYCHOANALYTIC CONCEPTIONS THAT HAVE INFLUENCED
LEARNING EXPERIMENTS AND THEORIES

In the foregoing account of parallels between Freudian theory and the work of academic psychologists, it should be evident that the two lines developed rather independently. That is, studies of the law of effect, of conflict, and of problem-solving were not undertaken to test Freudian theory, and Freudian theory was not developed in order to "explain" the results obtained by experimental psychologists. There are a number of topics within Freudian theory, however, that have definitely set problems for the experimental psychologist. We now turn to a review of some of these.

Anxiety as a Drive

Freud's views about anxiety evolved along with other aspects of his theory.[1] At first he thought that attacks of anxiety in his patients gave evidence of repressed instinctive (libidinal) excitation. That is, he thought that repressed libido was transformed into anxiety (1920a, pp. 347–349). Later, as he developed the theory of id, ego, and superego, he assigned anxiety production to the ego. When the ego perceives danger to itself, this perception arouses anxiety, and then steps are taken to reduce anxiety. Symptom formation may be one of these steps. Repression may also be one of the devices adopted by the ego, so that, instead of repression causing anxiety, we now have anxiety causing repression (1926).

Anxiety is closely related to fear, though fear usually has a specific object, whereas anxiety may be a vague apprehension of unknown danger. Three kinds of anxiety can be distinguished, the first of which is indistinguishable from fear:

1. *Objective anxiety* (also called realistic anxiety) depends upon real or anticipated danger whose source lies in the external world. To be afraid of a poisonous snake or a holdup man is to be anxious in this way. Objective anxiety implies a real, known danger.
2. *Neurotic anxiety* is in regard to an unknown danger. Upon analysis it is found that the danger is, as Freud put it, an instinctual one. That is, a person is afraid of being overpowered by some impulse or thought that will prove harmful to him. Sometimes there is a real or threatened danger but the reaction to it is excessive, thus revealing the neurotic element in the anxiety (1926, pp. 112–117).
3. *Moral anxiety* is aroused by a perception of danger from the conscience (superego). The fear is that of being punished (belittled, degraded) for doing or thinking something that is contrary to the ego ideal. Moral anxiety is experienced as feelings of *guilt* or *shame*.

Anxiety in later life was said to have two modes of origin, one involuntary and automatic whenever a danger situation arose, the second "produced by the ego when such a situation merely threatened, in order to procure its avoidance" (Freud, 1926, p. 109).

---

[1] An account of the changes in Freud's conceptions is given by R. May (1950, pp. 112–127).

Mowrer (1939) was the first of the experimenters on learning to see the possibility of studying an analog of anxiety in experiments on avoidance conditioning. He proceeded to show experimentally how rats that had experienced pain in the presence of certain cues could be led to make avoidance responses in the presence of those cues—that is, when the pain was merely threatened (1940). Thus he believed the anxiety-fear response to be the conditioned form of the pain response. Just as pain can be used as a drive to produce learning through escape, so anxiety can be used to produce learning. The anxiety can be reduced by appropriate avoidance responses just as pain can be reduced by escape responses. Hence these anxiety-reducing responses are learned by the ordinary reinforcement principle of tension reduction. Conceivably, defense reactions or neurotic symptoms might be acquired through this familiar learning pattern. This kind of acquired fear or anxiety has been extensively studied as a drive in animal learning, especially by N. E. Miller (1948a). The importance of fear as a drive is summarized in this way by Dollard and Miller:

One of the most important drives of all is fear, or "anxiety" as it is often called when its source is vague or obscured by repression (Freud, 1926). There are three main reasons why fear is so important: because it can be so strong, because it can be attached to new cues so easily by learning, and because it is the motivation that produces the inhibiting responses in most conflicts. (1950, p. 190)

A somewhat different, yet related, use of the concept of anxiety in learning experiments was introduced by Taylor (1951), when she classified human subjects in an investigation of eyelid conditioning according to their scores on a verbal self-report "anxiety scale." She found that the more anxious subjects conditioned more rapidly than the less anxious ones, and interpreted this characterological anxiety as drive—as the multiplier D in Hull's theory. A number of additional experimenters have used this "manifest anxiety" scale in testing various hypotheses about the relationship between anxiety and conditioning.[2]

Our review shows that anxiety concepts were originally introduced into learning theory by those who were interested in Freudian theory; and although they deviated from the details of Freud's anxiety theories, they indicated indebtedness to Freud's writings.

Unconscious Influences upon Word Associations

The free-association technique of psychoanalysis has found its representation in psychological experimentation chiefly through the diagnostic word-association test introduced by the Swiss psychiatrist Carl Jung. Many experiments have been carried out, acknowledging the importance of the emotional processes behind word associations (e.g., Hull & Lugoff, 1921). For instance, stimulus words that arouse some emotional response typically produce very slow, variable, and rare word associations. Recognition of words briefly flashed in a tachistoscope, which is also a form of associative reaction

[2] For an early review of both experiment and theory, see Farber (1954). The scale itself is described in Taylor (1953).

to the word, has been studied in relation to the affective significance of the words. These studies, often referred to as studies of perceptual defense, illustrate another influence of psychoanalysis upon the psychological laboratory. In the belief that perceptual recognition is, in fact, a lengthy process stretched out over time with many tiny sequential decisions, the further hypothesis was offered that emotionally taboo ("obscene") words would have higher recognition thresholds because their incipient unconscious identification arouses "perceptual defenses" against perceiving ego-threatening materials. Despite early favorable evidence, experimentation surrounding the hypothesis has not been much pursued recently since a large number of contaminating artifacts were found in the typical studies of recognition of briefly flashed taboo words. One major difficulty, for instance, was deciding whether the differing "report thresholds" for neutral versus dirty words were due to a real perceptual difference or to a greater unwillingness to guess a taboo word on the basis of fragmentary clues from the flashed word. The consensus (e.g., reflected in Neisser's review, 1967) is that "perceptual defense" is a weak and very elusive phenomenon to demonstrate after all artifacts have been removed from the experimental situation. However, Dixon (1971) provides a sympathetic review plus new experiments demonstrating "perceptual defense," and argues persuasively that earlier research on the problem was dropped prematurely and for inadequate reasons.

Repression, Forgetting, and Recall

Ever since Ebbinghaus, psychologists have made quantitative study of memorization and recall part of their laboratory practice. It was natural, therefore, that Freudian interpretations of memory lapses should have been seized upon as appropriate for experimental testing. At first, psychologists grasped only the forgetting aspect of repression, failing to take into account the motivational aspects. This was due, in part, to the rejection of the psychoanalytic theory of instincts, and in part to the absence of motivational concepts in prevailing studies of memory and forgetting.[3]

Freud distinguished between a *primal repression* and a second phase called repression proper (1915a). The primal repression consists in "a denial of entry into consciousness to the mental (ideational) presentation of the instinct." The ideational content then remains unaltered and the instinct remains attached to it. "The second phase of repression, *repression proper*, concerns mental derivatives of the repressed instinct-presentation, or such trains of thought as, originating elsewhere, have come into associative connection with it."

It is to be noted that repression proper assumes a primal repression, so that the pattern for all later repressions is set up early in life. Later events may be assimilated to these earlier ones. The activity of repression is not completed, however, at the time something is repressed.

The process of repression is not to be regarded as something which takes place once and for all, the results of which are permanent, as when some living thing has

---

[3] These points were made by R. R. Sears (1936) in an able review of Freud's theory of repression and the possibilities within experimentation.

been killed and from that time onward is dead; on the contrary, repression demands a constant expenditure of energy, and if this were discontinued the success of the repression would be jeopardized, so that a fresh act of repression would be necessary. (Freud, 1915a, p. 89)

R. R. Sears (1936) has summarized the characteristics of a repressed instinctual impulse, according to Freud, in six statements:

1. It is not represented in its true form in consciousness.
2. The instinct-presentation develops in a more luxuriant fashion than it would if it were conscious.
3. The resistance of consciousness against derivatives and associations of the instinct-presentation varies in inverse proportion to their remoteness from the ideas originally repressed.
4. Repression is highly specific to each idea and substitute idea.
5. Repression is very mobile.
6. The degree of repression varies with the strength of the instinctual impulse.

The feature of repression that has appealed most to psychologists is its relation to pleasure and pain. Freud says, for example, that in repression the avoidance of pain must have acquired more strength than the pleasure of gratification. Psychologists have often interpreted repression quite superficially to mean that pleasurable events will be remembered and distasteful ones forgotten. The first experiments used merely affectively pleasant or unpleasant materials, such as pleasant and unpleasant odors, or words such as *sugar* (pleasant) and *quinine* (unpleasant), to study whether or not such materials could be easily memorized or retained. Later studies have sought in one way or another to meet more squarely the demands of psychoanalytic theory. We shall return later to a consideration of some of them.

Fixation

Fixation has two closely related meanings in psychoanalytic theory. The first meaning is that of *arrested development*, so that an adult may be fixated at an infantile or adolescent level of psychological functioning. This usually implies an object choice (the mother or a like-sexed person) appropriate to the level of fixation, and the statement is then made that the person is fixated *at* such-and-such a level and fixated *upon* such-and-such an object. The second meaning is that of *fixed habits* leading to preferred modes of solving personal problems, such as a fixation upon a particular mechanism of defense or habitual means of coping with social stresses. The two meanings are not clearly distinguished in psychoanalytic theory because the stage of arrested development is so intimately related to the style of life. That is, habitual modes of reacting as an adult are likely to be described in developmental terms, for example, the "anal character," the "oral character."[4]

In his review of objective studies bearing on psychoanalytic concepts, R. R. Sears (1943) treated fixation as habit strength, and listed a dozen circum-

---

[4] Fenichel (1945, p. 523) writes that neurotics "are not only fixated to certain levels of instinctive demands but also to certain mechanisms of defense." He also includes "character attitudes" among the items to which they are fixated.

stances shown experimentally to modify the strength of instrumental acts. While aware of the problem, he failed to treat in any detail the qualitative features of transition from one stage of development to the next. The transition depends not only on the strength of the earlier fixation but on the hazards involved in transition to the next stage. If the next stage is attractive and nonthreatening, presumably the growing individual will enter upon it even though he showed strong attachments at the earlier stage. If some residue from the earlier stage makes entrance upon the later stage painful and anxiety producing (e.g., giving up a strongly held attachment), arrested development may occur. Habits at the different levels are not all-or-nothing affairs, for an adult who is grown up in some habits may be infantile in others.

Regression

Regression is related to fixation in that when an act is blocked or frustrated, some substitute will occur. The substitute is quite likely to be an act that was strongly established earlier in the individual's repertory. Such a substitution of an earlier habit for a contemporary one represents one kind of regression.

We may distinguish three kinds of regression:

1. Instrumental-act regression. When the organism is prevented from using one habit, an earlier learned habit is substituted. Many animal experiments have demonstrated this phenomenon.[5] For example, a rat might first learn to rotate a small wheel mounted on its cage to turn off an electric shock; then the wheel is made inoperative and the animal learns to depress a lever to turn off the shock. If lever-depressing is now extinguished (no longer terminates shock), it will be found that the rat readily returns to rotating the wheel, despite the futility of such old responses. These results provide an analogy to *object regression* in Freudian theory, the kind of regression in which gratification is gained by relinquishing a present object and returning to an earlier one.

2. Age regression. Under some circumstances the person returns to earlier modes of behavior and appears to obliterate his knowledge of events occurring since the age to which he has become regressed. If, for example, an adult who regressed under hypnosis to an early age began to speak in a language used in childhood but no longer available to him in his adult life, we could say that he had regressed (at least in this respect) to an earlier period in his life. Experiments under hypnosis have led to somewhat ambiguous results. Occasionally the functioning at the suggested (regressed) age resembles very closely the known historical circumstances in the person's life. When regressed subjects take intelligence and personality tests, their performances differ from those of actual children at the age levels represented by the suggested regression. Hence there appears to be a certain amount of role-playing going on.

---

[5] R. R. Sears (1943, pp. 89–96) has reviewed this literature.

3. Primitivation. Even though the regressed individual may not return either to instrumental acts once in his inventory of habits or to personality functioning characteristic of himself at some previous period, he may, under stress, show a kind of behavioral disorganization that can be characterized as primitive. This kind of regression has been studied with young children subjected to mild frustration. Barker, Dembo, and Lewin (1941) showed, regression by such indices as reduced constructiveness in play following the experienced frustration.

Aggression and Its Displacement

In his later years Freud became increasingly aware of aggression, hostility, and destructiveness. In discussing racial tensions and other intergroup antagonisms, he said:

We do not know why such sensitiveness should have been directed to just these details of differentiation; but it is unmistakable that in this whole connection men give evidence of a readiness for hatred, an aggressiveness, the source of which is unknown, and to which one is tempted to ascribe an elementary character. (1921, p. 56)

Freud recognized the importance of giving expression to hostility, rather than holding it back, and many contemporary analysts now give prominence to the role of repressed hostile impulses in neurosis.

While Freud, in his later writings, paid increasing attention to aggressiveness as something inherent in man, he had earlier suggested that interference with instinctual satisfaction leads to a hostile attack upon the source of the frustration. Symptoms of neurotic illness may be so directed as to cause distress to someone in the environment who is perceived as the agent of frustration. Building upon these suggestions (in Freud, 1915b), Dollard and his collaborators formulated the *frustration-aggression hypothesis* in a manner to make possible quantitative testing.[6] The general principle stated was that frustration leads to aggressive action; it was necessary later to correct the implication that aggression was the only (or even an inevitable) consequence.[7] The experimental evidence gave abundant support to the hypothesized linkage between experienced frustration and subsequent aggressive, hostile, or destructive behavior.

If the agent responsible for frustration is unknown or inaccessible as an object of attack (absent or protected through conflicting response tendencies), another object will be chosen. This is called *displaced aggression.* The object may be as innocent as the scapegoat which in the ancient Hebrew ritual was made to bear the nation's sins.[8] The word *scapegoat* has come into general use to refer to a victim of displaced aggression.

Neal Miller and his collaborators succeeded in relating displacement to stimulus generalization in learning theory (see the discussion in Chapter 6). In his original experiment, Miller taught rats to strike each other, as in

---

[6] Dollard et al. (1939).

[7] N. E. Miller (1941), R. R. Sears (1941).

[8] The Old Testament account of the scapegoat is in Leviticus 16:22.

fighting, in order to remove an electric shock. When a second rat was not present, a rat would "displace" the aggression to a toy doll or other object in the environment. The gain from Miller's theory is that certain quantitative predictions can be made about the occasions for displacement, the intensity of the reaction, and so on. Miller formulated eight specific deductions from his theory, of which the following three are illustrative:

When the direct response to the original stimulus is prevented by the absence of that stimulus, displaced responses will occur to other similar stimuli and the strongest displaced response will occur to the most similar stimulus present.

When the direct response to the original stimulus is prevented by conflict, the strongest displaced response will occur to stimuli which have an intermediate degree of similarity to the original one.

If the strength of the drive motivating the direct response to the original stimulus is increased, it will be possible for increasingly dissimilar stimuli to elicit displaced responses. (1948b, pp. 168, 170)

While Miller's experiments on displacement have been with animal subjects, he shows how the principles may apply to human behavior. In human beings, discriminations are aided by discriminating labels so that we narrow our meanings and reduce our generalizations. The reverse can also occur, as when we use words to generalize, to name classes of objects that belong together. At this point, however, we are interested in discrimination and how it breaks down. Suppose that Mr. Brown distinguishes among his new neighbors by calling them all by name. Because of a painful snub, he becomes very angry at Mr. Jones, one of these neighbors. Because Mr. Jones's social position is more secure than Mr. Brown's and Mr. Brown is new to the neighborhood, Mr. Brown may repress his anger. (This fits the suggestion that the expression of hostility may be prevented by fear of punishment.) In Miller's interpretation, what Mr. Brown represses is the sentence: "I am angry at Mr. Jones." Because this sentence is repressed, the anger is no longer tied directly to Mr. Jones, and it is more likely to generalize to another neighbor because discrimination through names has broken down.

Miller recognizes that the displacement problem is actually more complex than this. He points out that the *name* of Mr. Jones is not repressed when it is not in a sentence referring to anger. So Mr. Brown recognizes the neighbor's dog and says to himself: "This is Mr. Jones's dog." Because the name of Mr. Jones is attached unconsciously to hostile tendencies, he may give the dog a swift kick, which he would not do if he recalled that he was really angry at Mr. Jones, not at his dog. Thus Miller deduces some functional differences between consciously and unconsciously determined behavior. He restates his deduction succinctly:

To summarize, the repression of verbal responses specifying the source of the aggression may remove a basis for discrimination and allow the illogical generalization, or displacement, of that aggression to be mediated by a different verbal response which is not repressed. (1948b, p. 176)

Some closely related observations arise out of the study of doll play by young children. In respect to aggressive behavior (aggressive fantasy in this case), the choice of object tends to follow the principles of conflict outlined by Miller. That is, when anxiety is high, the object of aggression chosen is one less similar to the person who is the source of aggression than when anxiety is low. Consequently, as children play repeatedly in a permissive environment, their choice of object gradually shifts toward the parents, who have commonly been the authority figures responsible for some of their frustration.[9]

Learning as Related to Stages of Development

Writers on psychoanalysis often stress that it is a *genetic* (developmental) as well as a dynamic theory (Hartmann & Kris, 1945). That is, continuities in the life of the individual deriving from the past must always be taken into account along with what is happening in the present. At many points the theory suggests that the very young child is unusually susceptible to influences which leave a permanent mark on his personality, so that, for example, dreams throughout his life may be influenced by these earliest learnings. If this interpretation is true, it is important for a general psychology of learning, and the evidence needs to be specified.

While the problems have not been formulated clearly in terms of learning (i.e., why and in what way the results of childhood learning are more permanent than later learning), there are some kinds of evidence supporting the gross facts of consequences in adulthood of early childhood experiences. Among the early experiments with animals, the best known are the experiments of J. McV. Hunt (1941) on the effects of infant feeding frustration on adult hoarding in rats, and of Wolf (1943) on the effects of sensory deprivation in early life upon types of functioning under stress in later life, again with rats. While the results of these experiments are subject to some reservations, they are relevant to the genetic theory that early experiences may show their influences in the conflicts of later life. A considerable literature developed around this topic of early developmental stresses, not all, of course, motivated by psychoanalytic theory (e.g., F. A. Beach & Jaynes, 1954; Fiske & Maddi, 1961).

Some conjectures about child-training practices and personality in adult life were tested by Whiting and Child (1953). They went to the cross-cultural files, where anthropological reports on upwards of 200 cultures are summarized according to a great many categories. Then they asked certain questions about childhood practices and developed hypotheses about their consequences for adult experiences in those cultures. To take one illustration, they predicted that socialization anxiety established in early childhood should affect the interpretation of the causes of illness in adult life. Even in our own culture, with the emphasis on the germ theory of disease, we have many subordinate interpretations of illness: "It must have been something I ate," "I've been working too hard," "You have to suffer for your sins." Our remedies, too, show something of the magical quality: indiscriminate prescriptions of cure by rest, by liquids, by bland foods, by cathartics, by play,

[9] P. S. Sears (1951), R. R. Sears (1951), R. R. Sears et al. (1953).

by suntanning, by fasting, by religious observances. If a "scientific" culture such as ours has all these magical residues, it is not too much to expect that primitive interpretations of illness might be somewhat magical, too.

Whiting and Child specified five kinds of anxiety and developed criteria for rating these. The five were: oral, anal, sexual, dependence, and aggression anxieties. The assumption was that severity of socialization training and severity of punishment for infraction in these areas, or failures of gratification, would lead to anxiety. A culture might be severe in one of the areas and permissive in the others. In addition, Whiting and Child classified primitive interpretations of illness as derivatives of these five anxieties.

When the childhood rearing practices were correlated with adult interpretations of illness, some striking correspondences turned up. For example, 46 cultures could be classified with respect to degree of oral anxiety in childhood, and with respect to interpretations of illness with oral aspects, such as food poisoning. Of 20 cultures high in producing oral anxiety in children, 17 used oral interpretations of illness. Correspondingly, of 19 cultures low in oral anxiety, only 6 used oral interpretations of illness. This kind of correlational evidence does not prove a relationship between childhood anxiety and adult behavior, but it makes such a relationship plausible.

Another important suggestion from psychoanalysis is that of childhood amnesia. In later life we appear unable to recall events of our early childhood that must surely have impressed us at the time, and about which we must have talked. Because these events become secondarily linked with repression sequences, they too are repressed. Memories that are recalled are often trivial, and perhaps distorted, probably serving some of the purposes of repression. This whole field has been touched hardly at all by academic psychologists. The adult may be unable to revive experiences of very early childhood simply because (a) the perceptual-verbal skills needed to firmly encode the experience into a coherent, stable memory were lacking, (b) such memories as were recorded have decayed away by the natural processes of interference and disuse, and/or (c) the experiences were stored in a childlike code, and the adult has lost the ability to "think like a child," his thought categories having so changed that he can make no sense or real contact with the coding categories of his childhood memories (see E. G. Schachtel, 1947). It is difficult to know how to decide among these alternatives, or whether and to what degree all three are operative, especially since experiments with young preverbal children (before 18 months) encounter all sorts of logistical problems. So the matter is likely to remain one of speculation for some time.[10]

A further aspect of the developmental sequence posited by psychoanalysis, and relevant for learning, is the *latency period*, for it has been related to readiness for schooling (at about the age of 6) when the oedipal problems are temporarily solved and the ego is ready to feast its curiosity about the external world. After a few years adolescence produces a new threat, and learning may again be disrupted.

[10] For a discussion from the psychoanalyst's viewpoint, see A. Freud (1935, pp. 9–37). What data there were on the problem were reviewed by G. J. Dudycha and M. M. Dudycha (1941).

Psychodynamics of Thinking

The possibility of drawing upon psychoanalysis in studying the psychology of thinking was brought strongly to the fore by the appearance of a large volume assembling papers on the organization and pathology of thought (Rapaport, 1951). Especially important for the psychoanalytic influences are the sections devoted to symbolism (including experimentally produced dreams), and to motivation of thinking, fantasy thinking, and pathology of thinking.

A fundamental distinction within the psychoanalytic theory of thinking is that between *primary process* thinking, which is impulse-driven and largely irrational, seeking immediate gratification at all costs, even by way of hallucinations, and *secondary process* thinking, which is patient and logical, willing to postpone gratification for future gains. Adult thinking falls somewhere between these poles, either oscillating between the two modes or combining them in some manner (E. R. Hilgard, 1962). Kris (1952) stressed the importance for creativity of "regression in the service of the ego," by which he meant a partial and reversible regression in which the freedom of primary process thinking was utilized for assembling the fantasy material that could then be sorted out and refined by way of secondary process thinking. A similar idea was employed by Koestler (1964), who has given one of the more intelligible and respectable discussions of creative thinking.

In the current emphasis on general education programs in our colleges and universities we hear much about the integrative role of the arts and music. Yet as we look at artists and musicians we see truth in the popular conception that they are somehow different, and occasionally classify them as deviates. Hence the question recurs of the relationship between art and neuroticism. One form of putting it is this: Would the artist be less creative if he resolved his conflicts through psychoanalysis? Is not his neurosis precious to him? Possibly if we were successful in our mental hygiene programs, we would develop a class of very uninteresting normal and contented people; perhaps we are saved from this by the ineffectiveness of our measures. But there are more constructive possibilities. For one thing, artists and writers who come to analysis are those who find that they are afraid to practice their arts. For them, psychotherapy may give back their creativity. Again, the end of therapy is not necessarily to get rid of conflicts, but to find a way of living with them.

Therapy as Learning

The goal of psychoanalytic therapy is to give the person *insight* into the unconscious motives and conflicts underlying his neurotic symptoms. Furthermore, he is to emotionally accept these impulses and work through the conflict in some rational way, thus removing the sustaining motivation for the symptom. The main impediment to insight is the patient's own defensiveness, revealed in many forms of *resistance* to therapy. The process of working through and achieving insights was thought by Freud to grow out of the intense personal attachment the patient develops for the therapist, an affect which Freud called *transference*. Presumably, feelings and problems the person originally experienced during childhood in relations with parents (or siblings) are projected onto the therapist and the relationship is reestablished and worked out in that context.

The primary vehicle for psychoanalytic therapy is simply *talking*, between the analyst and the patient. The patient tells the analyst about his past history and past problems, about events of recent times, about his dreams, or sometimes he simply free associates, baring the flowing stream of his conscious thoughts without censorship. The analyst listens, asks questions, and suggests psychodynamic interpretations of the patient's problems.

Academic psychologists have been concerned to study patient-therapist interactions during therapy, and to relate these interactions to therapeutic outcome. Since the reports of conditioning of verbal response classes by subtle social reinforcers (e.g., Greenspoon, 1955, 1962), psychologists have begun to look upon the psychotherapeutic situation as ideal for the operation of verbal conditioning. The patient feels helpless, desires to please the "doctor," who is a prestigious authority figure, and so would seem to be readily conditionable. It has been shown repeatedly that abundant verbal conditioning occurs in such therapeutic interviews: the patient learns what is interesting to the analyst and what is disapproved, and he learns how to describe himself, his problems, and his "insights" in terms congenial to his analyst (see Bandura, 1969; Bergin & Garfield, 1971). As Mischel says:

> Thus clients whose therapists are Freudians may acquire Freudian insight; those treated by Jungians gain Jungian insights; those treated by Rogerians redefine their self-concepts and "self-actualize" according to Rogers, and so on. (1971, p. 440)

There has also been some research on moment-by-moment changes in the patient's verbal behavior as controlled by the analyst's reactions—whether he replies with encouragement ("Tell me more about that"), scorn ("That's irrelevant"), indifference, a bored yawn, or simply silent acceptance (e.g., Salzinger, 1969). Sufficient information exists to show that interpersonal contingencies of reinforcement play just as large a role in shaping the content and style of psychotherapeutic verbal interactions as in shaping behavior in any social dialogue. Such results fit in, of course, with the "operant conditioning" view of what transpires during the therapeutic interview (see Chapter 7). The claim is that whereas conventional psychotherapists manipulate verbal reinforcement contingencies unwittingly and unconsciously according to their personal ideologies, the behavior therapist ought to deliberately plan and exploit the reinforcement contingencies of the therapeutic interview so as to shape or alter certain verbal repertoires (e.g., self-descriptions). Be that as it may, it is the behavior therapists more than conventional psychotherapists who attempt explicitly to apply scientific methods to the "programming" of therapeutic procedures and to their assessment. A byproduct of this concern with verbal conditioning in the therapy setting is that the patient's self-report (or the therapist's report) of how much he has improved is not accepted as the sole criterion of "improvement," since such self-reports are notoriously susceptible to persuasion, modification, and suggestion. Instead, some kind of objective validation or actual behavior change in the problematic area is called for as an acid test of the alleged improvement brought about by psychotherapy.

In this instance it would seem that experimental psychology has much to contribute to the study of psychotherapeutic methods, both in assessing old methods and in proposing new programs. The approach does not simply record what goes on in a psychoanalytic session; rather, it assesses the effects of that and other therapies, and proposes self-corrective means for evolving more successful therapeutic programs.

EXPERIMENTS ON REPRESSION AS ILLUSTRATIVE OF THE LABORATORY USE OF PSYCHOANALYTIC CONCEPTS

Psychologists were quick to pick up the suggestion from Freud that affective factors might influence recall. Learning theorists have conceived of "repression" in terms of "avoidance of anxiety-provoking thoughts." Such phenomena can be plausibly reconstructed if one conceives of ideas in terms of "cue-producing responses." Just as an animal will learn to avoid (by "doing something else") behavior sequences ending in punishment, so should the person come to avoid (deflect his thoughts away from) verbal or ideational chains leading up to internal stimuli associated with unpleasantness and anxiety. Not only does a person avoid telling others about incidents which cast him in an extremely unfavorable light, he also comes to avoid telling himself about such incidents (rehearsing them) or will not even name them in the first place so that his self-image does not suffer. For so-called liberalized versions of S-R theory, these kinds of translations of Freud's "repression" hypotheses seem very reasonable.

There is, unfortunately, not much acceptable experimental evidence for ideational repression. Repression is distinguished somewhat inexactly from *suppression*; in suppression, the idea in question can be recalled covertly but its overt expression is "deliberately" blocked or prevented by a form of self-control (competing sentences, telling ourselves to "hold our tongues"). In repression, on the other hand, the ideational content itself is supposedly unconscious, blocked from awareness. The distinction between the two notions rests tenuously on a particular viewpoint of awareness or self-knowledge; but it is nonetheless a distinction that has been widely accepted in the literature of psychology. Demonstrations of suppression are very easy to arrange; for instance, one simply arranges payoff contingencies so that "not overtly remembering" is worth more than overtly recalling some material. On the other hand, demonstrations of unconscious repression appear to be considerably harder to arrange in the laboratory. In the following we shall review some of these tests which try to relate affect to ease of recall. These test the implication that anxiety or simply unpleasant affect may hinder recall in a manner analogous to Freudian repression.

An early review of the pertinent literature by Zeller (1950a) listed 93 references, suggesting how inviting this field had proved to be to investigators. We shall consider a few experimental reports typical of five approaches to the study of affective factors in recall.

1. Recall of associates to affectively toned sensory stimuli. The most satisfactory study of this type, following upon several earlier ones, is that of

Ratliff (1938). He had subjects rate the pleasantness and unpleasantness of odors, pitches, and colors. Then the subjects associated numbers with the affective items and later were tested for recall. The results with odors were against the hypothesis of the forgetting of the unpleasant, but with pitches and colors the recall of numbers associated with the pleasant items was superior to the recall of numbers associated with unpleasant ones. Because the pleasantness and unpleasantness of sensory stimuli have little personalized relevance, such experiments are no longer considered very pertinent as tests of Freudian theory.

2. Recall of memorized words with personal affective connotations. In order to introduce some kind of ego threat into the laboratory-type experiment, Sharp (1938) went to the case records of neurotic subjects to find words that would be emotionally unacceptable to them as individuals, and words that for them would express gratifications. She then compared their retention of unacceptable and acceptable words in a verbal learning task, and found the unacceptable words less well recalled. Unfortunately, the only reported repetition of portions of her work did not yield confirmatory results (Heathers & Sears, 1943; see R. R. Sears, 1943).

A study by Clemes (1964) showed the possibility of bringing repression somewhat under control through hypnosis. Clemes selected words with high or low "emotionality" for each subject by taking those to which the person gave either very slow or normal reaction times in a word association test. A list containing half critical (high emotionality) and half noncritical (nonemotional) words in random order was then memorized under hypnosis. The critical words in a list of this kind were memorized as readily as noncritical ones. The crucial test was then a suggested partial amnesia, in which the subject was told that he would forget an unspecified half of the list. The hypothesis was that the critical words would be the most likely targets for amnesia. The words were recovered later by means of a prearranged signal given within hypnosis, lifting the instructed amnesia. To be sure that the paradigm of repression was followed, the only words scored statistically were those that were forgotten in the amnesia test but recovered when the amnesia was lifted. Clemes found evidence for repression in that the critical words were disproportionately the targets for amnesia following the suggestion that half the words would be forgotten.

3. Recall of memorized items remotely associated with pain. Some experiments try to manipulate recall by associating pain and anxiety with a response to be recalled. An early example is an experiment by Eriksen and Kuethe (1956), who had students give free word associates to a set of 15 stimulus words, which was repeatedly presented for such free associates. While misinformed regarding the purpose of the experiment, the subject received an electric shock for the first associate (response word) he gave on trial 1 to a selected 5 of the 15 stimulus words. Moreover, on later trials shocks were again delivered if the same trial 1 associates were to be given to these five critical stimuli. Hence, to avoid shock to the critical stimuli, the subjects learned to give some associate different from their trial 1 associate to each critical word. So far, this is simply an experiment on avoidance conditioning of verbal responses. But Eriksen and Kuethe collected two further bits of information following avoidance conditioning: first, the electrodes were removed so that all threat of shocks should cease; then the subjects were presented with each stimulus word and asked to give a continuous chain of free associations for 15 seconds; finally, each subject was questioned intensively to determine how much he had figured out when or why shocks had occurred during the earlier "avoidance training" session. On the basis of this interview, subjects were categorized as "aware" or "unaware" of the correlation of the shocks with the critical words.

The results of this experiment showed, first, that all subjects learned to avoid giving the initial associate to the critical word (i.e., the punished response); this avoidance learning occurred regardless of whether or not the subject was categorized as aware of the specific shock contingency. A second finding was that in the chained associations test which occurred at the end of the experiment, the initial associates to the critical stimuli (which were shocked and presumably avoided) were very unlikely to occur, despite the removal of the threat of shock. This "repression" of the punished responses occurred whether or not the subject was categorized as "aware."

The Eriksen and Kuethe experiment seems to demonstrate two aspects of repression, that thoughts (words) associated with anxiety will tend to be eliminated, and that the repression process can occur without the person's awareness; repression is "automatic" in the sense that the person does not deliberately change his thoughts or word associations.

The experiment has interpretive difficulties, not the least of which is the difficulty of defining "awareness" appropriately and in operational terms. The fact that shocked associates appeared less in the shock-free, chained-associate test is easily explained. Trial 1 associates given to neutral (non-shocked) stimuli were typically repeated to that stimulus throughout the entire experiment, whereas trial 1 associates given to shocked stimuli were put aside and replaced by one or several competing responses to that cue. Therefore, according to simple principles of disuse or interference causing forgetting, the shocked associate would be expected to be less available later than the nonshocked trial 1 associate.

A recent experiment of a similar kind has been reported by Glucksberg and King (1967). They associated pain and anxiety with a remote associate of the response word to be repressed. The paradigm is illustrated in Table 11.1 reproduced from Glucksberg and King. The subjects first learned a list of syllable-word paired associates, denoted *A-B* in Table 11.1 (e.g., *DAX-memory*). From published association norms, it was known that the primary associates to the *B* words were those given in the *C* column (e.g., *mind* to *memory*), and the primary normative associates to the *C* words were those listed in the *D* column (e.g., *brain* to *mind*). The idea here is that following *A-B* learning, the syllable is also remotely associated to the *D* word through the chain *A-B, B-C, C-D*.

In the second phase of the experiment, the *D* words were presented and a painful electric shock was associated with three of the *D* words, the other seven *D* words being presented without shock. Two subsequent groups of subjects had different sets of three shock words as indicated in Table 11.1.

Table 11.1   Stimulus syllables and response words used, and inferred associative responses. The D words followed by (1) were the experimental
words for half the subjects; those followed by (2) were the experimental words for the remaining subjects. (From Glucksberg & King,
1967. Copyright 1967 by the American Association for the Advancement of Science.)

List 1		Inferred Chained Word	List 2	
A	B	C	D	
CEF	stem	flower	smell	(1)
DAX	memory	mind	brain	(2)
YOV	soldier	army	navy	
VUX	trouble	bad	good	(2)
WUB	wish	want	need	
GEX	justice	peace	war	(1)
JID	thief	steal	take	(2)
ZIL	ocean	water	drink	
LAJ	command	order	disorder	
MYV	fruit	apple	tree	(1)

The subject's task during this phase was to learn to anticipate shock or non-
shock upon presentation of each D word.

Following this shock learning phase, the subjects were tested for list 1
retention by presentation of the syllable (A) for recall of its associated word
(B). After the two subgroups of subjects were pooled, it was found that
when the D term was shocked, the A-B pair was "forgotten" 29 percent of
the time; when the D term was not shocked, the A-B pair was forgotten only
6 percent of the time. The difference favors the motivated forgetting explanation: the D term becomes associated to anxiety; therefore, A-B associates
which lead to the D term are also repressed, automatically and unconsciously.

The main problem with the Glucksberg and King result is that it has not
withstood "systematic replication," i.e., variation in what are believed to be
insignificant procedural details. For example, Weiner and Higgins (1969)
could not repeat the finding except by an *exact* replication of the Glucksberg
and King procedure, in particular, using the same D words in the shocked
and nonshocked subsets. Weiner and Higgins argue that initial differences
in retention are really due to the particular A-B and D items which were
shocked in the Glucksberg and King experiment. Specifically, they argue
that, by chance selection, the specific A-B pairs with a shocked D term were
harder to learn initially, and consequently had less overlearning on the
average than the A-B pairs which had an unshocked D term; therefore, the
differential retention of the two sets of A-B terms could really be due to item
differences in initial learning, not to motivated forgetting. Glucksberg and
Ornstein (1969) have disputed this argument. However, Wescourt (1971) was
unable to reproduce the "repression" finding of Glucksberg and King under
several conditions of close replication. The upshot in this case, then, is that

the effect has not stood up under systematic replication, under variation in what theorists believe to be insignificant details.

4. *Repression induced by experienced failure.* R. R. Sears (1937) suggested that an important element of the repressing anxiety is that it be personally related to the subject, that it be a harsh threat to his self-esteem. In his experiment, he had subjects learn a nonsense syllable list, then perform a card-sorting task on which they were made to experience admirable success or depreciatory failure and loss of self-esteem. A later recall test showed greater forgetting of the nonsense syllables by subjects experiencing failure on the interpolated task.

Zeller (1950a) pointed out that a complete test of repression ought to show *recovery* of the repressed material when the threat is removed. Several experimenters have attempted to demonstrate the two phases: induced repression followed by the lifting of the repression. Zeller (1950b), Aborn (1953), and D'Zurilla (1965) performed representative experiments of this type. Following learning, the subject is made to fail or in some way feel inadequate (e.g., led to believe he has neurotic tendencies). A subsequent retention test shows poor recall of the originally learned list; however, "debriefing" the subject and relieving his worries why he failed lead to an increase in the amount he can now recall from the original list.

The basic problem with these "failure" studies of repression—besides their poor representation of repression—is that they are readily interpretable in simple terms of distraction caused by competing thoughts. Thus, the subject who fails miserably on an interpolated task or is made in some way to doubt his normalcy may be expected to have gnawing, persisting worries. And it is easily demonstrated that if one is thinking or worrying about something else, he does poorly in concentrating on the task of recalling the original set of materials. Of course, when he is debriefed, his worries are laid to rest, so he can concentrate on the recall task and do better; consequently, his memory appears to recover by reason of the lifting of repression. This analysis of the "failure" studies, due to Holmes and Schallow (1969), was tested with uniformly confirmatory responses. The critical element was the amount (and not the content) of the interfering mental activity going on during the interpolated task and persisting through to the first retention test, when "repression" was shown. It would thus appear that the results of the "failure" experiments have a much simple interpretation and afford no evidence for the more elaborate repression theory.

5. *Recall of affectively toned life experiences.* In an effort to achieve more naturalness in experiments, many experimenters have abandoned the memorizing of material under the artificial conditions of the laboratory and turned instead to studying the recall of actual experiences met outside the laboratory.

Meltzer (1930) asked students who had just returned to college after the Christmas holidays to describe their vacations. He had them list their experiences, and asked them also to rate these as pleasant, unpleasant, or indifferent. Six weeks later he unexpectedly asked them to repeat the listing they had made on the day of their return. Not only had they listed more pleasant than unpleasant memories immediately after returning from vacation, but after six weeks the predominance of pleasant over unpleasant memories had increased. This finding is in accord with the interpretation of repression as an active process, continuing after the original event, and in one form or another has been repeatedly observed. Still, no one has seriously researched the possibility that this is a simple "suppression-like" effect arising from our general cultural habit of avoiding reporting to others experiences which cast us in an unfavorable light, involving loss of self-esteem. This generalized avoidance could operate as a differential "threshold" for reporting positive as against negative experiences. Soon after an experience, its "strength in memory" would be sufficiently high so that positive and negative experiences might be equally reported. But with the passage of time, when memory strengths had declined, the differential report threshold would produce an advantage for reports of weak "positive" experiences. This analysis in terms of a cultural habit of self-reporting suggests altering these reporting responses in a verbal-conditioning paradigm (see Chapter 7) by means of differential rewards and punishments for reporting positive versus negative experiences.

However, there is a second effect in such memory reporting experiments. Experiences associated with more intense affect, whether positive or negative, seem to be better remembered, or at least reported more frequently, than are drab, neutral experiences which entailed little or no affect. It is introspectively clear that we often do remember embarrassing or frightening experiences, whereas a simple repression theory would hold that we should forget such happenings. There is, in fact, much experimental evidence for this "intensity of affect" hypothesis, relating recall to amount rather than pleasantness of affect connected to the experience (see Dutta & Kanungo, 1967; Waters & Leeper, 1936).

Recently, Holmes (1970) has shown theoretically and experimentally how the two classes of data can be reconciled. Specifically, he assumes that recall depends on the intensity of affect associated with an experience *at the time of the recall test*. It is further supposed that the intensity of affect or emotions aroused by re-thinking about an experience decreases over time. The final and critical assumption is that the intensity of negative affects will decay faster or to a greater extent than will the intensity of positive affects. According to this assumption, starting with a collection of experiences, some positive and some negative but all with equally intense affect, a later test will produce more recall of the "pleasant" experiences.

Holmes (1970) collected data which confirmed each of these assumptions. College students kept a daily "affective experiences" diary for a week, rating the direction and intensity of each recorded experience immediately on a nine-point "pleasant-unpleasantness" scale. After turning in their diaries to the experimenter, the subjects waited a week, then recalled each experience they had recorded. This recall showed the usual two effects: better recall of experiences originally rated as having extreme affect (pleasant or unpleasant) and more probable recall of experiences rated as pleasant rather than unpleasant. Beyond these recall data, Holmes also obtained new affect ratings: the person was shown his earlier diary recording of each experience but not his affect rating, and was asked to rate again the direction and degree of affect he felt about the experience "right now." These second ratings showed the expected trends. Nearly all the experiences were rated as having less intense affect than when they were originally experienced, and the decrease in affect was greater for unpleasant, negative experiences than for pleasant, positive experiences. Further, these second affect scores and the recall data showed a firm correlation; recall was related to the intensity of the current affect rating, not to whether it was a pleasant or an unpleasant affect.

Holmes's hypothesis thus seems to account well for the pattern of results in his experiment as well as for the other results obtained by this method of "life-experiences" reporting. Of course, it is still to be explained why the intensity of negative affects declines faster than that of positive affects. Although this could be "denial" of negative affects, Holmes suggests several simpler, plausible explanations. For instance, given a lapse of time, a person may discover that the actual, eventual aversive consequences of an event turn out to be not nearly as bad as had been anticipated, so the earlier experience as a whole is remembered with less affect. Another consideration is that many of the things people list as "unpleasant" concern something which must be done (e.g., write a term paper, save enough money to pay taxes). Perhaps in the intervening time the appropriate action has been taken, thus alleviating the affect associated with thought of the impending event. Also, Zajonc (1968) has shown over a variety of situations that "mere repeated exposure of an individual to a stimulus object enhances his attitude toward it" (p. 23). That is, the more a person is exposed to or thinks about an item, the more *positive* he feels about it. Therefore, if a subject repeatedly thinks about an experience laden with negative affect, his attitude toward it should change in a positive direction. Of course, this factor, along with those mentioned earlier, would produce a greater net decrease in affect for unpleasant than for pleasant experiences.

Where do all these various laboratory studies of repression lead us? We seem to be left in the curious bind that it is very hard to produce unequivocal, replicable laboratory demonstrations of forgetting that clearly require an account in terms of unconscious repression rather than some more parsimonious explanation. On the other hand, we have many clinical reports of "hysterical" amnesia in which a person appears temporarily to lose a whole block of memories associated with a particularly traumatic event or time of stress; the memories are unretrievable at one time, but become retrievable en masse later. Grinker and Spiegel (1945a, 1945b) describe many cases of "traumatic war neuroses" surrounding an apparently repressed memory of traumatic anxiety episodes of an overwhelming nature; recall of the repressed event was presumably released by hypnosis or by narcoleptic drugs (sodium amytal, the so-called truth serum). Other hysterical amnesias include the cases of apparent multiple personality (e.g., Prince, 1905; Thigpen & Cleckley, 1957), in which the individual appears to have distinct "dissociated" personalities which alternate in consciousness, each with different sets of motives and memories. These cases are in fact very rare, being much more frequent in the dramatic theater than in the clinic. But localized, functional amnesias, in which the person simply forgets his personal identity for a while, are still occasionally reported in the clinical literature (for reviews, see Barbizet, 1970; Talland & Waugh, 1969). Most often, the hysterical amnesia does seem to be instrumental in helping the person escape from an unhappy or frightening life. Although these anecdotes and clinical reports regarding amnesia would seem to illustrate the Freudian idea of repression, they are in a sense a little too good, too massive and total. Freud had presumed that repression was discriminating, that it might affect a particular idea but not the entire stock of an individual's personal memories. At present, nobody really knows how to explain in acceptable terms the clinical phenomenon of hysterical amnesia. By and large, the clinical descriptions of the "symptoms" strive for dramatic impact rather than objective evaluation; relatively little has been done in the way of alternative and converging tests of memory. Too often the verbal self-reports of the patient about what he can or cannot remember are accepted at face value by the clinician without his ever checking other, more subtle or more sensitive measures of memory. Obviously, the experimental analysis of hysterical amnesia and other "dissociation" phenomena remains as an interesting and rewarding task for psychologists.

ESTIMATE OF FREUD'S CONTRIBUTION TO LEARNING

Freud's Position on the Typical Problems

The foregoing account shows many points at which Freudian theory has impinged on the psychology of learning. A recapitulation is in order to summarize his views as they relate to the several problems with which learning theories deal.

1. Capacity. As a developmental psychology, Freud's theory implies that the very young infant is most impressionable, so that primary repressions occur in the first years of childhood, and character syndromes find their origins in the conflicts over food, toilet training, sex, and aggression. The resolution of these conflicts takes place according to fundamental themes or styles of response, and the rest of life is spent in playing out these early themes with the assimilation, of course, of new content. Fundamental changes in the structure of the personality do not take place through ordinary education; such changes require the special kind of reeducation provided by in-depth therapy. Alongside these modes of conduct determined by instinctual conflicts are the conflict-free ego processes, which are the kinds dealt with in ordinary give-and-take with the real environment. At some stages of life the conflict-laden personal problems loom unusually large, and make difficult the adjustment to external reality implied in school learning. The easiest time for conflict-free learning should be during the "latency period," and after adolescent conflicts are resolved, but individual differences are to be expected throughout because some children do not outgrow their earlier fixations, and some conflicts remain active and disruptive at any age.

2. Practice. The principle of learning through practice is illustrated by "working through," that aspect of therapy in which the patient faces the same conflicts over and over again in the process of reeducation. Learning takes place in "working through" because the conflicts are faced from new angles, and the cues to faulty conduct become detected early enough so that the behavior can be deflected. Repetition is needed for learning, but for repetition to be effective it must be repetition with a difference.

3. Motivation. Freud's is chiefly a psychology of motivation, and he detected motivational control in kinds of behavior that others had thought of as trivial or accidental, such as minor forgettings and slips of speech. The first serious effort to incorporate psychoanalytical theory into general psychology recognized the Freudian wish as providing a theory of motivation (Holt, 1915). The motivational concepts that have impinged most directly upon contemporary learning theory are *anxiety* (as a learned drive), and the consequences of various *ego threats*, as in the studies of regression, aggression, repression, and the defense mechanisms generally. The emphasis on sex as a master drive has been less influential in learning theories than in other fields of personality study, although many of the ego-threatening situations considered have included sexual conflicts.

4. Understanding. Despite Freud's preoccupation with the irrational in human behavior, his theory lays great stress on the possibilities of cognitive control. We can even gain insight into our unconscious processes, if we work at it properly—no mean achievement for the intellect. The developing "ego psychology," playing up the "conflict-free ego sphere," allows even more room for rationality in the control of conduct.

The aim of psychoanalytic therapy is to eliminate self-deception and other blocks to rationality. To the extent that the methods are successful, they should provide some principles useful for learning and teaching.

5. Transfer. We must not permit verbal equivalences to lead us to assume identity where identity does not exist. "Transference" has a special meaning in psychoanalysis. It refers to the special role that the therapist plays for the patient as he stands from time to time for important people in the patient's life, perhaps the mother, or father, or older brother. The patient reacts to the therapist with the emotions appropriate in reacting to these other people. Thus psychoanalytic transference does share with transfer of training the fact of generalization of responses learned in one situation to novel but related stimuli.

Problems of equivalence loom large in psychoanalysis. By way of symbols, something commonly stands for something else and provokes the responses (especially affective responses) appropriate to that something else. We have seen this process at work in displaced aggression. Other processes of symbolization and condensation are relevant to the manner in which earlier and later learning come into psychological relationship.

6. Forgetting. Freud long championed the view that registration of early experiences persists throughout life, that forgetting is therefore chiefly the result of repression. Forgetting is mostly a kind of amnesia, and under appropriate circumstances (as in dreams) the persistence of these memories may be detected, while under other circumstances (as in psychoanalysis) the repression may be lifted and the memories restored to waking consciousness. Although the most important repressions take place first in early childhood, the repressive process continues throughout life, maintaining the original repressions, and adding new items to the unconscious store.

Significance of Psychodynamics for Learning Theory

One influence of psychoanalytic thinking has been to broaden the *topical content* studied within the field of learning. Psychoanalytical thinking has helped to erase the boundaries between the neurotic and the normal, so that what was once relegated to "abnormal psychology" now becomes part of general psychology. Because there is a recognized continuum between the neurotic and the normal, the learning of symptoms becomes continuous with the learning of mannerisms and the acquiring of attitudes. Symbolism in night dreams makes us look for symbolism in daydreams, and in other products of creative imagination and thought. What we learn from unusual perceptual distortions, hallucinations, and amnesias influences how we think about ordinary perception in relation to the needs of the perceiver, and ordinary forgetting as related to motivation. Hence the range of topics that interest students of learning has been extended to include perceptual distortion, repression, and symbolism, all implying personal and idiosyncratic modes of expressing the results of learning.

In one form or another the conception of *unconscious determination* made important changes in thinking about human motivation. Psychologists seeking to maintain the behavioristic orientation of the 1920s were somewhat resistant to consciousness and even more so to an unconscious. But even Watson was influenced strongly by Freudian doctrine and accepted "the unverbalized" as a substitute for the unconscious (Watson, 1924a). Thus the subjective-objective controversy did not turn out to be a decisive one, insofar as it concerned incorporating motives of which the learner was unaware (or which he could not describe). Freud can be credited with being the first to propose that repression leads to the inability to verbalize:

> Now, too, we are in a position to state precisely what it is that repression denies to the rejected idea in the transference neuroses—namely, the translation of the idea into words which are to remain attached to the object. (1915b, pp. 133–134)

Any appraisal of psychoanalytic influences would be most incomplete if it did not call attention to the emphasis upon unconscious processes and their derivatives. This is the most obvious way in which to acknowledge the dynamic contribution of psychoanalysis.

Finally, the genetic or developmental aspects of psychoanalysis have brought to the fore the need for an adequate *ego psychology*. If we are to understand the learner as he sets his goals and works realistically toward them, or as he is torn by conflicts that prevent his using his abilities, or as he burns himself out in the quest for futile objectives, we need a theory of personality organization incorporated within our general theory of learning.

The Anti-Freudian Tendency of Recent Years

Styles change in psychology as in other fields of endeavor, and as this is being written there is a widespread coolness toward Freudian concepts as compared to their enthusiastic acceptance in the years immediately following World War II.

The attack began with a disparagement of the results of psychoanalytic therapy, with which this chapter is, of course, little concerned. Statistical results were said to show little efficacy in psychoanalytic treatment, despite its time-consuming and costly character (e.g., Eysenck, 1952, 1965). Hence in psychiatric circles attention began to turn to the new "wonder drugs," particularly the tranquilizers, and recognition was given to the new biochemistry, so successful in the realm of genetics, including molecular diseases. In clinical psychology, attention turned to the objective "behavior therapies," drawing either on the classical conditioning concepts used by Wolpe (1958; discussed in Chapter 3) or upon the social learning methods deriving from Skinnerian studies of contingency management or Bandura's studies of modeling and imitation (reviewed in Chapter 7). Beginning from a small trickle, research by the "behavior modification" group developed into a large-scale flood which at this writing is practically dominating research on psychotherapy.

The earlier attacks on the relative ineffectiveness of psychoanalytic treatment presently spread to attacks on psychoanalytic theory generally. This is not the place to review those criticisms of psychoanalytic theory, because they are numerous, lengthy, somewhat disputatious, and off the topic of learning theory (for such critiques, see Bandura, 1969; Kanfer & Phillips, 1970; Salter, 1952). Suffice it to say that the arguments have carried great weight with academic psychologists, so that psychoanalysis and other "psychodynamic" theories of personality have fallen somewhat into disfavor.

A particularly telling criticism by the behavior therapists was aimed at learning theorists such as Mowrer (1950) and Dollard and Miller (1950). These latter theorists accepted the basic hypotheses and claims of psychoanalysis, and proceeded to translate them into the terms of modern learning theory—stimuli, responses, drives, rewards, conflicts, avoidance of anxiety, symptoms as learned habits, therapy as providing an arena for unlearning debilitating emotional conflicts and for learning to discriminate realistic from unrealistic emotions, and so on. But the critics (Bandura, 1969; Kanfer & Phillips, 1970; Salzinger, 1969) have argued that the translation went in only one direction; no substantial change in psychotherapeutic methods was either recommended or adopted widely as a result of such translations. Rather, the effect of such learning-theory translations was to lend some scientific legitimacy to psychoanalysis, to give some degree of "real-world relevance" to learning theory, but not to assess, evaluate, change, or improve upon psychoanalytic therapy. As Kanfer and Phillips stated the matter:

. . . it is equally noteworthy that [Dollard and Miller's] reformulation had little impact on therapeutic practices. . . . no radically new methods of treatment can be traced directly to the theoretical formulations by Dollard and Miller. More radical behavioristically and environmentally oriented clinicians have made little use in the newer forms of behavior modification of the reformulations offered by Dollard and Miller, Mowrer, and their colleagues. (1970, p. 83)

The current behavioristic groundswell should not be permitted to blind us to the truly seminal and significant ideas that Freud formulated, nor to the reality of many of the clinical phenomena to which he drew attention. Freud's genius has won him a permanent place in the history of psychology and in the intellectual history of the world, regardless of how he may be evaluated by contemporary behavior therapists. As psychologists, we need to continue to face the kinds of questions that Freud called to our attention, no matter how we redefine them in our own terms. A sympathetic but experimentally oriented reader of Freud can tease out many significant hypotheses that can be put to the test, as Sarnoff (1971) has recently illustrated with social-psychological experimentation. Perhaps what is ultimately needed is a close, sympathetic collaboration between the experimental psychologist and the psychotherapist who deals daily with individual problems of enormous complexity laden with intense emotional significance.

SUPPLEMENTARY READINGS

The collected works of Freud appear in many volumes, but a few of the shorter books give the essence of his theories as they bear upon the topic of this chapter:
FREUD, S. (1920b) *Beyond the pleasure principle*. Translation, 1950.
FREUD, S. (1923) *The ego and the id*. Translation, 1927.
FREUD, S. (1926) *The problem of anxiety*. Translation, 1936.
FREUD, S. (1940) *An outline of psychoanalysis*. Translation, 1949.

Freud's writings spanned many decades and are voluminous. A simple, succinct summary of Freud's "final system" is:
HALL, C. S. (1954) *A primer of Freudian psychology*.

A variety of viewpoints about psychoanalysis in relation to psychology can be found in the following paperbound books:
SARASON, I. (Ed.) (1965a) *Psychoanalysis and the study of behavior*.
SARASON, I. (Ed.) (1965b) *Science and theory in psychoanalysis*.

A reflective account of what Freud has meant to American psychology can be found in:
SHAKOW, D., & RAPAPORT, D. (1964) The influence of Freud on American psychology. *Psychological Issues*, 4, Monograph 13.

There are many biographies of Freud. The most definitive is the three-volume work by Ernest Jones, a disciple and long-time friend of Freud; a recent popular biographical novel is by Stone:
JONES, E. (1953–1957) *The life and work of Sigmund Freud*.
STONE, I. (1971) *The passions of the mind*.

Mathematical Learning Theory

Since the experimental method for the study of learning was first introduced, a tradition of quantitative methods for recording, processing, and describing behavioral data has been established. The common measures of response tendencies are numerical in nature: amplitude or latency of response or relative frequency of occurrence. Even the earliest experimental papers of Thorndike and Ebbinghaus reported learning functions and forgetting functions in which some quantitative behavioral measure, such as time to respond or percentage of items correctly recalled, was graphed against the independent variable, practice trials, or time elapsed since learning. This tradition has survived, and it is now standard practice to report the results of experiments in terms either of mathematical functions or of verbal descriptions of the general class of functions (e.g., "performance declines with an increase in x").

MATHEMATICAL MODELS AND MATHEMATICAL LEARNING THEORY

Since the mid-1950s, one trend in American psychology has been toward framing hypotheses regarding learning which take seriously the quantitative details of behavioral data. These *mathematical models* of learning seek to predict the exact numerical details of experimental results. A major historical impetus to this trend came from the writings and theoretical work of Clark Hull (see Chapter 6). Hull argued forcibly for the development of quantitative theories in learning. His own work in this respect was mainly programmatic and yielded few genuinely quantitative predictions of numerical data. However, the type of program for which Hull argued appeared in significant form in the work of Estes, Burke, Bush, and Mosteller after 1950 under the designation *stochastic learning models.* Since then, it has become a small, steady, and prominent focus of theoretical activity in learning research. In fact, a high proportion of theoretical articles in learning contain some equations or a model; it has become a common mode of expression.

In 1950, Estes published the initial theoretical paper on stimulus sampling theory (SST). Soon thereafter, Bush and Mosteller (1951) published their initial work on the linear learning model, which is quite similar to the central model used in SST (see below). Throughout the next 10 years, Estes and Burke at Indiana University and Bush and Mosteller at Harvard University worked in close collaboration on experimental and mathematical analysis of the linear model for learning. Many of the early developments are reviewed by Bush and Mosteller (1955) and Estes (1959a), and in the *Handbook of mathematical psychology* (Luce, Bush, & Galanter, 1963, 1965).

One important point to stress at the outset is that there is really no such thing as "mathematical learning theory." This term denotes a particular kind of approach to theory construction rather than a single, specific set of postulates that could be properly called "the theory." The use of mathematics is freely available to theorists of all persuasions. The mathematics involved is indifferent to the content of the psychological ideas expressed by it. That is, a diversity of substantive hypotheses about learning and behavior can be stated and analyzed in mathematical terms. Mathematical learning theory as a field is occupied by a loose confederation of workers, with different substantive ideas, whose only common bond is their use of mathematics as a vehicle for precise statement and for testing their hypotheses against data.

In overview, work in mathematical learning theory has concentrated around the experimental situations exploited by Hull, Skinner, and the functionalist tradition, namely, classical and instrumental conditioning, selective learning, and a major emphasis on human learning under laboratory conditions. By and large, too, most of the theoretical work has been predominantly in the vein of "stimulus-response associationism." However, this primarily reflects the background and predilections of workers in the mathematical idiom, since "cognitive" hypotheses can be and often have been represented in mathematical form.

Perhaps the signal contribution of mathematical learning theory has been to make us aware of the richness of relationships existing in our data. In its more successful instances, it has shown how this rich network of relationships in data is all perfectly predictable from a very simple conception of what rules (laws) govern the subject's behavior. To take a simple example, consider the data gathered from successive trials of a group of rats learning to turn right in a T-maze. For a given subject, the data consist of a trial-by-trial sequence of his errors and correct responses. Writing "C" for "correct" and "E" for "error," a particular protocol might be CEECCECEEECCCCECC . . . (all the rest C). We would have one such protocol for each of our N subjects. Reduced to its barest essentials, the job for an adequate theory is to describe and account for such sequences of Cs and Es. The best job of description, of course, is simply to reproduce the original sequences. Theories, as economical abstractions, do not seek to do this. However, they can try to predict the general statistical characteristics of a sample of such sequences. A partial list of such characteristics (or statistics) might include the average total errors before learning, the average trial number of the first success, of the nth success, of the last error, the average number of runs of errors, the number of alternations of successes and failures, and so forth. There is an indefinitely large number of such descriptive statistics that one may calculate. Each statistic asks a slightly different question of the data, and each provides us with a slightly different perspective upon (or snapshot of) the mass of data. A mathematical learning model tries to paint a simple hypothetical picture of the learning process and its interactions with the conditions of learning which will integrate into one these different snapshots of, or perspectives on, the data. The way it achieves this is by predicting, to within a hopefully small random error, the numerical value of any statistic you care to calculate from the data. When successful, such a model serves both as an economical description of the data and as an explanation of it. That is, the data are, in a sense, explained when we have expressed the rules of operation of a theoretical system (or machine) that produces results similar to those that we observe.

Practically all extant models treat learning and performance as a probabilistic (or stochastic) process. A stochastic process is simply a sequence of events that can be analyzed in probability terms. The main dependent variable of such theories is the probability of various responses of the subject at any point in time, given his particular learning history. For example, in our T-maze illustration, in the theory we would let $p_1, p_2, p_3, \ldots$ represent the subject's probability of making a correct response on trial 1, on trial 2, on trial 3, etc. The model might then consist of a set of assumptions about how this response probability changes from trial to trial as a result of the outcomes the subject experiences on each trial. Given this representation of learning and performance as a trial sequence of response probabilities, the business of predicting statistics of the data then consists only of mathematical work within the probability calculus, which itself has no psychological content or significance. Because frequent mathematical problems arise in making these derivations, a certain portion of the literature in the field is concerned with such purely mathematical problems and the techniques for solving them.

From the discussion above, it may be inferred that mathematical models are usually highly specific, local sets of assumptions designed to characterize learning in particular situations, and that different situations require somewhat different models. By and large, this is true. There are advantages and disadvantages in the specificity inherent in mathematical models. One advantage is that it allows a very close comparison between data and theory, so that more theoretical "mileage" is gained from a given set of data. A related advantage is that if the model is inadequate, comparison of its predictions with data is very likely to disclose its faults at once in a glaring way. Because of this, no model currently espoused goes for very long without being shown to be inadequate for some situation or other. Thus, a model originally formulated to fit data from situation A is found to fail on B, fit C well, describe D with partial success, and fail again on situation E. An alternative model may fail on A, fit B partially, succeed well on F and G, miss on D and be mediocre on C. And there are probably still more competitors in the marketplace.

Such mild cacophonies, conflicting patterns of fits and misfits of competing models, are commonplace in the field. No one theory dominates all others in all situations, for all have their failings and incompletenesses. It is characteristic that contemporary workers in the field have come to view this conflict with composure rather than alarm, as a state of affairs to be expected rather than an occasion for scientific revolution. The models are admittedly simplified, idealized, incomplete caricatures of the behaving organism, and once certain situational constraints are altered, the incompleteness of any one caricature becomes evident. But being incomplete or overly idealized is not the same as being dead wrong, because the model may work extremely well in restricted cases. The hope is that eventually we shall have a powerful supertheory that will be generally dominant, essentially reducing to model 1 for those cases where model 1 fits, reducing to model 2 for cases where model 2 fits, and so on. Such a powerful theory is not to be found in the contemporary scene, and very likely it will not be for some time to come. However, the theoretical activity on a lower level continues at a steady pace.

Stimulus sampling theory (SST; also called statistical learning theory) as developed by Estes and Burke was intended to be a high-level theory in the sense discussed above. Starting from a general set of theoretical assumptions, amounting essentially to a "viewpoint," specific models were to be derived to handle specific situations when various special assumptions were added to the general framework. Such a program is so flexible that, in one sense, it is difficult to decide whether it has succeeded or failed, or if indeed such a question is at all relevant. This general approach has certainly led to a proliferation of specific models and to much experimental testing of them, and the stimulus sampling framework appears to give them all a common origin.

Stimulus sampling theory has operated at several levels throughout its history: these may be called the quasi-quantitative and the specific-quantitative levels. In the quasi-quantitative mode, exemplified, say, in Estes's theory of drive or spontaneous recovery, the aim is to show how SST can explain the correct general trends of the empirical functions observed in previous work, but no strong emphasis is laid upon precise validation of the mathematical description. Most of Clark Hull's theoretical work was quasi-quantitative in this sense. In the specific-quantitative mode, however, it is intended that a specific model be put through the wringer of stringent tests, fitting many numerical aspects of a set of data, with attendant requirements that certain constants (parameters) of the model remain invariant as experimental conditions are varied that theoretically should not affect these parameters, and so on. Operation in this specific-quantitative mode can be a bone-crushing encounter for a plausible quasi-quantitative theory, and few will pass muster. In fact, few earlier theories about learning were formulated with sufficient precision to even permit a test of this nature. One virtue of SST is that specific models derived from it can be put to this kind of test. Some of the models have passed these stringent tests with sufficient regularity to warrant discussing them in our review.

STIMULUS SAMPLING THEORY

In many respects, SST represents a formalization of Guthrie's approach to stimulus-response associationism (see Chapter 4). The stimulus situation is represented as a population of independently variable components or aspects of the total environment, called stimulus elements. At any moment (experimental trial), only a sample of elements from the total population is active or effective. The less variable the experimental conditions, the less variable are the successive trial samples of stimulus elements.

Two sources of random variation in stimulation may be identified: the first arises from incidental changes in the environment during the experiment (extraneous noises, temperature fluctuations, stray odors, etc.); and the second arises from changes in the subject, either from changing orientation of his receptors (what he is looking at or listening to), from changes in his posture or response-produced stimuli, or from fluctuations in his sensory transmission system (e.g., the temporal and spatial pattern of electrical activity in the auditory cortex evoked by the sound of a bell). When verbal stimuli are presented in human subjects, variability in encoding may occur due to different implicit associations or interpretations aroused by the material upon different occasions (e.g., G. H. Bower, 1972d). There is no commitment to any fixed amount of such stimulus variability; that is to be estimated by the theory. Thus, in simple learning situations in which the experimenter is applying the "same" stimulus (say, the sound of a bell) at the onset of each trial, this may be represented simply as a potential population of N stimulus elements.

On each trial, only a sample of the N elements will be active or effective. If we think of the stimulus elements represented as N marbles in an urn, various sampling schemes are possible, but two simple ones have been most widely employed in theoretical discussions. One scheme supposes that each stimulus element has probability θ of being sampled, independently of how many other elements are sampled. According to this scheme, the number of elements in the sample will randomly vary from one trial to the next, with the average sample size consisting of $N\theta$ elements. The second scheme supposes that a fixed number of elements are drawn at random without replacement from the N elements of the population. If we let s represent the fixed sample size, then each element has an overall probability of s/N of appearing in the sample. The special models obtained when it is assumed that $s = 1$ are called "pattern" models. They have been much investigated, and are reviewed later.

The Conditioning Assumption

This much of the system tells us how the stimulus situation and trial sample are represented. To make contact with performance, the theory assumes that each stimulus element is conditioned to (connected to) one response. In a two-choice experiment, say, some elements would be connected to response alternative A_1 and some to the other alternative, A_2; in a free-operant situation, A_1 might be "pressing the lever" and A_2 would denote any behavior other than lever-pressing. The procedure for identifying the relevant response alternatives is simply that commonly used by experimenters. It is supposed that the conditional connection between a stimulus element and a response is unitary and at full strength, not varying in degree. According to this approach, we can characterize the subject's dispositions at any moment in our situation by listing the various stimulus elements and the relevant response which is currently associated with each element. Such a listing is the theoretical "state of the system" as it applies to an individual at this time. Throughout the course of learning, the elements will be changing their associations for this subject; alternatively, we would say that the state of the system is changing trial by trial.

Since the probabilities of the various responses depend on the state of the system, we have to calculate the state of the system as trials progress. Can we find a useful way to represent the state of the system so that these calculations can be simplified? Indeed we can, and the reason for this is that the sampling schemes mentioned above assign an *equal* sampling probability to each element. Because of this assumption, we do not need to know *which* elements are associated with which responses in order to predict response probability. All we really need to know is *what proportion* of the stimulus elements are associated with each response. For example, in a two-response experiment, we could let p denote the proportion of elements associated with response A_1 and $1 - p$ denote the remaining proportion of elements associated with response A_2. In this case, our description of the "state of the system" reduces to the single number, p. And calculations of this single number are considerably easier to follow than would be calculations on the changing listing of S-R associations.

Performance on any trial is determined by the elements which are experienced, or "sampled," on that trial. The probability of any response is assumed to be equal to the proportion of sampled elements on that trial that are connected to that response. If a sample of size 10 contains 5 elements connected to A_1, 3 to A_2, and 2 to A_3, then the probabilities are 0.5, 0.3, and 0.2, respectively, that the response will be A_1, A_2, or A_3. If the number of elements is large so that the statistical "law of large numbers" applies, this performance rule has the effect of setting the probability of response A_1 equal to p, the proportion of A_1-connected elements in the population. It is usually assumed that this is the case.

Having drawn a stimulus sample and responded, the subject then receives some reinforcing outcome. It is these outcomes that change the conditional connections of the elements sampled on a trial, thus altering the state of the system. In theory, if r response classes have been identified, then $r + 1$ theoretical reinforcing events are defined, denoted $E_0, E_1, E_2, \ldots, E_r$. It is supposed that exactly one of these reinforcing events occurs at the termination of the trial. Events $E_1, E_2, \ldots, E_r$ refer to reinforcement of responses $A_1, A_2, \ldots, A_r$, respectively, whereas E_0 denotes that none of the responses was reinforced. If a trial terminates with reinforcing event E_k, then all elements sampled on that trial become conditioned to response A_k if they were not already so conditioned. For example, if an element connected to A_1 is sampled on a trial when reinforcement E_2 occurs, then this element switches its conditional connection from A_1 to A_2 in an all-or-none manner. Finally, E_0 denotes a null event; occurrence of E_0 means that none of the responses was reinforced, so no change occurs in the conditional connections of the sampled elements.

Let us comment on these conditioning assumptions. First, these axioms presumably describe the dynamic changes in the state of the system over trials, and this is what learning is considered to be. By these rules, successive practice trials result in the attachment of the rewarded or "correct" response to progressively more stimulus elements sampled from the population, with the resultant detachment of "error" responses from these elements. The exact description of this process is given below. Second, we note that following Guthrie, SST assumes all-or-none conditioning of the sampled elements to the reinforced response. Conditioning of response A_1 is achieved at the expense of removing associations from alternative responses, and no special postulates regarding extinction are needed. Extinction is by "interference" in the sense that the probability of some reference response A_2 declines while the likelihood of a competing response A_1 increases.

This representation of reinforcing events is theoretically neutral. For particular applications, one must make substantive assumptions about the relationships between the hypothetical reinforcing events and the actual trial outcomes—food reward for a rat turning left in a T-maze, the unconditioned stimulus or its absence in classical conditioning, information about the correct answer in verbal learning, etc. Alternative interpretations are possible at this point. As a matter of personal preference, Estes began by trying consistently to apply Guthrie's contiguity theory of reinforcement to interpretation of the relationship between trial outcomes and the hypothetical reinforcing events.[1] The Guthrian assumption is that the last response (overt or covert) to occur in the presence of the trial stimulus sample is the one that becomes associated with the elements of that sample. The effect of an empirical reinforcing operation is either (a) to insure that the appropriate response is evoked at the end of the trial (e.g., the US in classical conditioning evokes the response to be conditioned, information evokes rehearsal of the correct response in verbal learning, etc.), or (b) to delay or prevent the occurrence of competing reactions before the subject is removed from the trial stimulation (e.g., feeding a hungry rat in the goal-box of a straight alley). This contiguity interpretation of reinforcement is not a necessary adjunct of stimulus sampling theory. More often, the users of the theory simply employ a general law of effect: if the outcome of a particular trial has the effect of increasing the probability of response A_1, then this trial's outcome is identified as E_1 in the model. Secondly, should one choose to do so, this scheme for representing reinforcing events can accommodate the quantitative effects of variations in the traditional "reinforcement parameters" such as magnitude, quality, and delay of reinforcement. This consists of postulating particular probabilistic relationships between the particular trial outcome (e.g., the amount of food given as a reward to a hungry rat) and the

---

[1] Estes's later views on reinforcement were reviewed in Chapters 2 and 3 and will be covered in the section entitled "The Scanning Model."

hypothetical reinforcing events. For example, it might be assumed that the more food given following an A_1 response, the more likely it is that an E_1 rather than an E_0 event occurs on that trial (see Estes, 1962).

Derivation of Basic Difference Equations

The state of the system, it will be recalled, is given by the fractions of stimulus elements conditioned to the various response alternatives. The assumptions of the theory permit us to derive how these proportions will change from trial to trial as a result of the reinforcing events. We will illustrate this for a two-alternative situation. Let p and $1-p$ denote the proportions of elements connected to responses A_1 and A_2. Since these proportions will be changing over trials, we use a subscript to denote the trial number in question. Thus, p_n will denote the proportion of A_1-connected elements at the moment of evocation of the response on the nth trial. p_n may also be interpreted as (a) the probability that any randomly selected single element in the population is connected to A_1, and as (b) the probability that the response on trial n will be A_1.

Suppose that an E_1 reinforcing event occurs in trial n. We wish to calculate p_{n+1}, the probability that an element is conditioned to A_1 at the beginning of the next trial, $n+1$. The equation may be written in two equivalent forms, where we recall that θ is the probability that a stimulus element is sampled on any given trial:

$$p_{n+1} = p_n + \theta(1 - p_n) \tag{1a}$$

$$p_{n+1} = (1 - \theta)p_n + \theta. \tag{1b}$$

Equation (1a) may be interpreted as follows: with probability p_n the element is already conditioned to A_1 and remains so conditioned when E_1 occurs on this trial; with probability $1-p_n$ the element was formerly connected to A_2 but it switches to an A_1 connection if it is sampled (an event having probability θ) on this E_1 trial. Equation (1b), which is identical to (1a), is interpreted slightly differently: with probability $1-\theta$ the element is not sampled, so its probability of being connected to A_1 remains at p_n; with probability θ the element is sampled, so the E_1 event conditions it to A_1 with certainty.

Let us note a few mathematical facts about equation (1) in either form. First, p_{n+1} will be greater than or equal to p_n, so an E_1 reinforcement increases the probability of an A_1 response. Second, p_{n+1} is a linear (straight line) function of p_n. From this fact comes the name "linear model," in reference to a system of such equations. Third, an E_1 event increases p to an eventual limit (or asymptote) of unity. That is, when $p_n = 1$, then equation (1) will give $p_{n+1} = 1$. In fact, the limit of any such equation may be generally defined as that value of p where $p_{n+1} = p_n$ (i.e., when p reaches its limiting value, it stops changing). If a consistent series of E_1 events were given, corresponding to repeated applications of equation (1), p would increase from some initial value and approach an asymptote of unity. Thus, equation (1) implies that consistent E_1 reinforcements would eventually lead to consistent occurrences of A_1 responses.

Suppose that an E_2 reinforcing event occurs on trial n. This should lower p_n and increase $1-p_n$, the probability that an element is connected to A_2. Two equivalent versions of this equation are

$$p_{n+1}=(1-\theta)p_n+\theta \cdot 0=(1-\theta)p_n \tag{2a}$$

$$(1-p_{n+1})=(1-\theta)(1-p_n)+\theta. \tag{2b}$$

The reader may prove for himself that these two equations are identical. To interpret (2a): with probability $1-\theta$ the element is not sampled and so remains connected to A_1 with the same probability as before, namely p_n; with probability θ it is sampled, and the E_2 event connects it to A_2 so that its connection to A_1 has probability zero. To interpret (2b): the probability, $1-p_n$, of an A_2 response is increased by an E_2 event by exactly the same reasoning that led to equation (1b) whereby an E_1 event increased p_n. That is, the effect of E_1 on p_n is the same as the effect of E_2 on $1-p_n$.

Examining equation (2a), it is seen that (a) p_{n+1} is less than or equal to p_n since $1-\theta$ is a fraction (a probability), (b) p_{n+1} is a linear function of p_n, and (c) the limit of this equation is zero. That is, a succession of E_2 reinforcing events, with correspondingly repeated applications of equation (2a), would reduce p_n to zero, where A_1 responses would cease and A_2 responses would consistently occur.

Finally consider that a null E_0 event occurs on trial n. This null event produces no change in conditioning of the sampled elements. An equation which expresses this preservation of the status quo is simply $p_{n+1}=p_n$.

To collect the equations into summary form, we use $E_{i,n}$ to denote the event of E_i occurring on trial n. We have

$$p_{n+1}=\begin{cases} (1-\theta)p_n+\theta & \text{if } E_{1,n} \\ (1-\theta)p_n & \text{if } E_{2,n} \\ p_n & \text{if } E_{0,n} \end{cases} \tag{3}$$

These equations constitute the core of the "linear model." We note that they are *difference equations*, expressing how a variable (p_n) changes its values from one discrete point in time (trial n) to the next point in time (trial $n+1$).

These equations express the trial-by-trial incremental or decremental effects of reinforcing events. A learning curve consists of a plot of the performance probabilities $p_1, p_2, p_3, \ldots, p_n$ over the successive practice trials $1, 2, 3, \ldots, n$ of the experiment. If we wish to predict the learning curve, we simply trace out the trial-by-trial effect of applying equation (1) or (2) to the initial value p_1 from which the process begins on trial 1. Suppose that we have a consistent sequence of E_1 events; then we would repeatedly apply equation (1). That is, p_2 is calculated from p_1 by equation (1). Then p_3 is calculated from p_2 using equation (1) again, etc. The result of doing this is the following general expression:

$$p_n=1-(1-p_1)(1-\theta)^{n-1}. \tag{4}$$

This expression gives p_n as a "negatively accelerated" function of practice trials, n. The limit of p_n is 1 since the fraction $1-\theta$ decreases to zero as it is raised to higher and higher powers. Some graphs of this function are shown in Figure 12.1. For these curves, $p_1 = 0.20$ and θ is 0.05, 0.10, and 0.20 for the three curves. The curve rises faster for larger values of θ. Recall that θ is the probability that a stimulus element is sampled; when θ is low, there will be much trial-to-trial variability in the composition of the stimulus sample; when θ is high, most elements will always be present, so one sample will vary little from another. We see in Figure 12.1 how this stimulus variability affects the rate of learning. The retarding influence of increased stimulus variability upon learning was first noted by Pavlov (the phenomenon of "external inhibition"). Later experiments by Wolfle (1936), E. J. Green (1956), and Burke, Estes, and Hellyer (1954) give results interpretable in terms of θ variations.

APPLICATION OF SST TO SELECTED PROBLEMS

Response to Stimulus Compounds

One standard question is whether we can predict the probabilities of the various responses to a compound of several stimuli given knowledge of how the individual elements of the compound are connected to the responses. If one set of elements, denoted S_1, is connected to response A_1, and another set, denoted S_2, is connected to A_2, how are we to predict response probabil-

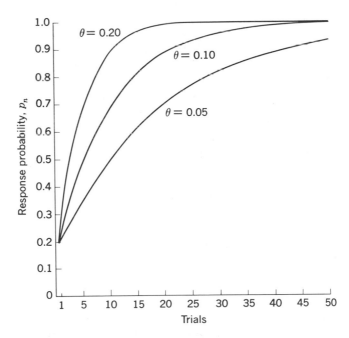

Figure 12.1. Graphs of the function p_n described by equation (4), where $p_1 = 0.20$ and the learning rate, θ, has the values of 0.05, 0.10, and 0.20 for the three curves.

ity to a compound or test pattern consisting of n_1 elements from S_1 and n_2 elements from S_2? The assumption of SST is that the response probabilities are determined by the proportions of stimulus elements in the sample connected to the various responses. In the test situation described above, the probability of response A_1 is expected to be $n_1/(n_1+n_2)$, and of A_2, $n_2/(n_1+n_2)$. Further, let S_3 be a third set of stimulus elements with a random one-half of the S_3 elements connected to A_1 and one-half of the elements connected to A_2. If the test compound consists of n_1 elements from S_1, n_2 from S_2, and n_3 from S_3, then the expected proportion of A_1 responses is

$$p = \frac{n_1 + \frac{1}{2} n_3}{n + n_2 + n_3}. \tag{5}$$

The $\frac{1}{2} n_3$ term in the numerator is the expected number of A_1-connected elements of the n_3 drawn from the S_3 stimulus set.

An experiment by Schoeffler (1954) provides a test of these predictions. The three sets of stimulus elements were identified as different sets of 8 small jewel lamps in a 24-lamp display in front of the subject. Subjects were first trained to move a switch in one direction (A_1) when elements of the S_1 set were presented, and to move it in the opposite direction (A_2) when elements of the S_2 set were presented. The S_3 lamps never were presented during this preliminary training, and the theory presupposes that these elements start off (and remain) randomly connected, half to A_1 and half to A_2. Following this preliminary training, subjects were tested for their response to different combinations of the S_1, S_2, and S_3 elements (lamps). During the test series, subjects were told to respond as they thought appropriate and there was no information feedback concerning the "correct" response.

The test combinations used and the results obtained are shown in Table 12.1 along with the predictions from three different combination rules. To illustrate how Table 12.1 is to be interpreted, consider the fifth test pattern (row 5) consisting of 8 bulbs of the S_1 set, 4 randomly selected bulbs of the S_2 set, and all 8 bulbs of the S_3 set. To this combination, the average relative frequency of response A_1 for the group of subjects was 0.62.

The column of predicted values labeled "Averaging Rule" uses the formula derived from SST above. For example, for test 6 consisting of 8, 2, and 8 elements from S_1, S_2, and S_3, respectively, the predicted value is

$$p_5 = \frac{8 + \frac{1}{2} \cdot 8}{8 + 2 + 8} = \frac{12}{18} = 0.67.$$

This predicted value is identical with the 0.67 value observed. In fact, except for the second test pattern, the predictions of the averaging rule are uniformly close to the observed values.

The "neutral elements" rule, an alternative suggested by LaBerge's work (1959), applies the averaging rule with the exception that S_3 elements are presumed to be neutral and to contribute to neither A_1 nor A_2. For instance, in test 6, the neutral-elements hypothesis deletes the 8 S_3 elements and predicts $p = 8/(8+2) = 0.80$. From Table 12.1 it is seen that in tests 5 through 8 where the two sets of predictions differ, the neutral-elements rule is consistently inferior to the averaging rule.

Table 12.1   **Proportions of A₁ responses, observed and predicted, to each of nine test patterns (rows). Composition of the test patterns is indicated by the column entries under S₁, S₂, S₃. See text for explanation of predictions. (Data from Schoeffler, 1954. Copyright 1954 by the American Psychological Association. Reprinted by permission.)**

| Test Pattern | No. of elements from | | | Observed $p(A_1)$ | Predicted by | | |
	S_1	S_2	S_3		Aver. Rule	Neutral Elements	Majority Rule
1	8	8	0	0.54	0.50	0.50	0.50
2	8	4	0	0.79	0.67	0.67	1.00
3	8	2	0	0.81	0.80	0.80	1.00
4	4	2	0	0.63	0.67	0.67	1.00
5	8	4	8	0.62	0.60	0.67	1.00
6	8	2	8	0.67	0.67	0.80	1.00
7	4	2	8	0.54	0.57	0.67	1.00
8	8	0	8	0.73	0.75	1.00	1.00
9	8	8	8	0.54	0.50	0.50	0.50

The last hypothesis, labeled "Majority Rule" in Table 12.1, assumes that the response is determined by whichever conditioned elements are in the majority in the sample. This rule, which at first thought seems plausible, is discredited by these data.

There are many other sets of data of this general type, in which the averaging rule is tested by its predictions about response proportions to novel combinations of conditioned stimuli. By and large, the averaging rule has fared quite well throughout these various tests, and it seems an excellent working assumption to handle these kinds of problems.

Probability Learning

A considerable portion of the early experimental work in SST was carried out in the probability learning situation. In its simplest arrangement, the task for the subject is to predict on each trial which one of two events is going to occur. After he has made his predictive response, the actual event is shown. The common feature of these experiments is that the events occur in a random sequence, and there is usually no information available to help the subject predict perfectly which event will occur. The label "probability learning" describes this fact about the situation.

We let A₁ and A₂ denote the subject's two predictive responses and E₁ and E₂ the two events, E_i meaning that response A_i was correct on a given trial. Suppose that π_n denotes the probability that the reinforcing event E₁ occurs on trial n, and $1 - \pi_n$ is the probability of an E₂ on trial n. If an E₁ event occurs, p_n is assumed to increase; if an E₂ event occurs, p_n is assumed to decrease. The average change in the A₁ response probability is obtained by weighting the two parts of equation (3) by π_n and $1 - \pi_n$ to obtain the following:

$$p_{n+1} = \pi_n[(1-\theta)p_n + \theta] + (1-\pi_n)[(1-\theta)p_n] = (1-\theta)p_n + \theta\pi_n. \tag{6}$$

There is a variety of procedures (or schedules) the experimenter can use to decide whether to show E_1 or E_2 on a given trial. To list a few examples, the probability of an E_1 on trial n might (a) be a constant π, (b) increase or decrease in some systematic manner as trials proceed, (c) vary depending on the response of trial n, (d) vary depending on the response or reinforcing event that occurred a few trials back in the sequence. Independently of how the sequence is generated, equation (6) makes the general prediction that the long-term average proportion of A_1 responses will eventually come to match (equal) the long-term average proportion of E_1 events. To show this, we take the average of both sides of equation (6) by summing over trials 1 to N, and dividing by N. The result is

$$\frac{1}{N}\sum_{n=1}^{N} p_{n+1} = (1-\theta)\frac{1}{N}\sum_{n=1}^{N} p_n + \theta\frac{1}{N}\sum_{n=1}^{N}\pi_n$$

$$\frac{1}{N}\left[p_{N+1} - p_1 + \theta\sum_{n=1}^{N} p_n\right] = \frac{\theta}{N}\sum_{n=1}^{N}\pi_n.$$

To take the long-term average, we let the number of trials N become very large. In this case, the term $p_{N+1} - p_1$ divided by N becomes negligible (zero) and our final result is

$$\frac{1}{N}\sum_{n=1}^{N} p_n = \frac{1}{N}\sum_{n=1}^{N}\pi_n. \tag{7}$$

This equation says that the average proportion of A_1 responses over a large number of trials should be equal to the average proportion of E_1 events over those trials. This is called the "probability matching" theorem and it results from assuming that E_1 and E_2 have symmetric effects in increasing p_n and $1 - p_n$.

This matching prediction has been tested for a variety of reinforcement schedules. By and large, the prediction has been confirmed; moreover, the theory's predictions are usually fairly accurate regarding the shape of the learning curve under particular schedules (see Estes, 1959a). The predictions are confirmed for the learning curves for individual subjects as well as for group averages. A paper by Estes (1964) reviews and systematically classifies those experiments which consistently yield matching results and those which yield results discrepant to some degree with matching. For example, it is known that the matching prediction is wrong when monetary payoffs and penalties are introduced for correct and incorrect predictions. We will consider a later generalization of SST that will handle these discrepant cases.

To illustrate a few cases of predictive success of the simple model, let us return to equation (6) and consider the schedule where the probability of the E_1 event varies depending upon the response made on that trial. Specifically, let us suppose that the probability of E_1 is π_1 if response A_1 is made, and is π_2 if response A_2 is made; otherwise, an E_2 event occurs. For this schedule, the average probability of an E_1 on trial n is seen to be

$$\pi_n = p_n\pi_1 + (1 - p_n)\pi_2.$$

The first term represents the probability of an A_1 response followed by an

E_1 reinforcing event; the second term represents the probability of an A_2 response followed by an E_1 event. If we substitute this expression for π_n into equation (6) and simplify, we arrive at the following result:

$$p_{n+1} = [1 - \theta(1 - \pi_1 + \pi_2)]p_n + \theta\pi_2$$

or

$$p_{n+1} = p_n + \theta[\pi_2 - (1 - \pi_1 + \pi_2)p_n]. \tag{8}$$

For this case, we ask, what is the limiting value attained when p stops changing? This limiting value is attained when the added term (inside the brackets) in equation (8) is zero, since at this value no more change in p occurs. Thus the asymptote is that value of p where

$$\pi_2 - (1 - \pi_1 + \pi_2)p = 0.$$

Hence, we have

$$p = \frac{\pi_2}{1 - \pi_1 + \pi_2}. \tag{9}$$

We note that, as in equation (7), the predicted asymptotic proportion of A_1 responses is independent of the learning rate θ. The asymptote depends on the relative "disconfirmation" probabilities: note that π_2 is the likelihood of an E_1 given an A_2 response, and the $1 - \pi_1$ term in the denominator is the likelihood of an E_2 given an A_1 response. An experiment by Suppes and Atkinson (1960) reports data relevant to these predictions. They ran three groups of 48 students on the π_1 and π_2 values specified in Table 12.2. The subjects were told to predict whether a left- or right-hand bulb would light on each trial. Each subject was run for 300 trials; the proportions shown in Table 12.2 are the group average proportion of A_1 responses over the last 100 trials, where performance was judged to have reached its limiting value. Examination of Table 12.2 shows that the theoretical predictions from equation (9) were very accurate in this case.

This probability matching result has been pursued in a variety of ways. Binder and Feldman (1960), for example, have shown that it predicts response frequencies on tests with single stimulus components which in previous training had been parts of stimulus patterns. To illustrate, suppose we let a, b, c represent three component elements. To the pattern ab we train response A_1; to the pattern cb we train response A_2. We unbalance the frequencies so that the ab pattern occurs, say, four times as frequently as the cb pattern. Binder and Feldman found that a later test to b alone resulted in approximately 80 percent A_1 responses and 20 percent A_2 responses. This result may be interpreted in SST by noting that when the b element occurred

Table 12.2   Average A_1 proportions at asymptote under response-contingent reinforcement schedules. (Data excerpted from Suppes & Atkinson, 1960, p. 253.)

π_1	π_2	*Observed*	*Predicted*
0.67	0.60	0.650	0.645
0.67	0.80	0.700	0.706
0.40	0.80	0.560	0.571

(within the training patterns), four out of five times response A_1 was reinforced. Hence, the probability that b is connected to A_1 would come to match this $4/5$ relative frequency of E_1 to E_2 reinforcements.

Another line of work investigates probability matching in elementary "interaction" situations involving two subjects at once. The two subjects work concurrently on probability learning tasks in lock-step trials. On each trial, each subject makes one of two responses and receives reinforcement for one of these. The new wrinkle is that the probabilities of the reinforcing events on each trial depend upon the responses of both subjects on that trial. The reinforcement schedules for the two subjects are interactive in the sense that the probability of an E_1 event for subject A depends on B's response as well as A's. Special mathematical techniques are required to apply the model to such situations, since both A's and B's behaviors are changing over trials. When applied to a variety of such interactive conditions, the asymptotic predictions come quite close to the obtained data (see Suppes & Atkinson, 1960). As before, the prediction is that both subjects will eventually match their A_1 response frequency to their E_1 event frequency. The only complication is the difficulty encountered in calculating this E_1 event probability in a given interactive situation.

Several generalizations of the probability learning experiment and theory have been investigated by a number of researchers. In one procedure (Suppes et al., 1964) the subject's response and the reinforcing event can vary over an entire continuum on which there are, in principle, an infinite number of response alternatives. In the task employed, the subject tries to predict where a spot of light will appear on the edge of a large circle before him. Suppes's generalization of the linear model to this situation appears to do a fairly good job of accounting for the mean response distributions. In a second variation (Suppes & Donio, 1967), discrete choice trials are eliminated. The situation is so arranged that the subject is always in either an A_1 or an A_2 "response state." For example, the subject might hold a toggle switch which he has to keep pushed to the left or the right side at all times. The subject is free to switch between response states at any time. The reinforcing events might be, for instance, left and right lamps which flash briefly at random intervals, with one point scored if the subject has his response switch on the same side as the lamp that flashes. In this situation, the primary dependent variable is the proportion of time the subject is in the A_1-response state. The setup, resembling a free-operant situation in many respects, has such independent variables as the time rate at which reinforcements are delivered and the proportion (π) of the reinforcements that are given on the A_1 side. The major prediction which has been confirmed is that the proportion of time that the subject spends in the A_1 state will converge asymptotically to π, the proportion of A_1 reinforcements, and this asymptote will be independent of the time rate at which E_1 or E_2 reinforcements are given. More detailed discussions of the models and the data in these several cases would take us too far afield for our present purposes.

A third variation of the standard probability learning task, studied by Neimark and Shuford (1959) and L. R. Beach et al. (1970), requires subjects to make trial-by-trial estimates of the probability that event E_1 either will occur on the next trial or has occurred over the past series of trials. Much like the average proportions of A_1 predictive responses, these probability estimates begin at around chance and then converge with continued practice to π, the true E_1-event probability. In further work, Reber and Millward (1968) showed that subjects could be brought rapidly to event-matching in their A_1 predictions by initially having them, rather than predict individual trials, merely *observe* a rapidly exposed series of E_1/E_2 events. What was important was simple exposure to the probabilistic information series rather than "rewards" and "punishments" for overt predictive responses.

A fourth variation studied by G. H. Bower (1966), had subjects attempt to predict which two (out of four) exclusive events (lights) would occur at the end of each trial. In this situation, subjects came eventually to treat *pairs* of prediction responses (e.g., 2-4, 1-3, 1-4, etc.) as patterned response units, so that asymptotic matching occurred between the proportions of $A_i A_j$ prediction pairs and the joint probabilities of $E_i E_j$ outcome pairs.

Sequential Statistics

In the discussion above, we were interested in discovering whether the model would predict the mean learning curve and the limiting value of the average response proportions as trials increase. Part of the power of stochastic learning models is that they permit us to predict much more than just these mean response curves. In principle, predictions may be derived for any feature of the data we care to examine.

An important source of information about the learning process is provided by *sequential statistics*. These gauge the extent to which a subject's response on trial $n+1$ is influenced by his responses and/or reinforcing events on one or more prior trials. The immediate history of events for a subject on trials n, $n-1$, etc., has a large effect upon his response probability on trial $n+1$. Sequential statistics enable us to examine these effects. The mean response curve is not informative on this score since in averaging over subjects we pool together those for whom different events occurred on trials n, $n-1$, etc. In this sense, sequential statistics provide a more detailed examination of learning than does the classical "learning curve." Additionally, sequential statistics continue to yield useful measures of the incremental and decremental effects of single trial events long after the average response probability has reached its limiting value and has ceased to provide any new information.

To illustrate these matters, we consider a two-response experiment where E_1 occurs with a fixed probability π and we examine the process after a large number of trials, after the mean response proportions have ceased changing. We will be concerned with the probability of an A_1 response given that a particular response-and-reinforcement combination occurred on the previous trial, namely A_1E_1, A_1E_2, A_2E_1, and A_2E_2. We will write the conditional probability of A_1 given that A_1E_1 occurred on the previous trial as $P(A_1|A_1E_1)$; similarly for the other three combinations. It is possible to derive a theoretical expression for each of these quantities, and they depend upon θ and π. Once a numerical value of θ has been estimated, predictions of these sequential probabilities are possible. For derivational details the reader may consult Atkinson, Bower and Crothers (1965) or Suppes and Atkinson (1960).

To illustrate the results of this procedure, we may review the results of an experiment by Suppes and Atkinson (1960). Thirty college students were run 240 trials in a two-choice probability learning task with $\pi = 0.60$. Tabulation of response frequencies over the last 100 trials, when mean performance had ceased changing, gave the results displayed in Table 12.3. The first entry shows that the observed mean A_1-response probability came to approximate closely the probability matching value $\pi = 0.60$. The next four entries show the A_1 probability conditional upon the four response-reinforcement events on the prior trial. The last four entries give A_1 proportions conditional upon only the prior response or the prior reinforcing event.

It is noteworthy that these conditional probabilities vary over a wide range (from 0.413 to 0.715) even though the mean response probability is relatively constant near 0.60. Thus, there are powerful sequential effects from trial to trial in these data. To get an intuitive understanding of these sequential statistics, let us consider which events on the prior trial promote or decrease the probability of A_1 on the current trial. First, an E_1 event will increase p_n, whereas an E_2 event will decrease it; the bottom two lines show this difference. Second, when we select out those trials following the occurrence of A_1 on the prior trial, we will be selecting out those cases (trials and/or subjects) where the past history of reinforcing events has produced a higher than average bias toward the A_1 response. Other things being equal, we would thus expect that the probability of response A_1 will be higher for those subjects who make A_1 on the previous trial than for those who make A_2. This effect is shown in lines 6 and 7 of Table 12.3. The probability of A_1 following a given combination of the response and reinforcing event on the prior trial may be considered the result of these two effects adding together or canceling each other out, depending on whether the A and E are the same or different.

Comparison of the observed proportions with those predicted by the theory shows them to be in excellent agreement. The predictions from the

Table 12.3   **Observed and predicted sequential statistics for the Suppes-Atkinson experiment (1960). These show the conditional probability that an A_1 response occurs following the specified events of the preceding trial. For the predictions, the θ estimate is 0.185. The first entry and the last four are derivable from the four joint probabilities and the fact that $\pi = 0.60$. Hence they are not independent predictions once the joint probabilities have been predicted.**

	Observed	*Predicted*
$P(A_1)$	0.596	0.600
$P(A_1|E_1A_1)$	0.715	0.708
$P(A_1|E_2A_1)$	0.535	0.524
$P(A_1|E_1A_2)$	0.603	0.624
$P(A_1|E_2A_2)$	0.413	0.439
$P(A_1|A_1)$	0.641	0.635
$P(A_1|A_2)$	0.532	0.550
$P(A_1|E_1)$	0.667	0.675
$P(A_1|E_2)$	0.488	0.490

theory depend upon getting a numerical estimate of θ from these various data. The estimate was $\theta = 0.185$. The linear model provides a very good fit to the details of these data. For more information on tests of the model in the probability learning situation, the reader is referred to papers by Estes (1964, 1972a) and Friedman, Podella, and Gelfand (1964).

Difficulties and Later Developments

Examination of such sequential statistics has uncovered several discrepancies from the predictions of the linear model. As one example, the model predicts that during a run of E_1 events the subject's probability of predicting E_1 should increase monotonically. But on the contrary, in early trials of an experiment the results often show the opposite pattern, with the subject becoming increasingly likely to predict E_2 the longer has been the current run of E_1 events (and vice versa for E_2 runs). It is as though the subject believed that the E_1 run made an E_2 event increasingly due to occur in order to even out the series' proportions. This odd belief is called the "negative recency effect" or the "gambler's fallacy," and it is indeed a firmly entrenched belief of most of us regarding real-world events.

A second set of discrepancies arises from the fact that subjects appear to be testing out "hypotheses" regarding the event series. That is, the typical subject has an implicit faith in the notion that the E_1/E_2 event series has a systematic though complex pattern; hence, he constructs, tries out, and evaluates a series of hypotheses regarding local trial-by-trial regularities in the event series. Examples of such hypotheses would be the belief that the events are scheduled for double alternation (as in 22112211), or that only runs of a length of two or four identical events are being used (as in 111122112222). In a truly random reinforcement schedule, these beliefs in local regularity amount to little more than elaborate superstitions, though, for all that, they are nonetheless persistent. In Chapter 13, we consider a computer simulation model by Feldman (1961) which is designed to deal with this hypothesis-testing approach to the probability learning situation.

Do these discrepancies mean that the SST account of probability learning is fundamentally incorrect, as N. H. Anderson (1964) has argued? Not necessarily. Rather, such results lead one to question the identification of the "stimulus elements" provided by the earlier linear model, and to search for a more plausible identification of the operative stimulus elements. Whereas the former linear model stemmed from the assumption that the stimulus elements were something like the "ready signal" initiating each trial, each element having equal sampling probability, perhaps it is more fruitful now to identify the stimulus elements with memories or traces of the past sequence of outcomes or responses (see Estes, 1972a). For each distinct sequence of prior outcomes (say, three trials back), we would identify in the mathematical model a corresponding "stimulus element." Perhaps it is more appropriate to call this composite memory trace a pattern. In any event, each such pattern is "sampled" as a single unit when its corresponding prior event sequence occurs. Needless to say, the "equal sampling probability" assumption is immediately abandoned when stimulus elements are identified with memories of the past few events.

There are certain advantages to this approach. First, it can be shown that with noncontingent random reinforcement, asymptotic probability matching will still be obtained. What differs are the predictions regarding sequential statistics and learning rate. The approach predicts a well-known fact, namely, that the average learning rate increases directly the nearer π is to 1 or 0. This fact is predicted now because the variability of the event sequence (i.e., the new "stimulus patterns") is related to the product $\pi (1 - \pi)$, which is smallest when π is near 1 or 0. Second, suppose that the stimulus elements correspond to runs of E_1s and runs of E_2s of varying lengths, and suppose that initially all these various stimulus elements are connected equally to A_1 and A_2 responses. Now, since long runs of E_1 or E_2 events are relatively rare in a random reinforcement schedule, stimulus patterns corresponding to these long runs are not sampled or conditioned as often in the experiment as are shorter run lengths. This state of affairs means that something like the negative recency effect will be predicted, at least early in the experiment before long runs of events have been encountered and conditioned in the expected way.

A third advantage of identifying the effective stimuli with patterns of past events is that it accounts for how subjects can learn systematic event sequences when these occur repeatedly in the series. People clearly can learn a double-alternation series like 11221122. This would be represented in the theory as the cyclic presentation of four stimulus patterns—those corresponding on the two preceding trials to events 1-1, events 1-2, events 2-2, and events 2-1. To these four stimuli, the correct reinforced responses are 2, 2, 1, and 1, respectively. Recently there have been many investigations of how subjects learn systematic binary sequences (see Myers, 1970; Vitz & Todd, 1967). The models used can be translated into the idiom of SST but with particular identifications of the operative stimulus patterns as event sequences. Restle (1970) and Simon (1972) have offered countervailing views and evidence to suggest that "hierarchic phrase-structures" are learned as higher-order descriptions of patterned sequences. A few of these notions will be reviewed in Chapter 13 when we discuss the work of Simon and Kotovsky (1963) concerning how people induce pattern descriptions from exposure to a rule-generated series.

Spontaneous Recovery and Forgetting

The phenomena of spontaneous recovery and forgetting have been recognized for a long time. Pavlov was the first to report facts regarding spontaneous recovery. Following experimental extinction of a conditioned response (CR), the CR showed some recovery if the dog was removed from the apparatus and allowed to rest in his home cage for a while before being returned to the experimental situation and tested. The CR had "spontaneously recovered" without any special reconditioning by the experimenter. Later studies have shown that the amount of recovery increases with the length of the rest interval between sessions. Pavlov and others have also performed experiments in which the CR is repeatedly extinguished over consecutive daily sessions. They report that the amount of recovery of the CR becomes progressively less as the extinction sessions proceed; eventually, the CR recovers not at all.

The salient facts about forgetting (spontaneous regression) are markedly similar to those that characterize spontaneous recovery (e.g., Ebbinghaus, 1885). The amount forgotten increases with the time that has elapsed since the end of practice, and the amount of session-to-session forgetting becomes progressively less as daily practice on a task continues. Apparently Estes (1955a) was the first to point out the apposition of spontaneous recovery and forgetting. Once it has been pointed out, the similarities of their functional laws are indeed apparent.

Estes (1955a) proposed to interpret these spontaneous changes in response probabilities as due, to some extent at least, to random changes in the stimulating environment from one experimental session to the next. In our previous discussion of stimulus sampling theory, it was assumed that the stimulus population was fixed and that random samples from this population were effective from trial to trial. Estes proposed to expand this representation by assuming that at any given time only a subset of the total stimulus population is available for sampling, the remainder not being available at this point in time. Over time, different stimulus elements become effective or available for sampling, whereas previously available elements may become temporarily unavailable. The type of factors Estes presumably has in mind can be illustrated by day-to-day fluctuations in the temperature and humidity of the experimental room, changes in the subject's internal milieu, in his postural sets or attitudes, in the sensitivity of various receptors, and the like. Such fluctuations in subtle stimuli are practically beyond control. There need be no commitment in the theory regarding the magnitude of these changes; the amount of such change is to be estimated by inference from the change in behavior.

It is clear that if such random stimulus fluctuations do occur, then they help account for spontaneous changes in response probabilities between experimental testing sessions. Regression would occur if available elements conditioned to the response are replaced during a rest interval by elements, previously unavailable, which have not been connected to the response. Spontaneous recovery will occur if those elements to which the CR has been extinguished (by the end of an extinction session) are replaced by elements previously conditioned to the CR. These two schemes are illustrated in Figure 12.2, where the "available" and "unavailable" sets of cues at the end of session n and beginning of session $n+1$ are shown.

To see some of the implications of this scheme, let us make the assumptions more explicit. The stimulus population is divided at any moment into a proportion J that are available for sampling and another proportion $1-J$ that are temporarily unavailable. The elements in these two sets are assumed to be interchanged randomly at some fixed rate. The probability of the CR is given by the proportion of conditioned elements at that moment in the set available for sampling. Suppose that our experimental procedures during some session have brought the proportion of conditioned elements in the available set to p_0; let p_0' denote the proportion of conditioned elements in the set of stimuli that were unavailable during this session. We now impose a rest interval and let the fluctuation process go on for some time t, at which time we test the subject again. Let p_t denote the probability of the response to the set of stimulus elements available at time t. The equation Estes derives for this situation is as follows:

$$p_t = p_0[J + (1-J)a^t] + p_0'(1-J)(1-a^t). \tag{10}$$

In this equation, J is the proportion of elements available from the total population, a is a fraction indexing the rate of interchange, and p_0 and p_0' are the proportions of conditioned available and unavailable elements at the beginning of the rest interval. We note that at time $t=0$, $p_t = p_0'$ since the a^t terms equal one when $t=0$. As time goes on and t becomes very large, a^t goes to zero and we will have $p_t = p_0 J + p_0'(1-J)$, which is the overall (population) proportion of conditioned elements. The effect of the fluctuation process is thus to modify the available set so that p_t changes over time from p_0 to the overall population mean. This diffusion causes a "homogenization" of effects of particular training, bringing the available and unavailable sets into equilibrium with respect to their proportions of conditioned elements. To give an analogy with diffusion, conditioning of the available set of elements is like introducing a concentrated dye into one of two solutions separated by a permeable membrane. With the passage of time, the

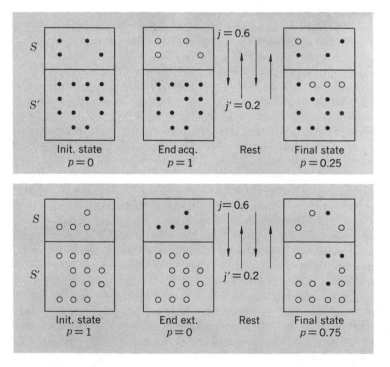

Figure 12.2.   Hypothetical picture of stimulus fluctuation producing forgetting (top panel) or spontaneous recovery (bottom panel). The sets of available (S) and unavailable (S') elements are divided graphically into two boxes. Stimulus elements are represented as dots. Open dots indicate elements conditioned to some reference CR; solid dots indicate elements connected to incompatible behaviors. (From W. K. Estes, Statistical theory of spontaneous recovery and regression. *Psychological Review*, 1955a, 62. Copyright 1955 by the American Psychological Association. Reprinted by permission.)

added dye is diffused throughout both compartments, reaching stable equilibrium when the dye is equally concentrated in both compartments.

The cases of interest to us fall out as special cases of equation (10). If $p_0 > p'_0$, then p_t decreases over time to a lower value and we call it forgetting; if $p_0 < p'_0$, then p_t increases over time to a higher value and we call it spontaneous recovery. Figure 12.3a shows some theoretical forgetting curves plotted from equation (10); Figure 12.3b shows some recovery curves. We can see from Figure 12.3a, for example, that the amount of forgetting decreases as we increase p'_0, the conditional strength of the elements unavailable during the previous session. These are the changes to be expected as the response is retrained over successive days. As the training sessions continue, it becomes more probable that every element in the population has been available at some time and been conditioned. Thus p'_0 increases over sessions and progressively less response decrement (forgetting) occurs between one session and the next. A similar interpretation applies to progressive decreases in spontaneous recovery of extinguished responses (Figure 12.3b) except that we interchange the role of conditioned and unconditioned stimulus elements.

We thus see that the fluctuation theory accounts for the usual shapes of forgetting and recovery curves, and for their progressive changes as retraining or extinction is continued. Estes (1955a, 1955b) uses the theory to interpret a number of other facts related to recovery and regression. In addition, Estes (1959a) has shown how the theory applies to experiments on forgetting involving retroactive and proactive interference (see Chapter 9). In terms of the model, the interference studies are not very different from the study of spontaneous recovery of a CR that has been conditioned and then extinguished (i.e., elements connected to a response differing from the first one learned). G. H. Bower (1967b) gives more explicit illustrations of how some findings of interference studies may be interpreted in these terms. The fluctuation theory has also been applied to experiments on verbal short-term memory (see Estes, 1971; G. H. Bower, 1972d; L. R. Peterson, 1963), in which single verbal items are forgotten over brief intervals of several seconds filled with rehearsal-preventing, interpolated activities. In this case it is supposed that the verbal item is associated to "background contextual stimuli," which are progressively altered during an interpolation interval before the retention test for the single item (see Falkenberg, 1972). The primary results in short-term memory studies seem interpretable in terms of this fluctuation theory. In summary, then, the concept of random stimulus fluctuation has been a very fruitful hypothesis, considering how many and diverse are the kinds of phenomena that it explains.

Other Response Measures

As we have seen, the sole dependent variable of SST is response probability. But experimenters frequently describe their subject's performance in terms of other measures such as response latency (or speed) response rate, or response amplitude. Much as Hull did with his $_sE_r$ construct, SST sets out to relate these other measures to its primary dependent variable, response probability. However, instead of simple postulating a particular relation

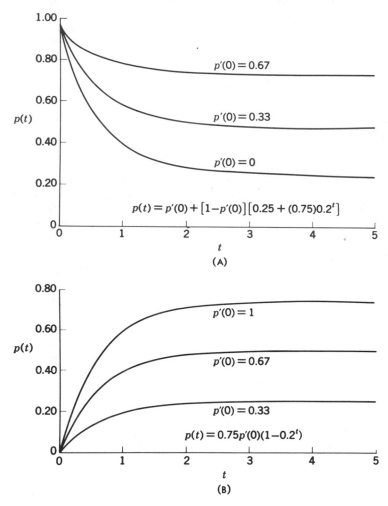

$$p(t) = p'(0) + [1-p'(0)][0.25 + (0.75)0.2^t]$$

(A)

$$p(t) = 0.75p'(0)(1-0.2^t)$$

(B)

Figure 12.3.   (a) Families of forgetting curves. The proportion of conditioned elements in the available set at the end of the learning session is unity; the parameter differentiating the curves is the proportion of conditioned elements in the unavailable set (p_0') at the end of the learning session.

(b) Families of spontaneous recovery curves. The proportion of conditioned elements in S at time 0 is zero; the parameter of the curves is p_0', the proportion of conditioned elements in S' at the end of the extinction session. (From W. K. Estes, Statistical theory of spontaneous recovery and regression. *Psychological Review*, 1955a, 62. Copyright 1955 by the American Psychological Association. Reprinted by permission.)

between response probability and these other measures, the strategy in this case has been to derive this relationship by an auxiliary model of the response-emission process. By this means, it is possible to detach the assumptions about response-emision from the remaining assumptions about learning and so test them separately. At present writing, the response models, while fairly good at the quasi-quantitative level, run into some difficulties at the specific-quantitative level of analysis.

Let us consider a very simple probability model for response latency. At the start of a trial, we present a signal, start a clock, and record the time elapsed before the subject performs some designated act. To be specific, suppose the act in question is getting a rat to run several steps down a straight alley (which has a food reward at the end) and interrupt a light beam outside the starting compartment. The latency measure is the time from the opening of the starting gate until the rat interrupts the light beam a few inches beyond the start-box. An elementary model of this process supposes that in each small unit of time (of length h seconds), the animal either performs the necessary act or does something else. We let p denote the probability that he performs the act in the next small unit of time if he has not already done so. The latency is then just the number of timed units of length h that pass before the act is performed. The probability that the latency is exactly $k \cdot h$ seconds is the likelihood that the subject lets $k-1$ intervals go by and then responds in the kth interval. The probability of this sequence of $k-1$ failures and then a success is

$$P(L=k \cdot h)=p(1-p)^{k-1} \text{ for } k=1, 2, 3, \ldots.$$

That is, with probability p, he responds in the first interval; with probability $(1-p)p$, he fails to respond in the first interval but responds in the second, and so forth. On the average, the response will occur in $1/p$ intervals, and so the average latency will be h/p.

This simple response model thus leads to a reciprocal relationship between average latency and response probability; as probability increases, latency decreases. In a learning experiment where we expect p_n to be changing over trials according to the learning function in equation (3), the average latency L_n will decline over trials. The equation would be:

$$L_n = \frac{h}{p_n} = \frac{h}{1-(1-p_1)(1-\theta)^{n-1}}.$$

The two right-hand panels of Figure 12.4 show two empirical curves that were fitted by choosing the parameters h, p, and θ in this function. The bottom right curve is the average starting latency over trials of a group of rats learning to run down a runway for food reward. The top right is the average duration that rats held down a lever in a Skinner box when reward depended on pressing, then releasing, the lever.

The top left panel of Figure 12.4 gives the average rate of lever-pressing (in responses per minute) of the same group of rats working for consistent reward in a free-operant Skinner box. To interpret the free-operant situation

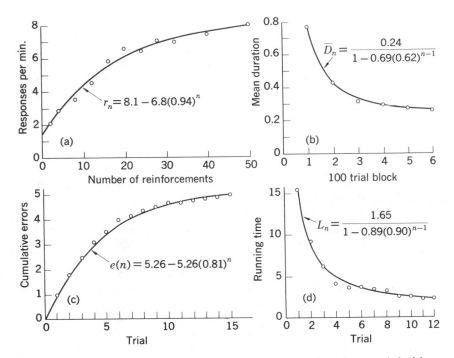

Figure 12.4. Four kinds of simple acquisition functions derived from statistical learning theory. Curves A, B, C, and D, respectively, represent rate of bar-pressing versus number of reinforcements, mean bar-press duration per 100-trial block, mean cumulative errors versus trials in T-maze learning, and median running time versus trials in a runway experiment. (From Estes, 1959a. By permission.)

in terms of the response-emission model, assume that each response resets the clock to zero and that h/p is the average time until the next response. If the average time between responses is h/p, then the average *rate* of responding is the reciprocal, namely, p/h. Given the theoretical equation for p_n as a function of the number of reinforcements n, the curve in the upper left panel may be fitted to the data. In that equation, 8.1 is the estimate of $1/h$, so $h = 0.123$ minute or 7.38 seconds.

We thus have seen how a probability theory can make contact with other measures of learned performance. Response amplitude has not been specifically considered in the literature of SST, although a model making amplitude proportional to p_n is easy to devise. In this case, learning curves of CR amplitude would be expected to look like the response rate curve in the upper left panel of Figure 12.4. In another vein, G. H. Bower (1959, 1962a) has developed probability models to describe vicarious trial-and-error (VTE) behavior of subjects just before they make a choice. The role of this behavior in guiding the eventual choice was emphasized by Tolman (see Chapter 5).

Although the simple latency or rate models introduced above appear adequate for fitting mean response curves in simple acquisition, they are easily shown to be inadequate at a more detailed level of quantitative testing. For example, the elementary model implies that when p_n reaches unity, all responses occur in exactly time h, which is absurd. Moreover, the relative frequency histogram of observed latencies seldom has the shape implied by the simple model. Discussions by Bush and Mosteller (1955) and McGill (1963) show some of the detailed issues involved in predicting exact latency distributions. A fair amount of work in mathematical psychology is centered on the problem of predicting reaction-time distributions across a number of experimental conditions. A paper by M. F. Norman (1964) applies the linear learning model to interresponse times (in the free operant situation) with the added assumption that the subject is learning which interresponse times will produce reward. This model is related to Logan's "micromolar" approach discussed in Chapter 6. Shimp (1969) has provided a more tractable model for interresponse time selection and fitted it to a wide range of data from performances of pigeons on various reinforcement schedules as well as their preferential choices between two concurrently operating schedules.

In the examples of verbal learning treated so far, the retention measure under discussion has been "response recall," and SST treats this case directly. However, an alternative retention measure is *recognition memory*: following exposure to a series of verbal items (e.g., words or nonsense syllables), the subject might be shown a long list of items, some old and some new, and be asked to check off the items he recognizes as having been presented in the study list. Memory is shown by the subject's ability to discriminate between old study items and new distractor items. One way to interpret recognition memory for single items within SST (see G. H. Bower, 1972d) is to suppose that presentation of a stimulus item causes a sample of its encodings to become associated with concurrent contextual events (e.g., thoughts). When the item is represented later on the retention test, the new encodings of the item at that time may reinstate to a greater or lesser degree the context in which that item was experienced earlier, leading to a recognition judgment of greater or lesser confidence. Bower shows how this idea, coupled with the fluctuation theory of forgetting, accounts for some of the standard findings on recognition memory, so-called memory operating characteristics, recency of experience judgments, list discrimination, and frequency of experience judgments. It would take us too far from our immediate concerns to discuss these matters in detail here.

Stimulus Generalization, Discrimination, and Motivation

No account of a learning theory is complete without at least brief mention of how it handles the issues of stimulus generalization, discrimination, and motivation. Although there is an extensive literature on these topics in SST, we will merely indicate the outlines of the approach here.

SST conceives of stimulus generalization along the lines of the "identical elements" theory of Thorndike (see Chapter 2). A response associated to stimulus population S_1 will generalize to a test stimulus S_2 to the extent that the S_2 population shares common stimulus elements with the S_1 population. The situation for two stimuli is illustrated abstractly in terms of Venn diagrams in Figure 12.5, where solid dots represent stimulus elements associated to some reference CR whereas open dots represent unconnected elements.

The sets labeled S_1 and S_2 contain totals of 20 and 16 elements, respectively, and they share a set of 8 common elements (in the intersection subset marked I in Figure 12.5). The figure shows the state of the system following training on S_1 which has brought the performance of the CR to 75 percent. Assuming homogeneous mixing of the elements in the unique and intersection subsets of S_1, this means that about $8(.75) = 6$ elements of the intersection set I will be associated to the CR. When we then test for generalization at S_2, the probability of the CR will be the proportion of conditioned elements (solid dots) in the entire S_2 set, which would be $6/(8+8) = .375$ in this example. Clearly the proportion of generalized CRs depends on the product of two factors: (1) the level of conditioning of the CR to the training stimulus, which level will be denoted as p_1, and (2) the proportion of the S_2 (test) population of stimulus elements which it shares with S_1, which will be denoted here as $s_{1,2}$ (s for *similarity* of S_2 to S_1). For the illustration above, $p_1 = .75$, $s_{1,2} = .50$, and so the CR probability to the generalized stimulus is $p_2 = p_1 s_{1,2} = (.75)(.50) = .375$, as illustrated numerically above. The similarity coefficients vary from zero (disjoint sets) to unity (complete overlap). But these coefficients are never observed directly; rather, they must be estimated from the ratio of the observed proportions p_2 and p_1, or by the ratio of *rates* of responding (see the earlier discussion relating free-operant rates to response probabilities). But once the $s_{1,2}$ coefficient is estimated, it may be used to predict generalized responding for any conditioning level, p_1, and be based on any kind of conditioned response. Or so the theory says.

This same set-theoretical analysis of the stimulus is used even when SST is dealing with simple "one-dimensional" stimuli like the loudness or pitch of a pure tone, the spatial position of a dot on a line, or any of hundreds of other quantitative as well as qualitative dimensions (see Atkinson & Estes, 1963; LaBerge, 1961; Carterette, 1961).

In *discrimination learning* of the simple variety, presentations of S_1 and S_2 occur in random alternation with, say, response A_1 reinforced to S_1 but either with A_1 not reinforced to S_2 or some other response A_2 reinforced to S_2. Assuming the usual laws of conditioning and extinction, inspection of Figure 12.5 suggests that the unique or distinctive elements of S_1 and S_2 will become readily associated to A_1 and to A_2, respectively. But problems arise with respect to the common elements in the intersection set, I. These com-

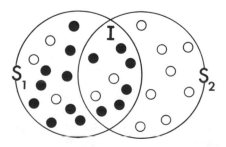

Figure 12.5.   Illustration of two overlapping sets of stimulus elements. Solid dots represent elements associated to some reference CR. The index of stimulus generalization is provided by the proportion of elements that a given set shares with another.

mon elements causing stimulus generalization also are responsible for failures to discriminate, making responding to S_1 a weighted mixture of the correctly conditioned unique elements and the "confusedly conditioned" intersection elements. In order to attain perfect performance in such a model, either the confusing common elements must be rendered nonfunctional (habituated or adapted out) by selective attention or else entire stimulus samples consisting of some unique and some common elements must be perceived as Gestalt patterns that are conditioned as configured units to responses reinforced in their presence. The former approach, dealing with selective attention to relevant cues, is exemplified in models proposed by Restle (1955), Lovejoy (1968), Sutherland and Mackintosh (1971), and Zeaman and House (1963). Selective attention to relevant cues is also the dominant theme in "hypothesis-testing" models of discrimination learning such as Restle (1962), M. Levine (1970), and Trabasso and Bower (1968). These will be discussed later in this chapter. The latter approach, which supposes that conditioning to Gestalt patterns preempts and has priority over the conditioning of individual elements, has been adopted in the so-called mixed model of SST (see Atkinson & Estes, 1963; Friedman, Trabasso, & Mosberg, 1967). Of these two approaches, the one based on selective attention concepts seems by far the more vigorous and viable avenue of attack on discrimination learning.

Finally, to round out this section, brief mention should be made of the conceptualization of motivation in SST. In an early, important statement, Estes (1958) attempted to handle the effect of drive level upon performance by assuming that deprivation operations (e.g., withholding water) cause certain intraorganismic sources of stimulation to become active (e.g., a dry mouth, stomach pangs), and the relative weight of these drive-stimuli in the total cue complex was assumed to increase with the time span of deprivation. By supposing that these internal drive-stimuli could themselves become associated to instrumental responses, Estes was able to account for many of the well-known facts relating motivation to performance. Also, the drive-stimulus approach has a natural way to handle findings regarding "drive discrimination" in which an animal learns to respond discriminately depending on the type or intensity of drive level he is currently experiencing. The illustrations above have been of "internal" drives such as hunger and thirst, involving deprivation of food or water. But it is clear that the theory applies just as well, if not better, to externally induced "drives" from noxious stimulation such as electric shock, loud noises, bright lights, temperature extremes, and the like. These are clearly instances in which the drive-inducing operation consists of increasing the intensity of a source of stimulation, which would be connected to some instrumental response. Estes's approach was to interpret the internal drives from deprivation in a fashion analogous to our intuitive interpretation of such external drives.

Responding to various deficiencies in this early formulation, Estes (1969b) has more recently proposed a second hypothesis regarding the role of internal drives in performance, and this was discussed earlier in Chapter 4. It is supposed that response evocation depends *jointly* upon input from discriminative stimuli and input ("facilitatory feedback") from a positive drive. Initially, the drive mechanism is activated only by a combination of internal conditions resulting from deprivation and an external unconditioned stimulus (e.g., taste of food). For example, the taste of food activates the drive mechanism (see panel [a] of Figure 12.6) which generates feedback elements that facilitate and maintain the consummatory behavior until the internal deprivation conditions have been materially altered. It is supposed that activation of this drive mechanism can be conditioned in the usual manner to external stimuli preceding the unconditioned response (which innately activates the drive mechanism). Thus, in the learning of instrumental appetitive responses, the discriminative stimulus (S^D in panel [b] of Figure 12.6) becomes associated not only to the reinforced response but also to activation of the positive drive mechanism. This provides facilitatory input (symbolized as + + in panel [b]), which summates with the association of the stimulus elements to the instrumental response, thus evoking the response. Due to the reinforcement contingencies, this response produces the reinforcer (say, food), which elicits consummatory behavior, which in turn activates the positive drive mechanism again, which further conditions this drive activation to the external stimuli of the reinforcing environment. Estes (1969b) makes further assumptions regarding noxious stimuli and their negative drive mechanisms, and how these determine escape and avoidance learning. It is assumed further that the negative and positive drive mechanisms exert mutually inhibitory influences on one another. In this way, Estes explains the phenomenon of "conditioned suppression" (see Chapter 7) wherein a stimulus that evokes fear (due to its past association with pain) will suppress responding for appetitive rewards.

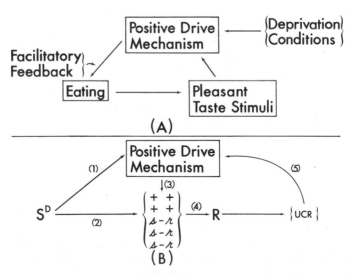

Figure 12.6.   Illustration of facilitatory feedback from positive drive amplifier elements. Panel (a) shows how internal deprivation conditions and unconditioned taste stimuli combine jointly to activate the positive drive mechanism, which provides feedback to maintain eating. Panel (b) illustrates the situation in instrumental conditioning after the discriminative stimulus has become associated both to responses and to activation of the positive drive mechanism.

As noted in Chapter 4, this theory of drive, its conditioning and its joint facilitation of S-R associations in generating performance, is remarkably like the Hullian theory of *incentive motivation,* in which anticipation of reward (by means of r_g) to discriminative stimuli is presumed to generate "excitement" which feeds in to facilitate or invigorate ongoing instrumental responses. What the Estes theory does (as did Sheffield's [1954], before that) is to eliminate the separate status of the drive (D) and incentive motivation (K) constructs in Hull's theory. Also, the assumption of reciprocal inhibition between positive and negative drive centers carries matters a step further.

The Scanning Model for Decision-Making

Hitherto we have been describing the subject as though his responses were simply a matter of stimulus-response connections. In many cases, this seems to be a serviceable approach to analyzing behavior. However, there are clearly other instances in which circumstances conspire to induce the subject to make a more deliberative choice. Such circumstances are typically arranged in studies of *decision-making,* and they are easily mimicked in the learning laboratory in studies of preferential choice. In the typical preferential choice experiment, the subject may be repeatedly offered a choice between two alternatives, A_1 and A_2 (or, more typically, a set of different pairs), each associated with a different rewarding outcome or set of outcomes. The subject's asymptotic choices reflect his particular "preference ordering" among the two or more rewards being compared.

As indicated in Chapter 2, Estes's approach to this situation treats the rewarding outcomes as informational stimuli, the representations of which can become associated with prior stimuli or responses that are temporally correlated with these reward magnitudes. For example, in a verbal discrimination task in which choice of nonsense syllable A_1 is followed by receipt of 5 points whereas choice of syllable A_2 (with which A_1 is compared) is followed by receipt of 3 points, the theory supposes that the person learns the response-to-payoff associations A_1-5 and A_2-3. This learning could be indexed by the person's ability to verbally predict or anticipate the points or value of each alternative response.

Given this knowledge of the payoffs, the subject is presumed to decide between A_1 and A_2 in three substages within a deliberative choice trial: first, he *scans* over the available responses A_1 and A_2, considering each in turn, and for each response he generates a prediction of the rewarding outcome ("points") to be obtained were that response to be chosen on this trial, and then he temporarily stores this predicted outcome; second, he *compares* the value or utility of the outcomes so predicted by the scanning process; and third, he *chooses* that response with the highest predicted value. These sets of assumptions are the core of what Estes (1962) calls the "scanning model." Thus, in the choice comparing A_1-5 points with A_2-3 points, the subject will eventually always choose the A_1 side once he has acquired the response-reward associations. The only cases where perfect preference will fail to be achieved are those in which the sensory *discrimination* between the rewarding outcomes is imperfect (e.g., a rat probably cannot reliably discriminate 5.02 grams of wet mash from 5.05 grams) or in which the outcomes themselves are complex "commodity bundles" or composite packages of many subcomponents about which evaluations fluctuate. Humans, of course, increase the discriminability of different quantities of reward by counting (e.g., counting pennies of a payoff), which is one illustration of a purely cue-producing response.

Consider the case in which the outcomes following each choice are probabilistic. To be concrete, let us suppose that the person is confronted with the choice situation diagramed in Figure 12.7. Choice of alternative A_1 is followed by a win of $w\cent$ on a random proportion π_1 of the trials, whereas it is followed by loss of $x\cent$ on the remaining $1-\pi_1$ proportion of the trials. Similarly, choice of A_2 wins $y\cent$ with probability π_2 and loses $z\cent$ with probability $1-\pi_2$. If the subject begins from total ignorance, then we may presume that through repeated experiences he gradually learns the outcomes which can follow each response and he also learns the probabilities π_1 and π_2. That is, this situation really has two smaller "probability learning" tasks contained within it, namely, learning the different outcome probabilities following A_1 choices, and, independently, learning the outcome probabilities following A_2 choices. We may suppose that both of these component learning processes are described by something like the linear model or the small-element pattern models to be given later.

Given this learning background, how ought the subject to choose? The scanning model attempts to predict this asymptotic choice probability from knowledge simply of the objective probabilities π_1 and π_2, and the payoffs w, x, y, z, all of which are under the experimenter's control. Let us consider a few special cases of how the scanning model operates. First of all, if every outcome that follows A_1 is favored over every outcome that follows A_2, then A_1 will obviously be the asymptotically dominant choice. Second, consider the symmetric case in which the wins and losses for the two alternatives are equal (i.e., $w=y$ and $x=z$) and their payoff probabilities differ. Asymptotically, the events within each choice trial go as follows: the subject generates a predicted win or loss for A_1 and similarly for A_2. This produces the four possible prediction pairs shown in Table 12.4. In the row of each prediction pair is also written the expected probability of that pair (based on the assumption of asymptotic probability matching of the two components), and

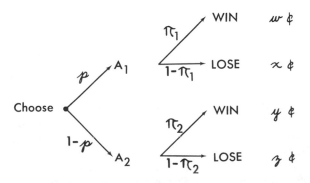

Figure 12.7.   Illustration of a choice situation with probabilistic payoffs and penalties.

Table 12.4 Possible prediction pairs for winning w¢ or losing x¢, their joint probabilities asymptotically, and the decision in the four cases.

Expected Outcome for		Probability of This Prediction Pair		Decision
A_1	A_2			
Win w	Win w	π_1	π_2	(Rescan)
Win w	Lose x	π_1	$(1-\pi_2)$	A_1
Lose x	Win w	$(1-\pi_1)$	π_2	A_2
Lose x	Lose x	$(1-\pi_1)$	$(1-\pi_2)$	(Rescan)

the indicated decision given that predicted pair of outcomes for this trial. The decision rule is to choose the unique winner if there is one; if a tie occurs, the person should rescan his memory, making a new independent pair of predictions for the two outcomes, and continue this until he generates a unique winner. This amounts to supposing that the subject continues scanning until he lands eventually in row 2 or row 3 of Table 12.4. Therefore, the expected asymptotic probability that he will choose A_1 will just be the likelihood of the row 2 prediction pair divided by the sum of the row 2 and row 3 probabilities, viz.,

$$P(A_1) = \frac{\pi_1(1-\pi_1)}{\pi_1(1-\pi_1)+\pi_2(1-\pi_1)}. \qquad (11)$$

Table 12.5 shows some predictions compared to proportions of A_1 responses observed in experiments by Atkinson (1962), by Siegel (1961), and by Friedman, Padilla, and Gelfand (1964). In each experiment subjects received 200 to 400 trials on a two-choice probability learning task, with a 5¢ payoff for each correct prediction and a 5¢ penalty (loss) for each incorrect predic-

Table 12.5 Asymptotic probabilities of A_1 responses, observed and predicted, in twelve conditions studied by Atkinson, by Siegel, and by Friedman, Padilla, and Gelfand (1964).

Exp.	Group	π_1	π_2	$P(A_1)$ Observed	Predicted
Atkinson	1	.60	.50	.60	.60
	2	.70	.50	.69	.70
	3	.80	.50	.83	.80
Siegel	1	.75	.25	.93	.90
	2	.70	.30	.85	.85
	3	.65	.35	.75	.77
Friedman, Padilla, and Gelfand	1	.80	.80	.47	.50
	2	.80	.50	.81	.80
	3	.80	.20	.94	.94
	4	.50	.50	.48	.50
	5	.50	.20	.82	.80
	6	.20	.20	.47	.50

tion (Friedman, Padilla, & Gelfand used only "points"). Different groups in each experiment corresponded to different values of π_1 and π_2 as shown in Table 12.5. The predictions are obtained *a priori* by simply substituting the values of π_1 and π_2 into equation (11). Note that the asymptotic response probabilities in the Siegel experiment (as in groups 3 and 5 in Friedman, Padilla, & Gelfand) exceed probability matching, which is a frequent finding when symmetric payoffs are used. The fit of the model's predictions are quite good in all cases.

The cases reviewed suggest the usefulness of the scanning model in predicting asymptotic choice probabilities in uniform ("riskless") situations as well as in probabilistic schedules with symmetric payoffs and losses. It has had a somewhat spottier record in predicting asymptotes when the payoffs are *asymmetric*, that is, when there is inequality of the amounts won and/or the amounts lost for the two response alternatives. In such cases, the payoff scanning model sometimes predicts the observed asymptotes successfully and sometimes not. Attempts to repair the discrepancies (unpublished work by Estes and Bower) either have concentrated on rescaling the values that are being scanned and compared (e.g., use the scale of *regret* rather than simple payoffs) or have tried reformulating the "memory process" by which the person remembers and compares the outcomes from past trials. An example of this latter approach would have the person, before choosing, recall k prior outcomes for each alternative, and assign to that alternative the sum (or average) of the values of the outcomes so recalled for it. Then the usual comparison process would intervene to select a unique winner, if any, as the choice. For $k = 1$, this is the scanning model as presented earlier. The discrepant results with asymmetric payoffs seem to be fit by assuming $k = 2$. However, these are tentative suggestions requiring further elaboration and testing.

In any event, we may conclude that the scanning model provides a viable approach to a process theory of decision-making. It has been used successfully for predicting individual behavior of animals and men in situations ranging from paired-associates to probability learning. It has been applied with success to two-person games in which payoffs depend on the joint actions of the two players (see Estes, 1962). It has been shown to follow logically from an earlier model for VTE behavior of a subject at a choice point (see G. H. Bower, 1959; Audley, 1960). All in all, the basic notions contained in the scanning model have proved to be exceedingly simple, elegant, and powerful in bringing orderliness into a range of data regarding choice behavior.

MARKOV MODELS

As we have seen, the earlier versions of SST represented the experimental situation as a very large set of N stimulus elements, only a sample of which affect the subject on any one trial. With a large population of stimulus elements, the assumption of all-or-none conditioning of the sampled elements leads to gradual change in the proportion of the population elements connected to the response. With N elements, the possible values of the A_1-response probability are $0, 1/N, 2/N, \ldots, (N-1)/N$, and 1. As the result of the reinforcing event on a trial, the response probability may change from one of these values to another. If N is large, then there are so many possible values of response probability that the "discreteness" of these changes cannot be detected by data analysis. In this case, one might as well represent learning as a change in a continuous variable p_n which can take on any possible value. This indeed is what is assumed once the linear model is used, and is the approach exemplified in Bush and Mosteller's work (1955).

Starting roughly in 1960 and continuing thereafter, a major trend in mathematical learning theory has been one of increasing disenchantment with the continuous linear model (including its several variants) and an increasing pursuit of alternative models. This disenchantment, which is not yet final, has come about for three reasons: first, because nearly all substantive hypotheses can be stated equivalently in terms of either "large N" or "small N" models indifferently; second, because the small-element models are mathematically more tractable; and third, because of frequent failures of the simple linear model to deliver accurate numerical predictions in various experiments. And one aim during these years has been to develop limited-scope models that operate accurately at the specific-quantitative level for particular classes of experiments. As one result of this emphasis, the literature contains many instances in which a specific model fits a wealth of descriptive statistics of a single experiment with dumbfounding accuracy. These instances of very accurate fit of a model's predictions to data have had the effect of raising the general standards for assessing whether the fit of a model's predictions is good or bad. An unfortunate side effect has been that a particular model is rather soon outdone by some alternative model, one perhaps contrived on the spot. This can lead to a proliferation of different models that are inadequately followed up with suitable experimental tests. And this proliferation may occur despite the fact that, in a rough sense, the fit of the first model to the data was really not all that bad.

The current trend toward Markov models as alternatives to the continuous models probably got its initial impetus from another classic paper by Estes (1959b).[2] This paper was soon followed by the related work of Suppes and Atkinson (1960). Estes showed essentially that learning models of a different type follow from SST if one supposes that the number of stimulus elements, N, is small, say, one to three or so. When the number of elements is small, then the discreteness of the changes in response probability ought to be detectable by suitably sensitive data analyses. Moreover, it was found that many of the detailed predictions of data (e.g., sequential statistics) depended in a dramatic way on the assumed number of stimulus elements. The main reason for the work on small-element models was the fact that such finer analyses of data yielded many instances in which the Markov models were clearly correct.

The N-Element Pattern Model

To exemplify the general approach, we discuss the axioms of the pattern model developed by Estes (1959b). The stimulus situation is represented by N patterns (functioning like the previous elements) exactly *one* of which is sampled randomly on each trial. The pattern is thought of as the total configuration of stimulation effective on a trial; different patterns may share

---

[2] The new directions were set off by the experiments of Rock (1957), which gave support to one-trial verbal learning.

some common components, but this fact is ignored in the simple version of the model. With probability c the sampled pattern becomes conditioned to the reinforced response in an all-or-none manner; with probability $1 - c$ reinforcement is ineffective and the pattern remains connected as it was before. In a two-response situation, the state of this system is indexed by the number of patterns connected to A_1 instead of A_2. The state can change by $+1$ or -1, or possibly remain the same from one trial to the next.

This system is best represented as a *Markov chain*, a class of probability processes that have been well analyzed by mathematicians. To characterize such processes briefly, let us suppose that we observe a random process at spaced time intervals (trials) and that it occupies one of several different "states" at each trial. Then the process is a Markov chain if the state it occupies on the current trial depends only upon its state on the previous trial and is independent of the history of the process before it arrived at that state on the previous trial. A chain is characterized by its transition probabilities, which are the probabilities that the process will go from any given state to any other state on the next trial. It is a simple matter to derive these transition probabilities for the pattern model discussed above, where the possible transitions from state k (i.e., number of A_1 elements) are to $k+1$, or to $k-1$, or to remain at k from one trial to the next. A one-trial transition from state k to state $k+1$ will occur if an A_2-conditioned pattern is sampled, an E_1 reinforcing event occurs, and the reinforcement is effective upon this occasion in conditioning response A_1 to the sampled pattern. This chain of events has probability $P(E_1) \cdot c \cdot (N-k)/N$. The other transition probabilities are similarly derived from the theory. This pattern model has been extensively tested in probability learning as well as other kinds of experiments. In the standard probability learning task, the linear model and the N-element pattern model (with equiprobable sampling of elements) predict the same sequential statistics and differ only in variance predictions. A special schedule called "noncontingent success" (i.e., either response is called correct) creates a distinction between the predictions of the two models (see Yellott, 1969), and in such experiments the N-element pattern model fares better. However, as we observed earlier, the equiprobable sampling assumption probably should be abandoned in favor of the idea that the stimulus patterns are comprised of traces from the past several outcomes. Such identification, of course, binds the stimulus pattern sampled on trial n to the outcomes occurring on trials $n-1$, $n-2$, etc.

A noteworthy general fact about the pattern models is that they imply an average learning curve that is identical with that of the linear model. For example, the equation for p_n following a consistent series of E_1 reinforcements is

$$p_n = 1 - (1-p_1)(1-c/N)^{n-1}. \tag{12}$$

If we interchange θ and c/N, we obtain equation (4) of the linear model. The parameters θ and c/N mean roughly the same thing: both are the probability that any particular stimulus element (or pattern) will be sampled and effectively conditioned on a given trial.

The identicalness of the linear and Markov models in this respect is surprising. Imagine that $N=2$ and that $p_1 = 0$. Then the pattern model says that there are only three possible values of A_1-response probability, namely, 0, 1/2, or 1. The subject starts in state 0 (has $p=0$), moves on some later trial into state 1 (has $p=1/2$), and moves on some still later trial into state 2 (has $p=1$). How fast he traverses the states depends on c, the effectiveness of reinforcement. The "waiting time" in each state before the transition is exponentially distributed, somewhat like the model given earlier for response latencies. A schematic representation of the "learning curve" for an individual subject is shown in Figure 12.8. For the one-element model ($N=1$), the individual "curve" is a step function, the step occurring on that random trial at which conditioning is finally effective. For the two-element model, the function consists of two discrete steps, from 0 to 1/2 and from 1/2 to 1. Despite these discrete steps in the individual curves, when we average together many subjects having their steps at different trials, we get an average or mean p_n curve that is smooth and described by equation (12). However, if the appropriate analyses were done on individual data, we should be able to detect the discrete steps in the individual curves. For example, if the one-step function were appropriate, then we should find no improvement in performance prior to the trial of the last error. If the two-step function were appropriate, then we should find no improvement in performance over trials between the first correct response (state 0 has been left) and the trial of the last error (state 2 has not yet been entered). Suppes and Ginsberg (1963) and G. H. Bower and Theios (1964) provide the rationale for these analyses and illustrate them with several sets of data that show such step functions.

One-Element Model

To show the range of successful predictions that are possible with a simple model, let us apply the one-element model to an unpublished experiment by G. H. Bower on an elementary paired-associates learning task. Thirty college students learned a list of 20 pairs in which the stimulus member of the pair was a Greek letter and the response was the digit 1 or 2. Response 1 was assigned to 10 of the 20 stimuli selected at random. The 20-item list was gone through in random order until each subject gave three consecutive perfect recitations of the whole list of associates.

To represent this task in the model, we consider the stimulus member of

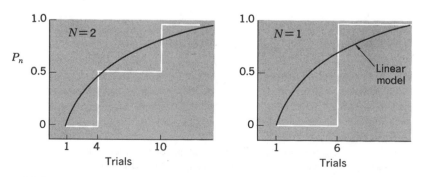

Figure 12.8. Examples of individual learning functions for the two-element and one-element models. The smooth curve is the learning function for the linear model.

each pair as a single pattern that is always sampled when that stimulus is presented. The pattern is considered to be in one of two states: either connected to the correct response, or, prior to that, in a guessing state wherein the probability of a correct response is $p = 0.50$. On each trial, following the subject's response the experimenter shows the correct response. We assume that with probability c this reinforcement is effective in conditioning the correct response to the stimulus pattern if it is not already so conditioned; with probability $1 - c$ the reinforcement is ineffective and the state of the stimulus pattern remains as it was at the start of the trial. Items begin in the guessing state on trial 1 and stay there until their reinforcement is effective; once that happens, they remain conditioned so that the subject will respond correctly thereafter.

This model is to be applied to the trial-by-trial sequence of correct responses and errors that a subject gives to a particular stimulus item. With 30 subjects each learning 20 items, there are 600 such "subject-item" sequences of data. In principle, the theory could be applied by estimating a value of c for each of these 600 sequences. However, to reduce computational labor, we will assume that all sequences reflect the same value of c. Proceeding on this assumption, it is found that a good estimate of c is 0.20. This means that, on the average, $1/c = 5.00$ reinforcements were required before an item was learned.

The observed and predicted results will be compared by means of two graphs and two tables of statistics. First, Figure 12.9 shows the mean proportion of correct responses over successive practice trials. The initial trial is a "pure guess" and the success rate starts at the *a priori* value of $1/2$ or 0.5. The theoretical curve fitted to the data in Figure 12.9 is equation (12), where $N = 1$, $p_1 = 0.50$, and $c = 0.20$. Figure 12.10 is a histogram of the relative fre-

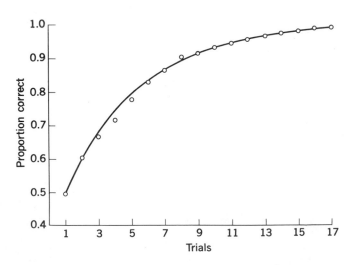

Figure 12.9.   Observed and predicted mean proportions of correct responses over trials. Predictions derived from the one-element model. (Data from G. H. Bower, unpublished.)

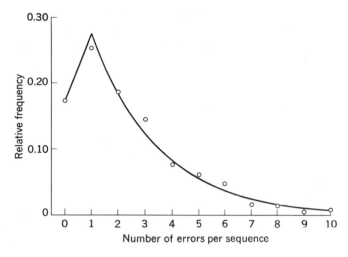

Figure 12.10. Probability distribution of the number of errors per subject-item sequence before learning. (Data from G. H. Bower, unpublished.)

quency of the total errors per subject-item sequence before learning. It shows, for example, that 17.3 percent (104 cases) of the sequences had zero errors, 25.0 percent (150 cases) had exactly one error, 18.2 percent (109 cases) had exactly two errors, and so on. Following the initial increase between zero and one errors, the predicted distribution follows an exponential decline for the proportions of sequences having more and more errors. Table 12.6 gives a different statistic, namely, the proportions of sequences that have no errors following their kth success, for k running from zero through eight. This proportion rises with k because the initial successes are likely to be guesses (followed by errors), whereas later successes are likely to be due to prior conditioning with the result that no errors will follow in the sequence. Finally, Table 12.7 gives a summary of various point predictions of the model. The last ten entries refer to sequential statistics. To explain two examples, a run of exactly two errors is counted once whenever a trial

Table 12.6   Proportion of sequences having no errors over those trials following their kth success for k = 0, 1, 2, . . . , 8.

k	*Observed*	*Predicted*
0	0.17	0.17
1	0.43	0.44
2	0.62	0.63
3	0.76	0.75
4	0.83	0.83
5	0.90	0.89
6	0.93	0.93
7	0.95	0.95
8	0.97	0.97

Table 12.7   Mean values of various statistics for the paired-associate experiment. The standard deviations refer to the statistic listed on the line above. Statistics calculated as mean per subject-item sequence.

Statistic	Observed	Predicted
Total errors	2.50	2.50
Standard deviation	2.34	2.50
Trial of first correct	1.92	1.84
Standard deviation	1.20	1.12
Trial of last error	4.18	4.17
Standard deviation	4.06	4.50
Prob. of error after an error	0.42	0.40
Total runs of errors	1.44	1.47
Runs of one error	0.85	0.87
Runs of two errors	0.33	0.35
Runs of three errors	0.13	0.15
Runs of four errors	0.08	0.06
No. pairs of errors:		
one trial apart	1.06	1.03
two trials apart	0.85	0.82
three trials apart	0.65	0.65
four trials apart	0.51	0.51

sequence of the form "...CEEC..." is encountered in a subject-item protocol. A pair of errors three trials apart (i.e., on trials n and $n+3$) is counted once whenever a trial sequence of the form "...EXXE..." occurs where the Xs may be correct or error responses.

The derivation of the theoretical predictions for such statistics is simple but lengthy and would serve no useful purpose here (see Atkinson, Bower, & Crothers, 1965; or G. H. Bower, 1961a). Though a variety of other statistics of the data could be calculated and predicted, the sample provided is sufficient to illustrate the accuracy of the model in this instance. Comparison of the observed and predicted values reveals that the model is astonishingly accurate. In fact, the fit of the theory in this case is probably as close as psychologists can ever expect to get in studies of learning. This is the more impressive because only one parameter c had to be estimated from the data before the predictions could start.

The close degree of correspondence between the obtained data and the predictions of a specific model as we have illustrated it above has come to be considered the attainable standard of success that we can hope for from an adequate model. Similar accurate fits of the one-element model to paired-associates data have been reported in several publications (e.g., Kintsch, 1964; L. Keller et al., 1965; Suppes & Ginsberg, 1962; G. H. Bower, 1961a, 1962b). In addition, analyses of response times in several experiments have shown results in line with this model; that is, (a) no differences in speeds of correct and incorrect responses, and relative constancy of these, over trials prior to the last error on an item, and (b) abrupt increases in speed of the correct response after the trial of the last error. These results are consonant with the assumption of a guessing state before conditioning occurs on or soon after the trial of the last error in a subject-item sequence.

In related work, Restle (1962) and G. H. Bower and Trabasso (1964) have used a slightly modified version of the model to account for an elementary form of learning to identify concepts in a discrimination task. In that work, the subject was assumed to be testing out various hypotheses regarding the solution to the problem (see the discussion in Chapter 5, p. 141). The "guessing" state corresponds to the subject's testing out irrelevant (incorrect) hypotheses, and the "conditioned" state corresponds to the subject's using the correct hypothesis for classifying the stimuli. This work is related to the earlier ideas of Lashley and Krechevsky (see Chapter 5). In the past 10 years, this research area has been extensively cultivated with mathematical models (see Trabasso & Bower, 1968) and already a "second-generation" of better models has arisen. Papers by Chumbley (1969), Falmagne (1970), and M. Levine (1970) use the basic hypothesis-testing theory, but suppose that the subject gradually learns to reject hypotheses that have been tried and failed, although he may forget that a given hypothesis was rejected some time ago. The correct hypothesis becomes increasingly likely to be selected because incorrect hypotheses are being increasingly eliminated as training proceeds. On the whole, the developments in this subarea have become quite compatible with the so-called information-processing approach to cognition (see Gregg & Simon, 1967), an approach to be discussed in Chapter 13. The papers cited may be consulted for further details.

The results confirming the one-element model in paired-associate learning have in common the fact that only two response alternatives are involved. Somewhat similar confirmatory results have been found in the case of recognition memory in which the subject says whether or not he has seen a particular stimulus (e.g., nonsense syllable) before in the preceding series (e.g., Kintsch & Morris, 1964; Bernbach, 1965; Olson, 1969). It is understood, of course, that paired-associates learning can be a complex tangle of processes involving stimulus discrimination, response learning, associative mediators, strategic guessing, and the like. The processes described in the one-element model can be clearly revealed only in specially simplified experimental situations which minimize these complicating factors. The hope is that these complicating factors and their interactions can eventually be included within the basic model by extension of the notion of all-or-none associations.

To illustrate the sorts of effects that can be handled in this way, let us consider the role of the number of known response alternatives in paired-associates learning. Suppose that stimulus differentiation and response learning have been minimized, so that only association formation is implicated. Now it happens that the accuracy of predictions from the one-element model usually breaks down for paired-associates learning involving more than two response alternatives (e.g., in learning a list with N stimuli and N different responses with one-to-one pairings). The reason for the breakdown is that performance improves somewhat over trials before the last error on an item. The one-element model supposes, instead, that the probability of a correct response will be constant over these trials. Various methods of testing by second guesses, ranking of responses, confidence ratings, and so on (see G. H. Bower, 1967a) lead to the conclusion that all-or-none description is probably wrong in these cases. That is, the performance is not always "all' or "none" but can be partial. In other words, as common sense would have it, something can be learned along the way before learning is complete.

One can react to this state of affairs in a variety of ways. One common interpretation is to say simply that the one-element model is wrong, that it fits the two-response data for irrelevant reasons, and that alternative conceptions should be pursued. An alternative reaction is to try to patch up the model, or to formulate it in a more general way, so that it covers, at least qualitatively, the main disconfirming results (cf. Greeno & Steiner, 1964; P. G. Polson & Greeno, 1965). A third alternative is to try to discover why the model fits when it does and fails when it does, and from an understanding of this pattern, to develop a more general theory which essentially reduces to the one-element model in the former cases and accounts for the discrepancies in the latter.

Let us consider one illustration of this third approach. Suppose we analyze each paired-associate (A-B) as involving two distinct associations, namely, a *forward* association from the nominal stimulus (A) to the response (B), and a *backward* association from the "response" term (B) to the stimulus (A). In a one-one pairing situation, the two associations can be assessed independently—for instance, by presenting B for recall of A or vice versa. The labels "forward" association and "backward" association have reality for the experimenter (in terms of which element is the prescribed cue), but not for the subject, who thinks he is simply learning which items are paired together. In our model, let us suppose that the "state of knowledge" of the subject with respect to each paired-associate refers to the presence or absence of the forward and the backward association. There are then four states of knowledge for a given pair: neither association yet formed (denoted $\bar{F}\bar{B}$), the forward association but not the backward ($F\bar{B}$), the backward but not the forward ($\bar{F}B$), and both forward and backward associations formed (FB). Let us assume further that on each reinforced trial (i.e., when the person rehearses the correct A-B pairing) prior to the learning of the indicated association, the subject has probability f of forming the forward association and, independently, probability b of forming the backward association. These learning assumptions imply the following matrix of probabilities for one-trial transitions between states:

		State on trial $n+1$			
		FB	$F\bar{B}$	$\bar{F}B$	$\bar{F}\bar{B}$
	FB	1	0	0	0
State on	$F\bar{B}$	b	$1-b$	0	0
trial n	$\bar{F}B$	f	0	$1-f$	0
	$\bar{F}\bar{B}$	fb	$f(1-b)$	$(1-f)b$	$(1-f)(1-b)$

The lower row of this transition matrix, for instance, displays the joint probabilities of the four states (listed in the column headings) following one trial which began with the pair in state $\bar{F}\bar{B}$. We may suppose that all items begin in state $\bar{F}\bar{B}$ at the outset of the experiment, and with repeated study trials eventually end up in state FB. The earlier one-element formulation referred only to the forward association; the new formulation would reduce to the previous one-element process either if $b=0$, in which case the only states are $\bar{F}\bar{B}$ and $F\bar{B}$, or if the forward and backward associations are perfectly correlated, in which case the only states are $\bar{F}\bar{B}$ and FB.

The interesting new development is the relationship between performance and these states of knowledge regarding a pair. In cued recall, if an association has been formed from the cue, then the associated term is given as a response, as was assumed previously. The significant cases arise in states $F\bar{B}$ or $\bar{F}B$ when recall is cued with either the backward (B) or forward (A) element of the pair, respectively. In these cases, given sufficient time, the person can "guess" in a very strategic manner guaranteed to give him a success rate far in excess of chance. To illustrate, suppose the subject learns five syllable-number pairs using the digits 1–5 as responses; suppose that after a small amount of training he knows DAX-2 in a backward but not a forward direction. Therefore, when presented with DAX as a test cue, the subject will fail to retrieve a forward association; however, he can now begin to generate implicitly the known list of response terms (the digits 1–5) and check each of these for a backward association to the test cue DAX. Should he find such a response, the subject can give it, knowing it must be the correct response. Similarly, should the scanned response have a backward association to some other stimulus syllable, then in the one-to-one list that response can be eliminated as a possible guess for the test cue DAX. After all responses have been scanned and possibly some eliminated, then the subject is presumed to guess from his remaining pool of uneliminated response candidates.

The effect of these several strategies is to improve the subject's correct responding to the "forward cue" DAX even before he has learned the forward all-or-none association. Moreover, the amount of improvement above chance guessing introduced by these strategies depends on the uniqueness of the "backward" associations, which of course varies with the number of response alternatives for a fixed list of stimulus items. In particular, with two response alternatives, the process reduces practically to the simple one-element model, since each response will have so many backward associations that little restriction of the guessing pool can be accomplished in this case. The backpath strategies also produce "improvements" in other performance measures of paired-associate learning such as second guesses after errors, rankings, confidence ratings, latencies after criterion, and recognition measures—all of which, it will be recalled, were producing discrepancies from the simple one-element model.

Let us consider pair recognition as one example of an earlier problem that is now handled by this distinct associations model. Wolford (1971), who originally formulated this model, explicitly tested its ability to interrelate associative recall to pair recognition. In his experiments, the student would study a list of pairs, each comprised of a word and a two-digit number such as *lamp*-43 and *rug*-86. The retention tests were of four different sorts: forward recall (*lamp*- ?), backward recall (? -43), recognition of correct pairing (*rug*-86?), and recognition of incorrect, reshuffled pairings (*rug*-43?). On such recognition tests, the subject said *Correct* or *Incorrect*, judging whether the test *pairing* was one he had studied. Wolford reasoned that a correct test pair could be recognized or accepted if the subject had formed and retained either the forward or the backward association. On the other hand, the subject could reject an incorrect pairing like "*rug*-43" either if he retained the correct forward association from the stimulus term ($rug \rightarrow 86$) or if he retained the correct backward association from the response term ($43 \rightarrow$

lamp). If the person cannot remember enough to definitely accept or reject a test pair, then it is presumed that he guesses *Correct* with some base rate (assumed to be one-half in Wolford's two-response experiment).

It is important that the forward and backward association probabilities can be estimated directly from the recall tests. These were $f = .47$ and $b = .25$. The probability of recognizing a correct old pairing is expected to be $1 - .5(1 - f)(1 - b)$, which computes to be .80 in this case. The observed probability of correct pair recognition was also .80, precisely as predicted. In this case, the predicted percentage of rejections of incorrect pairing was also .80, whereas .79 was observed. Obviously, the model is confirmed in these cases of Yes-No paired-associate recognition. Wolford also showed that the same model predicted performance as measured by multiple-choice recognition tests (e.g., was it 43 or 86 that was paired with *rug*?). In related unpublished work by Arnold and Bower, the distinct-associations model was extended to deal with triplets of elements (rather than pairs), symbolized as (*ABC*), (*DEF*), and so on. With triplets, there are two kinds of recall tests (single or double cues), and a variety of pairwise and triplet recognition tests, some correct and some incorrect. Estimating a single parameter (corresponding to an average of f and b above), Arnold and Bower successfully predicted the total pattern of results on all the recall and recognition tests. It would thus appear that the distinct-associations model has been well supported in these tests. But importantly, it also provides a useful (though by no means proven) analysis of why the simple one-element model worked when it did and failed when it did. It achieves this, it should be noted, by compounding two all-or-none learning processes, one describing the forward association, the other the backward association. This approach of modeling a theoretical process by compounding a few all-or-none components has provided a viable strategy for theorizing about a number of learning problems (see G. H. Bower & Theios, 1964; Restle, 1964a). A further illustration of this strategy is seen in the model relating short-term memory to long-term memory, to which topic we now turn.

Short-Term Memory Models

The decade of the 1960s might be described as that period when learning theorists finally "discovered" that short-term memory existed. In studies of "immediate" or "short-term" memory, a subject's recall of information is tested within a few seconds after he has briefly studied it. If only one or two items (words, nonsense syllables) are involved, then he usually shows perfect immediate recall. Moreover, he will show perfect recall over an interval of 30 to 60 seconds, provided he is not distracted. But if he is distracted by some means, say, by having to respond to other material, then his ability to recall the first material drops off precipitously within the space of a few seconds. Such phenomena are familiar to most of us; after looking up a telephone number or street address, we forget it if something distracts us before we have written it down or used it. Figure 12.11 below shows some measurements of this effect in the laboratory. In this particular experiment, by L. R. Peterson and M. J. Peterson (1959), the subject was briefly presented with a nonsense trigram (e.g., *CHQ*), and then engaged in doing mental arithmetic (successively subtracting three from a random number) before being asked to recall the trigram. The curve shows the decreased probability that the trigram was correctly recalled after intervals of up to 16 seconds devoted to successive subtracting.

Phenomena of this general type have stimulated much experimental research in recent times. In appearance, the findings seem to imply a *short-term* memory of extreme fragility, lasting only a few seconds when distracting material is presented. But what is the functional use of this short-term memory system in the overall economy of the mind? What relation does this short-term system have to our relatively "long-term" memories? How are we to describe the operation of this short-term system? What are its laws? These and other questions have inspired some interesting theoretical conjectures and a spate of experimentation.

With a growing body of systematic results, it was not long before mathematical psychologists began trying to answer theoretical questions. One can apply Estes's stimulus fluctuation model to such results, assuming that the verbal response is associated to a sample of contextual stimuli which are altered by the intervening activity. This is a viable approach with many merits, and it views short-term and long-term memory as being on a continuum with both affected by common variables (see G. H. Bower, 1967b; Falkenberg, 1972; L. R. Peterson, 1963; Rumelhart, 1967). However, the alternative and predominant approach has been to treat short-term memory as a separate "memory store" or information holder, distinct from long-term memory. The early formulations of this "two-store" model were by Broad-

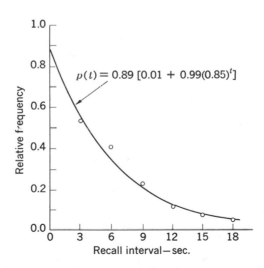

$$p(t) = 0.89\,[0.01 + 0.99(0.85)^t]$$

Figure 12.11. Percentage of correct recalls of a nonsense trigram after varying intervals of distraction by successively subtracting threes. The equation fit to the data points (open dots) is derived from Estes's stimulus fluctuation theory (see equation [10]). (From L. R. Peterson and M. J. Peterson, Short-term retention of individual verbal items, *Journal of Experimental Psychology*, 1959, 58. Copyright 1959 by the American Psychological Association. Reprinted by permission.)

bent (1957), Atkinson and Crothers (1964), Waugh and Norman (1965), and G. H. Bower (1967a). The most extensive and systematic statement of what was to become the "standard two-store" theory was given by Atkinson and Shiffrin (1965, 1968). Figure 12.12 may be used to illustrate the points, say, in reference to learning of word-digit paired-associates. This diagram depicts the "flow of information" through the various components of the total system. When a stimulus, such as the pair "*rug*-7," is presented to be studied and learned, it is supposed that this pair is entered into sensory registers which extract informative features from the stimulus. When attention is given to the input, it is "recognized" in the sense that the input contacts the internal representation of itself in memory. This internal representation then outputs some code indexing itself, which indexing code is entered into short-term memory. For instance, the input may be the visual grapheme "dog" whereas the output of the pattern recognizer might be the subvocal pronunciation "dawgh" or the articulatory parameters for constructing this pronunciation. Next it is supposed that short-term memory (abbreviated STM henceforth) is an active but limited capacity storehouse that can only hold a few items at any one time. The capacity is limited by the complexity or amount of information in each item. This STM is usually thought of as the place in which occurs active, subvocal rehearsal or "going-over" of verbal material; because this going-over of material takes time, there may be time enough to go over only a few items (say, two to four pairs) before the next items arrive to be dealt with. "Distracting" tasks like doing arithmetic or studying interpolated material is presumed to require attention, thus limiting the amount of processing effort left over for rehearsal of the material to be remembered.

Unless the person in some way gives especial priority in attention to a particular item, it is supposed that that item eventually becomes replaced or lost from the STM as a result of the necessity for the STM to deal with newly arriving information. The greater the demands of the interpolated material (e.g., the greater its difficulty), the more attention it takes away from rehearsal, and the sooner the material to be remembered will be

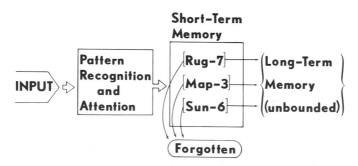

Figure 12.12.   Illustration of standard "two-store" model of short-term and long-term memory. Paired-associate items input to the system are attended to, recognized, and their codes are entered into the active short-term memory. Rehearsal or mnemonic organization is used to transfer information about the pairs from short-term to long-term memory.

removed from the STM. In circumstances involving homogeneous interpolated material, it is commonly supposed that each interpolated item (e.g., each successive step of subtracting by threes) has some fixed probability d of causing an item in STM to be displaced or removed from STM. This formulation leads to an exponential loss of items from STM, with the likelihood that a target item is still in STM after n interpolated items being $(1-d)^n$. As indicated, the loss of items from STM can be conceived along these lines: there are a fixed number of "slots" (items) that can be attended to, and once these slots are filled, a newly arriving item is inserted into the system only by "bumping out" or displacing the former occupant of a slot.

During the time an item resides in STM, there is an attempt to transfer some information about it to long-term memory (LTM). The LTM is conceived of as holding not only the semipermanent working memories being used in particular tasks, but also our permanent knowledge about the world, about our language, and so on. The LTM is, in fact, the memory system psychologists always talked about until the facts regarding immediate memory forced an appraisal of the STM-LTM distinction. The LTM is of unlimited capacity, and loss of information from it is very slow relative to the loss rate from STM; also, forgetting from LTM is usually conceived to follow rules of associative interference rather than autonomous decay.

The picture of learning that results, then, may be heuristically viewed along the lines of a "customer service" queue (see G. H. Bower, 1967a; J. S. Reitman, 1971). Customers, representing items to be stored, arrive periodically at the service counter, demanding immediate service from a limited supply of clerks (slots). An earlier customer (A) may have his service interrupted if a new customer (B) arrives before A's service has been completed, and A's server (slot) is elected to take care of the new arrival B. A customer who completes service to his satisfaction corresponds to an item that has been transferred to LTM before being bumped out of STM. A customer whose service is interrupted is presumed to leave dissatisfied, which event corresponds in the model to an item that is bumped out of STM before sufficient information about it can be transferred to LTM, so consequently it is forgotten.

Let us see if we can formulate this process mathematically, in terms compatible with the all-or-none model we have been discussing. (This follows similar discussions by Atkinson & Crothers, 1964, and Greeno, 1968). We may imagine that an item to be remembered is "unlearned" before presentation, but upon presentation it enters STM. Assume that at the moment of entry into STM, the item is either successfully copied into LTM (with probability c) or it is not so transferred (with probability $1-c$), in the latter case remaining for a while in STM. If an item is in STM when an interpolated event occurs, with probability d that event will cause the code of the target item to be lost from STM. Let $r_{1,n}$ denote the likelihood that an item will be retained throughout n interpolated events following its first presentation. Then the equation for $r_{1,n}$ derivable from the foregoing assumptions is

$$r_{1,n} = c + (1-c)(1-d)^n. \tag{13}$$

To interpret equation (13): with probability c the study trial causes the item to be transferred into LTM, from which it is not forgotten; with probability $1 - c$, the item fails to go into LTM, stays in STM, and the probability that an item in STM survives through n interpolated events is $(1 - d)^n$.

Equation (13) is an exponential decay curve (comparable to equation [10] derived from fluctuation theory), starting at 1.00 immediately following an item's presentation and declining with the number of interfering events to an asymptote of c. If an item is presented k different times at widely distributed intervals, this provides k opportunities for it to be transferred into LTM, much as in the one-element model. The likelihood of recall after n interpolated events and following the kth presentation of the same item will be

$$r_{k,n} = 1 - (1 - c)^k + (1 - c)^k (1 - d)^n. \tag{14}$$

This is a simple generalization of equation (13) with the $1 - c$ factor raised to the kth power reflecting the k opportunities for the item to enter LTM. The plots of equation (14) look like those in panel a of Figure 12.3, computed from stimulus fluctuation theory, having a higher asymptote with more study trials (larger values of k).

Such an equation is directly applicable to data derived from the typical short-term memory experiment—for instance, that of L. R. Peterson and M. J. Peterson (1959) displayed in Figure 12.11. In a standard "list-learning" experiment, say with paired-associates, the STM factor introduces slight complications since an item presented on trial k may not be learned (in LTM) but will still be in STM and recalled correctly when it is tested at the beginning of the list on trial $(k + 1)$. Thus, in terms of the earlier one-element model, allowance for the STM factor would produce a slight increase in the average success rate above the base guessing level before learning (LTM storage). This elevation, for example, would be greater for short lists of items than for long lists, a factor which in itself would account for part of the list-length effect, that is, that longer lists are more than proportionately hard to learn than shorter lists.

Although mathematical models such as this one describe the short-term retention curves, they do not particularly illuminate the nature of the process; that is, they do not tell us about the priority rules for insertion or deletion of material, the causes of forgetting, or the nature of the code which is entered into STM and which determines the nature of confusion errors in recall, nor do they tell us exactly what it is that is transferred to LTM. These "process" assumptions regarding the rules governing the operation of the STM system and the proper representation of the knowledge it acquires are typically stated verbally (see any of the references on STM, e.g., Atkinson & Shiffrin, 1968), but they appear only very indirectly in the mathematical statement. Much of the experimentation in this area, however, has been directed at these "process assumptions." Consequently, except in the work of Atkinson and Shiffrin (1968) and a few formal models described in a collected volume *Models of memory* (edited by D. A. Norman, 1970), the significant experimentation on STM has not been much guided by the availability of such mathematical models. These issues are reviewed later in this chapter and also in Chapter 15.

Compounds of All-or-None Processes

For the moment, we will merely note that again the elementary all-or-none learning model has permitted a ready extension so as to handle some of the phenomena of short-term memory. As in the "distinct associations" extension, we note that this new extension simply requires that we distinguish another "state of knowledge" and take account of its influence on performances of various kinds. But the new addition is just another state in a Markov process, derived by the compounding of several all-or-none processes operating successively or simultaneously. It is this strategy, first enunciated clearly by Restle (1964a), which has proven quite serviceable in developing models for other classes of learning.

In such models, knowledge relevant to performance of the criterion task is presumed to be analyzable into distinct parts or phases, the learning of which occurs in discrete stages or "steps." Various theories differ in the psychological constructs and assumptions used to rationalize this representation and the "stage" models. The theories differ in content, of course, depending on the nature of the learning task being analyzed, whether it be paired-associates or concept identification with humans, or Pavlovian or avoidance conditioning with animals. Typically, the learning process is represented as a three-state (or four-state) Markov process, with the psychological identification of the states varying across tasks. Typically, also, there is a beginning state in which the subject starts out before he learns much of anything; there are one or two intermediate states of knowledge into which he may move (as learning trials proceed), in which he knows something but not everything he needs to always respond correctly; then there is a final state in which the task has been learned, eventually arrived at after sufficient reinforced practice.

Let us briefly mention just a few of the many different theories and applications that have used this multistate representation. One situation concerns the relation between recognition of an item (e.g., a nonsense syllable) and its free recall when it is embedded in a list. Kintsch and Morris (1964) thought of the intermediate state as that in which an item can be recognized (as one studied earlier) but not yet free-recalled, whereas the terminal learning state corresponds to that in which the person is able to free-recall as well as to recognize the item. Their experiments gave presumptive evidence for these identifications.

Restle (1964a; see also M. C. Polson, Restle, & Polson, 1965) interprets the intermediate state in paired-associate learning as due to stimulus confusion errors arising because of similarity among stimuli to which different responses are being associated. The intermediate state is entered from the initial guessing state by associating a response to nondiscriminating aspects of a stimulus (i.e., aspects that this stimulus shares with others). The intermediate state is either bypassed or escaped when the response becomes associated to a unique feature of the stimulus. The data from these studies offer presumptive evidence that restricted confusions among similar stimuli produce the intermediate performance. In this theory, the one-element model describes paired-associate learning either if (a) stimulus-confusion errors are minimized, or if (b) there are two responses, in which case confusions and guesses cannot be distinguished.

In applying a three-state model to the simple avoidance conditioning of animals, Theios and Brelsford (1966) assume that two associations are involved: one between the warning signal and the emotional fear reaction; the other, between the cue of being afraid and the response of running from the shock compartment into the safety compartment. The intermediate state is entered once the latter habit is learned but while the former (emotional) habit is still vacillating in strength. A series of experiments by Brelsford (1967) provides considerable evidence for this interpretation of the task.

Finally, Trabasso and Bower (1964) used the three-state model in interpreting learning to identify concept instances in which two attributes (e.g., color and shape) had to be used for correct classification. The intermediate state was interpreted as one in which the subject has learned only one of the two relevant attributes so that his success rate improved above the chance level. Detailed internal analyses of the data plus subsidiary experiments provided evidence for this interpretation of the learning.

As pointed out before, in these applications a given learning task is conceived to involve several stages, with each stage being a unit of learning which supposedly the subject acquires in an all-or-nothing fashion. When the simple all-or-none (one-element) process is used to describe each state, then the multiprocess model conjoins end-to-end several all-or-none processes. The all-or-none process is used as a basic building block. The conjunction of several all-or-none processes yields a model which, in its gross properties, resembles a "continuous improvement" notion of learning. However, in comparison with the continuous linear model discussed earlier, the Markov models generally are favored in respect to both their accuracy of fitting data and the relative ease with which theoretical derivations can be carried through.

There is no way of knowing whether this strategy of using all-or-none building blocks will always be successful and fruitful. At present, several models of this kind seem to operate effectively. The question of validity always centers around the cogency and sharpness with which a theory identifies the various subparts of the task with their associated parameters, and how convincing the data are in supporting the proposed partitioning into subtasks. In some cases, at least, specially designed experiments or data analyses can produce strong evidence favoring the task analysis proposed by a particular model.

THE LIMITATION OF GOODNESS-OF-FIT CRITERIA

During the period from roughly 1959 through 1966, the emphasis was increasingly on fitting specific models to a large variety of descriptive statistics of each set of learning data. The theorists involved felt that it was important to demonstrate that detailed numerical accuracy in fitting a psychological theory was possible. The initial estimates of goodness of fit were only "ocular" tests; one simply looked at tables of predicted and observed statistics (like Table 12.7) and decided on some intuitive basis whether the overall fit was good, fair, or poor. This informal appraisal has in many instances been replaced by standard statistical tests of goodness of fit such as chi square.

However, workers gradually came to realize that a large experiment, with thousands of observations, would reject practically every model on the basis of such chi-square tests (Grant, 1962). The theory may predict the relevant data numbers with an average error of, say 3 percent; but given sufficient observations, that 3 percent discrepancy can become statistically significant. Yet though statistically significant, the discrepancy may be trivial in a practical sense. All scientists are willing to admit that their theories are not literal truth, but rather ideal abstractions (models) that approximate the data more or less closely. And what "close" means in this context is a comparative judgment; the model is closer to the data than are competing theories, or its relative error is near the standard expected by the scientific fraternity for theories in this particular area of specialization. The goodness-of-fit tests are thus seen as really relevant only when several models are being compared on predicting the same data.

As the goal of relatively accurate fit was achieved to a greater or lesser degree by many of the models being seriously proposed, goodness of fit as a theoretical decision strategy began to recede into its proper place. That is, relatively good fits to data are now viewed as an important though not overwhelming reason for favoring a particular model. This view was forced upon us by the fact that some types of standard learning data were fitted fairly well by abstract models that have neither a sensible psychological rationale nor clear identifications with psychological processes. They are models in search of a rationale, in search of a psychological analysis that will lend some sense to the mathematics that provide an abstract description of the behavior involved.

As a result of this changing perspective, mathematical psychologists have, by and large, become psychologists once again rather than mathematicians manipulating abstract symbol-structures. The trend has clearly been more toward an interest in the "internal processes" which mediate the effects of experience upon behavior, with less emphasis on stochastic models which "simply describe" data. Thus, the predominant sorts of concepts in use today refer to different cognitive processes engaged during learning, such as attending, grouping, classifying, encoding, rehearsing, mnemonically elaborating, storing information, and retrieving information to answer questions. More detailed assumptions are made and tested regarding the rules governing these various processes. The so-called information-processing language of computer simulation has provided an appropriate framework within which to talk about these processes and their complex interrelations. We shall explore these matters in Chapter 13.

Analysis of a particular behavioral phenomenon (e.g., hypothesis selection in concept identification tasks) typically begins with a set of theoretical ideas which are stated verbally; the theorist then determines how this set of theoretical mechanisms would combine with the experimental procedure, the net yield being a stochastic model presumably giving a formal description of the expected data protocols. Gregg and Simon (1967) have argued that the stochastic model is a hybrid aggregate of process assumptions and procedural details; moreover, the process assumptions which may be of primary concern are typically not formalized but rather serve as a verbal rationale in deriving the model. They therefore argue for a more explicit formalization of the process theory (insofar as this can be done), typically in the form of an explicit step-by-step algorithm (or computer program), and for separation of this formulation from the way the assumed processes combine with the experimental procedures to produce a net, aggregative description of the data. The value of a process theory is that it will frequently make more predictions and much stronger predictions about performance than will the stochastic model derived from it. The issues here are technical, complex, and depend in part upon which theoretical strategy individual scientists feel more comfortable with. The Gregg and Simon argument is acceptable in those cases in which there is some reasonable certainty about the processes involved (as is the case they selected for their argument), but it carries less force regarding initial exploratory efforts in a relatively new research area. In any event, arguments of this nature have had persuasive impact in leading mathematical learning theorists to become more concerned with internal representations and cognitive processes than with simple analysis of trial-by-trial changes in response probabilities. This shifting interest is evident in the recent annual review of mathematical learning theory by Greeno and Bjork (1973). In this respect, mathematical learning theorists have shifted increasingly to experimentation designed to get at a postulated process in a direct way or to show large qualitative differences. In this latter regard, the criteria for evaluating their theories is little different from the criteria by which qualitative theories have been generally evaluated throughout the history of psychology. The difference lies in the theory's potential for being translated into explicit models that operate accurately at the specific-quantitative level of prediction.

Range of Applicability of Mathematical Learning Models

Starting from a modest beginning in 1950, mathematical learning theories have been applied to an increasingly broader range of experiments. The specific ideas may vary from one application to another, but a common method of theory construction runs throughout. The range of behavioral phenomena investigated by these methods includes the traditional provinces of learning theory plus a few newly opened territories. We will list a sample of situations or phenomena for which mathematical models have been formulated and tested: classical conditioning, operant conditioning, stimulus generalization, mediated generalization, discrimination learning, partial reinforcement and extinction, rote serial learning, paired-associate learning, free verbal recall, short-term or immediate memory, attitude change, impression formation, concept identification of simple and complex sorts, probability learning, recognition memory, signal detection and recognition in psychophysics, imitation learning, avoidance conditioning, VTE and latency in choice situations, memory-search tasks, stimulus-compounding, correlated reinforcement and interresponse time distributions, paired-comparison choices, information integration, parametric investigations of drive, CS intensity, CS-US interval, and variations in reinforcement in conditioning situations, two-person interaction games, reaction time, spontaneous recovery and forgetting, retroactive interference experiments, and so forth. This list is representative but hardly exhaustive. Practically every domain of learning research has been infiltrated to some degree by quantitative theorizing.

The depth of the various applications differs considerably, some consisting only of a model for a single experiment, some amounting to a major line of continuing research. Some applications are of the quasi-quantitative variety in which it is shown that derivations from some general assumptions account for the major qualitative trends observed. Frequently a mathematical model simply leads to a reworking of data derived from some classical experimental situation, or leads to investigations of slight alterations of the standard situations. In its better moments, this reexamination of a familiar situation in terms of a mathematical model can bring to light new regularities in the data that had never before been suspected. For example, data analyses guided by the Markov learning models have shown the existence of performance plateaus or step functions in situations where it was previously thought learning was a continuous and gradual improvement in performance.

A recent application of mathematical learning models involves optimality questions about educational programs (see Restle, 1964b; Crothers, 1965; Smallwood, 1962, 1971; Atkinson & Paulson, 1972). The types of questions investigated include (1) how best to allocate study time to different independent materials in order to maximize the total amount learned in a fixed time; (2) the optimal rate for a teacher to present materials in a course in which understanding the nth unit requires that the student have learned the first $n-1$ units; and (3) the best way in which to divide a large group of students into smaller tutorial classes so as to minimize the total cost (in teachers' plus students' time) of teaching particular material. When such problems are clearly formulated (often with simplifying conditions), a learning model can be used to calculate the value of different programs, and thereby tell us which programs teachers should use if they wish to optimize certain goals. This kind of work is small in substance and has not yet achieved any spectacular successes in terms of optimality recommendations; however, we may expect it to be a continuing concern of learning theorists.

Concluding Comments

It is difficult to evaluate mathematical theory construction in psychology. It is a method or technique for formulating substantive theories, not a theory in its own right. Some of the uses are fitting and fruitful, some obviously are not, and each case must be judged more or less on its own merits. In general terms, it is fair to say that mathematical models have guided psychologists into more intensive analyses of learning data. The models have shown us the rich information that can be gathered from learning data by carrying out more refined analyses. They have also demonstrated that valuable understanding sometimes arises from suitably sensitive comparisons of several well-formulated theories on data derived from very elementary experiments.

A wholesome side effect of the work in mathematical models has been the realization that such theories *can* yield predictions of data of an accuracy that is on a par with the accuracy of the best physical theories. The many instances now available demonstrate that numerical accuracy of a learning theory is possible. Such demonstrations are important in helping us to establish the standards which we can realistically hope for our theories to achieve.

The problems that beset work in mathematical learning theory appear generally characteristic of the contemporary scene in learning theory. Many small-scale models or local hypotheses seem to be spawned at a fast rate, and many are inadequately followed up with exacting tests or integrated with a more general body of theories. The observer gets an impression of clutter, of disjointedness and fragmentation. One occasionally feels acutely the absence of any overall integrating scheme that guides these many efforts of model-building.

At one time, stimulus sampling theory appeared to be the most comprehensive scheme for integrating the fragmented efforts within mathematical learning theory. However, even this general viewpoint is professed by an increasingly smaller proportion of the active contributors to the field. For example, although the initial developments of Markov learning models were inspired by Estes's original paper on these, most of the later work has used different theoretical rationales to justify the particular Markov model being used. This change in theoretical base was apparent in our discussion of the rationales provided for various applications of the two-stage Markov models. Many theorists simply find it more convenient to think in terms of various subprocesses or stages in learning, frequently using the information-processing concepts current in computer simulation work (see Chapter 13). Moreover, in his recent writings, Estes (1972a, 1972b) has shown his tremendous versatility by presenting ideas that appear equally translatable into either information-processing heuristics or stimulus sampling terms.

Even on the basis of our selective review, it is clear that mathematical models have become thoroughly ingrained in many areas of learning research; they are definitely here to stay. We may expect that the contemporary models will soon be outmoded, but even so the enterprise as a whole can be expected to increase the quantity and the quality of its products, because more students of psychology are being mathematically equipped to do this kind of theoretical work. Though not obviously the "wave of the future" in learning research, mathematical theorizing will nonetheless continue as a prominent current. Their influence throughout later generations of psychologists will serve as sufficient tribute to the small band of founders in this area—Estes, Burke, Bush, Mosteller, Luce, Suppes, Restle—whose early efforts provided enough momentum to convert an ideal into an expanding scientific movement.

SUPPLEMENTARY READINGS

Elementary introductory textbooks that introduce quantitative descriptions of basic psychological concepts are:

GALANTER, E. (1966) *Textbook of elementary psychology.*

GREENO, J. G. (1968) *Elementary theoretical psychology.*

RESTLE, F. (1971) *Mathematical models in psychology: An introduction.*

More advanced textbooks are the following, with the first providing the most material on learning:

ATKINSON, R. C., BOWER, G. H., & CROTHERS, E. J. (1965) *Introduction to mathematical learning theory.*

COOMBS, C. H., DAWES, R. M., & TVERSKY, A. (1970) *Mathematical psychology: An elementary introduction.*

RESTLE, F., & GREENO, J. G. (1970) *Introduction to mathematical psychology.*

A text that stresses mathematical techniques of derivations with several classes of models is:

LEVINE, G., & BURKE, C. J. (1972) *Mathematical model techniques for learning theories.*

A collection of readings pertinent to the development of stimulus sampling theory is:

NEIMARK, E. D., & ESTES, W. K. (Eds.) (1967) *Stimulus sampling theory.*

The standard compendium of authoritative articles is the three-volume work (with associated volumes of readings):

LUCE, R. D., BUSH, R. R., & GALANTER, E. (Eds.) (1963, 1965) *Handbook of mathematical psychology.* Vols. I, II, III.

Information-Processing

Theories of Behavior

A recent technique in psychological theorizing is the formulation of theories in the format of *programs* that run on high-speed computers. The aim of the enterprise is to get such a programmed computer to go through a series of "actions" which in some essential ways resemble or simulate the cognitive and/or behavioral actions of a real subject performing some task. This chapter explores and hopes to clarify this brief introductory statement; primarily we will be reviewing some of the theories and models that have been formulated in this manner.

The historical antecedents of this theoretical technique are diverse, although many of the modes of thinking have been imported into psychology from engineering. Perhaps an appropriate way to begin is with a discussion of the age-old art of robotology. Men have long been fascinated by the similarities between the "behavior" of machines and the behavior of living organisms. All the analogies are there, implicit in our natural-language descriptions of what machines do. Robotology consists in the deliberate design of machines that mimic the behavior of living organisms. From a leisurely beginning, recent successful advances have made this enterprise nothing short of spectacular. It is now widely recognized that machines can be designed to perform many sorts of tasks previously done exclusively by humans. Indeed, the machine may often exceed the performance capabilities of the man it replaces. The effect of this engineering feat is apparent in the present concern about automation and the possible obsolescence of the human worker of the future.

During the 1950s a few behavioral scientists began to construct robots that were supposed to embody directly different principles about behavior

Included among these hardware models are W. R. Ashby's *homeostat* (1952) that seeks and maintains a favorable homeostasis of its "internal milieu," Walter's *Machina speculatrix* (1953) that imitates the actions of an animal foraging about its environment in search of food or shelter, Walter's (1953) and Deutsch's (1954) learning machines which mimic the maze learning of rats, Hoffman's machine (1962) that displays most of the phenomena of classical conditioning, and several others to be mentioned later.

One may ask whether these robots are to be considered seriously. What is their logical status? Are they to be viewed as serious explanations of behavior, or merely as amusing, but idle, curiosities? The prevailing consensus is that a machine which accurately simulates relevant aspects of some organism's behavior indeed constitutes a genuine explanation of that behavior. The idea is that the abstract principles involved in designing the machine— its functional components and their organization—could in fact be the same as those describing the design and functioning of the living organism. In designing and building a machine to simulate certain behaviors, one is, in effect, working out a physical embodiment of a theory about how that behavior is produced by that organism. Getting the machine to actually work and to simulate some interesting behavior is a way of demonstrating that the theory is internally consistent and that it has specified a sufficient set of mechanisms. Running the robot through one or another task is logically equivalent to deriving theorems about behavior from the theory that is modeled by the physical realization. Conversely, it is claimed that we have a fairly complete understanding of a piece of behavior when we know how to build a machine that would behave in just that way.

The distinction here between an abstract theory and a particular mechanical model of it is similar to the logician's distinction between an axiom system and various realizations of it. The theory or axiom system has the top logical priority; the particular physical realizations of it are secondary. In this sense, it is psychologically irrelevant what hardware is used to realize our robot, whether in terms of cogwheels, relays, vacuum tubes, transistors, electrochemical processes, or actual neurons (although the neurophysiologist is concerned with the actual hardware). All proper realizations of the theory will carry out isomorphic behaviors; that is, they will display a parallelism or point-to-point correspondence in the behavior path that they trace out over time. If two systems show this kind of functional parallelism, this point-to-point correspondence in critical features, then we shall say that one system is a *simulation* of the other. If the correspondence is sufficiently extensive, then we have some reason to believe that the two systems are different realizations of the same theory. In scientific practice, this means that a theory about behavior could be tested by constructing a machine designed in accordance with the theory, and then seeing whether this machine simulates the behavior of interest.

But having reached this point in the argument, we can begin dispensing with the actual hardware altogether. This paring away can be done simply by attending to what are the essential as opposed to the irrelevant features of the system to be simulated. This clearly is determined by one's goals. As an example, suppose that our goal were to simulate the behavior of a rat learning a maze. Then it is clearly immaterial whether our robot looks like a rat, or moves on wheels rather than legs, or, for that matter, merely informs us (by some means) what it would do if it had legs to run with. It would seem that all that a psychological explanation would require is that our robot be equipped with (a) a pseudosensory system whereby it receives stimulus information from its environment, possibly with additional elements sensitive to its "internal drive" states, (b) a central network of learning, storage, and decision-making mechanisms, (c) some way for the central mechanisms to deliver and/or sustain commands to a motor system (actual or imaginary), and (d) a means for relaying back to the sensory system the effects of its motoric actions. These components are essential; the rest of the rat's natural accoutrements would appear to be just excess baggage from a logical point of view. Nonetheless, even agreeing to this functional caricature of the rat-as-learner does not carry us very far. The major work still lies ahead, in specifying the design and organization of these components, their "rules" of operation, and how they are interconnected.

But we may now dispense with the physical machinery entirely. The robot is just a physical embodiment of a particular explanatory theory; putting it through its paces corresponds to making various deductions from the theory. But there are alternate ways to make deductions from a theory. If the theory is simple enough, specifying only a few parts that perform simple functions, then deductions can be made either verbally, in symbolic logic, or with mathematics. But if the theory is complicated, then verbal deductions become tedious and error-laden, whereas mathematical ones often cannot be pushed through at all. In these cases, we can have recourse to a high-speed computer.

By this approach, we would program a computer so that it goes through the same steps that we would if we were making a verbal deduction from the theory. The computer does the job for us in a short time and it makes no errors. When programmed to operate according to our theory, the computer then becomes just another realization of that theory. It is, however, an inexpensive and efficient realization, since it saves us time and labor. But to realize a behavioral theory in the form of a computer program is not to imply that the theorist conceives of the organism as computerlike. The computer is being used here merely as a tool for making deductions. And the fact that a theory is realized as a computer program does not tell us what type of theory it is, or lend any special credibility to it. Any theory that is sufficiently well specified can be realized as a computer program.

The foregoing passages outline some of the arguments for stating theories in the form of a computer program. The strategy itself is noncommittal about the types of theories or concepts that are programmed. It is a historical accident that most theories realized in this way have in fact had a distinctly "cognitive" bias. This results from the aims of the particular theorists involved; often those aims have been to simulate the "higher mental processes" of man, thinking and problem-solving. However, a good deal of work has been done also on programs to simulate learning. In this chapter we review some of the problem-solving programs as well as those directly concerned with learning. We have no hesitation in including discussion of the problem-solving programs, since they illustrate important concepts common to the general approach, and they demonstrate how past learning can be utilized in novel and ingenious ways to solve problems.

INFORMATION-PROCESSING CONCEPTS AND MODELS

Each new theoretical approach usually creates its own descriptive language, or jargon, and so it is with the computer-simulation approach. The jargon is that of "information processing," and it derives from the ways computer scientists generally describe what their machines do. Stimuli, data, instructions—the generic name is "information"—are *input* or *read in* to the computer; after more or less whirling, the computer *outputs* (*reads out*) some particular end result, usually by printing it or displaying a picture on a cathode ray tube. Between the input and output, the computer is described as performing a series of instructed manipulations of the input data. These manipulations may consist of altering or transforming the mass of data, calculating something from it, comparing it to something else, using the result to search for something previously stored in the computer, evaluating what is found at intermediate stages, making decisions about it, and so on. Each of these manipulations may require a short series of instructions in the computer program, called a *subroutine*. It is convenient to refer to subroutines in terms of the functions they perform with the information input to them. And from this, it is an easy step to begin referring to the subroutine as representing an *information-processing mechanism*. Thus, the computer-simulation theories of behavior may be generally described as postulating the existence within the organism of an array of information-processing mechanisms, each of which performs a certain elementary function, and these processes are assumed to be organized and sequenced in some particular way.

It is perhaps apt to describe most research in the information-processing (IP) area as a concerted effort toward the experimental synthesis of complex human behaviors. Some typical sorts of behaviors that are simulated include the reasoning of a chess champion in selecting his next move in a chess game, the generation of hypotheses by a subject solving a concept-formation task, the selection of stocks and other securities in which an investment broker can wisely invest his or his client's capital, and so forth. The models attempt to portray and understand the behavior of a man when he is using his rational capabilities to the utmost. Therefore, in conception and goals, IP models are separated by a wide gap from the traditional stimulus-response approach with its emphasis upon progressively finer analyses of simpler and smaller parcels of behavior. In revolt against this analytic tradition, the IP theorists have attempted to synthesize these complex behaviors, to construct models whose capabilities equal those of men.

To synthesize a complex piece of behavior (e.g., such as proving a theorem in symbolic logic), the theorist must specify many processes as well as a complex organization of all these processes; additionally, many conditional decision rules must be specified which stipulate how the model is to be switched one way or another in its search depending on the outcome of previous calculations. How are we to gather information about the performance capabilities of such a complex system? As mentioned earlier, we could arduously follow through its operation step by step using paper and pencil. But to shortcut this, the system is programmed as a sequence of instructions to be carried out by the computer. By running the program on a computer and having the computer print out its actions, we learn about its capabilities. First of all, we learn whether the system has been specified in sufficient completeness so that it will run at all; possibly more parts have to be specified or internal contradictions removed. Second, we can see whether the synthetic "behavior" it prints out displays the particular features we aimed to duplicate. Third, we can determine from different runs how the behavior of the entire program changes when we modify selected parts of it.

Computers are programmed by writing a usually long sequence of instructions which are to be carried out either on some input information or on information stored in the "memory" banks of the machine. The total sequence of instructions is called a program. Such programs have to be written in a precise format using some standardized language that the computer can "understand." (For a discussion of programming languages, see B. F. Green, 1963). The FORTRAN and ALGOL languages are in common use for programs that carry out ordinary numerical calculations. The flow chart of a simple program is shown in Figure 13.1. As data, we have the weights of 12 people; the program is to calculate their average weight. We let $x(I) = 1, 2, \ldots, 12$ represent the 12 numbers. These 12 numbers are punched into IBM cards and given to the computer. In the program, SUM is our label for a memory cell which we use as a temporary working space. The sequence of instructions is depicted in Figure 13.1. The main compo-

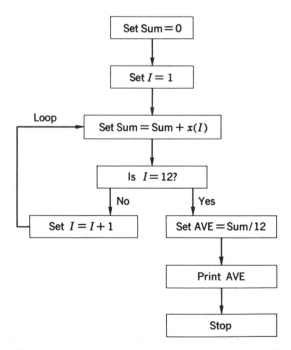

Figure 13.1.   Flow chart depicting the steps involved in calculating the average of 12 numbers labeled $x(1)$, $x(2)$, . . . , $x(12)$. A loop is used to calculate the sum of the numbers starting with $x(1)$. On each pass through the loop, the index I is increased by +1; after $x(12)$ has been added to the sum, the program exits from the loop, calculates the average value, and prints it out.

nent is the "loop" which adds $x(I)$ to SUM and increases I by 1. This loop is executed 12 times, and then the program goes on to the division and print-out operations.

A Simple Simulation

Although this example illustrates numerical calculation, a slight variant of the program that has psychological content would use a loop to search a memorized list of elements, checking to see whether it contains a critical target item. This task has been studied extensively by Sternberg (1969) and others as indicating how short-term memory is searched. The operative program for simulating performance in this "Sternberg task" is illustrated in Figure 13.2, where we have broken it down into microsteps. The typical trial begins by loading a small list of digits or letters into short-term memory; these elements are denoted $x(1)$, $x(2)$, . . . , $x(N)$ in Figure 13.2. For the moment, think of $x(1)$, $x(2)$, . . . , $x(N)$ as N different storage cells in memory that hold the items of the list, say, the letters Q, W, F, G. We then give the probe letter (e.g., T), and the subject is to decide as fast as he can whether the probe is a member of the memory set. Since we are interested in the time he takes to make this decision, in our model we set up an internal clock called RT to keep track of the time, and we start this clock at zero when the probe is presented. The operative program retrieves an element from the memory set (an operation which takes time r), compares this element to the probe (which comparison takes time c), responds Yes if it matches the probe, but continues on to scan the next element of the list if the current $x(I)$ mismatches. The query "Is $I=N$?" is used to decide whether the complete memory list has been scanned. If it has not, then the index is updated and the next element on the list is fetched; if the whole list has been scanned without finding an element matching the probe, then the program exits by printing a No response.

This flow chart diagrams the step-by-step operations in doing the task, and attaches time charges to the various operations (which explains the frequent instruction to set RT to RT plus some constant). This program exemplifies what is called a "serial self-terminating search"; it is *serial* in the sense that the elements of the list are retrieved and compared to the probe one at a time rather than simultaneously (in parallel or all at once); it is *self-terminating* in the sense that the process stops (exits from the scanning loop) as soon as it obtains a match to the probe stimulus rather than scanning *exhaustively* through to the end of the list regardless of whether an earlier match was obtained. Assuming a random (uniform) distribution of positive probe locations within the list, the *average* location will be at $(N+1)/2$ in a list of length N. With a self-terminating search, this $(N+1)/2$ will then be the average number of fetch-and-compare operations carried out on positive probe trials. The equations implied for average reaction times on positive probe (Yes) and negative probe (No) trials will be

$$RT(\text{Yes}) = (r+c)\frac{(N+1)}{2} + e\frac{N}{2} + y = \frac{(r+c+e)}{2}N + y + \frac{r+c}{2'}$$

and

$$RT(\text{No}) = (r+c+e)N + h. \tag{1}$$

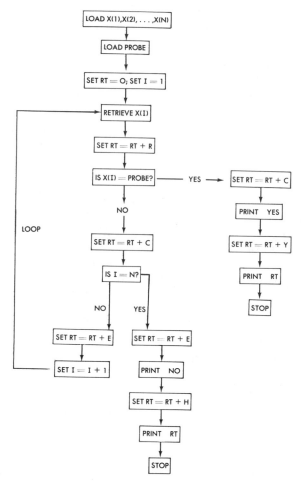

Figure 13.2.   Flow chart depicting a simulation model to predict reaction times in the Sternberg "memory-searching" task. The subject is to decide whether or not a given probe item is a member of a prescribed set of items in memory, denoted $x(1)$, $x(2)$, . . . , $x(N)$.

In each case, the reaction times are expected to increase as a straight line (or proportionately) as list length N is increased. The model programmed in Figure 13.2 expects the slope of the No line (the coefficient multiplying N) to be exactly twice the slope of the Yes line.

These are quite definite predictions from the "process model" in Figure 13.2. Though they serve to illustrate the approach, these particular predictions regarding the slopes are not always correct. Instead, the actual data (see Sternberg, 1969) often show *equal* slopes for the Yes and No lines. This could be produced by a model which scans exhaustively through all the memory-set items before exiting with the answer. This would require modifying the program diagrammed in Figure 13.2 so that it remembers any match encountered in its scan, but nonetheless completes the list scanning before responding Yes. Sternberg proposes essentially this model for his data; much experimentation has recently concentrated around this memory-search task and these kinds of models.

Now, the entire program in Figure 13.2, starting from the initializing statements, could be given a name (SCANLIST) and then treated as a unitary subroutine for embedding within any larger program that requires such a function. Furthermore, the $x(I)$ could also be the names of entire lists of symbols rather than single elements; then an instruction like "For $I = 1$ to K, SCANLIST $x(I)$" would essentially result in K successive calls to the subroutine in Figure 13.2, checking the different lists for a specified probe. The important point is to see that SCANLIST has now become an "automatic routine" that can be used repeatedly as a component process in solving other problems. This whole process, of making a program a component embedded within a larger program that may be embedded within a larger program yet, is *hierarchical* in nature. Looking at matters "from the top down," in order to do program ("job") A, we call in subroutine B; but B can call in subroutine C, and so on and on, until single, simple instructions are encountered. Once C "completes its job assignment," it passes its result back up to B, which may then do some more manipulations (e.g., collate results from several subroutines) before passing its result back up to A, which is the "top-level executive" program controlling or "supervising" the entire hierarchy. Such a hierarchical program is rather like the form of control and work allotment within a hierarchical business or governmental organization.

Figure 13.3 shows a schematic of a three-level hierarchy of a problem-solving or work-allotment program. To illustrate, suppose you want to attend a concert or other public event (goal A). To do so, you have to purchase tickets (subgoal B) and get yourself to the concert hall at the right time (subgoal C). To purchase tickets, you have to write a check and a letter (subgoal D) and mail it to the ticket office (subgoal E). Once you get the tickets, you must get to the concert hall at the correct time. You get dressed or otherwise prepared to leave home at the right time (subgoal F), walk or drive to the concert hall (subgoal G), then walk in and take your seat on time (subgoal H). By finishing subgoal H, we have simultaneously satisfied the next-higher subgoal C (getting to the concert hall on time), and put ourselves in a position to satisfy the highest goal A (to listen to the con-

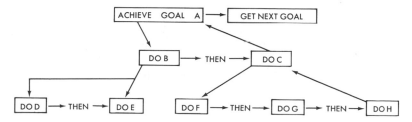

Figure 13.3. Schematic of a three-level hierarchical program in which achieving particular goals depends upon achieving a set of subgoals, which means "doing" a set of component activities. The arrows indicate the direction in which information and control passes through the system.

cert). Once that is completed, the next goal is loaded into the processor to be achieved—for instance, to find a coffee house for an after-concert drink.

Diagrams such as Figure 13.3 have an intuitive appeal to psychologists interested in analyzing behavior into its components and their organization. The subgoals and activities can be broken down into as fine and minute detail as the scientist desires, yet the "location" of a given component can be seen in terms of where it fits into and how it functions in the overall organization of the performance. The interpretation of arrows in Figure 13.3 and their direction is important. They indicate the direction of the flow of *control* by the central processor of the various activities; roughly speaking, the arrow mimics the brain shifting its "attention" and its processing effort to the activity at the tip of the arrow. This hierarchical analysis of psychological tasks derives directly from concepts of hierarchical computer programs, and it was imported into psychology by Simon, Newell, and other scientists working in computer simulation. A popular and accessible account of these ideas and their utility for psychological theory is contained in the book *Plans and the structure of behavior* by G. A. Miller, Galanter, and Pribram (1960). Their TOTE unit (for test-operate-test-exit) is merely the basic component of a hierarchical program. These ideas of Miller, Galanter, and Pribram were discussed earlier in Chapter 5.

To return to the SCANLIST program in Figure 13.2 for the Sternberg task, it should be noticed here that the computer is being used primarily as a symbol-manipulating device as well as a numerical calculator. For example, it fetches and compares two symbols for a match, as well as adding increments to the reaction-time counter. Within the IP literature, in fact, computers are viewed primarily as general-purpose symbol-manipulating devices. Mirroring this view, several "list-processing" languages have been developed to serve as convenient vehicles for formulation and expression of IP ideas into computer programs. Of the several list-processing languages available, LISP and IPL-V are the most often used in present IP work.

To illustrate just one of these languages, the basic objects of IPL-V are words (really, symbols) and names of lists of words. The operations that can be performed in IPL-V include adding or deleting a word on a particular list, reshuffling several lists, attaching a sublist onto another list, examining the words on a list to find matching words, describing the properties of a list and attaching this description list onto the first list, erasing a list, copying a list, and so forth. Such basic processes presumably form a natural language for the IP programs. In themselves, such small-scale operations appear not to impute any intelligence to the basic machinery that does it. However, when tens of thousands of such small-scale operations are cascaded within an organized program, the net performance characteristics of the machine change qualitatively into truly "intelligent" behavior, frequently of a variety unanticipated by the designer of the program.

Initial Developments

The years 1955–1960 marked the major beginning of modern IP models. Near the start of this period, Newell, Shaw, and Simon (1958; Newell & Simon, 1956) were beginning their work on the Logic Theorist, a program that proves theorems in symbolic logic. At the same time, a group of scientists at the Massachusetts Institute of Technology began work on automatic pattern recognition. Personnel in the Carnegie Tech–MIT–RAND Corporation combine worked cooperatively and exchanged many ideas and techniques during this formative period. More recently, large groups of scientists working on "artificial intelligence" have concentrated also at Stanford University and the Stanford Research Institute.

It is probably fair to say that the Logic Theorist set the basic mode for a large portion of the problem-solving programs that followed in the ensuing years, and that Selfridge's statement of the pattern recognition problem (1955, 1959) set forth the basic perplexities and tactics used to approach that problem. The Logic Theorist (LT) was designed to find proofs for theorems stated in the propositional calculus of symbolic logic. Such problems have a standard format. Some "givens," *A*, are provided, an end statement or theorem, *B*, is conjectured, and the problem for the theorem-prover is to try to transform the givens into the end statement. This has to be done by using the axioms of the system and the permissible transformation rules of the language (e.g., substitution, replacement, chaining, and detachment). As any student of logic can attest, theorem-proving is often a difficult and provocative task, and one in which failures are common. Since the axioms and transformation rules can be applied to the givens in a tremendous variety of sequential permutations, the problem is to select a path that leads to the given theorem.

A useful distinction may be made at this point between *algorithms* and *heuristic* methods of searching for an answer. An algorithm is a procedure or set of rules to follow that is guaranteed to lead eventually to the solution of a given kind of problem. It is like a flawless, sure-thing recipe. Many algorithms exist in mathematics, e.g., rules for solving a set of linear equations, for inverting a matrix, for doing long division, etc. But there are many more problems for which no algorithm is known, and some efficient strategy is needed to guide the search for a solution to such problems. Proving theorems in mathematics or the propositional calculus are examples.[1] To set out on a blind or even on a systematic search through all proper logical sequences that can be generated by the rules of the game, checking for one sequence that proves the theorem, would take a tremendously long time and be terribly inefficient. One could generate logical consequences of the givens for years in this manner without ever coming across a sequence that proves the theorem.

What obviously is needed is some means for directing the search toward a particular goal, one that has ways of detecting when it is getting close and what must be done to move still closer to the answer. In the Logic Theorist program, Newell, Shaw, and Simon used some *heuristics* to aid and guide the search process. Heuristics are rules of thumb telling one how to search in ways that are probably fruitful or efficient. When successful, these can reduce the search time considerably, though there is no guarantee that they will always be successful. In LT the main heuristic was "working backwards"

---

[1] More recently, algorithmic proof procedures have been developed for theorems in the propositional calculus (Wang, 1960, 1965) and in the first-order predicate calculus (see J. A. Robinson, 1970) based on "resolution principles." However, those mechanical algorithms are "brute-force" techniques that seem to be a very far cry from the heuristic methods used by a logician in proving a theorem.

from the theorem to be proved. One or more propositions, A', are sought which imply the theorem B by a simple transformation of A'. A subproblem is then set up, to deduce one of these A' statements from the given, A, by a simple transformation. If it cannot do so directly, then it works backwards from A' to another proposition A'' that implies A', and then tries to deduce A'' from the given, A. A number of subproblems may be generated in moving backwards each step; these are stored on a list of subproblems to be worked on. They are then edited by special routines which delete those that look nonprovable and promote those that look simple to prove and that are "similar" in a special sense to the given. LT works on the subproblems in order, seeking a proof. If one subproblem fails to yield a proof within a time limit, it goes on to try the next. If it runs out of subproblems to work on and can generate no more, then it gives up and fails to solve the problem. A great deal more than this goes on in the LT program, and the papers cited should be consulted for the richness of detail needed.

In one experiment with LT, the first 52 theorems of *Principia mathematica* (a standard classic in symbolic logic by Whitehead and Russell, 1925) were given to LT in the order they appeared. If LT proved a theorem, it was stored in its memory for possible later use. With this order of presentation, LT proved 38 (73 percent) of the 52 theorems. About half were solved in under a minute of computing time on the RAND JOHNIAC computer. Most of the remaining theorems took from 1 to 5 minutes each to solve. The amount of time to prove a given theorem increased sharply with the number of steps necessary to the proof. Other experiments showed that LT's ability to prove a given theorem depended on the order in which the theorems provided critical intermediate results for proving some of the more difficult theorems.

In discussing LT's performance as it was studied in several experiments, Newell, Shaw, and Simon (1958) point out numerous "human" characteristics of the model's problem-solving behavior. By way of summary, they say:

We have now reviewed the principal evidence that LT solves problems in a manner closely resembling that exhibited by humans dealing with the same problems. First, and perhaps most important, it is in fact capable of finding proofs for theorems—hence incorporates a system of processes that is sufficient for a problem-solving mechanism. Second, its ability to solve a particular problem depends on the sequence in which problems are presented to it in much the same way that a human subject's behavior depends on this sequence. Third, its behavior exhibits both preparatory and directional set. Fourth, it exhibits insight both in the sense of vicarious trial and error leading to "sudden" problem solution, and in the sense of employing heuristics to keep the total amount of trial and error within reasonable bounds. Fifth, it employs simple concepts to classify the expressions with which it deals. Sixth, its program exhibits a complex organized hierarchy of problems and subproblems. (p. 162)

It became clear very early that the advent of LT—more specifically, the methodology, aims, and strategies involved in the LT program—heralded a new era of conceptualizations and theorizing about complex mental processes—thinking, problem-solving, and the like. With rare exceptions (e.g., Duncker, 1945; DeGroot, 1946; Bruner, Goodnow, & Austin, 1956), previous psychological discussions of thinking and problem-solving had been characterized by serious vagueness and a baffling recognition of the incompleteness or insufficiency of any particular hypothesis, mechanism, or theory to account for the multiple richness of the phenomena. The behavior of the LT program constituted a big step in the right direction: it was completely and precisely specified, and the sufficiency of its mechanisms was determinable. It brought a new technology for theory construction to the study of complex human behavior, an area, it should be remembered, that had been scarcely touched by the behaviorists.

Since the year 1955, there has been a fast proliferation of programs for models that perform a variety of intelligent tasks. Minsky provides an early review (1961a) and a descriptor-indexed bibliography to the literature (1961b). An excellent collection of basic papers has been edited by E. A. Feigenbaum and Feldman (1963). Students unfamiliar with computers will find the texts by B. F. Green (1963) and Borko (1962) especially helpful in explaining computers, computer languages, and their usages in the behavioral sciences. This chapter is necessarily a limited review of what is going on in this rapidly expanding field. We shall select for discussion some of the work on models for pattern recognition (perceptual learning), problem-solving, and learning. Each system we shall review is in fact a very long and complex set of detailed instructions in a functioning program. This means that a brief description of each can merely touch upon the highlights of what a particular model does, and explain, in general terms, how it accomplishes this end.

A convenient, though frequently indefinite, classification of IP models divides them into those dealing with *simulation* and those dealing with *artificial intelligence*. The distinction hinges primarily on the expressed intent of the theorist. If his intention is that the model mimic step by step the processes he believes a person actually goes through in performing a task, then he is engaged in simulation of human behavior; if his intention is to design an efficient program that will perform some complex task, regardless of how a person might do it, then he is engaged in artificial-intelligence research. A radar-linked computer that calculates the trajectory of an approaching missile and fires off a countermissile to detonate it is an example of an artificially intelligent machine. What is wanted here is that the machine outperform the man, not simulate his behavior exactly. This distinction between the two research areas is not always clear-cut, however, and the principles used in constructing efficient automata are usually worth study, if only to see where or how a man falls short. Also, the principles incorporated in an artificially intelligent program to solve problems often derive from observation and introspection about how a man solves that problem. Man is far and away the most versatile, general-purpose problem-solver on this earth, so a model of man is often a good place from which to start in designing an artificially intelligent automaton. We may illustrate the problem of imitating man by considering pattern recognition.

Pattern Recognition

The problem is how to build a model, or write a program, or program a machine, that will display some of man's capabilities for classifying and discriminating the flux of environmental energies bombarding his sensors. One of the most basic skills is the classification of single units of input. To classify is to sort a series of things into separate classes, or what we may call "bins." Each bin has a name, and all things sorted into a given bin are given that name. The bin is an "equivalence" class; things sorted there must possess one or more features in common which constitute the criteria for equivalence, though they may at the same time differ in a number of aspects irrelevant to the current classification. For example, in identifying printed and handwritten letters of the alphabet, a child in elementary school learns to give one name, "A," to all the objects in Figure 13.4. After perceptual learning, the identifying label is *invariant* under a variety of transformations in size, shape, orientation, and alteration by extraneous cues in the external stimulus. The problem is to get a machine to do the same good job of classifying these inputs that a competent and careful child can do.

In a trivial sense, the problem of pattern recognition is solved if the stimulus objects are reduced to a constant, standardized format before being given to the machine. For example, business machines are in use that "read" alphanumeric characters (the alphabetic letters plus the numerals 0–9) by a light-photocell scanning process. The scanner reads a character by matching the standardized input to one of a number of "templates" or character prototypes that it has in store. The input is identified as that template which best matches it. But the input to such devices must be printed in a standardized type font with a fixed orientation, size, and location. Such sensing machines are of practical use in banks (reading checks, account numbers, etc.), in business firms, and in post offices (for sorting mail). However, they have almost no significance as solutions to the invariance problem outlined above.

A beginning step toward solution of the invariance problem is to write a program that carries out some simple cleaning-up and preprocessing on the stimulus input before it is fed to the more central machinery of the pattern recognizer. Such crude preprocessing might consist of smoothing out local irregularities, filling in small holes, dropping off excess curlicues, centering the stimulus on the receiving display, changing it to a standard size and orientation, and so on. Following such preprocessing, we might then try out the template-matching method in order to determine whether the whole system can now correctly identify all the stimuli. Figure 13.5 shows this

Figure 13.4. Sample of variations in handwriting of the capital letter A. The problem is to program a machine which discards irrelevant variations and identifies all these patterns as the letter A.

method and illustrates one of its main disadvantages. The difficulty at this point is that even after preprocessing, a sample input may still match a wrong template better than the right template. In Figure 13.5, for example, the *A* template produces a better match to the input *R* sample than it does to the two *A* samples.

An alternative attack on these difficulties is to supplement the preprocessing with a variety of other information-extracting procedures which may be called "feature counting." For example, a capital *A* usually has two mostly vertical lines, and one mostly horizontal line, is generally concave at the bottom, and so on. Such features together identify *A* rather than some other element. The feature count gives a standardized profile of an input and decisions may be made on the basis of this profile. The number and nature of such features counted are usually stipulated in advance by the model-builder.

Given a profile of features for the stimulus, there are two general schemes that can be used in coming to a decision about how to classify it: a *serial processor* and a *parallel processor*. To illustrate the serial processor, we use Selfridge and Neisser's (1960) example:

> . . . a program to distinguish the letters A, H, V, and Y might decide among them on the basis of the presence or absence of three features: a concavity at the top, a crossbar, and a vertical line. The sequential process would ask first: "Is there a

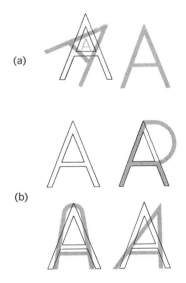

Figure 13.5.   (a) The match of the unknown letter (black) to the template (gray) will not succeed if the unknown is wrong in size, orientation, or position. The program must begin by adjusting the sample to a standard form. (b) Incorrect match may result even when sample (black) has been converted to a standard size and orientation. Here the sample letter R matches the A template more closely than do the other samples of the letter A. (From Pattern recognition by machine by O. Selfridge and U. Neisser. Copyright © 1960 by Scientific American, Inc. All rights reserved.)

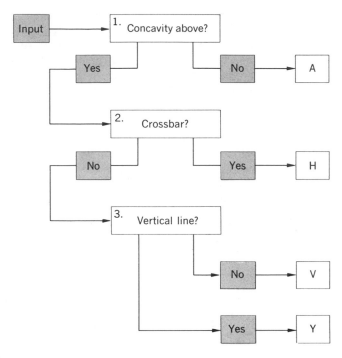

Figure 13.6.   Sequential-processing program for distinguishing four letters A, H, V, and Y, employs three test features: presence or absence of concavity above, crossbar, and a vertical line. The tests are applied in order, with each outcome determining the next step. (From Pattern recognition by machine by O. Selfridge and U. Neisser. Copyright © 1960 by Scientific American, Inc. All rights reserved.)

concavity at the top?" If no, the letter is A; if yes, then "Is there a crossbar?" If yes, the letter is H; if no, then "Is there a vertical line?" If yes, the letter is Y; if no, V. [See Figure 13.6] (p. 245)

A serial processing system of this kind (called a "sorting tree") is very efficient if the decision at each node (question) of the tree is almost certain to be correct.[2] But consider its behavior when the input data are noisy (sloppy) and each feature identifier is unreliable and uncertain in its output. If one feature is incorrectly identified, then the stimulus will be shunted off in the wrong direction through the sorting tree, and subsequent features that are correctly identified may not suffice to compensate for the misidentification of the initial features. The serial processor places too great a reliance upon the correctness of identifying each single feature. Perhaps a better decision process is one which pools together all of the feature-count information

[2] Careful inspection shows that Selfridge and Neisser's illustration does not use the features in the most efficient way. A more efficient tree asks first for presence of a crossbar, yielding the classes *H, A* and *V, Y*, and then asks for presence of a vertical line, which discriminates the elements within each pair. The tree in Figure 13.6 would be said to contain a *redundant* feature.

simultaneously; pooling many unreliable components may yield a total system whose reliability greatly exceeds that of any of its constituent parts. Parallel processors do just this.

In parallel processing, all the questions are asked at once, and all the answers presented simultaneously to the decision-maker (see Figure 13.7). Different combinations identify the different letters. One might think of the various features as being inspected by little demons, all of whom shout the answers in concert to a decision-making demon. From this concert comes the name "Pandemonium" for parallel processing (Selfridge & Neisser, 1960). A parallel processor of this nature is much less dependent on the reliability of the separate feature counters. The combination of many unreliable components may still give an overall reliable performance. Additionally, an important aspect of the parallel processor is that the features contributing to a particular pattern can be differentially weighted (by "amplifiers"), determining how loud the feature demons shout. Such differential weighting of the features by their importance cannot be done with a serial processor. For

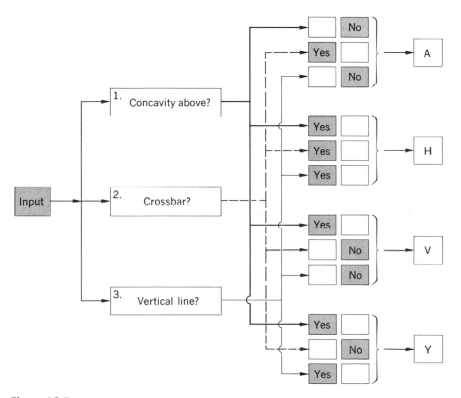

Figure 13.7.   Parallel-processing program uses the same test features as does the sequential program in Figure 13.6, but applies all tests simultaneously and makes decisions on the basis of the combined outcomes. The input is a sample of the letters A, H, V, or Y. (From Pattern recognition by machine by O. Selfridge and U. Neisser. Copyright © 1960 by Scientific American, Inc. All rights reserved.)

example, using the parallel processor, the weight of the "concavity above" feature to the A pattern could be adjusted to make its absence three times as important as the absence of the "vertical line" feature. These weights can be adjusted in trial-and-error fashion with experience until a maximally effective combination of the weighted features is achieved. The process is little different from the way psychologists find the "best linear discriminant function" to predict a criterion variable (A or not A) from a linear combination of predictor variables. In the early programs, this trial-and-error adjustment of the feature weightings was not done intrinsically by the model; rather, the human theorist did the adjustments for the machine. An alternative weighting scheme assigns weights to features according to Bayesian probabilities calculated from past experience. That is, the weight assigned to a given feature in calculating its contribution to, say, the A-pattern hypothesis, is the probability that, over past instances, the correct answer was A when that feature appeared. The sum of the probabilities of features contributing to each pattern is taken, and that pattern name with the largest sum is chosen as the identification of the input.

A computer program employing such notions was used by Doyle (1960) to recognize 10 capital letters hand-printed by several different persons. Doyle's program used 28 different features of hand-printed letters and weighted these by the Bayesian probabilities determined from a "training set" of the handwritten characters. Its later performance on a test set showed it to make only about 10 percent more errors than did human judges (whose error rate was about 3 percent). This is an impressive performance, though one which can be improved by further refinements.

One of the failings of Doyle's model is that the program-builder has to tell it what features to look at. It shows no perceptual learning in the sense of coming to extract those features from the samples which are particularly relevant to achieving a difficult discrimination. A fair amount of work on pattern recognition models has been concerned with the design of machines that construct their own feature counters, and that learn to keep good ones and discard poor ones as well as to adjust the weightings of the features as they contribute to discriminating among the several patterns.

A successful program of this type was devised by Uhr and Vossler (1963). The input to the program is an array of "on" elements in a 20×20 square array of photocells: an excited receptor cell is given the value 1 and an unexcited cell is given the value 0. This simulacrum of a retina is often used in pattern recognition studies. A set of operators (similar to the former feature counters) is used to characterize the input. An *operator*, in the Uhr-Vossler system, is simply a 5×5 matrix, each cell of which contains one element (1, on; 0, off). The center of this matrix is moved cell by cell over the 20×20 display containing the sample to be recognized, much like a mask passing over the surface of a picture. At each point, a check is made for an exact match of 1s and 0s between the 5×5 mask and the display cells below. At the end of a sweeping over the entire display, we have a listing of the number and locations at which the mask matched subparts of the display. A number of such operators (masks) are used by the program. The outputs from the operators may be considered as a list of characteristics of the shape displayed. These characteristics are then compared to the characteristics of patterns previously identified and stored in the machine's memory, and the name of the pattern most similar (in a complex sense) to the input is given as the response. Following the response, the environment feeds back information on the correct answer for the sample. The learning processes then take over: the operators are examined, and depending on whether they individually contributed to success or failure in the decision, their weighting (amplifier) is increased or decreased, respectively. If a particular operator is a poor one, it will eventually settle to a low weighting and will be discarded by the program and replaced by a newly generated operator. The new operators may be randomly generated or constructed within certain constraints.

One version of this model reported by Uhr and Vossler (1963) performed exceedingly well in discriminating several types of inputs which included hand-printed letters, outline pictures of faces and simple objects, random nonsense shapes, and the numbers *zero, one, two, three, four* spoken by different people. In this latter instance, the input to the program was a binary representation of the speech spectrogram which gives a moment by moment resolution of a complex speech sound into the amplitudes of the various frequency components. In each case, the machine achieved very high discriminative performance (95–100 percent) after only a few trials with feedback ("reinforcement") through the set of training materials. On later transfer tests with new materials from the same sources, it correctly identified between 55 percent and 97 percent of the various types of materials. In an experimental comparison, the program learned to identify the random nonsense shapes much more rapidly than did college students. The performance of this system gives us some indication of the power of "self-improvement" computer programs that learn in the sense of trying out features (even random features) by trial and error and then evaluating and adjusting their weights according to their contribution toward a successful performance.

It is clear that such work on pattern recognition is not simulation but mainly artificial intelligence. The relatively successful program of Uhr-Vossler clearly does not extract the same kind of attribute-value information from the stimulus as do the human eye and brain. In terms of simulation, the challenge is to build a machine that not only manufactures its own feature counters (i.e., shows perceptual learning) but that also converges onto roughly the same ones that human beings obviously do. A more modest solution is to start off the machine with a potentially vast storehouse of feature counters (supplied by the builder) and let some learning process modify the weights of these counters, in the hope that they will eventually converge on the same features that people customarily use, if the latter were known.

Despite these impressive accomplishments, there are several deficits to the Pandemonium model which prevent its being completely adequate. Most importantly, its strategy of "summing independent sources of evidence" misses the point that, for many concepts, one or more critical features *must* be present and others *must not* be present in order for the concept to apply. In distinguishing a *G* from a *C*, for instance, the crossbar is critical; a *G* must have one, and a *C* must not. No matter how great the evidence from the remaining features, it should not overwhelm this critical feature. The

Pandemonium model has no way to give obligatory status to absence as well as presence of a critical feature. A second failing is that Pandemoniums lack resources for describing relations among several features or for responding selectively only to a critical *pattern* of features. Minsky and Papert (1969) review the several weaknesses to which these failings lead. For example, an elementary Pandemonium would not learn an "exclusive disjunction" classification, such as to classify together geometric figures which are *blue* or *triangle* but not both. As a second example, Pandemoniums cannot "count," so would be unable to classify line grid patterns according to whether they have an odd or even number of lines. Pandemoniums generally lack relational descriptors of the most elementary kind, such as "line A is perpendicular to line B" or "surface C is co-planar to surface D." Yet these are the basic predicates needed to describe visual scenes, as will be discussed later.

A final problem, and one from which much of the field suffers, is that the programs are developed for identifying single, isolated characters input one at a time. But this is totally unrealistic for most circumstances. For example, cursive handwriting flows on continuously, and a major problem in analyzing it (for secretaries, paper graders, and computers alike) is finding a correct *segmentation*—that is, determining where are the boundaries at which one character stops and another one starts. This seems a trivial task for us most of the time because it is such an overlearned skill; but the problem shows up when we have to decipher an unfamiliar, nearly illegible hand. The same problem arises in speech recognition, where only an experienced listener can "hear" the pauses between word segments or between sentences. However, an acoustic recording of fluent speech reveals only a reasonably continuous stream of sound. The puzzle is how the speech-analyzing mechanisms can manage to segment this nearly continuous stream into phonemes, words, and phrases. The segmentation problem is very severe for character recognition programs, since without a segmentation routine they will never be able to analyze a complex pattern into its constituents. A machine that knew how to classify single alphabetic letters would, in the absence of a segmentation program, treat each two- or three-letter word as simply a novel pattern to be learned as a whole unit. A segmentation program would divide the scene into objects, describe and recognize these individual objects, and possibly describe their relationship to one another in the input scene. With such capabilities, the system would be able to perceive (describe) an infinite variety of scenes, all novel in one or another detail, using a relatively small vocabulary plus a few relations (much as many thousands of printed words are generated out of 26 letters plus a "right of" spatial relation).

One of the very early programs that dealt with this segmentation problem in an effective way was the program MAUDE (Gold, 1959), for automatic decoding of Morse code. Morse code is based entirely on discriminating the temporal durations of beeps and silent periods. In principle, a dash is to be three times as long as a dot; silent spaces between dashes or dots within a letter should be as long as a dot; silent spaces between letters should be three times as long; and silent spaces between words should be seven times as long as a dot. In practice, human code senders vary in producing these durations, and this variability is the source of confusion. The most difficult job in decoding is to separate the within-letter spaces from the between-letter spaces. MAUDE uses contextual information to decide this. Since no Morse character is more than five dots and/or dashes long, it is assumed that the longest of six consecutive spaces is a between-letter space and that the shortest is a within-letter space. The other four spaces of the six are classified according to whether they are above or below a threshold duration (continuously adjustable to the particular sender). If the tentative spacings do not make a permissible code letter in Morse, then the longest space is reclassified as a between-letter space. Similar processes are used to distinguish dots from dashes. In performance, MAUDE's error rate is only slightly higher than that of well-trained code receivers.

Scene Analysis

The programs reviewed above might be called "character recognition" machines since they classify symbols presented one at a time. MAUDE goes beyond that in handling the segmentation problem for a limited domain of input. More significant programs from a psychologist's viewpoint are recent ones by Guzman (1968) and Winston (1970) which analyze and describe visual scenes comprised of solid blocks in various relations. Figure 13.8 illustrates the type of block scenes which Guzman's SEE program will analyze. It consists of a variety of lines, angles, surfaces, and objects (cubes, bricks, wedges), arranged in various overlapping relations. Guzman's pro-

Figure 13.8.   Illustration of cluttered block scene analyzed by Guzman's SEE program. (From Winston, 1970. By permission.)

gram tries to isolate out objects and identify which surfaces belong together. It proceeds by first identifying various types of *vertices* between surfaces, each vertex type suggesting a particular sort of linkage of the surfaces into one or more objects. Figure 13.9 shows nine of the common vertices along with their names. To illustrate, the arrow provides evidence that the two regions bounded by the small angles are adjacent sides of one object. The fork suggests that the three pairs of sides are adjacent at each of the three edges. For an example of how these vertices are used to characterize an object, look at the solid cube in panel (a) of Figure 13.10. The critical vertices have been identified by heavy darkening. The corner "facing closest" to us is a fork vertex, with three arrow vertices below and to the right and left of the fork. The remaining three corners are L vertices. The fork and arrows provide the requisite information for segmenting this figure. Noticing

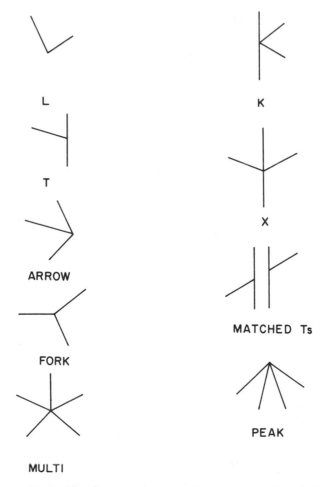

Figure 13.9.   Illustration of nine common vertices used by Guzman's program in segmenting block scenes. (From Winston, 1970. By permission.)

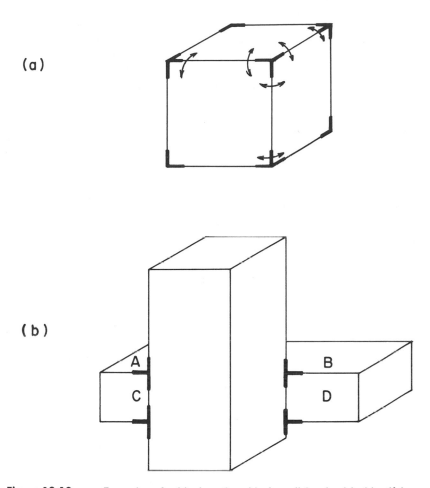

Figure 13.10. Examples of critical vertices (darkened) involved in identifying a cube (a), and one block occluding a second block (b). (Adapted from Guzman, 1968.)

these vertices and how they are connected, the SEE program will link together particular surfaces and decide which represent different sides of the same objects; these tentative linkages are indicated by the curved arrows in panel (a) of Figure 13.10. To take a second example, the T and matched-T vertices are important in suggesting that one figure is occluding another which extends behind it. This is seen in panel (b) of Figure 13.10 showing such a scene with the relevant T vertices emphasized. By a set of "good continuation" heuristics, the SEE program will identify the left- and right-hand Ts and thus aggregate together surface *A* with *B*, and surface *C* with *D*, and identify these as surfaces of a brick lying down which is occluded by the standing brick.

These brief descriptions cannot do justice to the range of heuristics SEE uses to segment and identify objects in a scene as jumbled and chaotic as that shown in Figure 13.8. Although SEE isolates surfaces and objects, it does not provide a very powerful *description* of a scene in terms of relations among identified objects. A program by Winston (1970) does just this, by imposing certain intelligent "assumptions" upon the visual world it is seeing (e.g., that blocks rest upon a table or other blocks rather than being suspended in midair). Winston takes the output of SEE as the input to his program, which then recognizes particular geometric relations between objects (such as *above, in front of, is supported by, abuts*) as well as properties of single objects. Winston's program builds up particular sorts of structural descriptions of a scene, represents these in terms of a particular formalism, and then tries to identify particular configurations with concepts and scenes with which it is familiar. Concepts are represented inside the memory as labeled relational networks; these serve as the "class prototypes" in memory for such concepts as *angle, arrow-vertex, T-joint, rectangle, triangle, wedge, brick, house, tent,* and *arch*. Figure 13.11 illustrates a fragment of the representation of intermediate-level concepts such as a *wedge* and an *arch*. The structural description of a wedge states that it comprises (to the eye of the viewer) three surfaces, two of which are a kind of rectangle whereas the third must be a triangle. This latter feature, of course, distinguishes a wedge from a brick. Thus, when shown a wedge, the lower-level program will first identify lines, edges, angles, and surfaces, and then rectangular and triangular surfaces, gradually building up a description of the scene. When this description is matched in memory to the set of known objects (concept descriptions), the best match occurs to the *wedge* concept. The same process applies to the *arch* concept illustrated in panel (b) of Figure 13.11.

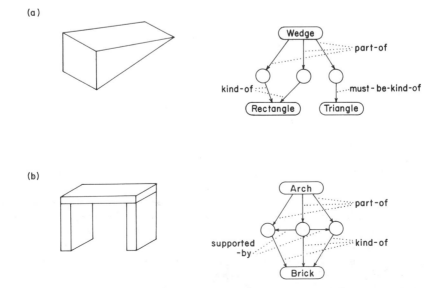

Figure 13.11.   Relational graph structures which characterize the concept of a *wedge* and an *arch*. (Adapted from Winston, 1970. By permission.)

In Winston's program, higher-order concepts are constructed out of relations between lower-order concepts. For example, a *stack* or *tower* is a set of rectangles aligned and supporting one another; a *tent* is two wedges that abut in a particular way; a *table* is a brick supported by upright bricks or wedges ("legs") at four corners, and so on. Winston's program also *learns* such concepts (relational descriptions) by being shown exemplars and close nonexemplars. We shall return later to the learning routines in Winston's program.

One reason for learning intermediate-level concepts is that they can simplify the description of a complex scene. For example, consider the scene in Figure 13.12, composed of a tent to the left of a house, both sitting on top of an arch. There are at least seven simple objects (bricks and wedges) in that scene, and they exhibit many interobject relationships. Before the system learns the intermediate-level concepts (of *tent, house, arch*), all of these parts and myriads of relationships would have to occur in the description of the scene. However, *after* the system has learned these concepts, they can be used as units to simplify the overall description to something approximating our English proposition "a tent to the left of a house both supported by an arch." Of course, following the system's exposure to this scene, the scene (or rather, its description) would be stored in memory like any other concept, and perhaps given an internal name (e.g., "Bill's architectural creation"). A later re-presentation of the scene would then lead to recognition memory; that is, the system would recognize that it has seen that scene before. On this account, then, recognition memory of individuals or individual scenes (or places) does not differ in essentials from classifying a pattern into a particular category.

Winston's program represents some of the more advanced and psychologically interesting work being done on scene analysis. It deals with an essentially static environment of toy blocks. The heuristics of Guzman's and Winston's programs are used in the "hand-eye" projects at Stanford and

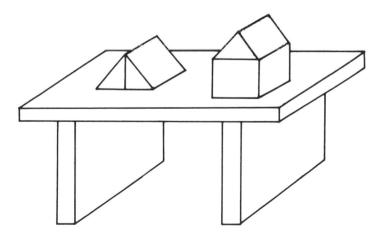

Figure 13.12.   Example of a complex scene composed of familiar intermediate-level concepts (parts) in specifiable relations. Such scenes evoke a hierarchical description from Winston's program.

MIT, and the "robot" project at the Stanford Research Institute. We postpone discussion of these projects to a later section.

Our review of programs dealing with pattern recognition has been brief but illustrates the main trends. Work on individual character recognition has been replaced by work on more complex scene analysis, which is cast in terms of deriving structural descriptions of the parts and their interrelations in the scene. The structural description must be economical (for storage in a finite memory), selective of relevant features, but also rich enough to support all sorts of visual problem-solving and reasoning (e.g., to solve geometric analogy problems). The present emphasis in research is on the difficult problems of segmentation, identification of relations, and the building of hierarchical descriptions, although the identification ("labeling") of particular objects still remains a standard component of all scene analysis programs.

These examples from pattern recognition have introduced us to other issues: for instance, is Winston's program a simulation or a piece of artificial intelligence? Just because a program solves some of the same problems as does a person does not mean that one is a decent simulation of the other. Other criteria of fittingness to actual data are required. Since most of the programs reviewed were intended simply to get a program to do some job intelligently, their "psychological reality" has not yet been put to really serious tests. What psychologists clearly need is some methodology for experimentally testing many of the very ingenious hypotheses and heuristics suggested by such programs as those reviewed.

PROBLEM-SOLVING PROGRAMS

We now turn to several kinds of programs that approximate the behavior of the human as he solves problems: theorem-provers, game players, and special problem-solvers.

Theorem-Provers

Following the lead of the Logic Theorist discussed earlier, other programs were devised to help along the development of mechanical mathematics. Gelernter (1959) wrote a program which constructs proofs of plane geometry theorems. The givens and the theorem to be proved are fed to the computer in the symbolic language of geometry, as line segments in various relations (e.g., parallel). A sample problem would be:

	SYMBOLIC	TEXT
Given:	$AB/\!/CD$	line AB is parallel to line CD
	$AD/\!/BC$	line AD is parallel to line BC
	$A\text{-}E\text{-}C$	form the line AEC
	$B\text{-}E\text{-}D$	form the line BED
Prove:	$AE = EC$	length of line AE = length of line EC
	$BE = ED$	length of line BE = length of line ED

After performing syntactic and semantic analysis of the input, the program uses the givens, much as does the geometry student, to construct a diagram and to label the points and line segments. The diagram in Figure 13.13 is consistent with the givens. As does LT, the geometry machine then tries to work backwards, looking for statements from which the theorem easily follows. In doing so, a number of subproblems may be generated as candidates to be worked on (e.g., prove that triangle 1 is congruent with triangle 2, and 3 is congruent with 4). A major heuristic of the program is to check out a subproblem by seeing whether it is true by measurement of the diagram. If it is, it is kept on the candidate list; if it is not true of the diagram, then it is discarded as a useless subgoal. Subproblems are further screened by a "similarity" analysis, and finally given to a subroutine that takes the input statements through a directed sequence of transformations permitted under the rules of plane geometry. In many respects, the program can be said to use the repertory of tricks taught to high school students for solving geometry problems, and it came out with a good grade on the final examination.

A program that performs integration of symbolic (nonnumerical) expressions in the calculus has been written by Slagle (1963). The main job is first to "parse" and identify the basic form (syntax) of a mathematical expression to be integrated. This often requires substitution of new variables and some algebraic cleaning up. Once this is done, a "dictionary-search" operation will often suffice to replace the standard form of the integrand by its indefinite integral. Of course, the program capable of achieving these ends is considerably more complicated than this brief description might suggest.

Game Players

The programming of a computer to play board games such as checkers or chess against an opponent shares many of the features found in programs that prove theorems. The arrangement of the pieces on the board at any moment constitutes the givens. The objective is to transform the givens into a winning final position by a sequence of moves permitted by the rules of the game. The permissible moves of the game play the same role as do the rules of inference in constructing logical arguments. Of course, in games, the program plays against an adversary who must be assumed to be at least as rational as the program.

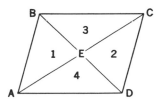

Figure 13.13.   A diagram constructed to be consistent with the givens of a geometry problem. The problem is to prove that line segments *AE* and *EC*, as well as *BE* and *ED*, are equal in length.

The basic unit for analysis is the individual move. The program, having an internal representation of the board and the location of all the pieces, looks ahead several moves—my move, his possible countermoves, my next move, his next possible countermoves to that, etc. How far ahead it looks is called the "depth" of its search. The "search tree" of possibilities can get very large if very many alternatives are considered at each move. The programs have to trade off the number of alternatives examined at each move for depth of search along particular branches of the tree. In general, programs that search deeply on a few "prosperous-looking" alternatives are more successful. Various heuristics are used to decide which alternatives one or two moves ahead warrant a deeper search.

Once a search tree of alternatives at a given move has been constructed, the program has to evaluate the various branches to discover their worth and to decide upon a move. The ultimate consequences of playing the entire game, to "win, lose, or draw," are usually too remote and too indeterminate to be of much help in evaluating a particular move. Thus, some *evaluation function* is needed that is sensitive to subgoals regarding a single, local move. Experts at the game can usually tell us a few generally desirable criteria to use in local evaluations in particular types of games, such as those that have a bearing on board control, piece advantage, king-piece exchange ratio, back row control, etc. In Samuel's checker-playing program (1959), a checker position was evaluated by computing a weighted average of the values of several such local characteristics. Each hypothetical position generated in a search tree was so evaluated.

In making a decision, the machine selects that move which has the highest value, where the value has been calculated by a "backwards minimax" procedure. Reference to Figure 13.14 will illustrate the procedure. This

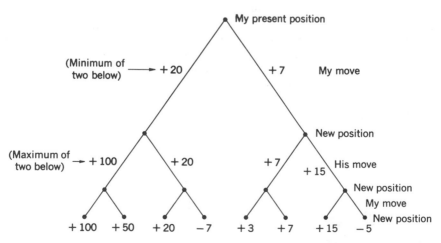

Figure 13.14.   A search tree of moves three levels deep, where only two moves are considered at each level. The positions at the deepest level searched are scored by the evaluation function. The score on a node at level 2 is the maximum of the scores on its two lower branches; the score on the level 1 node is the minimum of the score on its two lower branches.

shows a very simple search tree involving only two moves at each level (the computer may consider 10 to 20 moves at each level) and a search going only three levels deep (my move, his countermove, my next move). Each node on the tree represents a hypothetical state of the game. At the deepest level, the eight positions anticipated are scored by the evaluation function, with high positive scores indicating good positions for myself. Since I would choose the maximum scoring move on my second move, the value attached to the node above is the larger of the two lower scores. As to my opponent's move, we assume he would try to hold my gain to a minimum, so his choice would cause the minimum value to be attached to the node above. Backing up to my present position, the +20 branch is clearly a better move for me than the +7 branch, so that should be my choice.

This type of tree search and minimax backing-up analysis is done at every move of the game. Samuel's program for checker playing includes a variety of other features for improving the game it can play. Several are "learning" routines: one routine provides move-by-move feedback and correction of the weights assigned to the different subgoals in the evaluation function; the other involves a rote memory (on accessible magnetic tape) for all board positions previously encountered, searched, and evaluated. This omnibus memory helps reduce the search tree at each step to just those few branches that should be searched in greater depth.

Samuel performed many explorations with this program, trying different heuristics and self-improvement learning routines. The machine was trained by having it play checkers against human players and against published championship games from checkers books. The program improved its performance remarkably, eventually to the point where it could usually beat its human opponent. In the summer of 1962, a match was arranged between a former checkers champion, Mr. Robert W. Nealey, and the program. The machine won handily. At the conclusion of the game, Mr. Nealey commented:

> Our game . . . did have its points. Up to the 31st move, all of our play had been previously published, except where I evaded "the book" several times in a vain effort to throw the computer's timing off. At the 32-27 loser and onwards, all the play is original with us, so far as I have been able to find. It is very interesting to me to note that the computer had to make several star moves in order to get the win, and that I had several opportunities to draw otherwise. That is why I kept the game going. The machine, therefore, played a perfect ending without one misstep. In the matter of the end game, I have not had such competition from any human being since 1954, when I lost my last game. (Feigenbaum & Feldman, 1963, p. 104)

Since that time, Samuel (1967) has revised the scheme for evaluating positions and the attendant learning routines. The linear polynomial function of the prior work was abandoned in favor of a complex nonlinear evaluation process that involves hierarchical refinements of rough evaluations from many significant subpatterns or aggregations of "features" of given board positions. This new position evaluation function leads to many improvements in the checker playing of the program.

A variety of other theorem-provers and game-playing programs have been developed, but the ones reviewed suffice to characterize the undertaking in general. By and large, this is not simulation work and no one has seriously considered the programs as exact replicas of human thinking. The programs do have great intrinsic interest as fascinating intellectual performers that frequently beat their designers. Since chess is a tremendously rich, complex, and challenging game, it is no wonder that numerous projects have tried to design a chess program capable of playing a top championship game. Several chess-playing machines are already available, but as yet their performance is not near grand-master level of play (the program by Greenblatt et al., 1967, is one of the best available). The designing of a championship chess player can have little practical or even scientific significance, of course. Yet it would clearly constitute a major intellectual accomplishment on the part of the program writers. Fortunately, purely intellectual goals are highly esteemed and not at all rare in both mathematics and science.

Special Problem-Solvers

Many programs have been written that have a bearing on various problems of special interest to psychologists. Research in problem-solving (e.g., Duncker, 1945) has identified two areas of importance: the first, how a person sees, interprets, or represents a problem statement to himself and comes to understand what it is about; the second, the procedures he goes through in seeking a solution once he believes he understands the problem. The simulation models have bypassed the first, and in some ways more difficult, issue of how the problem gets interpreted by the subject; they have concentrated instead on the second issue. The problem is given to the program in a well-structured form and the programmer ensures that the problem is interpreted correctly by the model before it is set to work on it. The fuzzier issues of problem interpretation and representation have been given some thought and some special programs have been constructed. Language analysis programs, attached to so-called question-answering systems, are aimed at correctly interpreting problem statements (or questions), and these systems can be especially powerful when they have a well-defined semantic domain within which the problems are stated (e.g., a schematic picture of a scene or an electric circuit diagram; see Coles, 1968). The issue of representation of the problem space is of crucial importance, since it is well known that a given problem can be hard or easy depending on how the problem is represented internally. Although valuable discussions of this issue exist (see Amarel, 1968; Nilsson, 1971), there are no general procedures or rules to follow in concocting a good representation of a problem whereby its solution is transparent.

The programs by Simon and Kotovsky (1963) and by T. G. Evans (1968) attack conceptual problems familiar to all of us from various IQ tests. The Simon and Kotovsky program attempts to infer the rule generating successive letters in a short series. In the Thurstone Letter Series Completion Test, the subject is shown a letter series and asked to supply the correct next letter of the series. Examples are *cadaeafa__*, *atbataatbat__*, and *wxaxybyzczadab__*. Such series vary in difficulty, and some are sufficiently hard so that an appreciable proportion of college students fail them. The Simon-Kotovsky simulation program supposes that subjects solve such problems by developing a "pattern description" of the sequence and then using this description to generate the next member of the series. The model subject is assumed to have certain cognitive equipment to begin with, notably, the forwards alphabet, the backwards alphabet, the concept of "next successor" on a particular list, and the ability to store a pointer to a starting symbol and to detect and produce cycles through a list (e.g., in the simplest instances, a repetitive cycling through the list (b, a) yields the series bababa . . .).

A standard format is used to state pattern descriptions, and the main job of the program is to discover a suitable pattern description. It first looks for periodicities in the sequence by looking for relations that repeat at regular intervals. For example, axbxcx has period 2 based on the "next" relation in the forwards alphabet starting at a; qxapxboxc has period 3 in which the first element of each triple uses the backwards alphabet starting at q and the third letter of each triple uses the forwards alphabet starting at a. The relation repeating at period 3 is "next successor" of the corresponding element in the prior triple. If this simple periodicity cannot be found, then the program looks for a relation that is interrupted at regular intervals; for example, in aaabbbcccdd_, the relation "same letter" is interrupted in periods of 3. Once a basic periodicity has been found, the program makes a further analysis to uncover the details of the pattern, by detecting the relations—"next successor" or "same"—that hold between elements within a period or between corresponding elements in consecutive periods (as in the qxa . . . example above).

If such a generative rule is found, then it is used to extrapolate the next element. Several variants of the model differing in their power, i.e., in the richness of relations they can detect and use, were run and compared with the performance of college and high school students doing the same problems. A weak variant of the model did less well than the poorest subject, whereas a powerful variant did nearly as well as the best subject. There was considerable agreement among the subjects as a group and the program in ranking the problems in order of difficulty. Problem difficulty seemed correlated with the load on the subject's, and the model's, immediate memory. To solve the hard problems, the subject had to keep track in memory of his place on two separate lists (e.g., the forwards and the backwards alphabet), while for all easy problems he needed to keep track of his place on only one list.

Recently, Simon (1972) has shown how his earlier representation of serial pattern processing is consistent with other approaches which try to relate the structural complexity of a series pattern to the person's ability (a) to remember and reproduce a short sequence or to learn a cyclically recurring sequence (Glanzer & Clark, 1962; Restle, 1970), and (b) to judge, rate, or rank-order the psychological complexity of different sequences (Vitz & Todd, 1969). The basic measure of sequence complexity is the length of the internal code needed to describe the serial pattern in some appropriate representation. Simon argues that various theoretical approaches to serial pattern learning agree in supposing that subjects learn lawful sequences by inducing pattern descriptions which use the relations of "same" and "next successor" (in familiar numeric or letter "alphabets") between symbols, iteration of subpatterns, and hierarchic phrase structure. This analysis of the problem contrasts markedly with that given by statistical learning theory (see Chapter 12) for the learning of sequential patterns in the binary prediction (or "probability learning") experiments.

Another example of a program that performs a high-level intellectual task is one written by T. G. Evans (1968). Evans's program attempts to solve geometric-figure analogies of the type frequently encountered in various IQ tests. Two illustrative examples are shown in Figure 13.15 taken from tests prepared by the American Council on Education. The instructions to the subject (or program) are: "find the rule by which figure *A* has been changed to make figure *B*. Apply the rule to figure *C*. Select the resulting figure from figures 1–5." This task requires a considerable amount of information processing and transforming by human subjects, and it was of interest to Evans to see whether a heuristic program could be constructed which would arrive at the same answers that bright people do.

There are two main parts to Evans's program. The material given to the first part is a set of punched cards constructed by the experimenter giving a rather sketchy description of the outlined figures. For example, for figure *A* of Figure 13.15b it would identify a dot at a particular location in two-dimensional coordinates, a simple closed figure (triangle) with three vertices at specified locations, and another simple closed figure (rectangle) with four vertices at specified locations. The first part of the program performs analyses on these descriptions of the figures. It first labels the objects and then by various analytic geometry subroutines, provides various relational descriptions holding among parts of each figure. Thus, for figure *A* of Figure 13.15b, it would find that the dot is *above* the triangle and the rectangle, and that the rectangle is *inside* the triangle. Finally, part 1 of the program performs a "similarity calculation" on pairs of objects within each figure and between two figures (e.g., figure *A* to *B*, and figure *C* to figures 1, 2, 3, 4, 5). The similarity calculations on a pair of objects is done by a topological matching process which tries to find a set of transformations that take one object into another by horizontal or vertical reflection, rotation, translation, change of scale size, etc. Thus, in working on figures *A* and *B* of Figure 13.15b, it would find that the triangle in *A* matches the triangle in *B*, the rectangle in *A* matches the rectangle in *B*, etc. The object list, relational sentences, and similarity calculations are punched out and form the input to part 2 of the program.

The job of part 2 of the program is to find the answer to the problem. The first step is for it to generate one or more rules which transform figure *A* into figure *B*. Such rules specify how objects in *A* are to be removed, added to, or altered in their properties and relations to other objects to generate figure *B*. Such a rule relating *A* to *B* in Figure 13.15b would be "delete the dot and move the rectangle outside and to the left of the triangle." Each rule is generalized (if possible) so that it may be applied to figure *C*. It is performed on figure *C* and the program then checks to determine whether the transform of *C* matches one of figures 1–5. The method used deals generally with problems in which the number of objects added, removed, or altered in taking figure *A* into *B* is the same as the number of objects added, removed, or altered taking figure *C* into one of the answer

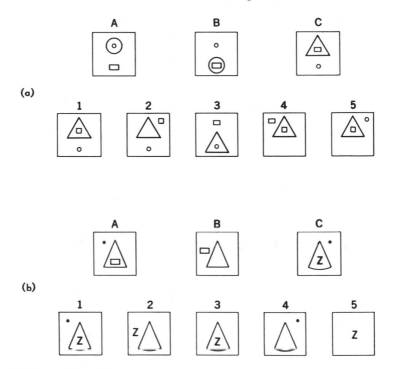

Figure 13.15.   Two illustrative problems solved by Evans's Geometric Analogies program. The question is: figure A is to figure B as figure C is to which one of the five answer figures? For problem (a), the answer is No. 3; for problem (b), the answer is No. 2.

figures. The routine may find two candidates for the answer. For example, several rules may be found taking figure A into B; more often the identification (or pairing) of A objects with C objects takes several forms (e.g., should we pair the Z with the rectangle or the triangle?), and depending on the pairings chosen, the rule formulated may transform C into something close to different answer figures. To select between answers (and identification pairings), the program selects (a) the rule that is the simplest in the sense of requiring the least alternation in the $A \rightarrow B$ rule to generalize it to the $C \rightarrow$ *some answer figure* rule, and (b) the rule that gives the better topological match of C transforms to some answer figure. These decision rules in the program enable it to mimic quite well the accepted answers to these problems as envisaged by the test's constructors. Over a number of such problems, the program's selected answer agreed with the accepted answer practically all of the time. In some cases where it differed, one could see grounds for a legitimate argument against the prescribed answers. In other cases, failure was clearly due to a poor degree of figure decomposition in part 1 of Evans's initial program. For example, in Figure 13.16 below, the program decomposes the representation into a square and three small triangles, located at the top and two sides of the square. But human subjects alternately can see the pattern as a square in the foreground superimposed

Figure 13.16.   An ambiguous figure that can be seen as a square with three small triangles, or as a square superimposed upon one large triangle.

upon a large triangle in the background. This is an instance where the Gestalt rule of "good continuity" of figures describes the phenomenon. If this latter description of the pattern is useful in later comparisons and rule-generating, then the person may find an answer where the program fails. Canaday (1962) at the Massachusetts Institute of Technology has worked with a pattern recognition program that operates on and analyzes such Gestalt features of figures, so that it indeed sees Figure 13.16 as "a square on top of a triangle."

As we mentioned earlier, Guzman's SEE program appears to do a better job of visual analysis than that available to Evans's analogies program when it was worked on in 1963. Winston (1970), building beyond Guzman's program, developed a very powerful way for describing visual scenes and the difference between two scenes. With this capability, his program gave very elegant solutions to geometric analogy problems involving toy-block scenes.

The General Problem-Solver

One of the most ambitious research programs on mechanical problem-solving is the General Problem-Solver (GPS), started by Newell, Shaw, and Simon (1959; Newell & Simon, 1961). GPS is a continuing project: since its conception in 1957, the program has existed in seven different "operating" versions, each version designed to handle a slightly different set of difficulties. The most recent versions are given in books by Ernst and Newell (1969) and Newell and Simon (1972). GPS was intended to be a core set of processes that could work on and solve a variety of problems involving different subject matters (proving theorems in logic, proving trigonometric identities, solving word puzzles, etc.). In setting up its operation on any particular problem, a "task environment" is to be provided by specifying for the machine the objects to be encountered and the transformation rules (moves) of the particular game.

The premises and the goal must be stated in comparable terms so that GPS seeks to transform the premises (or starting point) into the goal. It uses means-ends analyses, generating subproblems to work on, and builds up a tree of subproblems. There are general routines for comparing two expressions and detecting differences between them. If differences are detected, GPS then seeks some transformation which reduces these differences. Figure 13.17 gives a summary of three goals (or subgoals) and the associated methods GPS uses for working on them. The goals often occur recursively within a loop. Starting with the goal of transforming object A (e.g., premise) into object B (conclusion), the program may find one or more differences. If so, it sets up the goal of reducing the most important difference. This then goes to the goal of finding an operator (allowable transformation) which can be applied to the premises. If it cannot be so applied, then it sees whether A can be transformed into something to which the first operator can be applied. Part of the task environment supplied to GPS with the problem is an operator-difference (or "connection") table giving the permissible transformations that are relevant to reducing particular kinds of differences.

Goal I: Transform object A into object B

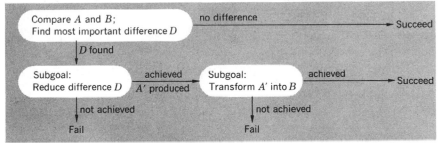

Goal II: Reduce difference D between object A and object B

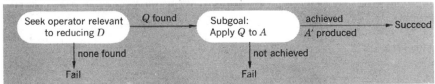

Goal III: Apply operator Q to object A

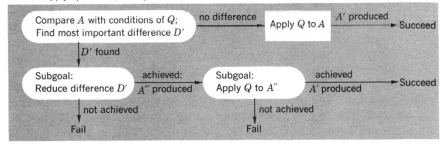

Figure 13.17.   A summary of the major goals and associated methods GPS uses to achieve these goals. The goals of transforming object A into B leads to the subgoal of reducing one or more differences between them. To reduce a given difference, a relevant operator is found. The next subgoal is to apply the operator to A. If that cannot be done, then the next subgoal is to see how A differs from something to which the operator can be applied. At this point the sequence will repeat at this lower level. (From B. F. Green, Jr., 1963. By permission.)

Because pursuit of each goal often leads to a proliferation of subgoals within subgoals, the GPS program has an executive routine that monitors the generation of new subgoals, evaluates them on multiple criteria, and then discards them or decides the order in which they will be worked on.

GPS involves considerably more processes and heuristics than this brief description conveys. In many respects, it is the most sophisticated of the simulation programs. It proves theorems, of course. Of perhaps greater interest to psychologists is the attempt by Newell and Simon (1972) to fit "thinking aloud" protocols taken from subjects who are encountering and solving logic and cryto-arithmetic problems for the first time, after only minimal training on the rules of the game. The subject is asked to think aloud, to say what he is looking for or considering at every step of the way while proving a theorem. Similarly, the internal workings (reasonings) of the computer program are printed out as it proceeds step by step to solve the problem. Analyzing numerous protocols, the authors point out a number of similarities in what the program and the subject are doing at various points along the construction of the proof. Newell and Simon conclude that the program's point-by-point behavior is a fairly accurate simulation of some of the significant features of the subject's verbal output and sequence of rule selections.

It is clear nevertheless that the General Problem-Solver is still very far from attaining the general capabilities of the human adult. It requires that the goal be described in exactly the same way as the givens of a problem. From this common description, it then tries to transform the givens into the goal. This constitutes a restriction, of course, on the class of problems it can attempt to solve. For example, the Letter Series Completion and the Geometric Analogies tasks have goals not describable in this manner, and it is clear that GPS would have no way of handling these or similar problems. In brief, GPS does not work on "ill-defined" problems for which the goal is not well specified.

Robot Projects

Perhaps of most interest to psychologists are the integrated "robot" projects that have developed at Stanford, MIT, and the Stanford Research Institute (SRI) over the past decade. The SRI robot appears the most ambitious of the several projects (see Fikes & Nilsson, 1971). It consists of a motor-driven cart with the following components:

(a) a television camera for taking a picture of its visual environment, a range-finder for triangulating the distance to any point from the robot, and a "cat whisker" that acts as a tactual sensor; these all relay afferent or sensory information to
(b) a computer holding a variety of programs for analyzing the afferent information, for planning out action sequences which will achieve certain effects upon its realistic environment, and
(c) a set of motors that can turn the cart, drive it forward or backward, and a set of bumpers that can be used to push boxes and other objects over a smooth floor.

The realistic environment provides a rich source of problems that can be posed for the robot to solve, as well as a fantastic number of engineering problems for the designers to solve. Let us consider just one problem to illustrate the nature of the system.

Consider Figure 13.18, which shows a schematic environment of five interconnected rooms with the robot in room 1 along with three boxes and a light switch. A first issue is to represent in the robot's memory information about the spatial layout of the environment. Some of this is relatively "permanent" information, such as where doors are and what rooms connect with other rooms. Included in this permanent information are also a number of physical laws about the environment (e.g., that an object in one place is not in another place) and rules of motion (e.g., that the robot cannot run over a box without moving it, or it cannot get into a room by going through brick walls, etc.). Some of the information in memory is "transient," such as the current location of the robot and the boxes. This information is acquired by the robot's video picture, which is analyzed by quite sophisticated "scene analysis" programs. The outcome of this transient analysis, plus the stable facts about the environment, are said to comprise the robot's "current model" of its world, call it M_0 (for initial model). For convenience, these facts are represented in terms of statements in the predicate calculus of logic. Thus, for example, the initial model (see Figure 13.18) would include the following statements regarding the locations of objects:

$$M_0: \begin{cases} \text{ATR } (e) \\ \text{AT (box 1, } A) \\ \text{AT (box 2, } B) \\ \text{AT (box 3, } C) \end{cases}$$

Suppose that the robot is now given the problem of gathering together the

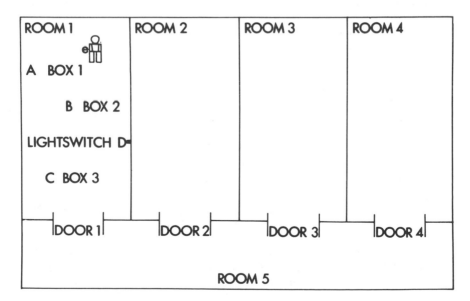

Figure 13.18. Room plan for the SRI robot. (From Fikes & Nilsson, 1971. By permission.)

three boxes. This goal is translated into a statement in the predicate calculus, to find a location x such that all three boxes are at x. A problem-solving program called STRIPS is the component that actually plans out the sequence of operators (steps or "motor commands") which the robot is to perform to achieve the goal state. STRIPS proceeds rather like GPS, using mainly the "means-ends" heuristic (for reducing differences), except that it has more powerful deductive capabilities than GPS. Beginning from its current "world model," M_0, STRIPS searches for a sequence of operators that will produce a new world model within which the goal statement is true. For the robot, the operators correspond to *action routines* whose execution causes the robot to take certain actions. Some of the action routines available to the SRI robot are as follows (consider the location constants to be two-dimensional vectors):

(1) go to $_1(m)$: robot goes to coordinate location m;
(2) go to $_2(m)$: robot goes *next* to item m;
(3) push to (m, n): robot pushes object m next to item n;
(4) turn on light (m): robot turns on light switch m;
(5) climb on box (m): robot climbs up on box m;
(6) climb off box (m): robot climbs off box m;
(7) go through door (d, m, n): robot goes through door d from room m into room n.

Each such operator has a set of *preconditions* which must be true of the world model before it can be applied. For example, the preconditions of *climb off box* (m) are that m is a box and that the robot is on m. Also, application of an operator causes the world model to change; these changes are handled by an *add* list and a *delete* list corresponding to each operator. The add list gives the new facts made true by the effect of the action on the world, whereas the delete list gives the prior true facts that have been canceled by the effect of the action. Two simple examples of add and delete lists for operators are the following:

(1) PUSH (k, m, n): robot pushes object k from place m to place n.
   precondition: AT (k, m): object k is at place m
                   ATR (m): robot at place m
   add list: AT (k, n): object k at place n
                   ATR (n): robot at place n
   delete list: AT (k, m): object k at place m
                   ATR (m): robot at place m

(2) GO TO (m, n): robot goes from place m to place n
   precondition: ATR (m): robot at place m
   add list: ATR (n): robot at place n
   delete list: ATR (m): robot at place m

STRIPS uses a theorem prover to try to show that the goal follows from the initial world model, M_0. If it cannot do this at once, like GPS it extracts from the uncompleted proof the difference between M_0 and the goal, and seeks an operator relevant to reducing this difference. If one is found, a subgoal is set up to prove that the preconditions of that operator (what must be true if it is to be applied) are satisfied by the current world model.

If so, then the operator is applied, the world model is updated (to M_1) by the add and delete lists of that operator, and the next step is to see whether M_1 satisfies the goal. If not, then the program takes the difference and applies the same routine again, and again in recursive fashion. If the precondition of a desired operator is not satisfied by the current world model, a subgoal will be set up to find an applicable operator which will imply a model that will satisfy the preconditions. This is, of course, the same sort of subproblem as the overall problem, and it illustrates the hierarchy of goals, subgoals, and models that may be generated by the search process. STRIPS evaluates particular continuations or lines of search by taking account of such factors as the number of subgoals remaining to be solved, the complexity of the differences among and types of predicates of these subgoals. It selects for development that search line having the better evaluation.

To return to the initial problem, the robot has been commanded to push together the three boxes (or has been given another goal which requires this as a subgoal). It might first determine to push box 1 from place A to place B near box 2. But a precondition for applying a PUSH (box 1, A, B) operator is that ATR(A). So a GO TO$_2$ (box 1) operator must be used to satisfy this precondition. Having moved behind box 1 and pushed it to box 2, the robot then applies a similar operator sequence to push box 3 to box 2, thus achieving its goal. Although this description is quite brief, the amount of problem-graph searching the robot (computer) does to achieve the task is quite large. But it must be remembered that the robot is rather like an uneducated baby in its initial performance of such tasks. Once it has carried out the task and similar ones several times, it will have learned a rather general subroutine for how to collect together various objects. The subroutine, somewhat like a human's, would be generalized over such particulars as how many objects are to be collected, what the objects are, and where they are located relative to the robot's initial position. Fikes (personal communication, 1972) is working on the question of how to generalize or abstract successful "action sequences" away from irrelevant particulars while capturing the relevant variables of each case (e.g., if one object is fixed, such as the light switch in Figure 13.18, then the pile of other objects must be collected around the stationary object).

The SRI robot has been tried out on a wide range of tasks, the programs revised and tried out again on harder tasks, and so on in successive cycles of refinement. It solves a number of problems. To list just a few of these in reference to the arrangements of Figure 13.18: the robot can go to a fixed location in another room; it can remove any pushable box that is blocking a doorway it has to go through; it can go to a specified room and push a box from there to another room; it can turn on the light switch by moving the tallest box to beneath the light switch then climbing up on it, and so on. It can perform a surprising range of effective actions, and its capabilities are expanding. An interesting and instructive movie is available from the Robot Project at SRI which illustrates the varieties of problems the robot solves and which provides some explanation of the scene analysis routines and the planning carried out by the STRIPS problem-solving program. This project and the "hand-eye" projects at MIT and Stanford University have been in the forefront in the past decade in proposing substantive problems and achieving significant results within the artificial intelligence field. Psychologists, particularly those professing a "cognitive bias," can be expected to show increasing interest in these bodies of substantial work.

Having in mind the various "special purpose" problem-solving programs we have reviewed, we may be tempted to imagine that a complete model of man would be a supersystem that somehow combines all these various programs into one. Few scientists have even attempted to suggest how this might be done in a really ingenious way. The trivial logical solution, of course, would be to have an executive program that is a pattern recognizer and dispatcher. All special programs would be linked to this dispatcher, either waiting on separate computers or in a call-up library. The executive program would recognize the problem type and dispatch it to the appropriate special purpose computer, which would work on it and relay back the answer. This is not an elegant solution to the dream problem of getting a general purpose machine. However, except for duplication of processes in the linked computers, it is difficult to say exactly how and where the dispatcher system differs very much from what humans do.

LANGUAGE-PROCESSING PROGRAMS

It is hardly possible to doubt that the unique capability of men is their competence in using language—listening to it, understanding it, using it for thinking and inference, and producing more of it in speech and writing. Modeling of these capabilities is currently the most formidable project confronting those at work in the simulation and artificial intelligence fields. The magnitude of this problem has resulted in its breakup into many splinter disciplines, each attacking a different aspect of the general problem. There are good general reviews of the chief issues and lines of research by Simmons (1970) and in books edited by Borko (1967), Simon and Siklossy (1972), and Minsky (1968). We shall touch briefly on three of the splinter areas.

Mechanical Translation

After giving the computer text in one language (e.g., Russian) the machine is to output an acceptable translation of it in another language (English). Because of the multiple meanings and usages of a given word in both languages, a simple dictionary-search program produces nothing but gibberish. Some syntactic and semantic (meaning) analysis is required, and this is exceedingly difficult to supply. About 1968 or so, a conference of experts on machine translations came to the conclusion that all efforts based on syntactic analysis and word-for-word substitution had failed, and that this approach should be abandoned. Obviously before one can translate, one must first correctly understand what is being said in the source language. But this itself is a vast problem, so efforts have been directed to designing programs which understand. The basic notion (e.g., Schank, 1972) is to have a conceptual base ("meaningful understanding") into which statements are translated and from which other statements are output. If the input and output are in different surface languages, then translation is occurring. One of the better new-generation programs which does this sort of translation (between English and French) is one by Wilks (1973).

Information Retrieval

A person places a request for all available documents on some particular topic (e.g., "simulation of learning by machines"). The ideal machine, having a large file of documents and their indexed listing, determines what the request is about and which documents are relevant to it, retrieves them from the files, and delivers them, or a list of their references, to the man making the request. Besides that of understanding the request, the problem here is to design a suitable classification and indexing system, since titles of papers are seldom informative of the range of topics discussed in the article. Another approach is not to store indexed titles of documents, but rather to take as one's data base the entire text itself. For instance, early versions of the PROTOSYNTHEX program of Simmons et al. (1966) began with the text of the children's Golden Book encyclopedia in memory, and requests were answered by retrieving relevant sentences from memory. The program first found the sentences in memory having the most words in common with the request, then performed some syntactic analysis to see whether the common words were in the right grammatical relationship to each other. If they were, then the selected text would be output as the answer. The problem with this approach is threefold: first, the request and the relevant target sentence in storage may be expressed in different paraphrases, so that literal word-matching fails to identify the answer; second, words can be quite ambiguous in having several meanings, and again simple word-matching will not necessarily select textual passages relevant to the requester's intended meaning (e.g., a request for information relevant to "banking" may retrieve facts about airplane flying, constructing raceways, and/or financial transactions); third, questions typically ask for inferences or deductions from a data base rather than for a simple spitting out of information from the store. Programs which can interpret questions and set up inferential procedures to compute answers are called question-answering systems. In many ways, they are the most interesting programs to psychologists. In more recent versions of PROTOSYNTHEX (Simmons et al., 1968) some of these inferential capabilities have been introduced, and the data base is now more conceptual and less literal in its form. This helps in recognition of paraphrases, but it does assign a heavy burden to the coding system (or "parser") which translates sentences into the conceptual base.

Understanding and Question-Answering Programs

The two areas of understanding and question answering will be treated together because one of the standard tests of understanding a sentence is that one be able to answer questions requiring use of the information in that sentence. However, much of the research has kept these two emphases somewhat distinct, possibly to the detriment of progress in the overall area. The better "understanding" programs appear to be precisely those that have a powerful question-answering component along with a realistic semantic-pragmatic basis (e.g., Winograd, 1972).

The basic components of all such systems are diagrammed in Figure 13.19. The user (or the environment) inputs statements which are either facts, questions, or commands. These statements are usually made in a restricted subset of English, with particular kinds of grammatical complexities disallowed. A translator or parser tries to convert the input statement into a coded version that is understandable and usable by the internal processes of the program. This is *the* primary difficulty, of course. Parsing is the procedure by which different elements in a statement are grouped together in a logical "deep structure." To illustrate, an ordinary sentence like "The man who was angered by it called the polluters up" involves a complex set of syntactic relations. The use of the definite article *the* signals that the speaker has a particular man and particular polluters in mind. Moreover, we know that the main verb is *called up* despite the fact that these two words are well separated in the surface sentence. In addition, we know that *called* is to be attached to *man* rather than to the pronoun *it* which is closest to the verb. We know that the phrase beginning "who..." is a relative clause modifying "the man" and that the relative clause is a passive construction that extends to the main verb. The relative clause itself is an embedded proposition, saying that "something angered the man." Moreover, the use of *it* in the relative clause, we know, probably refers to some adverse effect of the act of polluting (done by the polluters), which effect has angered the man. Thus, at a *conceptual* level the sentence is saying something like "Some persons or institutions polluted something, which caused the man to become angered, which caused him to telephone those persons or institutions"; presumably, he telephoned to complain to them about their polluting. Although an English speaker has the tacit knowledge to perform such parsing tasks effortlessly, it has proved inordinately difficult to program a computer to do it for a wide or general range of sentences. The most successful syntax parser is one programmed by Woods (1970), who was able to realize something close to a Chomskian transformational grammar as a simple recursive transition network.

A basic problem for syntactic parsers is that it does not suffice to simply

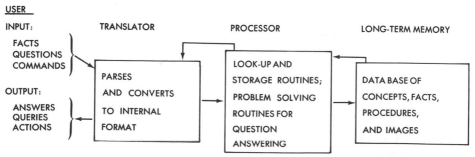

Figure 13.19.   Major components of a fact-retrieval and question-answering system.

look up the various meanings and grammatical parts of speech of the words in a sentence and then select combinations according to their fit to a host of standard grammatical frames. That approach quickly "explodes" into multiple parses of most sentences. As one example (cited in Quillian, 1968), Kuno's Harvard Multiple-Pass Syntactic Analyzer gave 120 different parsings to the definitional sentence "A *whip* can be a stick with a cord or leather fixed to the end of it, used to give blows in driving animals, etc., or as punishment." How can a dumb syntactic analyzer see 120 different parsings in that sentence, whereas we see only one? Because words have multiple meanings and syntactic form classes depending on their use in the sentence. For example, the word *fixed* in the definition can mean *repaired, altered, drugged, bribed, arranged,* or *attached,* and *stick* has even more meanings and syntactic forms. The meanings of words *multiply* in their sentential combinations, leading to the absurd proliferation of multiple interpretations of the sentence.

Clearly what is needed is some way to combine the meanings of the various words in a way that makes sense. That, of course, is what various "semantics-based" parsing systems attempt to do. In semantics-based parsers, such as Quillian's (1968), Schank's (1972), or Winograd's (1972), the general idea is to allow the context of the discourse as well as the meanings of the various words to act jointly along with a syntax analyzer to determine the most likely parsing and interpretation of the sentence. Winograd's parsing system is rather like Woods's in that it is written as a sequence of programs (one for each major grammatical group) which can recursively call one another during parsing. The advance of Winograd's system over Woods's is that there is a continuous interaction between grammatical evaluation and semantic evaluation (checks for meaningfulness of a tentative parsing). Winograd's system also differs in that much of the knowledge it has in long-term memory is not stored as simple facts but rather as procedures (or recipes) for proving or inferring certain consequences. For instance, instead of directly storing a universal fact like "All humans are mortal," Winograd's system would store this as a labeled "theorem" whose interpretation, is, roughly: "If I should ever wish to prove that X is mortal, then this can be done by proving that X is a human." The value of this representation is that it enormously facilitates inferences, such as the sophomoric logical syllogism "if Socrates is human, then Socrates is mortal."

In some of the more powerful question-answering systems (e.g., the QA-3 system of C. C. Green & Raphael, 1968, and C. C. Green, 1969a, 1969b), the translation goes from English into symbolic expressions in the predicate calculus. The facts that the system knows are then treated as a set of axioms, whereas a question to be answered is treated as a theorem to be proved by applying rules of inference to the axioms (the fact base). For example, if it knows facts such as IN (Bill, car), and IN (car, garage), and HAS (Bill, Jewels), then QA-3, through certain inferences permitted by IN and HAS predicates, can prove that the jewels are now in the garage. The query "Where are the jewels?" would create a program to find an X such that IN (jewels, X) is true. Green's QA-3 system uses J. A. Robinson's (1970) resolution principle in "mechanically deriving" the theorem (answer to question) from the axiom system (the set of facts known). Although resolution techniques are powerful derivational tools in logic, they clearly are inefficient and bear no resemblance to the way people reason from a fact base.

There are a variety of other question-answering systems available, programmed for special task environments and restricted subsets of English. In one by B. F. Green et al. (1961), basic factual data are put into the computer in well-organized, tabular form, and then questions are asked of the machine that require it to recombine or process the data in sometimes novel ways to compute the answer. Scores of baseball games played by the Yankees in July might be given as the basic data. A question asked might be, "In what percentage of their contests did the Yankees beat the Red Sox?" The main job, of course, is getting the machine to understand what is being asked for, and then proceed to find the data relevant to the answer. A program by R. K. Lindsay (1963) takes as input Basic English statements about kinship relations, constructs a meaningful model of the family tree, and then answers questions by inference from this kinship model. Given the data that Jane is Jim's sister and Mary's daughter, the computer, when asked, will infer that Mary is Jim's mother. If given many relational statements, the family tree may grow complex and inferences become difficult to draw out. Lindsay's aim was not to resolve kinship claims but rather to document his belief that realistic models of language must attribute to the subject (program) some ability to construct a usable representation of his (its) environment. The sentences processed by a person refer to things in the world and help him to construct by induction an internal "picture" of that world. Accordingly, questions are answered by referring to his "world view" rather than by scanning through a file of sentences he has stored away in his memory.

Another language-processing program by D. G. Bobrow (1964) solves word problems in algebra. Its main task is to perform a syntactic and semantic analysis of statements in English so as to effect a translation of them into a system of mathematical equations. Methods are employed to identify the mathematical variables and to translate relational statements ("Jim is twice as old as Jane") into equational form, and to interpret just what information is being requested. As most schoolboys know, once the translation has been successfully achieved, the solution of the system of linear equations is easy (as it is, too, for Bobrow's program).

Woods (1967) programmed a question-answering system that arranges airline flights for its user. The data base is the national airlines guide, giving direct flights and times between any two American airports. A typical problem solved by the program is when to schedule a person on a particular day for flights between two or more destinations, when he specifies desired approximate departure and arrival times. Difficulties can arise if one or more connecting flights must be scheduled through intermediate stops, all with appropriate time allowances. Woods's system was one of the first to define the meanings of primitive predicates like DEPART (flight A from place B) and CONNECT (place A to place B via flight C) in terms of programmed subroutines which the system is called upon to perform in doing inference and problem-solving. This same procedural approach to semantics is taken in Wonograd's program, which is presently the most powerful language-analysis program available.

Winograd's system handles discourse regarding a "toy world" comprised of a tabletop supporting wooden blocks and pyramids of various sizes and colors, and a large box in which objects can be placed. The discourse program drives a "mechanical hand" which can pick up blocks and move them about. The program has a number of primitive predicates for describing its visual world, and the actions it can perform with respect to that block world. Its approach to solving block-manipulation problems uses the PLANNER language, which allows easy formulation of recursive subgoals much as is done in the STRIPS program discussed earlier. Thus, given the command to GRASP (block B1), Winograd's program will first check for certain preconditions: "Is the hand already holding B1? Is B1 graspable? Is the hand holding something else? If so, get rid of it by finding a clear space on the table and putting the unwanted object there. Is the top of B1 cleared off so the hand can grasp it? If not, clear off the top of B1. How? By finding some clear space on the table, and. . . ." This sort of recursive programming of action routines to solve block manipulations is done with impressive efficiency in PLANNER, the goal-oriented programming language used by Winograd.

In carrying out a series of actions and subgoals along the way to carrying out a command, Winograd's program will store an explicit record of the sequence of intermediate-level events. This record comes in very handy in disambiguating anaphoric and/or pronominal reference, wherein later sentences refer back to earlier events in an opaque way. For example, after the program is told early on to pick up and move a block and subsequently to count the number of objects on the tabletop that are not in the box, it is then asked: "Is at least one of them narrower than the one I told you to pick up?" The problem here, which Winograd's program solves, is to understand that the pronoun "them" refers to the objects enumerated just previously. It also has a record of which block it was told to pick up earlier. Retrieving the block's measurements, the program then compares these to the blocks that are not in the box, finds a narrower one, and so outputs the answer, "Yes, the red one." This short-term event memory thus enables the program to resolve ambiguities of references and to answer questions regarding why or how some state of affairs came into existence. In brief, the program can recite its autobiography. In addition to these components, Winograd's program has a rich variety of inference-making capabilities; this allows it, for instance, to answer complex questions regarding a visual scene.

This is a most brief excursion through the rapidly developing field of computational linguistics and question-answering programs. The field is in ferment now with many ingenious and independent approaches to the problems of language analysis. This work is in many ways much more relevant to psycholinguists than is work in pure linguistics, because the computer simulators show more concern with synthesizing realistic models of linguistic performance than with stating abstract models of the linguistic competence of an idealized speaker-listener. Several groups of psychologists—for example, J. R. Anderson and Bower (1973), Kintsch (1972), and Rumelhart, Lindsay, and Norman (1972)—have developed models along these lines which make explicit contact with psychological results. The development and testing of simulation models for linguistic performance and the learning and retrieval of linguistic materials would appear to be a coming major effort within cognitive psychology.

LEARNING PROGRAMS

Relevant to the subject of this volume are the information-processing models aimed at understanding learning. In the preceding discussion of intelligent automata, we touched briefly on programs incorporating learning subroutines, which are used in modifying other parts of the program with the aim of effecting a better match between the program's response and an optimally intelligent one. Such subroutines indeed produce adaptive, responsive, optimizing machines. However, in many cases, simulation of how the actual subject might learn and improve his performance is not the goal. The information-processing models to be considered in this section were devised as first steps toward this aim. Accordingly, the theorists considered below have been more often concerned with describing and modeling experimental results than with actually producing an artificially intelligent machine.

Verbal Learning

A model of general interest to psychologists is the Elementary Perceiver and Memorizer (EPAM) of E. A. Feigenbaum and H. A. Simon. Their aim was to develop a model that simulates human behavior in a variety of experimental tasks involving associative learning. Included among these tasks would be paired-associate learning, rote serial learning, recognition learning, immediate or short-term memory tasks, and learning to read text, to name objects or pictures, to form concepts, and the like. In principle, the stimuli could be given directly to the machine in any form—visual or auditory. In fact, however, the present version of EPAM has no perceptual processor, so the programmer has to analyze the stimuli into distinctive features, punch this information onto IBM cards, and only then will EPAM be able to deal with the "stimuli."

Because of the comprehensive goals of the model, it is complicated and lengthy. The basic model (E. A. Feigenbaum, 1959) has undergone extensive testing and modification. The version to be discussed below is that described in a paper by Simon and Feigenbaum (1964). We consider its application to paired-associate learning. Specifically, suppose the model is learning a list of nonsense syllable pairs (*REH-GIJ, RUZ-FOT*, etc.). One part of the program simulates the experimental task; that is, it imitates a paced memory drum which exposes first a stimulus member, then the stimulus and response members together, repetitively cycling through all pairs in the list. The model's task is to anticipate (print out) the correct response when the stimulus is shown.

EPAM learns by building up a sorting tree or discrimination net that makes possible differentiation among the stimuli and responses. The sorting tree is a serial processing system much like that displayed previously in Figure 13.6. Stored at terminal nodes of this sorting tree are compound "images," which are more or less complete representations of the S-R pairs.

In general, neither the features used for sorting nor the information stored in the image is complete; that is, no more information is stored than is minimally needed to get by on the task at hand.

Two learning processes, image building (familiarization) and discrimination learning (tree growing) are postulated. When a stimulus S in view is sorted to a terminal node, it is compared with the stimulus image, S', residing there (from past experience). If no image is there, then part of S is copied as the image at that node. If an image is already there, a comparison of S and S' is made; if differences in detail only are detected, S' is changed or augmented to match S better. Thus is the S' image of S grown. If a positive difference (not just a lack of detail) between S and S' is detected, then the discrimination learning process takes over and constructs two new branches from the former terminal node, with S and S' separately as the images of the new terminals. To illustrate, suppose that we can arrive at a current terminal node by tests on the first letter R, and the current image at this node is R_H (see Figure 13.20a). Later RUZ is sorted to this node. In comparing RUZ to the image R_H, the program notes a difference in detail in the second position (not serious) and a positive difference (Z versus H) in the third position. It would then set up a third-letter test at this node as shown in Figure 13.20b. With this new node added to the tree, the stimuli REH and RUZ are no longer sorted to the same node and confusion errors between them will be avoided.

Although the sorting (recognizing) is done on the stimulus member of the pair, both the stimulus and response syllables are represented as a compound image S'-R' at the terminal node. The response image, R', is retrieved when S gets sorted to and makes contact with the stimulus image S'. The response image R' contains information enabling the program to locate another terminal node R'' in the net, and R'' will, after learning, contain the images of the three letters of the response syllables (G, I, J) and the information required to produce them (print them out). Eventually, then, presentation of stimulus REH causes the machine to print out GIJ and it has learned.

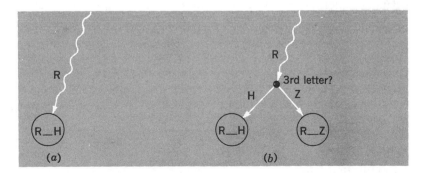

Figure 13.20.   An example of how a formerly terminal node in EPAM's discrimination net will be elaborated to differentiate previously confused stimuli. In (a), by first letter tests on R one arrives at a terminal node bearing the image R—H. Later, when RUZ is sorted to this node, causing a confusion error, a new test is added based on the third letter (b) and two lower nodes are sprouted from this terminal.

One virtue of this system is that it treats the nominal stimulus and response terms in comparable fashion, namely, as images to be built up in the sorting tree. Also the S-R pair to be associated requires no special representation as it is simply a compound image constructed from two simpler images. In addition to the recognition and learning processes mentioned above, EPAM has a higher-level executive routine that oversees and "runs the show." Part of its job is to keep the central processes in contact with the environment (e.g., "stop processing that last item; respond to the new S that has just appeared in the drum window"), to schedule where and how it shall distribute the processing effort and time at its disposal, since image building and net growing take processing time. It uses feedback about its current performance on an S-R pair to decide, roughly speaking, what is the matter and what part of the knowledge structure needs more polishing. These executive macroprocesses are responsible for some of EPAM's more interesting predictions—for instance, they allow it to predict serial position curves in rote serial learning (see E. A. Feigenbaum & Simon, 1962) and to account for the effect on serial learning of segmenting the series into groups of varying sizes (see Gregg, 1972). There are many more details to EPAM, but this sketch is not intended to do more than describe the basic processes it uses.

Simon and Feigenbaum (1964) have put the EPAM model through a variety of simulated learning experiments and compared its trial-by-trial output with that of human subjects. It shows a number of similarities to the data. Like human subjects, EPAM takes longer to learn a list in which the stimulus items are highly similar (many common letters). It displays positive or negative transfer in learning a second list depending on the stimulus-response relations of the two lists, in much the same way that the human data depends on these relations (see the reviews of work on transfer and retention in Chapter 9). It shows the beneficial effect of prior familiarization with the stimulus and response terms before these are used in a paired-associate learning task. The model shows stimulus confusion errors and retroactive interference to a degree depending on the similarity of stimulus items in the original learned list and the interpolated list. The simulation of the data is sometimes fairly accurate in a relative quantitative sense, i.e., the ratio of trials to learn under condition A to that for condition B is about the same for the model as for the human data. In an early paper, E. A. Feigenbaum and Simon (1961) showed that EPAM exhibited an interesting form of mediation (chained associations) seen in the training of reading. In phase 1, EPAM learned to associate acoustically coded properties of the spoken word *kahr* with symbolic pointing to a visually coded picture of a car. In phase 2, it learned to associate the visual word *car* with the acoustic pattern *kahr*. When later tested with the visual word *car* and required to point at a picture, it selected the car picture. This is a simple example of mediated transfer, and is of the elementary sort that most stimulus-response analyses would predict.

Hintzman (1968) has developed a series of models (dubbed SAL for Stimulus and Association Learner) based on the adaptive development of a discrimination net. The initial model (SAL-I), which simulates paired-associate learning, begins with essentially the same assumptions as EPAM except that net growth ("learning new discriminators") is considered to be a probabilistic process. In order to fit experimental results of various sorts, Hintzman introduced three further assumptions in SAL. First, it was supposed that even after perfect mastery of an item the program can still learn further descriptors about that item (i.e., growth of the net could occur on correct-response trials as well as on error trials.) This enables the theory to handle a variety of effects such as the effects of overlearning in reducing retroactive interference. Second, it was supposed that the "response" stored at the terminal node to which a stimulus is sorted could be a *list* or push-down stack of responses that have been reinforced to stimulus patterns sorted in that terminal. The rule for placing new responses on this push-down stack may be illustrated with respect to the terminal node denoted R_H in Figure 13.20a. This node was arrived at only by tests on the first letter, R. Suppose response A1 is attached to this stimulus terminal. A later pair RUZ-A2 will be sorted to this same terminal and an error (A1) will occur. But suppose that a new discriminator is not learned on this occasion; then Hintzman's SAL-III model would store the new response A2 in the top of a push-down stack attached to the terminal node R_H (with the old error A1 placed in the second slot in the stack). This assumption of a temporally ordered response hierarchy at "confused" stimulus terminals turns out to have a number of salutary implications that accord with details of verbal learning experiments (e.g., that pair recognition suffers far less interference than paired-associate recall). A third assumption of SAL-III is that, over time, responses residing at lower positions on a push-down stack will "spontaneously rise," and in so doing "push out" more recent responses and cause them to be forgotten. This *ad hoc* assumption, akin to the notion of "spontaneous recovery" of unlearned associations (see Chapter 9), enables SAL to account for several important facts regarding temporal changes in proactive and retroactive interference over a retention interval.

Hintzman's work is exemplary insofar as it utilizes relatively few assumptions, carefully delimits the range of phenomena to be explained, then proceeds systematically to explore the consequences of the simulated model in relation to a large number of different experimental results. The outcome is perhaps one of the most impressive examples we have of a simulation model being fit to a wide range of experimental results in learning. The EPAM and SAL models are surely not perfect nor complete theories, and they have been effectively criticized (e.g., see J. R. Anderson & Bower, 1973, Chapter 4). However, they are also clearly the sorts of serious models that a theoretical psychologist likes to have in his portfolio in trying to understand the nature of learning.

The Binary Choice Program

Feldman (1961, 1962) proposed a model to simulate the behavior of subjects in the binary experiment known as "probability learning." Such experiments were described earlier in Chapter 12 (see p. 385). In them, the subject tries to predict successive members in a sequence of binary events (e.g., C or P) that are shown to him one at a time. The sequences are constructed randomly (e.g., 70 percent C and 30 percent P events), although subjects frequently believe the sequence is lawful and orderly and they try to discover its pattern. The traditional account of behavior in this situation is that given by stochastic learning models (see Chapter 12), which suppose that the subject's probability of predicting C increases or decreases trial by trial depending on whether the C or P event occurs. It will be recalled from our review in Chapter 12 that these models have trouble accounting for sequential patterning in the subject's responses.

Feldman's model supposes that in this situation the subject is trying to discover local patterns (or trying out sequential hypotheses) to explain the event sequence and to extrapolate (predict) the next member of the series. To get information relevant to these notions, Feldman had his subjects "think aloud" and state their reasons trial by trial for the predictions they made. A subject's protocol consisted then of the sequence of his predictions and the reasons he gave for each. Feldman's model attempts to account for the sequence of reasons, since the subject almost always made a prediction that was consistent with the reason he gave. The model is tailored specifically to simulate a particular subject, and details of the program vary for different subjects.

The program proceeds by the testing out of hypotheses which are attempts to explain the event sequence. The trial-by-trial cycle for the model is as follows: use the current hypothesis to predict the next event; the next event occurs, and it is explained by an explanation hypothesis; a prediction hypothesis is developed, and is used to predict the next event; the next event occurs and the cycle repeats.

Each hypothesis consists of two components: an event-pattern hypothesis and a guess-opposite component. The event-pattern hypothesis is selected from a list of pattern hypotheses such as "progression of Cs," "alternation of two Cs and two Ps," and so forth. The patterns are placed on this list by the theorist after examining what types the subject said he used. The guess-opposite component may be either "on" or "off": if the pattern hypothesis is a progression of Cs and this component is off, the model predicts C; if the guess-opposite component is on, the model predicts P, the opposite of the pattern.

Various rules are employed whereby feedback from the event sequence is used to select, alter, or maintain the current hypothesis. If a hypothesis predicts correctly, it is retained for another trial. If it predicts incorrectly, it is likely to be replaced temporarily. In this case, the events from the last three or four trials are used to select the plausible candidates from the pattern-hypothesis list. If several candidates are plausible, the program chooses that pattern hypothesis which has been used most often in the past. The circumstances for modification of the guess-opposite component are more complicated and cannot be easily summarized.

Feldman (1962) has published the outcome of fitting the model to the behavior of one subject. His procedure was to continually revise the model until it gave a good fit. Feldman summarizes the process as follows:

The completion of the model was a lengthy task involving the iterative procedure of proposing a detailed model, testing the model against the data, modifying the model, testing again, and so on. During this procedure, almost every part of the model originally proposed was modified or replaced. (p. 342)

A unique feature of Feldman's model assessment was his use of "conditional prediction." If the model's prediction of the subject's hypothesis on trial n proved incorrect, then the model was set back on the correct track by replacing its "predicted" hypothesis with the subject's actual hypothesis. The supposition was that the model is strongly path-dependent, in the sense that if it is "off" on trial n, it will get progressively farther off from the data if it is not set back on the track.

These two methodological points, models tailored for individuals and contingent predictions, are novel to Feldman's work. They will be discussed later in the section on evaluation of simulation models. Suffice it to say that by using these techniques, Feldman demonstrated that his model was able to predict his subject's protocol with a high degree of accuracy.

Concept Learners

Psychologists have for many years carried out investigations of concept learning, most of the more recent ones falling within the framework of the kind of experimental tasks whose analysis was proposed by Hovland (1952). Stimulus objects or patterns are characterized according to a list of attributes, each with a number of values. For example, geometric patterns can differ in the attributes of size, color, shape, orientation, and so on. If there are n attributes with v values each, then there are potentially v^n patterns in all. A concept can be defined by a division of this set into two parts, with the patterns in one part belonging to class A and the remainder belonging to the complement class $\bar{A}$.

To illustrate, the universe of patterns might be four-letter nonsense strings; in each letter position ("attribute") any of three letters ("values") can appear. If the attribute-values are (X, Z, T), (P, M, K), (J, W, R), and (B, T, S), then $XPJB$ and $ZPRT$ are elements of the universe while $XZTP$ and $XPTW$ are not. For convenience, in the following we use abbreviations such as $3J$ to indicate the letter J at position 3. In Hovland's initial scheme, concepts were defined by specifying one attribute-value (e.g., $2K$) or several attribute values with a logical connective between them. In a *conjunctive* problem (e.g., $1X$ *and* $2P$), patterns containing both $1X$ and $2P$ go into class A; otherwise, into class $\bar{A}$. In other words, $1X$ (as is $2P$) is separately necessary but not a sufficient condition for class A. Several varieties of logical connectives are available besides these: exclusive disjunction ($2M$ or $4S$ but not both), implication ($4S$ or not $2M$ or both), and biconditional ($1X$ and $2P$, or not $1X$ and not $2P$).

E. B. Hunt (1962) and E. B. Hunt, Marin, and Stone (1966), following early notions of E. B. Hunt and Hovland (1961), developed an information-processing model which learns or solves such concept problems. Although the model uses several strategies that humans apparently also use (e.g., having a bias for conjunctive solutions), it contains features which humans quite certainly do not show (e.g., perfect memory for many previous patterns, perfect rationality, errorless checking and validation of a hypothesis).

The program proceeds roughly as follows: as successive instances of the A and $\bar{A}$ class are shown to the machine, they are stored away on two separate lists in memory. The model learns a concept by growing a sorting tree (serial processor); the sorting tree and the concept labels, A and $\bar{A}$, stored at its terminal nodes are then sufficient to classify all further instances. For example, a tree for the inclusive disjunction ($2M$ or $4S$ or both) is shown in Figure 13.21a, and one for exclusive disjunction ($2M$ or $4S$ but not both) in Figure 13.21b. The nodes of the tree ask a question about an attribute-value; depending on how an input pattern "answers" this question, it is shunted by the left or right branch to a lower node.

Hunt's concept learner is an algorithm embodying a "wholist strategy," which looks for common features of objects classified similarly. Given the current lists of A and $\bar{A}$ patterns, it looks for one or more characteristics always present in one list but not in the other. If such features are found, they are made the first node of the sorting tree and the problem is solved. This alone suffices if the concept is the affirmation or denial of either one element (e.g., not $2M$) or a conjunction of elements. If no such feature is found, then a first node is composed of that feature which occurs most frequently in the positive instances. This node produces two new pairs of sublists, namely, lists of positive and negative instances which do or do not have the first feature. Treating each pair of sublists as a separate problem, the program uses the wholist strategy again (recurses back to the beginning) on each subproblem, and from there constructs a second and third node for the sorting tree. The reader may verify that two such recursions will suffice to solve any two-element concept, e.g., the disjunctions in Figure 13.21. The recursion continues, or the decision tree grows, until all patterns in memory have been correctly classified.

In Hunt's program, the tree-growing routines will eventually come to a solution in the sense of correctly sorting all members of its A and $\bar{A}$ list. The decision tree it grows is not guaranteed to be the simplest in a logical sense but, in fact, it was so in most of the simulated runs of the program. E. B. Hunt, Marin, and Stone (1966) report results of conducting several experiments on the model's behavior. The main evidence offered for considering this as an initial candidate for simulation of how people solve concept problems is that the rank order of difficulty in solving concepts of different logical types turns out to be about the same for the program as for most people. At best, this is a weak constraint and not a very demanding test for a reasonable model to pass. The difficulty of acquiring a given concept is roughly correlated with the length of the logical statement required to define it. For example, "$2M$" is easiest, "$2M$ and $4S$" is next, "$2M$ or $4S$ or both" is next, and "$2M$ and $4S$, or not $2M$ and not $4S$" is hardest. A somewhat more convincing result is that a subject's trial-by-trial classifications of patterns (while learning) were predicted better by the model than by the responses of another subject going through the same problem.

The deficiencies of the model considered as a simulation are its large memory, its rationality, and its reliance upon a wholist strategy. Humans have error-prone memories, are not always rational, and have flexible search strategies that are easily modified by instructions or by a small amount of practice on problems of one type (e.g., Haygood & Bourne, 1965). A more realistic model incorporating short-term memory considerations has been proposed by G. F. Williams (1971). Her model assumes two memory stores: a short-term buffer for stimulus values to which it has recently attended, and

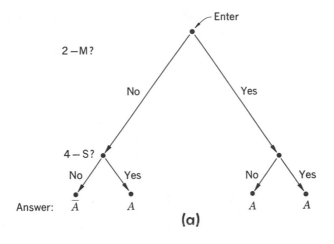

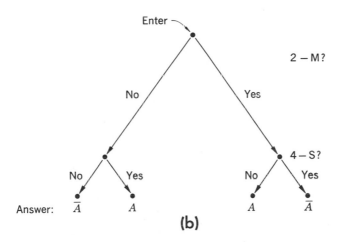

Figure 13.21.   Examples of optimally efficient binary sorting trees for classifying stimuli. In (a), the A concept is "2M or 4S or both." The first node asks whether the input pattern has an M in the second position; the second node asks whether it has an S in the fourth position. In (b), the A concept is "2M or 4S but not both."

a long-term memory that holds evaluations of stimulus dimensions which the subject has tested and rejected as irrelevant. The information in these two stores is assumed to interact; earlier decisions about what is irrelevant help determine the current hypothesis, which serves to focus attention and thus determine what new stimulus attributes are entered into the short-term buffer; the buffer information, in turn, is used to develop a new working hypothesis when the current one is shown to be incorrect. Stimulus dimensions which have been tested and found irrelevant have their "strengths" in long-term memory reduced almost to zero, from which they gradually recover (i.e., their irrelevance is forgotten). Williams programmed these focus and memory processes along with Hunt's earlier ideas regarding the way the subject selects a new hypothesis following an error. The model makes a number of strong trial-by-trial predictions regarding how the subject's hypothesis is altered depending on the nature of the mismatch between his current hypothesis and the pattern which he classifies incorrectly. Williams demonstrated the plausibility of her model in two experiments using practiced subjects who knew that the correct hypothesis involved a conjunction of two attributes (other concept rules can be handled by modifying the algorithm for constructing new hypotheses). In some respects, Williams's model is the most realistic one yet produced for the class of Boolean concepts which psychologists have studied in this tradition.

However, the fundamental deficiency of all such models stems from their restriction to only the Hovland type of concepts—that is, the format of attribute-value descriptions where the concepts are defined by Boolean operations on attribute-value pairs. Such description spaces are simply not rich enough to represent many of the concepts that people learn and use. For example, relational and metric notions, such as "*x* is *above y*," "*x* is *longer than y*," cannot be represented in these terms, nor can so many of our concepts that are defined by relations among their parts. The "concept" of the letter *E*, for instance, requires a listing of its parts (three horizontal short lines, one vertical long line) in certain relations to each other (horizontal lines above one another and parallel, their left ends making contact with vertical line, etc.).

Richer description spaces are provided in programs such as that of Winston (1970) discussed earlier. Objects and visual scenes are described in terms of properties and relations among parts, and the representations are in terms of labeled graphs. Winston was also interested in the problem of teaching the machine complex geometrical concepts like *arch, table, house, arcade,* and so forth. He developed a program which would learn from exposure to a series of instances and noninstances of the concept being taught. An initial positive instance leads to a hypothesized description of the concept, say, the concept of a house (see Figure 13.22a). Viewing the scene in Figure 13.22a, Winston's program would describe a house as a wedge supported by a brick. The next three panels of Figure 13.22 show what Winston calls "near misses"—that is, configurations that are close to a house but differ critically from it in one or another respect. When the machine is told that the configuration in panel (b) is "not a house," it describes the difference between panels (a) and (b), and attaches to its revised concept of a house that the wedge *must be* (emphatically) supported by the brick. Similarly, panel (c) informs the machine that the top object *must be* a wedge and not a brick, and panel (d) informs it that the bottom object *must be* a brick and not a wedge. These emphatic ("must be") markers are attached to the final concept description (Figure 13.23), and must be satisfied if the machine is to classify any new pattern as a house.

Winston's program brings up several interesting points. First is the question of how the concept learner assigns priority to given differences (between his current hypothesis and an instance which violates it). In reality, there are typically many differences; as experienced concept learners, we have

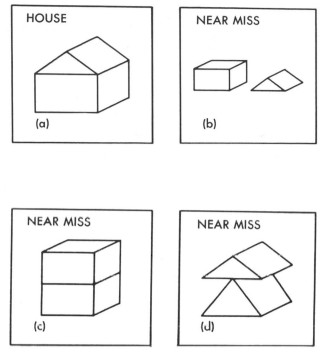

Figure 13.22.   An example of the concept of a *house* and three "near-miss" negative instances. (From Winston, 1970. By permission.)

tended to learn general strategies regarding what are likely to be important rather than irrelevant differences, and to use the high-priority differences to modify our earlier concept hypothesis. A second matter suggested by Winston's approach is the issue of optimal teaching sequences: given that we can specify the final form of a concept description, we should be able to arrange for presentation of a series of "near misses" which will most efficiently guide the learner to the correct concept. Child psychologists concerned with how the child develops certain Piagetian concepts (of conservation of mass, of volume, size, causality, time) have been quite interested in this matter of optimal training sequences.

Summary Comments

By way of summary, it may be seen that simulation models of learning have tended to tackle the more "complicated" learning situations and, generally speaking, have developed rather involved models of the subject. No efforts have been directed at modeling the so-called simple learning situations such as classical or instrumental conditioning. A significant distinction in strategy may be made between theorists who construct a model of subjects in general (Feigenbaum, Simon, Hunt, Williams) and those who tailor a

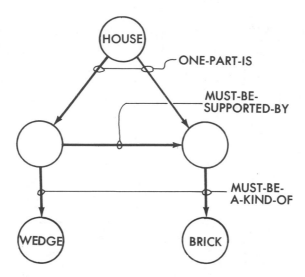

Figure 13.23.   A description of the concept of a *house* in terms of labeled relations among primitive concept nodes. Roughly, this says that a house has two parts, one part must be a kind of wedge and one a kind of brick, and the wedge must be supported by the brick. (From Winston, 1970. By permission.)

model for a specific subject (Feldman). The argument for the latter is that individuals differ, and may do so considerably, and it is wise not to ignore this fact. In constructing a model, one puts in various general processes or assumptions but then leaves it open with respect to a fringe of possible specific processes or their parameters which may be altered to model a particular subject. Hopefully, only these fringe processes will have to be changed to make the model fit other subjects. In a way analogous to factor analysis, the worth of the modeling enterprise depends on the weight of the common factors (general processes) relative to the specific or unique factors which are altered to produce the fits with different subjects. At present, the theorists have to admit that these relative weights are unknown.

DISCUSSION AND EVALUATION

Now that we have briefly described several of the information-processing models that have relevance to behavior theory, it may be helpful to discuss some of the advantages and accomplishments of this approach as well as a few of the problems connected with it. We take up the latter first, since we prefer to end the section in a positive forward-looking vein. The main problems are those of communication and evaluating goodness of fit.

The Communication Problem

The gap in communication between computer simulators and experimental psychologists is serious, but one which seems to be closing over time. Despite the obvious contributions of the developments in computer simulation, psychologists have been slow to adopt the techniques of simulation placed at their disposal. One obvious reason for the communication gap has to do with the differing backgrounds, skills, and languages of experimental psychologists and computer scientists. Simulation programs are comprised of exceedingly long sequences of instructions, with an almost dumbfounding welter of complex details, and all wrapped up and coded in a special programming language adapted to communication to an IBM 7090, not to a psychologist who understands nothing of LISP. As W. R. Reitman notes:

> . . . the description of a recent version of the Newell, Shaw, and Simon General Problem Solving program (GPS) runs to more than 100 pages and even so covers only the main details of the system. Furthermore, the discussion assumes a knowledge of an earlier basic paper on GPS and a knowledge of Information Processing Language V (IPL-V), the computer language in which it is written. Finally, the appendix, which simply *names* the routines and structures employed, takes another 25 pages. Unless one is familiar with similar systems, a thorough grasp of the dynamic properties of so complex a model almost certainly presupposes experience with the running program and its output. (1964, p. 4)

Acquiring facility with one or more of the list-processing languages is difficult and time-consuming, especially so for the older scientists who are very pressed for time by their usual research commitments. In place of a prolonged apprenticeship with a model's program and the computer, the ordinary experimentalist is dependent upon an intermediary to interpret the program for him. Because of the incompleteness of an "outsider's" knowledge of the program, he is unsure what the psychological assumptions in the theory are, or fails to grasp the importance and critical nature of one or another feature in the overall performance, such as the way a particular subroutine is coded.

But these problems are apparently being alleviated over the years, and for three reasons. First, new generations of graduate students in psychology are being trained in computer science, so that they can write simulation programs and understand those written by others. Second, the simulation theorists themselves (e.g., Gregg & Simon, 1967) have been rather vocal on the point that most simulation models are basically very simple in character, and that their length results only from necessary but psychologically irrelevant instructions for "housekeeping." Going along with this approach, published articles announcing new simulation programs frequently contain large sections flow-charting and describing the strategies, processes, and their basic operation, all in terms comprehensible to any psychologist. In principle, such program descriptions could be translated into a running program by any experienced programmer. A third reason for the narrowing of the communications gap is that the concepts and metaphors of information processing have by now thoroughly infused theoretical psychology, and have even become familiar pieces of jargon (see, for example, the texts by J. R. Anderson & Bower, 1973; P. H. Lindsay & Norman, 1972). The information-processing language—of programs, subroutines, conditional decisions, recursive subproblems and subgoals, searching through locations, associative memories, etc.—has been largely taken over, especially by cognitive psychologists, as an analogy to the way the mind works. Because psychological theories are increasingly being formulated in the idiom of information processing, the description of simulation programs is now in a vocabulary familiar and comprehensible to psychologists. Perhaps more than any other indicator, this wholesale adoption of information-processing metaphors within theoretical psychology reflects the major impact of the computer simulation movement.

Evaluating Goodness of Fit

The other major problem associated with computer *simulation* theories (which purport to be models of the person) lies in evaluating the goodness of fit of the model to the data. First, for the complex models such as GPS or EPAM, practically no *general* theorems can be proved regarding specific features of their behavior in particular situations. They differ in this regard from mathematical theories (at least those where explicit solutions can be obtained). Such general theorems are usually explicit equations of the form: "if the data statistics x_1, x_2, have known values, then the data statistics x_3 and x_4 should have the values $x_3 = f_1(x_1, x_2)$ and $x_4 = f_2(x_1, x_2)$." In the case of most information-processing theories, the results of a single simulation run are relatively uninformative about the general characteristics of the behavior the program can display. Hence, many simulation runs must be made, usually under slightly varying circumstances or model parameters, in the hope that one can infer some general properties of the behavior it exhibits by examining this sample of results. Newell and Simon note the issue as follows:

> . . . we can study the model empirically, exploring its behavior under variations of parameters and so on. But to date there is no body of theorems and general means of inference that allow us to derive general properties of the program given in symbolic form. Almost no interesting theorems, in the accepted mathematical sense of the word, have ever been proved about particular programs. (1963, p. 375)

The accumulation of knowledge about a program's specific capabilities by this method is often slow. In consequence of this slow accumulation the theorist often cannot answer specific questions about his model until he has run his program under just those specific conditions. Thus, information feedback to the questioning experimentalist is often much delayed.

In lieu of general theorems, the favored method for testing the validity of a simulation model of problem-solving is by direct comparison of the trial-by-trial statements of the subject while thinking aloud and the corresponding "reasonings" output by the computer program. Comparison with a single computer trace from the program will obviously not do if the program involves many probabilistic elements and, as a consequence, displays quite variable behavior over different runs. However, in the programs employing this "protocol-fitting" method (Feldman's binary choice machine and GPS), few or no probabilistic elements are involved, so the same trace is always obtained, given the same starting state and sequence of experimental events.

Despite its several advantages, the thinking-aloud technique also has some drawbacks. Often the subject's remarks have to be edited, "content analyzed," and coded in terms comparable to the computer's trace of GPS. Also, it must be assumed that the subject skips over or omits telling us about a number of processes that he must be running through. But which ones? In Feldman's binary choice situation, it may be plausibly argued that the format and content of the subject's "thinking aloud" statements are determined in part by incidental, selective reinforcements by the experimenter. For example, in one published protocol (Feldman, 1961), it would appear that during the early trials the subject was learning what kinds of "thinking aloud" statements were acceptable to the experimenter. The effect of casual reinforcement (through facial expression, tone of voice, etc.) upon behavior in such ambiguous situations is well established (see Krasner, 1958). If pressed, an S-R theorist might argue that the content of the thinking-aloud statements could be considered as rationalizations of the more primitive effects of reinforcement of prediction responses produced by the event series. The subject might "just feel that it'll be a C event," but learns to add on a rationalization of this ("You'll continue the progression"). Other studies argue for such "primitive" learning without awareness. Even more relevant is Verplanck's experiment (1962) showing that by incidental reinforcement the subject's motor responses and the content of his verbal rationalizing of them could be shaped almost independently of each other, even to the point of putting them entirely out of phase.

Skinner (1969) provides an illuminating perspective on several processes in problem-solving, including the person's ability (or inability) to verbalize all the steps he is "thinking through." Skinner also makes a very useful distinction between "rule-governed" behavior, which is mediated by explicit (verbalizable) rules, and behavior shaped by a long history of reinforcement contingencies which may be "unconscious, automatic, and unverbalizable." An example is the oft-cited discrepancy between the way grand masters actually play chess and the way they say that they do it; a program based on their prescriptions alone would be the rankest amateur. What is obviously missing is the fantastic detail of unverbalizable "situation-action" knowledge which they have accumulated in playing thousands of chess games. Computer simulation programs produce only "rule-governed" behavior; they have no "situation-action" repertoires based on tacit knowledge such as Skinner proposes. By the same token, they do not provide any useful account of how a verbal community teaches a child to verbalize about the sequence of "private events" we call thinking, or how we could teach an adult a richer, more discriminating verbal repertoire to describe his thought processes.

Setting aside these cautions, suppose we accept the validity of the thinking-aloud statements and ask about the goodness of fit of the model. Here Newell and Simon have made this succinct comment:

> Thus, in gaining a form of prediction (single trials of protocols) that seems hard to achieve by classical numerical models, we lose most of our standard statistical techniques for treating data and raise many difficult problems about assessing the goodness of our theories. (1963, p. 376)

Feldman (1962) lists three possible tests. The first, Turing's test (can an uninformed judge discriminate between a human protocol and the computer's protocol?), Feldman rejects as too weak, as it surely is. The second, simple difference counting (between the model's and subject's trial-by-trial output), he also rejects because of the strong path dependency implicit in certain models. The third method, contingent prediction, sets the model back on the right track each time it makes an error (i.e., replaces the model's prediction hypothesis with the subject's stated hypothesis). Feldman argues that only this method gives the model a fair chance. The fit of Feldman's model to one subject using this method is impressive, but this is difficult to assess when we recall how his model was repeatedly revised in terms of the data. Also, some of the more accurate predictions test only trivial aspects of the complex model (e.g., on 117 of 120 trials the subject kept his hypothesis for another trial when it was confirmed; in 193 of 195 trials he made his prediction consistent with his stated hypothesis, etc.).

It appears certain that alternative methods of testing goodness of fit must be developed as more simulation models get down to the hard business of exact trial-by-trial predictions, which after all is advertised as one of their chief merits. The conditional-prediction proposal will not be generally applicable (see W. R. Reitman, 1964). For some models, a given prediction depends upon such a complex network of prior decisions and arrangements of list structures that once the model errs (as it surely must, being only a model), it is not clear how to proceed in setting it back on the track of the subject.

Many recent simulation models are giving up the goal of predicting every response of every subject on a series of trials or series of problems. In some cases, such as Hintzman's work on SAL or Williams's work on concept learning, explicit probabilistic processes are introduced in the theory, thus leading to variability in outcomes of different simulation runs of the model. In such cases, the model is evaluated against group data by running a number of Monte Carlo simulations, calculating the *average* predicted performance on several measures, and comparing these to the observed averages. Frequently, the parameters of the model are varied and are so selected as to give the best fit of the predictions to the observed data. This is all in the same spirit as the way mathematical models are evaluated by Monte Carlo runs (see Chapter 12).

Advantages in Simulation

Let us conclude this section by mentioning a few of the accomplishments, benefits, and advantages of the simulation approach. First of all, the simulation approach has been a strong antidote to the predominately analytic trend that has generally characterized experimental psychology. The job of a scientist is only half done when he has carried through a thorough, analytic breakdown of a behavioral phenomenon. An equally important, and often neglected, part of his job is to show how to reconstruct or synthesize the behavior from his analytic units. If the behavior is complex, then there is all the more reason to demand a synthesis (a model) that can be proven sufficient unto the phenomena it purports to explain. The computer is a tool for helping us prove that our theory specifies enough parts, together with sufficient detail concerning their exact rules of operation to make it behave. There can be no hidden or implicit assumptions in the model; if it is not explicitly written in the program, the computer prints back "Garbage!" and throws you off, a sobering lesson in the necessity of explicitness and completeness.

A second point that we have learned is that the higher mental processes are neither so mysterious nor so complicated as to defy exact modeling, as had been formerly believed. Newell and Simon state this conclusion clearly:

The first thing we have learned—and the evidence is by now quite substantial— is that we can explain many of the processes of human thinking without postulating mechanisms at subconscious levels which are different from those that are partly conscious and partly verbalized. The processes of problem solving, it is turning out, are the familiar processes of noticing, searching, modifying the search direction on the basis of clues and so on. The same symbol-manipulating processes that partici- pate in these functions are also sufficient for such problem-solving techniques as abstracting and using imagery. It looks more and more as if problem solving is accomplished through complex structures of familiar simple elements. The growing proof is that we can simulate problem solving in a number of situations using no more than these simple elements as the building blocks of our programs. (1963, p. 402)

The general position that problem-solving involves organized sequences of only elementary processes is not itself a testable proposition. Rather, it is an orientation or strategy for undertaking the theory-constructing enterprise. In one sense, it is true that every complex process is eventually understood in terms of sequences of elementary (familiar) operations. So this position really reflects a confidence that the higher mental processes will eventually be understood by the rational methods of science.

A third benefit, as mentioned before, is that the computer and informa- tion-processing are providing exceedingly alluring metaphors and analogies for psychological interpretations (see Newell, 1970). Programmed machines are said to detect, identify, compare, and classify stimuli; to store and retrieve information; to learn and to answer questions; to think, solve problems, and decide which strategies to use, and so on. Because we can see mechanically how these processes are carried out in a computer program, we are lured into believing (a) that these terms have lost their mentalistic cast, and (b) that we now understand how real organisms do the things to which we give the same names. The first belief is undeniably valid, and it accounts for "information-processing concepts" being the accepted vernacular within modern cognitive psychology, totally replacing the "stimulus-response" terminology which formerly dominated discussions in experimental psychol- ogy. Whether such analogies produce real understanding is a matter over which there is still lively debate—possibly due to differing perspectives on what it means to "scientifically understand" some phenomenon. For exam- ple, a theorist like Skinner claims that the Inside Story of computer simula- tion tells us

nothing new about behavior. Only when we know what a man actually does can we be sure that we have simulated his behavior. The Outside Story must be told first. (1969, p. 295)

As we noted in Chapter 7, Skinner has some extreme views on what scien- tific understanding consists of. The alternative viewpoint, that situation- action correlations are only to be understood by rational theories about hypothetical information processing internal to the organism, is clearly the dominating theme in cognitive psychology. This shift in the paradigm of theoretical psychology is noted (and encouraged) in a recent overview by Newell (1970) on the relations between research in experimental psychology and artificial intelligence. After reviewing a number of uses of symbolic models in experimental psychology, he suggests that "a shift in the Zeitgeist in psychology has taken place toward a view of man as information processor" (p. 376). Later he writes

. . . if one looks at where the excitement has been over the last ten years in psychology—the places where rapid growth is taking place and which people talk about when asked "what's new"—a substantial fraction of these turn out to be connected to this shift towards information processing models. (p. 378)

A fourth benefit of unusually great importance is that the work on simulation has brought the study and explanation of complex cognitive processes within practicable reach. It has redressed the unbalanced trend of behaviorism toward the finer analysis and study of smaller units of behavior under artificial conditions. The argument had been that more complex behaviors—thinking and problem-solving—could be more easily understood only after simple behaviors under especially simplified conditions were better understood (e.g., rote learning, rats learning mazes, etc.). After some 30 to 40 years without striking advances in our understanding of the capabilities of the human mind, this argument began to have a hollow ring. It is one that certainly causes disillusion and discouragement in many students upon their first contact with a formal course in psychology. But the computer simulation technology has given us a tool for dealing with complexity in our theories, and has provided new impetus to the study of man's capabilities for thought. At the conclusion of a review of papers on simulation theories, Shepard cogently remarks:

. . . the start that is so admirably exemplified by many of the papers assembled by Feigenbaum and Feldman establishes a new direction in which those who aspire to precise, rigorous formulations may still find their way back to the heart of psychology—to the study of those processes that make man unique among known physical systems. Owing to the great complexities inherent in the problem, progress is bound to be slow—perhaps painfully slow. But, unless the goal itself is relinquished, what other alternative do we have? (1964, p. 65)

SUPPLEMENTARY READINGS

FEIGENBAUM, E. A., & FELDMAN, J. (Eds.) (1963) *Computers and thought.*
LINDSAY, P. H., & NORMAN, D. A. (1972) *Human information processing: An introduction to psychology.*
MINSKY, M. (Ed.) (1968) *Semantic information processing.*
NEWELL, A., & SIMON, H. A. (1972) *Human problem solving.*
NILSSON, N. J. (1971) *Problem-solving methods in artificial intelligence.*
REITMAN, W. R. (1965) *Cognition and thought.*
SHANK, R., & COLBY, K. M. (Eds.) (1973) *Computer models of thought and language.*
SIMON, H. A., & SIKLOSSY, L. (Eds.) (1972) *Representation and meaning: Experiments with information processing systems.*
SLAGLE, J. R. (1971) *Artificial intelligence: The heuristic programming approach.*

Neurophysiology of Learning

Nothing is more certain than that our behavior is a product of our nervous system. The proposition is almost more tautological than factual. This being the case, one may wonder why theories of learned behavior have not been more explicitly neurophysiological in their content, constructs, and referents. There are many historical reasons for this long-standing divorce between neurophysiology and behavior theory, and we will not attempt to discuss the cleavage here. For one thing, during the period 1930–1950 when most of the leitmotifs in our current approaches to learning were developing, it was felt that neurophysiology had very little that was relevant to offer on the psychological issues of the day. But with the explosion of neuropsychological research in the last two decades, this bias is fading away. Second, the major theories were never intended to describe the specific, actual events as they go on in the nervous system of their model learner. The tactics have been, and still are in large measure, those of descriptive behaviorism supplemented by intervening variable theorizing. The description of generic S-R relationships lies at one level: if you do such-and-so to your subject, he will behave in such-and-so way. The such-and-so in each instance may be replaced by a rather long listing of what are believed to be the relevant variables. At another level of theorizing, one simply postulates the existence within the organism of certain primitive mechanisms that carry out particular functions or that are governed by a particular set of "rules." The behavioral implications of the postulated mechanisms plus their rules of operation are then derived for varying sets of boundary conditions under which the model organism is to be observed.

Levels of Discourse

Such psychological theories operate at a completely different level of discourse than do physiological theories, and what are "primitive" notions at one level are exceedingly complex mechanisms when viewed from the other. To consider just one example, a computer program to simulate fact retrieval and question answering by humans must have differing components for (a) storing facts, (b) analyzing and interpreting questions, (c) searching memory for matching structures, (d) retrieving matching structures and composing acceptable answers. But even this brief characterization ignores the really difficult problems of inference and deduction which are inextricably tied up with question answering. Computer programs to simulate such activities (see Chapter 13) postulate a series of "information-processing" and storage mechanisms, and an organized sequence of operations carried out on a data base by a set of processes (the "program"). But now, imagine the task of trying to "understand" what the program is doing (or attempting) in terms of a moment-by-moment listing of the electrical charges on all the thousands of transistors and the field alignment of all the millions of magnetic core storage units in the computer. This vast amount of information and its fantastic complexity would be utterly dumbfounding to the observer; we could not hope to begin to make much of any order out of such vast quantities of particulate information. Rather, we would need some very powerful theories or ideas about how the particulate information was to be organized into higher-level concepts referring to structure and function (e.g., the notion of a bit, a "word," a register, an "address," an "instruction," etc.). Many psychologists feel that their task is to describe the "functional program" of the brain at the level of flow-charting information-processing mechanisms. What is important is the logical system of interacting parts—the model—and not the specific details of the machinery that might actually be functioning in a way that embodies it in the nervous system. As an abstraction, the logical system could possibly be realized either as sets of equations, or as a mechanical or electrical system, or as a program running inside a high-speed computer; the hardware embodiment is irrelevant to the main scientific question, which is whether the theoretical system gives an adequate explanation, description, or prediction of the primary facts relevant to it. If it does so, then psychologists, by and large, are satisfied with the theory and are willing to leave it at that. In fact, they claim that their theories, when substantiated, place strong constraints on what will be acceptable neuropsychological theories of behavior.

Neuropsychologists, on the other hand, are not satisfied to leave matters at that level. They are, in fact, dedicated to finding out about the specific hardware that evolution has tucked under our skulls. They wish to discover the actual machinery and how it works in getting an organism around in its everyday commerce with its environment. This is an exceedingly difficult goal because both the nervous system and its behavior are complicated and neither will be understood with any completeness for a long time. In this chapter we are concerned with learning; and the ability to store information about its history is perhaps the most remarkable capacity of the nervous system. It is also one of the least understood capabilities of nervous tissue.

An act of learning or an act of remembering probably involves many different parts of the nervous system. A performance of even the simplest conditioned response may fail because the organism does not see the stimulus, or does not attend to or register it with his sensory system; he may fail because he forgets how to interpret its meaning, because he never learned it at all, because he is momentarily unable to execute the motor units involved, or because he is no longer motivated to do so or is just not in the mood. This is a loose way to characterize the complex tangle of variables involved in whether and how often a learned act will be performed. It shows, too, the problems of delimiting the research area called the neurophysiology of learning. For example, should receptor physiology be included, since the retina has to transduce a photic signal before it can become a cue for a learned response? Should the study of muscle action be included, since muscles execute the learned performance? By convention such topics are excluded from the research area because these structures are presumed to function similarly whether or not learning is involved. It is usually assumed that a light flash is coded at the retina in an invariant manner whether the light flash is neutral or produces an expectation of reward or punishment due to past learning. Because of this functional distinction, the physiology of the receptors and effectors is usually not considered relevant to the study of learning; their normal operation is a necessary but not a sufficient condition for information storage.

The main search for learning structures, on the other hand, is directed inward from these peripheral structures to the central nervous system, to the brain in particular. The main question, of course, is what normally happens in the brain during learning. What processes and encoding are involved in storing information in the brain in a relatively permanent manner? Once stored, how is access to this information or retrieval of it achieved to guide later performance? What anatomical structures are involved and how do they operate? Can other structures substitute for them when the original ones are put out of commission? What gets changed during learning, and what is the nature of the change? How does it persist and what, if anything, destroys it? These and many others are the global questions that instigate brain research. Of course, none of them has yet been answered to anyone's satisfaction. Each poses a very large and complicated puzzle, and at any given moment we have only a few pieces of the puzzle before us to aid us in inferring its nature.

Technical Developments

Research into the neurophysiology of learning has been slavishly dependent upon the development of techniques for probing inside the brain. Until about the time of World War II, the technique most commonly used was *ablation,* in which a part of the brain is destroyed or cut out. Following ablation, the animal is observed for behavior deficits in one or more learning tasks. The hope is to infer whether the ablated brain structure is implicated in some way in the performances observed; but this inference is not definitive and it usually requires supporting evidence from other methods. Other techniques yielding information about the brain include electrical recording of the activity or artificial stimulation of selected components of the brain. On the electrical recording side, there are devices for amplifying and faithfully recording or displaying the tiny, rapidly changing electrical signals, which act as the "voices" of neural cells. Such amplifiers have made it possible to record a full range of electrical activity in the nervous system, from the gross electroencephalogram (EEG) obtained from the outer skull case down to the subminiature level which uses microelectrodes to record the activity of single neurons. Laboratory computers are also routinely used now to help the electrophysiologist record and detect regularities and lawful relations in certain forms of "noisy" EEG records in which the significant electrical events are often obscured by random electrical activity of no importance. On the stimulation side, the main techniques being currently exploited are those permitting direct electrical or chemical stimulation of a localized area of the brain of an intact animal that is awake, moving about, and behaving normally. Small bipolar electrodes may be implanted permanently in the animal's brain, with the animal living indefinitely with them in place. To stimulate the indicated brain structure, the wire tips of the electrodes protruding from the skull are connected to a source of electrical energy. Similarly implanted cannulae or tiny hypodermic needles may be used to inject chemical solutions or implant crystalline chemicals into a part of the brain. A technique has also been developed to provide for continuous sampling and measurement of various neural chemicals from the brain. Called the "push-pull" system, it involves two cannulae implanted side by side in the brain; a neutral "bathing" solution is slowly "pushed in" one cannula, while the solution plus the dissolved neural chemicals (from structures around the cannulae tips) are "pulled out" of the other cannula by a suction system. Neurally acting drugs can also be injected in tiny amounts, and their metabolites or other by-products can be collected after varying times, thus providing a picture of the time course of uptake and activity by the drug. The existence of many such techniques creates conditions that have indeed been exceptionally favorable for an expansion of research in neurophysiology.

The specific topics to be reviewed in this chapter are a selected sample of those cultivated mainly within the last 30 years. The work on attention, reward, and motivation is included because of the central influence of these factors upon learning and performance. In each case, our intention will be to give some idea of the type of findings relevant to each topic, describing these in relatively nontechnical language so that results may be understandable to readers unfamiliar with neurophysiology.

MOTIVATION, AROUSAL, AND ATTENTION

Motivation and learning are intimately related, no matter what position one takes with respect to the role of drive in habit acquisition and in the performance of learned acts. Hence we turn first to neurophysiological knowledge about drive, reward and punishment, arousal and attention, before turning to the more strict learning topics of memory and association.

Motivational Mechanisms in the Brain

Physiological research has been fairly successful in investigating the neurological mechanisms involved in the common biological motives. Most work has been done on thirst, hunger, and sex. The story is, of course, far from complete, but at least some headway has been made in understanding the brain centers involved. We will briefly review some of the evidence on the neural mechanisms in the brain subserving these consummatory activities.

Hunger. The study of hunger is by far the most difficult because of its many complex features. Organisms, in addition to being simply hungry for food in general, also regulate the amount of specific kinds of food they eat, and they do this according to their body's special requirements for carbohydrates, proteins, fats, minerals, and vitamins. A variety of diet-selection studies have shown that animals can detect their specific deficits and regulate their intake of appropriate substances with incredible accuracy. Recent studies have begun to clarify some of the mechanisms underlying this adaptiveness of diet selection. It has been found by Garcia and Koelling (1966) that a novel taste can become selectively associated with an internal physiological aftereffect (e.g., nausea or stomach sickness) at very long delays of several hours. This same type of association has been proposed to explain dietary selection by an animal with a particular dietary deficiency (see Rozin, 1965, 1967; Rozin & Kalat, 1972). The taste of a food rich in the needed substance is followed later by a beneficial internal effect; this results in that taste sensation's becoming a "good taste," which is then selected repeatedly by the animal.

Along with this enhanced understanding of selective subhungers, there is also rather extensive knowledge about the regulation of *how much* food in general is consumed. The primary neural structures involved lie within the hypothalamus, which is located at the base of the brain directly behind the throat. The *ventromedial nucleus* close to the midline of the hypothalamus appears to be primarily a "stop" or "satiation-detecting" center. That is, its normal functioning seems required to produce cessation of eating after the animal has consumed a sufficient amount to remove any deficit. This ventromedial nucleus may be destroyed by a localized electrolytic lesion; it is coagulated or "burnt out" by a strong electric current delivered through an implanted electrode. When this is done, the animal for a time does not "know how" to stop eating. He overeats by large amounts (hyperphagia) and soon becomes very obese, perhaps more than doubling his normal weight. The overeating really appears to stem from simple absence of an appropriate "stop" mechanism rather than from an increased hunger drive. Hyperphagic animals will not work very hard to get their food, and they will not tolerate much adulteration of their food with bitter quinine before they reject it, whereas normally hungry animals will both work hard and tolerate quinine in order to get something to eat.

Presumably the way the ventromedial nucleus normally functions is that signals from the mouth, stomach, and certain nutrients (e.g., glucose) circulating in the bloodstream or cerebrospinal fluid stimulate this structure, and its resulting activity, through some unknown means, stops the eating. It is known that if this structure is artificially stimulated by an electric current (by means of an implanted electrode) while a hungry animal is eating, the animal will be inhibited from further eating while the current is on (Wyrwicka & Dobrzecka, 1960). Learned responses rewarded by food are similarly inhibited by electrical stimulation of the ventromedial nucleus.

Likewise, injection of a minute quantity of a salty solution into this area (by means of an implanted cannula into which a hypodermic needle is fitted) produces inhibition of eating. On the other hand, a temporary increase in eating is produced when the substance injected is procaine (a local anesthetic commonly used by dentists). Presumably the procaine anesthetic temporarily mimics the effect of destruction of the tissue (see above). All these effects are consistent with the view that the ventromedial nucleus serves as a regulator to halt eating.

The "start" mechanisms for eating appear to lie in the lateral areas of the hypothalamus, one on either side of the midline. Destruction of the lateral hypothalamus on both sides (bilateral ablation) produces an animal that refuses to eat (or drink), and if special measures are not taken, it will starve to death in a cage filled with food. Teitelbaum and Epstein (1962) report that such animals go through several stages while being nursed back to recovery. For several days after the bilateral ablation, the animals (rats) refuse to eat or drink, and spit out substances placed in their mouths. They are kept alive by tube-feeding a nutrient liquid directly into their stomachs. After several days, they still refuse to drink but will eat highly palatable (sugary) foods. Later, they may eat regular lab food, though they still refuse to drink water. Still later, normal drinking may return in some animals. Whether or not and how much an animal will recover seems to depend on the completeness of the original destruction; the larger the lesion, the less the likelihood of significant recovery.

Thirst.   This ablation work seems to implicate the lateral hypothalamus in starting both eating and drinking. The two functions have been manipulated separately by localized electrical and chemical stimulation. Electrical stimulation in this area can cause a satiated animal either to eat or to drink depending on the precise location of the electrode. Injection of a tiny amount of a salty solution into this area of the brain will cause excessive drinking in a satiated animal; injection of pure water causes a thirsty animal to stop drinking. In the case of each of these kinds of stimulation, it has been shown that learned habits rewarded by food or water can be regulated (turned on or off) by the stimulation. A fair amount is known about the mechanisms involved in naturally occurring thirst and drinking. Water losses cause an increase in the concentration of electrolytes in the blood, with a resulting increase in its osmotic pressure. This in turn draws more water out of the cellular stores of the body. A set of neural cells lying in the vascular bed of the lateral hypothalamus puts out "thirst" signals when water is needed. These cells—called osmoreceptors—respond to an increase in osmotic pressure of the blood surrounding them. A minute injection of saltwater directly into this area mimics the effect of prolonged dehydration by raising the osmotic pressure in the tissue surrounding these osmoreceptors.

An interesting line of research begun by Grossman (1960) investigates differential chemical specificity of the feeding and drinking centers in the lateral hypothalamus of the rat. Grossman found that injection of certain chemicals (adrenergic drugs such as adrenaline) into the lateral hypothalamus greatly increased food consumption but did not increase the drinking of water. Injection of other chemicals (cholinergic drugs like carbachol) produced the opposite effect—increased drinking with no increased eating. Many other chemical effects of this kind have been reviewed by N. E. Miller (1965) and Grossman (1967). Of interest here is the fact that the adrenergic drugs used by Grossman (adrenaline and noradrenaline) have been identified as the neural transmitter substance for the sympathetic nervous system, whereas the transmitter for the rest of the nervous system is acetylcholine, a cholinergic substance. The selective sensitivity to adrenergic and cholinergic drugs by the drinking and eating centers suggests another basis for the functional differentiation of these drive systems despite their anatomical overlap in the hypothalamus.

Sexual behavior.   Finally, we consider the brain centers involved with sexual behavior. The pattern of results here is not clearly interpretable from the work on brain lesions. Ablations in some areas produce a complete loss of sexual behavior, whereas ablations in other areas have produced exaggerated, hypersexual behaviors (see Morgan, 1965, for a review). However, direct electrical and chemical stimulations of the hypothalamus have produced somewhat clearer results. Vaughan and Fisher (1962) elicited exaggerated sexual behavior in male rats by electrical stimulation in the anterior dorsolateral region of the hypothalamus. The electrical stimulus elicited persistent mounting of a female and produced an excess number of ejaculations, far beyond the satiating requirement of a normal male. Earlier work by Fisher (1956) in which the male sex hormone testosterone was injected into the hypothalamus of the male rat produced similar results. When the hormone was applied in one area (lateral preoptic), exaggerated male sexual behavior was elicited from both male and female rats. When injected in a slightly different area (medial preoptic area of the hypothalamus), both male and female rats would engage in "maternal" behaviors such as building a home nest and retrieving baby rats from outside the nest. These behaviors normally appear only in female rats after giving birth to a litter. When the testosterone hormone is delivered to a site between these two areas, mixed behavior may result: a male rat may alternate between nest-building and mating with an available female. Similar enhancement of sexual behavior in female cats has been reported by Michael (1962), who implanted small paraffin pellets containing estrogen into the hypothalamus. This caused the female to become sexually receptive ("in heat") for a period of 50 to 60 days, as the drug was absorbed very slowly. Though she was sexually receptive, the female cat's vagina and uterus were not in an estrous condition; she would be described as in heat behaviorally but not physiologically. From such results, it seems safe to conclude that sex drive and receptivity can be induced by direct hormonal stimulation of the hypothalamus.

More reliable sexual responsiveness to electrical stimulation has been reported by Caggiula (1970). Electrical stimulation to the posterior hypothalamus of male rats produced stimulus-bound copulation; if a receptive female were present, the male would readily mount and copulate when the brain stimulation was initiated, continuing repeatedly, possibly through several ejaculations, as long as the brain stimulation continued. Caggiula also showed that male rats receiving such brain stimulation would readily learn and perform a bar-pressing response reinforced by access to a receptive female. But the copulatory behavior was not a simple reflexive reaction. Rather, it depended on the convergence of appropriate external supporting stimuli (i.e., a receptive female had to be present to elicit the behavior) and brain tissue that had been appropriately primed through the body's standard supply of sex hormone. If the male rat was castrated, the frequency of sexual behavior "elicited" by the electrical stimulation gradually dwindled over a period of days (presumably as the remaining endogenous sex hormone was metabolized), and eventually the brain site was "sexually inert." Replacement of testosterone would, presumably, bring back the electrically controlled sexual behavior.

In concluding this brief sketch of neural drive centers, it is worth remarking that important structures for each drive system are found in the hypothalamus, a very small but phylogenetically very old part of the brain. In addition to the functions mentioned above, the hypothalamus is known to control other behaviors (e.g., aggressiveness) and to regulate various physiological functions (e.g., regulation of body temperature). Also, as we shall see, electrical stimulation in this area often produces either rewarding or punishing effects. The effectiveness of the rewarding brain shock to these sites can be enhanced or diminished by increasing or decreasing, respectively, the levels of hunger, thirst, or sex drive (e.g., Hoebel & Teitelbaum, 1962). Indeed, the hypothalamus might be called the "motivational center" of the brain. It now appears plausible that a remarkable range of psychologically significant variables have their eventual impact upon this small, well-packaged nub of neural tissue.

Controversial issues.   There are currently two controversies regarding interpretation of the types of results reviewed above under the heading of "drive centers" in the hypothalamus. One controversy concerns whether the motivated behavior elicited by brain stimulation is really very much the same as that exhibited during the normal operation of the drive, or whether instead there is simply a topographic resemblance to the consummatory behavior. To illustrate, we can teach a rat to lick water from a drinking spout in order to escape and avoid electric shock, but occurrence of such drinking would not suffice to infer a natural state of thirst. The issue perhaps resolves into comparing a variety of drive indicators under the "natural" and the "artificially stimulated" conditions. When this is done, several differences emerge in the detailed behavioral patterns. For example, an experiment by Franklin and Quartermain (1970) compared various indices of "thirst" induced by water deprivation as against minute injections of the drug carbachol into the lateral preoptic area of the hypothalamus of rats. Hours of water deprivation were adjusted until the amounts of water drunk *ad lib* under the two conditions were equal. Nonetheless, under three other tests for thirst—including bar-pressing for water and the amount of bitter quinine tolerated in water—the carbachol-elicited behavior was significantly weaker than that produced by water deprivation. It is likely that deprivation produces a stronger drive because it activates a number of different related systems (e.g., osmolarity of body fluids, intravascular fluid volume), whereas the carbachol injection operates only at the selected spot in the brain to control drinking. Similar differences between natural and artificially stimulated drives are known for sexual behavior (Caggiula, 1970) and for feeding (Valenstein, Cox, & Kakolewski, 1969).

A second controversy concerns the motivational *specificity* of the alleged "drive centers." The issue here was brought to the fore by some rather startling findings by Valenstein et al. (1968, 1969). After first noting that there is relatively little *anatomical* differentiation of the sites within the rat's hypothalamus which elicit eating, drinking, or both, or neither activity, Valenstein et al. went further and demonstrated that by environmental manipulations one and the same electrode (or anatomical site) can be made to act as a "feeding" electrode in a "hunger center" on one occasion and a "drinking" electrode in a "thirst center" on another occasion. The method is simple: take a hypothalamic electrode which reliably elicits, say, stimulus-bound eating when food and water are available; then remove the food and provide many long hours of periodic stimulation with only water available. In many cases the animal eventually comes to drink rapidly to the onset of the brain stimulation. Moreover, if following satiation on both food and water the animal is stimulated and given a choice between food and water, he is likely now to show a preference for stimulus-bound drinking, or at least alternate between eating and drinking. So what was formerly an "eating" electrode has been converted into a "drinking" or a "mixed" electrode. This conversion may be quite stable, unless a further bout of training in an environment without water returns the electrode's preference to food. Valenstein et al. (1969) conclude "that hypothalamic stimulation probably does not evoke natural motivational states when eliciting stimulus-bound behavior." The results argue for some kind of practice or learning component in associating arousal of a particular hypothalamic area with a specific motivated behavior. In extreme form, this hypothesis would say that much hypothalamic tissue begins as "equipotential" for controlling any or all drive-motivated behaviors, and that other internal conditions, together with a particular learning history, have conjoined to make one or another consummatory behavior prepotent for stimulation at specific loci.

However, this viewpoint has met with some resistance. First, Roberts (1969) has argued that there really is innate specificity of drive circuits, that they are anatomically overlapping so that large electrodes may activate several drive systems concurrently (with one possibly stronger than the other), and that smaller electrodes can elicit smaller, incomplete parts of the total consummatory chain (e.g., chewing, lip smacking). Although the different drive systems may overlap anatomically (like a tangle of spaghetti), the systems do seem differentially sensitive to adrenergic versus cholinergic drugs; also, the different systems have different refractory periods, since electrical stimulation at different frequencies can elicit different consummatory behaviors. A second problem with the extreme learning hypothesis is that subsequent research (e.g., Valenstein & Cox, 1970) has failed to find any other strong "experiential" determinants of which consummatory response occurs to a given brain stimulus. For instance, a hypothalamic electrode that is motivationally neutral cannot be converted into a "drinking" electrode by pairing its stimulation with drinking produced by natural deprivation, nor can a mixed food-water electrode be trained out of its dual effect by an external stimulus (the test cage) with a history of exclusive association either with stimulus-bound eating or with stimulus-bound drinking.

It rather looks as though only the original procedure of Valenstein et al. is effective in producing "motivational shifts," and then only with certain electrodes. But it is not yet clear whether the equipotentiality or the anatomical specificity viewpoint will come to prevail in neuropsychology. The trend of tradition and contemporary consensus is against "equipotentiality" notions, whether dealing with perception, learning, or motivation. The search for anatomical and biochemical specificity and differentiation of different "drive systems" will probably continue unabated despite Valenstein's very crucial critique of the primary basis for such an approach. However, it might be mentioned that Valenstein's basic position, that "drive expressions" are malleable, is compatible with recent work on the so-called cognitive control of motivation in human subjects (see Schachter, 1964, 1967; Zimbardo, 1969). These studies show how the motivation or emotion that a person feels, or the quantity of motivated behavior that he will display, depends in a critical way on social and situational variables rather than on particular conditions of physiological arousal, deprivation, or pain. Such findings warn us against the overzealous extrapolation to humans of studies on drive localization and motivational determinates in subhuman species.

Reward and Punishment by Brain Stimulation

The significance of the hypothalamus has been enhanced by another set of studies concerned with the effects of reward and punishment. A significant line of research in the last 20 years has been the mapping of the locations of reward and punishment centers in the mammalian brain. The initial observations on the reward effect were made by Olds and Milner (1954) and on the punishment effect by Delgado, Roberts, and Miller (1954). The experimental subject—typically a rat, cat, or monkey—is prepared with a two-pole electrode implanted so that it remains in its brain, with the tiny, stimulating tip of the electrode aimed at a particular structure of the brain. By means of this electrode, a small electric current can be delivered to that part of the brain surrounding the electrode tip, thereby artificially firing off a probably large population of neural cells in the neighborhood of the electrode tip. In the typical reward experiment, the subject is permitted to operate a switch that delivers brief electric shocks to his brain. If he learns to do this repeatedly, operating the lever at an appreciable rate, then stimulation at that brain site is said to be rewarding. Conversely, if he refrains from stimulating his brain under optimal conditions of learning, the stimulation could be either neutral or punishing. If it is punishing (aversive), then he will learn some response to turn off (escape) the brain shock once it is presented. By means of tests such as these, brain structures may be classified as rewarding, neutral, or punishing.

Upon investigation, it has been found that reward sites are densely and widely scattered throughout the subcortex of the rat's brain. The schematic drawing in Figure 14.1 shows one of the major positive reward systems (labeled FSR), a large "tube" of fibers on the lower floor extending from the hindbrain through the midbrain (hypothalamus) forward to the fore-

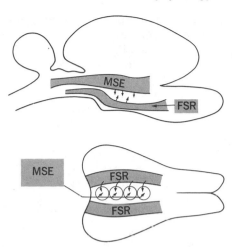

Figure 14.1.   Schematic sections of the rat's brain showing locations of major positive and negative reinforcement centers determined by electrical stimulation. The top figure is a sagittal section, slicing fore and aft from the top of the brain to the bottom. The bottom figure is a horizontal section, looking down upon the middle interior of the brain. Pure punishing effects were produced by stimulation of the periventricular system of fibers, here labeled MSE (for midbrain substrate of escape); pure positive rewarding effects were produced by stimulation of the lateral hypothalamic tube, here labeled FSR (forebrain substrate of reward). The nuclei (circled in lower figure) into which both these systems project yield ambivalent, that is, positive-negative, reactions. (From "Drives, Rewards, and the Brain" by James and Marianne Olds, in *New Directions in Psychology II*, by Frank Barron, William C. Dement, Ward Edwards, Harold Lindman and Lawrence D. Phillips, and James and Marianne Olds. Copyright © 1965 by Holt, Rinehart and Winston, Inc. Reprinted by permission of Holt, Rinehart and Winston, Inc.)

brain. Sites in which electrical stimulation produces punishing effects are situated above these reward fibers. They are labeled MSE in Figure 14.1. These effects depend, of course, on the intensity and other characteristics of the electrical stimulation to the brain. The intensity of the stimulation must exceed some threshold value before its behavioral effect is seen, and response rate typically increases with stimulus intensity up to some optimal level. Roberts (1958) and G. H. Bower and Miller (1958) first reported on electrode placements (in cats and rats, respectively) in which the onset of brain stimulation appeared to be rewarding, but if the stimulation was left on, it apparently became aversive after a few seconds or so. Thus, the animals would learn to perform one response to turn on the stimulus and another response to turn it off. These dual effects apparently arise because, although the electrode tip is located among positive reward cells, there are negative cells in the vicinity, so that during the few seconds of shock the effective site of stimulation spreads out from the electrode tip and activates the negative cells. Some of these ambivalent sites are circled in Figure 14.1. An alternate interpretation is that the electrical stimulus self-adapts to neutrality as the stimulation continues, and it is terminated simply in order to release the system from adaptation and to get another rewarding onset of stimulation. Recent experiments by Deutsch (1973) make this latter interpretation somewhat more plausible.

A number of interesting features regarding the electrical reward effect have been uncovered. First, the self-stimulating behavior does not satiate, whereas most naturally occurring positive reinforcers do, as in eating or drinking. This absence of satiation is inferred from the fact that animals will continue to stimulate their brains at a high rate for very many hours, until they drop from fatigue. Second, the behavior generally extinguishes very rapidly when the electrical stimulation is shut off, despite the fact that very high response rates had been generated by it. Third, in discrete-trial learning situations (e.g., a runway), performance is generally poorer the longer is the intertrial interval. At many brain sites, the animal must be "primed" with one or more free brain shocks before it goes into its act of rapid self-stimulation. Fourth, the reward effect at some locations appears to depend on the state of one or another motivational (drive) system. Rates of self-stimulation at some sites seem to depend on the animal's hunger drive (i.e., satiation lowers self-stimulation rate), and at other sites to depend on the level of circulating sex hormones (i.e., castration lowers self-stimulation rate). These drive-related effects do not appear at all rewarding sites in the brain. However, practically all hypothalamic electrodes that elicit motivated consummatory responses—feeding, drinking, or copulation—also prove to be rewarding at somewhat lower intensities (see, e.g., Caggiula, 1970; Hoebel, 1968).

Deutsch and Howarth (1963) have advanced a theory about brain stimulation reward which attempts to handle many of the pertinent facts. The gist of the theory is that the electrical stimulation in these "reward" experiments is actually serving two functions: reward for the immediate response and motivation for the next response in the series. Each brain shock produces some motivation for the habit which produced the brain shock. The motivation produced by a brain shock decays with the time elapsed since the brain shock, eventually diminishing to zero. The stronger the brain shock, the longer it takes the motivation to decay. The postulated effect of brain-shock reward may be aptly compared with the familiar effect of eating salted peanuts; the behavior is practically self-perpetuating, having a peanut keeps the "desire" for another going, but the urgency of the want declines with the lapse of time since consumption of the previous peanut.

Deutsch and Howarth present several experimental results consistent with their hypothesis, all essentially showing that the strength of behavior established with a brain-shock reward declines with time since the last brain shock. Gallistel (1966, 1969a) has confirmed and extended these drive-decay findings. He has also found (Gallistel, 1969b) that in rats implanted with two functional reward electrodes, the priming provided on one electrode still injects motivation for getting electrical stimulation (ESB) through the other as well. Since the theory postulates a dual effect of electrical stimulation—excitation of reward and motivational pathways—Deutsch and his associates have investigated means for separating these two effects. Results of a series of experiments are consistent with the assumption that the sensitivity of the two systems differs as stimulation parameters (current intensity, pulse frequency) are varied. Observations in one experiment suggested that the motivational pathway had a lower threshold than the reward pathway. Thus, a brain shock of low intensity could have a motivating but not a rewarding effect. In another experiment, frequency (pulses per second) of the brain shock was manipulated along with intensity. Frequency-intensity pairs found to be equally preferred (rewarding) in a T-maze preference test turned out to be unequally motivating in a simple runway test. This suggests that the reward and motivation pathways are maximally sensitive to different frequencies of electrical stimulation. In another set of experiments (Deutsch, 1964), evidence was adduced for the view that the neural "refractory period" of reinforcement pathways is shorter than that of the motivational pathways. The term *refractory period* refers to a very brief time following the firing of a neuron during which a second stimulus is ineffective and cannot fire the neuron again. By purely behavioral tests, Deutsch inferred that the refractory period for the reward pathway was about four-tenths of a millisecond, whereas that for the motivational pathway was about six- or seven-tenths of a millisecond.

This series of experiments certainly provides rather impressive evidence for Deutsch's hypothesis about brain stimulation reward. However, data inconsistent with the drive-decay hypothesis have continued to arise. The most common discrepancy is reports of rats who will self-stimulate without requiring "priming" brain shocks to get them started (e.g., Pliskoff, Wright, & Hawkins, 1965). The discrepancies have been made especially clear in work by Kent and Grossman (1969), who find two distinct populations of reward electrode placements, those that require priming (and which follow the drive-decay hypothesis) and those that do not. A single animal could have one electrode that required priming and a second electrode that did not require priming to initiate self-stimulation. Typically, however, Kent and Grossman experimented only with animals having a single electrode. Animals having nonpriming electrodes (called "nonprimers") show persistent self-stimulation performance independent of the intertrial interval between stimulations. The electrode placements also differed slightly for primers (animals with priming electrodes) and nonprimers. Of more interest was the hypothesis offered by Kent and Grossman that brain stimulation always produces a hedonically ambivalent mixture of affects, but with the negative (aversive) component of the mixture being relatively higher for the primers than for the nonprimers. For example, animals with priming electrodes would sometimes cringe and squeal during each stimulation, occasionally showing coordinated escape behavior, and yet they would continue to self-stimulate once they were started. Figure 14.2 summarizes the conflict interpretation of the hedonic complex provided by ESB. A temporal gradient of approach and avoidance behavior is presumed to extend backward in time and/or space relating to earlier components of the instrumental chain leading up to initiation of self-stimulation (point of ESB in Figure 14.2). By algebraic summation of the two affects (see Miller's conflict theory, Chapter 6), it will be seen that a subject who is a primer will not initiate the beginnings of the approach to the lever (or to the self-stimulation place), but will maintain close, persistent contact once brain stimulation has been delivered. This much of the diagram simply restates in another idiom the

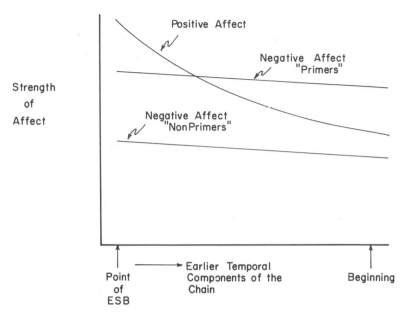

Figure 14.2. The positive and negative hedonic components aroused by electrical stimulation of the brain at "reward" sites, illustrating the conflict hypothesis due to Kent and Grossman (1969).

facts currently available. However, Kent and Grossman saw a further implication of this theory, namely, that nonprimers could be made to behave like primers if one could somehow increase the negative (aversive) component delivered for each self-stimulation response. They did this by arranging for a stationary rat to receive a moderately painful shock to its tail each time it pressed a lever to receive the pure ESB reward. The independent variable was the intertrial interval, the dead time during which the drive from the preceding ESB was decaying and before the lever was reinserted into the rat's cage. With the added tail shock, the nonprimers now began to show an intertrial interval function indistinguishable from that of the primer subjects, namely, fast return to the lever at a short intertrial delay but greater hesitancy to return for another ESB plus tail shock the longer was the interval since the preceding ESB. This result differs from the outcome to be expected in standard approach-avoidance conflicts involving conventional reinforcers.

The result does not uniquely support the conflict formulation of Kent and Grossman, since Deutsch's theory would expect the same outcome were the drive of nonprimers to decay over time since the preceding ESB. Perhaps the real value of the Kent and Grossman paper is in clearly identifying these two populations of reward sites and detailing their anatomical and behavioral properties. (Priming is a characteristic of an electrode placement.) As have others before them, Kent and Grossman found that reward electrodes not requiring priming were well within the lateral hypothalamic area, whereas reward electrodes requiring priming were located on the boundaries overlapping the lateral hypothalamus and surrounding structures; hypothalamic electrodes outside this area showed either no effect or an aversive effect of stimulation. In retrospect, however, the difference in behavior produced by priming and nonpriming electrodes may be only a quantitative one, referring to the asymptote of the curve relating reaction time to time since stimulation.

In passing, we might mention that human patients who have received stimulation to alleged "pleasure centers" of their brains often report the stimulation as satisfying or joyful or relaxing, without unpleasant after-effects, and will willingly take more (Heath & Mickle, 1960).

The largest bundle of reward fibers in the mammalian brain is the medial forebrain bundle, whereas the periventricular system of the diencephalon and midbrain appears to be the principal pathway of the punishment system. It is believed that natural rewards and punishments exert their influence through these major brain structures. In a series of provocative experiments, Stein (1964, 1969) has pursued the hypothesis that these two systems are biochemically differentiated, varying in terms of the major transmitter substances utilized predominately in synapses (neuronal junctures) of the two systems. Stein infers these biochemical properties of the two systems by injecting a variety of neurally active drugs and noting their effects on thresholds of rewarding self-stimulation and on blocking or enhancement of rewarding or punishing effects from electrodes in the two systems. Details will be discussed later when we turn to the topic of neurochemistry.

Arousal and Attention

Electrophysiological studies have brought forth many facts about arousal and attention. The arousal dimension includes variations ranging from euphoric excitement, to alert attentiveness, to relaxed wakefulness, to drowsiness, to deep sleep, and these are closely correlated with phenomenal impressions of conscious awareness. The varying states of arousal are associated with distinctive patterns in the electroencephalogram (EEG) of the subject. We can gauge the depth of sleep from the EEG. We can determine, too, at what times the sleeper is dreaming, for during dream episodes, the eyes move rapidly, as though the person were watching a visual scene unfold before him (see Kleitman 1963).

A host of studies have implicated the reticular activating system (RAS) of the brain stem as of paramount importance in arousal. This system seems to be involved in sleeping, wakefulness, and in fine gradations in attention. Anatomically, this system, which in man is about the size of the little finger (see Figure 14.3), is located at the core of the brain stem just above the spinal cord and below the thalamus and hypothalamus.

A number of important facts regarding the RAS are well established. First, selected cells of the RAS are aroused or alerted when signals are being transmitted through sensory input cables from the skin, ear, nose, etc. These sensory input cables send their information to specific "projection" areas in the cerebral cortex, all (except smell) doing so through specific relay nuclei in the thalamus. On the way in, however, these input

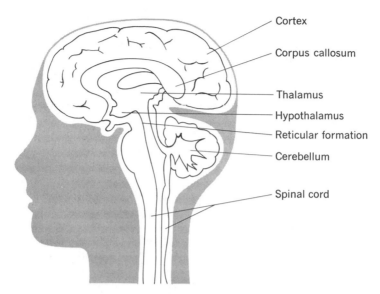

Figure 14.3.   Schematic sagittal section of the brain in man. (From D. P. Kimble, 1963. By permission.)

cables send off collateral branches into the RAS. These collaterals are shown schematically in Figure 14.4. Within the RAS, the collaterals from the various sensory channels are intermingled and lack specificity. Second, the RAS projects its unspecific messages to broad, diffuse areas of the cerebral cortex (see Figure 14.4). Research has indicated that the probable operation of this system is as follows: new sensory information stimulates the RAS, which relays the presence of some kind of stimulation to various sensory receiving areas of the cortex. This diffuse stimulation alerts the cortex, essentially telling it that some kind of news is arriving. The alerted cortex is then better able to deal with or process the specific information arriving over the specific sensory input channel to the cortex.

This story has been slowly pieced together. The alerting function of the RAS has been inferred from the fact that direct electrical stimulation of the RAS will awaken a sleeping cat and produce EEG brain waves characteristic of alertness and excitement. If the RAS is destroyed, a profound and enduring coma results; for all practical purposes, the animal is reduced to a sleeping vegetable. Anesthetic drugs that produce unconsciousness appear to act by depressing the RAS. The coma produced by either the ablation or the anesthetic endures despite the intactness of the sensory projection pathways. Though sounds, touches, lights, etc., still evoke definite electrical responses at the cortex while the animal is comatose, the subject is unaware of these inputs because the RAS switch controlling "consciousness" has been turned off. Nonspecific stimulation from the RAS thus apparently prepares the cortex to process the incoming sensory information.

Some indirect evidence of the perceptual efficiency of an alerted cortex is

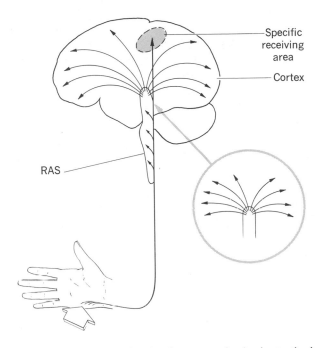

Figure 14.4. Schematic drawing showing how a touch stimulus to the hand is relayed to a specific receiving area in the cerebral cortex. The sensory channel also sends collateral branches into the reticular activating system (RAS), which in turn projects alerting stimulation to many areas of the cerebral cortex. The inset shows the cortical projections arising from the forward end (thalamic section) of the reticular formation. (From D. P. Kimble, 1963. By permission.)

seen in experiments by Lindsley (1958) and Fuster (1958). The Lindsley study showed that the cortex was better able to resolve and discriminate two successive light flashes if it were brought into an appropriate state of alert readiness by prior RAS stimulation. Fuster's study showed that prior RAS activation enabled monkeys to pick up more discriminating information from a very brief glimpse of a visual array.

Sensory Gating

In recent years a number of experiments have made it clear that the waking brain exerts considerable control over its sensory input channels. An electrical signal coursing inward from a particular receptor may be subject to modulating influences all along its sensory pathway to the primary receiving area at the cortex. These influences may either enhance or inhibit the inward-coursing signal, although inhibition seems to be the predominant mode. Enhancement and inhibition effects may be seen in the changes in the electrically evoked response recorded from various relay stations (synapses) along the sensory input cable. These effects are probably mediated by fibers from the cortex to relay stations near the receptors. A number of sensory inhibition effects can be produced by electrical stimulation in certain parts of the reticular formation.

The main function of these brain-to-periphery neural circuits appears to be that which is ascribed roughly to "attention." By this means the brain can attenuate or "gate out" sensory signals that are of no interest to it at the moment, while at the same time amplifying that sensory channel (if any) upon which attention is concentrated. The evidence for this generalization comes from studies of habituation and distraction, and the influence of brain stimulation upon evoked responses to sensory stimulation.

Consider first the phenomenon of *habituation*. When a novel stimulus of sufficient intensity impinges on a receptor, it evokes a strong and definite electrical response in the relays of that input channel, in the primary sensory cortex for that input channel, and in the reticular formation. This is the electrical accompaniment of the "orienting reflex" discussed by Pavlov and Sokolov (see Chapter 3). However, if the stimulus is repeated in a regular, monotonous series, the evoked response diminishes to a low, stable level, often not even detectable. The response has habituated. This habituation can be seen not only at the cortex but also far downstream, at essentially the first sensory relay station beyond the receptor. Such habituatory control is presumably designed to disengage the high brain centers from dealing with stimuli that have ceased to have any significance for it. The habituation can be temporarily lifted by disturbing the animal (e.g., by electric shock to the feet or an arousing reticular shock). Also, it is released to some extent by making some alteration in the stimulus pattern. The release of habituation seems to follow a regular generalization gradient related to the amount of stimulus change. Also, habituation will not occur if the stimulus is converted through conditioning into a signal of biological importance (e.g., by pairing a click with a painful shock or with food). In fact, the evoked electrical response is even larger than normal in this case. Thus, the significance of an input signal is crudely coded almost at once from the receptor inward.

A second set of observations relates to *selective attention*. It is well known that human adults can attend selectively to one stimulus and ignore others that are concurrently presented. A large number of psychological experiments have been done with such selective attention tasks, and the relevant variables have been reasonably well mapped out (see Moray, 1969, 1970, for reviews). Several EEG studies (using scalp electrodes with human adults) have examined changes in the average cortical response evoked by a given stimulus depending on whether it is or is not attended to. An initial study was done by Spong, Haider, and Lindsley (1965); their subjects were presented with concurrent series of light flashes and of auditory clicks, the two occurring independently in time. When subjects were instructed to attend to and count the light flashes, the evoked responses produced by flashes and recorded from the visual cortex (occipital area) were large, whereas the evoked responses produced by the clicks and recorded from the auditory cortex (temporal area) were small. When the instruction was reversed, and the subjects were requested to count clicks and ignore the light flashes, the magnitudes of the respective cortical evoked responses were reversed. This illustrates selective attention using stimuli of two different modalities. Later, Donchin and Cohen (1967) showed that, by means of instructions, cortical evoked responses could be selectively facilitated to one visual stimulus and inhibited to a second visual stimulus which occurred at different times mixed among the first stimulus and falling on roughly the same retinal locations as the facilitated stimulus. Thus the differential responses at the visual cortex evoked by the two visual stimuli had to result from central mechanisms assigning different weights for the two stimuli according to their relative importance rather than to good or poor peripheral adjustment of the receptor registering the two stimuli.

Consider a third set of observations on *distraction*. Hernandez-Peon, Scherrer, and Jouvet (1956) recorded in a cat the evoked response to an auditory click at the dorsal cochlear nucleus, a low-level relay station in the auditory pathways. Before habituation occurred, presentation of distracting visual or olfactory stimuli (a mouse or the odor of fresh fish) greatly reduced the evoked auditory response produced at that time by the click. A similar effect was produced by a novel smell or sound upon the evoked response to a light flash in the optic pathways. These observations suggest that the novel stimulus attracted the cat's attention, that stimuli in the input channel attended to were amplified, whereas stimuli in other input channels not attended to were flattened and blocked out. Moreover, this blockage can go on downstream at sensory relay stations near the receptor. Hernandez-Peon proposed that this blockage was carried out by efferent inhibitory fibers from the reticular formation to sensory relays; that is, when input in the visual channel captures attention, the reticular formation sends out impulses that temporarily inhibit neuronal activity in other input channels. He reported that direct electrical stimulation of the reticular formation sometimes has such suppressive effects on cochlear potentials. Similar suppression due to reticular stimulation (in other areas) has been reported for the visual pathways (see Deutsch & Deutsch, 1966, for a review).

A standard view of such results is to suppose that sensory information, possibly in degraded form, gets transmitted to central analyzers and is there weighted for its importance or novelty. During habituation, the reduced signal is fed to a higher-level comparator; if the input matches some stored replica or model of recent signals, a diminished evoked response occurs and the efferents sustain their inhibitory influence on that input channel. If the input does not match recent signals, then a difference detector remits the efferent inhibition and may activate the RAS so that the next stimulus in the series evokes strong electrical activity. Depending on the complexity of the input stimulus, the comparison of input to stored replica goes on at different levels of the brain. The assumption would be that the neural structures responsible for habituation to a particular stimulus are at the same level as those required for its discrimination. Deutsch and Deutsch (1963) propose a simple mechanism whereby the more important of a group of signals might be selected for attention. Inputs arriving over this selected channel would then be connected to further memorial or motor processes, whereas the remaining signals are not reacted to.

What may we conclude from the studies reviewed? First, it is clear that variations in reticular activation correlate with levels of wakefulness and arousal. Second, the RAS serves a usually facilitatory role in preparing the cortex for processing sensory information. Third, the RAS probably serves as a nonspecific governor or threshold determining the overall level of "importance" any stimulus must have to attract attention. In sleep or drowsiness, only the most important signals will be reacted to, for example, a baby's cry for its mother. As a parallel example, a sleeping cat will not be aroused by a neutral tone but will be awakened by a slightly different tone that evokes anxiety because of its previous pairing with shock. Fourth, the RAS and other parts of the brain control and modulate afferent inputs by way of a system of efferent networks. This modulation is usually inhibitory, attenuating channel A when channel B is being listened to. Effects of learning, or associating significance to a stimulus through conditioning, can be seen near the receptor or almost as soon as the signal enters the input channel. These brain-to-periphery influences provide some basis for speculation on the perceptual changes that occur during learning, on the attachment of "meaning" to stimuli, and on how stimulation, rather than effecting a passive registration, is selectively edited, discarded, and reworked for the purposes of the waking organism.

LEARNING AND MEMORY

An organism that could not learn might still behave differentially under various conditions of motivational arousal, might withdraw from noxious stimuli and continue to react to favored ones. Such behavior becomes important for learning only when change occurs with experience, that is, when past experiences are somehow stored in memory, so that when stimuli are again encountered, reaction to them is altered in light of what went before. Hence we need to supplement the foregoing account of brain activity with what is known about the changes that take place when learning occurs, and about memory storage and retrieval.

Consolidation of Memory Traces

In broad outline, there are basically two kinds of views about the neural basis for the retention of experience or learning. One view supposes that an experience sets up a continuing electrical activity in appropriate neural circuits and that the persistence of these active circuits is coordinate with the persistence of our memory of the experience coded in this way. When this active trace process stops, we lose that memory. We may call this the "dynamic" view of the engram or memory trace. Opposed to it is the "structural" view, that learning consists in some enduring physical, structural, or biochemical change in the nervous system, and that this physical change will persist even when the original neuronal circuits responsible for its having been established in the first place have returned to relative quiescence following the initial experience.

It takes very little thought or experiment to reject the "dynamic" view of memory. For example, cooling a hamster down to 5°C causes it to hibernate, during which time very little, if any, electrical activity can be recorded from its brain. However, when warmed up and tested, it still retains what-ever old habits were taught it before the hibernation period. As another example, consider the electrical "brainstorms" of *grand mal* epileptic seizures in human patients. Such seizures begin when a local epileptogenic focus (caused by a brain injury or tumor, for example) starts to recruit neighboring clumps of neurons into its abnormal discharge pattern. They fall into lock-step synchrony in firing with the epileptic focus, and then still more areas are recruited. The effective firing area spreads, and soon most of the cortex is being driven in synchrony with the epileptic focus; the seizure is in full swing, with practically all the brain participating in the paroxysmal activity. This full-blown seizure may last for a few minutes. Upon recovery from such a seizure, the patient is not devoid of memories of his past, as the "dynamic" view would suggest; in fact, it is difficult to detect that the seizure has produced any loss of memory. There are a variety of other lines of evidence that rule out the dynamic view that memory lives in a continual spinning circuit, so this view assumes prac-tically the status of a straw man.

By a process of elimination, then, we arrive at the accepted view that memory involves a relatively permanent physical or structural change in the nervous system. Though we cannot prejudge what the nature of this physical change is, it may be innocuous to assume that the change takes place over some span of time following the learning experience, possibly even increasing in magnitude with time. If the time span involved is extremely brief—say only a few *milliseconds* is required to complete the change—then the notion of temporal change is irrelevant to behavioral experiments. However, the notion does have behavioral implications of interest if the time span involved is fairly long—say, many seconds, min-utes, hours, or days. It is just this notion that has been pursued under the label of the "consolidation" hypothesis.

One form of such a hypothesis was proposed long ago by Müller and Pilzecker (1900). They suggested that the neural activity responsible for storing a physical change encoding an experience persists for some time after that experience, and as a consequence of the perseverating neural activity, the physical changes become more firmly fixed or of greater magnitude. This progressive fixation with time is called *consolidation*. If this persisting neural activity is soon interrupted by the intrusion of interfering activity, then the physical change is of small magnitude, and retention of the experi-ence should be poor. Hebb (1949) restated this hypothesis and gave a more detailed neurophysiological model for it. The Müller-Pilzecker hypothesis was originally proposed to account for retroactive interference in recall of verbal materials by human subjects. In that context, it was not very fruitful and has been eclipsed by associative interference theory (see Chapter 9). which proved to be more adequate to the factual details in that area. Con-tinuing interest in the consolidation hypothesis stems partly from clinical observations but primarily from experiments with animals.

To begin with a clear prototype, we consider a rudimentary form of "posture persistence" that has a clear consolidation period (Gerard, 1963). If a lesion is made on one side of the cerebellum of a rat, a postural asym-metry of the legs results, due to asymmetrical conduction of motoric impulses down the spinal cord. Cutting the spinal cord below the cerebellar lesion abolishes this asymmetrical discharge down the spinal cord. If done soon enough, this spinal section also abolishes the postural asymmetry of the legs. But if the cord is not cut until the lapse of a critical period of time after the lesion, then the asymmetric posture persists indefinitely despite sectioning of the spinal cord. In this instance, then, we have a relatively permanent change in neuronal circuits of the spinal cord that takes some time to occur. The fixation time turns out to be fairly sharp, about 45 minutes from the first appearance of asymmetry following the cerebellar lesion until spinal sectioning. Figure 14.5 shows a graph of the results of one experiment. In most cases of spinal-cord sectioning before 45 minutes, the asymmetry was abolished by the section, while for almost all cases of sectioning after 45 minutes, the postural asymmetry persisted after the cord sectioning. The critical fixation time could be increased or decreased by administration of drugs which either retard or enhance, respectively, the rate of protein synthesis in neural cells. We shall look further into the role of drugs in our later discussion of neurochemistry.

This experiment is mentioned because it presumably indicates a definite time period during which particular neuronal circuits (in this case, from the spinal cord of a rat to the legs) undergo a kind of permanent change. One might consider the cerebellar preparation as a primitive model of learning from the viewpoint of consolidation theory. It must be admitted, however, that it is only an analogy to learning as we ordinarily conceive of it. The

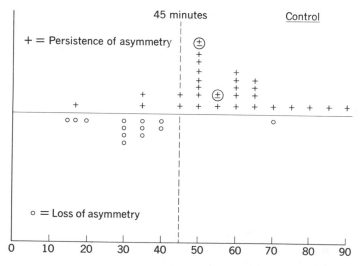

Figure 14.5.   Each symbol, + or o, represents one animal. + represents animals for whom the postural asymmetry persisted following sectioning of the spinal cord; o represents animals for whom the asymmetry disappeared upon cord sectioning. The time (in minutes) between development of postural asymmetry and sectioning of the spinal cord is indicated on the lower axis of the graph. For all but one animal, asymmetry persisted when the cord section occurred at or after 45 minutes; for 12 of 15 animals sectioned before 45 minutes, the asymmetry was lost. (From Gerard, 1963. By permission.)

main evidence for the consolidation theory of memory comes from studies of disturbing or traumatizing the brain shortly after registration of an experience. In theory, this disruption should prevent consolidation of the neural analogue of the memory, so no learning should be demonstrable at a later test.

In this regard, let us consider the striking clinical phenomenon of retrograde amnesia. After a person receives a hard knock on the head or some traumatic brain injury (such as a combat wound) producing unconsciousness and a coma, he is very likely when he awakens to be unable to recall the events immediately connected with and just prior to the injury. In the more severe and dramatic instances (W. R. Russell & Nathan, 1946), the events preceding the trauma by several hours, days, or months may be lost to recall, and such a patient is said to have amnesia. In most of these amnestic cases, the person eventually recovers his memories, and the events more remote in time from the injury seem to be recovered first. As recovery continues, events closer in time to the accident can be recalled; yet there usually still remains an unrecoverable portion of those events just immediately prior to the injury. Similar effects in milder degree caused by deep anesthesia, insulin- or metrazol-induced convulsions, and electroconvulsive shock have been reported in human patients. The consolidation hypothesis would interpret such amnestic phenomena roughly as follows: the injury or trauma prevents the process of consolidation of recent material and additionally raises the threshold for recall of older memories. The older memories, having had more time to consolidate, are stronger. During recovery, the threshold for recall declines so that the older, stronger memories return first.

In the experimental work on amnesia in animals (typically rats), most of the early experiments investigated how learning is disrupted when the subject receives an electroconvulsive shock (ECS) shortly after a learning trial. The convulsion, similar in many respects to the synchronized brainstorm in an epileptic seizure, is readily induced by briefly passing a strong electric current between electrodes clipped to the ears of a rat. Starting with work by Duncan (1949), a long series of studies have shown that ECS given to a rat soon after a learning trial interferes with its performance of the appropriate habit when it is tested the next day after recovery from the short-lived convulsion. Moreover, the closer in time the ECS comes to the end of the learning trial, the greater is the disruption in performance that appears in the subsequent test.

The effect can be illustrated by Duncan's initial experiment. Rats were trained on an active avoidance habit at the rate of 1 trial a day for 18 days. The trial started by placing the rat on the "danger" side of a two-compartment box. If it did not cross over to the "safe" compartment within 10 seconds, its feet were shocked until it did. Following its crossing over to the safe compartment, the rat received an ECS. The delay between the response and the ECS was varied for different animals, and was either 20, 40, or 60 seconds, 4 or 15 minutes, or 1, 4, or 14 hours. The ECS treatment was given following each of the training trials. A group of control subjects received no ECS. The effect of the delay between response and ECS is depicted in Figure 14.6, which shows the average number of avoidance responses over the 18 trials for animals given the ECS after each length of delay. The logarithm of the delay before ECS is plotted on the abscissa. Figure 14.6 shows a marked retrograde effect of ECS upon learning. At the shortest interval, 20 seconds, very little learning occurred. As the time before ECS is lengthened, less decrement occurs. With an ECS delay of 1 hour or more, the subjects receiving ECS perform as well as the controls receiving no ECS.

These results may be interpreted as reflecting a process of memory consolidation that goes on over about a 60-minute period following each learning trial. The ECS is assumed to interrupt this process, with the amount learned per trial increasing with the time for consolidation before the process is interrupted by ECS.

Unfortunately, an alternative hypothesis would also explain Duncan's finding, namely, the delay-of-punishment gradient. We might assume that the ECS is aversive, so that it punishes and inhibits responses which it shortly follows, doing so according to a typical delay gradient. This would explain Duncan's findings without requiring the consolidation hypothesis. Later experiments have indeed shown that a series of electroconvulsive shocks begins to act like an aversive event to be avoided; however, relatively little aversion is evident after just one ECS. For this and various other reasons, it is now believed that the best paradigm for showing amnestic

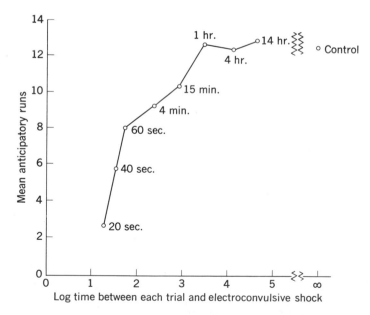

Figure 14.6.   The average number of anticipatory runs (avoidance responses) for all 18 trials, related to the logarithm of the delay time between the trial and electroconvulsive shock. Different points on the curve (with delay times indicated) represent different groups of subjects. (From C. P. Duncan, The retroactive effect of electroshock on learning, *Journal of Comparative & Physiological Psychology*, 1949, 42. Copyright 1949 by the American Psychological Association. Reprinted by permission.)

effects of ECS is a "one-trial learning" situation into which a single ECS is introduced.

A situation presently in use which meets these requirements is a passive avoidance situation. A rat or mouse is placed upon a small raised platform above a grid floor. If this is done with naive animals, they will step down off the small platform within a few seconds. If they are painfully shocked from the grid floor when they step down, a later test will show that they now refuse to leave the platform. They have learned a passive avoidance response in one trial. However, animals given an ECS soon after the foot shock seemingly "forget," so that on the next day's test they still step quickly off the platform (e.g., Chorover & Schiller, 1965). A graded amnesia effect is again obtained, although the time constants seem generally lower than those obtained by Duncan. For example, Chorover and Schiller report practically no ECS-induced amnesia when the ECS is delayed as much as 30 seconds following the learning trial; shorter delays (.5, 2, 5, 10 seconds) had stronger amnestic effects. A recent review of this literature may be found in McGaugh and Herz (1972).

The retrograde effect of ECS has by now been repeatedly observed. Similar amnestic effects have been produced by convulsant drugs, heat narcosis, hyperoxia, and certain anesthetic drugs which produce unconsciousness or convulsions. Over the last two decades, developments have followed three main lines. First, the retrograde amnestic effect has been studied in greater detail yielding deeper empirical knowledge of the phenomenon. Second, a variety of alternative hypotheses have been offered to explain the amnestic effect of ECS, and these often provoke experiments which try to differentiate the new hypothesis from the old memory-consolidation hypothesis. Third, the search for neurological structures implicated in the amnestic effect has proceeded to finer detail and to more discriminating knowledge of brain events that disrupt consolidation. Just a few results of each kind will be mentioned here.

First, empirical studies have turned up several phenomena in the ECS situation that create some difficulties for a simple consolidation theory. For one thing, there are frequent reports of ECS-induced amnesia which "spontaneously lifts" with time after the one-trial learning event followed by ECS. But if immediate ECS has really prevented any learning, then there should be no habit to recover over time. However, such recovery is not always obtained; the relevant variables determining recovery are the species (rats recover more often than mice) and, in the passive avoidance situation, the severity of the initial foot shock and of the ECS intensity.

A second embarrassing fact is that different indices of remembering following ECS do not always agree. For example, an animal receiving foot shock followed by ECS may readily "step down" the next day, apparently showing amnesia for the shock, and yet its heart rate will be accelerated in the test situation, indicating some association of fear to the situation (Hines & Paolino, 1970). Or if the animal received foot shock and ECS for stepping down onto the white side rather than the dark side of a two-compartment floor, on the next test day it may step down readily, apparently showing amnesia for the foot shock; yet it will strongly prefer to step down to the side of the nonshocked color, apparently remembering where it received the painful shock the day before (Carew, 1970). These matters could perhaps be handled by supposing that learning involving autonomic responses is more quickly consolidated than is learning involving instrumental responses, although this is clearly *ad hoc* and unpalatable.

A third discomforting fact for the hypothesis that ECS disrupts consolidation is that memory for the response apparently remains for a few hours after ECS, only to disappear 24 hours later—which test interval is the one typically used in such studies (Geller & Jarvik, 1968; McGaugh & Landfield, 1970). Such findings appear paradoxical for a simple consolidation theory, which would suppose that ECS produces total forgetting immediately and permanently. Perhaps it is fairer to say that ECS simply accelerates the rate of forgetting rather than causing immediate loss of the experience.

As mentioned above, the second line of research development is one which proposes and tests alternative interpretations of ECS-induced amnesia. An early one proposed by Lewis and Maher (1965) was that ECS should be viewed as an unconditioned stimulus causing unconsciousness and generalized inhibition to become conditioned in Pavlovian fashion to cues of the situation paired with ECS. Although this interpretation led to a series of interesting experiments (reviewed in Lewis & Maher, 1965, and in Lewis, 1969), it has not been generally accepted since it fails to account for those passive avoidance cases where ECS produces forgetting which is inferred from the shocked animal's now *actively* doing something—namely, stepping down onto the floor where it had received painful shock the day before rather than passively freezing on the ledge where it is placed like the control animal who only received foot shock. A more recent and interesting perspective on effects of ECS or similar brain traumas is that these may involve *retrieval* difficulties rather than *learning* difficulties (see G. H. Bower, 1972d, pp. 117–120; DeVietti & Larson, 1971; Lewis, 1969; Nielson, 1968). One possibility, for example, is that ECS following a learning event causes memory for that experience to be repressed, much as is supposed in the Freudian theory of repression. Such memories could then be evoked or assessed later only under special circumstances. One experiment suggesting this analysis is by Misanin, Miller, and Lewis (1968). The critical learning event was the pairing of a tone with a painful foot shock to rats. The next day, the group of rats was presented with the tone followed by ECS. This delayed experience of tone-ECS seemed to interfere with memory of the earlier tone-shock event (despite its having 24 hours "consolidation time"), for on the following day the tone did not elicit much fear as measured by its suppression of drinking. The idea is that, during the second day's treatment, the tone at first reinstated the memory of the tone-shock pairing; however, the ECS following revival of the tone-shock memory allegedly caused something like repression or inhibition to become attached to that memory in such manner as to block its subsequent retrieval to the tone stimulus. Dawson and McGaugh (1969) were unable to replicate this study, although DeVietti and Holliday (1972) reported a successful replication of it. The factors responsible for this discrepancy are not clear at present.

A second variant of the retrieval hypotheses uses the notion of state-dependent learning; it is presumed that the interaction of foot shock and ECS produces a change in brain excitability (or "brain state") for several days, during which time material learned in the normal brain state is not retrievable. When the state of brain excitability returns to that prevailing during original learning, the ability to retrieve and use the memory (of the foot shock) should return. Nielson (1968) found data supporting this thesis. Also, the foot shock–ECS interaction idea is not totally *ad hoc* since Chorover and DeLuca (1969) found that the electrocorticograms recorded during ECS not preceded by foot shock were decidedly different from those for ECS following foot shock, and that the disruption of normal ECoGs was greater the closer in time was the foot shock to the ECS.

Experiments by DeVietti and Larson (1971) and Schneider and Sherman (1968) have also cast some light on this state-dependency hypothesis regarding ECS effects. In the DeVietti and Larson experiment, thirty rats were first trained to drink in a distinctive test box, then received a painful foot shock paired with a tone. This procedure will usually condition the tone to fear, so that its presentation will inhibit drinking during tests given 48 hours later, reflecting fear and remembering of the tone–foot shock pairing. However, a novel treatment was interpolated between foot shock and test; namely, after 1 day the animal was placed in a new, different box and given a foot shock followed immediately by an ECS (without the tone's being presented). Then, after a 1- or 4-day delay, these animals were tested for inhibition of drinking to the tone. The result was that at the 1-day interval, these rats did not "remember" the tone–foot shock pairing very well as indicated by fairly rapid drinking (and little fear), whereas they did remember that experience at the 4-day interval, at which time they inhibited their drinking. Controls receiving foot shock alone or ECS alone showed either no change or a decline in fear over the same interval from 1 to 4 days. The interpretation in terms of the state-dependency hypothesis is that the foot-shock-then-ECS episode altered the brain state of the animal for several days, so that on the test a day later the rat could not readily retrieve the memory of the earlier tone–foot shock pairing. However, the brain state would have returned to normal after 4 days, so that the memory (fear) stored initially in that normal state was now once again retrievable. In a further test of these ideas, DeVietti and Larson showed that after fear training to the tone, a set of fear-extinction trials (tone but not shock) carried out a day following an isolated foot-shock-then-ECS episode had no effect on these animals' fear behavior 3 days later, whereas foot-shock-trained controls receiving fear-extinction trials showed the expected decline in anxiety and inhibition of drinking during the tone. This lack of transfer of extinction effects from extinction at a 1-day interval to a test session 3 days later is comprehensible if one believes that the brain state following a foot-shock-then-ECS episode is altered for 1 or 2 days, and that any learning experiences occurring during this altered state will not be retrievable in the normal state of excitability to which the brain returns after about 4 days.

Although hypotheses and investigations such as these are valuable in guiding a deeper empirical analysis of a given phenomenon, in the case of ECS-induced amnesia the alternative hypotheses tend not to be able to explain nearly so much as the original consolidation theory. That is, one can quickly cite data which are difficult for the alternative theories to handle. For example, the state-dependency theory ascribes special causal status to foot shock–ECS interactions, but it is not clear how to extend the hypothesis to amnesia caused by drugs like ether or fluorothyl or by localized brain stimulation (to be reviewed next); nor is it obvious how to extend it to deal with amnesia for appetitive habits or active escape habits learned without a discrete foot-shock event just preceding the ECS. Until such explanations can be provided, the new alternative is unlikely to be adopted as a general theory in the same sense as is the consolidation theory.

The third line of research development on amnesia is concerned with more closely mapping out the brain events crucial for disrupting memory consolidation. Some of this research seeks to specify more precisely the critical brain-component reaction to ECS or to anesthetics which is responsible for producing graded amnestic effects. For example, recent findings by Landfield and McGaugh (1972) and Landfield et al. (1972) suggest that degree of ECS-induced amnesia in rats is correlated with the length of time during which theta waves are absent in the hippocampus following ECS. Little or no amnesia was found for rats for whom theta activity quickly returned following ECS. Another kind of research seeks to interfere with memory consolidation by applying discrete, localized electrical stimulation to specific brain sites through implanted electrodes. A variety of brain sites have been found in which single electrical pulses applied soon after a learning event will prevent consolidation of a memory. Such stimulation can be weak and brief but selectively destructive in contrast to the "block-buster" devastation produced by a severe ECS. Interference with learning has been produced from discrete electrical stimulation to the dorsal hippocampus, the caudate putamen, and frontal cortex, among other sites, whereas *facilitation* in learning has been obtained from post-trial stimulation in the mesencephalic reticular formation and the ventral hippocampus, among other places (see McGaugh & Herz, 1972, for a review). At present, this research is not particularly illuminating since few experimenters have shown *temporal* gradients of effects, as required by the consolidation hypothesis. Moreover, the studies generally used massed trials, so that post-trial effects of stimulation cannot be easily separated. Thus, for instance, a particular type of brain shock may not prevent learning, but rather its persisting aftereffects may impair sensory discrimination so that the animal performs poorly on trials that follow soon after such stimulation. A proper psychological analysis of the effects of such brain stimuli is just beginning in earnest, and we can anticipate that the tracking down in this manner of the critical structures subserving memory consolidation is likely to be a long, slow, and probably indefinite process.

Neurological Patients

Some rather dramatic results have been obtained recently from electrical stimulation and selective ablation in the case of human patients undergoing brain surgery for medical reasons (typically, for removal of epileptogenic foci causing frequent seizures). Bickford et al. (1958) and Chapman et al. (1967) have reported that electrical stimulation to the temporal lobe of the brain of the waking patient (during surgery under local anesthesia) produces a temporary retrograde amnesia. The patient may be unable to retrieve events up to 2 weeks past, and the length of this memory gap increases with the duration of the hippocampal stimulation. The amnesia is temporary, however, with memory being recovered completely a few hours after stimulation. Although the patients were unable during stimulation to retrieve memories several hours or several days old, they were able to perform quite capably on short-term or immediate memory tasks, such as repeating back a short series of digits.

The critical role of the hippocampus in memory consolidation has been suggested by the peculiar disabilities of human patients who have suffered damage or ablation of the hippocampus bilaterally (on both sides of the midline). Although such patients appear to have normal short-term or immediate memory and can recall their life before their brain injury, they seem unable to retain new information for any great length of time (Milner, 1966). For instance, such a patient cannot remember a person he met and conversed with only a few minutes before. He will repeatedly introduce himself and ask the same questions as at the earlier encounters, with a perfect confidence that the current meeting is the first one. Such patients, of course, soon become quite disoriented as to where they are (in the hospital), how long they have been there, how they came to be there, or what has happened to them or to the world since their brain trauma (see Talland, 1965). For them, the elapsed time and the events which fill that time do not exist; regardless of how long ago they came to the hospital, in their memory it is always "yesterday."

This dramatic syndrome is consonant with the dual-memory hypothesis, which proposes a short-term and a long-term memory system. We might suppose that in these patients the mechanism for transferring representations of experience into long-term memory has been put out of commission, although their short-term memory is unimpaired, as is retrieval of the long-term memories they had preoperatively. Such patients have been studied extensively by Baddeley and Warrington (1970). On the other hand, Warrington and Shallice (1969) describe a brain-injured patient (not with hippocampal damage) who has just the opposite symptom, namely, a very deficient short-term memory (average digit span of 1.5 in contrast to a span of 6 to 8 digits for normal adults); yet this patient has no impairment in his ability to process new information into "long-term memory." Such cases suggest the view that the short-term and long-term storage mechanisms operate simultaneously, in *parallel*, rather than the standard view that short-term memory precedes and is the "entrance" to long-term memory. In the latter, sequential view, a deficit in short-term memory should necessarily cause a deficit in acquisition (learning) rate.

Despite these drastic effects of bilateral hippocampectomy in human patients, such lesions in lower animals do not appear to have nearly such extreme or dramatic effects upon learning. The literature regarding behavioral effects of hippocampal lesions in animals is diversely inconsistent, and cannot be simply summarized. In any event, it is clearly a gross oversimplification to claim that the hippocampus is the "doorway" to long-term memory in the mammalian brain. Would that life were so simple!

Variables Affecting Consolidation Rate

According to the hypothesis of a short-term and a long-term memory store, the input of stimulation supposedly produces "reverberating" neural activity, representative of that experience, which persists for a while. This dynamic neural trace is coincident with our short-term memory. While this reverberatory activity lasts, the permanent structural change underlying the long-term memory is slowly developing. Once the reverberatory trace dies out, the structural change stops and remains at the level attained. It is plausible, in this theory, to look for variables that influence reverberation rate or the length of time before the short-term trace dies out, since these should affect how much will be consolidated into long-term memory from a learning trial.

McGaugh (1965, 1968) has investigated two general classes of variables that may be interpreted by this means, namely, drugs and the genetic constitution of the animals. In one line of experiments, he has shown that certain CNS-stimulating drugs such as strychnine, diazamantan, amphetamine, and picrotoxin given in low doses speed up maze learning of rats when injected either before or after the one trial of each day. Such results have by now been replicated many times for many learning tasks (see McGaugh & Herz, 1972). It is presumed that these stimulants either increase the consolidation rate or prolong the short-term activity trace, which results in more consolidated learning per trial. A standard finding, for instance, is that post-trial injections facilitate learning only if they are given within 15 minutes or so after the day's learning experience. In the other line of work, McGaugh used genetic strains of rats that had been selectively inbred by Tryon (1942) to be either bright or dull in learning various maze problems. He tested the implications of the idea that the maze-bright and maze-dull strains differ in their neural reverberation rates or times. For example, one implication he confirmed is that in the one-trial learning ECS situation, ECS can be delayed longer yet still produce greater memory deficits in the maze-dull rats. Also, if maze trials are given widely spaced in time, the maze-dulls can learn as fast as the maze-bright rats, the difference appearing only with massed trials. This is understandable if it is assumed that maze-dulls consolidate more slowly and the consolidation of learning from trial n is cut short when trial $n + 1$ starts under the massed condition. Further, it was found that injection of the neural stimulant picrotoxin facilitated massed-trial learning of the maze-dulls (in fact, makes them learn as fast as the maze-brights) more than it facilitates the maze-bright animals. These observations and several others seem consistent with the view that the two genetic strains differ in rate of memory consolidation.

It is proper to note that the dual system hypothesis employs a "conceptual" nervous system to advantage, without specifying the neural circuitry involved. There is, to be sure, firm evidence of persisting reverberatory neural circuits in the cortex. For example, Burns (1958) reported that a few electrical shocks applied to an isolated slab of quiescent cortex will produce bursts of neural activity that may persist for minutes (sometimes as long as an hour) after stimulation has stopped. But little is really known of these persisting effects in nonisolated tissue. Nor is much known of the effect on the brain of the drugs like picrotoxin, etc., which facilitate learning, and we are only now slowly accumulating facts about the neurological effect of ECS upon the metabolism and general functioning of the brain. Our point in noting this is that the consolidation hypothesis derives its major, if not its sole, evidential support from "behavioral" studies, not from the observation of events in the central nervous system.

Although the consolidation hypothesis has proven itself to be a viable theory, a variety of further questions will have to be asked and answered by experiments. What causes differences in the time required to consolidate different learning tasks? Is the change gradual, all-or-none, or gradual with a threshold? How do we distinguish poor storage from poor access to a stored engram? What is the generic nature of the sorts of events that disrupt consolidation? How are proactive interference effects on retention to be explained in these terms? How can animals learn to avoid a place where ECS is delivered if that ECS prevents storage of the memory that it was unpleasant? Does consolidation stop when the short-term trace dies out or does it continue if not interfered with? How do we account for long-term recovery of a memory disrupted by ECS? What are the neural events that are facilitated when post-trial drug injections enhance learning? These and other questions come to mind, and future research will be directed at answering them in detail.

Physiological Changes in Learning

So far we have managed to discuss the neurophysiology of learning by skirting what is surely the central issue, namely, the nature of the physiological change that occurs during learning. The reason for skirting the issue is simple. The nature of this change is far from being understood. A number of speculative hypotheses have been offered over the years, but the evidence for any one of them is very limited, and little agreement exists even about what are the more promising leads. The hypotheses, such as there are, vary in their degree of elaboration, from one-line "suggestions" to more elaborate systems of postulates; but for none has it been demonstrated that the hypothesis is sufficient to account for a substantial range of the known facts about learning. This is a sorry state of affairs, but one that seems imposed on us by the difficulty of the problem. It certainly cannot be attributed to any lack of industry or ingenuity by experimenters in the field. In this section, we will touch briefly on a diverse miscellany of facts and ideas that are relevant to information storage in the nervous system, and also mention a few of the earlier, more prevalent ideas regarding the physical change in learning, not so much to point to the evidence supporting them but rather to the lack of it.

Let us begin with the example of a Pavlovian conditioned reflex. Next to habituation, classical conditioning is about the simplest context in which to place various notions about the physical change effected by learning. A bell (CS) is paired repeatedly with an electric shock (US) to the forepaw of a dog, eliciting a limb flexion (UR) until, with training, the bell alone serves to elicit the response (CR). When the process is viewed from the anatomical side, at least three classes of structures or cell populations are involved: (a) cells all along the sensory input channel excited by the CS, (b) cells along the sensory input channel excited by the US, and (c) cells along the motor output channel initiating and controlling the response (UR). We will call these multiple structures the CS, US, and UR sites or centers. Because of innate connections, there already exists a strong tendency for activation of the US center to produce activation of the UR center. Most neurophysiological theories of conditioning employ one or another modified version of the *substitution* notion of conditioning. By virtue of many contiguous pairings of activity in the CS center and the US (or UR) center, the former through some means gets "connected" to the latter so that activation of the CS now transmits effective excitation to the US (or UR) center. Thereupon the CS alone mimics or substitutes in some degree for the action of the US. Various hypotheses are then offered regarding the nature of this functional connection and the processes involved in its formation.

One class of hypotheses has to do with a selective increase in the efficiency of existing neural pathways connecting the CS and US centers, which may be assumed to involve many central synapses linked in a chain. Given good conduction between the CS and US centers, it is conceivable that the CS might fire the US center and thus evoke an anticipatory CR. In this case it is supposed that there is some anatomical or biochemical change at the synapses along such critical pathways. Some possibilities are that the presynaptic axon terminals either swell in size, grow in length, or multiply in numbers to make better contact with the postsynaptic neuron, thus aiding future transmission across the synapse.[1] There is slight evidence for the swelling notion and practically none for the growth or the multiplication suppositions. One problem is that normal stimulation across a synapse does not appear to change its efficiency (Brink, 1951). Efficiency can be enhanced, usually for only brief periods (a few minutes), if the synapse is bombarded with a volley of high-frequency impulses (e.g., 400 pulses per second), but the relevance of this particular result for normal learning has not been elaborated.

An alternative idea, proposed by Pavlov (see Chapter 3) and investigated by the Russians, is cortical irradiation of extraneuronal electrical fields. When activated, the cortical sites of the CS and US centers supposedly radiate electrical excitation, spreading out in all directions with diminishing intensity. Because the CS excitation is the weaker of the two, it is supposedly drawn toward the US excitation center by some method unspecified. As a consequence, some kind of cortical pathway (unspecified) would get established between the CS and US center. Beritoff (cited in Konorski, 1948) elaborates on the hypothesis further. However, two immediate problems are encountered by this notion of spreading intracortical electrical fields. First, it is known that animals (dogs) can learn simple conditional reflexes even after the cortex has been totally removed. Second, an experiment by Sperry and Miner (1955) showed that learning was essentially undisturbed in animals whose cortices had been altered by cross-hatching knife cuts or implantation of wires and mica sheets that serve as electrical conductors or insulators. Such devices must have distorted or destroyed any existing or

---

[1] The notion of a biochemical change at the synapse is discussed in a later section of this chapter.

generated electrical fields in the cortex. Yet they did not interfere at all with the learning of fairly complicated CRs.

As noted earlier in our discussion of consolidation, it has been proposed that a sequence of stimulus inputs sets up a short-term activity (memory) trace based on reverberatory neuronal circuits involving elements excited by the CS and US inputs. Neuron A excites neuron B, which, through some more or less direct path, excites A again; hence, the loop of A to B to A activity is alleged to perseverate for a time after the inputs. This persisting reverberatory activity is presumed to induce a more enduring structural change (of unknown nature) so that the A-B neural centers will now be aroused as a unit. The fairest statement we can make concerning this notion is that no convincing evidence has been adduced for the existence of reverberatory circuits in the intact brain that (a) are clearly implicated in learning, or that (b) last long enough to have the properties ascribed to them. Although, as mentioned earlier, Burns (1958) did report fairly persistent neural activity following stimulation of the cortex, that was in an isolated slab of material not subject to dissipating forces from other parts of the brain. In any event, the reverberation idea, even if true, still tells us nothing about the nature of the change effected by learning.

Model Preparations

Instead of speculating about the neural changes involved in CR learning, the strategy preferred by many investigators is to search for experimental preparations wherein a few neurons modify their behavior in a way that mimics learning. The hope is that by studying a primitive form of information storage or learning at the level of the single neural cell, we may come up with some fruitful hypotheses about the physical changes in learning. In line with this policy, there have been many efforts to devise preparations that show simple learning in a few neurons. We will review several preparations, two of which, devised by Morrell (1960, 1961a), appear very interesting in this respect.

The first Morrell preparation is the "mirror focus" epileptiform phenomenon whereby a cluster of normal brain cells learns to behave in an abnormal way. It has been observed that an abnormally discharging group of brain cells in the cortex of one cerebral hemisphere (the primary focus) will fire off a similar discharge in a corresponding area of the opposite hemisphere (the secondary focus). The main links connecting the two foci probably pass through the corpus callosum. The primary focus may be produced by local application of various chemicals (ethyl chloride or aluminum hydroxide) to the brain site or by an injury or tumor (as in epilepsy). Initially, discharge of the secondary focus is dependent upon discharge in the primary focus. However, after a time (about 8 weeks in the monkey), the secondary focus begins abnormally discharging on its own, independently of the primary focus. The primary focus can now be ablated, and the secondary focus continues its pattern of paroxysmal discharging. It has "learned" to discharge in an abnormal way. Moreover, if the secondary focus is neuronally isolated by cutting it away from surrounding tissue (but leaving its blood supply intact) and left in a quiescent state for some months, later stimulation of the tissue will still set off the abnormal discharge pattern. Apparently the tissue slab has "retained" this discharge pattern after months of inactivity. The importance of this preparation is that learning of a primitive sort has been shown to occur in a relatively small group of cortical cells.

The second preparation was devised in the course of pursuing some interesting developments concerning the relation between learning and steady electrical potential shifts in the surface of the cortex. Interest in this latter line of work stems from the fact, observed by Rusinov (1953) and others, that shifts in the steady electrical potential of the brain surface can be recorded during the course of classical conditioning. The supposition is that extraneuronal electrical fields exerting an electrotonic influence on neural cell populations would probably play some important role in the conditioning process. Such shifts in cortical steady potentials have been found to result from direct electrical stimulation of the brain. Indeed, Morrell (1961b) found that a shift of cortical potential elicited by a thalamic electric shock could be conditioned as a "response" to a tone stimulus. Of interest in this respect are studies of the effect of directly modifying the steady potential on the cortical surface. Rusinov modified the steady electrical potential of the brain of rabbits by applying a weak anodal constant direct current to a part of the motor cortex controlling forelimb flexion. Though such a current did not itself produce a motor response, nevertheless, while the polarizing current was acting and for up to 30 minutes after it terminated, neutral sensory stimuli such as a light, sound, or touch would produce flexion of the appropriate forelimb. It was as though the brain had been primed in readiness to make this motor response given any sudden sensory signal. Morrell (1961b) replicated these findings and extended them in several ways. In one experiment, it was shown that if a stimulus had been thoroughly habituated, as judged by the eventual absence of an EEG change to its presentation, then that stimulus would not elicit the limb flexion during the heightened excitability period after the polarizing stimulus is switched off. However, novel stimuli that had not been habituated would still trigger the response.

A miniature "learning" preparation was discovered in the course of further study of anodal polarization. In this experiment, a tiny microelectrode was used to record evoked electrical activity in single neurons of the visual cortex (see panels [a] and [b] of Figure 14.7). During anodal polarization of the cortex, it was easy to "drive" such cells in synchrony with a flashing light delivered to the eye. "Driving" in this context means that the cell in the visual cortex responds with a short burst of activity for each flash to the eye; for example, if the light flashes three times per second, then the driven cell responds in brief bursts three times per second. Such driving may be seen in panel (c) of Figure 14.7.

The interesting observation made by Morrell is that such neural cells can learn and retain for a while the particular driving frequency to which they have been exposed. When a cell was driven at three per second during anodal polarization, it would later respond to a *single* flash by prolonged three-per-second bursts of activity. The effect is seen in panel (d) of Figure 14.7. The cell apparently learned and retained the specific firing frequency imposed upon it during the "conditioning" phase carried out under anodal polarization.

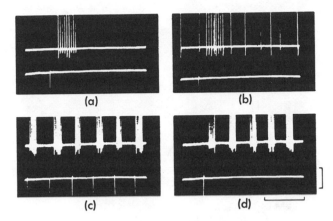

Figure 14.7.   Firing of a single neuron in the visual cortex induced by flashes of light. The flash is indicated by the pips on the lower line of each panel; the firing of the neurons is indicated by the pips on the top line of each panel. Time (.5 second in [a] and [b], 1 second in [c] and [d]) reads from left to right. A single flash elicited a single burst when the cell was quiescent (panel [a]) or randomly firing (panel [b]). Flashes occurring at a rate of three per second resulted in unit discharges at a rate of three per second (panel [c]). A single flash (panel [d]) delivered 3 seconds after termination of the rhythmic flashes produced repetitive unit discharge at a rate of about three per second. (From Morrell, Frank, "Information Storage in Nerve Cells." In Fields, W. S., and Abbott, W. (Eds.), *Information Storage and Neural Control*, 1963. Courtesy of Charles C Thomas, Publisher, Springfield, Illinois.)

This conditioned rhythmic response was retained over several minutes following the training phase. The three-per-second response to a single flash became progressively less reliable as time elapsed after the conditioning. The forgetting curve for the neuron is shown in Figure 14.8, depicting the declining percentage of three-per-second responses to a test flash as time passed. This preparation, then, provides another example of how information about the firing pattern can be retained by the brain, showing up in single neurons an appreciable time after the training phase. The anodal polarization of the cortex enhances the cell's ability to be so modified by input stimulation. Of course, there is no guarantee in this work that learning has occurred in the very cell from which the microelectrode records are taken. Possibly the learning occurs in structures remote from this cell, but if this is the case they project their response to the cortical cell from which the record is taken. Thus, one may have here not a cell that learns but rather one that is ganged with others that do learn.

A variety of further experiments have investigated the effects on learning and performance of conditioned responses of altering the steady electrical potential of the cortex. The technique has interesting consequences; for example, cathodal polarization seems to produce a functional ablation of a cortical area, yet one which is temporary and reversible. It is a technique that is being currently exploited as a method to learn more about brain functions (see Rowland, 1968, for a review).

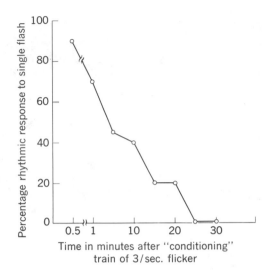

Figure 14.8.   Time course of "forgetting" of conditioned rhythmic response of a single cortical neuron. As time passed following the three-per-second flashes, a single flash was less likely to elicit the three-per-second pattern of unit activity. (From Morrell, Frank, "Information Storage in Nerve Cells." In Fields, W. S., and Abbott, W. (Eds.), *Information Storage and Neural Control*, 1963. Courtesy of Charles C Thomas, Publisher, Springfield, Illinois.)

Concerning "model preparations" which are proposed as ideal for studying learning processes, mention may be made of two further preparations because of their especial simplicity. One of these is *habituation* of a flexion reflex of an animal—typical examples are flexion of the hind leg of a spinally sectioned cat (see Thompson & Spencer, 1966) or the gill withdrawal reflex of the mollusk *Aplysia* (see Kandel & Spencer, 1968). These are especially simple neuronal reflexes, involving a sensory neuron from the skin, a motor neuron to the recorded muscle, and either zero, one, or at most two interneurons (and synaptic connections). Because of their simplicity, it is argued that such preparations are ideal for detailed electrophysiological and biochemical studies of learning phenomena. Habituation, assuredly one of the simplest forms of learning (it is comparable to "stimulus recognition" in humans), follows these nine empirical laws in most cases (adapted from Thompson & Spencer, 1966, pp. 18–19):

1. Repeated application of a stimulus results in progressive decrease of the usual response it elicits. This is called habituation.
2. The response spontaneously recovers over time without the stimulus.
3. When habituation series and recovery intervals are repeated, habituation proceeds progressively more rapidly.
4. Generally, the higher the rate of stimulation, the more rapid and extensive is habituation.
5. The weaker the stimulus, the quicker habituation occurs to it. Very intense stimuli may not habituate.

6. The effects of habituation training can proceed beyond the "zero" response level; that is, additional habituation trials given after the response has momentarily stopped will nonetheless cause slower recovery from habituation.

7. Habituation of a response to a given stimulus exhibits stimulus generalization to other stimuli.

8. A habituation response can be recovered by momentary presentation of another "surprising" or strong stimulus. This is called dishabituation.

9. Repeated use of the dishabituating stimulus (see 8 above) results in *that* stimulus's losing its dishabituating effect.

These nine characteristics may serve as the operational definition of habituation. Once several of these criteria have been satisfied by a given preparation, the neurophysiological correlates of habituation in that preparation may begin to be studied. Generally, habituation in polysynaptic preparations (like the spinal preparation in cats) is correlated with a decrease in transmission measurable by microelectrodes at interneuronal synapses. In nonsynaptic preparations such as the gill withdrawal reflex of *Aplysia*, habituation appears in attenuated transmission at the presynaptic terminal of the stimulated sensory neuron. Dishabituation occurs by stimulating any sensory neuron that synapses on the same motor unit.

The work on *Aplysia* has used the isolated abdominal ganglion, a cluster of large nerve cells consisting of motor neurons, interneurons, and neurosecretory cells. These cells mediate such diverse behaviors as egg laying, inking (darkening the surrounding water), and gill movement. A few giant nerve cells can be easily seen, stimulated, and recorded from. They show habituation to a repetitive stimulus. They also show nonspecific facilitation ("sensitization") in that repeated firing of a cell by a strong stimulus will "sensitize" the cell so that a weak (previously ineffective) stimulus that reaches the cell by a different synapse will now fire the cell (see Kandel & Tauc, 1965a, 1965b). The period of heightened excitability of the stimulated cell may last from 10 to 30 minutes. This particular phenomenon does not depend on a specific temporal pairing of weak (CS) and strong (US) stimuli; the effect is nonspecific. Whether and how much truly *specific* facilitation can be obtained (requiring CS-US pairings) is still a controversial issue. The plausible models for learning at the single synaptic level have been systematically presented by Kupfermann and Pinsker (1969), with special consideration of the invertebrate evidence.

The problem with studying the physiological substrates of learning or other behavioral phenomena with such simple preparations is that generalization of the results to higher, more complex organisms can be hazardous. Three hurdles must be passed to legitimize the generalization. First, the behavioral properties of learning in the model system must correspond to those found in more complex, intact vertebrates. Second, the neural mechanisms underlying learning in the model system must be simple enough to allow a detailed analysis. Third, the neural mechanisms subserving learning in the model systems must also be demonstrated for learning in the intact higher organism. In their review of such work, Thompson et al. (1972, p. 86) comment as follows: "This fundamental problem of inference is the greatest weakness of the model systems approach—there is no guarantee that the models will yield anything but interesting games quite irrelevant to an understanding of learning in higher vertebrates." In a similar vein, Kupfermann and Pinsker (1969, p. 382) urge, "It cannot be overemphasized that there is an enormous gap between knowledge of the plastic [learning—*Eds.*] properties of neurons studied in simple preparations, and knowledge of the physiological basis of reinforcement and learning in intact animals." However, this is an area in which intensive neurophysiological studies may be expected, based on the argument that we have little chance of understanding complex systems unless we can first thoroughly analyze and understand the simple case.

Neurochemistry and Experience

One appealing general hypothesis to explore is that individuals differ in their learning capabilities because of differences in the biochemistry of their brains. This is not an implausible supposition to follow up since developments in neurochemistry have supplied strong evidence that the transmission of neural signals is largely a chemical affair. Perhaps bright and dull individuals differ in the amount or manner of distribution over the brain of particular essential chemicals, or they may differ in the distribution of antagonistic chemicals which must be maintained in delicate balance for the proper functioning of the mind. The known effects of powerful hallucinogenic and psychotomimetic drugs such as mescaline and LSD offer some support for this thesis. These drugs have powerful and far-ranging effects on mental life, producing some of the bizarre subjective phenomena characteristic of patients during psychotic episodes. Because some psychotomimetic drugs have structural resemblances to chemicals found normally in the brain, much research has been aimed at discovering whether psychotics suffer from some disturbance in the biochemical system that produces these chemicals. Kety (1959) and Rinkel (1958) provide early reviews of the research bearing on this subject, while the most recent provocative work has been done by Stein and Wise (1971).

If we follow up the general idea of seeking to discover how brain chemistry is related to behavior, the first questions to be decided are what chemicals to look for and where in the brain to look for them. One approach is to measure the total amount of some chemical in gross areas of the brain, for example, in the whole cortex of a rat. An alternative might be to measure its amount and how it changes in a few neural cells located in specific brain structures implicated in the behavior we are studying. Another line of research uses brain chemistry alternately as an independent variable and as a dependent variable. In the first case, the aim is to find out how behavior varies on some standard task for individuals known to have different distributions of brain chemicals (e.g., because of age or of genetic differences). In the second case, the rearing and learning experiences of animals from a common genetic pool are manipulated, and then whether or not their brain chemistry has been changed as a result of experience is determined. Still another approach is to manipulate neurochemical processes at synapses by injection of centrally acting drugs, and then see whether hypothesized behavior effects follow. In most instances, several approaches are used by the same investigator. In what follows, we shall review one line of work representative of the relatively "gross" approach to brain chemistry and two that are representative of the synaptic approach.

1. Acetylcholine and cholinesterase. As indicated earlier, nerve cells may be thought of as telephone transmission lines that connect with one another functionally at junctures known as synapses. Line *A* connects with line *B* across a synapse, and the synapse is responsible for transmitting to *B* any nerve impulse (signal) traveling down line *A*. Nerve *B* has a threshold which the amount of stimulation must exceed in order to make *B* fire. However, several subthreshold impulses from *A* occurring in rapid succession will "temporally summate" in their effects and thus fire *B*; or subthreshold impulses arriving on *B* simultaneously from several different synapses will "spatially summate" to fire *B*. The transmission of a nerve impulse actually results from the impulse in *A* causing a shift in the membrane potential of nerve *B* on the other side of the synaptic gap. This transmission is largely a matter of biochemistry (see Figure 14.9, p. 533). An impulse in line *A* releases, literally squirts out at its end, a small amount of a substance called acetylcholine (ACh); this chemical crosses the tiny gap between *A* and *B* and is absorbed by the membrane of nerve *B*, causing a momentary shift in the membrane potential of nerve *B*. If the shift is large enough, it causes an electrical impulse to be generated and propagated down *B*. ACh is called the *transmitter* substance because of its essential role in this process. Following the firing of *B*, the enzyme cholinesterase (ChE) comes into play at the synapse. This enzyme works by hydrolizing (neutralizing) the ACh released at the synapse during transmission. In this manner, the ACh is cleared away and the synapse is returned to its prior state, ready to conduct further signals. The biochemical reactions here are extremely fast, requiring but a few milliseconds, and the interplay of the ACh and ChE systems is in a synchronized and delicate balance at a normal synapse. Small changes in the availability of or speed of access to one or the other chemical could result in malfunctioning, or at least in reduced efficiency in transmission of finely modulated, temporal patterns of neural impulses across the synapse. We will later discuss drugs whose major effects are to alter the availability of these transmitter substances.

A group of scientists at the University of California—psychologists Krech and Rosenzweig and biochemist Bennett—carried out a research program on ChE concentrations in rat brains. ChE is used because measurements of it are relatively easy to obtain, whereas reliable assays of ACh are difficult. Over a long period of research, these investigators gradually shifted their emphasis (because of the incoming data) concerning what brain chemistry measure should be used to find reliable correlations with behavior. The measure that seems most discriminating is the ratio of total cortical ChE activity to total subcortical ChE activity, called the C/S ratio (for cortical/subcortical). Low values of this C/S ratio are associated with quick learning of maze problems. In one study (Krech, Rosenzweig, & Bennett, 1960), rats reared in an "enriched" sensory environment, one filled with playground toys as well as other rats, had lower adult C/S ratios than rats reared under conditions of relative "isolation," where they were kept in small, enclosed cages devoid of other objects and fellow rats. On later tests of maze learning (Krech,

Rosenzweig, & Bennett, 1962), the "enriched" subjects also learned more rapidly. Within each rearing condition, individual differences in C/S ratio were correlated with errors in the maze-learning problem. The correlation was .81 for animals reared in the enriched environment and .53 for those reared in isolation. This shows a rather strong correlation between brain chemistry and speed of learning.

In other studies, rats of different genetic strains were examined for differences in C/S ratio. A series of studies was carried out with the Tryon maze-bright and maze-dull genetic strains of rats (see p. 518). Examination of the brains of these rats showed that the C/S ratio was lower for the maze-bright than for the maze-dull subjects. This finding is consistent with the previous results—that is, lower C/S ratios make for faster learning. In a genetic experiment by Roderick (1960), rats were selectively bred, some for high cortical ChE levels, some for low. After several generations of inbreeding highs with highs and lows with lows, there was little overlap in the distributions of cortical ChE levels in the two populations. Thus, brain chemistry was shown to be manipulable through genetic selection starting from a common genetic stock.

Although these studies were generally successful in disclosing individual and strain differences in brain chemistry that correlate with learning, the research ran into an interpretative problem. Though the C/S ratio "worked" empirically, no one was able to figure out a very convincing explanation for why it did so. Later studies, however, have provided an explanation. Their results showed, quite simply, that the cerebral cortex of "enriched-reared" (ER) rats is *bigger* than that of rats in the "isolation-reared" (IR) condition! Bennett et al. (1964) found that the cortex of the ER rats is both heavier and thicker. Because the increase in cholinesterase activity of the cortex is relatively less than the increase in its weight, the ChE activity per unit of weight decreases in the cortex of the ER rats. The ChE activity of the subcortex remains about the same, whereas the subcortex weight is slightly lower for ER rats, thus making for a higher subcortex ChE activity per unit weight. This explains why the C/S ratio of ChE activity is lower in the ER rats.

This discovery of a change in size of the cortex came as a complete surprise to those familiar with brain research. Before this, few experts would have believed that the effects of a sensorily enriched environment could induce so "obvious" a change in the brain. But the effect has by now been replicated about eight times, and is present each time in the ER-IR comparison. The magnitude of the change varies in different areas over the cortex, being largest (about 10 percent by weight) in the visual cortex. But it will be recalled that complexity of visual input is one of the main factors differentiating the two rearing conditions. In a further study (Rosenzweig et al., 1964), two groups of animals were reared in the same environment, the usual colony room, until they were 105 days of age, making them, roughly, adolescents, and then were separated, some to live in the enriched environment and some in the impoverished environment. After 85 days of such living, the two groups of rats were found to differ significantly in cortical weight and in ChE activity, much as when the differential rearing was done from birth onward. Thus, the brains of rats that have suffered an impoverished early life can be enlarged by placing them in an enriched environment at adolescence. This shows that there is no "critical period" before which the animal must be exposed to the enriched environment in order to produce an increase in the size of its cortex.

These findings instigated a number of follow-up studies investigating individual and strain differences in cortical size and visual learning ability, which have been reviewed by Rosenzweig and Leiman (1968). To date, no explanations have been offered, however, for (a) how a stimulating environment leads to a selective increase in cortical size, or (b) why individuals with a slightly larger cortex learn maze problems faster than do their slimmer-brained species fellows. Apparently, we may think of neural tissue much as we think of muscles which increase in size with exercise. Such a view would, until very recently, have been considered incredible nonsense in any respectable neurological discussion.

2. Cellular neurochemistry. One active line of contemporary research stems from the hypothesis that the physical basis for memory resides in some relatively enduring change in the biochemical constituents of a neuron which selectively control its response. This would suggest that an engram might be built up by certain biochemical changes occurring selectively in the cells of a neuronal circuit activated by the learning experience.

For various reasons, ribonucleic acid (RNA) was thought to be the logical candidate to assume this role of the memory molecule. It occurs in abundance in neural cells, it contains within its structure a potentially large storehouse for holding encoded information (explained below), and it determines and controls the specific form of proteins that are synthesized within a cell. RNA is a first cousin of DNA (deoxyribonucleic acid), which has been established to be the gene-carrying hereditary material in the chromosomes of each cell. DNA contains within its complex structure sufficient coded information to specify the genotypic character of an organism (i.e., its appearance), and it exercises its influence by controlling biochemical reactions in complex ways.

RNA is a very large, single-strand molecule (a polymer) consisting of a recurring sequence of a phosphate and sugar pair connected to any one of four bases, adenine, guanine, uracil, and cytosine. One of the four bases followed by a phosphate and a sugar may be considered as one of four types of links used to compose a long, beaded chain. The RNA molecule is very long (probably several thousand units), so that the number of possible sequential combinations of the four bases is very large. To illustrate, suppose each molecule were 2000 links long and at each position any of the four bases could occur. Then the number of different varieties of the molecule would be 4^{2000}, which is indeed a large number. This is important because it shows how much information could potentially be encoded in an RNA molecule. This capacity can be appreciated when it is recalled that Morse code translates a letter of the alphabet into a mere string of four or five binary units (dots and dashes). To compare it to the Morse code, an RNA strand consisting of 2000 units with four alternatives at each unit could encode and store a message about 1000 letters or 200 words long. Whether and how biological information is coded in RNA, and what the code is, are at present unanswered questions. However, the point here is that RNA has the potential for filling the role of a biological information storehouse.

If this were all there is to say about RNA, then it would have remained merely the subject of idle speculation. But a rash of behavioral evidence appeared to implicate RNA as a possible memory molecule. For one thing, its concentration in human brain cells first increases with age and then decreases, much as learning ability does. It has been reported that adding RNA supplements to the diet of aged persons improves their immediate memory; however, this result has not been obtained in attempted replications. Of more direct relevance is the fact that the concentration of RNA in neural cells increases when they are repetitively stimulated.

When the stimulation is to a cell importantly involved in learning some skill, the RNA in that cell not only increases but also changes its character as indexed by the amounts of the four bases (the "base ratio") found in RNA analysis following learning. In one study by Hydén and Egyhâzi (1962), rats were trained to balance upon and walk up an inclined tightrope to get a food reward. Following learning, the RNA in the vestibular nucleus was examined. This is a bundle of fibers that relays signals to the brain from the semicircular canals, which are receptor organs involved in maintaining postural balance. RNA in the nucleus of cells at this site was increased by the learning experience, and the dominant species of RNA was of a different kind (different base ratio) than that in control rats subjected to stimulation of their semicircular canals but not given the special training in tightrope balancing and walking. These control rats were instead merely rotated about in a small oscillating cage, movement that stimulates the semicircular canals. An interpretive problem with this study was that no one could figure out the adaptive significance of change in such a low-level sensory relay station.

In a further study (Hydén & Egyhâzi, 1964), right-"handed" rats were trained to use their left "hands" to grab food pellets from a food dispenser. Neural cells taken from certain layers of the opposite (right) cerebral cortex showed increases in nuclear RNA concentration and changes in the base ratio of the dominant RNA species. The particular cells were taken from cortical areas involved in use of the left hand; this is inferred from the report that destruction of this cortical area would disable the rat from learning the left-handed grasping skill.

A few difficulties arise in interpreting these results. First is the adequacy of the controls. Since stimulation or exercise *per se* enhances RNA in the neurons involved and the pattern of exercise may alter the type of RNA, the problem is to design the experiment so that the learning subjects and the nonlearning controls receive about the same pattern of input stimulation. The controls typically run are not adequate in this sense. Second, the changes with learning in the dominant species of RNA are confined only to what is found in the cell's nucleus, not in its cytoplasm. Third, the changes in nuclear RNA are found immediately after the animal has been performing in the learning situation, but are no longer detectable if one waits 24 hours after the learning sessions before sacrificing the animal and examining its RNA (see Hydén, 1965); that is, after 24 hours, differences in RNA between the learning subjects and the controls can no longer be detected.

Depending on one's attitude, these facts can be interpreted in terms that are either critical of, or sympathetic to the "RNA memory" hypothesis.

Other lines of evidence offered for the RNA memory hypothesis have been of two sorts: alleged biological transfer of RNA and memory from one individual to another, and behavioral effects of drugs which inhibit the action of RNA in synthesizing cellular proteins. In the transfer studies initiated by McConnell (1962) and his associates, one subject is trained until he has learned a habit. Then some of his RNA is extracted and injected into a naive subject, and thereafter the naive subject demonstrates that he too can perform the habit significantly more than can controls who received RNA from untrained donors. This transfer effect has been reported for planaria (flatworms), goldfish, rats, and mice (see Gaito, 1966, and Fjerding-stad, 1971, for reviews). The dramatic nature of such transfer effects provoked much subsequent research and a spate of conflicting outcomes. Whether such transfer was found seemed to vary with the species used, exact details of the procedure, methods for extracting RNA and other proteins from the brains of the trained donors, and the site of its injection into the recipient. For example, in rats it is clear that very little of an intraperitoneal injection of RNA actually reaches the brain of the recipient. The most reliable effects seem obtainable with brain injections in goldfish when the solution injected is made up of all the proteins extracted from the brains of trained goldfish (rather than just RNA). Experiments by Braud (1970) and Braud and Hoffman (1973) are especially noteworthy in supporting the hypothesis that specific stimulus-response habits (or memories) are transferred through such injections. Doubters had earlier conjectured that what might be transferred from donor to recipient is either (a) a generalized, increased responsiveness to any form of stimulation (such as to a CS), or (b) an enhanced general capability for learning any new habit, possibly through an enhanced sensitivity to the reinforcers used in training. The first alternative was ruled out in Braud's experiments by showing that "inhibitory habits," such as those produced by extinction or habituation, could also be transferred through chemical injections. The second alternative was excluded by showing that positive (approach) or negative (extinguished) habits were exhibited appropriately by recipients even in nonreinforced test situations. The evidence reviewed by Braud and Hoffman (1973) strongly implicates transfer of a specific stimulus-response habit, although the effect is often small and transient and its phylogenetic generality is unknown. Many researchers remain skeptical of the reliability or generality of positive transfer effects, although frequent defenses of the phenomena are mounted (see McConnell et al., 1972).

In an attempt to affect learning and memory by manipulating availability of RNA at critical synapses some experimenters have used antibiotic drugs (puromycin, cycloheximides, actinomycin) that inhibit protein synthesis. The hypothesis is that consolidation and maintenance of a memory requires continued protein synthesis (i.e., continued manufacture of neuronal proteins of a special type selected during conditioning), and that disrupting or inhibiting such synthesis should produce some loss of recent memories. For example, mice receiving puromycin injections into the brain before training will learn a maze habit as fast as controls but they appear to forget it much more readily (see Barondes & Cohen, 1966). At a 3-hour retention (relearning) test, for instance, savings were 91 percent for controls as against only 7 percent for the puromycin-injected mice. However, these investigators found virtually no effect on retention from injections of cyclohexamide, a drug similar to puromycin in inhibiting protein synthesis. Cohen, Ervin, and Barondes (1966) suggest that puromycin may be effective on memories whereas cyclohexamide is not because the former drug induces abnormal electrical activity in the hippocampal region and the latter does not. The other RNA synthesis inhibitor, actinomycin, has had inconsistent effects on learning depending on the task and the species. Gaito (1966, p. 165) states the evident conclusion from surveying a large experimental literature concerned with memory impairments produced by inhibitors of RNA synthesis: ". . . there is no crucial experiment which has unequivocally implicated RNA uniquely in memory functions." The credibility of the hypothesis is further reduced by the absence of a plausible, articulated theory which explains exactly how RNA and memory are, or could be, related. For instance, by what means and by what steps is the RNA in a neuron altered by experience? Since electrical impulses of a particular temporal pattern and frequency are the only information arriving at a neuron, how is this information translated into a biochemical code within RNA? How is this information retrieved? How does the dominant RNA species in the nucleus of a neuron selectively control the transmission properties or responsivity of the cell membrane? These are difficult questions; but the failure to answer them adequately, as well as the conflicting empirical results, has reduced the plausibility of the RNA memory hypothesis.

Efficiency of Cholinergic Synapses

Whether or not RNA changes comprise the biochemical substrate of learning, the most plausible general hypothesis is that learning involves enhanced efficiency of those synapses involved in mediating the successful, learned response. A series of experiments by Deutsch and his associates (reviewed in Deutsch & Deutsch, 1973) has tested a special form of this hypothesis. Specifically, it is proposed that learning experiences initiate processes that cause *cholinergic* synapses in the reinforced neuronal pathways (of the S-R chain) of the brain to produce more effective concentrations of acetylcholine during transmission. Learning is thus identified with the gradual growth in the efficiency of transmission, whereas forgetting is the reverse of this process. Deutsch has investigated this hypothesis by noting the influence on memory of drugs which are known to affect transmission at cholinergic synapses.

The details of the synaptic mechanisms may be explicated by the diagram in Figure 14.9, which idealizes a single synapse. An electrical impulse traveling down the presynaptic axon causes packets of acetylcholine (ACh) to be released from tiny vesicles of the presynaptic terminal. These move across the synaptic cleft to fit neatly into a population of tailor-made receptor sites on the postsynaptic terminal, each generating small shifts in electrical potential across the postsynaptic membrane. If enough transmitter is absorbed, an appreciable potential shift is integrated so that an impulse will be generated

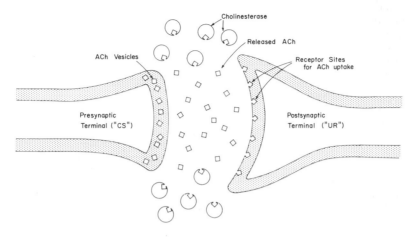

Figure 14.9.   Illustration of biochemical events involved in synaptic transmission.

down the postsynaptic neuron. The ACh is neutralized or "eaten up" by cholinesterase (see Figure 14.9) soon after it is released. We may think of the cholinesterase molecules as being continuously available in some concentration in the solution surrounding the synapses. If the ACh is produced in excess or is *not* destroyed by cholinesterase, then the UR cell will be "locked up" (hyperpolarized) and unable to fire again until the excess ACh has been cleared away.

By what means can we enhance the ability of the presynaptic terminal (call it the CS) to fire the postsynaptic cell (call it the UR)? One way would be to have the CS terminal release *more* ACh when it is stimulated, so that a previously totally ineffective CS cell now becomes completely effective in firing the UR cell by itself. A second way would be to increase the sensitivity or responsiveness of the postsynaptic membrane to a fixed amount of transmitter released at the presynaptic terminal. This could be done either by increasing the number of effective receptor sites which take up ACh or by lowering the threshold potential required in order to fire the UR neuron.

With this background, let us now consider the action of two types of drugs on this synaptic transmission. First are the anticholinesterase drugs (like physostigmine and DFP) which reduce the cholinesterase in the synapses. This has the secondary effect of increasing the amount of ACh (released by the CS terminal), which then becomes absorbed by the UR terminal. The effect of this increase in effective ACh on synaptic transmission is not a simple enhancement. If ACh levels are low, then anticholinesterase drugs will increase firing efficiency of the UR cell for a given CS input. But if the ACh levels to CS stimulation are already quite high, then addition of the anticholinesterase increment may cause hyperpolarization ("locking out") with a consequent *lowering* of net synaptic transmission.

Next consider *anticholinergic* drugs such as scopolamine and atropine; these molecules are taken up by receptor sites on the postsynaptic terminal, thus excluding ACh from these sites; yet the uptake of the anticholinergic drugs causes no electrical impulses to be generated in the UR neuron. These are called *blocking* drugs because they block or reduce the normal action of ACh. Their effect on the synapse is to reduce its firing efficiency for a given amount of ACh released by the CS terminal.

Deutsch has used anticholinesterase drugs and blocking drugs to track hypothetical changes over time (following learning) in the efficiency of transmission across a synapse contained in the successful, learned neuronal circuit. The predictions as well as the empirical data may be organized according to the diagram in Figure 14.10. This shows effective level of acetylcholine (ACh) transmitter released by a CS stimulation, when tested at varying times after initial learning. To explain the various parts of this figure, consider the normal (no-drug) curves first, the short-term component on the left and the long-term component moving to the right. The net total transmission is supposed to drop from 0 to 1 day, since the level of ACh accumulated by repeated training trials dissipates over this time much as does a short-term memory. Second, there is increasing consolidation of a "long-term" change in effective ACh at the learning synapses. In Deutsch's view, this consolidation is autonomous and continues over a few weeks. After a few weeks without further use, the ACh substrate of the habit begins to diminish, leading to "forgetting" due to disuse of the habit. The relation between effective ACh level and synaptic efficiency is complex, as we noted before: below a lower threshold, there has not been sufficient change in the synaptic efficiency to successfully fire the synapses involved throughout the circuit mediating successful performance of the learned act; above an upper threshold (denoted as the "blocking level" in Figure 14.10), there is more ACh than can be neutralized by cholinesterase, producing hyperpolarization and "locking up" of the synapse. The behavioral effect in this latter case is alleged to be a weakening of the response or an inability to perform the learned habit. Thus, optimal performance should occur when the effective ACh is in the

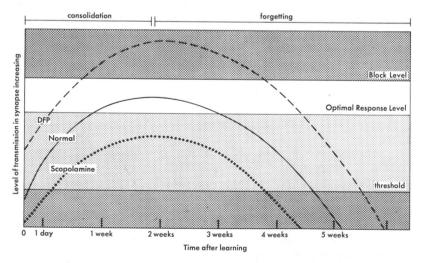

Figure 14.10.   The hypothesized changes in "memory" synapses, with time after training and with pharmacological intervention. (Adapted from Deutsch, 1971. Copyright 1971 by the American Association for the Advancement of Science.)

middle range. The effect of an anticholinesterase drug (DFP or physostigmine) is to elevate the entire curve for "effective ACh" in Figure 14.10,
whereas a cholinergic blocking agent (scopolamine) lowers the entire curve.
These dashed curves are to be interpreted as the effective amount of ACh
released by the CS in the context of the injection of the indicated drug at
varying times after initial learning. The amount of shift from normal (nondrugged) in the two cases depends, of course, on the dosage of the drug
injected.

This set of interlocking assumptions is quite complex; nevertheless, the
data appear to support most of the assumptions. A first set of facts concerns
injections of DFP versus scopolamine at varying times after learning. In the
typical experiment, a rat is trained in one session with massed trials in a
Y-maze to escape electric shock by turning into the lighted arm and avoiding
the darkened arm of the maze. Typically, training is carried to a criterion of
ten consecutive correct choices. Following a rest interval of either half an
hour, 1 day, 3 days, 1 week, 2 weeks, or 4 weeks, a number of rats are injected
either with DFP or with scopolamine, and control animals receive an injection of a neutral solution. Different groups of animals are tested at each
retention interval, and given one of the three injections. Soon after injection,
the animal is tested for retention in the Y-maze, relearning the originally
trained habit. The effective retention observed for the three classes of animals is depicted schematically in Figure 14.11. The retention scores confirm
the theory in detail. First, the controls having already learned a strong habit
initially simply show gradual forgetting over time before testing. Animals

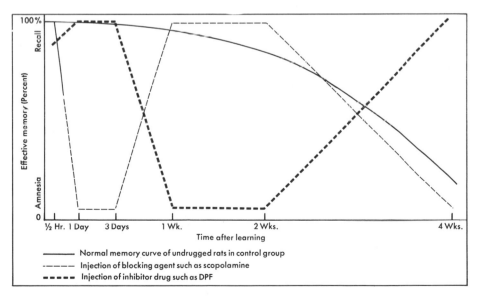

Figure 14.11.   Effect on memory. Results from rat experiments in Y-mazes show how
two types of drugs—blocking agents (anticholinergics) and inhibitors (anticholinesterases)
—can each produce amnesia or recall, depending upon the time of injection after
learning. (From Deutsch, 1968. By permission.)

receiving an anticholinesterase like DFP, which elevates the amount of effective ACh available, show good memory if injected and tested at 1 day and 3 days, poor retention at 1 week or 2 weeks, but good retention if injected and tested after a 4-week delay. Animals receiving the cholinergic blocking agent, scopolamine, show nearly the reverse of the DFP effects: memory is seriously impaired when the scopolamine injection and test occur after 1 or 3 days, is nearly perfect when the injection and test occur after 1 or 2 weeks, but is impaired again when the injection and test occur at 4 weeks after original learning. These effects are those predicted by the hypothetical curves of "synaptic transmission" in Figure 14.10. For instance, DFP produces poor performance at the 2-week interval because it elevates the amount of effective ACh at the synapse to above the blocking level, producing hyperpolarization and poor transmission.

In order to check on the consolidation hypothesis of spontaneous memory improvement over time without drugs, animals were undertrained with only a small number of reinforced trials (shock escapes) on the original habit After a fixed period, varying from 1 day to several weeks, these undertrained rats were returned to the maze to relearn the original habit. As expected, animals tested at 7 or 10 days showed better memory than animals tested after 1 or 3 days, or after several weeks (see Huppert & Deutsch, 1969). Later experiments by Huppert found a similar "reminiscence" effect on appetitively motivated habits reinforced with food rewards.

Further evidence was obtained from animals either undertrained or overtrained on the original habit; we may assume that these differences correspond to different degrees of "consolidation" effected by the end of training. Injections of DFP or a neutral solution and testing occurred 5 or 6 days later. For undertrained animals, DFP increased their memory performance above that of the undrugged controls; but for overtrained animals, DFP caused them to perform much worse than their undrugged controls. This is attributable to the blocking (hyperpolarization) of a well-consolidated habit by the excess ACh accumulated when much of the cholinesterase has been inactivated by DFP. A similar result occurs if animals are given a *fixed* number of training trials but with a difficult as opposed to an easy brightness discrimination. Animals learning the easier discrimination should have more consolidated memory after a fixed number of trials than would animals learning the difficult discrimination. Therefore, the prediction is that a DFP injection after 6 days would cause forgetting by the group with the easy, well-learned habit, but an enhancement in a performance by the group with the difficult, partially learned habit. This prediction was confirmed.

These drug effects on memory are only temporary, and memory returns to its "normal" level when the drug wears off. This is certainly true for habits that have been blocked by DFP injections. Prediction regarding the influence of the intertrial interval on performance is somewhat more subtle. If the DFP in the dosage used is not sufficient to inactivate all the cholinesterase, the ACh released at the synapse on one trial may be hydrolized ("eaten up") if enough time elapses without the synapse's firing again. On the other hand, if trials are massed, occurring quickly one after another, then the reduced cholinesterase permits the accumulation of ACh at the postsynaptic terminal, leading to hyperpolarization and the "locking up" of the synapse. The prediction, then, is that DFP injected 7 days after original training will have a devastating effect on performance if trials are massed, but relatively little effect if trials are spaced (most of the studies reviewed earlier used massed test trials). This prediction was confirmed too: DFP-injected rats showed nearly complete amnesia when tested with short (25-second) intertrial intervals, whereas those tested with longer (50-second) intervals between trials showed relatively little impairment (see Deutsch & Deutsch, 1973, for a review).

Deutsch's hypothesis of the efficiency of transmission seems to give a good account of these data, and it promises to be a viable explanation for other research. However, the details of the results are only now being subjected to systematic replication, and that very necessary step may turn up unexpected findings. One preliminary result, for example, is that these drug effects on memory are easier to demonstrate with rats than with mice (Deutsch, personal communication, 1972), and much exploratory work is required to find the "right" drug dosage for the latter so as to duplicate the effects produced with rats. One disturbing feature of the hypothesis is that it rests very heavily on an analogy between processes occurring at single synapses and the percentage of correct choices made by a rat in a maze. The gap between those two domains is filled with only hopeful promises. Moreover, all the evidence for the hypothesis rests on drug manipulations of retention. But it is well known that the drugs used by Deutsch have a multiplicity of effects (e.g., scopolamine is often used as a mild sedative or tranquilizer), and it is not known to what extent these other direct and indirect effects influence the results. Another problem is that it is known that many of the synapses in the central nervous system use a different transmitter, norepinephrine (adrenaline), which is not affected in nearly the same way as ACh is by anticholinesterase drugs and cholinergic blocking drugs. Should these cells be found to predominate in, say, the limbic system subserving behavioral reward effects, then Deutsch's biochemical conjectures would not be a plausible description of the alterations in *these* central synapses underlying reward expectancy and incentive motivation. All the tests of the hypothesis to date have used brightness discrimination by rats in a Y-maze. Autonomic indices of classical conditioning need to be studied, too, to see whether they agree with the forgetting assessed from instrumental choices. A final problem with Deutsch's hypothesis is that it is very complex and has a large number of arbitrary parameters or constants; looking at Figure 14.10, for instance, we see that only order information is critical to it. But after examining the results of an experiment, one can then select a lower threshold, an upper threshold, a "normal" consolidation curve with a peak and flatness as needed, an increment for the DFP-injection curve, and a decrement for the scopolamine-injection curve—all of these selected so as best to fit the observed results. The issue is whether the data can provide a very strong test of the model, which has so many arbitrary constants. Apparently so; but it is surely much more difficult to disprove a model with so much flexibility in its quantitative details. Despite these criticisms, however, it is fair to say that Deutsch's work represents some of the more significant and influential extensions available today for the general thesis that learning involves improved efficiency of certain neuronal pathways.

This concludes our brief tour around the fringes of the neurochemistry of learning. This is a very young field, full of many surprises, perplexities, and promises. There are major technical difficulties in doing research or theorizing at this level, and progress has to be slow. In order to understand the work at all well, one needs a fairly detailed knowledge of biochemistry, and for this reason psychologists are unlikely to rush into this research area in large numbers. It should be clear enough that at this early stage of development, no detailed biochemical account can be given for even the simplest learned act. However, we may look forward to major strides in this area in the next few decades.

TWO HEADS IN ONE SKULL: INTERHEMISPHERIC TRANSFER

One of the more striking features of the vertebrate brain is its bilateral symmetry. Brain structures appear to be duplicated nearly perfectly in homologous positions around the midline of the sagittal plane (i.e., the plane cutting fore and aft from the top of the head to the chin). This bilateral representation of function raises interesting possibilities for research on the localization of the memory trace.

To see some of these possibilities, consider the bilaterality of the visual system in mammals (see Figure 14.12). Visual information is picked up by the retina of each eye and transmitted along separate optic tracts. These tracts meet at a juncture called the optic chiasm. After the juncture, the tracts separate again, the left one coursing through various relay stations to project eventually onto the left cerebral hemisphere, the right one coursing similarly to project onto the right cerebral hemisphere. At the chiasm there is appreciable crossing-over of fibers from the two entering tracts, approximately half the fibers of each tract crossing over to the opposite tract as they emerge from the chiasm juncture. The fibers that cross are those that arise mainly from the half of the retina nearest the nose. Because of this cross-over of fibers at the chiasm, information from the nose side of the left retina is projected mainly to the right cortex, whereas information from the lateral left retina is projected to the left cortex. Moving on to the cerebral cortex, the two hemispheres are in direct communication with one another through a series of commissures, the fiber bundles that connect homologous structures on the two sides. The largest of these connecting commissures is the *corpus callosum*, a massive bundle of fibers interconnecting many parts of the two hemispheres.

Interocular Transfer and Its Surgical Abolition

Given this anatomical knowledge, let us now consider the phenomenon of interocular transfer of a visual discrimination that an animal (say, cat or monkey) has learned while using only one eye. The animal is forced by some means, such as the use of an occluding contact lens, to learn a visual discrimination using only one eye, with the other eye never seeing the discriminative stimuli. Following learning with the use of but one eye, the animal is tested with the opposite eye open and the trained eye occluded. Under normal circumstances, the animal will show practically perfect transfer of the habit from the trained to the untrained eye. A series of experiments by Sperry (1961) and his colleagues makes plausible the assumption

that in this case the visual knowledge (or engram) mediating the discriminative performance has been laid down in both visual hemispheres during
training, and that during testing with the untrained eye its afferent connections with the brain make contact with either one or both of the trained
hemispheres, thus retrieving and using the engram to guide correct responses.
Let us begin tracking down the systematic evidence for this interpretation.

Consider first the effect of cutting the optic chiasm in the sagittal plane
(as shown in Figure 14.12), in such a manner that each eye projects only to
its corresponding visual cortex on the same side. This sectioning of the

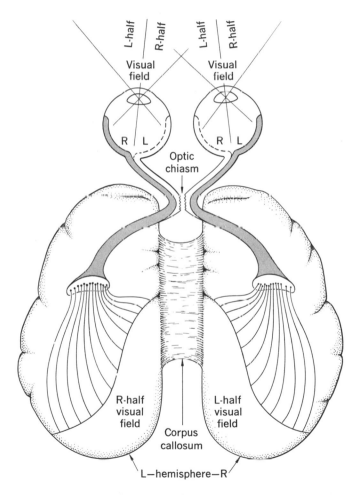

Figure 14.12.   Schematic drawing of visual system showing retina, optic chiasm, and
projections to visual receiving areas in cerebral cortex. In the figure, the optic chiasm
has been sectioned, thus eliminating that half of the visual field normally transmitted
by the cross-over fibers from the eye opposite to a cerebral hemisphere. Visual inflow
from each eye is restricted to the hemisphere on the same side as the eye. The corpus
callosum is shown intact. (From Sperry, 1961. Copyright 1961 by the American Association for the Advancement of Science.)

chiasm produces a hemianopia, which means that when only one eye is used, about half of the visual field (the peripheral edge that projects to the nose side of the retina) is blurred, though all aspects can be seen clearly by moving the eye. Surprisingly, cutting the chiasm in this manner does not affect interocular transfer, regardless of whether the cut is made before or after one-eyed training. Although training has restricted visual input to, say, the left hemisphere, later tests with the right eye (projecting to the right hemisphere) show that information along that channel in some way makes contact with the engram.

This contact of right eye with engram is made possible in either of two ways. One possibility is that the engram is laid down only in the left hemisphere that gets direct sensory input during training. The right eye and right hemisphere, however, can make use of this engram during testing by virtue of the callosal communication networks connecting the two hemispheres. The other possibility is that while the primary engram is being established in the left hemisphere during training, the connections through the callosum at the same time permit a duplicate or carbon copy of the engram to be laid down in the right hemisphere. The later test with the right eye would then use this carbon-copy engram established in the right hemisphere.

Two experiments indicate that the carbon-copy supposition is more likely the correct one. Suppose that following left-eye training of a chiasm-sectioned cat, we then ablate the visual cortex on the left side. According to the former view, this should disable performance with the right eye because the "informed source" is no longer available to feed information to the naive right hemisphere. But in fact, it is found that animals so treated still show substantial transfer when tested with the right eye. In a second experiment, the callosum is cut following left-eye training of a chiasm-sectioned animal. This should cut the communication lines, so on the basis of the first view we would expect no transfer on tests with the right eye. But such transfer is found. From these experiments, we infer that a duplicate copy of the engram is normally set up via the callosum during one-eyed training of a chiasm-sectioned animal.

With these facts in hand, the reader can readily guess what has to be done to abolish interocular transfer. The effective operation, of course, would be to cut both the chiasm *and* the callosum before the one-eyed visual training begins. And in fact, performing this dual operation before training virtually abolishes interocular transfer; the unseeing eye and hemisphere remain naive about the visual problem learned by the trained eye. This surgical preparation, called the *split brain*, apparently establishes two independent visual systems, one on either side of the brain, and the two sides no longer communicate with one another. For example, by successively occluding one and then the other eye, the animal may easily be trained to conflicting habits to the two eyes—in one case to choose vertical and avoid horizontal stripes when seen by the left eye, and in the other to do the opposite when seen by the right eye. Such conflicting training is extremely difficult for the normal intact animal but is learned with ease by the split-brain cat or monkey. It appears that all of the callosal fibers must be cut to obtain this remarkable independence of visual systems. If even a small portion of callosal fibers are spared, then transfer will still result.

Somewhat similar results have been discovered for transfer of a touch discrimination from one hand to the other, although there are several important differences from the visual system. A touch discrimination (e.g., rough versus smooth surface of objects) learned with the right hand will normally transfer to the left hand. However, if the corpus callosum is cut before the one-hand training, then intermanual transfer is abolished. This is consistent with the anatomical evidence that most somesthetic input lines cross over the midline and are projected to the contralateral hemisphere (i.e., touch on left hand projects to right cortex).

The interhemispheric transfer discussed above has involved, in each case, an active instrumental response, often one controlled by a relatively complicated discriminative stimulus. There is some evidence that conditioned emotional reactions (fear), especially those cued by a simple stimulus (e.g., a change in brightness), can be learned subcortically. Animals learn such CRs despite removal of both cerebral hemispheres. As this suggests, callosal section does not prevent the transfer of such classically conditioned "emotions" (see McCleary, 1960). It is known, too, that simple instrumental brightness discriminations can be learned subcortically—that is, without benefit of cortex. Consequently, it is not too surprising to find that such habits transfer between the eyes despite chiasm and callosal section before one-eyed training (Meikle, 1960; Meikle & Sechzer, 1960). Thus the dramatic absence of transfer from callosal section is seen only for those relatively more complex habits that depend upon a functioning cerebral cortex. This is a small restriction on the generality of the results, but nonetheless a significant one. It tells us that the emotional concomitants of learned instrumental responses are represented subcortically, whereas the refined "knowledge" guiding the selective response is likely to be stored cortically.

The split-brain preparation has illuminated many facts about bilaterality of storage in the visual and somesthetic systems, and the important role played by the corpus callosum in providing the connections that permit making a "carbon copy." Additionally, Sperry (1961) points out the many advantages of the split-brain preparation for the investigation of numerous questions regarding brain functions. For one thing, one brain-half can serve as an effective control when lesions and the like partially incapacitate the other brain-half. For another, radical surgical procedures can be carried out on one side only, when doing these bilaterally would seriously disable the animal as a useful experimental subject. Sperry describes a number of novel and ingenious uses that can be made of this split-brain preparation to investigate age-old problems of how the brain functions.

Split-Brain Humans

Gazzaniga (1967, 1970, 1972) and Gazzaniga and Sperry (1967) have investigated behavioral deficits of several human patients who have had practically all their corpus callosum removed surgically in order to alleviate severe epilepsy. In the visual problems encountered in the normal day-to-day living, these people appear to perform adequately—but this is because they are able to move both eyes repeatedly over any given visual stimulus. To detect their special deficit, Gazzaniga and Sperry would flash visual stimuli for a fraction of a second, projected to the left (or right) of the visual field. It should be noted that, for split-brain subjects, a stimulus flashed to the left visual field will be relayed primarily to the right cortex (hemisphere), whereas right-field visual stimuli go to the left cortex (see Figure 14.12); this procedure is used to "confine" the entry of a visual stimulus to the left or the right cerebral hemisphere. A series of tests carried out by Gazzaniga and Sperry show that the left cerebral hemisphere in split-brain patients is relatively specialized for active speech (e.g., reading, talking, writing), whereas the right hemisphere is more specialized for nonverbal perception and spatial reasoning. The left hemisphere can read words and act upon printed commands, either by speaking or by using the right hand to select named objects by touch. However, the right hemisphere in these split-brain patients appears unable to *say* what word or what picture has been flashed it; usually the patient says that he saw nothing or maybe "a flash." However, if he is forced to select a word from a small test array, he will unerringly "recognize" the correct item despite his earlier inability to say its name (see Gazzaniga, 1970, 1972). Further, the word projected to the right hemisphere may even guide the tactile search (with the left hand) for the correct object (e.g., a spoon) among a collection of objects hidden from the subject's view. Even after picking up in the left hand the object corresponding to the flashed word, the right hemisphere is unable to verbalize the object's name.

Such observations suggest that the right hemisphere has a crude capability for passive visual (verbal) recognition and comprehension; its comprehension, in fact, appears best with pictures, next best with concrete nouns, poorer with verbs, and poorest with abstract nouns derived from verbs (e.g., *painter*, *trooper*). The observations also suggest a curious form of split consciousness or dissociation. At one level of awareness, the person is unable to say which test object he is to pick up; however, at another level, he unerringly selects the correct object with his left hand by touch alone. Thus, two behavioral indices of "awareness" or stimulus control have been effectively dissociated by the split-brain procedure. The paradoxical nature of the dissociated performance rests on the ambiguity of the term "awareness"; we say someone is "aware of" a stimulus (event, state of affairs, etc.) either if he can verbally label it or if he behaves in a way which shows that he "takes account of" that event. For example, a person absorbed in a conversation or a radio program while driving a car is aware of the curves and stop signs along the road in the second sense but not in the first. The difference between this common case and that of the split-brain patient is that the patient seems almost incapable of "being aware" in the speech sense of a stimulus pattern projected only to his right cerebral hemisphere.

While somewhat deficient in active speech, the right cerebral hemisphere seems more specialized for handling nonverbal information, such as spatial or geometric figures or musical melodies. For instance, the left hand (controlled by the right hemisphere) is better than the opposite hand in carrying out solutions to puzzles requiring spatial reasoning, or in reconstructing the parts of a block scene or jigsaw puzzle, etc. A variety of evidence suggests that the left and right hemispheres in man become relatively specialized for perceiving, utilizing, and storing verbal and nonverbal (analogical, imaginal) information, respectively. A recent study by Galin and Ornstein (1972) showed that there was relatively greater EEG activity from the left than from the right hemisphere when a person was working on a verbal task (like composing a letter), but the relative EEG activity in the two hemispheres was reversed when the subject was doing a task involving "mental imagery." Along other lines, papers by Kimura (1963) and Milner (1968) report that patients with brain injury to the left temporal cortex show selective deficits in verbal but not nonverbal memory tasks, whereas patients with injury to the right temporal lobes have nonverbal but not verbal memory deficits. Nonverbal memory was tested by recognition or recall of pictures or melodies presented earlier; verbal memory was tested by recognition or recall of numbers, words, and word pairs. A further note on lateral specialization is that in right-handed children active speech develops primarily in the left hemisphere (the pattern is less clear for left-handed children). If the left hemisphere suffers severe injury or damage before the age of 8 to 14 (the exact "critical age" is in dispute), the child nonetheless regains adequate speech, but it is represented now in the right hemisphere. However, if the left hemisphere damage occurs *after* the critical age, then speech is grossly impaired and, depending on the extent of damage, only insignificant recovery of speech functions may ever occur (see Lenneberg, 1967). These brain injuries in their differing extents are responsible for the various speech aphasias. A common cause of small, localized aphasias is cerebral strokes, though the damage done in these cases is usually not so extensive as to prevent recovery of normal speech by other parts of the brain.

This whole line of evidence seems to tie up in a reasonably tidy package. We now know a lot about the two cerebral hemispheres, what specialized functions they perform, and how they tend to communicate with one another. This has been an area where much progress has been made, starting with the elementary split-brain preparation devised by Sperry. It illustrates how a physiological finding can ramify into a host of psychological studies (regarding lateralization of function), and can turn up results which clarify fundamental issues regarding perceptual experience and consciousness.

Chemical Dissociation of Cerebral Hemispheres

Bureš and Burešova (1960) and Bureš et al. (1964) have utilized a technique called *spreading depression* through which we may *temporarily* alter the normal functioning of one cerebral hemisphere. This procedure produces an altered animal for a few hours before recovery from the spreading depression occurs. To induce this effect, a small amount of a potassium chloride solution is applied locally through a small hole in the skull to the surface of the dura membrane surrounding the cortex. Within a short time, the normal electrical activity of the treated hemisphere of the cortex becomes depressed. The depression will persist for roughly as long as the chemical solution is applied. When it is removed, normal electrical activity in the depressed hemisphere is soon restored. In the rat, the depression spreads only over that cortical hemisphere to which the chemical has been applied. The effect is not that of a complete anesthetic since even with both hemispheres depressed the animal can still move about; however, it is likely that the animal experiences some numbness and partial paralysis of the arms and legs contralateral to each depressed hemisphere. Of most interest, however, is the finding of Bureš that, while depressed, a hemisphere gives no sign of retaining habits learned when it was intact. Access to the engram has somehow been blocked by the depression. Of further interest is the fact that an animal whose cortex is functioning normally apparently does not remember events that happened when its cortex was depressed.

The simplest demonstration of this is the absence of interhemispheric transfer of a learned habit. On day 1, a rat is trained to a simple light-shock avoidance habit with, say, its right hemisphere depressed. On day 2, it is tested with either its right or left hemisphere depressed. If the same hemisphere is functioning both days, then the animal shows retention of the habit; if a different hemisphere is functioning on the two days, then it shows little or no retention. I. S. Russell and Ochs (1961) have reported similar results for a bar-pressing habit taught to rats for food reward. The theoretical interpretation is that the hemisphere functioning during the training session stores the engram, while the depressed hemisphere remains naive. On the following test day when the trained hemisphere is depressed, the functioning (but naive) cortex has no access to the engram stored on the depressed side. As with the split-brain monkey, it is also possible, by alternately depressing first one and then the other hemisphere, to train the two hemispheres to conflicting stimulus-response habits, and there is relatively little interference between the two sides and their conflicting habits.

An intriguing question is why the educated hemisphere does not transmit its engram (via callosal connections) to the uneducated hemisphere after its depression has worn off and while the rat is just sitting around in its home cage. The lack of interhemispheric transfer shows that this does not happen. However, it turns out that something like this "cross-callosal tutoring" goes on if the rat is replaced in the learning situation and experiences a few rewarded trials while both hemispheres are functioning. I. S. Russell and Ochs (1961) reported that one trial was sufficient to effect substantial cross-callosal tutoring of the uneducated side; Travis (1964) found less dramatically that four or five trials were needed to get good transfer of an active avoidance habit. These results suggest that stimulation in the learning situation reactivated the engram in the educated cortex, setting up a persisting activity trace, and by way of the callosal links the engram was communicated to and consolidated in the alternate hemisphere.

However, Schneider (1967, 1968) has offered a more parsimonious explanation of these various results with spreading depression, namely, conditioned stimulus generalization. It is assumed that the "state" of spreading depression prevailing during original training, namely, left, right, neither, or both hemispheres depressed (L, R, N, or B), constitutes part of the total stimulus complex to which the response becomes associated. The most obvious peripheral components of the depressed cortical states are slight numbness and limb paralysis on the side opposite the depressed hemisphere. We may think of the similarity of any two brain states as determined by the overlap in zero, one, or two hemispheres being in the same normal or depressed condition; thus the normal state is equidistant from the state where either the left or the right hemisphere is depressed, but farthest from the state where both are depressed. Similarly, left-depressed is farthest from right-depressed but closer to both-depressed than to neither-depressed conditions. In this perspective, when the animal is tested under a different brain state the habit suffers "stimulus-generalization decrement" due to the changed internal, contextual stimuli. The greater the change in the amount of depression from acquisition to retention, the greater the impairment in test performance—a well-documented fact. Schneider found, for instance, that animals trained when their left hemisphere (L) was depressed retained the most when tested in state L, next most in state B, next in state N, and least in state R. This ordering differs from that expected from the alternate hypothesis that the original habit was confined to the right hemisphere and is available for retrieval whenever that hemisphere is normal. A second fact related to the stimulus-control hypothesis is that animals can be successfully trained to an operant discrimination for which the discriminative stimulus is the presence (versus absence) of unilateral spreading depression.

Schneider explains the "habit-transfer" results of I. S. Russell and Ochs (1961) and Travis (1964) in terms of new acquisition during the so-called transfer trial. In this view, the important relation is between the brain states on the transfer and retention-test trials; the more similar they are, the more "stimulus generalization" between the two hemispheres will be enhanced by the single transfer trial. To test this prediction, Schneider and Ebbeson (1967) repeated the Russell and Ochs study with an added condition for the "transfer trial." Following bar-press training with the left hemisphere L depressed, the transfer trial occurred either with neither hemisphere depressed (N) or with the right hemisphere depressed (R), and later retention for both groups was tested with the right hemisphere depressed (R). The results showed that the single transfer trial produced significant later interhemispheric transfer of bar-pressing for both groups; as expected by the stimulus-control argument, the group receiving the transfer trial in state R showed greater transfer to the later R testing situation than did the group receiving the transfer trial in state N. The alternative hypothesis that the original habit was confined to the right, nondepressed hemisphere has no resources to explain why transfer of the habit to the untrained hemisphere is best when the *trained* hemisphere is depressed, which event should inhibit the habit's retrieval and block its interhemispheric transmission.

These and other results provide rather convincing support for Schneider's stimulus-control theory of effects due to cortical spreading depression. The theory is parsimonious in using familiar concepts; it is also intuitively satisfying since it removes some of the mystical awe surrounding initial reports of dissociated states of consciousness provided by spreading depression. Although Schneider supposes that spreading depression alters the physiological locus of engram storage (from cortical to subcortical mechanisms on the depressed side), his hypothesis is readily understandable in purely psychological terms. A second effect of spreading depression, not reviewed here, is that it can be used, like electroconvulsive shock, as a means of interrupting consolidation of earlier learning experiences (see Albert, 1966). However, there is no need to follow out that line of research here.

Drug-Induced Dissociation

In the split-brain preparation, we have managed to dissociate various parts of the brain from one another. Metaphorically speaking, through the dissociation they are forced to lead separate lives, get educated in different schools, and have separate personalities. A related dissociation or split-personality effect has been reported in a fascinating series of drug studies, starting with observations on curare by Girden and Culler (1937). Later experiments by Overton (1964) showed the effect dramatically, using a different drug and testing somewhat more interesting behavior. His work will be reviewed briefly.

Overton found that the drug sodium pentobarbital produces dissociation in rats. This drug, similar to the popularly known "truth serum," is an anesthetic and, in sufficient dosage, puts the rat to sleep. Depending on the strength of the dose, the animal will begin to awake and become mobile within 15 to 45 minutes following the injection. At this time the animal can be run through various learning tasks; although somewhat lethargic, it will nevertheless learn such simple tasks as to turn left in a T-maze to escape shock delivered to its feet from a grid floor.

Overton reported that habits learned during this drugged state do not transfer to the nondrugged state, although the habit can be reactivated after putting the animal back into the drugged state. The dissociation works as well in the other direction: a habit learned in the nondrugged state is not available to the subject while it is in the drugged state. The habits are drug-state specific. By giving and withholding the drug on alternate days, Overton trained his rats to turn left to escape shock when drugged and to turn right when not drugged. The two habits were learned rapidly and independently, with little or no interfering cross-talk between the two states. Overton showed that complete dissociation is only the extreme pole of a graded continuum. He could obtain more or less dissociation depending on the amount of drug given, with larger dosages yielding a greater degree of dissociation.

With regard to this evidence, the explanation that immediately comes to mind is something like Schneider's stimulus-control hypothesis. In this perspective, the drugged and nondrugged states are differentiated in terms of differences in (a) how external stimuli are perceived, e.g., vision might be blurred in the drugged state, and (b) the presence or absence of distinctive interoceptive stimuli, as in the different "feelings" we have when we feel drowsy or alert or thirsty or whatever. If these kinds of stimuli were radically different in the drug and nondrug states, then the lack of transfer might be explained. The presence and absence of pentobarbital (and its internal effects) come to be discriminative stimuli to which different responses are attached.

Overton anticipated this "stimulus" interpretation and ran several control conditions to try to assess its plausibility. Discrimination learning of conflicting habits to presence versus absence of pentobarbital was compared to that obtained with presence versus absence of the following "stimuli": the drug Flaxedil (a muscle relaxant), thirst and hunger, an ambient light over the maze, a light and a tone and a stronger shock. Only in the last condition did any significant discrimination learning ("dissociation") occur, and then at a markedly slower rate than under pentobarbital.

To this evidence we can react in either of two ways. The first is to stick to the "stimulus" interpretation and exclaim with wonder at what a strong, effective stimulus a pentobarbital injection is. The other is to reject the stimulus interpretation as *ad hoc* and barren and to seek alternative explanations. One alternative sketchily advanced by Overton is that by modifying the thresholds and firing patterns of neurons, the drug may cause different neural circuits to become active from those that are active in the nondrug state. In this case the differences might consist in different patterns or timing of neural firing so that different circuits or routes of a complex neural network are used. Other speculative hypotheses are available but, unfortunately, further research on the issue has not brought any interpretive breakthroughs.

There have been several attempts to produce state-dependent learning in humans with different drugs. Goodwin et al. (1969) apparently produced slight alcohol-induced dissociation (drunk versus sober) for several verbal recall measures of memory but not for picture recognition. On the other hand, Osborn et al. (1967) found the more typical result with thiopental, a drug similar to the one Overton had used. The Osborn study showed that subjects could recall under the drug material learned in the undrugged state; but recall of material learned while drugged was not facilitated by reinstatement of the drugged state. The general conclusion from subsequent research is that "drug-state" dependency rests on precarious grounds, and is difficult to show unequivocally over and above the operation of several simple "main effects." A first simple effect is that material learned while the subject is drugged is poorly learned; it is often learned slowly, and appears easily forgotten regardless of the state at the time of testing. This is understandable enough if the drug simply blocks storage or consolidation of material into long-term memory. Second, there is typically some direct effect of the drug on test performance. In some cases this effect is facilitatory, as when alcohol reduces excessive fear and enables more efficient performance of an active avoidance response (e.g., eliminates unadaptive "freezing"); in others, the effect can be mildly debilitating, as when alcohol in humans reduces their concentration and performance on a recall test.

Deutsch and Roll (1973) have argued that these simple main effects suffice to account for the typical results that are claimed as evidence for state-dependent learning and/or recall under drugs. In those cases where there is a residual "true interaction" between presence versus absence of the drug during training and testing, the stimulus-control hypothesis (see above and Schneider, 1967) may be brought in to interpret the results. That is, it would be supposed that recall is best when the contextual stimuli present during learning are reinstated as completely as possible during the retention test. This is a very old and revered principle in studies of human retention (see Pan, 1926; McGeoch & Irion, 1952). It is used, for example, to isolate interpolated material and prevent it from creating interference in recall of some originally learned material. In an early illustrative study, interpolated learning occurred while the subject was in a hypnotic trance, whereas the original list was learned and later recalled in the normal waking state. The reverse sequence of states—original learning and retesting done while the subject was in a trance with interpolated learning occurring while awake—also drastically reduced retroactive interference. These and many other studies illustrate the potent influence on recall of reinstatement of the original context of learning.

In summary, then, the notions of dissociated states and state-dependent learning as unique physiological preparations have not been generally accepted or supported by later research. There are sufficient simple explanations around for the available data, so that parsimony demands that the more "exciting, dramatic" hypothesis of dissociation be held in abeyance until new evidence clearly demands something like that hypothesis.

CONCLUDING REMARKS

When we look back over our survey, it is apparent that large-scale advances in neuropsychology have been made over the last few decades. Truly, it is impossible to enter upon a thorough discussion today of such topics as consciousness, set, discrimination, pattern recognition, attention, arousal, drive, reward, and many others without giving a prominent place to the contributions of neuropsychological experimentation to what we know about these subjects. This has indeed been a grand accomplishment, for which praise should be bestowed on hundreds of research workers. However, from the point of view of this book, the most refractory problem of them all for neuropsychology has been our prime topic—learning, or information storage by the nervous system. With a few exceptions, the main lines of neuropsychological research on learning have been touched on here.

When things are viewed in neuronal terms, as we do in this chapter, the central question remains that of identifying the physiological basis for association. Assuming multiple connections between diverse populations of neurons (structures), we know that temporally proximate activity in two of them causes them to become associated in some primitive or basic manner, so that one is now able to excite the other, whereas formerly it did not do so. Several suggestions as to how this might occur have been mentioned. The most likely explanation still is some form of the hypothesis that the "efficiency" of particular neuronal circuits is somehow increased; Deutsch's pharmacological studies suggest further details of this increased efficiency.

Lest the reader think that our discussion of the role of neurons is too far removed from the behavior in which he or she may be primarily interested, it is apposite to note that appropriate networks of "model neurons" can be easily designed that display rather amazing discrimination and performance capabilities. This general line of theorizing, modeling performance capabilities by designing nerve networks, began with an early paper by Pitts and McCulloch (1947) and has been carried further since then. A book by Culbertson (1962) includes a review of some of the results. Roughly speaking, given any transfer function taking various input information (stimulation) into output information (response), a static nerve network can be designed to yield that transfer function. The hypothetical neurons in such nets all function by the same simple principles, which are derived more or less from neurophysiological research. Moreover, if certain premises are granted relating to how the efficiency of neural pathways is changed by feedback from the environment (through reward and punishment), then the nerve-net models will show adaptive learning in various situations. Rosenblatt (1958, 1962) shows how orderly discriminative performance can be produced (through reinforcement) by a large neuron network that begins with completely random interconnections. He also gives us the rationale for this general approach to the construction of models of behavior.

By and large, the people who construct nerve-net automata do not claim that their design represents exactly the way that the nervous system achieves what it does in a characteristic performance. They remain content rather with showing that starting with simple neuron elements, networks not obviously contradicted by neurophysiological evidence can be designed to show some of the capabilities of organisms. As such, the automata are "sufficiency proofs," meaning that they prove that interesting behavior *can* be produced out of constellations of simple on-off neural elements. Though the products of such labors are appreciated in some scientific quarters, the fact is that they are not esteemed in others. From the viewpoint of those working on computer simulation of human intelligence (Chapter 13), the nerve-net automata have only primitive intelligence, and their accomplishments are considered to be rather dull. Minsky and Papert (1969) have investigated in mathematical detail the limitations of such pattern-classifying machines. Then from another side, from the viewpoint of many neurophysiologists, the nerve-net theories are held to ignore too much of what is known about the neuron and the structure of the nervous system. Be that as it may, it seems obvious that if neurophysiology is to have an explicit theory capable of making contact with behavioral data, the form of it will be little different from the kinds of schemes presently being designed by those working on nerve-net automata.

Research on the neurophysiology of learning continues at an accelerating pace. Judging from the recent past, its future is likely to be filled with exciting discoveries, the devising of novel techniques, and profound alterations in our conceptions of the nervous system and its relation to behavior. In fact, in few other areas of psychology has there recently been such a high production rate of significant empirical discoveries as in physiological psychology. The pearls are easier to find in a new field than in the older fields that have been intensively cultivated for so many years.

SUPPLEMENTARY READINGS

There are a number of excellent textbooks in physiological psychology, each of which contains a quite detailed review of results on learning. Some of these are:

DEUTSCH, J. A., & DEUTSCH, D. (1973) *Physiological psychology* (2nd ed.).

GROSSMAN, S. P. (1967) *A textbook of physiological psychology*.

MORGAN, C. T. (1965) *Physiological psychology* (3rd ed.).

THOMPSON, R. F. (1967) *Foundations of physiological psychology*.

WOOLDRIDGE, D. E. (1963) *The machinery of the brain*.

Theoretically oriented treatises on the brain and behavior are:

HEBB, D. O. (1949) *The organization of behavior*.

JOHN, E. R. (1967) *Mechanisms of memory*.

McGAUGH, J. L., & HERZ, M. J. (1972) *Memory consolidation*.

PRIBRAM, K. (1971) *Languages of the brain*.

Recent Developments

Research on the learning process continues at an accelerating pace, and has expanded in a number of directions. Several thousand psychologists and scientists in related fields are doing research that can be roughly classified as investigations of learning. It is next to impossible to characterize the entire field, to cover the full range of phenomena under investigation, and to say where the whole enterprise is leading us. Indeed, this chapter merely touches upon a selected sample of recent developments. In many respects, research on learning has become more applied, with the development of related behavioral technologies as one consequence. For example, a number of psychologists are engaged in applying learning principles to the acquisition of language, to educational programs for teaching children various intellectual skills, to the modification of undesirable attitudes and behaviors of psychoneurotic patients and of problem children in classroom settings, to the efficient training of complex skills for military or industrial personnel, and to school-room behavioral management and the training of retarded children in simple skills. Chapter 16 discusses some of the work on programmed instruction, an important area of behavioral technology. Such behavioral engineering has immediate practical goals, and while not irrelevant to theory, it can be carried on without becoming distracted by unresolved theoretical issues. The value of learning research lies in its development of techniques of behavioral control, in the general frame of reference it provides and the concepts to be used in analysis, and, finally, in the factual knowledge obtained as the product of particular investigations.

The main trend in nonapplied ("pure") research in learning has been away from the large, comprehensive theories of the 1930s and 1940s toward the deeper experimental and theoretical analyses of the salient phenomena of learning. There has been intensive investigation of particular experimental tasks and paradigms which tap some kind of learning ability, with the consequence that the empirical mapping of many phenomena is now quite thorough. Many theoretical developments have stemmed from correcting earlier theoretical misconstructions, and from an increase in the definiteness, clarity, and precision of theoretical explanation.

The lines of demarcation between the historical positions have softened, faded, and become all but indistinguishable. The debates have subsided. Increasingly experimentalists talk the same language and listen to one another. There is an increasing unity of language and understanding among experimentalists working on learning. It is not uncommon for an experimentalist to operate within many of what were formerly considered to be somewhat differing theoretical orientations, ranging from Hullian theory to computer simulation. Each empirical subarea has its special phenomena to captivate interest, and one can soon learn the necessary dictionary of concept equivalences to permit moving among subareas.

In this chapter, we shall review a few of the prominent lines of recent research and theorizing in learning. The topics selected are among those in which there have been important developments since the previous edition of this text (E. R. Hilgard & Bower, 1966). In that edition, two chapters were devoted to "recent developments," and they can be read profitably to obtain a background for most of the material in the present chapter. The major conceptual division within research on learning is still the cleavage described by the contrasting terms "animal conditioning" and "human memory." Investigators working in the former area study animals in simple experimental arrangements and responses, and tend to describe their results in terms of the stimulus-response-reinforcement concepts of modern behaviorism. Workers in the "human memory" idiom tend to study adults and how they utilize their vast intellectual capabilities in learning and remembering verbal materials; the language of these workers is increasingly that of information-processing concepts and cognitive psychology. To be sure, there are minority voices against this cleavage—investigators in the two subareas who use predominantly the concepts derived from the other area (the work on the interference theory of forgetting is an example)—but these do not appear to be the prevailing voices. There are increasing attempts, nevertheless, to build bridges between theories in these two areas, and indeed some of the more fascinating work of the present and future promises to lie in this direction.

The organization of this chapter is along the lines of this cleavage for the simple reason that the contextual meaning of terms is preserved as long as discussion remains within one domain. The first half of the chapter deals with "animal conditioning" and reviews new work on operant conditioning of autonomic responses, on the role of biofeedback in learning, on changing conceptions of reinforcement and nonreinforcement, and on stimulus selectivity in learning. The last half of the chapter deals with human memory and reviews work on short-term memory, on so-called episodic memory, on organizational and imaginal factors in memory, on memory for linguistic materials, and on models for semantic memory. The section ends with a synopsis of social learning theory and its relation to the developing field of cognitive psychology. The treatment of these major topics must necessarily be brief and selective, but it should provide the student with some perspective on modern developments in learning theory.

ELEMENTARY CONDITIONING PROCESSES

Voluntary Control of Involuntary Responses

One of the oldest distinctions in philosophical psychology is that between voluntary and involuntary responses: voluntary responses are those that we consciously "will" and control; involuntary ones are those that occur unconsciously, automatically, without our willing. Innate reflexes—the breathing of air, the pumping of the heart, the blinking of the eye to a punch, the wetting of dry food in the mouth by saliva, the digestive processes set in motion by food in the intestines—these and a host of others are involuntary, "unwilled." It is just as well that such routine processes are carried on automatically outside of conscious awareness. Their automaticity is in fact an enormous convenience, since our attention can then be disengaged from seeing that all these matters are taken care of. Volitional behavior, on the other hand, is that which is conscious, is willed and purposive, is an expression of one's intentions.

Understandably, behavioral psychologists have been opposed to assigning conscious volitions and intentions to their animal subjects; and with animal subjects, the notion of volitional control could not be identified with the subject's verbal descriptions of his acts and their motives. Instead, the voluntary-involuntary distinction has become translated in behavioral psychology into a distinction between two distinct "response systems," each presumed to be learned and governed according to two different principles of learning. This is the distinction, explicated clearly by Skinner (see Chapter 7), between operant and respondent behavior, and their corresponding laws of conditioning. Operant responses involve the large skeletal muscles, innervated by the central nervous system, which are used to operate instrumentally upon the environment. Respondents are typically "innate reflexes" that involve smooth muscles of the glands or viscera, that are innervated by the autonomic nervous system, and are often involved in maintaining the homeostasis or equilibrium of the internal vital processes. Skinner and others proposed that such respondents could be learned *only* by the law of classical (Pavlovian) conditioning, by pairing the neutral stimulus to be conditioned with an adequate stimulus for eliciting the reflex; operant responses, on the other hand, could be learned *only* by the law of operant (reward) conditioning, by making some reinforcement contingent upon occurrence of the response to be conditioned. Although voices were often raised against this "two-factor" theory, the fact is that it maintained a position of prominence within learning theory for 30 years or so.

Within two-factor theory, there was a way to explain how a person could acquire "voluntary" control over a bit of respondent behavior, namely, by use of an intermediate operant response which either innately or through Pavlovian conditioning had come to control the respondent. For example, a person can learn to control his GSR (sweating of palms) either by tensing the muscles of his legs and torso on cue, or by saying to himself a word (e.g., *shock*) that he has earlier paired with an electric shock, thus evoking a galvanic skin reflex (GSR). Thus, were it to the person's advantage (say, to fake a "lie detector" test), he might learn *operantly* to control his GSR by saying "Shock" to himself or by moving some striated muscle group that causes GSR increases.

Everyone saw that in order to contradict the two-factor hypothesis, it would be necessary to show that respondents, such as heart-rate changes, visceral movements, or glandular secretions, could be learned according to the law of operant conditioning. Moreover, the demonstration had to be done in such a manner that an explanation in terms of an "operant mediator" was not plausible. It was this latter requirement that stymied the obvious projects. How to rule out intermediate instrumental behavior? The solution to this problem required the confluence of several significant technologies which have become available only over the last 15 years or so.

First, the drug curare (or *d*-tubocurarine) can be used to knock out the skeletal musculature. Curare acts to block the action of acetylcholine at the neuromuscular junctures of the striated musculature. In adequate doses, the entire musculature loses tonus, becomes flaccid and immobile; drugged animals cannot even breathe, so must be kept alive by artificial respiration. Curare was used on "poison" arrows of primitive hunters because it killed by paralyzing the respiratory apparatus. A human who is given curare and respirated is fully conscious and aware of what is happening about him; he can learn, think out, and remember solutions to language puzzles given to him (see Leuba et al., 1968). He cannot talk or move while under the drug, of course, but he can report these events several hours later when the drug wears off.

So a prospective preparation for our critical experiment would be a curarized animal. But a second problem arises: since such animals are totally immobile, how are they ever to be rewarded when their viscera perform the right trick? The technological solution was to use electrical stimulation to "pleasure centers" of the brain (ESB) by means of implanted electrodes (see Chapter 14 on ESB reinforcement). Thus the appropriate preparation would be an animal (typically, a rat) having permanently implanted electrodes of proven rewarding quality, immobilized with curare, kept alive by artificial respiration, and with one or more electronic devices attached for recording some respondent activity such as cardiac, vasomotor, or visceral responses. This preparation is shown in Figure 15.1 from DiCara (1970). Such are the artificial "ideal preparations" occasionally needed to answer scientific questions.

By the late 1960s, this preparation had begun to be studied by Neal Miller and his associates at Rockefeller University (see N. E. Miller, 1969). They tried to condition operantly various visceral responses. To illustrate the procedure, consider the way one would try to condition an increase in the heart rate of an animal. The heart rate of a rat is around 400 beats per minute, but its moment-by-moment rate fluctuates considerably; the momentary rate can be estimated by setting a digital counter to count the number of beats in successive 5-second intervals. Suppose we wished to oper-

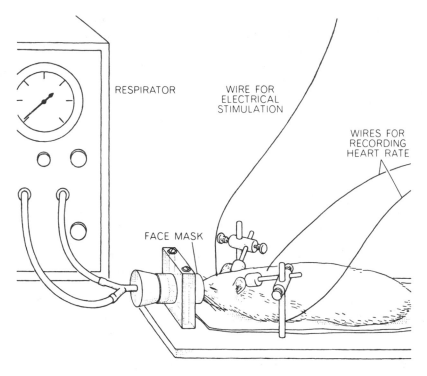

Figure 15.1. Illustration of a curarized rat fitted with a face mask connected to a respirator and with an electrode in a reward center of its brain. (From Learning in the autonomic nervous system by L. V. DiCara. Copyright © 1970 by Scientific American, Inc. All rights reserved.)

antly condition our animal to increase its heart rate when a tone sounds, but to maintain a normal rate when the tone is off. The method of shaping and response differentiation (see Chapter 7) can be used. Following recording of baseline heart rate to the tone, conditioning might begin by turning on the tone for 2 minutes every 4 minutes and delivering a rewarding ESB at the end of each 5-second observation interval during which the momentary heart rate is above a criterion rate. The criterion for reinforcement is initially low (say, 1 percent higher than the base rate); but over trials the criterion for reward is advanced to more extreme settings as the animal learns to increase its heart rate during the tone in order to get the ESB reward.

That is the general procedure. Perhaps the major result to report is that the procedure succeeds; that is, animals can learn reliably to change cardiovascular and visceral responses that are instrumental in getting rewards. The research being done on this presently is accomplishing several further ends. First, much research has aimed to establish the generality of the result with a variety of response systems. The list of visceral responses that have been successfully conditioned operantly in the curare preparation includes heart-rate increases or decreases, changes in blood pressure, control of blood vessel diameter (e.g., the vessels in the tail or ear of a rat), contractions of the large intestine, salivary secretion, and rate of formation of urine by the kidneys. This list is not exhaustive and doubtless will increase with further research. Second, there has been a concern to show that such conditioned operants follow pretty much the same laws as does any other learned response—that such responses show acquisition, extinction, retention, transfer, stimulus generalization, and discrimination. Third, much of the research has been concerned with establishing that these procedures produce "true" associative learning and not just sensitized responding, and that the learning changes are highly specific to the particular response reinforced and not just a *general* arousal or relaxation pattern of the entire autonomic system. The way the first issue was answered, for example, was by modifying the rate of the response in opposite directions to two different discriminative stimuli. Thus a rat might be conditioned to *increase* the rate and intensity of its intestinal contractions above normal when a tone sounds, but to *decrease* them when a light comes on. The opposing responses to differential stimuli would seem to rule out explanations of results based on general sensitization of one class of responses due to the rewarding ESB or other, nonspecific artifacts. The second issue, the specificity of the learning changes, has been assessed by monitoring two different visceral response systems such as heart rate and intestinal motility. ESB reward would be made contingent on changes in one of these responses but not contingent on the other response; yet this other response system would be observed for correlated changes. An example of such results is shown in Figure 15.2 from an experiment by N. E. Miller and Banuazizi (1968). The graph shows heart rate and intestinal contractions plotted over approximately 500 training trials for two groups of animals, half rewarded (during the S^D or time-in stimulus) for speeding up their heart rate and half rewarded for slowing it down. During training, appropriate changes in heart rate occur for these two groups. Also shown in Figure 15.2 are concurrent measurements of intestinal contractions during the S^D for the two groups. The important point is that these contraction measures do *not* change progressively or differentially as the heart rate changes are learned. Thus the response changes are quite specific to that system on which reward is contingent, and do not reflect a generalized "autonomic" arousal. The *tour de force* on this specificity issue was scored by DiCara and Miller (1968), who trained rats to produce on cue relatively greater vasoconstriction ("blanching") of the skin on their left ear than on their right ear (or vice versa). Such results show much greater specificity of the actions of the sympathetic nervous system than we would have believed possible before now.

Given the malleability of autonomic responses, one may suppose that they are playing a significant adaptive function in helping to maintain homeostasis, a stable internal environment. This suggests experiments (see DiCara, 1970) in which the correction of a deviation from homeostasis by an internal glandular response is shown to serve as a reward to reinforce learning. Thus, if internal responses are learnable and if removal of a deviation from homeostasis is rewarding, then internal responses whose effect is to remove deviations from homeostasis could be learned, at least to within the limits tolerated by the innate homeostatic mechanisms.

A further implication of this research on autonomic conditioning is that it suggests how physical symptoms of psychosomatic illnesses could be learned

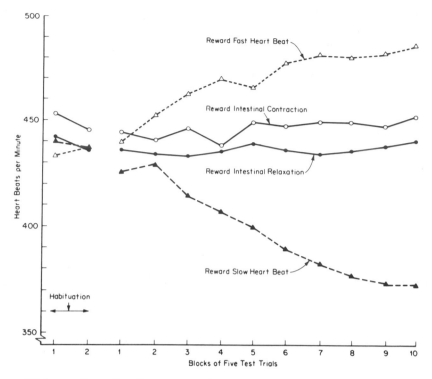

Figure 15.2.   Rewarding increases or decreases, respectively, in heart rate produces changes in the appropriate direction, but rewarding a different response, intestinal contractions, produces no changes in heart rate. (From N. E. Miller & A. Banuazizi, Instrumental learning by curarized rats of a specific visceral response, intestinal or cardiac, *Journal of Comparative and Physiological Psychology*, 1968, *65*, pp. 1–7. Copyright 1968 by the American Psychological Association. Reprinted by permission.)

because of their instrumental value. Psychiatrists call these benefits the "secondary gains" of the psychosomatic symptom. Thus, a child who is allowed to stay home from school because of a stomach upset and who is reinforced by avoiding an unpleasant situation at school may learn to have "genuine" stomach upsets whenever he wishes to avoid other unpleasant or anxious situations. The techniques of visceral learning combined with bio-feedback (to be discussed below) hold out the prospects for helping to cure patients suffering from such disorders as cardiac arrhythmia (extreme irregularity of heart beat), high blood pressure, tension headaches, and epileptic seizures.[1]

---

[1] Preliminary efforts along these clinical lines with human patients have met with only limited success in lowering blood pressure, somewhat more success in steadying irregular heartbeat, and best success with training relaxation of forehead and neck muscles to reduce the incidence of tension headaches. A disturbing note out of Miller's lab (N. E. Miller, 1972) is that in more recent experiments with animals, the size of the operant conditioning effect has diminished, especially with heart rate changes. The reasons for this are presently under investigation.

Neuronal Conditioning

Concomitant with these demonstrations of the operant conditioning of visceral and cardiovascular responses, there also began to appear reports of the operant conditioning of "neuronal responses" in the brain, measured either by macroelectrodes recording from populations of brain cells or by microelectrodes recording the firing of just a few neurons. Olds (1965, 1969) was one of the first workers to report altering the spontaneous firing rate of single cells in the motor cortex of rats by delivering an ESB reward whenever the firing rate went above a preset criterion; in other series, a reduction of the spontaneous firing rate of the cell would be rewarded, effecting the appropriate changes. Similar procedures have now been used with several measures of neuronal responsivity, including theta waves recorded from the hippocampus (Black, 1972), EEG spindles in the sensorimotor cortex (Wyrwicka & Sternman, 1968), the firing rate of single units in the motor cortex dissociated from a muscle group which they usually control (Fetz & Finocchio, 1971), and the amplitude of certain components of the evoked cortical response to a flash of light (Fox & Rudell, 1970).

The significance of such results is still in question—again, because of something like the old "mediation" argument. The neuron from which the recording is taken may not be the one that learns, but rather either (a) one involved in carrying out efferent commands to the motor system (i.e., most successful neuronal conditioning has been done with units in the *motor* cortex), or (b) one that receives sensory feedback from a motor operant that is controlled by the usual reinforcement contingencies. Thus, a monkey may alter a component of its evoked response to a flash by defocusing its eyes, staring at a dark corner, or squinting; therefore, in reinforcing the monkey "for altering its visual evoked response," the experimenter may in actuality only be reinforcing "squinting" in an exceedingly indirect manner. Again, use of curare preparations can help rule out some of these mediation arguments; but then the thesis just moves inward and asserts that "efferent commands" are being recorded, reinforced, and learned.

At some point in such discussions, someone is almost sure to notice that such procedures are rather like reinforcing the curarized animal for thinking certain thoughts, and it is an accepted commonplace that certain thoughts (e.g., daydreams or fantasies) can be increased in their frequency because of their pleasant consequences. The most cogent and careful discussion of these issues of methodology, interpretation, and significance of the neuronal conditioning work is given by Black (1972). He concludes that such work is important for illuminating brain processes and brain-behavior covariations, and that the mediation question is not nearly so critical as a generation of psychologists had been led to believe.

Biofeedback

It is perhaps not a coincidence that the "involuntary" responses are the ones that we ordinarily do not see or feel, whereas the "voluntary" responses of large skeletal muscles are out in the open for our continuous inspection. It seems likely that it is the absence of continuous information about internal responses that causes them to be beyond our volitional control. After all, we ordinarily learn responses and learn to guide our behavior by observing what we do, seeing its consequences, and making appropriate adjustments. Knowledge of the response and its consequences is carried in what are called "feedback stimuli," and they are exceptionally important in learning skilled movements. As one illustration, our normal speech can be seriously disrupted if an electronically controlled delay of about half a second is interposed by means of earphones between our speaking a word and hearing ourselves speak it. We begin to stammer, stutter, and slur our speech in a totally disorganized manner.

It would appear that many internal behaviors could be made more discriminable, and hence learnable or controllable, if their activity were to be fed back to the conscious person through amplifiers. The initial work along these lines was done by Kamiya (1962, 1969), who sounded a tone as a feedback stimulus to a human subject whenever his scalp EEG showed an amount of alpha-wave activity above a criterion baseline. Alpha is a brain wave of about 8–10 cycles per second, which is correlated roughly with the subjective state of "detachment, unconcern, or inner contemplation." Nonalpha, or the "blocking of alpha," is caused by the person's either going into a light sleep (brain waves get even slower) or becoming very alert and attentive to some outside stimulus (brain waves become faster, more desynchronized). Kamiya found that after several minutes to several hours of correlation of a feedback stimulus with presence versus absence of alpha activity, most subjects learn to discriminate presence versus absence of their own alpha without the external tone. Furthermore, if subjects were asked to produce alpha (or to produce nonalpha) or were given rewards for doing so, they could produce alpha (or nonalpha) at a rate in excess of the normal baseline. There is also evidence that by use of similar feedback techniques subjects can learn to discriminate and to control another type of EEG pattern called theta waves.

Studies of the EEG and its control have also been done with experienced practitioners of meditation according to the Zen or Yoga discipline (see Kasamatsu & Hirai, 1966; Anand et al., 1961). During both forms of meditation, the practitioners show almost continuous alpha waves (normally associated with a state of relaxed alertness) if they are not disturbed. If an external sensory signal is presented, the Zen monks show nearly unvarying blocking of alpha ("arousal") to the signal; the remarkable report is that this blocking or cortical arousal response does not habituate with repeated trials for the Zen monks as it does for ordinary subjects. The Yogins, on the other hand, are almost totally unresponsive electrically to sensory stimulation, continuing in the alpha state. There are known to be a variety of other physiological changes during "transcendental meditation," the changes reflecting a general slowing down of metabolic processes (see Ornstein, 1972). The suggested inference from the EEG observations is that *one* of the things Zen monks and Yogins learn to do in their years of meditation practice is to maintain the alpha state. The second inference is that one may be able to hasten training in meditation (where the novice is trying to achieve an ill-defined "meditative state") by providing EEG feedback to "shape" more frequent attainment and improved maintenance of the "alpha-wave state."

These EEG feedback techniques have been hailed as a powerful new tool for helping a person to expand his range of consciousness, to learn more about various "altered states of consciousness" and how to produce them. These are currently fashionable topics among college students. For example, this enthusiasm is seen in the following quote from E. E. Green et al.:

> The importance to our culture of this now developing technology for enhancing voluntary control of internal states can hardly be overstated. . . . Without stretching the imagination, the long-range implications and the effects for society of a population of self-regulating individuals could be of incalculable significance. (1970, pp. 1–2)

This goal of obtaining greater self-control over one's internal processes ("brain states") appears laudable, but some caution is surely needed in assessing and placing in perspective the findings on alpha control.

First, the evidence to date suggests that "alpha control" may be little more than inexplicit control of eye-movements or eye-focusing. The most alpha that can be produced occurs when you are relaxed with your eyes closed in a dark room. If you open your eyes in dim light, alpha activity is blocked; the reduction in alpha activity is greater with greater visual scanning of the room or with greater emotional tension. Most of the earlier successful demonstrations of "alpha control" are deficient in several respects: first, they typically did not control or measure eye movements (or even whether the subject's eyes were opened or closed); second, there usually was no control for the upward drift in the baseline level of alpha activity as the subject adapts over time to the initial arousal (and low alpha) caused by being hooked up to the experimental apparatus; third, the early experiments mainly demonstrated a difference in amount of alpha activity during the instructed "alpha-on" periods versus the "alpha-off" periods of the experimental session. But a simple difference can be produced not by enhancing alpha to above the normal baseline during "alpha-on" periods but by reducing alpha to below the baseline (by visual scanning) during the "alpha-off" periods. It might be further objected that people already know a variety of "mental tricks" which will either enhance or reduce alpha activity, at least to a limited extent. To produce nonalpha, just scan your visual environment. To increase alpha, just relax, defocus your eyes and stare fixedly into the distance; then imagine that you are staring at a blank wall or that your eyes are covered with halves of ping-pong balls which produce diffuse nonpatterned light. Thus, by instructions alone, most people are able to produce large differences in amount of alpha activity. Without such instructions, one can suppose that telling the person to learn to "keep the tone on" (which means to produce nonalpha, say) is similar to giving him an ill-defined trial-and-error problem to be solved. He will cast about until he strikes upon some "mental act" he does which turns on the tone and keeps it on. Has he learned to "enter a different state of consciousness"? Has he learned to control his "brain state"? Or has he simply learned that what turns the tone on is moving his eyes and looking about the lab room?

Evidence for this less flattering conclusion comes from a well-controlled experiment by Paskewitz and Orne (1973), who tried to train many subjects over many days to enhance their amount of alpha activity. They found, first, that if subjects were tested in a dark room and told to keep their eyes open, then no alpha enhancement could be produced above the baseline drift. If tested in a lighted room, they could "learn" to show a difference in alpha between "on" versus "off" periods. However, the most alpha activity obtained this way was barely half as much as was recorded before training when the subjects were told merely to relax and close their eyes. That is, training of alpha never came close to producing the alpha occurring simply with eyes closed. Secondly, the alpha difference achieved by subjects trained in the light completely disappeared when these subjects were tested in the dark (with eyes open in both conditions). It thus appears that the opportunity for scanning over a visual field is a necessary prerequisite for producing an alpha difference through such training. And clearly, it is a mistake to label this practice as training for deeper awareness of one's brain states or different levels of consciousness. The latter, flamboyant talk just leads to the muddled linguistic absurdity that every activity is correlated with a unique brain state or altered state of consciousness. But surely this is just a peculiar restatement of the standard brain-behavior hypothesis and of little interest.

Despite the advertising claims of uniform success, biofeedback training methods meet with mixed success (see Paskewitz & Orne, 1973; Mulholland, 1972) and many individuals fail to learn to control alpha or fail to experience the benefits for which it is advertised. Similarly, with visceral conditioning, as noted in footnote 1, attempts to teach hypertensive patients to lower their blood pressure have typically met with only limited or temporary success. Such findings suggest rather sporadic and inconstant results. A sensible position is that the techniques might be made uniformly successful when applied properly and for long enough periods. As positive evidence for uniformity, we can cite two visceral responses of people, namely, urination and defecation, which are uniformly and successfully controlled by everyone through extensive cultural training. Those successes make plausible the hypothesis that other internal responses can be similarly controlled given sufficiently pervasive and persistent training conditions. Clearly, much research remains to be done to explore the limits within which the responsiveness of internal processes can be altered by learning, and what are the effective parameters for doing so.

Despite these critical remarks, it should be noted that this research has been significant in altering our conceptions of self-control, awareness, and the nature of "private events." Perhaps internal reactions, including our emotions and other affective moods, are normally difficult for us to control because they are usually not observed and discriminated as such; they are vague and undifferentiated stimulus patterns. If one were to make such internal reactions discriminable through feedback—to "expand one's inner awareness"—this should increase the possibility of self-labeling and self-control of these emotions. Although such procedures would not appreciably alter the relationship between stimulation and physiological effect, they could alter the relation between that physiological effect and the emotion associated with it. In the extreme, one can envision a "stoical" training regime whereby one is able to decide cognitively how he will react to what ordinarily would be an emotionally upsetting event.

An intriguing hypothesis is that we can control only those behaviors which we can discriminate (technically, we can discriminate a behavior if its occurrence can serve as an S^D for later behaviors such as labeling). In other words, if you cannot discriminate when you are or are not doing some "act," then you cannot learn to control that act. This thesis could be advanced even for skeletal responses. The intuition behind the hypothesis can be appreciated if you try to teach a small child to wink with one eye, or try to teach yourself to wiggle your left ear (a trick Neal Miller learned in order to prove the point): the best procedure is to stand in front of a mirror and watch yourself carefully, shaping by self-reward any small movement in the correct direction.

To return to the larger issue, we may finally ask whether the Zen meditator or the ear wiggler or a good golfer or painter is expanding his awareness and reaching a higher state of consciousness. Perhaps it is better to talk about most such matters of "awareness" in terms of skills—perceptual skills, motor skills, self-descriptive skills, and the like—that are taught to the person by subcommunities which apply highly discriminated contingencies. But these are matters for more general discussion than is feasible in this textbook.

CONCEPTIONS OF REINFORCEMENT AND NONREINFORCEMENT

The Relativity of Reinforcement

The law of reinforcement, or law of effect, is one of the more important principles in all learning theory. It is a rule for shaping behavior by the use of rewards (reinforcers). We train a rat to press a lever by giving it a bit of food when it does so. Because of the central significance of the principle, there have been attempts to state it in a general yet precise way. One commonly accepted formulation is this: a learnable response followed by a reinforcing event (stimulus, state of affairs) will receive an increment in its strength or probability of occurrence. Critics of the law of effect have argued that this formulation is not an empirical law but rather a definition of a reinforcing event. Let us see. If a reinforcer is defined as something that strengthens a response, then by substitution in the statement of the law, it becomes: a learnable response followed by something that strengthens a response will receive an increment in its strength! But this is just vacuous circularity. Surely there must be more to the principle than the trivial tautology that "a rose is a rose."

The question of whether or not the law has any empirical content was considered by Meehl (1950) in a key paper entitled "On the circularity of the law of effect." Meehl concluded that the law does have empirical content, and that its content concerns the generality of a reinforcer. If I find that scratching a dog behind its ears will reinforce the behavior of lifting a paw to shake hands, then the law of effect makes the prediction that ear scratching can also be used to reinforce other sorts of canine responses—hand licking, tail wagging, ball rolling, stick retrieving, and so forth. The law of effect is used in a "definitional" mode in the initial discovery of ear scratching as a reinforcer; but it is used in an empirical, predictive manner when testing ear scratching as a reinforcer for later responses. Meehl's reformulation of the law of effect is: all reinforcers are transituational. An equivalent, and more understandable, version is: a reinforcer can be used to increase the probability of *any* learnable response.

Meehl's analysis resolved the circulatory charge, and psychologists went on their way satisfied with this formulation of the general law of effect. One implication of Meehl's or Thorndike's statement of the law of effect (see Chapter 2) is what may be called an "absolutist" classification of events as reinforcing or not reinforcing. That is, given a particular state of the subject (his conditions of deprivation, past training, etc.), we can roughly divide stimulus events into two lists: those that act upon him as reinforcers and those that do not. A list of reinforcers commonly contains biological items like food, water, and sexual contact for appropriately deprived individuals, together with learned (secondary) reinforcers like money, praise, social approval, attention, dominance, the spoken exclamation "good," etc., and a variety of manipulation-curiosity-novelty satisfying types of activities. Given such a partial listing, some psychologists were challenged to try to guess what all these reinforcing things have in common—what is the common essential ingredient that makes them all reinforcers? A plausible idea, for example, is Hull's conjecture that all primary reinforcers serve to reduce drives or biological needs, and that secondary reinforcers such as praise derive their value from having been associated with many instances of drive reduction, perhaps during the child's early rearing. This conjecture, as well as others like it, has been extensively researched and argued pro and con. G. A. Kimble (1961) gives a useful summary of this evidence for the interested student.

In this context, Premack (1959, 1965) offered a useful reappraisal of reinforcement and the law of effect which increases its generality. As with many useful insights, Premack's argument stems from noting an implicit assumption contained in previous formulations of the law of effect. This implicit assumption is that the response or activities which are to be reinforced are neutral or of no intrinsic value to the subject. But suppose that we take an opposite viewpoint, that the organism engages in a variety of activities (including eating, manipulating, playing, etc., *ad infinitum*) that vary in their intrinsic value for it. Imagine further that by some means we have ordered these activities in a ranking from most to least preferred, in the order $A, B, C, D, \ldots$.

Given this ranking of activities (considered in this general sense), what is now an appropriate way to formulate the law of effect? Premack argues that the only sensible formulation ties the reinforcement relation to this preference ordering: a given activity can be used to reinforce those of lesser value but not those of higher value. In our $A > B > C > D$ ranking, we can use B to reinforce C or D, but B will not reinforce A. But acceptance of this point commits us to a "relativity" view of reinforcement. A given event or activity can be used to reinforce some responses but not others. C can reinforce D

but not B, even though B is learnable, as we would find when we made A contingent upon B. Thus, not all reinforcers are "transituational"; a given reinforcer cannot be used to strengthen any learnable response whatever. Rather, an activity will reinforce only those activities of lesser value, not those of higher value.

An important question is, does this revision of the law of effect now make it completely circular? If Meehl's transituational idea is altered, is there any empirical content left to the law of effect? We can avoid the circularity, but it now requires two observations (rather than one) to make an empirical prediction. If we find that activity R reinforces A and that A reinforces Z, then the law predicts that R will reinforce Z. That prediction has empirical content and could possibly be false, and so would test the proposed law. Readers familiar with logic will recognize this as a test of the *transitivity* assumption about the reinforcement relation. So the law is testable even if we could find no independent way to assess value or preference.

A central issue is whether we can find an independent way to assess a subject's preference ordering for a set of activities. With human subjects, a verbal estimate of liking or attractiveness would probably serve as a valid index, though a slight hitch arises from the fact that people are occasionally unaware (unconscious) of what kinds of events can reinforce their behavior. But suppose that we wish to have some index of wide application, one that could be used with animals, or nonverbal mental defectives, and so forth. The search for an index of such generality constitutes a real challenge. Premack (1959) proposes that a generally valid index of value would be response rate (or momentary probability) in a "free-operant" situation in which the commodity or activity is freely available to the subject. This is a plausible index: the more a person likes an activity, the more often he engages in it when it is freely available with no constraints attached.

To illustrate by a concrete example, suppose the values of four different activities are to be assessed for a kindergarten child: playing a pinball machine (PB), looking at a movie cartoon (M), eating small chocolate candies (C), and hammering on a wooden pegboard (H). The assessment would consist of measuring how frequently (by count or by total time so spent) the child engages in each activity in a standard test room in which opportunity for engaging in each activity is introduced singly and separately. Suppose that the independent rates for a particular child come out in the rank order PB>M>C>H, from highest to lowest. Thus, we would predict that the opportunity to play with the pinball machine can be used to reinforce or increase the rate of either the M, C, or H activities; M can reinforce C or H but not PB; and C can reinforce H but neither M nor PB. The contingent test situation would involve one activity freely available; when it is performed, the other activity becomes available for a brief time and then turns off. For instance, in the M>C test, candy would be freely available at one location. When a candy has been eaten, a movie projector in another part of the room would turn on, showing, say, a 30-second segment of a cartoon. A reinforcing effect would be inferred if the rate of candy eating increased above its baseline rate when this contingency was introduced. Premack (1959, 1963, 1965) has presented data from children, monkeys, and rats indicating that predictions of this sort are generally accurate.

In some cases, we know that the relative value of two activities or commodities can be altered by altering relevant conditions of deprivation. Thus, I can alter your relative preference for eating versus sleeping by depriving you of food or sleep, respectively. Therefore, we should be able to reverse the reinforcement relation between two activities by altering motivation. Premack (1962) demonstrated this effect in rats using water ingestion and running in an activity wheel. The ingestion rate was altered by water deprivation, and the running activity by depriving the rat of access to an activity wheel in an otherwise confining living quarter. When deprived of water but not of activity, water ingestion would reinforce running but not vice versa. When deprived of activity but not water, running would reinforce drinking but not vice versa. Thus, the reinforcement relation was reversible.

Having described Premack's analysis and his experimental methods of checking it, let us go on to evaluate the idea and some of its implications for reinforcement theory. First, on the positive side, Premack's approach has the advantage of supplying an apparently valid, operational specification of what contingency arrangements will be reinforcing. The assessment of independent rate and prediction of reinforcement is sensitive to the individual characteristics of a subject and also to his current state (deprivation, past training, etc.). Second, Premack's rule appears to accurately characterize many "reinforcers" that are in common use in everyday life, in the school and home environments. Examination of many practical reinforcement procedures shows that the operation of a rule like this covers a variety of activities beyond the ingestive or consummatory responses most prototypic of the classical view of reinforcement. A common example is not permitting children to watch television until they finish eating their dinner, or telling them they cannot have dessert unless they finish their meat and potatoes. The principle has also been put to ready use in many practical contexts by behavior modifiers, therapists, and teachers (Homme et al., 1963). Third, acceptance of the rule, or the data reported in support of it, renders inconsequential any efforts to identify some essential property of absolute "reinforcing events" considered as isolated elements outside the relational context of the activity that is to be reinforced.

On the negative side of the ledger, several unresolved difficulties still remain for Premack's proposal. One is the problem of generality; another, the validity of response rate as an index of preference. The problem of generality arises when we notice that in almost all human learning studies the reinforcing operation is "information about which is the correct response." Through his motivating instructions, the experimenter or teacher has made being "correct" a reinforcing event for the subject, so that nothing else need be added to promote learning. The effectiveness of this operation probably depends upon a long history of cultural training in which being "correct" and similar achievements have been associated with parental praise and approval. For instance, in the case of very young preschool children, instructions and information are sometimes not enough, so that material rewards (trinkets, gold stars, candy) must be added if they are to be kept working at difficult learning tasks. In any event, it is unclear how or whether such reinforcement by mere information is or can be covered by what Premack proposes should be done. The same can be said for the topic of vicarious or observational learning.

The other problem is the general validity of the response rate index of preference. Premack admits that it is difficult to get comparable measures on independent rates of different activities; it will not do just to let the calculated rates depend on arbitrary units imposed upon the behavior by the recording system. Conceived in a general sense, our activities and/or inter-actions with goal-object vary in multiple ways—in duration of each contact, rate of interaction during contact, time between contacts, and so forth, and it is not at all clear how to combine these features into a single index. Consider, for example, the difficulties of getting comparable measures by which to arrange in rank order the three activities of reading a book, playing a piano, and sleeping. Other problems arise in connection with the rate index (e.g., it can be differentially trained by reinforcement) and this specific proposal seems to be threatened by endless troubles and unavoidable limitations. A less objectionable criterion of relative value would be preferential *choice*, which is the behavioral index most used in discussions of utility and decision-making. If in a free choice between activities *A* and *B*, the subject consistently chooses *A* over *B*, then we would predict that in a contingent situation we could reinforce activity *B* by making *A* contingent on *B*. This choice index would seem to resolve some of the difficulties encountered by the index of response rate.

Despite these difficulties in the way of carrying out Premack's specific proposal, there seems no escaping the fact that the law of effect must be amended to cover the relativity of the reinforcement relation. Certain kinds of evidence pointing to this necessity have been around for many years in studies on "affective contrast" (see Helson, 1964, for a review). Such studies tend to show that the same stimulus may be judged as pleasant or unpleasant depending on whether the subject has just been experiencing other stimuli which are relatively unpleasant or pleasant, respectively, in relation to the one being judged at the moment. Likewise, in studies of learned performance, a given reward for a response may have either an incremental or a decremental effect upon performance depending on what reward the subject expects or on the range of alternative rewards the subject has been receiving in similar contexts. If a person is expecting a one-cent payoff, getting ten cents is going to be positively rewarding; if he is expecting a dollar payoff, then ten cents is frustrating and may have the effect of a punishment. Effects such as these have been observed with animals as well as humans (e.g., G. H. Bower, 1961b, 1962c; Bevan & Adamson, 1960). They can all be interpreted in terms of Helson's concept of adaptation level. The rewards obtained over the past trials in a given context determine, by some averaging process, an internal standard or norm called the adaptation level. Each new reward is evaluated in relation to this adaptation level, having a positive influence on behavior if it is above the norm, a negative influence if it is below.

Premack's results can be interpreted in terms of adaptation level. In the *A*, *B*, *C* situation, suppose activity *B* is made freely available. Then, we expect the subject's adaptation level to adjust to a value near *B*. Since, if we make *A* contingent on *B*, the value received is higher than the adaptation level, a positive (reinforcing) effect on the B response will be observed. If we make C contingent on B, the value received is lower than the adaptation level and therefore no reinforcing effect is observed. Thus, the idea of adaptation level implies a relativistic view of reinforcement.

If this line of reasoning is accepted, it becomes apparent that we are moving away from a strict stimulus-response interpretation of the law of effect and toward a more "cognitive" point of view. The latter, in some ways, seems closer to common sense. It is a conception that makes contact also with the economists' notion of utility and even more obviously with the cognitive theorists' notion of expectancy. The effect on behavior of a given outcome is seen as dependent upon its relation to an internal norm derived through a pooling process from the series of prior outcomes encountered in a given situation. Papers by Bevan (1963) and Bevan and Adamson (1963) provide a tentative reinforcement model based on adaptation level theory. They use it to explain a number of observed relationships between reinforcement and performance. Whether these models will stand up under stringent experimental tests is not currently known. But it appears likely that an adaptation level model of this general sort is going to be needed to handle the range of results on reinforcement. Looking backward to Muhl's and Thorndike's earlier formulations of the law of effect, we seem to have made some progress in formulating the law in a more general and valid way.

Nonreward and Extinction

Along with developments in the contemporary conception of reinforcement and the law of effect, there have also been changes in the interpretation of nonreward and extinction. Almost all of this theory stems from work on nonreward and extinction with animal subjects, although it is presumed that similar ideas apply to at least some types of human learning. Certain earlier interpretations of nonreward of a previously rewarded response had assigned to it an essentially passive role. For example, Tolman supposed that nonreward served simply to disconfirm and weaken an S-R-S_G expectancy. Thorndike gave little systematic consideration to nonreward, and as best we can tell, he thought of it as essentially a neutral event. In Hull's theory (Chapter 6), nonrewarded trials are believed to permit inhibitory factors to build up without being offset by a corresponding increase in reaction potential. Hull's ideas about extinction were worked out only in very sketchy fashion and were never really adequate to a very wide range of data on extinction. In the last 20 years, a number of hypotheses have been proposed regarding nonreward and extinction. Most of these hypotheses have aimed at explaining the increased resistance to extinction in animals trained with a partial reward schedule. That is, a rat rewarded on only, say, 30 percent of its runs down a straight alley will persist longer in going to the goal-box during extinction than will another animal trained with 100 percent rewarded trials. This simple fact, embellished with many ancillary results, has constituted a perennial challenge to theorists. Not that explanations do not abound; it is sorting them out with critical experimental tests that has proved a demanding, though also informative, task. In Chapter 6 we reviewed Amsel's frustration theory of nonreward. In this section we review Capaldi's "sequential patterning" theory of nonreward and how it explains extinction phenomena.

The Sequential Hypothesis

Capaldi's theory (1966, 1967) of the partial reinforcement extinction effect is a sophisticated elaboration and refinement of two earlier ideas: (1) the *discrimination* or generalization hypothesis (see Chapter 5), which supposes that subjects will persist responding as long as they cannot discriminate the extinction series from an unfortunate run of nonreinforcements embedded within the training series; and (2) the *stimulus aftereffects* hypothesis (V. F. Sheffield, 1949), which supposes that reward (R) and nonreward (N) events on one trial set up distinctive stimulus traces which persist over the inter-trial interval and are part of the stimulus complex at the time the next response occurs. The stimulus aftereffects hypothesis supposes that during partial reinforcement training, traces from nonreinforced trials (denoted S^N) become conditioned to the response because of frequent NR transitions (i.e., a reinforced trial following a nonreinforced trial), and therefore the S^N stimuli prevalent during extinction will maintain responding.

Capaldi elaborates these ideas in several directions. First, he supposes that a run of k consecutive nonreinforced trials sets up a distinctive stimulus trace, denoted S^{N_k}. The S^{N_k} stimuli ($k - 1, 2, 3, \ldots$) form a stimulus continuum along which there will be generalization of habit strength from a run length experienced and conditioned during training to other run lengths experi enced during extinction. When a run of k N-trials terminates with a rein-forced trial, an increment in habit strength (see Hull, Chapter 6) accrues between S^{N_k} and the instrumental response, with the asymptote of that habit being higher the greater the amount of reward provided on that trial. Sec-ond, Capaldi supposes that extinction is simply the presentation of a sequence of stimuli $S^{N_1}, S^{N_2}, S^{N_3}, \ldots$, and is formally like testing for stimulus generalization: an animal will respond to S^{N_k} during extinction if S^{N_k} has sufficient habit strength either established during training or borrowed by generalization from neighboring N-lengths involved in training. In this view of matters, the significant variables characterizing a partial reinforce-ment training schedule are (1) the particular S^{N_k} stimuli which occur during training, and (b) the frequency with which they occur and are reinforced during training. These factors will determine the "habit profile" associated to the set of S^{N_k} stimuli at the beginning of extinction; that habit profile and its generalization of response tendencies to other S^{N_j} encountered during extinction jointly determine the "resistance to extinction" produced by a given training schedule.

In order to illustrate these notions, let us examine the 8-trial sequence in Table 15.1. Let us suppose that this sequence is repeated four times, for a total of 32 acquisition trials; after the first cycle, later cycles may be con-ceived to begin with an S^R stimulus on trial 1 due to carry-over from the R on trial 8 of the prior cycle. The four rewards cause conditioning of the instrumental response to three patterns: S^R (on trials 1 and 6), S^{N_1} (on trial 8) and S^{N_3} (on trial 5). After four cycles through this series, the animal

Table 15.1   Illustration of stimulus aftereffects analysis of an 8-trial sequence of rewarded (R) and nonrewarded (N) trials.

	1	2	3	4	5	6	7	8
Reward event	R	N	N	N	R	R	N	R
Stimulus trace from prior trial	S^R	S^R	S^{N_1}	S^{N_2}	S^{N_3}	S^R	S^R	S^{N_1}
Conditioning on this trial?	+	−	−	−	+	+	−	+

would have had seven reinforcements on S^R (recall that trial 1 of the first cycle was not preceded by an R), and four each on S^{N_1} and S^{N_3}. The profile of the three habits and their separate generalization tendencies to other S^{N_R} stimuli are illustrated in Figure 15.3. The habit strength above S^R is higher than that above S^{N_1} and S^{N_3} because of its having more reinforced trials. The S^{N_R} stimuli are spaced logarithmically along the axis, and the habit generalization gradients are assumed to be linear on that log scale. In this illustration, it may be seen that generalized habit from S^R alone would have been too weak to sustain performance at $S^{N_{50}}$ (on the fiftieth extinction trial), but the generalization of habit established at S^{N_3} would do so. In general, resistance to extinction produced by given training conditions depends upon the summated habit strength that is generalized to the right in this graph. The greater the N-length which can still evoke the instrumental response, the greater is the number of extinction trials for which the response persists.

This is a somewhat novel perspective on reinforcement schedules; it fits in very well with current "sequential pattern" models of probability learning such as those of Estes (1972a) and Myers (1970) (see discussion in Chap-

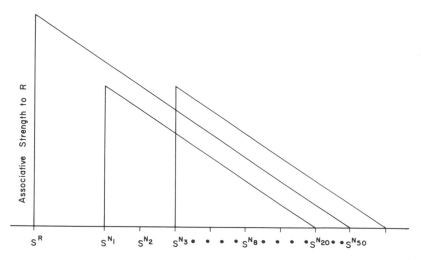

Figure 15.3.   Plot of habit profile to the three reinforced sequential patterns illustrated in Table 15.1, and the generalization of these habits to other run lengths of N trials.

ter 12). But the obvious payoff for this novel perspective is that it can account for a vast range of experimental results comparing resistance to extinction following training on the hundreds of variants of partial reinforcement schedules. The range of results is reviewed in Capaldi's papers (1966, 1967) and cannot be reiterated here. One bit of supporting data, for instance, is that with a small number of training trials resistance to extinction is higher with more frequent occurrences of short N-lengths and fewer occurrences of long N-lengths (holding number of N trials constant), whereas with many training trials the most persistence occurs in that schedule having the longer N-lengths. Capaldi has also extended the hypothesis to handle the effects of other goal-box events, such as different confinement durations in a nonrewarded goal-box, different magnitudes of reward, and different delays of reward. His treatment explains the fact that animals trained with a large reward on every trial extinguish faster than those trained with small reward because S^{large} is farther from S^N than is S^{small}. On the other hand, under random reward-nonreward schedules, greater persistence occurs for animals receiving the large reward because S^N is conditioned to a greater extent by the large reward on NR transitions. The transitions are shown to be important since animals receiving repeated cycles of SNL trials (small reward, then nothing, then large reward) proved to be much more resistant to extinction than those receiving the reverse sequence LNS (see Capaldi & Capaldi, 1970; Leonard, 1969).

A novel technique introduced by Capaldi (1966) is "intertrial reinforcement" (ITR), during which the animal is placed directly into the goal-box of the runway and rewarded. The ITR event functions within Capaldi's theory to establish the stimulus trace to be S^R for the next running trial regardless of whether the prior *running* trial had been N or R. The ITR, in other words, is the way to interject a different stimulus just before a given trial. Several ingenious experiments were done with ITR. Consider the five-trial schedule RNNNR, and let an ITR event be interposed for different groups of subjects after either the first, second, or third N event of the cycle. A control group receives no ITR. The prediction from the sequential hypothesis is that the controls will be most resistant to extinction, next will be the group receiving ITR after the first N trial, next those receiving it after the second N trial, while the poorest persistence will obtain for the group receiving ITR after the third N trial. This ordering is predicted because the ITR cuts short the N-length which can be conditioned by the R on trial 5 of the cycle. The control subjects experience S^{N3} on trial 5, and it becomes associated with the reinforced response. The subjects receiving ITR after the first N trial will then have S^R on trial 3, then S^{N1} on trial 4, then S^{N2} on trial 5 (see Table 15.1 above). The subjects receiving ITR after the third N trial will have S^R on trial 5. The groups thus differ in the longest N-length that becomes conditioned to the response, and their resistance to extinction varies accordingly.

One point at which Capaldi's theory deviates from the earlier aftereffects hypothesis of V. F. Sheffield concerns the time decay of information about the reinforcing event of the prior trial. Sheffield had assumed that R or N events set up relatively short-term stimulus traces which decay away after a few minutes. The problem with that idea is that it has no way to handle partial reinforcement effects that are obtained with widely spaced trials, say one trial every 24 hours. Capaldi assumes, on the contrary, that a trace of the prior R or N event persists indefinitely until it is modified or replaced by the next event to happen in the goal-box of this situation. Clearly, for Capaldi, the prior R or N stimuli are now available in something like a *memory* which is reactivated when the animal is placed back in the stimulus situation of the maze. Thus, an alternative way to discuss the theory is to say not that S^N is a persisting stimulus from a prior N trial (say, 24 hours ago), but rather that S^N is a stimulating effect from the subject now recalling the N event from the prior trial. This memory interpretation is in some ways more heuristic than the stimulus trace interpretation. In any event, what is needed is some theoretical mechanism ("information carrier") that is instantaneously responsive to the most recent reward outcome, that encodes that information in a discriminative manner (this is where the r_g mechanism fails), and which retains that discriminative information over time until the next trial. This temporal retention is required because most of the usual partial reinforcement phenomena (see Capaldi & Capaldi, 1970) occur whether the training trials are massed (one trial every 15 seconds) or widely spaced (one trial per day). Of course, the construct of a memory for an event (the substrate of the S^R or S^N) is what is embarrassingly clumsy to formulate in S-R behavior theory.

Capaldi (1967) applies his hypothesis to explain a wide range of different phenomena of scheduling, including the speeded up relearning and extinction that occur with multiple blocks of acquisition and extinction trials, the effects of patterned schedules and their discrimination (e.g., double alternation), the effects of varied magnitude and varied delay of reward, contrast effects due to shifts in reward magnitude, the effects of differing intertrial intervals (conceived as components of the stimulus complex), and so on. The theory has also been applied with considerable success to human probability learning and to resistance to extinction in that context; and a mathematical model casting the main constructs of the hypothesis within the framework of statistical learning theory has been recently developed (Koteskey, 1972). The consensus of researchers is that the sequential theory is the best one currently available for predicting the resistance to extinction produced by most reinforcement schedules. Surprisingly, it does not use any concepts of inhibition, frustration, or competing responses; rather, responses stop during extinction because the S^{Nk} stimuli become sufficiently remote on a generalization gradient from those conditioned to the response during training. The theoretical problem for the next decade is to combine the sequential hypothesis in some creative way with the concepts of frustrative nonreward and inhibition (these are simply undeniable effects) so as to produce a more general and complete theory of nonreinforcement and extinction effects.

INFORMATIONAL VARIABLES IN CONDITIONING

A view that is gradually becoming accepted is that in order to produce effective conditioning, even of the simple Pavlovian variety, more is required than simple temporal contiguity of the conditioned stimulus (CS) and the unconditioned stimulus (US). Rather, evidence is accumulating that, in order to become conditioned, the CS must impart reliable information about the occurrence of the US; it must be a useful predictor of the time, place, and quality of the US. Moreover, even if a given CS is predictive, it still may not become conditioned to the US if its usefulness has already been pre-empted by another redundant stimulus which is a better predictor or which has had a longer history of successfully predicting the US. These remarks are in regard to conditioning of excitation to cues predicting the US, but they also hold true for conditioning of inhibition to cues predicting the absence of the US in a situation in which the US otherwise occurs.

The basis for these conclusions is contained in a remarkable series of research papers by Rescorla and Wagner (for reviews, see Rescorla, 1972a; Rescorla & Wagner, 1972) studying classical conditioning, typically in the CER ("conditioned suppression") paradigm. They also develop a simple but intuitively compelling theory to knit together the diverse range of results they and other investigators have turned up. The basic notion is that the effectiveness of a reinforcement in producing associative learning to a prior stimulus depends not upon that reinforcement itself but upon the relationship between the reinforcement and the outcome that the subject anticipates. Thus one and the same US occurrence can have either no effect or a strong conditioning effect depending on whether the organism expected it. The principle that applies to excitation due to expecting a US also applies to inhibition due to omission of the US. And if the subject anticipates a given US on a given trial due to past learning with respect to one CS, then the reinforcing effect of the US on that trial is altered with respect to other simultaneously present stimuli. The theory can be stated more precisely:

Consider a situation in which a compound stimulus, AX, is followed by a given reinforcer, US_1. The equations below describe the theoretical change in conditioning to the component stimuli, A and X, as a result of a single such trial. V_A represents the associative strength, or amount of conditioning to A, and is presumed to be monotonically related to such dependent measures as probability of response or latency of response.

$$\Delta V_A = \alpha_A \beta_1 (\lambda_1 - V_{AX}) \tag{1a}$$

$$\Delta V_X = \alpha_X \beta_1 (\lambda_1 - V_{AX}) \tag{1b}$$

The parameter λ_1 represents the asymptote of conditioning supportable by the applied US_1; it is US-dependent and is subscripted to indicate that. The α and β are learning-rate parameters dependent, respectively, upon the qualities of the CS and the US. (Rescorla, 1972a, p. 11)

Study of these equations brings out a number of salient points. The change in conditioning of a given cue depends largely on the difference between the potency of the US (λ) and the associative strength to the stimulus *compound*, denoted V_{AX}. As a first approximation, it is supposed that $V_{AX} = V_A + V_X$—that is, the strength of the compound is just the sum of the strengths of its components. Thus, the smaller is the difference between λ and V_{AX}—the better the US is predicted—the less will be the change ΔV_A resulting from another pairing of AX with the US. The Vs in this equation can be negative, representing the case of conditioned inhibition. These equations are similar to the linear operators used in stimulus-sampling theory (see Chapter 12) to describe trial-to-trial learning changes. We now consider the application of this model to several cases of experimental interest.

Blocking. Suppose that stimulus A alone has already been conditioned to the US, so that $V_A = \lambda$. Assuming that V_X begins at zero strength, we now introduce the compound stimulus AX paired with the same US. But since $V_{AX} = V_A = \lambda$, the incremental equation (1b) for ΔV_X equals zero. The prediction is that no conditioning will occur to cue X. This result, originally suggested by Pavlov's work on "overshadowing" of one cue by another, has been much researched recently (Kamin, 1969b). It is called the "blocking" effect because prior acquisition of the A-US association blocks later learning of the X-US association in the AX compound. The effect was at one time claimed by selective attention theories (see Trabasso & Bower, 1968); however, it seems due instead to the "unsurprisingness" of the US following A in the AX compound. If the shock intensity used as the US is increased between the A training and the AX training, a higher value of λ would now prevail, so that equation (1b) expects (and one now finds) some learning (V_X) to occur to cue X during the AX training. This learning is assessed when cue X is presented by itself after the AX training.

Concurrent training of other stimuli. Consider again the case where compound AX-US trials occur; alternating with AX trials are trials on which A alone occurs, and for different subjects A alone is either paired with the US or is not so paired. The model predicts that the group receiving concurrent A-US trials will show much less conditioning to cue X than the other, unpaired group. Why? Because the A-US trials cause V_A and hence V_{AX} to be large, thus by equation (1b) reducing the increment ΔV_X, the conditioning of cue X.

Extinction by continued reinforcements. By judicious selection of a stimulus schedule, one can *extinguish* a prior habit to cue X by pairing the compound AX with the US! To illustrate, suppose the shock intensity supports a λ of 1.0, and we begin by pairing cue A with the US, applying equation (1a) until, say, the value of V_A increases to .5. At this point we now give a block of single cue X-US trials sufficient to bring $V_X = 1$. We now proceed to give a few AX-US compound trials interspersed among many X-US trials. On the AX-US trials, we will have $V_{AX} = V_A + V_X = .5 + 1.0 = 1.5$, so that $\alpha\beta(-.5)$; hence, ΔV_A will be negative. So pairing A with a stronger cue X on AX-US trials has the effect of *weakening* V_A, the associative strength of cue A. This kind of prediction has now been confirmed several times by Rescorla (1972a) and Kamin (personal communication, 1972). It shows the utter inappropriateness of the simplistic doctrine that temporal contiguity of a CS and US is all that is necessary and sufficient to obtain strong conditioning.

CS-US correlations. Earlier experiments by Rescorla (1968) had shown that conditioning of a CS (say, a tone) to a shock depended on the probability of the US in the presence of the CS relative to the probability of the US in the absence of the CS (when the rat was merely sitting in the experimental chamber). The higher the *correlation* between CS and shock, the better the conditioning. For a given US probability to the CS, conditioning to the CS was made poorer by increasing the US probability in the absence of the CS. In the extreme case where shocks never occurred when the CS was on but occurred often in its absence, the CS was converted into a conditioned *inhibitor* of fear; it became a signal for safety rather than fear. These results, apparently showing the effect of the CS-US correlation, are consistent with the conditioning equations above. Identify A with the background stimuli of the conditioning box, and let X denote the brief tone interjected into the situation, thus making up conceptually an AX compound. The greater the shock rate to A alone (in the absence of the tone), the greater V_A will become; consequently, by arguments similar to those above, the less will cue X become conditioned through pairing of the compound AX with a particular shock rate. Furthermore, if the shocks occurring in the absence of X (the tone) are always preceded by a second cue, B (a clicking noise), then B in the BA compound picks up some of the conditioning, depleting it from A (the background alone), with the result that cue X in the compound XA can now acquire some associative strength in its pairings with the US. So, all these results fit together neatly.

Inhibitory blocking. The results above have all concerned blocking or alteration of excitatory conditioning. It is also possible to arrange to block the learning of inhibitory properties by a cue (Suiter & LoLordo, 1971). In a CER situation, cue A is first made a conditioned inhibitor in the sense that A occurs without shock in a background situation where shocks otherwise occur frequently. Once A is established as a safety signal, cue X is now introduced in the compound AX paired with the absence of shock. However, later tests reveal that cue X does not acquire inhibitory properties in this procedure. Its learning has been "blocked" by the presence of the redundant inhibitory cue A. This is consistent with equation (1) if the Vs and λ are given a negative ("inhibitory") sign.

To summarize, then, equations (1a) and (1b) provide a very economic description of many important results in conditioning (see the papers cited for many more results). It is clear that the effectiveness of a reinforced pairing depends upon the strength of other cues presented simultaneously in the compound. Although it is convenient in talking about the theory to use the intuitive notion of "expectancy" and "information" value (e.g., a US causes conditioning only to the extent that it was unexpected), Rescorla (1972a) points out the pitfalls in this intuitive notion. For instance, the "predictive validity" intuition has no way to account for the substantial conditioning of a CS which is presented briefly in the middle of a lengthy shock. For the moment, we do best to simply rest with the implications of these equations (and their theoretical translation). Rescorla acknowledges a few phenomena not covered by the theory, such as transient second-order conditioning. However, progress is also occurring in the experimental analysis of that phenomenon (Rescorla, 1972b).

Selectivity by Innate Fittingness

One of the earlier principles of learning theory was what may be called "equipotentiality," the belief that any discriminable stimulus could be associated to any motor response of which the animal was capable. To be sure, the learning depended on the goodness of the cue, the ease of the response, and the goodness of the reinforcement condition. But the actual identities of the cues and responses were supposed to be irrelevant; any elements could be picked to be connected together.

This has turnd out to be a naive and false assumption. In Chapter 2 we reviewed the evidence against this equipotentiality thesis; there we argued instead for a "preparedness to associate" dimension (Seligman, 1970; Seligman & Hager, 1972) which was innately specified. This simply says that, by their innate makeup, animals are more prepared to make certain cue-response associations than others and are prepared against making still others, and this ordering will be reflected in the ease of training the animals to particular associations. One might say that the animal is innately programmed to see certain cues and responses as "naturally fitting" together, so that they are readily learned.

One of the more startling cases of this stimulus fittingness principle is illustrated in the work by Garcia and his associates on conditioned aversions to tastes (for a review, see Revusky & Garcia, 1970). An animal who drinks a tasty but harmless solution is later made to feel sick, either by X-irradiation or by injection of a drug causing nausea. The rat will selectively associate the internal upset with the earlier taste, despite the fact that very many external stimulus events may have occurred to the animal in the intervening time. But these external events which are closer in time to the illness are passed over by the innate "connector mechanism"; it "knows innately" that it is looking for a taste stimulus in the recent past to hook up to the illness. We would say that there is an innate selective association of flavors with physiological aftereffects, despite very long delays. Importantly too, internal toxicosis is *not* easily associated with an external, phasic stimulus. To illustrate the complete flip-over of the results, a novel taste cannot be associated over a long delay with an electric shock to the feet of the animal, whereas an earlier tone or light may be readily associated to the shock. Matters seem governed by some kind of "natural fittingness" principle rather than equipotentiality. In brief, tastes go with internal effects, whereas external stimuli become selectively hooked up to external reinforcing events. Such results have been shown now with a variety of tastes and smells and internal effects, beneficent ones (a thiamine injection to a thiamine-deficient animal) as well as noxious ones. If a novel taste is followed hours later by a beneficent internal effect (e.g., correction of a vitamin deficiency), then the substance with that taste is sought out and consumed by the animal at the next opportunity. If the taste is followed by an unpleasant sickness, then it is avoided at later encounters.

Apparently, when the animal experiences some internal upset, it retrieves memories of things recently tasted and looks for a novel one to "blame" for its sickness. Revusky and Garcia (1970) report several "retroactive interference" studies along these lines. A rat is repeatedly familiarized with drinking coffee-flavored water. On a critical day, it drinks some novel saccharine solution, and 50 minutes later receives either no treatment, a drink of its familiar coffee-water, or a drink of a new novel substance (weak vinegar solution). Then 50 minutes after that, internal sickness is induced by injection of a lithium chloride solution. Later aversion (avoidance) of the novel saccharine solution is greatest for the control animals and for those drinking the familiar solution after the saccharine, and least for those that drank another novel taste between the saccharine and the toxicosis. Apparently, the second novel taste acquires some of the associative strength to the sickness, doing so at the expense of the earlier novel taste. It is worth noting that familiar tastes, when paired alone with toxicosis, can acquire aversions, but they tend to acquire none when they are presented along with a novel taste. Again, it is the novel taste and not the "old, safe one" which gets selected for associating to the internal upset. The results are rather like those seen in the work on blocking of conditioning of the less salient stimulus by the more salient cue. The general results on remembering of tastes by a rat over a long delay link up, too, with Capaldi's ideas about how memories of S^R or S^N events (tastes) can persist for some time until the next trial.

These ideas have also been applied to explain specific subhungers. Thus, an animal deficient in a given vitamin will learn to associate a specific taste with either a good effect (from a vitamin-rich food) or a bad effect (from a vitamin-impoverished food), learning to eat more or less of it to alleviate his vitamin deficiency (see Rozin & Kalat, 1972). Revusky and Garcia (1970) take the hypothesis a step further and tentatively propose that eating in general is a *discriminated operant* response which is reinforced only by its delayed, beneficial consequences. Internal stimuli correlated with deprivation serve as discriminative stimuli or "S^Ds"; eating is not "innately hooked up" to hunger, but rather eating in the presence of greater or lesser internal hunger stimuli is rewarded more or less according to the subsequent changes in the need state due to nutritive aftereffects of eating. In this way the animal learns the relationship between the internal cues signaling the "degree of its need" and how much food it should eat to reduce just that amount of need. This is a novel hypothesis regarding a possible associative component in how need states are expressed; Revusky and Garcia use it to speculate about a number of findings in the literature regarding biological motivations.

Response Fittingness

The Garcia-Revusky work on taste-sickness associations illustrates selectivity between an unconditioned reaction and an earlier stimulus, the novel taste. There seems also to be a specific "fittingness principle" illustrated when we try to use particular reinforcers to condition certain classes of *behaviors* which are or are not appropriate for receiving or dealing with that particular reinforcer. Recent work on this problem has been summarized by Bolles (1970, 1972), although he confines himself largely to the procedural problems in teaching rats a discrete response to a CS in order to avoid a painful electric shock. In traditional theory, any response which terminates the CS should be reinforced and strengthened by fear reduction. But alas, experimenters began to find some responses which rats were loath to make to avoid shock (for instance, lever-pressing in a Skinner box to avoid shock); most animals could not be conditioned at all, and those that did condition gave relatively poor performances which just as often ceased as training continued. All efforts at manipulating the effectiveness of the experimental parameters were to little avail; something was just wrong with the theoretical analysis, at least of such lever-box situations. However, in other situations such as one in which the rat can jump completely out of the shock-box, or another in which it merely has to "freeze" and remain motionless, the learning of avoidance responses is exceedingly rapid. Such observations on variations in ease of training different classes of avoidance responses have been made with a variety of mammalian species.

Bolles proposes a generalization to cover such variations. He refers first to a class of responses, termed "species-specific defense reactions" (SSDRs), meaning that animal's repertoire of innate defensive reactions to a threatening situation; for the rat frightened by shock, such reactions include fleeing, freezing, aggressively attacking some object, leaping up, circling about, screaming. The hypothesis is that an animal will readily learn a specific avoidance response to shock if the response is one of its SSDRs (or a component of one), such as fleeing or freezing, but will not readily learn a response which is not an SSDR. Bolles (1972) shows how a shift to this perspective materially alters the traditional theoretical analysis of avoidance learning. This newer analysis does not premise a direct association from the CS to an avoidance response; rather, the CS makes the animal frightened, which then brings out a repertoire of SSDRs. The "correct" SSDR gets selected from among the others not so much because it removes the CS but because all the others are ineffective (inappropriate) in a given experimental situation and are "punished." The cited papers should be consulted for the complexities of and arguments for this interpretation.

Coping.   In connection with these innate reactions to fear, a number of recent findings suggest that animals have a complex range of internal reactions to stress. But how devastating and debilitating a given stress is psychologically depends markedly on whether the animal can "prepare itself" for the stressor and whether the animal "thinks" it has a way to *cope* with the stress when it arrives. Experiments by Weiss (1971a, 1971b) illustrate these effects with rats receiving frequent electric shocks over many hours while strapped down on a table. If the shocks occurred often and at random unexpected times, most of the rats soon developed severe stomach ulcers. If occurrences of shocks were signaled by a warning tone, fewer ulcers appeared. The fewest ulcers developed when not only did the warning signal occur but the rat could also perform a simple response to avoid and/or escape shock. So the availability of a coping response appears to be a large factor in the amount of psychological stress caused by a given physical stress. However, if performance of the coping response itself involves conflict (e.g., if it sometimes leads to further shock), ulceration still occurs (Weiss, 1971b). Weiss has also studied the physiology of these stress reactions, finding that animals with an available coping response to relieve stress have lower corticosterone levels in the bloodstream and elevated levels of norepinephrine (a biochemical transmitter) in the brain. In humans, drugs which elevate norepinephrine at the synapse are associated with activation and a euphoric mood, whereas mental depression is associated with depressed norepinephrine levels much like those of the "helpless" animal during stress.

Other research by Seligman, Maier, and Solomon (1971) has shown similarly devastating *behavioral* effects of not being able to cope or of being helpless in stressful situations. In preliminary training of a dog or a rat, the animal received shocks; the "copers" could remove these shocks by performing a simple but distinct escape response; the "noncopers" could do nothing to escape or avoid the shocks. By a "matching" procedure, the two groups of animals received the same number and durations of shocks. Yet there was a substantial difference in the two "personalities" produced by this experience. In new situations, the copers would now readily learn new escape and avoidance responses, whereas the noncopers would not easily learn active coping responses under stress. They had learned to be "helpless," to believe that all efforts to get away from stress would be ineffective, so they might as well be passive and take their punishment. They could be brought to learn coping responses only very gradually by special guidance procedures. These laboratory results on stress, coping patterns, and learned helplessness have obvious parallels in the psychiatric clinic.

HUMAN MEMORY

The second half of this chapter will briefly review some of the major theoretical trends in research on human learning and memory. Prior to about 1965, most research on human learning was in what was called the "rote verbal learning" tradition (and/or the "psychomotor skills" tradition). The research rather explicitly followed the concepts of stimulus-response associationism with a strong behavioristic, functionalistic bias (see McGeoch & Irion, 1952, for a good example). The primary dependent variable was response probability—the likelihood that the subject would recall the correct response under specified conditions of practice and testing—and there was relatively little concern for the internal processes mediating the observed response probabilities. These probabilities were alleged to be a function of stimulus-response verbal habits, all of which were assumed to follow the laws laid down in the prevailing learning theories of the day, such as those of Hull or Guthrie. An excellently serviceable representative of this general approach still exists in the interference theory of forgetting which was reviewed in Chapter 9. But in recent times there has been a clear conceptual shift away from that older tradition. Contemporary theorists are more concerned with "cognitive" aspects of remembering, and show more interest in internal processes that occur during acts of memorizing and remembering. These "memory theorists" are also more likely to derive inspiration from the older Gestalt psychology or cognitive psychology than from Hull or Skinner; they are also likely to express their theories in the idiom and jargon of information-processing concepts, possibly with a computer simulation program implicitly in mind. In their major review of the current scene, Tulving and Madigan (1970) outline this division between "verbal learning" and "memory" theorists. However, it would be unproductive to emphasize the differences here, since most of the viable approaches today try to make use of concepts and data from both orientations (e.g., see J. R. Anderson & Bower, 1973; Tulving & Donaldson, 1972). In any event, the topics to be reviewed here include several themes from this newer approach to memory.

One of these concerns elaboration of operations in short-term memory, to be discussed first. Then we shall examine the issue of organization in memory, mnemonics, and mental imagery; finally we cover the "episodic versus semantic" memory distinction, and discuss plausible representations of knowledge in long-term memory and how it is retrieved, added to, and used.

Short-Term Memory

The topic of immediate or short-term memory was introduced in Chapter 12 (see Figure 12.12). The Atkinson-Shiffrin buffer model was briefly described, and a simple mathematical description of an item's fate in the system was briefly presented. For convenience of reference in the current context, Figure 15.4 shows a simplified block diagram of the memory stores typically assumed in the theoretical discussions. A stimulus item input to the perceptual system is first analyzed, then identified, and if attended to (by the control processes) an internal code for it is entered into an active short-term memory (abbreviated STM). The STM is of limited capacity, holding at most only a few items of information. If the items in STM are to be retained, the control processes initiate some sort of mnemonic activity such as rehearsal. For verbal materials, such rehearsals doubtless consist of subvocally going over the names of the items. The usual assumption is that each rehearsal cycle may transfer into a more permanent long-term memory (LTM) information about the item's presence on the list to be memorized. For concreteness, let us follow through an illustrative example. (1) Visual presentation of the letter *L* in a letter list to be memorized in serial order would be identified as a familiar letter (pattern), and be coded if possible as the vocal name *ell*; (2) this pronunciation code *ell* would be rehearsed subvocally in STM along with several other letter items of the input list to be memorized, and (3) the memory structure established in LTM might be

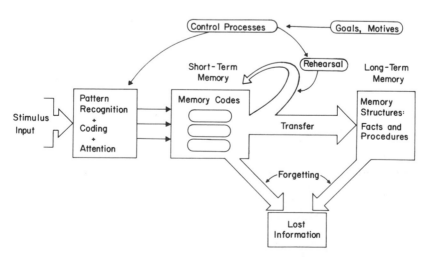

Figure 15.4.   Diagram of storage components and control processes that are commonly assumed in modern theories of memory. See text for explanation.

a factual proposition of the form "L was presented in the most recent list." To the extent that this structure is successfully built up, it is retrieved and used when the experimenter later asks the subject to name the letters presented on the most recent list he had studied. So much for the preliminaries. Let us now go somewhat deeper into the details and the research surrounding them.

Coding. The memory code is the temporary "name" or internal representation assigned to the stimulus item and deposited in STM. For vocal subjects dealing with verbal materials, this is most often the sound of the name of the stimulus or of a verbal description of it or (if it is a familiar picture) a label for it. The effect of this vocal naming is to convert a visual stimulus into an internal articulatory form. If, however, the speech apparatus is otherwise engaged or inoperative at the time the stimulus to be remembered is visually presented, then this visual-to-articulatory conversion cannot occur and the presented stimulus appears to be retained in terms of its physical (visual) properties. As a second example of nonverbal coding, deaf persons dependent on manual sign language will use manual coding when they are to remember visually presented letters. In any event, the form of this internal representation of a target item determines (1) what other kinds of materials will interfere with or cause forgetting of the target, and (2) the kinds of confusion errors the person will make when he misremembers the target item. If he has coded an item according to its sound, then sound-alike materials will interfere and errors in recall are likely to sound like the target (e.g., he will recall T when it should have been P or V or B). If articulatory coding is prevented so that the person is forced to encode visually presented letters in terms of their visual characteristics (Kroll et al., 1970; Salzberg et al., 1971), then greatest interference is caused by interpolated material that is visually similar to the item to be remembered (e.g., R is visually but not acoustically similar to P). In like manner, for deaf persons using manual signs to encode items to be remembered, greatest interference will come from interpolated materials that involve signs that are manually similar to the item to be remembered (Locke & Locke, 1971).

The memory codes in STM are quickly available to retrieval. This quick retrieval from STM is studied in the task devised by Sternberg (1969, see Chapter 13). The subject hears a small set of one to six "target" items to place in his STM, and then hears a "probe" item; he is to decide whether the probe matches one of the target items. It is presumed that in this task the subject stores in STM the codes of the target items, and then, when the probe occurs, scans for a code that matches it. In this view, reaction time for probes will increase linearly with the number of items in the memory list (provided the list is shorter than STM capacity), and this is the standard finding. The more complex the items (e.g., nonsense syllables rather than letters), the more "space" they take up in the limited-capacity STM, requiring the overflow from big lists to be retrieved from LTM, all making for slower reaction time in the Sternberg task (Cavanaugh, 1972).

If we ask what events cause removal of items from STM, the answer is that removal results when the STM becomes engaged in dealing with other, new material so that rehearsal of the old material stops and its trace fades away. Research shows that the new material apparently displaces or knocks the old items out of STM. If attention is engaged in alert monitoring, but without new inputs, the old items seem to just "stick in STM" even though they are not rehearsed explicitly (see J. S. Reitman, 1971). As noted above, the more similar the new material to the item to be remembered (e.g., it sounds nearly the same), the more it tends to knock out the old material in STM.

If a person wants to forget something in STM—or rather, wants not to remember it—he has merely to stop rehearsing it and its memory code will fade away. A number of studies have been done on this "directed forgetting," and the procedure works rather well (see Bjork, 1970; Epstein, 1972). For example, in a free-recall situation in which single words are presented every 2 seconds to be learned, with the whole list to be recalled later, the person may be informed at some point during input that he is not responsible for the earlier items (he can "forget" them) and will have to recall only those that will follow (Bruce & Papay, 1970). A variety of follow-up tests, among which is an unexpected request for the subject to now try to recall items he was told earlier to forget, suggest that the "forget cue" is a signal to the subject to dump out of STM all those items he does not have to remember, so that they receive less rehearsal and are therefore weaker than they normally would have been. The subject is able to edit his recall for only those items that occurred after (rather than before) the "forget" cue; moreover, the data suggest that when recalling the terminal sublist, the subject can "set aside" the memory traces of those earlier items so that they do not compete with the items to be recalled.

Another way to cause forgetting of an item or an input series (for free recall) is to follow it with a high-priority item to which the subject can be expected to pay special attention. The high-priority item preempts storage space in STM, with the result that later items in the list (1) are somewhat less likely to be entered into STM, and (2) if entered, are likely to bump out the earlier memory codes of lesser priority, namely, those that entered just before the high-priority item. Experiments by Ellis et al. (1971) show both such decremental effects on recall of the immediately preceding (and several following) names of common line drawings in a list in which the special high-priority item was a photograph of a nude. Their results are shown in Figure 15.5; the critical item is recalled much above normal, while items immediately before and after it are depressed in recall. Tulving (1969) observed only a prior item decrement by putting into a list of unrelated words to be remembered the name of a famous person which the subject had been especially urged to recall. These effects may be interpreted as resulting from either rehearsal prevention or rehearsal enhancement. Monetary payoffs yield similar effects; if the person is told during study of an item that its later recall will be worth a lot of money, he will concentrate harder (rehearse more, maintain that item in STM for a longer time) and remember it better. The payoff affects the assignment of a priority and amount of rehearsal to the item, and that rehearsal in turn affects the strength of the memory trace laid down (see, for example, Atkinson & Wickens, 1971; Loftus, 1972).

We have implied that various mnemonic effects are due to differential

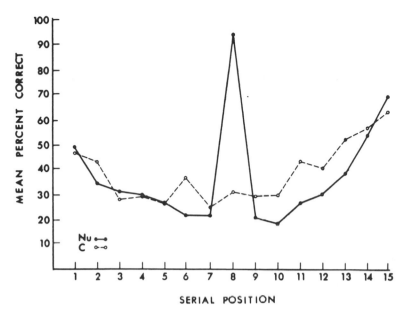

Figure 15.5.   Percentage recall of names of pictures according to their serial position in the list. The "critical" list (solid curve) contained a photograph of a nude woman in serial position 8, whereas the "noncritical" list (dashed curve) used only the familiar, unemotional pictures. (From Ellis et al., Amnesic effects in short-term memory, *Journal of Experimental Psychology*, 1971, 89, p. 358. Copyright 1971 by the American Psychological Association. Reprinted by permission.)

rehearsal of the appropriate material. A simple way to operationalize rehearsal processes is to have the subject "think aloud" as he is studying the list (Rundus & Atkinson, 1970; Rundus, 1971). If the subject is presented with a list of 20 unrelated words which he is to free-recall, and if the items occur singly at a leisurely 5-second rate, his moment-by-moment rehearsals might look like the protocol in Table 15.2. During each 5-second interval, he is overtly rehearsing about four tokens (covert rehearsal could be much faster). As each new word occurs, it is entered into the ongoing rehearsal set, others are dropped, and earlier ones may be picked up again in later rehearsals. Of the many descriptions one might give of such a protocol, perhaps the simplest statistic is just the number of times a given item (say the *k*-th item in the list) receives a rehearsal. Thus, in the hypothetical protocol in Table 15.2, the item that occurred in the first position (*dog*) received 8 rehearsals, the second (*rug*) also received 8, the third (*book*) received 1, and so on.

The dashed curve in Figure 15.6 shows the average number of rehearsals received by each of the 20 successive items in a study list; this is averaged over 25 subjects, each performing one trial on 11 different free-recall lists. The values are given on the right-hand ordinate of the graph, and vary from a mean of 12 rehearsals for the first item to 2 rehearsals for the twentieth and last. Immediately following presentation of the list of words, the

Table 15.2   Hypothetical example of overt rehearsal of items during input of list for free recall; procedure devised by Rundus & Atkinson (1970).

Item Presented	Items Rehearsed (Rehearsal Set)
1. dog	dog, dog, dog
2. rug	$\overset{1}{\text{rug}}$, dog, $\overset{2}{\text{rug}}$, dog
3. book	book, $\overset{3}{\text{rug}}$, dog
4. pen	pen, pen, $\overset{4}{\text{rug}}$, dog
5. ship	ship, $\overset{5}{\text{rug}}$, pen, dog
6. wall	wall, $\overset{6}{\text{rug}}$, wall, $\overset{7}{\text{rug}}$
7. key	key, ship, wall, $\overset{8}{\text{rug}}$
8. bag	bag, key, ship, wall
. .	.
. .	.
. .	.
20. hair	hair, sock, paper, hair

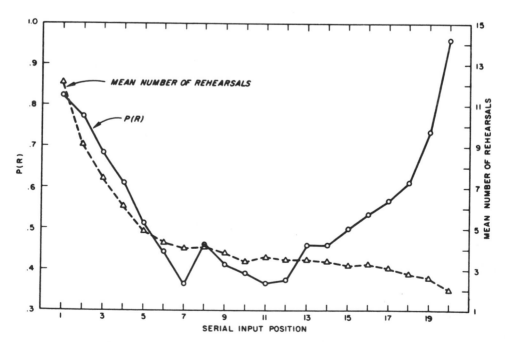

Figure 15.6.   The mean probability of recall, P(R), and the mean number of rehearsals of an item as a function of its serial input position. (From D. J. Rundus, Analysis of rehearsal processes in free recall, *Journal of Experimental Psychology,* 1971, 89, No. 1. Copyright 1971 by the American Psychological Association. Reprinted by permission.)

subjects free-recalled as many of them as they could in any order they wanted. The probability of recall of the word in each serial input position is graphed in the solid line labeled $P(R)$.

Several features of this serial position curve can be noted. First, the last few items of the list are well recalled—a so-called recency effect—and the theory supposes that these most probably were in the twentieth rehearsal set (see Table 15.2) and were retrieved from STM when recall was requested. Second, the initial items in the list are better recalled than the middle items —a so-called primacy effect. Of interest here is the fact that the number of rehearsals of an item correlates with its probability of recall, at least for items up to above serial position 14 (STM enters to enhance recall of later items). This correlation is quite strong even if one considers only items whose last appearance in a rehearsal set was four to seven items back, before recall commenced.

The standard two-store interpretation of such results is that the earlier "primacy" items are well recalled because they have a high strength in long-term memory (due to their extra rehearsals), whereas the later "recency" items are well recalled because they are in STM. An implication is that recall of these recency items is more fragile, more easily disrupted. This is true; if a distracting arithmetic task is interpolated for 30 seconds between list input and recall, the items in STM are removed and the "recency effect" in recall is wiped out. But the level of the primary effect is not much disturbed by such interpolation. A further implication comes from the slight downturn in the rehearsal curve for items at the end of the list. If these items have lesser strength in LTM due to the fewer rehearsals, then a similar downturn should be detected in long-delayed recall of such lists. Such a delayed recall downturn was found by Craik (1970), but it is not yet certain that "differential rehearsal" is the correct interpretation of the result.

Problem boxes. The evidence reviewed makes plausible the general "boxes diagram" in Figure 15.4 showing STM, LTM, and the flow of information between them by a rehearsal. But there are a few conceptual problems with that general view which require ironing out. First, the layout of the "boxes" seems askew inasmuch as information in long-term memory is always used for pattern recognition during initial perception and coding, whereas the diagram suggests that LTM is entered only much later. Second, equating STM with active rehearsal leads to an inability to handle the facts regarding memory for nonverbal stimuli. Third, it may *not* be subvocal rehearsal that causes transfer of an item to a more permanent store, but rather other elaborative and organizing activities which may be only roughly indexed by overt rehearsal. Certainly in instances where various learning strategies are compared, subjects using simple rote repetition of the individual items recall the poorest. Rather, various organizational or imaginal elaborations seem to promote memorizing, as we shall see later. In any event, that rehearsal helps at all may not be due to its providing an opportunity for the system to transmit information to LTM about an item, but may rather be because rehearsal itself constitutes practice at retrieving the item from memory, and perhaps it is this retrieval practice that is beneficial. Fourth, there is really little strong qualitative evidence that requires the sequential view that residence of an item in STM is a necessary prerequisite for establishing its trace in LTM. Most of the STM evidence is quite compatible with the notion of two *parallel* stores; that is, the input item would be recorded simultaneously in two separate stores (an STM and an LTM) with the two traces having different decay constants (see Shallice & Warrington, 1970). Fifth, the STM-LTM models are for the most part rather vague regarding the way in which new information arriving in STM is first compared to material stored in LTM, so as to assess what is old and what is new about the current input. This identification enables the learner to shunt aside redundant material he already knows and to concentrate on the new information to be learned. Thus, if I already know that "John Smith is a thief," then I need not spend further time on that subproposition when I am asked to remember "John Smith is a thief but nonetheless a good father." The new predicate "is a good father" is extracted from the input, and attached in memory to my former concept of John Smith, the thief. But this sifting and selection among the input propositions to determine what is old (i.e., is already retrievable from memory) and what is new would seem to require much more interaction between the "two stores" than is envisioned in the "boxes" diagram. Sixth, the boxes approach does not easily accommodate to the finding that the subject's later incidental memory for some items depends upon the "depth of processing" he had given to the item as it was presented (see Craik, 1973; Craik & Lockhart, 1972; Hyde & Jenkins, 1969). Having the subject categorize a word semantically ("It is a flower") produces better delayed recall than having him tag it in terms of its superficial features ("It is printed in capital letters"; "It rhymes with *bank*"). Perhaps some of the differential properties ascribed to STM versus LTM (see Glanzer, 1972; Murdock, 1972) have to do with strategic variation by the subject in this "depth of processing"; items that the person expects to retain only briefly may be processed only superficially, in terms of their physical characteristics rather than in terms of the semantic referents for which they are symbols. These are questions which future research will be addressing and trying to answer.

Organization and Memory

In reviewing Gestalt theory in Chapter 8, we discussed the role Gestalt theorists assigned to organization as a determinant of memory and recall. We reviewed there several findings concerned with the coherence in memory of elements organized together by various conditions of grouping. The Gestalt view was that the perceptual or conceptual groupings of the material would become the "psychological units" in memory and recall.

This theme was echoed in a seminal paper by G. A. Miller (1956) in which he suggested, among other things, that immediate reproductive memory would be limited in terms of the number of "chunks" of elements rather than the number of single elements. Thus, a list of 7 two-syllable words is remembered just as well as one of 7 one-syllable words or of 7 single letters, because they are all treated as single units. The psychological unit is that amount of material which the person already knows (e.g., a word or cliché).

The conjecture was that immediate recall was limited to about 7 or so chunks. In this view, the way a person learns a longer list, say of 14 unrelated words, is to *organize* the lower-order units into 7 or fewer higher-order units or "chunks." Learning, then, was to be viewed as a matter of segregating, classifying, and grouping the elementary units into a smaller number of richer, more densely packed chunks.

This hypothesis, along with several others, motivated research on *free recall* and later on mnemonic devices. In free recall, as exemplified in the Rundus experiment reviewed above (see Figure 15.6), the subject is exposed to a list of words and then tries to recall as many of them as he can in any order. What is "free" about free recall is the order in which the person recalls the items from the set to be remembered. Such latitude permits us to attribute any systematic stereotypy and patterning of the subject's recall to the organizational processes the subject uses to learn the material. It may be noted that free recall does not obviously fit the standard stimulus-response paradigm, since there is no specific stimulus, only the unhelpful injunction from the experimenter to recall the word list just presented.

Starting with seminal papers by Bousfield (1953), Tulving (1962, 1966, 1968), and G. Mandler (1967, 1968), free recall has been intensively studied as a test situation for revealing organizational processes in memory. A recent book edited by Tulving and Donaldson (1972) reviews and evaluates many branches on a large research tree regarding this topic. Investigations of free recall have shown repeatedly that subjects systematically group words together during recall despite the fact that these words were presented far apart during the input of the list. The subject's groupings most often tend to be on the basis of the words' similarity of meaning, i.e., their semantic associations. If the list is composed of words from several semantic categories (e.g., animals, cities, vegetables, cars), the words belonging to a given category will be especially likely to be grouped together during recall. On this hypothesis, the effect of repeated practice on a list of words is to increase the size and stability of these "subjective groups," which are sets comprised of several list words each. If the subject is forced to change his groupings every time he studies the list (by having him form mental images to represent varying quartets of list items), then improvement in his recall of that list is seriously retarded (see G. H. Bower, 1970b). It appears that inter-item grouping of list words is both necessary and sufficient to promote free-recall learning: simple exposure to a list of words without instructions to learn promotes very little free recall (Tulving, 1966), whereas having the person simply sort the list words into categories on the basis of meaningful similarities promotes as good incidental recall later as when he is told to learn the words during sorting (G. Mandler, 1967). Such results suggest the view that learning is accomplished by *organizing* the materials.

As noted earlier, the "constant chunk" hypothesis is that immediate recall cannot exceed a constant number of chunks (four to eight—the hypothetical number varies from one theorist to another). If the number of chunks becomes too large, they will have to be grouped in turn into a hierarchy of higher-order units. Figure 15.7 shows a hypothetical hierarchy of subjective units. The words of the list are indexed as W_1 through W_{27}. The nodes

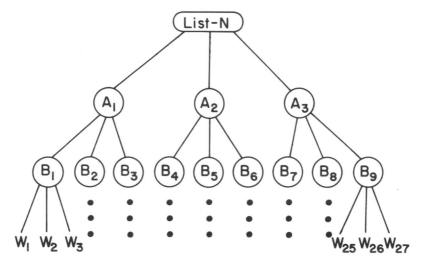

Figure 15.7.   Illustrative hierarchy of higher-level chunks, encompassing into groups the 27 list word indexed W_1, W_2, . . . , W_{27}. The B_i index groups of words; the A_i index groups of B groups. The top node, list N, stands for the entire list in memory.

marked B_i are internal names, nodes, or codes in memory which stand for the word groups they dominate in the hierarchy; the A_i nodes stand for a collection of B_i nodes. This is the presumptive memory structure.

The important thing about such a hierarchy is that the top node (code, chunk) can serve as the name held in short-term memory standing for the complete information structure in long-term memory. Thus, list N could be retrieved by cueing the subject with "List N" (or having him cue himself); this cue can then be "associatively unpacked" in terms of chunks A_1, A_2, and A_3; the A_i can be unpacked in terms of the B_i, which then lead to generation of the words on the list. Johnson (1970) provides the most explicit model and tests of how a hierarchical memory structure could be retrieved. Johnson's tests involved *serial* recall of chunked (grouped) letter series, but his general model can be applied to unordered, free recall.

A hierarchy can be a powerful retrieval scheme, since it can readily span a number of elements (27 or 3^3 in the small hierarchy shown in Figure 15.7). Moreover, G. H. Bower et al. (1969) showed that free-recall subjects greatly benefited from having their word lists "preorganized" for them in a hierarchical fashion revealing the semantic hierarchies available in the carefully constructed word lists. The subjects appeared to use the hierarchical tree as a retrieval plan, starting at the top and unpacking successive levels in recursive fashion. Although these are interesting demonstrations of the power of hierarchical organizations in memory, they in no way prove that this is what subjects are in fact doing while they are learning lists of allegedly "unrelated" words. Regarding that issue, the jury is still out. Recent computer simulation models of free recall (J. R. Anderson, 1972; G. H. Bower, 1972c) are explicitly *not* hierarchical in their basic character. The papers cited should be consulted for details.

Mnemonic Devices

With the growing interest in organizational factors in memory, it was perhaps inevitable that psychologists would turn to the analysis of mnemonic devices. Mnemonic devices are those which enable the person to enrich or elaborate upon the material to be learned, all with the aim of helping him to remember it better. They typically help the person to classify and organize the material. There are a variety of mnemonic devices, varying according to the types of materials and recall requirements for which they are appropriate, and a number of semipopular books describe many of these (e.g., Furst, 1958; M. N. Young & Gibson, 1966).

One mnemonic device that has been analyzed extensively (e.g., G. H. Bower, 1970b) is the "pegword" method for learning ordered lists of items such as shopping lists, errands, historical events, sets of laws in psychology, etc. The technique is briefly illustrated in Table 15.3. The person first learns a list of rhyming pegwords, pairing concrete images with the first 20 or so integers. In learning a new list of items, the person then uses successive pegwords as imagined pegs upon which to hook the successive items of the list. As the first list word occurs (*cigar*), the person is to call to mind his first pegword, and form a mental image of some vivid scene of interaction between the two objects. Examples are shown in the right-hand column in Table 15.3. The images may be as bizarre as one wishes—their effectiveness seems independent of that aspect. This same procedure for imaginal pairing is followed for each of the list words in turn. To revive the list in memory, the person needs only to go through his already well-learned list of pegwords, and as he considers each one in turn he tries to re-create or recall the imaginal scene elaborated around that pegword image; from this remembered scene, he can usually name the desired item ("cigar").

This and similar schemes are exceedingly effective, at least in comparison to normal free recall of subjects not taught to use any special tricks. Recall might be improved by a factor of two or three times as much as normal. One of the main reasons the device works so well is that the person has a systematic *retrieval scheme*; he knows how to cue himself with the items (the pegwords) to which he has explicitly associated the list words as they were presented. The usual free-recall subject, on the other hand, simply does not know how to remind himself of all the list words he knows. We know that

Table 15.3   **Illustration of first four pegword images and their use in learning the first four items on a shopping list.**

Pegword	List Word	Mnemonic Image
one—bun	cigar	bun smoking a cigar
two—shoe	butter	spreading butter on shoe sole
three—tree	chicken	chicken sitting up in a tree
four—door	nails	hammering nails into front door
.	.	.
.	.	.
.	.	.

if we give the ordinary subject various hints, especially semantic clues ("One of the list words was a dairy food"), he can recall a great deal more than he can free-recall on his own (see Tulving & Pearlstone, 1966; Tulving & Psotka, 1971). The advantage for the pegword user, therefore, is partly the result of his knowing how to systematically cue each of the words from each input-list position. The second advantage of the pegword method undoubtedly stems from its deployment of mnemonic imagery. Since mental imagery has become a topic of recent concern in research on human memory, we will briefly review some of that research.

Mental Imagery

Mental imagery, or the "pictures of the mind's eye," was one of those introspectionist concepts that John Watson and other radical behaviorists found no use for in an objective psychology. Not that they denied the subjective experiences people describe as "having images"; rather, they argued that "public behavior" had to be analyzed first in its own right rather than only as an index of the subjective counterpart—which, in the behaviorists' lexicon, might just be excess baggage anyway. In any event, and for whatever reason, human memory came to be viewed through the somewhat distorted lenses of "verbal-motor habits" (see Watson, 1924b; Hull et al., 1940). In their classic and monumental survey of the field of human learning, McGeoch and Irion (1952) did not even mention the topic of mental imagery or imagination or visualization.

The tide has clearly turned, and "mental imagery" is now a popular research topic. This turnabout has been caused partly by the aforementioned splinter movement of "memory researchers" away from the "verbal learning" movement. Sustained and effective arguments have been given (see G. H. Bower, 1972b; Cooper & Shepard, 1973; Paivio, 1971; Richardson, 1969) for recognizing mental imagery (or the "imaginal system") as one of the primary modes of representation of information in memory, and a variety of features have been suggested for distinguishing the imaginal from the verbal-symbolic mode of representation. For example, the imagery system seems specialized for dealing with information presented simultaneously, in parallel, from sources distributed about in space, whereas the verbal system would appear specialized for dealing with information presented sequentially, in series, from sources distributed over time. In brief, the imagery system (particularly *visual* imagery) represents information as distributed in space, whereas the verbal system deals best with information distributed in time.

A large number of learning experiments have now been done indicating that imaginal and/or pictorial representation of information usually facilitates memory, by factors ranging from 1.5 to 3 or so. For example, students told to concoct mental images so as to learn arbitrary pairs of concrete words will recall about 1.5 to 2 times more paired-associates than will uninstructed controls. In extensive studies examining various attributes of words and how a person's learning of the words varies with these attributes, Paivio (1971) and his associates have found that the concreteness of a word's referent (or the vividness of the imagery it arouses) is the most powerful predictor of the word's memorability. This generalization held true in a variety of verbal learning tasks, even when the imagery concreteness of words was compared to such other measures as meaningfulness, number of associations, familiarity, emotionality, and semantic-differential ratings. Moreover, standard verbal learning results that historically have been attributed to verbal factors like word meaningfulness may in actuality be due to an imagery effect (see Paivio, 1971, for examples), since imagery correlates fairly highly with a word's meaningfulness or the number of associates it elicits.

Why are pictures, then images, and then concrete words remembered in that order, with all remembered so much better than abstract words? The current conjecture is what is called the "dual-trace" hypothesis (see G. H. Bower, 1972b; Paivio, 1971). It supposes that there are two distinguishably different forms of representation, the imaginal and the verbal, and that concepts within these systems are usually closely connected, much like equivalent words in two languages (e.g., French and English). When a word to be remembered is shown, the subject enters a memory trace of that event in his verbal store. If it is a concrete word, then the corresponding nodes (concepts) in the imaginal system are activated, the person "experiences the corresponding imagery," and a trace of the event is laid down in the imagery system. So a word (or word pair) that is imaged or a picture that is named has the advantage of having two, redundant copies of the memory trace laid down. The redundancy prolongs memory in comparison to abstract items, since the second, imaginal trace is likely to survive after the initial, verbal trace has decayed. That is, not only are there two traces, but the one in the imaginal system seems more resistant to forgetting.

Although this is not a particularly deep or revealing hypothesis, it has led to a lot of supportive research (e.g., Paivio, 1971; Paivio & Csapo, 1972). It has also guided a large number of practical efforts to use imagery, pictorial representations, and special audiovisual aids in boosting learning in primary school settings (e.g., Jensen & Rohwer, 1970; Rohwer, 1970). It now seems reasonably certain that all efforts at audiovisual instruction, plus teaching the pupil techniques of mnemonic elaboration and imagery of materials to be learned, are likely to maximize the amount of learning obtainable within the least time, and with the least repetitive drill and difficulty. However, much research is still going on to further clarify the relation between imagery and language, particularly the role imagery has to play in conceptions of semantic meaning.

EPISODIC VERSUS SEMANTIC MEMORY

As is perhaps becoming apparent to the student, investigators of human memory like to propose distinctions between various types of memories—short term versus long term, acoustic versus visual, imaginal versus verbal, and many more unmentionables. These are helpful classifications in delimiting the domain over which empirical generalizations may be true; they are also quite heuristic in suggesting new questions to investigate as well as new answers to old questions. Most often such distinctions evolve gradually out of a body of experimental work, when the investigators realize that they are dealing with memory phenomena that differ in critical properties from those ascribed to other regular memories.

Tulving (1972) has recently summarized and stated such a distinction now prevalent in memory research, namely, that between *episodic* memory and *semantic* memory. To quote Tulving,

> Let us think of episodic and semantic memory as two information processing systems that (a) selectively receive information from perceptual systems or other cognitive systems, (b) retain various aspects of this information, and (c) upon instructions transmit specific retained information to other systems, including those responsible for translating it into behavior and conscious awareness. The two systems differ from one another in terms of (a) the nature of stored information, (b) autobiographical versus cognitive reference, (c) conditions and consequences of retrieval, and probably also in terms of (d) their vulnerability to interference resulting in transformation and erasure of stored information, and (e) their dependence upon each other. In addition, psychological research on episodic memory differs from that on semantic memory in several respects. (1972, p. 385)

Thus, episodic memory records information about temporally dated events which have particular sensory attributes, and which always have autobiographical reference. Examples would be that I remember just having heard thunder, or I remember seeing a bear in Yellowstone Park last summer, or I remember that the word *rug* appeared next to the number 14 in the list of pairs I just studied. A specification of semantic memory is as follows:

> Semantic memory is the memory necessary for the use of language. It is a mental thesaurus, organized knowledge a person possesses about words and other verbal symbols, their meaning and referents, about relations among them, and about rules, formulas, and algorithms for the manipulation of these symbols, concepts, and relations. Semantic memory does not register perceptible properties of inputs, but rather cognitive referents of input signals. The semantic system permits the retrieval of information that was not directly stored in it, and retrieval of information from the system leaves its contents unchanged, although any act of retrieval constitutes an input into episodic memory. The semantic system is probably much less susceptible to involuntary transformation and loss of information than the episodic system. Finally, the semantic system may be quite independent of the episodic system in recording and maintaining information since identical storage consequences may be brought about by a great variety of input signals. (Tulving, 1972, p. 386)

Typically, semantic memories are in "long-term memory," have lost all autobiographical reference or information about their mode or context of learning, and would be said to constitute part of our permanent knowledge. Examples of semantic knowledge are verbal relations like "Lions are mammals," "*Man* means *male human*"; facts like "Chicago is in Illinois"; laws like "A physical object cannot be located in two places at once"; and inference rules like "If object A is with object B, and A is located at place C, then B is also located at place C."

It takes little reflection to note that nearly all laboratory research on memory has been exclusively concerned with episodic memory. The subject is exposed to a series of discrete events (presentations of words or pictures in a list), and later is tested for the verbatim *accuracy* of his reproduction or identification of it. Most often the cue for reproduction refers to the temporal-spatial context of the events to be recalled, as in "Recall the names of the pictures you just saw in the experimental list." Of course, in encoding or learning events, the person may make use of knowledge in his semantic store. For example, if in a list of paired-associates the subject sees the pair *robin-bird*, that is already a preestablished relation in his semantic memory. In this case, then, he need only tag this old, known relation with the new autobiographical information that it was presented in a particular experimental context.

Context, Recency, and Frequency Judgments

Events recorded in episodic memory are presumed to contain some description of their context of presentation. This context contains not only the perceptual characteristics of the item's physical mode of presentation but also such incidental matters as *where* and *when* it was said or done and *by whom*. We may think of these contextual elements as features associated to the internal representation of the event, features that are potentially retrievable when the person is asked to remember or recognize the event (see J. R. Anderson & Bower, 1972a). Experiments have indeed shown that subjects automatically record all sorts of such incidental information; for instance, they can remember whether a word was presented visually or auditorily, whether it was spoken by a male or female voice, whether it was presented as a word or a picture, whether it was presented on the left or right display screen, and so on (e.g., see Light et al., 1973). Of special interest is that subjects can also judge how *recently in time* a given event occurred. Since such recency judgments obviously involve remembering, the main theories to explain recency judgments have been concerned with memory (see Hinrichs, 1970; Ornstein, 1969). One model that does a reasonably serviceable job supposes that presentation of an item establishes an association to a set of contextual elements and that the strength of this association declines systematically over time as other events are interpolated. When the item is re-presented for test, the person assesses the item's strength in memory, and on this basis decides on a recency-of-experience judgment for it. On this theory, one expects that items that are presented several times to strengthen their memory trace will, as a consequence, tend to be judged as having occurred more recently than weaker, once-presented items. Although this model has certain obvious faults, a better way to conceptualize recency judgments from memory is not yet obvious.

Another type of information available from episodic memory is the *frequency* with which an event has occurred in a given context, or the frequency with which events of a general class or type have occurred. An example of the first type would be the judgment that the word *dog* appeared three times scattered throughout an input list of words; an example of the second would be the judgment that there were approximately six animals mentioned in the input list. People are fairly accurate in these sorts of judgments regarding event memories whether or not they know during the study trial that such frequency information will be tested. The prevailing hypothesis regarding how frequency judgments are implemented in episodic memory is that subjects try to retrieve and count the different local contexts in which the test item has occurred (see J. R. Anderson & Bower, 1972a). Something like this counting process occurs for small frequencies (say, six or less), but a "retrieval sampling-plus-estimation" procedure is used for higher frequencies (e.g., comparing frequencies of occurrence of gasoline stations versus delicatessens in America).

One of the significant applications of this context-retrieval technique has been to the issue of deciding how repetition of an event improves its recall. There have been essentially two alternative proposals regarding why repetition enhances memory. One view is that a second presentation makes contact with and *strengthens* the trace of the initial presentation of the item, and recall reflects this enhanced memory strength. The other is that the second presentation lays down further information about the initial event, information detailing the context of its occurrence. Recall then improves because the person has more access routes to the event information or because the event information has been "multiply copied" in connection with several retrieval cues. An experiment by Hintzman and Block (1971) provides striking evidence for the latter view. They found that subjects could retrieve differential and veridical information about the successive repetitions of a single item. Following presentation of a 100-item list, for instance, subjects would be able to remember accurately that the word *dog* appeared twice, that its first occurrence was visual and was in the initial fifth of the input list, while its second occurrence was auditory and was in the third fifth of the input list. Such discriminative information could not be provided by a mechanism which deals with repetition by simply incrementing a "habit strength" for the word *dog*. It is instructive to point out that this very question of how the memory deals with repetition could not even have been clearly posed, let alone answered, within the framework of S-R behaviorism with its emphasis on verbal habits. This illustrates the type of questions of concern to "memory theorists" today.

Semantic Memory

As noted earlier, semantic memory includes our knowledge of word meanings, of our language, of procedures for doing things (e.g., "action recipes"), and strategies for solving problems; it also includes our factual knowledge about the world, its individual events, personages, places, and laws. The domain is simply too vast to begin to enumerate exhaustively. Studies of semantic memory are just now in the formative, groping stages, but certain questions are clearly dominating the research on the topic. One question concerns the way in which the information in memory is organized. A second issue concerns how the mind gains access to particularly relevant information and retrieves it in the course of answering a question. Another issue concerns how already known information is used for detecting redundancy in newly arriving inputs in order to decide what is really novel and should be recorded in memory. A further and critical issue is how we would try to represent, in our psychological theories, the information which a person has regarding a particular domain of concepts. The decision on how to represent the subject's knowledge has implications regarding his behavior in answering questions or drawing inferences or performing effective actions with respect to that domain.

There are currently two major methods for representing semantic knowledge, both of which are exemplified in current computer simulation programs. One supposes that most knowledge can be represented as a *labeled graph structure*, wherein the points or nodes represent universal concepts ("dogs") or particular individuals ("Spot") and the links between nodes represent labeled semantic relationships between the concepts or individuals. We shall further elaborate this notion below. The second approach, represented largely in T. Winograd's (1972) program for language understanding (see Chapter 13), tries to represent concepts in terms of decision routines ("To decide if X is a Republican, first check to see if it has properties p, q, r, . . .") and to represent knowledge generally in terms of action recipes or procedures for how to bring about some consequence or make some decision. Thus, a simple universal statement like "All men are mortal" would be encoded in terms of a small program encoding a procedure—to wit, that should one ever wish to find out whether X is mortal, it is sufficient merely to prove that X is a man.

Psychologists have been more attracted by the former representations, those using networks of labeled semantic relationships, on the belief that action recipes are easily "written" from static knowledge of what is the case and what the person wants to achieve. (Curious how the refrains of the Tolman versus Guthrie debates regarding knowledge versus action keep echoing through later works!) Networks of labeled relations among semantic concepts are not really all that different from the earlier notions of the British associationists regarding how "complex ideas" were to be built up by associating simpler ideas together. What differs in the modern accounts is, first, the notion of the labeling of the association with the logical (or semantic) type it exemplifies; and, second, the notion that a complex idea need have no direct correspondence to an observable stimulus or response, and yet can still be represented as a single unit in memory, a unit about which further information can be predicted. For a detailed discussion of these philosophical points and their ramifications throughout associationistic psychology, see J. R. Anderson & Bower (1973, Chapters 2 and 4).

One elementary approach to representing concepts and meanings in terms of graph structures can be illustrated by a semantic memory model being developed by David Rumelhart, Peter Lindsay, and Donald Norman at the University of California at San Diego (see Rumelhart, Lindsay, & Norman, 1972; P. H. Lindsay & Norman, 1972). First, the model distinguishes between concepts and events. A concept corresponds roughly to an idea; a concept is introduced into the system by way of definitions which give its relations to other concepts in the system. Typically, we mention the type or more general class to which the concept belongs, we mention one or more distinguishing properties of the concept, and perhaps we list several examples or instances of the concept. Thus, Figure 15.8 shows the simplest graphic information defining the concept of a *bird*: it is a kind of animal, has feathers, has wings, can fly; examples of birds are robins, canaries, and so on. The number of properties, superordinates, and subordinates can be extended

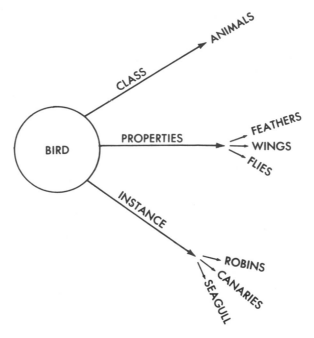

Figure 15.8.   Illustration of a labeled graph defining the concept of *bird*. The labeled associations point to properties, to supersets, and to subsets of the concept.

indefinitely. The elementary graph in Figure 15.8 exemplifies two aspects: that the relations are directional and that they are labeled. For example, we know that the relation of *bird* to *animal* is one of subordinate class (or "subset of").

A realistic memory, of course, contains many thousands of such concepts, each with very many connections, so that the actual topographical representation would look like a huge "wiring diagram." But a fantastic amount of information is inherently encoded in such graph structures. To see just a hint of this, consider the fragment of a semantic network surrounding the concept of a *tavern* as shown in Figure 15.9. This graph implicitly encodes the information that a tavern is a kind of business establishment (as is a drugstore), which has beer and wine, and Luigi's is an example of a tavern. It also gives some properties of beer, wine, and Luigi's. This is only a fragment, of course, and much more information could and would be in a realistic memory. But notice how very many questions one is enabled to answer with just this fragment. For example, it can answer questions that require chains of subset relations, such as that "Luigi's is an establishment" or that "A drugstore is a place." It can also read out the properties or classes that any two concepts have in common. Thus, if we ask the system to compare the similarities and differences of *wine* and *beer*, it would quickly find that the similarities are that they are both beverages sold at taverns, but one is made from fermented grain while the other is made from fermented fruit. The number of factual relationships derivable and possible

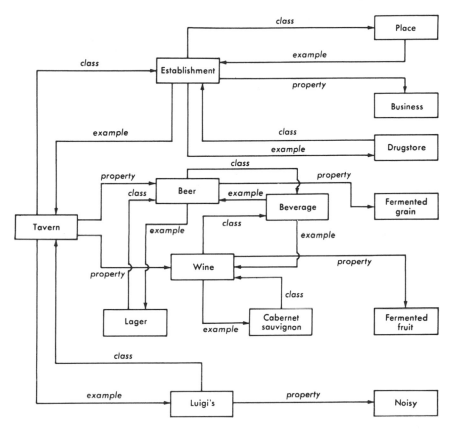

Figure 15.9. Fragment of a semantic network surrounding the concept of a *tavern*. The linkages between concepts are labeled according to their type. (From P. H. Lindsay & D. A. Norman, 1972. By permission.)

questions that can be answered increases exponentially as the number of encoded predicates or "bits of knowledge" increases.

Concepts and their definitions in terms of class, examples, and properties are quite serviceable for many purposes, but still further distinctions and rules are needed for building up second-order concepts from more elementary ones. Rumelhart et al. (1972) provide a set of such rules for forming second-order concepts, including rules of *qualification* (lamb → *young* sheep), *quantification* (crowd → *many* people), *location* (*under*water, *after*noon), and conjunction (ham *and* eggs). For encoding complete events, they use the notion of a *proposition*; the event is action based, denoting a scenario with agents, actions, and objects. For representing such events, Rumelhart et al. use the "Case Grammar" of the linguist Charles Fillmore (1968) as the formalism of their syntactic deep structure. Some of the major distinctions in Case Grammar are illustrated in Figure 15.10, which shows the proposed encoding of the event of the police rapidly chasing bank robbers with a car yesterday down Baker Street. The action centers around the main verb

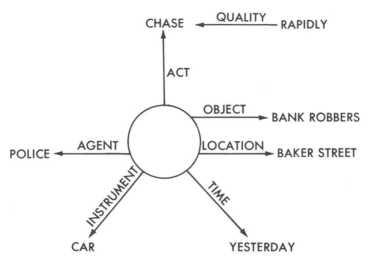

Figure 15.10.   A graph structure depicting Case Grammar relations among various nouns and the main verb. This graph is encoding in memory the event of the police rapidly chasing bank robbers in a car yesterday down Baker Street.

chased, which requires an agent (someone who performs the action), an object, and implicitly a means or instrument of the action. The act itself can be modified by an adverb of manner, such as *rapidly,* and time and location information can also be attached to the event. Linguistic propositions which we hear would have a similar encoding to that of actual events. Of course, most propositions we hear do not fill in so many details—they are elliptical or shortened in many ways by reference to earlier parts of an ongoing speech or dialogue.

It should be appreciated that such information structures as that shown in Figure 15.10 are assumed to be "anchored into" the already known concepts of memory (such as police, Baker Street, etc.): the new propositional information or event is simply a new set of temporary, labeled connections between these preexisting concepts. Once such a proposition is encoded and learned, the person can later use it to answer various questions. Questions typically specify *part* of the desired information, and leave blank the elements which are to be filled in by the answer. Questions such as, "What happened on Baker Street yesterday?" or, "How, where, and when did the police chase the bank robbers?" are rather like compound retrieval cues by which we probe the system for desired information. Most retrieval systems operate on a "pattern-matching" or similarity principle. The question is first analyzed into its Case Grammar format, and then memory is searched for the best-matching memory structure that can be found for the probe. Particular linkages between concepts in memory will be retrieved and used only when the relations among the concepts are the same as in the probe question. Thus, in answering questions about whom the police chased yesterday, the system will pass over facts about police and chasing that did not happen yesterday, and will also discard retrieved instances where the police might have been the objects rather than the agents of the chasing action (e.g., wild lions were loose and chasing policemen down Baker Street yesterday). If the original propositional information has been recorded ("learned") successfully, if the question probe stipulates sufficient retrieval cues, and if the memory search proceeds rapidly and efficiently enough, the simulation model should come up with the right answer to the question. At present, the system that has been most implemented and tested for psychological plausibility in this respect is one by J. R. Anderson and Bower (1973); however, it would take us too far afield to go into details of their theory and the range of psychological evidence they use to enhance its scientific credibility.

Two further matters require brief mention. First, it is understood that in such representational systems, entire propositions, once encoded, can now be treated as units in their own right, so that predications or comments can be made about them. For example, the system may record that "*John regrets that* such-and-such is true," that "such-and-such *is false*," or that "something happened *just in the nick of time*." Also, propositions can enter into propositional *conjunctions*, by the use of connectives like *and*, *then*, *while*, and *causes*. Thus, a sequence of events, as contained for instance in a story, would be recorded in memory as a chain of propositional events of the general form, "event 1, then (event 2 while event 3) cause event 4, then event 5. . . ."

The second matter to be mentioned is the issue of inference and deduction in question answering. Very often in discourse we are asked questions for which we do not have answers directly stored; rather, we must interpret the question and then try to infer the answer from other things we know. Thus we can answer the query, "Did Aristotle have a liver?" by retrieving the relevant facts that Aristotle was a human, and all humans have a liver, and by then applying the logical rule that a property true of a whole class is true of each member of the class. Similarly, if asked whether any part of the country of Chile is cold, we might retrieve the fact that the high Andes Mountains run through Chile and that the tops of mountains are usually cold; so even if Chile is near the equator, it still probably has some very cold locations. In this last illustration, the inference is starting to look more like "problem-solving," where a number of different facts have to be retrieved and their combination evaluated in order to come up with an answer. (For more discussion of question-answering, see Chapter 13.) Although each of us has developed a varied and complex repertoire for solving such inferential problems, psychologists still do not understand how to write a program to simulate the way the person does this. At present, we are still groping about, beginning to collect and classify protocols and types of question-answering procedures (see J. R. Anderson & Bower, 1973; Collins & Quillian, 1972; Meyer, 1970; D. A. Norman, 1972).

The Future of Such Models

It is not possible in a brief survey to provide the full rationale, intuitive evidence, and motivation underlying the work on models of semantic information processing. The book by J. R. Anderson and Bower (1973) or the papers by Kintsch (1972) and by Rumelhart et al. (1972) should be consulted for the underlying rationales. However, several comments are appropriate regarding the significance of these theories. First, they are theories which for the first time bring learning research into rather direct and fruitful contact with research in linguistics and psycholinguistics. It has always seemed that any sensible reconstruction of human memory must be able to make some reasonable remarks about how language is used to learn and to remember propositions, episodes, stories, plays, factual materials, and the like. But S-R theory and the "verbal learning" tradition have not built sturdy bridges from their laboratory base to the problem of the understanding of language; the persuasive and devastating criticisms of those older accounts made by the linguist Noam Chomsky, and by his associates, were reviewed in Chapter 7. Psycholinguistics as an intellectual movement was largely born out of Chomsky's critiques as well as his systematic insights about language. While psycholinguistics has been a most vigorous research area, it has remained largely divorced from the more traditional research on human memory (e.g., for reviews, see G. A. Miller & McNeill, 1969, or Slobin, 1971). These new theories of semantic memory reviewed briefly above provide common grounds of contact and mutual interest between psycholinguistics, artificial intelligence, and the experimental psychology of memory. This is exemplified, for example, in the book by J. R. Anderson and Bower (1973) which explicitly reviews and combines research work in these several areas. They propose a theory of an operational system for cognition (realized as a computer simulation program) which (1) carries out a linguistic analysis of sentences given to the system, (2) provides a means for looking up what is already known about the newly arriving information so as to decide what parts of old memories can be reused in recording the new information, (3) provides a mathematical description of the process by which new informational structures such as that in Figure 15.10 are acquired, and (4) describes and experimentally tests a plausible retrieval mechanism whereby a question or retrieval probe gains access to information that is relevant to constructing an answer. Practically all of the experimental evidence cited by Anderson and Bower as favoring their model comes from their own and others' research on memory for propositional materials, on confusion errors in sentence recognition memory, on difficulties people experience in comprehending sentences and in verifying sentences against pictures or known facts, and on distortions of memory for thematically related textual materials. However, they also make very explicit efforts to show how their theory stems from the associationist tradition in psychology, how the theory would operate in standard verbal learning tasks, and how it encompasses the standard results supporting the interference theory of transfer and forgetting. The significance of the Anderson and Bower book is its detailed and serious attempt to bring together these two research areas and two traditions (associative memory and psycholinguistics), and to place in perspective their respective contributions to understanding human memory.

As mentioned earlier, theoretical work on models of long-term memory is still in the formative, searching stage (see Freija, 1972, for a review). Without doubt this is an area that will undergo a tremendous upswing in scientific activity within the next decade, and the modest theories being tentatively offered currently will probably soon be outdistanced. But the important thing about the development is that it represents the "coming home" finally of the prodigal psychologist to the tough but fascinating problems of understanding how the human mind uses its linguistic knowledge and intellectual skills in learning and remembering. Such problems cannot be avoided indefinitely; the promise of recent models of semantic memory and question-answering is that they are at least leading us once again into these paths, to ask the significant and fundamental questions. The road is rocky and progress is difficult; but we have the assurance that we are studying fundamental processes of the intellect. The development of performance models for language comprehension and memory, and their utilization, may very well constitute the number one problem for cognitive psychology in the coming decade.

SOCIAL LEARNING THEORY

A book such as this one which reviews different theoretical approaches must give the impression that the present theoretical scene is seriously fragmented into a multitude of warring camps, all in contention for dominance. But that impression is terribly misleading; indeed, nothing could be further from the truth. Although disagreement exists within almost any collection of scientists, among learning theorists the disagreements usually concern not basic findings or fundamental principles but rather the interpretation to be placed upon certain facts. Within the contemporary scene in learning theory, disagreements are not over fundamentals except for the major division that still remains between Skinnerian behaviorists and cognitive psychologists. These two approaches involve somewhat different methodological orientations, different commitments regarding the proper subject matter of psychology, and different restrictions on what kinds of theories are admissible. This distinction was discussed in our review of Skinner's position (Chapter 7), and of the "behavior modification" movement within clinical and educational psychology which has derived its impetus from operant conditioning concepts. The reader may have gotten the impression that modern cognitive psychology (see P. H. Lindsay & Norman, 1972; Neisser, 1967) deals only with human memory and perceptual processes and not with other factors such as motivation, reward, and contingency management of behavior. But this is not true. Social learning theory, a systematic position advanced by Bandura (1969, 1971a, 1971b) and many others (e.g., Mischel, 1968; N. E. Miller & Dollard, 1941; Rotter, 1954), tries to provide a more balanced synthesis of cognitive psychology with the principles of behavior modification. It is a selective distillation of what is probably a "consensus" position of moderation on many issues of importance to any theory of learning and behavior modification. Social learning theory not only deals with the usual set of learning principles but also adds several new ones, and attempts to describe in detail how a set of social and personal competences (so-called personality) could evolve out of the social conditions within which this important learning occurs. It also deals rather explicitly with techniques of "personality assessment" (Mischel, 1968) and behavior modification in clinical and educational settings (Bandura, 1969; Krumboltz & Thoresen, 1969).

Although the social learning theorist accepts the usual injunctions of the behaviorist against invoking psychodynamic "inner causes" of disturbed behavior, he tempers the injunction with a counteremphasis on man's cognitive-symbolic functioning in acquiring new behaviors and in regulating the frequency and occasions of their appearance.

A valid criticism of the extreme behavioristic position is that, in a vigorous effort to eschew spurious inner causes, it neglected determinants of man's behavior arising from his cognitive functioning. Man is a thinking organism possessing capabilities that provide him with some power of self-direction. To the extent that traditional behavioral theories could be faulted, it was for providing an incomplete rather than an inaccurate account of human behavior. The social learning theory places special emphasis on the important roles played by vicarious, symbolic, and self-regulatory processes. (Bandura, 1971a, p. 2)

As is well known, the traditional theories of learning had placed great emphasis on learning by direct experience, by the application of reinforcement contingencies to practiced responses. This is wrapped up in the notions of "learning by doing," of response differentiation, and of the shaping of complex behavior chains by successive approximation. Social learning theory accepts such shaping principles although it tends (much as did Tolman) to see the role of rewards in this process as both conveying information about the optimal response in the situation and as providing incentive motivation for a given act because of the anticipated reward. And in contrast to the learning-by-doing emphasis, social learning theory holds that a large amount of human learning is done *vicariously*, through *observing* another person making the skilled responses (or reading about it or viewing pictures of it) and then by trying to imitate the response of the model. By this means, the observer can often learn and some time later perform novel responses without ever having made them before or having been reinforced for them (since they have never occurred before). It is obvious that many human skills (e.g., pronunciation of foreign words) could not be acquired at all without this observational learning, and that most other skills, such as driving, which *could* be learned laboriously (though dangerously) by reinforcing successive approximations alone, are in practice taught more efficiently through verbal instructions and demonstrations by a "model performer." Although these teaching techniques are used routinely and are familiar to all of us, the reader should realize how very discrepant they actually are from the paradigm of training recommended by exclusive use of operant reinforcement procedures.

Observational Learning

In a fertile series of research papers and books, Bandura (1962, 1965, 1969, 1971a, 1971b) has pointed out the ubiquity and efficiency of such observational learning in humans and has emphasized its unique features not found in the standard paradigms of shaping and instrumental conditioning. He has also carried out an admirable series of studies, mostly with young children, that throw light on the variables influencing such observational learning.

In the typical experiment, a kindergarten child (the subject) sits and watches some person (the model) perform a particular behavioral sequence. Later the subject is tested under specified conditions to determine to what extent his behavior now mimics that displayed by the model. What he does is compared to what control subjects who are tested without having observed the model do. A number of factors can be varied in this situation, and many are shown to affect the extent of imitative behavior performed by the subject. We list a few of those studied by Bandura:

A. Stimulus properties of the model
   1. The model's age, sex, and status relative to that of the subject are varied. High-status models are more imitated.
   2. The model's similarity to the subject: the model may be either another child in the same room, or a child in a movie, or an animal character in a movie cartoon, etc. Imitation induced in the subject decreases as the model is made more dissimilar to a real person.
B. Type of behavior exemplified by the model
   1. Novel skills are compared to novel sequences of known responses. The more complex the skills, the poorer the degree of imitation after one observation trial.
   2. Hostile or aggressive responses. These are imitated to a high degree.
   3. Standards of self-reward for good versus bad performances. The subject will adopt self-reward standards similar to those of the model. Also, the subject will imitate the type of moral standards exhibited by an adult model. Techniques of self-control can be transmitted in this manner.
C. Consequences of model's behavior
   1. Whether the model's behavior is rewarded, punished, or "ignored" (neither reinforced nor punished) by other agents in the drama is varied. Rewarded behaviors of the model are more likely to be imitated.
D. Motivational set given to the subject
   1. Instructions given to the subject before he observes the model provide him with high or low motivation to pay attention to and learn the model's behavior. High motivation might be produced by telling the subject that he will be rewarded commensurate with how much of the model's behavior he can reproduce on a later test. Under minimal instructions, learning is classified mainly as "incidental."
   2. Motivating instructions may be given after the subject views the model and before he is tested. This aids in distinguishing learning from performance of imitative responses.

This listing of variables in the observational learning situation is hardly exhaustive, and is intended only to show the range of possibilities. A wide range of behaviors can be transmitted under these conditions by the model, and the fidelity of the subject's mimicry (even under incidental learning conditions) is often remarkable.

As mentioned above, the model's behavior is more often imitated when the model has been rewarded rather than punished. Bandura was able to show that this reward-punishment variable affected the subject's *performance* of imitative responses but not his *learning* of them. After the observation trial, attractive rewards were offered to the subjects if they would reproduce the model's responses. This increased the display of imitative responses and totally wiped out the differential effect of having seen a rewarded versus a punished model. Thus it was found that the observer had learned the "bad guy's" responses even though he did not perform them until the incentive to do so was offered.

Mechanisms of Observational Learning

The mechanisms required for such observational learning have begun to be rather extensively analyzed by Bandura and his associates. A recent volume (Bandura, 1971b) describes the research, but it can be briefly noted and contrasted to the Skinnerian view (see Gewirtz & Stingle, 1968). The operant conditioning analysis of modeling relies on the standard three-term paradigm S^d-R-S^r, where S^d denotes the modeling stimulus (e.g., the model touching his left ear), R denotes the overt matching response performed by the observer, and S^r denotes the reinforcement provided by some agent for matching ("imitative") responses. As Bandura says about this paradigmatic reconstruction:

The scheme above does not appear applicable to observational learning where an observer does not overtly perform the model's responses in the setting in which they are exhibited, reinforcements are not administered either to the model or to the observer, and whatever responses have been thus acquired are not displayed for days, weeks, or even months. Under these conditions, which represent one of the most prevalent forms of social learning, two of the factors ($R \rightarrow S^r$) in the three-element paradigm are absent during acquisition, and the third factor (S^d, or modeling stimulus) is typically missing from the situation when the observationally learned response is first performed. . . . Skinner's analysis clarifies how similar behavior that a person has previously learned can be prompted by the actions of others and the prospect of reward. However, it does not explain how a new matching response is acquired observationally in the first place . . . such learning occurs through symbolic processes during exposure to the modeled activities before any responses have been performed or reinforced.[1]

In his analysis of observational learning, Bandura emphasizes four interrelated subprocesses. First are *attentional* processes: the model stimulus must be attended to by the subject if he is to learn from the model; a number of factors are known to influence this attention, including, for example, the past functional value of attention to models of a particular type and competence. Second are *retention* processes, and the study of these has been the special province of researchers on human memory. If the model's behavior is to exert influence upon the observer's behavior at a much later point in time, then the model's behavior as a stimulus event has to be coded, symbolically represented, and retained over that interval.

To elaborate on this latter point, observational learning in humans involves two representational systems—an imaginal and a verbal one. During exposure to modeling stimuli, sequences of corresponding sensory experiences (images) occur and appear to become associated or integrated by mere contiguity; for example, see the discussion in Chapter 3 of F. D. Sheffield's (1961) analysis of the learning of "perceptual blueprints." Later, the revival of the integrated sensory experiences will guide the observer's behavior in imitation. The abundant research on mental imagery in human memory (reviewed earlier in this chapter) lends special credence to this form of cognitive maps. The second representational system, verbal coding, can be designed to be of varying levels of efficiency. At the simplest level, once verbal labels ("names") are available for the subject, he can describe to himself the model's behavior as it unfolds, and can then rehearse and learn these verbal descriptions. Their later recall can serve as cues for directing or guiding the subject through the imitative responses. An experiment by Bandura, Grusec, and Menlove (1966) manipulated this factor by having children view a model (shown in a film) under three different conditions. In one, the subject verbalized aloud the sequence of novel responses performed by the model. In another, the subject was instructed merely to observe carefully. In the third, the subject was required to count rapidly while watching the film, and this presumably interfered with his implicitly verbalizing and learning the model's behavior. A later performance test, under either high or low incentive for imitation, showed the three groups ranked in the order in which we listed them in their ability to imitate the model's behavior. That is, subjects who described in words the model's behaviors learned best, and those who had to engage in the interfering counting task during observation learned the least.

Related experiments by Bandura and Jeffery (1973) and by Gerst (1971) pretrained subjects to use a special vocabulary for verbally coding complex perceptual events. In the Bandura and Jeffery experiment, the subject learned a verbal name for each of several two-component movements describing the model person's path in moving a stylus through a visual maze; the criterion task required the subject to learn and reproduce a sequence of 12 movements (6 two-link movements). In Gerst's study, subjects were taught labels for components of the manual sign language of the deaf, and were then compared to nonpretrained subjects in their ability to learn from a visual demonstration of hand signs how to reproduce a set of signs. As would be expected, subjects who had been taught a special verbal code for specific components of the movements of the model easily segmented the criterion modeled sequence into these components, labeled them, rehearsed the labels, and were far superior to untrained controls in their later ability to reproduce the model's criterion performance.

None of this is surprising, especially not to researchers who study the role of cognitive representations in human memory. The experimental situation is really not much different from the typical laboratory study in verbal learning where a subject observes verbal items exposed by a memory drum and later recites them back (and if they are familiar patterns—words—they are more easily acquired than if they are unfamiliar nonsense). To a large extent also, variables similar to those found to influence verbal learning will apply to learning by observation (e.g., competitive sources of control, proactive and retroactive interference, complexity of the material, etc.). That is, if the subject is exposed to a "cast" of several models performing several different actions, we can well expect him (as does the paired-associate learner) to become confused in remembering which model did what performance with what consequences.

To return to Bandura's analysis of imitative learning, the third subprocess he emphasizes is *motoric reproduction* skills. A child or adult may know "cognitively" and roughly what is to be done (can "recognize" a correct performance) but nonetheless be relatively unskilled at the performance itself. Skilled acts like auto driving, ballet dancing, or golfing typically require many small components; even though the sequence of acts may be communicated by observation, the fine motor coordination required within the components themselves may be absent in the novice, so that the entire performance appears quite amateurish. Often the relevant parts of the skilled movement (e.g., tipping a shoulder while swinging a golf driver) are not conspicuous to the casual observer or even to the performer himself, and considerable motor practice with feedback of results is needed to gradually shape the motor skills. But to soften this point, it is known that with some motor skills such as basketball shooting, driving, and dart throwing, covert "cognitive rehearsal" or "imaginery practice" can often produce significant improvements in actual performance (for a review, see Richardson, 1969).

The fourth subprocess in Bandura's analysis of observational learning is the role of *reinforcement*. He treats the anticipation of reinforcement as a motivational factor determining expression of cognitions and behaviors learned earlier. A person will tend to perform or inhibit a vicariously learned response to the extent that he believes he will be rewarded or punished for performing the act. Reinforcement may also alter the level of observational learning by affecting who or what the observer will attend to (e.g., stimulus properties of attractive, prestigious models) and how actively he codes and rehearses the modeled behavior. This conception of reinforcement is rather like that adopted by most modern learning theorists with the conspicuous exception of the Skinnerians; they would still hold to a "direct strengthening" view of reinforcement, and would account for "incentive motivation" in terms of the discriminative-stimulus character of verbal "anticipations" of reinforcement.

As a final word on the topic, it is important to point out that in a practical sense an optimal training program for transmitting many behaviors to human beings would use the observational method in conjunction with differential reinforcement. By having the person observe a model, we increase the initial probability that a response pattern resembling the one desired will occur. After it occurs, the response can be further refined or differentiated and its rate stepped up by reinforcement. For some finely skilled performances, once the activity has been initiated, more benefit derives from actual practice in the skill than from further observing of the model. The division and order of allotment of time for observing a model versus practicing with reinforcing feedback will surely have different optimal arrangements depending on the nature of the particular task performance to be shaped. Such questions concerning what is optimal would seem, at present, to have no general answers, and each must be worked out under appropriate field conditions.

We have discussed the social learning theory analysis of observational learning in some detail not only because of the intrinsic interest of the topic but also because it highlights one of the differences between social learning theory and a straightforward operant conditioning analysis of the same phenomenon. The salient difference from the current viewpoint is that Bandura willingly admits cognitive processes (coding, imagery, symbolic representations, problem-solving) into his theoretical accounts of observational learning, planning, and action evaluation. He illustrates through example and experimentation how such cognitive processes are involved in controlling the influence of reinforcement contingencies, in controlling or reinforcing one's own actions, in thinking out and evaluating alternative actions, and in supporting or altering one's self-concept. The principles are applied with ingenuity to a considerable range of social behaviors such as competitiveness, expressions of aggression, adoption of sex roles, psychiatric deviancy, and "pathologically disturbed" behavior (see Bandura & Walters, 1963; Bandura, 1969). In broad outline, social learning theory provides the best integrative summary of what modern learning theory has to contribute to solutions of practical problems. It also provides a compatible framework within which to place information-processing theories of language comprehension, memory, imagery, and problem-solving. These theories, for their part, fill in the details of the "representational systems" and "symbolic processes" which are employed for explanatory purposes in applications of social learning theory. For such reasons, social learning theory would appear to be the "consensus" theoretical framework within which much of learning research (especially that on humans) will evolve in the next decade.

SUPPLEMENTARY READINGS

An annual volume of novel theoretical and experimental work is edited by G. H. Bower; these volumes cover major areas within learning and have been published regularly since 1967.

BOWER, G. H. (Ed.) *The psychology of learning and motivation: Advances in research and theory.* Vol. 1 in 1967 through Vol. 7 in 1973, and continuing.

For recent research in conditioning and animal learning, the reader may refer to:

BLACK, A. H., & PROKASY, W. F. (Eds.) (1972) *Classical conditioning. II: Current theory and research.*

BOAKES, R. A. & HALLIDAY, S. (Eds.) (1972) *Inhibition and learning.*

GILBERT, R. M., & MILLENSON, J. R. (Eds.) (1972) *Reinforcement: Behavioral analyses.*

GILBERT, R. M., & SUTHERLAND, N. S. (Eds.) (1969) *Animal discrimination learning.*

HONIG, W. K., & MACKINTOSH, N. J. (Eds.) (1969) *Fundamental issues in associative learning.*

SUTHERLAND, N. S., & MACINTOSH, N. J. (1971) *Mechanisms of animal discrimination learning.*

For recent theory and research on human memory, the following books are appropriate:

ANDERSON, J. R., & BOWER, G. H. (Eds.) (1973) *Human associative memory.*

BANDURA, A. (1969) *Techniques of behavior modification.*

KINTSCH, W. (1970) *Learning, memory, and conceptual processes.*

LINDSAY, P. H., & NORMAN, D. A. (1972) *Human information processing.*

MELTON, A. W. & MARTIN, E. (Eds.) (1972) *Coding processes in human memory.*

NORMAN, D. A. (Ed.) (1970) *Models of memory.*

PAIVIO, A. (1971) *Imagery and verbal processes.*

STAATS, A. W. (1968) *Learning, language and cognition.*

TULVING, E., & DONALDSON, W. (Eds.) (1972) *Organization of memory.*

Theory of Instruction

Any isolation of basic science from applied science, when it persists, is unfortunate. Over the years the advances in science have occurred in intimate relation with advances in technology. The instrument makers (producing microscopes, telescopes, transistors, computers) have opened new fields of basic research; invention has all along gone hand in hand with scientific discovery. If we were to apply the historical lessons from astronomy, physics, biology (and their related technologies) to the psychology of learning, we would expect an equal intimacy between theory and research in the basic processes of learning and the applied aspects of instruction in the schools.

Educational institutions are under a large measure of social control, whether they are public or private; hence they are open to improved methods of teaching if it can be demonstrated that these methods are an outcome of scientific research. Because of this, it might be assumed that the psychologist interested in the study of learning would be very eager to have his theories embodied in the arts of instruction and validated by the greater efficiency and effectiveness of teaching techniques that result from his findings.

While many students of learning are indeed interested in instruction, this is not universally true. The uneven interest in applications comes about in part through division of labor and specialization of knowledge: there are "pure" science aspects to the study of learning, just as in other fields of inquiry, and the scientist delving into basic problems may not be concerned with applying what he knows. Thus one does not expect every geneticist to be interested in the breeding of farm animals, even though what he learns may ultimately be useful to the animal breeder. While many investigators of learning are interested in pure science, apart from applications, some investigators are very much concerned with the technology of instruction. The range of such interest is reflected in review chapters devoted specifically to the psychology of instruction (Gagné & Rohwer, 1969; Glaser & Resnick, 1972). In this chapter we wish to examine some of the problems that are involved in bridging the gap from the laboratory to the classroom, in the conviction that a sound theory of learning may be validated by its influence upon the arts of practice.

To move from theory to practice is not all that easy. The naive view is that the basic researcher stocks a kind of "medicine cabinet" with aids to solve the problems of the teacher. When a problem arises, the teacher can take a "psychological principle" from the cabinet and apply it like a bandage or an ointment to solve the educational problem. It is increasingly recognized that in order to move soundly from basic research to practice we need a theory of application, which in this case is a *theory of instruction* to complement our theories of learning. A theory of instruction differs both in its goals and in its content from a theory of learning. It seeks to move beyond the descriptive and explanatory to the *prescriptive*, that is, to procedures to be recommended in practice. Its content, therefore, must take into account the actual curriculum of the school and the social contexts in which learning occurs.

THE DIRECT APPLICABILITY OF LEARNING "PRINCIPLES" AND OF LEARNING THEORIES

While we do not support the "medicine cabinet" view of application, the direct application of knowledge from the laboratory to the classroom is not to be entirely rejected. Very often the laboratory knowledge helps us to understand what some of the important variables and influences are, even before these have been formulated in a more prescriptive form. A skilled teacher may understand better why some practices work and others do not because of acquaintance with basic learning principles. Such principles permit a better analysis by pointing out where to look and what to expect.

Some "Principles" Potentially Useful in Practice

The reason for writing "principles" in quotation marks is that the generalizations to be listed are mere summarizations of empirical relationships that hold rather widely, and many of them are not stated with sufficient precision to be considered "laws" of learning. Students of learning who have not devoted themselves primarily to problems of instruction can still give some very useful advice. Some of this advice comes from those oriented toward S-R theories, some from those who tend more toward cognitive theories, some from those whose concern is with motivation and personality. The following suggestions for practice are in large part acceptable to all parties (with some reservations); the assignment to one or another source is a matter of emphasis (and vocabulary) rather than an indication that the statement is controversial.

A. Principles emphasized within S-R theory.

1. The learner should be *active*, rather than a passive listener or viewer. The S-R theory emphasizes the significance of the learner's *responses*, and "learning by doing" is still an acceptable slogan.

2. *Frequency of repetition* is still important in acquiring skill, and in bringing enough overlearning to guarantee retention. One does not learn to type, or to play the piano, or to speak a foreign language, without some repetitive practice.

3. *Reinforcement* is important; that is, repetition should be under arrangements in which desirable or correct responses are rewarded. While there are some lingering questions over details, it is generally found that positive reinforcements (rewards, successes) are to be preferred to negative reinforcements (punishments, failures).

4. *Generalization* and *discrimination* suggest the importance of practice in varied contexts, so that learning will become (or remain) appropriate to a wider (or more restricted) range of stimuli.

5. *Novelty* in behavior can be enhanced through imitation of models, through cueing, through "shaping," and is not inconsistent with a liberalized S-R approach to learning.

6. *Drive conditions* are important in learning, but not all personal-social motives conform to the drive-reduction principles based on food-deprivation experiments. Issues concerning drives exist within S-R theory; at a practical level, it may be taken for granted that motivational conditions are important.

7. *Conflicts* and *frustrations* arise inevitably in the process of learning difficult discriminations and in social situations in which irrelevant motives may be aroused. Hence these have to be recognized and provision made for their resolution or accommodation.

B. Principles emphasized within cognitive theory.

1. The *perceptual features* according to which the problem is displayed to the learner are important conditions of learning (figure-ground relations, directional signs, "what-leads-to-what," organic interrelatedness). Hence a learning problem should be so structured and presented that the essential features are open to the inspection of the learner.

2. The *organization of knowledge* should be an essential concern of the teacher or educational planner. Thus the direction from simple to complex is *not* from arbitrary, meaningless parts to meaningful wholes, but is from *simplified wholes* to *more complex wholes*. The part-whole problem is therefore an organizational problem, and cannot be dealt with apart from a theory of how complexity is patterned. Also, studies of cognitive growth inform us that the appropriate organization of knowledge may depend on the developmental level of the learner.

3. *Learning with understanding* is more permanent and more transferable than rote learning or learning by formula. Expressed in this form, the statement belongs in cognitive theory, but S-R theories make a related emphasis on the importance of meaningfulness in learning and retention.

4. *Cognitive feedback* confirms correct knowledge and corrects faulty learning. The notion is that the learner tries something provisionally and then accepts or rejects what he does on the basis of its consequences. This

is, of course, the cognitive equivalent of reinforcement in S-R theory, but cognitive theory tends to place more emphasis on a kind of hypothesis-testing through feedback.

5. *Goal-setting* by the learner is important as motivation for learning, and his successes and failures are determiners of how he sets future goals.

6. *Divergent thinking*, which leads to inventive solutions of problems or to the creation of novel and valued products, is to be nurtured along with *convergent* thinking, which leads to logically correct answers. Such divergent thinking requires appropriate support (feedback) for the person's tentative efforts at originality so that he may perceive himself as potentially creative.

C. Principles from motivation, personality, and social psychology.

1. The learner's *abilities* are important, and provisions have to be made for the slower and the more rapid learners, and for those with specialized abilities.

2. *Postnatal development* may be as important as hereditary and congenital determiners of ability and interest. Hence the learner must be understood in terms both of inherent maturational factors and of special influences that have shaped his development.

3. Learning is *culturally relative,* and both the wider culture and the subculture to which the learner belongs may affect his learning.

4. *Anxiety level* of the individual learner may determine whether certain kinds of encouragements to learn will have beneficial or detrimental effects. The generalization appears justified that with some kinds of tasks high-anxiety learners perform better if *not* reminded of how well (or poorly) they are doing, while low-anxiety learners do better if they *are* interrupted with comments on their progress.

5. The same objective situation may tap *appropriate motives* for one learner and not for another, as, for example, in the contrast between those motivated by affiliation and those motivated by achievement.

6. The *organization of motives and values* within the individual is relevant. Some long-range goals affect short-range activities. Thus college students of equal ability may do better in courses perceived as relevant to their majors than in those perceived as irrelevant.

7. *Self-esteem* and its related manifestations (self-confidence, level of aspiration, self-awareness) cannot be overlooked.

8. The *group atmosphere* of learning (competition versus cooperation, authoritarianism versus democracy, individual isolation versus group identification) will affect satisfaction in learning as well as the products of learning.

If one reviews such a list of suggestions as the foregoing, it becomes apparent that laboratory knowledge does not lead automatically to its own applications. Any teacher reading the list will say: "How can I do these desirable things, with the many pupils in my classes, and with the many demands upon me?" Or even: "How would I do it if I had only a single student to tutor?" As in the development of any technology, further steps are needed between the pure science stage and the ready application of what has been found out. Yet it is still worthwhile to attempt to assemble such suggestions from the general knowledge of learning, for then the steps of application will presumably be taken more economically.

Approaches to Practical Problems by Means of Unified Theories

The effort to arrive at unified conceptions of learning is commendable. The scientific enterprise tends in general to favor elegant and simple theories; parsimony and aesthetic appeal help guide the search for comprehensive theories. Within applied science, however, the constraints are somewhat different. For one thing, applied science cannot wait for the answers of pure science to come in: crops must be planted and gathered, the sick must be treated, and children must be taught with whatever tools and knowledge are available at the time. It is natural that in the early development of the relevant sciences, the appliers, the technologists, will tend to be eclectic, picking up a plausible idea here and there, and using it somewhat inventively in the practical situation. Skilled teachers contribute to educational advance, with students of the psychology of learning sometimes bringing up the rear. Only when science has progressed further can pure science take the lead in developing practice, as it does in the aiming of rockets at the moon.

The option is still open of attempting to guide practical developments by way of one or the other of the prevailing theories, or by developing some new model which has more unity than a set of eclectic "principles." Some psychologists have chosen this approach, and a number of their positions may be examined briefly in turn. The classical position in this respect was, of course, that of Thorndike, for his position on learning was developed as an educational psychology, with its emphasis upon elements, transfer, measurement, and the law of effect. The functionalism of John Dewey, although a related viewpoint, had a very different influence upon the schools; while his position was called "experimentalism," it was not synonymous with the "experimentation" of Thorndike, and, while victorious over Thorndike in some respects (McDonald, 1964), it did not lead to much research within educational psychology. The exciting newcomer on the field in the 1930s was Gestalt psychology; it became the accepted educational psychology for a time, but its excesses in the hands of some of its educational enthusiasts, who were not experimentally oriented, led to its declining influence (E. R. Hilgard, 1964b). We may, for illustrative purposes, consider three of the views represented in earlier chapters (Guthrie, Skinner, and Hull) in terms of some contemporaries who have attempted to use these theories in relation to practical problems.

1. Applications of Guthrie's contiguous conditioning.   In giving a rationale for their applied psychological research, Lumsdaine, F. D. Sheffield, and Maccoby, all at one time students of Guthrie, have deferred repeatedly to his theoretical position.

Lumsdaine (1964), for example, believes that much that is done in programmed learning can be better accounted for according to Guthrie's views than according to Skinner's. The chief issue is over *prompting versus shaping*.[1] According to Guthrie, one learns by assimilating cues to responses, so that the *cueing* of responses follows directly from his theory. The program-

---

[1] The notions of *prompting, shaping,* and *fading* are all within Skinner's conceptions of programming. We are concerned here with the theory of their operation.

mer frequently does just that: he tries to give enough cues to guarantee a high probability of successful responses. Maintaining the responses with fewer stimulus supports ("fading") is also coherent with Guthrie's theory. This emphasis on the *responses* of the learner, reflected in the title of one of the books that Lumsdaine edited, *Student response in programmed instruction* (1961), follows from Guthrie's position that we learn what we do. Skinner's concentration on the role of reinforcement, by contrast, emphasizes the rewarding of approximate responses, and then, through differential reinforcement, the strengthening of those responses that better meet the specifications of what is wanted. While this works pretty well in free-operant behavior, the programmed type of learning is more constricted, and, according to Lumsdaine, the practice accords more to cueing and prompting than to shaping.

F. D. Sheffield (1961) outlined the theory guiding the work that he and Maccoby and their collaborators carried out on the learning of complex sequential tasks from combinations of filmed demonstrations and practice. Sheffield's theory is pure Guthrie[2] (association by contiguity, referred to as conditioning), except for an important amendment: perceptual responses are said to follow the same principles as motor responses. It must be noted that this does *not* mean that perceptual responses *are* motor responses (e.g., discriminatory reactions, subvocal speech, etc.), but rather that one can take them for what they are phenomenally, and then apply the associative rules to them.

The position taken here is that what is usually called "perception" refers to cases in which the immediate sensory stimulation is not only eliciting its innate sensory response, but is also eliciting other sensory responses which have been conditioned to the immediate stimulation in past experience. (F. D. Sheffield, 1961, p. 15)

The word *response* has here lost its original behaviorist meaning of a muscular movement or a glandular secretion; a new category of innate response, *sensory response*, has been added, which, through conditioning, becomes a perceptual response. This gives Sheffield great freedom in introducing cognitive processes into an essentially S-R type of system. For example:

In the same vein, a wristwatch is completely "transparent" to a skilled watch repairman. From the outside he can note the distinctive brand and model; this is sufficient for him to "fill in" all of the internal parts—their sizes, shapes, arrangements, and so forth. When he takes the watch apart he is completely prepared for everything he sees because his anticipatory conditioned sensory responses correspond with his immediate unconditioned sensory responses when he opens it and makes the inner works visible. (F. D. Sheffield, 1961, p. 16)

Without questioning either the validity or the usefulness of the ideas embodied here, we may note that this is the kind of statement which, had it been expressed in terms of sensations and their revival as images, would have been most repugnant to an early behaviorist. It is clear enough that a functionalist would accept such a statement, but even a contemporary S-R

---

[2] See earlier discussion in Chapter 4.

theorist must have some trouble with this kind of response. Having ignored this hurdle, Sheffield is able to do some very cogent theorizing about what goes on in sequence learning and in response organization. Many of his conceptions have overtones of Gestalt or cognitive theory, such as the distinction between *imposed* and *inherent* organization, "natural units" of a sequential task, perceptual "blueprinting." The concept of natural structure was much emphasized by Wertheimer, and the notion of mapping, as mentioned earlier, by Tolman. Although, in Sheffield's opinion, he has gone beyond Gestalt or cognitive psychology in deriving their truths from conditioning theory, the major leap is to the interpretation of organization in perception as the conditioning of innate sensory responses. Whether or not one sees these additions as natural extensions or consequences of Guthrie's theory, from a practical standpoint one can only applaud the trend toward consensus on some of the implications for instruction.

2. *Applications of Skinner's operant conditioning.*   Part of Skinner's success in gaining adoption for programmed learning (originally for the teaching machine) was due to his insistence that he was basing this instructional device strictly on what had been discovered from his experiments on rats and pigeons. The major concepts of emitted response and its strengthening through carefully timed reinforcement, of the importance of reward over punishment, of shaping through small-step gains, of the subject's control of his own pace, all came from the experimental background of operant conditioning. In his original announcement of programmed learning, Skinner was very clear that he was deriving the principles of programmed learning from his laboratory work; the child was simply a new organism to be studied:

> There are certain questions which have to be answered in turning to the study of any new organism. What behavior is to be set up? What reinforcers are at hand? What responses are available in embarking upon a program of progressive approximation which will lead to the final form of the behavior? How can reinforcements be most efficiently scheduled to maintain the behavior in strength? These questions are all relevant in considering the problem of the child in the lower grades. (1954, p. 93)

The notion of shaping through reinforcement is clearly set forth. One of Skinner's associates enunciated the laboratory principles as they applied to programmed learning in terms of the following six topics (Holland, 1960):

1. Immediate reinforcement.
2. Emitted behavior.
3. Gradual progression to complex repertoires.
4. Fading; gradual withdrawal of stimulus support.
5. Control of observing (attentive) behavior.
6. Discrimination training (abstractions; concepts).

There can be little doubt that what was earlier done in Skinner's laboratory contributed to programming as he developed it.

Several comments are in order. In the first place, the direct application of these principles has not proved universally to be the only efficient way to proceed. Reservations apply to immediate reinforcement, the necessity to emit behavior (in the form of constructed responses), even to some aspects of gradual progression. Others have noted, too, that Skinner has not moved as directly from his free-operant model as his writings sometimes have suggested; for example, Zeaman (1959) showed that it would be possible to consider programmed learning as an illustration not of a free operant but of a controlled operant, and in some respects similar to classical conditioning. Moreover, specific inventiveness, ingenuity, and empiricism (revising programs through tryout) have played a role equal to that of any generalizations from the animal laboratory. Hence all credit is due to Skinner, but not necessarily on the basis of the authority of any principles learned from the rat or the pigeon. In his later book, Skinner (1968) provides a larger context to the relationship between his position and the task of schooling.

3. Hull's drive-reinforcement theory applied in the Miller-Dollard version.
N. E. Miller and Dollard (1941) introduced a simplified version of a theory very near to that of Hull in which they stressed the sequence "drive-cue-response-reward," a theory later developed more fully by Miller (1959). Miller has shown that his less mathematical version of a theory similar in type to Hull's can be used to derive practical consequences. This is best illustrated by way of a small book on graphical methods in education that Miller edited, and much of which he wrote (N. E. Miller, 1957).

In applying his theory to propose the conditions for maximum learning from motion pictures, Miller used the four-stage analysis he and Dollard had originally proposed:

1. Drive: The student must want something.
2. Cue: The student must notice something.
3. Response: The student must do something.
4. Reward: The student must get something he wants.

This manner of discussing what Hull would have talked about in terms of stimuli, reaction potential, habit strength, and drive permits Miller to summarize experimental findings in a very sensible manner. The outline proved not quite sufficient, however, and he added another chapter to the four discussing each of these stages. The additional chapter discussed such issues as the specificity versus generality of the influence of watching a teaching film, the superiority of logical over rote learning, meaningfulness and organization of material, forgetting and review, the value of demonstrating errors (as well as correct responses) in the visual material, dramatic versus expository presentation, types of audience, and the need to train students to profit from films.

While the theory provides a structure around which to give an exposition of research, a reader cannot help noting how few of the principles give any very direct guidance for motion picture learning, and how other principles, besides the more formal ones, seem necessary when a practical instructional situation is to be faced. What is shown is that a major theory can indeed provide a vocabulary that will allow one to talk sensibly about practical learning situations. However, the heavy reliance on sheer empiricism to supplement derivations from theory suggests the need for an explicit theory of instruction which takes these empirical steps into account.

THEORIES OF INSTRUCTION

Most of the earlier theories of instruction were embodied in curriculum theory, a discipline within the study of education that seeks to organize the materials of instruction in some orderly manner for effective teaching and learning. It would take us afield to attempt a summary of this literature (e.g., McClure, 1971); our interest is rather in a number of recent developments in which psychologists concerned with learning theory or aspects of cognitive development have turned their attention to improving or optimizing instruction when both subject matter and guided learning are under scrutiny. What they have developed is, of course, relevant to curriculum, for a theory of instruction is in some sense a theory of curriculum development. At the present time, however, the instructional theories tend to deal with more limited aspects of schooling than do curriculum theories.

A clear call for such a theory was stated by Gage (1964), who lamented the failure of psychological investigators in the field of learning to concern themselves more directly with a theory of teaching. Gagné (1962a) had already expressed interest in these problems. Carroll (1963a) had proposed an instructional model, and Bruner (1964a) was beginning to offer steps toward a theory of instruction, making use of such concepts as the organization of knowledge and principles of cognitive development. For many reasons, the time appeared to be ripe. The development of programmed learning in which experimental psychologists played a large part had clearly been one instigation, inasmuch as a program designed for the schools had to reflect actual content of school learning and was no longer limited to the familiar and artificial laboratory materials. Some of those who during World War II had been deeply immersed in the actual problems of training airplane pilots, or teaching exotic languages, were eager to see some of the lessons they had learned applied outside the armed services. The upsurge of interest in educational advancements after the Sputnik launching in 1957 had brought scholars from mathematics, physics, biology, and other areas into the design of instructional materials. One might say that the scholarly community decided that schooling could not be left to professional educators alone, and, as many more were drawn into the act, the interest spread to a number of psychologists whose earlier work had been remote from schooling. Professional educators welcomed these new allies, and considerable collaborative work has resulted.

Theory of instruction has not yet settled down into an accepted system refined by the give and take of theory, experiment, and dialogue, so that the best we can do at present is to give some illustrations of contemporary developments as indications of what is to come. For this purpose, we have chosen three "models," assigned to the three theorists proposing them, no one of whom is committed to a global theory of learning as described in earlier chapters. The theories are not proposed as alternatives; they do not deal with exactly the same problems, and those proposing one model have had little to say about the models that the others have put forward. Hence we are at an early stage in the development of such theories.

Gagné's Hierarchical Theory

Robert M. Gagné was one of those who had turned from the study of basic problems in the laboratory to the practical tasks of training in the air force during World War II, where he worked especially (though not exclusively) on various devices for simulating the task of the pilot. He emerged from this experience somewhat disillusioned about the applicability of the psychology of learning. He found the best-known psychological principles of learning (practicing a response, reinforcement, distribution of practice, meaningfulness) "strikingly inadequate to handle the job of designing effective training situations" (1962b, p. 85). He notes that in several specific tasks (gunnery, procedures of switch-pressing, trouble-shooting complex equipment), practice, even under presumably favorable conditions (according to established "principles"), was not very effective; the learner instead had to learn what to look for, what was to be done, and what classes of situations were likely to be encountered. To meet this circumstance, Gagné first proposed that all learning was not alike; he divided learning into eight types or categories, arranged in a hierarchy because each implies the earlier ones. His eight types, with a brief description, are listed in Table 16.1.

It is intuitively clear that Gagné, having proposed so many different kinds of learning, should find it relatively easy to describe many kinds of school learning according to one or another of his types. As for hierarchy, two con-

Table 16.1   **Gagné's eight types of learning. (Modified from Gagné, 1970, pp. 63–64.)**

Type	*Brief Description*
1. Signal learning	The classical conditioned response of Pavlov, in which the individual learns to make a diffuse response to a signal.
2. Stimulus-response learning	The connection of Thorndike, the discriminated operant of Skinner; sometimes called an instrumental response.
3. Chaining	Two or more stimulus-response connections are joined together.
4. Verbal association	Chains that are verbal.
5. Multiple discrimination	Identifying responses to stimuli that resemble each other, such that some interferences occur.
6. Concept learning	A common response to a class of stimuli.
7. Rule learning	A chain of two or more concepts; reflected in a rule such as "If *A*, then *B*," where *A* and *B* are concepts.
8. Problem-solving	Thinking is involved; principles are combined according to a "higher-order" rule.

ceptions must be distinguished in his writing. One is the hierarchy of learning types (from type 1 through type 8); the other is the organization of knowledge according to a hierarchy of subcomponent skills and learned rules. How Gagné deals with these matters can best be shown by an example.

Gagné has illustrated the hierarchical organization of school instruction, according to his types, for mathematics, science, foreign languages, and English (1965, pp. 175–203; 1970, pp. 246–274). One structure for reading is reproduced in Figure 16.1; while there is a certain plausibility to such an outline, it is by no means clear that a sequence of instruction can be designed upon it, or that the basic notion is sound that the lower steps of the hierarchy must be mastered before the higher steps can be learned.

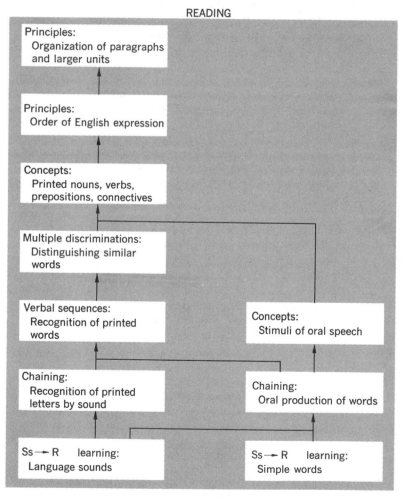

Figure 16.1.   A learning structure for the basic skills of reading. (From *The Conditions of Learning* by Robert M. Gagné. Copyright © 1965 by Holt, Rinehart and Winston, Inc. Reprinted by permission of Holt, Rinehart and Winston, Inc.)

There may well be a kind of cyclical development in learning, in which the various stages repeatedly assert themselves.

Gagné has continued to work on these problems, and recently with Briggs has addressed himself directly to the task of designing instructional sequences (Gagné & Briggs, 1974). In this he is dealing explicitly with the problem of the curriculum. He finds it useful to refer repeatedly to a hierarchy of levels, for example, in sequencing a course, a topic within that course, a lesson within that topic, a component within that lesson. None of the steps can be circumvented, whether or not everything is written down in planning the curriculum. To keep this discussion within the context of learning theory, we may consider how he applies sequencing principles to some outcomes expressed as learning outcomes rather than as knowledge specific to some subject matter. One of his summary tables is reproduced as Table 16.2. It will be noted that in this table the hierarchical design is implied for each type of learning outcome, although the learning outcomes themselves are not here arranged in hierarchical order.

It is evident that in any theory of instruction, there must remain a large element of empiricism in the decision as to just how much time and effort must be expended on each step of a sequence. The main point is that Gagné has found the hierarchical principle a useful one for moving from learning

Table 16.2   **Desirable sequence characteristics associated with five types of learning outcome. (Gagné & Briggs, 1974.)**

Type of Learning Outcome	Major Principles of Sequencing	Related Sequence Factors
Motor skills	Provide intensive practice on part-skill of critical importance, and practice on total skill.	First of all, learn the "executive routine" (rule).
Verbal information	For major subtopics, order of presentation not important. Individual facts should be preceded or accompanied by meaningful context.	Prior learning of necessary intellectual skills involved in reading, listening, etc., is usually assumed.
Intellectual skills	Presentation of learning situation for each new skill should be preceded by prior mastery of subordinate skills.	Information relevant to the learning of each new skill should be previously learned, or presented in instructions.
Attitudes	Establishment of respect for source as an initial step. Choice situations should be preceded by mastery of any skills involved in these choices.	Information relevant to choice behavior should be previously learned, or presented in instructions.
Cognitive strategies	Problem situations should contain previously acquired intellectual skills.	Information relevant to solution of problems should be previously learned, or presented in instructions.

principles to the sequencing of instruction. In this sense he has made hierarchy the basis for his approach to a theory of instruction.

Bruner's Cognitive-Developmental Theory

Jerome S. Bruner came strongly to the attention of the education profession with the publication of his book *The process of education* (1960), which was the outcome of a conference devoted to educational problems, attended by many who had not had strong prior identification with professional education. He later prepared a chapter in which some theorems regarding instruction were proposed, illustrated by the teaching of mathematics, and moved further toward a theory of instruction in a subsequent collection of essays (Bruner, 1966). In the latter, he points out that a theory of instruction is *prescriptive* in that it proposes rules for achieving knowledge or skill and provides techniques for measuring or evaluating outcomes. It is also *normative*, in that it sets goals to be achieved and deals with conditions for meeting them.

> . . . A theory of instruction, in short, is concerned with how what one wishes to teach can best be learned, with improving rather than describing learning.
>
> This is not to say that learning and developmental theories are irrelevant to a theory of instruction. In fact, a theory of instruction must be concerned with both learning and development and must be congruent with those theories of learning and development to which it subscribes (Bruner, 1966, p. 40)

He goes on to specify four features that a theory of instruction must encompass:

1. *Predisposition to learn.* A theory of instruction must be concerned with the experiences and contexts that will tend to make the child willing and able to learn when he enters school.
2. *Structure of knowledge.* A theory of instruction must specify the ways in which a body of knowledge should be structured so that it can be most readily grasped by the learner.
3. *Sequence.* A theory of instruction should specify the most effective sequences in which to present the materials.
4. *Reinforcement.* A theory of instruction should specify the nature and pacing of rewards, moving from extrinsic rewards to intrinsic ones.

Each of these points needs elaboration (which he provides), particularly with respect to the individual differences among children at any given age, the differences to be expected with growth, the differences in structure within various fields of knowledge, necessary flexibility of sequencing to meet individual differences in rate of learning as well as in preference, and so on. Bruner has taken the position that, with sufficient understanding of the structure of a field of knowledge, something anticipating the later, more advanced concepts can be taught appropriately at much earlier ages. His aphorism has been widely quoted: "Any subject can be taught effectively in some intellectually honest form to any child at any stage of development" (1960, p. 33).

The developmental aspect of Bruner's theory lies in his interest in cognitive development, originally stimulated by Piaget. This has led him to emphasize three modes of representation in a developmental sequence: the *enactive*, the *iconic*, and the *symbolic* (1964b). The enactive mode is learning through action, an essentially wordless learning, such as learning to ride a bicycle. The iconic mode is based on representation through perceptual means (hence the "icon" or image standing for something). A mental map that permits us to follow a route from where we are to where we are going constitutes such an iconic representation. Finally, the symbolic mode enables the translation of experience into words, and these permit eventually the kinds of transformations that at the later stages become of so much interest to Piaget. In relation to learning theory Bruner notes that much of the conditioning or S-R learning appears appropriate to the enactive mode, Gestalt psychology was concerned very largely with the iconic mode, and the new concern with the symbolic mode brings in the psycholinguists and many others besides Piaget.

As with all of those who become interested in the concrete problems of instruction, Bruner is insistent on the empirical steps necessary before the theory can prescribe the practice. Psychological explanation, at the level of practice, has to account for the ways in which children actually deal with the problems before them; he believes, for example, that Piaget's theory, with its heavy emphasis on epistemology, is too formal to provide a psychological description of the processes of growth (Bruner, 1966, p. 7).

Atkinson's Decision-Theoretic Analysis for Optimizing Learning

Richard C. Atkinson came to instructional psychology from an interest in mathematical learning theory (e.g., Atkinson, Bower, & Crothers, 1965), which he applied to computer-assisted instruction (CAI). Through actual use of the computer in schools across the country for the teaching of reading and spelling, he became interested in the broader context of instruction, including such practical matters as the amount of time the pupil should spend with the computer and the amount with the live teacher, the costs of computer instruction, and so on. With a number of collaborators, he has gradually been formalizing a theory of instruction (Atkinson, 1972; Atkinson & Paulson, 1972).

Atkinson (1972) proposes four criteria that must be satisfied prior to a precise derivation of an optimal instructional strategy:

1. A model of the learning process.
2. Specification of admissible instructional actions.
3. Specification of instructional objectives.
4. A measurement scale that permits costs to be assigned to each of the instructional objectives.

It is possible at this stage to follow Atkinson's model for rather specific instructional tasks; the collection of such task-specific models should lead to a more general theory of instruction. The model is, in fact, a special case of *optimal control theory* as it has been developed in the mathematical and engineering fields (e.g., Kalman, Falb, & Arbib, 1969).

As a first example, Atkinson makes use of data from initial reading instruction in regular classrooms in which CAI supplements the work of the teacher (Atkinson & Fletcher, 1972). The optimizing task that is set is to use the computer most efficiently, granted a specific total amount of computer time available, and in full awareness that not all the pupils are at the same level to begin with or learn at the same rate. The four criteria can be met, at least provisionally. There is a model of learning that is reasonably satisfactory for giving the information required; the instructional actions have already been programmed on the computer, so that all that is now necessary is to allocate time on the computer among the pupils in an optimal way; the third criterion, the instructional objective, will be discussed below in more detail; costs and payoffs are readily taken care of because computer time (hence computer cost) is a constant, and the payoff can be defined as the performance on the end-of-the-year reading test.

The instructional objectives for a class, given the individual differences in learning, may not be the same as those for an individual. Atkinson considers four possibilities:

(a) To maximize the mean performance over the class.
(b) To minimize the variance in performance over the class.
(c) To maximize the number of students who score at grade level at the end of the year.
(d) To maximize the mean performance without increasing the variance above what it would have been without CAI.

It is very easy to make glib statements about the successes of one school over another, based solely on mean performance on some sort of test. That would rely on objective (a), but note that it *might* mean that the procedures would then favor working with the most promising students, pushing them far ahead and permitting those most likely to fail to end up as failures. Or, in the interests of having everyone come out more or less alike (a romantic interpretation of the democratic ideal), objective (b) might be chosen, with the consequence that the more rapid learners would be held back and all effort spent on the slow learners.

Because of the known parameters for individual students' learning according to the existing computer program, it was possible to simulate an experiment on the computer, to see what the consequences would be of adopting each of the four objectives, without actually conducting the experiment in the schools. The results are presented in Figure 16.2, which plots the gains (or losses) through maximizing each objective.

If objective (a) were adopted, calling for maximum mean gain, reading averages would go up about 15 percent by the end of the year, but the variance would also go up about 15 percent. What this means is that the average gain would be at the expense of a greater spread between the more successful and the less successful students—hardly a result to be celebrated. If objective (b) or (c) were chosen, the average performance would be reduced, a consequence of holding back the more rapid learners in order to reduce variability. Objective (d), requiring a program allowing equal time for each student, raises the mean about 8 percent, less than objective (a), but without the unfortunate side effect of increased variability. Hence, in this comparison, objective (d) would seem to be the one to favor.

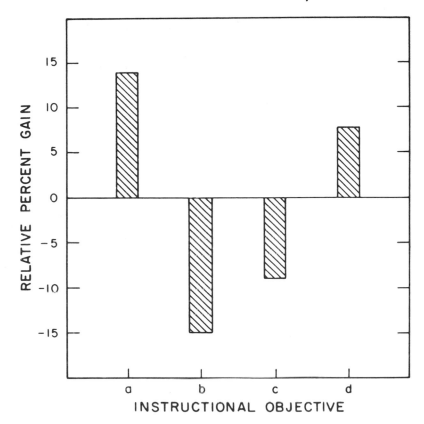

Figure 16.2.   Gains or losses to be expected through maximizing each of four objectives. (From R. C. Atkinson, Ingredients for a theory of instruction, *American Psychologist*, 1972, 27, pp. 921–31. Copyright 1972 by the American Psychological Association. Reprinted by permission.)

The important point here is to show how a decision-theoretic model can indeed lead to practical decisions.

As another illustration of the approach in action, we may review briefly the second example Atkinson (1972) uses: the learning of a foreign language vocabulary (German) by English-speaking college students. Three instructional strategies were employed in an experimental comparison: a *random-order strategy*, in which selected German words are presented in a random order; a *learner-controlled strategy*, in which the learner decides which items require more practice and hence should be presented; and a *response-sensitive strategy*, in which the computer has been programmed to present materials according to the prior successes and failures of the individual student in line with a decision-theoretic analysis of the task.

The instruction is controlled by a computer in an instructional session of approximately 2 hours and a briefer delayed-test session a week later. To permit a comparison of the three strategies, the presentation is made as follows. A list of 12 German words (one of seven lists) is displayed, and then one item from the list is selected for test and study. After an item is selected, the student attempts a translation and receives feedback regarding the correct translation. This item can be selected at random, by the learner, or according to the model designed to be optimal. Each subject is assigned to one of these treatment procedures. The delayed test, the same for all students, tests the entire vocabulary of 84 words making up the seven lists. The results, as presented in Figure 16.3, came out essentially as predicted, with the designed strategy (the response-sensitive strategy) the most successful on the criterion (delayed) test. The different orders were to be predicted, for the designed strategy calls for most practice during the instructional sessions on the items causing most trouble; the learner-controlled strategy is to do something similar to this, but is less efficient. The optimal strategy was derived on the basis of a learning theory in its mathematical form, and is explained in the original account; its details are not required for our purposes. It is based on the conception that an item can be in state U (unknown), in state T (temporary storage in memory), or in state P (relatively permanent memory storage). The learning model has to account precisely for changes from one state to another, and can be used to derive equations that compute

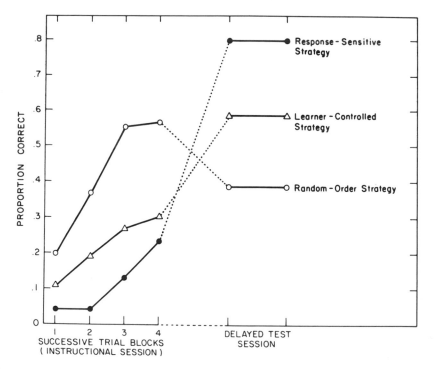

Figure 16.3.   Proportion of correct responses with three learning strategies. (From R. C. Atkinson, Ingredients for a theory of instruction, *American Psychologist,* 1972, *27,* pp. 921–31. Copyright 1972 by the American Psychological Association. Reprinted by permission.)

the probabilities of being in each of the states for each of the items at the start of any one trial, given some empirical parameters and the student's response history (Atkinson & Crothers, 1964). The computational procedure is then implemented on the computer.

This example is somewhat incomplete from the point of view of fully practical instructional theory in that it is a little too close to a typical laboratory experiment on learning, being conducted over a short time and with college students not enrolled in a language course. It has the virtue, however, of using school-relevant materials (a foreign language vocabulary), and of testing some theories about instruction by comparing student choice with a systematic choice in sequencing learning. It is clear in this setting that the student is not the most efficient guide to optimal learning.

Atkinson points out that an all-inclusive theory of learning is not a prerequisite for the development of optimal procedures; in fact, formulation of a theory of instruction would be stymied if a complete theory of learning were a prior necessity. Rather, advances in learning theory will affect the development of a theory of instruction, and conversely the development of a theory of instruction will influence research on learning (Atkinson, 1972, p. 929).

Atkinson's theory deriving from work with the computer is, of course, only one among several approaches (the others not dependent upon the computer) to the problem of how to deal effectively with individual differences in learning. Carroll (1963a), for example, proposed a model in which the individual would be allowed enough time to learn what he needed to learn as a background for the next stage, interpreting aptitude for a task as essentially the time required for the individual to master that task. This approach was adopted by Bloom and his associates and developed into an instructional plan known as *mastery learning*, based on the guiding principle that the learner should achieve mastery at one stage before going on to the next (Bloom, 1968; Block, 1971). Another approach has been that known as *individually prescribed instruction* (IPI), developed by Glaser and his associates at Pittsburgh (e.g., Lindvall & Bolvin, 1967; Lindvall & Cox, 1969). Utilizing materials arranged in progressively more difficult units, the school using IPI tries to meet individual differences in mathematics, reading, and science by permitting each student to work with appropriate materials after he has taken a placement test to prescribe the proper unit. Still another approach is *aptitude-treatment interaction* (ATI), which proposes that individual differences be met by different approaches to instruction for students of different aptitude (e.g., Cronbach, 1967; Cronbach & Snow, 1969). Adapting instruction to the individual is a basic problem in the design of the curriculum, and it is to be expected that various approaches will be invented to meet this need.

The three theories of instruction presented here (Gagné's hierarchical model, Bruner's cognitive-development model, and Atkinson's decision-theoretic optimization model) serve to illustrate contemporary explorations toward a prescriptive theory of instruction. The history of these attempts in anything like their current form is a short one, and we can look forward to a number of developments in the years immediately ahead.

TECHNOLOGICAL AIDS IN TRAINING AND INSTRUCTION

Teachers have always used such aids to instruction as were available to them: slates, blackboards, libraries, textbooks, workbooks, laboratories, studios, stages, playgrounds. There have been educational innovations over the years, and educational technology, as such, is not new. What is new is the pace at which new devices have been developed, and a better opportunity to ask what research tells us about their effectiveness. In turn, because of the clarity with which they proceed, they may also contribute to instructional theory, as in the preceding account of Atkinson's work with the computer.

Simulators

Gagné (1962b) has reviewed the successful use of simulators in military training, not only aircraft simulators for training pilots, but trainers for aircraft controllers and control tower operators, missile guidance operators, and technicians of various kinds. He points out that it is not necessarily the device that is simulated, but the *operations* or *tasks* related to it: procedures, skills, identifications, trouble shooting, and team skills such as communication of information.

He believes that the educational use of simulators should be at fairly advanced stages of instruction, as in the training of civilian technicians, and perhaps in some kinds of performance assessment (e.g., assessment of automobile-driving skill).

The generalizations, as far as theory of learning is concerned, again bear more upon task analysis than upon learning processes involved, though of course problems of degree of similarity between simulated and real situation must be considered. This is essentially a practical matter, however, and is not helped too much by theories of generalization and transfer.

Films and Television

Films and television are similar in that both use animated pictures with sound. Films may of course be presented over closed-circuit television sets, with some advantage in that room darkening is less necessary and remote projectors or video tape recorders can present the films. Television may also be "live," again either from a remote source or over closed-circuit from near sources, including the lecturer's own desk if he wishes to permit a room full of students to look over his shoulder as he carries out a dissection or performs some other demonstration. We are not interested here in how the equipment can be made more convenient, although that of course has something to do with its use. Instead, our concern is with the kind of teaching that takes place with such audiovisual aids.

In a very incisive review of the research on learning from films, Hoban (1960) classified the results of some 400 investigations of teaching films into three zones of certainty with respect to the findings: low, intermediate, and high certainty. To achieve high certainty, results had to satisfy four criteria: (1) they should be intuitively reasonable, (2) they should have been reported by a competent and constructively imaginative investigator, (3) they should be related to some systematic formulation, and (4) the investigation should have been replicated. Other degrees of certainty were attached to those findings which did not satisfy these four criteria. Skipping over the findings of low and intermediate certainty (areas in which more research is urgently needed) we may examine the results that Hoban felt met his high-certainty criteria. These can be stated fairly concisely:

1. People learn from films.
2. Learning from films varies in amount with audience characteristics, such as age and formal education.
3. The amount of learning from films can be increased by the use of one or more of the following tested mechanisms and methods:
   a. *Redundancy*. Filmmakers (and English teachers) make the use of redundancy an uphill fight, according to Hoban, yet repetition of information, even repetition of whole films, can be demonstrated to provide increments in learning.
   b. *Participation*. If student activity, such as answering questions inserted in a film, can be encouraged, learning is enhanced, particularly if there is some feedback so that the student knows whether or not he answered correctly. Experimentation has shown that this is not merely a motivational device (to be sure that the student notices what is going on) but that there is a genuine practice from making relevant responses.
   c. *Attention-directing devices and methods*. A motion picture can use arrows that appear on a chart (or picture) to call attention to some feature, or in other ways can help the student search out the desired critical information. Such devices and teaching methods appropriate to them produce gains in learning films.

Again, using this summary to ask about the background of learning theory, we find that the basic principles are familiar and not, as principles, very incisive: individual differences, repetition of presented materials and ideas, practice in making responses that are desired, paying attention to what is relevant. Of greater importance, as the actual research is studied, is how these principles are embodied in detail, taking into consideration again the structure of what is being taught.

Television came rapidly to the fore as a possible means of teaching after receiving sets became widely available in homes and schools, and after the development of artificial satellites led to the practical possibility of directing programs to widely separated targets, including developing areas where textbooks and teachers might be scarce. In a comprehensive review of studies of the effectiveness of television in instruction, Chu and Schramm conclude:

> . . . it has become clear that there is no longer any reason to raise the question whether instructional television can serve as an efficient tool of learning. This is not to say that it always *does*. But the evidence is overwhelming that it *can*, and under favorable circumstances that it does. This evidence comes now from many countries, from studies of all age levels from preschool to adults, and from a great variety of subject matter and learning objectives. (1967, p. 98)

The peculiar advantages which they point out are that television allows a good teacher to be shared by a number of classes, it provides a variety and quality of experiences that would otherwise be impossible, and it can carry teaching to areas in which there are no schools. It also frees the local teacher to use available time for working with smaller groups and for giving individual guidance. The chief disadvantage is that it is a one-way system, and in fact there has been some experimentation with call-back or talk-back systems (e.g., Greenhill, 1964), but cost considerations have thus far made them not generally feasible.

The Language Laboratory

While in World War I we tended to show our distaste for the enemy by burning books and eliminating the teaching of the enemy's language, in World War II the importance of language learning was emphasized, and considerable effort was expended on ways to facilitate such learning. Here, if anywhere, we should expect a payoff for education, because language teaching has always been one of the standard school tasks, although there has been some vacillation between teaching the language as something to be spoken or as something to be read. The military training emphasized the spoken language; now the emphasis has shifted within schools and colleges back to the spoken language and away from reading knowledge. This has come about in part because better devices are available for bringing acceptably pronounced utterances to students in smaller schools who might lack teachers fully proficient in the language being taught. The language laboratory was rapidly adopted after World War II (Haber, 1963).

A language laboratory is simply a class of devices which allow speech, recorded on electromagnetic tape, to be used in instruction. The more elaborate contemporary devices permit the student to imitate what is heard, and then to listen to his own production or to have the teacher monitor what he has said. The console at which the teacher sits may allow two-way communication with a number of students at once.

Sometimes the public impression is that the methods developed during the war were so revolutionary that language learning had become easy. This is by no means the case. In the Army Language School at Monterey, California, a student typically spent nearly all of his time for 8 months working on a language, and 12 months if it was one of the more difficult ones. Even so, many were unsuccessful. In one of the earlier studies of language learning in the armed services, S. B. Williams and Leavitt (1947) reported that 80 percent of those who undertook to learn Japanese dropped out before they completed mastery of the language. There are no easy roads to the mastery of any difficult learning task.

Carroll (1963b), reviewing research on foreign language teaching, gives the impression that we know next to nothing about the effectiveness of the procedures that have been adopted in language laboratories, such as the student's hearing his own speech, practice on particular patterns of speech, and so on. Very little help has come from conventional laboratory learning experiments. For example, it might be supposed that the work on paired-associate learning is directly relevant to vocabulary learning, but as Carroll points out, vocabulary is not actually learned this way (particularly when the "natural method" is used in which only the language to be learned is the vehicle of communication). Furthermore, it assumes a one-to-one correspondence of words, which is inappropriate; a good bilingual speaker does not translate word for word.

There have been some reasonably satisfactory comparisons of the language laboratory type of teaching with conventional methods. Thus, a study carried out by faculty members at Antioch College compared conventional teaching of 20 students in a class taught six times a week by a regular instructor with teaching in a language laboratory in which 60 students met twice a week with a regular instructor and four times a week with student laboratory assistants (Antioch College, 1960). The experimental procedures saved about 12 hours per week of the time of the regular instructors. The laboratory periods of 1½ hours each were divided into the presentation of audiovisual materials (slides and accompanying tape-recorded sound), individual work in language laboratory booths, and drill and practice in face-to-face contact with the student assistants. In two separate years, achievement tests at the end of the year showed no significant differences to be attributed to the two forms of instruction; because the laboratory method was better liked by the students and saved the time of regular instructors, it still had something to recommend it. Pickrel, Neidt, and Gibson (1958) showed that teachers untrained in Spanish could teach conversational Spanish to seventh-grade students effectively if they based their teaching on tapes prepared by a specialist in Spanish; the children did not differ in oral fluency from those taught by the regular Spanish teacher. Thus the new methods offer promise, but no great revolution in teaching effectiveness. In the study just cited, the groups taught by the Spanish teacher were superior to those taught by tapes on written tests of Spanish.

In his analysis of what is involved in foreign language learning, Carroll (1962) identified the following aspects of foreign language aptitude: phonetic coding, grammatical sensitivity, rote memory for foreign language materials, and inductive language learning ability. It may be noted that the ordinary verbal factor or verbal knowledge factor (tested often by vocabulary in the familiar language) is not a good predictor of ability to learn a foreign language, in part because in the first stages of learning a foreign language it is not necessary to master a large vocabulary. In his model of the learning process as it applies to foreign language learning. Carroll (1962, 1963b) proposes that success is a function of the following five elements, the first three of which are qualities of the learner, the final two, of the instructional process:

1. The learner's language aptitude.
2. The learner's general intelligence.
3. The learner's perseverance.
4. The quality of the instruction.
5. The opportunity for learning afforded the student.

Again we note the importance of analyzing the nature of the performance in order both to specify the requisite component abilities and to design an appropriate instructional program.

Programmed Learning

Attention to programmed learning began with the introduction of the teaching machine as a technological aid, although the essence of programming does not reside in the particular kind of equipment used. The first of these machines was developed by Sidney L. Pressey at Ohio State University many years ago (Pressey, 1926, 1927). While originally developed as a self-scoring machine to facilitate the taking and scoring of objective examinations, the machine soon demonstrated its ability to actually teach. The student reads the question presented in the aperture of the machine, selects an answer from among several alternatives, and then presses the button corresponding to this chosen answer. If he is correct, the next question appears in the slot; if he has made a mistake, the original question remains. The machine counts his errors and the tape does not move on to the next question until the right button has been pressed. Because the student knows that he is correct when the question moves, he has immediate information (reinforcement, feedback) and thus learns while testing himself. Because the machine has counted his errors, his score can be read off as soon as he has finished taking the test. This machine of Pressey's did not become popular, although a number of studies by him and his students showed it to be effective as a teaching device.

A new forward push was given to the idea of automatic self-instruction by the publication of a paper by Skinner (1954), whose operant conditioning work had already given him authority in the field of learning. The time was now right, and work on teaching machines and programmed learning flourished shortly thereafter. Now it is a very large-scale international scientific, educational, and commercial enterprise. Skinner's machine differed from Pressey's chiefly in that the student was not given alternatives to choose from but instead was asked to write his own response in the spaces provided, and then, as a printed tape advanced, the correct answer appeared for comparison with what he had written. He thus "emitted" his own response to be "reinforced" by the comparison response. A further difference is involved: the material is so planned that it is not essentially a review of partially learned material, but rather a "program" in which the responses of the learner are "shaped" as he learns. We shall return to the problems of programming after considering another set of technological aids.

Far more complex instructional devices have been developed beyond those of Pressey and Skinner. Quite different sets of devices were developed somewhat earlier in the U.S. Air Force. Lumsdaine, who had a prominent role in their development, has given a description of some of them (Lumsdaine, 1959). For example, in one arrangement, a step-by-step film projection is used to teach a technician how to operate a piece of electronic equipment. A single demonstrational segment appears on the screen until the learner has mastered it. He then presses the button to bring on the next illustration, and so on, until he has learned the complete operation. Modern electronic computers have been brought into the picture, occasionally to combine slide projection, motion picture projection, and other materials within the program for a single learner, occasionally to allow the management of learning for a group of learners. The flexibility provided makes possible almost any arrangement that the investigator desires, as long as the costs can be met.

The essence of learning by means of a teaching machine lies not in the machinery but in the material to be presented, and it has been found that properly designed programmed books can serve about the same purpose as the simpler forms of teaching machines. The simple machines are sometimes derogated as "mechanical page-turners" because they do little more than the student can do as well for himself. Obviously, the more complex machines go well beyond this, and the belittling of the simple machine is intended to point to the importance of the program over the technology. The programmed book is not to be confused with the earlier "workbook" in common educational use; the "workbook" was primarily a place to practice on examples of what had been taught by the teacher or a textbook, but the program is designed to do the teaching itself. Hence the program necessarily must begin with what the learner already knows, and it then adds to this by supplying answers that are at first *hinted at* or *prompted* in order to make the correct answers highly probable. These answers, once "reinforced," are then overlearned through their repeated use as new material is grafted onto that already learned. It is evident that the person who constructs a program must be aware of the *organization of knowledge,* both its logical organization and its psychological organization, in order to build knowledge and understanding in this way. The programmer does his best to anticipate what will happen, then in practice he corrects the program through tryout until it can be mastered by its intended learners with a minimum of errors, usually in one run through the program. The result of the learning is then tested by a conventional-type examination to see if the material has indeed been mastered and can be applied appropriately in new contexts.

In order to correct misapprehensions about programming's being just another form of mass education, Skinner (1958) made the case for a similarity between programmed instruction and individual tutoring. He pointed out several resemblances to a tutor:

1. A good tutor begins where the pupil is, and does not insist on moving beyond what the pupil can comprehend.
2. A good tutor moves at the rate that is consistent with the ability of a pupil to learn.
3. A good tutor does not permit false answers to remain uncorrected.
4. A good tutor does not lecture; instead, by his hints and questioning he helps the pupil to find and state answers for himself.

According to Skinner, these qualities are all found in a good program.

Varieties of programming.   The type of program advocated by Skinner, that which moves step by step through a single set of materials, has come to be called linear programming. Another type, commonly associated with the name of Norman Crowder, is known as a *branching program.*[3] In the programmed books which use this method (e.g., Crowder & Martin, 1961), multiple-choice answers are provided, and the answer the student selects directs him to a different page in the book. The book is thus a "scrambled one" which is read most irregularly. The correct answer leads to a page on which the next bit of instruction is given, with new alternatives. An incorrect answer is pointed out, with some comments as to why this might have

---

[3] Another name is *intrinsic* programming. Although this is Crowder's own term for his program (e.g., Crowder, 1959), it is less descriptive than *branching.*

been selected, and then the learner is sent back to make another choice. Crowder believes that students who are ill prepared should always have a way to go back to simpler materials, and those who are well prepared should be able to bypass some of the material; hence his later developments provide for these alternative paths through the material. Linear programs of a more modern sort also provide for some kind of review for those who wish to go back to earlier parts of the program, and some kind of skipping for those ready to go ahead. Computer-based programs provide the maximum amount of flexibility in these respects, including alternative paths and different examples for those who may need them. Thus programming is no more a single line of development than the teaching machine is a single type of equipment.

Computer-Assisted Instruction (CAI)

Computer-assisted instruction has by now taken on so many dimensions that it can no longer be considered a simple derivative of the teaching machine or of the kind of programmed learning that Skinner introduced. The teaching machine and the linear or branching programs are, to be sure, its immediate ancestors, but it has evolved rapidly.

One great advantage of the computer over other kinds of educational technology lies in the nature of the device: it computes! Hence, it not only can provide a very flexible presentation of materials to the learner, but can keep track of the progress of a number of learners at the same time. A "readout" from the computer can show where all the learners are at a given time, and what their progress has been from some earlier point of reference.

Several modes of computer-assisted instruction have come into use (Atkinson & Wilson, 1969). The first is the tutorial drill-and-practice procedure, as an outgrowth of programmed learning; this is doubtless the most prevalent mode, and the one used in the systems developed by Atkinson and by Suppes at Stanford. This mode is, of course, commonly used by teachers without the computer; the computer has the advantage of individualizing the activities and of introducing greater learning efficiency through the management of the learning by the computer. A somewhat different method has been used in the teaching of statistics at the University of California at Los Angeles. The student learns a computer language through which he can manipulate large bodies of data, and hence come out of the statistics course able to handle data. Another use is in connection with games that simulate actual problems, whereby complex decisions in relation to metropolitan problems or political control systems can be made and their consequences studied. One such system developed by the Board of Cooperative Educational Services in Westchester County, New York, deals with economic problems through the game called the Sumerian game. The student rules a mythical empire and allocates manpower and other resources; the computer estimates the interactive consequences of his decisions. Even laboratory experiments in chemistry can be carried out without the student's handling equipment and chemicals (Bunderson, 1967). The flexibility of the computer is enormous; hence, any preconception as to the inherent limitations of computer-assisted instruction is likely to be false.

The development of CAI at Stanford University provides a representative case history of the growth of both the technology and the acceptance of CAI. A small system was developed beginning in 1963, and then a large-scale program was undertaken after funds became available under the Elementary and Secondary Education Act of 1965. A system making use of the IBM 1500 was developed jointly by IBM and the Stanford group and became operative in 1966. From the small start of computer drill for 41 fourth-grade children in one school in 1965, the system grew until by the year 1967–68 approximately 3000 students received daily lessons in initial reading, arithmetic, spelling, logic, and elementary Russian in seven nearby schools and in locations as far distant from California as McComb, Mississippi, and Morehead, Kentucky. All instruction was controlled by one central computer located at Stanford.

The original 1500 Tutorial System for reading instruction had a complex station or terminal at which the student worked, consisting of a screen on which images could be projected from frames randomly accessed under computer control, a cathode-ray tube on which material could be presented, a light pen by which touch-probe responses on the cathode-ray tube could be made and recorded, a typewriter keyboard, a set of earphones, and a microphone (Figure 16.4). This device, a kind of virtuoso of instructional technology, served its purpose in showing what could be done; however, as so often happens with new products, it has gradually become simplified without much loss in effectiveness (Atkinson & Fletcher, 1972) (Figure 16.5).

The motivational problems with the computer turn out to be different

Figure 16.4. Student terminal used for tutorial instruction in initial reading. (Courtesy of R. C. Atkinson.)

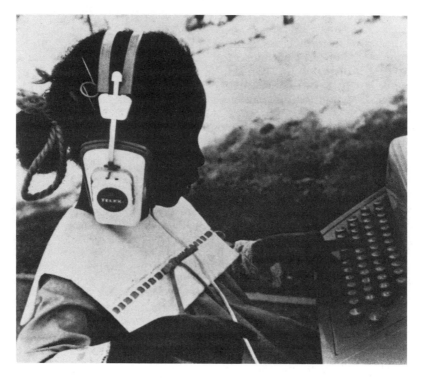

Figure 16.5.   Simplified terminal later used for instruction in initial reading. (Courtesy of R. C. Atkinson.)

from what might have been expected. Instead of the computer's seeming mechanical and forbidding, because it is responsive, the student often becomes very fond of it; one form of motivation may be to deny him the opportunity to use it, which he will interpret as deprivation or punishment (Hess & Tenezakis, 1970).

A lingering problem is always that of costs. Economic feasibility depends on sufficient use of the computer to reduce the hourly cost per student. It has been estimated that for a single system serving 500 terminals (enough for a small elementary school, a junior high school, and a high school in close proximity), the cost could be kept to $.11 per student hour, about what is now spent on traditionally administered instruction in rural schools (Kopstein & Seidel, 1969).

THE RESEARCH DEVELOPMENT PROBLEM IN RELATING LEARNING TO EDUCATION

The brief characterizations of the research on simulators, teaching by films and television, the language laboratory, programmed learning, and computer-assisted instruction help to create a context in which to discuss the role of research in relation to practical problems. It is abundantly clear that each new device requires research to find its most appropriate use, and it is now commonly recognized that there is no linear progression from basic science to applied science to development and dissemination. Instead, there is a complex division of labor in which original work goes on at various stages between basic research and utilization, with complex feedbacks all along the line, so that basic research contributes to applied research and applied research to practical utilization; at the same time, the reverse is also true—applied research contributes to basic understandings, and technological applications and inventions affect the course of pure science. We have already noted that many efforts have been made to leap the gap from basic learning theories to instructional practices, but when the situation is examined closely, it can be seen that there are many empirical steps to be taken. It was for this reason that the idea of a theory of instruction developed, going at its problems somewhat differently than does a theory of learning.

In order to consider the role of research and development in producing modification of educational practices, we do well to examine a classification of the kinds of research that go on in the spectrum from the most basic to the most practical, recognizing that we are *not* dealing with a linear model, in which each step implies the preceding one.

A Taxonomy of Basic Learning Research and Instructional Research and Development

The U.S. government, in its reports of research expenditures, classifies research as basic, applied, and development. In the physics-engineering field, these distinctions are fairly clear: work on solid-state physics is basic research, study of how a transistor can be made to do the work formerly done by vacuum tubes is applied research, and mass-production of transistors and their packaging into electronic devices belongs in development. In the field of education, the distinctions are more difficult to make, for the technological products are commonly not that tangible. An audiovisual aid can of course be treated the same as any other engineered product, but a new curriculum or a new type of school organization (such as an ungraded school) does not automatically fit the conventional scheme. Even in the engineering field there is a good deal of arbitrariness in differentiating between basic and applied, but this does not mean that there is no usefulness in the distinctions, particularly as they refer to the motivations and responsibilities of the scientists engaged in different kinds of tasks. For our purposes we may conveniently divide research on learning and instruction into seven types according to their relevance to the educational enterprise. Three of these may be placed within the "basic learning research" end of the continuum, and four within the "instructional research and development" end, as shown in Figure 16.6.

Basic-science research on learning. By basic-science research is meant that which is guided by the problems that the investigator sets himself, without regard for the immediate applicability of the results to practical situations. This does not mean that the investigator has no practical interests, or that

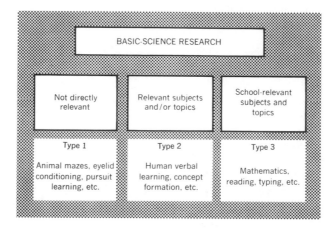

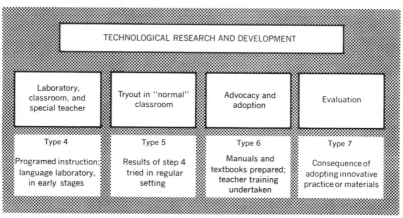

Figure 16.6.   Taxonomy of basic research and instructional research and development.

he does not want his results used; it is only that he is patient and uses the methods and procedures appropriate to the topic on which he works. Within learning research we may divide the stages of relevance to learning into the following three, expanding somewhat the left-hand three boxes of Figure 16.6.

Basic-Science Research on Learning

Type 1. Research on learning with no regard for its educational relevance, for example, animal studies, physiological and biochemical investigations. Learning in the flatworm and learning in the rat with transected spinal cord classify here.

Type 2. Research on learning which is not concerned with educational practices but which is more relevant than that of type 1 because it deals with human subjects and with content that is nearer to that taught in school, for example, nonsense-syllable memorization and retention. The principles being tested are likely to be theoretical ones, such as the relative importance of proactive and retroactive inhibition.

Type 3. Research on learning that is relevant because the subjects are school-age children and the material learned is school subject matter or skill, though no attention is paid to the problem of adapting the learning to school practices, for example, foreign language vocabulary learned by the paired-associate method with various lengths of list and with various spacing of trials.

These three types of relevance all classify as basic-science research because the problems are set by the investigators in relation to some theoretical issue and do not arise out of the practical needs of instruction. Of course there may be bridges from any basic-science project to a practical one: perhaps drugs discovered in brain studies of rats may aid remedial learning; studies of interference may suggest optimal intervals between classes or what should be studied concomitantly; and language-vocabulary results obtained in a laboratory context may guide language acquisition in schools. The main point is that the scientist has not committed himself to relevance.

The difficulty of deciding just where a study belongs is well illustrated by the example previously given of the optimizing of the learning of some foreign language words by college students in the experiment by Atkinson (1972). The study has relevance to instruction (and was presented in that context); at the same time, such a study would be a very incomplete guide as to the best way to teach a foreign language, because vocabulary learning, as noted by Carroll (1963b), is a small part of the process.

Instructional research and development. We are now ready to consider what happens on the right-hand side of Figure 16.6, in the types having to do with applied rather than basic-science research. The types may be described as follows:

Technological Research and Development

Type 4. Research conducted in special laboratory classrooms, with selected teachers, for example, bringing a few students into a room to see whether or not instruction in set theory or symbolic logic is feasible, granted a highly skilled teacher.

Type 5. A tryout of the results of prior research in a "normal" classroom with a typical teacher. Whatever is found feasible in type 4 must be tried out in the more typical classroom, which has limited time for the new method and may lack the special motivation on the part of either teacher or pupil. What is tried out may also be a "hunch" or an "invention" by the teacher, without prior research. Initiative may be taken within *any* of the types listed.

Type 6. Developmental steps related to advocacy and adoption. Anything found to work in types 4 and 5 must be "packaged" for wider use, and then promoted through the processes by which new methods or procedures are adopted by those not party to the experimentation.

Type 7. The goal of instruction has to do with changes in the learner in desirable directions, so that educational materials or practices that have been widely disseminated should be studied according to their consequences. There are many subordinate questions here. Were the materials actually used as intended? Did the teachers change in their practices? Did the pupils show signs of learning improvement over what was expected of them before? What suggestions were there for further modification or improvement? Were the materials or practices appropriate for some classes and not for others?

It is evident that the mood has changed in the transition from basic-science research to technological research.

If one were to review the experimentation on learning by psychologists in its relation to education over past decades, it would be fair to say that too much of the research has fallen under types 1 and 2 to be educationally relevant; educational psychologists, too, have tended to work at this end of the spectrum and then to jump, by inference, to type 6, without being sufficiently patient about types 4 and 5. In this respect, the new interest in the psychology of instruction has been helpful, because of the serious concern both with the structure of subject matter and with the individual learner for whom the program is designed.

The Problem of Educational Innovation

In something as complex as a school system, we need at a high level a special research strategy which may be called the *strategy of innovation*. The best of equipment may lie idle, the best of resources remain unused, the best of techniques sabotaged, unless there is care in introducing the new methods or new materials to all concerned. Once the basic-science principles have been established and the applications validated in practice schoolrooms, their more widespread adoption is by no means guaranteed, nor, if the adoption is forced, is there assurance that the desired results will be forthcoming. Abstractly, the steps of innovation are clear enough: provide (a) a sound research-based program, validated in tryout; (b) the program packaged in such a way that it is available, as in good textbooks, supplementary readings in the form of pamphlets, films, programs for teaching machines, and guides for the teacher; (c) testing materials by which it can be ascertained if the objectives of the program have indeed been realized, with appropriate normative data on these evaluative instruments; (d) in service training of the teacher to overcome the teacher's resistance to new methods and materials and to gain his enthusiastic acceptance of the program as something valuable, as well as to train him in its use;[4] and (e) support for the program from the community, school boards, parents, and others concerned with the schools.

We have not done very well in appraising carefully our strategies of innovation. We have sometimes gone overboard for the novel and untried, just to keep up with the Joneses ("we have teaching machines, too"); at other times we have been very resistant. Commercialism and vested interests enter in unpleasant ways, sometimes supported, unfortunately, by factions of the educational profession itself. Here, then, is a task calling for wisdom and sensitivity. The psychological contributions to the task may come more from social psychology than from the psychology of learning, for the processes are those of social control and attitude change; but unless there is serious concern about the appropriate ways in which to bring about innovation, schools are likely to be the victims of whims, rather than the heirs of the best tradition we can establish through cooperative effort.

---

[4] A puzzling problem with respect to innovations arises, on the one hand, from resistance by both teachers and students to something untraditional, and, on the other, from a "placebo" or "Hawthorne effect" due to the hope and enthusiasm developed by something new and promising. Care must be taken to avoid either distortion. For a relevant discussion, see Miles (1964).

There are some specific suggestions that might be given consideration. It would be desirable, for example, for every school system, of whatever size, to have somewhere within it a school building, or at least a set of school-rooms, devoted to in-service training of teachers and to innovation; these are ongoing matters important at the community level and cannot be left to teacher-training colleges or universities. Both children and teachers could be rotated through these rooms in order to try out innovations before there is firm commitment to them. A few teaching terminals for computer-assisted instruction or some closed-circuit television projectors could be tried out without investing in them for a whole school system; teachers could have a voice in saying whether or not they wanted the new devices, or in selecting among various possibilities. Usually no harm would be done in waiting for a while if teachers were not ready, for methods imposed on teachers are unlikely to prove successful. Some of the innovations to be tried out might be those of successful local teachers themselves, here given the opportunity to show their colleagues how they do it in their own class-rooms. Members of the school board and representatives of the parents could be brought in also to observe such testing. The principles of tryout before acceptance, of choice by those who are to use the method, seem to be sound ones. If the new methods are indeed good, they will find acceptance.

In order to build a sound connection between the experimental studies of learning and the classroom, we need a series of steps, for applied science consists of more than applying principles to practice. The main point is that in the research and development phases a collaboration is called for between psychologist, subject-matter specialist, and teacher; beyond this, careful consideration must be given to techniques of innovation. If we achieve success in integrating these phases, we will move toward that improvement of education which will be satisfying to us all.

The Role of Major Research and Development Centers

The history of research on the technology of education suggests that the approach through multitudinous small research projects does not yield satisfactory consequences. For example, the thousands of small studies that have been done on the teaching of reading have yielded remarkably little in the way of sound knowledge (Chall, 1967). What is apparently needed are large-scale programs which will do for teaching and learning what large-scale testing enterprises, such as the Educational Testing Service, have done for evaluation. Educational measurements have been improved through basic studies in statistics, theory of scaling, factor analysis, and so on; at the same time, the arranging of materials and the determination of norms have proceeded only because the applied aspects were taken as seriously as the basic-science aspects. Until recently, little of this kind of effort has gone into the problems of providing better teaching materials and tested instructional methods. We now have a number of experiences of large-scale cooperative efforts in producing better teaching materials through the collaboration of subject-matter experts, learning specialists, and teachers. The U.S. Office of Education has seen fit to establish large research and development centers in universities, and substantially financed regional laboratories. More recently, a National Institute of Education has been established by the federal government. The prior large-scale experience in the military establishments shows that results do not come either quickly or cheaply, and there appears to be no alternative to carefully conceived massive attacks on the learning problems involved in instruction.

SUPPLEMENTARY READINGS

The following books are helpful in attempting to appraise theories of instruction, educational technology, and educational research.

Theories of Instruction
BLOCK, J. H. (Ed.) (1971) *Mastery learning.*
BRUNER, J. S. (1966) *Toward a theory of instruction.*
GAGNÉ, R. M. (1970) *The conditions of learning.*
HILGARD, E. R. (Ed.) (1964a) *Theories of learning and instruction.*
SKINNER, B. F. (1968) *The technology of teaching.*

Educational Technology
ATKINSON, R. C., & WILSON, H. A. (Eds.) (1969) *Computer-assisted instruction: A book of readings.*
CARNEGIE COMMISSION ON HIGHER EDUCATION (1972) *The fourth revolution: Instructional technology in higher education.*
CHU, G. C. & SCHRAMM, W. (1967) *Learning from television: What the research says.*
LANGE, P. C. (Ed.) (1967) *Programed instruction.*
LEVIÈN, R. E. (1972) *The emerging technology: Instructional uses of the computer in higher education.*
SUPPES, P., JERMAN, M., & BRIAN, D. (1968) *Computer-assisted instruction: Stanford's 1965–66 arithmetic program.*
SUPPES, P., & MORNINGSTAR, M. (1972) *Computer-assisted instruction at Stanford, 1966–68.*
TICKTON, S. G. (Ed.) (1970) *To improve learning: An evaluation of instructional technology.*

Educational Research
CRONBACH, L. J., & SUPPES, P. (Eds.) (1969) *Research for tomorrow's schools.*
GAGE, N. L. (Ed.) (1963) *Handbook of research on teaching.*
GAGNÉ, R. M., & GEPHART, W. L. (Eds.) (1968) *Learning research and school subjects.*

References

ABERNETHY, E. M. (1940) The effect of changed environmental conditions upon the results of college examinations. *J. Psychol.*, 10, 293–301.—*301*

ABORN, M. (1953) The influence of experimentally induced failure on the retention of material acquired through set and incidental learning. *J. exp. Psychol.*, 45, 225–231.—*366*

ACH, N. (1906) Uber die Willenstätigkeit und das Denken. Göttingen: Vanderhoeck and Rerprecht, 1905. Reprinted as "Determining Tendencies" in J. Mandler & G. Mandler (Eds.), *Thinking: From association to Gestalt.* New York: Wiley, 1964, 201–207.—*9–10*

ADAMS, J. A. (1967) *Human memory.* New York: McGraw-Hill.—*312, 316*

AEBLI, H. (1951) *Didactique psychologique: Application à la didactique de la psychologie de Jean Piaget.* Neuchâtel: Delachaux et Niestlé.—*340*

ALBERT, D. J. (1966) The effect of spreading depression on the consolidation of learning. *Neuropsychol.*, 4, 49–64.—*544*

ALLEN, G. A., & ESTES, W. K. (1972) Acquisition of correct choices and value judgments in binary choice learning with differential rewards. *Psychon. Sci.*, 27, 68–72.—*50*

ALLPORT, G. W. (1937) *Personality: A psychological interpretation.* New York: Holt, Rinehart and Winston.—*221*

ALLPORT, G. W., & POSTMAN, L. (1947) *The psychology of rumor.* New York: Holt, Rinehart and Winston.—*270*

AMAREL, S. (1968) On representations of problems of reasoning about actions. In D. Michie (Ed.), *Machine Intelligence.* Vol. 3. New York: American Elsevier.—*456*

AMMONS, R. B. (1962) Psychology of the scientist. II: Clark L. Hull and his "Idea Books." *Percept. Mot. Skills*, 15, 800–802.

AMSEL, A. (1958) The role of frustrative nonreward in noncontinuous reward situations. *Psychol. Bull.*, 55, 102–119.—*130, 166, 192*

AMSEL, A. (1962) Frustrative nonreward in partial reinforcement and discrimination learning. *Psychol. Rev.*, 69, 306–328.—*130, 166, 192*

AMSEL, A. (1965) On inductive versus deductive approaches and neo-Hullian behaviorism. In B. B. Wolman (Ed.), *Scientific Psychology.* New York: Basic Books, 187–206.—*174*

AMSEL, A. (1967) Partial reinforcement effects on vigor and persistence. In K. W. Spence & J. T. Spence (Eds.), *The psychology of learning and motivation.* Vol. 1. New York: Academic Press.—*192, 195–98*

AMSEL, A., & WARD, J. S. (1965) Frustration and persistence: Resistance to discrimination following prior experience with the discriminanda. *Psychol. Monogr.*, 79, No. 4 (Whole No. 597).—*193*

ANAND, B. K., CHHINA, G. S., & SINGH, B. (1961) Some aspects of electroencephalographic studies in yogis. *Electroencephalography and Clinical Neurophysiology,* 13, 452–456. Also in C. T. Tart (Ed.), *Altered states of consciousness: A book of readings.* New York: Wiley.—*558*

ANDERSON, J. R. (1972) FRAN: A simulation model of free recall. In G. H. Bower (Ed.), *The psychology of learning and motivation: Advances in research and theory.* Vol. 5. New York: Academic Press.—*279, 586*

ANDERSON, J. R., & BOWER, G. H. (1972a) Recognition and retrieval processes in free recall. *Psychol. Rev.,* 79, 97–123.—*297, 591, 592*

ANDERSON, J. R., & BOWER, G. H. (1972b) Configural properties of sentence memory. *J. verb. Learn. verb. Behav.,* 11, 594–605.—*280*

ANDERSON, J. R., & BOWER, G. H. (1973) *Human associative memory.* Washington, D.C.: V. H. Winston.—*7, 9, 23, 280, 310, 311, 471, 475, 483, 577, 592, 597, 598*

ANDERSON, N. H. (1959) Temporal properties of response evocation. In R. R. Bush & W. K. Estes (Eds.), *Studies in mathematical learning theory.* Stanford: Stanford Univ. Press.—*171*

ANDERSON, N. H. (1964) An evaluation of stimulus sampling theory: Comments on Professor Estes' paper. In A. W. Melton (Ed.), *Categories of human learning.* New York: Academic Press.

ANDERSON, R. C., & CARTER, J. F. (1972) Retroactive inhibition of meaningful-learned sentences. *Am. Ed. Res. J.* 9, 443–448.—*310, 311*

ANDERSON, R. C., & MYROW, D. L. (1971) Retroactive inhibition of meaningful discourse. *J. ed. Psychol., Monogr. Suppl.,* 62, 81–94.—*310*

ANDERSON, R. C., & WATTS, G. H. (1971) Response competition in the forgetting of paired associates. *J. verb. Learn. verb. Behav.,* 10, 29–34.—*303*

ANGELL, J. R. (1907) The province of functional psychology. *Psychol. Rev.,* 14, 61–91.—*284*

Antioch College (1960) *Experiment in French language instruction: Second report, 1959–1960.* Yellow Springs, Ohio: Antioch Press.—*627*

ARNOLD, P. G., & BOWER, G. H. (1972) Perceptual conditions affecting ease of association. *J. exp. Psychol.,* 93, 176–180.—*264*

ASCH, S. E. (1969) Reformulation of the problem of association. *Amer. Psychol.,* 24, 92–102. —*264–67*

ASCH, S. E., CERASO, J., & HEIMER, W. (1960) Perceptual conditions of association. *Psychol. Monogr.,* 57 (Whole No. 3).—*264*

ASHBY, E. (1967) Machines, understanding, and learning: Reflections on technology in education. Austin, Tex.: *Grad. J.,* 7, No. 2.

ASHBY, W. R. (1952) *Design for a brain.* New York: Wiley.—*429*

ATKINSON, R. C. (1962) Choice behavior and monetary payoffs. In J. Criswell, H. Solomon, & P. Suppes (Eds.), *Mathematical methods in small group processes.* Stanford: Stanford Univ. Press.—*405–6*

ATKINSON, R. C. (1968) Computerized instruction and the learning process. *Amer. Psychol.,* 23, 225–239.

ATKINSON, R. C. (1972) Ingredients for a theory of instruction. *Amer. Psychol.,* 27, 921–931. —*619, 621–23, 634*

ATKINSON, R. C., BOWER, G. H., & CROTHERS, E. J. (1965) *Introduction to mathematical learning theory.* New York: Wiley.—*389, 412, 619*

ATKINSON, R. C., & CROTHERS, E. J. (1964) A comparison of paired associate learning models having different acquisition and retention axioms. *J. math. Psychol.,* 1, 285–315.—*418, 419, 623*

ATKINSON, R. C., & ESTES, W. K. (1963) Stimulus sampling theory. In R. D. Luce, R. R. Bush, & E. Galanter (Eds.), *Handbook of mathematical psychology.* Vol. 2. New York: Wiley.—*400, 401*

ATKINSON, R. C., & FLETCHER, J. D. (1972) Teaching children to read with a computer. *The Reading Teacher,* 25, 319–327.—*619–20, 631*

ATKINSON, R. C., & PAULSON, J. A. (1972) An approach to the psychology of instruction. *Psychol. Bull.,* 78, 49–61.—*425, 619*

ATKINSON, R. C., & SHIFFRIN, R. M. (1965) *Mathematical models for memory and learning.* Technical Report #79, Psychology Series, Institute for Mathematical Studies in the Social Sciences. Stanford: Stanford Univ. Press.—*250, 418*

ATKINSON, R. C., & SHIFFRIN, R. M. (1968) Human memory: A proposed system and its control processes. In K. W. Spence & J. T. Spence (Eds.), *The Psychology of Learning and Motivation.* Vol. 2. New York: Academic Press.—*418, 420*

ATKINSON, R. C., & WICKENS, T. D. (1971) Human memory and the concept of reinforcement. In R. Glaser (Ed.), *The nature of reinforcement*. New York, Academic Press.—*48, 138, 580*

ATKINSON, R. C., & WILSON, H. A. (Eds.) (1969) Computer-assisted instruction. In *Computer-assisted instruction: A book of readings*. New York: Academic Press, 3–14.—*630*

AUDLEY, R. J. (1960) A stochastic model for individual choice behavior. *Psychol. Rev.*, 67, 1–15.—*406*

AZRIN, N. H. (1964) Aggression. A speech to American Psychological Association, Sept. 6, 1964, Los Angeles. Title listed in *Amer. Psychol.*, 17, 501.—*194, 223*

AZRIN, N. H., HAKE, D. F., & HUTCHINSON, R. R. (1965) Elicitation of aggression by a physical blow. *J. exp. Anal. Behav.*, 8, 55–57.—*223*

AZRIN, N. H., & HOLZ, W. C. (1966) Punishment. In W. K. Honig (Ed.), *Operant behavior: Areas of research and application*. New York: Appleton-Century-Crofts, 380–447.—*213, 224–25*

BABKIN, B. P. (1949) *Pavlov; a biography*. Chicago: Univ. of Chicago Press.—*63*

BADDELEY, A. D., & WARRINGTON, E. K. (1970) Amnesia and the distinction between long- and short-term memory. *J. verb. Learn. verb. Behav.*, 9, 176–189.—*517*

BANDURA, A. (1962) Social learning through imitation. In M. R. Jones (Ed.), *Nebraska Symposium on Motivation: 1962*. Lincoln: Univ. of Nebraska Press, 211–269.—*600–601*

BANDURA, A. (1965) Vicarious processes: A case of no-trial learning. In L. Berkowitz (Ed.), *Advances in experimental social psychology*. Vol. 2. New York: Academic Press.—*600–601*

BANDURA, A. (1969) *Principles of behavior modification*. New York: Holt, Rinehart and Winston.—*241, 288, 349, 361, 372, 599, 600–601, 605*

BANDURA, A. (1971a) *Social learning theory*. New York: General Learning Press.—*239, 242, 599, 600–601*

BANDURA, A. (1971b) *Psychological modeling: Conflicting theories*. New York: Aldine-Atherton.—*599, 600–601, 602*

BANDURA, A., GRUSEC, J. E., & MENLOVE, F. L. (1966) Observational learning as a function of symbolization and incentive set. *Child Devel.*, 37, 499–506.—*245, 603*

BANDURA, A., & JEFFERY, R. W. (1973) Role of symbolic coding and rehearsal processes in observational learning. *J. Pers. soc. Psychol.*, in press *26, 122 30, 603*

BANDURA, A., & McDONALD, F. J. (1963) The influence of social reinforcement and the behavior of models in shaping children's moral judgments. *J. abnor. soc. Psychol.*, 67, 274–281.—*349*

BANDURA, A., & WALTERS, R. H. (1963). *Social learning and personality development*. New York: Holt, Rinehart and Winston.—*605*

BARBIZET, J. (1970) *Human memory and its pathology*. San Francisco: W. H. Freeman.—*369*

BARKER, R. G., DEMBO, T., & LEWIN, K. (1941) Frustration and regression: A study of young children. *Univ. Ia. Stud. Child Welf.*, 18, No. 1.—*356*

BARNES, J. M., & UNDERWOOD, B. J. (1959) Fate of first-list associations in transfer theory. *J. exp. Psychol.*, 58, 97–105. *302, 304, 312*

BARONDES, S. H., & COHEN, H. D. (1966) Puromycin effect on successive phases of memory storage. *Science*, 151, 594–595.—*532*

BARRETT, R. J., PEYSER, C. S., & McHOSE, J. H. (1965) Effects of complete and incomplete reward reduction on a subsequent response. *Psychon. Sci.*, 3, 277–278.—*193*

BARTLETT, F. C. (1932) *Remembering*. London: Cambridge Univ. Press.—*270, 343*

BEACH, F. A. (1955) The descent of instinct. *Psychol. Rev.*, 62, 401–410.—*18*

BEACH, F. A., & JAYNES, J. (1954) Effects of early experience upon the behavior of animals. *Psychol. Bull.*, 51, 239–263.—*358*

BEACH, L. R., ROSE, R. M., SAYEKI, Y., WISE, J. A., & CARTER, W. B. (1970). Probability learning: Response proportions and verbal estimates. *J. exp. Psychol.*, 86, 165–170.—*388*

BEM, D. J. (1967) Self-perception: An alternative interpretation of cognitive dissonance phenomena. *Psychol. Rev.*, 74, 183–200.—*238*

BEM, D. J. (1972) Self-perception theory. In L. Berkowitz (Ed.), *Advances in experimental social psychology*. Vol. 6. New York: Academic Press.—*238*

BENNETT, E. L., KRECH, D., & ROSENZWEIG, M. R. (1964) Reliability and regional specificity of cerebral effects of environmental complexity and training. *J. comp. physiol. Psychol.*, 57, 440–441.—*528*

BENTHAM, J. (1789) *The principles of morals and legislation*. London.—*13*

BERGIN, A. E., & GARFIELD, S. L. (Eds.) (1971) *Handbook of psychotherapy and behavior change*. New York: Wiley.—*239, 361*

BERLYNE, D. E. (1960a) Conflict, arousal, and curiosity. New York: McGraw-Hill.—*81*

BERLYNE, D. E. (1960b) Les équivalences psychologiques et les notions quantitatives. In D. E. Berlyne and J. Piaget, *Théorie du comportement et operations*. Paris: Presses Universitaires de France.—*337*

BERLYNE, D. E. (1965) *Structure and direction in thinking*. New York: Wiley.—*337–40*

BERNBACH, H. A. (1965) Stimulus learning and recognition in paired-associate learning. Doctoral dissertation, Univ. of Michigan. Also Technical Report #05823-7-T under Contract No. AF 49(638)-1235.—*413*

BERNOULLI, D. (1738) Specimen theoriae novae de mensura sortis. *Commentari academiae scientiarum imperiales petropolitanae*, 5, 175–192. (Translated by L. Sommer in *Econometrika*, 1954, 22, 23–36.)—*13*

BERSH, P. J. (1951) The influence of two variables upon the establishment of a secondary reinforcer for operant responses. *J. exp. Psychol.*, 41, 62–73.—*220*

BEVAN, W. (1963) The pooling mechanism and the phenomena of reinforcement. In O. J. Harvey (Ed.), *Motivation and social interaction: Cognitive determinants*. New York: Ronald Press, 18–44, 453–472.—*566*

BEVAN, W., & ADAMSON, R. (1960) Reinforcers and reinforcement: Their relation to maze performance. *J. exp. Psychol.*, 59, 226–232.—*565, 566*

BEVAN, W., & ADAMSON, R. (1963) Internal referents and the concept of reinforcement. In N. F. Washburne (Ed.), *Decisions, values and groups*. Vol. 2. New York: Pergamon.

BEVER, T. G. (1968) Associations to stimulus-response theories of language. In T. R. Dixon & D. L. Horton (Eds.), *Verbal behavior and general behavior theory*. Englewood Cliffs, N.J., Prentice-Hall.—*247*

BEVER, T. G., FODOR, J. A., & GARRETT, M. (1968) A formal limitation of associationism. In T. R. Dixon & D. L. Horton (Eds.), *Verbal behavior and general behavior theory*. Englewood Cliffs, N.J.: Prentice-Hall.—*247*

BEVER, T. G., FODOR, J. A., & WEKSEL, W. (1965a) On the acquisition of syntax: A critique of contextual generalization. *Psychol. Rev.*, 72, 467–482.—*234–35*

BEVER, T. G., FODOR, J. A., & WEKSEL, W. (1965b) Is linguistics empirical? *Psychol. Rev.*, 72, 493–500.—*234–35*

BICKFORD, R. G., MULDER, D. W., DODGE, H. W., SVIEN, H. J., & ROME, P. R. (1958) Changes in memory function produced by electrical stimulation of the temporal lobe in man. *Res. Pub. Assoc. for Res. in Nerv. and Ment. Dis.*, 36, 227.—*516–17*

BINDER, A., & FELDMAN, S. E. (1960) The effects of experimentally controlled experience upon recognition responses. *Psychol. Monogr.*, 74, No. 496.—*387*

BIRCH, H. G. (1945) The relation of previous experience to insightful problem-solving. *J. comp. Psychol.*, 38, 367–383.—*273*

BIRNBAUM, I. M. (1972) General and specific components of retroactive inhibition in the A-B, A-C paradigm. *J. exp. Psychol.*, 93, 188–192.—*304*

BITTERMAN, M. E. (1965) The CS-US interval in classical and avoidance-conditioning. In W. F. Prokasy (Ed.), *Classical conditioning: A symposium*. New York: Appleton-Century-Crofts.—*171*

BITZER, D. L., & SLOTTOW, H. G. (1968) Principles and application of the plasma panel. *Proceedings of the OAR Research Applications Conference*, Vol. 1, a1–a43. Washington, D.C.: Institute for Defense Analyses.

BJORK, R. A. (1970) Positive forgetting: The noninterference of items intentionally forgotten. *J. verb. Learn. verb. Behav.*, 9, 255–268.—*580*

BLACK, A. H. (1972) The operant conditioning of central nervous system electrical activity. In G. H. Bower (Ed.), *The psychology of learning and motivation: Advances in research and theory*. Vol. 6. New York: Academic Press.—*557*

BLACK, A. H., & PROKASY, W. F. (Eds.) (1972) *Classical conditioning. II: Current theory and research*. New York: Appleton-Century-Crofts.

BLOCK, J. H. (Ed.) (1971) *Mastery learning: Theory and practice*. New York: Holt, Rinehart and Winston.—*623*

BLODGETT, H. C. (1929) The effect of the introduction of reward upon the maze performance of rats. *Univ. Calif. Publ. Psychol.*, 4, 113–134.—*134*

BLODGETT, H. C., & McCUTCHAN, K. (1947) Place versus response-learning in the simple T-maze. *J. exp. Psychol.*, 37, 412–422.—*131–32*

BLODGETT, H. C., & McCUTCHAN, K. (1948) The relative strength of place and response learning in the T-Maze. *J. comp. physiol. Psychol.*, 41, 17–24.—*131–32*

BLOOM, B. S. (1968) Learning for mastery. *Evaluation Comment*, 1, No. 2, Univ. of California at Los Angeles. (Reprinted in Block, 1971, 47–63.)—*623*

BLOUGH, D. S. (1961) Experiments in animal psychophysics. *Sci. Amer.*, 206, July, 113–122. *—261*

BLOUGH, D. S. (1966) The study of animal sensory processes by operant methods. In W. K. Honig (Ed.), *Operant behavior: Areas of research and application*. New York: Appleton-Century-Crofts.*—231*

BOAKES, R. A., & HALLIDAY, S. (Eds.) (1972) *Inhibition and learning*. New York: Academic Press.

BOBROW, D. G. (1964) Natural language input for a computer problem-solving system. Project MAC—Technical Report No. 1. Cambridge: MIT, Sept. Unpublished Ph.D. thesis, MIT, 1964.*—470*

BOBROW, S. A. (1970) Memory for words in sentences. *J. verb. Learn. verb. Behav.*, 9, 363–372.*—311*

BOLLES, R. C. (1970) Species specific defense reactions in avoidance learning. *Psychol. Rev.*, 71, 32–48.*—575–76*

BOLLES, R. C. (1972) The avoidance learning problem. In G. H. Bower (Ed.), *The psychology of learning and motivation: Advances in research and theory*. Vol. 6. New York: Academic Press.*—175, 178, 575–76*

BORING, E. G. (1950) *A history of experimental psychology* (2nd ed.). New York: Appleton-Century-Crofts.*—6, 347*

BORING, E. G., LANGFELD, H. S., WERNER, H., & YERKES, ROBERT M. (Eds.) (1952) *A history of psychology in autobiography*. Vol. 4. Worcester, Mass.: Clark University Press.*—346*

BORKO, H. (Ed.) (1962) *Computer applications in the behavioral sciences*. Englewood Cliffs, N.J.: Prentice-Hall.*—439*

BORKO, H. (Ed.) (1967) *Automated language processing*. New York: Wiley.*—466*

BOUSFIELD, W. A. (1953) The occurrence of clustering in the recall of randomly arranged associates. *J. gen. Psychol.*, 49, 229–240.*—585*

BOWER, G. H. (1959) Choice-point behavior. In R. R. Bush & W. K. Estes (Eds.), *Studies in mathematical learning theory*. Stanford. Stanford Univ. Press, 109–124.*—143, 398, 406*

BOWER, G. H. (1960) Partial and correlated reward in escape learning. *J. exp. Psychol.*, 59, 126–130.*—191, 197*

BOWER, G. H. (1961a) Application of a model to paired-associate learning. *Psychometrika*, 255–280.*—412*

BOWER, G. H. (1961b) A contrast effect in differential conditioning. *J. exp. Psychol.*, 62, 196–199.*—565*

BOWER, G. H. (1962a) Response strengths and choice probability: A consideration of two combination rules. In E. Nagel, P. Suppes, & A. Tarski (Eds.), *Logic, methodology, and philosophy of science: Proceedings of the 1960 International Congress*. Stanford: Stanford Univ. Press, 400–412.*—398*

BOWER, G. H. (1962b) An association model for response and training variables in paired-associate learning. *Psychol. Rev.*, 69, 34–53.*—143, 412*

BOWER, G. H. (1962c) The influence of graded reductions in reward and prior frustrating events upon the magnitude of the frustration effect. *J. comp. physiol. Psychol.*, 55, 582–587.*—193, 565*

BOWER, G. H. (1964) Drive level and preference between two incentives. *Psychon. Sci.*, 1, 131–132.*—190*

BOWER, G. H. (1966) Probability learning of response patterns. *Psychon. Sci.*, 4, 215–216.*—389*

BOWER, G. H. (1967a) A descriptive theory of memory. In D. P. Kimble (Ed.), *The organization of recall*. Vol. 2 of series. New York: New York Academy of Sciences.*—413, 418, 419*

BOWER, G. H. (1967b) Verbal learning. In H. H. Helson & W. Bevan (Eds.), *Contemporary approaches to psychology*. Princeton: Van Nostrand.*—395, 417*

BOWER, G. H. (1970a) Analysis of a mnemonic device. *Amer. Sci.*, 58, 496–510.*—150, 266*

BOWER, G. H. (1970b) Organizational factors in memory. *Cog. Psychol.* 1, 18–46.*—272, 279, 585, 587*

BOWER, G. H. (1972a) Perceptual groups as coding units in immediate memory. *Psychon. Sci.*, 27, 217–219.*—258–59*

BOWER, G. H. (1972b) Mental imagery and associative learning. In L. W. Gregg (Ed.), *Cognition in learning and memory*. New York: Wiley.*—588, 589*

BOWER, G. H. (1972c) A selective review of organizational factors in memory. In E. Tulving & W. Donaldson (Eds.), *Organization of memory*. New York: Academic Press.*—272, 586*

BOWER, G. H. (1972d) Stimulus-sampling theory of encoding variability. In E. Martin & A. Melton (Eds.), *Coding theory and memory*. Washington, D.C.: V. H. Winston.—*297, 378, 395, 398, 514*

BOWER, G. H., CLARK, M. C., WINZENZ, D., & LESGOLD, A. (1969) Hierarchical retrieval schemes in recall of categorized word lists. *J. verb. Learn. verb. Behav.*, 8, 323–343.—*279*

BOWER, G. H., LESGOLD, A., & TIEMAN, D. (1969) Grouping operations in free recall. *J. verb. Learn. verb. Behav.*, 8, 481–493.—*279, 586*

BOWER, G. H., MCLEAN, J., & MEACHAM, J. (1966) Value of knowing when reinforcement is due. *J. comp. physiol. Psychol.*, 62, 184–192.—*211*

BOWER, G. H., & MILLER, N. E. (1958) Rewarding and punishing effects from stimulating the same place in the rat's brain. *J. comp. physiol. Psychol.*, 51, 669–674.—*499*

BOWER, G. H., & SPRINGSTON, F. (1970) Pauses as recoding points in letter series. *J. exp. Psychol.*, 83, 421–430.—*257*

BOWER, G. H., STARR, R., & LAZAROVITZ, L. (1965) Amount of response-produced change in the CS and avoidance learning. *J. comp. physiol. Psychol.*, 59, 13–17.—*99–100*

BOWER, G. H., & THEIOS, J. (1964) A learning model for discrete performance levels. In R. C. Atkinson (Ed.), *Studies in mathematical psychology*. Stanford: Stanford Univ. Press.—*409, 416*

BOWER, G. H., & TRABASSO, T. R. (1964) Concept identification. In R. C. Atkinson (Ed.), *Studies in mathematical psychology*. Stanford: Stanford Univ. Press, 32–94.—*312–13*

BOWER, G. H., & WINZENZ, D. (1969) Group structure, coding, and memory for digit series. *J. exp. Psychol. Monogr.*, 80, No. 2, Part 2, 1–17.—*257, 269*

BOWER, T. G. R. (1965) Stimulus variables determining space perception in infants. *Science*, 149, 88–89.—*8*

BOWER, T. G. R. (1966) Slant perception and shape constancy in infants. *Science*, 151, 832–834.—*8*

BOWER, T. G. R. (1967) The development of object-performance: Some studies of existence constancy. *Percept. Psychophys.*, 2, 411–412.—*325*

BRAINE, M. S. (1959) The ontogeny of certain logical operations: Piaget's formulations examined by non-verbal methods. *Psychol. Monogr.*, 73 (Whole No. 475).—*336*

BRAINE, M. S. (1963) On learning the grammatical order of words. *Psychol. Rev.*, 70, 323–348.—*234*

BRAINE, M. S. (1964) Development of a grasp of transitivity of length: A reply to Smedslund. *Child Devel.*, 35, 799–810.—*336*

BRAINERD, C. J. (1973) Order of acquisition of transitivity, conservation, and class inclusion of length and weight. *Devel. Psychol.*, 8, 105–116.—*331*

BRAUD, W. G. (1970) Extinction in goldfish: Facilitation by intracranial injection of RNA from brains of extinguished donors. *Science*, 168, 1234–1236.—*531*

BRAUD, W. G., & HOFFMAN, R. B. (1973) Response facilitation and response inhibition produced by intracranial injections of brain extracts from trained donor goldfish. *Physiol. Psychol.*, 1, 169–173.—*531*

BREITENFELD, F., JR. (1970) Instructional television: The state of the art. In S. G. Tickton (Ed.), *To improve learning: An evaluation of instructional technology*. Vol. 1. New York: Bowker, 137–160.

BRELAND, K., & BRELAND, M. (1951) A field of applied animal psychology. *Amer. Psychol.*, 6, 202–204.—*231*

BRELAND, K., & BRELAND, M. (1960) The misbehavior of organisms. *Amer. Psychol.*, 16, 661–664.—*85, 244*

BRELSFORD, J. W., JR. (1967) Experimental manipulation of state occupancy in a Markov model for avoidance conditioning. *J. Math. Psychol.*, 4, 21–47.—*422*

BRESSON, F., & DE MONTMILLON, M. (Eds.) (1966) *Psychologie et epistemologie genetique: Themes Piagetiens*. Paris: Dunod.—*346*

BRIGGS, G. E. (1954) Acquisition, extinction and recovery functions in retroactive inhibition. *J. exp. Psychol.*, 47, 285–293.—*305–6*

BRIGGS, G. E. (1957) Retroactive inhibition as a function of original and interpolated learning. *J. exp. Psychol.*, 53, 60–67.—*301–3*

BRINK, F., JR. (1951) Synaptic mechanisms. In S. S. Stevens (Ed.), *Handbook of experimental psychology*. New York: Wiley, 94–120.—*520*

British Medical Bulletin (1971) Vol. 27, Whole Number 3, "Cognitive Psychology."

BROADBENT, D. E. (1957) A mechanical model for human attention and immediate memory. *Psychol. Rev.*, 64, 205–215.—*417–18*

BROWN, J. S. (1969) Factors affecting self-punitive locomotor behavior. In B. A. Campbell & R. M. Church (Eds.), *Punishment and aversive behavior*. New York: Appleton-Century-Crofts.—*101*

BROWN, J. S., & JACOBS, A. (1949) The role of fear in the motivation and acquisition of response. *J. exp. Psychol.*, 39, 749–759.—*178*

BROWN, P. L., & JENKINS, H. M. (1968) Auto-shaping of the pigeon's key-peck. *J. exp. Anal. Behav.*, 11, 1–8.—*244*

BROWN, T. (1820) *Lectures on the philosophy of the human mind*. 4 vols., 16th ed. Edinburgh: William Tait, 1846.—*63, 289*

BRUCE, D., & PAPAY, J. J. (1970) Primacy effect in single-trial free recall. *J. verb. Learn. verb. Behav.*, 9, 473–486.—*580*

BRUNER, J. S. (1960) *The process of education*. Cambridge: Harvard Univ. Press.—*618*

BRUNER, J. S. (1964a) Some theorems on instruction illustrated with reference to mathematics. In E. R. Hilgard (Ed.), *Theories of learning and instruction*. Chicago: Univ. of Chicago Press, 306–335.—*614*

BRUNER, J. S. (1964b) The course of cognitive growth. *Amer. Psychol.* 19, 1–15.—*619*

BRUNER, J. S. (1966) *Toward a theory of instruction*. New York: Norton.—*618, 619*

BRUNER, J. S., GOODNOW, J., & AUSTIN, G. (1956) *A study of thinking*. New York: Wiley.—*438*

BRUNER, J. S., OLVER, R. R., & GREENFIELD, P. M. (1966) *Studies in cognitive growth*. New York: Wiley.—*334*

BRUNSWIK, E. (1939) Probability as a determiner of rat behavior. *J. exp. Psychol.*, 25, 175–197.—*139*

BRUNSWIK, E. (1955) Representative design and probabilistic theory in a functional psychology. *Psychol. Rev.*, 62, 193–217.—*317*

BRYAN, W. L., & HARTER, N. (1897) Studies in the physiology and psychology of the telegraphic language. *Psychol. Rev.*, 4, 27–53.—*31*

BRYAN, W. L., & HARTER, N. (1899) Studies on the telegraphic language: The acquisition of a hierarchy of habits. *Psychol. Rev.*, 6, 345–375.—*31*

BUCHWALD, A. M. (1967) Effects of immediate vs. delayed outcomes in associative learning. *J. verb. Learn. verb. Behav.*, 6, 317–320.—*49, 50–51*

BUCHWALD, A. M. (1969) Effects of "right" and "wrong" on subsequent behavior: A new interpretation. *Psychol. Rev.*, 76, 132–143.—*49*

BUGELSKI, B. R. (1956) *The psychology of learning*. New York: Holt, Rinehart and Winston.

BUGELSKI, B. R. (1964) *The psychology of learning applied to teaching*. Indianapolis: Bobbs-Merrill.—*312*

BUNDERSON, V. (1967) The role of computer-assisted instruction in university education. *Progress Report to the Coordination Board of the Texas College and University System*. Austin: University of Texas.—*630*

BUREŠ, J., & BUREŠOVÁ, O. (1960) The use of Leao's spreading depression in the study of interhemispheric transfer of memory traces. *J. comp. physiol. Psychol.*, 53, 558–563.—*543*

BUREŠ, J., BUREŠOVÁ, O., & FIFKOVÁ, E. (1964) Interhemispheric transfer of a passive-avoidance reaction. *J. comp. physiol. Psychol.*, 57, 326–330.—*543–44*

BURKE, C. J., ESTES, W. K., & HELLYER, S. (1954) Rate of verbal conditioning in relation to stimulus variability. *J. exp. Psychol.*, 48, 153–161.—*383*

BURNS, B. D. (1958) *The mammalian cerebral cortex*. London: Edward Arnold.—*518, 521*

BUSH, R. R., & MOSTELLER, F. (1951) A mathematical model for simple learning. *Psychol. Rev.*, 58, 313–323.—*375, 399, 407*

BUSH, R. R., & MOSTELLER, F. (1955) *Stochastic models for learning*. New York: Wiley.—*375*

BYKOV, K. M. (1957) *The cerebral cortex and the internal organs*. (Translated by W. H. Gantt.) New York: Chemical Publishing.—*74, 212*

CAGGIULA, A. R. (1970) Analysis of the copulation-reward properties of posterior hypothalamic stimulation in male rats. *J. comp. physiol. Psychol.*, 70, 399–412.—*495–96, 497, 500*

CALDWELL, W. E., & JONES, H. B. (1954) Some positive results on a modified Tolman and Honzik insight maze. *J. comp. physiol. Psychol.*, 47, 416–418.—*134*

CANADAY, R. H. (1962) The description of overlapping figures. Unpublished master's thesis in electrical engineering, MIT.—*460*

CAPALDI, E. J. (1966) Partial reinforcement: An hypothesis of sequential effects. *Psychol. Rev.*, 73, 459–477.—*567–70*

CAPALDI, E. J. (1967) A sequential hypothesis of instrumental learning. In K. W. Spence & J. T. Spence (Eds.), *The psychology of learning and motivation: Advances in research and theory.* Vol. 1. New York: Academic Press.—*140, 197, 567–70*

CAPALDI, E. J., & CAPALDI, E. D. (1970) Magnitude of partial reward, irregular reward schedules, and a 24-hour ITI: A test of several hypotheses. *J. comp. physiol. Psychol.,* 72, 203–209.—*569, 570*

CAREW, T. J. (1970) Do passive avoidance tasks permit assessment of retrograde amnesia in rats? *J. comp. physiol. Psychol.,* 72, 267–271.—*513–14*

Carnegie Commission on Higher Education (1972) *The fourth revolution: Instructional technology in higher education.* New York: McGraw-Hill.

CARR, H. A. (1925) *Psychology, a study of mental activity.* New York: Longmans.—*287–88*

CARR, H. A. (1930) Teaching and learning. *J. genet. Psychol.,* 37, 189–219.—*288*

CARR, H. A. (1931) The laws of association. *Psychol. Rev.,* 38, 212–228.—*285, 289*

CARR, H. A. (1938) The law of effect. *Psychol. Rev.,* 45, 191–199.—*288*

CARROLL, J. B. (1962) The prediction of success in intensive foreign language training. In R. Glaser (Ed.), *Training research and education.* Pittsburgh: Univ. of Pittsburgh Press, 87–136.—*627*

CARROLL, J. B. (1963a) A model of school learning. *Teachers Coll. Rec.* 64, 723–733.—*614, 623, 627*

CARROLL, J. B. (1963b) Research on teaching foreign languages. In N. L. Gage (Ed.), *Handbook of research on teaching.* Chicago: Rand McNally, 1060–1100.—*626, 627, 634*

CARTERETTE, T. S. (1961) An application of stimulus sampling theory to summated generalization. *J. exper. Psychol.,* 62, 448–455.—*400*

CAVANAUGH, J. P. (1972) Relation between the immediate memory span and the memory search rate. *Psychol. Rev.,* 79, 525–530.—*579*

CHALL, J. (1967) *Learning to read: The great debate.* New York: McGraw-Hill.—*637*

CHAPMAN, L. F., WALTER, R. D., MARKHAM, C. H., RAND, R. W., & CRANDELL, R. H. (1967) Memory changes induced by stimulation of hippocampus or amygdala in epilepsy patients with implanted electrodes. *Trans. Amer. Neurol. Assoc.,* 92, 50–56.—*516–517*

CHOMSKY, N. (1957) *Syntactic structures.* The Hague: Mouton.—*148, 247*

CHOMSKY, N. (1959) Review of Skinner's *Verbal Behavior. Language,* 35, 26–58.—*234, 246–47*

CHOMSKY, N. (1965) *Aspects of the theory of syntax.* Cambridge: MIT Press.—*247*

CHOMSKY, N. (1967) Review of Skinner's *Verbal Behavior.* In L. A. Jakobovits & M. S. Miron (Eds.), *Readings in the philosophy of language.* Englewood Cliffs, N.J.: Prentice-Hall.—*248*

CHOMSKY, N. (1971) The case against B. F. Skinner. *N.Y. Rev. Books,* Dec. 30, 1971, 18–24. Also published as "Psychology and Ideology." *Cognition,* 1972, 1, 11–46.—*246*

CHOMSKY, N. (1972) *Language and Mind* (Enlarged ed.) New York: Harcourt Brace Jovanovich. (1st ed., 1968.)—*11–12*

CHOROVER, S. L., & DeLuca, A. N. (1969) Transient change in electrocorticographic reaction to ECS in the rat following footshock. *J. comp. physiol. Psychol.,* 69, 141–149.—*515*

CHOROVER, S. L., & SCHILLER, P. H. (1965) Short-term retrograde amnesia in rats. *J. comp. physiol. Psychol.,* 59, 73–78.—*513*

CHU, G. C., & SCHRAMM, W. (1967) *Learning from television: What the research says.* Stanford: Institute for Communication Research.—*625*

CHUMBLEY, J. (1969) Hypothesis memory in concept learning. *J. math. Psychol.,* 6, 528–540. —*413*

CLEMES, S. R. (1964) Repression and hypnotic amnesia. *J. abnorm. soc. Psychol.,* 69, 62–69. —*363*

COAN, R. W., & ZAGONA, S. V. (1962) Contemporary ratings of psychological theorists. *Psychol. Rec.,* 12, 315–322.—*88*

COFER, C. N. (Ed.) (1961) *Verbal learning and verbal behavior.* New York: McGraw-Hill.

COGHILL, G. E. (1929) *Anatomy and the problem of behavior.* New York: Macmillan.—*319*

COHEN, H. D., ERVIN, F., & BARONDES, S. H. (1966) Puromycin and cycloheximide: Different effects on hippocampal electrical activity. *Science,* 154, 1157–1558.—*532*

COHEN, L. H., HILGARD, E. R., & WENDT, G. R. (1933) Sensitivity to light in a case of hysterical blindness studied by reinforcement-inhibition and conditioning methods. *Yale J. Biol. Med.,* 6, 61–67.—*114*

COLEMAN, E. B. (1962) Sequential interference demonstrated by serial reconstruction. *J. exp. Psychol.,* 64, 46–51.—*309–10*

COLES, L. S. (1968) An on-line question-answering system with natural language and pictorial input. *Proceedings of ACM 23rd National Conference*, 157–167. Princeton: Brandon Systems Press, 1968.—*456*

COLLINS, A. M., & QUILLIAN, M. R. (1972) How to make a language user. In E. Tulving & W. Donaldson (Eds.), *Organization of memory*. New York: Academic Press.—*597*

COOK, S. W., & SKINNER, B. F. (1939) Some factors influencing the distribution of associated words. *Psychol. Rec.*, 3, 178–184.—*233*

COOMBS, C. H., DAWES, R. M., & TVERSKY, A. (1970) *Mathematical psychology: An elementary introduction*. Englewood Cliffs, N.J.: Prentice-Hall.

COOPER, L. A., & SHEPARD, R. N. (1973) Chronometric studies of the rotation of mental images. In W. G. Chase (Ed.), *Visual information processing*. New York: Academic Press. —*588*.

CORMAN, H. H., & ESCALONA, S. K. (1969) Stages of sensorimotor development: A replication study. *Merrill-Palmer Quart.*, 15, 352–361.—*333*

CORNSWEET, T. N. (1970) *Visual perception*. New York: Academic Press.—*20*

COTTON, J. W. (1955) On making predictions from Hull's theory. *Psychol. Rev.*, 62, 303–314. —*174*

COWLES, J. T., & NISSEN, H. W. (1937) Reward expectancy in delayed responses of chimpanzees. *J. comp. Psychol.*, 24, 345–358.—*130*

CRAIK, F. I. M. (1970) The fate of primary memory items in free recall. *J. verb. Learn. verb. Behav.*, 9, 143–148.—*583*

CRAIK, F. I. M. (1973) Levels of analysis: A view of memory. In P. Pliner, L. Krames, & T. M. Alloway (Eds.), *Communication and affect: Language and thought*. New York: Academic Press.—*584*

CRAIK, F. I. M., & LOCKHART, R. S. (1972) Levels of processing: A framework for memory research. *J. verb. Learn. verb. Behav.*, 11, 671–684.—*584*

CRONBACH, L. J. (1964) Learning research and curriculum development. In R. E. Ripple & V. N. Rockcastle (Eds.), *Piaget rediscovered*. Ithaca, N.Y.: Cornell Univ. Press.—*341*

CRONBACH, L. J. (1966) The logic of experiments on discovery. In L. S. Shulman & E. R. Keislar (Eds.), *Learning by discovery*. Chicago: Rand McNally.—*345*

CRONBACH, L. J. (1967) How can instruction be adapted to individual differences? In R. M. Gagné (Ed.), *Learning and individual differences*. Columbus, Ohio: Merrill, 23–29.—*623*

CRONBACH, L. J., & SNOW, R. E. (1969) *Individual differences in learning ability as a function of instructional variables*. Stanford: Stanford School of Education.—*623*

CRONBACH, L. J., & SUPPES, P. (Eds.) (1969) *Research for tomorrow's schools*. New York: Macmillan.

CROTHERS, E. J. (1965) Learning model solution to a problem in constrained optimization. *J. math. Psychol.*, 2, 19–25.—*425*

CROUSE, J. H. (1971) Retroactive interference in reading prose materials. *J. ed. Psychol.*, 62, 39–44.—*310, 311*

CROWDER, N. A. (1959) Automatic tutoring by means of intrinsic programming. In E. H. Galanter (Ed.), *Automatic teaching: The state of the art*. New York: Wiley, 109–116.—*629*

CROWDER, N. A., & MARTIN, G. (1961) *Trigonometry*. Garden City, N.Y.: Doubleday.—*629*

CULBERTSON, J. T. (1962) *The Minds of Robots*. Urbana: Univ. of Illinois Press.—*548*

DALY, H. B. (1969) Learning of a hurdle-jumping response to escape cues paired with reduced reward or frustrative nonreward. *J. exp. Psychol.*, 79, 146–157.—*193*

DALY, H. B. (1970) Combined effects of fear and frustration on acquisition of a hurdle-jump response. *J. exp. Psychol.*, 83, 89–93.—*193*

DASHIEL, J. F. (1949) *Fundamentals of general psychology* (3rd ed.). Boston: Houghton Mifflin.—*286–87*

DAWSON, R. C., & McGAUGH, J. C. (1969) Electroconvulsive shock effects on a reactivated memory trace: Further examination. *Science*, 166, 525–527.—*514*

DEESE, J. (1965) *The structure of associations in language and thought*. Baltimore: Johns Hopkins Press.—*298*

DEESE, J., & HULSE, S. H. (1967) *The psychology of learning* (3rd ed.). New York: McGraw-Hill.

DEGROOT, A. (1946) *Het Denken van den Schaker*. Amsterdam: Noord-Hollandsche Uitgevers Maatschappij.

DEGROOT, A. D. (1965) *Thought and choice in chess*. New York: Basic Books.—*9, 438*

DE LEMOS, M. M. (1969) The development of conservation in aboriginal children. *Internatl. J. Psychol.* 4, 255–269.—*327*

DELGADO, J. M. R., ROBERTS, W. W., & MILLER, N. E. (1954) Learning motivated by electrical stimulation of the brain. *Amer. J. Physiol.*, 179, 587–593.—*498*

DELPRATO, D. J. (1972) Pair-specific effects in retroactive inhibition. *J. verb. Learn. verb. Behav.*, 11, 566–572.—*304*

DeNIKE, L. D., & SPIELBERGER, C. D. (1963) Induced mediating states in verbal conditioning. *J. verb. Learn. verb. Behav.*, 1, 339–345.—*55–56*

DEUTSCH, J. A. (1954) A machine with insight. *Quart. J. exp. Psychol.*, 6, 6–11.—*146, 429*

DEUTSCH, J. A. (1960) *The structural basis of behavior.* Chicago: Univ. of Chicago Press. —*146*

DEUTSCH, J. A. (1964) Behavioral measurement of the neural refractory period and its application to intracranial self-stimulation. *J. comp. physiol. Psychol.*, 58, 1–9.—*501*

DEUTSCH, J. A. (1968) The neural basis of memory. *Psychol. Today*, 1, No. 12, 56–61.—*535*

DEUTSCH, J. A. (1971) The cholinergic synapse and the site of memory. *Science*, 174 (19 November), 788–794.—*534–36*

DEUTSCH, J. A. (1973) Prolonged rewarding brain stimulation. In G. H. Bower (Ed.), *The psychology of learning and motivation.* Vol. 7. New York: Academic Press.—*500*

DEUTSCH, J. A., & CLARKSON, J. K. (1959) Reasoning in the hooded rat. *Quart. J. exper. Psychol.*, 11, 150–154.—*134, 146–47*

DEUTSCH, J. A., & DEUTSCH, D. (1963) Attention: Some theoretical considerations. *Psychol. Rev.*, 70, 80–90.—*507*

DEUTSCH, J. A., & DEUTSCH, D. (1966) *Physiological psychology* (1st ed.). Homewood, Ill.: Dorsey.—*507*

DEUTSCH, J. A., & DEUTSCH, D. (1973) *Physiological psychology* (2nd ed.). Homewood, Ill.: Dorsey.—*532, 537*

DEUTSCH, J. A., & HOWARTH, C. I. (1963) Some tests of a theory of intracranial self-stimulation. *Psychol. Rev.*, 70, 444–460.—*500*

DEUTSCH, J. A., & ROLL, S. K. (1973) Alcohol and asymmetrical state-dependency: A possible explanation. *Behav. Biol.*, 8, 273–278.—*547*

DeVIETTI, T. L., & HOLLIDAY, J. H. (1972) Retrograde amnesia produced by electrocon-vulsive shock after reactivation of a consolidated memory trace: A replication. *Psychon. Sci.*, 29, 137–138.—*514*

DeVIETTI, T. L., & LARSON, R. C. (1971) ECS effects: Evidence supporting state-dependent learning in rats. *J. comp. physiol. Psychol.*, 74, 407–415.—*514, 515*

DEWEY, J. (1929) The quest for certainty. New York: Minton, Balch.—*317*

DEWS, P. B. (Ed.) (1970) *Festschrift for B. F. Skinner.* New York: Appleton-Century-Crofts.

DiCARA, L. V. (1970) Learning in the autonomic nervous system. *Sci. Amer.*, 222, 30–39.—*553, 554, 555*

DiCARA, L. V., & MILLER, N. E. (1968) Instrumental learning of vasomotor responses by rats: Learning to respond differentially in the two ears. *Science*, 159, 1485–1486.—*555*

DINSMOOR, J. A. (1954) Punishment: I. The avoidance hypothesis. *Psychol. Rev.*, 61, 34–46. —*178, 213*

DINSMOOR, J. A. (1955) Punishment: II. An interpretation of empirical findings. *Psychol. Rev.*, 62, 96–105.—*213*

DIXON, N. F. (1971) *Subliminal perception: The nature of a controversy.* London: McGraw-Hill.—*353*

DOLLARD, J., DOOB, L. W., MILLER, N. E., MOWRER, O. H., SEARS, R. R., FORD, C. S., HOVLAND, C. I., & SOLLENBERGER, R. T. (1939) *Frustration and aggression.* New Haven: Yale Univ. Press.—*356*

DOLLARD, J., & MILLER, N. E. (1950) *Personality and psychotherapy.* New York: McGraw-Hill.—*73, 177, 235, 350, 352, 372*

DONCHIN, E., & COHEN, L. (1967) Averaged evoked potentials and intramodality selective attention. *EEG and clin. Neurophysiol.*, 22, 537–546.—*507*

DOYLE, W. (1960) Recognition of sloppy hand-printed characters. *Proceedings of the Western Joint Computer Conference.* New York: IRE, 133–142.—*444*

DREYER, P., & RENNER, K. E. (1971) Self-punitive behavior—masochism or confusion? *Psychol. Rev.*, 78, 333–337.—*102*

DUDYCHA, G. J., & DUDYCHA, M. M. (1941) Childhood memories: A review of the literature. *Psychol. Bull.*, 38, 668–682.—*359*

DULANY, D. E. (1968) Awareness, rules and propositional control: A confrontation with S-R behavior theory. In T. R. Dixon & D. L. Horton (Eds.), *Verbal behavior and general behavior theory.* Englewood Cliffs, N. J.: Prentice-Hall.—*56, 246*

DUNCAN, C. P. (1949) The retroactive effect of electroshock on learning. *J. comp. physiol. Psychol.*, 42, 32–44.—*511–13*

DUNCKER, K. (1945) On problem-solving. (Translated by L. S. Lees from the 1935 original.) *Psychol. Monogr.*, 58, No. 270.—*9, 275, 280, 438*

DUTTA, S., & KANUNGO, R. (1967) Retention of affective material: A further verification of the intensity hypothesis. *J. Pers. soc. Psychol.*, 5, 476–480.—*367*

D'ZURILLA, T. (1965) Recall efficiency and mediating cognitive events in "experimental repression." *J. Pers. soc. Psychol.*, 9, 253–257.—*366*

EBBINGHAUS, H. (1885) *Memory.* (Translated by H. A. Ruger & C. E. Bussenius.) New York: Teachers College, 1913. Paperback ed., New York: Dover, 1964.—*6–7, 31, 289, 393*

EDWARDS, W. (1954) The theory of decision making. *Psychol. Bull.*, 51, 380–417.—*146*

EDWARDS, W. (1962) Utility, subjective probability, their interaction, and variance preference. *J. Conflict Resolution*, 6, 42–51.—*146*

ELKIND, D. (1967) Piaget and Montessori. *Harvard ed. Rev.*, 37, 535–545.—*342*

ELKIND, D., & FLAVELL, J. H. (Eds.) (1969) *Studies in cognitive development: Essays in honor of Jean Piaget.* New York: Oxford Univ. Press.

ELLIOTT, M. H. (1928) The effect of change of reward on the maze performance of rats. *Univ. Calif. Publ. Psychol.*, 4, 19–30.—*130*

ELLIS, N. R., DETTERMAN, D. K., RUNCIE, D., McCARVER, R. B., & CRAIG, E. M. (1971) Amnesic effects in short-term memory. *J. exp. Psychol.*, 89, 357–361.—*580–81*

ELLISON, G. D. (1964) Differential salivary conditioning to trace. *J. comp. physiol. Psychol.*, 57, 373–380.—*77*

EPSTEIN, W. (1972) Mechanisms of directed forgetting. In G. H. Bower (Ed.), *The psychology of learning and motivation: Advances in research and theory.* Vol. 6. New York: Academic Press.—*580*

ERIKSEN, C. W., & KUETHE, J. L. (1956) Avoidance conditioning of verbal behavior without awareness: A paradigm of repression. *J. abnor. soc. Psychol.*, 53, 203–209.—*363–64*

ERIKSON, E. H. (1963) *Childhood and society* (2nd ed.). New York: Norton.—*324*

ERNST, G. W., & NEWELL, A. (1969) *GPS: A case study in generality and problem solving.* New York: Academic Press.—*460*

ESTES, W. K. (1950) Toward a statistical theory of learning. *Psychol. Rev.*, 57, 94–107.—*110, 115, 375*

ESTES, W. K. (1955a) Statistical theory of spontaneous recovery and regression. *Psychol. Rev.*, 62, 145–154.—*393–96*

ESTES, W. K. (1955b) Statistical theory of distributional phenomena in learning. *Psychol. Rev.*, 62, 369–377.—*395*

ESTES, W. K. (1958) Stimulus-response theory of drive. In M. R. Jones (Ed.), *Nebraska Symposium on Motivation.* Vol. 6. Lincoln: Univ. of Nebraska Press.—*401*

ESTES, W. K. (1959a) The statistical approach to learning theory. In S. Koch (Ed.), *Psychology: A study of a science.* Vol. 2. New York: McGraw-Hill.—*375, 386, 395, 397–98*

ESTES, W. K. (1959b) Component and pattern models with Markovian interpretations. In R. R. Bush & W. K. Estes (Eds.), *Studies in mathematical learning theory.* Stanford: Stanford Univ. Press.—*407–8*

ESTES, W. K. (1962) Theoretical treatment of differential reward in multiple-choice learning and two-person interactions. In J. Criswell, H. Solomon, & P. Suppes (Eds.), *Mathematical methods in small group processes.* Stanford: Stanford Univ. Press.—*144, 381, 403, 406*

ESTES, W. K. (1964) Probability learning. In A. W. Melton (Ed.), *Categories of human learning.* New York: Academic Press.—*386, 391*

ESTES, W. K. (1969a) Reinforcement in human learning. In J. Tapp (Ed.), *Reinforcement and behavior.* New York: Academic Press.—*46, 49, 51–54, 144, 246*

ESTES, W. K. (1969b) Outline of a theory of punishment. In B. A. Campbell & R. S. Church (Eds.), *Punishment and aversive behavior.* New York: Appleton-Century-Crofts. —*105, 223, 401–3*

ESTES, W. K. (1970) *Learning theory and mental development.* New York: Academic Press. —*104*

ESTES, W. K. (1971) Learning and memory. In E. F. Beckenbach & C. B. Tompkins (Eds.), *Concepts of communication.* New York: Wiley, 282–300.

ESTES, W. K. (1972a) Research and theory on the learning of probabilities. *J. Amer. Statis. Assoc.*, 67, 81–102.—*391, 426, 568*

ESTES, W. K. (1972b) An associative basis for coding and organization in memory. In A. W. Melton & E. Martin (Eds.), *Coding processes in human memory.* Washington, D.C.: V. H. Winston.—*426*

ESTES, W. K., KOCH, S., MACCORQUODALE, K., MEEHL, P. E., MUELLER, C. G., JR., SCHOENFELD, W. N., & VERPLANCK, W. S. (1945) *Modern learning theory.* New York: Appleton-Century-Crofts.

ESTES, W. K., & SKINNER, B. F. (1941) Some quantitative properties of anxiety. *J. exp. Psychol.,* 29, 390–400.—*104–5, 223*

ESTES, W. K., & STRAUGHAN, J. H. (1954) Analysis of a verbal conditioning situation in terms of statistical learning theory. *J. exp. Psychol.,* 47, 225–234.—*139*

EVANS, S. (1936) Flexibility of established habit. *J. gen. Psychol.,* 14, 177–200.—*134*

EVANS, T. G. (1968) A program for the solution of geometric-analogy intelligence test questions. In M. Minsky (Ed.), *Semantic information processing.* Cambridge: MIT Press.—*456, 458–60*

EYSENCK, H. J. (1952) The effects of psychotherapy: An evaluation. *J. consult. Psychol.,* 16, 319–324.—*372*

EYSENCK, H. J. (1965) The effects of psychotherapy. *Internatl. J. Psychiat.,* 1, 99–142.—*372*

FALKENBERG, P. R. (1972) Recall improves in short-term memory the more recall context resembles learning context. *J. exp. Psychol.,* 95, 39–47.—*301, 395, 417*

FALMAGNE, R. (1970) Construction of a hypothesis model for concept identification. *J. math. Psychol.,* 7, 60–96.—*413*

FARBER, I. E. (1954) Anxiety as a drive state. In M. R. Jones (Ed.), *Nebraska Symposium on Motivation: Current theory and research on motivation.* Lincoln: Univ. of Nebraska Press, 1–46.—*352*

FEIGENBAUM, E. A. (1959) An information processing theory of verbal learning. RAND Corp. Paper, P-1817, Oct.—*472*

FEIGENBAUM, E. A., & FELDMAN, J. (1963) *Computers and thought.* New York: McGraw-Hill. —*439, 455*

FEIGENBAUM, E. A., & SIMON, H. A. (1961) Performance of a reading task by an elementary perceiving and memorizing program. RAND Corp. Paper, P-2358, July.—*474*

FEIGENBAUM, E. A., & SIMON, H. A. (1962) A theory of the serial position effect. *Brit. J. Psychol.,* 53, 307–320.—*474*

FEIGENBAUM, K. D. (1963) Task complexity and IQ as variables in Piaget's problem of conservation. *Child Devel.,* 34, 423–432.—*333*

FELDMAN, J. (1961) Simulation of behavior in the binary choice experiments. *Proceedings of the Western Joint Computer Conference.* New York: IRE, 133–144.—*391, 475–77, 485*

FELDMAN, J. (1962) Computer simulation of cognitive processes. In H. Borko (Ed.), *Computer applications in the behavioral sciences.* Englewood Cliffs, N.J.: Prentice-Hall.—*475–77, 485–86*

FELSINGER, J. M., GLADSTONE, A. I., YAMAGUCHI, H. G., & HULL, C. L. (1947) Reaction latency (StR) as a function of the number of reinforcements (N). *J. exp. Psychol.,* 37, 214–228.—*166*

FENICHEL, O. (1945) *The psychoanalytic theory of neurosis.* New York: Norton.—*354*

FERSTER, C. S., & SKINNER, B. F. (1957) *Schedules of reinforcement.* New York: Appleton-Century-Crofts.—*216–19*

FESTINGER, L. (1942) Wish, expectation, and group standards as affecting level of aspiration. *J. Abnorm. soc. Psychol.,* 37, 184–200.—*148*

FESTINGER, L. (1957) *A theory of cognitive dissonance.* New York: Harper & Row.—*147, 343*

FESTINGER, L. (1961) The psychological effects of insufficient rewards. *Amer. Psychol.,* 16, 1–11.—*148*

FETZ, E. E., & FINOCCHIO, D. V. (1971) Operant conditioning of specific patterns of neural and muscular activity. *Science,* 174, 431–435.—*557*

FIELD, W. S., & ABBOTT (Eds.) (1963) *Information storage and neural control.* Springfield, Ill.: Charles C. Thomas.—*522–24*

FIKES, R. E., & NILSSON, N. Y. (1971) STRIPS: A new approach to the application of theorem proving to problem solving. *Sec. Intern. Conf. Art. Intell.*—*461–65*

FILLMORE, C. (1968) The case for case. In E. Bach & R. T. Harms (Eds.), *Universals in linguistic theory.* New York: Holt, Rinehart and Winston.—*595*

FISHER, A. E. (1956) Maternal and sexual behavior induced by intracranial chemical stimulation. *Science,* 124, 228–229.—*495*

FISKE, D. W., & MADDI, S. R. (Eds.) (1961) *Functions of varied experience.* Homewood, Ill.: Dorsey.—*358*

FJERDINGSTAD, E. J. (Ed.), *Chemical transfer of learned information.* New York: American Elsevier, 1971.—*531*

FLAVELL, J. H. (1963) *The developmental psychology of Jean Piaget.* Princeton: Van Nostrand.—*326, 329, 330*

FLAVELL, J. H. (1970) Concept development. In P. H. Mussen (Ed.), *Carmichael's manual of child psychology.* Vol. 1. New York: Wiley.

FLAVELL, J. H., & WOHLWILL, J. F. (1969) Formal and functional aspects of cognitive development. In D. Elkind & J. H. Flavell (Eds.), *Studies in cognitive development: Essays in honor of Jean Piaget.*—*336*

FOX, S. S., & RUDELL, A. P. (1970) Operant controlled neural event: Functional independence in behavioral coding by early and late components of visual cortical evoked response in cats. *J. Neurophysiol.,* 33, 548–561.—*557*

FRANKENBURG, W. K., & DODDS, J. B. (1967) The Denver developmental screening test. *J. Pediat.,* 71, 181–191.—*324*

FRANKLIN, K. B. J., & QUARTERMAIN, D. (1970) Comparison of the motivational properties of deprivation-induced drinking with drinking elicited by central carbachol stimulation. *J. comp. physiol. Psychol.,* 71, 390–395.—*496*

FREIJA, N. H. (1972) Simulation of human memory. *Psychol. Bull.,* 77, 1–31.—*598*

FREUD, A. (1935) *Psychoanalysis for teachers and parents.* New York: Emerson.—*359*

FREUD, S. (1915a) Repression. In *Collected papers.* London: Hogarth, 1925, Vol. 4, 84–97.—*353–54*

FREUD, S. (1915b) The unconscious. In *Collected papers.* London: Hogarth, 1925, Vol. 4, 98–136.—*356, 371*

FREUD, S. (1920a) *A general introduction to psychoanalysis.* New York: Liveright.—*351*

FREUD, S. (1920b) *Beyond the pleasure principle.* Translation, 1950. New York: Liveright.—*348*

FREUD, S. (1921) *Group psychology and the analysis of the ego.* Translation, 1922. New York: Liveright. *356*

FREUD, S. (1923) *The ego and the id.* Translation, 1927. London: Hogarth.

FREUD, S. (1926) *The problem of anxiety.* Translation, 1936. New York: Norton.—*351, 352*

FREUD, S. (1940) *An outline of psychoanalysis.* Translation, 1949. New York: Norton.

FRIEDMAN, M. P., PADILLA, G., & GELFAND, H. (1964) The learning of choices between bets. *J. math. Psychol.,* 1, 375–385.—*391, 405–6*

FRIEDMAN, M. P., TRABASSO, T., & MOSBERG, L. (1967) Tests of a mixed model for paired-associates learning with overlapping stimuli. *J. math. Psychol.,* 4, 316–334.—*401*

FROLOV, Y. P. (1937) *Pavlov and his school.* New York: Oxford Univ. Press.—*63*

FURST, B. (1958) *Stop forgetting: How to develop your memory and put it to practical use.* Garden City, N.Y.: Doubleday.—*587*

FURTH, H. G. (1970) *Piaget for teachers.* Englewood Cliffs, N.J.: Prentice-Hall.—*341*

FUSTER, J. M. (1958) Effects of stimulation of brain stem on tachistoscopic perception. *Science,* 127, 150.—*505*

GAGE, N. L. (Ed.) (1963) *Handbook of research on teaching.* Chicago: Rand McNally.

GAGE, N. L. (1964) Theories of teaching. In E. R. Hilgard (Ed.), *Theories of learning and instruction.* 63rd Yearbook of the National Society for the Study of Education, Part I. Chicago: NSSE, 268–285.—*614*

GAGNÉ, R. M. (1962a) The acquisition of knowledge. *Psychol. Rev.,* 4, 355–365.—*614*

GAGNÉ, R. M. (1962b) Simulators. In R. Glaser (Ed.), *Training research and education.* Pittsburgh: Univ. of Pittsburgh Press, 223–246.—*615, 624*

GAGNÉ, R. M. (1965) *The conditions of learning.* New York: Holt, Rinehart and Winston.—*616*

GAGNÉ, R. M. (1970) *The conditions of learning* (Rev. ed.). New York: Holt, Rinehart and Winston.—*26, 312, 615–16*

GAGNÉ, R. M., & BRIGGS, L. J. (1974) *Principles of instructional design.* New York: Holt, Rinehart and Winston.—*617*

GAGNÉ, R. M., & GEPHART, W. L. (Eds.) (1968) *Learning research and school subjects.* Itasca, Ill.: Peacock.

GAGNÉ, R. M., & ROHWER, W. D., JR. (1969) Instructional psychology. *Ann. Rev. Psychol.,* 20, 381–418.—*607*

GAITO, J. (1966) *Molecular psychobiology: A chemical approach to learning and other behavior*. Springfield, Ill.: Charles C Thomas, 1966.—*531, 532*

GALANTER, E. (1966) *Textbook of elementary psychology*. San Francisco: Holden-Day.

GALIN, D., & ORNSTEIN, R. (1972) Lateral specialization of cognitive mode: An EEG study. *Psychophysiol.*, 9, 412–418.—*542–43*

GALLISTEL, C. R. (1966) Motivating effects in self-stimulation. *J. comp. physiol. Psychol.*, 62, 95–101.—*500*

GALLISTEL, C. R. (1969a) The incentive of brain-stimulation reward. *J. comp. physiol. Psychol.*, 69, 713–721.—*500*

GALLISTEL, C. R. (1969b) Self stimulation: Failure of pre-trial stimulation to affect rats' electrode preference. *J. comp. physiol. Psychol.*, 69, 722–729.—*500*

GANTT, W. H. (1965) Pavlov's system. In B. B. Wolman & E. Nagel (Eds.), *Scientific Psychology*. New York: Basic Books, 127–149.—*73*

GARCIA, J., & KOELLING, R. (1966) Relation of cue to consequence in avoidance learning. *Psychon. Sci.*, 4, 123–124.—*85, 493*

GARDNER, B. T., & GARDNER, R. A. (1971) Two-way communication with an infant chimpanzee. In A. Schrier & F. Stollnitz (Eds.), *Behavior of non-human primates*. Vol. 3. New York: Academic Press.—*85, 234*

GAZZANIGA, M. S. (1967) The split brain in man. *Sci. Amer.*, 217, No. 2, 24–29.—*541*

GAZZANIGA, M. S. (1970) *The bisected brain*. New York: Appleton-Century-Crofts.—*541–42*

GAZZANIGA, M. S. (1972) One brain—two minds? *Amer. Sci.*, 60, 311–317.—*541–42*

GAZZANIGA, M. S., & SPERRY, R. W. (1967) Language after section of the cerebral commissures. *Brain*, 90, 131–148.—*541–42*

GEIS, G. L., STEBBINS, W. C., & LUNDIN, R. W. (1965) *Reflexes and conditioned reflexes: A basic systems program*. New York: Appleton-Century-Crofts.

GELERNTER, H. (1959) Realization of a geometry-theorem proving machine. *Proceedings of the International Conference on Information Processing*. New York: UNESCO, 273–282.—*452–53*

GELLER, A., & JARVIK, N. E. (1968) The time relations of ECS-induced amnesia. *Psychon. Sci.*, 12, 169–170.—*514*

GENGERELLI, J. A. (1928) Preliminary experiments on the causal factors in animal learning. *J. comp. Psychol.*, 8, 435–457.—*91*

GERARD, R. W. (1963) The material basis of memory. *J. verb. Learn. verb. Behav.*, 2, 22–33.—*509–10*

GERST, N. S. (1971) Symbolic coding processes in observational learning. *J. Pers. Soc. Psychol.*, 19, 7–17.—*603*

GESELL, A. (1929) Maturation and infant behavior pattern. *Psychol. Rev.*, 36, 307–319.—*319*

GESELL, A., & THOMPSON, H. (1941) Twins T and C from infancy to adolescence: An experimental study by the method of co-twin control. *Genet. Psychol. Monogr.*, 24, 3–121.—*323*

GEWIRTZ, J. L., & STINGLE, K. G. (1968) Learning of generalized imitation as the basis for identification. *Psychol. Rev.*, 75, 374–397.—*602*

GIBSON, E. J. (1969) *Principles of perceptual learning and development*. New York: Appleton-Century-Crofts.—*8*

GILBERT, J. A. (1894) Researches on the mental and physical development of school-children. *Studies from the Yale Psychological Laboratory*, 2, 40–100.—*327*

GILBERT, R. M., & MILLENSON, J. R. (Eds.) (1972) *Reinforcement: Behavioral analyses*. New York: Academic Press.

GILBERT, R. M., & SUTHERLAND, N. S. (1969) *Animal discrimination learning*. New York. Academic Press.

GIRDEN, E., & CULLER, E. A. (1937) Conditioned responses in curarized striate muscle in dogs. *J. comp. Psychol.*, 23, 261–274.

GLADSTONE, A. I., YAMAGUCHI, H. G., HULL, C. L., & FELSINGER, J. M. (1947) Some functional relationships of reaction potential (rEs) and related phenomena. *J. exper. Psychol.*, 37, 510–526.—*166*

GLANZER, M. S. (1972) Storage mechanisms in recall. In G. H. Bower (Ed.), *The psychology of learning and motivation: Advances in research and theory*. Vol. 5. New York: Academic Press.—*584*

GLANZER, M. S., & CLARK, H. H. (1962) Accuracy of perceptual recall: An analysis of organization. *J. verb. Learn. verb. Behav.*, 1, 289–299.—*457*

GLASER, R., & RESNICK, L. B. (1972) Instructional psychology. *Ann. Rev. Psychol.* 23, 207–276. *—607*

GLEITMAN, H. (1971) Forgetting of long-term memories in animals. In W. K. Honig & P. H. R. James (Eds.), *Animal memory.* New York: Academic Press.

GLEITMAN, H., NACHMIAS, J., & NEISSER, U. (1954) The S-R reinforcement theory of extinction. *Psychol. Rev.*, 61, 23–33.—*165*

GLUCKSBERG, S., & KING, L. J. (1967) Motivated forgetting mediated by implicit verbal chaining: A laboratory analog of repression. *Science*, 158 (October), 517–519.—*364–65*

GLUCKSBERG, S., & ORNSTEIN, P. A. (1969) Reply to Weiner and Higgins: Motivated forgetting is not attributable to a confounding of original learning with retention. *J. verb. Learn. verb. Behav.*, 8, 681–685.—*365*

GOLD, B. (1959) Machine recognition of hand-sent Morse code. *IRE Trans. on Inform. Theory*, IT-5, 17–24.—*446–47*

GOLDSTEIN, H., KRANTZ, D. L., & RAINS, J. D. (1965) *Controversial issues in learning.* New York: Appleton-Century-Crofts.

GOODNOW, J. J., & BETHON, G. (1966) Piaget's tasks: The effects of schooling and intelligence. *Child Devel.*, 37, 573–582.—*333*

GOODWIN, D. W., POWELL, B., BREMER, D., HOINE, H., & STERN, J. (1969) Alcohol and recall: state-dependent effects in man. *Science*, 163, 1358–1360.—*547*

GRANT, D. A. (1962) Testing the null hypothesis and the strategy and tactics of investigating theoretical models. *Psychol. Rev.*, 69, 54–61.—*423*

GRAY, J. A. (Ed.) (1964) *Pavlov's typology: Recent theoretical and experimental developments from the laboratory of B. M. Teplov.* New York: Macmillan.

GREEN, B. F., JR. (1963) *Digital computers in research.* New York: McGraw-Hill.—*432, 439, 462*

GREEN, B. F., WOLF, A., CHOMSKY, C., & LAUGHERY, K. (1961) Baseball: An automatic question-answerer. *Proceedings of the Western Joint Computer Conference.* New York: IRE, 219–224.—*470*

GREEN, C. C. (1969a) Application of theorem proving to problem solving. *Proceedings of the International Joint Conference on Artificial Intelligence.* Bedford, Mass.: Mitre Corp., 219–240.—*469*

GREEN, C. C. (1969b) Application of theorem proving to question-answering systems. Unpublished doctoral dissertation, Stanford Univ. Technical Report CS-138, Computer Science Dept., Stanford.—*469*

GREEN, C. C., & RAPHAEL, B. (1968) The use of theorem-proving techniques in question-answering systems. *Proceedings of the 23rd National Conference of the Association of Computing Machinery.* Washington, D.C.: Thompson.—*469*

GREEN, E. E., GREEN, A. M., & WALTERS, E. D. (1970) Voluntary control of internal states: Psychological and physiological. *J. transper. Psychol.*, 2, 132–147.—*559*

GREEN, E. J. (1956) Stimulus variability and operant discrimination in human subjects. *Amer. J. Psychol.*, 69, 269–273.—*383*

GREENBERG, J. H. (Ed.) (1962) *Universals of language.* Cambridge: MIT Press.—*12*

GREENBLATT, G., EASTLAKE, D., & CROCKER, S. (1967) The Greenblatt chess program. *Proceedings of the Fall Joint Computer Conference.* Anaheim, Calif.—*456*

GREENFIELD, P. M. (1966) On culture and conservation. In J. S. Bruner, R. R. Olver, & P. M. Greenfield, *Studies in cognitive growth.* New York: Wiley.—*334–35*

GREENHILL, L. P. (1964) Penn State experiments with two-way audio systems for CCTV. *NAEB J.*, 23, 73–78.—*626*

GREENO, J. G. (1968) *Elementary theoretical psychology.* Reading, Mass.: Addison-Wesley.—*419*

GREENO, J. G., & BORK, R. A. (1973) Mathematical learning theory and the new "mental forestry." *Ann. Rev. Physiol.*, 24, 81–116.—*424*

GREENO, J. G., & STEINER, T. E. (1964) Markovian processes with identifiable states: General considerations and application to all-or-none learning. *Psychometrika*, 29, 309–333.—*414*

GREENSPOON, J. (1955) The reinforcing effect of two spoken sounds on the frequency of two responses. *Amer. J. Psychol.*, 68, 409–416.—*361*

GREENSPOON, J. (1962) Verbal conditioning in clinical psychology. In A. J. Bachrach, *Experimental foundations of clinical psychology.* New York: Basic Books.—*361*

GREGG, L. W. (1972) Simulation models of learning and memory. In L. W. Gregg (Ed.), *Cognition in learning and memory.* New York: Wiley.—*474*

GREGG, L. W., & SIMON, H. A. (1967) Process models and stochastic theories of simple concept formation. *J. math. Psychol.*, 4, 246–276.—*413, 423–24, 483*

GRINGS, W. W. (1965) Verbal perceptual factors in the conditioning of autonomic responses. In W. F. Prokasy (Ed.), *Classical conditioning: A symposium.* New York: Appleton-Century-Crofts.

GRINKER, R. R., & SPIEGEL, J. P. (1945a) *Men under stress.* New York: Blakiston.—*368*

GRINKER, R. R., & SPIEGEL, J. P. (1945b) *War neuroses.* New York: Blakiston.—*368*

GROSSMAN, S. P. (1960) Eating or drinking elicited by direct adrenergic or cholinergic stimulation of the hypothalamus. *Science*, 132, 301–302.—*494–95*

GROSSMAN, S. P. (1967) *A textbook of physiological psychology.* New York: Wiley.—*495*

GRUSEC, T. (1965) Aversive conditioning and peak shift in stimulus generalization. Unpublished doctoral dissertation, Stanford Univ.—*227*

GUTHRIE, E. R. (1930) Conditioning as a principle of learning. *Psychol. Rev.*, 37, 412–428.—*115*

GUTHRIE, E. R. (1934) Pavlov's theory of conditioning. *Psychol. Rev.*, 41, 199–206.—*92*

GUTHRIE, E. R. (1935) *The psychology of learning.* New York: Harper & Row.—*92, 95, 98–103, 105, 118–20*

GUTHRIE, E. R. (1936) Psychological principles and scientific truth. *Proc. 25th Anniv. Celebr. Inaug. Grad. Stud.* Los Angeles: Univ. Southern California.—*105*

GUTHRIE, E. R. (1938) *The psychology of human conflict.* New York: Harper & Row.

GUTHRIE, E. R. (1940) Association and the law of effect. *Psychol. Rev.*, 47, 127–148.—*98*

GUTHRIE, E. R. (1942) Conditioning: A theory of learning in terms of stimulus, response, and association. Chapter 1 in *The psychology of learning.* 41st Yearbook of the National Society for the Study of Education, Part II, 17–60. Chicago: Univ. of Chicago Press.—*92, 97*

GUTHRIE, E. R. (1952) *The psychology of learning* (Rev. ed.). New York: Harper & Row.—*109, 128*

GUTHRIE, E. R. (1959) Association by contiguity. In S. Koch (Ed.), *Psychology: A study of a science.* Vol. 2. New York: McGraw-Hill, 158–195.—*110–11*

GUTHRIE, E. R., & EDWARDS, A. L. (1949) *Psychology: A first course in human behavior.* New York: Harper & Row.—*105*

GUTHRIE, E. R., & HORTON, G. P. (1946) *Cats in a puzzle box.* New York: Rinehart Press.—*97, 105, 106–9*

GUTHRIE, E. R., & POWERS, F. F. (1950) *Educational psychology.* New York: Ronald Press.—*105*

GUZMAN, A. (1968) *Computer recognition of three-dimensional objects in a visual scene.* MIT Artificial Intelligence Laboratory, Project MAC-TR-59. Cambridge.—*447–49*

GWINN, G. T. (1949) The effects of punishment on cats motivated by fear. *J. exp. Psychol.*, 39, 260–269.—*101*

HABER, R. N. (1963) The spread of an innovation: High school language laboratories. *J. exp. Ed.*, 31, 359–369.—*626*

HALL, C. S. (1954) *A primer of Freudian psychology.* Cleveland: World.

HALL, J. F. (1966) *The psychology of learning.* Philadelphia: J. B. Lippincott.

HALL, J. F. (1971) *Verbal learning and retention.* Philadelphia: J. B. Lippincott.—*312, 316*

HARLOW, H. F., & HARLOW, M. K. (1966) Learnng to love. *Amer. Sci.*, 54, 244–272.—*18*

HARSH, C. M. (1937) Disturbance and "insight" in rats. *Univ. Calif. Publ. Psychol.*, 6, 163–168.—*134*

HARTMANN, H., & KRIS, E. (1945) The genetic approach in psychoanalysis. *Psychoanal. Stud. Child*, 1, 11–30.—*358*

HAYGOOD, R., & BOURNE, L. E. (1965) Attribute and rule learning aspects of conceptual behavior. *Psychol. Rev.*, 72, 175–195.—*478*

HAYS, R. (1962) Psychology of the scientist: III. Introduction to "Passages from the 'Idea Books' of Clark L. Hull." *Percept. Mot. Skills*, 15, 803–806.

HEATH, R. G., & MICKLE, W. A. (1960) Evaluation of seven years' experience with depth electrode studies in human patients. In E. R. Ramey and D. S. O'Doherty (Eds.), *Electrical studies on the unanesthetized brain.* New York: Harper & Row, 214–247.—*503*

HEATHERS, L. B., & SEARS, R. R. (1943) Experiments on repression: II. The Sharp technique. (Unpublished: see Sears, 1943.)—*363*

HEBB, D. O. (1949) *The organization of behavior.* New York: Wiley.—*509*

HEFFERLINE, R. F., & KEENAN, B. (1963) Amplitude-induction gradient of a small-scale (covert) operant. *J. exp. Analy. Behav.*, 6, 307–315.—*57*

HEFFERLINE, R. F., KEENAN, B., & HARFORD, R. A. (1959) Escape and avoidance conditioning in human subjects without their observation of the response. *Science*, 130, 1338–1339. —*57*

HELSON, H. (1964) *Adaptation-level theory*. New York: Harper & Row.—*186*

HENLE, M. (1961) *Documents of Gestalt psychology*. Berkeley and Los Angeles: Univ. of California Press.

HERBERT, J. A., & KRANTZ, D. L. (1965) Transposition: A re-evaluation. *Psychol. Bull.*, 63, 244–257.—*187*

HERENDEEN, D. L., & SHAPIRO, M. M. (1971) Classical and DRO discrimination of salivary responding. Paper presented at meetings of the Western Psychological Association, April 1971.—*211*

HERENDEEN, D. L., & SHAPIRO, M. M. (1972) A within- and between-subjects comparison of the effects of extinction and DRO on salivary responding. Paper presented at meetings of the Midwestern Psychological Association, May 1972.—*211*

HERNANDEZ-PEON, R., SCHEERER, H., & JOUVET, M. (1956) Modification of electric activity in cochlear nucleus during "attention" in unanesthetized cats. *Science*, 123, 331–332.—*507*

HERRNSTEIN, R. J. (1969) Method and theory in the study of avoidance. *Psychol. Rev.*, 76, 49–69.—*214*

HERRNSTEIN, R. J. (1970) On the law of effect. In P. B. Dews (Ed.), *Festschrift for B. F. Skinner*. New York: Appleton-Century-Crofts.—*219*

HESS, E. H. (1958) "Imprinting" in animals. *Sci. Amer.*, 198, 81–90.—*18*

HESS, R. D., & TENEZAKIS, M. D. (1970) *The computer as a socializing agent: Some socio-affective outcomes of CAI*. Stanford: Stanford Center for Research and Development in Teaching.—*632*

HILGARD, E. R. (1931) Conditioned eyelid reactions to a light stimulus based on the reflex wink to sound. *Psychol. Monogr.*, 41, No. 184.—*114*

HILGARD, E. R. (1956) *Theories of learning* (2nd ed.). New York: Appleton-Century-Crofts. —*136, 167*

HILGARD, E. R. (1962) Impulsive versus realistic thinking: An examination of the distinction between primary and secondary processes in thought. *Psychol. Bull.*, 59, 477–488.—*360*

HILGARD, E. R. (Ed.) (1964a) *Theories of learning and instruction*. 63rd Yearbook of the National Society for the Study of Education, Part I. Chicago: Univ. of Chicago Press, 1–418.—*312*

HILGARD, E. R. (1964b) The place of Gestalt theory and field theories in contemporary learning theory. In *Theories of learning and instruction*. 63rd Yearbook of the National Society for the Study of Education, Part I, 54–77. Chicago: Univ. of Chicago Press.—*610*

HILGARD, E. R., & BOWER, G. H. (1966) *Theories of learning* (3rd ed.). New York: Appleton-Century-Crofts.—*45, 71, 125, 174, 182, 183, 551*

HILGARD, E. R., & CAMPBELL, A. A. (1936) The course of acquisition and retention of conditioned eyelid responses in man. *J. exp. Psychol.*, 19, 227–247.—*95*

HILGARD, E. R., & MARQUIS, D. G. (1940) *Conditioning and learning*. New York: Appleton-Century-Crofts.—*63, 68–69, 78, 170, 208*

HILGARD, J. R. (1933) The effect of early and delayed practice on memory and motor performances studied by the method of co-twin control. *Genet. Psychol. Monogr.*, 14, No. 6. —*323*

HILL, W. F. (1963) *Learning: A survey of psychological interpretations*. San Francisco: Chandler.

HILL, W. F. (1971) *Learning: A survey of psychological interpretations* (Rev. ed.). Scranton, Pa.: Chandler.

HINDE, R. A. (1966) *Animal behavior: A synthesis of ethology and comparative psychology*. New York: McGraw-Hill.—*18*

HINDE, R. A., & TINBERGEN, N. (1958) The comparative study of species-specific behavior. In A. Roe & G. G. Simpson (Eds.), *Behavior and evolution*. New Haven: Yale Univ. Press, 251–268.—*18*

HINES, B., & PAOLINO, R. M. (1970) Retrograde amnesia: Production of skeletal but not cardiac response gradients by electroconvulsive shocks. *Science*, 169, 1224–1226.—*513*

HINRICHS, J. B. (1970) A two-process memory strength theory for judgment of recency. *Psychol. Rev.*, 77, 223–233.—*297, 591*

HINTZMAN, D. L. (1968) Explorations with a discrimination net model for paired-associate learning. *J. math. Psychol.*, 5, 123–162.—*474–75*

HINTZMAN, D. L., & BLOCK, R. A. (1971) Repetition in memory: Evidence for a multiple trace hypothesis. *J. exp. Psychol.*, 88, 297–306.—*592*

HOBAN, C. F. (1960) The usable residue of educational film research. In W. Schramm (Ed.), *New teaching aids for the American classroom.* Stanford: Institute for Communication Research, 95–115.—*624–25*

HOBBES, T. (1840) *Human nature.* Reproduced in W. Molesworth (Ed.), *The English works of Thomas Hobbes.* 4 vols. London: Bohn, 1839. (Originally published in 1650.)—*4–5*

HOBBES, T. *Leviathan.* Reproduced in W. Molesworth (Ed.), *The English works of Thomas Hobbes.* 4 vols. London: Bohn, 1840. (Originally published in 1651.)

HOCHBERG, J. E. (1964) *Perception.* Englewood Cliffs, N.J.: Prentice-Hall.—*8*

HOEBEL, B. G. (1968) Inhibition and disinhibition of self-stimulation and feeding: Hypothalamic control and post-ingestional factors. *J. comp. physiol. Psychol.*, 66, 89–100.—*500*

HOEBEL, B. G., & TEITELBAUM, P. (1962) Hypothalamic control of feeding and self-stimulation. *Science*, 135, 375–376.—*496*

HOFFDING, H. (1891) *Outlines of psychology.* New York: Macmillan.—*266–67*

HOFFMAN, H. S. (1962) The analogue lab: A new kind of teaching device. *Amer. Psychol.*, 17, 684–694.—*429*

HOLLAND, J. G. (1960) Teaching machines: An application of principles from the laboratory. In A. A. Lumsdaine & R. Glaser (Eds.), *Teaching machines and programmed learning: A source book.* Washington, D.C.: National Education Association, 215–228.—*612*

HOLLAND, J. G., & SKINNER, B. F. (1961) *The analysis of behavior: A program for self-instruction.* New York: McGraw-Hill.—*232*

HOLLINGWORTH, H. L. (1928) General laws and redintegration. *J. gen. Psychol.*, 1, 79–90.—*117*

HOLMES, D. S. (1970) Differential change in affective intensity and the forgetting of unpleasant personal experiences. *J. Pers. soc. Psychol.*, 15, 234–239.—*367–68*

HOLMES, D. S., & SCHALLOW, J. R. (1969) Reduced recall after ego threat: Repression or response competition? *J. Pers. soc. Psychol.*, 13, 145–152.—*366*

HOLT, E. B. (1915) *The Freudian wish and its place in ethics.* New York: Holt, Rinehart and Winston.—*370*

HOMME, L. E., C'DEBACA, P., DEVINE, J. V., STEINHORST, R., & RICKERT, E. J. (1963) Use of the Premack principle in controlling the behavior of nursery school children. *J. exper. Analy. Behav.*, 6, 544–545.—*564*

HONIG, W. K. (1962) Prediction of preference, transposition, and transposition-reversal from the generalization gradient. *J. exp. Psychol.*, 64, 239–248.—*185*

HONIG, W. K. (Ed.) (1966) *Operant behavior: Areas of research and application.* New York: Appleton-Century-Crofts.—*232*

HONIG, W. K., & JAMES, P. H. R. (1971) *Animal memory.* New York: Academic Press.—*298*

HONIG, W. K., & MACKINTOSH (Eds.) (1969) *Fundamental issues in associative learning.* Halifax: Dalhousie Univ. Press.

HONZIK, C. H. (1936) The sensory basis of maze learning in rats. *Comp. Psychol. Monogr.*, 13, No. 64.—*93*

HOROWITZ, L. M., NORMAN, S. A., & DAY, R. S. (1966) Availability and associative symmetry. *Psychol. Rev.*, 73, 1–15.—*42*

HOVLAND, C. I. (1937) The generalization of conditioned responses: I. The sensory generalization of conditioned responses with varying frequencies of tone. *J. gen. Psychol.*, 17, 125–148.—*65–67*

HOVLAND, C. I. (1952) A "communication analysis" of concept learning. *Psychol. Rev.*, 59, 461 472.—*477*

HULL, C. L. (1928) *Aptitude testing.* Yonkers-on-Hudson: World Book.—*156*

HULL, C. L. (1929) A functional interpretation of the conditioned reflex. *Psychol. Rev.*, 36, 498–511.—*156*

HULL, C. L. (1932) The goal gradient hypothesis and maze learning. *Psychol. Rev.*, 39, 25–43.—*172*

HULL, C. L. (1933) Differential habituation to internal stimuli in the albino rat. *J. comp. Psychol.*, 16, 255–273.—*164*

HULL, C. L. (1934a) The concept of the habit-family hierarchy and maze learning. *Psychol. Rev.*, 41, 33–54.—*173*

HULL, C. L. (1934b) Learning: II. The factor of the conditioned reflex. In C. Murchison (Ed.), *A handbook of general experimental psychology*. Worcester, Mass.: Clark Univ. Press, 382–455.—*65*

HULL, C. L. (1935) The conflicting psychologies of learning—a way out. *Psychol. Rev.*, 42, 491–516.—*153, 156*

HULL, C. L. (1937) Mind, mechanism, and adaptive behavior. *Psychol. Rev.*, 44, 1–32.—*153, 156, 173*

HULL, C. L. (1938) The goal-gradient hypothesis applied to some "field-force" problems in the behavior of young children. *Psychol. Rev.*, 45, 271–299.— *172, 173*

HULL, C. L. (1943) *Principles of behavior*. New York: Appleton-Century-Crofts.—*156, 159–64, 166–68, 189, 198, 202*

HULL, C. L. (1945) The place of innate individual and species differences in a natural-science theory of behavior. *Psychol. Rev.*, 52, 55–60.—*201*

HULL, C. L. (1950) Behavior postulates and corollaries—1949. *Psychol. Rev.*, 57, 173–180.—*166*

HULL, C. L. (1951) *Essentials of behavior*. New Haven: Yale Univ. Press.—*156, 166, 167*

HULL, C. L. (1952a) *A behavior system: An introduction to behavior theory concerning the individual organism*. New Haven: Yale Univ. Press.—*156, 166–68, 171, 172, 174, 203*

HULL, C. L. (1952b) Autobiography. In Carl A. Murchison, ed., *A history of psychology in autobiography*. Vol. 4. New York: Russell & Russell Press.

HULL, C. L. (1962) Psychology of the scientist: IV. Passages from the "Idea Books" of Clark L. Hull. *Percept. Mot. Skills*, 15, 807–882.—*156*

HULL, C. L., FELSINGER, J. M., GLADSTONE, A. I., & YAMAGUCHI, H. G. (1947) A proposed quantification of habit strength. *Psychol. Rev.*, 54, 237–254.—*166*

HULL, C. L., HOVLAND, C. I., ROSS, R. T., HALL, M., PERKINS, D. T., & FITCH, F. G. (1940) *Mathematico-deductive theory of rote learning*. New Haven: Yale Univ. Press.—*156–59, 558*

HULL, C. L., & LUGOFF, L. S. (1921) Complex signs in diagnostic free association. *J. exp. Psychol.*, 4, 111–136.—*352*

HUMPHREYS, L. G. (1939) Acquisition and extinction of verbal expectations in a situation analogous to conditioning. *J. exp. Psychol.*, 25, 294–301.—*139–40*

HUNT, E. B. (1962) *Concept learning*. New York: Wiley.—*477–78*

HUNT, E. B., & HOVLAND, C. I. (1961) Programming a model of human concept formation. *Proceedings of the Western Joint Computer Conference*. New York: IRE, 145–156.—*477–78*

HUNT, E. B., MARIN, J., & STONE, P. (1966) *Experiments in induction*. New York: Academic Press.—*477–78*

HUNT, J. McV. (1941) The effects of infant feeding frustration upon adult hoarding in the albino rat. *J. abnorm. soc. Psychol.*, 36, 338–360.—*358*

HUNT, J. McV. (1961) *Intelligence and experience*. New York: Ronald Press.—*319*

HUNT, J. McV. (1969) The impact and limitations of the giant of developmental psychology. In D. Elkind & J. H. Flavell (Eds.), *Studies in cognitive development: Essays in honor of Jean Piaget*. New York: Oxford Univ. Press, 3–66.

HUPPERT, F. A., & DEUTSCH, J. A. (1969) Improvement in memory with time. *Quart. J. exp. Psychol.*, 21, 267–271.—*536*

HYDE, T. A., & JENKINS, J. J. (1969) Differential effects of incidental tasks on the organization of recall of a list of highly associated words. *J. exp. Psychol.*, 82, 472–481.—*584*

HYDÉN, H. (1965) Activation of nuclear RNA in neurons and glia in learning. In D. P. Kimble (Ed.), *Learning, remembering, and forgetting*. Vol. 1. *The anatomy of memory*. Palo Alto: Science and Behavior Books, 170–239.—*530*

HYDÉN, H., & EGYHÁZI, E. (1962) Nuclear RNA changes of nerve cells during a learning experiment in rats. *Proc. Nat. Acad. Sci. U.S.*, 48, 1366–1373.—*530*

HYDÉN, H., & EGYHÁZI, E. (1964) Changes in RNA content and base composition in cortical neurons of rats in a learning experiment involving transfer of handedness. *Proc. Nat. Acad. Sci. U.S.*, 52, 1030–1035.—*530*

INHELDER, B. (1936) Observations sur le principe de conservation dans la physique de l'enfant. *Cashier Pédagogiques Experimentale Psychologique Enfant*, No. 9.—*327*

INHELDER, B. (1944) *Le diagnostic du raisonnement chez les debiles mental*. Neuchâtel: Delachaux et Niestlé.—*328*

INHELDER, B. (1969) Memory and intelligence in the child. In D. Elkind & J. Flavell (Eds.), *Studies in cognitive development: Essays in honor of Jean Piaget*. New York: Oxford Univ. Press.—*343-44*

INHELDER, B., & PIAGET, J. (1958) *The growth of logical thinking from childhood to adolescence*. New York: Basic Books.—*331*

ITARD, J. M. G. (1932) *The wild boy of Aveyron*. (Translated by George Humphrey & Muriel Humphrey.) New York: Century.—*19*

IVANOV-SMOLENSKY, A. G. (1927) On the methods of examining the conditioned food reflexes in children and in mental disorders. *Brain*, 50, 138–141.—*80*

JACKSON, T. A. (1942) Use of the stick as a tool by young chimpanzees. *J. comp. Psychol.*, 34, 223–235.—*273*

JAKOBSON, R. FANT, C. G. M., & HALLE, M. (1963) *Preliminaries to speech analysis: The distinctive features and their correlates*. Cambridge: MIT Press.—*11*

JAMES, H. (1953) An application of Helson's theory of adaptation level to the problem of transposition. *Psychol. Rev.*, 46, 345–351.—*186*

JAMES, W. (1890) *The principles of psychology*. New York: Holt, Rinehart and Winston.—*63*

JENSEN, A. R., & ROHWER, W. D., JR. (1970) An experimental analysis of learning abilities in culturally disadvantaged children. Final Report, Contract No. OEO-2404 to Office of Economic Opportunity. Univ. Cal., Berkeley, July.—*589*

JOHN, E. R. (1967) *Mechanisms of memory*. New York: Academic Press.

JOHNSON, N. F. (1970) The role of chunking and organization in the process of recall. In G. H. Bower (Ed.), *Psychology of learning and motivation: Advances in research and theory*. Vol. 4. New York: Academic Press.—*586*

JONCÍCH, G. (1968) *The sane positivist: A biography of Edward L. Thorndike*. Middletown, Conn.: Wesleyan Univ. Press.

JONES, E. (1963) *The life and work of Sigmund Freud*. 3 vols. New York: Anchor. (Paper.) Hardcover, New York: Basic Books, 1953, 1955, 1957; abridged ed., 1961.

JONES, E. E., KANOUSE, D., KELLEY, H. H., NISBETT, R. E, VALINS, S., & WEINER, B. (Eds.) (1971) *Attribution: Perceiving the causes of behavior*. New York: General Learning Press. —*238*

JUDSON, A. J., COFFER, C. N., & GELFAND, S. (1956) Reasoning as an associative process: II. "Direction" in problem solving as a function of prior reinforcement of relevant responses. *Psychol. Rep.* 2, 501–507.—*235-36*

KAGAN, J. (1966) Learning, attention, and the issue of discovery. In L. S. Shulman & E. R. Keislar (Eds.), *Learning by discovery*. Chicago: Rand McNally.—*346*

KALMAN, R. E., FALB, P. L., & ARBIB, M. A. (1969) *Topics in mathematical system theory*. New York: McGraw-Hill.—*619*

KAMIN, L. J. (1965) Temporal and intensity characteristics of the conditioned stimulus. In W. F. Prokasy (Ed.), *Classical conditioning*. New York: Appleton-Century-Crofts.—*223*

KAMIN, L. J. (1969a) Selective association and conditioning. In N. J. Mackintosh & W. K. Honig (Eds.), *Fundamental issues in associative learning*. Halifax: Dalhousie Univ. Press. —*223*

KAMIN, L. J. (1969b) Predictability, surprise, attention, and conditioning. In B. A. Campbell & R. M. Church (Eds.), *Punishment*. New York: Appleton-Century-Crofts.—*572*

KAMIYA, J. (1962) Conditioned discrimination of the EEG alpha rhythm in humans. Paper presented at the Western Psychological Association Meeting, San Francisco.—*558*

KAMIYA, J. (1969) Operant control of the EEG alpha rhythm and some of its reported effects on consciousness. In C. T. Tart (Ed.), *Altered states of consciousness*. New York: Wiley.—*237, 558*

KANDEL, E. R., & SPENCER, W. A. (1968) Cellular neurophysiological approaches in the study of learning. *Physiol. Rev.*, 48, 65–134.—*524*

KANDEL, E. R., & TAUC, L. (1965a) Heterosynaptic facilitation in neurones of the abdominal ganglion of *Aplysia depilans*. *J. Physiol.*, 181, 1–27.—*525*

KANDEL, E. R., & TAUC, L. (1965b) Mechanism of heterosynaptic facilitation in the giant cell of the abdominal ganglion of *Aplysia depilans*. *J. Physiol., Lond.*, 181, 28–47.—*525*

KANFER, F. H. (1968) Verbal conditioning: A review of its current status. In T. R. Dixon & D. L. Horton (Eds.), *Verbal behavior and general behavior theory*. Englewood Cliffs, N.J.: Prentice-Hall.—*57*

KANFER, F. H., & PHILLIPS, J. S. (1970) *Learning foundations of behavior therapy*. New York: Wiley.—*372*

KANT, I. (1781) *Kritik der reimen Vermunft.* Leipzig: P. Reclam., English ed., *Critique of pure reason.* (Translated by J. M. D. Meiklejohn.) London: George Bell, 1887.—*7–8, 12*

KASAMATSU, A., & HIRAI, T. (1966) An electroencephalographic study on the Zen meditation (Zazen). *Folio of Psychiatry and Neuropsychology, Japonica,* 20, 315–336. Also in C. T. Tart (Ed.), *Altered states of consciousness: A book of readings.* New York: Wiley, 1969.—*558*

KASWAN, J. (1957) Association of nonsense figures as a function of fittingness and intention to learn. *Amer. J. Psychol.,* 70, 447–450.—*260*

KATONA, G. (1940) *Organizing and memorizing.* New York: Columbia Univ. Press.—*271–72, 279*

KATZ, J. (1966) *The philosophy of language.* New York: Harper & Row.—*10–11*

KELLER, F. S., & HILL, L. M. (1936) Another "insight" experiment. *J. genet. Psychol.,* 484–489.—*134*

KELLER, F. S., & SCHOENFELD, W. N. (1950) *Principles of psychology.* New York: Appleton-Century-Crofts.—*220, 229–231, 243*

KELLER, L., COLE, M., BURKE, C. J., & ESTES, W. K. (1965) Paired associate learning with differential reward. Technical Report No. 66, Psychology Series, Institute for Mathematical Studies in the Social Sciences. Stanford Univ., Sept. 3.—*412*

KENDLER, H. H. (1971) Environmental and cognitive control of behavior. *Amer. Psychol.,* 26, 962–973.

KENDLER, T. S., & KENDLER, H. H. (1970) An ontogeny of optional shift behavior. *Child Devel.,* 41, 1–27.

KENT, E., & GROSSMAN, S. P. (1969) Evidence for a conflict interpretation of anomalous effects of rewarding brain stimulation. *J. comp. physiol. Psychol..* 69, 381–390.—*501–3*

KEPPEL, G. (1968) Retroactive and proactive inhibition. In T. R. Dixon & D. L. Horton (Eds.), *Verbal behavior and general behavior theory.* Englewood Cliffs, N.J.: Prentice-Hall. —*304*

KEPPEL, G., POSTMAN, L., & ZAVORTINK, B. (1968) Studies of learning to learn: VIII. The influence of massive amounts of training upon the learning and retention of paired-associate lists. *J. verb. Learn. verb. Behav.,* 7, 790–796.—*308–9*

KETY, S. S. (1959) Biochemical theories of schizophrenia. *Science,* 129, 1528–1532.—*526*

KIMBLE, D. P. (1963) *Physiological psychology: A unit for introductory psychology.* Reading, Mass.: Addison-Wesley.—*504–5*

KIMBLE, G. A. (1961) *Hilgard and Marquis' conditioning and learning* (2nd ed.). New York: Appleton-Century-Crofts.—*63, 69, 78, 87, 93, 182, 212, 562*

KIMBLE, G. A., & PERLMUTER, L. C. (1970) The problem of volition. *Psychol. Rev.,* 77, 361–384.—*80*

KIMMEL, H. D. (1966) Inhibition of the unconditioned response in classical conditioning. *Psychol. Rev.,* 73, 232–240.—*76–77*

KIMURA, D. (1963) Right temporal lobe damage. *Arch. Neurol.,* 8, 264–271.—*543*

KINTSCH, W. (1964) Habituation of the GSR component of the orienting reflex during paired associate learning before and after learning has taken place. *J. math. Psychol.,* 2, 330–341.—*412*

KINTSCH, W. (1970) *Learning, memory, and conceptual processes.* New York: Wiley.

KINTSCH, W. (1972) Notes on the structure of semantic memory. In E. Tulving & W. Donaldson (Eds.), *Organization of memory.* New York: Academic Press.—*23, 471, 598*

KINTSCH, W., & MORRIS, C. J. (1964) Application of a Markov model to free recall and recognition. *J. exp. Psychol.,* 69, 200–206.—*413, 421*

KLEITMAN, N. (1963) *Sleep and wakefulness* (Rev. ed.). Chicago: Univ. of Chicago Press.— *503*

KLEITMAN, N., & CRISLER, G. (1927) A quantitative study of a salivary conditioned reflex. *Amer. J. Physiol.,* 79, 571–614.—*65*

KLING, J. W., & RIGGS, L. A. (1971) *Experimental psychology.* New York: Holt, Rinehart and Winston.

KOCH, S. (1954) Clark L. Hull. In W. K. Estes, S. Koch, K. MacCorquodale, P. E. Meehl, C. G. Mueller, W. N. Schoenfeld, & W. S. Verplanck, *Modern learning theory.* New York: Appleton-Century-Crofts, 1–176.—*165, 174, 203*

KOCH, S. (Ed.) (1959) *Psychology: a study of a science.* Vol. 2. New York: McGraw-Hill.

KOESTLER, A. (1964) *The act of creation.* New York: Macmillan.—*360*

KOFFKA, K. (1924) *The growth of the mind.* (Translated by R. M. Ogden.) London: Kegan Paul, Trench, Trubner.—*252, 254*

KOFFKA, K. (1935) *Principles of Gestalt psychology.* New York: Harcourt, Brace & World.—*255, 267*

KÖHLER, W. (1971) *Intelligenz-prufungen an Menschenaffen.* See Köhler, 1925.

KÖHLER, W. (1918) Nachweis einfacher Strukturfunktionen beim Schimpansen und beim Haushuhn. *Abb. d. königl. Preuss. Ak. d. Wissen,* Phys. Math. Klasse, Nr. 2, 1–101. Transslated and condensed as "Simple structural functions in the chimpanzee and in the chicken," in W. D. Ellis, *A source book of Gestalt psychology.* New York: Harcourt, Brace & World, 1938, 217–227.—*183*

KÖHLER, W. (1920) Die physische Gestalten in Ruhe und in stationären Zustand, Ein naturphilosophische Untersuchung. Braunschweig Verlag. Portions condensed and translated in W. D. Ellis, *A Source book of Gestalt psychology.* New York: Harcourt, Brace & World, 1938, 17–54.—*278*

KÖHLER, W. (1925) *The mentality of apes.* (Translated by E. Winter.) New York: Harcourt, Brace & World.

KÖHLER W. (1929) *Gestalt psychology.* New York: Liveright.—*270*

KÖHLER, W. (1938) *The place of value in a world of facts.* New York: Liveright.—*263–64*

KÖHLER, W. (1940) *Dynamics in psychology.* New York: Liveright.

KÖHLER, W. (1941) On the nature of associations. *Proc. Amer. Phil. Soc.,* 84, 489–502.—*270*

KÖHLER, W., & HELD, R. (1949) The cortical correlate of pattern vision. *Science,* 110, 414–419.—*278*

KÖHLER, W., HELD, R., & O'CONNELL, D. L. (1952) An investigation of cortical currents. *Proc. Amer. Phil. Soc.,* 96, 290–330.—*278*

KÖHLER, W., & RESTORFF, H. VON (1935) Analyse von Vorgangen im Spurenfeld. *Psychol. Forsch.,* 21, 56–112.—*270–71*

KOHNSTAMM, G. A. (1967) *Teaching children to solve a Piagetian problem of class inclusion.* Uitgevers: Mouton.—*336*

KONORSKI, J. (1948) *Conditioned reflexes and neuron organization.* Cambridge, Eng.: Cambridge Univ. Press.—*520*

KONORSKI, J. (1964) On the mechanism of instrumental conditioning. *Proceedings of the 17th International Congress of Psychology.* Amsterdam: North-Holland Publishing Co., 45–59.—*78*

KONORSKI, J., & MILLER, S. (1937a) On two types of conditioned reflex. *J. gen. Psychol.,* 16, 264–272.—*78*

KONORSKI, J., & MILLER, S. (1937b) Further remarks on two types of conditioned reflex. *J. gen. Psychol.,* 17, 405–407.—*78*

KOOISTRA, W. H. (1963) Developmental trends in the attainment of conservation, transitivity, and relativism in the thinking of children. Unpublished doctoral dissertation, Wayne State Univ.—*328*

KOPSTEIN, F. F., & SEIDEL, R. J. (1969) Computer-administered instruction versus traditionally administered instruction: Economics. In R. C. Atkinson & H. A. Wilson (Eds.), *Computer-assisted instruction.* New York: Academic Press, 327–362.—*632*

KOTESKEY, R. L. (1972) A stimulus sampling model of the partial reinforcement effect. *Psychol. Rev.,* 79, 161–171.—*570*

KRANTZ, D. L. (1971) The separate worlds of operant and non-operant psychology. *J. appl. behav. Anal.,* 4, 61–70.—*249*

KRASNER, L. (1958) Studies of the conditioning of verbal behavior. *Psychol. Bull.,* 55, 148–170.—*485*

KRASNER, L. (1962) The therapist as a social reinforcement machine. In H. H. Strupp & L. Luborsky (Eds.), *Research in psychotherapy.* Vol. 2, Baltimore: French-Bray.—*57*

KRASNER, L. (1965) Verbal conditioning in psychotherapy. In L. Krasner & L. P. Ullman (Eds.), *Research in behavior modification.* New York: Holt, Rinehart and Winston, 211–228.—*79*

KRECH, D., ROSENZWEIG, M., & BENNETT, E. L. (1960) Effects of environmental complexity and training on brain chemistry. *J. comp. physiol. Psychol.,* 53, 509–519.—*527*

KRECH, D., ROSENZWEIG, M., & BENNETT, E. L. (1962) Relations between brain chemistry and problem solving among rats raised in enriched and impoverished environments. *J. comp. physiol. Psychol.,* 55, 801–807.—*527–28*

KRECHEVSKY, I. (1932a) "Hypotheses" in rats. *Psychol. Rev.,* 39, 516–532.—*140–41*

KRECHEVSKY, I. (1932b) "Hypotheses" versus "chance" in the presolution period in sensory discrimination-learning. *Univ. Calif. Publ. Psychol.,* 6, 27–44.—*140–41*

KRECHEVSKY, I. (1933a) Hereditary nature of "hypotheses." *J. comp. Psychol.*, 16, 99–116.— *140–41*

KRECHEVSKY, I. (1933b) The docile nature of "hypotheses." *J. comp. Psychol.*, 15, 429–443.— *140–41*

KRETSCHMER, E. (1925) *Physique and character.* (Translated from 2nd ed.) New York: Harcourt, Brace &World.—*72*

KRIS, E. (1952) *Psychoanalytic explorations in art.* New York: International Universities Press.—*360*

KROLL, N. E. A., PARKS, T., PARKINSON, S. R., BIBER, S. L., & JOHNSON, A. L. (1970) Short-term memory while shadowing: Recall of visually and of aurally presented letters. *J. exp. Psychol.*, 85, 220–224.—*579*

KRUMBOLTZ, J. D., & THORESEN, C. E. (Eds.) (1969) *Behavioral counseling: Cases and techniques.* New York: Holt, Rinehart and Winston.—*241, 600*

KUHN, T. S. (1962) *The structure of scientific revolutions.* Chicago: Univ. of Chicago Press. —*151*

KUO, Z. Y. (1937) Forced movement or insight? *Univ. Calif. Publ. Psychol.*, 6, 169–188.—*134*

KUPFERMANN, I., & PINSKER, H. (1969) Plasticity in *Aplysia* neurons and some simple neuronal models of learning. In J. T. Tapp (Ed.), *Reinforcement and behavior.* New York and London: Academic Press.—*525, 526*

LABERGE, D. L. (1959) A model with neutral elements. In R. R. Bush & W. K. Estes (Eds.), *Studies in mathematical learning theory.* Stanford: Stanford Univ. Press.—*384*

LABERGE, D. L. (1961) Generalization gradients in a discrimination situation. *J. exp. Psychol.*, 62, 88–94.—*400*

LANDFIELD, P. W., & McGAUGH, J. L. (1972) Effects of electroconvulsive shock and brain stimulation on EEG cortical data rhythms in rats. *Behav. Biol.*, 7, 271–278.—*516*

LANDFIELD, P. W., McGAUGH, J. L., & TUSA, R. J. (1972) Theta rhythm: A temporal correlate of memory storage processes in the rat. *Science*, 175, 87–89.—*516*

LANGE, P. C. (Ed.) (1967) *Programed instruction 66th Yearbook of the National Society for the Study of Education*, Part II. Chicago: NSSE.

LASHLEY, K. S. (1924) Studies of cerebral function in learning: V. The retention of motor habits after destruction of the so-called motor area in primates. *Arch. neurol. Psychiat.*, 12, 249–276.—*115*

LASHLEY, K. S., & BALL, J. (1929) Spinal conduction and kinesthetic sensitivity in the maze habit. *J. comp. Psychol.*, 9, 71–105.—*131*

LASHLEY, K. S., CHOW, K. L., & SEMMES, J. (1951) An examination of the electrical field theory of cerebral integration. *Psychol. Rev.*, 40, 175–188.—*278*

LAURENDEAU, M., & PINARD, A. (1962) *Causal thinking in the child.* New York: International Universities Press.—*333*

LAWRENCE, D. H., & DERIVERA, J. (1954) Evidence for relational discrimination. *J. comp. physiol. Psychol.*, 47, 465–471.—*186*

LAWRENCE, D. H., & FESTINGER, L. (1962) *Deterrents and reinforcement: The psychology of insufficient reward.* Stanford: Stanford Univ. Press.—*147–48*

LENNEBERG, E. H. (1967) *The biological foundations of language.* New York: Wiley.— *11, 19, 85, 543*

LEONARD, D. W. (1969) Amount and sequence of reward in partial and continuous reinforcement. *J. comp. physiol. Psychol.*, 67, 204–211.—*569*

LEUBA, C., BIRCH, L., & APPLETON, J. (1968) Human problem-solving during complete paralysis of the voluntary musculature. *Psychol. Rep.*, 22, 849–855.—*553*

LEVIÉN, R. E. (1972) *The emerging technology: Instructional uses of the computer in higher education.* New York: McGraw-Hill.

LEVINE, G., & BURKE, C. J. (1972) *Mathematical model techniques for learning theories.* New York: Academic Press.

LEVINE, M. (1965) Hypothesis behavior. In A. M. Schrier, H. F. Harlow, & F. Stollnitz (Eds.), *Behavior of nonhuman primates.* Vol. 1. New York: Academic Press.—*141, 401*

LEVINE, M. (1969) Neo-noncontinuity theory. In G. H. Bower & J. T. Spence (Eds.), *The psychology of learning and motivation.* Vol. 3. New York: Academic Press.—*141*

LEVINE, M. (1970) Human discrimination learning: The subset sampling assumption. *Psychol. Bull.*, 74, 397–404.—*141–43, 246, 413*

LEVY, N., & SEWARD, J. P. (1969) Frustration and homogeneity of rewards in the double runway. *J. exp. Psychol.*, 81, 460–463.—*197*

LEWIN, K. (1935) *A dynamic theory of personality*. (Translated by D. K. Adams & K. E. Zener.) New York: McGraw-Hill.—*175*

LEWIN, K. (1942) Field theory and learning. Chapter 4 in *The psychology of learning*. 41st Yearbook of the National Society for the Study of Education, Part II, 215–242.

LEWIS, D. J. (1969) Sources of experimental amnesia. *Psychol. Rev.*, 76, 461–472.—*514*

LEWIS, D. J., & KENT, N. D. (1961) Attempted direct activation and deactivation of the fractional anticipatory goal response. *Psychol. Rep.*, 8, 107–110.—*191*

LEWIS, D. J., & MAHER, B. A. (1965) Neural consolidation and electroconvulsive shock. *Psychol. Rev.*, 72, 225–239.—*514*

LIDDELL, H. S. (1936) Pavlov, the psychiatrist of the future. *J. Mt. Sinai Hosp.*, 3, 101–104.—*72*

LIDDELL, H. S. (1961) Pavlov, the psychiatrist of the future. In N. S. Kline (Ed.), Pavlovian Conference on Higher Nervous Activity. *Ann. N.Y. Acad. Sci.*, 92, 981–983.—*72*

LIGHT, L. L., & CARTER-SOBELL, L. (1970) Effects of changed semantic context on recognition memory. *J. verb. Learn. verb. Behav.*, 9, 1–11.—*268*

LIGHT, L. L., STANSBURY, C., RUBIN, C., & LINDE, S. (1973) Memory for modality of presentation: Within-modality discrimination. *Mem. and Cog.*, 1, 395–400.—*591*

LINDSAY, P. H., & NORMAN, D. A. (1972) *Human information processing: An introduction to psychology*. New York: Academic Press.—*483, 593, 595, 599*

LINDSAY, R. K. (1963) Inferential memory as the basis of machines which understand natural language. In E. A. Feigenbaum & J. Feldman (Eds.), *Computers and thought*. New York: McGraw-Hill.—*470*

LINDSLEY, D. B. (1958) The reticular system and perceptual discrimination. In H. H. Jasper et al. (Eds.), *Reticular formation of the brain*. Boston: Little, Brown, Chap. 25.—*505*

LINDVALL, C. M., & BOLVIN, J. O. (1967) Programed instruction in the schools: An application of programing principles in "individually prescribed instruction." In P. C. Lange (Ed.), *Programed instruction*. 66th Yearbook of the National Society for the Study of Education, Part II, 217–254. Chicago: NSSE.—*623*

LINDVALL, C. M., & COX, R. C. (1969) The role of evaluation in programs for individualized instruction. In R. W. Tyler (Ed.), *Educational evaluation: New roles, new means*. 68th Yearbook of the National Society for the Study of Education, 156–188. Chicago: NSSE.—*623*

LOCKE, J. (1690) *An essay concerning human understanding*. London: T. Basset. Recent edition is by A. S. Pringle-Pattison. Oxford: Clarendon Press, 1924.—*5–6*

LOCKE, J., & LOCKE, V. L. (1971) Deaf children's phonetic, visual, and dactylic coding in a grapheme recall task. *J. exp. Psychol.*, 89, 142–146.—*579*

LOFTUS, G. (1972) Eye fixations and recognition memory for pictures. *Cog. Psychol.*, 3, 525–551.—*48, 580*

LOGAN, F. A. (1956) A micromolar approach to behavior theory. *Psychol. Rev.*, 63, 63–73.—*198*

LOGAN, F. A. (1959) The Hull-Spence approach. In S. Koch (Ed.), *Psychology: A study of a science*. Vol. 2. New York: McGraw-Hill, 293–358.—*198*

LOGAN, F. A. (1960) *Incentive*. New Haven: Yale Univ. Press.—*54, 191, 198, 199, 218*

LOGAN, F. A. (1965) Decision making by rats. *J. comp. physiol. Psychol.*, 59, 1–12, 246–251.—*192, 198*

LOGAN, F. A. (1968) Incentive theory and changes in reward. In K. W. Spence & J. T. Spence (Eds.), *The psychology of learning and motivation*. Vol. 2. New York: Academic Press.—*191–92*

LOGAN, F. A. (1969) The negative incentive value of punishment. In B. A. Campbell & R. M. Church (Eds.), *Punishment and aversive behavior*. New York: Appleton-Century-Crofts.—*192, 198*

LOGAN, F. A. (1970) *Fundamentals of learning and motivation*. Dubuque, Iowa: Brown.—*198*

LOGAN, F. A., & WAGNER, A. R. (1965) *Reward and punishment*. Boston: Allyn & Bacon.—*198*

LORENZ, K. Z. (1952) *King Solomon's ring*. New York: Crowell.—*18*

LOUCKS, R. B. (1933) An appraisal of Pavlov's systematization of behavior from the experimental standpoint. *J. comp. Psychol.*, 15, 1–47.—*71*

LOVEJOY, E. (1968) *Attention in discrimination learning*. San Francisco: Holden-Day.—*189, 401*

LOVELL, K. (1962) *The growth of basic mathematical and scientific concepts in children*. New York: Philosophical Library.—*341*

LUCE, R. D. (1959) *Individual choice behavior.* New York: Wiley.—*190–91*

LUCE, R. D., BUSH, R. R., & GALANTER, E. (Eds.) (1963) *Handbook of mathematical psychology.* Vols. 1 and 2. New York: Wiley.—*375*

LUCE, R. D., BUSH, R. R., & GALANTER, E. (Eds.) (1965) *Handbook of mathematical psychology.* Vol. 3. New York: Wiley.—*375*

LUMSDAINE, A. A. (1959) Teaching machines and self-instructional materials. *Audiovisual Communica. Rev.,* 7, 163–172.—*628*

LUMSDAINE, A. A. (Ed.) (1961) *Student response in programmed instruction: A symposium,* Washington, D.C.: National Academy of Sciences–National Research Council.—*611*

LUMSDAINE, A. A. (1964) Educational technology, programmed learning, and instructional sciences. In E. R. Hilgard (Ed.), *Theories of learning and instruction.* Chicago: Univ. of Chicago Press, 371–401.—*610–11*

LUNZER, E. A. (1960) *Recent studies in Britain based on the work of Jean Piaget.* London: National Foundation for Educational Research.—*341*

LURIA, A. R. (1961) *The role of speech in the regulation of normal and abnormal behavior.* New York: J. B. Lippincott.—*80*

LURIA, A. R. (1966) *Higher cortical functions in man.* New York: Plenum.

MACCORQUODALE, K. (1969) B. F. Skinner's *Verbal Behavior:* A retrospective appreciation. *J. exp. anal. Behav.,* 12, 831–841.—*235, 248*

MACCORQUODALE, K. (1970) On Chomsky's review of Skinner's *Verbal Behavior. J. exp. anal. Behav.,* 13, 83–100.—*248*

MACCORQUODALE, K., & MEEHL, P. E. (1953) Preliminary suggestions as to a formalization of expectancy theory. *Psychol. Rev.,* 60, 55–63.—*125, 126–29*

MACCORQUODALE, K., & MEEHL, P. E. (1954) Edward C. Tolman. In W. K. Estes, S. Koch, K. MacCorquodale, P. E. Meehl, C. G. Mueller, W. N. Schoenfeld, & W. S. Verplanck, *Modern learning theory.* New York: Appleton-Century-Crofts, 177–266.—*125, 136*

McCLEARY, R. A. (1960) Type of response as a function of interocular transfer in the fish. *J. comp. physiol. Psychol.,* 53, 311–321.—*541*

McCLURE, R. M. (Ed.) (1971) *The curriculum: Retrospect and prospect.* 70th Yearbook of the National Society for the Study of Education, Part I. Chicago: Univ. of Chicago Press. —*614*

McCONNELL, J. V. (1962) Memory transfer through cannibalism in planarians. *J. Neuropsychiat.,* 3 (Suppl. 1), 542.—*531*

McCONNELL, J. V., BRYANT, R. C., GOLUB, A. M., & ROSENBLATT, F. (1972) Nonspecific behavioral effects of substances from mammalian brain. *Science,* 178, 521–523.—*531*

McDONALD, F. J. (1964) The influence of learning theories on education. In E. R. Hilgard (Ed.), *Theories of learning and instruction.* 63rd Yearbook of the National Society for the Study of Education. Chicago: Univ. of Chicago Press, 1–26.—*610*

MACFARLANE, D. A. (1930) The role of kinesthesis in maze learning. *Univ. Calif. Publ. Psychol.,* 4, 277–305.—*131*

McGAUGH, J. C. (1965) Facilitation and impairment of memory storage processes. In D. P. Kimble (Ed.), *Learning, remembering, and forgetting.* Vol. 1. *The anatomy of memory.* Palo Alto: Science and Behavior Books, 240–291.—*518*

McGAUGH, J. C. (1968) Drug facilitation of memory and learning. In D. H. Efron et al. (Eds.), *Psychopharmacology: A review of progress, 1957-1967.* PHS publication 1836, 891–904. Washington, D.C.: U.S. Govt. Printing Office.—*518*

McGAUGH, J. L., & HERZ, M. J. (1972) *Memory consolidation.* San Francisco: Albion.—*513, 516, 518*

McGAUGH, J. L., & LANDFIELD, P. W. (1970) Delayed development of amnesia following electroconvulsive shock. *Physiol. and Behav.,* 5, 751–755.—*514*

McGEOCH, J. A. (1932) Forgetting and the law of disuse. *Psychol. Rev.,* 39, 352–370.—*291, 300*

McGEOCH, J. A. (1936) The vertical dimensions of mind. *Psychol. Rev.,* 43, 107–129.—*285*

McGEOCH, J. A. (1942) *The psychology of human learning.* New York: Longmans.—*288*

McGEOCH, J. A., & IRION, A. L. (1952) *The psychology of human learning* (Rev ed.). New York: Longmans.—*312, 313, 314, 316, 547, 577, 588*

McGILL, W. J. (1963) Stochastic latency mechanisms. In R. D. Luce, R. R. Bush, & E. Galanter (Eds.), *Handbook of mathematical psychology.* Vol. 1. New York: Wiley.—*399*

McGOVERN, J. B. (1964) Extinction of associations in four transfer paradigms. *Psychol. Monogr.,* 78 (Whole No. 593).—*305*

MACINTOSH, N. J., & HONIG, W. K. (Eds.) (1971) *Fundamental issues in associative learning.* Halifax: Dalhousie Univ. Press.

MCNEILL, D. (1970) *The acquisition of language.* New York: Harper & Row.—*11*

MADDEN, E. H. (1962) *Philosophical problems of psychology.* New York: Odyssey.—*256*

MANDLER, G. (1967) Organization and memory. In K. W. Spence & J. T. Spence (Eds.), *The psychology of learning and motivation: Advances in research and theory.* Vol. 1. New York: Academic Press.—*585*

MANDLER, G. (1968) Association and organization: Facts, fancies, and theories. In T. R. Dixon & D. L. Horton (Eds.), *Verbal behavior and general behavior theory.* Englewood Cliffs, N.J.: Prentice-Hall.—*279, 585*

MANDLER, J. M., & MANDLER, G. (1964) *Thinking: From association to Gestalt.* New York: Wiley.—*9*

MARLER, P. (1970) A comparative approach to vocal learning: Song development in white-crowned sparrows. *J. comp. physiol. Psychol.,* 71, No. 2, Part 2 (monograph).—*18*

MARTIN, E. (1965) Transfer of verbal paired associates. *Psychol. Rev.,* 72, 327–343.—*296–97*

MARX, M. H. (Ed.) (1963) *Theories in contemporary psychology.* New York: Macmillan.

MASSERMAN, J. H. (1943) *Behavior and neurosis.* Chicago: Univ. of Chicago Press.—*73*

MAY, R. (1950) *The meaning of anxiety.* New York: Ronald Press.—*351*

MAYHEW, K. C., & EDWARDS, A. C. (1936) *The Dewey school: The Laboratory school at the University of Chicago, 1896–1903.* New York: Appleton-Century-Crofts.—*283*

MECHNER, F. (1958) Probability relations within response sequences under ratio reinforcement. *J. exp. anal. Behav.,* 1, 109–122.—*216*

MEEHL, P. E. (1950) On the circularity of the law of effect. *Psychol. Bull.,* 47, 52–75.—*561–63*

MEIKLE, T. H. (1960) Role of corpus callosum in transfer of visual discrimination in the cat. *Science,* 132, 1496.—*541*

MEIKLE, T. H., & SECHZER, J. A. (1960) Interocular transfer of brightness discrimination in "split-brain" cats. *Science,* 132, 734–735.—*541*

MELTON, A. W. (1941) Learning. In W. S. Monroe (Ed.), *Encyclopedia of educational research.* New York: Macmillan.—*285*

MELTON, A. W. (1950) Learning. In W. S. Monroe (Ed.), *Encyclopedia of educational research* (Rev. ed.). New York: Macmillan.—*285, 286, 288–89, 291*

MELTON, A. W. (Ed.) (1964) *Categories of human learning.* New York: Academic Press.

MELTON, A. W., & IRWIN, J. McQ. (1940) The influence of degree of interpolated learning on retroactive inhibition and the overt transfer of specific responses. *Amer. J. Psychol.,* 53, 173–203.—*302*

MELTON, A. W., & MARTIN, E. (Eds.) (1972) *Coding processes in human memory.* Washington, D.C.: V. H. Winston.

MELTZER, H. (1930) Individual differences in forgetting pleasant and unpleasant experiences. *J. educ. Psychol.,* 21, 399–409.—*366–67*

MERRYMAN, C. T. (1969) Effects of strategies on associative symmetry. Indiana Mathematical Psychology Program Rep. No. 69-6. Bloomington: Univ. of Indiana Press.—*42*

MERRYMAN, C. T. (1971) Retroactive inhibition in the A-B, A-D paradigm as measured by a multiple-choice test. *J. exp. Psychol.,* 91, 212–214.—*304*

MEYER, D. E. (1970) On the representation and retrieval of stored semantic information. *Cog. Psychol.,* 1, 242–300.—*597*

MICHAEL, R. P. (1962) Estrogen-sensitive neurons and sexual behavior in female cats. *Science,* 136, 322–323.—*495*

MICHOTTE, A. (1954) *La perception de la causalité* (2nd ed.). Louvain: Publications Univ. de Louvain.—*8*

MILES, M. B. (Ed.) (1964) *Innovation in education.* New York: Teachers College, Columbia Univ.—*636*

MILLER, G. A. (1956) The magical number seven plus or minus two: Some limits on our capacity for processing information. *Psychol. Rev.,* 63, 81–97.—*584–85*

MILLER, G. A., GALANTER, E., & PRIBRAM, K. H. (1960) *Plans and the structure of behavior.* New York: Holt, Rinehart and Winston.—*148–50, 436*

MILLER, G. A., & MCNEILL, D. (1969) Psycholinguistics. In G. Lindzey & E. Aronson (Eds.), *The handbook of social psychology* (2nd ed.). Vol. 3. Reading, Mass.: Addison-Wesley.—*598*

MILLER, N. E. (1941) The frustration-aggression hypothesis. *Psychol. Rev.,* 48, 337–342.—*356*

MILLER, N. E. (1944) Experimental studies in conflict. In J. McV. Hunt (Ed.), *Personality and the behavior disorders.* New York: Ronald Press, 431–465.—*175–76*

MILLER, N. E. (1948a) Studies of fear as an acquired drive: I. Fear as motivation and fear-reduction as reinforcement in the learning of new responses. *J. exp. Psychol.*, 38, 89–101. —*352*

MILLER, N. E. (1948b) Theory and experiment relating psychoanalytic displacement to stimulus-response generalization. *J. abnorm. soc. Psychol.*, 43, 155–178.—*177, 356–58*

MILLER, N. E. (1951) Learnable drives and rewards. In S. S. Stevens (Ed.), *Handbook of experimental psychology.* New York: Wiley.—*175*

MILLER, N. E. (1957) *Graphic communication and the crisis in education.* Washington, D.C.: National Education Association.—*613*

MILLER, N. E. (1958) Central stimulation and other new approaches to motivation and reward. *Amer. Psychol.*, 13, 100–108.—*177*

MILLER, N. E. (1959) Liberalization of basic S-R concepts: Extensions to conflict behavior, motivation and social learning. In S. Koch (Ed.), *Psychology: A study of a science.* Vol. 2. New York: McGraw-Hill, 196–202.—*175, 177, 613*

MILLER, N. E. (1965) Chemical coding of behavior in the brain. *Science*, 148, 328–338.—*177, 495*

MILLER, N. E. (1969) Learning of visceral and glandular responses. *Science*, 163, 434–445.— *209, 222, 244, 553*

MILLER, N. E. (1972) Two psychosomatic effects of learning. Speech delivered at the International Congress of Psychology, Tokyo, Japan, 1972. (Published as LS10-2 in Proceedings of the International Congress of Psychology, 1972.)—*556*

MILLER, N. E., & BANUAZIZI, A. (1968) Instrumental learning by curarized rats of a specific visceral response, intestinal or cardiac. *J. comp. physiol. Psychol.*, 65, 1–7.—*555–56*

MILLER, N. E., & DOLLARD, J. (1941) *Social learning and imitation.* New Haven: Yale Univ. Press.—*177, 178, 599, 613*

MILLER, N. E., & MURRAY, E. J. (1952) Displacement and conflict: Learnable drive as a basis for the steeper gradient of avoidance than of approach. *J. exp. Psychol.*, 43, 227–231. —*176*

MILLER, S., & KONORSKI, J. (1928) Sur une forme particulière des réflexes conditionnels. *C. R. Soc. Biol. Paris*, 99, 1155–1157.—*78, 88*

MILNER, B. R. (1966) Amnesia following operation on temporal lobes. In C. W. N. Whitty & O. L. Zangwill (Eds.), *Amnesia.* London: Butterworths.—*517*

MILNER, B. R. (1968) Visual recognition and recall after right temporal-lobe excision in man. *Neuropsychol.*, 6, 191–209.—*543*

MINSKY, M. (1961a) Steps toward artificial intelligence. *Proc. of Inst. of Radio Engineers*, 49, 8–30. Also reprinted in E. Feigenbaum & J. Feldman (Eds.), *Computers and thought.* New York: McGraw-Hill, 1963.—*439*

MINSKY, M. (1961b) A selected descriptor-indexed bibliography of the literature on artificial intelligence. *IRE Transactions on Human Factors in Electronics*, 2, 39–55. Reprinted in E. Feigenbaum & J. Feldman (Eds.), *Computers and thought.* New York: McGraw-Hill, 1963.—*439*

MINSKY, M. (Ed.) (1968) *Semantic information processing.* Cambridge: MIT Press.—*466*

MINSKY, M., & PAPERT, S. (1969) *Perceptions: An introduction to computational geometry.* Cambridge: MIT Press.—*446, 549*

MISANIN, J. R., MILLER, R. R., & LEWIS, D. G. (1968) Retrograde amnesia produced by electroconvulsive shock after reactivation of a consolidated memory trace. *Science*, 160, 554–555.—*514*

MISCHEL, W. (1968) *Personality and assessment.* New York: Wiley.—*239, 599–600*

MISCHEL, W. (1971) *Introduction to personality.* New York: Holt, Rinehart and Winston.— *239, 241, 350, 361*

MOLTZ, H. (1957) Latent extinction and the fractional anticipatory response mechanism. *Psychol. Rev.*, 64, 229–241.—*137*

MONTADA, L. (1970) *Die Lernpsychologie Jean Piagets.* Stuttgart: Ernst Klett.—*337*

MONTESSORI, M. (1946) *Spontaneous activity in education.* Cambridge: Robert Bentley.—*342*

MORAY, N. (1969) *Listening and attention.* Baltimore: Penguin Books.—*506*

MORAY, N. (1970) *Attention: Selective processes in vision and hearing.* New York: Academic Press.—*506*

MORGAN, C. T. (1965) *Physiological psychology* (3rd ed.) New York: McGraw-Hill.—*495*

MORRELL, F. (1960) Secondary epileptogenic lesions. *Epilepsia*, 1, 538–560.—*521–22*

MORRELL, F. (1961a) Effect of anodal polarization on the firing pattern of single cortical cells. *Ann. N.Y. Acad. Sci.* 92, 860–876.—*521–522*

MORRELL, F. (1961b) Electrophysiological contributions to the neural basis of learning. *Physiol. Rev.*, 41, 443–494.—*522*

MORRELL, F. (1963) Information storage in nerve cells. In W. S. Fields & W. Abbott (Eds.), *Information storage and neural control.* Springfield, Ill.: Charles C Thomas.

MORSE, W. H. (1966) Intermittent reinforcement. In W. K. Honig (Ed.), *Operant behavior: Areas of research and application.* New York: Appleton-Century-Crofts.—*218*

MOWRER, O. H. (1939) A stimulus-response analysis of anxiety and its role as a reinforcing agent. *Psychol. Rev.*, 46, 553–565.—*352*

MOWRER, O. H. (1940) Anxiety reduction and learning. *J. exp. Psychol.*, 27, 497–516.—*352*

MOWRER, O. H. (1947) On the dual nature of learning—A re-interpretation of "conditioning" and "problem-solving." *Harv. educ. Rev.*, 17, 102–148.—*78–79, 102, 178*

MOWRER, O. H. (1950) *Learning theory and personality dynamics.* New York: Ronald Press. —*372*

MOWRER, O. H. (1956) Two-factor learning theory reconsidered, with special reference to secondary reinforcement and the concept of habit. *Psychol. Rev.*, 63, 114–128.—*178–79*

MOWRER, O. H. (1960) *Learning theory and behavior.* New York: Wiley.—*54, 104, 144, 175, 179–82*

MUELLER, C. G., JR., & SCHOENFELD, W. N. (1954) Edwin R. Guthrie. In W. K. Estes, S. Koch, K. MacCorquodale, P. E. Meehl, C. G. Mueller, W. N. Schoenfeld, & W. S. Verplanck, *Modern learning theory.* New York: Appleton-Century-Crofts, 345–379.—*109, 120–21*

MUENZINGER, K. F. (1935) Motivation in learning: I. Electric shock for correct response in the visual discrimination habit. *J. comp. Psychol.*, 17, 267–277.—*138*

MUENZINGER, K. F. (1938) Vicarious trial and error at a point of choice: I. A general survey of its relation to learning efficiency. *J. genet. Psychol.*, 53, 75–86.—*143*

MUENZINGER, K. F., BROWN, W. O., CROW, W. J., & POWLOWSKI, R. F. (1952) Motivation in learning: XI. An analysis of electric shock for correct responses into its avoidance and accelerating components. *J. exp. Psychol.*, 43, 115–119.—*138*

MUENZINGER, K. F., KOERNER, L., & IREY, E. (1929) Variability of an habitual movement in guinea pigs. *J. comp. Psychol.*, 9, 425–436.—*138*

MULHOLLAND, T. B. (1972) Occipital alpha revisited. *Psychol. Bull.*, 78, 176–182.—*560*

MÜLLER, G. E., & PILZECKER, A. (1900) Experimentelle Beiträge zur Lehre vom Gedachtnis. *Z. Psychol.*, Ergbd. I.—*291, 509*

MURDOCK, B. B., JR. (1972) Short-term memory. In G. H. Bower (Ed.), *The psychology of learning and motivation: Advances in research and theory.* Vol. 5. New York: Academic Press.—*584*

MURPHY, G. (1949) *Historical introduction to modern psychology.* New York: Harcourt, Brace & World.—*6*

MYERS, J. L. (1970) Sequential choice behavior. In G. H. Bower (Ed.), *The psychology of learning and motivation: Advances in research and theory.* Vol. 4. New York: Academic Press.—*392, 568*

MYROW, D. L., & ANDERSON, R. C. (1972) Retroactive inhibition of prose as a function of the type of test. *J. educ. Psychol.*, 63, 303–308.—*310*

NAGGE, J. N. (1935) An experimental test of the theory of associative interference. *J. exp. Psychol.*, 18, 663–682.

NEIMARK, E. D., & ESTES, W. K. (Eds.) (1967) *Stimulus sampling theory.* San Francisco: Holden-Day.

NEIMARK, E. D., & SHUFORD, E. H. (1959) Comparison of predictions and estimates in a probability learning situation. *J. exp. Psychol.*, 57, 294–298.—*388*

NEISSER, U. (1967) *Cognitive psychology.* New York: Appleton-Century-Crofts.—*148, 250, 353, 599*

NEWELL, A. (1970) Remarks on the relationship between artificial intelligence and cognitive psychology. In R. Banerji & M. D. Mesarovic (Eds.), *Theoretical approaches to non-numerical problem solving.* New York: Springer-Verlag.—*487–88*

NEWELL, A., SHAW, J. C., & SIMON, H. A. (1958) Elements of a theory of human problem solving. *Psychol. Rev.*, 65, 151–166.—*148, 436–38*

NEWELL, A., SHAW, J. C., & SIMON, H. A. (1959) A report on a general problem-solving program. *Proceedings of the International Conference on Information Processing.* New York: UNESCO, 256–265.—*460*

NEWELL, A., & SIMON, H. A. (1956) The logic theory machine. *IRE Transactions on Information Theory*, IT-2, 61–69.—*436*

NEWELL, A., & SIMON, H. A. (1961) Computer simulation of human thinking. *Science*, 134, 2011–2017.—*460*

NEWELL, A., & SIMON, H. A. (1963) Computers in psychology. In R. D. Luce, R. R. Bush, & E. Galanter (Eds.), *Handbook of mathematical psychology*. Vol. 1. New York: Wiley.—*484, 485, 487*

NEWELL, A., & SIMON, H. A. (1972) *Human problem solving*. Englewood Cliffs, N.J.: Prentice-Hall.—*236, 280, 460, 461*

NEWTON, J. M., & WICKENS, D. D. (1956) Retroactive inhibition as a function of the temporal position of interpolated learning. *J. exp. Psychol.*, 51, 149–154.—*295*

NIELSON, H. C. (1968) Evidence that electro-convulsive shock alters memory retrieval rather than memory consolidation. *Exp. Neurol.*, 20, 3–20.—*514–15*

NILSSON, N. J. (1971) *Problem-solving methods in artificial intelligence*. New York: McGraw-Hill.—*456*

NORMAN, D. A. (1965) *Attention and memory*. New York: Wiley.—*150*

NORMAN, D. A. (Ed.) (1970) *Models of memory*. New York: Academic Press.—*420*

NORMAN, D. A. (1972) Memory, knowledge, and the answering of questions. Paper presented at the Loyola Symposium on Cognitive Psychology, Chicago. Also Technical Report #25, Center for Human Information Processing. University of California, San Diego, May 1972.—*597*

NORMAN, M. F. (1964) *A probabilistic model for free-responding*. Technical Report #67, Psychology Series, Institute of Mathematical Studies in the Social Sciences. Stanford Univ., Dec. 14.—*399*

NOTTEBOHM, F. (1970) Ontogeny of bird song. *Science*, 167, 950–956.—*18*

NOTTERMAN, J. M., & MINTZ, D. E. (1962) Exteroceptive cueing of response force. *Science*, 135, 1070–1071.—*229*

NUTTIN, J. (1949) "Spread" in recalling failure and success. *J. exp. Psychol.*, 39, 60–69.—*17*

NUTTIN, J. (1953) *Tâche, réussite et échec*. Louvain: Publications Univ. de Louvain.—*47*

OLDS, J. (1965) Operant conditioning of single unit responses. *Excerpta Medica, Foundation International Congress Series*, 87, 372–380.—*557*

OLDS, J. (1969) The central nervous system and the reinforcement of behavior. *Amer. Psychol.*, 24, 114–132.—*557*

OLDS, J., & MILNER, P. (1954) Positive reinforcement produced by electrical stimulation of septal area and other regions of rat brain. *J. comp. physiol. Psychol.*, 47, 419–427.—*498*

OLDS, J., & OLDS, M. (1965) Drives, rewards, and the brain. In *New directions in psychology*. Vol. 2. New York: Holt, Rinehart and Winston.—*498–99*

OLSON, G. M. (1969) Learning and retention in a continuous recognition task. *J. exp. Psychol.*, 81, 381–384.—*413*

ORNSTEIN, R. E. (1969) *On the experience of time*. London: Penguin Books.—*591*

ORNSTEIN, R. E. (1972) *The psychology of consciousness*. San Francisco: W. H. Freeman.—*558*

OSBORN, A. G., BUNKA, J. P., COOPER, L. M., FRANK, G. S., & HILGARD, E. R. (1967) Effects of thiopental sedation on learning and memory. *Science*, 157, 574–576.—*547*

OSGOOD, C. E. (1949) The similarity paradox in human learning: A resolution. *Psychol. Rev.*, 56, 132–143.—*293–95*

OSGOOD, C. E. (1953) *Method and theory in experimental psychology*. New York: Oxford Univ. Press.—*316*

OSGOOD, C. E., SUCI, G. J., & TANNENBAUM, P. H. (1957) *The measurement of meaning*. Urbana: Univ. of Ill. Press.—*314*

OVERTON, D. A. (1964) State-dependent or "dissociated" learning produced by pentobarbital. *J. comp. physiol. Psychol.*, 57, 3–12.—*546–47*

PACKARD, R. G. (1970) The control of "classroom attention": A group contingency for complex behavior. *J. appl. behav. Anal.*, 3, 13–28.—*240*

PAIVIO, A. (1971) *Imagery and verbal processes*. New York: Holt, Rinehart and Winston.—*266, 588–89*

PAIVIO, A., & CSAPO, K. (1972) Picture superiority in free recall: Imagery or dual coding? Research Bulletin #243. Department of Psychology, University of Western Ontario, Aug. 1972.—*589*

PAN, S. (1926) The influence of control upon learning and recall. *P. exp. Psychol.*, 9, 468–491.—*301, 547*

PARSONS, C. (1960) Inhelder and Piaget's *The growth of logical thinking: II. A logician's viewpoint. Brit. J. Psychol.*, 51, 75–84.—*331*

PASCAL, G. R. (1949) The effect of relaxation upon recall. *Amer. J. Psychol.*, 62, 32–47.—*300*

PASCUAL-LEONE, J., & BOVET, M. C. (1966) L'apprentissage de la quantification de l'inclusion et la théorie opératoire. *Acta psychol.*, 25, 334–356.—*336*

PASKEWITZ, D. A., & ORNE, M. T. (1973). Visual effects on alpha feedback training. *Science*, 181, 360–363.—*559–60*

PAVLIK, W. B., & CARLTON, P. J. (1965) A reversed partial-reinforcement effect. *J. exper. Psychol.*, 70, 417–423.—*197*

PAVLOV, I. P. (1902) *The work of the digestive glands.* London: Griffin.—*62*

PAVLOV, I. P. (1903) Experimental psychology and psychopathology in animals. In Pavlov (1928), 47–60; also in Pavlov (1955), 151–168.

PAVLOV, I. P. (1927) *Conditioned reflexes.* London: Clarendon Press.—*63, 66, 77, 84, 152, 210*

PAVLOV, I. P. (1928) *Lectures on conditioned reflexes.* (Translated by W. H. Gantt.) New York: International Publishers.—*63, 64, 84*

PAVLOV, I. J. (1932) The reply of a physiologist to psychologist. *Psychol. Rev.*, 39, 91–127.—*92*

PAVLOV, I. P. (1941) *Conditioned reflexes and psychiatry.* New York: International Publishers.—*63*

PAVLOV, I. P. (1955) *Selected works.* Moscow: Foreign Languages Publishing House.—*63, 70–72, 86*

PAVLOV, I. P. (1957) *Experimental psychology and other essays.* New York: Philosophical Library.—*63*

PERKINS, C. C., JR. (1955) The stimulus conditions which follow learned responses. *Psychol. Rev.*, 62, 341–348.—*211*

PETERSON, J. (1922) Learning when frequency and recency factors are negative. *J. exp. Psychol.*, 5, 270–300.—*91*

PETERSON, L. R. (1963) Immediate memory: Data and theory. In C. N. Cofer & B. S. Musgrave (Eds.), *Verbal behavior and verbal learning.* New York: McGraw-Hill.—*395, 417*

PETERSON, L. R., & PETERSON, M. J. (1959) Short-term retention of individual verbal items. *J. exp. Psychol.*, 58, 193–198.—*416–17, 420*

PHILLIPS, J. L., JR. (1969) *The origins of intellect: Piaget's theory.* San Francisco: W. H. Freeman. (Paper.)—*341*

PIAGET, J. (1950) *The psychology of intelligence.* New York: Harcourt Brace Jovanovich.

PIAGET, J. (1952) Autobiography. In C. Murchison & E. G. Boring (Eds.), *A history of psychology in autobiography.* Vol. 4. Worcester, Mass.: Clark Univ. Press, 237–256.

PIAGET, J. (1954) *The construction of reality in the child.* New York: Basic Books.—*342*

PIAGET, J. (1957) *Logic and psychology.* New York: Basic Books.—*344*

PIAGET, J. (1969a) *Psychologie et pedagogie.* Paris: Denoel.—*341*

PIAGET, J. (1969b) *The mechanisms of perception.* Trans. by G. N. Segram. New York: Basic Books.—*337*

PIAGET, J. (1970a) *Science of education and the psychology of the child.* New York: Viking. —*337, 340, 341–42*

PIAGET, J. (1970b) Piaget's theory. In P. H. Mussen (Ed.), *Carmichael's manual of child psychology.* Vol. 1. New York: Wiley.—*318–23, 329, 336, 339*

PIAGET, J. (1971) *Psychology and epistemology.* New York: Grossman.—*344*

PIAGET, J., & INHELDER, B. (1941) *Le développement des quantités chez l'enfant.* Neuchâtel: Delachaux et Niestlé.—*327, 328, 330*

PIAGET, J., & INHELDER, B. (1962) Le développement des images mentales chez l'enfant. *Journal de psychologie, normale et pathologique*, 59, 75–108.—*339*

PIAGET, J., & INHELDER, B. (1969) *The psychology of the child.* New York: Basic Books.

PIAGET, J., INHELDER, B., & SINCLAIR, H. (1968) *Memoire et intelligence.* Paris: Presses Universitaires de France.—*343*

PICKREL, G., NEIDT, C., & GIBSON, R. (1958) Tape recordings are used to teach seventh grade students in Westside Junior-Senior High School, Omaha, Nebraska. *Nat. Assoc. Sec. Sch. Principals Bull.*, 42, 81–93.—*627*

PINARD, A., & LAURENDEAU, M. (1964) A scale of mental development based on the theory of Piaget: Description of a project. *J. Res. Sci. Teaching*, 2, 253, 260.—*332*

PINARD, A., & LAURENDEAU, M. (1969) "Stage" in Piaget's cognitive-developmental theory: Exegesis of a concept. In D. Elkind & J. H. Flavell (Eds.), *Studies in cognitive development: Essays in honor of Jean Piaget.* New York: Oxford Univ. Press.—*333, 336*

PITTS, W., & McCULLOCH, W. S. (1947) How we know universals, the perception of auditory and visual form. *Bull. Math. Biophys.*, 9, No. 3, 127–147.—*548*

PLISKOFF, S. S., WRIGHT, J. E., & HAWKINS, T. D. (1965) Brain stimulation as a reinforcer: Intermittent schedules. *J. exp. anal. Behav.*, 8, 75–88.—*501*

POLSON, M. C., RESTLE, F., & POLSON, P. G. (1965) Association and discrimination in paired-associates learning. *J. exp. Psychol.*, 69, 47–55.—*421*

POLSON, P. G., & GREENO, J. G. (1965) Nonstationary performance before all-or-none learning. Paper read at Midwestern Psychological Association Meetings, Chicago, May 1. (Reprints available from J. G. Greeno.)—*414*

POPPEN, R. L. (1968) Counterconditioning of conditioned suppression. Unpublished doctoral dissertation, Stanford Univ.—*97*

POSTMAN, L. (1961) The present status of interference theory. In C. N. Cofer (Ed.), *Verbal learning and verbal behavior*. New York: McGraw-Hill, 152–179.—*300*

POSTMAN, L. (1962) Rewards and punishments in human learning. In L. Postman (Ed.), *Psychology in the making*. New York: Alfred A. Knopf, 331–401.—*28, 45*

POSTMAN, L. (1971) Transfer, interference, and forgetting. In J. W. Kling & L. A. Riggs (Eds.), *Woodworth and Schlosberg's experimental psychology* (3rd ed.). New York: Holt, Rinehart and Winston.—*293, 294, 296, 300, 301, 312*

POSTMAN, L., & STARK, K. (1969) Role of response availability in transfer and interference. *J. exp. Psychol.*, 79, 168–177.—*295, 302–5*

POSTMAN, L., STARK, K., & FRASER, J. (1968) Temporal changes in interference. *J. verb. Learn. verb. Behav.*, 7, 672–694.—*307*

POSTMAN, L., STARK, K., & HENSCHEL, D. (1969) Conditions of recovery after unlearning. *J. exp. Psychol. Monogr.*, 82 (Whole No. 1).—*307*

PREMACK, D. (1959) Toward empirical behavior laws: I. Positive reinforcement. *Psychol. Rev.*, 66, 219–233.—*562, 563*

PREMACK, D. (1962) Reversibility of the reinforcement relation. *Science*, 136, 255–257.

PREMACK, D. (1963) Rate differential reinforcement in monkey manipulation. *J. exp. anal. Behav.*, 6, 81–89.—*563*

PREMACK, D. (1965) Reinforcement theory. In M. R. Jones (Ed.), *Nebraska Symposium on Motivation: 1965*. Lincoln: Univ. of Nebraska Press.—*562, 563*

PREMACK, D. (1969) A functional analysis of language. Invited address to Meetings of American Psychological Association, Washington, D.C.—*234*

PREMACK, D. (1970) The education of S*A*R*A*H*. *Psychol. Today*, 4, 54–58.

PRENTICE, W. C. H. (1959) The systematic psychology of Wolfgang Köhler. In S. Koch (Ed.), *Psychology: A study of a science*. Vol. 1. New York: McGraw-Hill, 427–455.

PRESSEY, S. L. (1926) A simple apparatus which gives tests and scores—and teaches. *Sch. and Soc.*, 23, 373–376.—*628*

PRESSEY, S. L. (1927) A machine for automatic teaching of drill material. *Sch. and Soc.*, 25, 549–552.—*628*

PRIBRAM, K. (1971) *Languages of the brain*. Englewood Cliffs, N.J.: Prentice-Hall.

PRINCE, M. (1905) *The dissociation of a personality*. New York: Longmans.—*368*

PROKASY, W. F. (Ed.) (1965) *Classical conditioning: A symposium*. New York: Appleton-Century-Crofts.

QUILLIAN, M. R. (1968) Semantic memory. In M. Minsky (Ed.), *Semantic information processing*. Cambridge: MIT Press.—*469*

RAPAPORT, D. (1951) *Organization and pathology of thought*. New York: Columbia Univ. Press.—*360*

RATLIFF, M. M. (1938) The varying function of affectively toned olfactory, visual, and auditory cues in recall. *Amer. J. Psychol.*, 51, 695–699.—*362–63*.

RAZRAN, G. (1939) A quantitative study of meaning by conditioned salivary technique (semantic conditioning). *Science*, 90, 89–91.—*79*

RAZRAN, G. (1961a) The observable unconscious and the inferable conscious in current Soviet psychophysiology. *Psychol. Rev.*, 68, 81–147.—*79*

RAZRAN, G. (1961b) Recent Soviet phyletic comparisons of classical and of operant conditioning: Experimental designs. *J. comp. physiol. Psychol.*, 54, 357–367.—*78*

RAZRAN, G. (1965) Russian physiologists' psychology and American experimental psychology. *Psychol. Bull.*, 63, 42–64.—*87–88*

RAZRAN, G. (1971) *Mind in evolution: An East-West synthesis of learned behavior and cognition*. Boston: Houghton Mifflin.—*83–84, 212*

REBER, A. S., & MILLWARD, R. B. (1968) Event observations in probability learning. *J. exp. Psychol.*, 77, 317–327.—*389*

REIFF, R., & SCHEERER, M. (1959) *Memory and hypnotic age regression.* New York: International Universities Press.—*300*

REITMAN, J. S. (1971) Mechanisms of forgetting in short-term memory. *Cog. Psychol.*, 2, 185–195.—*419, 580*

REITMAN, W. R. (1964) Information-processing models in psychology. *Science*, 144, 1192–1198.—*483, 486*

REITMAN, W. R. (1965) *Cognition and thought.* New York: Wiley.

RESCORLA, R. A. (1966) Predictability and number of pairings in Pavlovian fear conditioning. *Psychon. Sci.*, 4, 383–384.—*75–76*

RESCORLA, R. A. (1968) Probability of shock in the presence and absence of CS in fear conditioning. *J. comp. physiol. Psychol.*, 66, 1–5.—*572–73*

RESCORLA, R. A. (1969a) Conditioned inhibition of fear. In N. J. Mackintosh and W. K. Honig, eds., *Fundamental issues in associative learning.* Halifax: Dalhousie Univ. Press. —*74*

RESCORLA, R. A. (1969b) Pavlovian conditioned inhibition. *Psychol. Bull.*, 72, 77–94.—*223*

RESCORLA, R. A. (1972a) Informational variables in Pavlovian conditioning. In G. H. Bower (Ed.), *Psychology of learning and motivation: Advances in research and theory.* Vol. 6. New York: Academic Press.—*571, 572, 573*

RESCORLA, R. A. (1972b) Second order conditioning: Implications for theories of learning. Paper presented at Conference on Contemporary Views of Learning and Conditioning, North Carolina State Univ., May.—*573*

RESCORLA, R. A., & SOLOMON, R. L. (1967) Two-process learning theory: Relationships between Pavlovian conditioning and instrumental learning. *Psychol. Rev.*, 55, 151–182.—*209*

RESCORLA, R. A., & WAGNER, A. R. (1972) A theory of Pavlovian conditioning: Variations in the effectiveness of reinforcement and nonreinforcement. In A. Black & W. F. Prokasy (Eds.), *Classical conditioning: II. Current research and theory.* New York: Appleton-Century-Crofts.—*571*

RESTLE, F. (1955) A theory of discrimination learning. *Psychol. Rev.*, 62, 11–19.—*401*

RESTLE, F. (1957) Discrimination of cues in mazes: A resolution of the "place-vs.-response" question. *Psychol. Rev.*, 64, 217–228.—*132–33*

RESTLE, F. (1962) The selection of strategies in cue learning. *Psychol. Rev.*, 69, 329–343.—*141, 401, 412–13*

RESTLE, F. (1964a) Sources of difficulty in learning paired associates. In R. C. Atkinson (Ed.), *Studies in mathematical psychology.* Stanford: Stanford Univ. Press.—*416, 421*

RESTLE, F. (1964b) The relevance of mathematical models for education. In E. R. Hilgard (Ed.), *Theories of learning and instruction.* 63rd Yearbook of the National Society for the Study of Education. Chicago: Univ. of Chicago Press.—*425*

RESTLE, F. (1970) Theory of serial pattern learning: Structural trees. *Psychol. Rev.*, 77, 481–495.—*392, 457*

RESTLE, F. (1971) *Mathematical models in psychology: An introduction.* Baltimore: Penguin Books.

RESTLE, F., & BROWN, E. (1970) Organization of serial pattern learning. In G. H. Bower (Ed.), *The psychology of learning and motivation: Advances in research and theory.* Vol. 4. New York: Academic Press.—*261*

RESTLE, F., & GREENO, J. (1970) *Introduction to mathematical psychology.* Reading, Mass.: Addison-Wesley.

RESTORFF, H. VON (1933) Analyse von Vorgangen in Spurenfeld. 1. Über die Wirkung con Bereichsbildungen im Spruenfeld. *Psychol. Forsch.*, 18, 299–342.—*270–71*

REVUSKY, S., & GARCIA, J. (1970) Learned associations over long delays. In G. H. Bower (Ed.), *The psychology of learning and motivation: Advances in research and theory.* Vol. 4. New York: Academic Press.—*574–75*

RICHARDSON, A. (1969) *Mental imagery.* London: Routledge & Kegan Paul.—*604*

RILEY, D. A. (1958) The nature of the effective stimulus in animal discrimination learning: Transposition reconsidered. *Psychol. Rev.*, 65, 1–7.—*186*

RILEY, D. A. (1963) Memory for form. In L. Postman (Ed.), *Psychology in the making.* New York: Alfred A. Knopf, 402–465.—*270, 299*

RINKEL, M. (Ed.) (1958) *Chemical concepts of psychosis.* New York: McDowell, Oblensky.—*526*

RIPPLE, R. E., & ROCKCASTLE, V. N. (Eds.) (1964) *Piaget rediscovered.* Ithaca, N.Y.: Cornell Univ. Press.—*341*

ROBBINS, D. (1971) Partial reinforcement: A selective review of the alleyway literature since 1960. *Psychol. Bull.,* 76, 415–431.—*198*

ROBERTS, W. W. (1958) Both rewarding and punishing effects from stimulation of posterior hypothalamus of cat with same electrode at same intensity. *J. comp. physiol. Psychol.,* 51, 400–407.—*499*

ROBERTS, W. W. (1969) Are hypothalamic motivational mechanisms functionally and anatomically specific? *Brain, Behavior, and Evolution,* 2, 317–342.—*497*

ROBINSON, E. S. (1927) The "similarity" factor in retroaction. *Amer. J. Psychol.,* 39, 297–312. —*291–93*

ROBINSON, E. S. (1932a) *Association theory today.* New York: Appleton-Century-Crofts.— *285, 289–90*

ROBINSON, E. S. (1932b) *Man as psychology sees him.* New York: Macmillan.—*315*

ROBINSON, E. S. (1935) *Law and the lawyers.* New York: Macmillan.—*315*

ROBINSON, J. A. (1970) An overview of mechanical theorem proving. In R. Banerji & M. Mesarovic (Eds.), *Theoretical approaches to non-numerical problem solving.* New York: Springer-Verlag.—*437, 469*

ROCK, I. (1957) The role of repetition in associative learning. *Amer. J. Psychol.,* 70, 186–193. —*407*

RODERICK, T. H. (1960) Selection for cholinesterase activity in the cerebral cortex of the rat. *Genetics,* 45, 1123.—*528*

ROGERS, C. R., & SKINNER, B. F. (1956) Some issues concerning the control of human behavior. *Science,* 124, 1057–1066.

ROHWER, W. D., JR. (1970) Mental elaboration and learning proficiency. In J. P. Hill (Ed.), *Minnesota Symposium on Child Psychology.* Vol. 4. Minneapolis: Univ. of Minnesota Press.—*589*

ROSENBLATT, F. (1958) The perceptron: A probablistic mode for information storage and organization in the brain. *Psychol. Rev.,* 65, 386–407.—*549*

ROSENBLATT, F. (1962) *Principles of neurodynamics.* Washington, D.C.: Cornell Aeronautical Laboratory, Report 1196-G-8.—*549*

ROSENZWEIG, M. R. (1962) The mechanisms of hunger and thirst. In L. Postman (Ed.), *Psychology in the making.* New York: Alfred A. Knopf.—*64*

ROSENZWEIG, M. R., BENNETT, E. L., & KRECH, D. (1964) Cerebral effects of environmental complexity and training among adult rats. *J. comp. physiol. Psychol.* 57, 438–439.—*528–29*

ROSENZWEIG, M. R., & LEIMAN, A. L. (1968) Brain functions. *Ann. Rev. Psychol.,* 19, 55–98.—*529*

ROSS, R. R. (1964) Positive and negative partial-reinforcement effects carried through continuous reinforcement, changed motivation, and changed response. *J. exp. Psychol.,* 68, 492–502.—*195–97*

ROTTER, J. B. (1954) *Social learning and clinical psychology.* Englewood Cliffs, N.J.: Prentice-Hall.—*146, 599*

ROWLAND, V. (1968) Cortical steady potential (direct current potential) in reinforcement and learning. In E. Stellar & J. M. Sprague (Eds.), *Progress in physiological psychology.* Vol. 2. New York: Academic Press.—*523*

ROZIN, P. (1965) Specific hunger for thiamine: Recovery from deficiency and thiamine preference. *J. comp. physiol. Psychol.,* 59, 98–101.—*493*

ROZIN, P. (1967) Specific aversions as a component of specific hungers. *J. comp. physiol. Psychol.,* 64, 237–242.

ROZIN, P., & KALAT, J. W. (1972) Learning as a situation-specific adaptation. In M. E. P. Seligman & J. L. Hager (Eds.), *Biological boundaries of learning.* New York: Appleton-Century-Crofts.—*493, 575*

RUJA, H. (1956) Productive psychologists. *Amer. Psychol.,* 11, 148–149.—*204*

RUMELHART, D. E. (1967) The effects of interpresentation intervals on performance in a continuous paired associate task. Unpublished doctoral dissertation, Stanford Univ.—*417*

RUMELHART, D. E., LINDSAY, P. H., & NORMAN, D. A. (1972) A process model for long-term memory. In E. Tulving & W. Donaldson (Eds.), *Organization of memory.* New York: Academic Press.—*23, 471, 593, 595, 598*

RUNDUS, D. J. (1971) Analysis of rehearsal processes in free recall. *J. exp. Psychol.,* 89, 63–77. —*271, 581–82*

RUNDUS, D. J., & ATKINSON, R. C. (1970) Rehearsal processes in free recall: A procedure for direct observation. *J. verb. Learn. verb. Behav.,* 9, 99–105.—*581–82*

RUSINOV, V. S. (1953) An electro-physiological analysis of the connecting function in the cerebral cortex in the presence of a dominant area. *Communications at the XIX International Physiological Congress, Montreal.*

RUSSELL, I. S., & OCHS, S. (1961) One-trial hemispheric transfer of a learning engram. *Science,* 133, 1077–1078.—*544, 545*

RUSSELL, W. R., & NATHAN, P. W. (1946) Traumatic amnesia. *Brain,* 69, 280–300.—*511*

RYLE, G. (1949) *The concept of mind.* London: Hutchinson.—*312*

SACKETT, G. P. (1967) Some persistent effects of different rearing conditions on preadult social behavior of monkeys. *J. comp. physiol. Psychol.,* 64, 363–365.—*18*

SALTER, A. (1952) *The case against psychoanalysis.* New York: Citadel Press. (Rev. ed., 1963.) —*372*

SALZBERG, P. M., PARKS, T. E., KROLL, N. E. A., & PARKINSON, S. R. (1971) Retroactive effects of phonemic similarity on short-term recall of visual and auditory stimuli. *J. exp. Psychol.,* 91, 43–46.—*579*

SALZINGER, K. (1969) The place of operant conditioning of verbal behavior in psychotherapy. In C. M. Franks (Ed.), *Behavior therapy: Appraisal and status.* New York: McGraw-Hill.—*361, 372*

SAMUEL, A. L. (1959) Some studies in machine learning using the game of checkers. *IBM J. Res. Devel.,* 3, 210–229. Also reprinted in E. A. Feigenbaum & J. Feldman (Eds.), *Computers and thought.* New York: McGraw-Hill, 1963.—*454–55*

SAMUEL, A. L. (1967) Studies in machine learning using the game of checkers: II. Recent progress. *IBM J. Res. Devel.,* 11, 601–617.—*455*

SARASON, I. (Ed.) (1965a) *Psychoanalysis and the study of behavior.* Princeton: Van Nostrand.

SARASON, I. (Ed.) (1965b) *Science and theory in psychoanalysis.* Princeton: Van Nostrand.

SARNOFF, I. (1971) *Testing Freudian concepts: An experimental social approach.* New York: Springer.—*373*

SASMOR, R. M. (1966) Operant conditioning of a small-scale muscle response. *J. exp. anal. Behav.,* 9, 69–85.—*57*

SCHACHTEL, E. G. (1947) On memory and childhood amnesia. *Psychiatry,* 10, 1–26.—*359*

SCHACHTER, S. (1964) The inter-action of cognitive and physiological determinants of emotional states. In P. H. Leiderman & D. Shapiro (Eds.), *Psychological approaches to social behavior.* Stanford: Stanford Univ. Press.—*498*

SCHACHTER, S. (1967) Cognitive effects of obesity on bodily functioning: Studies of obesity and eating. In D. C. Glass (Ed.), *Neurophysiology and emotion.* New York: Rockefeller Univ. Press and Russell Sage Foundation.—*498*

SCHACHTER, S., & SINGER, J. E. (1962) Cognitive, social, and physiological determinants of emotional state. *Psychol. Rev.,* 69, 379–399.—*238*

SCHANK, R. C. (1972) Conceptual dependency: A theory of natural language understanding. *Cog. Psychol.,* 3, 552–631.—*466, 469*

SCHANK, R. C., & COLBY, K. M. (Eds.) (1973) *Computer models of thought and language.* San Francisco: W. H. Freeman.

SCHLOSBERG, H. (1937) The relationship between success and the laws of conditioning. *Psychol. Rev.,* 44, 379–394.—*78–79*

SCHNEIDER, A. M. (1967) Control of memory by spreading cortical depression: A case for stimulus control. *Psychol. Rev.,* 74, 201–215.—*544–45, 547*

SCHNEIDER, A. M. (1968) Stimulus control and spreading cortical depression: Some problems reconsidered. *Psychol. Rev.,* 75, 353–358.—*544–45*

SCHNEIDER, A. M., & EBBESON, E. (1967) Interhemispheric transfer of lever pressing as stimulus generalization of the effects of spreading depression. *J. exp. anal. Behav.,* 10, 193–197.—*545*

SCHNEIDER, A. M., & SHERMAN, W. (1968) Amnesia: A function of the temporal relation of foot shock to electroconvulsive shock. *Science,* 159, 219–221.—*515*

SCHOEFFLER, M. (1954) Probability of response to compounds of discriminated stimuli. *J. exp. Psychol.,* 48, 323–329.—*384–85*

SCHOENFELD, W. N. (1970) "Avoidance" in behavior theory. In P. B. Dews (Eds.), *Festschrift for B. F. Skinner.* New York: Appleton-Century-Crofts, 351–356.—*214*

SCHOENFELD, W. N., ANTONITIS, J. J., & BERSH, P. J. (1950) A preliminary study of training conditions necessary for secondary reinforcement. *J. exp. Psychol.,* 40, 40–45.—*220*

SCHULMAN, L. S., & KEISLAR, E. R. (Eds.) (1966) *Learning by discovery: A critical appraisal.* Chicago: Rand McNally.

SEARS, P. S. (1951) Doll play aggression in normal young children: Influence of sex, age, sibling status, father's absence. *Psychol. Monogr.,* 65, No. 6.—*358*

SEARS, R. R. (1936) Functional abnormalities of memory with special reference to amnesia. Psychol. Bull., 33, 229–274.—*353, 354*

SEARS, R. R. (1937) Initiation of the repression sequence by experienced failure. *J. exp. Psychol.,* 20, 570–580.—*366*

SEARS, R. R. (1941) Non-aggressive reactions to frustration. *Psychol. Rev.,* 48, 343–346.—*356*

SEARS, R. R. (1943) *Survey of objective studies of psychoanalytic concepts.* New York: Social Science Research Council.—*354–55, 363*

SEARS, R. R. (1951) Effects of frustration and anxiety on fantasy aggression. *Amer. J. Orthopsychiat.,* 21, 498–505.—*358*

SEARS, R. R., WHITING, J. W. M., NOWLIS, V., & SEARS, P. S. (1953) Some child-rearing antecedents of aggression and dependency in young children. *Genet. Psychol. Monogr.,* 47, 135–236.—*358*

SECHENOV, I. (1935) *Selected works.* Moscow: State Publishing House.—*64*

SELFRIDGE, O. G. (1955) Pattern recognition and modern computers. *Proceedings of the 1955 Western Joint Computer Conference,* 85–111.

SELFRIDGE, O. G. (1959) Pandemonium: A paradigm for learning. In D. V. Blake, & A. M. Uttley (Eds.), *Proceedings of the Symposium on Mechanization of Thought Processes.* London: H. M. Stationary Office.—*437*

SELFRIDGE, O., & NEISSER, U. (1960) Pattern recognition by machine. *Sci. Amer.,* Aug., 203, 60–80.—*437, 441–44*

SELIGMAN, M. E. P. (1970) On the generality of the law of learning. *Psychol. Rev.,* 77, 406–418.—*84–86, 244, 574*

SELIGMAN, M. E. P., & HAGER, J. L. (Eds.) (1972) *Biological boundaries of learning.* New York: Appleton-Century-Crofts —*574*

SELIGMAN, M. E. P., MAIER, S. F., & SOLOMON, R. L. (1971) Unpredictable and uncontrollable aversive events. In F. R. Brush (Ed.), *Aversive conditioning and learning.* New York: Academic Press.—*576–77*

SELZ, O. (1927) Die Umgestaltung der Grundanschauungen vom intellektuellen Geschehen. Kantstudien, 32, 273–280. Translated as "The revision of the fundamental conceptions of intellectual processes," in J. Mandler & G. Mandler (Eds.), *Thinking: From association to Gestalt.* New York: Wiley, 1964, 225–234.—*9*

SEWARD, J. P., & LEVY, N. J. (1949) Sign learning as a factor in extinction. *J. exp. Psychol.,* 39, 660–668.—*137*

SHAKOW, D., & RAPAPORT, D. (1964) The influence of Freud on American psychology. *Psychol. Issues,* 4, Monogr. 13.

SHALLICE, T., & WARRINGTON, E. K. (1970) Independent functioning of verbal memory stores: A neuropsychological study. *Quart. J. exp. Psychol.,* 22, 261–273.—*584*

SHAPIRO, M. M. (1961) Salivary conditioning in dogs during fixed-interval reinforcement contingent upon lever pressing. *J. exp. anal. Behav.,* 4, 361–364.—*209*

SHARP, A. A. (1938) An experimental test of Freud's doctrine of the relation of hedonic tone to memory revival. *J. exp. Psychol.,* 22, 395–418.

SHEFFIELD, F. D. (1949) Hilgard's critique of Guthrie. *Psychol. Rev.,* 56, 284–291.—*102, 567*

SHEFFIELD, F. D. (1954) A drive-induction theory of reinforcement. New Haven: Yale Univ. (Mimeographed manuscript.)—*403*

SHEFFIELD, F. D. (1961) Theoretical considerations in the learning of complex sequential tasks from demonstration and practice. In A. A. Lumsdaine (Ed.), *Student response in programmed instruction.* Washington, D.C.: National Academy of Sciences–National Research Council, Pub. 943, 13–32.—*116–18, 602, 611*

SHEFFIELD, F. D. (1965) Relation between classical conditioning and instrumental learning. In W. F. Prokasy (Ed.), *Classical conditioning: A symposium.* New York: Appleton-Century-Crofts.—*77, 103–4, 211*

SHEFFIELD, V. F. (1949) Extinction as a function of partial reinforcement and distribution of practice. *J. exp. Psychol.,* 39, 511–526.

SHEPARD, R. N. (1964) Review of computers and thought. *Behavioral Sci.,* 9, 57–65.—*488*

SHERRINGTON, C. S. (1906) *The integrative action of the nervous system.* New Haven: Yale Univ. Press.—*103*

SHIMP, C. P. (1969) Optimal behavior in free-operant experiments. *Psychol. Rev.*, 76, 97–112. *—200, 218, 399*

SHULMAN, L. S., & KEISLAR, E. R. (Eds.) (1966) *Learning by discovery: A critical appraisal.* Chicago: Rand McNally.—*320, 345*

SIDMAN, M. (1960) *Tactics of scientific research: Evaluating experimental data in psychology.* New York: Basic Books.—*219, 249–50*

SIEGEL, S. (1961) Decision making and learning under varying conditions of reinforcement. *Ann. N.Y. Acad. Sci.*, 89, 766–783.—*405–6*

SIGEL, E. G. (1969) The Piagetian system and the world of education. In D. Elkind & J. H. Flavell (Eds.), *Studies in cognitive development: Essays in honor of Jean Piaget.* New York: Oxford Univ. Press.—*341*

SIGEL, I. E., & HOOPER, F. H. (Eds.) (1968) *Logical thinking in children: Research based on Piaget's theory.* New York: Holt, Rinehart and Winston.—*341*

SIMMONS, R. F. (1970) Natural language question-answering systems: 1969. In R. Banerji & D. Mesarovic (Eds.), *Theoretical approaches to non-numerical problem solving.* New York: Springer-Verlag.—*466*

SIMMONS, R. F., BURGER, J. F., & LONG, R. F. (1966) An approach toward answering English questions from text. *Proceedings of the Fall Joint Computer Conference*, 357–363.—*467*

SIMMONS, R. F., BURGER, J. F., & SCHWARZ, R. (1968) A computational model of verbal understanding. *Proceedings of the Fall Joint Computer Conference*, 441–456.—*467*

SIMON, H. A. (1972) Complexity and the representation of patterned sequences of symbols. *Psychol. Rev.*, 79, 369–382.—*392, 457–58*

SIMON, H. A., & FEIGENBAUM, E. A. (1964) An information-processing theory of some effects of similarity, familiarization, and meaningfulness in verbal learning. *J. verb. Learn. verb. Behav.*, 3, 385–396.—*472–74*

SIMON, H. A., & KOTOVSKY, K. (1963) Human acquisition of concepts for sequential patterns. *Psychol. Rev.*, 70, 534–546.—*392, 456*

SIMON, H. A., & SIKLOSSY, L. (1972) *Representation and meaning: Experiments with information processing systems.* Englewood Cliffs, N.J.: Prentice-Hall.—*466*

SINGER, E. A. (1911) Mind as an observable object. *J. Phil. Psychol. Sci. Meth.*, 8, 180–186.— *90*

SKAGGS, E. B. (1925) Further studies in retroactive inhibition. *Psychol. Monogr.*, 34, No. 161. *—291–92*

SKINNER, B. F. (1935) Two types of conditioned reflex and a pseudo type. *J. gen. Psychol.*, 12, 66–77.—*88*

SKINNER, B. F. (1936) The verbal summator and a method for the study of latent speech. *J. Psychol.*, 2, 71–107.—*233*

SKINNER, B. F. (1937a) Two types of conditioned reflex: A reply to Konorski and Miller. *J. gen. Psychol.*, 16, 272–279.—*77, 78–79*

SKINNER, B. F. (1937b) The distribution of associated words. *Psychol. Rec.*, 1, 71–76.—*233*

SKINNER, B. F. (1938) *The behavior of organisms: An experimental analysis.* New York: Appleton-Century-Crofts.—*74, 199, 207–9, 213, 214, 223–24, 225, 229, 231*

SKINNER, B. F. (1948a) *Walden two.* New York: Macmillan.—*207*

SKINNER, B. F. (1948b) Superstition in the pigeon. *J. exp. Psychol.*, 38, 168–172.—*209–10*

SKINNER, B. F. (1950) Are theories of learning necessary? *Psychol. Rev.*, 57, 193–216.—*95, 213, 215, 221*

SKINNER, B. F. (1951) How to teach animals. *Sci. Amer.*, 185, Dec., 26–29.—*231*

SKINNER, B. F. (1953) *Science and human behavior.* New York: Macmillan.—*210, 213, 214, 220–21, 222, 229, 235,238, 242, 243, 248, 317*

SKINNER, B. F. (1954) The science of learning and the art of teaching. *Harvard educ. Rev.*, 24, 86–97.—*612, 628*

SKINNER, B. F. (1957) *Verbal behavior.* New York: Appleton-Century-Crofts.—*233–35, 246–47*

SKINNER, B. F. (1958) Teaching machines. *Science*, 128, 969–977.—*232*

SKINNER, B. F. (1961) *Cumulative record* (Rev. ed.). New York: Appleton-Century-Crofts.

SKINNER, B. F. (1968) *The technology of teaching.* New York: Appleton-Century-Crofts.— *613*

SKINNER, B. F. (1969) *Contingencies of reinforcement: A theoretical analysis.* New York: Appleton-Century-Crofts.—*485, 487*

SKINNER, B. F. (1971) *Beyond freedom and dignity.* New York: Alfred A. Knopf.—*207, 246*

SLAGLE, J. R. (1963) A heuristic program that solves symbolic integration problems in freshman calculus. In E. A. Feigenbaum & J. Feldman (Eds.), *Computers and thought*. New York: McGraw-Hill.

SLAGLE, J. R. (1971) *Artificial intelligence: The heuristic programming approach*. New York: McGraw-Hill.—*453*

SLAMECKA, N. J., & CERASO, J. (1960) Retroactive and proactive inhibition of verbal learning. *Psychol. Bull.*, 57, 449–475.—*301*

SLOBIN, D. I. (1971) *Psycholinguistics*. Glenview, Ill.: Scott, Foresman.—*248, 598*

SMALLWOOD, R. D. (1962) *A decision structure for teaching machines*. Cambridge: MIT Press.—*425*

SMALLWOOD, R. D. (1971) The analyses of economic teaching strategies for a simple learning model. *J. math. Psychol.*, 8, 285–301.—*425*

SMEDSLUND, J. (1961) The acquisition of conservation of substance and weight in children. *Scan. J. Psychol.*, 2, I, 11–20; II, 71–84; III, 85–87; IV, 153–155; V, 156–160; VI, 203–210.——*334*

SMEDSLUND, J. (1962) The acquisition of conservation of substance and weight in children. *Scan. J. Psychol.*, 3, VII, 69–77.—*334*

SMEDSLUND, J. (1963) Development of concrete transitivity of length in children. *Child Devel.*, 34, 389–405.—*336*

SMEDSLUND, J. (1964) Internal necessity and contradiction in children's thinking. In R. E. Ripple & V. N. Rockcastle (Eds.), *Piaget rediscovered*. Ithaca, N.Y.: Cornell Univ. Press.—*333*

SMEDSLUND, J. (1965) The development of transitivity of length: A comment on Braine's reply. *Child Devel.*, 36, 577–580.—*336*

SMITH, C. B. (1956) Background effects on learning and transposition of lightness discriminations. Unpublished doctoral dissertation, Univ. of Texas.—*186*

SMITH, S., & GUTHRIE, E. R. (1921) *General psychology in terms of behavior*. New York: Appleton-Century-Crofts.—*91–92, 103, 105*

SOKOLOV, E. M. (1963) Higher nervous functions: The orienting reflex. *Ann. Rev. Physiol.*, 25, 545–580.—*20, 81*

SPENCE, K. W. (1936) The nature of discrimination learning in animals. *Psychol. Rev.*, 43, 427–449.—*166, 182–83, 187–88*

SPENCE, K. W. (1937) The differential response in animals to stimuli varying within a single dimension. *Psychol. Rev.*, 44, 430–444.—*184–85*

SPENCE, K. W. (1942) The basis of solution by chimpanzees of the intermediate size problem. *J. exp. Psychol.*, 31, 257–271.—*184–86*

SPENCE, K. W. (1947) The role of secondary reinforcement in delayed reward learning. *Psychol. Rev.*, 54, 1–8.—*168, 171–72*

SPENCE, K. W. (1952) Clark Leonard Hull: 1884–1952. *Amer. J. Psychol.*, 65, 639–646.—*204*

SPENCE, K. W. (1956) *Behavior theory and conditioning*. New Haven: Yale Univ. Press.—*54, 104, 114, 175, 189*

SPENCE, K. W. (1960a) The roles of reinforcement and nonreinforcement in simple learning. In *Behavior theory and learning: Selected papers of K. W. Spence*. Englewood Cliffs, N.J.: Prentice-Hall, Chap. 6.—*189, 192*

SPENCE, K. W. (1960b) *Behavior theory and learning: Selected papers*. Englewood Cliffs, N.J.: Prentice-Hall.—*143, 175*

SPERRY, R. W. (1961) Cerebral organization and behavior. *Science*, 133 (2 June), 1749–1757. —*538–41*

SPERRY, R. W., & MINER, N. (1955) Pattern perception following insertion of mica plates into visual cortex. *J. comp. physiol. Psychol.*, 48, 463–469.—*278, 520*

SPONG, P., HAIDER, M., & LINDSLEY, D. B. (1965) Selective attentiveness and evoked cortical responses to visual and auditory stimuli. *Science*, 148, 395–397.—*506*

STAATS, A. W. (1968) *Learning, language and cognition*. New York: Holt, Rinehart and Winston.—*234, 236*

STAATS, A. W., & STAATS, C. K. (1963) *Complex human behavior*. New York: Holt, Rinehart and Winston.—*235–36*

STADDON, J. E. R., & SIMMELHAG, V. L. (1971) The "superstition" experiment: A re-examination of its implications for the principles of adaptive behavior. *Psychol. Rev.*, 78, 3–43.— *79, 209, 210*

STALNAKER, J. M., & RIDDLE, E. E. (1932) The effect of hypnosis on long-delayed recall. *J. gen. Psychol.*, 6, 429–459.—*300*

STEA, D. (1964) The acquired aversiveness of a cue contiguously associated with the removal of positive reinforcement. Unpublished doctoral dissertation, Stanford Univ.—*181*

STEIN, L. (1964) Reciprocal action of reward and punishment mechanisms. In R. G. Heath (Ed.), *The role of pleasure in behavior.* New York: Hoeber, 113–139.—*223, 503*

STEIN, L. (1969) Chemistry of purposive behavior. In J. T. Tapp (Ed.), *Reinforcement and behavior.* New York: Academic Press.—*503*

STEIN, L., & WISE, C. D. (1971) Possible etiology of schizophrenia: progressive damage to the noradrenergic reward system by 6-hydroxydopamine. *Science,* 171, 1032–1036.—*526*

STERNBERG, S. (1969) Memory scanning: Mental processes revealed by reaction-time experiments. *Amer. Sci.,* 57, 421–457.—*250, 433–36, 579*

STEVENS, S. S. (1939) Psychology and the science of science. *Psychol. Bull.,* 36, 221–263.—*317*

STONE, C. P., & NYSWANDER, D. B. (1927) Reliability of rat learning scores from the multiple T-maze as determined by four different methods. *J. genet. Psychol.,* 34, 497–524.—*134–35*

STONE, I. (1971) *The passions of the mind: A biographical novel of Sigmund Freud.* New York: Doubleday.

STRASSBURGER, R. C. (1950) Resistance to extinction of a conditioned operant as related to drive level at reinforcement. *J. exp. Psychol.,* 40, 473–487.—*221*

STRATTON, G. M. (1919) Retroactive hypermnesia and other emotional effects on memory. *Psychol. Rev.,* 26, 474–486.—*300*

SUITER, R. D., & LoLORDO, V. M. (1971) Blocking of inhibitory Pavlovian conditioning in the conditioned emotional response procedure. *J. comp. physiol. Psychol.,* 76, 137–144.—*573*

SUPPES, P., & ATKINSON, R. C. (1960) *Markov learning models for multiperson interactions.* Stanford: Stanford Univ. Press.—*387, 389–90, 407*

SUPPES, P., & DONIO, J. (1967) Foundations of stimulus-sampling theory for continuous-time processes. *J. math. Psychol.,* 4, 202–225.—*388*

SUPPES, P., & GINSBERG, R. (1962) Application of a stimulus sampling model to children's concept formation with and without overt correction responses. *J. exp. Psychol.,* 63, 330–336.—*412*

SUPPES, P., & GINSBERG, R. (1963) A fundamental property of all-or-none models. *Psychol. Rev.,* 70, 139–161.—*409*

SUPPES, P., JERMAN, M., & BRIAN, D. (1968) *Computer-assisted instruction: Stanford's 1965–66 arithmetic program.* New York: Academic Press.

SUPPES, P., & MORNINGSTAR, M. (1972) *Computer-assisted instruction at Stanford, 1966–68: Data, models and evaluations of the arithmetic program.* New York: Academic Press.

SUPPES, P., ROUANET, H., LEVINE, M., & FRANKMANN, R. W. (1964) Empirical comparison of models for a continuum of responses with noncontingent bimodal reinforcement. In R. C. Atkinson (Ed.), *Studies in mathematical psychology.* Stanford: Stanford Univ. Press.—*388*

SUPPES, P., & ZINNES, J. (1963) Measurement theory. In R. D. Luce, R. R. Bush, & E. Galanter (Eds.), *Handbook of mathematical psychology.* Vol. 1. New York: Wiley.—*191*

SUTHERLAND, N. S., & MACKINTOSH, N. J. (1971) *Mechanisms of animal discrimination learning.* New York: Academic Press.—*189, 401*

TALLAND, G. A. (1965) *Deranged memory: A psychonomic study of the amnesic syndrome.* New York and London: Academic Press.—*517*

TALLAND, G. A., & WAUGH, N. (Eds.) (1969) *The pathology of memory.* New York: Academic Press.—*369*

TAYLOR, J. A. (1951) The relationship of anxiety to the conditioned eyelid response. *J. exp. Psychol.,* 41, 81–92.—*352*

TAYLOR, J. A. (1953) A personality scale of manifest anxiety. *J. abnorm. soc. Psychol.,* 48, 285–290.—*352*

TEITELBAUM, P., & EPSTEIN, A. N. (1962) The lateral hypothalamic syndrome. *Psychol. Rev.,* 69, 74–90.—*494*

TERRACE, H. S. (1963a) Discrimination learning with and without errors. *J. exp. anal. Behav.,* 6, 1–27.—*226*

TERRACE, H. S. (1963b) Errorless transfer of a discrimination across two continua. *J. exp. anal. Behav.,* 6, 223–232.—*226–27*

TERRACE, H. S. (1964) Wavelength generalization after discrimination learning with and without errors. *Science,* 144 (April), 78–80.—*227–28*

TERRACE, H. S. (1973) Classical conditioning. In G. S. Reynolds, C. Catania, & B. Schard (Eds.), *Contemporary experimental psychology.* Chicago: Scott, Foresman.—*79, 209, 211, 244*

THEIOS, J. & BRELSFORD, J., JR. (1966) Theoretical interpretations of a Markov model for avoidance conditioning. *J. math. Psychol.*, 3, 140–162.—*422*

THIGPEN, C. H., & CLECKLEY, H. A. (1957) *The three faces of Eve.* New York: McGraw-Hill. —*368*

THISTLETHWAITE, D. L. (1951) A critical review of latent learning and related experiments. *Psychol. Bull.*, 48, 97–129.—*136*

THOMPSON, R. F. (1967) *Foundations of physiological psychology.* New York: Harper & Row.

THOMPSON, R. F., PATTERSON, M. M., & TAYLOR, T. J. (1972) The neurophysiology of learning. *Ann. Rev. Psychol.*, 23, 73–104.—*525–26*

THOMPSON, R. F., & SPENCER, W. A. (1966) Habituation: A model phenomenon for the study of neuronal substrates of behavior. *Psychol. Rev.*, 73, 16–43.—*524–25*

THOMSON, D. N., & TULVING, E. (1970) Associative encoding and retrieval: Weak and strong cues. *J. exp. Psychol* , 86, 255–262.—*269*

THORNDIKE, E. L. (1898) Animal intelligence: An experimental study of the associative processes in animals. *Psychol. Rev., Monogr. Suppl.*, 2, No. 8.—*7, 28–31*

THORNDIKE, E. L. (1903) *Educational psychology.* New York: Lemcke and Buechner.—*37*

THORNDIKE, E. L. (1911) *Animal intelligence.* New York: Macmillan.—*29, 78, 84*

THORNDIKE, E. L. (1913) *Educational psychology: The psychology of learning.* Vol. 2. New York: Teachers College.—*29, 31–37, 60*

THORNDIKE, E. L. (1922) *The psychology of arithmetic.* New York: Macmillan.

THORNDIKE, E. L. (1931) *Human learning.* New York: Century Co., (Paperback ed., Cambridge: MIT Press, 1966).—*42–43, 48–50*

THORNDIKE, E. L. (1932a) *The fundamentals of learning.* New York: Teachers College.—*38, 40, 41–42*

THORNDIKE, E. L. (1932b) Reward and punishment in animal learning. *Comp. Psychol. Monogr.*, 8, No. 39.—*39*

THORNDIKE, E. L. (1933a) A proof of the law of effect. *Science*, 77, 173–175.—*43*

THORNDIKE, E. L. (1933b) An experimental study of rewards. *Teachers Coll. Contr. Educ.*, No. 580.—*43*

THORNDIKE, E. L. (1933c) A theory of the action of the after-effects of a connection upon it. *Psychol. Rev.*, 40, 434–439.—*40*

THORNDIKE, E. L., (1935) *The psychology of wants, interests and attitudes.* New York: Appleton-Century-Crofts.—*35, 40*

THORNDIKE, E. L. (1949) *Selected writings from a connectionist's psychology.* New York: Appleton-Century-Crofts.

THORNDIKE, E. L., et al. (1927) *The measurement of intelligence.* New York: Teachers College.—*58*

THORNDIKE, E. L., et al. (1928) *Adult learning.* New York: Macmillan.

THORNDIKE, E. L., & WOODWORTH, R. S. (1901) The influence of improvement in one mental function upon the efficiency of other functions. *Psychol. Rev.*, 8, 247–261, 384–395, 553–564.—*37*

THUNE, L. E., & UNDERWOOD, B. J. (1943) Retroactive inhibition as a function of degree of interpolated learning. *J. exp. Psychol.*, 32, 185–200.—*302*

THURSTONE, L. L. (1927) A law of comparative judgment. *Psychol. Rev.*, 34, 273–286.—*168*

TICKTON, S. G. (Ed.) (1970) *To improve learning: An evaluation of instructional technology.* 2 vols. New York: Bowker.

TILTON, J. W. (1939) The effect of "right" and "wrong" upon the learning of nonsense syllables in multiple choice arrangement. *J. educ. Psychol.*, 30, 95–115.—*43–44*

TILTON, J. W. (1945) Gradients of effect. *J. genet. Psychol.*, 66, 3–19.—*43–44*

TINKLEPAUGH, O. L. (1928) An experimental study of representative factors in monkeys. *J. comp. Psychol.*, 8, 197–236.—*130*

TITCHENER, E. B. (1898) Postulates of a structural psychology. *Philos. Rev.*, 7, 449–465.—*281–282*

TOLMAN, E. C. (1917) Retroactive inhibition as affected by conditions of learning. *Psychol. Monogr.*, 25, No. 107.—*145*

TOLMAN, E. C. (1922) A new formula for behaviorism. *Psychol. Rev.*, 29, 44–53.—*145*

TOLMAN, E. C. (1932) *Purposive behavior in animals and men.* New York: Appleton-Century-Crofts. Reprinted, Univ. of California Press, 1949.—*122, 129*

TOLMAN, E. C. (1938) The determiners of behavior at a choice point. *Psychol. Rev.*, 45, 1, 1–41.—*28, 125*

TOLMAN, E. C. (1939) Prediction of vicarious trial and error by means of the schematic sowbug. *Psychol. Rev.*, 46, 318–336.—*143*

TOLMAN, E. C. (1942) *Drives toward war*. New York: Appleton-Century-Crofts.—*145*

TOLMAN, E. C. (1948) Cognitive maps in rats and men. *Psychol. Rev.*, 55, 189–208.—*117, 124*

TOLMAN, E. C. (1949) There is more than one kind of learning. *Psychol. Rev.*, 56, 144–155.—*145*

TOLMAN, E. C. (1951) *Collected papers in psychology*. Berkeley: Univ. of Calif. Press.—*123*

TOLMAN, E. C. (1959) Principles of purposive behavior. In S. Koch (Ed.), *Psychology: A study of a science*. Vol. 2. New York: McGraw-Hill, 92–157.

TOLMAN, E. C., & BRUNSWIK, E. (1935) The organism and the causal texture of the environment. *Psychol. Rev.*, 42, 43–77.—*139, 146*

TOLMAN, E. C., & GLEITMAN, H. (1949) Studies in learning and motivation: 1. Equal reinforcements in both end-boxes, followed by shock in one end-box. *J. exp. Psychol.*, 39, 810–819.—*137*

TOLMAN, E. C., HALL, C. S., & BRETNALL, E. P. (1932) A disproof of the law of effect and a substitution of the laws of emphasis, motivation and disruption. *J. exp. Psychol.*, 15, 601–614.—*138*

TOLMAN, E. C., & HONZIK, C. H. (1930a) "Insight" in rats. *Univ. Calif. Publ. Psychol.*, 4, 215–232.—*133–34, 146*

TOLMAN, E. C., & HONZIK, C. H. (1930b) Introduction and removal of reward, and maze performance in rats. *Univ. Calif. Publ. Psychol.*, 4, 257–275.—*134–35*

TOLMAN, E. C., RITCHIE, B. F., & KALISH, D. (1946) Studies in spatial learning: II. Place learning versus response learning. *J. exp. Psychol.*, 36, 221–229.—*131–32*

TOLMAN, E. C., RITCHIE, B. F., & KALISH, D. (1947) Studies in spatial learning: V. Response learning vs. place learning by the non-correction method. *J. exp. Psychol.*, 37, 285–292.

TRABASSO, T. R., & BOWER, G. H. (1964) Component learning in the four-category concept problem. *J. math. Psychol.*, 1, 143–169.

TRABASSO, T. R., & BOWER, G. H. (1968) *Attention in learning: Theory and research*. New York: Wiley.—*143, 189, 401, 413, 422, 572*

TRAVIS, R. P. (1964) The role of spreading cortical depression in relating the amount of avoidance training to interhemispheric transfer. *J. comp. Psychol.*, 57, 42–46.—*544–45*

TRONICK, E., & GREENFIELD, P. M. (1973) *Infant curriculum: The Bromley-Heath guide to the care of infants in groups*. New York: Media Projects.—*341*

TROWBRIDGE, M. H., & CASON, H. (1932) An experimental study of Thorndike's theory of learning. *J. gen. Psychol.*, 7, 245–258.—*39*

TRYON, R. C. (1942) Individual differences. In F. A. Moss (Ed.), *Comparative psychology*. Englewood Cliffs, N.J.: Prentice-Hall.—*518*

TUDDENHAM, R. D. (1966) Jean Piaget and the world of the child. *Amer. Psychol.*, 21, 207–217.—*333*

TULVING, E. (1962) Subjective organization in free recall of "unrelated" words. *Psychol. Rev.*, 69, 344–354.—*279, 585*

TULVING, E. (1966) Subjective organization and effects of repetition in multi-trial free recall learning. *J. verb. Learn. verb. Behav.*, 5, 193–197.—*585*

TULVING, E. (1968) Theoretical issues in free recall. In T. R. Dixon & D. L. Horton (Eds.), *Verbal behavior and general behavior theory*. Englewood Cliffs, N.J.: Prentice-Hall.—*279, 585*

TULVING, E. (1969) Retrograde amnesia in free recall. *Science*, 164, 88–90.—*580*

TULVING, E. (1972) Episodic and semantic memory. In E. Tulving & W. Donaldson (Eds.), *Organization of memory*. New York: Academic Press.—*590*

TULVING, E., & DONALDSON, W. (Eds.) (1972) *Organization of memory*. New York: Academic Press.—*150, 280, 577, 585*

TULVING, E., & MADIGAN, S. A. (1970) Memory and verbal learning. *Ann. Rev. Psychol.*, 21, 437–484.—*577*

TULVING, E., & PEARLSTONE, Z. (1966) Availability versus accessibility of information in memory for words. *J. verb. Learn. verb. Behav.*, 5, 381–391.—*588*

TULVING, E., & PSOTKA, J. (1971) Retroactive inhibition in free recall: Inaccessibility of information available in the memory store. *J. exp. Psychol.*, 87, 1–8.—*588*

TULVING, E., & THOMSON, D. N. (1971) Retrieval processes in recognition memory: Effects of associative context. *J. exp. Psychol.*, 87, 116–124.—*268–269*

TYLER, F. (1964) Issues related to readiness to learn. In E. R. Hilgard (Ed.), *Theories of learning and instruction*. 63rd Yearbook of the National Society for the Study of Education, Part I. Chicago: Univ. of Chicago Press.

UHR, L., & VOSSLER, C. (1963) A pattern-recognition program that generates, evaluates, and adjusts its own operators. In E. A. Feigenbaum & J. Feldman (Eds.), *Computers and thought*. New York: McGraw-Hill.—*444–45*

ULRICH, R. E., & AZRIN, N. H. (1962) Reflexive fighting in response to aversive stimulation. *J. exp. anal. Behav.*, 5, 511–520.—*223*

ULRICH, R. E., STACHNIK, T., & MABRY, J. (1966) *Control of human behavior*. Vol. 1. Glenview, Ill.: Scott, Foresman.—*241*

ULRICH, R. E., STACHNIK, T., & MABRY, J. (1970) *Control of human behavior*. Vol. 2. Glenview, Ill.: Scott, Foresman.—*241*

UNDERWOOD, B. J. (1957) Interference and forgetting. *Psychol. Rev.*, 64, 49–60.—*308*

UNDERWOOD, B. J. (1966) *Experimental psychology*. (2nd ed.) New York: Appleton-Century-Crofts.

UNDERWOOD, B. J., & POSTMAN, L. (1960) Extra-experimental sources of interference in forgetting. *Psychol. Rev.*, 67, 73–95.—*308–9*

UNDERWOOD, B. J., & SCHULZ, R. W. (1960) *Meaningfulness and verbal learning*. Philadelphia: J. B. Lippincott.—*314*

UZGIRIS, I. C. (1964) Situational generality of conservation. *Child Devel.*, 35, 831–841.—*334*

VALENSTEIN, E. S., & COX, V. C. (1970) Influence of hunger, thirst, and previous experience in the test chamber on stimulus-bound eating and drinking. *J. comp. physiol. Psychol.*, 70, 189–199.—*497*

VALENSTEIN, E. S., COX, V. C., & KAKOLEWSKI, J. W. (1968) Modification of motivated behavior elicited by electrical stimulation of the hypothalamus. *Science*, 159, 1119–1121.—*197–98*

VALENSTEIN, E. S., COX, V. C., & KAKOLEWSKI, J. W. (1969) The hypothalamus and motivated behavior. In J. Tapp (Ed.), *Reinforcement and behavior*. New York: Academic Press.—*497*

VAUGHN, E., & FISHER, A. E. (1962) Male sexual behavior induced by intracranial electrical stimulation. *Science*, 137, 758–760.—*495*

VERHAVE, T. (Ed.) (1966) *The experimental analysis of behavior: Selected readings* New York: Appleton-Century-Crofts.

VERNON, P. E. (1961) *Intelligence and attainment*. New York: Philosophical Library.—*319*

VERPLANCK, W. S. (1962) Unaware of where's awareness: Some verbal operants—notates, monents, and notants. In C. W. Eriksen (Eds.), *Behavior and awareness*. Durham, N.C.: Duke Univ. Press.—*485*

VINH-BANG (1957) Elaboration d'une échelle de développement du raisonnement. *Proceedings of the 15th International Congress of Psychology*, 333–334.—*332*

VITZ, P. C., & TODD, R. C. (1967) A model for simple repeating binary patterns. *J. exp. Psychol.*, 75, 108–117.

VITZ, P. C., & TODD, R. C. (1969) A coded element model of the perceptual processing of sequential stimuli. *Psychol. Rev.*, 76, 433–449.—*392, 457*

VOEKS, V. W. (1948) Postremity, recency, and frequency as bases for prediction in the maze situation. *J. exp. Psychol.*, 38, 495–510.—*93, 112–13*

VOEKS, V. W. (1950) Formalization and clarification of a theory of learning. *J. Psychol.*, 30, 341–363.—*93, 111–12*

VOEKS, V. W. (1954) Acquisition of S-R connections: A test of Hull's and Guthrie's theories. *J. exp. Psychol.*, 47, 137–147.—*113–14, 312*

VOEKS, V. W. (1964) *On becoming an educated person*. Philadelphia: Saunders.

VON NEUMANN, J., & MORGENSTERN, O. (1944) *Theory of games and economic behavior*. Princeton: Princeton Univ. Press.—*146*

WAGNER, A. R. (1963) Conditioned frustration as a learned drive. *J. exp. Psychol.*, 66, 142–148.—*192, 193*

WAGNER, A. R. (1966) Frustration and punishment. In R. N. Haber (Ed.), *Research on motivation*. New York: Holt, Rinehart and Winston.—*192, 194*

WALLACE, J. G. (1965) *Concept growth and the education of the child: A survey of research and conceptualization*. Slough, Eng.: National Foundation for Educational Research.—*341*

WALTER, W. G. (1953) *The living brain*. New York: Norton.—*429*

WANG, H. (1960) Towards mechanical mathematics. *IBM J. Res. Devel.*, 4, 2–22.—*437*

WANG, H. (1965) Games, logic, and computers. *Sci. Amer.*, 98–107.—*437*

WARREN, H. C. (1921) *A history of association psychology*. New York: Scribner's.—*6*

WARRINGTON, E. K., & SHALLICE, T. (1969) The selective impairment of auditory verbal short-term memory. *Brain*, 92, 885–896.—*517*

WATERS, R. H., & LEEPER, R. (1936) The relation of affective tone to the retention of experiences in everyday life. *J. exp. Psychol.*, 19, 203–215.—*367*

WATSON, J. B. (1907) Kinesthetic and organic sensations: Their role in the reactions of the white rat to the maze. *Psychol. Monogr.*, 8, No. 33.—*91, 93*

WATSON, J. B. (1914) *Behavior, an introduction to comparative psychology.* New York: Holt, Rinehart and Winston.—*91*

WATSON, J. B. (1916) The place of the conditioned reflex in psychology. *Psychol. Rev.*, 23, 89–116.—*73, 91*

WATSON, J. B. (1919) *Psychology from the standpoint of a behaviorist.* Philadelphia: J. B. Lippincott.—*91*

WATSON, J. B. (1924a) The unverbalized in human behavior. *Psychol. Rev.*, 31, 273–280.—*371*

WATSON, J. B. (1924b) *Behaviorism.* New York: Norton.—*588*

WAUGH, N. C., & NORMAN, D. A. (1965) Primary memory. *Psychol. Rev.*, 72, 89–104.—*418*

WEAVER, G. E., DUNCAN, E. M., & BIRD, C. P. (1972) Cue-specific retroactive inhibition. *J. verb. Learn. verb. Behav.*, 11, 362–366.—*304*

WEBB, W. B., & NOLAN, C. Y. (1953) Cues for discrimination as secondary reinforcing agents: A confirmation. *J. comp. physiol. Psychol.*, 46, 180–181.—*220*

WEINER, B., & HIGGINS, J. (1969) A mediational paradigm for the study of motivated forgetting: A critical analysis. *J. verb. Learn. verb. Behav.*, 8, 677–680.—*365*

WEISS, J. M. (1971a) Effects of coping behavior in different warning conditions on stress pathology in rats. *J. comp. physiol. Psychol.*, 77, 1–13.—*577*

WEISS, J. M. (1971b) Effects of punishing the coping response (conflict) on stress pathology in rats. *J. comp. physiol. Psychol.*, 77, 14–21.—*577*

WENDT, G. R. (1937) Two and one-half year retention of a conditioned response. *J. gen. Psychol.*, 17, 178–180.—*95*

WERTHEIMER, M. (1923) Untersuchung zur Lehre von der Gestalt, II. *Psychol. Forsch.*, 4, 301–350. Translated and condensed as "Laws of organization in perceptual forms," in W. D. Ellis, *A source book of gestalt psychology.* New York: Harcourt, Brace & World, 1938, 71–88.—*256–63*

WERTHEIMER, M. (1945) *Productive thinking.* New York: Harper & Row.—*274–76, 280*

WERTHEIMER, M. (1959) *Productive thinking* (Enlarged ed.). New York: Harper & Row.—*274, 280*

WESCOURT, K. T. (1971) Studies of motivated forgetting. Unpublished senior honors thesis, Princeton Univ.—*365*

WHITE, A. R. (1967) *The philosophy of mind.* New York: Random House.—*313*

WHITE, R. W. (1964) *The abnormal personality.* New York: Ronald Press.—*350*

WHITEHEAD, A. N., & Russell, B. (1925) *Principia mathematica* (2nd ed.). Vol. 1. Cambridge: Cambridge Univ. Press.—*438*

WHITING, J. W. M., & CHILD, I. L. (1953) *Child training and personality.* New Haven: Yale Univ. Press.—*358–59*

WHYTT, R. (1763) *An essay on the vital and other involuntary motions of animals* (2nd ed.). Edinburgh: J. Balfour.—*64*

WICKENS, D. D. (1938) The transference of conditioned excitation and conditioned inhibition from one muscle group to the antagonistic muscle group. *J. exp. Psychol.*, 22, 101–123.—*115*

WILKS, Y. (1973) An artificial intelligence approach to machine translation. In R. Shank & K. Colby (Eds.), *Computer models of thought and language.* San Francisco: W. H. Freeman.—*467*

WILLIAMS, D. R. (1965) Classical conditioning and incentive motivation. In W. F. Prokasy (Ed.), *Classical conditioning.* New York: Appleton-Century-Crofts.—*209*

WILLIAMS, D. R., & WILLIAMS, H. (1969) Auto-maintenance in the pigeon: Sustained pecking despite contingent non-reinforcement. *J. exp. anal. Behav.*, 12, 511–520.—*244*

WILLIAMS, G. F. (1971) A model of memory in concept learning. *Cog. Psychol.*, 2, 158–184.—*478–80*

WILLIAMS, S. B., & LEAVITT, H. J. (1947) Prediction of success in learning Japanese. *J. appl. Psychol.*, 31, 164–168.—*626*

WINOGRAD, T. (1972) Understanding natural language. *Cog. Psychol.*, 3, 1–191.—*468, 469, 471, 593*

WINSTON, P. H. (1970) *Learning structural descriptions from examples.* Cambridge: MIT Artificial Intelligence Laboratory, Project MAC-TR-231.—*447–48, 450–52, 460, 480–82*

WITTGENSTEIN, L. (1953) *Philosophical investigations.* Oxford: Blackwell.—*313*

WITTROCK, M. C. (1966) The learning by discovery hypothesis. In L. S. Shulman & E. R. Keislar (Eds.), *Learning by discovery.* Chicago: Rand McNally.—*345*

WOLF, A. (1943) The dynamics of the selective inhibition of specific functions in neurosis. *Psychom. Med.,* 5, 27–38.—*358*

WOLFE, J. B. (1934) The effect of delayed reward upon learning in the white rat. *J. comp. Psychol.,* 17, 1–21.—*172*

WOLFF, P. H. (1960) The developmental psychologies of Jean Piaget and psychoanalysis. *Psychol. Issues,* 2, Monogr. 5.—*325*

WOLFLE, D. L. (1936) The relative efficiency of constant and varied stimulation during learning: III. The objective extent of stimulus variation. *J. comp. Psychol.,* 22, 375–381.—*383*

WOLFORD, G. (1971) Function of distinct associations for paired-associate performance. *Psychol. Rev.,* 78, 303–313.—*415–16*

WOLPE, J. (1958) *Psychotherapy by reciprocal inhibition.* Stanford: Stanford Univ. Press.—*96–97, 372*

WOODS, W. A. (1967) *Semantics for a question-answering system.* Report No. NSF-19, Aitken Computation Laboratory. Harvard University, Sept.—*471*

WOODS, W. A. (1970) Transition network grammars for natural language analysis. *Communications of the Association for Computing Machinery,* 13, 591–606.—*468*

WOODWARD, M. (1959) The behavior of idiots interpreted by Piaget's theory of sensorimotor development. *Brit. J. educ. Psychol.,* 29, 60–71.—*328*

WOODWORTH, R. S. (1918) *Dynamic psychology.* New York: Columbia Univ. Press.—*103, 284–85, 286*

WOODWORTH, R. S. (1929) *Psychology.* (Rev. ed.). New York: Holt, Rinehart and Winston.—*153*

WOODWORTH, R. S. (1937) Situation- and goal-set. *Amer. J. Psychol.,* 50, 130–140.—*287*

WOODWORTH, R. S. (1938) *Experimental psychology.* New York: Holt, Rinehart and Winston.—*315*

WOODWORTH, R. S. (1958) *Dynamics of behavior.* New York: Holt, Rinehart and Winston. —*284–85*

WOODWORTH, R. S., & SCHLOSBERG, H. (1954) Experimental psychology. (Rev. ed.). New York: Holt, Rinehart and Winston.—*316*

WOOLDRIDGE, D. E. (1963) *The machinery of the brain.* New York: McGraw-Hill.

WRIGHT, J. C. (1960) Problem solving and search behavior under noncontingent reward. Unpublished doctoral dissertation, Stanford Univ.—*210*

WULF, F. (1922) Über die Veränderung von Vorstellungen (Gedächtnis und Gestalt). *Psychol. Forsch.,* I, 333–373. Translated and condensed as "Tendencies in figural variation," in W. D. Ellis, *A source book of gestalt psychology.* New York: Harcourt, Brace & World, 1938, 136–148.—*269–70*

WYRWICKA, W., & DOBRZECKA, C. (1960) Relationship between feeding and satiation centers of the hypothalamus. *Science,* 123, 805–806.—*493*

WYRWICKA, W., & STERNMAN, M. B. (1968) Instrumental conditioning of sensorimotor cortex EEG spindles in the waking cat. *Physiol. & Behav.* 3, 703–707.—*557*

YAMAGUCHI, H. G., HULL, C. I., FELSINGER, J. M., & GLADSTONE, A. I. (1948) Characteristics of dispersions based on the pooled momentary reaction potentials. $(_s\bar{E}_R)$ of a group. *Psychol. Rev.,* 55, 216–238.—*166*

YELLOTT, J. I., JR. (1969) Probability learning with noncontingent success. *J. math. Psychol.,* 6, 541–575.—*408*

YERKES, R. M. (1927) The mind of a gorilla: I. *Genet. Psychol. Monogr.,* 2.—*273*

YNTEMA, D. B., & TRASK, F. P. (1963) Recall as a search process. *J. verb. Learn. verb. Behav.,* 2, 65–74.—*302*

YOUNG, M. N., & GIBSON, W. B. (1966) *How to develop an exceptional memory.* Hollywood: Wilshire Press.—*587*

YOUNG, R. K. (1968) Serial learning. In T. R. Dixon & D. L. Horton (Eds.), *Verbal behavior and general behavior theory.* Englewood Cliffs, N.J.: Prentice-Hall.

ZAJONC, R. (1968) Attitudinal effects of mere exposure. *J. Pers. and Soc. Pers.,* Monogr. Suppl., 9 (2, Pt. 2). 1–27.—*368*

ZEAMAN, D. (1959) Skinner's theory of teaching machines. In E. H. Galanter (Ed.), *Automatic teaching: The state of the art.* New York: Wiley, 167–176.—*613*

ZEAMAN, D., & HOUSE, B. J. (1963) The role of attention in retardate discrimination learning. In N. R. Ellis (Ed.), *Handbook of mental deficiency.* New York: McGraw-Hill, 159–223.—*401*

ZEILER, M. D. (1963) The ratio theory of intermediate size discrimination. *Psychol. Rev.,* 70, 516–533.—*186–87*

ZELLER, A. F. (1950a) An experimental analogue of repression: I. Historical summary. *Psychol. Bull.,* 47, 39–51.—*362, 366*

ZELLER, A. F. (1950b) An experimental analogue of repression: II. The effect of individual failure and success on memory measured by relearning. *J. exp. Psychol.,* 40, 411–422.—*366*

ZENER, K. (1937) The significance of behavior accompanying conditioned salivary secretion for theories of the conditioned reflex. *Amer. J. Psychol.,* 50, 384–403.—*209*

ZIMBARDO, P. G. (1969) *The cognitive control of motivation.* Glenview, Ill.: Scott, Foresman. —*498*

ZIRKLE, G. A. (1946) Success and failure in serial learning: I. The Thorndike effect. *J. exp. Psychol.,* 36, 230–236.—*47*

Index